D1223765

"The combination of substantial reflective essays on major themes in Christian spirituality and sharply focused articles on major figures and topics provides a rich mixture of insight, information, and inspiration. 'Spirituality' can be a subject that wafts into the ether, but in this broadly ecumenical and very well-balanced work, it is presented with real substance and genuine edification."

—**Mark A. Noll**, *Francis A. McAnaney Professor*
of History, University of Notre Dame; author,
Jesus Christ and the Life of the Mind

"The very publication of this work speaks to the contemporary interest in spirituality. So much spirituality, however, is uninformed, shallow, and vague. All the more reason to welcome this important dictionary. It is impressive in its scope, wide in what is included, and deep in the intent to strengthen life in the Spirit of Christ. Scan a few entries, and it will be evident what a valuable resource this can be. I cannot imagine a dictionary on spirituality that is all prose. So I was delighted to see the entries on, for example, Poetry, and Hopkins. Don't miss them."

—**Leighton Ford**, *President, Leighton Ford Ministries*

"The *Dictionary of Christian Spirituality* is a well-researched, comprehensive study of Christian Spirituality from a broad evangelical perspective. Particularly insightful are the thirty-four extensive 'Integrative Essays' that cover nearly the first third of the book. The almost 700 alphabetized entries fill in multiple details and make connections between movements, ideas, and significant leaders throughout Christian history. While covering the entire range of Christian spirituality, special attention is given to persons of evangelical persuasion who have had significant impact over the centuries. This distinguishing characteristic provides an important corrective to a long-neglected omission. I give the *Dictionary of Christian Spirituality* my highest recommendation."

—**Richard J. Foster**, *author of Celebration of Discipline*

"Engaging, comprehensive, informative, broad in perspective. Who thinks it is fun to read a dictionary? This one is! This is a dictionary to be read for enjoyment as well as information. The essays and articles are freshly written, thorough but concise. The *Dictionary of Christian Spirituality* reflects the deep respect and appreciation the writers have for their topics. Reading this dictionary is like taking a finely tuned course in the topics included. The essays and dictionary entries portray the complex and diverse history of the Christian church embodied in women and men and the contexts of their times and cultures. Many readers will delve into these volumes seeking information about particular topics. I was fascinated and drawn from article to article … appreciating the fine scholarship, depth of research reflected, and careful writing that make the *Dictionary of Christian Spirituality* an excellent resource."

—**Jeannette A. Bakke**, *author of Holy Invitations:*
Exploring Spiritual Direction; retired professor,
Bethel Seminary

"This is not the only dictionary about Christian spirituality in town. There are many around and some of them very good. But this one, with its global interests and spiritual zeal, has an energy and breadth that lifts it into a new league. Moreover, as well as making a very good job of expanding our knowledge of Christian spirituality and all the sources that have shaped it, this important volume steers the reader through the people, movements, and issues with a reliable, generous, and grace-focused wisdom. It is a source not just of information about Christian spirituality but of real formation, through the Spirit, in the life of Christ."

—**Christopher Cocksworth**, *Bishop of Coventry,*
Church of England

"The more I read in the *Dictionary of Christian Spirituality*, the more I wanted to read more! The initial essays provide a thoroughly excellent foundation, and the alphabetized entries that follow leave us intrigued to read others. I highly recommend this dictionary for all Christians, especially those who want to grow in their active practices of various spiritual disciplines, their devoted love for God and neighbor, and their fervent thanksgiving for global saints and the myriad ways God works in the world."

—**Marva J. Dawn**, *Teaching Fellow in Spiritual Theology*
at Regent College, Vancouver, BC

"Scholarship with a soul! This is a book like no other—scholarly breadth with spiritual depth in a dictionary. So many have written so much about Christian spirituality that it is difficult to connect the parts. Here is a readable resource that brings everything together. I kept turning the pages ... not to read through, but to explore. Every article led me to another journey on a different page."

—**Leith Anderson**, *President,*
National Association of Evangelicals

"The *Dictionary of Christian Spirituality* is a remarkable balance of broad, integrative essays and more than 700 succinct, informative dictionary entries. It combines a wide survey of the great movements in Christian spirituality while giving attention to the main contributors from all parts of the globe, past and present. The contributors include some of the great heavyweights of the movement while also incorporating significant voices from a variety of related disciplines and perspective. The work is a must-have resource for every able scholar, pastor, and follower of Jesus."

—**Gayle D. Beebe**, *President, Westmont College*

ZONDERVAN

DICTIONARY of
CHRISTIAN SPIRITUALITY

ZONDERVAN

DICTIONARY of CHRISTIAN SPIRITUALITY

General Editor
Glen G. Scorgie

Consulting Editors
Simon Chan
Gordon T. Smith
James D. Smith III

ZONDERVAN®

ZONDERVAN.com/
AUTHORTRACKER
follow your favorite authors

ZONDERVAN

Dictionary of Christian Spirituality
Copyright © 2011 by Glen G. Scorgie, Simon Chan, Gordon T. Smith, and James D. Smith III

This title is also available as a Zondervan ebook. Visit www.zondervan.com/ebooks.

This title is also available in a Zondervan audio edition. Visit www.zondervan.fm.

Requests for information should be addressed to:

Zondervan, *Grand Rapids, Michigan 49530*

Library of Congress Cataloging-in-Publication Data

Dictionary of Christian spirituality / Glen G. Scorgie, general editor ; consulting editors: Simon Chan, Gordon T. Smith, James
D. Smith III.
     p. cm.
   ISBN 978-0-310-29066-7 (hardcover, printed)
    1. Spirituality. I. Scorgie, Glen G. II. Chan, Simon. III. Smith, Gordon T., 1953- IV. Smith, James D., 1951 Jan. 12-
BV4501.3.D545 2011
  248 — dc22
                                                        2010037314

Other versions of Scripture are listed on page 12, which hereby becomes a part of this copyright page.

Cover and interior design: Kirk DouPonce

Printed in the United States of America

11 12 13 14 15 16 17 /DCI/ 23 22 21 20 19 18 17 16 15 14 13 12 11 10 9 8 7 6 5 4 3 2 1

CONTENTS

Part 2: Dictionary Entries

PREFACE

This volume was prepared with the conviction that the way to really live is to do so before God in the transforming and empowering presence of his Spirit. The key is to cultivate consciousness of and willing alignment with the presence and grace of God in all things. At this point in history, this has become more than a "quality of life" issue. Many insightful observers of our times agree with Thomas Cahill in his assessment that "the twenty-first century will be spiritual or it will not be." The crises of the modern, materialist world suggest that spirituality may now matter more than ever before. The problems of our times are too deep-seated to allow for merely political or economic solutions.

But then we must also frankly ask: Does the Christian faith still possess the resources necessary to satisfy the spiritual needs of the human race? We are convinced that it does. And we also believe that today the Spirit of God is prodding the amnesiac people of God to reclaim the spiritual resources that have inspired and sustained believers through the centuries. The future is ominous for all forms of organized religion that in their worldly calculus cut themselves off from the transcendent.

One scholarly critic of the "spiritual scene" today has described spirituality, as popularly conceived, as a marketable commodity for individuals, one that amounts to little more than "wafting experientialism." Admittedly, much of the devotional literature produced by Christian publishers is of precisely this vague and fluffy nature. One of the purposes of a reference volume like this is to help Christians reunite their heads with their hearts (and also with their hands, as Dennis Hollinger would have us add). Christian spirituality is about more than having warm feelings toward Jesus.

A new volume like this is not created from scratch. It utilizes resources already available, and we acknowledge with gratitude our indebtedness to so many of these. For example, we have profited from numerous efforts to publish English translations of important primary sources in Christian spirituality. The most impressive of such efforts is the Classics of Western Spirituality (CWS) series that was launched by the Paulist Press in the 1980s. Since then the series has grown to well over one hundred volumes and continues to expand. Also since then HarperCollins has spun off a sixteen-volume series of abridged versions of selected texts from the larger CWS series.

The sheer quantity of such material can be daunting to navigate. For this reason a number of abbreviated one-volume anthologies have been published. Among these there are F. Magill and I. McGreal, eds., *Christian Spirituality* (1988); R. Foster and J. B. Smith, eds., *Devotional Classics* (1993); and A. Holder, ed., *Christian Spirituality: The Classics* (2009).

Certain works have earned the status of milestones in the history of the disciplines of spirituality and spiritual theology. Some of these are not yet available in English, but among those that are, we acknowledge in particular the translated three-volume *History of Christian Spirituality* (1963–1969), written by Louis Bouyer and others, as well as the three historically sequenced volumes on *Christian Spirituality* (1985–1989), edited by Bernard McGinn, John Meyendorff, and others, in the World Spirituality series.

In recent years a number of significant reference works in Christian spirituality have been published. *The New Dictionary of Catholic Spirituality* (1993), edited by Michael Downey, represents a Roman Catholic perspective. On the Protestant side there are *The Westminster Dictionary of Christian Spirituality* (1983), edited by Gordon Wakefield, and its successor, *The New Westminster Dictionary of Christian Spirituality* (2003), edited by Philip Sheldrake. *The Study of Spirituality* (1986), edited by Cheslyn Jones and others, is a substantive and supplementary collection of historical and thematic essays with rich bibliographic suggestions for further study.

The field has been further enriched with *The Story of Christian Spirituality* (2001), edited by Gordon Mursell, an accessible volume with colorful visuals. From the Wesleyan tradition has come *The Upper Room Dictionary of Christian Spiritual Formation* (2003), a helpfully concise work edited by Keith Beasley-Topliffe, and from Oxford, *The Blackwell Companion to Christian Spirituality* (2005), prepared by Arthur Holder, dean of the Graduate Theological Union at Berkeley.

Since the field of Christian spirituality is already so well resourced with excellent English-language reference works, the question surfaces: Why produce yet another?

The short answer is: Christian spiritual theology, spirituality, and spiritual formation have now become familiar terms in the global evangelical community. Consequently, an accessible and reliable academic resource is needed on these topics — one that will offer a discerning orientation to the wealth of ecumenical resources available while still highlighting the distinct heritage and affirming the core grace-centered values of classic evangelical spirituality. While a number of scholarly reference works on Christian spirituality are already available, the need exists for a high-quality reference volume with the following features:

1. Biblically engaged
2. Accessible and relevant to contemporary Christian practitioners
3. Generous in its regard for the full range of Christian traditions of spirituality
4. Attentive to otherwise neglected topics, concerns, and formative figures in the evangelical tradition of spirituality
5. Global and international in both topical scope and contributors
6. Reflective of interdisciplinary engagement with related fields of inquiry
7. Reasonably priced

This volume has two main divisions: (1) thirty-four larger "integrative perspective" essays followed by (2) nearly seven hundred smaller alphabetized entries of varying lengths. Each of the integrative perspective essays has been written with an awareness of the other briefer but related articles included. These shorter articles provide more details on particular topics than was possible to include in the integrative essays themselves. Believing as we do that history is shaped by individuals as well as by larger movements, we make no apology for including many succinct biographical entries in our mix.

Preparing this volume has been a stretching experience for everyone involved. Some contributors — specialists in their own biblical, historical, or theological fields — have been obliged for the first time to think carefully about the links between subjects familiar to them and the discipline and dynamics of Christian spirituality. To some degree, therefore, the present volume reflects "the state of the union" in emergent evangelical study of Christian spirituality. The reader will be able to tell some things about us by what we have included and what we have left out. The volume is not presented as the definitive work on this topic; it is our hope, however, that it will prove to be immediately helpful and a serviceable benchmark for future editions.

In terms of our intended audience, contributors to the volume have been encouraged to address their peers in ways that will also be accessible to a larger audience of thoughtful readers. As editors and writers who have made substantial investments in this volume, we naturally hope that it will be well received and favorably reviewed. Positive response from people "in the know" will naturally be most welcome. But deeper down, I think we identify with the great American theologian Jonathan Edwards, who resolved fairly early on in his own career to be "useful rather than conspicuous." We are hopeful that the volume may influence the understanding — and even more importantly, the actual dynamics — of Christian spirituality in many churches, colleges, and seminaries for years to come.

Glen G. Scorgie
Beijing, July 5, 2010

ACKNOWLEDGMENTS

This volume has been a collaborative effort. I am especially grateful to our three consulting editors — Simon Chan, Gordon Smith, and Jim Smith — for their wisdom, scholarship, global and historical perspectives, and faithful commitment to this project. For the last two years or more, this trio has weighed in via email from all over the world — Oxford and Hanoi, Bangalore and Nairobi, Manila and Pittsburgh. In many instances, they pointed toward neglected literature, refined draft statements, and preempted serious gaffes. They have enriched the content of this volume in countless ways; the task simply could not have been completed with anything near the same quality without them. Their advice was not taken in every instance, however; so they cannot be held responsible for the errors that will inevitably surface.

I also wish to acknowledge our first Zondervan editor, David Frees, for his originating vision of this reference work and navigating the many administrative steps required to move it forward. We also thank our follow-up editors at Zondervan, Jim Ruark and Laura Weller, who took the completed contents from David and shaped them into their final, published form. Among the many other Zondervan people who worked on this project to whom I wish to express my special appreciation are Stine May and Sue Johnston in the contracts office — it was no easy job superintending the flow of contracts for all our contributors.

J. D. Douglas was a remarkably gifted, somewhat reclusive Scottish church historian and editor, who now, "from the heavenlies," still inspires through the memory of his character and work ethic. Years ago, during our graduate student days at St. Andrews, he voluntarily took it upon himself to watch out for our little family. Each quarter he invited us over to his home for tea on a Sunday afternoon. There he would regale us with witty anecdotes and inquire concerning our welfare. The sitting room in which we met was encircled with books, many of them with his name on the spines and dust jackets. "Dr. Douglas, did you actually write all these?" someone once asked with amazement. Eager to demonstrate my own knowledge of the scholarly world, I interrupted dismissively: "No, no. He gets other people to write all this stuff. He just puts it together." The conversation continued right on, but I had a vague sense even then that I may have slightly underestimated the editorial task. Well, for what it's worth, now I know.

Yet back then in Dr. Douglas's parlor I had been basically right. An edited reference work consists of contributions from a host of qualified scholars; they provide the real substance of the thing. Throughout this endeavor it has been a privilege to interact with so many such special people, most of whom we would not have otherwise had any excuse to bother. They include high-profile persons who have left their mark on the life of the church and have been mentors to some of us. They also include younger, lesser-known but gifted and diligent contributors who are emerging as the next generation of spiritual writers and leaders.

This particular volume has been a collaborative venture among more than two hundred contributors in all — women and men, and the whole representing the inhabited continents of the world. We feel gratified that this group encompasses the full spectrum of Protestants, including Calvinists and Wesleyans, Episcopalians and Anglicans, Pentecostals and Baptists, Seventh-day Adventists and Dispensationalists; also some Roman Catholics and Eastern

Orthodox; and even a few who are not going to church at all right now. We want to express our special gratitude toward those who distinguished themselves by writing large numbers of entries: among them Bruce Demarest, Brad Holt, Evan Howard, Todd Johnson, Glenn Myers, Dennis Okholm, Tom Schwanda, Carole Spencer, Ruth Tucker, and Jason Zuidema. Thanks to all of them for going well beyond minimalist definitions of duty.

One of the raps against Christian spirituality, as it is often practiced and articulated, is that it is disconnected from real life. This is not the brand of spirituality presented in this volume, and it is worth noting that the contributions to this volume have been forged in the crucible of real life. The contributors have often written amid the press of ministerial demands or from difficult corners of the earth; those with whom we have been in contact have experienced the anguish of a child's suicide, debilitating stroke, parenting children with severe disabilities, exhaustion, diagnosis of terminal illness, job termination, spousal abandonment, care for dependent spouses, depression, and many other challenging realities of life — in short, their fair share of "the thousand natural shocks that flesh is heir to." These entries were not written for the superficial purposes of impressing or entertaining their readers. And yet there is for all of that a spirit of resilient joy evident throughout, which we hope readers will be able to detect.

As general editor, I am grateful to Bethel Seminary for awarding me a sabbatical in which to complete this work, and for Bethel San Diego dean John Lillis's enthusiastic support of this release time during a period of financial belt-tightening for the institution. My teaching assistant, Johanna Vignol, has been an enormous help with all the administrative and editorial tasks associated with this project — her perfectionist instincts were precisely what we needed most month after month. There ought to be a special category of Pulitzer Prize for a contribution like hers. I am also indebted to Dr. André Ong for stepping in during my sabbatical and carrying my teaching load in such an enthusiastic and capable manner. Bethel San Diego's remarkable triumvirate of librarians — Mary-Lou Bradbury, Mariel Voth, and Françoise Anderson — has served once again as indispensable counselors and colleagues.

BIBLE VERSIONS

ABBREVIATIONS

Sources

ACCS   Ancient Christian Commentary on Scripture
ACW   Ancient Christian Writers
ANF   *Ante-Nicene Fathers*
BibSac   *Bibliotheca sacra*
CE   *The Catholic Encyclopedia*
CFS   Cistercian Father's Series
CRS   Classics of Reformed Spirituality
CWS   Classics of Western Spirituality
MSMS   Modern Spiritual Masters Series
NT   New Testament
NCE   *New Catholic Encyclopedia*
OT   Old Testament
SAS   Sources of American Spirituality Series
TDNT   *Theological Dictionary of the New Testament* (Kittel)
TDOT   *Theological Dictionary of the Old Testament* (Botterweck and Ringgren)
WSEH   *World Spirituality: An Encyclopedic History of the Religious Quest* (Cousins)
WTJ   *Westminster Theological Journal*

Terms

AT   Author's translation or paraphrase
ed(s).   editor(s)
Gr.   Greek
Heb.   Hebrew
Lat.   Latin
trans.   translated by

Publication Dates

The date of a work cited in the text of an entry is normally the date of its original publication. The date of a work cited in For Further Reading is normally the date of the translation or edition quoted in the article or recommended to the reader. The specific number of an edition (e.g., 5th ed.) is not provided.

CONTRIBUTORS

Bernard Adeney-Risakotta (Ph.D., Graduate Theological Union, Berkeley) is director of the Indonesian Consortium for Religious Studies at Gadjah Mada University in Yogyakarta, Indonesia.

Ray Aldred (M.Div., Ambrose Seminary) is assistant professor of theology at Ambrose Seminary in Calgary, Canada.

Carl E. Armerding (Ph.D., Brandeis University) is formerly professor and president of Regent College, director of Schloss Mittersill Study Centre, and Fellow of the Oxford Centre for Mission Studies.

Chris R. Armstrong (Ph.D., Duke University) is associate professor of church history at Bethel Seminary in St. Paul, Minnesota.

Clinton E. Arnold (Ph.D., University of Aberdeen) is professor of New Testament language and literature, and chair of the Department of New Testament at Talbot School of Theology in La Mirada, California.

Diane S. George Ayer (M.A.R., Ambrose Theological Seminary) is circulation supervisor of Ambrose Library at Ambrose University College in Calgary, Canada.

Lynne M. Baab (Ph.D., University of Washington) is the Jack Somerville Lecturer in Pastoral Theology at the University of Otago in Otago, New Zealand.

Jeff Bach (Ph.D., Duke University) is director of the Young Center for Anabaptist and Pietist Studies at Elizabethtown College in Elizabethtown, Pennsylvania.

Jo-Ann Badley (Ph.D., University of St. Michael's College, Toronto) is professor of New Testament at Mars Hill Graduate School in Seattle, Washington.

Catherine M. Barsotti (M.Div., Pacific School of Religion) is a doctoral candidate at Fuller Seminary and a professor at Centro Hispano de Estudios Teologicos in Bell Gardens, California.

Ruth Haley Barton (B.A., Wheaton College) is a writer and the founder of The Transforming Center.

Timothy J. Becker (M.Div., Pittsburgh Theological Seminary) is a doctoral candidate at Union Theological Seminary in New York.

Nancy E. Bedford (Th.D., University of Tübingen) is Georgia Harkness Professor of Applied Theology at Garrett-Evangelical Theological Seminary in Evanston, Illinois.

Matthew Bell (M.Div., Pittsburgh Theological Seminary) is a doctoral candidate at University of Durham in the United Kingdom.

Michael Bergmann (Ph.D., University of Notre Dame) is professor of philosophy at Purdue University in West Lafayette, Indiana.

James A. Beverley (Ph.D., University of St. Michael's College, Toronto) is professor of Christian thought and ethics at Tyndale Seminary in Toronto, Canada, and associate director of the Institute for the Study of American Religion in Santa Barbara, California.

Cynthia Hyle Bezek (M.A., Syracuse University) is senior editor and prayer resources director for NavPress, the publishing division of the Navigators.

Michael Birkel (Ph.D., Harvard University) is professor of religion and director of the Newlin Center for Quaker Thought and Practice at Earlham College in Richmond, Indiana.

Mark J. Boda (Ph.D., University of Cambridge) is professor of Old Testament at McMaster Divinity College and professor, Faculty of Theology, McMaster University in Hamilton, Ontario, Canada.

Arthur Paul Boers (D.Min., Northern Baptist Theological Seminary) holds the R. J.

Bernardo Family Chair of Leadership at Tyndale Seminary in Toronto, Canada.

Radu Bordeianu (Ph.D., Marquette University) is assistant professor of systematic theology at Duquesne University in Pittsburgh, Pennsylvania.

Jeannine K. Brown (Ph.D., Luther Seminary) is professor of New Testament at Bethel Seminary in St. Paul, Minnesota.

Bogdan G. Bucur (Ph.D., Marquette University) is assistant professor of theology at Duquesne University in Pittsburgh, Pennsylvania.

Marcia J. Bunge (Ph.D., University of Chicago) is professor of humanities and theology at Christ College, the Honors College of Valparaiso University in Indiana.

Gary M. Burge (Ph.D., University of Aberdeen) is professor of New Testament at Wheaton College and Graduate School in Wheaton, Illinois.

Nancy R. Buschart (M.A., Denver Seminary) is director of mentoring at Denver Seminary in Littleton, Colorado.

W. David Buschart (Ph.D., Drew University) is professor of theology and historical studies at Denver Seminary in Littleton, Colorado.

Heidi Campbell (Ph.D., University of Edinburgh) is assistant professor of communication at Texas A&M University at College Station, Texas.

Julie Canlis (Ph.D., University of St. Andrews) is a Templeton Scholar living in Methlick, Scotland.

G. William Carlson (Ph.D., University of Minnesota) is professor of history and political science at Bethel University in St. Paul, Minnesota.

Mark J. Cartledge (Ph.D., University of Wales) is senior lecturer in Pentecostal and charismatic theology at the University of Birmingham in the United Kingdom.

Simon Chan (Ph.D., Cambridge University) is professor of systematic theology at Trinity Theological College, Singapore.

Minoa Chang (Ph.D., Alliant International University) is a psychologist and faculty associate at Bethel Seminary in San Diego, California.

Cynthia Cheshire (B.A., North Park University) is a graduate student in church history.

Alexander Chow (Th.M., Regent College) is a doctoral candidate in theology at the University of Birmingham in the United Kingdom.

David K. Clark (Ph.D., Northwestern University) is provost of Bethel University in St. Paul, Minnesota.

John H. Coe (Ph.D., University of California, Irvine) is director of the Institute for Spiritual Formation at Talbot School of Theology and professor of spiritual theology and philosophy at Rosemead School of Psychology in La Mirada, California.

Charles J. Conniry Jr. (Ph.D., Fuller Theological Seminary) is vice president and dean of George Fox Evangelical Seminary in Portland, Oregon.

Kelby Cotton (M.Div., Princeton Theological Seminary) is pastor of spiritual formation at South Suburban Christian Church and adjunct professor of spiritual formation at Denver Seminary in Littleton, Colorado.

Dan R. Crawford (D.Min., Southwestern Baptist Theological Seminary) is senior professor of evangelism and missions, and chair of prayer emeritus at Southwestern Baptist Theological Seminary in Fort Worth, Texas.

Carla M. Dahl (Ph.D., University of Minnesota) is professor of formation and lead faculty for marriage and family therapy at Bethel Seminary in St. Paul, Minnesota.

Kimberly Dawsey-Richardson (M.Div., Bethel Seminary) is a minister at Fletcher Hills Presbyterian Church in San Diego, California.

Joshua Dean (B.A., North Park University) is a recent university graduate.

Bruce A. Demarest (Ph.D., University of Manchester) is professor of Christian theology and spiritual formation at Denver Seminary in Littleton, Colorado.

Margaret Diddams (Ph.D., New York University) is chair of psychology at Seattle Pacific University in Seattle, Washington.

Allan Effa (Ph.D., Fuller Theological Seminary) is the Ray and Edith DeNeui Professor of Intercultural Studies at Taylor Seminary in Edmonton, Canada.

Matthew A. Elliott (Ph.D., University of Aberdeen) is the president of Oasis International in Chicago, Illinois.

Christopher J. Ellis (Ph.D., University of Leeds, United Kingdom) pastors a Baptist church and teaches at the University of Nottingham in the United Kingdom.

Leif Gunnar Engedal (Ph.D., University of Oslo) is professor of practical theology at the Norwegian Lutheran School of Theology in Oslo, Norway.

Victor I. Ezigbo (Ph.D. University of Edinburgh) is assistant professor of theology at Bethel University in St. Paul, Minnesota.

David Frees (M.Th., Cornerstone University) is former senior acquisitions editor for Zondervan in Grand Rapids, Michigan.

Sharon Gallagher (M.T.S., Graduate Theological Union, Berkeley) is associate director of New College Berkeley and editor of *Radix* magazine.

Timoteo D. Gener (Ph.D., Fuller Theological Seminary) is associate professor at Asian Theological Seminary in Quezon City, Philippines.

Linde J. Getahun (Ph.D., University of Minnesota) is associate professor of psychology at Bethel University in St. Paul, Minnesota.

Kevin Giles (Th.D., Australian College of Theology) is vicar of St. Michael's Church in North Carlton, Australia.

Catherine Gunsalus González (Ph.D., Boston University) is professor emerita of church history at Columbia Theological Seminary in Decatur, Georgia.

Justo L. González (Ph.D., Yale University) is a church historian who has taught at many institutions, including the Evangelical Seminary of Puerto Rico and Emory University in Atlanta, Georgia.

Ondina E. González (Ph.D., Emory University) is a specialist in colonial Latin America who has taught at, among other institutions, Emory University and Agnes Scott College in Atlanta, Georgia.

Emilie Griffin (B.A., Tulane University) is an independent scholar and author.

Steven R. Guthrie (Ph.D., University of St. Andrews) is associate professor of theology and directs the Religion and the Arts program at Belmont University in Nashville, Tennessee.

Christopher A. Hall (Ph.D., Drew University) is chancellor of Eastern University in St. Davids, Pennsylvania, and dean of its Templeton Honors College.

Geordan Hammond (Ph.D., University of Manchester) is tutor in church history and administrator of the Manchester Wesley Research Centre at Nazarene Theological College in Manchester, United Kingdom.

Maxine Hancock (Ph.D., University of Alberta) is professor of interdisciplinary studies and spiritual theology at Regent College in Vancouver, Canada.

Wayne S. Hansen (Ph.D., Drew University) is professor of theology at Bethel Seminary of the East in Willow Grove, Pennsylvania.

Michael A. G. Haykin (Ph.D., University of Toronto) is professor of church history and biblical spirituality at the Southern Baptist Theological Seminary in Louisville, Kentucky.

Elaine A. Heath (Ph.D., Duquesne University) is McCreless Assistant Professor of Evangelism at Southern Methodist University in Dallas, Texas.

Natalie Hendrickson (M.Div., Bethel Seminary) is director of Supervised Ministry and Student Assessment at Bethel Seminary in San Diego, California.

Bruce Herman (M.F.A., Boston University) is Lothlórien Distinguished Chair in the Fine Arts at Gordon College in Wenham, Massachusetts.

Wil Hernandez (Ph.D., Fuller Theological Seminary) is owner and manager of the Nouwen Legacy.

Joshua L. Hickok (M.B.A., North Park University) is a recent university graduate.

D. Bruce Hindmarsh (D.Phil., Oxford University) is James M. Houston Professor of Spiritual Theology at Regent College, Vancouver, Canada.

E. Glenn Hinson (D.Phil., University of Oxford) is senior professor of church history and spirituality at Baptist Seminary of Kentucky in Lexington, Kentucky.

Dennis P. Hollinger (Ph.D., Drew University) is president and the Coleman M. Mockler Distinguished Professor of Christian Ethics at Gordon-Conwell Theological Seminary in South Hamilton, Massachusetts.

Bradley P. Holt (Ph.D., Yale University) is professor of religion at Augsburg College in Minneapolis, Minnesota.

James M. Houston (D.Phil., Oxford University) is Board of Governors' Professor of Spiritual Theology and the first principal of Regent College in Vancouver, Canada.

David M. Howard Jr. (Ph.D., University of Michigan) is professor of Old Testament at Bethel Seminary in St. Paul, Minnesota.

Evan B. Howard (Ph.D., Graduate Theological Union) is director of Spirituality Shoppe: An Evangelical Center for the Study of Christian Spirituality, in Montrose, Colorado.

Edith M. Humphrey (Ph.D., McGill University) is William F. Orr Professor of New Testament at Pittsburgh Theological Seminary in Pittsburgh, Pennsylvania.

Klaus Issler (Ph.D., Michigan State University) is professor of Christian education and theology at Talbot School of Theology of Biola University in La Mirada, California.

Peter J. Jankowski (Ph.D., Texas Tech University) is associate professor of psychology at Bethel University in St. Paul, Minnesota.

L. Paul Jensen (Ph.D., Fuller Theological Seminary) is founder and director of the Leadership Institute in Orange, California, and an adjunct professor at Fuller Theological Seminary in Pasadena, California.

R. Boaz Johnson (Ph.D., Trinity International University) is associate professor and chair, Department of Biblical and Theological Studies, North Park University in Chicago, Illinois.

Todd E. Johnson (Ph.D., University of Notre Dame) is the Brehm Chair of Worship, Theology and the Arts at Fuller Theological Seminary in Pasadena, California.

Robert K. Johnston (Ph.D., Duke University) is professor of theology and culture and co-director of the Reel Spirituality Institute at Fuller Theological Seminary in Pasadena, California.

Richard F. Kantzer (M.Phil., Yale University) is professor of theology at Bethel Seminary of the East in Willow Grove, Pennsylvania.

Matthew Kemp (B.A., North Park University) is currently a graduate student.

Mabiala Justin-Robert Kenzo (Ph.D., Trinity Evangelical Divinity School) is professor of systematic theology at Ambrose Seminary in Calgary, Alberta, and at the Faculté de Théologie Evangélique de Boma in the Democratic Republic of Congo.

Norm Klassen (D.Phil., University of Oxford) is associate professor and chair of the Department of English at St. Jerome's University in Waterloo, Ontario, Canada.

Alan Kolp (Ph.D., Harvard University) holds the Moll Chair in Faith and Life at Baldwin-Wallace College in Berea, Ohio.

Gisela H. Kreglinger (Ph.D., University of St. Andrews) is assistant professor of spiritual formation at Beeson Divinity School in Birmingham, Alabama.

Kiem-Kiok Kwa (Ph.D., Asbury Theological Seminary) is lecturer at East Asia School of Theology in Singapore.

Brian C. Labosier (Ph.D., Westminster Theological Seminary) is professor of biblical studies at Bethel Seminary of the East in Willow Grove, Pennsylvania.

Joel Lawrence (Ph.D., Cambridge University) is assistant professor of theology at Bethel Seminary in St. Paul, Minnesota.

John R. Lillis (Ph.D., Michigan State University) is dean and executive officer at Bethel Seminary in San Diego, California.

Ben K. Lim (Ph.D., Texas Tech University) is associate professor of marriage and family therapy at Bethel Seminary in San Diego, California.

Michael Lodahl (Ph.D., Emory University) is professor of theology and world religions at Point Loma Nazarene University in San Diego, California.

Heather Looy (Ph.D., McMaster University) is associate professor of psychology at the King's University College in Edmonton, Canada.

Kin-Yip Louie (Ph.D., University of Edinburgh) is assistant professor of theological studies at China Graduate School of Theology in Hong Kong.

Nora O. Lozano (Ph.D., Drew University) is associate professor of theological studies at Baptist University of the Américas in San Antonio, Texas.

Wonsuk Ma (Ph.D., Fuller Theological Seminary) is executive director of the Oxford Centre for Mission Studies in Oxford, England.

Frank D. Macchia (Th.D., University of Basel) is professor of systematic theology at Vanguard University of Southern California in Costa Mesa, California.

Michael Mangis (Ph.D., University of Wyoming) is professor of psychology at Wheaton College and cofounder of the Center for Rural Psychology in Elburn, Illinois.

Kevin W. Mannoia (Ph.D., University of North Texas) is chair of the Wesleyan Holiness Consortium and chaplain at Azusa Pacific University in Azusa, California.

Dennis D. Martin (Ph.D., University of Waterloo) is associate professor of theology at Loyola University in Chicago, Illinois.

William R. McAlpine (Ph.D., University of Aberdeen) is associate professor of practical theology at Ambrose University College in Calgary, Canada.

Mark W. McCloskey (Ph.D., University of South Florida) is professor of ministry leadership at Bethel Seminary in St. Paul, Minnesota.

Martin Mittelstadt (Ph.D., Marquette University) is associate professor of New Testament at Evangel University in Springfield, Missouri.

David Montzingo (M.Div., Gordon-Conwell Theological Seminary) is rector of Holy Spirit Anglican Church and Faculty Associate at Bethel Seminary in San Diego, California.

David Morris (M.T.S., Southern Methodist University) is a graduate student at Bethel Seminary in San Diego, California.

Christopher Morton (Ph.D., University of Manchester) is the chief theological and cultural researcher for the Navigators and theological reviewer with NavPress in Colorado Springs, Colorado.

Terry C. Muck (Ph.D., Northwestern University) is dean and professor of mission and world religion at Asbury Theological Seminary in Wilmore, Kentucky.

John M. Mulder (Ph.D., Princeton University) is the former president of Louisville Presbyterian Theological Seminary in Louisville, Kentucky.

M. Robert Mulholland Jr. (Th.D., Harvard University) is professor of New Testament at Asbury Theological Seminary in Wilmore, Kentucky.

John Mustol (M.Div., Bethel Seminary San Diego) is a graduate student at Fuller Theological Seminary in Pasadena, California.

Glenn E. Myers (Ph.D., Boston University) is professor of church history and theological studies at Crown College in St. Bonifacius, Minnesota.

David S. Nah (Ph.D., Claremont Graduate University) is assistant professor of theology at Bethel Seminary in St. Paul, Minnesota.

Bradley Nassif (Ph.D., Fordham University) is professor of biblical and theological studies at North Park University in Chicago, Illinois.

Paul L. Neeley (Ph.D., University of Ghana) is president of the International Council of Ethnodoxologists and teaches at various schools and seminaries.

Holly Faith Nelson (Ph.D., Simon Fraser University) is associate professor of English at Trinity Western University in Langley, British Columbia, Canada.

Charles W. Nienkirchen (Ph.D., University of Waterloo) is professor of Christian history and spirituality at Ambrose University College in Calgary, Canada.

Dennis Okholm (Ph.D., Princeton Theological Seminary) is professor of theology at Azusa Pacific University in Azusa, California.

Kim Olstad (M.A., University of San Francisco) is a graduate student at Bethel Seminary in St. Paul, Minnesota.

André Ong (Ph.D., Claremont Graduate University) is founding and senior pastor of International Christian Church, and faculty associate at Bethel Seminary in San Diego, California.

Julie Oostra (B.A., North Park University) is a recent university graduate.

J. I. Packer (D.Phil., University of Oxford) is the Board of Governors' Professor of Theology at Regent College in Vancouver, Canada.

Renē Padilla (Ph.D., University of Manchester) is international president of Tearfund in Buenos Aires, Argentina.

Gino Pasquariello (Ed.D., Azusa Pacific University) is professor of theological and historical studies at Horizon College in San Diego, California.

Richard V. Peace (Ph.D., University of Natal, South Africa) is the Robert Boyd Munger Professor of Evangelism and Spiritual Formation at Fuller Theological Seminary in Pasadena, California.

Carrie Peffley (M.Phil., Cambridge University) is instructor in philosophy at Bethel University in St. Paul, Minnesota.

Timothy Scott Perry (Ph.D., Durham University) is associate professor of theology and ethics at Providence Theological Seminary near Winnipeg, Canada.

Greg Peters (Ph.D., University of St. Michael's College) is assistant professor of medieval and spiritual theology at Biola University in La Mirada, California.

Eugene H. Peterson (M.A., Johns Hopkins University) is professor emeritus of spiritual theology at Regent College in Vancouver, Canada.

Paul Peucker (Ph.D., University of Utrecht) is archivist at the Moravian Archives and teaches Moravian History at Moravian College in Bethlehem, Pennsylvania.

Susan S. Phillips (Ph.D., University of California, Berkeley) is executive director and professor of sociology and Christianity at New College Berkeley, an affiliate of Berkeley's Graduate Theological Union in California.

Richard V. Pierard (Ph.D., University of Iowa) is Stephen Phillips Professor of History at Gordon College in Wenham, Massachusetts.

Clark H. Pinnock (Ph.D., University of Manchester) was the professor emeritus of systematic theology at McMaster Divinity College in Hamilton, Ontario, Canada.

Steve L. Porter (Ph.D., University of Southern California) is associate professor of theology and philosophy at Biola University Institute for Spiritual Formation, Talbot School of Theology, and at Rosemead School of Psychology in La Mirada, California.

T. C. Porter (M.Div., Bethel Seminary San Diego) is an urban missionary and founding pastor of Adams Avenue Crossing in San Diego, California.

Brian Post (Psy.D., Wheaton College) is a licensed clinical psychologist and visiting assistant professor of psychology at Wheaton College in Wheaton, Illinois.

John P. Powell (D.Min., Fuller Theological Seminary) is senior pastor of the Point Loma Community Presbyterian Church in San Diego, California.

Pamela Baker Powell (D.Min., Pittsburgh Theological Seminary) is faculty associate in pastoral theology at Bethel Seminary in San Diego, California.

Robert V. Rakestraw (Ph.D., Drew University) is professor emeritus of theology at Bethel Seminary in St. Paul, Minnesota.

Kevin S. Reimer (Ph.D., Fuller Theological Seminary) is professor of graduate psychology at Azusa Pacific University in Asuza, California.

Wyndy Corbin Reuschling (Ph.D., Drew University) is professor of ethics and theology at Ashland Theological Seminary in Ashland, Ohio.

Bruce Rideout (Ph.D., University of California, Davis) is director of Wildlife Disease Laboratories at the San Diego Zoo's Institute for Conservation Research in San Diego, California.

Debra Rienstra (Ph.D., Rutgers University) is associate professor of English at Calvin College in Grand Rapids, Michigan.

Kyle A. Roberts (Ph.D., Trinity Evangelical Divinity School) is assistant professor of systematic theology at Bethel Seminary in St. Paul, Minnesota.

David L. Rowe (Ph.D., University of Virginia) is professor of history at Middle Tennessee State University in Murfreesboro, Tennessee.

Leland Ryken (Ph.D., University of Oregon) is professor of English at Wheaton College in Wheaton, Illinois.

Steve J. Sandage (Ph.D., Virginia Commonwealth University) is associate professor of marriage and family studies at Bethel Seminary in St. Paul, Minnesota.

Cheryl J. Sanders (Th.D., Harvard University) is professor of Christian ethics at Howard University School of Divinity and senior pastor of Third Street Church of God in Washington, D.C.

Fred Sanders (Ph.D., Graduate Theological Union) is associate professor of the Torrey Honors Institute at Biola University in La Mirada, California.

Mary E. Sanders (M.A.M.F.T., Bethel Seminary) is associate dean for Student Learning Outcomes and director of Spiritual and Personal Formation Programs at Bethel Seminary in St. Paul, Minnesota.

Alethea Savoy (B.A., North Park University) is currently a graduate student.

Tom Schwanda (Ph.D., Durham University) is associate professor of Christian formation and ministry at Wheaton College, Wheaton, Illinois.

Glen G. Scorgie (Ph.D., University of St. Andrews) is professor of theology at Bethel Seminary in San Diego, California.

Kate Scorgie (Ph.D., University of Alberta, Canada) is professor of advanced education studies at Azusa Pacific University in Azusa, California.

Sarah G. Scorgie (B.A., San Diego State University) is a recent university graduate.

Myrla Seibold (Ph.D., Fuller Theological Seminary) is a licensed psychologist and professor of psychology at Bethel University in St. Paul, Minnesota.

Herman Selderhuis (Th.D., Theologische Universiteit Apeldoorn) is professor of church history at the University of Apeldoorn in the Netherlands.

Peter M. Sensenig (M.Div., Palmer Theological Seminary) is a doctoral student at Fuller Theological Seminary in Pasadena, California.

Joseph Shao (Ph.D., Hebrew Union College) is president and professor of the Hebrew Bible at the Biblical Seminary of the Philippines in Manila, and general secretary of the Asia Theological Association.

Gerald L. Sittser (Ph.D., University of Chicago) is professor of theology at Whitworth University in Spokane, Washington.

Aaron T. Smith (Ph.D., Marquette University) is assistant professor of theology at Colorado Christian University in Lakewood, Colorado.

Gordon T. Smith (Ph.D., Loyola School of Theology, Ateneo de Manila University) is president of reSource Leadership International in Richmond, British Columbia, Canada.

Ian Smith (B.A., North Park University) is a recent university graduate.

James D. Smith III (Th.D., Harvard University) is professor of church history at Bethel Seminary in San Diego, California.

Rebecca Wilds Smith (B.A., Bethel University) is a teacher in Minneapolis, Minnesota.

Robert M. Solomon (Ph.D., University of Edinburgh) is bishop of the Methodist Church in Singapore.

Carole Dale Spencer (Ph.D., University of Birmingham, United Kingdom) is director of the Friends Center and adjunct professor of church history and spiritual formation at George Fox Evangelical Seminary in Portland, Oregon.

Mark Stanton (Ph.D., Fuller Theological Seminary) is dean and professor of behavioral and applied sciences at Azusa Pacific University in Azusa, California.

Glen Harold Stassen (Ph.D., Duke University) is Lewis B. Smedes Professor of Christian Ethics at Fuller Theological Seminary in Pasadena, California.

Todd Statham (M.Div., The Presbyterian College, Montreal) is a doctoral candidate at McGill University in Montreal, Canada.

Carrie Steenwyk (M.T.S., Calvin Theological Seminary) is coordinator of research and publications at the Calvin Institute of Christian Worship at Calvin College in Grand Rapids, Michigan.

R. Paul Stevens (D.Min., Fuller Theological Seminary) is emeritus professor of marketplace theology at Regent College in Vancouver, Canada.

Diane B. Stinton (Ph.D., University of Edinburgh) is associate professor of theology at the Africa International University and Nairobi Evangelical Graduate School of Theology in Nairobi, Kenya.

Mark L. Strauss (Ph.D., University of Aberdeen) is professor of New Testament at Bethel Seminary in San Diego, California.

Brad D. Strawn (Ph.D., Fuller Theological Seminary) is dean of the chapel and vice president for Spiritual Development at Southern Nazarene University in Bethany, Oklahoma.

Jane Strohl (Ph.D., University of Chicago) is professor of Reformation history and theology at Pacific Lutheran Theological Seminary in Berkeley, California.

Steven M. Studebaker (Ph.D., Marquette University) is assistant professor of historical and systematic theology, and Howard and Shirley Bentll Chair of Evangelical Thought at McMaster Divinity College in Hamilton, Ontario, Canada.

Sarah Sumner (Ph.D., Trinity Evangelical Divinity School) is dean of A. W. Tozer Theological Seminary in Redding, California.

Scott W. Sunquist (Ph.D., Princeton Theological Seminary) is professor of world Christianity at Pittsburgh Theological Seminary in Pittsburgh, Pennsylvania.

Lynn R. Szabo (M.A., University of British Columbia) is associate professor and chair of the English department at Trinity Western University in Langley, British Columbia, Canada.

Rosalind Lim Tan (Ph.D., Asia Graduate School of Theology) is director of the Holistic Child Development Institute at Malaysia Baptist Theological Seminary in Penang, Malaysia.

Sunny Boon Sang Tan (Ph.D., Asia Graduate Baptist Theological Seminary) is academic dean at Malaysia Baptist Theological Seminary in Penang, Malaysia.

John Christopher Thomas (Ph.D., University of Sheffield) is Clarence J. Abbott Professor of Biblical Studies at the Church of God Theological Seminary in Cleveland, Tennessee.

Judith Tiersma-Watson (Ph.D., Fuller Theological Seminary) is associate professor of urban mission in the School of Intercultural Studies at Fuller Theological Seminary in Pasadena, California.

Terrance L. Tiessen (Ph.D., Ateneo de Manila University) is professor emeritus of systematic theology and ethics at Providence Theological Seminary near Winnipeg, Canada.

Ruth A. Tucker (Ph.D., Northern Illinois University) is teacher, author, and conference speaker in Grand Rapids, Michigan.

John Tyson (Ph.D., Drew University) is professor of theology at Houghton College in Houghton, New York.

Melvin P. Unger (D.M.A., University of Illinois at Urbana-Champaign) is a choral conductor and director of the Riemenschneider Bach Institute at the Baldwin-Wallace College Conservatory in Berea, Ohio.

Heidi Unruh (M.A., Palmer Theological Seminary) is director of the Congregations, Community Outreach and Leadership Development Project of Evangelicals for Social Action.

Bernie Van De Walle (Ph.D., Drew University) is associate professor of historical and systematic theology at Ambrose University College in Calgary, Canada.

Mary M. Veeneman (Ph.D., Fordham University) is assistant professor of biblical and theological studies at North Park University in Chicago, Illinois.

Johanna Knutson Vignol (B.A., Point Loma Nazarene University) is a teaching assistant at Bethel Seminary in San Diego, California.

John A. Vissers (Th.D., University of Toronto) is principal of The Presbyterian College, Montreal, and adjunct professor of Christian theology at McGill University in Montreal, Canada.

James L. Wakefield (Ph.D., Marquette University) is associate professor of biblical and spiritual theology at Salt Lake Theological Seminary in Salt Lake City, Utah.

Douglas D. Webster (Ph.D., University of St. Michael's College) is professor of pastoral theology and Christian preaching at Beeson Divinity School in Birmingham, Alabama.

Roy Whitaker (M.A., Harvard University) is lecturer of religious studies at San Diego State University in San Diego, California.

Loren Wilkinson (Ph.D., Syracuse University) is professor of interdisciplinary studies and philosophy at Regent College, Vancouver, Canada.

Mary Ruth K. Wilkinson (M.A., University of Illinois) is sessional lecturer at Regent College in Vancouver, Canada.

Dallas Willard (Ph.D., University of Wisconsin) is professor of philosophy at University of Southern California in Los Angeles, California.

Edwin M. Willmington (D.M.A., University of Arizona) is director of the Fred Bock Institute of Music at the Brehm Center for Worship, Theology and the Arts at Fuller Theological Seminary in Pasadena, California.

Christian T. Collins Winn (Ph.D., Drew University) is assistant professor of historical and systematic theology at Bethel University in St. Paul, Minnesota.

John D. Witvliet (Ph.D., University of Notre Dame) is director of the Calvin Institute of Christian Worship and professor of worship at Calvin College and Calvin Theological Seminary in Grand Rapids, Michigan.

J. Dudley Woodberry (Ph.D., Harvard University) is dean emeritus and senior professor of Islamic studies, School of Intercultural Studies, at Fuller Theological Seminary in Pasadena, California.

John E. Worgul (Ph.D., Dropsie College) is an Anglican priest and dean of Holy Trinity Theological College and Seminary in Towson, Maryland.

Wendy M. Wright (Ph.D., University of California, Santa Barbara) is professor of theology at Creighton University in Omaha, Nebraska.

Hing-Kau (Jason) Yeung (Ph.D., London University) is professor and director of the Chinese Culture Research Centre at China Graduate School of Theology in Hong Kong.

Amos Yong (Ph.D., Boston University) is J. Rodman Williams Professor of Theology and director of the Doctor of Philosophy Program in the School of Divinity of Regent University in Virginia Beach, Virginia.

Ronald F. Youngblood (Ph.D., Dropsie College) is professor emeritus of Old Testament and Hebrew at Bethel Seminary in San Diego, California.

Jason Zuidema (Ph.D., McGill University) is lecturer in historical theology at Farel Reformed Theological Seminary in Montreal, Canada.

Phil C. Zylla (Th.D., University of South Africa) is academic dean and associate professor of pastoral theology at McMaster Divinity College in Hamilton, Ontario, Canada.

PART ONE

INTEGRATIVE PERSPECTIVES

CHAPTER 1

OVERVIEW OF CHRISTIAN SPIRITUALITY

GLEN G. SCORGIE

Terms such as *spirituality*, *spiritual theology*, and *Christian formation* circulate freely now. While they may sound novel to some, the things in themselves, to which the terms refer, are as old as the faith itself and familiar terrain for devout believers.

Christian spirituality is the domain of lived Christian experience. It is about living *all of life*— not just some esoteric portion of it—before God, through Christ, in the transforming and empowering presence of the Holy Spirit. And precisely because this lived experience of the Christian is the existential heart of the faith, its careful examination and nurture are vitally important.

Admittedly, *spiritual* (adjective) and *spirituality* (noun) have been slippery concepts with, as is so often the case with venerable terminology, somewhat quirky histories. In the past, they have been used to differentiate the otherworldly from the concrete, church-related matters from those of the state, or people in religious orders from ordinary laypersons. But spirituality began its semantic journey in the New Testament itself, where the apostle Paul used *pneumatikoi* (literally, spiritual persons) to describe people who keep in step with the *pneuma* (Spirit) of God. This canonical point of departure for spirituality-talk is instructive, for it reminds us, all subsequent permutations of the word notwithstanding, that Christian spirituality is ultimately about being attentive to the Holy Spirit's voice, open to his transforming impulses, and empowered by his indwelling presence. It is always *Spirit*-uality (Fee, 5).

But spirituality, as it is used in general discourse, has a somewhat different meaning. Spirituality in its generic sense is about connecting with the transcendent and being changed by it. It involves an *encounter* with the transcendent (or the numinous, the Real, or whatever is ultimately important) and then the beneficial *effects* of that encounter on a person or a community. It is about establishing a transforming connection to something more—a connection that will shape who we become and how we will live.

Christians affirm a distinct version of this definition. Through the corrective lens of biblical revelation, the transcendent reality of generic spirituality comes into focus as the living, personal triune God. And the effects of encounter include growing in Christlikeness and participating in the larger purposes of God.

Two concepts of Christian spirituality—one narrow, the other holistic—now circulate. The narrow version is concerned with experiencing the presence, voice, and consolations of God in a direct, right-here-right-now way. It pursues what have been aptly called "esoteric moments" and "points of wonder" (Humphrey, 5).

Authentic Christianity has always celebrated the possibility of experiencing God in this direct and interactive manner. At the same time, it has insisted that there is more to being a Christian than this. Holistic spirituality is about living *all of life* before God. It retains an important place for experiences, but it involves more. It also includes things like repentance, moral renewal, soul crafting, community building, witness, service, and faithfulness to one's calling.

Spirituality can be difficult to conceptualize if we are accustomed to thinking of Christianity as chiefly a matter of doctrines to believe and duties to perform. To be sure, it is grounded in convictions—and ones with behavioral implications. Yet above all it is a lived experience, one that involves a unique way of seeing, a special gestalt of emotions, values, and aspirations, and a distinct consciousness and sensibility.

To mention the human spirit is not to suggest that there is a mysterious extra component—a special "God chip"—embedded in or alongside the human soul. It signifies, rather, our unique human capacity to connect with the transcendent in that interior space where deep calls to deep. Nor is this interior domain some privatized region sealed off from, and largely irrelevant to, the more important world of "real life." Rather, this region of the heart, as Jesus said, constitutes the very wellspring of our responses to life (Luke 6:45). It is decisive and determinative of everything else.

Spirituality, precisely because it is a historical and experiential phenomenon, lends itself to descriptive, nonevaluative study. By contrast, *spiritual theology* is prescriptive, constructive, and prophetic. The former describes what has been and what is, while the latter proposes what ought to be. Spiritual theology summarizes the implications of relevant scriptural teaching, probes the doctrinal foundations of a genuinely Christian spirituality, and recommends means to achieve the prescribed goals.

The popular term *spiritual formation* properly signals the importance of soul crafting and positive change in individual believers. It is through disciplined, attentive dependence on the impulses of the indwelling Holy Spirit that believers are privileged to participate in the renewing work of God within them. Yet formation should probably not be treated as a synonym for the totality of Christian spiritual-

ity, because the latter is a broader reality. Whenever formation is dislocated from its proper relational context and neglectful of the necessary divine impulses, it becomes a mere portfolio of spiritual disciplines and another grinding self-improvement project.

Evangelical Commitment

Christian spirituality is embedded in traditions and fostered in communities. It is impossible, even if it were desirable, to approach the matter from a completely detached point of view. Each of us is necessarily located in a tradition and will reflect something of its shared assumptions, perspectives, and sensitivities in our work. While not all its contributors identify themselves as evangelicals, this reference work reflects in general terms an evangelical consciousness and commitment.

The term *evangelical* is fraught with ambiguity today. Here it is employed to designate a broad tradition of experiential religion rooted in the Protestant Reformation and its Bible-centered approach to the Christian faith (Bebbington; Haykin and Stewart). At the heart of evangelical spirituality, as articulated by Jonathan Edwards, John Wesley, and others, is a liberating consciousness of unconditional grace and divine embrace, and an expectation that this God of grace will continue to be encountered, and his voice heard, chiefly through Scripture. Also central to evangelical spirituality is a perception of God's pleasure when the gospel, the biblical narrative of grace, is shared with others, or when believers otherwise contribute to its credible dissemination. There is a shining brightness, as well as a shadow side, to the evangelical inclination toward activism. Often the contours of evangelical spirituality are manifested less in formal creeds and confessions, and more in the hymnody and songs of the movement. In many ways, evangelical spirituality follows its own singing or, to use Mark Noll's felicitous phrase, *lex cantandi* (Noll and Thiemman, 10).

The evangelical tradition has its own distinct spirituality, and the distinctive themes and key figures of this tradition will receive a degree of recognition in this volume that has not always been accorded them elsewhere. At the same time, a generous evangelical spirituality acknowledges the limitations of its own history and identity, and seeks to incorporate everything from the wider ecumenical tradition of Christian spirituality that is good and consistent with its own core consciousness.

To be a Christian is not to craft a customized personal spirituality, but to find one's place in a larger movement. There is a broad and generous Christian tradition that goes back two millennia to its roots in the biblical writers' encounters and journeys with God. The Christian faith spread outward from its Judean birthplace, most notably in northerly and westerly directions. As it did so, it took on the color and nuance of the regions and cultures into which it flowed. Divisions within the church also contributed to its diversification. In the 11th century, the church fractured along a roughly east-west fault line, and nearly five hundred years later the Protestant Reformation split the Western church. Out of all this dividing, multiple trajectories of Christian spirituality were launched.

Today Roman Catholic, Orthodox, and Protestant (including evangelical) believers in quest of spiritual renewal are reconnecting with long-lost relatives. Each of these three great streams possesses a distinct character and grace. East and West offer rich mystical and juridical orientations to the Christian life, while the Protestant tradition celebrates the joyful and transforming experience of Christ's forgiveness and righteousness. Each possesses resources to be selectively appropriated by previously estranged members of the one Christian family.

Christianity has become a global religion. Consequently, no serious conversation about Christian spirituality can remain merely Western or otherwise parochially bounded, but now must include diverse and insightful voices from around the world. The globalization of Christianity also means that Christian spirituality is acquiring new faces as it becomes contextualized into various cultures.

Within this newer context of shared insights and practices, evangelicals are drawn especially to resources that resonate with the spirituality of the biblical writers themselves (Bowe), and are "accessible" to the whole people of God. They identify most readily with motivations that are consistent with their own assurance of grace and are compelled by the same gratitude they feel. They tend to take ownership of those elements of the Christian spiritual heritage that celebrate the cross of Christ as a saving death, highlight liberating encounter with the living Christ, and attend carefully to the disposition of one's heart (Spener).

Dynamics of Christian Spirituality

From an evangelical perspective, the mystery of a life lived before God through Christ and in the power of the Holy Spirit cannot be reduced to a "one size fits all" formula. The Spirit remains free like the wind that "blows wherever it pleases" (John 3:8). The best we can do is to identify some pervading themes and recurring emphases. The encouraging thing is that through it all the Holy Spirit manifests a signature style.

Despite the diversity of historic Christian spirituality, certain recurring dynamics or themes become obvious. We will better appreciate these dynamics if we recall first of all what it means to be human and then remember Scripture's analysis of what is wrong with us now. As we shall see, each dynamic of Christian spirituality addresses an aspect of our pathological condition and thereby renews a dimension of God's original design for us.

We were created for community, but our sin has produced alienation. By his Spirit, Christ is restoring our intimacy with God, others, and nature. The first dynamic then is a *relational* one. There is a God, and there are people like us; and as humans we share this world with a myriad of other creatures. The fact is that we are not alone. The impulses of this dynamic move vertically and horizontally. The Bible attaches great importance to relationship with God, and prayer is preeminently the practice of keeping company with him.

Once we open ourselves up to God, other things begin to change as well. The life of God, which is characterized by self-giving love, turns out to be mysteriously contagious (Rom. 5:5). Experiencing it creates a *general* disposition within the soul to embrace rather than exclude other human beings as well (Volf). Love for God and love for neighbor are both expressions of the same divine impulse.

We were also created holy and whole, but our sin has damaged us. By his Spirit, Christ is purifying and healing our true selves. This is the transformational dynamic of Christian spirituality. True friendship with God is always *transforming* friendship (Houston). It never sanctions the status quo.

Classic Christian spirituality has taken the challenge of the sinful self seriously, practiced self-examination, intentionally cultivated virtue, and embraced spiritual disciplines. The goal is the transformation of the inner command center of one's being. But there is another side to this whole story as well. Sin is never good for us. It always injures and disfigures. Part of the good news is that God is also our Healer (Ex. 15:26). By his grace we are destined to become whole as well as holy. And so the Christian tradition abounds with imagery of soul surgery and medicine as well as rigorous conditioning and training.

We were created for joyful participation in God's work in the world, but sin has made our existence seem futile. By his Spirit, Christ is rebuilding purpose and meaning into our lives. Thus, the Christian life is also about doing. The third dynamic of true Christian spirituality is the *vocational*. In other words, we have a calling on our lives to participate in the purposes of God. Authentic Christian spirituality follows the pattern of the incarnation—it becomes flesh. Vocation is following the heart of God into the world.

These three dynamics are more than sequential steps to spiritual growth; they are ongoing realities of the Christian life. The relational, transformational, and vocational are always vitally connected, overlapping, and interdependent. It is not possible to choose one and neglect the others. In summary, authentic Christian spirituality (or the Christian life, which is the same thing) is a Spirit-enabled relationship with the triune God that results in openness to others, healing progress toward Christlikeness, and willing participation in God's purposes in the world.

The longings of the human spirit are most fully satisfied in Jesus Christ, as we encounter him through his Holy Spirit. From a Christ-centered perspective, the first dynamic is about Christ *with* us. The second concerns Christ *in* us, and the third is about Christ working *through* us. By his Spirit, then, Christ is inviting people to come to him, submit to his transforming influence, and then follow him into the world. The pattern is always the same. True spirituality involves continuous cycles of encounter, change, and action. The three are interconnected, and each is essential to life as God intended it to be.

The Cloud of Witnesses

The literature of Christian spirituality provides ample resources for nourishing all three aforementioned dynamics. It is also worth noting that different writers and spiritual traditions tend sometimes to emphasize different dynamics and give priority to one over the others.

First there are the mystical writers. These contemplative figures have left a great legacy of insight into the nature of deep communion with God. Often they were women who responded to the gender restrictions imposed on them in patriarchal societies by cultivating their interior life with

God—to the blessing of women and men ever since.

The monastic tradition has explored the transformational impulse with great passion. To the ranks of monastic figures through the centuries we would also add Protestant Puritans, and later on John Wesley, and after him numerous Holiness figures who sought entire sanctification and perfect love. Into this same transformational category we can add those who work at the intersection of Christian faith and therapy to bring healing to wounded souls.

Finally, there are the mission-focused writers. These are the visionary spiritual leaders whose compassion, evangelistic zeal, or sensitivity to the demands of justice has led them to attempt great things for God in the world. The passion of their work is to be obedient in service and to do ministry in the name of Christ.

We are wise to embrace the full scope of our spiritual heritage. The mystics inspire us by their passion for God and teach us about creating space for him. But by itself the mystical pursuit can become self-serving and even narcissistic. The call to holiness is central to the biblical revelation and key to our liberation and the restoration of God's image in us. But on its own, to the neglect of everything else, this impulse can breed legalism. Authentic spirituality finds its completion in eager, obedient action. Nevertheless, an exclusive fixation on mission and doing can also have negative results. Divorced from the other two dimensions, it can lead to secularized activism.

The history of Christian spirituality is a vast panorama. It includes martyrs who embraced death to be closer to Christ, people who sought soul-purification in the isolated dunes of the Egyptian desert, and others like the judicious Benedict who commended a rhythmic life of work and prayer. It embraces the celebration of God's presence in nature by Francis and Clare of Assisi, the passionate imitation of Christ practiced by Thomas à Kempis, the baptized imagination of Teresa of Avila, the mystical wisdom of Julian of Norwich, the cultivated stillness of the Hesychasts, the moral outrage of abolitionist Quakers, the intrepid adventures of Amy Carmichael, the fortitude of Wang Ming Dao, and the self-forgetful raptures of modern Pentecostals. Out of all of this has emerged a kaleidoscope of enduring schools and traditions of Christian spirituality. Each has its distinctive grace and special testimony to the larger community of faith.

Across the years, Christians have embraced different inspirational profiles of the ideal Christian. They have likewise emphasized different means by which grace is mediated to us, including art and music, poetry, liturgy, and sacred space. The portals to transformation have been variously identified. Everyone agrees that sin should be resisted and virtue cultivated. But which sins should be most resisted and which virtues most nurtured are subjects of considerable difference of opinion. The same has been true of Christian understandings of what it means to imitate Christ and how to pursue this goal with disciplined intent.

Certain tensions persist through the years. For example, there is an intuition that spirituality is to be cultivated by the whole people of God, regardless of their vocation, and not just for an elite group of exceptional "athletes of the spirit." This was a celebrated theme of the Reformation, and recently Vatican II affirmed the "universal call to holiness" (Abbott, 65–72). Yet there remains a pressing need for inspirational models and heroes—for saints, if you will—to withstand the pervasive pressures to downsize Christian spirituality to a lowest common denominator.

Another persistent tension comes from the fact that human beings are cosmic amphibians—wired to connect to the transcendent while being rooted in the material world. There is a deep strain of "other-worldliness" in the history of Christian spirituality, an inclination to withdraw from the temptations, distractions, and banalities of everyday life to focus on things perceived to matter more. This ascetical impulse is frequently blamed on the persistent shadow of Plato, yet this may not be entirely fair. The call to detachment from the world is embedded deeply in the Scriptures themselves. Yet equally so is the call to active service in the world — living out the principle of the incarnation that Jesus himself embodied. Indeed, Jesus as portrayed in the Gospels demonstrated a rhythmic life of renewing retreat and active social engagement. But how this ideal is approximated in the lives of Christians is shaped by numerous considerations.

Peripheral Vision

Contemporary Christian spirituality cannot remain healthy or sustainable if sequestered in a protective greenhouse, cut off from the rest of human existence and enquiry. Psychology, for example, is a natural and increasingly necessary conversation partner for Christian spirituality. The quest for personal authenticity and self-awareness, which Augustine of North Africa exemplified early on in his *Confessions*, is essential to spiritual growth and an exploration greatly aided by contemporary psychological insights. Similarly, Christian spirituality should not evade the hard epistemological questions that philosophers of religion may pose to it. It must be able to offer a credible defense of its claim to genuine encounters with the transcendent rather than mere self-referential experiences.

The same may be said of other social sciences, as well as neuroscience and the "hard" sciences that continue to shape the contemporary worldview. Likewise, advances in technology have done far more than enrich our lifestyles with a plethora of convenience. Such advances are actually altering our collective consciousness and the ways we experience life, providing significant implications for our spiritual existence.

It is widely assumed that while doctrine divides, a common spirituality can unite human beings, even across the lines that traditionally have divided the world religions one from another. Comparative examination of their different spiritualities reveals significant similarities of aspiration and experience but also brings into focus many clearly distinctive features of the Christian tradition. Interfaith encounter is certainly one of the most important frontiers for Christian spirituality.

Conclusion

Certainly there is a place for highlighting the strengths of our own denominations and church traditions. This volume does so for the evangelical movement. Even so, the spiritual experience of the people of God is enriched, stimulated, and typically guided back on track by listening to the diverse voices of the larger harmony. It is "together with all the Lord's people" that we are able to grasp the full dimensions of the love of God (Eph. 3:18 TNIV).

Ultimately we believe there is one holy, catholic, and apostolic church — one people of God who live and move in his transforming and empowering presence. Beneath many surface idiosyncrasies are the strong, subterranean continuities of a shared life with God. The dynamics of Christian spirituality are known to all those who are embraced by the Father, redeemed by the Son, and open to the Holy Spirit.

Sources Cited

Abbott, W., ed. *The Documents of Vatican II* (1966).

Bebbington, D. *Evangelicalism in Modern Britain* (1989).

Bowe, B. *Biblical Foundations of Spirituality* (2003).

Fee, G. *Listening to the Spirit in the Text* (2000).

Haykin, M., and K. Stewart, eds. *The Advent of Evangelicalism* (2008).

Houston, J. *The Prayer: Deepening Your Friendship with God* (2007).

Humphrey, E. *Ecstasy and Intimacy* (2006).

Noll, M., and R. Thiemman, eds. *Where Shall My Wond'ring Soul Begin?* (2000).

Spener, P. *Pia Desideria*. Trans. T. Tappert (1964).

Volf, M. *Exclusion and Embrace* (1996).

For Further Reading

Chan, S. *Spiritual Theology* (1998).

Collins, K. ed. *Exploring Christian Spirituality* (2000).

Foster, R. *Prayer* (1992).

————. *Streams of Living Water* (1998).

George, T., and A. McGrath, eds. *For All the Saints* (2003).

Holder, A., ed. *The Blackwell Companion to Christian Spirituality* (2005).

Howard, E. B. *Brazos Introduction to Christian Spirituality* (2008).

Nouwen, H. *Reaching Out* (1975).

Peterson, E. *Christ Plays in Ten Thousand Places* (2005).

Scorgie, G. *A Little Guide to Christian Spirituality* (2007).

Sheldrake, P. *A Brief History of Spirituality* (2007).

CHAPTER 2

APPROACHES TO THE STUDY OF CHRISTIAN SPIRITUALITY

JOHN H. COE

Some may think it inappropriate, even pointless, to engage in the academic investigation of Christian spirituality. After all, is the faith not for the foolish so that they might shame the wise of the world (1 Cor. 2:6–16)? And cannot the uneducated and simplest of believers become holy and devout without a technical, academic study of spirituality?

It is true that one does not need to engage in rigorous investigation of spirituality to have a profound spiritual life. That is part of the genius of the Christian faith. It is not fundamentally reserved for the intellectually elite but is a way of living in response to God that is available to all. Neither is true spirituality just for the few dedicated ascetics who have discovered some secret, rigorous path to the divine. Rather, it is revealed to those in every walk of life who have, in Jesus' words, ears to hear.

The study of Christian spirituality is not a substitute for spirituality, but rather the means by which the dynamics of such spirituality can be understood more deeply, and thus commended more clearly and facilitated more effectively. To these ends, there are things helpful for ears to hear and minds to grasp.

The Logic of Christian Spirituality as Something to Study

Christianity is most fundamentally a *revealed* faith or religion. This is the starting point that makes all the difference. Believers do not ascend to God primarily through meditative-intellectual techniques or ascetic practices to discover God. Rather, God descended to humanity to reveal himself: through mighty acts in history, by becoming human, by indwelling believers, and by providing an authoritative interpretation in Scripture of these realities and the spiritual life. Humanity has not been left to guessing the best interpretation of the acts of God in history and the best ways to a relationship with him.

Four implications relevant to the study of spirituality emerge from the fact that Christianity is a revealed faith. First, teaching has always been emphasized in the Christian faith (2 Tim. 2:2). There is a revealed word from God that is to be understood and passed down through generations. It speaks of the work of God and what our spiritual response to him should be (2 Tim. 3:14–15). As a result, the church has always been interested in the study and teaching of that revealed word from God.

Second, the Scriptures being the authoritative divine interpretation of certain realities gives a centrality and importance to studying the Bible above all other things in understanding the spiritual life. In this case, biblical exposition — and doctrine in general — will be central to the church's understanding of the spiritual life.

Third, because God not only revealed himself in history and in his Word in the past, but also continues to reveal himself in the lives of believers through the indwelling Spirit, the church has also been interested in understanding the lives of the saints and the present work of the Spirit. In that sense, we should expect that comprehensive investigation of the spiritual life will integrate study of the Scriptures with study of his extracanonical work in human lives (which two things, taken together, comprise *spiritual theology*).

Fourth, God not only must reveal himself for people to know him, but God by his Holy Spirit must do a work in the human heart for people even to "receive" his Word and work. According to Paul, the unregenerate do not accept the things of God revealed, but the believer possesses "the mind of Christ" through the illumination of the Holy Spirit, who influences hearts to receive and wills to follow the Word of God (1 Cor. 2:14–16).

The Scriptures' Own Testimony on Studying Spirituality

While it is true that the Scriptures do not explicitly advocate academic study of spirituality, they clearly imply in certain biblical narratives, and elsewhere explicitly prescribe, that the church is to study, teach, observe, and understand the truth about life in Christ. Paul wrote that Christ has given gifted individuals to the church, some as teacher-shepherds to assist believers to become mature persons "to the measure of the stature which belongs to the fullness of Christ" (Eph. 4:11–13 NASB). Paul further encouraged Timothy to retain the sound teaching and words that Paul taught him (2 Tim. 1:13), and as a pastor to be diligent in "accurately handling the word of truth" (2 Tim. 2:15 NASB), to preach the Word (1 Tim. 4:13–15; 2 Tim. 4:2), and to pass these teachings on to others who could teach (2 Tim. 2:1–2). Similarly, Luke commended the synagogue at Berea upon hearing the teaching of Paul, "Now these were more noble-minded than those in Thessalonica, for they received the word [Paul's teaching] with great eagerness, examining the Scriptures daily to see whether these things were so" (Acts 17:10–11 NASB). It is not fundamentally from human intuition or self-discovery that we learn of true spirituality, but (1) in the light of God's revelation in Scripture, which provides an authoritative interpretation of the spiritual life ("In your light we see light," Ps. 36:9), and (2) on account of the Spirit opening within believers the "mind of Christ" by which we receive his revelation (1 Cor. 2:16).

The *Telos* or Goal of Studying the Spiritual Life

As important as study of the spiritual life from Scripture is to the believer, it turns out that the goal of all study and teaching is beyond mere cognitive apprehension of the truth. In Thomas Aquinas's words, "God destines us for an end beyond the grasp of reason" (1a.1)—or in Paul's word's, God destines us for a relationship with the living God by the indwelling Spirit that goes beyond the pages of Scripture and what can be taught to a love that surpasses knowledge by being filled with the fullness of God (Eph. 3:17–19). In that case, the goal of all Christian teaching and study of the Scriptures and the spiritual life (and all that we do) is a cluster of ultimate ends that extend well beyond study: that believers will love God and neighbor (1 Tim. 1:5), be complete or mature in Christ (Col. 1:28–29), be trained in righteousness (1 Tim. 4:7–8), and glorify God in all things (1 Cor. 10:31). However, there has always been a temptation to divorce doctrine, teaching, and study from transformation.

Unhealthy Approach to the Study of Christian Doctrine

According to the Fathers of the church and medieval theologians, to do theology apart from transformation and the *telos* of loving God is to commit the intellectual vice of "curiosity" (Lat. *curiositas*, cf. Thomas Aquinas, 2a.2ae, Q 166–67). Curiosity as an intellectual vice has at least two forms: (1) the desire to know what should not be known (e.g., astrology, pornography) and (2) the desire to know something in a manner in which it should not be known, namely, for the sake of knowing itself apart from loving and glorifying God. Teachers and students can be tempted to turn aside to lesser goals and divorce doctrine from transformation.

In that case, various spiritual-epistemological disciplines are important in order to aim intentionally in all studies at love and transformation and to avoid self-indulgent curiosity. Such spiritual disciplines (including honesty, truthfulness, prayer, and contemplation) assist the person in opening to the truth of what God intends in the manner in which God intends (filled with the Spirit) and honestly attending to his or her motivations for study. The spiritual-epistemological disciplines also protect the researcher from unhealthy influences. They guard the learner from unwillingness to acknowledge the truth before them and against false agendas, fantasy, grandiosity, overconfidence, timidity, arrogance, and pride.

Historical Musings on the Study of Christian Spirituality

Evagrius Ponticus, in the 4th century, best summed up the early church and church fathers' approach to studying Scripture and spirituality: "A theologian is one who prays truly, and one who prays truly is a theologian" (Ponticus, 65). Many historians of Christian spirituality believe that during the first four centuries of the church there was no impulse to separate study of Scripture and theology from the spiritual life of prayer and transformation. The two were usually linked.

Exactly when and how the change occurred is obscure. Nonetheless, by the late medieval period, a change had definitely begun. Schoolmen such as Thomas Aquinas attempted to retain a holistic approach to sacred doctrine; however, the separation of theology in the first part of his *Summa* from moral theology and the spiritual life in the second part became a pattern for subsequent theology in the West. Moreover, the separation of moral theology from spiritual theology in subsequent centuries ultimately became an unhelpful divorce of morality and virtue from a spirituality that focused more and more on religious experience in prayer.

Spirituality itself became further fragmented into "ascetic" and "mystical" divisions. Sometimes the two were conflated; more often rigorous moral-spiritual training of the religious (ascetical theology) was differentiated from the special ecstasies and stages of those having extraordinary religious experiences (mystical theology).

Consequently, the disciplines of studying doctrine, morality, and the spiritual life/experience gradually separated from one another, with the latter becoming chiefly the concern of clergy and monks. Numerous suggestions for these splits have been suggested, including the rise of scholastic theological method, and later Protestant Scholasticism; the eclipsing of spirituality by dogmatic theology as a response to the threat of heresy; the slow divorce of theology from pastoral concerns; the modernist university and response of theology to critical studies; and others. Over time there developed a clear academic-theological dividing of the faith into fields of discourse, with some identified as more important to the faith itself.

By the 20th century, the church and academy in the West were fractured by numerous splits: science and the humanities separated from theology; theology separated from pastoral and moral theology, which was further divorced from a spirituality that more and more focused on extraordinary growth and spiritual experiences. Often moral and spiritual issues were cut off from serious theological concern and relegated to a piece of pastoral theology or merely a part of praxis and the personal.

This is most clearly seen in many prestigious universities and schools of theology in which scholarly work became preoccupied with higher critical concerns. But even in conservative seminaries, one can see this divorce evident in the split between theology, exegesis and historical studies on the one hand, and praxis-oriented disciplines like pastoral theology, counseling, and Christian education on the other—with spiritual formation relegated to the latter or absent from the curriculum altogether.

Nevertheless, interest in spirituality and spiritual formation in these last decades, in both Roman Catholicism and Protestantism, particularly evangelicalism, has prompted a renewed interest in the academic understanding of the spiritual life. This movement has encouraged a renaissance in studying the history of spirituality and in bringing back some rigor to the study of the spiritual life itself. This is a good direction that needs to be sustained if the church is to provide an understanding of the spiritual life that is biblically grounded, historically informed, and intellectually and experientially vital.

Varieties of Approaches to the Study of Spirituality

A variety of manners or methods has emerged in the study of spirituality. Evan Howard notes two broad approaches: (1) the descriptive approach, with an emphasis on the historical, phenomenological, and psychological analysis of spirituality; and (2) the normative approach, emphasizing the theological, philosophical, and application-oriented approach (Howard, 25). Michael Downey discerns four methods: the theological, the historical, the anthropological and the appropriative (Downey, 123–31). Along another vein, Bruce Demarest has classified possible approaches according to their degrees of openness to interdisciplinary understandings of spirituality, and the datum of science and religious experience. He locates three groups along this continuum: those most open to interdisciplinary insights; moderates who are somewhat welcoming interdisciplinary insights, but still with strong doctrinally normative leanings; and conservatives who are only receptive to the Scriptures and the application of biblical examples to the spiritual life (Demarest, 74–79).

After surveying the variety of approaches to studying the spiritual life, Howard recommends a cautious interdisciplinary approach that looks at (1) biblical-theological-philosophical-normative issues, (2) historical-phenomenological–human scientific–descriptive issues, and (3) personal-applied-social-relational issues. Given that God has revealed himself in Christ, in word, in nature, and in his people through history; and given the *telos* of loving and glorifying God, it is essential for the church to explore a robust, integrative and appropriative understanding of the spiritual life. These qualities are keys to an intellectually and existentially rich spiritual theology.

Spiritual Theology and "The Sanctification Gap"

What is needed is a theological-experiential methodology for addressing what Richard Lovelace described as "the sanctification gap" (Lovelace, 365). Indeed, a serious gap exists in the minds of many believers between what they know to be the goal of sanctification and growth, the spiritual ideal clearly set forth in the Bible, and where they know they actually are in their lives. A robust spiritual theology, whose goal is both understanding and experience of transformation, can help equip the church to address this sanctification gap.

Spiritual theology can be understood in two senses that are logically interconnected. First, spiritual theology, in its broadest and most minimal sense, involves the task of drawing out the spiritual and existential implications of doctrine to better understand and participate in the process of real life transformation. In that sense, all responsible Christian teaching involves doing spiritual theology.

Second, spiritual theology proper can be understood as a first order theological discipline of its own with its own unique data for study, domain of investigation, methodology, and aim (as in the case of systematic theology, New Testament studies, and other related disciplines). This more robust form of spiritual theology encompasses and entails the minimal form as application but goes beyond it in terms of scope, content, methodology, and rigor. As a theological discipline in its own right, spiritual theology is interdisciplinary in scope by integrating (1) the scriptural teaching on sanctification and growth from a biblical and systematic theology perspective with (2) observations and reflections (an empirical study) of the Spirit's actual work in the believer's spirit and experience. Deficiencies in recent theological education have been due largely to (a) the assumption that this is the task of someone other than the theologian and/or (b) the incorrect assumption that understanding the process of spiritual growth is solely a biblical-textual study that involves no reflection on human experience.

The Scriptures are certainly the central and controlling datum for understanding the dynamics of Christian spirituality. However, this needs to be combined with an understanding of how the realities discussed in the Bible actually work in real life. Here spiritual theology also pays attention to the datum of the work of the Spirit in human experience and practice. Both kinds of data are essential preconditions of a full understanding of sanctification and the work of the Spirit in growth. This approach is based on a realist pneumatology in which, in dependence on the Spirit, we need to study the Spirit's work not only from the Bible but also as he works within the space-time continuum of human lives, just as the Scriptures indicate he does ("However, you are not in the flesh but in the Spirit, if indeed *the Spirit of God dwells in you*," Rom. 8:9 NASB, emphasis added). Whereas systematic theology's peculiar task, for example, includes the systematic study of transformation in the Bible, spiritual theology's peculiar task is to combine this with study of the Spirit's actual work in the human soul and experience, grounded in dependence on the Spirit to receive his teaching. Thus, the study of spiritual theology is a (1) textual, (2) empirical-reflective, and (3) existential-reflective enterprise involving study, observation, reflection and opening the heart to both the Bible and the Spirit's work in human experience.

The following, then, is a definition of spiritual theology proper as a peculiar branch of theological investigation and knowledge (adapted from Aumann, 22). Spiritual theology is that part of theology that brings together (1) a study of the truths of Scripture with (2) a study of the ministry of the Holy Spirit in the experience of human beings (3) in dependence on the illuminating work of the indwelling Christ, in order to (a) define the *nature* of this supernatural life in Christ, (b) explain the *process* of growth by which persons advance from the beginning of the spiritual life to its full perfection in the next life, and (c) formulate *directives* for spiritual growth and development.

In the first place, spiritual theology is not merely an academic or intellectual enterprise, but involves the indwelling Spirit giving us the "mind of Christ," so that over time the believer's heart is more and more inclined to receive and gain wisdom from the revelation of God (1 Cor. 2:14–16). This implies that the spiritual theologian must nurture a relationship with Christ by the Spirit and Word, to know the love of Christ beyond knowledge (Eph. 3:16–19), to see that in Christ are "hidden all the treasures of wisdom and knowledge" (Col. 2:2–3 NASB) and to understand more deeply the transforming work that is from God and unattainable through autonomous human intellect and effort (Col. 2:8, 18–19; cf. Phil. 2:12).

Second, the study of spiritual theology is, in part, a textual enterprise, with the Scriptures as the central, most important, and highest authoritative datum. The method of investigation in this aspect consists of literary tools and the principles of interpretation (hermeneutics). Much work has been done recently in theology and biblical interpretation to achieve clarity on these matters, and evangelical theologians in particular have been making great strides in clarifying the nature of robust hermeneutics and helpful exegesis in light of faith and an inspired revelation from God.

Third, whereas the interpretive-literary-textual dimension of the methodology in spiritual theology has been highly developed, this is much less the case with the empirical aspect of its methodology. Spiritual theology uniquely involves observation and reflection on the Spirit's work in the life of the believer and the church corporately, the dynamics of sin and the Spirit's indwelling work in one's own life and that of other believers, resistant and healthy responses to the Spirit's work, the psychological dynamics of legalism, and helpful models and examples of growth. Spiritual theology also reflects on the lives of saints who have gone before and of what has been written about them. These aspects are in accordance with Paul's admonition to "join in *following my example*, and *observe* those who walk according to the pattern you have in us" (Phil. 3:17 NASB, emphasis added).

Fourth, insofar as spiritual theology studies human phenomena relevant to sin, growth, and the Spirit's work, it also attends to those creation disciplines that are empirical in nature, that have to do in the best sense with commonsense observation and reflection (e.g., Christian philosophy, psychology, sociology, literature) and have something relevant to say on the nature of persons and the dynamics that govern the soul. Of course, these theoretical disciplines will be truncated whenever they are divorced from the insights of the Bible.

Consequently, spiritual theology takes the fruit of biblical and doctrinal studies and brings it all to bear on our grasp of the manner in which the Spirit works in human lives. This is much like the Old Testament sage in Proverbs, who brought together wisdom gained through observation of, and reflection on, both the Scriptures and real life (Prov. 24:30–34). Of course, spiritual theology raises a number of epistemological- and justifica-tion-related questions that theologians and Christian academics have been concerned with over the centuries, and which will need to be addressed, particularly when apparent tensions emerge between the Bible, human reason, and experience.

Conclusion

Because the whole of the believer's spiritual life involves dependence on and response to the indwelling Spirit of God (Gal. 5:16; Eph. 5:18), the Christian life itself is a form of "doing spiritual theology" involving the commonsense practices of watching, waiting, and listening for the Spirit's work in real life on the basis of the Scriptures. Spiritual theology could go a long way to providing a theory-praxis of transformation that will be helpful to all believers, a practice of formation that is theoretically connected to the Bible, theology, and what is going on in human experience.

Sources Cited

Aumann, J. *Spiritual Theology* (1980).

Demarest, B. *Satisfy Your Soul* (1999).

Downey, M. *Understanding Christian Spirituality* (1997).

Howard, E. *The Brazos Introduction to Christian Spirituality* (2008).

Lovelace, R. "The Sanctification Gap." *Theology Today* 29, no. 4 (1973): 363–69.

Ponticus, Evagrius. *Practicos and Chapters on Prayer*. Ed. and trans. J. Bamberger (1972).

Thomas Aquinas. *Summa Theologiae*. Ed. Blackfriars. Vol. 44 (1972).

For Further Reading

Chan, S. *Spiritual Theology* (1998).

Coe, J. "Spiritual Theology." *Journal of Spiritual Formation and Soul Care* 1, no. 2 (2008): 4–43.

McIntosh, M. *Mystical Theology* (1998).

Porter, S. "Sanctification in a New Key." *Journal of Spiritual Formation and Soul Care* 1, no. 2 (2008): 129–48.

Sheldrake, P. *Spirituality and History* (1998).

———. *Spirituality and Theology* (1998).

Thornton, M. *English Spirituality* (1963).

CHAPTER 3

OLD TESTAMENT FOUNDATIONS OF CHRISTIAN SPIRITUALITY

MARK J. BODA

The following article sketches a biblical foundation of spiritual theology in the Old Testament. Following the canonical shape of the Old Testament, it highlights the diverse perspectives on spiritual theology within the various canonical units without losing sight of their unified witness to the relationship between Yahweh and humanity.

Torah

In the opening chapter of the book of Genesis, God creates the cosmos by lexical fiat and, at its rhetorical height, forms humanity, identifying both male and female as made in God's image. It is this image that qualifies humanity to function as God's vice-regents on earth, ruling the earth and filling it (Gen. 1:26–28). While all of creation declares its origin in the Divine One who created it through word, humanity in a unique way reflects the image of this one who is spirit. Genesis 2 reveals the intimacy of relationship between God and humanity. From the beginning, humanity is reliant on the combining of divine breath and created matter, an act that forms what is called in Genesis 2:7 a living soul. This is foundational to Old Testament anthropology, explaining humanity's position between material creation and spiritual Creator. The emphasis throughout this key chapter is on fellowship with Yahweh as humanity participates with Yahweh in caring for creation. Yahweh's legal declaration ("you may eat … you shall not eat," 2:16–17 NASB) and invitation to name the animals (2:19) is a reminder that the relationship between God and humanity will be typified by freedom and will require reciprocation on humanity's part. Genesis 3 highlights the fundamental break in the cosmic order introduced through humanity's rebellion against Yahweh. The divine-human relationship is estranged, typified, first, in the human shame experienced by both male and female who hide from God and one another, and second, in the divine curses that hinder fulfillment of the creation mandate (ruling the earth, filling it) as God's vice-regents. The enmity created between land and man, and between the seed of woman and serpent highlights the broader implications of this breach in humanity's relationship with God for creation (both inanimate and animate) as a whole. Creation itself is estranged from humanity and, because of humanity's role as vice-regent of God, also estranged from God.

It is clear from the chapters that follow Genesis 3 that God's restoration of this broken relationship will be accomplished through the provision of a human community that seeks after God (Boda 2009, 33). The texts of Genesis 4–11 reveal two fundamental human genealogies, one typified by rebellious independence and the other by relational intimacy. The fundamental human impulse for a spiritual relationship with the Creator is showcased from the outset in Genesis 4 as Cain and Abel bring sacrifice to God, but throughout Genesis 4–11 humanity that flows from the godly line of Seth is depicted as calling upon God (Gen. 4:26;

cf. 12:8). While the domination of creation by the rebellious line prompts the judgment of the flood (Gen. 6:1–7), returning creation to a state akin to Genesis 1:2 (cf. Gen. 7–8), this opens the opportunity for renewal of relationship between God and humanity. This time that relationship is guided by a covenant that will extend to all of humanity (8:20–9:17). It is clear, however, that there remains estrangement between humanity and God (compare 8:21 with 6:5). The flood was not designed to eradicate this estrangement, but to recalibrate the relationship through the structure of covenant.

It was the line of Shem and ultimately the clan of Abraham through Isaac and then Jacob that would provide a way for restoration of relationship between God and humanity. The stories of Genesis 12–50 reveal the initial steps in the formation of this redemptive community, and key to this story is the relationship between God and these families. It is clear that covenant is key to this relationship, one that was initiated by God (Gen. 12; 15) but also demanded human reciprocation (Gen. 17; 22). These redemptive clans are depicted as constantly relating to God who passionately pursues them. Abraham is presented as one whose faith in God is foundational to the establishment of covenant (Gen. 15:6) and yet at the same time one who struggles to trust (Gen. 16). He is one in whom God confides (e.g., Gen. 18:17–19). Jacob typifies Israel as a nation in his nocturnal struggle with God (or his representative; Gen. 32:24–32), foreshadowing future challenges to the fulfillment of the redemptive purposes of God through this community. For these key figures in Israel's history, altars were important to the rhythm of relationship with Yahweh, a means by which one could "[call] on the name of the LORD" (Gen. 13:4).

While Genesis provides orientation to the broader drama of relationship between God and humanity and the foundational steps taken to make possible a redemptive community, Exodus depicts the formative redemptive and revelatory events that would provide structure for the relationship between God and the redeemed community. Throughout the depiction of the salvation of Israel from Egypt in Exodus 1–15, readers are consistently reminded that the purpose of this salvation for the community is the covenant relationship that would be established at Sinai (cf. Ex. 3:12; 9:1; 10:3). So also when the relationship is inaugurated in Exodus 20, it is the salvific event of the exodus that is identified as the foundation for the relationship (20:2). The Decalogue (20:3–17) and the Covenant Code that follows it (21:1–23:33) make clear that relationship with Yahweh will be structured by moral principles. This relationship thus has an ethical dimension that encompasses humanity's relationship with God, one another, and all of creation. It also has a missional dimension — that is, God saves Israel and enters into covenant with them so that they may function as priests among the nations of the world and make possible a relationship with God for all humanity (19:5–6; C. Wright). Israel's mediatorial role among the nations, foreshadowed already in the mediation of Abraham and Joseph in Genesis, is showcased in Moses' mediatorial role within Israel itself (esp. Gen. 32–34). It is clear in the depiction of the establishment of relationship with God in Exodus that such a relationship is communal in character. Even in Genesis, although the relationship was focused on a particular clan head like Abraham, Isaac, and Jacob, these figures functioned as representative of their own present and future communities of faith.

The bulk of the book of Exodus is comprised of the revelation and construction of the tabernacle. Placed after the establishment of covenant, these texts remind the reader that the goal of the covenant is the presence of God with this covenant community. The spatial shift from Exodus 19 to 40 is that of a God who moves from the transcendent place on top of the mountain to an immanent place at the heart of the camp. This shift establishes an important principle at the outset of Israel's existence, that is, God's enduring passion to be present among the redeemed community, even though he is truly a consuming fire. The revelation of the tabernacle showcases God's meticulous attention to a ritual aesthetic that is highly symbolic, suggesting a return to the garden where fellowship was possible (Longman). At the center of the tabernacle account, one finds one of the greatest crises in Israel's history, that is, the golden calf rebellion (Ex. 32–34). And yet, ironically, it is at this dire moment of need that Israel experiences the greatest revelation of the character of God in the Old Testament, as Yahweh declares the significance of his name to Moses, a goal foreshadowed at the outset of the book of Exodus (see Ex. 3:13–14; 6:1–8). This revelation has significant implications for spiritual theology in the Old Testament, as it reappears throughout the Old Testament witness as the foundation for praise and penitence (e.g., Num. 14:18; Neh. 9:17; Ps. 86:5; Joel 2:13).

A priestly ritual aesthetic dominates the spiritual theology of the books of Leviticus and Numbers. Legislation contained in these books is designed to ensure the enduring presence of Yahweh in the midst of the camp (Ex. 25–40) and to nurture the covenant relationship established at Sinai (Ex. 19–24). The book begins by providing key legislation for the sacrificial rites that would nurture this relationship. The burnt, grain, and peace offerings were voluntary sacrifices primarily enabling Israelites to express their praise, commitment, and thanks to Yahweh (Lev. 1–3). While there was an atoning dimension to the burnt offering (Lev. 1:4), atonement was the dominant focus of the required sin and guilt offerings (Lev. 4–6; cf. Sklar). The sacrificial system provided a means for nurturing the relationship between God and his people. While the legislation in Leviticus 1–7 was focused more on the individual family/clan, it is clear from the history of Israel that these various sacrifices were also practiced on the national level in communal settings. Leviticus 16 provides legislation for the key Day of Atonement rituals, which involved a complex of sacrificial and symbolic acts designed to ensure God's enduring presence and nurture Israel's relationship with their God.

The ritual dimension of the priestly legislation extends into all of life (see Milgrom; D. P. Wright). Leviticus 10:10–11 instructs the priests to distinguish between holy and common, unclean and clean (see Jenson; Nelson 1993). Through these categories the priestly legislation created a ritual world defined by the presence of the Creator God who dwelled at the heart of Israel, with holy categorizing that which was closest to Yahweh's manifest presence and unclean the furthest from it. Human sin and impurity removed Israel from the realms of the holy, while priestly rituals (sacrifice, anointing, shaving, washing) moved Israel toward the realms of the holy. This categorization extended to all areas of life and creation, from activities in the bedroom, to bodily emissions, childbirth, and even eating, because, as Jacob Milgrom has wisely noted, "the Decalogue would fail were it not rooted in a regularly observed ritual, central to the home and table, and impinging on both senses and intellect, thus conditioning the reflexes into patterns of ethical behavior" (Milgrom, 191). The priestly legislation thus created a symbolic ritual universe in which Israel was constantly reminded of the presence of their God and their opportunity to commune with Yahweh in covenant relationship.

The book of Deuteronomy not only brings closure to the Torah but also functions as an important segue into the rest of the Old Testament, where it dominates the theological landscape. The spiritual theology expressed in this book is significantly different from that articulated in the priestly legislation. In Deuteronomic perspective, communion with God is based on internal and external covenantal response. This response is based on God's acts of love, election, covenant loyalty, jealousy, discipline, and holiness and must engage the community's internal affection as well as external behavior. Thus, relationship with God demands a love with all one's heart, soul, and might, but also obedience to the commandments, statutes, and judgments. In Deuteronomic theology there is great concern for the who, where, and how of worship. Worship must be restricted to the one God, Yahweh, alone. Worship must be expressed at one place of Yahweh's choosing. Worship must be practiced in appropriate ways, eschewing inappropriate practices of the surrounding nations.

The rhetoric of the book focuses on the importance of decision for Israel's relationship with Yahweh (Nelson 2002, 11). Expressed in the form of a sermon delivered by Moses to the people about to enter the Promised Land, it is filled with exhortations calling Israel to choose the way of life rather than death, through loving, clinging to, worshiping, serving, fearing, listening to, obeying, and knowing Yahweh by walking in God's ways, observing God's commandments, and keeping God's statutes (e.g., Deut. 10:12 – 13). Although the covenant in view is that established at Sinai, that covenant is not merely a past event, but rather a present reality, not a relationship established merely with the generation now gone, but with "us" who stand here today (see Deut. 29:14 – 15). Accountability to this covenant relationship is ensured through the blessings and curses, that is, privileges and disciplines, articulated in Deuteronomy 27 – 28.

Prophets

It is this Deuteronomic theology of relationship with Yahweh that dominates the books of the Former Prophets (Joshua, Judges, Samuel, Kings). These books are filled with Israel's struggle to remain faithful in relationship with Yahweh as they run after other gods, worship at unsanctioned high places, and utilize pagan practices. Throughout these books, God consistently calls to this community of faith through the Torah, his direct voice, or his prophets, and ultimately it is the curses or disciplines articulated in Deuteronomy that Yahweh must use to draw Israel back to God in covenant relationship (see Deut. 30:1 – 8). Not only prophets, but also sacred and civil leaders were to play a role in nurturing this covenant relationship. Various models can be discerned in this civil leadership, ranging from the theocracy to monarchy as the story shifts from Moses to Joshua to the judges to the kings. Although not ideal, Davidic kingship holds out the greatest hope, especially as it upholds the Deuteronomic values of passion and purity in worship. The one place of worship presaged in Deuteronomy 12 is identified ultimately as Jerusalem where Solomon builds a temple for the manifest presence of God. The function of this temple according to Solomon's dedicatory prayer in 1 Kings 8 is to nurture the relationship between Israel and Yahweh, making it primarily a place of prayer where Israel can seek God.

The Latter Prophets exhort and encourage the community to embrace God in faithful relationship. They consistently express concern over the violations of the basic stipulations articulated in the Torah, especially idolatry (loving God with one's heart, soul, and might) and social injustice (loving one's neighbor as oneself). The dominant call in the book of Isaiah is to trust in Yahweh alone in the face of the nations, in the book of Jeremiah to a heart response that leads to repentance, and in the book of Ezekiel to a relationship with God that heightens his glory within the world. Throughout the Book of the Twelve prophets (Hosea – Malachi), Yahweh consistently cries for response from the people based on the invitation of grace, even though this invitation is backed up with the threat of discipline. A common thread throughout all of the prophetic traditions is the call to repentance (Zech. 1:3), expressing hope that such penitence will prompt the gracious response of God. Ultimately, however, such repentance is not forthcoming, leading to the development especially in Jeremiah and Ezekiel that Yahweh must perform an internal work through the Spirit that will enable his covenant people to fully experience the kind of relationship envisioned at creation.

The Latter Prophets express a spiritual theology not only through their preaching, but also through their own experience with Yahweh. In the accounts of their commissioning (Isa. 6; Jer. 1; Ezek. 1–3), readers are given a glimpse of the experience of a human in the manifest presence of the Creator. The prophetic response is often one of self-deprecation, questioning how they could act on behalf of this transcendent God. And yet their calling is evidence of Yahweh's passion to extend grace to the covenant people. Caught as intermediary between this covenant community and their God, prophets are often depicted as tragic figures, and in this the reader catches glimpses of a relationship with God typified by honesty. From Isaiah's "How long?" to Jeremiah's "confessions" to Habakkuk's confrontation, the prophets display a spirituality akin to the protest traditions related to Moses, David, and Job.

Writings

Often accused of being secular, the wisdom tradition is undeniably theological in character (Waltke). The fear of God is the beginning (Prov. 1:7) and goal (2:5) of wisdom and represents the covenantal orientation of all wisdom. The foundational corpus in Proverbs 1–9 orients the reader to a spirituality designed to function in everyday life. Proverbs 10–31 articulates a pragmatic spirituality, as the fear of Yahweh is applied to the realms, for example, of relationships, commerce, and leadership. Qoheleth showcases the frustrating search of an ancient sage in order to exhort the young to remember their Creator by fearing God and keeping Torah while in their youth. Job reveals a form of intimacy with God that is only accessible when humanity reaches its intellectual limits, encountering the one whose ways and character are beyond human comprehension.

Within the book of Psalms, one finds a liturgical spirituality that is diverse in its expression. The Psalms give voice to a breadth of human expression (Brueggemann)—from expressing the experience of those living in equilibrium (orientation), to those living in times when equilibrium has been disturbed (disorientation), to those who live in the wake of such disorientation (new orientation). Not surprisingly it is the second category that dominates the Psalter, even if there is a noticeable shift in the Psalter toward orientation so that disorientation is not considered the ideal or goal of the Psalms, even if it is a legitimate expression to which God listens. The spirituality of the Psalter is both individual and communal. At times the community as a whole expresses the cry of their collective heart to Yahweh, while at other times it is the individual crying out. Many times the individual expression of the cry of the soul moves toward the community as a whole, such as the confession of sin in Psalm 51 that recognizes the impact that such confession can have on the entire community. The Psalms are dominated by the voice of humanity expressed to a listening God from a variety of life settings, but at times the voice of God breaks into the Psalter (Bellinger; Tournay), and in this the Psalter encourages a dialogic spirituality in which both human and divine voices converse and characters meet.

The book of Chronicles provides the most intricate depiction of the spirituality practiced within the temple in Jerusalem. It describes the origins of the priestly and Levitical orders responsible for the sacrificial and musical practices that came to typify the community's worship at the temple sponsored by the Davidic dynasty. This sponsorship encouraged and enabled the development of a musical tradition superintended by Levitical musicians that would fill the once silent sanctuary with the glorious tones of music that would match the breadth of human experience (1 Chron. 16:4). Chronicles also encourages a spirituality of immediate covenantal response. Through speeches and prayers embedded in Israel's monarchic story, the chronicler exhorts his audience living in the wake of the exilic nightmare to humble themselves, pray, seek God's face, and turn from their wicked ways (see esp. 2 Chron. 7:13–15; Dillard). Such responses would prompt reciprocity from Yahweh, who was offering this new generation a new lease on life through a spirituality of covenantal intimacy. The spirituality articulated by the chronicler is showcased in the key restoration narratives of Ezra-Nehemiah. The community that emerges from exile is one focused at the outset on the reconstruction of the temple and its services (Ezra 1–6) before relating a story punctuated by accounts of a spirituality of penitential response (Ezra 9; Nehemiah 1; 9; Duggan).

Such attention to repentance showcases a response to the earlier guidance for restoration provided by the voice of Moses in Deuteronomy 30 and Solomon in 1 Kings 8 (Boda 2006).

The Old Testament clearly provides diverse perspectives on spiritual theology and a variety of ways to relate to God. Yet at its center is God's passionate pursuit of a people who would love him with all their heart, soul, and might.

Sources Cited

Bellinger, W. *Psalmody and Prophecy* (1984).

Boda, M. "Confession as Theological Expression." In *Seeking the Favor of God*, ed. M. Boda et al. Vol. 1 (2006, 21–50).

———. *A Severe Mercy* (2009).

Brueggemann, W. *The Message of the Psalms* (1984).

Dillard, R. "Reward and Punishment in Chronicles." *WTJ* 46 no. 1 (1984): 164–72.

Duggan, M. *The Covenant Renewal in Ezra-Nehemiah* (2001).

Jenson, P. *Graded Holiness* (1992).

Longman, T., III. *Immanuel in Our Place* (2001).

Milgrom, J. "Ethics and Ritual." In *Religion and Law*, ed. E. Brown Firmage (1989), 159–92.

Nelson, R. *Deuteronomy* (2002).

———. *Raising Up a Faithful Priest* (1993).

Sklar, J. *Sin, Impurity, Sacrifice, Atonement* (2005).

Tournay, R. J. *Seeing and Hearing God with the Psalms* (1991).

Waltke, B. "The Book of Proverbs and Old Testament Theology," *BibSac* 136 (1979): 302–17.

Wright, C. *The Mission of God* (2006).

Wright, D. P. "Observations on the Ethical Foundations of the Biblical Dietary Laws." In *Religion and Law*, ed. E. Firmage (1989), 193–98.

For Further Reading

Brueggemann, W., and P. D. Miller. *The Psalms and the Life of Faith* (1995).

Curtis, E. M., and J. J. Brugaletta, eds., *Discovering the Way of Wisdom* (2004).

Gane, R. *Cult and Character* (2005).

Hagelia, H. *Coram deo* (2001).

Kleinig, J. W. *The Lord's Song* (1993).

Millar, J. G. *Now Choose Life* (1999).

CHAPTER 4

NEW TESTAMENT FOUNDATIONS OF CHRISTIAN SPIRITUALITY

JEANNINE K. BROWN

The New Testament portrays spirituality as the human journey toward deeper participation with and experience of God in Christ, initiated and infused by God's Holy Spirit. This journey is a communal one; it is the journey of the church. Although this discussion centers on a spirituality *informed* by the New Testament, it is also the case that the church's spirituality is *formed* by the New Testament and Scripture more broadly.

There are three hallmarks of New Testament spirituality when viewed in light of the overarching biblical storyline. New Testament spirituality is Messiah-shaped, eschatological, and marked by the Holy Spirit. The New Testament also witnesses to a number of spiritual practices that did and should characterize the church.

New Testament spirituality cannot be understood apart from Israel's story portrayed in the Old Testament. Three particular facets are important for understanding New Testament spirituality. First, Israel's God is a covenanting God, providing the relational context for Israel to experience God's presence in spite of the human propensity toward idolatry (Ex. 19:3–6). This means that God is the (repeated) initiator of their divine experience. Second, Israel's experience of Yahweh is thoroughly communal, mediated through community structures such as family, temple, and Torah (Deut. 6:1–9). Third, God's covenant with Israel is fundamentally missional (Gen. 12:1–3; Deut. 4:5–7). These facets of the Old Testament story provide important continuity for New Testament

authors and underwrite an understanding of New Testament spirituality, which claims that God has broken into human history in a breathtakingly new way in the person of Jesus Christ.

New Testament Spirituality as Messiah-Shaped

If spirituality is understood broadly as experiencing God's activity and presence, then the New Testament writers uniformly understand spirituality to be *Messiah-shaped*. That is, New Testament spirituality centers on Jesus Christ, as revealer of God and redeemer of those who trust in him, and as the human expression of full covenant loyalty.

Jesus reveals the true God. According to Matthew's gospel, Messiah Jesus is the manifestation of God's presence. Matthew frames his story of Jesus by beginning and ending with this foundational affirmation (Matt. 1:23; 28:20; cf. 18:20). John begins his gospel by claiming that to see Jesus is to know the unseen God (John 1:18). New Testament writers indicate that Jesus is rightly worshiped and experienced as the living Lord (Matt. 28:17–20; John 20:28; 1 Cor. 8:5–6; 1 Peter 3:15; cf. Bauckham, 127–51). "In Jesus' life, death, and resurrection, people … are granted an encounter with God" (Koester, 27).

The narrative shaping of the Gospels indicates *how* Jesus reveals God. The gospel writers tell the story of Jesus in a way that leads to and climaxes in the cross (e.g., Mark 8:31; 9:31; 10:33–34;

15:21–41). "The cross is the surest, truest and deepest window on the very heart and character of the living and loving God" (Wright, 94). This theological affirmation derived from the narrative contours of the Gospels is echoed in Paul's story of Jesus in Philippians 2:5–11. Jesus, who was "in very nature God," then "made himself nothing" by becoming human (2:5–6). As a human being, "he humbled himself and became obedient to death … on a cross" (2:8). As a result, he is now exalted by God, demonstrating that Jesus in his self-emptying truly reveals God's nature (2:9–11). Experiencing God's presence in Jesus, then, is to experience a God defined by self-giving (by "cruciformity"; Gorman, 33).

Christian spirituality is a life lived in intimate relationship with Christ—a life defined by salvation and self-giving. Because they are "in Christ," believers participate in all that Messiah Jesus has accomplished on their behalf. Paul uses this phrase (*en Christô*, "in the Messiah") along with language of participation (*koinonia*) to signal both the benefits of salvation that believers receive and their ongoing relational experience of the crucified and resurrected Christ. Those who repent and trust in Jesus receive and participate in eternal life (Rom. 6:23) and every spiritual blessing, including forgiveness of sin (Eph. 1:3–10).

Jesus, as Messiah, both enacts God's restoration of humanity and represents humanity as the utterly faithful one. According to the biblical story, because of idolatry and sin, humanity, and even Israel—God's chosen people—fall short of living out their true calling and identity. God's intentions for Israel and so for humanity more broadly are concentrated in the person of Jesus, the one who is truly faithful (Wright, 81–82). Those who trust in his work and give their allegiance to him participate in *his* faithfulness, and the life of Christ becomes their reality and the pattern of their existence. "I have been crucified with [the Messiah] and I no longer live, but [the Messiah] lives in me" (Gal. 2:20). *In the Messiah*, believers receive Jesus'

faithfulness as their own and are enabled to live out his faithfulness. This intimate relationship is wonderfully captured by the words of Colossians 3:3: "your life is now hidden with Christ in God."

John's gospel provides some of the most potent metaphors to express the intimate relationship between Christ and believers. For John, Jesus is the very real sustenance for believers. He is bread (6:35) and water for them (4:10). As branches, they are sustained by Jesus, the vine (15:1–8). In fact, Jesus is life itself for them (1:4; 14:6). Jesus also nurtures and protects his followers: he is the Good Shepherd and the gate for the sheep (10:1–18). As the true light, he is their guide and source of knowledge and power (1:4–5; 8:12; 9:5). Jesus' prayer in John 17 communicates this sense of relational intimacy. "I pray also for those who will believe in me through their message, that all of them may be one, Father, just as you are in me and I am in you. May they also be in us so that the world may believe that you have sent me. I have given them the glory that you gave me, that they may be one as we are one" (vv. 20–22).

New Testament Spirituality as Eschatological

Because the New Testament authors claim that Messiah Jesus inaugurates God's final restoring work, their understanding of spirituality is fundamentally eschatological. According to Matthew, Mark, and Luke, the center of Jesus' preaching is the nearness of the kingdom of God (cf. Matt. 4:17; Mark 1:15; Luke 4:43; 8:1). Luke's Jesus announces the arrival of the kingdom of God, being witnessed by the generation who observes his powerful deeds (Luke 11:14–20). New Testament authors, broadly speaking, call their audiences to live in light of the Christ-event, which "has brought the end into the *now* of human history" (Brown et al.).

For New Testament authors, spirituality flows from understanding and living in this time of "already and not yet." Matthew's beatitudes, the hallmark blessings of Jesus' followers, introduce Jesus' teaching on discipleship or spirituality (Matt. 5:3–10). The eight blessings begin and end with an emphasis on the present realization of blessing ("for theirs *is* the kingdom of heaven"; 5:3b, 10b, emphasis added). Inside this framing device, the emphasis lands on kingdom experience as future (e.g., "for they *will be* comforted"; 5:4b, cf. 6b–9b). This "already and not yet" reality sets the tone for the rest of the sermon (Matt. 5–7), which calls disciples to covenantal identity and loyalty (5:14–48; 7:15–27); covenantal practices of giving, prayer, and fasting (6:1–18); trust and loyalty versus worry (6:19–34); and prayer and discernment (7:1–14).

In his exhortations to churches, Paul navigates the already–not yet dimensions of God's restoration by calling believers to live in light of the eschatological reality of the Messiah to which they already belong. They are to discard the ways of the old person (*anthrōpos*; an allusion to *Adam*/humanity of Gen. 1:27) and put on the new person — Christ (Col. 3:9–10). Since believers have already died with Christ (at baptism; Rom. 6:1–10; cf. 2 Cor. 5:14–15), Paul exhorts them to "count [themselves] dead to sin but alive to God in Christ Jesus" (Rom. 6:11). Paul can even speak of believers already experiencing "new creation" (eschatological language): "If anyone is in the Messiah, new creation!" (2 Cor. 5:17; my translation; cf. Gal. 6:15). This evokes a vivid picture of God's renewal of creation already having begun in the work of the Messiah and already being experienced in some way within the Christian community. Present living is marked by the reality of God's restoring work in Christ.

For these and other New Testament writers, already and not yet overlap. This means that the metaphor of journey is supremely appropriate to New Testament spirituality (cf. Brown et al.). Because humans are finite and because they live in the time when full restoration has not yet occurred, they are on a journey of formation. Yet because the new time of the Messiah has begun, their journey is guided by the sure hope of the final restoration of God's people and all of creation (Rom. 8:18–22).

Although the New Testament testifies to the inauguration of God's final restoration in Jesus the Messiah, it is not naively triumphalistic in its spirituality. Instead, a powerful undercurrent of suffering as part of Christian spirituality flows through its pages. For instance, the author of 1 Peter frames his understanding of suffering eschatologically. He assures suffering and slandered churches in Asia Minor that they are living in the time of the Messiah and so at a privileged point in history (1:10–12). As he helps them understand their suffering, he confirms their suffering as arising from allegiance to Christ as a sign that the end is imminent. God's final judgment and vindication of those faithful to Christ has already begun, as evident in their suffering, and signals the proleptic beginning of final consummation (4:12–19; cf. 4:7). This coheres with Paul's conception of suffering as a sharing in the sufferings of the Messiah in anticipation of believers' glory or vindication (Rom. 8:17–18; 2 Cor. 4:16–18; Phil. 3:10–11). "We have heard the end of the story, and it is resurrection" (Moe-Lobeda, 193).

New Testament Spirituality as Lived in the Holy Spirit

If New Testament spirituality is fundamentally eschatological, then it is spirituality marked by the Spirit. In the Old Testament prophets, the outpouring of God's Spirit was part of a composite of eschatological hopes for Israel's restoration (Isa. 42:1–4; Ezek. 36:26–27; Joel 2:28–29). New Testament authors draw upon this connection to demonstrate that through Jesus the time of the Spirit's outpouring has begun, signaling God's restoration. At Pentecost, Peter's speech connects fulfillment of Joel 2:28–32 with the outpouring of the Holy Spirit upon the fledgling church (Acts 2:16–21). In the rest of Acts, the Holy Spirit (or "the Spirit of Jesus"; cf. 16:6–7) directs the church to witness to and embody the gospel of Jesus as Lord of all (cf. 10:36). The time of the Messiah is the time of the Spirit.

Paul identifies the Holy Spirit as a down payment (*arrabōn*) who guarantees now the fullness of future restoration (2 Cor. 1:22; 5:5; Eph. 1:13–14). For Paul, living in light of and in line with this "Spirit reality" is the essence of spirituality ("spiritual," *pneumatikos*; 1 Cor. 2:13; 3:1; Gal. 6:1). Paul refers to *walking* by the Spirit (Rom. 8:4 NRSV) and *keeping in step* with the Spirit (Gal. 5:25) as ways to describe this "new eon" spirituality. Through these metaphors, Paul indicates that spirituality is not a prepackaged template that predetermines how believers are to live in particular contexts and situations. Instead, spirituality is a lifelong journey of discernment (Brown et al.). Walking in step with the Spirit necessarily means relating to God's Spirit in ways that are often beyond our experience of human relationships. Because of this, Christian spirituality, as the experience of the risen Christ through the Spirit, dwells in mystery.

Yet there are clear indicators of the Holy Spirit's work. The Holy Spirit guides believers into love, joy, peace, patience, kindness, goodness, faithfulness, gentleness, and self-control ("the fruit of the Spirit"; Gal. 5:22–23). The Spirit empowers holy and just living, giving believers freedom to live a life of service patterned after Christ (Gal. 5:13–14, 24). The Spirit also leads the church into witness and mission (Acts 1:8; 10:19–20, 44; 16:6–7). Most centrally, believers personally and corporately experience the very presence of the triune God "in the person of the Spirit" (Fee, 34).

Spiritual Practices

Central spiritual practices indicated by New Testament authors include worship and prayer, baptism and the Lord's Supper, hospitality and common meals, witness and mission, service and giving.

New Testament writers envision local churches living out each of these practices communally and in ways that contribute to the common good and the unity of the church. These practices are tangible expressions of God's restoring kingdom work, and as such, they tend toward the breaking down of social status barriers ubiquitous in the first-century Greco-Roman world (cf. Resseguie, 86–87). These spiritual practices are necessarily "bodily" practices. The modifier "spiritual" is not the opposite of "physical." Instead, these "embodied" practices involve the whole person with God and with their Christian community (Clapp).

Like the act of drawing breath, communal worship and prayer are reflexive practices for the church, fostering its relationship with the triune God. Colossians 3:16 portrays the rich texture of Christian worship: "Let the word of Christ dwell in you richly as you teach and admonish one another with all wisdom, and as you sing psalms, hymns and spiritual songs with gratitude in your hearts to God." Prayer permeates the New Testament writings. The Gospels, Epistles, and Revelation themselves contain prayers (Matt. 6:9–13); their authors exhort believers to pray (at all times! Luke 18:1; 1 Thess. 5:17; James 5:13–16). Epistle authors indicate both that they pray for their recipients (Phil. 1:3–11; 3 John 2) and that they need their prayers (Eph. 6:20; Col. 4:4; Heb. 13:18).

Baptism and the Lord's Supper—communal acts of worship—are celebratory rites that signal believers' participation with Christ in his death and resurrection. The initiatory covenantal sign of baptism indicates that believers in Christ are symbolically buried and raised to new life with him (Rom. 6:3–4; Col. 2:11–12). As a result, the believing community no longer participates in the distinctions that once characterized humanity: Jew/Gentile, slave/free, male/female are one in the Messiah through baptism (Gal. 3:26–29; cf. Rev. 7:9–10). The Lord's Supper is to be celebrated regularly by believers as an act of participation in Christ's body and blood—the embodiment of his self-giving sacrifice (1 Cor. 10:16–17). This practice centers on the remembrance and proclamation of the death of Jesus (1 Cor. 11:23–26) and is an embodiment of believers' unity in the Messiah (1 Cor. 10:16–17; 11:17–22).

Common meals and the broader practice of hospitality were important practices in the first-century church that could inform contemporary Christian spirituality. "Meals are profound expressions of our spirituality" (Resseguie, 1; cf. related issue of fasting, 82–84). Jesus' pattern of eating with "tax collectors and sinners" as narrated in the Gospels (Luke 5:30; 7:34; 15:1) sets the tone for shared meals in the church that often transgressed social or cultural boundaries (Acts 2:42–47; 11:1–3; 15:1–35; cf. also Gal. 2:11–14; 1 Cor. 11:17–34; Jude 12). The significance of these meals is rooted in the notion of believers' corporate participation in the Messiah (1 Cor. 10:16–17). As Johnson concludes, the New Testament evidence "emphatically support[s] the understanding of Christian meals … as a fellowship in the powerful life of God mediated through the resurrected Jesus and proleptic of his future triumph" (Johnson 1998, 176–77). In and beyond their common meals, early Christians were expected to share life with each other through the practice of hospitality (Rom. 12:13; Heb. 13:2; 1 Peter 4:9; 3 John 5–8; cf. Brown et al.).

Witness and mission are also New Testament spiritual practices. In calling disciples to love even their enemies, Matthew's Jesus connects this mission to Christian identity as God's covenant children: "that you may be children of your Father in heaven" (Matt. 5:43–48 TNIV). Covenantal relationship results in mission (cf. 5:14–16). In Acts, Christian witness is propelled by the Holy Spirit (Acts 1:8) and focused on proclamation of the gospel to both Jews and non-Jews—the good news that Jesus the Messiah was crucified but is now resurrected and so is Lord of all (Acts 2:36; 10:36). The letter of 1 Peter provides a fascinating case study in Christian mission, as it is written to Chris-

tians trying to live godly lives in a social context that is prone to interpret their behavior as suspect (2:11–12; 4:1–3). The author calls them to embody their allegiance to Jesus as Lord, being careful to avoid any impropriety that might call into question the goodness of their behavior (3:15; cf. 3:1, 13–17). By living rightly, some will inquire about their common hope in Christ, providing opportunity to give their reasons for their hope (3:15).

As the church lives out the life of the Messiah, service will be a hallmark of their community (Matt. 20:25–28). Service to others is a spiritual practice, since it is a path toward deeper participation with and experience of God in Christ and with the church. In fact, according to Matthew 18, Jesus' community is defined by their care for the most vulnerable ("little ones"; vv. 6–9 TNIV) and those who have fallen prey to sin (vv. 15–20), as they live out the values of status renunciation and unlimited forgiveness (Brown 2002, 69–76). At the climax of Matthew's five discourses of Jesus' teaching, we hear the fate of all humanity decided on their identification and service to "the least of these," those in need of food, clothing, and hospitality (25:40, 45). "Especially in the world's oppressed and outcast and marginalized, the face of Jesus is to be discerned" (Johnson 1999, 55). This value of caring for the needy and providing for them permeates the New Testament (Luke 6:20; 12:33; 18:22; Acts 9:36; 10:31; Rom. 15:26; Gal. 2:10; James 2:1–12; 5:1–6).

In conclusion, New Testament spirituality is Messiah-shaped, eschatological, and lived in the Spirit. God's covenantal community—reconstituted around and shaped by Messiah Jesus—lives by the Spirit in the inaugural time of God's restoration. Their spirituality is a journey of discernment as the church learns to keep in step with the Spirit between the time of the not yet and the already. Through their participation in the Messiah, God works to conform the community of faith into the image of Jesus as they pursue faithful living in worship, service, and mission.

Sources Cited

Bauckham, R. *Jesus and the God of Israel* (2008).

Brown, J. *Disciples in Narrative Perspective* (2002).

Brown, J., W. Corbin-Reuschling, and C. Dahl. *Becoming Whole and Holy* (2011).

Clapp, R. *Tortured Wonders* (2004).

Fee, G. *Paul, the Spirit, and the People of God* (1996).

Gorman, M. *Inhabiting the Cruciform God* (2009).

Johnson, L. T. *Religious Experience in Earliest Christianity* (1998).

———. *Living Jesus* (1999).

Koester, C. *A Theology of John's Gospel* (2008).

Moe-Lobeda, C. "A Theology of the Cross for the Uncreators." In *Cross Examinations*, ed. M. Trelstad (2006), 181–95.

Resseguie, J. *Spiritual Landscape* (2004).

Wright, N. *The Challenge of Jesus* (1999).

For Further Reading

Barton, S. *The Spirituality of the Gospels* (1992).

Bouyer, L. *The Spirituality of the New Testament and the Fathers.* Trans. M. Ryan (1982).

Fee, G. *Listening to the Spirit in the Text* (2000).

Howard, E. *The Brazos Introduction to Christian Spirituality* (2008).

Humphrey, E. *Ecstasy and Intimacy* (2006).

CHAPTER 5

SPIRITUAL THEOLOGY

SIMON CHAN

Joseph de Guibert defines spiritual theology as "the science which deduces from revealed principles what constitutes the perfection of the spiritual life and how man can advance towards and obtain it" (Guibert, 11). This definition highlights two main foci in spiritual theology. First, it traces the progress of the spiritual life from its beginning to its final perfection, and second, it studies various means needed for progress to be realized. Most standard works of spiritual theology basically follow these two divisions.

Its nature and function become clearer in comparison with other theological disciplines. Spiritual theology is closely related to systematic or dogmatic theology but also differs in approach to its subject matter. The subject matter dogmatic theology covers a range of doctrines organized around broad loci, such as God, creation, man and sin, Christ and salvation, and so on. Doctrines are formulations derived from the church's experience of God, primarily its experience of the worship of and communion with God. Doctrines in turn regulate the church's experience and help to distinguish right experiences of worship (*orthodoxia*; lit., "right worship") from wrong ones. Spiritual theology covers the same ground but from the perspective of the church's experience itself. Spiritual theology is the flip side of dogmatic theology. It focuses on the experiential reality underlying the concepts of systematic theology. Again, spiritual theology differs from practical theology in that the latter seeks to draw out practical applications from theology. For example, in practical theology the doctrine of the love of God may provide the motive for loving others, practicing hospitality and pacifism, but spiritual theology seeks to understand and cultivate the love of God itself as an experience. The love of God, in fact, is the definitive characteristic of the believers' communion with God.

The study of spiritual theology has undergone important changes over the years. Traditional spiritual theologies tend to view the Christian life from the perspective of the individual, focusing on the cultivation of certain qualities, virtues, and graces in individual souls. This approach in the past has resulted in a tendency to divorce the moral life from dogmatics, and in an excessive focus on one's personal relationship with God (Hughes). But more recent developments have come to see that Christian life is essentially ecclesial, lived out in relation to the triune God in the ecclesial community into which Christians are baptized, and in which they are continually nourished by word and sacrament. In other words, the underlying theological anthropology is not the individual as a unique being made in the image of God who possesses independent qualities like freedom, self-consciousness, and rationality, but persons existing in freedom and communion in Christ and his body, the church. The cultivation of virtues in individuals is still important, since it is through such efforts that one participates more actively in the ecclesial community, but virtues cannot be pursued independently of life in the church. Thus, ecclesiology is seen as the more basic category under which the doctrine of the salvation and development of individuals is subsumed. Since the ecclesial life is formed and expressed primarily in worship, the study of liturgical spirituality has become an increasingly important part of spiritual theology (Pfatteicher; Saliers). In short, the newer approach acknowledges that the Christian life must be understood relationally, especially in relation to its divine source.

The Source of Spiritual Life

The spiritual life has its source in the Holy Spirit, "the Lord and giver of life." But life in the Spirit cannot be understood apart from the works of the Father and the Son. Thus, spiritual theology may be understood as the exploration of the nature of life in relation to the Trinitarian economy. A Trinitarian spirituality has been characteristic of Eastern Orthodoxy, but its full ramifications have only become more widely appreciated in relatively recent times, especially with the revival of interest in Trinitarian theology in the second half of the 20th century.

Christians are called not only to pattern their lives after the Trinitarian pattern, but also to share in the very life of the Trinity, to be partakers of the divine nature (2 Peter 1:4), which the Eastern church calls *theosis* or deification. The life of the Trinity is essentially a relationship of love in which each person gives freely to the others. Thus, as Bernard of Clairvaux taught during the Middle Ages, growth in the spiritual life may be understood in terms of growth in love.

The spiritual life may be further explicated in relation to the distinct works of the persons of the Trinity. The divine acts appropriate to the Father are creation and love for his creatures; the act appropriate to the Son is his *kenōsis*, or self-emptying, for the redemption of the world; and the act appropriate to the Holy Spirit is *episkiasis*, his "coming upon" to give new life. A spirituality that focuses on the Father as "maker of heaven and earth" recognizes the goodness of creation and hence of life as essentially sacramental. The Father's sending the Son for the world's redemption highlights the evangelical dimension of the spiritual life centering in the gospel-events of Jesus' life, death, resurrection, ascension, and coming again. The continuation of the Trinitarian story in the sending of the Holy Spirit at Pentecost to indwell the church (the "second sending") underscores its charismatic dimension. The spiritual life could therefore be characterized as sacramental, evangelical, and charismatic. A sacramental spirituality presupposes an indirect working of grace through created things. An evangelical spirituality is marked by a warm and intimate relationship with Jesus Christ as Lord, Savior, friend, etc., while a charismatic spirituality is open to the direct workings of the Spirit coming from "beyond history" (Zizioulas) in surprising ways, such as prophecies and healings. In the past, these three dimensions have been kept more or less distinct in the Catholic, Protestant, and Pentecostal traditions. But there is now a growing awareness that these are not inherently incompatible but must be brought together precisely because they reflect the works of the triune God. Some evangelicals and charismatics have formed "communions," such as the International Communion of the Charismatic Episcopal Church and the Communion of the Evangelical Episcopal Church, which seek to bring about the convergence of these three streams of spirituality. Convergence is the practice of Trinitarian spirituality that finds concrete expression in the liturgy. The liturgy is sacramental in structure, evangelical in content, and charismatic in orientation. The structure of the liturgy consisting of Word and sacrament underscores its sacramental character. The basic content of the liturgy is the celebration of the paschal mystery, while the direction of the liturgy is pneumatologically conditioned. The Spirit as the firstfruits of the new creation and the gift of the last days orients the liturgy toward the eschaton and mission. As firstfruits the Spirit inspires hope (Rom. 5:1–5) and gives to the church its characteristically already–not yet eschatological existence. As gift the Spirit distributes the charisms in the church, making it a charismatic body to fulfill the *missio Dei*.

Different understandings of the order of the Trinitarian relations affect the way the Christian communal life is conceived. In Catholicism and Orthodoxy the revelation of the triune God is seen as entailing a certain hierarchical order expressed in the phrase "the monarchy of the Father." The Father is the "source" from whom the Son is generated and the Spirit is spirated. This is reflected in the ancient church's liturgy where the doxological response is expressed "*to* the Father, *through* the Son, *by* the Holy Spirit." All things lead back to the Father ("to the praise of his glory," Eph. 1:6, 12, 14), through the Son, the mediator, and by the power of the Holy Spirit. In contrast, modern Protestantism conceives of the Trinity as an egalitarian society resulting in a view of the church as a strictly egalitarian community (Moltmann).

Progress in the Spiritual Life

All Christian traditions recognize that the spiritual life must undergo development, but how it progresses is differently understood. The resources for understanding spiritual progress have traditionally come from Scripture and the Christian tradition, but nowadays increasing use is made of the social sciences, especially in the field of developmental psychology (Fowler; Kohlberg; Loder).

In Catholic spiritual theology, progress is usually explicated in terms of the Three Ways of purgation, illumination, and union. Within this process two elements are distinguished: the ascetical and the mystical. The ascetical has to do with training or discipline (*askēsis*) in order both to purify the heart through prayer, meditation, and mortification of sin (purgation), and to acquire and strengthen the virtues or good habits so as to become more Christlike (illumination). Illumination is so called because it is when a person becomes more dependent on the illumination of the Spirit than on *askēsis* to further strengthen the virtues. One begins to experience what is traditionally called infused grace rather than grace acquired through spiritual discipline. It is a transition from the more active, ascetical phase to the more passive, mystical phase.

The latter is marked by contemplative prayer of increasing depth, which leads to the achievement of mystical union. Modern discussions on spiritual progress have generally moved away from viewing the Three Ways as discreet, sequential steps to seeing them as simultaneous and continuing processes.

In Protestantism, progress is usually understood in terms of an order of salvation (*ordo salutis*), which is variously defined but broadly consisting of three stages—conversion, sanctification, and glorification—which roughly parallel the Three Ways. Conversion occurs when one turns from sin to God in repentance. The believer is given new life by the Spirit, or "born again." The emphasis on the gift of new life in Christ has been the great strength of evangelical spirituality, especially in mission situations. Evangelicals, however, have tended to view conversion as a crisis experience, although more recently it is also being recognized as a continuing demand.

Sanctification is a lifelong process of growing in holiness that is usually understood as conformity to the image of Christ. If the content of sanctification is expressed in terms of some specific virtues, it is usually linked to the fruit of the Spirit (Gal. 5:22–23) but seldom to the theological and cardinal virtues. This reflects the evangelical preference for scriptural rather than traditional resources. Sanctification will only be completed at death (glorification). Glorification is strictly a future event, so that the possibility of mystical experiences as an actual foretaste of the heavenly life is not envisaged.

However, in the history of Protestantism, this was not always the case. Some of the English Puritans in the 17th century seemed to entertain a concept of the Christian life as progressing from an ascetical to a more mystical phase. They drew freely from medieval mystical writers, especially Bernard of Clairvaux. Joseph Hall (1574–1656) not only wrote an ascetical work, *The Art of Divine Meditation* (1606), which was an adaptation of an elaborate method of meditation from Johannes Mauburnus's *Rosetum exercitiorum spiritualium et sacrarum meditationum* (1494), but in later life wrote a number of devotional works with a strong mystical strain, such as *The Breathings of the Devout Soul* (1651) and *An Holy Rapture or Pathetical Meditation on the Love of Christ* (1654). Hall envisaged the possibility of "seeing" the invisible God through deep contemplation: "And if in the seeing of God we be (as the School[men] hath taught us to speak) unitively carried into him, how can we choose but in this act be affected with joy unspeakable and glorious?" Similarly, Richard Baxter not only enjoined "heavenly meditation" in his earlier work, *The Saints' Everlasting Rest* (1650), but toward the end of his life, he also wrote some moving mystical works, such as *The Divine Life* (1664), urging Christians to go beyond just being "related" to God and to embark on "a course of complacential contemplation."

The progressive concept of the Christian life continued in John Wesley's doctrine of entire sanctification, or Christian perfection, as a second work of grace beyond conversion. This Wesleyan idea had had a powerful impact on the Holiness and Keswick movements in the 19th-century and Pentecostalism in the 20th century. While their understanding of the Christian life as progressing in precise stages may be questioned, the underlying concern for the "higher life" or "baptism in the Spirit" has deeply shaped these later expressions of Wesleyan spiritualities.

But these spiritual impulses exist uneasily with modern evangelicals whose understanding of spiritual progress is seldom clearly spelled out, and whose spirituality tends to be defined by activism and evangelism. The result is what Richard Lovelace calls "the sanctification gap," where one moves from conversion (conceived as a crisis experience) to activism (primarily evangelism and mission) without the mediation of the sanctified life found in the Puritan and Wesleyan traditions. But this weakness is being corrected as evangelicals learn the importance of cultivating the traditional spiritual disciplines (Foster; Willard).

Although attempts have been made to describe evangelical spirituality (Gillett; Parker), evangelical spiritual theology is still largely undeveloped. Some suggestive implications for spiritual theology, however, can be discerned in recent evangelical thinking on ecclesiology. Webster, for example, argues that the relationship between the church and God must be predicated on the distinction rather than similarity between humans and God. The relationship is basically covenantal, resulting in "fellowship" with God rather than participation in the divine life as found in the Orthodox doctrine of deification.

The Means of Spiritual Progress

The second major focus of spiritual theology is how individuals are assisted to advance in their spiritual life. Mortification of sin and growth in virtue, that is, the ways of purgation and illumination, cannot be properly achieved without dealing with specific vices and virtues. The task of spiritual theology includes identifying and studying the nature of these vices and virtues, often using "templates" taken from Scripture and traditional sources. The seven deadly sins and the three enemies of the soul (the world, the flesh, and the devil) are traditional ways of explicating the nature of sin. A scriptural template for the virtues is the sevenfold "gifts of the Spirit" (Isa. 11:2), while from traditional sources there are the theological virtues (faith, hope, and charity) and the cardinal virtues (prudence, justice, temperance, and fortitude). Such an approach is based on a perceptive insight that difficulties in the Christian life are not just a matter of sin in general but of having to deal with specific besetting sins and cultivating specific virtues to overcome them.

Spiritual theology, further, includes the study of the nature and purpose of various personal and corporate spiritual practices. Some methods are tried and tested over the centuries, e.g., the Ignatian method of meditation and the monastic practice of *lectio divina*. These have been adapted for use in various times and contexts even to this day. Others have more limited application, such as anchoritism. Basic to one's spiritual development is the practice of prayer. The whole growth process could be seen as growth in prayer. In Teresa of Avila it is delineated in nine stages beginning with vocal prayer and ending in the prayer of transforming union. Prayer broadly conceived includes spiritual reading, meditation, self-examination, and participation in common worship. Since the Christian life is defined by relationship with other Christians in the body of Christ and expressed in mission in the world, practices like fellowship, hospitality, and social engagement are important means of developing a holistic life. And since the corporate life is supremely realized in the church especially in its liturgical celebration, increasing focus has been given to practicing the "marks of the church," such as proclamation of the Word, baptism, Eucharist, and catechesis (Braaten and Jenson). The aim is to form an ecclesial "community of character."

The study of spiritual progress is not complete without considering the problems that hinder progress, such as distractions, temptations, and sins, and how to deal with them. For example, how does one deal with distraction during meditation, distinguish temptation from sin, overcome a besetting sin? Many spiritual writers are of the view that the very nature of the growth process entails trials that include experiences of a sense of divine absence. These periods of "dark night" (John of the Cross) occur at the higher levels of the spiritual life and are the means to an even deeper relationship with God.

The range of means for advancing the spiritual life and the problems that hinder it is quite limitless. What spiritual theology does as a theological discipline is to study the underlying theological rationale of the various spiritual experiences, bring out their interconnectedness, and relate them to other disciplines, especially the social sciences. For example, the possibility of spiritual formation through the spiritual disciplines is predicated on a doctrine of the means of grace (Protestant), some form of sacramental theology (Catholic), or the doctrine of synergy (Orthodoxy); the nature of temptation needs to be seen in relation to the three enemies of the

soul; a particular besetting sin may be the result of social and childhood conditioning, which in some instances may require "inner healing" (Seamands).

As each person is different, spiritual theology seeks to develop approaches that take individual uniqueness into consideration. This is the work of spiritual direction. In this work, discernment is critical. Discernment draws on the spiritual director's intimate knowledge of spiritual principles as well as knowledge of the directee's personality. The director helps the directee to discern God's will with respect to choices concerning his or her life's basic direction and also to distinguish between what is and what is not from God's Spirit. Discernment is even more crucial as the spiritual life deepens and a person sometimes encounters baffling experiences, such as a prolonged period of the dark night, extraordinary phenomena such as revelations, visions, and unusual bodily sensations. In this connection, an intimate knowledge of similar experiences in the Christian tradition is most helpful. Discernment also extends to specific issues, such as whether a particular spiritual exercise and its duration is suitable for a certain personality type or for one at a particular stage of spiritual maturity.

Contexts and Types of Spiritual Theology

Just as theology in general is shaped by the social-political and ethnographic contexts, the same could be said of spiritual theology in particular. The spiritual life is lived in specific contexts, and the diverse contexts in the world affect the way the Christian life is concretely expressed. Thus, various forms of liberation spiritualities have emerged in contexts of extreme poverty resulting from unjust distribution of resources, corruption, nepotism, and other forms of structural evils. Similarly, feminist and black spiritualities represent responses to perceived inequalities with respect to gender and race. In situations of relative affluence, the call is made to voluntary poverty and simplicity as valid forms of spirituality. In these spiritualities, the issues addressed are predominantly sociopolitical in nature. But in places where the ethnographic and religious contexts play a critical role in shaping one's worldview, the resulting spirituality may be quite different, as can be seen in the predominance of Pentecostal-type spiritualities in much of the global south. They show deep affinities with primal spirituality and its essentially sacramental worldview (Turner). They also have much in common with the premodern worldview of the Bible so that the Bible is often taken at face value (Jenkins). Not only do contexts shape spirituality, personality types are just as determinative. It explains why some are drawn to a more "active" spirituality while others prefer a more "contemplative" type, why some prefer a more structured worship while others the "free" forms. Questions, however, persist regarding the extent to which different spiritual expressions could be taken in light of the norms of Scripture and the Christian tradition. In a world that celebrates "multiculturalism," there is a danger of treating all types of spiritualities as equally valid even if they are inherently incompatible with doctrinal norms or with each other.

Sources Cited

Braaten, C., and R. Jenson, eds. *Marks of the Body of Christ* (1999).

Foster, R. *Celebration of Discipline* (1978).

Fowler, J. *Stages of Faith* (1981).

Gillett, D. *Trust and Obey: Explorations in Evangelical Spirituality* (1993).

Guibert, J. de. *The Theology of the Spiritual Life* (1953).

Hughes, R. D., III. *Beloved Dust: Tides of the Spirit in the Christian Life* (2008).

Jenkins, P. *The New Faces of Christianity* (2006).

Kohlberg, L. *The Psychology of Moral Development* (1984).

Lovelace, R. *Dynamics of the Spiritual Life* (1979).

Loder, J. *The Logic of the Spirit* (1998).

Moltmann, J. *The Church in the Power of the Spirit* (1977).

Parker, D. "Evangelical Spirituality Revisited." *Evangelical Quarterly* 63, no. 2 (1991): 123–48.

Pfatteicher, P. *Liturgical Spirituality* (1997).

Saliers, D. *Worship and Spirituality* (1984).

Seamands, D. *Healing of Memories* (1985).

Turner, H. *The Roots of Science* (1998).

Webster, J. "The Church and the Perfection of God." In *The Community of the Word*, ed. M. Husbands and D. Treier (2005), 75–96.

Willard, D. *The Spirit of the Disciplines* (1988).

Zizioulas, J. *Lectures in Christian Dogmatics*. Ed. D. Knight (2008).

For Further Reading

Chan, S. *Spiritual Theology* (1998).

Groeschel, B. *A Still Small Voice* (1993).

Hambrick-Stowe, C. *The Practice of Piety* (1982).

Kelsey, M. *God, Dreams and Revelation* (1974).

Kilmartin, E. *Christian Liturgy* (1988).

CHAPTER 6

JESUS

DALLAS WILLARD

Christian spirituality has at its center Jesus of Nazareth, acknowledged by believers to be both Savior and Lord. To be a Christian, then, is to follow this Jesus. To appreciate what this has involved, and must continue to involve, it may be helpful to consider very briefly the dynamics that explain and shape all human spiritualities. For spirituality, viewed broadly, is indeed a universal dimension of human life. It arises out of the human quest for a *place*, an *identity*, and *powers* that are more than the "mere facts" of human existence. It seeks to make meaningful contact with, and draw substance from, that "more," that "higher power." Such a quest is the source of religions as we find them in our world, but it is not limited to religion. It constantly overflows and renews religion—very often by opposing what religion has become.

In their origin and development, religions are profoundly shaped by the spiritual journeys of individuals. In the case of Christianity, this has been supremely the life story of Jesus. In turn, each religion, as a concrete social reality, makes a distinct spirituality available to those in significant contact with it, and that spirituality always has two main dimensions. These two dimensions are dependent on and simultaneously in tension with each other. They are first, the *human forms*, outwardly recognizable patterns of behavior, events, and equipage, that yield the many different "spiritualities" familiar to us; and second, the *transcendental interconnection* that lies outside of and within human forms and institutions, inhabiting them but always challenging, correcting, and modifying them.

Through the centuries, distinctively Christian spirituality has involved the endeavor to conform individual and social life to what Jesus did and said—more deeply still, to who he was and is. He lived out in his own person a spirituality that had both a human and a transcendental dimension. His followers through the ages, in adoration of him, have sought to penetrate to the core of his spirituality and to make it their own. Sometimes this has been a very explicit quest, as in the famous work of Thomas à Kempis on *The Imitation of Christ* (1471), and in the *Imitatio Christi* tradition generally, but it has always been an implicit reality of the Christian life.

In its outward dimension (that is, in the part necessarily expressed in human society and culture), the spirituality of Jesus was that of a serious Jewish young man—eventually a rabbi—living in the period of mature, postexilic Judaism. He was brought up and lived for the most part in outlying areas of the Jewish homeland under Roman occupation, but he was thoroughly immersed from his youth in the teachings, traditions, and official practices of the Jewish religion of his day. He lived and died within the outward forms of that religion, even while, as a true son of Israel, he drew from the Law and the Prophets a vision of the whole world under God's rule (Ps. 46:10; Isa. 49:6).

Freeing human life from the tyranny of certain specific cultural—especially religious—forms was one of the main thrusts of his life and ministry as well as a major part of the task his followers inherited from him. Staying, himself, within the Jewish forms of his day, at many points he challenged those forms as practiced around him, but always from within the resources of the Law and the Prophets. He constantly contrasted the heart of the law, or God's intent with his laws, to the distortions and misapplications those laws had undergone at the hands of the "power people" or authorities of his day — "the scribes and the Pharisees." They used and abused "the law" to shut people away from God and to impose, for their own advantage, impossible burdens upon the masses of simple people they were supposed to serve. By critiquing them, Jesus continued the ancient prophetic tradition of Israel: that of the insider who is also an outsider, standing among people in the presence and power of God.

The spirituality of Jesus Christ was in that precise sense *incarnational*. To use that word, however, is not to refer only to the metaphysical nature of Christ, as is usually done. Rather, it is an indication of two different realms coming together to form a unique kind of life, in which human life *in* the world is an expression of divine life surpassing the world. The fullest expression of this "incarnation" is perhaps given in Jesus' prayer of John 17: "I have given them your word, and the world has hated them because they do not belong to the world, just as I do not belong to the world.... As you, Father, are in me and I am in you, may they also be in us, so that the world may believe that you have sent me" (vv. 14, 21 NRSV). Christ followers are, it is often said, "in the world but not of it." In the words of the apostle Paul, "our citizenship is in heaven" (Phil. 3:20).

The spirituality of Jesus Christ and of his followers is therefore a twofold life. It is, on the one hand, an ordinary human existence of birth, family and social context, work, and death, shared by all human beings, including Jesus himself. That is what it means to be "in the world." The spirituality

of Jesus is not flight from the world. But it is also a life of knowing God by interactive relationship with him as we live in the world. It is eternal living (*aionios zoe*, John 17:3) here and now. It expresses itself within ordinary human life through understandings, events, and characteristics that cannot be explained by natural capacities of human beings or the natural course of events in "the world." It is accordingly "of the spirit and not of the flesh." This distinction, along with the warfare of spirit and flesh, is a focal point of the spirituality of Christ and the Christ follower, and a direct consequence of its incarnational nature.

The language Jesus used to express the spiritual side of the twofold life was the language of "the kingdom of the heavens" or "the kingdom of God." The kingdom of God, which is exercised from "the heavens" around us, is the domain of God's action: it is where what he wants done is actually done. Jesus worked and spoke in terms of the kingdom of God. He *proclaimed* or "preached" the direct accessibility to all of life in this "kingdom of heaven" (Matt. 4:17; Mark 1:15), he *manifested* the presence of God's action with him through deeds of power, and he *taught* about how things were done, what life would be like, for those living under the rule of God. (On this threefold ministry of proclaiming, manifesting, and teaching, see Matt. 4:23; 9:35.) Thus, one of his most oft-repeated phrases is: "The kingdom of the heavens is like...." After his resurrection he was in and out among his friends "over a period of forty days and spoke about the kingdom of God" (Acts 1:3). The message of the kingdom's presence and availability through faith in Christ was committed to the disciples and carries on through the book of Acts (28:23, 31) and beyond.

So the spirituality of Jesus was a twofold life; Jewish in outward form, but drawn, on the divine side, from the kingdom of the heavens, as a domain of reality in which one lives now. In the life of Jesus as presented in the Gospels, his spirituality was characterized by a number of traits that have also been prominent in the lives of his followers.

Independence from Human Authority

That he had authority—that is, the power, and not just the right, to direct thought, action, and events around him—was never in doubt. The effects of his power were obvious, and that is repeatedly brought out in the Gospels. That it did not derive from human sources was also obvious, for human authority was mainly set against him and eventually caused his death. He was questioned concerning the source of his authority (Luke 20:2), but no one doubted he had authority. His implicit reply to the question was that his authority came from heaven. John the Baptizer had authority from heaven, and his "endorsement" of Jesus put the stamp of "heaven" on Jesus.

Jesus was, however, not the disciple of John, or of any other prophet or rabbi. Jesus' effects in speaking and acting manifestly originated from the God who was "with him" (Acts 10:38). That was an essential part of his spirituality. He endowed his followers with that same authority (Luke 9:1–2; Acts 1:7–8). Independence of human authority—so often exercised, unfortunately, in the name of God, yet in a manner contrary to his character and purposes—is nonetheless a constant factor in Christian spirituality, from Jesus and his first followers up to the present day. Its watchword in this respect is always, "We must obey God rather than any human authority" (Acts 5:29 NRSV; cf. 4:20).

The Great Inversion

"What is prized by human beings is an abomination in the sight of God" (Luke 16:15 NRSV). And, it was also clear to Jesus that what is prized by God is often an abomination in the sight of men. The two sides of the twofold life offer very different vantage points on what is good and what is important—of what "success" in life really amounts to. This was a note often struck in the Old Testament, but Jesus relentlessly drives it home in every aspect of his life and teaching. He repeatedly empha-

sizes that "many who are first will be last, and the last will be first" (Matt. 19:30 NRSV). His most remarkable statements on this point—and perhaps the most misunderstood—are the "beatitudes" of Matthew 5 and Luke 6. He himself was among the humanly "unblessables" in his birth, life, and death—as the great "kenosis" passage of Philippians 2:7–8 so clearly spells out. But he was blessed before God nonetheless. Down in the human order (poor, mournful, etc.) may well be up (among the blessed) in the divine order. Up in the human order (rich, popular) may well be down ("Woe to …") in God's order. Well-being is not at all what humans routinely take it to be. But those alive in the kingdom of God, no matter what their circumstances may be, are blessed, well-off. The servant is regarded by human beings as among the lowest of the low. But in the spirituality of Jesus, "The greatest among you must become like the youngest, and the leader like one who serves. For who is greater, the one who is at the table or the one who serves? Is it not the one at the table? But I am among you as one who serves" (Luke 22:26–27 NRSV).

The Practice of the Presence of God

The spirituality of Jesus is unthinkable apart from the presence of God with him. In the times when he was alone from the human point of view, God was with him (John 8:16, 29; 16:32). On the cross, apparently, he was allowed to experience being forsaken by God, as he "taste[d] death for everyone" (Heb. 2:9). But his oneness with the Father was unbroken. The covenant people from Abraham onward had lived interactively with the God who was with them. That accounted for the manifold types of extra-human effects and accomplishments that characterized individuals as well as the people of Israel together. The tabernacle in the wilderness was an arrangement made in order for God to dwell among the children of Israel and be their God. "And they shall know that I am the LORD their God, who brought them out of the land of Egypt that I might dwell among them; I am the LORD their God" (Ex. 29:46 NRSV). God was so manifestly with Isaac, for example, that his powerful neighbors asked him to move away—and then came to ask him to move back, because "We see plainly that the LORD has been with you" (Gen. 26:16, 28 NRSV). Looking back upon the career of Jesus, the apostle Peter explains "how God anointed Jesus of Nazareth with the Holy Spirit and with power; how he went about doing good and healing all who were oppressed by the devil, for God was with him" (Acts 10:38 NRSV). The "practice of the presence" is today one of the strongest themes in Christian spirituality.

Complete Security and a Worry-free Existence

Jesus taught and practiced a life of peace and joy in the knowledge of God's complete nearness and care, and he offered that life to his disciples as well. Such life lay at the very heart of his own spirituality. His mastery over events and people through faith in God, and the presence of God with him, never left him at a loss, no matter the situation. Though sometimes saddened to tears or exasperated by the ineptitude of his students, only in the supernatural struggle with evil in Gethsemane, on the way to the cross, and then upon the cross do we witness his vulnerability—his "passion" (John 12:27). No doubt it was from him that Paul learned how to be "afflicted in every way, but not crushed; perplexed, but not driven to despair" (2 Cor. 4:8 NRSV).

He could enjoy the company of "publicans and sinners." He could continue his nap in the storm, though the boat was filling with water and his disciples were scared out of their wits. After calming the storm he asked them: "Why are you afraid? Have you still no faith?" (Mark 4:40 NRSV). Surely his friends must have wondered at these questions. They simply did not yet see what he saw.

He knew that there was no reason to be afraid

of those who can kill the body but after that have no more that they can do (Luke 12:4). "Whoever keeps my word," he said, "will never see death" (John 8:51 NRSV). "Keepers of his word" will have already passed from death to life. There also is no need for them to worry about food or clothing or the material provisions for life (Luke 12:22–31). One has only to devote oneself to living in the kingdom and every provision will be made— though perhaps not to the world's taste. Provisions for this life and beyond are made by the father, who watches over everything and is always with us. Joy, the pervasive sense of well-being, is the condition in which we live the kingdom life.

The early believers knew the secret: "Keep your lives free from the love of money, and be content with what you have; for he has said, 'I will never leave you or forsake you.' So we can say with confidence, 'The Lord is my helper; I will not be afraid. What can anyone do to me?'" (Heb. 13:5–6 NRSV). Writing to the Philippians from his prison cell, citing the fact that "the Lord is near," Paul echoed the instruction of Jesus (Matt. 6:25–34) not to worry about anything. Rather "in everything by prayer and supplication with thanksgiving let your requests be made known to God. And the peace of God, which surpasses all understanding, will guard your hearts and minds in Christ Jesus" (Phil. 4:4–7 NRSV).

Subversive of "The World"

The picture of Jesus' spirituality that emerges from the above points naturally leads to appropriate subversion of merely human arrangements, which are largely based on fear. Subversion was the charge that led to the death of those early Christians who would not worship Caesar, and it is the charge that has been repeated through the ages up to today in many parts of the world. The charge upon which Jesus was crucified was, essentially, that of subversion of the religious and political orders. In his encounter with Pilate, Pilate said to Jesus: "'Do you not know that I have power to release you, and power to crucify you?' Jesus answered him: 'You would have no power over me unless it had been given you from above'" (John 19:10–11 NRSV). The source of governmental power is the same as the source of the "new birth" (it is *anōthen*, Gr. "from above").

Then Jesus proceeded through death to destroy the one who has the power of death, and thus to set "free those who all their lives were held in slavery by the fear of death" (Heb. 2:15 NRSV). The primary human instrument of repression and control, the fear of death, is set aside by Jesus and his good news about eternal living now in the kingdom of God. He "abolished death and brought life and immortality to light through the gospel" (2 Tim. 1:10 NRSV). The Christ follower honors those to whom honor is due, but always "under God." It is because they stand under eternal authority and power that they more than any others stand for what is good, whether with or against those who have responsibility in human affairs. This, too, is the spirituality of Jesus Christ, and it is radically subversive. The ultimate "subversion" would of course be at the coming of "the day of the Lord," when the "kingdoms" of this world would have become the kingdom of our God and of his Christ.

Death to Self

Unlimited abandonment to God is essential to the spirituality Jesus lived and taught. He did not have to go to the cross. No one made him. It was his choice when there were other paths he could have taken. Choice is sacred to God, but what is best to choose? Faced with options, he saw that "Unless a grain of wheat falls into the earth and dies, it remains just a single grain; but if it dies, it bears much fruit. Those who love their life lose it, and those who hate their life in this world will keep it for eternal life. Whoever serves me must follow me" (John 12:24–26 NRSV). Abandonment to God is the fruitful way to experience good under

God. It means relinquishing "our way." It means not being angry or resentful when things do not go our way. It means that in God's hands we are content for him to take charge of outcomes. And in that posture we make way for him to occupy our lives with us and achieve what is best for us and for others far beyond anything we can even imagine. "I have been crucified with Christ." His abandonment becomes our abandonment. "[Nevertheless,] I live" (Gal. 2:19–20). His resurrection becomes our resurrection—even before our "physical" death (Col. 3:1–4). Death to self is not ultimately a negation, but a rising up into the very life of God (2 Peter 1:4). Thus, our life is saved by his life (Rom. 5:10).

The positive aspect of the "if it die" is "bringing forth much fruit." The death he chose was for the sins of the world. It was not just to lose life, but also to give life. This is what prevents his death, and Christian "death to self," from being morbid. It was for the "joy that was set before him" that he "endured the cross, disregarding its shame" (Heb. 12:2 NRSV). According to the ancient prophecy, he saw the work accomplished by his suffering and was satisfied (Isa. 53:11). "He died for all, so that those who live might live no longer for themselves, but for him who died and was raised for them" (2 Cor. 5:15 NRSV). The mark of his disciples, accordingly, that they love one another just as he loved them (John 13:34), is simply the outflow of transcendent life that comes through self-giving death.

These are a few outstanding points in the incarnational spirituality of Jesus Christ, which he shares with us today. Many people will find them surprising, because they have come to think of him and his spirituality, roughly speaking, in "monastic" terms. This widely shared vision of him sees him as withdrawing from the world and from "natural" human existence in order to be "spiritual." But for all of the virtues that may be found in monasticism, Jesus and his students were not monastics. Theirs was a spirituality of engagement with the world—a spirituality of stewardship, which hears the words "Do business with these until I come back" (Luke 19:13 NRSV) and rises up, in the face of all opposition, to conduct normal human affairs in the power of God.

To succeed with this indeed requires a life disciplined under grace. We learn to follow Jesus by entering into the activities he practiced. Effectual spirituality in the manner of Jesus demands wise, nonlegalistic spiritual disciplines that nurture spiri-tual formation in Christ. But practicing spiritual disciplines is not itself spirituality. Spirituality is the life from God flowing through our life, which spiritual disciplines, rightly used, can help to facili-tate. Indeed, the kingdom walk with Christ is no life as usual among human beings, but an intel-ligent and spiritually informed course of regular activity that maximizes interactive relationship with the Trinity in the twofold life.

For Further Reading

Barclay, W. *Jesus as They Saw Him* (1978).

Edersheim, A. *The Life and Times of Jesus the Messiah*, 2 vols. (1993).

Francis of Assisi. *The Little Flowers, Legends, and Lauds.* Trans. M. Wydenbruck (1947).

Muggeridge, M. *Jesus* (1984).

Pelikan, J. *Jesus through the Centuries* (1999).

Ratzinger, J. *Jesus of Nazareth* (2007).

Willard, D. *The Spirit of the Disciplines* (1988).

Wright, N. T. *Jesus and the Victory of God* (1997).

CHAPTER 7

THE HOLY SPIRIT

CLARK H. PINNOCK AND GLEN G. SCORGIE

The Holy Spirit is the flame of God's love, the ecstasy of the divine life, the uniting bond within the Trinity, the overflowing abundance of God outwardly. He is the one who sweeps us up into the love of God. Christian spiritual theology affirms that human persons are revitalized by faith in Jesus Christ and by the power of the Holy Spirit. Yet through the centuries, the doctrine of the Holy Spirit, vital though it is, has often been neglected or treated in a slipshod manner. Making things worse, the church has too often neglected movements of revival and reform. Thankfully things are improving; efforts are now being made to relate the Spirit to all other facets of reality, including the Christian life — often spurred on by the expansion of the Pentecostal impulse. Hopefully this will translate into real and deepened practice of life in the Spirit.

Water, Breath, and Fire

The Bible does not reveal the character of the Holy Spirit in the manner of a systematic theological treatise with terse definitions of terms. Instead, the wonder of the Spirit is evocatively revealed through elemental symbols. One of these is water. We find this imagery used in the Old Testament in places like the prophecies of Isaiah (44:3; 55:1) and Ezekiel (47:1 – 12). Especially to a people who lived in a hot, dry, and often desert climate, water was a compelling image of what was life giving and soul nourishing. And Jesus later picked up on this when he engaged the Samaritan woman at the well. He

spoke to her of the possibility of "living water" springing up within her to satisfy her thirst forever. Later on the apostle John explained that his comments about water are actually references to the Holy Spirit (John 7:39). It is a reminder that the Spirit sustains and nourishes life and satisfies thirst.

Another important biblical image for the Holy Spirit is a word (Heb. *ruach*, Gr. *pneuma*) that can mean either wind or breath. There are enough similarities between wind and breath that we should not be surprised that these ancient peoples used one word for both phenomena. The image of wind conveys the truth that the Spirit's operations are invisible and mysterious, as Christ himself pointed out in John 3:8. Yet they have noticeable, sometimes powerful, effects.

But *ruach* and *pneuma* can also mean breath. Such breath was life giving in the Genesis account of Adam's creation (2:7). God fashions an inert body for the first man, but it is when God breathes into him that he stirs, his eyes open, and he becomes a living soul. Likewise, it is the breath of God in Ezekiel (37:9) that revitalizes the valley of dry bones and restores life to corpses and skeletons. It is almost certainly the significance of the resurrected Christ breathing on the disciples prior to his ascension (John 20:22). The intent of these images can be summed up in the words of Paul: "The Spirit gives life" (2 Cor. 3:6). Surely this inspired imagery of oasis water and animating breath is instructive for churches that want to live and not die.

The Holy Spirit is also represented by fire, as when John the Baptist predicted that Jesus would baptize with the Holy Spirit and with fire (Luke 3:16); tongues of fire settled on each person in the upper room at Pentecost (Acts 2:3); and the apostle Paul urged believers not to quench the Spirit's fire (1 Thess. 5:19). In the Old Testament, fire was associated with God's presence (e.g., Ex. 3:1–6); in this instance fire may also symbolize divine power, the Spirit's refining and purifying force, and the ardor of burning love (Pinnock).

Pentecost and the Church

Pentecost was a Trinitarian event, and the apostolic community spoke about it in personal terms — Father, Son, and Spirit, three persons in loving community. The Son receives the gift of the Spirit from the Father and pours it out on the peoples (Acts 2:33). This language reveals the structure of the gospel in which God sends his Son and Spirit to bring about the salvation of the world. It creates a vision of the Spirit within the liveliness of the Trinitarian mystery. "Spirit" speaks of the serendipitous power of divine creativity within the relationality of God. The Spirit participates in the communion of loving persons overflowing with divine life. The church fathers sometimes pictured it as a dance, a coming and a going, a circling around of Trinitarian life that calls upon everyone to join in. We imagine that there exists a perfect communion in the heavenly sphere into which we are being summoned to enter. When we speak about the Trinity, we confess our faith, not in a solitary God, but in God who is a loving communion. We recognize a "three-ness" in the mystery of God and believe that it provides a symbolic picture of totally shared life at the heart of the universe.

The Christian faith is not an individual affair; Christians are a people who allow themselves to be built up into a *Spirit*-ual house (1 Peter 2:5). Historically evangelical spirituality has emphasized direct and personal relationship with God, unme-diated by the church per se. It has appreciated how the Spirit's freedom makes it impossible to contain or restrain the Spirit's movements within any humanly constructed, legally registered, visible-from-the-freeway institutional structure. Nonetheless, the church is more than a hollow shell where humans dream moral dreams and do good deeds; it is the house where God by his Spirit has chosen to live and enliven. The people of God are more than a tribe coalescing around shared values; together they constitute a "temple" of the Holy Spirit (Eph. 2:21–22) (Badcock). In it the presence of God's Spirit is experienced more as communion and community than as structures and forms. Since the Holy Spirit is by nature a uniting impulse and has made a commitment to the nurturing of this unique community, believers who choose to disassociate from it will necessarily also experience some measure of disconnect from the Spirit's presence and grace. The imagery of the Spirit's advent — immersion, deluge, pouring out, infilling — suggests an act of divine generosity and plenitude to meet the needs of the church. Even so, the church's desire remains for even greater filling — ever more fulsome animation with the Spirit's transforming and empowering presence (Eph. 5:18).

Growing Clarity Concerning the Spirit

One of the earliest and most enduring summaries of what Christians believe became known as the Apostles' Creed. The riches of the Christian belief system were distilled into a series of short affirmations — nonnegotiable convictions without which Christianity could not carry on. After declaring belief in God the Father Almighty and in Jesus Christ, his only Son, our Lord, the Apostles' Creed (like the Nicene Creed, which followed it) takes a deep breath and adds: "I believe in the Holy Spirit."

Were the early Christians simply acknowledging that the Holy Spirit existed? If that were all that they meant, it would still have been significant.

The sheer existence of the Spirit—the fact that he is here—changes our perception of reality. During the patriarch Jacob's first night as a fugitive, he had a vision of God and bright angels descending on a ladder to the exact place where he rested on the ground. In the morning, Jacob exclaimed, "Surely the Lord is in this place, and I was not aware of it" (Gen. 28:16). He had a spine-tingling awareness that the supernatural presence of God had been brooding over the entire scene all along. When we grasp that we are not alone either—that the invisible Spirit is a real and pervading presence all around us, our sense of wonder is aroused. And we are unable to live like secular materialists anymore.

The Spirit early believers acknowledged was always the *Holy* Spirit. This signature attribute ensured that in the Christian tradition, as in the Jewish tradition before it, spirituality and morality would be joined at the hip. Holiness is intrinsic to the Spirit's disposition, so there are always ethical impulses associated with his presence and influence. He is the agent of sanctification, the instigator of outrage against injustice, the manifestation of divine hostility against all that threatens human well-being.

But the early Christians, in affirming that they *believed* in the Holy Spirit, were saying more. They knew that biblical faith combines believing *that* (*assensus*) with believing *in* (*fiducia*). They recognized that genuine faith is first a matter of intellectual assent, but it is also a matter of personal trust. In confessing "I believe in the Holy Spirit," they were declaring their full confidence in the unseen reality of the Holy Spirit, and counting on him to make the decisive difference in their lives and communities. The early Christians recognized the Spirit as the indispensable presence and power in their lives and knew that without him Christianity simply could not, and would not, long survive.

The words of Hilary of Poitiers, from the 4th century, still ring true. In response to the calling upon his life, he prayed: "If I am actually to do it, I must ask for your help and mercy, ask you to fill with wind the sails I have hoisted for you and to carry me forward on my course—to breathe, that is, your Spirit into my faith … and to enable me to continue" (Hamman, 194). Like Hilary, we must become sailors, hoisting our sails so that the empowering wind, the very breath of God, can move us forward. The prophetic Scripture comes to mind that it is " 'not by might nor by power, but by my Spirit,' says the Lord Almighty" (Zech. 4:6).

No Second-Class Holy Spirit

Christology was the consuming focus of 4th-century Christian theology. Yet concurrently there was growing consciousness of the fully divine nature and crucial role of the Holy Spirit as well. By the end of the century, the so-called Nicene Creed (in its AD 381 form) added these confessional descriptors of the Spirit: "The Lord, the giver of life … who with the Father and Son together is adored and honored" (Burns and Fagin, 155–204). This magisterial consensus statement carried at least two significant implications. First, the Spirit was no mere sentimental feeling or commodity to be managed. The Spirit, being *the Lord*, possessed ultimate gravitas, and a fitting spirituality therefore needs to respond to the Spirit's impulses with respect and careful regard—indeed, with all that was implied by the classic phrase "the fear of the Lord."

On one occasion, Jesus explained to his disciples that the promised Holy Spirit would take it as his mission to glorify the risen Christ (John 16:14). In light of this text, some Christians have felt uncomfortable about directing any worship toward the Spirit. Such hesitancy reflects a misunderstanding of the text. The real point is that the Spirit, who came in fullness at Pentecost, had no intention of establishing a new, Spirit-centered religion. The Spirit was not a replacement or an upgrade on Jesus Christ. The Spirit, as Bruce Milne has noted, is "that member of the eternal Godhead who brings to bear in the life of God's people the fruits of the victory won by Christ in his life, death and resurrection" (Milne, 180). This is all profoundly important to the unity of the faith, but now we are clear to embrace the complementary truth that the Holy Spirit has every claim upon our worship by reason of his essential divinity. The Spirit is more than God's aide; he is God-with-us now. When we sing the concluding words of the doxology, "Praise Father, Son, and Holy Ghost," we are worshiping aright. The Holy Spirit is in no way a second-class or inferior member of the Holy Trinity. For this reason he has every claim upon our obedience and respect.

The Giver of Life

In the second place, the creedal phrase "giver of life" underscores how crucial the Spirit is to the natural life of the whole creation, as well as to the spiritual vitality of the church and the regenerated people who comprise it. He is indeed the life-giving breath of God. Sometimes we restrict our thinking of the Spirit to the sphere of redemption and cut him off from bodily life and nature. We need a vision of the Spirit that corresponds to the breadth of the biblical concept of Spirit. We must not lose the continuity of the work of the Spirit in creation and in new creation. Spirit has roles to play in all of creation and is not a mere ornament of piety. It is the life of creation itself—in the vitality and joy, in the radiance and beauty. The Spirit is God's energy for life and the ecstasy that triggers the divine abundance. In the biblical traditions, the Spirit is God's breath that breathes life into the creation. From the dust humankind lives and breathes. Spirit animates all of the wonderful and diverse creatures that run and hop and swim. Everything comes from God's breathing. Spirit is a way of talking about God's creative and energizing power (Ps. 104). All of the creatures look to God to give them food in due season. When God sends forth his Spirit, they are created, and God renews the face of the ground. The Spirit is also involved in the creation of the nonhuman universe, bringing beauty and grace into the whole world.

The life-giving character of the Spirit is admirably illustrated in his enlivening of the written Word. Past revelation in the form of Scripture is God-given and profitable (2 Tim. 3:16), but how does it become timely? The Spirit is the key to making the word contemporary and living. The Spirit of truth leads the community into more and more truth as it moves forward in mission. The apostles asked not only what the text had said in its original context, but also what was now crucial for their time and place. The Spirit of God makes the text revelatory and an effective witness. He searches the deep things of God and gives us the mind of Christ.

Sometimes we boast about the Bible, as something sacrosanct and fixed, and fail to notice how Jesus and the apostles interpreted Scripture. Scripture for them was not like a set of rational propositions in need of logicians to grasp the truth and sort it out. Rather, they themselves were grasped by the power of the text and were transformed by a demonstration of the Spirit and power. Jesus and the apostles interpreted the Old Testament as if it were a dynamic text. For them, having a high view of Scripture did not mean rote submission; it meant much more. They sought guidance concerning what texts mean now. They had a dynamic concept of revelation. God might be showing us something fresh through it.

This does not diminish or deny the authority of the Bible. Rather, it sets texts free to function as the word of the Lord for today. We can exalt the letter above the Spirit and miss the point. The biblical authors were not always in a position to grasp the full meaning and implications of the truths they articulated. There is a surplus of meaning, thanks to the nature of texts and to the Spirit. Scripture is ever open to fresh (though always chastened and circumspect) interpretations.

Jesus and the Spirit

Prior to the outpouring of Pentecost, Jesus was subordinate to the Spirit. His life was controlled and led by the Spirit so that he could carry out his messianic vocation. Thus, the life-giving breath of God, who enables the universe of creatures to unfold and enables human beings in grace, brings about the event to which both creation and grace are directed—the Christ event. The Son is subordinated to the Spirit so often in the gospel narratives that we can speak of "the lordship of the Spirit" in relation to Jesus. Christ performed all his work in the power of the Spirit—a supreme example of what is possible in a human life that is dependent on the Spirit. Thus, he passes the Spirit along to the disciples who also need to be empowered for mission. The outpouring of the Spirit on the disciples at Pentecost gives them the power that was promised, and not just once but repeatedly. Jesus was a charismatic and his church a charismatic community.

At Pentecost there was a role reversal. The Son was no longer subordinate to the Spirit. The bearer of the Spirit became the bestower of the Spirit. In his state of humiliation, the Messiah was directed by the Spirit; in his exaltation, the Spirit is at his disposal. Jesus tells the disciples that God is going to give them "another paraclete," just like Jesus, who will be with them forever, a never-failing friend. This Spirit of truth will convict the world and will lead us more and more deeply into the truth. Then Jesus breathed on them, signifying new creation (John 14–15). Henceforth, the *fruit* of the Spirit would characterize the transformed character of believers, and the *gifts* of the Spirit their empowered ministries.

A new period in history opened up. We have been baptized in the Spirit; the power has been poured out. "As the Father has sent me," said Jesus, "I am sending you" (John 20:21). The Spirit gives us what we need. This is not a single experience, but a continuing relationship. There is always subsequence, always more. There is no rigid order here; there is room for variation, room for breakthroughs. That which God did once at Pentecost, he can still do again. There can be new stirrings of the hearts of God's people, new times of refreshing from the Lord.

Purposes of the Spirit

Christian spirituality has three distinct yet interwoven dynamics—three impulses that mix and move together as a single living thing. The first is relational in character (about connecting), the second is transformational (about becoming), and the third is vocational (about doing). These are the basic ongoing realities of the Christian life, and the Holy Spirit actively encourages all three. He encourages the *relational* dynamic through his assuring and uniting work. He actively assures us that the relationship we are counting on is real, and we do belong to God. He testifies to our spirits that we are the children of God (Rom. 8:15–16). He also nurtures unity—arresting the alienating impulses of sin, prompting grace and forgiveness, and restoring harmony and shalom to human relationships. As Irenaeus winsomely envisioned, the Holy Spirit is the moisture that softens souls in order to knead them together in Christ (Burns and Fagin, 34–35, 208). It is by the Spirit that we were all baptized so as to form one body (1 Cor. 12:13). Little wonder, then, that the Scriptures urge us to "make every effort to keep the unity of the Spirit through the bond of peace" (Eph. 4:3).

Likewise, the Spirit promotes the *transformational* impulse of Christian spirituality. He does so by his works of moral refining and soul-healing. The Spirit's work of moral renewal is beautifully described in Galatians 5, where the fruits of the Spirit stand in striking contrast to the acts of the sinful flesh. After agonizing struggles with his own sinful nature, Paul finally discovered that the Spirit had set him free from the law of sin and death (Rom. 8:2). Both Peter and Paul refer to the sanctifying work of the Spirit (1 Peter 1:2; 2 Thess. 2:13). With respect to healing, the anointing oil used in the healing ordinances of the church (James 5:14) is also a symbol of the Holy Spirit.

Finally, the Spirit contributes to the *vocational* dynamic by guiding, equipping, and empowering believers. His ministry of guidance is apparent throughout the book of Acts, from the story of how he led Philip to appear alongside the Ethiopian eunuch's chariot, to Paul's decision, following the Macedonian call in a vision, to venture beyond Asia to bring the gospel into Europe for the first time. When the Spirit came at Pentecost, the disciples acquired power for effective service that Jesus had promised to them (Acts 1:8). The subsequent ministries of the early church were conducted in the power of the Spirit. Where the Holy Spirit is a manifest presence in lives, these three elements—the relational, the transformational, and the vocational—all seem to be naturally present as well. And the appropriate response on our part, as the apostle Paul explains, is to "keep in step" with the Spirit (Gal. 5:25).

Keeping in Step with the Spirit

What are the keys to fuller experience of the uniting, purifying, and empowering presence of the Spirit? On our part, it comes to the dispositions of the heart, in particular to attentiveness and hospitality. Many spiritual disciplines are simply proven practices for *tuning out* the distractions and noise of creature-centered existence, and *tuning in* to the unseen reality and persistent voice and nudges of the Spirit. The ability to listen with discernment is a cultivated skill, but it is more than a technique. Listening requires sacrifice and the relinquishment of other priorities, and our practice will be shaped not so much by what we understand as by what we care about most.

Miroslav Volf has eloquently presented our two options when faced with otherness: either exclusion or embrace. The first is an unflinching will to exclude, symbolized by arms tightly crossed and closed. The alternative of embrace involves two body movements. Open arms, reminiscent of Christ's outstretched arms on the cross, and the Father's welcome home of the prodigal son, illustrate the desire for inclusion—the "sign of discontent at being myself only." But there is also a closing of the arms around the other, symbolizing both incorporation and enrichment. The one embraced, he maintains, not only enters within the circle of care but "become[s] part of me so that she can enrich me with what she has and I do not" (Volf, 29). It is the same with the Holy Spirit. We must create space in our lives for him by being attentive and welcoming. The pace and rhythms of our lives, no less than the disposition of our hearts, must reflect a posture of invitation to the Spirit—because, as Philip Yancey has remarked, God goes where he's wanted (Jenkins, 15). And so believers echo in their own spirits such great 19th-century hymn-prayers as "Spirit of God, descend upon my heart" and "Breathe on me, breath of God."

Conclusion

The Holy Spirit is the life-giving "breath" of God and Christ's great gift to the church (Luke 11:13). Christians must not focus on only one or two of the divine persons, but worship and serve as Trinitarians who revere and passionately care about all three divine persons—the Father, the Son, and the Holy Spirit. Indeed, the church, according to the benediction of 2 Corinthians 13:14, is to be nourished by the grace of our Lord Jesus Christ, the love of God the Father, and the fellowship of the Holy Spirit—that exquisite foretaste of the eternal dance of reciprocating delight.

Sources Cited

Badcock, G. *The House Where God Lives* (2009).

Burns, J. P., and G. Fagin. *The Holy Spirit* (1984).

Hamman, A., ed. *Early Christian Prayers* (1961).
Jenkins, P. *The Next Christendom* (2002).
Milne, B. *Know the Truth* (1982).
Pinnock, C. *Flame of Love* (1996).
Volf, M. *Exclusion and Embrace* (1996).

For Further Reading

Bloesch, D. *The Holy Spirit* (2000).
Cole, G. *He Who Gives Life* (2007).
Edwards, D. *Breath of Life* (2004).
Ferguson, S. *The Holy Spirit* (1996).
Green, M. *I Believe in the Holy Spirit* (1985).
Kärkkäinen, V. M. *Pneumatology* (2002).
Macchia, F. *Baptized in the Spirit* (2006).
Moltmann, J. *The Spirit of Life* (1992).
Welker, M. *God the Spirit* (1994).

CHAPTER 8

HUMAN PERSONHOOD

BRUCE A. DEMAREST

Christian spirituality has been defined as "lived experience of God in Christ through the Spirit and reflection on this experience" (Callen, 17). Spiritual formation, on the other hand, involves the shaping and nurturing of the Christian's inner being after the pattern of Jesus Christ for the blessing of others. Since the domain of spirituality and spiritual formation is man and woman, it is necessary to explore the nature of human personhood as a matter of foundational importance to Christian spirituality and spiritual formation.

Beginning of Human Life

The creation account in Genesis 1 states that "God created human beings in his own image, in the image of God he created them; male and female he created them" (Gen. 1:27 TNIV). Scripture provides a second and complementary account of Adam's creation in Genesis 2:7. Most leading Christians throughout history, such as Clement of Alexandria, Tertullian, Jerome, Luther, Calvin, and evangelicals today are persuaded that human life begins not at birth or postbirth at some level of functional ability, but at conception. In modern scientific terms, conception occurs at completion of the fertilization process at about twenty-four hours, when sperm and ovum unite, fuse nuclei, and join chromosomes to form a zygote of a particular sex.

That human life begins in the womb is substantiated by biblical evidence. When Jacob's wife, Rebekah, became pregnant "The babies [Jacob and Esau] jostled each other within her ..." (Gen. 25:22 TNIV). The Lord then said to her, "Two nations are in your womb, and two peoples from within you will be separated" (Gen. 25:23 TNIV). The psalmist David testified that God ordained the course of his life as he was being formed in his mother's womb (Ps. 139:13–16). Furthermore, God called Isaiah and Jeremiah to prophetic ministry while they were yet unborn (Isa. 49:1; Jer. 1:5). Luke indicates that both Jesus in Mary's womb (Luke 1:31) and John the Baptist in Elizabeth's womb (Luke 1:41) were human beings. Abortion thus represents the morally blameworthy act of destroying a human life.

Essential Composition

Scripture is not silent regarding the essential composition of the human person. Figuratively interpreting the terms *soul*, *spirit*, and *body* as descriptive of the entire person, substance monism claims that the human person consists of a single substance, either spiritual soul (idealism) or material body (materialism, Marxism). Much of nonevangelical theology (Bultmann; J. A. T. Robinson) subscribes to substance monism. Some evangelical thinkers (Ray S. Anderson; G. C. Berkouwer), together with much modern psychology influenced by brain science, proffer this position. Trichotomy, on the other hand, claims that the terms *soul*, *spirit*, and *body* refer to distinct substances, each with different functions. Guided by 1 Thessalonians

5:23, "May your whole spirit, soul and body be kept blameless at the coming of our Lord Jesus Christ" (cf. Heb. 4:12), Christian trichotomists (Delitzsch, J. N. Darby, and C. I. Scofield of the influential *Scofield Reference Bible*) distinguish between the substances of the rational soul, the immortal spirit, and the physical body. The human soul is said to be the seat of self-consciousness; the spirit, God-consciousness; and the material body, world-consciousness.

Other authorities subscribe to substance dualism (Augustine, Tertullian, Aquinas, Luther, Carl Henry), sometimes represented as dualistic holism or holistic dualism (John W. Cooper). This position argues that the human person is a differentiated whole, consisting of a single immaterial soul/spirit united with a material body. "Soul" (*nepeš, psychē*) in Scripture occasionally denotes the whole person (Gen. 2:7) and the life force that animates the body (Isa. 42:5). But more frequently it signifies the functional seat of the intellect, will, emotions, and desires (Job 7:11; Ps. 10:3; Prov. 2:10). The soul may be said to be the immaterial self-relating horizontally to oneself and others. Spirit (*rûah, pneuma*) in Scripture likewise occasionally refers to the whole person (Ps. 31:5) and the vital power from God that animates the body (Job 27:3). But more frequently it signifies the faculty that responds to the Almighty (Ps. 51:10; Isa. 26:9). Spirit may be regarded as the immaterial self-relating vertically to God, particularly so in the New Testament following the outpouring of the Spirit at Pentecost. Soul and spirit, though sometimes exercising different functions, consist of the same immaterial reality, for Scripture often uses soul and spirit interchangeably (Job 7:11; Isa. 26:9; Luke 1:46–47), indeed, as quasi-synonyms (1 Thess. 5:23; Heb. 4:12).

"Body" (*bāśār, sōma*) in Scripture occasionally refers to the whole person (Ps. 16:9). But more commonly it denotes corporeal, material substance (Gen. 17:14; Job 19:26; Gal. 6:17). The important biblical term *heart* (*lēb, kardia*) commonly refers to the integrating center of humans or "the wellspring of life" (Prov. 4:23). From the heart emerge thoughts, intentions, desires, emotions, moral sentiments, and spiritual life (Rom. 10:9–10; Col. 3:16). Further supporting holistic dualism is the Bible's differentiation between inner (immaterial) and outer (material) aspects of the human person (Rom. 7:22–23; 2 Cor. 4:16; 5:1–9). Further evidence is provided by the doctrine of redemption; although believers' material bodies decay, their soul/spirit is being renewed by the Holy Spirit (see Rom. 8:23; 2 Cor. 4:16). Likewise, the doctrine of the intermediate state holds that at death the immaterial soul/spirit separates from the material body and enters either the intermediate heaven (Luke 23:43; Acts 7:59–60; Phil. 1:22–24) or provisional hell. See Jesus' parable of the rich man and Lazarus (Luke 16:19–31). Cooper concludes: "The biblical view of human nature is both holistic—emphasizing the religious, phenomenological, and functional integration of life—and dualistic—asserting that persons are held in existence without fleshly bodies until the resurrection" (Cooper, 231).

Likeness to God

"God created human beings in his own image, in the image of God he created them; male and female he created them" (Gen. 1:27 TNIV). The *imago Dei* concerns humans' likeness or similarity to their Creator, which distinguishes them from all other creatures. Guided by God's command to the first pair, "fill the earth and subdue it. Rule over the fish in the sea and the birds in the sky and over every living creature that moves on the ground" (Gen. 1:28 TNIV), some authorities (D. J. A. Clines, Dale Moody, G. von Rad) interpret the *imago* as humans' exercise of dominion over the earth and its inhabitants. On this showing, functionality is substituted for ontology; the human being *is* what he or she *does*. Moreover, from the statement "male and female he created them" (Gen.

1:27), other authorities (Barth, Bonhoeffer, Stanley Grenz) proffer the relational view. This affirms that, analogous to relations among the persons of the Trinity, the *imago* represents humans' freedom to *relate* to self, spouse, neighbors, and God. Here relationality is substituted for ontology; the human person *is* insofar as he or she *relates*.

The traditional view on human composition focuses on substance (spiritual and material) and capacities. Augustine, Aquinas, Luther, Calvin, and most evangelicals identify the *imago* as humans' soul/spirit that endures beyond the grave (Eccl. 12:7) together with capacities of intellect, volition, emotion, morality, relationality, and activity in the world. This interpretation reflects humans sharing God's communicable (but not incommunicable) attributes. Calvin distills this view thusly: "God's image was visible in the light of the mind, in the uprightness of the heart, and in the soundness of all the parts" (Calvin, 1.15.3). Although Scripture offers no systematic exposition of the *imago*, the New Testament sheds light on its nature by highlighting the restoration in Christ of aspects thereof that were marred by humanity's fall into sin. Such features include knowledge of God, reasoning powers, righteousness and holiness, and pious devotion (Rom. 12:2; Eph. 4:23–24; Col. 3:10). Since God created humans to resemble himself in important respects, defamation of persons (James 3:9) and acts of murder (Gen. 9:6) are forbidden.

Human Functioning

Humans function holistically out of the created capacities that constitute the *imago Dei*. Biblically, human functioning represents the soul, mind, or heart working through the body. Intellectually, human functioning includes consciousness (awareness of oneself, others, the world, and God), reason (drawing conclusions from facts and experiences), imagination (forming mental images of things not present to the senses), and memory (recollection of past experiences and persons). Volitionally, humans are capable of self-determination (the freedom to be who I am) and of choosing goals and strategies for accomplishing these goals. "In their hearts human beings plan their course" (Prov. 16:9 TNIV). As put by Calvin, the will's function is "to choose and follow what the understanding pronounces good, but to reject and flee what it disapproves" (1.15.7).

Emotionally, humans possess the capacity to experience inward-oriented feelings (pride, embarrassment, shame), outward-oriented emotions (joy, fear, anger), passions (intense emotions), desires (emotionally laden longings), and sensations (hunger, fatigue, pain). Morally, humans possess the capacity to differentiate between good and evil (Gen. 3:5, 22). Solomon prayed for "a discerning heart … to distinguish between right and wrong" (1 Kings 3:9). Conscience (*syneidēsis*, "coknowing")—the moral evaluator of the heart—dialogues between God's law implanted on the heart and written in the Scriptures and thoughts and behaviors. Paul wrote that Gentiles who do not have the law "show that the requirements of the law are written on their hearts, their consciences also bearing witness, and their thoughts now accusing, now even defending them" (Rom. 2:15).

Relationally, God created humans for relationship, defined as emotionally freighted connections between persons or objects. Philosophically, the theory of external relations, held by most orthodox Christians, posits that relations are accidents that do not define personhood essentially. The theory of internal relations, held by some postmoderns, posits that the nature of persons depends on the relation they sustain to other persons. Thus, without relating to another person, Mary or John would not be a human person. On this showing, a fetus, a newborn baby, or a senile elder would not be human. A person is an embodied soul/sprit with the capacity, among other things, to relate to one's internal and external worlds. Humans relate authentically (Lev. 19:18) to themselves, to spouses and family members, to other persons, to the inanimate world, and supremely to God himself. Helen Perlman identifies characteristics of a healthy relationship as "warmth, loving, caring, acceptance, responsiveness, empathy, genuineness, attentiveness, concern, support [and] understanding" (Perlman, 23). Sexuality is a good gift of God, not only for reproduction (Gen. 1:28), but also for completeness (cf. Gen. 2:20) and for the strengthening of love between the sexes.

Functionally, the human person is capable of performing many worthy works, such as working at creative employment, tending the home, cultivating the ground, constructing cities, governing subjects, developing technologies, and engaging in the fine arts—in short, fulfilling God's cultural mandate (Gen. 1:28–30; cf. Ps. 8:6–8). All created human capacities and functions cited above operate interdependently. For example, the intellect informs the will; the will evokes emotions; conscience directs behaviors; behaviors enhance knowledge; and so on. No one function dominates the others.

Personhood Degraded by Sin

To understand the condition of humans in the present, we observe that God placed Adam and Eve in a pristine garden where they enjoyed unbroken communion with himself as well as the delicious fulfillment of every human need. Yet motivated by pride and the quest for self-autonomy, the first pair disobeyed God and as a result experienced alienation from their Creator, objective guilt, and temporal and eternal judgment. The progenitors of the race tragically forfeited the noble purpose for which they were created. The consequences of the first pair's sin passed down upon the entire human race by generation and by personal choice.

Intellectually, sin distorts human reasoning processes, particularly in spiritual matters. "The god of this age has blinded the minds of unbelievers, so that they cannot see the light of the gospel of the glory of Christ" (2 Cor. 4:4). Spiritual verities

appear to the unregenerate as "foolishness" (*môria*) because they are spiritually discerned (1 Cor. 2:14). The condition of the unsaved thus is one of epistemic blindness spiritually (Eph. 4:17–18; Titus 1:15). Volitionally, the unregenerate are disposed to sinful motives and choices. Instead of choosing to love and serve God, sinners decide for themselves (2 Tim. 3:2), the world system (1 John 2:15), wickedness (2 Tim. 2:12), and misdirected pleasures (2 Tim. 3:4). Biblical data suggest the bondage of the unregenerate will in spiritual matters (Rom. 6:16, 20; Titus 3:3; 2 Peter 2:19).

Emotionally, human feelings, affections, and desires are disordered (James 1:14), reflected in the form of sinful pride (Prov. 16:18), arrogance (Dan. 5:20), envy (James 4:5), jealousy (Rom. 13:13), lust (1 Peter 4:3), and so on. Morally, sin objectively incurs guilt before the righteous God (Jer. 2:22), and subjectively, an accusing conscience (Isa. 57:20–21), loss of moral sensitivity (Eph. 4:19), and lack of peace (Isa. 48:22). Behaviorally, the unsaved bring forth corrupt speech and conduct. They are "filled with every kind of wickedness, evil, greed and depravity. They are full of envy, murder, strife, deceit and malice. They are gossips, slanderers, God-haters, insolent, arrogant and boastful; they invent ways of doing evil" (Rom. 1:29–31). Relationally, the unregenerate are conflicted within themselves (Isa. 57:21) and with family members and neighbors (James 4:1–2), and they are tragically estranged from their Creator and Redeemer (Isa. 59:2; Eph. 2:12). In the fallen state, God's good gift of sexuality is conflicted with shame (cf. Gen. 3:7). In sum, the *imago Dei* in holistically depraved pre-Christians (Jer. 17:9) is corrupted, albeit not altogether destroyed (James 3:9).

Personhood Renewed in Christ

Reversal of the debilitating effects of the fall is accomplished by the redemptive life and work of Jesus Christ. Spiritual transformation begins with the renewal of the mind (Rom. 12:2; cf. Eph. 4:23; Col. 3:10). Intellectually, through the restorative work of the Spirit together with the exercise of spiritual disciplines such as study and meditation, believers are renewed in knowledge, understanding, and wisdom (Eph. 1:17; James 3:17). Christians put on the mind of Christ (1 Cor. 2:16; Phil. 2:5) by bringing all thoughts, images, and memories under his dominion. Volitionally, believers submit to Christ's control by allowing the Spirit to order their intentions, decisions, and choices. Thereby freedom of the will in the spiritual realm is restored. Transformed Christians prove to be self-controlled because they are God-controlled (Gal. 5:23). Moreover, since love primarily is a choice, not a feeling or emotion, renewed believers are empowered to love God, brothers and sisters in Christ, all persons, and all things noble.

Emotionally, carnal feelings, emotions, and affections are put to death (Col. 3:5, 8). Renewed hearts bring forth healthy inner responses, such as longing for fulfilling intimacy with God (2 Cor. 7:11), tenderness (Phil. 2:1), compassion (Eph. 4:32; 1 Peter 3:8), and joy (Rom. 14:17). Morally, spiritually renewed people pursue holiness of life in accord with God's command (1 Peter 1:15–16). The goal of the renewed life is to become "perfect" (*teleios*, Matt. 5:48), not in the sense of sinless perfection achieved in this life, but in terms of soundness, wholeness, and ethical maturity (1 Cor. 2:6; Eph. 4:13). The outcome of such is a clear conscience (1 Tim. 1:19; 1 Peter 3:16). Moral transformation involves putting off the "old self" dominated by sinful passions and putting on the "new self, created to be like God in true righteousness and holiness" (Eph. 4:22, 24). Holiness of life means that believers are sanctified not only de jure but also de facto.

Relationally, saints in Christ accept themselves as a valued image of God graciously adopted into his family (Rom. 8:15–17). Believers experience trustful and loving relationships with spouses and other family members (Col. 3:18–21), with Christian brothers and sisters (Rom. 12:16), and with all persons, even those who cruelly mistreat them (Luke 6:27–28). Supremely, believers experience loving relations with the triune God. By virtue of Christ's redemption, Christians are caught up in the reciprocity of life and love between the three divine persons (John 17:21, 23), represented in the ancient church by the term *perichorēsis*, meaning "dance around." Eastern Orthodoxy depicted believers' dynamic participation in the relational life of the Trinity by the term *divinization* (*theōsis*), meaning sharing in the life of God through the energy of the Spirit as a result of which we become new creations in Christ (2 Cor. 5:17). In the realm of sexuality, as in all areas of existence, God calls believers to pursue purity of life (1 Thess. 4:7).

Functionally and behaviorally, believers offer the members of their bodies not as instruments of wickedness but of righteousness (Rom. 6:13, 19). The tongue speaks the truth rather than lies (Eph. 4:25); the hands serve the poor and needy in Jesus' name (Eph. 6:7); and the feet walk the path of God-honoring obedience (Ps. 119:101). Renewed humans exercise faithful stewardship of the earth and its resources for the glory of God and the good of the human family, thereby fulfilling the Genesis cultural mandate.

The upshot of holistic transformation of human personhood is the progressive renewal of the *imago Dei*. Peter expressed this goal as participation in the divine nature (*theia physis*; 2 Peter 1:4), equivalent to sharing in Christ (Heb. 3:14) or sharing in his holiness (Heb. 12:10). Via holistic transformation, the goal of human existence is realized: the reshaping of the total person into the likeness of Jesus Christ, the true image of God (Rom. 8:29; 2 Cor. 3:18) and the prototype of the new humanity (1 Cor. 15:47–49). Complete conformity to Christ—the ultimate attainment of human destiny—will occur when we see the Savior face-to-face (1 John 3:2), either at death or at his second coming.

Sources Cited

Callen, B. *Authentic Spirituality* (2001).

Calvin, J. *Institutes of the Christian Religion*, 2 vols. Trans. J. McNeill (1960).

Cooper, J. W. *Body, Soul and Life Everlasting* (1989).

Perlman, H. *Relationship: The Heart of Helping People* (1979).

For Further Reading

Allen, R. B. *The Majesty of Man: The Dignity of Being Human* (2000).

Berkouwer, G. C. *Man: The Image of God* (1962).

Brown, W. S., N. Murphey, and H. Newton Maloney, eds. *Whatever Happened to the Soul? Scientific and Theological Portraits of Human Nature* (1998).

Willard, D. *Renovation of the Heart* (2002).

CHAPTER 9

SPIRITUALITY IN COMMUNITY

GLEN G. SCORGIE AND KEVIN S. REIMER

Christian spirituality is about life with God—that is, in his presence, with a welcoming and reverent regard for his person and claims. This divine-human link constitutes the core of Christian spirituality. Regardless of how profound such an experience of union with God may be, despite the level of self-forgetful submission or ecstasy to which some believers may attest, the relationship remains a differentiated one. The Christian is not absorbed into the oneness of all things—he or she does not forfeit personal identity. The Christian will never become God. For all these reasons, we can safely conclude that Christian spirituality is irreducibly relational in nature.

From the earliest days of Christianity, there were believers who sought God in isolation from others—in the desert, in wilderness huts, in sealed up enclosures. To this day, Christian history is salted with disappointing, even disturbing instances of "spiritual autism," when zealous believers claim to love God but disdain human fellowship or pursue God by means of radical dissociation from others. The 4th-century shift from eremitical to monastic forms of spirituality indicates the presence of spiritual instincts whereby the people of God affirm the value of "horizontal" human relationship and social context. We consider this horizontal dimension together with vertical orientation, a bidirectional frame for identity as created in God's image.

The Case for Relational Spirituality

Thomas Merton was a sophisticated, well-traveled young man when he was finally accepted into the order of Trappist monks and confirmed into a life of rigorous disciplines and protracted silences. His acceptance came as an enormous joy and relief, "the sweet savor of liberty" (Merton, 409). The variety of Christian spiritual traditions offers space for diverse individual temperaments and varying personal inclinations along a broad continuum between sociability and privacy. Transcending personality variables, the human propensity for relationships is the essence of our experience, and consequently, our spirituality. We offer four observations to support this thesis.

The first argument for being attentive to communal dynamics is a pragmatic one—namely, that as humans we are already embedded in relational networks. We have others all around us, people who are proximate to us, people who qualify as our "neighbors." These are contexts in which our spirituality is to be lived out. Spirituality is never a disembodied experience or something to be undertaken by escaping from the quotidian realities of our lives. Rather, it is meant to touch all aspects of our ordinary lives; it is to be lived out in the framework of our actual circumstances. The goal is not to escape our relational reality, but to engage it meaningfully and navigate it successfully. To be spiritual requires the presence of others—individuals who mirror back features of personal identity aligned with Christ's kingdom or requiring additional divine grace.

The second reason the scope of our spirituality must encompass human relationships is that "being-in-relation" stands at the center of eternal reality. Since before time, God has been a tri-unity of differentiated persons. As image-bearers of a relational God, we were designed for relationships following those enjoyed among the persons of the holy Trinity. Humans are like God in a number of ways, and not least among these we bear a social likeness to the divine. We were designed to "do relationships" like God does, and we become more fully human—that is, we enter most fully into the experience for which we were originally designed—when we do. The 20th-century theologian Emil Brunner was among those who highlighted the social meaning of the *imago Dei*. It has also been emphasized in a host of more recent works, including Stanley Grenz's *The Social God and the Relational Self* (2007). Today there is a transdisciplinary acknowledgment of the relational character of human nature.

Through increased conformity to the relational nature of God, we find our own broken humanity progressively restored. Consequently, Christians should be attentive to how they interact with others—in short, how they navigate the interpersonal realities of life. What we can achieve and accomplish in life is of course important, but *how* we go about it relationally may prove equally or more significant. Christians can learn to relate to others following God's own ways of relating. Doing so is crucial to our deliverance from painful alienation, loneliness, relational wounds, and dysfunctions. Our personal growth is significantly contingent upon the quality of our relationships. Christian identity matures not through navel-gazing, but engagement with God's larger interest in the reconciliation and healing of a wounded humanity.

The third rationale for a relational spirituality is that love for God and love of others are naturally and organically linked. Jesus was once asked to identify the greatest commandment of all. His answer has two parts: love God and love one's neighbor as oneself (Matt. 22:34–40). He did not really offer two answers, as is often assumed.

Rather, he gave a single answer with two parts. Love for God and love for others are actually two vectors from a single matrix. The underlying logic is that by its very nature, self-giving love requires "openness" to the other. As Miroslav Volf has pointed out, it involves a willingness to embrace rather than exclude. Love requires the transcendence of narrow self-interest. We must enlarge our hearts and widen our concerns to encompass what is beyond ourselves. This certainly is true when it comes to loving God; it requires that we overcome the inward curve of the sinful self, our ingrained disposition toward pride, selfishness, and narcissism. To experience intimacy, we must embrace ecstasy (*ek-stasis*, moving outside ourselves) (Humphrey).

Once such a disposition of "openness to the other" becomes habituated, it is potentially applicable to other persons. Openness grows into a more generalized, instinctive, and dispositional response to life. The enlarged heart stays enlarged, so to speak, and offers space into which human neighbors can also be welcomed. When the needs of another impose, it no longer lashes back: "Am I my brother's keeper?" Such thinking seems to undergird the apostle John's insistence that those who feel no love for their neighbor cannot really love God (1 John 4). Pointing out this connection certainly indicts those of us who privately identify with a man in a recent *New Yorker* cartoon, who, as he is leaving church, complains to his wife, "How can I love my enemies when I don't even like my friends?" As it turns out, love for God and openness to others are mutually reinforcing dispositions of the heart. As James Houston observes, "If we find it hard to form lasting relationships with those we see around us, then we will find it very hard to relate in any depth to the God we cannot see" (Houston 1996, 21–22).

The fourth reason for valuing human relations in Christian spirituality is that the transformation of such relationships happens to be a high priority of the Holy Spirit. The Spirit is a uniting force—countering the centrifugal tendencies of sin, and creating intimacy, community, and communion where alienation and mistrust previously dominated (Eph. 4:3). To "keep in step with the Spirit" involves aligning with, rather than resisting, the Spirit's reconciling impulses and uniting mission in the world. This drawing-together, bringing-near ministry of the Holy Spirit operates like a magnetic force along vertical and horizontal vectors.

Meanwhile, the Spirit is also drawing people into healthy associations in the contexts of friendship, home life, marriage, and the marketplace. Additionally, the Spirit is bringing believers together so that they can become a *temple*—a sacred dwelling place—for his own presence (Eph. 2:21–22; 1 Peter 2:5). Since the Holy Spirit has made a commitment to the nurturing of such community, and to locating himself in it, believers who choose to associate with it enjoy special access to the Spirit's presence and blessing. Conversely, those who disdain or disassociate from such community will experience some measure of disconnect from the Spirit. It is one measure of the Spirit's success in creating spiritual community that the church has been attesting since its earliest creeds that it recognizes and treasures "the communion of saints."

In summary, human relationships are important to Christian spirituality for at least four reasons. First, humans are already relational, meaning that authentic spirituality must address this reality. Second, people as divine image-bearers find their own human fulfillment as they align with and echo in their own relationships the paradigmatic community of the triune God. Third, openness to God naturally grows into a disposition that influences how we respond to others. Finally, since the cultivation of relationships is a high priority of the Spirit, it is important to those who are attuned to his will and ways.

Contours of Christian Community

As human beings, we are relational by nature. The primary issue, then, is whether the dynamics of our human relationships will remain essentially sinful ones—self-aggrandizing, manipulative, deceitful, controlling, and so forth—or whether they will be transformed into healthy, loving, satisfying, and mutually empowering ones. The vocabulary of the Christian faith contains many descriptors for relationships of superior quality. It includes, for example, *shalom*, that wistful desideratum of the ancient Jews. In the New Testament the descriptive language includes fellowship or *koinonia*; later it has come to contain community and communion, with their etymological suggestions of intimate sharing. The best words are not the hierarchical ones (*arch*-this and *uber*-that), but the *co*-words of mutuality and partnership. An absence of power struggles and competitiveness is the hallmark of the genuine image of God. The great Catholic humanitarian Jean Vanier challenges Christian communities to live accordingly, embracing relationships of downward mobility. Community is not just any old relationship, but a particular kind of being-in-relationship. No church-based activity or group exercise should be labeled *communal* just because more than one person is involved in it.

Throughout Scripture, and in the Christian spiritual tradition extending from it, communal relationships are portrayed in imagery of marital and familial intimacy, friendship, musical symphonies and nature's harmonies, and the compelling unity of common cause and shared allegiance. Repeatedly the biblical vision celebrates reciprocity and mutuality operating against a backdrop of justice. The relational ideal is captured in the psalmist's grateful insight, "How very good and pleasant it is when kindred live together in unity! It is like the precious oil on the head, running down upon the beard, on the beard of Aaron, running down over the collar of his robes" (Ps. 133:1–2 NRSV).

Life in the Spirit is designed to cultivate these positive relational dynamics. The Holy Spirit is continually at work to foster empathy, generosity, and sensitivity, and to restrain the divisive impulses of the sinful nature. So many of the fruits of the

Spirit seem designed to blunt our human capacities for hurtful, alienating words and actions. The basic contours of the Spirit's uniting actions are consistent through the centuries.

Nonetheless, each historical era and culture poses special challenges to his reconciling ministry, and so we must ask what these special challenges might be for our own day. We suggest that in our contemporary context it is of great importance how a Christian community acknowledges and handles the dynamics of power in its midst; how it practices leadership and models transparency; how it empowers all its members; and how it protects the weaker, renounces exploitation, and shows regard for diverse perspectives.

The communal dimension of Christian spirituality means that Christian leaders cannot justify their management decisions purely by appeals to a "bottom line" of achieving measurable organizational goals. Spirit-directed relationships involve noninstrumental regard for others as subjects rather than objects. In God's economy, people should never be exploited or sacrificed for a cause, however grandiose the rhetoric used to commend it. They should be treated as *persons*. In his Sermon on the Mount, Jesus depicted the church as "a city on a hill" (Matt. 5:14), and by that image of a city—a complex, interacting *polis* of persons in multiple associations—he signaled the importance of Christian relational dynamics to the credibility of the gospel itself. The gospel is in part the good news of a new, alternative way of doing life together.

Beyond Self

We know from Scripture that God's heart goes out to all humanity, and it reaches out in a special way to the entire Christian community. Simply acknowledging this fact can be positively transforming for an individual Christian. The reason is that the sheer existence of a Christian community amounts to "proof positive" that I am not the only one God loves. He loves others too. Like an only child who has to come to terms with the arrival of a newborn sibling, and the subsequent diffusion of parental love on multiple children, the individual Christian must accept that God loves many, while also realizing that God's love for and delight in individuals is not diminished by its expanded scope. The spiritual theologian Henri Nouwen once observed that our chosenness does not obfuscate the chosenness of others (Nouwen, sermon, 7 Sept. 1996).

Envy seems to be the default setting of those who are anxiously self-absorbed. With insight the German pastor-theologian Helmut Thielicke confessed, "As soon as I look at my 'dear' neighbor and realize that he too is included in God's generosity, I feel some slight pangs in the region of the heart." We tend to repeat one "dismal song [that] always has the same refrain, and it goes like this: God's goodness comes to the wrong person because it doesn't come to me" (Thielicke, 122–23). To transform the habits of our hearts, and to put such attitudes behind us, Jesus taught us to begin our prayers with "*Our* Father"—not "*My* Father," but the plural possessive of Father—as if to underscore that none of us is any longer a separate entity. As the truth implicit in this language takes root in our souls, we will slowly begin to change. By this means and others like it, God's Spirit draws us out of ourselves and "into the grand objective realm of the *not merely me*" (Wood, 95). With enlarged souls, we can more honestly own the apostle Paul's words, "Who is weak, and I do not feel weak? Who is led into sin, and I do not inwardly burn?" (2 Cor. 11:29 TNIV).

One common vestige of hubristic pride is a stubborn sense of spiritual self-sufficiency. It manifests itself in the persistent notion that we don't need any help from all these other (largely hapless, we assume) Christians on our own journey toward God. For a number of reasons, we actually do need them. As individual Christians, we each are in some ways incomplete and must depend on others to help us, through their strengths and insights, with our own weaknesses or blind spots. Poet Luci

Shaw articulates the positive side of all this: "The body of the church reinforces its individual parts when they are weak, including me, just as when I have a toothache on the right side of my mouth I am prompted to let the left side take over the chewing for a while. Often I have felt this strength of being 'carried along' like a small boat in a flowing current, by the community of faith" (Shaw, 45).

Within the community of faith, there will be some who are especially gifted and informed by their own unique experience to assist us in our spiritual formation. David Benner addresses this category of fellow believers in his work *Sacred Companions* (2002). In addition to those who provide pastoral care, we can profit from the presence, wisdom, and prayers of spiritual directors, spiritual mentors, and spiritual friends. Each of these relationships is slightly different in its structure and degree of formality, but each embodies the truth that God's transforming wisdom and grace are often mediated to us through others. God has evidently designed the channels or delivery systems for grace so that we cannot pretend to have no need of others.

We also receive considerable inspiration from heroes of the faith — people who have embodied on a large stage certain Christian virtues (like courage) that we aspire to emulate. These may not be people we know personally, or who necessarily lived in our time, but like Christ they show us how to live and evoke within us the desire to emulate. Sometimes it is the ordinary or even "weaker" members of our communities that function as inspirational exemplars of the highest ideals of our faith, through their joyful service, sacrificial giving, determined persistence, and fortitude in the face of suffering and disability. They teach us what is most important in life and help us view it from a different and truer perspective altogether.

Formational Communities

Supplementing these observations is the fact that social communities function as powerful agencies of personal formation. Through community we not only naturally absorb a first language (or languages) as children, but we are socialized throughout life into a set of culturally approved virtues, into assumptions of what is plausible and implausible, into tastes and estimates of worth. Human beings are shaped more by social dynamics than by pointed instruction or formal education. Families, schools, offices, gangs, sport teams, and churches all function as more or less powerful cultures of formation.

This is true of spiritual formation as well. Instructional practices like Bible study, catechism, teaching, and preaching all have positive influence, but persons are formed even more significantly by the life practices of influential others, and they are profoundly shaped by the collective ethos of their communal environments. For example, the way a Christian community treats the weaker and more vulnerable members (such as children or persons with developmental disability) is crucial to the spiritual formation of all who are associated with it. Perhaps the ultimate test of character for any formational community is how it treats its weakest members. From the beginning, the biblical revelation has underscored protecting "the widow and the orphan," the alien and those oppressed by injustice. Today a chorus of credible voices — from theologians such as Jon Sobrino and Jürgen Moltmann to champions of persons with disability, such as Jean Vanier and Henri Nouwen, to researchers in the field of disability studies — reminds us that care for our weaker brothers and sisters is not only beneficial to them but also key to our humanization and to our own spiritual renewal. In his signature style, the Spirit often uses the "weak" and "foolish" things of this world to redeem the strong and the wise.

Quaker spiritual writer Parker Palmer agrees that formation is "soul work done in community," observing that leadership is crucial to this process. "Transformational crucibles are shaped and maintained by the relational expectations and example of community leaders." This is not to legitimize forceful, top-down approaches to spiritual formation. Rather, the environments that are most transformational are those in which participants "refrain from fixing, saving, or setting straight others in the group." Thus, "all of our relationships would be deepened if we could play the fixer role less frequently" (Sandage et al., 203).

When Christian Community Disappoints

It is easy to articulate high ideals for Spirit-empowered Christian community but considerably more difficult to deal with the disillusion that can set in when mean-spirited behavior and evil emerge through our structured life together. Two truths must be held in tension: that the Spirit is indeed present in the church, and that the church itself is a flawed and imperfect community. Believers must accept that the church really is the body of Christ, *and* that it will sometimes disappoint. It is the place where God dwells by his Spirit, *and* it is a collecting point for difficult people. Thomas Merton wrote that "one of the most important aspects of any religious vocation ... is the willingness to accept life in a community in which everyone is more or less imperfect" (Merton, 419). This is true not just of monasteries, but also of Christian communities generally.

Ultimately the unity of the Spirit is not preserved by the social intelligence of its leaders or the ethnic and socioeconomic homogeneity of its members, but by grace to forgive, courage to speak truth, faithfulness to covenant commitments, and respect for the vulnerable. Through it all, we should be able to see glimpses of Christ in others. We must live for each other, following the kenotic example of Christ who emptied himself with our brokenness squarely in view. The Spirit upholds unity not through imposition, but through invitation arising from sacrificial intent. This is crucial, even though many times the presence of the Spirit will remain relatively hidden to the unpracticed eye.

It is prudent not to expect everything of the church. Evangelical spirituality has been wise to reject the notion that the organized, institutional structures of the Christian religion can in any way contain or control the dispensing of God's grace, or exclusively mediate his presence to others. Yet it is also important to expect something of it. The Holy Spirit continues to build such communities, and he is still especially present wherever there is genuine communal coalescing around shared faith in Christ.

Rhythms of Solitude and Community

Through the gift of Spirit-created community, Christians are able to make the healing journey "from individualism to personhood" (Houston 2002). Whenever this journey is successfully navigated, the believer's identity will flourish rather than be crushed. Healthy Christian community is not cultlike in its inner workings; it is not a homogenizing cauldron, but a milieu in which diversity is permitted and even welcomed—and all this without, amazingly enough, the whole breaking apart. Christian community is a place where respect is conferred upon others with love and reciprocity.

On this journey to wholeness, believers must learn to live according to the rhythms of solitude and community. Jesus was deeply committed to others, but he accepted and embraced these rhythms of human life before God, as periodically he paused to reconnect, be renewed, and regain perspective in the focused presence of his Father. It is possible to have an unhealthy dependency on Christian community—to the extent that we feel desperate without an ever-present shoulder to lean on or a chattering voice to entertain. Such needy persons are rarely able to contribute much to the community to which they are so incessantly, even desperately attached.

We are meant to live our lives with a disposition of openness to others. To live this way is key to becoming fully human. Our personal fulfillment and destiny are found in taking our place and playing our part before God in a larger web of relationships. We may initially hesitate to move into this larger sphere from fear that we may be diminished. But such fear is misplaced. Moving in this direction is essential to our own fulfillment and joy.

Sources Cited

Houston, J. *The Mentored Life* (2002).
———. *The Transforming Power of Prayer* (1996).
Humphrey, E. *Ecstasy and Intimacy* (2006).
Merton, T. *The Seven Storey Mountain* (1998).
Sandage, S., et al. "Relational Spirituality and Transformation." *Journal of Spiritual Formation and Soul Care* 1, no. 2 (2008): 182–206.
Shaw, L. "Words along the Way." In *Nouwen Then*, ed. C. de Vinck (1999), 40–55.
Sobrino, J. *The Principle of Mercy* (1994).
Thielicke, H. *The Waiting Father.* Trans. J. Doberstein (1959).
Vanier, J. *Becoming Human* (1999).
Volf, M. *Exclusion and Embrace* (1996).
Wood, R. "Outward Faith, Inward Piety." In *For All the Saints,* ed. T. George and A. McGrath (2003), 91–108.

For Further Reading

Balswick, J., et al. *The Reciprocating Self* (2005).
Buber, M. *I and Thou.* Trans. R. G. Smith (1958).
Chan, S. "New Directions in Evangelical Spirituality," *Journal of Spiritual Formation and Soul Care* 2, no. 2 (2009): 219–37.
Erikson, E. *The Life Cycle Completed* (1997).
Houston, J. *Joyful Exiles* (2006).
Nouwen, H. *Reaching Out* (1975).
Reimer, K. *Living L'Arche* (2009).
Shults, L. *Reforming Theological Anthropology* (2003).
Shults, L., and S. Sandage. *Transforming Spirituality* (2006).
Wilhoit, J. *Spiritual Formation as if the Church Mattered* (2008).

CHAPTER 10

EDUCATION AND SPIRITUAL FORMATION

GORDON T. SMITH

Education—teaching and learning—is a vital part of the Christian spiritual tradition, a feature that is shared with and inherited from the church's Jewish roots. We note the emphasis on teaching in the Scriptures and its role in the mission and purposes of God in the church and in the world. The book of Deuteronomy highlights the place of teaching within families and the religious community; and the book of Nehemiah profiles the work of Ezra, a scholar (Ezra 7:11, 25), and other scribes, whose teaching brought understanding and deep joy (see Neh. 8). And the book of Proverbs emphasizes that this teaching and learning has a specific objective: that individuals and that the people of Israel would grow in wisdom and understanding.

But most of all, the Christian heritage revels in the wonder of Jesus himself as the divine teacher. The life and ministry of Jesus centered around his illuminating and liberating teaching. He taught old and young, educated and unlearned, women and men. He taught with compassion and authority. He taught by way of parables—stories that illustrated the meaning of the kingdom of God. He taught by way of simple aphorisms, along the way as with his disciples he wandered from town to town. He taught in large and expansive settings to crowds that gathered. And he taught individuals (Nicodemus, John 3; the Samaritan woman, John 4), groups of as few as two (Martha and Mary, Luke 10 and John 11; the pair on the road to Emmaus, Luke 24). He taught prior to and leading up to his passion; indeed, it would appear from John 14–16 that his last hours with his disciples prior to the cross were spent in intense teaching. And he taught them after the resurrection prior to his ascension and the sending of the Spirit. He taught the crowds, certainly; but his focus was on his immediate disciples. They became his followers, his disciples, by agreeing to learn from him—to attend to his teaching, to hear and then to live in obedience to this teaching. To be a follower of Jesus was to be a learner. Jesus was a teacher; one was only his follower, a disciple, if one was a learner.

What makes John 14–16 so significant in the biblical canon is the recognition that Jesus is recorded in these chapters as declaring that this teaching ministry continues after the ascension—after his return to the immediate presence of the Father. Jesus the Teacher continues to be Teacher through the Spirit who guides the disciples, the Christian community, into all truth (John 16:13–14). This work of the Spirit is manifested specifically, though not exclusively, through the work of the apostles and the teaching office or ministry of the church. Immediately prior to the ascension, Jesus calls his disciples to the work of making disciples, and they are to do so specifically by baptizing and teaching others—indeed, the nations—all that Jesus has commanded (Matt. 28:19–20). Thus, we read that the newly baptized Christians devoted themselves to the apostles' teaching (Acts 2:42).

This teaching ministry of the apostles is then handed on to those who would succeed them.

Nowhere is this more powerfully evident than in the Pastoral Epistles; clearly the work of the pastor is the work of teaching—as Timothy is mandated to teach others, who are in turn capable of teaching others (2 Tim. 2:2). There is certainly more to the pastoral office than teaching; and there is more to congregational life than teaching-learning. The church is not merely a school. And yet it is a school, as something central to its way of being. A church is a learning community, which in its learning is forming disciples into the image of Christ Jesus.

In other words, Christian spirituality is sustained by the teaching ministry of the church. We cannot conceive of the one without the other. There is no growth in faith, hope, and love without teaching. The Christian knows the transforming grace of God through the renewing of the mind (Rom. 12:2); Christians are "sanctified," made holy, transformed, by the truth (John 17:17).

Thus, the Christian spiritual tradition takes the truth seriously and takes the mind seriously. Truth is anchored in the revelation of God. True spirituality is one of attentiveness to God as the source of all understanding; and to be a learner, then, demands meekness (James 1:21)—literally, submission to the truth, as divinely revealed, as embodied in Christ Jesus (who is the truth incarnate, John 14:6) and as passed down through the apostles.

The church has always recognized that "spiritual" education includes critical engagement with the whole of God's revelation—the panoply of the heavens, the wonder of life on earth (the sciences); the relations of humans to each other, to their own selves, and to their environment (the social sciences). Such learning is worship: a delight in and honoring of the Creator as the source of all wisdom, understanding, and truth. The pursuit of truth is itself a spiritual journey.

The teaching ministry of Christ, by and in the Spirit, finds primary expression first in the Scriptures and then, secondarily, in the creedal history of the church. The Christian spiritual heritage has always recognized the primary place of Bible study, the teaching and learning of the Scriptures for the spiritual life. When accompanied by prayer and other spiritual disciplines, the study of the Scriptures is the very lifeblood of the Christian believer and of the Christian community. And the necessary complement to the Scriptures is the historic teachings of the church; the two complement each other—the primacy of the Scriptures grounded in the creedal heritage of the church as this heritage always tested against the enduring witness of the Scriptures. Thus, catechesis is a twofold exercise: to know the Scriptures and to know the "faith" of the church.

Education begins early in one's Christian journey. For the children of the church, raised within Christian homes and within the faith community, education is a central feature of their nurture. Similarly, for one who becomes a Christian as an adult, one is taught the faith as one comes to Christ; thus education and evangelism are integrally linked. While distinct, there is no evangelism without teaching; true evangelism is grounded in the teaching ministry of the church. Thus, catechesis—instruction in preparation for baptism—authenticates and is integral to conversion. Conversion is, then, a decision to become a learner, a disciple, who attends to the teaching ministry of Jesus as revealed or communicated by the Spirit through the Scriptures and the faith tradition of the Christian community.

This honored place given to teaching comes in recognition of the vital place of the mind in Christian spirituality—evident in the full corpus of the biblical canon but perhaps most notably in the writings of the apostle Paul, who speaks of transformation coming specifically through the renewal of the mind (Rom. 12:2). For spiritual growth depends on growth in understanding—insight and illumination; for one only truly lives when one lives in the light. Thus, for the Christian spiritual tradition, truth is powerful; it sanctifies (John 17:17). Teaching and understanding are essential to the process of coming to faith and then just as critical to the process of spiritual growth toward maturity in Christ. The apostle Paul depicts the human condition or predicament as one in which the world is "darkened in understanding" and contrasts this with the life to which the Christian is called: not unstable, blown here and there by every wind of teaching (Eph. 4:14) but rather rooted and grounded in Christ and growing up into Christ who is the head of the church (v. 15), and this comes specifically through the process of teaching and learning.

There is no spiritual maturity without wisdom; indeed, wisdom is the mark of this maturity. And there is no wisdom without knowledge. While it may be possible to have knowledge without wisdom, the converse is not possible. There is only wisdom when there is knowledge. And knowledge comes through education — through teaching and learning. There is hardly a greater gift that Christ can give the church than gifted scholars and teachers who explain the Scriptures and the faith of the church — patiently, compassionately, speaking the truth in love (Eph. 4:15), engaging the mind, and fostering depth of understanding and empowering the Christian and the church to walk in truth.

These scholars and teachers are at their best, as gifts to the church, when they recognize that the Christian spiritual tradition affirms teaching and the life of the mind with three distinctive caveats.

First, authentic teaching engages both heart and mind. Christian spirituality has consistently recognized that the polarization of head and heart impoverishes both; it is not true learning if it does not foster love of God and joy in the Spirit. It is a misunderstanding of true learning to suggest that education must bracket out the emotions. Affect is integral to intellectual development. Emotion does not merely modify thinking, reasoning, and the development of insight; it is integral to the reasoning process. True instruction in the faith frees the learner from fear and anxiety and nurtures faith in the living Christ; it fosters faith and is sustained by joy. Thus, wise teachers give attention to the emotional dynamics of the teaching-learning process. Many integrate hymns and songs of faith into their teaching as a means of encouraging a more full-orbed response to the instruction that is given.

Second, genuine teaching fosters obedience. Christian spirituality recognizes that teaching is not an end but a means to an end: to walk in the light and live in the truth. Jesus encouraged his disciples for obedience (Matt. 28:20); and this is but an affirmation that the illumination of the mind demands repentance: to repent, or turn, from walking in darkness and walk in the light. Christian spirituality is thus a journey of conversion — constant and in many ways persistent as the Spirit continually calls the church and the individual Christian more and more into the light. The process is interactive: as the Christian walks in the light, she is more and more able to see the truth and respond more fully to the light. We do not receive more light until and unless we walk in the light already received; and when we walk in obedience, we see more and understand more deeply and are thus empowered by the Spirit to grow more fully in the wisdom of God (2 Cor. 3:18). But it requires obedience; the Christian attends to the teaching of the church, not as a dilettante, but as one eager to live in the truth.

And third, Christian spirituality recognizes that the interplay between education and spirituality is essentially communal. This is not a denial of the very legitimate place of the solitary learner; indeed, all learning at some point requires solitude, and the church has always affirmed the spiritual value of being alone, perhaps in a library with a classic text or with the Scriptures, as the individual diligently pursues some dimension of truth or understanding. And yet even in solitude we recognize the communal character of effective teaching-learning, for the solitary learner draws on the wisdom and confessional heritage of the Christian community.

Christian education is communal in that it is intergenerational. As noted above, the book of Proverbs demonstrates that wisdom is passed down from one generation the next (1:8; 4:1). Timothy is specifically instructed to teach those who are in turn capable of teaching others (2 Tim. 2:2). And wise Christians foster their capacity to learn from the generations that have preceded them — whether it is their immediate forbearers (the generation of their parents) or the generations of wise teachers who continue to be gifts to the church through their writings. Christians read and learn from the Fathers of the church, from her "doctors" — everyone from Teresa of Avila to Calvin, from Augustine to Julian of Norwich to A. W. Tozer.

But Christian education is also communal in that learning and growth in wisdom are often best fostered in ways that promote the capacity of Christians to learn together. While many streams of Christian spirituality have recognized the vital place of small groups, perhaps no one has integrated this principle into the process of spiritual formation quite as emphatically as did John Wesley with the establishing of the classes and bands for spiritual learning, nurture, conversation, and accountability. Early in his ministry, Wesley visited Herrnhut, a Moravian community in Germany. He was deeply impressed with the corporate spiritual discipline that marked their common life, and he adapted this so that it became a characteristic mark, indeed a cornerstone, of his own model for spiritual formation. Wesley was convinced that spiritual growth required mutual encouragement and accountability as the context or setting for effective teaching-learning.

Just as education is vital to authentic spirituality (as has been implied and perhaps needs to be made explicit), spirituality is, in turn, integral to authentic education. It is a false notion that vital spiritual devotion is a threat to teaching-learning. To the contrary, just as critical theological reflection fosters depth of heart and devotion and thus informs worship and service, similarly worship and prayer open the heart and mind to the truth. Thus, it is fitting in the context of formal education, for example, to appreciate the essential dynamic that is represented by the chapel — as the space and

place of worship and liturgy and the classroom or the library as the place of learning. The interplay between the two is essential to both. The learning community moves from study and learning to the place of worship, eager to allow the truth to inform worship, resolved that understanding will inform devotion and prayer. Worship is informed by theology — by teaching and learning; even more, worship is theology in practice. But the converse is equally true: the community moves from worship to the classroom or the library, allowing the prayers of the community to foster the capacity for growth in understanding. Education is animated through prayer and worship and generous service.

Spirituality without education is mere sentimentality — religious feelings, perhaps, but not authentic devotion; education without the spiritual dynamic is one-dimensional and cerebral at best, but not ultimately transformational and thus not authentic education.

This vision for the interplay between education and spirituality is nowhere more evident than in the process of ministerial formation for those whose education is preparing them for religious leadership within the church. The pastoral office is certainly not the sole arbiter of the teaching ministry of the church. Yet few are so uniquely positioned to model and nurture the vital link between education and spirituality. As is implied in Ephesians 4:11 and as is explicitly clear in even a cursory reading of the Pastoral Epistles (1 and 2 Timothy and Titus). Pastors are teachers. They are called of Christ to be the teaching ministry of Christ to the church; for this they are trained and equipped, and for this they are anointed by the Spirit. As noted above, there is more to the pastoral office than teaching; but without teaching the rest of pastoral ministry is merely religious activity. It is by teaching that the whole of the pastoral office has integrity and purpose, assuring that each dimension of pastoral ministry is anchored in the theological heritage of the church.

Perhaps the greatest threat to the vital place of education in ministerial formation is the pragmatic orientation that permeates the church, seemingly in each culture, but particularly in the West. The extraordinary push to make pastors effective at a particular task or responsibility often subverts the slow and deliberate process of intellectual formation. It is not that pastors do not need to be effective in their responsibilities; it is rather that lifelong effective ministry is necessarily rooted in breadth and depth of understanding of the faith of the church, the Christian Scriptures, and the nuances of cultural mores and perspectives. Further, a good education, at its best, fosters the capacity for continuous learning so that pastors are always learning. Their education is lifelong and continually informing their life, work, and ministry.

One of the challenges that evangelical Christians face is a religious heritage or tradition, particularly in the West, that has consistently displayed ambivalence regarding the life of the mind. This hesitancy was perhaps to some degree rooted in a legitimate concern for a one-dimensional use of the mind that subverted authentic Christian devotion. But this reaction was unfortunately itself misguided; and it has led to what Mark Noll has aptly called the "scandal of the evangelical mind." Such a propensity to discount the integral role of the mind in the life of the church has made evangelical Christians vulnerable to both sentimentalism and pragmatism.

There are two voices that for many Christians have provided an antidote to the ambivalent view of the intellect. Simone Weil, in her remarkable essay "Reflections on the Right Use of School Studies," observes that the heart of Christian spirituality is attentiveness and that, indeed, this is prayer: attention to God. And then she goes on to suggest that our studies—everything from the study of geometry to learning an ancient language—fosters this very attentiveness and thus nurtures within the Christian a capacity for prayer.

But she also adds that the joy of study and learning and discovery are integral to true learning and thus to education. The intellect is led by desire; and there is therefore joy in learning and discovery. And this is particularly critical early in one's life to develop the joy-filled power of attention. Education, therefore, brings one nearer to God.

The other voice is that of Harry Blamires, who published *The Christian Mind* in the early 1960s; therein he argued that it is vital to develop a Christian mind in contrast to the prevailing secular mind that has so deeply shaped the church, and he went on to identify the marks of a Christian mind and to demonstrate how the development of a Christian mind is integral to the life and witness of the church and of the individual Christian.

In other words, the antidote to the misuse of the intellect is not to discount or dismiss the mind, but rather to affirm its rightful place in the life of the Christian and the life of the church. This will be evident when the historic vehicles of Christian education—creed and catechism—are restored to their rightful and integral place in congregational life.

For Further Reading

Blamires, H. *The Christian Mind* (1963).
Groome, T. *Christian Religious Education* (1980).
Leclercq, J. *The Love of Learning and the Desire for God* (1961).
Moore, M. *Teaching from the Heart* (1991).
Noll, M. A. *The Scandal of the Evangelical Mind* (1994).
Palmer, P. J. *The Courage to Teach* (1998).
Weil, S. *The Simone Weil Reader* (1977).

CHAPTER 11

ESCHATOLOGY AND HOPE

KYLE A. ROBERTS

Hope, one of the three great Christian virtues (1 Cor. 13:13), is the confident anticipation of a positive future. Eschatology, the theology of final things (Gr. *eschata*), is intricately connected to the Christian experience of hope. Eschatology explores the meaning, direction, and goal of history and probes the mystery of what might come after this history. Creation is filled with ambiguity, suffering, and anxiety. The apostle Paul noted that such turmoil testifies to the incomplete and unredeemed nature of this present world; and he proclaimed the good news that God will redeem it (Rom. 8:19–22). With similar logic, the Bible sets the tragedy and difficulty of the present world alongside a new restored and completed one. The theology of final things elucidates this juxtaposition by pointing to God's promises of a new and better future, and by describing the biblical ground for hope in a broken world.

In relational terms, spirituality is the form of life, "whether anemic or energetic, anxious or peaceful," in which a person relates to oneself, to others, and to God (Shults and Sandage, 59). Christian spirituality in particular can be thought of as the "lived reality" that grows out of a response to the animating principles of Spirit and Word and is ultimately formed in accordance with the story of the life, death, and resurrection of Jesus (Chan, 16, 20). Hope is deeply ingrained in the story of Jesus and in the narratives of the Christian church. To live apart from Christ is to be "without hope and without God in the world" (Eph. 2:12).

In the resurrection of Jesus, Christians have been newly born "into a living hope" and an irrepressible inheritance (1 Peter 1:3–4). Christian hope is neither an object to possess nor a skill to master; rather, it is a gift that comes through Christ and is sustained by the Spirit. It is animated by the irruption of God's kingdom into this present world of ambiguity, difficulty, and suffering. Hope is the comforting, illuminating presence of the Spirit during the dark interim of Holy Saturday—that period of uncertainty between Good Friday and Easter—and is given its material content in the promises of God in the gospel. Christian spirituality depends on hope for its survival. A posture of praise, thanksgiving, prayer, and obedience could not be sustained for long in a chaotic and pointless world with no good end in sight. Eschatology, grounded in Christian hope, softens the soil for the development of spirituality—and for the continual renewal of hope—in the face of an otherwise uncertain, fragmented, and hopeless future. In the words of theologian Gerhard Sauter, eschatology asks: What dare we hope? This essay explores the basis and content of that hope.

The Story of Eschatology

Christianity has long depended on eschatology for its coherence and vibrancy. Scripture located the source of hope in a faithful God and in a future that will eclipse present trials and sufferings. In the Old Testament, eschatological promises justified hope (Jer. 29:11) and were consistently ratified by God's covenantal faithfulness. From Abraham and Noah to the exodus and exile, the historical narratives testify to the hope of Israel in their God. Israel believed that God would care for them, protect them from their enemies, and establish them in the land. Hope in an individual afterlife was only embryonic in the Old Testament, reflecting common Near Eastern perspectives.

The Old Testament implied an inchoate hope in a life beyond death, which pointed toward a deeper and more complete expression in the New Testament. The Gospels offer the life, death, and resurrection of Jesus as both the paradigm and the source of hope. The resurrection of Jesus signaled the triumph of God over sin, death, and hell. With the Christ-event, eschatology took on its fullest significance as the sign of the breaking in of the kingdom of God and as the power of the resurrection (1 Cor. 15:20–22). Jesus' resurrection was the "proleptic anticipation" of the kingdom of God (Pannenberg). Identification with Jesus in suffering was understood as a necessary condition for sharing in his glory at the *parousia* (1 Peter 4:12–13). Jesus warned his disciples to "be on guard" and to keep watch, because no one knows the time of the eschatological judgment and renewal of all things (Mark 13:32–37; Luke 21:36). In the garden of Gethsemane, facing his greatest spiritual trial, Jesus reminded his disciples to "watch and pray" (Mark 14:38). Hope is kept alive by constant alertness and prayer that God's will be done on earth as it is in heaven. Peter also connected eschatology and prayer, pointing out that the imminence of the end requires alertness and sobriety of mind "so that you can pray" (1 Peter 4:7). The admonitions of Jesus and Peter highlight the tensions within which Christians must live. The Christian anticipates, prays, and works in the present for what they hope will come about in the future—ultimately and finally by God's agency. This instigates constructive anxiety, joy, and a sense of hopeful responsibility among God's people.

The Revelation of John presented an apocalyptic, symbolic glimpse into God's activity behind the scenes of history. The *Pantocrator*, the heir to the throne, is "making everything new" (Rev. 21:5) and will overcome the powers of evil. This hope for the future bore dramatic political, social, and spiritual implications. Creation will be restored when God comes to earth to dwell with humanity (Rev. 21:4). This suggests that the sufferings of the present are "not worth comparing with the glory that will be revealed in us" (Rom. 8:18). Biblical eschatology is neither escapist nor unconcerned with the present. Rather, God's plan for restoration gives history meaning. Eschatology is God's invitation to live in the kingdom in light of God's glorious future (Grenz, 652).

The Nicene Creed links eschatology to Christology and to Trinitarian action. Christ was resurrected on the third day, ascended to the Father, and will return in the power of the Spirit to judge the living and the dead. The creed concludes with affirmation of the coming general resurrection and a hopeful anticipation of "the life of the world to come." This reminds believers that this present life does not constitute the whole of reality. God's judgment will make right what is wrong and will bring injustice to light. Those who have been mistreated and oppressed for the sake of righteousness will be vindicated. The incompleteness of history will find its ultimate fulfillment in a new day in which God reigns.

While Christianity has expressed general agreement along these broad themes, theologians have interpreted the meaning of the particulars of eschatology in a variety of ways. Does resurrection imply the inherent immortality of the soul as distinct from the body? What happens to a person immediately after death: soul sleep, purgatory, or something else? Is hell a "place" of eternal, conscious torment? If so, will persons in heaven be consciously aware of it? Must there be a "double outcome" of final judgment, or might God's salvation eventually be universal in its efficacy?

Speculation on the nature of God's plans for human history has taken Christians in a number of directions. Millennial eschatology, for example, views the reign of Christ as constituting a thousand-year period of peace on the earth (Rev. 20), which would either follow (premillennial) or precede (postmillennial) the second coming of Christ. Amillennialists reject the notion of a literal thousand-year reign, viewing the kingdom of God as a present, spiritual reality and the church as the primary locus of Christ's lordship.

Points of contention between eschatological positions can be found in the extent to which they view current historical and human experience as continuous or discontinuous with what is to come. *Present evolutionary* approaches take an optimistic view of the future of the universe and of the progress of the human race. God is immanently at work in human and cosmological history. Nineteenth-century liberal theology generally held that the kingdom of God is not an anticipated cataclysmic event; rather, "the kingdom of God is within you" (Luke 17:21). The spiritualities attending these approaches tend to be inward and focused on ethical, cultural, and human development. They are less attuned to apocalyptic perils, to the severity of sin, and to ultimate questions of personal, eternal destiny—thus, they lack the existential rigor of other kinds of eschatological reflection and are less motivated by the material content of the Gospels.

The *existential-encounter* approach, exemplified by the dialectical theologians Rudolf Bultmann and Karl Barth, explores the eschatological nature of encounter with God. In the context of social and political turmoil in war-torn Europe, what pastoral benefit is hope in the goodness of humanity and the progress of culture? Hope, for Barth, had to be grounded in Christology and in God's Word to humankind. For Barth (though not for Bultmann) Christ's historicity matters because it provides eschatology with its substantive content. The spiritualities generated by this approach are heavily driven by both symbol and narrative; as such they are deeply theologically informed and derive their energy from personal encounter with God mediated through the Word and the church.

A third approach, the *futurist-historical,* has been advocated by such contemporary theologians as Wolfhart Pannenberg and Jürgen Moltmann. They have sought to revitalize eschatology by demonstrating its forceful implications for the present. For Moltmann, the *advent* of God should revitalize and overturn human expectations. From the future, God brings about something new, inviting all people into the liberating power of the kingdom in the present. For Pannenberg, the kingdom of God and human history should be understood from the perspective of God's future relation to creation. History will come to its end and achieves its full meaning in God's end-time kingdom and universal rule. In the hands of Moltmann, in particular, the implications for spirituality turn in a very concrete and social direction. Spirituality is a communal form of life energized by the transformational, liberating, and politically confrontational coming of God.

In its most creative forms, evangelical eschatology has combined elements of all three of these models, though with particular focus on the "already but not yet" theme prevalent in the New Testament. Jesus called for a reorientation of priorities in the present. His ministry focused on the sick, the oppressed, and the outcast—those without hope in the world. The traditional focus of evangelical eschatology on individual, future salvation needs a continual reminder that the ministry of Jesus included the proclamation of good news to the poor and restoration for the broken (Luke 4:18). While the church waits for the ultimate fulfillment of God's kingdom, God's people are called to "hopeful involvement" and to "realistic engagement" (Grenz, 657–58).

Hope, Eschatology, and Salvation

Theological reflection on individual salvation and the corporate restoration of all things is a time-honored and deep source of spiritual renewal. In this respect, Catholic spiritual tradition has encouraged devotional reflection on the Four Last Things: death, judgment, hell, and heaven. The bishop and spiritual writer Alphonsus Liguori (1696–1787) recommended regular meditation on one's final eschatological destination in light of the transiency of life and the certainty of death. While troubling for its heavy emphasis on the judgment of God and the horrors of hell, Martin von Cochem's devotional *The Four Last Things* is at the least an unsettling reminder of the biblical witness to judgment and of God's ultimate oversight of humanity's final destination. These and other devotional reflections give rise to more theoretical contemplations as well.

For example, in light of the eschatological hope of resurrection, what ought we to think of the nature of the human being? Throughout much of Christian history, eschatology has operated under the assumption that a human being is a composite of two essences, soul and body. This assumption has undergirded the notion that upon death the soul is extracted from the body and either relocated to a spiritual dimension called heaven or placed in a state of soul sleep until its reunion with the body in the general resurrection. The *Catechism of the Catholic Church* teaches that in purgatory souls are cleansed from impurity and prepared for eternal bliss in heaven. The seeds of the full-orbed medieval view of purgatory can be partly located in apocryphal texts of early Judaism and in liturgical prayers for the dead, a practice common to the patristic age. The doctrine has been nuanced in contemporary theology by Pope Benedict XVI to highlight the purifying efficacy of the soul's union with Christ at death through the transitional "fire" of purgatorial judgment (Ratzinger, 228–33).

Some contemporary theologians have identified a Hellenist metaphysic underlying anthropological dualism and rediscovered the Hebraic view that a human being is a "psychosomatic unity" (Polkinghorne; Shults). Though a person consists of spiritual and physical aspects, these are not to be thought of as distinct essences. The biblical notion of life necessitates embodiment. Jesus Christ, the firstfruit of the resurrection, appeared in a transformed, spiritual body. Embodiment secures continuity between the life of a person before and after death. Immortality is not inherent to humanity as such; rather, resurrection is the miraculous act of God granting continuance of life beyond death. This individual dimension of eschatology should be coupled with the cosmic and the communal. At the *eschaton* God will restore all of creation to perfection. A prevalent misconception in popular eschatology is that the earth will be destroyed and Christians will be transported to a different and better one in "heaven." As N. T. Wright has recently pointed out, this notion is far from the biblical portrayal of the "new heavens and new earth" as a renewed but not completely different creation. The marriage feast of Christ with his church will take place on the earth, where God will dwell with humanity.

But Who Will Be Saved?

The concept of *apokatastasis*, or the restoration of all things, has had a long (though not dominant) history in Christian theology. Origen of Alexandria believed that God would not possibly consign to eternal destruction any rational, sentient creature he had made. God's justice is not a retributive justice, but a reconciling one. Evangelical theology has traditionally rejected universalism largely on the basis of its commitment to biblical authority and the presence of texts suggesting the necessity of personal relationship with God in Christ and the irrevocability of judgment for those who spurn God's offer. The freedom to choose how one relates to God requires the possibility of eternal separation. In the most positive expressions of evangelical salvation doctrine, hell is not considered so much a direct result of God's wrath as a consequence of the misuse of human and angelic freedom. Nonetheless, the doctrine of eternal separation remains a difficult one for many evangelicals and a challenging hurdle in apologetic contexts. This has led some evangelicals to suggest that unbelievers will be annihilated after judgment. They argue that the biblical association of hell with fire implies an eventual destruction of the person. Others have suggested that immortality is not an inherent characteristic of human nature, but a *conditional* gift offered through faith in Christ. Those without salvation simply cease to exist when they die.

Evangelicals rightly empathize with the existential difficulties implied by the doctrine of eternal separation. God's goodness renders the notion of everlasting punishment difficult to swallow. God's power and eventual triumph over evil make the eternal existence of hell problematic. Nonetheless, the freedom and responsibility God has granted to angels and humans, the finality and efficacy of the Christ-event, and the urgency of the biblical witness should prevent a hasty dismissal or minimization of the possibility of hell as part of God's eschatological economy. The mere possibility that unbelievers will be eternally separated from God provides a deep (though not exclusive) motivation for evangelism and discipleship — practices close to the heart of evangelical, Christian spirituality.

Hope, Eschatology, and Theodicy

Apart from a connection to eschatology, responses to the problem of evil and suffering seem shallow. Confidence in God's eschatological victory enables those who embrace it in faith and hope to endure patiently the ominous and pervasive threat of suffering and evil. Christians are called to overcome evil with righteousness, to defeat injustice with justice, and to help others bear the burden of suffering, thereby "fill[ing] up ... what is still lacking in regard to Christ's afflictions" (Col. 1:24). All are invited to join the Trinitarian life and the Trinitarian project of making God's kingdom a present reality, while acknowledging that only God can bring it about in full. Eschatology should never encourage the deferral of action against injustice and unrighteousness in the present. Neither should it neglect the powerful biblical notion that God is present in the midst of suffering.

In the midst of suffering and tragedy, eschatology inspires hope. This hope takes shape in the spiritual practices of prayer, worship, and bold action. Jesus' eschatological warnings conclude with a command to watch and pray. Prayer is in part the trusting anticipation that God will fulfill his promises to restore all things and bring justice on the earth. As such prayer should include a personal attentiveness to our own holiness — or lack thereof — and to the ways in which our lives may be held up to the light of God's judgment. Prayer should incorporate requests for forgiveness and appeals to the never-failing mercies and promises of God. In worship the Christian participates in the sacraments of God; these serve as symbolic reminders of eschatological realities. Baptism and the Eucharist, as N. T. Wright points out, connect eschatology to Christian spirituality. Baptism reveals the connection of heaven and earth in the reality of the new birth while the Eucharist discloses "the arrival of God's future in the present" in the communion meal (Wright, 271–74). Corporate worship in song can also reflect eschatological hope as Christians voice in unity their anticipation of God's renewal of creation and their faith in Christ for salvation. Finally, in bold action, Christian spirituality is given its most concrete, real-world expression. True Christian hope takes root in transformation at an individual and a societal level and is predicated on the future reaching into the present, effecting repentance, redemption, and restoration. Those who have bought into the promises of the gospel are empowered through it to work for the redirection of human history — away from hopelessness and toward hope. As von Balthasar has pointed out, Christian hope differs from secular hope in that its source and goal lie in Christ. In the power of the resurrection, Christian hope overcomes the ambiguity and despair caused by the universality of death. In consequence, no practice of care for any segment of society—whether the sick, dying, or mentally ill—seems "not worth the trouble." On the basis of Christian hope, bold action in the present is "undertaken as a challenge to the meaninglessness of this world" (von Balthasar, 60–61).

God has promised that the present reality is not the final one. It is not supposed to be this way, and it will not finally be this way. Eschatology joins human agency to the infinitely loving and powerful agency of God, inviting the future into the present. Eschatology turns the attention of the sufferer—and of all Christians—to the God whose faithfulness, love, and promise invite worship. The worshiper knows that things are not supposed to be this way; but by opening oneself to God, one finds hope, strength, and courage. The discord, anxiety, anger, and fear—which so often characterize the experience of temporality—are countered by God's gracious, eschatological presence. Hope for the future lies in the promise that the future does not lie outside of God. Paul wrote, "I consider that our present sufferings are not worth comparing with the glory that will be revealed in us" (Rom. 8:18). "*In hope,*" he went on to say, "... the creation itself will be liberated from its bondage to decay and brought into the glorious freedom of the children of God" (Rom. 8:21, emphasis added). Hope for creation is located in the eschatological coming of the fullness of God.

Sources Cited

Balthasar, H. U. von. *Engagement with God* (1986).

Chan, S. *Spiritual Theology* (1998).

Grenz, S. *Theology for the Community of God* (2000).

Moltmann, J. *The Coming of God.* Trans. M. Kohl (1996).

———. *Theology of Hope.* Trans. M. Kohl (1995).

Pannenberg, W. *Metaphysics and the Idea of God.* Trans. P. Clayton (2001).

Polkinghorne, J. *Exploring Reality: The Intertwining of Science and Religion* (2005).

Ratzinger, J. *Eschatology: Death and Eternal Life* (1988).

Shults, L. *Reforming Theological Anthropology* (2003).

Shults, L., and S. Sandage. *Transforming Spirituality* (2006).

Wright, N. T. *Surprised by Hope* (2008).

For Further Reading

Bauckham, R., and T. Hart. *Hope against Hope* (1999).

Florovsky, G. *Creation and Redemption* (1976).

Ladd, G. E. *Gospel of the Kingdom* (1959).

Peters, T. *God: The World's Future* (2000).

Polkinghorne, J. *The God of Hope and the End of the World* (2002).

Schillebeeckx, E., and B. Willems, eds. *The Problem of Eschatology.* Concilium 41 (1969).

Volf, M., and W. Katerberg. *The Future of Hope* (2004).

Walls, J. *The Oxford Handbook of Eschatology* (2008).

CHAPTER 12

SURVEY OF THE HISTORY OF CHRISTIAN SPIRITUALITY

GERALD L. SITTSER

There has never been, nor ever will be, a "golden age" of Christian spirituality, not even during the apostolic period, as evidenced, for example, by the difficulties the church in Corinth faced. Christians have always been a flawed people, which is why they are Christian in the first place. Likewise, the church has always been a flawed institution. Still, Christians living today can profit from the inspirational examples and helpful practices of the past by studying and appropriating—critically, of course—their "useable history." This essay will explore the usable history of Christian spirituality, giving voice to Christian ancestors who have something to say about their beliefs, convictions, and practices. The assumption is that chronology can play to the advantage of those living in the present, for though people living today cannot speak to those who have gone before, they can certainly listen to and learn from that "great cloud of witnesses."

Ancient Christianity

The earliest confession found on the lips of Christians was "Jesus is Lord!" It was an unusual confession, because during his earthly life, Jesus seemed so unworthy of the appellation. Jesus had only a brief public ministry before Roman authorities, needled by Jewish leaders, put him to death. The primary symbols of Jesus' earthly life—a stable and a cross—hardly seem to warrant the title of "Lord." If his life had ended at that moment, Jesus simply would have become another in a long line of failed messiahs, and the movement he started would have soon fizzled out. But the opposite occurred. Having witnessed his bodily resurrection, Jesus' earliest followers proclaimed him Lord and devoted themselves to him.

The Christian movement posed a threat to the Roman world from the very beginning. Though comprising far less than 1 percent of the population of the Roman Empire at the end of the 1st century (which numbered some 60 million), Christians aroused the fury of emperors because of their exclusive commitment to Jesus. Such conflict with the state continued until the 4th century. Martyrdom became a means of witnessing to the lordship of Christ. For example, the stories of the martyrdoms of Ignatius of Antioch; Polycarp, bishop of Smyrna; Justin Martyr; Blandina of Lyons; and Perpetua all demonstrate a commitment to honor and serve Jesus over Caesar. Thus, at the public execution of Polycarp, the proconsul charged, "This fellow is the teacher of Asia, the father of the Christians, the destroyer of our gods, who teaches numbers of people not to sacrifice or even worship" (Richardson, 153). Christianity was both compelling and threatening because it exalted Jesus as Lord. Rome put thousands of Christians to death for that very reason.

The early Christians also cultivated a communal life that made the Christian movement unusually attractive and competitive in the ancient religious world. Christians practiced a faith that won ordinary people and met concrete needs, which are two reasons why the movement grew steadily for nearly three centuries. Christians met in homes, which made it easier to reach their friends and neighbors, and they followed a strict morality that differed sharply from the permissiveness of Roman society. They treated women well, cared for children, attended to the needs of widows and orphans, and nursed the sick and dying—most notably during two plagues that swept through the Roman world in 165 and 250. The community of the church itself became a second form of witness to the lordship of Christ. Written in the first half of the 2nd century, the *Epistle to Diognetus* describes this peculiar kind of community among Christians: "They dwell in their own countries, but only as aliens. As citizens, they share in all things with others, and yet endure all things as foreigners. Every foreign land is to them as their native land, and every land of their birth is as foreign land to them" (Tyson, 59).

The era of martyrdom came to an end when Constantine, the first Christian emperor, granted the church legal status in 313. For the next twenty-five years, Constantine showed increasing favoritism toward the church. One of his successors, Theodosius I, made Christianity the official religion of the empire. These decisions had a huge and enduring impact on Christianity. The number of catechumens swelled; worship became increasingly ornate, clergy increasingly worldly, and church buildings ever larger and more opulent. Not everyone was pleased with these developments. Founded largely as a protest movement, the desert tradition of spirituality tried to maintain the old standards of discipleship under new conditions. Following the example of the famous Antony, these ascetics—known by their paradoxical title "bloodless martyrs"—withdrew into the deserts of Egypt, Palestine, Syria, and Cappadocia, and submitted to the guidance of an *abba* or *amma* to learn how to live as true disciples. They sought after God, fought the devil, prayed, meditated on Scripture, and practiced the ascetic disciplines (e.g., fasting and poverty).

These early Christians tried to live as "resident aliens" in the world, which surfaced in extreme devotion to Jesus and engendered distance from the world. Such distance became more pronounced in the case of the desert fathers and mothers after Christianity emerged as the privileged religion of the empire in the 4th century.

Augustine, bishop of Hippo, turned this radical discipleship in an interior direction. Though reared by a godly mother, Augustine rejected the religion of his youth as intellectually crude and morally restrictive and pursued a worldly life. After becoming a teacher of rhetoric in Rome and then Milan, he began his long and tumultuous journey back to Christianity, which culminated when Ambrose baptized him in 387. He served as bishop of Hippo from 395–430, where he became involved in many of the major theological, moral, and political controversies of his day. Augustine explored the interior landscape of Christian spirituality, especially in *The Confessions*. He believed that the soul remains unfulfilled and restless until it finds its rest and fulfillment in God. However hard people try to put something in God's place, which is the essence of idolatry, in the end they fail until they turn to God and order their lives under him. Typical of his writing is this poem:

> Late have I loved you, Beauty so ancient and
>   so new, late have I loved you!
> Lo, you were within,
> but I was outside, seeking there for you,
> and upon the shapely things you have made I
>   rushed headlong,
> I, misshapen.
> You were with me, but I was not with you.
>
>   (Augustine, 262)

The Middle Ages

The invasion of various tribal groups and the rapid rise of Islam caused significant disruption in the Mediterranean world, which in turn created a vacuum that the church was poised to fill. That occurred in at least two ways. First, the dominant institution that emerged during this period was the monastery. However large or small, every monastery was organized according to a rule—a set of guidelines governing how life should be lived in obedience to God and in communion with fellow believers. In the 4th and 5th centuries, Pachomius, Basil the Great, and Augustine of Hippo wrote such rules; but it was Benedict of Nursia who compiled and edited the one that has been used with minimal modifications for centuries. His rule outlined a seamless rhythm of life that included three basic activities: prayer or worship (e.g., the Divine Office), manual labor, and study.

Over the course of several centuries, literally thousands of monasteries sprang up across Europe and the Middle East. Though functioning as cloistered communities, they nevertheless provided a number of vital services to the surrounding population. They served as libraries and schools, pharmacies and hostels, and centers for scholarship and mission work. The spirituality of the medieval period, therefore, tilted in a monastic direction. It was ascetic, rhythmic, and hierarchical. *Religious* referred to monks and nuns, whose pattern of life was perceived as nearest and dearest to God; *secular* applied to priests, many of whom were uneducated and unqualified; while *laypeople*—everyone who did not serve the church as monk, nun, or clergy—occupied the bottom of this spiritual hierarchy.

Second, the church provided a concrete and tangible means of access to grace for a largely illiterate, immobile, and vulnerable population, the majority of which worked the land as peasants. From birth to death, the church served as a powerful benefactor through the administration of the seven sacraments, which were regarded as concrete, tangible, and effectual signs of God's generosity. In fact, the entire religious world of the medieval period was saturated with the sacramental. The faithful embarked on pilgrimages to important religious sites, such as Jerusalem and Rome; emulated the lives and venerated the relics of saints; and

sought spiritual refuge in churches and cathedrals, whose size and symbolism overwhelmed them with a sense of the power of God.

During the early Middle Ages, the eastern and western halves of the Roman Empire drifted apart, which eventually resulted in the formation of two distinct church traditions as well, the Eastern Orthodox and the Roman Catholic. Though similar in origin, beliefs, and practice, they gradually developed differences. One difference in particular shaped the respective spiritualities of these two Christian communities. The Greek-speaking East emphasized Christ in his *glorified* state, which can be seen very clearly even today in the ubiquitous presence of the icon of Christ the Pantocrator (Ruler of All) in the domes of Orthodox churches. The Latin-speaking West focused attention on the *suffering* Christ, which explains why cruciform art forms predominated there.

Subtle differences of spiritual practice naturally followed. The East lavished its churches with icons because these depicted figures—Jesus, Mary, the apostles and saints—in their exalted state, mediated between heavenly and earthly realities. Influenced by Neoplatonism, the East also gravitated toward mysticism, which promised union with God who, as impenetrable and incomprehensible as he is, can only be known in darkness, silence, and mystery, as is evidenced in the writings of mystics like Origen, Evagrius of Pontus, Gregory of Nazianzus, and Pseudo-Dionysius. Finally, the East stressed the doctrine of *theosis* or deification, which refers to human participation in the divine glory. The West did not deny these, to be sure. For example, it had its mystics, too, most notably Bernard of Clairvaux, Bonaventure, and Julian of Norwich. But the preoccupation with the cross of Christ made sin, suffering, and atonement dominant features of its spirituality, which in turn affected its art (e.g., the crucifix), its music (e.g., "O Sacred Head, Now Wounded"), and its spiritual practices (e.g., the festival of Corpus Christi).

In the 12th century, laypeople began to emerge as a more powerful force in the Western church.

An increasing number (still small by our standards) took advantage of the market economy that was just emerging in Europe. They moved to cities, made money as merchants, bankers, and traders, and enrolled in one of the new universities that dotted the late medieval landscape. They wanted to experience a more active and accessible spiritual life, and thus expected more from the church. It took the genius of Francis and Dominic to address their concerns and to set a new trajectory for spirituality. They left the isolated cloister of the monastery and traveled as itinerants to the city, Francis to serve the poor and to preach, Dominic to teach the orthodox faith and to combat heresy. They were known not as monks but as mendicants (beggars), for they lived among urban laypeople and depended on them for their very survival. What followed in their wake was a burst of new religious movements, such as the Beguines, Third Order Franciscans, and Brethren of the Common Life, which inspired laypeople to pursue the spiritual life with the zeal and discipline of monks, though without taking formal vows or withdrawing so completely from secular life.

The spirituality of the later Middle Ages had to address misery and death too. Two catastrophic events occurring in the 14th century — the Hundred Years' War and the Black Death — made this palpably necessary. People became acutely aware of their own mortality. Various artistic creations and spiritual practices associated with *Memento Mori* enabled monks, clergy, and the laity to "remember their death," escape judgment, prepare for eternity, and rely on the mediation of the church for protection, which only reinforced the power of the saints and their relics, the use of papal indulgences to reduce years in purgatory, and the obsession with heaven and hell, often at the expense of discerning what it meant for them to live for God in this world.

The Reformation

The Reformers simplified Christian spirituality by emphasizing that there is only one mediator between God and humanity, the Word of God, the divine self-revelation of God in Jesus Christ. In their minds, Scripture was central because it tells the story of God's self-revelation; likewise, baptism and the Eucharist were important because they serve as the concrete manifestations of God's self-revelation. The Reformers were notable preachers of the Word of God, for they believed that proclamation *is* the Word. In their preaching they aimed to build faith, for faith in Christ draws all attention away from the self. "This is the reason," Luther wrote, "why our theology is certain; it snatches us away from ourselves and places us outside ourselves, so that we do not depend on our own strength, conscience, experience, person, or works but depend on that which is outside ourselves, that is, on the promise and truth of God, which cannot deceive" (Wicks, 136–37).

The Reformers encouraged the laity to practice a spirituality that celebrated ordinary life in this world. For example, most of the Reformers married and had children, thus setting them apart from their celibate Catholic counterparts. Moreover, they encouraged the laity to serve God in their secular vocations, which they defended as legitimate spheres of spiritual influence. As Calvin stated, gratitude and stewardship should mark how laypeople live in the world. "We are the stewards of everything God has conferred on us by which we are able to help our neighbor, and are required to render account of our stewardship. Moreover, the only right stewardship is that which is tested by the rule of love" (Calvin, 3.7.5).

The Lutherans and Calvinists, however, were not the only catalysts for reform in the 16th century. The English wing emphasized the centrality of liturgy, especially under the leadership of Thomas Cranmer, archbishop of Canterbury and the primary author of the *Book of Common Prayer*. The Anabaptist movement urged the faithful to be rebaptized as believers and to turn to Jesus as an example to follow. The Sermon on the Mount became as authoritative to them as the book of

Romans was to Luther. Their commitment to simplicity, pacifism, egalitarianism, and separation of church and state cut a unique path in the 16th century. Finally, Catholics initiated several reforms too. The papacy clarified church doctrine at the Council of Trent (1545–1563) and imposed higher standards on the clergy. Meanwhile, two Spanish mystics, Teresa of Avila and John of the Cross, both members of the Carmelite order, laid out a pathway to God that required the experience of the "dark night of the soul." Ignatius of Loyola founded the Society of Jesus in 1540 to create a disciplined religious force that dispatched missionaries around the world and established hundreds of schools and universities to educate leaders for the church. His *Spiritual Exercises* is still used around the world today. But Catholics were sensitive to the needs of the laity too. For example, Francis de Sales, bishop of Geneva, wrote his *Introduction to the Devout Life* to make the spiritual life more accessible to all people, regardless of their station, thus enabling them to find and follow God right where they lived and worked.

Evangelicalism

But the Reformation divided the church in Europe too. Discipleship often deteriorated into debates over doctrine. Finally, religious rivalry, entangled with state corruption and ambition, erupted into a series of brutal religious wars that devastated Europe in the 17th century. This dark period of history set the stage for the rise of both the Enlightenment and evangelicalism. The precursors of the modern evangelical movement, such as Pietist leader Philip Jacob Spener and Moravian leader Nicolas Ludwig von Zinzendorf, believed that it was not enough to have correct belief. True faith requires piety, moral purity, missionary outreach, and sacrificial service. A generation later John and Charles Wesley, George Whitefield, and Jonathan Edwards became catalysts for the First Great Awakening. Their commitment to the centrality of the cross, the authority of Scripture, compassionate activism, and the necessity of a conversion experience unleashed a movement that has continued to thrive to this day. John Wesley preached some 40,000 sermons, often before people who were alienated from the established church; his brother Charles wrote more than 6,000 hymns for use in worship; Whitefield relied on open-air and extemporaneous preaching to win converts among the masses; and Edwards developed tests or criteria by which to discern whether a particular religious revival was a genuine work of God. These evangelical leaders established a vast network of small groups (*collegia pietas*, "bands," "holy clubs," or "class meetings," as they were called), often outside official church structures, that introduced ordinary believers to spiritual disciplines, such as confession, Bible study, and prayer, and held them accountable to a concrete practice of faith.

The evangelical movement formed voluntary societies to do the work of ministry, too, often through the initiative of the laity. Many early temperance and abolitionist societies were founded by evangelicals. One evangelical in particular, William Wilberforce, a member of the British Parliament for forty-five years, led the crusade to abolish slavery in the British Empire and supported dozens of other causes to reform the morals of England. Other evangelicals started missionary societies to spread the gospel (and sometimes Western culture too) to the uttermost parts of the world.

Thus, the evangelical movement only added to the momentum the Jesuits and Moravians had created, helping to spread Christianity around the world. Once largely European, it now encircles the globe. In fact, it is growing most rapidly south of the equator. The Pentecostal movement serves as both symbol and catalyst of that growth. Exploding on the historical stage in the early 20th century, it now numbers some half billion followers, most of whom are non-Western. Like evangelicalism, the Pentecostal movement calls for an experience of conversion; but it also emphasizes a second experience of Spirit baptism, which manifests itself in tongues, healings, and prophecy. The Pentecostal movement claims that it is a fulfillment of the Joel prophecy, which promises the outpouring of the Holy Spirit on *all* believers, regardless of gender, age, wealth, status, or education.

Conclusion

If anything characterizes the Christian movement in the past two hundred years, it is this orientation toward addressing the needs of ordinary believers, sometimes by appropriating the wisdom of the ancient past. In the past two hundred years, for example, Catholics have founded a number of new religious orders, such as the Sisters of Charity, to serve the needs of a suffering world. Vatican II (1962 – 1965) surprised nearly everyone by making worship and Christian education more accessible to laypeople. Its "Dogmatic Constitution on the Church" defined the church not as a hierarchy of church offices but as the *Laos*, the people of God. A decade later the pope initiated the reform of the catechumenate, too, which culminated in the publication of the Rites of the Christian Initiation of Adults. The Eastern Orthodox Church, though facing enormous pressure under the expansion of Islam and the menace of communism, rediscovered ancient wisdom and practice when two monks from Mount Athos published the *Philokalia*, which contains the writings of the major spiritual masters of Eastern Orthodoxy, thus making these writings accessible to those who live outside the walls of the monastery. Protestants, too, have turned to history as a rich resource of spirituality. Richard Foster's *The Celebration of Discipline* has introduced millions to the major spiritual exercises, like meditation and fasting, that the church has used through the ages.

This cross-fertilization underscores certain tensions that have often run through the history of Christian spirituality. The first concerns the degree to which Christian spirituality borrows from and adapts to larger cultural trends. The desert fathers and mothers were no doubt motivated by the teachings of Scripture, but they also practiced an asceticism that pagan philosophers valued too. Medieval mystics found biblical support for the contemplation of the ineffable God, but Neoplatonism shaped their thought as well. The Reformers studied and preached the Bible as the Word of God, but the humanist movement inspired them to "return to the ancient sources" (*ad fontes*!), which included the Bible. Evangelicals want to reach the lost, calling them to conversion, but that very impulse, good in itself, plays into the subjectivism and consumerism that characterizes Western society.

A second tension has to do with the role of the earthly in the spiritual life. By its very nature, spirituality addresses a reality that transcends space and time. When Christians worship, pray, and meditate, for example, they focus their attention on transcendent reality. Yet they cannot entirely escape the material world either. The incarnation reminds Christians that God himself took on materiality for humanity's sake. The sacraments, secular vocation, and activism, all of which take the material world seriously, are inherently and profoundly earthly — and Christian too. In Christian spirituality, divine and human, soul and body, spiritual and material achieve a perfect unity in the person of Jesus Christ, which also shapes the way Christians practice their spirituality in the world.

A third tension involves how often Christians have reached across traditional barriers to expand their understanding and experience of the spiritual life, even when those barriers seem insurmountable. That is especially true today. Some Protestants, for example, have followed the example of Kathleen Norris, author of *The Cloister Walk*, and become *oblates* — lay members — of a religious order such as the Benedictines, though still remaining Protestant. Others have begun to read the great theologians of Eastern Orthodoxy, such as Athanasius, Gregory of Nyssa, and John of

Damascus, due largely to the efforts of St. Vladimir's Seminary Press. But the traffic is moving in both directions. Many Catholics have gained a new appreciation for "personal devotions," a standard evangelical discipline, recognized the importance of personal evangelism, and embraced the power that has become available, especially to the poor, through the Pentecostal movement.

A final tension revolves around the uneasy relationship between the religious elite and ordinary believers. Much of the writing on Christian spirituality has come from the pen of these elites—monks, mendicants, ministers, missionaries, and professors—who had the time and opportunity to pursue the spiritual life with unusual rigor. The desert fathers and mothers are an extreme example of such elitism. How many Christians could ever hope to live as they did? How many would want to? Often marginalized by elites, ordinary believers—the laity—have had to figure out how to access, appropriate, and apply these various spiritual traditions to mundane life in the world. In fact, the strength of evangelical spirituality resides in that practical orientation. It has excelled at reaching the masses, though sometimes at the expense of intellectual sophistication and cultural impact.

Sources Cited

Augustine. *The Confessions* (1997).
Calvin, J. *Institutes of the Christian Religion,* 2 vols. Trans. J. McNeill (1960).
Richardson, C., ed. *Early Christian Fathers* (1996).
Tyson, J., ed. *Invitation to Christian Spirituality* (1999).
Wicks, J. *Luther and His Spiritual Legacy* (1983).

For Further Reading

Bouyer, L., et al. *A History of Christian Spirituality*, 3 vols. (1977).
Duprē, L., and D. Saliers. *Christian Spirituality.* Vol. 3 (1989).
Maas, R., and G. O'Donnell, eds. *Spiritual Traditions for the Contemporary Church* (1990).
McGinn, B., et al., eds. *Christian Spirituality.* Vol. 1 (1985).
Raitt, J., ed. *Christian Spirituality.* Vol. 2 (1987).
Sheldrake, P. *Brief History of Spirituality* (2007).
Sittser, G. *Water from a Deep Well* (2007).
Wilken, R. *The Spirit of Early Christian Thought* (2003).

CHAPTER 13

ANCIENT CHRISTIAN SPIRITUALITY (AD 100 – 600)

CHRISTOPHER A. HALL

Ancient Christian spirituality—the spiritual perspectives and practices during the period roughly covering the 2nd through the 7th centuries of the church's history—is marked by a distinct emphasis on worship and prayer as the heart of healthy spiritual life. Ancient Christians were first and foremost worshipers. Many ancient Christians' minds and hearts were captured and enraptured by the wonder and beauty of God made known to them in Jesus Christ and in his body on earth, the church. Every key distinctive of ancient Christian spirituality mentioned in this essay—*ascesis*, the purposeful imitation of Christ, the sacramental perspective and practice of the early church, the communal nature of ancient Christian spirituality, and the centrality of Scripture—is enlivened by worship and prayer. Indeed, from an ancient Christian viewpoint, prayer and worship are well nigh indistinguishable.

Years before the first great church council—the Council of Nicea (AD 325)—ancient Christian leaders such as Tertullian, Origen, and Cyprian were writing significant treatises on the Lord's Prayer, the fundamental pattern of prayer for the ancient church. Tertullian, for instance, viewed the Lord's Prayer as a wonderful "summary of the whole gospel.... In these summaries of a few words, how many sayings of the prophets, evangelists, and apostles are touched on—sermons of the Lord, parables, examples, precepts! How many duties at the same time are captured!" (Ferguson, 252).

Cyprian observed that the Lord's Prayer invites all believers to call God "Father," a privilege of God's children given to them in Christ (Ferguson, 253), while Origen discerned the ethical implications of the Lord's Prayer's petition for the coming of God's kingdom. "It is clear that he who prays for the coming of the kingdom of God rightly prays that the kingdom of God might be established, and bear fruit and be perfected in himself" (Origen, 85). In fact, Origen believed that a life lived well before Christ was actually a form of prayer.

The Union of the Mind and Heart

The spirituality of early Christian pastors and teachers was communally formed and shaped in the church. As early Christians met weekly for worship, heard the Scripture read and taught, sang the psalms, shared the Eucharist together, and celebrated the baptism of new Christians, they pondered the process involved in leading human beings into an ever-deepening relationship with the incarnate source of all truth—Jesus Christ—and with each other through the power of the Holy Spirit.

Ancient Christian leaders were convinced that more than intellectual prowess alone was necessary to approach and worship the mystery of God; the wonder of the incarnation, ministry, crucifixion, resurrection, and ascension of the Son of God; the intricacies of human relationships; and the complexities of the created order. Holy living, disciplined thinking, feasting upon Christ in the Eucharist, keen observation of human society and the natural world, and continual prayer were key aspects of ancient Christian spirituality's approach to growing into the truth.

The wise development and nurture of key virtues, such as patience, holiness, stability, self-control, gentleness, kindness, perseverance, discretion, and peace (cf. Gal. 5:22)—all summed up in the word *love*—were viewed as essentials in spiritual development. The healing and union of the mind and the heart—the intellect and the affections—enabled Christians to move ever more deeply into the mystery of Christ, "in whom," as Paul puts it, "are hidden all the treasures of wisdom and knowledge" (Col. 2:3).

Ancient Christians fervently believed genuine holiness manifested itself in wisdom, love, and spiritual knowledge. In turn, love, knowledge, and wisdom established holiness ever more deeply, all wonders of the treasure hidden in Christ. Maximus the Confessor expressed this insight well: "If, as Paul says, Christ dwells in our hearts through faith (Eph. 3:17), and all the treasures of wisdom and spiritual knowledge are hidden in him (Col. 2:3), then all the treasures of wisdom and spiritual knowledge are hidden in our hearts. They are revealed to the heart by means of the commandments" (Maximus the Confessor, 49).

The Role of Ascesis

The Greek noun *ascesis* is related to the Greek verb *askeo*, which in a secular context meant "to exercise." All Greek athletes maintained a strict *ascesis* or training regimen that included a specific diet, certain specific exercises depending on the athlete's particular sport, hours of training on a daily basis, and so on. For athletes, then as today, most *ascesis* took place behind the scenes, apart from the public's gaze. *Ascesis* was often boring, repetitive, grueling, and difficult. But apart from this specific, disciplined regimen, an athlete would be naïve to expect to win in the stadium or arena. Specific training honed the athlete's innate athletic abilities and gifting and enabled him to perform at his peak in the midst of competition.

Ancient Christians transferred the importance of *ascesis* or a strict training regimen for athletes to the context of spiritual formation, with the metaphor of the Christian as athlete frequently employed in discussions of the spiritual life. Though ancient Christian *ascesis* sometimes fell into legalism, at its best moments it represents the insight that spiritual formation requires effort, discipline, and constant reliance on the grace of God through the power of the Spirit. Early Christians understood that intellectual and spiritual growth were nurtured by key dispositions, habits, and spiritual disciplines, such as prayer, meditative reading of Scripture—often involving significant and lengthy memory work—and fasting. If Christians were to become like Christ—the image of God—purposeful imitation of Christ's perspectives and behaviors, often modeled in the lives of the apostles, was absolutely necessary.

Key Elements of Ancient Christian Spirituality

How can we best describe ancient Christian spirituality? First and foremost, spiritual perspectives and practices in the early church were grounded in the worship of the incarnate, crucified, risen Christ. At the heart of ancient Christian spirituality is a deep belief and commitment to Christ, the Son of God, the Son of Man. Early Christians affirmed, embraced, and worshiped the Word made flesh (John 1:1, 14, 18). Athanasius, archbishop of Alexandria in the 4th century, observed that "the Word of the Father is himself divine. . . . By what seems his utter poverty and weakness on the cross, he overturns the pomp and parade of idols, and quietly and hiddenly wins over the mockers and unbelievers to recognize him as God" (Athanasius, *On the Incarnation*, 25).

Though the Council of Nicea (AD 325) was the first council of bishops to affirm the full deity of the incarnate Word, the church in its practice from the 1st century forward worshiped Christ as Lord (*kurios*) and God. Prayers, for example, were offered to Christ as well as the Father. With further reflection, the church also recognized the deity of the Holy Spirit and the role of the Spirit in forming Christians into the image of Christ. Basil, writing in the 4th century, taught that the Holy Spirit "perfects all other things, and is never depleted.... He is the source of sanctification, spiritual light, who gives illumination to everyone using his powers to search for the truth—and the illumination he gives is himself" (Basil the Great, 43).

Ancient Christian spirituality was sacramental. In part, the church's sacramental perspective was shaped in response to the gnostic attempt to spiritualize the gospel and denigrate the goodness of matter. The early church firmly believed that God delights in using very tangible means to communicate his presence to his people—means and matter as earthy as water, wine, and bread. The sacramental realism of the ancient church is evident in the realistic—indeed graphic—language early Christians frequently employed in speaking of the Eucharist as a feeding on the blood and body of Christ. Justin Martyr, writing in the 2nd century, noted: "We do not receive these gifts as ordinary food or drink. But as Jesus Christ our Savior was made flesh through the word of God, and took flesh and blood for our salvation; in the same way the food over which thanksgiving has been offered through the word of prayer that we have from him—the food by which our blood and flesh are nourished through its transformation—is, we are taught, the flesh and blood of Jesus who was made flesh" (Justin Martyr, 66).

Ancient Christians did not attempt to analyze or describe how God's grace or Christ could actually be present in the baptismal waters or consecrated bread. We don't find theories of transubstantiation or consubstantiation, for instance, in the Eucharistic theology of the ancient church. Instead, on the basis of the incarnation itself (what we might call the *incarnational principle*), Christians believed that God delighted to dwell with his people in a manner that was earthy, tangible, and concrete, though how God could do so was left up to God. "I venerate the fashioner of matter, who became matter for my sake and accepted to dwell in matter and through matter worked my salvation, and I will not cease from reverencing matter, through which my salvation was worked" (John of Damascus, 29). The union of the Son's divine nature with human nature in the incarnate Christ demonstrated that God came to his church through very real, substantial, earthy means. The efficacy of a sacrament, however, was linked to an individual's personal faith. Ancient Christians had a strong abhorrence for anything that smacked of the superstition and magic so prevalent in the Roman world.

Tertullian, writing in the 3rd century, highlighted the sacramental link between the material and the spiritual in baptism and the eschatological fulfillment of the old covenant given to Israel in the new covenant given to the church in Christ. In baptism the believer is "plunged in water. Yet, its effect is spiritual, in that we are freed from sins" (Tertullian, 672). In addition, the entire baptismal service, the key initiatory rite of the ancient church, reminded Tertullian of previous old covenant practices and their fulfillment in Christ.

The laying on of hands—subsequent to baptism—and the entire liturgy of the baptismal service brought to Tertullian's mind key old covenant types and "sacramental" rites that pointed to Christ and found their fulfillment in him. Jacob, for instance, laid his hands on the heads of both Ephraim and Manasseh as he blessed them. When Jacob did so, though, he crossed his arms (Gen. 48:12–14). Tertullian argued that the Old Testament narrative drew the discerning reader to think of its eschatological fulfillment in Christ, "with his hands laid on them and interchanged, and indeed so transversely slanted one over the other, that, by delineating Christ, they even portended the future benediction of Christ" (Tertullian, 672). *The Epistle of Barnabas*—which may be dated as early as AD 90—also draws our attention to the Christian symbolism present in Jacob's blessing of Ephraim and Manasseh, demonstrating how early eschatological and sacramental themes appeared and intersected in ancient Christian spirituality (Holmes, 180).

Ancient Christian spirituality was strongly communal and largely unmarked by the individualism that characterizes the evangelical scene in North America today. Especially before the conversion of Constantine in the 4th century, to become a Christian was a dramatic move from one world and community to another, a commitment to follow Christ in a life of discipleship that had financial, familial, and vocational implications; certain vocations, for example, were off limits for ancient Christians. Actors, gladiators, athletes, charioteers, and occasionally soldiers—for at least the first four hundred years of the church's history—were required to leave their vocations behind if they were to be baptized.

Early Christian spirituality was rooted in the Scripture. On Sundays the Hebrew Scriptures (in the Greek Septuagint form) and the writings of the apostles were read and explained in the context of worship. The praying of the Psalms was an important aspect of early Christian praise, much as it had been in the synagogue. The earliest monastic communities prayed all 150 psalms in a single day! By the time of Benedict of Nursia in the 6th-century, monastic communities prayed the entire Psalter over seven days.

Athanasius wrote on the importance of praying the Psalms and, through their constant recitation, committing them to memory. In doing so, worshipers formed their consciousness—their way of viewing God, the world, worship, issues of justice, questions concerning suffering—around the consciousness of the psalmist, in many cases David himself. "He who recites the Psalms is uttering the rest as his own words, and each sings them as if they were written concerning him, and he accepts them and recites them not as if another were speaking, nor as if speaking about someone else. But he handles them as if he is speaking about himself. And the things spoken are such that he lifts them up to God as himself acting and speaking them from himself" (Athanasius, *To Marcellinus*, 110).

Memory, recitation, and conscious imitation, then, were important aspects of ancient Christian spirituality. Libanios, John Chrysostom's secular tutor, taught John and other students to "Install Demosthenes in your soul." That is, know Demosthenes so well that you and he are virtually inseparable in thought and practice. Chrysostom took this principle seriously but applied it to Christ and the apostles. He spent two years in a cave above Antioch memorizing huge quantities of Paul, John, Peter, and of course Jesus. The result, from Chrysostom's perspective, was that his mind and heart had merged with that of the apostles, and through the apostles, with Christ through the power of the Holy Spirit.

Ancient Christian spirituality was forged and molded in the fires of suffering and persecution for the first three hundred years of its history. Though Roman persecution of the church was sporadic, harassment could be quite vicious. Possible outbreaks of violence always hung over the ancient Christian community. The Romans, who viewed themselves as tolerant of a vast variety of religious perspectives, simply couldn't comprehend the much narrower perspective and commitment of the church, particularly regarding the exclusive nature of its devotion to Christ. Thus, baptism was a spiritual and political act; in baptism Christians crossed a line in the sand between the broader Roman culture and the new, distinct community of the church.

When persecution did occur, Christians were often asked to sacrifice to the emperor as a god, a seemingly innocuous act in Roman eyes but a grave sin from a Christian perspective. Martyrs for the faith—those who bore witness to Christ by their words, lives, and deaths—became valued models of faithful discipleship for ancient Christians; the martyrs had faithfully and literally obeyed Christ's call to take up one's cross and follow him (Mark 8:34). In a manner of speaking, martyrs were the Christians par excellence.

The Holy Spirit was believed to be especially active and vibrant in the martyrs, supplying supernatural strength and courage, not only to the martyrs' minds and souls, but also to their bodies. Because of the ancient church's sacramental and incarnational worldview, the bodies (often ashes) of the martyrs were venerated as still holy and powerful, on the pattern of biblical narratives. Just as the bones of Elisha possessed supernatural power from God (cf. 2 Kings 13:21)—the result of the Spirit resting on Elisha throughout his life—so the bodies and ashes of ancient Christian martyrs were treasured as spiritually powerful and the day of martyrs' deaths celebrated as their "birthday."

The Conversion of Constantine

The conversion of Constantine—AD 312—marks an extremely important juncture in the history of the church and in ancient Christian spirituality. Up to this point, the church had been a cohesive, highly committed community, largely marked by a history of faithful discipleship to Christ and willingness to die rather than compromise its commitment to its incarnate Lord. With Constantine's conversion, though, the church passed from being a persecuted community to being a privileged one. The implications of this transition should not be exaggerated, but it is fair to say that some people became Christians as the political and religious winds shifted. It was more convenient and tactful to follow the example of the emperor, though Constantine's own faith appears sincere and committed. Thus, early believers after Constantine's conversion faced spiritual dangers of a new kind: complacency, a mechanical view of the sacraments, spiritual lethargy, spiritual flimsiness—in a word, the threat of cultural Christianity.

In a reaction to this trend, some Christians—first individually and then in groups, migrated to the desert environment of Egypt, Syria, and Palestine. These believers moved into the rugged environment of the desert for a variety of reasons; a primary motivation was to find intense, unremitting solitude and silence. In this unique geographical learning milieu, Christians attended carefully to Scripture, to the voice of God in prayer and worship, and to their habitual thoughts and practices. In the desert Christians learned to study with the mind in the heart, a phrase that is indicative of the ancient Christian concern that the unregenerate mind and heart can easily mutate into a world unto themselves, attracted to what kills and resistant to what brings life.

To draw close to God, these early Christians believed, is to encounter love and truth. Divine love is always a holy love, a love grounded in truth: astringent, bracing, achingly attractive, amazingly beautiful, and insistent in its desire to overcome any roadblocks to the reception of what divine love offers and longingly desires to be received. In the desert environment a fundamental movement of the spiritual life was birthed and nourished with the wise direction of experienced guides (the *abbas* and *ammas*) and through the practice of key spiritual disciplines. This was the movement from self-deception to self-awareness, with safe, sane, healthy, robust love the result, along with love's corresponding insights.

To admit the truth about oneself is always a harrowing and, sometimes, horrifying experience. Some monks lived in the desert for years and never changed. The self-awareness that nurtures the growth of love was simply too threatening for some to face. This refusal to accept God's grace-filled call to change short-circuited the healing process entailed in moving into God's love. If a monk persisted in lying to himself, others, and God about the condition of his own personality and its habitual patterns of life, his spiritual and emotional growth was stunted rather than enriched in its desert environment. Indeed, the monk's rugged learning context—the tensions, demands, and difficulties of the desert—actually widened the cracks in the self-deceived monk's personality. We find disintegrated as well as integrated personalities in the desert.

The silence, solitude, heat, nighttime cold, and barrenness of the desert functioned like a spiritual nutcracker for those who would invade its spaces in search of a closer relationship with God. Desert dwellers learned quickly how helpless, weak, and dependent they were—on God and on others—and how the diversions and delights of town and city life had buffered them from recognizing their innate helplessness and the stark disjunction between their thoughts and actions. There were few alternatives for the desert fathers and mothers: remain where you are and learn the lessons God desires to teach, remain where you are and continue to flee from God internally, or return to the wider world, the very world that had driven you to search for God in the isolation of the desert.

The goal of desert spirituality and ancient Christian spirituality as a whole was transformation. In fact, we can sum up the heart of ancient Christian spirituality in this phrase: "ever-deeper transformation into the image of Christ," known in the ancient church as deification. Early Christians knew they would never become God, but they surely realized they were called to be faithful image-bearers of the image of God himself, Jesus Christ (cf. Col. 1:15).

Sources Cited

Athanasius: *The Life of Antony and the Letter to Marcellinus*, CWS (1980).

———. *On the Incarnation*. Trans. a religious of C.S.M.V. (1982).

Basil the Great. *On the Holy Spirit*. Trans. D. Anderson (1980).

Ferguson, E. *Inheriting Wisdom* (2004).

Holmes, M., ed. *Apostolic Fathers* (1989).

John of Damascus. *Three Treatises on the Divine Images*. Trans. A. Louth (2003).

Justin Martyr. *First Apology*, ANF (1956).

Maximus the Confessor: *Selected Writings*, CWS (1985).

Origen. *Prayer, Exhortation to Martyrdom*, ACW 19 (1954).

Tertullian. *On Baptism*, ANF (1994).

For Further Reading

Bouyer, L. *The Spirituality of the New Testament and the Fathers* (1982).

Brown, P. *The Body and Society* (1988).

Burton-Christie, D. *The Word in the Desert* (1993).

Byassee, J. *An Introduction to the Desert Fathers* (2007).

Clement, O. *The Roots of Christian Mysticism* (1993).

Hall, C. *Worshiping with the Church Fathers* (2009).

Harmless, W. *Desert Christians* (2004).

McGinn, B., et al., eds. *Christian Spirituality*: *Origins to the Twelfth Century*, WSEH (1985).

Oden, T., and C. Crosby. *Ancient Christian Devotional* (2007).

Reardon, P. H. *Christ in the Psalms* (2000).

CHAPTER 14

BYZANTIUM AND THE EAST (600–1700)

BRADLEY NASSIF

This essay focuses on the spirituality of the Eastern Orthodox Church in the Byzantine (330–1453) and Russian (988–1917) empires between AD 600 and 1700. Byzantine and Slavic Christianity are intimately tied to their political and social histories.

The Orthodox Church itself, however, is not identical with these political realities, for by its very nature the church transcends historical particularity of any kind—be it Byzantine, Russian, or any other culture. Nevertheless, the spirituality of Eastern Christianity was articulated within the context of these empires and continues to shape the spiritual ethos of the church to this day.

Centrality of the Gospel

The central reality that governed the spiritual tradition of the Orthodox Church between 600 and 1700 was the same one that inspired the early apostolic preaching, namely, the victory of the gospel. By 600 many of the central themes of Orthodox spirituality were already in place. The legacy of those themes is so foundational to the period under consideration that a brief overview of them is required.

Christification (deification). The goal of the gospel in every life-giving action of the church was the "deification" of the human person into Christlikeness in anticipation of the ultimate transformation of the cosmos. The term *deification* is a translation of the Greek word *theosis*. Athanasius speaks for the entire Greek patristic tradition in his affirmation, "God became humanized so that humans might become divinized." By virtue of the incarnation and the "communication of idioms" between Christ's divine and human natures, Christians were called to participate in the deified humanity of Christ. They were called not merely to imitate Jesus' moral life, but to participate *in* Christ through baptism, Eucharist, and the sacramental life of the church. Such was the goal of Orthodox spirituality, which the following sought to attain.

Trinity and Christology. The foundations of deification rested upon the dogmas of the Trinity and Christology as expounded by the Councils of Nicea (325), Constantinople (381), Ephesus (431), and Chalcedon (451). These provided the theological foundations for the later debates over icons (726–843), the church's mystical theology, and the role of the body in prayer (10th–14th centuries). A special position of honor was also given to Mary in worship and devotion because of her relation to Christ as the *Theotokos* ("God-Bearer").

Monasticism. The primitive simplicity of monastic life from 300 to 500 continued to occupy a central role in the Eastern Church from 600 to 1700. Monastic ideals were described in the classic biography *The Life of Antony* by Athanasius; an anonymous book titled *The Sayings of the Desert Fathers*; and *The Ladder of Divine Ascent* by John Climacus, the abbot of Mount Sinai. These and other writings contained famous sayings and stories from the desert fathers (*abbas*) and mothers (*ammas*) of

Egypt, Palestine, and Syria. Evagrius of Pontus and (Pseudo) Macarius of Egypt emphasized "prayer of the mind" and "prayer of the heart" respectively. They contributed to the development of the famous Jesus Prayer that was at the center of the Hesychast controversy in the 14th century (see Gregory Palamas below). Monastic principles such as humility, fasting, contemplation, repentance, and others permeated Orthodox spirituality and worship.

Liturgical and sacramental life. The gospel was supremely manifested in the church's liturgical and sacramental life. Orthodox worship was mystical and doxological. The shape and experience of the church's sacred space was designed to transport believers from the cares of this world to the mysteries of heaven. The connection between prayer and faith is best summarized by the dictum, "The rule of prayer is the rule of faith" (*lex orandi lex est credendi*). The main Sunday service, called the Divine Liturgy of St. John Chrysostom, consisted of the preaching of Scripture and, especially, partaking of the heavenly meal, the Eucharist. An annual cycle of feasts and fasts centered on Pascha, the Easter celebration of Christ's resurrection from the dead. The victory of life over death became a constantly recurring theme throughout the church's hymnography.

Compassionate activism. The social relevance of the gospel inspired the physical ministries of the early and Byzantine church. Despite the Christian veneer that resulted from the new alliance between church and state in the 4th century, the Roman Empire was a world of tensions, social injustices, and love of money. In this context, Basil the Great (of Caesarea) and John Chrysostom—two of the greatest church fathers—stressed the urgency of Christian philanthropy. Hospitals, schools, orphanages, hospices, and other forms of social work were practical expressions of the gospel's emphasis on love for the neighbor. The church's liturgy and belief in the incarnation inspired love for the poor and fostered spiritual growth in the likeness of Christ.

Byzantine Christianity (600–1453)

Byzantine spirituality from the time of Maximus the Confessor to the fall of the Byzantine Empire (1453) flowed from the preceding centuries of patristic tradition. Church dogmas, such as the coequality of the Father and Son (described by the Aristotelian term *homoousios*), were often expressed in philosophical language that had been given explicitly Christian meanings. Byzantine iconographic style also adapted the conventions of late Greco-Roman art that mixed naturalism with philosophical abstraction. These and other cultural adaptations of the age were put in the service of the gospel.

Collectively, bishops, monks, hymnographers, poets, and iconographers created a coherent synthesis that would define the particularity of Orthodox spirituality and worship up to the present day. The following are a selection of some of the leading personalities and issues that shaped the ethos of the period in roughly chronological order.

Romanos the Melodist (died c. 555) was a Syrian writer who was one of the greatest poets and musicians of the Byzantine church. His special contribution was the development of the *kontakion* (meaning "from the pole"). The *kontakion* was a long biblical hymn or sermon that was so long it was rolled up on a pole for use in church services. Theology was often expressed musically by juxtaposing a series of complementary or opposing ideas. Over time, the *kontakion* was greatly abbreviated. The following Christmas *kontakion* by Romanos, from the *Divine Services of the Eastern Orthodox Church*, is still sung at Christmas services:

> Today the Virgin gives birth to the Transcendent One,
> And the earth offers a cave to the Unapproachable One!
> Angels with shepherds glorify Him!
> The wise men journey with a star!
> Since for our sake the Eternal God was born as a little child! (372)

Even more influential than Romanos was John of Damascus. John's theology and poetry expressed the heart of Byzantine spirituality. The incarnation of the Word stood at the very center of the church's sacramental life, which transfigured believers into the divine likeness. The classic teaching of Athanasius and the entire Greek patristic tradition on *theosis* (noted above) permeates his theology, songs, and prayers. In the *Service Book of the Holy Eastern Orthodox Church*, John's funeral hymns highlight the mystery of death: "I weep and lament when I think upon death, and behold our beauty created in the likeness of God lying in the tomb disfigured, bereft of glory and form" (194).

John is most famous for opposing the heresy of the iconoclasts. The iconoclasts rejected religious images on the grounds that they violated the second of the Ten Commandments ("You shall make no graven images"). They wanted to destroy all religious icons, mosaics, and statues. John of Damascus defended the use of sacred images. He explained that the respect given to them is really given to the person they represent. Theodore the Studite (759 – 826) and Patriarch Nicephorus (758 – 828) added further refinements to John's arguments on the basis of the Christology of the Council of Chalcedon (451). Sophisticated arguments based on Scripture, tradition, and Christology coalesced in a formidable defense of icons that eventually led the Seventh Ecumenical Council (787) officially to proclaim their validity in worship and devotion. The Council supported the veneration or reverencing of icons (*proskynesis*) while sternly forbidding their worship (*latreia*). A feast, known as the Triumph of Orthodoxy, was commissioned by Empress Irene in 843 and is celebrated annually to this day at the start of Great Lent.

Icons continue to play a central role in the liturgy and personal piety of Orthodox Christians. They edify the faithful by creating an intimate link of communication between believers and the ones who are portrayed in the images. As "books for the illiterate" (John of Damascus), icons instruct others in Bible stories and the church's faith. When the faithful contemplate the meaning of icons, the icons inspire them to imitate the holy lives of the saints portrayed; but above all, icons bear witness to the incarnation of the Word made flesh (John 1:14). Icons are eschatological witnesses to the incarnation and the reality that Christ will one day transform the entire cosmos into "a new heaven and a new earth" (Rev. 21:1). All this contributes to the deification or Christification of believers.

Another writer, Pseudo-Dionysius the Areopagite, had an enormous influence on the spiritual tradition of Byzantine Christianity. His true identity is completely unknown, but his works hint that he was a Syrian bishop and monk. His writings were enormously influential in both Eastern and Western Christianity. In the Eastern Church he is quoted by Maximus the Confessor, John of Damascus, Symeon the New Theologian, and Gregory Palamas.

The impact of Dionysius lies chiefly in his teachings on celestial and ministerial hierarchies, the three stages of growth, and a style of theology known as the apophatic method. His teaching on hierarchies discusses ranks of angels, church ministries, sacraments, and the three ways of spiritual life (purification, illumination, and union with God). Like the teachings of Origen and Evagrius of Pontus, Dionysius's doctrines were modified and integrated into the church's tradition, though serious questions remain. Perhaps his greatest impact, however, was his massive use of apophatic theology (literally a "turning away from speech"). According to Dionysius, the Christian experience of God is essentially unknowable: "Everything can be affirmed of God at one and the same time, and yet he is none of these things" (Pseudo-Dionysius, 27). Negative theology affirms and denies assertions about God while simultaneously leading one to a positive encounter with him.

Maximus the Confessor wrote extensively on Christology and the spiritual life. His writings influenced the subsequent Greek tradition. The title "confessor" indicates his survival of martyrdom after state authorities cut off his tongue and right hand for speaking and writing in support of the human and divine wills of Christ. A brilliant thinker, he wrote extensively on the integration of theology and the spiritual life. He synthesized the preceding centuries of teaching on prayer with the theological orthodoxy of the church. He believed that the purpose of theology was to deepen communion with God. Origen, Gregory of Nazianzus, and Pseudo-Dionysius provided the sources for much of his thought.

Maximus argued that Christ had two wills, human and divine, that worked in perfect harmony with one another. Like Christ, believers are to bring their human wills, choices, and actions into harmony with God's will. Human perfection, therefore, is linked to the proper use of human freedom. Maximus has also been known for his stress on the cosmic dimensions of salvation. Following the christological maximalism of the apostle Paul in the book of Colossians, the healing of humankind embraces the entire cosmos on the basis of the incarnation.

After the church had gone through the great Trinitarian, christological, and iconoclastic debates (325–787), orthodox dogma emerged triumphant. A general attitude of self-assuredness prevailed in the Orthodox Church. Consequently, the church became heavily institutionalized. Theology began to be divorced from personal experience. The liturgy was often reduced to barren ritualism. People affirmed that a conscious experience of God's grace in the heart was possible in the days of the great church fathers, but not in their day. It was in this context that Symeon the New Theologian emerged.

Symeon was a prophet of Christian experience. He strongly cautioned believers against substituting barren ritualism for a "conscious experience of God in the heart." Those who lacked this conscious awareness should not and could not serve as ministers, be they priests, bishops, or patriarchs. For this, Symeon was branded a heretic, to which he replied: "Here are those whom I call heretics: Those who say that there is no one in our time in

our midst who would observe the commandments of the gospel and become like the holy Fathers.... These people have not fallen into some particular heresy, but into all the heresies at once, since this one is worse than all in its impiety!" (Symeon, 9).

Repentance was the key to obtaining a conscious knowledge of God in the heart. Water baptism that is unaccompanied by a "conscious experience" of the Holy Spirit cannot save. Rather, a "baptism of the Holy Spirit" was given by God to all those who shed the tears of true repentance. By his poetic enthusiasm, Symeon seemed formally to deny the sacraments and authority of the hierarchy. But baptism and Eucharist were actually the foundations for Symeon's doctrine of personal experience. He believed there was no contradiction between the church's "spiritual" and "institutional" ministries, because the same Spirit checks and balances both.

The theological foundations of how one comes to know God were developed by Gregory Palamas. He was a bishop and monk from Mount Athos, which was the monastic center of Orthodox spirituality from the 10th century onward. He and other monks practiced a method of prayer known as hesychasm ("holy silence"). Hesychasm combined breathing techniques with a short petition known as the Jesus Prayer: "Lord Jesus Christ, Son of God, have mercy on me." By looking at the heart or navel, regulating one's breathing, and reciting this prayer, some monks experienced a vision of the visible but uncreated light that radiated from Christ when he was transfigured on Mount Tabor (Matt. 17:2).

Hesychasm soon came under attack by Barlaam of Calabria, a fellow Orthodox theologian who was well versed in Western Scholasticism and the Renaissance. They disagreed over how the unknowable God can also be known. Barlaam denied the monks' claim of having a direct, personal experience of God. However, the church in Constantinople sided with Gregory and condemned Barlaam in a series of councils throughout the 14th century. Gregory synthesized the previous one thousand years of patristic theology by distinguishing between God's "unknowable essence" and his "knowable energies." This gave the Orthodox Church a common spirituality that crossed geographic and cultural boundaries by confirming that humans can indeed know God personally and partake of the divine glory in this life. Hesychast practices, however, were not required of all Christians, nor were they the only legitimate forms of Orthodox mysticism.

Russian Christianity

The Byzantine legacy described above was transplanted on Russian soil with the conversion of Prince Vladimir in 988. The essential content of the Byzantine spiritual tradition remained rigorously the same in Russia, with but a few changes. In the new environment, Russian saints were less interested in speculative theology than the Greeks, hermit monks emphasized more of the social implications of the gospel than their predecessors, and iconographers adapted Byzantine themes and style to fit their Russian culture. Andrew Rublev (d. 1427) was one of the best examples.

Russians highly valued the place of suffering in the Christian life. This can be seen early in Russian history through the lives of Vladimir's two sons, Boris and Gleb. At the death of Vladimir in 1015, their older brother attempted to seize their principalities, but Boris and Gleb refused to resist him based on a literal reading of the gospel to "turn the other cheek." Each in turn was murdered. They preferred that their blood be shed rather than the blood of others. Soon after, the church bestowed on them the title of "Passion Bearers," because through their innocent and voluntary suffering, they shared in the passion of Christ.

Monasteries played an important part in old Russia just as they did in Byzantium. The most influential of them all was the Monastery of the Caves in Kiev. One of its most illustrious leaders was Theodosius of the Caves (d. 1074). Theodosius was keenly aware of the social implications

of the gospel and so lived a life of humility and extreme poverty, much as Francis of Assissi did in the Christian West. He wore old clothing, worked with the slaves, and avoided the use of power.

This theme of humility through suffering was to capture the Russian soul for centuries. The familiar saying "No temptation, no salvation" (a paraphrase of Antony of Egypt in the 4th century) became widely quoted by the Russian people. Later writers such as Tolstoy and Dostoevsky developed the theme in their writings.

Serge of Radonezh (c. 1314 – 1392), Russia's greatest national saint, followed a similar path of humility and founded the Holy Trinity monastery near Moscow. His spiritual children, however, engaged in a major dispute over the use of monastic property. Joseph of Volokolamsk (1439 – 1515) and his followers were called the "Possessors," while Nil Sorsky (1433 – 1508) and his disciples were called the "Non-Possessors." The Possessors emphasized the social obligations of the gospel to care for the sick and poor with the money gained from monastic lands. "The riches of the church are the riches of the poor," they argued. The Non-Possessors opposed this by emphasizing prayer as the primary calling of monks along with their life of poverty and detachment from worldly possessions. Their main function was to be a prophetic witness to others that the kingdom of God is not of this world. In the end, the Possessors won. Regrettably, the church became too closely tied to the state, thus creating a spiritual imbalance in the centuries that followed.

The church establishment of the 16th century rigorously followed the tradition of the Possessors. A protest movement arose, therefore, among the monks in reaction to the injustices and hypocrisies of church and state leaders. They became known as "holy fools" (from 1 Cor. 4:10) for their bizarre behavior. While never harming anyone, they confronted those who lied or did violence to others. One of these "fools" was Basil the Blessed (d. 1552), after whom the Kremlin cathedral now takes its name. Basil once dared to warn Czar Ivan the Terrible that his unjust killing of others would condemn him to hell. During Lent, Basil confronted Ivan for abstaining from meat while at the same time murdering people. Ivan lived in fear of Basil and refused to bring him harm.

Conclusion

Our brief pages on the history of spirituality in the Eastern Orthodox tradition from 600 – 1700 show that "catholicity" was the essential element in the church's message. Catholicity is understood here in a broad sense that embraces truth, fullness, and continuity with the apostolic faith. Despite its human failures across the centuries, the church's catholicity was manifested in the dogmas, prayers, hymns, sacraments, iconography, and liturgical services that originated from the gospel of Jesus Christ. Communion with God through the incarnate Christ was the ultimate inspiration and goal of human existence. The church's task was to bear witness to that fullness at all times, in all cultures, and in all countries.

Sources Cited

Athanasius. *On the Incarnation of the Word*. Christian Classics Ethereal Library (2007).
Divine Services of the Eastern Orthodox Church (1959).
John of Damascus. *Three Treatises on the Divine Images*. Trans. A. Louth (2003).
Maximus the Confessor. *Selected Writings*. Trans. G. Berthold, CWS (1985).
Palamas, Gregory. *The Triads*. Trans. N. Gendle, CWS (1983).
Pseudo-Dionysius. "Mystical Theology." In *The Complete Works*, CWS (1987).
Service Book of the Holy Eastern Orthodox Church. Ed. Antiochian Orthodox Archdiocese (1960).
Symeon the New Theologian. *The Discourses*. Trans. C. J. De Catanzaro (1980).

For Further Reading

Holder, A., ed. *Christian Spirituality: The Classics* (2009).
McGinn, B. *Essential Writings of Christian Mysticism* (2006).
McGinn, B., and J. Meyendorff. *Christian Spirituality*. Vols. 1 and 2 (1986).
McGuckin, J. A. "Christian Spirituality in Byzantium and the East (600 – 1700)." In *The Blackwell Companion to Christian Spirituality*, ed. A. Holder (2005), 90 – 105.
———. *Standing in God's Holy Fire: The Byzantine Tradition* (2001).
Nassif, B. "Kissers and Smashers." *Christian History* 16, no. 2 (1997): 20 – 23.
Pelikan, J. *The Christian Tradition*. Vol. 2 (1977).
Rentel, A. "Byzantine and Slavic Orthodoxy." In *The Oxford History of Christian Worship*, ed. G. Wainwright and K. Westerfield Tucker (2006): 254 – 306.

CHAPTER 15

THE MEDIEVAL WEST (600–1450)

DENNIS D. MARTIN

Salvation in Christ transforms the Christian believer by Christ's grace from a sinner alienated from God to a participant—as an adopted child and coheir with Christ—in the inner life of the Trinity (e.g., Rom. 8:17; Eph. 1; Col. 1; 1 Peter 1:4; 2 Peter 1:4). Medieval Christians in Western Europe lived within this framework. In the East it was called *theosis*; in the West it was known as deification (Keating). Saving grace comes to the believer in and through Christ's mysterious body, his spouse (Eph. 5), that is, through the church and its sacraments. Thus, spirituality in the medieval West was fundamentally sacramental; contemplative or "mystical" union was actually secondary. Visions and other spiritual gifts (Rom. 12; 1 Cor. 12–14; 1 Peter 4) are decidedly secondary to general salvation, whether anticipated in mystical union or not. Such charisms are given to an individual for the edification of others, not for the recipient's aggrandizement.

Sacramental means of grace were primary even for monks, nuns, and members of mendicant religious orders. Married folk, as well as monks and nuns, lived the sacramental life, and disciplined (i.e., regular—from *regula*, meaning "rule") prayers and devotions were expected of both, though at different intensities. By freeing themselves from the obligations of married life in the world, monks and nuns did indeed open space in their daily lives for intensified, "professional" growth in holiness. They understood themselves to be anticipating, as watchers and vigil-keepers, for Christ's return, heaven's more perfect communion in Christ. Their "professional" focus did, however, mean that many of the deepest insights and writings about spirituality arise from monastic circles. Yet the instructions for Christian living outlined by Benedict in his 6th-century *Rule for Monks* are the same as the virtues and "fruit of the Spirit" that all Christians were supposed to pursue. In that sense, lay spirituality was modeled on monastic spirituality, and that modeling was by no means unrealistic, because monastic spirituality simply followed Scripture on these points.

In addition to the sacraments, Christian life in the medieval West was marked above all by liturgy, and the liturgy consisted of almost nothing except Scripture, woven together to express the ineffable mysteries of the faith. Beyond the eucharistic liturgy, the daily round of prayers at cathedrals and in monastic houses, which involved the recitation of the entire book of Psalms at least weekly, as well as daily readings from both Testaments, was attended by at least some of the devout laypeople. The spiritual life of those Christians who took their baptismal faith seriously was also marked by springtime rogation processions to beg (*rogare*) God to bless the crops and fields; prayers and processions in communion with deceased members of the church in heaven (Feast of All Saints, November 1) or on the sure path to heaven (Feast of All Souls on November 2); the Candlemas procession for the Feast of Jesus' Presentation in the Temple (February 2); the blessing of flowers at the

Feast of the Assumption of Mary (August 15); the autumn remembrance of Michael the Archangel who defends in dark days against the devil (September 29); and other feasts of Christ and Mary (Annunciation, March 25; Mary's Conception, December 8; Mary's Nativity, September 8). Even the more nominal Christians could scarcely remain unaffected by the public nature of these celebratory liturgical events.

The Continuum from Sacraments to Contemplative Union

Christian spirituality in this period cannot be understood without first grasping the communal nature of salvation in the mystical body of Christ, the church (de Lubac; cf. Lewis, 2.5; 4.4). Baptism, Eucharist as the saving sacrifice of Christ, reception of Communion as an even more intimate aspect of Eucharist, and God's restoration of a fallen sinner to baptismal grace in the sacrament of Confession were the main means of participation in Christ. As reception of Communion became more infrequent, presence at the eucharistic sacrifice of the Mass became the most important ongoing means of grace for most people. But even the anointing of the (deathly) sick was publicly and communally visible. As the priest hurried through the streets to bring Communion to a dying person, bells rang out, informing everyone of an imminent death, and people knelt as Christ himself passed by in his hidden but real eucharistic presence.

Since the invisible things of God are understood by the things that are made (Rom. 1:20), water, bread, wine, and oil can be employed by God as vehicles of his supernatural grace. In his *Confessions*, Augustine turned to all the creatures and asked who God is. They replied, "We are not God, but God made us"; that is, Christians do not worship the creatures, but the creatures are signs and vehicles that efficaciously point to their Creator. In the early 1200s, Francis of Assisi's *Canticle of the Sun* shows the persistence of this principle:

rather than monistic nature mysticism, Francis articulated an ancient Jewish and Christian appeal to Brother Sun and Sister Moon and to all of creation to praise God (Ps. 148).

Therefore, laypeople in the world need not devalue their activity in deference to supposedly "higher" spiritual callings. We find this explicitly stated by Hugh of Lincoln (d. 1200):

> "The kingdom of God is not confined only to monks, hermits and anchorites. When at the last, the Lord shall judge every individual, he will not hold it against him that he has not been a hermit or a monk, but will reject each of the damned because he had not been a real Christian." [Hugh] ... taught that even married people, who never rose above the natural obligations of their state, should not be considered to be devoid of the virtue of chastity but equally with virgins and celibates would be admitted to the glory of the heavenly kingdom. (Adam of Eynsham, 4.9)

The notion that life "in religion" is simply superior to life in the world arises only in the later Middle Ages, among some of the mendicants.

Since sin had distorted and disintegrated the movements of the human spirit, had destroyed the likeness to God while disfiguring but not destroying the image of God, the goal of the sacramental and spiritual life was reintegration of the passions (Gr. *apatheia*, and *puritas cordis* in John Cassian's Latin; see Bell). No one can achieve this by his or her own effort: one finds God only because God was always already out ahead seeking those lost in the "land of unlikeness" (Augustine, *Confessions* in general; Bernard of Clairvaux, *On Loving God*, 7.22).

This, then, is the broader context for the specific spirituality of "contemplative union" and "mystical union" with God. Union with God here on earth is granted solely at God's pleasure and thus represents one of the charisms or special gifts. But because contemplative union constitutes an anticipation of the same heavenly bliss to be enjoyed by all the saints in heaven, it exists in continuity with the saving grace communicated in baptism and the other sacraments. Medieval spiritual writers repeatedly insist that one must first deal with one's own serious sin by sacramental confession before the gift of contemplative union may be granted.

Among many descriptions of contemplative union, in Gregory the Great (preceded by Gregory of Nyssa and Pseudo-Dionysius) we find the notion that the closer one approaches to the blinding light that is God, the more one enters into a fog of darkness. (The "stages" or "rungs of ladders" employed by most medieval spiritual authors in the summaries that follow are not simply sequential stages. One might be on several rungs at once or move back and forth from a higher to a lower rung.)

Bernard of Clairvaux wrote a classic work on contemplative union, *On Loving God*. We first love not God but (1) ourselves for our own sake, then realize that we are creatures of God and that we must (2) love God for what God does for us. Next (3) one loves God for God's sake alone. Most readers might think that reaching this stage constitutes reaching perfection. But Bernard goes further, to (4) love of ourselves for God's sake alone. This fourth stage, characteristic of Christians in heaven, can be anticipated by God's grace on earth. It is mystical or contemplative union. In it, yearning for God does not cease; rather, for all eternity God's saints will satisfyingly long for God. Dynamic, satiated but unending, yearning union with God is more perfect than any static merger with the One or the Absolute could ever be.

Contemplative union of this sort is a form of deification. In his *Mirror of Faith*, Bernard's fellow Cistercian William of St. Thierry wrote:

> And such is the astounding generosity of the Creator to the creature; the great grace, the unknowable goodness, the devout confidence of the creature for the Creator, the tender approach, the tenderness of a good conscience, that man somehow finds himself in their midst, in the embrace and kiss of

the Father and the Son, that is, in the Holy Spirit. And he is united to God by that charity whereby the Father and Son are one. He is made holy in Him who is the holiness of both. (chap. 17, par. 32)

Many scholars argue that the 12th-century devotion to the humanity of Christ, which, via the hypostatic union in Christ, brings union with Christ, represents a turning point from a more cosmic to a more this-worldly spirituality. Certainly with Francis of Assisi in the early 1200s, the patristic Western inclination toward Christ's passion in his human nature reached a fiery climax when Francis received the stigmata or wounds of Christ in his experience on Mount Alverno. His fellow Franciscan Bonaventure, in his *Soul's Journey into God* (mid-1200s), integrated two Augustinian principles — that all creatures bear vestiges of the Trinity, and that the human creature bears the image of God — into a breathtaking Christocentric passion mysticism. Bonaventure's achievement restates and transforms the thought of Pseudo-Dionysius. This caps a process of Western appropriation of the latter that began with new translations and the writings of the Canons Regular Hugh and Richard at the monastery of St. Victor in Paris in the 1100s.

Bonaventure maintained that we begin to know God by employing natural reason to observe all creation outside of us, then extend this knowledge by observing the image of God within us both naturally and in the image's restoration by Christ's grace, which enlightens our reason. We then move beyond and above ourselves by receiving contemplative understanding of the Trinity, first in its unity and then in its plurality, the latter in the summit of the human spirit, the *apex mentis* or *synderesis*. But all of this understanding can take us only so far. In the seventh stage, one leaves all of the previous understandings behind. In this final rapture, one must ask for grace, not learning; desire, not understanding;

> groaning of prayer, not diligence in reading; the Bridegroom, not the teacher; God, not man; darkness, not clarity; not light, but

the fire that wholly inflames and carries one into God through transporting unctions and consuming affections.... Let us, then, die and enter into this darkness. Let us silence all our care, our desires, and our imaginings. With Christ crucified, let us pass out of this world to the Father, so that, when the Father is shown to us, we may say with Philip: It is enough for us. (*Soul's Journey* 7.6)

In the 1100s and 1200s, when the university scholastic theologians, such as Bonaventure and Thomas Aquinas, were developing more refined understandings of human nature and human knowing, Western European population, cities, economies, and political structures were expanding. With that expansion came a growing vernacular culture in Italian, French, German, and English. The Dominican Meister Eckhart tried to express mystical theology in the vernacular but in his inventiveness risked being misunderstood as teaching a kind of union with God that eliminated the individuality of the human person, merging monistically into the Godhead. The contents of the Scriptures had always been known in the vernacular, since preaching to the uneducated was always done in the vernacular, aided by vernacular translations and paraphrases like the *Heliand* (see below), found in all periods of medieval Christendom. What was new with Eckhart was the attempt to put the deepest, highest level of scholastic-mystical theology into the vernacular. But until the rise of wider literacy in the early modern period, knowledge of Scripture was mediated by educated elites, which was no less true for Wycliffe's disciples than it was for the 9th-century Saxons learning the Jesus story from the monks and their *Heliand* book.

In less rarified form, Johannes Tauler, Catherine of Siena, the Flemish Beguine Hadewijch, Walter Hilton, the anonymous author of *The Cloud of Unknowing*, and Julian of Norwich contributed to this new vernacular spirituality (McGinn). In the early 1400s, Jean Gerson at the University of Paris wrote handbooks of mystical theology both at a high level for experts inside and outside the monasteries, and also at "entry level" in both Latin and French for uneducated devout people like his own sisters, taking care to draw clear lines against monism. Gerson's Latin handbooks and writings by Bernard of Clairvaux and others were valued by Protestant Pietists in the early modern era (Erb).

At the end of the Middle Ages, Nicholas of Cusa wove a number of threads together, drawing directly on Pseudo-Dionysius and Eckhart, but also on the classic "union of spirit" Latin spirituality of Bernard, William, and others. In Nicholas's Latin work, *The Vision of God* (1453), one finds a paradigmatic restatement of contemplative union as a passing over from language and signs characteristic of this world into ineffable, heavenly union by way of the ladder of Christ. Its foundational imagery plays on the double meaning of *visio Dei*: God's vision of us, our vision of God. Thomas à Kempis, a member of the more monastic branch of the *Devotio Moderna*, also offers us, in his *Imitation of Christ* (c. 1420), a convenient summary of the patristic-monastic traditions on cultivating, by grace, the Christian virtues. As written it took a liturgical and sacramental framework for "interior communion with Christ" for granted. Editions with this dimension deleted became very popular among Protestants, inasmuch as the *Imitation* appeared, by this editorial sleight of hand, to be concerned only with one's "interior" relationship with Christ.

Spirituality as Practiced in the World

The treatises on mystical or contemplative union described above were known to the very devout and (semi)literate circles of medieval Western Christians. Monks, nuns, and members of religious orders wrote most of the formal treatises on how to love and be united with God. Yet the basic principles of loving God, lived out in daily life through the virtues of gentleness (expected even of noblemen, i.e., of *gentlemen*), humility, chastity, patience, zeal for God, etc., were accessible to and pursued by devout laypeople. In the mid-800s, we find a remarkable work by the noblewoman Dhuoda, written for her son William, who had to live amid the intrigues and power politics of the Carolingian court. Her grasp of theology and spiritual virtues is quite remarkable, and she seems to have acquired it from a thorough education that included theology and spirituality, presumably an education received from monks, as well as from paying close attention to the daily liturgy, rich in Scripture. Prayer was an indispensable part of a Christian's life, she reminded her son, and her recommendation that he pray as much of the monastic daily round of prayer (Divine Office) as he could seems to have been characteristic of devout laypeople throughout most of the period under consideration here.

Both in early medieval Ireland and on the Continent during the 7th through 9th centuries, monastic life and the life of "average" Christians intersected at many points. Monks and nuns carried out the evangelization of northern Europe and the countryside of Mediterranean Western Europe (Head and Noble). Since Irish spirituality laid great emphasis on going into exile as a form of penance, Irish monks founded many of the great Continental monasteries. At the same time, the exceptionality of Irish spirituality should not be overstated; for example, Patrick himself was formed in the indigenous Gallo-Roman monasticism of Germanus's (d. 448) monastery at Auxerre, which itself arose from the tradition of Martin of Tours (d. 397).

Closer to the end of the Middle Ages, we encounter Francis of Assisi, formally uneducated, yet possessing a thorough grasp of classic, patristic (and therefore highly scriptural) Christian theology and spirituality. Presumably he acquired much of it from paying close attention to the Latin liturgy. Laypeople outside monasteries frequently had siblings or cousins inside monasteries, especially in the earlier Middle Ages up to about 1000, when most monks and nuns entered monastic life

as young children, echoing Hannah's offering of the young Samuel to the holy man Eli (De Jong; 1 Sam. 1–2).

Monks and nuns lived under a rule, a structuring of their daily lives that assisted them, crutch-like, in doing right. Laypeople outside monasteries also were encouraged to establish regular, rule-based patterns. Among these structural aids, one finds the lists of the Corporal and Spiritual Works of Mercy: aid the hungry, thirsty, naked, and homeless; visit the sick; ransom captives; bury the dead (corporal); instruct the ignorant; counsel the doubtful; admonish sinners; bear wrongs patiently; forgive offenses willingly; comfort the afflicted; pray for the living and the dead (spiritual).

But actions alone were not the goal. A Christian ought to move beyond merely doing right to develop virtues, that is, develop firm dispositions to do the right thing so that, when confronted with temptation to do wrong, one is already inclined toward the right because of habits formed by prior acts. Remembering constantly that life on earth prepares for death and face-to-face encounter with Christ (*memento mori*), offered one important aid to developing virtues.

To assist his people in this goal, a Christian king like Alfred the Great in the later 800s, despite preoccupation with defense against invaders, translated or caused to be translated into Anglo-Saxon several manuals for Christian living: Gregory the Great's *Pastoral Care* (a leadership manual for bishops), Gregory's *Dialogues* (lives of monks interacting with the world), Boethius's *Consolation of Philosophy* (Why do bad things happen to good people?), Augustine's *Soliloquies* (basic spirituality), and the first fifty psalms. On the Continent, at about the same time as Alfred's work, *The Heliand* (The Savior) gave German expression to the Sermon on the Mount's selfless *agape* love in the midst of a warrior culture. (*The Heliand* was essentially a vernacular paraphrase, in Saxon-German poetic form, of the Gospels.) At the end of our period, Carthusian monks invented the meditative rosary as a methodical means of contemplative prayer based on the life of Christ. It became widespread among the populace in the late 1400s (Martin, sec. 4).

The lives of saints played an important role in encouraging popular spirituality, exhibiting the Christian virtues of humility, selfless love, generosity, and utter dedication to God in memorable and entertaining forms. From the lives of the desert fathers, which became "bedtime reading" for monks and nuns, to classic saints' lives from all centuries collected in the *Golden Legend* (c. 1260) by Jacobus de Voragine, these entertaining stories underwent secularizing, even bawdy, transformation to produce some of Boccaccio's *Decameron* and Chaucer's *Canterbury Tales*.

Living the Christian life in the medieval period was understood to be possible solely by God's grace (Froehlich). At the Carthusian monastery in Basel, Martin Ströulin prepared to take his solemn vows around 1450 by drawing up this expression of his belief: "For all these my many and great transgressions and sins I offer you, most loving God, for satisfaction, the most precious and overflowing treasure of the most innocent passion of our Lord Jesus Christ, the crucified, your most beloved Son, since I know that I can be saved and satisfy you in no other way than by the merit of his innocent suffering and death" (*Basler Chroniken* 1:514–15). The members of the monastic community of Walkenried in northern Germany in the 1460s recited communally a reminder that only "through Christ are we truly justified in faith . . . not through monastic vows, not through the cowl, nor by fasting or any other human work, can man be saved" (Heutger, 56).

Finally, medieval Western spirituality was deeply embedded in the reality of human life through devotion to Mary. Not to honor the mother of the divine Logos become incarnate would have seemed counterintuitive to medieval Christians (Luke 11:27–28, interpreted via Luke 2:19 and parallels). Marian spirituality in the West drew heavily on Eastern Christian stories about Marian miracles, but the Western tradition was also very down to earth. Philip of Seitz's German-language rhyming *Life of Mary* in the 1300s carefully maintains both the divine and human natures of the child and man Jesus while presenting his mother as a real, practical, devout, human woman. It was so successful that it became the basis for vernacular, illustrated "world history" books in the 1400s (Martin, sec. 2).

Sources Cited

Augustine, *King Alfred's Version of St. Augustine's Soliloquies*. Ed. T. Carnicelli (1969).

Adam of Eynsham. *Magna Vita Sancti Hugonis* [Great Life of Saint Hugh] (1985).

Basler Chroniken, vol. 1. Ed. W. Vischer et al. (1872).

Bell, D. "*Apatheia*: The Convergence of Byzantine and Cistercian Spirituality." *Cîteaux* 38 (1987): 141–63.

Bernard of Clairvaux. *On Loving God*, CFS (1995).

Bonaventure. *The Soul's Journey into God*, CWS (1978).

De Jong, M. *In Samuel's Image* (1996).

Dhuoda, *Handbook for William*. Trans. C. Neel (1991).

Erb, P. *Pietists, Protestants, and Mysticism* (1989).

Fox, S. *King Alfred's Anglo-Saxon Version of Boethius De consolatione philosophiae*, with English trans. (1864).

Froehlich, K. "Justification Language and Grace." In *Probing the Reformed Tradition*, ed. E. A. McKee and B. Armstrong (1989), 27 – 47.

Gregory the Great. *Dialogues*. Trans. O. Zimmerman (1959).

———. *Pastoral Care*. Trans. H. Davis (1978).

Head, T., and T. Noble, eds. *Soldiers of Christ* (1995).

The Heliand. Trans. G. R. Murphy (1992).

Heutger, N. *850 Jahre Kloster Walkenried* (1977).

Jacobus de Voragine. *The Golden Legend*. Trans. W. G. Ryan (1995).

Keating, D. *Deification and Grace* (2007).

Lewis, C. S. *Mere Christianity* (1952).

Martin, D. "Behind the Scene: The Carthusian Presence in Late Medieval Lay Spirituality." In *Nicholas of Cusa and His Age*, ed. T. Izbicki and C. Bellitto (2002), 29 – 62.

McGinn, B. *Meister Eckhart and the Beguine Mystics* (1997).

Nicholas of Cusa. *Vision of God*. In *Selected Spiritual Writings*, trans. H. L. Bond (1997).

Thomas à Kempis, *The Imitation of Christ* (c. 1420, innumerable editions and translations).

William of St. Thierry, *Mirror of Faith*. (1979).

For Further Reading

Aelred of Rievaulx. *The Mirror of Charity*. Trans. E. Connor (1990).

Durandus, W. *Rationale Divinorum Officiorum*. English trans. of prologue, bk. 1. Trans. T. Thibodeau (2007).

Guigo II the Carthusian. *The Ladder of Monks*. Trans. E. Colledge (1981).

Hugh of St. Victor. *Didascalicon*. Trans. J. Taylor (1991).

———. *On the Sacraments of the Christian Faith*. Trans. R. Deferrari (1976).

McGinn, B. *The Presence of God: A History of Western Mysticism*, 4 vols.+ (1991 –).

William of St. Thierry. *The Golden Epistle*. Trans. T. Berkeley, CFS (1971).

CHAPTER 16

EUROPEAN REFORMATION AND COLONIAL EXPANSION (1450 – 1700)

CATHERINE G. GONZÁLEZ, JUSTO L. GONZÁLEZ, AND ONIDA E. GONZÁLEZ

As Western Europe reached the middle of the 15th century, there was great dissatisfaction with the church. This is not surprising, since the Avignon papacy and the Great Schism undermined the authority of the hierarchy and its ability to foster spiritual life. Early in the 15th century, monk Thomas à Kempis wrote *The Imitation of Christ*, a book that expressed much of the unease many felt over the manner in which spirituality was experienced. Three quotations from that book show its thrust: "What good does it do, then, to debate about the Trinity, if by a lack of humility you are displeasing to the Trinity?" (Thomas, 30). Theology in the universities was dismal. It had little, if any, connection to the experiences of laypeople and their churches. Equally problematic was the lack of training of many of the priests serving parishes.

A second quote says, "Do not rely on friends and neighbors, and do not put off your soul's welfare to the future, for people will forget you sooner than you think. It is better to take care of yourself now and to send some good along ahead of you than to trust in the help of others [praying for you after you die]" (Thomas, 56). Much of the actual life of Christians was geared to being as secure as possible in the world to come. The church had rules to follow, ways of gaining merit for later, but how to become closer to God in this life seemed of little concern to the official structures of the church.

And finally, "Many people scurry about to various places to visit the relics of the saints.... But look! You are present to me here on the altar.... Often curiosity and the desire to see new things lead people to make pilgrimages. They seldom change their lives as a result" (Thomas, 166). The stress on gaining merits that could help in the life to come also meant going to various places to see relics. For Thomas, receiving communion was not a means of gaining merit, but of growing closer to Christ, of experiencing the presence of Christ, and therefore an essential part of faithfulness. This was in contrast to the usual pattern of attending Mass but receiving communion only once a year.

The group that Thomas à Kempis represented, the Brethren of the Common Life, was a reform group, calling into question many of the current practices and attitudes of the church, without openly challenging official theology or actions. It stressed the way of the cross and simplicity, seeking to live a life that was honest and charitable and to come closer to God through prayer and sacraments. Its members, both men and women living in separate communities, supported themselves largely by teaching in day schools they opened across much of Europe for the children of the rising commercial class. They taught their own simple piety along with reading, writing, and arithmetic in the vernacular. They were therefore a significant force for the spiritual development of those they taught.

Their writings showed what they opposed as well as what they supported. In various ways, they influenced the childhoods of Erasmus, Luther, Loyola, and Calvin. The popularity of Thomas à Kempis's book in the late 15th and early 16th centuries showed the desire for reform within the church, particularly among those with a measure of education.

In spite of the unease of the times and the quest for deeper forms of spirituality, most of the people probably expected life—and particularly the life of spirituality—to continue much as it had been for centuries. Then came two unforeseen and momentous events that would forever change the life of Christians in Western Europe and would eventually bring about new dimensions in Christian spirituality: the colonial expansion that began late in the 15th century and the Protestant Reformation that began early in the sixteenth.

Colonial Expansion

The so-called discovery of the New World was a great shock to a Europe that had to confront the fact that it was science and not revelation that had exposed half the globe. Traditional theology held that the three parts of the world—Europe, Asia, and Africa—were a sign of the Trinity, but now this was proven wrong.

Profound as were the changes in Europe, they were much more drastic in the Western Hemisphere. As Spanish conquistadors and priests crossed the Atlantic, they brought their world with them, including the militant and religious zeal of the myth of the *reconquista*—the story of the reconquest of Iberia from the Moors by Christians guided by God—that permeated Spanish society. They viewed their mission as bringing the cross—if necessary by means of the sword—to the peoples they encountered in the Indies. The *reconquista* had resulted in the melding of military endeavors with the Christian rebirth of the peninsula, and now the "spiritual conquest" of the Americas

would bring forth another new form of spirituality. This spirituality would evolve constantly through the contributions of the various components of the population—indigenous, European, and later, African.

Unlike the Spanish, the Portuguese enterprise in the Americas was primarily an economic partnership between individuals and the crown. Then, as the latter's interest in Brazil grew—largely because of the region's economic value—so, too, did its control and concern over the spiritual formation of its colonists and the indigenous communities. In both Spanish and Portuguese America, the process of colonization reveals a spirituality that was molded by the circumstances it encountered, often taking on the contours of its environment. In that context, spirituality was a cohesive factor in society, for all aspects of the colonial Latin American world were bound up with the spiritual.

Among the earliest European arrivals, there was a conviction of the rightness of the conquest itself. Much of this rested on the understanding of the conquest as just and on the assurance of the salvific properties of ritual. Two examples illustrate these points. The first, the *requerimiento* (1514), was a declaration read in Spanish to Indians immediately before they were attacked. This statement explained that were the Indians not to accept the Spanish king as their sovereign and Christianity as the one true faith, this would justify an imminent assault and their subsequent enslavement. For many Spaniards (both military and clerical), the assurance that their violence was part of God's work justified their actions. The second example is the mass baptisms performed by Franciscans—the first religious order to arrive in the Americas. For the missionaries performing these rituals, often on thousands at one time, the act meant that they, the friars, had accomplished their most important function: bringing the Indians into the family of God. The *requerimiento* and mass baptisms provide us a window into the spirituality of the earliest Europeans: conversion, however achieved, was the goal.

Neither the *requerimiento* nor mass baptisms went unchallenged by other Spaniards. The best known of many critics of the Spanish conquest and treatment of the Indians is Bartolomé de Las Casas (1484–1566), a Dominican who argued that the only "just" war was being waged by the Indians *against* the invaders. He—along with other Dominicans as well as Augustinians and eventually Jesuits—also called into question the efficacy of mass baptisms. How could one truly become a Christian without some semblance of Christian education? Debates of this sort would plague the church and its adherents with little, if any, resolutions.

Such conflicts, however, did not stop friars from traveling to and throughout the Americas seeking to convert the indigenous population and to train it in the Christian faith. Fairly quickly, the friars realized that their efforts were futile if they did not speak indigenous languages or understand indigenous cultures. By the mid-16th century, bilingual dictionaries and compendiums of American traditions and histories were in print throughout the Indies. At the same time, missionaries also realized that imagery culturally bound to Spain made no sense to indigenous communities. In the Andes, for example, the missionaries began using the condor in flight and the constellation of the Southern Cross as symbols of God's ownership. In the entire process, the church was becoming "Americanized."

The quintessential symbol of the "Americanization" of Spanish spirituality is the Virgin of Guadalupe. As the story goes, in 1541, at the ancient sacred site of Tepeyac in the outskirts of Mexico City, where an Indian goddess was worshiped as "the mother of the gods," a dark-skinned Virgin Mary dressed in Indian garb appeared to converted Aztec Juan Diego. After much skepticism, Bishop Juan de Zumárraga accepted Juan Diego's story, especially after the image of the Virgin appeared on the Indian's cape. Soon a small shrine was built at Tepeyac, but the full impact of the Virgin's appearance would not begin until more than a century later with the publication of an account of the miracle (1648). Soon American-born priests pointed to the Virgin's appearance as clear evidence of her blessing the Mexican church. The dark-skinned Virgin became the symbol of a church and a nation in which indigenous and Spanish elements merged into a new whole.

The influence of the seemingly suppressed culture on spirituality is also evident in church architecture and religious images. Because of a shortage of Spanish artisans—particularly in the 16th century—church officials relied heavily on indigenous workers and artisans who, even though trained in Spanish techniques and style, imbued their creations with distinctly indigenous motifs. Once again, the mixing of cultural expressions reveals the birth of a unique American Christian spirituality.

The New World, however, was also populated by Spaniards and those of Spanish descent who replicated much of the spirituality from the mother country. This was especially evident in the relationship between towns and convents. In what has been termed a "spiritual economy," these two institutions developed symbiotic relationships: the towns provided economic sustenance and protection for the nuns in exchange for prayers and financial credit, with the convents often loaning money acquired through bequests and donations. The intricate link between the everyday life of the secular community and the everyday life of the convent ironically belies the cloistered nature of these convents. Yet it also points to the understanding of spirituality as deeply imbedded in all facets of life, both within and beyond convent walls.

In colonial Brazil, Christianity's strongest presence was always through the religious orders, especially the Jesuits. Arriving in the mid-16th century, the Society of Jesus quickly turned its attention to protecting the Indians from the excesses of the colonists. As a result, in Brazil the mixture of the indigenous with the European was less intense than in Spanish America. Even so, in Brazil something new was also being created. Europe, the Americas, and soon Africa were all contributing to the new spirituality of the Americas.

The Reformations

The weaknesses of the late medieval church and the widespread desire for a reformed spirituality culminated around the person of Martin Luther in 1517. The floodgates opened, and the rest of the 16th century saw a variety of spiritualities develop among both Roman Catholics and Protestants. Aided by the printing press, the lack of serious theological education for clergy as well as for laity was addressed. Catechisms were developed by most churches as a means for training children. But this required the training of parents, thus resulting in the education of two generations at the same time. In addition, seminaries were developed so that those called to serve as pastors would have sufficient education.

There was also a reformation of Roman Catholicism. In that reformation, the problematic theology of the late Middle Ages was replaced by the work of Thomas Aquinas, whose theology had been largely neglected. Particularly in Spain, there was a renewal of monastic spirituality led by such figures as Teresa of Avila, John of the Cross, and Ignatius Loyola, founder of the Society of Jesus. Ignatius's *Spiritual Exercises* and Teresa's *Interior Castle* provided the paradigms for the new Catholic piety. This spirituality, affirmed and sustained by the reforms of the Council of Trent, centered on the sacraments, especially frequent Communion, and well-trained pastors who used the confessional for spiritual guidance. Thus, the criticisms raised earlier by Thomas à Kempis and others were addressed.

For its part, Protestant spirituality centered on reading the Bible, often in private, with examination of conscience through individual prayer. Family prayers were also important, as was teaching the catechism to younger family members. In Anglican circles, the *Book of Common Prayer* took center stage. It was a compilation of morning and evening prayer adapted from the monastic offices, with daily Scripture lessons and prayers, all of which could be used both in congregational worship and for private devotion and family prayers.

By the end of the 16th century, there were five distinct groups: Lutherans, Reformed, Anglican, the smaller groups of more radical Protestants such as the Mennonites, and Roman Catholics. The lines separating churches hardened, leading to greater emphasis on detailed theology, showing how each religious tradition differed from the others. The theology of this period, known as "Protestant Orthodoxy," often led to a loss of spirituality in the pursuit of accurate doctrine. A reaction would not be long in coming. In the early 18th century, Pietism responded to Protestant Orthodoxy by lessening the interest in theology and stressing the life of prayer.

Geographically, the limits of the old Roman Empire in Western Europe held, so that generally those areas that had been part of the empire remained Catholic. These lines were fixed more permanently at the end of the Thirty Years' War in the 17th century. England, with its distinct history, had its own indigenous mix of Protestantism and Catholicism. This shows that there were many nontheological forces at work. Except for the radical wing of the Reformation, which rejected the notion of a state church, all of the churches stemming from the Reformation were state churches.

Later Colonial Enterprises

Just as the 16th century had seen the great expansion of Spain and Portugal, the seventeenth saw the birth of new colonial empires, each taking with it its own spiritual traditions. Thus, British and Dutch colonial expansion spread various forms of

Protestantism, while the French contributed to the spread of Catholicism.

The English colonies that would later become the United States were first populated with a mixture of people, chiefly from the Reformed tradition: Dutch Reformed, Puritans—both Congregationalists and Presbyterians—Huguenots, a few English Baptists, and some among the Anglicans. There were also smaller groups of Mennonites, Quakers, Roman Catholics, and Jews, among others. The *Book of Common Prayer* was used by all Anglicans, but a wide variety of theological traditions could be supported by it. While the actual theology of these Anglicans could vary, many were strongly influenced by the Reformed tradition.

However much the theology and church structures differed among these churches, a free-flowing, common Reformed theology was being created in the colonies that affected almost all Protestant churches. Its spirituality was generally centered on the Bible, so that schools were needed to teach people to read and write. Education was an absolute necessity. There was also a strong sense that the highest calling of a Christian was to public service, especially to elected office, where the common good could be served. At the same time, there was great fear that tyranny could hinder the spiritual freedom of believers. Joined to the Reformed emphasis on the sinfulness of human nature, this led to the conviction that any governmental power needed to be limited and checked. The main opponents to this view were often among the Anglicans, especially those who directly represented the king. Since no institutional church could be identified as its sole source, the emerging common spirituality could be free of any church domination. In a sense, it was a noninstitutional spiritual ethos.

This spirituality was so commonly held that public events could have prayers from ministers of any of the generally recognized churches, and schools could promote spirituality without much conflict with the churches themselves. One of the main results of this common spirituality was that the various denominations on the American side of the Atlantic grew to resemble each other, often more than they resembled their European progenitors.

The African Presence

As native labor proved insufficient, first in the Portuguese and Spanish colonies, and then in the British colonies, slaves were imported from Africa. In Brazil, the presence of black slavery permeated the region sooner than it did in Spanish America. It is in the spiritual interactions between Africans and people of African descent with white Brazilians that we best see the "Americanization" of Christian spirituality in Brazil. Early in the history of Brazilian Christianity, Catholic saints took on attributes of African deities, Christian festivals were celebrated with African instruments and dance, and black religious confraternities were established. Similar developments would also take place in the Spanish colonies, particularly in the Caribbean. The result was a spirituality that combined traditional Christian elements with others brought from Africa, to the point that in some areas these combinations became distinct religious traditions.

Catholic spirituality in Latin America was also shaped by the need to respond to the presence and suffering of African slaves. Foremost in this new spirituality was Pedro Claver (1528–1610), who became famous for both his defense of the weak and his criticism of the powerful—emphases that in the 20th century would come to the foreground of Latin American Catholic spirituality.

In the British colonies, some of the first African slaves coming from the Congo were Roman Catholic. But the vast majority continued many of the practices of their ancestral African religions. An African-American Protestant spirituality did not develop until the early 18th century, when the majority of slaves were born in the colonies.

Sources Cited

Thomas à Kempis. *The Imitation of Christ*. Trans. W. C. Creasy (1989).

For Further Reading

Dupré, L., and D. Saliers, eds. *Christian Spirituality: Post-Reformation and Modern,* WSEH (1989).

González, O., and J. González. *Christianity in Latin America: A History* (2008).

Lippy, C. H., R. Choquette, and S. Poole. *Christianity Comes to the Americas, 1492 – 1776* (1992).

Raitt, J., ed. *Christian Spirituality: High Middle Ages and Reformation,* WSEH (1987).

CHAPTER 17

EUROPE AND NORTH AMERICA (1700–PRESENT)

EMILIE GRIFFIN

Conversion, for many Christians today, is a necessary, momentous, and generally once-in-a-lifetime experience. But transformation (sometimes called "turning" or "ongoing conversion") is equally important. And what is true of individuals may also influence whole Christian communities. In short, conversion and transformation are the distinctive traits of Christian spiritual life in Western society today. John Wesley's experience at Aldersgate Street in London in 1738, in which he heard a reading of Martin Luther's preface to the epistle to the Romans and found his heart "strangely warmed" (Wesley, 103), sets the tone of modern Christian spirituality. But such times of grace and transformation recur throughout Christian lives. Thomas Merton, in a famous letter to Jacques Pasquier, observed that "we are converted, not once in our life, but many times" (Merton, back cover). Such recurring experiences of conversion, he suggested, will lead to our transformation in Christ. This insight is akin to what John Henry Newman preached about Christian repentance: namely, that "we are ever but beginning ... the most perfect Christian is to himself but a beginner" (Newman, 90). Christian spiritual life is dynamic, not static, and this has certainly been true in Europe and North America over the last three centuries.

Is this a modern understanding? Not entirely. It is rooted in the apostle Paul's personal conversion and teaching. As he told the Galatians, by joining themselves to Christ crucified they entered into a world of transformed and transforming life. Yet today's language and practice of Christian spirituality are also shaped by historical circumstances, both at the grassroots level and within the institutional church.

Four major influences have been at work in the spiritual development of Christian Europe and North America since the 18th century. One is John Wesley's emphasis on the life of holiness and perfection. Wesley himself, by his high Oxford education and his love for the common person, bridged both the social divide and the conflict between the Enlightenment, the revolutionary spirit of the times, and deep allegiance to historical Christianity. A second is the Pietist impulse, broadly felt throughout the series of spiritual awakenings that ebbed and flowed through the Western world in the 18th and 19th centuries. A third is an intense emphasis, particularly among Roman Catholics and Quakers, on the mystical life and prophetic action. And a fourth is the powerful influence of preaching and evangelism in the spread of the gospel and the transformation of society. The power of Christian zeal to transform society is exemplified by abolitionists such as William Wilberforce, justice advocates such as Quaker John Woolman and civil rights leader Martin Luther King Jr., and influential evangelists such as Billy Graham.

In the 1700s the word *spirituality* had not yet come into common use. "Devotion" or perhaps "the devout life" came closer to what is now meant by spirituality. But in spite of the Enlightenment, the politics of revolution, the challenge of modern science, and the encroachment of secularization,

Christian spirituality has remained a vital force. To be sure, it has also been affected by modern culture and psychological influences. Early twenty-first-century spirituality urges progress, not perfection. This is not an overturning of Wesley's proposed life of perfection, but a modernization of it. Christians are encouraged, through participation with others in groups, spiritual direction, and worship to understand their own vulnerability and the power of God's grace. This grassroots endeavor relies not on the size of church membership, but rather on small group efforts that often cross over denominational lines. Nondenominational Christianity seems more and more viable. Today's Christian spirituality is energetic and practical, and less and less institutional. Spiritual formation has a definite role to play. To borrow a phrase from the psychologist William James, authentic spirituality has "cash value" (James, 88). These four influences find expression in a number of Christian movements.

Pietism and the Wesleyan Movement

Pietism, a powerful Christian movement in Europe and America, lasted from the late 17th century to the late 18th, and continues to have an impact today. It emerged as a protest against the lack of true piety in institutional religion. Initially its subversive influence was felt by many continental Lutherans, but soon it also touched the Moravians, and through them the Wesleyan movement, and still later the entire evangelical movement. Pietism put strong emphasis on personal conversion, individual piety, and a vital, heart-felt Christian life.

John Wesley, himself an Anglican priest and an Oxford-educated intellectual, helped to shape Christian spiritual life both in England and America. He insisted on preaching the gospel to the people outside the walls of the established church. His itinerant, open-air preaching throughout the British Isles created an atmosphere of Christian enthusiasm and fervor. Wesley did not stop there, however, but created "societies" in which Christians could meet, study Scripture, and share experience. These societies have a parallel in today's "accountability groups." Through them, the Wesleyan movement encouraged all Christians to pursue holiness and the life of perfection.

The vision for Wesleyan societies stemmed from the idea of *ecclesiola in ecclesia* (the little church within the larger church) that had been advocated by somewhat early Pietist thinkers. Ultimately, of course, small group development cannot be ascribed to any one Christian movement, for it gains its inspiration from the earliest Christian church as described in the book of Acts and in the New Testament epistles. While such groups were based on the social structure of the "household" as it existed in the ancient Graeco-Roman world, the idea of small group meetings and mutual support recurs throughout Christian history.

In Roman Catholicism after 1700, standard approaches to cultivating spiritual life were sharply divided between those for laypersons and those for individuals who had taken religious vows (that is, the "religious" — priests, brothers, and sisters). Such religious communities saw themselves as coming together through a charism, or special grace, granted to a founder or a founding group. Such was the experience of the Jesuits (founded earlier by Ignatius Loyola) and the Religious of the Sacred Heart (founded in the 19th century by Madeleine-Sophie Barat). But some Roman Catholic writers were like Francis de Sales, whose *Introduction to the Devout Life* (1609), published a century earlier, held that the life of religious devotion was open to all baptized Christians. De Sales taught that the method of prayer and spiritual formation would vary according to one's state in life, but all were called to practice spiritual disciplines and grow in the life of grace. This idea grew in plausibility in the centuries to follow.

Spiritual Leadership by Women

After 1800 the leadership of women was felt both in Protestant and Catholic spirituality. Women were active in writing devotional literature, composing hymns and spiritual songs, practicing philanthropy, and serving heroically in missionary service. In America, Phoebe Palmer (1804 – 1874), the wife of a Methodist clergyman, became widely influential as an author and conference speaker. Her bestselling books focused on commitment and surrender to the godly life. Women's leadership found its Catholic expression chiefly in religious communities. Mother Frances Cabrini (1850 – 1917), an Italian immigrant to the United States, was known for her works of radical compassion and charity. She founded the Missionary Sisters of the Sacred Heart of Jesus, a society of women religious in America dedicated to establishing orphanages and caring for the poor and sick. Another striking example of spiritual leadership by a woman is Mother Cornelia Connelly (1809 – 1879). A married woman, mother of five, and the wife of an Episcopal clergyman, Cornelia followed her husband into the Roman Catholic Church. Surprisingly, the Roman hierarchy chose Cornelia (not her husband) for the high task of founding a new vowed religious community, the Sisters of the Holy Child Jesus, which today has a presence in Britain, Africa, and the United States.

In the 19th and 20th centuries, several Catholic women were towering spiritual figures. These included Therese of Lisieux, who advocated "the Little Way," and Dorothy Day, cofounder of the Catholic Worker movement, who responded to the challenge of Marxism through compassionate Christian practice. Day is remembered as a pacifist and social activist who saw Christ in the faces of the poor. Therese, a Carmelite nun and contemplative, became known after her death for her simple, childlike way of prayer and service and her bestselling autobiography, *The Story of a Soul.* In 1925 she was canonized and named a Doctor of the Roman Catholic Church, one of only three women to receive this honor. Mother Teresa of Calcutta, world famous for her work in India with the dying, is a remarkable example of the connection between humanitarian work and constant practice

of the spiritual life. Since her death, she has been proclaimed Blessed Teresa of Calcutta. Her writings, in which she frankly acknowledges long periods of spiritual darkness, are now read by millions.

Revivalism and Preaching

Christian zeal has long been fostered by revivalism, which has flourished in informal and unconventional settings: the frontier, the rural camp meeting, or on a sawdust trail drawn out beneath the canvas of a makeshift tent. In settings like these, out under the stars, countless North Americans (some without much education) encountered a transforming elemental holiness and responded to it with deeply felt emotion.

For such vitality revivalism has always depended on strong preaching. Two preachers who became legendary for their widespread efforts are Billy Sunday (1862 – 1935) and Billy Graham. Their names remain well known today. Both of them stand in a long tradition of revivalist preaching, largely geared toward personal conversion to Jesus Christ. Billy Sunday was also known for his advocacy of Prohibition and support of the temperance movement. Another example of the decisive influence of preaching is the civil rights campaigning of Dr. Martin Luther King Jr. in the mid-20th century.

African-American Spirituality and Social Change

American Christians of African heritage are often Bible-centered Christians with distinctive styles of worship and praise. Devotional singing (frequently called "gospel music") is associated with African-American church worship and additionally has had a broad influence over the whole of American Christianity. Still another powerful rhetorical device comes out of African American churches, the custom known as "call and response." The preacher or leader issues a challenging question to the congregation. The congregation responds with a powerful answer. This device, embedded in black preaching, is often very compelling and persuasive; repetition heightens the effect. By incorporating this rhetorical device into his speeches, Martin Luther King Jr. effectively influenced both church congregations and a wider American audience.

King also exemplified the way this tradition changed in the 20th century. Like Wesley, he bridged the Enlightenment gap by employing both advanced theological education and a simple confidence in God's prophetic action in society. King studied Gandhi and admired the revolutionary ideals of the American founders but chose Jesus as his teacher and prophet. "It was the Sermon on the Mount," he wrote, "rather than a doctrine of passive resistance, that initially inspired the Negroes of Montgomery [Alabama] to dignified social action. It was Jesus of Nazareth that stirred the Negroes to protest with the creative weapon of love" (Foster and Griffin, 279).

Pentecostal and Ecstatic Spirituality

While ecstatic behavior has been part of Christianity since early days, in the 20th century it is associated with the Pentecostal movement. This community pinpoints its origins in a prayer meeting at a small Holiness Bible school in Topeka, Kansas, on January 1, 1901. There, many who were present judged that speaking in tongues was the biblical sign of the Holy Spirit's baptism. The founder of this school, Charles Parham, later moved to Houston, Texas, where, despite segregation, an African-American preacher, William J. Seymour, attended his Bible classes. Seymour later traveled to Los Angeles where, in 1906, his preaching gave rise to the Azusa Street Revival. Though the Pentecostal movement in the United States is the product of many streams of influence, it is generally acknowledged that it began with Seymour's Azusa Street Revival. The Azusa revival received significant press attention and gained national and worldwide influence.

Although the Pentecostal movement has no central authority and has spawned many churches with different theologies, it has been influential in celebrating the work and life of the Holy Spirit. The early movement was also countercultural: African-American men and women had major leadership roles, and early on the movement was racially integrated.

The charismatic renewal is a second Spirit-driven renewal movement. Celebrating the manifestation of the supernatural as the sine qua non of God's real presence in a skeptical age, and seeking to cultivate spiritual gifts for the edification of the body of Christ, it developed in the mid-20th century and quickly spread across Protestant and Catholic denominational lines. Charismatic groups are focused on the spontaneous reception of the Holy Spirit, typically manifested by speaking in tongues, and may thus be taken as an extension of the Pentecostal twentieth-century stream. An equally important aspect of charismatic spirituality is its emphasis on healing, especially emotional healing, through prayer.

Oxford Group, Moral Re-Armament, and Twelve-Step Spirituality

In the 19th century, numerous efforts to oppose drunkenness were organized under Christian auspices. Chiefly, this is known as the temperance movement, based on a belief that total abstinence could be secured by an adherence to Christian principles. Early in the 20th century, the United States Congress attempted to buttress this movement by passing the Eighteenth Amendment to the United States Constitution. Taking effect in 1920, the amendment ushered in an era known as Prohibition, in which sale and consumption of alcoholic beverages became illegal in the continental United States. Prohibition, a colossal failure, was repealed in 1933. However, abstinence from alcohol was considered mandatory for many virtuous conservative Christians throughout the following decades.

In sharp contrast to this failed public policy effort, a group called Alcoholics Anonymous emerged in 1935, based on spiritual principles known as "the Twelve Steps." Influenced by an existing Christian movement of the 1920s and 1930s, first called the Oxford Group and later known as Moral Re-Armament, Alcoholics Anonymous relies on spirituality (trusting a "Higher Power") and mutually supportive group interactions that establish confidentiality and trust. They also exert a power of example. Through AA's custom of sponsorship, a newcomer is paired with an established AA member who will help to guide the newly sobered-up person through a process of abstinence, self-examination, and spiritual restoration.

Despite its origins, AA cannot be said to be a Christian program, since it endorses no religious program or theology. However, many Christian churches have advocated and supported this evidently viable method for gaining and maintaining sobriety. Through acknowledgment of vulnerability and brokenness, the recovery movement has profoundly influenced Christian spirituality as a whole.

Hesychast Spirituality and Contemplation

Many factors have converged in reclaiming contemplation as a broadly practiced style of prayer. Not least has been the influence of hesychast spirituality, long associated with the desert fathers and mothers of early Christianity, and later with the spiritual practices of Eastern Orthodoxy. However, the use of contemplative prayer in many monastic Anglican and Roman Catholic communities has been equally influential. What underlies this trend is the soul hunger of people caught up in the intense distractedness of competitive, urban, high-tech existence.

Henri Nouwen, a Dutch Roman Catholic priest who lived most of his life in the United States and Canada, was a persuasive voice for "desert spirituality," especially through his slender volume *The Way of the Heart* (1991). From the Protestant side, the Quaker pastor Richard Foster has been an advocate of silence, solitude, and the contemplative life. Other writers in this vein include Kathleen Norris, a Presbyterian, who celebrated Benedictine spirituality in her New York Times bestseller, *A Cloister Walk* (1997), and Dennis Okholm, an evangelical theologian at Azusa Pacific University, who has written *Monk Habits for Everyday People* (2007). Thomas Keating and Basil Pennington, both Cistercians, have popularized hesychast spirituality as "centering prayer."

The Ecumenical Movement and Vatican II

Christian ecumenism has long been a goal for established churches, pursued principally through formal efforts to reconcile the doctrinal differences that arose at the European Reformation. Not surprisingly, this approach has had limited success. But after the Second Vatican Council (1962 – 1965), a common spirituality began to spring up, much of it influenced by North American experience. Wherever Catholics and Protestants were living side by side, new perceptions arose of common Christian values. More important, the Second Vatican Council, through its liturgical reform, introduced hymns into Catholic worship that previously had been thought Protestant. In English-speaking Catholic churches, hymns by John and Charles Wesley rang out. From the Protestant side, some leaders began to encourage spiritual practices that had been thought Catholic: retreats, contemplative prayer, fasting, silence, and solitude.

But among Roman Catholics there has been a countering movement to such relaxed grassroots ecumenism. Opus Dei, founded in 1928 by the Spanish priest and writer Josemaría Escrivá, has distinct parallels to the original founding of the Jesuits by Ignatius Loyola. Loyola's mystical experience at Manresa is thought by many to have been the source of his drive to found the Society of Jesus and a worldwide spiritual renewal. Like Loyola, Escrivá claimed divine inspiration for the founding of Opus Dei, widened it (under divine guidance) to include women, and then married people. Opus Dei encourages a spirituality of daily work and the active life, and is established in sixty-six countries worldwide. Escrivá (1902 – 1975) was canonized in 2002.

Spiritual Formation: Recovering Ancient Spiritual Practices

In 1979 a surprise bestseller by Richard Foster, *A Celebration of Discipline*, encouraged a restored practice of some ancient Christian disciplines. Among these were meditation, fasting, Bible study, solitude, confession, guidance, and celebration. Many of these practices were long established among Protestant evangelicals. Others seemed novel, even though they had ancient roots within Christian practice. Out of the ferment and enthusiasm caused by Foster's book came a fresh approach to Christian life, shaped and taught by Renovaré, the organization he founded in 1988. Based in Denver, Colorado, with an international scope and an ecumenical focus, Renovaré is currently led by Anglican clergyman Christopher Webb, who succeeded Foster in 2007. With expressions in North America, Britain, Ireland, Africa, South America, and Korea, it teaches and encourages spiritual formation and transformation.

Since 1700 Christianity has shown a knack for adaptation, especially through the practice of the spiritual life. The Enlightenment and its rationalism attacked the foundations of belief. The political revolutions of the 18th century undermined authority. But spirituality, moving at the grassroots level, has met these challenges. In their search for spiritual freedom, Christians are not consciously attempting to break loose from the past. If anything, Christian believers cherish their heritage and long to recover many ancient practices with a strong biblical warrant. The yearning for prayer and contemplative worship, a sense of the Holy Spirit in community, an attachment to music and hymn singing are part of the effort of contemporary Christians to remain rooted in the faith of their ancestors. In his study *Streams of Living Water* (1998), Richard Foster

names six Christian traditions that are strongly linked to the past yet viable today. They are the contemplative, holiness, charismatic, evangelical, justice, and incarnational traditions. All six of these dimensions are drawn from the example and practice of Jesus and tend to complement one another.

Today's Christian spirituality is searching for a deeper historical consciousness. Influential spiritual teachers stress the power of Christian devotional writers before and after the Reformation, suggesting that God has been present to his people throughout history. In this, the words of C. S. Lewis seem prophetic: "It is a good rule ... to keep the clean sea breeze of the centuries blowing through our minds, and this can be done only through reading old books" (Lewis, 201 – 2). Lewis is elaborating the thought of Paul the apostle in his letter to the Philippians: "Finally, beloved, whatever is true, whatever is honorable, whatever is just, whatever is pure, whatever is pleasing, whatever is commendable, if there is any excellence and if there is anything worthy of praise, think about these things" (Phil. 4:8 NRSV). In both Europe and North America, intentional communities, joined in common styles of worship, Bible study, and spiritual friendship, bear witness to the vigor and liveliness of today's spirituality.

The New Challenge of Secularization

In today's world, the spirituality of Eastern Orthodoxy is gaining ground. Orthodox spirituality has been one of resilient suffering, most notably in the face of its brutal twentieth-century suppression and expulsion from Turkey, and by surviving the atheistic regimes of Soviet communism in Slavic countries.

This tradition holds the allegiance of many millions of Europeans and North Americans, particularly in Eastern Europe, but also elsewhere through immigration and conversion. In fact, until 1867 Alaska was a Russian territory, and the Orthodoxy established along its western shoreline continues to be a presence there even today. Today in post-communist

European countries, citizens are returning to their Orthodox spiritual roots in significant numbers.

Nonetheless, it is clear that by the year 2000 the configurations of European and American Christianity had already entered into radical change. The Christian Europe of our historical memory is not the Europe of today. The established churches of Europe, despite their rich theological history, are up against a loss of attendance and belief, not a profound atheism but instead a casual dismissal of Christian truth and lived Christianity. If spirituality and renewal are forces of adaptation, as history suggests they are, then the new century must rely on an energy that stems from surprising and unexpected pockets of grace, functioning within rapidly changing cultures. The remarkable vision and ministry established by Brother Roger Schultz at Taize, France, is a notable case in point.

George Weigel, an American social critic, has explored the current spiritual crisis in Europe in his book *The Cube and the Cathedral*. Influenced by the teaching of John Paul II, Weigel celebrates Europe's spiritual heritage as one of Christ-centered humanism. When he reflects on the apparent decline of a Christian Europe, he asks, "Are movements for spiritual renewal perhaps the way forward?" Weigel sees Opus Dei, Focolare, and a handful of other renewal movements as more likely to strengthen Christianity from below than institutional action from above. This promising dynamic within the locus of Roman Catholicism appears to be at work throughout European and North American Christianity as a whole.

Spirituality's aim is not cultural adaptation, but transformation in Christ. However, Christians who are actively practicing their faith — especially in recognizable groups and associations — are a force for adaptation to the challenges and shifts of culture. Such renewal and revival — conversion and transformation — are the dominant motifs of Christian spirituality today.

Sources Cited

Foster, R., and E. Griffin, eds. *Spiritual Classics* (2000).

James, W. *Pragmatism and Other Essays* (1963).

Lewis, C. S. "On the Reading of Old Books." In *God in the Dock*, ed. W. Hooper (1970), 200–207.

Merton, T. Letter to Jacques Pasquier. *Informations Catholique Internationales* (April 1973), back cover.

Newman, J. H. "On Christian Repentance." In *Parochial and Plain Sermons*. Vol. 3 (1835).

Wesley, J. *The Works of John Wesley*. Vol. 1 (1979).

For Further Reading

Abbott, W., ed. *Documents of Vatican II* (1966).

Barry, W., and W. Connolly. *The Practice of Spiritual Direction* (1986).

Beebe, G., and R. Foster. *Longing for God* (2009).

Dupré, L., and others, eds. *Christian Spirituality* (1989).

Foster, R. *Celebration of Discipline* (1978).

Griffin, E. *Turning: Reflections on the Experience of Conversion* (2003).

May, G. *Addiction and Grace* (1991).

Polkinghorne, J. *The Faith of a Physicist* (1994).

Weigel, G. *The Cube and the Cathedral* (2005).

Willard, D. *Renovation of the Heart* (2002).

CHAPTER 18

GLOBAL CHRISTIANITY (1700 – PRESENT)

SCOTT W. SUNQUIST

From 1700 to 2000 Christian spirituality, along with its theology and practitioners, shifted from the North Atlantic to the non-Western world. This global Christian shift brought about a tremendous diversification of Christianity as a result of the many new cultural encounters. The shift has been dramatic and was never predicted. In 1500 only 1.6 percent of Christians were African, and the percentage actually dropped slightly by 1900. In 2000, however, 18 percent of the world's Christians were found in Africa. Looked at from another perspective, as late as 1900, 90 percent of Christians were of European stock (Europe, North America, New Zealand, and Australia). Today 70 percent of Christians live in the non-Western world. Christian life and worship are now predominately a non-Western affair, and Christian prayers are predominately given in African and Asian-Pacific languages. Christian spirituality has become a form of African religious spirituality, Chinese spirituality, and Indian spirituality.

We can look at the changes that took place in three chronological stages. In some regions (such as the Roman Catholic Church in Sabah and Sarawak, or the Chinese church under Mao), all three periods were passed through in a single generation. In other regions and under other conditions, the changes were very gradual, taking up most of the time period in question. However, as a general guide we can call the first stage Western missionary spirituality, the second stage resistant and transitional, and the third stage local-global spirituality.

The first stage of global spirituality (Western missionary spirituality) is generally the pioneering period when Western missionaries provided patterns for spiritual practice that they used themselves. Worship in a Scottish Presbyterian Church in Malawi looked like and sounded like worship in a *kirk* in Edinburgh or Glasgow. A Roman Catholic Mass in Mexico City was virtually identical with one in Madrid. In all cases, there were some necessary adaptations, and we will look at these below. The second stage, resistant and transitional, is a mixed period where many of the North Atlantic patterns are continued, but local church leadership is either now in control or eager for more control. This brings about greater affirmation of local cultural customs generally with some resistance to foreign leadership and patterns (missionary as well as colonial). The final stage of local-global spirituality is where the church is fully under indigenous leadership and local Christians affirm appropriate spiritual practices and patterns. We call this local-global because many of the patterns will be local (using local instruments, dance, early morning prayer, local poetry, or music), but many of the patterns may be global (traditional liturgies, Pentecostal patterns, shared global Christian music, cell group Bible study). In the following paragraphs, we will look at each of these stages, citing examples from the global church.

Western Missionary Patterns

In the first decades of the 18th century, most all non-Western Christians were Roman Catholic or Orthodox (Western and Southern Asia, Egypt, and Ethiopia). Their patterns of spiritual practice were mostly European. Approval was briefly given for the Roman Catholic Mass to be said in some local languages in Latin America and Asia. For example, in China, worship was conducted partly in Chinese during much of the 17th century, for in 1615 Pope Paul V approved the use of Chinese for the administration of the sacraments. However, the translation of liturgical books lagged behind, and by the middle of the 18th century, the Chinese language liturgy was denounced along with compromises on Chinese rites. In Latin America, there was also some translation work done in the earlier stages (16th and 17th centuries), but most of the church worship and practices were merely reproduced Iberian practices by 1700. Certain elements of Spanish spirituality, notably devotion to Mary and to the saints, took on greater importance and a different significance, but this development will concern us in the next section. The reason we focus on languages is that Christian spirituality is a matter of communication and personal relationship with a living God. If the Mass, or other prayers and devotion, are done in a different language, then Christian spirituality often becomes more a matter of magic and mysterious ritual than relationship.

In some countries, colonial powers brought about unity through the European language (English in India and East Africa, Spanish and Portuguese in Latin America and most of the Caribbean), and so spirituality grew with the use of a new language. However, in all of these regions, the mother tongue continued to be used, but only later became significant in Christian devotion. Filipino patterns of spirituality followed the pattern of Latin America in large part because the Philippines were considered an extension of New Spain (Mexico) in the Spanish Conquest. In this first stage, Christian spirituality followed the basic pattern of the West so only a few differences from Western spirituality (Iberian) would be seen: language, ethnic diversity, converts, and adult baptisms. One other difference that would eventually affect the spirituality is that all of the priests and most of the monks in the Spanish lands and Portuguese lands (including Goa and Malacca) would be

Iberian males. Very few *peninsulare* women settled in the Americas, Africa, and Asia until the 19th century. Thus, most of the women were *mestizo* or indigenes, and so they brought indigenous approaches and sensitivities that were not European. This became more significant in the second stage of development.

Resistance and Transitional Stage

In this second stage of non-Western Christian spirituality, two major changes took place. First, indigenous church leaders were generally more ready to take over churches and provide leadership than the missionaries were willing to allow. Second, Protestants began a slow work of missionary activity, and by the late 19th century, their work—especially their work of translation—would transform non-Western spirituality. In this transition period, we see many indigenous forms of spirituality being expressed, some in more Christian ways than others. For example, in Latin America indigenous and African belief in fetishes continued, as did belief or worship of certain spirits. But now the fetishes became the Christian statues and holy water, and the spirits became the Christian saints. Since literacy was still very low in this transition period, spirituality was often visual (statues of saints and religious paintings) and experiential (pilgrimages, Mass, festivals). In Latin America and the Philippines, spirituality centered upon the cult of saints, festivals, and pilgrimages. These were all indigenous patterns that took on more or less Christian expressions. Women's devotion was often modeled on the life and devotion of *beaterios*, congregations of laywomen who lived out a disciplined life, generally in community. A *beata* often entered the semi-cloistered life as a refuge, in devotion to Christ, Mary, and the church. Part of their devotion was to offer prayers and to serve local churches in areas of basic needs (cleaning churches, providing candles, etc.).

In the Caribbean, Protestant Christians brought a new form of spiritual development. The fastest-growing Protestant churches (Moravian, Methodist, and Baptist) had come out of awakenings and revivals in Europe and North America. Consequently, there was a greater emphasis on personal experience of grace in Christ, reading the Bible, and attending to preaching. In addition, many of the early leaders were abolitionists or were themselves of African descent, and so social reform was also an important part of the Christian life. The early Moravians came specifically to minister to slaves on plantations, and the first ordained Afro-Caribbean woman (1746), Rebecca Protten, was herself a freed slave. In Afro-Caribbean cultures, many of the patterns from the African religious soil were expressed from the seeds of awakened and revivalist Protestantism. Such patterns include movement in worship (or even dancing) and the use of drums and "conjuring," though now it was a matter of conjuring up the Holy Spirit rather than ancestors. With the arrival of Pentecostalism in the 20th century, both Afro-Caribbean and African Christian spirituality found more affinity than they ever had with high church or more rationalistic forms of Christianity.

One of the more significant transformations of Asian Christian spirituality occurred during the Great Korean Revival of 1907. Two important spiritual patterns came out of that revival period: the Korean "day break prayer meetings" (*saebyok kido*) and vocalized communal prayer. During the revival, whole congregations would pray out loud at the same time, and this later became a pattern in Korea as well as in other countries of East Asia. The Korean day break prayer meeting, begun by the man considered the "father of Korean Christianity, Rev. Kil Son-ju, had its roots in both Korean Confucian and Buddhist patterns of early-morning piety. Kil and others of this stage of development also promoted the use of local Korean instruments and melodies in worship.

Another way Christian spiritual practices were absorbed and refashioned in local contexts is in the understanding of sacred space. In Pakistan, in the last decade of the nineteenth-century, Catholic missionaries established a Christian village devoted to Mary. Maryabad soon became a sacred place of pilgrimage for faithful Catholics and even non-

Catholics. In Latin America, devotion to Mary was taken over with great zeal so that "Our Lady of" became the most popular prefix for churches and holy places. There are many sacred places in Latin America that claim their sacredness because of the appearance of Mary or one of the saints; but two of the most popular places of pilgrimage in the world are Mexico City where Our Lady of Guadalupe is housed, and Aparecida, Brazil, where Our Lady of Aparecida is located. In Africa also, sacred places developed mostly in the early 20th century, attracting Catholics to come and lay their requests before the Virgin Mother. One pilgrimage site in Africa is much newer — the basilica for the twenty-two known Ugandan martyrs (1885 – 1886), built on the site where one of the young boys was killed at Namugango, near Kampala.

Another spiritual development at this stage, which also produced sacred pilgrimage sites, are independent churches. In Africa, independency came about in the late 19th century and became stronger in the first three decades of the 20th century.

One of the earliest modern indigenous Christian movements, however, was that of Ntsikana, a Xhosa from South Africa. Lead by a vision from God, his early indigenous movement became a model for later Ethiopian and Zionist movements in South Africa. All African Christian independency is marked by music. Ntsikana (c. 1815), the pioneer Xhosa Christian leader, was also a hymn writer. These movements are generally started by a prophet or prophetess who responds to a vision or a dream. In obedience, they call people to holiness and faithfulness to Christ. African Independent Church leadership is often hereditary, and leaders are less concerned with church order than with evangelistic outreach and experiencing the presence of God. Their very African spirituality (music, prophecy, dreams, visions, dance, ritual) speaks to the African soul in the ways that much Western spirituality does not. AICs recovered a more biblical understanding of resisting evil powers, healing, and dream interpretation than was taught by

Western Christianity. Because their spirituality does not assume the Western dichotomy between the sacred and the secular, there was a more natural acceptance of spiritual powers and the immediacy of spiritual experience. The Bible was the one spiritual book, and the Old Testament took on greater importance because of elective affinities between many African cultures and the cultures and stories of the Old Testament.

Independency also took place in Asia as local leaders began to assert their own ideas and practices. A number of independent churches (Jesus Only Church, Jesus Family, China Independent Christian Church, etc.) began to develop in China in reaction to the liberalizing trends the Chinese Christians saw in Western Christianity. Spiritually, these movements had greater emphasis on prayer (both group and individual or private prayer), much greater devotion to and study of the Bible, and less political involvement as a part of their Christian calling. A number of great Chinese evangelists and preachers arose who gave credence to this form of Chinese spirituality, including Wang Ming Dao, John Sung, and Watchman Nee. Today we can better understand that these leaders spoke out of the East Asian Confucianist concern for right relationships and doing one's duty. Expressed as concern for righteous living and holiness, their impact was felt throughout East Asia.

Local-Global

The last stage is where we are today in global spirituality. Except in smaller towns in poorer countries, Christian spirituality in the non-Western world is a local expression but is shaped by the global culture. Seminary students may read their Bible on a computer or a hand phone in Malaysia or India, but then in chapel they will sing in a local language and hear local instruments unknown of in New York or Newcastle. Where technology is available, Christian spirituality has common global elements shared through publications, translations, and through technology. However, where technol-

ogy is not available, and where the illiteracy rate is still very high (mostly in Africa and South Asia), patterns of spirituality are more localized and communal. In places where people don't have the skill to read the Bible, spirituality is passed on through worship and through stories and communal activities. In rural areas of India, Malaysia, Indonesia, or Africa, Christian spirituality is expressed through group prayer (or all night prayer meetings), through interpretation of dreams and visions, listening to testimonies, experiencing healings or cleansings, or listening to and memorizing Bible stories. Because of the high rate of illiteracy in many countries, Christianity is experienced not in reading; it is what we do and feel more than what we think and read. As a result, spirituality is often expressed as lifestyle changes, as observable behavior, both in sacred times and places and in secular or daily life.

If, for example, traditional culture was marked by alcoholism and poverty, Christian spirituality will be understood to be a rejection of all alcohol and acceptance of the responsibility to take care of family and crops. Christian longhouses among the Iban in Sarawak can be identified not only by the cross over their doors (rather than fetishes), but also by the healthy animals and clean property. All of life is a matter of spirituality for all Christians, but especially for the semiliterate and more isolated peoples of the world: how one lives reveals one's relationship with God. What might be viewed as legalism by Western Christians, for indigenous Christians in the non-Western world is a sign of liberation that has come through the preaching of the gospel.

Two other important elements of global spirituality are characteristic of this third stage of global spirituality. First are the physical expressions of Christian life and worship. Christian buildings express the spirituality of a people. In many cultures, Christian worship is much more a matter of communal prayer, repentance, and praise than a time of teaching or preaching. In this case, the church buildings will be more open, allowing for movement, including dancing. There may be two or three different choirs in a worship service, so the buildings reflect the communal participation in praise. In some villages the place of worship is more a matter of space than of buildings, and so worship is a matter of bringing sacredness to a village or to a home. Local skills and crafts are brought to honor God in Christ through tapestries, beadwork, carvings, and buildings. What in past generations was seen as dedicated to the worship of demons or idols now is generally accepted as something that can and should be dedicated to God in Christ. Drums may have been used to conjure up the spirits of the ancestors in the past, but now they can be used to lift up praise to God. Dancing or carving images, activities that had strong associations with the non-Christian past, are now skills dedicated to Christian worship.

The second common theme of spirituality is the strong dimension of Christian witness that is central to one's identification with Jesus Christ. African Independent Churches are, by their very nature and purpose, witnessing communities. Men and women (separately) will go out after worship to minister in local communities and villages the Spirit of Christ to Christians and non-Christians. Chinese Christianity is evangelistic in its very DNA. Chinese Christians not only see it as their calling to give Christian witness to their family, but also to the other villages or provinces in China, as well as in Central Asia and the Middle East. Latin American indigenous churches, as well as charismatic Catholics are marked by a strong evangelistic zeal.

Christian life in most of the non-Western world is evangelistic and outward moving. Nigerian church planters are found in the Ukraine, Western Europe, and in North America, but Chinese evangelists are working in factories and shops planting churches throughout Asia. Christian faith, for these rapidly growing churches, overflows to global witness.

The above paragraphs describe regions of the world where Christianity developed from the 15th century on. In parts of India and Persia, as well as in Egypt and Ethiopia, there were existing churches (various Orthodox branches) whose spiritual practices were marked more by consistency than innovation. The Coptic Church (Egypt), for example, worships facing the East, using the human voice for music, follows one of three liturgies that have existed since the early church (St. Basil, St. Gregory, or St. Cyril), and is marked by the use of icons for corporate and private worship. In Orthodox churches an iconostasis, or a screen made up of icons, is at the front of the sanctuary, and only the priest and deacon may pass through. Icons are also reminders of the spiritual qualities of the saints though the ages and are used as windows or guides in prayer. Worship continues to be the central element in the spiritual life of the Orthodox, whether in Western Asia, Eastern Europe, or Africa. Such traditions are now being encountered by newer Christian communities giving a newer dimension to the local-global, what we might call the contemporary-traditional.

For Further Reading

Fernando, L., and G. Gispert-Sauch. *Christianity in India: Two Thousand Years of Faith* (2004).

Hanciles, J. *Beyond Christendom* (2008).

Irvin, D., and S. Sunquist. *History of the World Christian Movement*. Vol. 2 (2010).

Jenkins, P. *The Next Christendom* (2002).

McLeod, H., and W. Ustorf, eds. *The Decline of Christendom in Western Europe, 1750–2000* (2003).

Sanneh, L. *Disciples of All Nations: Pillars of World Christianity* (2008).

Sanneh, L., and J. Carpenter, eds. *The Changing Face of Christianity: Africa, the West, and the World* (2005).

CHAPTER 19

A COMPARISON OF MAJOR CHRISTIAN TRADITIONS

W. DAVID BUSCHART

The Christian tradition consists of a number of smaller traditions, each bound by its limitations and each offering its own contributions to spirituality (see, e.g., Buschart, 255–61, 278–80). This essay introduces and compares Christian spirituality as it is conceived and practiced in the three major traditions: Eastern Orthodox (Orthodox), Roman Catholic (Catholic), and Protestant. It is important to note that attributing a characteristic belief or practice to one of these traditions does not necessarily mean that it is not also present in the other traditions. Furthermore, there is great diversity within each of the traditions, and this diversity must be acknowledged when making generalized observations. Nonetheless, there is sufficient commonality and unity within each tradition to be able to make meaningful observations.

Each of these traditions traces its historical origins to the life and work of Jesus Christ. When describing the historical path from these origins to today with particular attention to the relationships between Orthodoxy, Catholicism, and Protestantism, the most commonly cited landmarks are the so-called East-West "Great Schism," which culminated in the 11th century, and the era of reformation in the Western church of the 16th century, which gave birth to Protestantism. Significant differences, many of which are directly or indirectly related to these historical turning points, unquestionably remain, and at the same time, recent decades have seen a significant increase in dialogue and mutual understanding between Orthodox, Catholics, and Protestants, not least with respect to spirituality.

The Context of Spirituality

All three traditions hold certain fundamental beliefs about God and the human condition — thus, the context in which spirituality is realized and experienced. The Orthodox, Catholic, and Protestant traditions all affirm that the triune God is the Creator of all that is, including and especially human beings, and this has at least three implications with respect to spirituality.

First, human beings exist *coram deo* ("before God"). They are not alone; they have been created by God and live their lives before him. Furthermore, in addition to being made *by* God and living *before* God, humans are made by God's creation design to live *for* God.

Second, human beings live as creatures within a world designed, created, and sustained by God. This is of significance in several respects. Human beings themselves are complex, multidimensional creatures, consisting of both the corporeal and the spiritual. Thus, "it is crucial to acknowledge the significance of both matter and spirit in spiritual development" (Driskill, 10). Furthermore, the lives of human beings are inextricably linked to the rest of the created order. Human beings were created "in friendship with God and in harmony with creation" (*USCCA*, 67). Creation, in part or in whole, is never to be confused with the Creator, and spiritual life transcends created reality. However, human spirituality can never be rightly understood nor properly lived apart from the created order. Preeminent among all created realities are human beings. Without reducing nonhuman creation to insignificance, relationships with other human beings occupy a uniquely integral role in spirituality. In sum, in affirming that human beings live as creatures within a created order designed by God the Creator, all three traditions affirm that human spirituality entails being rightly related to God, to oneself, to other people, and to the rest of the created order.

Third, human beings, as well as the rest of creation, were created good. Thus, for example, according to Orthodoxy's sacramental view of the world, "nothing in life is ultimately profane or secular" (Bartholomew, 85; see Gen. 1). And God created human beings *uniquely* "good." Not only were we made "in a state of original holiness and justice" (*USCCA*, 67), but human beings alone were made in the image of God. While being creatures and, thus, inextricably connected to other creatures and the rest of creation, human beings are gloriously spiritually unique, "different from and superior to all other living creatures on earth" (ibid.).

This recognition of divinely created origins and design, and divinely created goodness, provides context and foundation for each tradition's understanding of human spirituality. However, each tradition also views human spirituality in light of "the fall" (see Gen. 3). As a result of rebelling against God's original design, the *imago Dei* has been corrupted or horribly distorted, and all of human being's relationships—with self, with others, with the creation, and most significantly with God—have been shattered. With the entry of sin into the human race, human beings' spiritual needs increased while human capacities, including spiritual capacities and context, were now corrupted.

The Trajectory of Spirituality

All three traditions envision a similar overall trajectory for human spirituality, that is, a path from a corrupted self and broken relationships with God, self, others, and the creation to a restoration or renewal of self and these relationships. However, each tradition's vision of this spiritual path reflects its own distinctive history, theology, terminology, and emphases.

The Orthodox tradition speaks of the trajectory of Christian spirituality as one of *theosis* (or "deification," "divinization"). While occupying a place in the scheme of salvation somewhat analogous to the Protestant notion of sanctification, or growth in holiness, *theosis* "goes beyond" this. Without losing their individuality, human beings actually participate in God's divine "energies" (as distinct from the divine "essence"), thereby realizing a "personal and organic union" (Tibbs, 245). One contemporary Orthodox writer describes *theosis* as "the perfection of the power of grace so irradiating the being of the redeemed saints that they too become light-filled, perfected by the mercy of God, in order to be conformed to the divine presence" (McGuckin, 198–99). The "chasm" between God and human beings narrows and is bridged as humans become "[participants] in the divine nature" (2 Peter 1:3–4). This is a lifelong process in which the spiritual dimensions of the human person gain ascendancy over the more material dimensions (McGuckin, 196).

Union with Christ, also a theme in Orthodox and Protestant spirituality, is central to the Catholic vision of Christian spiritual life, in which "spiritual progress tends toward ever more intimate union with Christ" (*CCC*, 435, par. 2014). Not unlike the Orthodox tradition, a mystical "participation" in the Godhead is associated with an increased realization of this union; and, not unlike the Protestant tradition, spiritual progress is associated with growth in "holiness." While the contemplative dimensions of spirituality have long been and continue to be important, spiritual growth is also understood as having an outward orientation, entailing "perfection of one's relationship with others … rather than personal sanctification rooted in an ever-deepening inner gaze" (Downey, 45).

Within Protestantism the spiritual life is most commonly conceptualized, whether explicitly or implicitly, with respect to justification (being rightly related to God) and sanctification (growth in holiness). Justification is not the result of sanctification; rather, it is the point of entry to the process of sanctification. Views vary within Protestantism as to the pattern of sanctification and the degree to which it can be realized in this life. While acknowledging these and other differences, the three traditions share in common a vision of the Christian spiritual life as one of increasing holiness as modeled in the person and life of Jesus Christ.

The Way of Spirituality: God and Human Being

Most Christians acknowledge that the precise delineation of the respective roles of divine work and human effort in Christian spirituality is, to a considerable degree, a mystery. Yet each of the traditions does seek to shed light and hence offer spiritual guidance regarding this divine-human dynamic.

The range of views can be thought of in terms of a continuum, from synergistic to monergistic views, with variations in between. The Orthodox, Catholic, and some Protestant traditions believe that the Christian spiritual life arises and continues through processes entailing divine-human synergism. That is, God and human persons work together. Spirituality is conceived as a form of collaboration between God and human being. However, even the capacity for this participation is itself a function of the grace of God (*USCCA*, 168). Enabled by grace and exercising free will, individual persons cooperate and participate with God in spiritual life.

Some Protestant traditions (e.g., those that hold to Reformed theology) have a monergistic view, believing that the entrance into spiritual life is solely and exclusively the result of the work of God. Believing that human free will was lost in the fall, entrance into spiritual life is achieved solely by divine working. In some traditions (e.g., Lutheran) this takes place in infant baptism, while in others (e.g., Baptists who hold to Calvinist theology) this takes place in regeneration and conversion prior to baptism. In either case, human beings do not participate, because they are "dead in . . . transgressions and sins" (Eph. 2:1). Once made spiritually alive by God, however, they can cooperate with God in the sense of being submissive and responsive to his work.

However the relationship between God's work and human work is conceived, God's work is understood to be Trinitarian. Generally speaking, God the Father originates and, in a sense, orchestrates, divine work in the spiritual life. God the Son makes spiritual life possible by his redeeming work, his union with Christians, and his mediation between human beings and God. God the Holy Spirit applies Christ's work to human beings and guides and energizes.

Over the course of the 20th century, there was a virtual explosion of spirituality that gave particular prominence, in both belief and practice, to the person and work of the Holy Spirit. The two largest streams of such spirituality are the charismatic movement(s) and Pentecostal Christianity. These forms of spirituality continue to flourish today, not least in the global south. Charismatic types of spirituality, with an emphasis on direct encounter with the Holy Spirit and his supernatural working in the otherwise natural world, can be observed at points throughout the history of Christianity. In the 20th century, charismatic spirituality generally emerged from within or "came alongside" of existing ecclesiastical traditions, including—admittedly in different ways—Orthodoxy, Catholicism, and many of the subtraditions within Protestantism. Thus, in the latter half of the century, these forms of spirituality were often described in hyphenated terms, such as charismatic-Catholic, charismatic-Lutheran, or charismatic-Anglican. Believing that most forms of Christian spirituality are good but incomplete, charismatic spirituality pursues a more holistic approach, sometimes described as "the full gospel," which seeks to embrace fully the present-day working of the Holy Spirit, including his work with respect to the material world, including the physical dimensions of being human.

Pentecostalism shares this pursuit of a holistic spirituality, but with several distinctive characteristics and emphases, two of which can be noted here. One of the hallmarks of classical Pentecostalism has been the belief that, in addition to justification, God calls Christians to experience an associated yet distinct miraculous work usually referred to as "baptism in the Holy Spirit." And, for classical Pentecostals, speaking in unknown languages (*glossolalia* or evidential "tongues") has been evidence of this baptism. This new relationship with the Holy Spirit, in conjunction with being rightly related to Christ through justification, is then the source of spiritual power and enablement for Christian life and ministry. A second distinctive of Pentecostalism is that, unlike the charismatic hyphenated identification with other Christian traditions, Pentecostals have generally formed their own churches and denominations, usually viewed as subtraditions of Protestantism.

The Way of Spirituality: Resources

Each tradition commends some and requires other resources and corresponding practices for nurturing spiritual life. Many of the differences among the traditions are grounded in differing understandings of the authority (or authorities) for spiritual life, or in differing understandings of the means (or lack thereof) by which the relationship between God and human beings is mediated.

The Orthodoxy tradition's resources can be viewed as elements of tradition. These "great legacies" include the "mysteries" (often a preferred term for the sacraments), the liturgy, the Bible, prayer, the apostolic faith, and guidance for the spiritual life, such as that gathered in the *Philokalia*, a col-

lection of ascetic and mystical writings (Coniaris, 9). Each of these resources is available through the living tradition of the Orthodox Church. In particular, the first eight centuries following the time of Christ provided wise and essentially normative guidance for the spiritual life in the form of confessions of doctrine, liturgical forms and practices, sacramental forms and practices, the use of icons, and specific forms of prayer. These ancient resources are part of the tradition that is handed down by and through the Orthodox Church, and that is "living" by virtue of the Holy Spirit's continuing work through it.

Catholicism's resources can be most readily understood in relation to its understanding of the church. Resources for spiritual life are to be found in and through the Catholic Church. Foundational for and central to all of these resources are the liturgy and the sacraments, particularly the Eucharist. "The other sacraments, and indeed all ecclesiastical ministries ... are bound up with the Eucharist and are oriented toward it. For in the blessed Eucharist is contained the whole spiritual good of the Church, namely Christ himself." Thus, the Eucharist is "the source and summit" of the spiritual life (*CCC*, 368–69, par. 1324). It is through the Eucharist and the other sacraments that "divine life is dispensed to us" by the Catholic Church (*CCC*, 320, par. 1131).

Acknowledging that this mediation is richly complex and multifaceted, two observations can be noted here. First, God's grace is primarily communicated to humankind, and spiritual life is fundamentally nurtured in and through the church. In both the Orthodox and the Catholic traditions, spirituality is inextricably grounded in and mediated through the Orthodox or the Catholic Church respectively (*USCCA*, 167; Ware, 107). Second, both the Orthodox and the Catholic traditions grant a significant role for what is sometimes referred to as the "church triumphant," that is, those Christians who have lived and died on earth but are now alive with Christ. This is expressed most notably in the roles given to "saints," including, particularly in Catholicism, special devotion to Mary *Theotokos*, "Mother of God" (Council of Ephesus, AD 431; *USCCA*, 145). Having lived lives of uncommon holiness, these individuals can now serve as both spiritual models and intercessors.

There is greater diversity among Protestant views of the resources; yet some emphases are characteristic of most, if not all, of Protestantism. The Bible has a more prominent role, and this role is both formal and material. Formally, the Bible provides information about and guidance for spiritual life. Materially, reading the Bible and listening to it being preached are spiritual exercises that become, by virtue of the work of the Holy Spirit, occasions or "events" through which spiritual life is nurtured. Such notions are not absent from either Orthodoxy or Catholicism, but they are noticeably more prominent and pervasive within Protestantism.

A second contrast centers on the ways in which spiritual life with God is, and is not, mediated. Some Protestant traditions (e.g., Lutheran, Anglican, many Presbyterian) give a prominent and determinative role to the sacraments, which in Protestantism are two: baptism and the Lord's Supper. To be sure, these sacramental traditions view the spiritual life as more than receiving the sacraments (as do also Orthodoxy and Catholicism). At the same time, in viewing baptism and the Lord's Supper as sacraments, these traditions are somewhat similar to Orthodoxy and Catholicism in viewing spiritual life as in this way mediated in and through the church.

Many Protestant traditions (e.g., Baptist, Anabaptist, most nondenominational churches) have a much different, and more limited, view of the role of the church in the mediation of the spiritual life. These churches place much greater emphasis on a direct relationship between individual persons and God. Baptism and the Lord's Supper are viewed as "ordinances," practices ordained or instituted by Christ, but they are not viewed chiefly as means of spiritual grace from God to us. Rather, they are forms of testimony to God and others of the spiritual life God has already given. Life with God is experienced directly, apart from any particular means or church ritual. God's Spirit speaks directly to our spirits (Rom. 8:16). To the degree that God employs some other "means," this is most often the Bible or another Christian communicating biblical teaching.

The Way of Spirituality: Practices

The practices of the spiritual life correspond in many ways to the resources commended or required. Thus, participating in the life of the church, particularly though not exclusively the liturgy and sacraments, is fundamental to spirituality as conceived and practiced in Orthodoxy and Catholicism (e.g., *CCC*, 320, par. 1131; Ware 107–8).

Beyond the sacraments, other church-based and church-guided practices are essential to spiritual life. For example, prayer is significantly shaped through liturgy and tradition. "The prayer of Orthodox Christians was primarily formed in the liturgy of the community, rather than inside the walls of monasteries or in the hearts of individual saints" (Bartholomew, 75), and in Catholicism, "all Christian prayer finds its source and goal" in the liturgy (*CCC*, 303, par. 1073). There are specific prayers—such as the Jesus Prayer (Orthodoxy) and the rosary (Catholicism)—that have been recited for centuries.

Many other practices, grounded in liturgy and prayer, both express and nurture spiritual growth. Asceticism is perhaps most fully expressed in various forms of monasticism. However, the discipline associated with daily "taking up one's cross" (see Luke 9:23)—an ascetic path—is not confined to those in monasteries. Many spiritual practices involve the use or sacralizing of some created entity, such as time (e.g., the liturgical year), space (e.g., pilgrimages), and material culture (e.g., icons, relics).

The mediation of the church and its sacraments is important to spirituality in sacramental Protestant traditions (e.g., Anglican, Lutheran, Presbyterian). By contrast, many Protestant traditions (e.g., Anabaptist, Baptist, Free Church, Pietist, nondenominational) stress a Christian's direct, unmediated "personal relationship" with Jesus Christ. Either explicitly or implicitly, the role of the church in the spiritual life is minimized or regarded as optional. The practices of spirituality are often anchored in personal Bible reading and prayer. The church's primary roles include, then, providing biblical teaching, spiritual instruction, and community. The church is often viewed primarily as a venue for community or fellowship, and participating in this "priesthood of all believers" (see 1 Peter 2:5–9) is viewed as important for the encouragement of spiritual growth.

Conclusion

In conclusion, here are some observations about recent developments in spirituality across the major traditions and about evangelical Protestantism. First, there is a growing emphasis on "horizontal" dimensions of spirituality. This includes a growing emphasis on the connections between spirituality and social justice, and spirituality and the natural environment. Spiritual life is increasingly understood as being both nurtured by and expressed in care for fellow human beings and care for the natural world. Second, Orthodox, Catholics, and Protestants are becoming better acquainted with and increasingly open to learning from one another. Significant theological differences and organizational separations remain. There is, however, increasing openness to learning from one another regarding the Christian life.

Perhaps no tradition has experienced a greater change in this regard than evangelical Protestantism. Because evangelicalism is associated with experiential religion and religion "of the heart," spirituality has long been part of its fabric. Nevertheless, the evangelical inclination toward activism or "doing," combined with a relative neglect of historical tradition, has often resulted in little reflection about and attention to spirituality qua spirituality. Since the late 1980s, however, evangelicals have devoted increasing explicit attention to spirituality. (This dictionary is one expression of this development.) And one of the hallmarks of this renewed evangelical interest in spirituality has been openness to learning from a wider range of authors and sources. This wider range has included both greater historical depth — learning from sources that predate modern evangelicalism by centuries — and greater trans-traditional breadth — learning from authors and sources that until recently had been ignored (or simply unknown) because they were Orthodox or Catholic.

At the same time, evangelicalism continues to offer its own insights and commend its emphases to the larger Christian church. The supreme authority and guide for spiritual life is the Bible, the written Word of God that is employed by the Holy Spirit. Spiritual life should be more than but it can never be less than "a religion of the heart." And grounding it all is life with God the Father through a personal relationship with Jesus Christ empowered by the Holy Spirit.

Sources Cited

Bartholomew, Ecumenical Patriarch of Constantinople. *Encountering the Mystery* (2008).
Buschart, W. D. *Exploring Protestant Traditions* (2006).
Catechism of the Catholic Church (2000).

Coniaris, A. *Philokalia: The Bible of Orthodox Spirituality* (1998).

Downey, M. *Understanding Christian Spirituality* (1997).

Driskill, J. *Protestant Spiritual Exercises* (1999).

McGuckin, J. *The Orthodox Church* (2008).

Tibbs, E. M. "Eastern Orthodoxy Theology." In *Global Dictionary of Theology*, ed. W. Dyrness and V-M. Kärkkäinen (2008), 244–51.

Ware, K. *The Orthodox Way* (1995).

United States Catholic Catechism for Adults (2006).

For Further Reading

Anonymous (a monk of the Eastern church). *Orthodox Spirituality* (1978).

Bacik, J. *Catholic Spirituality* (2002).

Collins, K., ed. *Exploring Christian Spirituality* (2000).

Foster, R. *Streams of Living Water* (1998).

Howard, E. *The Brazos Introduction to Christian Spirituality* (2008).

McGinn, B., et al., eds. *Christian Spirituality*, 3 vols., WSEH (1985–1989).

Mursell, G., ed. *The Story of Christian Spirituality* (2001).

Senn, F., ed. *Protestant Spiritual Traditions* (1986).

CHAPTER 20

CONTOURS OF EVANGELICAL SPIRITUALITY

D. BRUCE HINDMARSH

Evangelical is the adjective that corresponds to the noun *gospel*, but because the adjective derives from Greek and the noun from Old English, it is easy to miss the connection between the terms nowadays when the word *evangelical* has become highly politicized. The close relationship between *evangelical* and *gospel* was explained in the 16th century by William Tyndale: "Evangelion (that we call the gospel) is a Greek word; and signifieth good, merry, glad and joyful tidings, that maketh a man's heart glad, and maketh him sing, dance, and leap for joy" (Tyndale, 8). While Tyndale could not have envisioned the explosion of hymn singing that would emerge in the later evangelical movement, or the erudite analysis of religious emotion that would appear in the writings of Jonathan Edwards, and while he most certainly would not have imagined the Welsh jumpers of the 1760s or Pentecostal dancing in the Spirit in the 20th century, he did appreciate what the apostle Paul called the power, or dynamic, of the gospel to generate confidence and set people in joyful motion. This relationship between word and life, message and experience, doctrine and devotion, has been central to evangelical spirituality from its earliest days.

A Modern Form of Traditional Spirituality

As the quotation from Tyndale illustrates, the word *evangelical* was used during the Reformation and applied to the churches of the Protestant Reformation and their teaching, especially the Lutheran *evangelische* church. But the origins of modern evangelicalism, as it is generally understood in the English-speaking world, are to be found in the revivals in the North Atlantic region in the early 18th century as antecedent movements of devotion, such as Pietism, Puritanism, and the Anglican holy living tradition, coalesced to generate a general spiritual awakening on both an Anglo-German and Anglo-American axis. What resulted was a form of Christian spirituality with roots in earlier traditions of Christian spirituality that was nevertheless highly adapted to the conditions of the emerging modern world.

In the middle third of the 18th century, a number of figures in England and Wales, who would later be drawn into evangelical preaching, passed through a crisis of personal conversion. For example, the future evangelist George Whitefield was converted in 1735, and the future Methodists John and Charles Wesley were converted in 1738, and all three went on to remarkable careers as evangelical leaders. But these are only the most famous examples. Most of those thus converted were already baptized and highly observant Christians who nevertheless each came to a crisis of conscience and spiritual insufficiency that seemed to demand a new and more deeply personal experience of repentance and faith in Christ. They each likewise discovered a new impulse to preach, travel, organize, and campaign for widespread evangelical renewal within their own spheres, whether Anglicans, Methodists, Moravians, Presbyterians, Congregationalists, or Baptists. When they witnessed large numbers of men and women experience a personal conversion similar to their own, such as George Whitefield witnessed at Cambuslang in Scotland in 1742, they typically spoke of this as a remarkable "work" of God. This is where the American and Scots-Irish experience of corporate renewal in local communities influenced the emergent sense of a broader transatlantic evangelical awakening. Jonathan Edwards gave public attention to the conversion of some three hundred persons in the Connecticut Valley Revival of 1734–1735 in his *Faithful Narrative of a Surprising Work of God* (1737), and the case studies of individual conversion he recounted, as well as his analysis of spiritual awakening as a general phenomenon among the populace, established a paradigm that was applied to the wider North Atlantic region as evangelicals reflected on news of spiritual concern from places near and far. In 1745 Wesley identified with this North Atlantic movement, marveling, "In what age has such a work been wrought, considering the *swiftness* as well as the *extent* of it?" (Wesley, 9.276).

The new evangelical piety evident in this spiritual awakening was international and interdenominational, and it was characterized by a focus on "true religion" over against nominal affiliation to church establishments and a religion of law and custom. Moreover, the evangelical movement had the mobility and democratic appeal of its modernizing context, and it gained many of its adherents through itinerant preaching in open public spaces. Across this whole region, evangelical devotion centered on the atoning death of Christ and the necessity of personal conversion, and it drew laypeople into practices of Bible reading, small group fellowship, extempore prayer, personal testimony, and hymn singing—all of which have remained central to evangelical spirituality throughout its history. Evangelicalism emerged on the trailing edge of Christendom and the leading edge of

modernity as a spiritual movement concerned to spread "real Christianity" among a populace that thought of itself as Christian even as social change was devolving more weight upon individual agency in spheres such as commerce, the press, and politics. As the *ancien régime* was superseded by the modern world with its constitutional guarantees of freedom of religion, its democratic ideals and commercial freedoms, its industry and technology, its enlarged print and other public media, and its efficient and long-distance communication and trade, evangelicals would increasingly appeal to women and men as personal agents and connect them in intimate small groups and larger associations that were voluntary, rather than mandated by corporate hierarchies or social custom.

For this reason, it is important to appreciate that evangelicalism is, above all, *a form of spirituality*. The field of spirituality is especially concerned with "lived experience," rather than doctrine or practices in isolation from their embodiment and expression in real life in real time (Schneider, 6). And it was precisely a focus on "lived experience" that united evangelicals in a common mission from the outset of the movement. "Lived experience" could have been their motto. The evangelical Joseph Milner wrote a *History of the Church of Christ* and remarked in the preface that he wanted to celebrate what he called "genuine piety." Johann Arndt had earlier written a book that would be foundational for the movement for piety in Germany, and its title suggested the same theme: *True Christianity*. In the middle of the 18th century, Joseph Bellamy wrote *True Religion Delineated*, and at the close of the century, William Wilberforce wrote *A Practical View of . . . Real Christianity*. "Genuine piety," "true Christianity," "true religion," "real Christianity"—all of these terms signal what was the central preoccupation of the leaders of the evangelical movement, namely, that men and women who had a merely formal relationship with the church and its teaching come to a real experience of Christian faith.

Despite the surprising work of God in their own times, the first generation of evangelicals saw themselves in continuity with earlier generations of Christians in their concern for true religion. When the evangelical clergyman John Newton wrote a general letter to his parishioners in London in 1781 and sought to explain to them why he might be called a Methodist, he said that men of the same spirit had earlier been branded as Pietist and Puritan, and even earlier they were called Lollards and Gospellers (Newton, 6.271). He understood that his contemporary evangelical experience was in continuity with traditions of piety in late medieval protest, the Reformation, and post-Reformation devotional movements. He also made good use of continental Catholic sources, saying:

> If such persons as De Fenelon, Paschall, Quenell, and Nicole (to mention no more), were not true Christians, where shall we find any who deserve the name? In the writings of these great men, notwithstanding incidental errors, I meet with such strains of experimental Godliness, such deep knowledge of the workings of the Spirit of God and the heart of man, and such masterly explications of many important passages of Scripture, as might do honour to the most enlightened Protestant. (Newton, 5.29)

It was the "experimental godliness," spiritual insight, and devotional use of Scripture in these Catholic spiritual writings that made them good sources for evangelical spirituality. Thus, evangelicals since John Wesley have been readers of Thomas à Kempis's *Imitation of Christ* and other continental Catholics, such as the Quietist writer Madame Guyon, who has reappeared at many points on the reading lists of evangelicals, from the eighteenth-century poet William Cowper to the twentieth-century pastor and devotional writer A. W. Tozer. For all their adaptations to modernity, evangelicals have drawn deeply from the wells of earlier Protestant and Catholic spirituality. They have also actively reprinted, abridged, and popular-ized this devotional literature in collections such as Wesley's *Christian Library* in the 18th century or James M. Houston's *Classics of Faith and Devotion* in the twentieth.

Three Centuries of Evangelical Spirituality

The phenomenon of evangelical renewal in the 1730s and '40s was not the work of one generation but rather the emergence of a religious movement that would endure for three centuries and spread around the world through the missionary movement and globalization. Put differently, there is a complex genealogy or family tree of evangelicals that can be traced back to the revivals of the 18th century. From the teaching of John and Charles Wesley on Christian perfection emerged the Holiness movement of the 19th century, and then later, within this milieu, modern Pentecostalism. Again, one can trace a genealogy of public evangelists (and the revivals associated with them) from George Whitefield to Charles Finney to Dwight L. Moody to Billy Sunday to Billy Graham. But there is no one line of evangelical history to be traced from the past to the present. Like the phenomenon of a braided river, with its multiple strands, there are many crisscrossing streams that can be followed down the generations.

There are various interpretations of the phases of evangelical history. From an American point of view, some, such as William McLoughlin, have seen evangelical history in terms of a series of *revivals* from the Great Awakening in the 18th century to the Second Great Awakening at the turn of the century through the Prayer Meeting Revival at midcentury and the transatlantic urban revivalism of the Gilded Age, and so on. From a British perspective, David Bebbington has interpreted evangelicalism as a movement with a core of characteristics that have remained constant in the midst of *cultural change* from Enlightenment in the 18th century, through romanticism in the nineteenth, to modernism in the twentieth. Again, Joel Carpenter has presented evangelicalism as a coalition of groups with shared concerns and who form something like a changing kaleidoscope rather than a fixed mosaic. The relative influence of one group over another, and of some ideals over others, has given a *thematic unity* to different periods, rather like the pieces in a kaleidoscope overlap, change position, and form new patterns, so that new colors come to the fore and cast their hues over the whole field (Carpenter, 238). From this angle of vision, one can discern after the transatlantic awakening of the 18th century a "Methodist era" on the American frontier that corresponded to the growth of evangelical nonconformity and the mid-Victorian heyday of evangelicalism in Britain, and also a "Holiness era" in the mid-to-late 19th century in which the Methodist doctrines of perfection were taken up more widely, especially through the influential Keswick Conferences, into ideals of the victorious or higher Christian life and consecration for missionary service. The early 20th century was a "Fundamentalist era" that merged into the neo-evangelical postwar revival associated with Billy Graham. The late 20th century introduced a Pentecostal-charismatic impulse that has become perhaps the most influential form of evangelical religion worldwide—a "Pentecostal-charismatic era."

Because evangelicalism has been populist and concerned, as Wesley said, with "plain truth for plain people," it has not produced an extensive or sophisticated body of spiritual theology, compared with, say, the traditions of monastic theology. Most of its spiritual theology is *kerygmatic*, literally preached in sermons, proclaimed in songs, announced in testimonies, or jotted down in letters. Yet each of the periods outlined above have produced some spiritual writings of lasting value. The most important has probably been the hymns, and these are a good example of a genre that teaches about prayer and the spiritual life in the form of prayer. *Lex orandi, lex credendi* (roughly paraphrased, "the way of worship is the way of

belief") is not just an ancient principle. John Wesley described the standard Methodist hymnbook as a "little body of experimental and practical divinity," and the same could be said about the whole corpus of evangelical song, from the Methodist and Victorian hymnbooks to the shape-note choruses and camp meeting and gospel songs, from the Sunday school hymns and the African-American spirituals to the Jesus music of the 1960s and '70s or the Vineyard songs of the '80s.

Autobiography and biography have also been a way of presenting the spiritual life for evangelicals. In the 18th century, the *Journal* of John Wesley or the *Authentic Narrative* of the converted slave trader John Newton or the *Life* of the missionary David Brainerd by Jonathan Edwards each taught readers about the goals, the shape, the obstacles, and the resources for Christian living, as did later classics, such as *The Memoir and Remains of Robert Murray McCheyne* (1844) by Andrew Bonar.

The evangelical concern for a life of holiness was expressed in John Wesley's *Plain Account of Christian Perfection* (1777) and reprised in different ways in the Holiness movement in popular works such as Phoebe Palmer's *Way of Holiness* (1843), Hannah Whitall Smith's *The Christian's Secret of a Happy Life* (1875), or Andrew Murray's *Abide in Christ* (1882). A bridge figure between these Holiness writers and the era of the Fundamentalist-Modernist controversies was the influential Chinese evangelist Watchman Nee, whose books *The Spiritual Man* (1928) and *The Normal Christian Life* (1938) were widely read by Christians from East and West. Similarly, the devotional writings of A. W. Tozer, *The Pursuit of God* (1948) and *The Knowledge of the Holy* (1961), have sustained attention to the themes of holiness and the mystical presence of God in the life of the believer.

Calvinist evangelicals since the 18th century have continued the tradition of practical divinity and pastoralia that was so evident in Puritans such as Richard Baxter. From Jonathan Edwards's unsurpassed analysis of the nature of religious experience, *A Treatise Concerning Religious Affections* (1746) or William Romaine's trilogy *The Life, Walk, and Triumph of Faith* in the 18th century, to Bishop J. C. Ryle's work on *Holiness* (1877) in the 19th century and J. I. Packer's *Knowing God* (1973) in the 20th century, there has been a steady stream of Calvinist and neo-Calvinist spiritual literature.

While Pentecostal-charismatic evangelicalism has not been expressed primarily through an extensive literature, it has produced widely read writings on the spiritual life by leaders such as David Watson, Michael Green, and John Wimber. The most influential expression of the spirituality of charismatic evangelicalism is the Alpha Course, which was begun in the 1970s in London but spread internationally in the 1990s to reach millions of people. Like the Jesus film that was first released in 1979 and has since been shown worldwide to millions of people in hundreds of languages, the Alpha Course illustrates the missional and innovative impulses of evangelical spirituality, as well as the evangelistic concern to reach out to as many as possible with a simple but life-giving message of salvation through personal faith in Christ. The popularity among evangelicals of John Stott's *Basic Christianity* and C. S. Lewis's *Mere Christianity* likewise point to this anti-elitist interest in a simple accessible outline of the spiritual life, rather than a complex mystagogy of ascent.

Since the early 1970s there has been a growing interest in classical spirituality among evangelicals, and the pioneering works of writers such as Richard Foster (especially his *Celebration of Discipline* in 1978), James Houston, Dallas Willard, and Eugene Peterson have been followed by a host of others. In fact, most evangelical publishers now have an active list of titles or special series on spirituality or spiritual formation.

Interpreting Evangelical Spirituality

The very diversity of these writings and this evangelical history raises the question of whether there is a core to the evangelical tradition. If evangelicalism cannot be identified as a church or denomination with any kind of consistent visible church order, how are you to understand and identify it? Everyone knows what a Jesuit is, but how do you know what an evangelical is?

Therefore, the most common way to define evangelicalism is by trying to determine the distinctive, universally shared characteristics of the movement. This can be done from the inside, as it were, by an evangelical theologian such as J. I. Packer, who writes from conviction about what evangelicalism *ought* to be, or from the outside, by a historian such as David Bebbington, mentioned above, who describes from a more neutral point of view what it seems the movement *is* (or what it *was*). Whereas Packer identifies a syllabus of ten doctrinal convictions that *ought* to characterize evangelicals, such as the authority of Scripture, the supremacy of Christ as Savior and Lord, the necessity of faith and holiness, and so on, Bebbington argues that only four characteristics have really distinctively characterized evangelicals throughout their history, namely, their emphasis on personal conversion, the Bible, the cross of Christ, and active Christian service (Bebbington, 1–19; Packer, 179–81). Thus, while evangelicals are orthodox Christians with a Protestant heritage like many other Christians, these four characteristics together set them apart and hold them together as a movement through time and change.

Indeed, the four characteristics emphasized by David Bebbington describe a simple and popular form of Christian spirituality. Moreover, the structures of evangelicalism as a social movement of the sort studied by Charles Tilly and other sociologists—which are generally understood to have taken their modern form in the mid-to-late 18th century—highlight the mobility and modernity of this form of spirituality (Tilly, 1–7). As Martin Marty has asserted, "Evangelicalism is the characteristic Protestant way of relating to modernity" (cited in Carpenter, 235). Evangelicalism was modern, not in the sense accommodating its doctrines to progressive intellectual thought, but in the sense of being adapted to modern social conditions on the ground.

Three analogies might help us to appreciate the character of evangelical spirituality as it has appeared in the modern era. The notion of a new "work of God," as evangelicals described the spiritual awakening in the 18th century, has its theological analogue in the idea of a "founding charism" for *a religious order*. Interpreting the movement in this way, evangelicalism appears less as a sectarian alignment in Protestant Christianity than as something like a religious order in the Catholic Church, a sodality or confraternity that arises at a particular time with a particular purpose within the wider church. Comparing early evangelicalism to a Roman Catholic religious order is not as farfetched as it might at first seem. Thomas Babington Macaulay wrote that the Roman Church would have known exactly what to do with John Wesley: he would have been made the first director general of a new religious society (Trevelyan, 246).

To use a similar analogy to that of a religious order, the early evangelical movement appears as a new *school* of spirituality within the church universal. The nineteenth-century historian John Henry Overton often used the term *school* when he wrote about the Evangelical Revival. He wrote of "the Evangelical school in the last century," and so on (Overton, 78). This nomenclature has also appeared in the history of Christian spirituality, so that it is common to speak especially of Counter-Reformation movements as schools: the Spanish school after St. Teresa, the French school after Francis de Sales, or the Italian school in the 16th century, and so on (Pouratt, 3.x–xii). Raymond Deville provides an account of a school of spirituality: "A spirituality or a spiritual tradition is a certain, symbolic way of hearing and living the Gospel. This 'Way' is conditioned by a period, a 'fertilized soil' the particular influence of a specific milieu. It can be incarnated in a clearly identified group of human beings and can continue,

historically, enriched or impoverished.... In this way, a 'spiritual tradition' or a 'school' of spirituality comes to be" (Deville, 153–54). Evangelicals likewise insisted that their first concern was with a "way" of life itself—true religion or real Christianity—more than with a system of ideas, and their concern was that women and men be formed or "schooled" within this way. The period that conditioned them, the soil in which they were planted, was modernity itself, and they were therefore highly attuned to the needs and conditions of modern women and men.

Third, evangelicalism may be understood as a form of life within the wider confession of catholic Christian identity. Evangelicals have always been most themselves when seeking to be Christians, not when seeking to be evangelicals. J. I. Packer thus describes evangelicalism as an ethos of convertedness within a larger ethos of catholicity (Packer, 182). Convertedness is a divine dynamic generated by an understanding of the gospel and issuing in a renewal of life. It is a form of life. It is like *a mainstream current* within the great Mississippi River, a mainstream that flows onward, despite eddies and bayous, mudflats and reed beds. Creeds and councils mark the banks of the river. Faith, repentance, fellowship, communion, holiness, and service are all the while being renewed by the coursing life of the Spirit.

All three of these analogies—a religious order, a school, or a current—point to the same insight that while evangelicalism is a robust form of Christian living, it has always been nested within or contingent upon a wider and deeper Christianity, or what has been called the Great Tradition. Whenever evangelicals sheer away from this deep connection to the historic faith of the church, they are like a stream that seeks to run on without its source. But evangelical spirituality at its best presses beyond doctrinal precision, ecclesiastical observance, or moral rectitude to experience nothing less than what one of their favorite writers called "the life of God in the soul of man."

Sources Cited

Bebbington, D. W. *Evangelicalism in Modern Britain* (1988).

Carpenter, J. *Revive Us Again* (1997).

Deville, R. *The French School of Spirituality* (1994).

McLoughlin, W. *Revivals, Awakenings, and Reform* (1978).

Newton, J. *Works* (1808).

Overton, J. H. *The Evangelical Revival in the Eighteenth Century* (1886).

Packer, J. I. "Reflections and Response." In *J. I. Packer and the Evangelical Future,* ed. T. George (2009), 171–85.

Pouratt, P. *Christian Spirituality* (1953).

Schneider, S. "The Study of Christian Spirituality." In *Minding the Spirit,* ed. E. A. Dreyer and M. S. Burrows (2005), 5–24.

Tilly, C. *Social Movements, 1768–2004* (2004).

Trevelyan, G. O., ed. *Selections from the Writings of Lord Macaulay* (1876).

Tyndale, W. *Doctrinal Treatises,* ed. H. Walter (1848).

Wesley, J. *Works* (1976–).

For Further Reading

Bebbington, D. W., and M. A. Noll, eds., *A History of Evangelicalism,* 5 vols. (2004–).

George, T., and A. McGrath, eds. *For all the Saints: Evangelical Theology and Christian Spirituality* (2003).

Gordon, J. M. *Evangelical Spirituality* (1991).

Houston, J. "Spiritual Theology." *CRUX,* no. 2 (1991): 2–8; no. 3 (1991): 25–33.

Larson, T., ed. *Biographical Dictionary of Evangelicals* (2003).

Lovelace, R. "Evangelical Spirituality: A Church Historian's Perspective." In *Exploring Christian Spirituality*, ed. K. J. Collins (2000), 214–26.

Parker, D. "Evangelical Spirituality Revisited." *Evangelical Quarterly* 63, no. 2 (1991): 123–48.

Peterson, E. *Christ Plays in Ten Thousand Places* (2005).

CHAPTER 21

PATHWAYS TO REFORM AND RENEWAL

JAMES D. SMITH III

In pursuing spiritual "reform" and "renewal," Christians engage two of the most compelling change concepts in the human experience. These terms join others in English that (expressing Latin roots) feature the *re-* prefix: e.g., remembrance, repentance, reconciliation, restoration, and reunion. Each suggests a valued antecedent seeking current expression: a past moment of truth gaining fresh attention, a turning toward previous virtue, a wounded relationship now healed, something fallen into disrepair upgraded, fragmented pieces finding new wholeness together.

Such experiences involve a personal and social process: valuing an earlier standard or state now evidencing departure or decay, choosing anew to embrace essential qualities, and pursuing a preferred outcome. The work of Gerhard Ladner has been influential in exploring these concepts and informing dialogue. Broadly speaking, *reformatio* denotes intentional efforts toward restored ideals while *renovatio* suggests a more spontaneous revitalization. While these dynamics are present across cultures, it is the community confessing Jesus Christ as Lord that singularly moves beyond nostalgia and novelty to pursue this numinous life.

Christian Distinctives

The distinctive of reform and renewal in the Christian experience lies first in its return to a *standard*. The Scriptures, as the authoritative Word of God, correct human life (2 Tim. 3:16). Woman and man, created in the image and likeness of God, pursue their full recovery (Gen. 1:26–27). Jesus Christ as perfect moral example, loving Savior, and faithful Lord (2 Peter 1:2–11) calls all back from wandering. The kingdom of God is the plumb line for recapturing true community (Matt. 5–7). Faith, hope, and love are eternal values and spiritual dynamics (1 Cor. 13).

Christian reform and renewal also acknowledge, on the basis of authoritative Scripture, the role of *sin* in "the gap" between ideal and realization. At the personal level, all have sinned and fallen short of God's glory (Rom. 3:23). Too often, one who knows the right still doesn't do it (James 1:22; 4:17). Creation itself groans under the outcomes of human brokenness (Rom. 8:18–25). Ignorance, woundedness, and the ecological crisis are indeed issues, with education, peacemaking, and living green as initiatives inviting attention. But deeper than mistakes and missteps in human spiritual DNA is the sin issue affecting all others — and requiring authentic repentance for cleansing and healing.

Finally, the Scriptures affirm the *living hope* that authentic reform and renewal are possible. The Word of God invites all: "I have set before you life and death, blessings and curses. Now choose life" (Deut. 30:19). Jesus' life and atoning sacrifice invite all by faith to return to God and a "forever family" — reconciled, new creations, ambassadors for God's kingdom reign (2 Cor. 5:14–21). None need live as pawns of determinism, oppression, or strange spirits, for Jesus as "full of grace and truth" (John 1:14) brings exactly what is needed to truly be alive and in community.

The next step in reform and renewal is, as noted earlier, to choose anew to embrace the revealed standard. Envisioning this plane of living, the church, the people of God, recommits to becoming what it is called to be: a missional, worshiping community, "salt and light" in the world. The Nicene Creed declared this identity and aspiration in "Four Notes" of the church: one, holy, catholic, and apostolic. In the 16th century, the Protestant tradition emerged, one expression of the church-wide call to continuing reform "in head and members"—*sui et ecclesia semper reformanda*. In the 19th century, Joseph Milner's multivolume *History of the Church of Christ* (1794–1809) presented an evangelical view of the church's past as a history of renewal and reform. In the 1960s, Kenneth Cober's hymn began: "Renew Thy church, her ministries restore: both to serve and adore."

Whether as impulse, orientation, or program, reform and renewal are vital dynamics within the larger narrative of progressive development or spiritual maturation in Christian life. In contrast, for example, with mystical visions, management by spiritual objective and more existentialist or pragmatic voices, "R&R" advocates manifest an "ancient-future" approach, a usable past informing a hopeful prospect, *ad fontes et fidelitas*. As individuals and in community, they hear a prophetic call: you've rejected your first love, remember from where you've fallen, repent of this, and redo the earlier virtue—or the Lord will remove you. In peril, choose paradise (Rev. 2:4–7).

Pathways of Spiritual Reform and Renewal

Reform and renewal suggest the imagery of spiritual *pathways*. Moving upward from how things are to recapturing the divine intention of how they ought to be, God's Word offers a "lamp to my feet" and "light for my path" (Ps. 119:105). Believers ask, "Where have we been and come to, and what's our best next step?" They seek to trust in the Lord, acknowledge him in all things, and find direction into a straightened path (Prov. 3:5–6). Jesus Christ, in whom the image of God was perfectly fleshed out in human form, offers to all a luminous "example, that you should follow in his steps" (1 Peter 2:21). Metaphor may locate the returning disciple's feet on holy ground up-thrust by seismic spiritual movements, but more often it calls for what Eugene Peterson calls "a long obedience in the same direction." Those seeking reform and renewal in their world (per John Bunyan) are most often—via bracing step or breakthrough— *pilgrims seeking progress back home.*

Evident are nine spiritual pathways in which believers, in community, have pursued becoming what they are called to be, initiatives seeking to make spiritual life more authentic and vital; that is, reformed and renewed.

1. *The anointed leader.* This pathway involves realistic assessment of the moment, belief that God calls and sends leaders into challenging situations, attentiveness to those so called to lead, and discerning "followership." From Scripture, many have echoed the words of Mordecai to Esther: "Who knows but that you have come to royal position for such a time as this?" (Est. 4:14). In the tradition, Nathan saw this anointing in David, John the Baptist in Jesus, Eusebius in Constantine, thirteenth-century Italians in Francis of Assisi, sixteenth-century German peasants initially in Martin Luther, and twentieth-century American civil rights advocates in Martin Luther King Jr. The study of such lives reveals an imperfect but inspiring "cloud of witnesses" leading within their sphere of influence. As John Henry Newman declared in his *Parochial Sermons*, "Once it was the apostles' turn ... and down to this very time, when faith has well-nigh failed, first one and then another have been called out to exhibit before the Great King.... Now it is our turn" (Newman, 6:230–31).

2. The inspired meeting. This pathway identifies issues, believes in a Spirit-led process rediscovering God's way, identifies divergent parties positioned to make wise decisions, and convenes a gathering to pursue thoughtful, prayerful resolution. The New Testament spiritual ancestor of these meetings is the Jerusalem Council. The church, pulled by both "Judaizers" and "Gentilizers," called all back to essentials: heed the Word (Acts 15:19–21) and work (15:4–12) of God. Their rationale: "It seemed good to the Holy Spirit and to us" (15:28). This practice anticipates those at Nicea in 325, the Synod of Whitby, the Second Council of Nicea in 787, Lateran IV, the late medieval conciliar movement, the Westminster Assembly, the Edinburgh Conference of 1910, the initial World Council of Churches convocation, Vatican II's *aggiornamento*, and Lausanne Conferences in 1974 and following.

3. A prophetic asceticism. This pathway recognizes sin or complexities (e.g., money, sex, and power) that threaten fellowship with God. These may be overcome through pursuing simplicity, purity, and spiritual virtue in solitude and fellowship. The awareness of "sin in the camp" (Josh. 6:18; 7:10–11) as affront to God's holiness quickens this path of renunciation, as do Jesus' teachings that disciples "deny themselves and take up their cross and follow me" (Mark 8:34 TNIV) and his needs-based lifestyle (Matt. 10:9–10). In *The Idea of Reform*, Ladner suggests that the monastic way of life—focusing on the contemplation of God in and through his Son and the building of the divine kingdom and city (ideally the goals of all Christians)—from antiquity became the principal agent of reform in the Christian world. Other voices include Jeremy Taylor, Keswick conference attendees, and Quaker divines. In "purifying the church," some have not only sought to be rid of sin but also of sinners—thereby crossing the line from a healthy church discipline to the tragedy of religious persecution.

4. An institutional correction. This pathway affirms the importance of group structures and institutions and, seeing things improper or inefficient, seeks to work "within the system" to recover core values and reorganize for better stewardship of time, talent, and treasure as divine gifts. Many have been inspired by the Old Testament text in which the recovery of the Book of the Law in the house of the Lord under King Josiah (2 Kings 22–23) led to extensive public correction, complemented by prophetic ministry from Jeremiah. In this tradition, Jesus ministered in the synagogues, John Chrysostom preached and purged abusive clergy under his care, Gregory VII sought "top down" church reforms, as did the late medieval curialists, and several stayed in their "home churches" to bring renewal—Luther the Catholic, John Wesley the Anglican, Richard Allen the Methodist-Episcopalian—until stirred like the nineteenth-century Restorationists to begin movements becoming denominations, requiring their own correction.

5. The enlightened mind(s). This pathway views intellect and rationality—the life of the mind—as God's greatest gifted faculty, foundational to corrected/corrective steps. "As [a man] thinketh in his heart, so is he" (Prov. 23:7 KJV). Jesus called us to love God with our "mind" (Mark 12:29–30). When Paul's "be transformed by the renewing of your mind" (Rom. 12:2) was, as Brad Gregory notes, preached by Catholic humanist John Colet in 1510, he "ripped into his clerical colleagues" for their pursuit of honors, pleasures, and earthly entanglements as betraying true church teachings (Gregory, 589). University learning was meant to refine one for service. Envisioning unity through like-mindedness, Erasmus patiently remained Catholic, publishing his Greek New Testament edition in 1516 while envisioning vernacular translations, the increase of literacy, and all people reading God's Word for themselves. Visual arts may inspire the mind: Alexander Nagel's studies of Michelangelo note that artistic restorations and archaizing style often evidence a preoccupation with reform, and Henri Nouwen's reflections on Rembrandt's "Prodigal Son" reveal a theology of roles and return. Though at times individualistic (as in William of Occam), many, such as C. S. Lewis, have informed the church and ecumenical Christian unity through their insights.

6. *Doing justice.* This pathway holds that each human being, made in the image of God, has an inherent dignity that requires he or she be treated justly in personal relationships and social systems. Across cultures—given the inclination to measure human value by appearance, possessions, and status—living out this conviction has often meant a countercultural commitment to reform. God alone judges perfectly. The Old Testament prophets proclaim this: "Let justice roll on like a river, righteousness like a never-failing stream" (Amos 5:24), for "What does the LORD require of you? To act justly and to love mercy and to walk humbly with your God" (Mic. 6:8). Jesus declares the blessedness of those who are poor, hungry, mournful, and despised (Luke 6:20–22) finding companionship with those loving and generous to "the least of these" (Matt. 25:40). Reformation may involve reparation. Social reformers in the church have included Constantine's mother Helena, those who have endowed and enhanced service in hospitals, Vincent de Paul, William Wilberforce, Sojourner Truth, William and Catherine Booth, Dorothy Day, Martin Luther King Jr., Mother Teresa, Jean Vanier, and Bono.

7. *Seasons of revival.* This pathway anticipates that central to God's kingdom coming on earth are visible spiritual movements, within which notable numbers of people hear the Word, experience personal repentance and conversion, and show lasting fruits of new life in Christ. Peter's preaching to "brothers and sisters" called them to remember the prophets, recognize the Messiah, repent of their sin, and be redeemed as a blessing to all peoples (Acts 3:11–4:4). With five thousand believing, this "season of refreshing from the Lord" suggests other moments. William McLoughlin has utilized this dimension of reform to structure his history of evangelicalism in America. J. Edwin Orr (com-

poser of "Search Me, O God") was a keen student. Whatever the details—surprising like the Great Awakening (Jonathan Edwards, 1740s) or anticipated due to prayerful preparations (Charles Finney, 1820s), emphasizing the Holy Spirit (Wales, 1904–1905) and sign gifts (Azusa Street, 1906) or expressing a counterpoint-completion to other religious traditions (East Africa, 1930s); evidencing more "first-time" decisions or "rededications" to deeper life—God's gracious, refreshing "showers of blessing" outpoured result in changed lives, lifestyles, and cultures.

8. *Spiritual warfare.* This pathway carries the conviction that this world has become deformed and deranged by strange spirits and can only be reformed and redeemed by spiritual encounters confronting these powers. Scripturally, the believer is to take up the "armor of God" as sure defense, and the "sword of the Spirit, which is the word of God" as weapon, "for our struggle is not against flesh and blood, but against the rulers, against the authorities, against the powers of this dark world and against the spiritual forces of evil in the heavenly realms" (Eph. 6:10–20). As Charles Kraft has observed, there may be three types of encounter (whatever the starting point) in which sin, Satan, and false self are confronted: the foundational truth encounter, the relational allegiance encounter, and the potential power/signs encounter. By God's grace, people are set free as his people oppose the lie, the crowd, and the show. Recently, figures like Neil Anderson and John Wimber have led in these areas, as worldwide notably Pentecostals and charismatics proclaim the Lord's deliverance (Luke 11:20) as well.

9. *Mystical union.* This pathway embraces what has often been called the threefold-path of personal Christian renewal: purgation, illumination, and finally union. As LeRon Shults has noted, these are not linear steps but interrelated moments within an ongoing process of intensification. Created in the image of God, and by regeneration a "partaker of the divine nature" (2 Peter 1:4 KJV), this one

with unveiled face contemplating the Lord's glory is being transformed into his image with ever-increasing glory from the Lord, the Spirit (2 Cor. 3:18). Though not typically called a mystic, Irenaeus of Lyons provided the theological path: it is fitting that humanity be created, receive growth, be strengthened, abound, then recover [from the disease of sin], and having recovered should be glorified, and being glorified should see his Lord. In his theory of recapitulation, "Christ became as we are that we may become as he is." Those in this tradition include Pseudo-Dionysius, Symeon the New Theologian, and John of the Cross—and disciples for whom retreat may be a necessary step toward reform. By grace, the dangers of this mystical approach can be overcome: e.g., individualism (by Catherine of Siena) and anti-intellectualism (by John Wesley). Each contributed to Christian reform and renewal in his or her day and continues to inspire others.

Non-Christian Concepts

Early Christian thought and life were embedded in a Greco-Roman culture with alternative concepts of renewal—several of which have variants today. Drawing upon Ladner's detailed discussions, these may be briefly summarized. *Cosmological* views focus on repetitive cycles and recurrent themes (e.g., the earth turning and the seasons), which lack an appreciation of the gift of human freedom to intervene meaningfully. *Vitalistic* views emphasize physical renewal (e.g., plant and animal life), and employ the language of personal "revival" and "renaissance," but fall short spiritually apart

from Christ's redemptive action and one's intentional pursuit of his person and ways. *Messianic/millenarian* renewal uplifts an ideal plane of perfection and progress but admits counterfeits and absolutist agendas if not exalting Christ's kingdom. A *distinctly Christian view* is cognizant of the others but singularly identified with the realities of God's grace in the conversion, baptism, repentance, and restoration of the believer. For the individual and Christian community, the reconstitution of divine life necessitates reform to the image and likeness of God (Gen. 1:26–27).

Authentic reform and renewal call for contemplation and action, *theoria* and *praxis*, affirmation and negation in both the individual and community. John O'Malley, in exploring Western civilization, has identified "prophecy and reform" together as one of four major cultures, expressing contempt for worldliness by pursuing corrective action in the world. Once again, the Lord's apocalyptic words to the seven churches (popular in "reform to the better" preaching) include a prophetic call: "You have forsaken the love you had at first. Consider how far you have fallen! Repent and do the things you did at first. If you do not repent, I will come to you and remove your lampstand from its place.... Whoever has ears, let them hear what the Spirit says to the churches. To those who are victorious, I will give the right to eat from the tree of life, which is in the paradise of God" (Rev. 2:4–7 TNIV). In this remembrance, repentance, and renewal, human efforts can only cooperate with the character and all-sufficient grace of God. In this there is, with each summons to faithfulness, a lively hope—fully realized only in new heavens and earth.

Sources Cited

Gregory, B. "Christian Reform and Its Discontents." In *The Renaissance World*, ed. J. J. Martin (2007), 589–604.

Kraft, C. "Three Encounters in Christian Witness." In *Perspectives on the World Christian Movement*, ed. R. Winter, S. Hawthorne, et al. (2009), 408–14.

Ladner, G. *The Idea of Reform* (1959).

McLoughlin, W. *Revivals, Awakenings and Reform* (1978).

Newman, J. H. "Warfare the Condition of Victory." In *Parochial and Plain Sermons*. 8 vols. (1907).

O'Malley, J. *Four Cultures of the West* (2004).

Peterson, E. *A Long Obedience in the Same Direction* (1980).

Shults, L., and S. Sandage. *Transforming Spirituality* (2006).

For Further Reading

Bellitto, C. *Renewing Christianity: A History of Church Reform from Day One to Vatican II* (2001).

Foster, R. *Streams of Living Water* (1998).

Lovelace, R. "The Sanctification Gap." *Theology Today* 29, no. 4 (1973): 363–69.

McNally, R. *The Unreformed Church* (1965).

Melloni, A. "Christianisme et reforme." In *Reformes: Comprendre et comparer les religions*, ed. P. C. Bori et al. (2007), 37–63.

Nouwen, H. *The Return of the Prodigal Son* (1992).

Nagel, A. *Michelangelo and the Reform of Art* (2000).

O'Malley, J. *What Happened at Vatican II* (2008).

Ozment, S. *The Age of Reform, 1250–1550* (1980).

Strauss, G. "Ideas of *Reformatio* and *Renovatio* from the Middle Ages to the Reformation." In *Handbook of European History 1400–1600*, ed. T. Brady (1995), 1–30.

Stump, P. "The Influence of Gerhard Ladner's *The Idea of Reform*." In *Reform and Renewal in the Middle Ages and the Renaissance*, ed. T. Izbicki (2000), 3–17.

Trinkaus, C. *In Our Image and Likeness: Humanity and Divinity in Italian Humanist Thought* (1970).

Van Engen, J. *Sisters and Brothers of the Common Life* (2008).

Williams, G. H. *Wilderness and Paradise in Christian Thought* (1962).

CHAPTER 22

LITURGICAL SPIRITUALITY

JOHN D. WITVLIET AND CARRIE STEENWYK

Corporate worship gatherings are an indispensable dimension of a faithful Christian way of life. Whether conducted in grand cathedrals or prison camps, in public or in secret, in vast congregations or in small assemblies, these gatherings enact relationships that are fundamental to Christian life, both within the community of believers and between the community and the triune God.

While nearly every Christian community practices corporate worship in some form, liturgical spirituality refers to an approach that particularly emphasizes the nourishing value of corporate worship, is intentional about cultivating well-grounded worship practices that express the faith of the church throughout time and space, and invites worshipers to explicitly link these practices with a grateful, obedient, Christ-centered, Holy Spirit—led way of life.

Liturgical spirituality is grounded in the conviction that these corporate actions are occasions for not only human, but also divine activity, where the triune God speaks to the assembly through the reading, preaching, singing, and contemplating of the Word of God; feeds the assembly through the Lord's Supper; and is further active not only in receiving, but also in prompting and perfecting the prayers and responses of the assembly, a Trinitarian vision of divine activity that invites worshipers to think of themselves as caught up in the ongoing action and relationships of divine persons. In this view, corporate worship practices simultaneously enact the relationship that Christians have with God and each other, renew and transform believers by shaping how believers imagine God and the world, and serve as a means through which God calls believers to new discipleship. This means that a liturgical spirituality is fundamentally grounded in acts of waiting, receiving, and celebrating the sovereign grace and actions of the triune God, and thus is not an achievement but a gift. Liturgy is, etymologically and experientially, the "work of the people," but in a Trinitarian context this can only mean the congregation's grateful and obedient participation in the redemptive acts of proclamation, prayer, and celebration that God makes possible, and indeed perfects through the ongoing priestly work of Jesus Christ.

Liturgical spirituality is also grounded in the conviction that corporate worship must not be viewed merely as an expressive act (reflecting only the prior experience of the community), but also as a formative one (generating new and deeper experiences of God's grace, judgment, promises, and calling for the community over time). Grounded in biblical patterns and in the wisdom of the church of all ages, corporate worship, by the power of the Holy Spirit, stretches a community's capacity both to receive God's grace and to speak to God in ever deeper and more transparent expressions of praise, lament, confession, and testimony — whether offered with words or in silence, with music or artworks, with movement or in stillness. This formative view of worship is implied in the detailed instructions for tabernacle and temple worship in the Old Testament and in Jesus' introduction to the Lord's Prayer ("pray in this way," or, in other words, "apprentice yourself to this text"). In the history of the church, formative accounts of worship extend from early church references to the Psalms as the "gymnasium of the soul" (Ambrose) to the famous testimony of Dietrich Bonhoeffer that "all singing together that is right must serve to widen our spiritual horizon, make us see our little company as a member of the great Christian Church on earth, and help us willingly and gladly to join our singing, be it feeble or good, to the song of the Church" (61). Such a vision depicts worship as a kind of pedagogy of desire, shaping the central orienting loves that guide human thought and action. This explains how Alexander Schmemann, echoing the testimony of the psalmist, could describe corporate worship as "a vantage point from which we can see more deeply into the reality of the world" (27, cf. Ps. 73:17). These observations mean that participation in worship is not only an occasion to express sentiments to God, but also to be formed or sculpted by God as if by a master potter.

Central Practices of Christian Corporate Worship

While particular expressions of Christian liturgical spirituality vary widely among Orthodox, Catholic, and Protestant traditions across centuries and continents, nearly all the vigorous expressions embrace the following common practices.

One central practice is that of blessing, thanking, and adoring the triune God. While all Christian communities express such praise, those known for a liturgical spirituality are particularly intentional about offering praise for the entire sweep of God's actions in history and for the entire range of divine excellencies revealed in Scripture, thus "condensing into prayer the entire body of religious truth" (Guardini, 24). This intentionality is often aided by the disciplined recitation of the biblical Psalter and use of classic canticles of praise, such

as the *Te Deum Laudamus* ("We praise you, O God"), *Gloria in excelsis Deo* ("Glory to God in the Highest"), and the *Sanctus* ("Holy, Holy, Holy"). Such full-orbed praise decenters the human person, resists the idolatry of self and society, and forms a receptive community of believers. As Dallas Willard explains, "Worship is the single most powerful force in completing and sustaining restoration of our whole beings to God. Nothing can inform, guide and sustain pervasive and radiant goodness in a person other than the true vision of God and the worship that spontaneously arises from it" (Willard, 128).

Such praise and thanks is often practiced through remembering and rehearsing God's action in history. Astute readers of the Bible notice that many biblical sermons and prayers are essentially mini history lessons, recounting the history of God's covenant faithfulness (e.g., Josh. 24; Ps. 136; and Acts 2). By echoing this narrative pattern, worshiping communities contemplate the meaning of these historical events, appropriate these events as identity-shaping experience, and encourage a hope for the future based on God's faithfulness in the past. This narrative pattern is found in prayers of thanksgiving at baptisms, in biblical psalms, and in ancient creeds that name key historical acts of God, and is particularly prominent in the "Great Prayer of Thanksgiving" of historic Lord's Supper liturgies. Prominent works in liturgical spirituality—including those of Orthodox Alexander Schmemann, Catholic Romano Guardini, and Protestants Robert Webber and James White—nearly all call for deeper understanding and engagement with these acts of corporate memorializing.

A second central practice is that of beseeching, lamenting, interceding, and confessing to God. Whether spoken or sung, these prayers express dependence on God and longing for the fullness of God's reign. While all Christian communities practice prayer, those known for liturgical spirituality are particularly concerned to ensure that the entire range of human experience is expressed in worship, often through the disciplined use of the Psalms, through expansive intercessory prayers, and through classic canticles, such as *Kyrie eleison* (Lord, have mercy), and *Agnus Dei* (Lamb of God).

An especially important type of intercession asks God to be active, not only in receiving, but also in prompting and perfecting worship. Such prayers, known as epicletic prayers, acknowledge that worshipers cannot create or engineer God's presence and work, but rather celebrate God's presence and work in the liturgical assembly as a gift. Examples of this type of prayer include prayers for God's active presence, which often begin public worship (e.g., "open [our] lips, and [our] mouths will declare your praise" (Ps. 51:15), prayers for illumination prayed before the reading and preaching of Scripture, and prayers for the Holy Spirit's work in and through the celebration of baptism and the Lord's Supper. Liturgical spirituality is intentional about making this historic practice a daily discipline, a fitting dimension of devotional prayer and Scripture study.

Third, corporate Christian worship is a natural home for the reading and preaching of God's Word. While these are central actions in many Christian communities, those that cultivate an intentional liturgical spirituality are particularly concerned about ensuring that the community hears a balanced diet of scriptural readings over time, that portions of the Bible are read in illuminating juxtaposition with each other, and that worshipers have the opportunity to correlate their own private devotional reading of Scripture with that of public worship. These goals are often met through the use of a set lectionary of assigned readings for each Sunday and weekday, whether the approved lectionaries of various denominational bodies or the ecumenical Revised Common Lectionary. Liturgical preaching is also concerned with ensuring that the Bible texts read in worship are not merely explored in terms of their implications for private and family life, but also are appropriated in terms of their cosmic and communal significance as the grand narrative of the drama of divine redemption. Liturgical spirituality also recognizes the important place of Scripture in many liturgical elements, including calls to praise and repentance and words of assurance and blessing.

Fourth, corporate worship in all Christian traditions includes the celebrations of baptism and the Lord's Supper. Many traditions also practice other ritual actions described in Scripture, including anointing with oil and foot washing. While the categories and language for interpreting these actions varies widely, each Christian tradition calls attention to the fact that these are embodied actions involving ordinary material objects (water, wine, bread, and oil), which simultaneously enact a constellation of meanings by means of physical actions. A liturgical spirituality invites worshipers to revel in these multivalent actions and to recognize, for example, how the Lord's Supper is at once a meal of spiritual nourishment, Christian unity, remembrance, a proclamation of the gospel to the world, and an anticipation of the feast of the coming kingdom. A liturgical spirituality is also intentional about the movement, gestures, and postures that most fittingly shape participation in these actions, and about how these actions form worshipers for new patterns of hospitality and faithfulness in the Christian life.

A fifth common dynamic in classic Christian worship involves the ordering and shaping of each of these elements in ways that call attention to the nature of God and God's redeeming work. The Psalms suggest that worship is not an act of obeisance to placate a deity, but rather is a holy conversation between covenant partners. Psalmic poetry offers scripts for a personal covenantal encounter, including both God-humanward actions of promise and warning and human-Godward expressions of adoration, intercession, dedication, confession, and lament. Similarly, nearly every classic Christian liturgy involves the intentional interplay between Scripture texts and congregational response so that, for example, a divine invitation to worship elicits congregational praise, a call to repentance leads to the confession of sin, an assurance of pardon evokes a response of thanksgiving, and the preaching of God's Word leads to the congregations' testimony of faith. A liturgical spirituality fosters awareness of this relational pattern and seeks to replicate it in personal devotional actions. In the context of the bustle of contemporary culture, liturgical spirituality is also particularly attentive to meaningful periods of silence that contribute to this relational exchange, call worshipers to "find rest ... in God alone" (see Ps. 62), recalibrate each worshiper's perspective toward his or her relationship with God, and deepen the interior life.

Because all of these relational actions are accomplished or enacted through the senses — through speaking and listening, seeing, gesturing, singing, tasting, smelling — each of them is essentially an artistic act and can be deepened by intentional artistic craft, whether determined ahead of time (such as a well-rehearsed song of praise or a well-crafted communion vessel) or extemporaneous (like an improvised sermon or song). Thus, an act of confession can be deepened by means of a poignant song; an act of testimony can be sharpened by the use of ancient words; an act of proclamation can be strengthened by a stained-glass window or by a child's drawing of a biblical narrative. A liturgical spirituality is intentional about deepening these artistic expressions, learning their unique languages and capacities, and sensing how these artistic expressions can be echoed outside of formal worship services, so that corporate worship can function as the "soundtrack by which believers live their entire life before God" (Long, 47). A liturgical spirituality is attentive to how these artistic expressions serve the function of worship, directing the attention of worshipers, not to the artistic expressions in and of themselves, but rather through them — iconically — to the cruciform glory and beauty of God.

Sixth, individual worship services are also caught up in larger patterns that extend over time.

Christian corporate worship has long featured the rhythmic marking of time, observing how daily, weekly, and yearly patterns can rehearse the gospel of Jesus, drawing on and transforming the Old Testament patterns of daily prayer, Sabbath observance, and annual festivals. The Christian calendar has, for example, been described as "time to inhabit the story of God" (Gross, i), not merely serving as an invitation to observe a few holidays that ornament a way of life more fundamentally shaped by the calendars of schools, athletics, and cultural observances, but rather as an invitation to orient every aspect of life to the narrative of God's work accomplished in Jesus. When fully celebrated in this immersive way, the events of the Christian year promise, in the memorable words of N. T. Wright,

> to function as a sequence of well-aimed hammerblows which knock at the clay jars of the gods we want, the gods who reinforce our own pride and prejudice, until they fall away and reveal instead a very different god, a dangerous god, and subversive god, a god who comes to us like a blind beggar with wounds in his hands, a god who comes to us in wind and fire, in bread and wine, in flesh and blood: a god who says to us, "You did not choose me; I chose you." (Wright, 24)

A liturgical spirituality is intentional about explaining how the disciplines of daily prayer, weekly worship, and the Christian calendar protect the community from the whims of a given leader, free leaders and worshipers from the notion that worship depends on their own fickle emotional states, and enable rather than restrict authentic spontaneity.

For each of these practices to be genuinely "liturgical," they must be fundamentally communal and not merely in the sense of reflecting the experiences and patterns of a local congregation. As Romano Guardini noted, simply, "The liturgy does not say 'I,' but 'We'" (Guardini, 36), and the "we" refers to the vast communion of saints across time and place. This corporate vision of piety matches the unmistakably corporate language that the Bible uses to describe the church as the people of God, the body of Christ, and the temple of the Spirit. This communal vision is further enhanced by the use of time-tested liturgies and creeds, songs from various cultures and historical periods, and processes for worship preparation that do not rely on the whims or preferences of a given leader. At their best, these practices offer worshipers a sense of being immersed in a rich, flowing, multigenerational, cross-cultural communion of saints that provides balance and poise for a long journey through a culture of sound bites. And this communion of the saints is, in turn, bound up in the praise of God offered by the entire creation, including all creatures on and under the earth (Rev. 5), the trees of the field, the ocean, the sky, and all that is in them (Ps. 104). This means, experientially, that worshipers are invited to rehearse and celebrate this grand drama of redemption with an all-encompassing engagement, the kind of engagement that signals that God's story of redemption in Jesus Christ is the source of Christian identity and hope.

This broad vision also reorients every specific action of worship, including those that have sometimes been radically individualized. For example, the commands in 1 Corinthians 11 concerning table participation ("doing this in remembrance of Jesus," "proclaiming the Lord's death," "examining ourselves," "discerning the body," and "waiting for one another") not only call for personal introspection (a typical evangelical concern), but also call for intentional hospitality, serving at once as a call to renewed personal piety and to corporate acts of justice that refuse any distinctions in the Christian community between the wealthy and the poor.

Liturgical Spirituality Crosses Christian Traditions

Throughout history, there have been noteworthy streams of liturgical spirituality within all the great Christian traditions, Catholic, Orthodox, and Protestant. To be sure, liturgical practices among these traditions vary widely from culture to culture and century to century, shaped through the complex interplay of practices, theological convictions, and cultural patterns. There are many particular communities known for their own robust form of liturgical spirituality, including Roman Catholic monastic communities (the Benedictines, Cistercians, and many others), Orthodox renewal movements (represented by the ecumenical councils and noteworthy writers such as Symeon the New Theologian), and twentieth-century ecumenical communities of renewal (the Taizé and Iona communities). Further, the history of nearly every Protestant tradition—Anglican, Lutheran, Anabaptist, Reformed, Methodist, Pentecostal, and more—includes examples of communities that practiced worship with thoughtfulness, disciplined creativity, and integrity, and thereby leaving for subsequent generations such gifts as the prayers of Thomas Cranmer, the music of J. S. Bach, the sermons of John Donne, the church buildings of Christopher Wren, the psalms and hymns of Isaac Watts and Charles Wesley, and thousands of other liturgical resources. These resources demonstrate that there is potential for enhanced spirituality and spiritual formation in all the Christian traditions, with unique opportunities for deeper understanding and renewal made possible through the vast amount of historical information available and the opportunities for cross-cultural encounter available to believers in the Internet age.

Evangelicalism is arguably one of the traditions least associated with the term *liturgical spirituality*, in part because of the traditional evangelical concern to resist anything that implies or suggests formalism or ritualism. However, although the term *liturgy* is often associated with formal orders of worship or the use of set prayers, it can also be used to refer to the practices, patterns, and shared expectations that inevitably shape communal worship in any congregation. In this sense, every

Christian community—including "free church" and "low church" traditions and all those who resist the term *liturgy*—nevertheless inevitably develops some form of recurring practices (a liturgy), which in turn shape particular expressions of piety (a liturgical spirituality). Further, every community develops an implicit awareness of the function and relative significance of corporate worship in the Christian life, as well as characteristic dispositions, symbols, and expressions that form Christian experience and shape Christian life in the world. The primary question for all communities, then, is not whether to have a liturgical spirituality, but rather how adequate that spirituality is or could be—how attuned it is to the fullness of the gospel and how adequate is it for forming full-orbed Christian disciples.

Strengthening Liturgical Spirituality

This question invites every Christian community to strengthen and deepen its own implicit liturgical spirituality. One place to start is by articulating the implicit wisdom of existing corporate worship practices and comparing them to practices found in various Christian traditions. While understanding the historical background and theological rationale for the elements of worship is not necessary for engaging in worship, it is immensely generative and constructive, inviting worshipers to deeper levels of engagement.

Second, liturgical spirituality is strengthened by approaching worship as a spiritual discipline, an ordered set of practices (including extemporaneous ones) to which the community commits, and which it practices regardless of the whims of the moment. Such disciplines "protect certain essential aspects of reality from being reduced to the dimensions of my interest or intelligence or awareness" (Peterson, 205), and free worshipers from the kind of endless innovation that can leave a worshiping community reeling with uncertainty.

Third, liturgical spirituality is strengthened when a community understands the value of genuinely corporate action. Corporate worship inevitably entails that not every text or prayer matches the mood or experience of each worshiper in the moment. Participating in corporate worship is inherently decentering, an act of subordinating individual preferences or experiences to corporate expressions, of apprenticing oneself to expressions led by someone else. It is realizing that worship is not about individual desires but "is the primary means by which we immerse ourselves in the rhythms and stories of God's work" (Peterson, 112). At the same time, this submission ought to be paired with active accountability in Christian communities to resist coercive or manipulative exercise of authority and imposition of liturgical expressions that are misleading, overstated, or heretical.

Fourth, liturgical spirituality is strengthened when worshipers are helped to perceive the relationship between embodied experience and divine action. On the one hand, worshipers are perennially tempted to attend to the sights, sounds, and gestures of worship more than to God, limiting their awareness of the material actions of worship. This concern leads renewalists to insist that worshipers be invited to perceive God's actions in and through it all, following the example of John Wesley, who summoned worshipers to "have an eye to God in every word you sing." On the other hand, worshipers can also be tempted to minimize the inherently sensory and bodily acts of worship, yearning for a spiritualized or unmediated glimpse of divine glory. This concern, which replicates the gnosticism rampant in the early church, leads renewalists to insist that worship is an inherently bodily, multisensory experience, which is immeasurably enriched by deep attention to other worshipers, to the sounds of speech and music, to the sight of symbols and artwork, to the gestures and postures offered, and to the taste and fragrance of bread and cup.

Fifth, liturgical spirituality is strengthened by recognition that worship is simultaneously transcultural and contextual, cross-cultural, and countercultural. This vision of worship as "in but not of" the world (cf. John 17:14 – 19; 1 Peter 2:11 – 12), is grounded in the person and ministry of Jesus, who came to all cultures, was incarnate in one specific context, and came both to resist aspects of culture that did not comport with the kingdom of God and to reach out to express hospitality to those in other cultural contexts (Lutheran World Federation). This vision calls into question any approach that emphasizes the "relevance" of worship at the expense of biblical faithfulness, or the "timeless" quality of right worship apart from any specific local context.

Finally, liturgical spirituality is strengthened by full, conscious, and active participation in the community's liturgy, expressing love for God with heart, soul, mind, and strength (Mark 12:30), protesting both intellectualism and anti-intellectualism, both cultural activism and cultural retreat. A faithful Christian liturgical spirituality shapes both contemplation and active service; it expresses and forms the community for both fellowship (*koinonia*) and service (*diaconia*); it not only forms a community to participate in God's mission in the world, but also serves as a part of that mission. It is, in sum, a spirituality that promises to be at once corporate, formative, holistic, in-but-not-of-the-world, missional, sanctifying, and eschatological — a spirituality that stretches to be as expansive as the gospel itself.

Sources Cited

Bonhoeffer, D. *Life Together* (1954).

Gross, B. *Living the Christian Year* (2009).

Guardini, R. *The Spirit of the Liturgy* (1998).

Long, T. *Testimony* (2004).

Lutheran World Federation. *Nairobi Statement on Worship and Culture* (1996).

Peterson, E. *Christ Plays in Ten Thousand Places* (2005).

Schmemann, A. *For the Life of the World* (1973).

Wesley, J. "Instructions for Singing," in *Select Hymns* (1761).

Willard, D. *The Great Omission* (2006).

Wright, N. T. *For All God's Worth* (1997).

For Further Reading

Boers, A. *The Rhythm of God's Grace* (2003).

Chan, S. *Liturgical Theology* (2006).

Ellis, C. *Gathering: A Theology and Spirituality of Worship in the Free Church Tradition* (2004).

Guardini, R. *The Art of Praying* (1994).

Pfatteicher, P. *Liturgical Spirituality* (1997).

Saliers, D. *Worship and Spirituality* (1984).

Smith, J. *Desiring the Kingdom* (2009).

Webber, R. *The Divine Embrace* (2006).

CHAPTER 23

PRAYER

CHARLES W. NIENKIRCHEN

The impulse to pray is universal. It is not dependent on religious affiliation. The irrepressible yearning for "the beyond" that resides in every soul certifies that all human beings are bearers of the *imago Dei*. Definitions of prayer accumulated over centuries of Christian tradition are both prescriptive and descriptive. They are multitudinous in number and myriad in their metaphorical nuances. From antiquity to the present, Christian writers have composed a cacophonous and arrhythmic chorus of comment in response to the timeless question What is prayer? The ever elusive, conclusive answer, which perhaps unlocks the door to the essence of what it means to be a finite and fragile human being in relationship with a transcendent and omnipotent deity, has been deemed by many devout practitioners to be worth the search.

The voices of a caravan of prayer pilgrims stretching interminably through time and traversing an array of ecclesiastical landscapes often sharply differentiated by conflicting, theological contours, testify eloquently to the richly textured nature of what is ostensibly designated "Christian prayer." They speak luminously of prayer as a "dialogue with God" (Clement of Alexandria), a "continual intercourse of the spirit with God" (Evagrius of Pontus), "raising of the mind and heart to God" (Augustine of Hippo), an "altar to God in your mind" (John Chrysostom), "formal words or expressions" (Martin Luther), a "special friendship" (Teresa of Avila), "always believing" (E. M. Bounds), a "deepening of the soul's unseen attachments" (Evelyn Underhill), "the real I who speaks" (C. S. Lewis), "the highest form of communication" (Ellul), an "attentiveness to God's Spirit" (Wendy Wright), an "inner Sabbath" (Marjorie Thompson), a "way of living in awareness of the Presence" (Richard Rohr), a "currency of a relationship" (Philip Yancey), a "daring venture into speech" (Eugene Peterson), a "remedy for world-weariness" (Emilie Griffin), "an exploration of all our faculties as channels towards God" (Margaret Hebblethwaite), a "homesickness for God" (James Houston), and a "human readiness to hear" (Simon Chan).

In their totality, the diverse definitions of prayer served up by devoted Christian pray-ers of all centuries envision a dynamic, transformative, dialogical relationship between humans and the triune God, one to which humans are graciously invited by God. The conversation at the heart of the relationship is quintessentially modeled in the earthly life of Jesus Christ as described in sacred Scripture. It engages the lips, mind, and heart and is not governed necessarily by any prescribed forms or rituals. In fact, it embraces the breadth of life's circumstances, penetrates the depths of the human soul, and evokes an uncensored expression of human pains, passions, and perplexities. Divine responses can come from time to time by mysterious and unpredictable visitations. Prayer is empowered by the Holy Spirit and emboldened by the confidence that whatever the unfathomable, metaphysical abyss between God and humanity, one can be certain of the divine intention to draw near and communicate with humans who take the risk of entering such a dialogue. The ultimate purpose of a life of prayer, energized and renewed continually by both inflamed and quiescent psychological rhythms, is the hallowing of life and the cultivation of holiness—a transfiguration of the pray-er's desires, motives, and behaviors in accordance with the perfection of the divine character and will incarnated in Jesus Christ.

Current writers often complicate further the task of defining prayer by reducing it to a matter of personal preference. As a result, in the marketplace, prayer has become many things to many people—a descent into the subconscious, an opening up to paranormal voices from the beyond, a reflection of one's unique temperament, an expression of the deepest longings of the soul, a journey in personal transformation, a conduit for the release of repressed emotions, a tool for vocational discernment, and a source of spiritual and physical healing—to identify but a few of the motifs that dominate popular prayer literature. Such prayer themes, once regarded as theologically suspect, are making inroads among evangelicals.

In the evangelical world, both the theology of prayer and prayer practices are presently in transition. Growing numbers of "convergent" evangelicals exiting from the fractured world of denominational sectarianism have aligned themselves with liturgically structured Anglican, Catholic, and Orthodox churches that claim a continuous link with Christian antiquity. For them, having reconnected with ancient prayer forms has expanded their prayer experience beyond the confines of words and rationality. Rather, in its most visceral form, it is about movements of the heart, often in silence, using intentional postures, meditation techniques, sacramental symbols, and icons as external aids to prompt such interior movements.

The yearning of these pilgrims to find a direct connection with the transcendent, spiritual world predisposes them to be enthusiastic practitioners of novel prayer practices once alien to them. It is now popular for them to spend time in a retreat center or monastery to receive spiritual direction for one's inner life, walk the stations of the cross as part of observing the Christian calendar, say the daily office, sing the Psalms, and cultivate an inner capacity for sustained silence in which to listen to God. New prayer forms offer refreshment for a parched soul denuded of vitality by a previous lifestyle of prayerless activism in which faith was more a system of belief than a way of life.

The theological and historical implications of this burgeoning convergence movement for redefining the evangelical prayer experience warrant careful attention. It is now in vogue for convergent evangelicals who have both left their churches and remained within to engage in multilateral dialogue with multiple prayer traditions. They are apparently at ease with a cross-pollinated prayer conversation in which ancient church fathers from the Roman Catholic West and the Orthodox/non-Chalcedonian East (such as Greeks, Syrians, Copts, Ethiopians, and Armenians), desert fathers and mothers, Celtic solitaries, medieval Latin monks and mystics, Protestant and Catholic Reformers, Puritans, Quakers, Quietists, evangelical Protestant revivalists, Pentecostals and charismatics, Messianic Jews, and perhaps even "insider," Christ-following Muslims are accepted as bona fide participants. In this dialogical context, prayer elicits the strongest of evangelical, ecumenical intentions.

A biblically based, evangelical perspective on prayer is necessarily Christocentric. The prayer-saturated lifestyle of Jesus Christ, the Spirit-filled God-man, as described in Scripture, is exemplary in every respect to Christians in all traditions. The Lord's Prayer (Matt. 6:9–13; Luke 11:2–4), which Jesus taught to his followers was the verbal encapsulation of his lifestyle, empowered by a relentless passion to live in union with his invisible Father (John 5:30). It was never intended to be a formulaic and trivialized recitation for the ages, though early Christians did pray it three times a day.

Jewish-Christian scholarship has shown the evident parallelism between it and preexisting Jewish prayers.

There was nothing about God being at arm's length in Jesus' prayer experience. The Father of Jesus was "other" but not remote. The Gospels portray Jesus' relationship with his Father as exuding a startling kind of dialogue characterized by intimacy, candor, respect, trust, and affection, which must have scandalized those who watched. Prayer served as the daily sanctuary of his life in which he found rest, consolation, direction, and rejuvenation in the fulfillment of his messianic mission. There was no "wimpiness" in his collaboration with the divine will, progressively revealed throughout his lifetime. As the wellspring of his earthly pilgrimage, prayer was the key to the temporal unfolding of his eternally predetermined role in the redemption of humanity. It served as the source of daily wisdom for his interaction with an assortment of individuals, the origin of discernment that guided his responses to the mundane and the unseen and the source of the authoritative faith with which he engaged the hostile forces of nature. It was also the lifeline of his spiritual energy, the agent for the synergetic release of the charismatic power of the Holy Spirit in his life. He attributed the ministerial impotence of his disciples to their lack of prayer and chided them for it (Mark 9:28–29). The post-Pentecost church of Acts followed in his footsteps in their devotion to prayer (Acts 2:42), even normalizing ecstatic, glossalalic prayer speech, an effusion of otherworldliness at the moment of a convert's initial reception of the Spirit, which continued in private prayer and public worship (Acts 10:46–47; 19:5–7; 1 Cor. 14). Through a constant regimen of prayer in the Spirit, early believers were drawn into an organic union with the resurrected Christ, hence the apostle Paul's designation of the church as the "body of Christ" (1 Cor. 12:27) in which the divine presence was supernaturally manifested.

The mysterious fusion of divinity and humanity in Jesus did not compromise the authenticity of his prayer experience. Jesus' prayer journey, the subtext of his life, transported him through a kaleidoscope of complex life circumstances framed by the full spectrum of human emotions. The pain that issued from his vocational fidelity and infused his prayers was not artificially alleviated by his divine essence. In fact, his own soul was transformed through the prayerful process of learning obedience in suffering (Heb. 5:7–8). Prior to the horribly violent termination of his life, he endured an anguished, temporary suspension of his "abba culture," which unleashed a terrifying, psychological freefall into an abyss of desolation poignantly captured in a tortured wail of grief (Matt. 27:46). Restored just at the point of death, Jesus' shockingly transparent communion with his Father, which had radically distinguished him from his religious contemporaries, retained its centrality in the spirituality of the early church (Gal. 4:6; Rom. 8:15).

The sometimes designated "minor prayers" of Jesus are few in recorded number due perhaps to the fact that he prayed frequently in solitude. However, those that have been preserved are brief and pithy. They demonstrate conclusively that prayer for Jesus was not motivated by religious obligation. Rather, it was the warp and woof of his existence shaped by the vicissitudes of his life. It flowed vibrantly from a collage of real situations—an exuberant eruption of joyful praise upon rejection (Matt. 11:25–26; Luke 10:21), a generous request for the forgiveness of his abusers (Luke 23:34), spiritual combat on behalf of a friend (Luke 22:31–32), the endearing blessing of children (Mark 10:16), an agonizing plea to evade a cataclysmic circumstance (Matt. 26:39, 42; Mark 14:36; Luke 22:42; Heb. 5:7), a haunting lament of abject despair in the face of life coming apart at the seams (Matt. 27:46), and a serene relinquishment into the jaws of death (Luke 23:46).

Jesus' private prayers, often in the predawn and after sunset, also took the form of all night vigils.

Additionally, they were preludes to pivotal events in his life—his baptism, which incorporated a visionary experience (Luke 3:21–22); the choosing of the Twelve (Luke 6:12); the transfiguration (Matt.17:1); and his ascension (Luke 24:51). Nothing fell beyond the scope of his prayerfulness. His personal prayer agenda evinced a deep sensitivity to the spiritual needs of his close companions (John 17), a city, and his nation (Luke 19:41–42).

Extemporaneity and learned liturgy both characterized the prayer experience of Jesus. The Gospels confirm that Jesus, though an incarnation of divinity, was nonetheless the inheritor of a Jewish prayer tradition formed over the generations. Reared by pious Jewish parents, he was likely introduced to a life of prayer through specific benedictions at the outset and close of meals. In manhood his daily prayer experience revolved around the daily morning and evening routines of Jewish prayer, which included the repetition of the Shema (Deut. 6:4). There is also a biblical hint that "as was his custom," he participated in the prayers of the weekly synagogue Shabbat service—possibly the Shema, the *Tephillah*, and the *Kaddish*, which provided a structural backdrop for the Lord's Prayer (Luke 4:16). The Psalms, the prayer book of his people, gave formational definition to his humanity. As death approached, he breathed the nighttime prayer of Jewish boys and girls falling off to sleep (Luke 23:46; Ps. 31:5). Such was the abiding strength of the prayer formation he received in his earliest years.

The multifold traditions of Christianity that emerged over time forged their own distinctive prayer paths to God, each of which could claim a seminal connection with the prayer habits of Jesus. Systematic discussions of prayer first appeared in the 3rd century when three prayer treatises were authored by three North African church fathers within fifty years of each other. Tertullian, Origen, and Cyprian each composed full-length prayer treatises that included a commentary on the Lord's Prayer, extolled as the perfect condensation of the gospel. Additionally they addressed a growing body of questions about the theology and practice of prayer as a spiritual event that occurs in time and space. How can prayer without ceasing be accomplished according to the apostolic injunction (1 Thess. 5:17)? In what sense is time sanctified through the observance of fixed prayer hours? Are virtuous works an expression of prayer? Do physical postures and formal gestures contribute to the efficacy of prayer? Should prayer be a private or public exercise (1 Tim. 2:8; Matt. 6:5–6)? Augustine broadened the patristic discussion on prayer with the innovative suggestion that desires could also be prayers.

In the 3rd and 4th centuries, monasticism flourished as an ascetic protest movement against the legalized and morally diminished urban Christianity of the Roman Empire. Desert fathers and mothers, devoted to ceaseless prayer, inhabited the most inhospitable, liminal landscapes of Syria, Egypt, and Palestine where wild nature surrounded their lifelong quest for spiritual martyrdom and transformation of the heart in solitude and silence. *The Sayings of the Desert Fathers* (*Apothegmata*) (see Ward) drew heavily from the New Testament as inspiration for the one-sentence, ejaculatory prayers used by anchorites in spiritual warfare (Matt. 9:27; 15:22; Mark 10:48). Prominent in this genre of desert prayer was the Jesus Prayer, which developed between the 5th and 8th centuries. It prescribed the repeated invocation of the name of Jesus, synchronized with breath rhythms (hesychasm) as a medium of protection, illumination, and joyful consolation. The anonymous nineteenth-century Russian classic *The Way of a Pilgrim* heralded the Jesus Prayer as a superior method of ceaseless prayer that enabled one to maximize an interior sense of the divine presence.

While evangelicals have tended to regard prayer solely as monologue, that is, humans speaking to God, there is evidence of transdenominational stirrings of interest in the practice of listening prayer that has deep roots in Christian prayer history. The sixth-century Benedictine practice of *lectio divina* (holy reading) is undergoing a renaissance in evangelical circles. Benedict's monks regarded meditative prayer as a relaxed process of intentional listening to the Word of God with a view to obeying what they heard. This was central to their spiritual formation. Contemplative prayer developed through stages. It commenced with *lectio* (reading and listening to the Scriptures), deepened to *meditatio* (repeating and reflecting on the Word), progressed to the penultimate state of *oratio* (spontaneous, responsive praying from the heart), and climaxed in mystical *contemplation*, which heightened the pray-er's awareness of the sacredness of all of life. Contemplation, the prayer of being, was understood as a passive sensation of permeation by the divine presence while enwrapped in interior silence. It was not uncommon for contemplatives, while enraptured in this wordless state, to be the recipient of visions, locutions, and other ecstasies. In their often erotic accounts of union with the divine after advancing through purgation and illumination, numerous medieval male and female mystics testified to such suprarational phenomena.

While evangelical Protestants often oppose mystical prayer because it allegedly undermines the foundational Protestant belief in salvation by grace alone, mystical prayer experiences are not unknown to certain traditions of Protestantism. Significantly, Martin Luther's prayer treatise *A Simple Way to Pray* (1535) harmonized the ancient pre-Reformation monastic *lectio divina* prayer tradition with the Protestant notion of *sola scriptura*. It also endorsed direct communications from the Holy Spirit in punctuated moments of silence as preferable to one's own prayerful thoughts. George Muller (1805–1898), lauded by evangelicals for his extraordinary faith demonstrated in the care of Bristol's orphans, unwittingly followed Luther's prayer instruction. With no evident knowledge of *lectio divina*, he adjusted his personal prayer habits after ten years of ministry to align them with what

was in effect the ancient monastic prayer tradition in which Scripture reading and meditation preceded prayers of response to the biblical text. Muller was confident of being guided in practical matters by the divinely originated impressions of the heart, which arose from his prayers.

Catholic prayer themes also surfaced among evangelical descendants of John Wesley who advocated kindred versions of holiness and the deeper/higher life in the later 19th century. They crossed the Reformation divide and drank deeply at the wells of Catholic Quietism and were theologically comfortable with marrying the classic Catholic mystical themes of silence and contemplation to the Protestant prayer practices of intercession and petition. Friedrich Heiler, the Roman Catholic turned Lutheran religious phenomenologist, constructed a systematic classification of "mystical" and "prophetic" types of prayer. He observed that "mystics" often disdained "prophets" for their infantile and inferior kind of prayer preoccupied with personal desires and requests. By contrast, mystics in all eras, claiming a higher degree of self-abnegation, have sought the allegedly loftier attainment of the union of the soul with God in the *Mysterium Tremendum et Fascinans*. Such a hierarchy of prayer styles is problematic for evangelicals. It smacks of a spiritual elitism incompatible with the biblical witness.

Despite intrinsic tensions between mystical and prophetic conceptions of prayer, some recent evangelical writers have suggested the possibility of enriching one's personal prayer experience through the creative, nonsubordinate integration of the best elements of the two traditions. They envision incomprehensible, numinous moments of transcendence as enhancing the passion-filled, robust, verbal outpourings of the heart and vice versa. In short, they propose that mystics and prophets can indeed complement each other's prayer experience. Their dialectical relationship preserves the integrity of prayer as a genuine dialogue in which both God and humans converse. In biblical terms,

Psalm 46:10a and James 5:16b belong together in the canon of evangelical prayer experience.

At the outset of the third millennium, labels such as "evangelical," "mystical," "contemplative," and "charismatic" are no longer mutually exclusive. The evangelical Quaker Richard Foster, a prolific proponent of cross-denominational spiritual renewal, assumes that evangelicals can confidently claim as their rightful heritage and learn from all the major prayer traditions of the Christian church. For him and a significant portion of the North American evangelical constituency, the doctrinal convictions and ecclesiastical identities of the spiritual masters who frequently appear together in edited anthologies of thematically assembled spiritual texts is of limited concern.

In the same assimilative vein, convergent evangelicals enthusiastically draw guidance and inspiration from an enormous and inclusive Christian prayer treasury to which Christ followers in all ages have made their distinctive contributions. The hymn prayers of Ephrem the Syrian, fourth-century exegete and poet, lead into the impassionate celebration of divine self-abasement. The *Breastplate* of Patrick of Ireland, Celtic monk and bishop-evangelist, teaches how to invoke boldly the angels and Christ to protect against the assaults of evil. *The Prayer to Christ* of Anselm, archbishop of Canterbury, combats spiritual lethargy by arousing a deeper love of God that pervades the intellect, emotions, and will. Francis of Assisi's *Canticle of Creatures* anticipates the new creation and inspires the musical praise of God's presence in nature. The prayers of numerous late medieval male and female mystics encourage emotion-charged expressions of love for the divine while journeying deeply into the mystery of Christ for the sake of transforming self and society.

Contemporary evangelical eclectics also value prayer traditions closer to home. The Anglican *Book of Common Prayer* offers an enduring, non–Roman Catholic template for those evangelicals entering the liturgical world of morning and evening prayers and the sacramental. Protestant Reformers of the sixteenth-century and their eighteenth- and nineteenth-century Methodist, revivalist, and missionary grandchildren inspire ardent involvement in faith-based intercession. English Puritans of the 16th and 17th centuries substantiate the practice of meditation as the necessary formational bridge between Scripture reading and prayer. Modern-day Pentecostals, and charismatics in all Christian traditions, invite experimentation with glossalalic prayer beyond learned speech, which the convergent, evangelical pray-er easily integrates with saying the "Lord, make me an instrument of your peace" prayer (wrongly attributed to Francis of Assisi) or the Serenity Prayer used in Twelve-Step programs. All the foregoing prayer traditions are interknit in the devotional culture of twenty-first-century evangelicalism.

In summary, the current widespread appreciation of prayer as a total experience, engaging body, mind, and spirit in an age of globalization, has birthed a postmodern, nonparochial prayer culture that is overtaking segments of evangelicalism. Consequently, there are many who, while claiming to be evangelical in their core beliefs, have nevertheless rejected the sectarian, evangelical culture once deemed indispensable to safeguarding those beliefs. In fact, it is difficult to speak anymore of a homogeneous, evangelical prayer culture. For spiritually adventurous evangelicals seeking fresh, metamorphic religious experiences beyond traditionally sanctioned, theological boundaries, prayer has become a multifaceted and many-splendored affair. Meditation techniques, body postures, pilgrimages (prayer by feet), ancient chants, ecstatic speech, silent retreats, prolonged fasting and vigils, inner impressions, extrasensory visions, instantaneous healings, prayer walks, and empowered intercessions on behalf of others and against the cosmic powers of darkness are all colorful pieces in an emerging new evangelical prayer mosaic.

Sources Cited

Foster, R. *Prayer* (1992).

Heiler, F. *Prayer* (1932).

Luther, M. *A Simple Way to Pray*. Ed. M. Thompson (2000).

Pokrovsky, G., trans. *The Way of a Pilgrim* (2001).

Ward, B., trans. *The Desert Christian: Sayings of the Desert Fathers* (1975).

For Further Reading

Bradshaw, P. *Daily Prayer in the Early Church* (1982).

Buttrick, G. *Prayer* (1942).

Casey, M. *Sacred Reading* (1995).

Deiss, L. *Springtime of the Liturgy* (1979).

Gire, K., ed. *Between Heaven and Earth* (1997).

Jungmann, J. *Christian Prayer through the Centuries* (2007).

Leech, K. *True Prayer* (1980).

Magdalen, M. *Jesus, Man of Prayer* (1987).

Payne, L. *Listening Prayer* (1994).

Squire, A. *Asking the Fathers* (1973).

Ware, T., ed. *The Art of Prayer* (1966).

CHAPTER 24

EXPERIENCE

EVAN B. HOWARD

The people of God have characteristically exhibited an experiential relationship with God. From Adam's walk with God in the garden, to Jacob's dream, to Moses' face-to-face conversations, to the glory of the temple and the prophets' encounters, God was experienced. This experiential dimension was intensified when the Holy Spirit filled the gathering of Jesus' followers on the first Pentecost after Jesus' resurrection. And ever since, the Christian faith birthed from this church has exhibited an experiential relationship with God. The church's appropriation of this experiential dimension, however, has not been without difficulties. Conflicts and councils have wrestled with the church's experience over the centuries. Furthermore, the topic of experience is particularly relevant today. With the recent "turn to experience" in theological circles and popular interest in spiritual experience generally, the church is pressed to clarify the place of experience in Christian spirituality. This article will review the history of the church's experience, clarify the meanings of the term *experience* and their significance for spirituality, develop an approach to experience rooted in Christian theology, and explore a few pastoral concerns relevant to the experiential dimension of the Christian faith.

History

However defined, the Christian church has exhibited a distinctly experiential relationship with — and knowledge of — God. The experience of the living presence of God was, for the New Testament church, the fulfillment of the promises made to Israel and the taste of a much larger restoration to come. The early Christians acknowledged the presence of the Holy Spirit as they were moved to speak (Acts 2:4, 11; 4:31; 1 Cor. 12:8 – 10). They perceived the influence of God as they struggled toward unity (Acts 15:28; Eph. 4:3; Jude 19). They experienced personal transformation as a work of the Spirit (Acts 6:3, 5; 11:24; Rom. 8:3 – 4, 13) and social transformation as evidence of God's grace (Acts 4:33 – 35). Their gospel was proclaimed "not simply with words, but also with power, with the Holy Spirit and with deep conviction" (1 Thess. 1:5; see Rom. 15:18 – 19; 1 Cor. 2:4) and was confirmed with "signs" and "wonders" (Heb. 2:4; see Acts 14:3).

Yet even at its inception, the community of Christ found the experiential dimension of its faith to be a periodic difficulty as well as a source of blessing. False prophets also felt moved to speak (Acts 13:6; 1 John 4:1). Some took their experience as a sign of God's special favor and became self-absorbed or used their experience to legitimize factions within the body of Christ (1 Cor. 1 – 3; 12 – 14). Even angelic experiences or miraculous signs and wonders were not exempt from the misleading influence of the enemy of the faith (2 Cor. 11:13 – 15; 2 Thess. 2:9). Thus, the Christian church emerged as a people who not only experienced the living God but were also obliged to *discern* their experience of God.

The church of the first centuries was a charismatic church. Writers such as Irenaeus (c.130–200) and stories such as the *Martyrdom of Perpetua and Felicitas* (c. 203) recounted healings, prophecies, and deliverances through the ministry of the Holy Spirit. Theologians such as Augustine and Athanasius spoke openly of encounters with the Holy Spirit and with unholy spirits. Some Christians devoted themselves to a monastic life of prayer and spiritual disciplines, facilitating both deepened experience and careful reflection on experience. Movements such as Montanism (2nd century) emphasized the experiential over the institutional, forcing the church to consider its relationship to experience. Similarly, the council of Gangra (c. 341) clarified the place of spiritual disciplines within the Christian faith. And the Iconoclast controversy (c. 725–842) compelled the Eastern church to explore the relationship between experience of God and the means used to facilitate it (such as icons for meditation).

While one finds less record of tongue-speaking or public prophetic expression, the church of the Middle Ages was still experiential. The medieval Celtic church manifested a unique sense of the divine in the midst of the ordinary. By the 11th century an interest in feeling was having its effect on the Western church's sense of divine experience. The works of Bernard of Clairvaux are a prime example of the deeply felt devotion of this period. Words such as *rapture, ecstasy*, and *union* characterized medieval experience of God. Similarly, in light of a growing interest in order and technique, methods and manuals of devotion multiplied. Some explored maps of the spiritual life. Others, however, such as the early Dominicans, made little of the stages and methods of devotion, preferring to see prayer as the simple turning to God in petition and thanksgiving in the context of ministry and life. Francis of Assisi encountered God not only through tender devotion and piercing stigmata, but also in the midst of humble service to the poor. The Eastern church affirmed the

vital place of experience as a consequence of the Hesychast controversies.

The Reformation(s) of the 16th century brought further developments in the church's experience of God. Martin Luther encouraged Christian faith as a heartfelt trust and not merely an intellectual assent, while at the same time he tried to steer his followers away from an "enthusiastic" abandonment to spiritual impressions. Other reformers, such as Hans Denck (c. 1500–1527), placed even greater emphasis on the role of the Spirit, urging Christians to drink "from the invisible chalice the invisible wine" (Denck 25). The first generation of Protestants hammered out doctrinal foundations. Later generations—particularly the Pietists, Puritans, and other kindred spirits—explored how Christianity was experienced. The "pious communities" of Philip Spener, for example, established a network of small groups that recovered the patristic vision for prayerful, experiential reflection on Scripture. While early Lutherans emphasized Scripture, Quakers stressed the Inner Word. Baptists emphasized Word and Spirit. While Socinians argued for the centrality of reason, Anglicans stood upon the "three legged stool" of Scripture, tradition, and reason. Methodists expanded this stool into a "quadrilateral": Scripture, tradition, reason, and experience.

Through the writings of Ignatius of Loyola, Teresa of Avila, and John of the Cross, the methods of Roman Catholic spiritual experience were charted with meticulous precision. Tensions arose within the Roman Catholic community as they struggled to articulate their approach to experience in the seventeenth-century controversies regarding Quietism. The monastic communities of the Eastern church exhibited competing trends toward either a communal/liturgical experience or a more private and contemplative experience of God (Hackel, 158–60).

In the modern era (c. 1750–1950), three aspects received attention. One was the personal-interior aspect. The exploration of "infused contemplation" in the Roman Catholic West or "the prayer of the heart" in the East became the fascination of many. It was here that the term *mysticism* began to be used. Similarly, Protestants were caught up in "revival," "entire sanctification," "second blessings," "the deeper life," or "baptisms in the Spirit." The second aspect of experience explored was the rational. Biblical, philosophical, and scientific studies forced many to rethink — and to reexperience — their relationship with God. Deism, for example, was not merely a matter of theology. A central belief of many Deists was the minimizing of divine intervention. This, in turn, required a personal suppression of the perception or expectation of divine experience apart from one's participation in the laws of nature and morality. The third aspect developed in the modern era was the social, as Christians of all varieties discovered experience of God in the midst of compassionate service and social reform. Needless to say, each of these aspects has involved the church in many difficult discernments. And with the emergence, somewhere around 1950, of a postmodern culture, factors such as globalism, pluralism, technology, and pace of change are precipitating a contemporary overhaul of the church's experience of God.

Definition

It is one thing to review the church's experience of God. But this exercise is itself shaped by one's understanding of just what *experience* is. Consequently, our sense of the role(s) of experience in Christian life is bound up with our understanding of the meaning of experience.

From a commonsense perspective, experience refers to a practical wisdom gained from exposure (e.g., the experienced master). Richard of St. Victor used this definition when he distinguished one who knows spiritual truth "by knowledge" from one who knows "by experience." A related use of *experience* is to designate an encounter with something (for example, I "experienced" seasickness). The Pietists of the 17th century employed this

definition to speak of the need for experience as an essential component of the Christian faith. A more precise definition of *experience* appeared in the philosophy of John Locke (1632 – 1704). Locke argued that the foundation of all human knowledge was in experience, by which he meant the perception of either sense data or the operations of the human mind. Jonathan Edwards, and Puritans more generally, developed Locke's notion with reference to the Christian faith. Edwards emphasized the "sense of the heart" or "religious experience": a perception of the excellencies of God granted to humans upon conversion (Miller). Puritan diaries of religious experience recounted the nuances of this spiritual perception as the believer matured through life.

William James broadened the definition of experience even further. His *Varieties of Religious Experience* (1902) introduced particular encounters as case studies, "religious experiences," data in a science of religious phenomena. Yet James himself saw experience not merely in terms of isolated events, but also as an ongoing succession of mental phenomena. Hence his aim was to account for "the religious" within the entire flow of human consciousness. More recently, liberation theologians have identified experience with the economic struggles of people, transcendental Thomists (followers of Karl Rahner and Bernard Lonergan) have directed Christians to a primordial experience of God behind human cognition, and process theologians have identified experience with the changing character of reality itself.

Our understanding of the role of experience in the Christian life depends on our use of the term *experience*. Our approvals or condemnations of experience reflect both our circumstances and the uses of the term at our disposal. What is needed in order to clarify the place of experience in Christian spirituality is theological reflection that honors the historical and semantic diversity of Christian experience in the context of a basic theology of the Holy Spirit and the Christian life.

Theology

We must begin with an understanding of human experience that is broad enough to encompass a wide range of meanings and yet definite enough to clarify particular doctrines of the faith. Hence, *human experience* will be defined here as *the particular presence and interactive entirety of any and all dimensions of human life* (see Howard, 77–111). Our bodies are part of our experience. Yet there is more than "body" to human experience; we are also soul, mind, and spirit. Our thoughts, feelings, and intentions each contribute to the richness of human experience. Our awareness, whether foggy or clear; our perceptions; our decisions; our actions; and our relationships with God, spiritual beings, nature, others, and self all play a part in this broad character of human experience.

This broad understanding of experience, in turn, comprehends other definitions. The experienced master is one who has given thought, action, or attention over time to something such that his or her predispositions or experience are shaped accordingly. A *particular* experience is a perceptual encounter that introduces something to human experience more generally. And while Locke's "sense" and "reflection" are certainly significant, a broader understanding of "experience" sees them as just two components, along with states of awareness, worldviews, moods, possibilities, etc. of a much larger universe. Human experience includes economic struggles, barely perceived depths, and the continuity of change itself.

Religious experience, then, designates human thought, feeling, action, relationships, economic realities, and so on insofar as these involve the divine. And *Christian* experience means the interaction of the living Christ with each and all dimensions of human existence. We see evidence of this Christian experience in the artifacts of ordinary life. For example, the practice in evangelical Christianity of writing conversion narratives or journals of personal examen has often served to process and document the effects upon heart and mind of interaction with God.

The primary theological foundation of Christian experience is the Christian Godhead. The Father sends, reveals. The Son hears the Father. The Spirit glorifies the Son. The divine life is itself an experienced life. And this mutually experienced life of the Three-in-One is expressed through and to creation. God is present to creation through miraculous appearances, through prophetic revelations, through the Word made flesh, and through the Spirit of Christ. Moreover, God is *actively* present. God reveals both himself and our own hope through the sending of Jesus. God initiates relationship through the sending of the Spirit. As we respond to the invitation of God and God responds to our response, we learn to share in the very experience of the Trinitarian Godhead.

A second theological foundation is humanity itself. We resemble God ("image and likeness"), yet God's ways are incomprehensible to us. We share, with God, creative dominion and care for the earth, yet we do so as part of the earth. Furthermore, our image and dominion involve the full richness of human experience: thought, feeling, the senses, relationship, body, and more. Human experience is a great thing; hence we can celebrate our unique place in creation. But human experience is also a tragic affair. We suffer from the consequences of sin, from sinful social forces, and from the powers of the devil. Our thoughts become twisted and our relationships become fractured. Nevertheless, human experience is also a thing of hope. Through the life of Jesus, we are confronted with the dream of something more. Through the work of Christ, we anticipate the restoration of human experience, to the "bringing to right" of every dimension of our personal and social existence: forgiveness of sin, reconciliation of hostile factions, healing of the land. And for those who receive the living Christ, it is not merely hope, but an experienced reality (Howard, 145–93).

God offers the gospel through Jesus Christ. And this offer is given in a tangible and ongoing manner through the ministry of the Holy Spirit.

The Spirit brings thoughts to our minds, reminding us of what is of Christ (John 14:26). The Spirit softens our hearts, pouring out God's love (Rom. 5:5). The Spirit guides our wills, leading us to embody the righteousness of God (Rom. 8:4). The Spirit guides the gathered church into courageous evangelism (Acts 13:2) and into harmonious decisions (Acts 15:28). At times the voice of God is a still, small voice. At other times it is a mighty wind, tearing us from our not-so-stable foundations.

The Christian experience of God, then, invites us into the depths of interiority, inviting us to see the false selves we may have constructed, giving us a profound felt-touch of Christ's love for us or stimulating heartfelt repentance. But the Christian experience of God also draws us out to the margins of exteriority, demanding the reconstruction of economic relations as our divinely inspired hatred for injustice and our awareness of unrighteous relationships around us guide us into new habits of life and action. Our experience of God is found in sudden events and developing life habits. Christian experience reveals the power of God; it also reveals the ordinary frailties of people.

Pastoral Concerns

Experience, in this broader sense, has an important place in the Christian life. Indeed, Christianity is seen from this perspective as an *experienced* life in the Spirit, in all its rich dimensions. How then are we to address the significant problems that have faced and still face the church with regard to "experience"? Two examples must suffice.

A first problem is the tendency for some to become self-absorbed in introspection or even prideful of their religious experiences. This problem is countered by respecting the breadth of experience. Yes, there are times when relationship with God is nourished through self-examination or powerful experiences. Nonetheless, God desires that we love the Lord with heart, soul, mind, and strength (Mark 12:30). We cannot mature in the Christian life unless we allow our experiences to broaden. Authentic experience of God cannot be reduced to *my* experience of God here and now.

The Bible recounts a wide range of experiences: seeing God (Matt. 5:8), knowing the unknowable God (Eph. 3:16–19), sharing in the divine nature (2 Peter 1:4), experiencing things "in the spirit/Spirit" (Rev. 1:10; 4:1–2), visions, dreams, appearances, convictions, consolations, and so on. While it appears universal *that* humans are meant to experience God, just *what* that experience "must" look like is never specified.

A second problem is the potentially misleading character of experience. If we permit ourselves to be guided by experience, aren't we opening ourselves to unreliable or even deceptive influences? What about *false* prophets? As mentioned above, ecclesial factions in the 16th and 17th centuries struggled to clarify the relationship between Scripture, reason, tradition, and experience. And we have seen, even within Scripture, that God's people have both been guided and misled through experience. God's Spirit can enlighten our minds through reflection on the Bible (2 Peter 1:19–21). Satan can tempt us through the same means (Matt. 4:6). Every dimension of our lives is available to God's transformation and to our own and even demonic misunderstanding. Thus, we are called not only to follow the Spirit, but also to "test the spirits" (1 John 4:1). Authentic Christian experience is *discerned* experience, and Christian history is full of wisdom regarding the virtues that promote discernment, the criteria used to measure discernment, and the nature of the discernment process itself. Needless to say, Christian regard for sacred Scripture arises, in part, in the context of this need to discern experience.

Other problems could be explored similarly. Those presented merely illustrate that experience is central to the Christian faith, present in many forms, reflecting both the grace of God and the character of human life, and therefore requiring the wisdom of the church in ongoing discernment.

Sources Cited

Denck, H. "The Nuremberg Confession." In *Schriften II* (1956).

Hackel, S. "The Russian Spirit." In *The Story of Christian Spirituality* (2001), 151–64.

Howard, E. *The Brazos Introduction to Christian Spirituality* (2008).

James, W. *Varieties of Religious Experience* (1902).

Miller, P. "Jonathan Edwards on the Sense of the Heart," *Harvard Theological Review* 41, no. 2 (1948): 123–46.

For Further Reading

Fee, G. *God's Empowering Presence* (1994).

Gelpi, D. *The Gracing of Human Experience* (2001).

———. *The Turn to Experience in Contemporary Theology* (1994).

Johnson, L. T. *Religious Experience in Earliest Christianity* (1998).

Lovelace, R. *Dynamics of Spiritual Life* (1979).

Smith, J. "The Reconception of Experience in Peirce, James, and Dewey." In *America's Philosophical Vision* (1992), 17–35.

Willard, D. *Renovation of the Heart* (2002).

CHAPTER 25

MYSTICISM

EVAN B. HOWARD

The language of the mystical and the aspects of spirituality described by such language have been essential to Christianity from its beginnings to the present. This vocabulary, however, has been variously defined, and even today there is no consensus regarding what mysticism means. The clarification of mysticism's meaning and value involves examining the history of mystical vocabulary and the framework of mystical theology. Here mysticism will be explored as an opening to divine reality, access to which or the meaning of which is gained through a unique participation with God, a transforming participation that both mediates and is itself the fruit of this opening.

History

One way the New Testament church described its experience of the saving presence of Christ was through the language of mystery (*mysterion*). The apostle Paul wrote, "God has chosen to make known among the Gentiles the glorious riches of this mystery, which is Christ in you, the hope of glory" (Col. 1:27). Some religions of Paul's day claimed to initiate people into the "mysteries" of salvation. Philosophers advertised their views as revealing "mysteries" hidden to the unenlightened. Paul cleverly reapplied this language to describe the precious, tangible, yet not altogether comprehensible reality of the indwelling Christ, which had previously been hidden from the Gentiles but was now accessible to believers — an opening into divine reality that both requires and *is* a mutual participation ("Christ in you"). Else-

where Paul spoke of the acceptance of the Gentiles, the ministry of Christ, and the intimacy of Christ and the church all as mysteries (Eph. 3:3–9; 1 Tim. 3:16; Eph. 5:32; see also Eph. 1:9; 6:19). These mysteries were learned in ordinary community life and in extraordinary experiences of participation with God when, for example, Paul was "caught up to paradise" and "heard inexpressible things" (2 Cor. 12:4; cf. 1 Cor. 13:2; 14:2). After clarifying the "mystery" of Gentile salvation, Paul closes his theoretical section of Romans with a doxology proclaiming God's "unsearchable ... judgments" (Rom. 11:25–36).

In the first centuries of the church, the terms *mysteries* or *mystical* usually referred to gospel realities mediated through reflection on Scripture or through the gathered congregation. Through spiritual reading, writers like Origen claimed, the people of God received the mystical meaning of the Scriptures, hidden to those who approached them merely as historical stories or moral philosophy. Likewise, early Christian writings such as the Apostolic Constitutions (c. 350) often spoke of being initiated through baptism and the Lord's Supper into the mysteries of the gospel. The sacraments, administered in the context of the gathered body of Christ, softened hearts, enlightened minds, and transformed lives.

Augustine of Hippo developed a Trinitarian theology of experience, clarified the character of impressions and ecstasies, and shared his own participation with God in his *Confessions*. The writings attributed to Dionysius the Areopagite (5th or 6th centuries) coined the phrase *mystical theology*. For the author of these writings, *mystical* theology—unlike other ways of knowing God—begins from the assumption that God is beyond our comprehension. What is "mystical" about mystical theology is that it bypasses ordinary, rational means (later labeled *kataphatic*) and approaches God and participates in God-transcending categories (thus, *apophatic*). Maximus the Confessor (580–662) is less known in the West but is recognized as a synthesizer of Eastern Christian thought. Maximus reflects on the character of the mutual participation of humans and Christ, flowing from Christ's participation with the life of God in the Trinity. His book *The Church's Mystagogy* portrays the initiation of the church into the mysteries of the gospel through congregational worship.

Between the 11th and 15th centuries, a number of what later were labeled distinct forms of "mysticism" emerged—among them the *affective* mysticism of the Cistercians, women's *visionary* mysticism, and the *speculative* mysticism of Meister Eckhart. The character of these expressions influenced the late medieval debates regarding mystical theology. Jean Gerson, for example, argued that thought and feeling are *both* involved in mystical theology for, "although no one perfectly attains mystical theology who ignores its principles, which are received through inner experience, there should be no refusal from presenting and receiving its teaching" (Gerson, 268). While the roles of the faculties involved in attaining mystical theology were disputed, all those involved in the debate were in agreement that whatever "mystical theology" was, it was accessed through an experienced participation in the divine life.

The Protestant Reformation also used and developed the language of mysticism. John Calvin, for example, saw "mystical union" with God as a central principle. He writes of mystical union in the language of medieval bridal mysticism: "To this is to be referred that sacred marriage, by which we become bone of his bone, and flesh of his flesh, and one with him (Eph. 5:30), for it is by the Spirit alone that he unites himself with us" (Calvin,

3.1.3). Roman Catholic writers of this period, such as Teresa of Avila, specified "mystical theology" as an experience of participation in God's presence that arises apart from reason or vision. It was in this Catholic context that the terms *mystic* and *mysticism* were first used. The noun *mystic* designated those who were masters of "mystical theology," who reached the heights of Christian prayer. *Mysticism* referred to the interests of those who explored special experiences of God. These terms were employed both by people who appreciated mysticism as well as by those who did not. Later, in the 18th century, John Wesley, for example, warned of "the mystics" and of "mysticism," while simultaneously promoting an "experimental" (mystical) faith.

As the modern era developed, Puritans analyzed "conversion" into a finely tuned precisionism, developing their own set of "mystics" (Schwanda). Protestants opened themselves to the mystical realities of participation with Christ—though without using the common language of mysticism—through "entire sanctifications," "second blessings," and "deeper life" encounters. Roman Catholics further specialized their understanding of mysticism by distinguishing between ascetical and mystical theology, identifying the latter with so-called infused contemplation—"those supernatural acts or states which our own industry is powerless to produce, *even in a low degree, even momentarily*" (Poulain, 1). Students of philosophy, psychology, and comparative religion also became fascinated with the mystical. By the mid-20th century, mysticism identified—for those who welcomed it and those who condemned it—content-less union, altered states of consciousness, or parallel experiences in non-Christian religions. In recent decades there has been a broadening of perspective and a reappropriation of biblical and patristic approaches to the mysteries of the faith.

Certainly, the vocabulary of mysticism developed through the centuries, as did the church's experience of Christ. Yet throughout this history of mystical vocabulary and experience, one perceives a people discovering God: not merely through ordinary analysis or ritual, but also through a unique participation with the indwelling Christ.

Theology

Our understanding of this participation in Christ—which opens us to reality and is itself the reality to which we are opened—is explored through theological reflection. Such reflection attends not only to the past, but also to the ways in which participation in Christ is and can be lived out today. A preliminary outline of such a theology may be summarized in three statements:

First, *as a divine-human encounter, Christian mysticism manifests the characteristic presence of the Christian God.* A few matters related to this must be addressed. One is the question of the "common ground" of mysticism. Does the mere fact—or the character—of global religious experience ("mysticism") suggest a common Source of the experiences? Some see religious experience as essentially one: we are all experiencing the same Absolute. Others see it as essentially plural: Buddhists have Buddhist experiences, Christians have Christian experiences. Still others would say that some are experiencing the One True God; the rest are experiencing demons. An authentically Christian approach to the "common ground" question assumes that the almighty Creator simply *is* the ground of all experience. Further, whether through the character of the natural world, the utterances of prophetic revelation, the historical Jesus, or the movings of the Spirit, God the Redeemer initiates transforming participation. In this sense the Creator-Redeemer is the ground of all authentic mysticism. Yet Christianity also affirms the existence of malevolent spiritual beings, some that appear even to Christians "as an angel of light." In addition, Christians believe that God's invitations to humans are subject to the various forces that shape all of human life. Consequently, Christians do believe in a common plurality of factors shaping mystical experience: the almighty and inviting Trinity, the angelic/demonic forces, and the complexities of human experience itself.

Another matter regarding the divine character of Christian mysticism is that specifically Christian mysticism is characteristically personal. Insofar as opening to reality is associated with participation in the Christian God, it will be essentially an encounter with the one *personal* God, with the three-*personed* God. As transcendent, God surpasses all categories, but as immanent, God meets us person to person. Consequently, as a divine-human participation, Christian mysticism is not merely an exercise of the mind, but an encounter with the Master.

An additional matter regarding Christian mysticism as divine regards the availability of mystical experience. Is mysticism only meant for a few special Christians, or is it offered to all? For those who saw mysticism as a particular experience given at the pinnacle of Christian maturity, it was easy to see it as the calling of a few. For others, such as the Second Vatican Council, God's universal call to holiness was primary. After Vatican II, the Catholic Church's expectations regarding the availability of mystical experience were forced to change. As participation in the God of the Christian Scriptures, mysticism was understood to be for everyone. God may offer the participation of infused contemplation to one, entire sanctification to another, ordinary obedience to another, and the darkness of faith to still another. Who is to say which is higher or holier? Christian mysticism involves a divine-human encounter, and as such it will reflect God's infinitely gracious invitation.

Second, *as a divine-human encounter, Christian mysticism manifests humanity.* As human, Christian mystical experience is inescapably diverse. Scholars of mysticism disagree on the definition of mysticism. This disagreement becomes visible as one notices who is, or is not, included as an example of mysticism. Those who approve of mysticism may see it as the highest form of prayer and so present examples of mystics in light of this assumption, and those who don't approve present examples in light of their assumption. Scholars identify the essential characteristics of mysticism variously. The point is that our lived relationship with God is diverse. One Christian is inflamed with the heat of God's fiery love while another is caught up in heady reflection on the character of God, and still others discover the divine presence while doing God's will. Some struggle toward maturity of spiritual experience through particular means and methods. Others following the same path grow pharisaic or find themselves buried under guilt.

What, then, are the essential characteristics of mystical experience? Only this — the authentic meeting of Spirit with spirit. And that is the point. Christian experience is mystical because it can be reduced to no single faculty, no prescribed characteristics. The mysteries of the gospel are mysterious because they are revealed only through a unique participation with Christ, a participation that, divinely adapted to each of us, can never be fully prescribed or even described.

Furthermore, as human, Christian mysticism involves a cycle of interpretation and encounter. Some see mysticism as a primordial encounter to which conceptual interpretation is subsequently given. Others emphasize the priority of the interpretive frameworks out of which experience is encountered *as this* or that. Still others discuss the possibility of an interpretation-free experience of "pure consciousness." Can we become present to God in such a way — if only for a moment — that culture and language are simply left behind as we hear "inexpressible things"?

Well-known nineteenth-century hymn writer Fanny Crosby confessed, "The most enduring hymns are born in the silences of the soul, and nothing must be allowed to intrude while they are being framed into language.... Sometimes the song without words has a deeper meaning than the more elaborate combinations of words and music. But in the majority of instances these two must be joined in marriage" (Crosby, 186). When we meet God in transforming participation, our categories of thought, feeling, and language are exposed in all their shallowness. Nonetheless, as humans, we find ourselves speaking. Christian mysticism, *as human*, will necessarily involve interplay between encounter and interpretation.

Finally, mysticism, because it has a human dimension or component, will necessarily be subject to the follies of humanity. Some will reduce participation in Christ to a private interiority and, in the name of mysticism, will neglect compassion, evangelism, or broader restoration. Some will misinterpret the character of mystical participation with God, concluding that means of grace are unnecessary to the Christian life when, on the contrary, God ordinarily chooses means of grace through which to communicate heart, will, and life. Consumers will try, like Simon Magus, to buy the Spirit. Intellectuals will try to master mysticism. Religious managers will try to manufacture it. Those in power will try to control it, but always in vain, for the mysteries of God are not taught by human wisdom but rather are "taught by the Spirit, explaining spiritual realities with Spirit-taught words" (1 Cor. 2:6–13 TNIV).

Third, *the character of experience as human-divine participation necessitates a practice of Christian discernment.* "Do not put out the Spirit's fire," Paul exhorted the church at Thessalonica. "Do not treat prophecies with contempt but test them all" (1 Thess. 5:19–21 TNIV). As both *human and divine*, mysticism involves us in unclearness. Is this an angel of light? Is my prayerful insight from Scripture a leading from God? Is my discomfort with a certain social situation a participation in God's own discomfort?

Philosophers of religion frequently ask a particular discernment question: Does mystical experience in any way validate belief in God? The "religious experience argument for God's existence," as it has become labeled, was developed most significantly by William James in his *Varieties of Religious Experience*. He reasoned that the pervasiveness and value of mysticism throughout human history offered sufficient warrant to believe that there was at least a "something more" experienced. Whether one accepts James's argument, it confronts us with the global presence of mystical experience. The mere fact of mysticism demands our discerning response.

Discernment was a common theme of Old Testament prophets, desert elders, medieval confessors, Puritan divines, and many others, creating a heritage of wisdom. A central criteria of Christian discernment presented in this heritage is Scripture. More generally we see this criterion expressed today with regard to mysticism in the question, "Is mysticism biblical?" And as we have seen, our answer will depend on how we define *mysticism*. If by *mysticism* we refer to a pursuit of a content-free mental state informed by pantheistic assumptions, then mysticism is certainly not "biblical." If, however, by *mysticism* we understand the mystery of the gospel expressed as "Christ in you the hope of glory," or as the pursuit of a lived experience of the indwelling Christ, then mysticism is clearly biblical (Howard, 326–27).

Conclusion

One issue that remains is the question of mysticism as the aim of the Christian life. Many throughout Christian history have asserted that spiritual union—identified as a contemplation of absorption and then labeled "mysticism"—is the goal of Christian spiritual life. Is this claim correct? How might one respond to it? We have been exploring mysticism as arising from and leading to a profound *participation* in Christ. But what exactly does this participation look like and how might it influence our idea of mysticism as the aim of the Christian life? Clearly, participation is a matter of spiritual union. But full participation with God is a matter of the union of *all* of human experience. True, God wants us to share in his heart. Yet God also wants to share our actions with his, so that we live in true union (right-relatedness or "righteousness") with nature and with others. God wants mystical union, yet this mystical union is not merely a felt oneness of interior experience, but a real harmony of *all* experience, every aspect of our lives: personal, doctrinal, social, ecological. God desires that we share in the divine life so fully that our very actions and character display the divine: a "mystical life." But is this really mysticism? It is the opening of humankind to reality through the unique and transforming participation in Christ's own life—an opening hidden from those who do not know the gospel and the Spirit of God, but now available to those who do. At times our participation in Christ is perceived in special instances or encounters. Perhaps we can call these times "deeply mystical moments." But if so, then this mysticism simply highlights what is common to all of Christian spirituality: Christ present in and to all believers in the midst of everyday life—"Christ in you the hope of glory."

Sources Cited

Calvin, J. *Institutes of the Christian Religion.* 2 vols. Trans. J. McNeill (1960).

Crosby, F. *Fanny J. Crosby: An Autobiography* (1986).

Gerson, J. "On Mystical Theology: The First and Speculative Treatise." In *Jean Gerson: Early Works,* trans. B. P. McGuire (1998), 262–87.

Howard, E. *The Brazos Introduction to Christian Spirituality* (2008).

Poulain, A. *The Graces of Interior Prayer: A Treatise on Mystical Theology.* Trans. L. L. Yorke Smith (1928).

Schwanda, T. "Soul Recreation: Spiritual Marriage and Ravishment in the Contemplative-Mystical Piety of Isaac Ambrose" (Unpublished dissertation, Durham University, 2009).

For Further Reading

Certeau, M. *The Mystic Fable* (1992).

Houston, J. "Reflections on Mysticism: How Valid Is Evangelical Anti-Mysticism." In *Gott lieben und seine Gebote halten*, ed. M. Bockmuehl and H. Burkhardt (1991), 163–81.

James, W. *Varieties of Religious Experience* (1997).

Katz, S. *Mysticism and Philosophical Analysis* (1978).

Louth, A. *The Origins of the Christian Mystical Tradition* (2007).

McGinn, B. *The Presence of God: A History of Western Christian Mysticism*, 4 vols. (1991–2005).

Woods, R., ed. *Understanding Mysticism* (1980).

CHAPTER 26

MUSIC AND THE ARTS

STEVEN R. GUTHRIE

As long as there has been a Christian church, the devotion of godly men and women has found expression in paint, wood, and stained glass, their prayers and praises articulated in melodic lines and poetic cadences. As long as there has been a gospel to announce, that proclamation has been embodied in song and story, verse and image. Whether in public worship or private contemplation, the arts have been the persistent and spontaneous companion of Christian spiritual practice.

A Song-Saturated Church

Among the arts, singing has had an especially important role, and again, this has been the case since the earliest days of the church. The Last Supper concludes with a hymn (Matt. 26:30). Paul observes as a matter of course that when the church gathers, they sing (1 Cor. 14:26). The apostle himself, when imprisoned with Silas, turns not only to prayer but to song (Acts 16:25). James, likewise, can suggest no more natural expression of joyful praise than singing (James 5:13). The song-saturated life of the Christian is depicted warmly by the Christian theologian Clement of Alexandria, writing in the early 3rd century: "Throughout our entire lives, then, we celebrate a feast, persuaded that God is present everywhere and in all things; we plough the fields while giving praise, we sail the seas while singing hymns, and on every other public occasion we conduct ourselves skillfully" (McKinnon, 36).

The importance of music and the arts for Christian spirituality is nowhere more evident than in the early church's reverence for the Old Testament psalms. The psalms are, along with Isaiah, the biblical texts most frequently cited by New Testament authors (Moyise and Menken, 2). The Psalter profoundly shaped Christian spiritual practice, serving as the "foundational and paradigmatic prayer book of the Christian church" (Witvliet, 13). Patristic writers were extravagant in their commendations of the Psalms. Basil declares that while all of Scripture is inspired, "the Book of the Psalms embraces whatever in all the others is helpful" (Stapert, 150). This same devotion to the psalms persists into the medieval era, and the regular recitation of the psalms emerges as the cornerstone of monastic spirituality. The psalms are familiar enough to us that it is worth underlining the obvious point that these are works of art. It is from the poetry and song of the Psalter that the church learned "the vocabulary and grammar of worship" (Witvliet, 12).

A Profound Ambivalence

This account of the enthusiastic reception of the arts is incomplete, however. It is not the case that the church has always and everywhere welcomed music and the other arts. If the arts have been a persistent feature of Christian spirituality, so have been the controversies and suspicions surrounding their practice.

A revealing instance of this ambivalence is Augustine's tormented deliberation over music in Book X of the *Confessions*. The problem is not that Augustine is indifferent to music; rather, he worries that his love of music is excessive, that it competes with rather than nurtures his love of God. On the one hand, he remembers the warm tears of devotion the songs of the church drew from him when he was first returning to faith. He also recognizes that in song "our souls are moved and are more religiously and with a warmer devotion kindled to piety" (Augustine, 207). On the other hand, Augustine is troubled that at times he finds himself more delighted with the sensual beauty of the melody than with the truth of the words he is singing. When this happens, "I confess myself to commit a sin deserving punishment, and then I would prefer not to have heard the singer" (Augustine, 208). And there is another way in which music may mislead us: Augustine worries that music encourages the worshiper to follow the lead of the physical senses, rather than acting on (what Augustine believes to be) the higher faculty of reason. Augustine recognizes that at times music, the physical senses, and song *may* be a powerful means of directing our attention to what is higher—words, contemplation, and the love of God. At other times, however, these same aids to devotion may draw our attention *away* from higher things, leaving us entranced by the lower and lesser goods of music and sensual pleasure. It is a dilemma that leads Augustine, once again, to tears. "See my condition! Weep with me, and weep for me, you who have within yourselves a concern for the good" (Augustine, 208).

In this struggle (as in so many other ways) Augustine anticipated the passions and concerns of the church that would come after him—a church in which the arts would find both lavish patronage and deep suspicions. The 8th and 9th centuries would give rise to violent disputes over the contemplation of icons, while the 11th and 12th centuries would give rise to richly decorated prayer books, tapestries, brightly colored mosaics, and elaborate works in stained glass. One of the great achievements of Luther's and Calvin's reforms was the introduction and promotion of congregational song; one of the great embarrassments of the Reformation was the regular eruption of iconoclastic vandalism. The Puritans assiduously cultivated the devotional practices of spiritual writing, poetry, and song, while on the other hand gaining a reputation (though, some would argue, undeserved) for plainness and extreme aesthetic austerity. Throughout its history, the church has both embraced the arts as an ally in the spiritual life and restricted their practice as a threat.

Certainly within contemporary evangelicalism this same ambivalence has persisted. On the positive side, evangelical churches are very often distinguished by the emphasis they place on musical worship. Twentieth-century evangelicals inherited the song services and impassioned singing of nineteenth-century revivalists. And while the fundamentalists of the early 20th century became increasingly isolated from culture, the neo-evangelicals of the 1950s and 1960s—figures like Harold Ockenga, Carl F. H. Henry, and Billy Graham—made a deliberate effort to "engage culture." Evangelicals of Graham's generation pioneered the use of film, drama, and popular music in worship and evangelism. This use of media has sometimes been dismissed as nothing more than crass religious marketing, but it is better understood as a genuine expression of evangelical spirituality. Active participation in culture—including its art and media—is one of the ways evangelicals have actively lived out their Christian identity.

Nevertheless, like Augustine, evangelicals have continued to worry over the place of the arts in the spiritual life. We are concerned about "emotionalism" and "experientialism" in worship; we debate the appropriateness of new forms and artistic styles. Our churches focus on proclamation, teaching, and training, and so our artists, working in media that tend to be more allusive, sometimes feel the need to justify their existence within the body of

Christ. And—perhaps because the first generation of evangelical theologians emphasized the "propositional truths" of Scripture so strongly—forms of devotion that are more poetic than propositional are sometimes treated with suspicion.

The Gifts of Art

The church's ambivalence toward the arts has arisen in a variety of specific cultural and historical situations. Nevertheless, it is possible to identify three regular criticisms of the arts, namely, their (1) *irrationality*, (2) *sensuality*, and (3) *triviality*. Of course, these concerns are for the most part out of step with the prevailing attitude and temper of our own time; contemporary Western culture is not generally characterized by an overwhelming anxiety over the dangers of sensuality and triviality. For just this reason, we should not be too quick to dismiss these concerns. Anyone who has served on a church music committee can testify to the danger of giving a central place to trivial concerns. Augustine worries that his worship sometimes descends into self-indulgent pleasure, and again, Christians should recognize this as a perennial temptation—in both private devotion and public worship. Our orientation subtly shifts from seeking God to seeking a certain *experience*. Augustine likewise confesses that at times he finds himself far more interested in the shape and presentation of the melody he is singing than in the one to whom he is singing. Can any professional musician or church minister of music hear this confession without at least some sympathy?

And yet, in keeping with the paradoxical history we have described, the qualities that have aroused Christian anxiety also turn out to be among the principal gifts that the arts offer to Christian spirituality.

Holism, Not Irrationality

Augustine worried about the irrationality of music; that rhythm and melody do not speak to our rea-son, but to our physical senses. Too often in the case of music, he observed, "the perception of the senses is unaccompanied by reason and is not content to be in a subordinate place. It tries to be first and to be in the leading role, though it deserves to be allowed only as secondary to reason" (Augustine, 208). However, it is precisely the capacity to enlist the whole person that makes music and art such a valuable resource for the spiritual life. What Augustine feared as irrationality in worship may be understood positively as a holistic spirituality. Apart from practices that engage the body and the senses, the spiritual life is much more prone to sterile abstraction.

Evangelicals in particular have—very rightly—insisted upon the importance of doctrine and correct belief. Conversion, according to this way of thinking, includes the recognition of important truths about God and humanity (that Jesus Christ is God's Son, for instance, or that Jesus is God's perfect provision for a fallen humanity). While this emphasis is appropriate, it may be misunderstood. A garbled version of this affirmation is that conversion is nothing more than adopting right beliefs, that the Christian life is merely a matter of placing check marks beside the appropriate doctrinal affirmations. Our encounter with poetry, music, and images is a persistent reminder, however, that we are more than our thoughts and ideas, and that the appropriate response to what is good and beautiful includes more than bare intellectual assent.

Not only do the arts demonstrate the inadequacy of a wholly abstract faith; they also offer a means of bringing theological convictions to lived expression. If Christian spirituality is the domain of *lived* Christian experience, then clearly the arts are a valuable asset in the spiritual life. In song and dance, in sculpture and drama, inward convictions are drawn *out* into the realm of action and motion; into the lived world of time and mass and extension in space. Conversely, by enlisting sense and imagination the arts draw God's truth *in* more deeply; embedding and incarnating belief at many levels of one's person. Richard Mouw observes that the poetic imagery of a hymn text "impresses [a] theological point on your consciousness as no scholarly treatise can do." Through melody and verbal imagery the theological truth "becomes graphic" (Mouw and Noll, xiv).

Responsiveness, Not Sensuality

The arts' appeal to our physical senses has given rise to a second, closely related concern. If we devote attention to and find pleasure in the senses, then perhaps (some Christians have reasoned) there is a danger that we will be led into "sensuality." If we feed the senses, they may grow more and more ravenous, and we may become people who live only to gratify sensual cravings. In his reflections on Eden, the church father Ambrose associates Adam with reason and the mind. Eve on the other hand is associated with the aesthetic, the senses—and notably—with temptation and moral error. "We maintain that the figure of the serpent stands for enjoyment and the figure of the woman for the emotions of the mind and heart. The latter is called by the Greeks *aesthesis*. When according to this theory the senses are deceived, the mind, which the Greeks call *nous*, falls into error" (Thiessen, 58).

In fact—and in contrast to this negative assessment—the *sense*-uality of the arts is one of their great gifts to the spiritual life, a valuable counterbalance to the mystical tendency toward inwardness and isolation. Spirituality is sometimes described as "the inner path," or "the interior life." Certainly, spiritual vitality will include self-examination, a willingness to be alone in the presence of God and a careful attention to the inward movements of one's soul. But just as attentiveness to doctrine may descend into its caricature of intellectual sterility, so in the same way solitude and self-awareness may decay into insularity and self-absorption. Moreover, the larger goal of the Christian life is not to move ever inward, but rather to unfold outward in love, toward God and our neighbor. Indeed, a classic theological definition of sin is *incurvatus in se*—being turned in upon oneself.

Reciting a poem, following a melody, or enjoying a painting, on the other hand, necessarily means being moved outside of oneself. The work of the bodily senses is to perceive and respond to the outside world. As they engage our senses, the arts invite us to attend to and appreciate the distinctive character of sounds, colors, cadences, movements, and shapes; and this sort of seeing and valuing of the external world may act as a prelude to loving and serving it.

Even more, physicality is the necessary condition of community. We participate in human society through sound, gesture, and touch. When Christian devotion is embodied in song or dance or image, it can be shared. Perhaps the most obvious example of this artistic sharing is communal song. When I sing, I "out" what is most inward. This is true figuratively in the case of heartfelt worship, as my inner devotion is given expression in a sensible form. This "outing of the inward" is also true physically. As I sing, breath from my lungs is forced out into the room around me, carrying a sounding image of myself—my voice—into the surrounding space. Likewise, the tune I had heard "inside" my head is now a thing outside of me, carried through the air, both to others and to me. If I am singing with others, the sound of my voice becomes one element in a single sound that is simultaneously my voice and the voice of the community. This communal song only continues if its members continue to listen carefully to one another, adjusting moment by moment to stay "in tune" and "in sync." Nor does the song of the community remain outside of me, but it likewise is carried back "inside" as I listen. No wonder Simon Chan believes that singing "underscores more strongly than any other act of worship our life in Christ as one community.... In singing together the whole community can speak the same word and pray the same prayer" (Chan, 118).

Gratuity, Not Triviality

Another persistent concern about the arts is that they seem to be a luxury rather than a necessity of human existence. Evangelical spirituality has often had an active and even pragmatic character. We want to be about the serious work of evangelism, of bringing gospel light to a dark world, of serving the needs of those who are broken. In such an environment, a concern with form, beauty, and aesthetic delight may seem to be a distraction at best, trivial and self-indulgent at worst. Generations of Christian artists have heard variations on the objection: "Couldn't that time and money be better devoted to missions?" Though he was writing about physical adornment, Clement of Alexandria voiced a version of this concern: "We make no allowance for pleasure not connected with a necessity of life … let us choose only what is useful…. [I]f Christ forbids solicitude once and for all about clothing and food and luxuries, as things that are unnecessary, do we need to ask Him about finery and dyed wools and multicolored robes, about exotic ornaments of jewels and artistic handiwork of gold?" (Thiessen, 50).

While a concern for good stewardship of resources is commendable, a wholly pragmatic spirituality is wildly out of step with a God of *gratuity*, whose actions toward us are marked above all by *gratia* (grace) — unnecessary, excessive goodness. This God creates a garden named "delight" (the meaning of the Hebrew *Eden*) and crowns his creation work with a wonderfully inefficient day of Sabbath rest. The very gratuity of the arts offers a corrective to the North American orientation toward functionalism, utilitarianism, business models, and church growth techniques. The arts' association with feasting, enjoyment, and delight are also a helpful counterpart to the austerity and severity of ascetical practices, a reminder that there is such a thing as "the beauty of holiness."

Art and a New Creation

Not only do the arts point back to the creation of the world in all its gratuitous goodness, but in a very significant way they point forward to its completion. Artistry is an image of, and — in some

cases — a participation in the Spirit's work of transforming and redeeming all things.

Paul describes the Holy Spirit as the "first-fruits" of this great redemption (Rom. 8:23), and "a deposit guaranteeing our inheritance" (Eph. 1:14). By the Spirit we experience *now* the power and presence of God that will one day be fully manifest in all of creation. The Spirit's work, in other words, is eschatological. And if it is the case that Christian spirituality is always in the first instance "*Spirit*-uality," then spirituality can be said to have an eschatological character as well. In the spiritual life, we experience now some portion of the promised new creation. Through prayer and meditation, we experience now the presence of God; through community and spiritual discipline we are more and more changed into the likeness of Christ (whose likeness we will reflect perfectly when we see him face-to-face — 1 John 3:2); through service and proclamation we begin to see even now a world in which "the poorest of the poor will find pasture" (Isa. 14:30) and in which people of all nations say, "Let us go … and seek the LORD Almighty" (Zech. 8:21).

When art is used in contemplation, prayer, mission, and worship, it is one further instance of this eschatological work of making "the kingdoms of this world" into "the kingdoms of our Lord, and of his Christ" (Rev. 11:15 KJV). In liturgical and contemplative art, time, space, and the material stuff of this world are transformed and offered up to God as a place of his habitation. The Psalms and Prophets speak often of all of creation being enlisted in worship — of trees shouting with joy (Ps. 96:12), of mountains announcing peace and justice (Ps. 72:2), and of the sky rejoicing. In music, poetry, sculpture, and other arts, these words are in fact realized, as wood and air, stone and metal are made the resonating body of God's praise.

Of course, it is not only the nonhuman creation that is to be transformed; this renewal is meant for humanity as well. The work of artistry then, gives us a picture of the spiritual life itself, a powerful analogy of the work God's Holy Spirit is bringing about in us. As the Spirit transforms us "into [Christ's] likeness with ever-increasing glory" (2 Cor. 3:18), the ordinary stuff of the world — our own humanity — is taken up, beautified, and sanctified in the praise of God. In the spiritual life, we creatures offer ourselves to God to be filled with his presence; and without any diminishment of our humanity or individuality, we are made whole and perfect. So then, while the arts are a perennial dimension of human devotion, it is ultimately the Spirit who is the great artist, and his surpassing masterpiece is men and women remade in the image of the perfect humanity of Jesus Christ.

Sources Cited

Augustine. *Confessions.* Trans. H. Chadwick (1998).

Chan, S. *Spiritual Theology* (1998).

McKinnon, J. *Music in Early Christian Literature* (1987).

Mouw, R., and M. Noll, eds. *Wonderful Words of Life* (2004).

Moyise, S., and M. Menken. *The Psalms in the New Testament* (2004).

Stapert, C. *A New Song for an Old World* (2007).

Theissen, G. *Theological Aesthetics* (2004).

Witvliet, J. *The Biblical Psalms in Christian Worship* (2007).

For Further Reading

Begbie, J. *Resounding Truth* (2008).

Begbie, J., and S. Guthrie, eds. *Resonant Witness* (2010).

Best, H. *Music through the Eyes of Faith* (1993).

Brand, H., and A. Chaplin. *Art and Soul* (1999).

Brown, F. B. *Good Taste, Bad Taste, and Christian Taste* (2003).

Guthrie, S. *Creator Spirit: The Holy Spirit and the Art of Becoming Human* (2011).

Jensen, R. *The Substance of Things Seen* (2004).

Kroeker, C. *Music in Christian Worship* (2005).

Westermeyer, P. *Te Deum* (1998).

CHAPTER 27

SPIRITUALITY IN RELATIONSHIP TO PSYCHOLOGY AND THERAPY

STEVEN J. SANDAGE

The historical relationship between psychology and spirituality has been complex, interspersed with periods of mutual suspicion, disinterest, or romantic fascination. But there is evidence the field of psychology is moving toward a maturer and more respectful and integrative stance in the quest for the sacred. Over the past three decades, the fields of psychology and psychotherapy have experienced a transformation in relation to the topic of spirituality. Throughout most of the 20th century, the dominant perspectives in North American and European psychology and psychoanalysis portrayed antagonistic or disinterested attitudes toward religion and spirituality. The antagonistic stance was reflected in the writings of major thinkers like Sigmund Freud and Albert Ellis, who argued that religiosity was an illusion, mostly pathological or immature, and deleterious to mental health. Behaviorists such as B. F. Skinner promoted a logical positivistic approach to science that called for ignoring "nonobservables" in favor of a focus on observable behavior. This philosophy of science contributed to the neglect of empirical research on spiritual or religious constructs that were thought to be difficult or impossible to operationalize and measure.

There has always been a remnant of psychologists who have held more positive attitudes toward the empirical study and health potential of spirituality and religion. While psychological methods cannot verify metaphysical realities or directly measure the Holy Spirit, authentic spirituality can be expected to create measurable traces in a person's life. William James helped pioneer the modern psychological study of religion and spirituality by actually interviewing people reporting profound spiritual experiences. James was quite sympathetic to the possible transformative benefits of religious and spiritual experience on psychological functioning given his own mystical and healing experiences. Carl Jung countered his mentor Freud in suggesting that internalized religion and spirituality can provide archetypal symbols that facilitate the quest for wholeness, though Jung was more ambivalent about religious orthodoxy based on disappointments in his father's uninspiring example as a Swiss Reformed pastor. Gordon Allport also explored forms of *intrinsic* faith that could be (a) consistent with psychological health and development and (b) differentiated from conformity to religious prejudice and racism. Object relations theorists, such as Harry Guntrip, Donald Winnicott, and Ana-Maria Rizzuto, continued the post-Freudian reevaluation of spirituality and religion by suggesting that individual differences in images of God (e.g., God as warmly available or hostile and punitive) are shaped, in part, through relational experiences during development and can be more or less healthy (Sorenson). These theorists helped shape a more complex landscape for the psychological study of spirituality as a valuable part of human experience and a clinically useful phenomenon.

During the 1980s and 1990s, psychological researchers increased the quantity, quality, and breadth of the empirical study of religion, spirituality, and health. Martin Seligman galvanized the positive psychology movement by encouraging the field to move beyond a focus on the scientific study of mental illness to consider age-old questions of human flourishing and the constructive roles of spirituality, religion, and character strengths or virtues, such as forgiveness, gratitude, wisdom, compassion, and hope. Empirical studies have found positive relationships between many indices of religion and spirituality and measures of mental and even physical health (Hill and Pargament). The scientific data shows that Freud and Ellis were far too pessimistic in their global pathologizing of religion and spirituality, even leading Ellis to moderate his views late in his career. A recent survey of American Psychological Association members showed the vast majority regarded religion as beneficial (82 percent) rather than harmful (7 percent) to mental health (Delaney et al.).

Christian Approaches to Relational Integration

Christians have historically also taken a variety of relational postures with regard to psychology. Pastoral theologians have been engaging in informal psychology for centuries through concern for human struggles and the practice of Christian soul care. The 1980s and 1990s were also a fertile period for spiritual directors such as Henri Nouwen, Alan Jones, and David Benner, who advanced the integration of spiritual formation and psychology. Evangelicals (such as Gary Collins, Mary Stewart Van Leeuwen, Larry Crabb, and Siang Yang Tan) also offered numerous integrative models of psychology and Christian faith during this time.

Contemporary Christian approaches to the formal discipline of psychology have been grouped into four primary views (Johnson and Jones). The *Biblical Counseling* tradition views psychology as largely antithetical or irrelevant to Christian spirituality, given the sufficiency of Scripture. The view formally designated as *Christian psychology* allows a secondary place for empirical research but privileges theology over psychology in the foundations of knowledge. The *levels of explanation* view differentiates separate levels or dimensions of reality and heralds the value of the humility of science and rigorous empirical research to complement or even revise theological understandings. The *integration* view starts with the understanding that psychology and theology are both hermeneutical or interpretive disciplines that can be mutually enriched by interpenetrating dialogue rather than prearranged hierarchy or exclusionary boundaries.

All of these Christian views have tended to approach psychology and theology as abstract bodies of knowledge. More recently, Shults and Sandage have suggested a *relational integration* approach that moves relational dynamics between psychologists, theologians, and pastors to the foreground in understanding Christian spirituality. It is people who attempt (or resist) the work of cooperative integration. From a theological perspective, the realities of the fall mean that it is easier to suspect one another and compete across disciplines than it is to partner together in mutual respect. A Christian approach to spiritual formation can also frame the ultimate goal of integrating psychology and theology as one of developing Christlike relational virtues, such as love, compassion, honesty, and justice, between persons rather than simply the logical consistency of ideas. So, relational integration offers a framework that can illuminate the relational barriers and pathways to integrative spiritual formation.

Relational integration also suggests that psychology and theology are unavoidable parts of human experience and spirituality. Everyone makes interpretations, however unconscious or implicit, about human behavior and about ultimate theological concerns. Psychology is valuable for hermeneutical understanding of what we each "bring to the text" of Scripture and spiritual experience. For example, personality traits have been found to predict beliefs about the characteristics of Jesus (Piedmont, Williams, and Ciarrocchi). If personality influences one's Christology, then an important part of Christian spiritual formation is growth in the self-awareness to responsibly manage projections onto scriptural interpretations. While the Christian tradition clearly teaches that God exists beyond the boundaries of the human psyche, human spiritual experience is always mediated through our neurobiological and psychological structures (Sandage et al.). In contrast to Gnostic dualism, which sought to spiritually bypass embodiment, Judaism and Christianity have held incarnational views of human spirituality that value the sacredness of personhood and everyday life.

From a Christian perspective, psychological science is aimed at understanding the general revelation of God's wisdom in creation. Psychology can be described as "the empirical study of God's masterpiece," that is, humanity. Epistemologically, theology and social science can be relationally integrated toward a healthy partnership. In general, theology tends to focus on prescription (how things should be) and psychology focuses on description (how things are). This is obviously an oversimplification, because theology can also be rooted in history and addresses human realities, and psychological models also convey certain values and "metaphors of ultimacy" embedded in larger theories (Browning and Cooper). But there is a difference in emphases and methodology. A Christian spirituality should value description as well as prescription to empirically test for discrepancies between the ideal and the actual. Spiritual traditions always claim benefits for adherents, but not all traditions embrace empirical accountability for assessing spiritual fruit. A Christian approach to psychology will also value ethical and supernatural

perspectives imported from theological reflection for fidelity to Christian ideals. Kierkegaard called for balancing the dialectic of the finite and infinite, which is a wise invitation to spiritual integration of the actual and the ideal.

Spirituality and Human Development

Like Kierkegaard, psychologists view spiritual experience as embedded within the finitude of human development. Hill and Pargament offered a descriptive and psychological definition of spirituality as the "search for the sacred," highlighting the active quest of humans to discover the divine or ultimate truth within their developmental contexts. Shults and Sandage (2006) adapted this definition to fit an integrative relational framework by defining *relational spirituality* as "ways of relating to the sacred" (161). Humans relate to God and the sacred in a variety of ways, such as devotion, mistrust, avoidance, surrender, and so on. An emphasis on relational spirituality is useful since a wealth of psychological data now confirms the impressions of psychoanalysts that relational experiences shape neurobiological templates used in forming God images and theological beliefs (Sorenson). For example, those who had a distant relationship with their parents are more likely to experience God as distant than those whose parents were consistently warm and responsive. Relational factors can also influence self-identification with certain narrative themes in the development of personality. For example, those who experience early traumatic disappointments in parents may develop a tragic worldview and need a form of Christian spirituality that involves authentic lament. While some psychological theories and theologies can be critiqued as excessively individualistic, numerous theories are more communitarian in considering the relational matrix of human life (Balswick et al.).

A relational perspective on spirituality is also consistent with Trinitarian theology—God always exists in relationship. God as Trinity exemplifies *differentiated relationality*, that is, separate persons existing in intimate and cooperative relationship. In an analogous fashion, family systems researchers have defined *differentiation of self* as an ability to balance intimacy and autonomy, or community and solitude, in relationships. Differentiation of self involves the mature capacity to value both unity and diversity similar to Paul's instruction in 1 Corinthians 12. High levels of differentiation involve emotional and relational wholeness, which carries semantic resonance with the biblical maturity constructs of *shalom* and *teleios* (Sandage et al.). Low levels of differentiation result in the relational extremes of either enmeshment or estrangement that can sabotage spiritual growth in families and faith communities.

A relational approach to human development can also support models of spiritual formation by identifying family transitions and interpersonal factors that encourage or inhibit growth and maturity. For example, narcissism is a trait that inhibits spiritual maturity and virtue, while the developmental achievement of empathy correlates with numerous measures of spiritual health and maturity. A developmental framework can also help tease apart the egocentrism that could be normal for a child from the pathological grandiosity that is immature in an adult. In the person of Jesus, God submitted to human development and the process of growing "in wisdom and stature" (Luke 2:52). Jesus' developmental growth in reasoning and autonomy at age twelve was confusing and frustrating to his parents, and families continue to be challenged to appreciate the changes necessitated by adolescence and other developmental transitions.

Spirituality and Virtue

The positive psychology of virtue is one of the other promising areas for integrating psychology and spirituality. Research on human well-being and virtue has been exploding in recent decades.

A biblical spirituality will certainly emphasize the "fruit of the Spirit," such as love, joy, peace, patience, generosity, and self-control (Gal. 5:22), which are all robust topics within contemporary psychology. Forgiveness, hope, and gratitude are three other virtues generating fascinating empirical connections to spiritual and psychological well-being. Interpersonal forgiveness has been one of the most widely studied virtues in psychology with over twelve hundred empirical studies in the past twenty years. For example, studies have identified developmental and personality correlates of forgiving others, including empathy or compassion as a key causal mechanism (Shults and Sandage 2003). Based on measures of relational spirituality, those with a secure emotional attachment with God also tend to have a more forgiving disposition than those with an insecure emotional attachment with God (Davis et al.), again highlighting the importance of relational development.

Positive psychologists study well-being and the virtues of maturity, but the differences between well-being and maturity are sometimes overlooked. Some theorists define well-being hedonically as "happiness" or "life satisfaction." Others, typically those using the language of virtue and a developmental lens, point out that well-being and maturity are not synonymous (Shults and Sandage 2006). Growth in maturity can involve temporary reductions in well-being, particularly as idealistic notions about life and spirituality are surrendered. The ancient Greek concept of *eudaimonia* has been reengaged by some positive psychologists who are interested in a mature and less-hedonistic form of well-being that involves fulfilling one's purpose or *telos* in community with others. In a parallel way, some Christian spiritualities seem to focus on simply feeling better or enjoying life, while other approaches describe a developmental trajectory toward mature virtue.

Discerning Christians will recognize that virtues are not generic. Virtues are construed in a narrative context and shaped by cultural and religious meanings. Buddhist and Christian understandings of a virtue like forgiveness will likely be different, though we can find different catalogs of virtue and nuances of meaning even within the Christian tradition. For example, a study of Reformed and contemplative writers on the virtue of humility can reveal interesting differences. In a similar way, psychological theories are diverse and will lead to somewhat differing virtue constructions. So, the overall task is not simply integrating a generic Christian theology with psychology. The process involves clarifying a particular Christian tradition and a particular psychological theory, for example, Pietism and attachment theory on the virtue of love. Theology is useful for deepening the rather "thin" meaning that psychologists sometimes use in their definitions of virtue. Psychological methods can then serve to empirically test models and interventions to promote these virtues.

Spirituality and Psychology

Spiritual leaders and psychotherapists each have much to offer and much to gain by progress in relational integration, as both disciplines are concerned with transformative change. Rich traditions of pastoral soul care and communal practice have helped suffering individuals for centuries, and surveys show that clergy are typically the first line of intervention with mental health problems. The field of psychotherapy has generated empirically supported interventions for fourteen mental disorders and a host of individual, couple, and family struggles over the past fifty years. Spiritual leaders can benefit from collaborating with theologically informed therapists in the community, because pastors and other ministry leaders typically do not have the time or competence to deal with the volume and complexity of all mental health and relational problems. Moreover, it is valuable for some people, including Christian leaders, to have the resources of professional therapy in the community so help can be obtained within safe boundaries of privacy. While some readily find spiritual and emotional growth in church or spiritual direction contexts, those who have experienced spiritual abuse may need to pursue healing for a period in a therapy context that is less likely to reactivate traumatic associations. And psychotherapists can benefit from healthy collaboration with religious communities since most clients will engage those systems of communal support long after they finish therapy.

It can be tempting to try to differentiate problems that are "spiritual" from those that are "psychological." However, neither a biblical view of personhood nor contemporary psychological research supports those simple distinctions. Emotional and relational dynamics will typically influence one's experience of the sacred and vice versa. Mental health problems, such as depression or posttraumatic stress disorder, are often socially isolating and will negatively impact spiritual functioning. Therapeutic interventions that alleviate mental health problems will typically contribute to the potential for healthier relational spirituality. In fact, studies have shown that even secular psychotherapy for depression can improve spiritual well-being in Christian clients (Worthington and Sandage).

Of course, well-informed and spiritually-sensitive therapists can potentially contribute to even greater levels of integration with their clients. For example, spiritually-integrative therapy has been found to improve both mental health and positive God images, and numerous spiritual practices are showing promising results in clinical research. Some therapists may avoid discussing spiritual issues with clients due to their own limited familiarity or spiritual conflicts. However, surveys show most clients are interested in discussing spiritual and religious concerns in therapy (Rose et al.). While respect for client boundaries is healthy, neglecting the topic of spirituality when clients want to discuss it is not.

Depression and anxiety are topics that reveal the complexity of spiritual and psychological integration. Some positive-minded approaches to both spirituality and psychotherapy promote a linear goal of alleviating symptoms of depression or anxiety as quickly as possible. Other developmental or "depth" approaches to spirituality and psychotherapy have suggested a potentially constructive place for crucibles of emotional and spiritual darkness (Schnarch). For example, the contemplative tradition of viewing "dark nights of the soul" as a time of weaning from spiritual idealizations and a pruning of distortions can be paralleled in the psychoanalytic emphasis on surrendering immature defense mechanisms and grieving prior illusions (Jones). Relational approaches to both spirituality and psychotherapy can also find convergence in highlighting the pivotal role of interpersonal dynamics in healing and transformation.

Spirituality and Social Justice

The constructive relational integration of spirituality and psychology can also contribute to social justice. Participation in the advancement of social justice is a vital dimension of Christian spiritual maturity, and the field of psychology has developed substantive bodies of research and organizational initiatives aimed at social justice. For example, psychological research has shown that the dynamics of racism, sexism, and other forms of discrimination are often subtle and preconscious, echoing the biblical truth that our own motives can be hidden (Prov. 20:5). In North America, psychologists and therapists also include a higher percentage of women and persons of color than the current cadre of evangelical Christian leaders. So collaboration can enrich the diversity of the Christian community. At the same time, the disciplines of both

psychology and theology can be practiced in ethnocentric ways, so the challenge is to develop culturally sensitive approaches to therapy and spiritual formation (Dueck and Reimer).

Those with serious mental illness are also one of the underserved and often stigmatized populations in our churches and larger communities. Interpreting the relationship between mental illness and spiritual warfare raises challenging worldview questions and practical dilemmas. However, the demonization of all mental illness runs risk of oppressing vulnerable persons who may be helped through psychiatric treatment for schizophrenia, bipolar disorder, or other mental illnesses. Rather than reducing all suffering to a single etiology, integrative Christian spirituality can retain a place for supernatural, systemic, psychological, and biological influences on suffering and healing.

Finally, voices from the social sciences, even non-Christian ones, can provide a prophetic critique of the church from "outside the system." John Wesley said, "Even to imagine that those who are not saved cannot teach you is a very great and serious mistake. Dominion is not found in grace. Not observing this has led some into many mistakes and certainly pride." Listening to "pagan prophets and poets" does call for critical reflection and wise appropriation (Dan. 1; Acts 17). But to exclude all outside voices runs the fundamentalist risk of a narcissistic implosion, which typically most disadvantages women and other nondominant groups within a system. Ultimately, the relational integration of Christian spirituality and psychology is a challenging and formative process that both requires and cultivates the *integrity* of wholeness and holiness in union with Christ. The "field is ripe."

Sources Cited

Balswick, J., et al. *The Reciprocating Self* (2005).

Browning, D., and T. Cooper. *Religious Thought and Modern Psychologies* (2004).

Davis, D., et al. "Relational Spirituality and Forgiveness." *Journal of Psychology and Christianity* 27, no. 4 (2008): 293–301.

Delaney, H., et al. "Religiosity and Spirituality among Psychologists." *Professional Psychology: Research and Practice* 38, no. 5 (2007): 538–46.

Dueck, A., and K. Reimer, *A Peaceable Psychology* (2009).

Hill, P., and K. Pargament, "Advances in the Conceptualization and Measurement of Religion and Spirituality." *American Psychologist* 58, no. 1 (2003): 64–74.

Johnson, E., and S. Jones, eds. *Psychology and Christianity* (2000).

Jones, A. *Soul Making* (1985).

Kierkegaard, S. *The Sickness unto Death* (1980).

Piedmont, R., et al. "Personality Correlates of One's Image of Jesus." *Journal of Psychology and Theology* 25, no. 3 (1997): 364–73.

Rose, E., et al. "Spiritual Issues in Counseling." *Journal of Counseling Psychology* 48, no. 1 (2001): 61–71.

Sandage, S., et al. "Relational Spirituality and Transformation." *Journal of Spiritual Formation and Soul Care* 1, no. 2 (2008): 182–206.

Schnarch, D. *Passionate Marriage* (1997).

Seligman, M. *Authentic Happiness* (2002).

Shults, F. L., and S. Sandage. *The Faces of Forgiveness* (2003).

———. *Transforming Spirituality* (2006).

Sorenson, R. *Minding Spirituality* (2004).

Wesley, J. *A Plain Account of Christian Perfection* (1767).

Worthington, E., Jr., and S. Sandage. "Religion and Spirituality." In *Psychotherapy Relationships That Work*, ed. J. Norcross (2002), 383–400.

For Further Reading

Aten, J., and M. Leach, eds. *Spirituality and the Therapeutic Process* (2009).

McMinn, M., and C. Campbell. *Integrative Psychotherapy* (2007).

Miller, W., and H. Delaney, eds. *Judeo-Christian Perspectives on Psychology* (2005).

Pargament, K. *Spiritually Integrated Psychotherapy* (2007).

CHAPTER 28

SPIRITUALITY IN RELATION TO CREATION

LOREN WILKINSON AND MARY-RUTH K. WILKINSON

Christian spirituality is founded on the belief that God is Creator and we are creatures. But the spirituality evoked by creation is not limited to Christians, for all people live in a cosmos that is sheer gift—which we could not have imagined and certainly could not have created. The universe, and our conscious presence in it, is a miracle, acknowledged or not, which ought to evoke wonder, praise, worship, and care.

Such general awareness of the Creator through creation has evoked all sorts of spiritualities, including the generic spiritualities of these late modern times, many associated with "deep ecology" (a religious dimension of the environmental movement). The incompleteness of such "creation spiritualities," and the fact that they sometimes see only creation, not the Creator, has understandably made many Christians ambivalent about them. The term *creation spirituality* was championed by Matthew Fox, a former Catholic (and now Episcopal) priest. Fox has been influenced by another controversial Roman Catholic thinker, Thomas Berry, who has argued that Christians ought to set the Bible aside for a generation and learn only from creation. The thoroughly heterodox ideas of these proponents of "creation spirituality" have made the term very difficult for evangelical Christians to use. Hence, the circuitous title of this article!

Nevertheless, the Spirit who opens people to the glory of God through creation is the same Spirit who opens Christians to the love of God in Jesus. A major challenge for contemporary Christians, therefore, is to learn that any genuine Christian spirituality will also involve a "creation spirituality." This requires thoughtful reading of both creation and Scripture, but Scripture is the necessary starting point.

The Biblical Basis for Creation Spirituality

The biblical story is fundamentally about God's purpose in creation: the important human role in that purpose, the way that role is restored to us through the costly love of God in Jesus, and the ultimate fulfillment, heralded by the resurrection, of God's purpose of sharing his love with a renewed creation. All Christian spirituality is informed by our participation in this great story.

The biblical narrative begins with the creation. Several themes in the Genesis Creation story are important for understanding biblical spirituality. First is the announcement of the *goodness* of creation. Less obvious, perhaps, but crucial for fully understanding the text, is the fact that the biblical creation story is itself a kind of argument *against* the surrounding "creation spiritualities" of ancient Near Eastern cultures. Neither sun nor moon nor sea nor any other creature is to be worshiped, as in animisms primeval and contemporary; these good things are all creations of the transcendent God.

Another crucial theme for Christian spirituality in the biblical creation account is the close relationship of human persons to the rest of creation on the one hand and to their Creator on the other.

Humans are *adam*, from the Hebrew *adamah*, meaning "earth," a wordplay that suggests we really ought to call "Adam" (and ourselves) something like "earthling(s)." One powerful implication for biblical "spirituality," therefore, is its affirmation of the material. We share our good material existence with everything else on earth. Human uniqueness in creation resides in our responsibility *to* the Creator *for* the rest of creation (both ruling it and taking care of it). Being made in "the image of God" implies our relationship of responsibility to the Creator: whether clearly or with distortion, we represent his presence and character to the rest of creation. It is this privilege of being that unique part of creation called into personal relationship with the triune God, rather than the possession of some uniquely spiritual quality, that is the foundation of Christian spirituality. Wendell Berry eloquently describes this deep biblical unity of body and soul:

> The formula given in Genesis 2:7 is not man = body + soul; the formula there is soul = dust + breath. According to this verse, God did not make a body and put a soul into it, like a letter into an envelope. He formed man of dust; then, by breathing His breath into it, He made the dust live. The dust, formed as man and made to live, did not *embody* a soul; it *became* a soul.... Humanity is thus presented to us, in Adam, not as a creature of two discrete parts temporarily glued together but as a single mystery. (Berry, 106)

The other major creation-related theme from early Genesis is the recognition that though we are made for intimate relationship with God, we are alienated from God—and hence from ourselves, from each other, and from the rest of creation generally. Careful reading of Genesis 3 suggests that what has come to be called "the fall" describes not an ontological change in the creation, but a relational change in Adam, "earthling," imager of God. The implications for Christian spirituality are profound. First, such an understanding of sin refutes the idea, inherited from Platonism and restated in mythological terms by the Gnostics, that in order to be "spiritual" one should shun the physical world. Second, to understand sin as broken relationship with creation implies that redemption means a healed relationship with creation. Thus, an authentic Christian spirituality should root us more deeply in material creation, not separate us from it.

No part of the story of redemption in Scripture leaves creation behind. The first biblical covenant (in Gen. 9) is not only with Noah, but with "every living creature of all flesh," and follows God's promise:

> "As long as the earth endures,
> seedtime and harvest,
> cold and heat,
> summer and winter,
> day and night
> will never cease."
>
> (Gen. 8:22)

The better-known covenant with Abraham and his descendants is a promise that God's people are to be given a *place* where the fruits of creation are abundant: "For the LORD your God is bringing you into a good land ... with wheat and barley, vines and fig trees, pomegranates, olive oil and honey.... When you have eaten and are satisfied, praise the LORD your God for the good land he has given you" (Deut. 8:7–10). As Christopher Wright has pointed out, this picture of a three-way harmony between God, people, and a particular place in creation is intended, from Eden on, to be an emblem of God's purpose for the whole earth (174–76). No spirituality that leaves out creation does justice to the biblical vision.

This essential role of creation in our experience of the purposes and promises of God is particularly evident throughout the Psalms. We see it metaphorically in the picture of the righteous man as a fruitful tree planted by abundant waters (Ps. 1). In Psalm 19 "the heavens declare the glory of God." Throughout the Psalms, that glory is usually manifested through creation as God's continuing goodness and care: "You care for the land and water it...."

The streams of God are filled with water" (65:9). In Psalm 104 the order of creation from Genesis 1 is repeated, but mainly as what God is doing *now*, continuously: "He makes grass grow for the cattle, and plants for people to cultivate—bringing forth food from the earth: wine that gladdens human hearts, oil to make their faces shine, and bread that sustains their hearts" (vv. 14–15 TNIV). And at the end of the Psalter (Ps. 148), humanity is invited to join with sun, moon, water, weather, trees, birds, and animals in their praise of the Creator.

We find a different sort of instance of the role of creation in biblical spirituality in God's answer to the repeated pleas of Job for God to explain his undeserved suffering. When God finally speaks, from the whirlwind, his answer to Job's spiritual anguish is a detailed challenge to look at creation, which God proceeds to show him in detail. The whole book seems to carry the message that an experience of creation as the work of God is a better answer to some spiritual questions than any amount of theological explanation (which is amply provided by Job's friends). Creation testifies to the fact that God's purpose for good is still there behind the mystery and the pain, whether or not we see it.

Sometimes Christians pass over this abundant Old Testament witness to the spiritual value of creation by placing more emphasis on the New Testament. However (quite apart from the danger of trying thus to drive a wedge between the testaments), a little reflection shows how thoroughly the story of Jesus in the New Testament reaffirms the spiritual value of creation that is so clearly set forth in the Old. The central Christian affirmation—that in Jesus, God himself has become an "earthling"—profoundly reaffirms the worth of creation. This mighty "yes!" through the incarnation to the goodness of creation is reaffirmed in the resurrection and ascension, which show us a physical Jesus: changed, but still very much a part of creation, which is now taken up into God. As N. T. Wright puts it in *Surprised by Hope*: "The gospel of Jesus Christ announces that what God did for Jesus at Easter he will do not only for all those who are 'in Christ' but also for the entire cosmos. It will be an act of new creation, parallel to and derived from the act of new creation when God raised Jesus from the dead" (Wright, 99). Wright's words on the meaning of the resurrection make plain another truth, which has sometimes been overlooked in Christian spirituality: that God's ultimate purpose for creation is not its destruction and replacement, but its renewal and transformation. Just as we look forward, not to an eternally disembodied spiritual existence, but to a resurrected life in the body, so our glimpses of "new creation"—whether in Isaiah, Ezekiel, or Revelation—show us a physical world changed but recognizably continuous with the creation, which, from the beginning, God has always maintained in its goodness. The highly figurative language of Revelation shows us a city descending to a renewed earth, into which the "glory and honor of the nations" are gathered (Rev. 21:26).

Underlying these New Testament affirmations of the everlasting goodness and value of creation is a foundational New Testament teaching that makes an even more startling claim on the Christian to affirm the value of creation: that is the close causal link between Christ and creation. In some mysterious way, the Christ we are called to identify with is described as the *means* of creation. Thus, John begins his account of Jesus' life by saying that "Through him all things were made" (John 1:3). Even earlier, in his first letter to the Corinthians, Paul speaks of the "one Lord, Jesus Christ, through whom all things came and through whom we live" (8:6). The writer of the letter to the Hebrews speaks of Jesus as the Son of God "through whom he made the universe" (1:2). And Paul in his letter to the Colossians says of Jesus, "In him all things were created.... In him all things hold together" (1:16–17 TNIV). He continues by stressing that just as Christ is involved in the creation of all things, so he is also involved in their redemption: "God was pleased to have all his fullness dwell in him, and through him to reconcile to himself all things" (1:19–20 TNIV).

As "co-heirs with Christ" (Rom. 8:17), we inherit a familial role of bringing order into chaos — especially the chaos that we ourselves have brought by not heeding the original mandate to "take care of" the garden (Gen. 2:15). Bringing healing to creation seems to be the implication of Jesus' words when he claimed that in healing a person with disability he worked as his Father works (John 5:17). As God's (Father, Son, and Holy Spirit's) creation, we have thwarted the continual action of Father, Son, and Holy Spirit in making and sustaining creation. This mandate is a spiritual task: Jesus said, "All who have faith in me will do the works I have been doing, and they will do even greater things" (John 14:12 TNIV). Thus, a Christian spirituality implies that we join the triune God in healing the creation we have harmed.

Creation in Christian Tradition and Spiritual Practice

As we have seen, Scripture carries a powerful message to the Christian about creation. But it is a double message. On the one hand, all creation points to the Creator, so involvement with creation should draw one closer to God. But because reconciliation with God should involve as well our reconciliation with other creatures, and because in Christ we meet the very agent of creation, the Christian's life "in Christ" should open one up toward creation. Closeness to creation should result in openness to God; conversely, closeness to God should result in openness to creation. Christians have always recognized that to be reconciled to God in Christ implies love and care for one's neighbor. In the 21st century, the groaning of a suffering creation (Rom. 8:22) makes it clear that a true Christian spirituality implies love and care for the rest of creation as well. Thus, Christian spirituality carries with it strong implications about how we should treat creation.

Yet the history of Christian attitudes toward creation shows much evidence of the first message, but very little of the second. One reason for this asymmetry is probably that Scripture itself encourages the believer to put restored relationship with God first and sometimes seems to treat creation, "the things of the world," as an impediment. The most severe form of this spiritual error is idolatry, the worship of the creature instead of the Creator. We have already seen how the Genesis 1 creation account stresses the power and otherness of God the Creator, who spoke and things were made, precisely because in the surrounding culture those things — sun, moon, trees, animals — were worshiped as divine. Thus, God gave the second commandment: "You shall not make for yourself an image in the form of anything in heaven above or on the earth beneath or in the waters below. You shall not bow down to them or worship them" (Ex. 20:4–5 TNIV). In the same vein, the Hebrew people were commanded to destroy the "groves," to tear down the altars in "high places," since these were sites for the worship of things in "nature" misperceived as divine. Similarly in the New Testament, reconciliation with God is the most urgent human need. Even Paul's affirmation in Romans 1 that "since the creation of the world God's invisible qualities ... have been ... understood from what has been made" is tempered by the warning that therefore people are "without excuse" for worshiping instead the images of created things — "birds and animals and reptiles" (vv. 20–23 TNIV).

Such words have given rise to a long *contemptus mundi* ("contempt for the world") tradition in Christianity. We see it early in the desert fathers, who withdrew into the desert — not to get closer to creation, but to flee from anything that would hinder relationship to the Creator. Pseudo-Dionysus, around AD 500, produced a hugely influential argument for a "negative way" of approach to God, which saw everything in creation as a weight to be left behind in the spiritual "flight of the alone to the Alone." And though the Reformation in many ways opened the world up again to the recognition that it is a good and healthy place (John Calvin often referred to the world as a "theater for the mighty acts of God"), the tradition of suspicion toward creation continued, precisely because creation is not God, and hence of infinitely lower worth. We encounter this suspicion toward creation in popular evangelical songs of the 19th and 20th centuries, such as "This world is not my home; I'm just a-passing through," or

> Turn your eyes upon Jesus,
> Look full in His wonderful face,
> And the things of earth will grow strangely dim,
> In the light of His glory and grace.

Similarly, much recent worship music is generally about unmediated connection between the worshiper and God: there is much encouragement for the worshiper to exalt God "to lift up his name"—but rarely because of God's work in creation. And hardly ever does the invitation to worship God turn us back to our task in creation. As a general rule, the more that contemporary worship songs speak of Christ or of the Spirit, the less they involve creation. They rather link the worshiper and God in a kind of sacred bubble from which the rest of creation is excluded. This mistake is evident throughout much of Christian spirituality, past and present: the closer one is to God, the more creation seems to recede.

Yet balancing this venerable "negative way" is a Christian "affirmative way," which proceeds on the assumption that everything in creation is capable of being a pointer to God, of value both for its own sake and for what it can tell us of its Creator. The one early pioneer of such a recovery of the place of creation in Christian spirituality was Francis of Assisi. His clear understanding that the incarnation affirms the creation is evident in his bringing animals into the church at the celebration of the nativity of Christ—the beginning of the "Christmas crèche" tradition. Even more significant is Francis's great hymn "Canticle of the Sun," familiar today as "All Creatures of Our God and King," which is still one of the few Christian hymns that

(in the spirit of Psalm 148) joyfully gathers the human worshiper, together with the rest of creatures ("brothers" sun, wind, and fire; "sisters" moon, stars, water) in praise of their Creator.

One of the eventual consequences of that recovered openness to the goodness of creation is the whole tradition of science. Though the origins of science are complex, an essential root was the recognition by devout Christians like Johannes Kepler that to study creation was to "think God's thoughts after him."

Today a failure to recognize that science has deep Christian roots is widespread and has tragic consequences. One of these is the effective dwindling of the meaning of "creation" to a particular theory of how and when God created. Debates that pit creation against evolution are symptoms of a double failure. On the part of many Christians, it is the failure to recognize the richness of the biblical teaching outlined earlier: that creation is the ongoing relationship of the triune God, through the Spirit who brings life, to a cosmos, which "holds together" in Christ. On the part of a science that is ideologically atheistic—or entirely pragmatic—it is a forgetfulness of the wonder and awe in which science is rooted. Christians should recognize that to understand creation as part of a describable process extending over time is not in any way inconsistent with viewing creation as the action of God. Scientists, on the other hand (Christian or not), should recognize that no matter how exhaustive an explanation might be, it is still an explanation of a miracle—the foundational miracle that there is anything at all, let alone the deluge of sound, scent, color, complexity, and life that pours over and sustains us.

Thinking about creation in the light of the full story of revelation leads to theology; thinking about creation in terms of the story it tells about itself leads to science. And yet the relationship between science and theology has often been troubled and adversarial. Some have been content to leave the two stories disconnected—from the science side, for example, Steven Jay Gould, who called them "non-conflicting magisteria"; from the theology side, Karl Barth, who said a resounding "no" (in a famous argument with Emil Brunner) to any attempt at a "natural" theology.

But an authentic Christian spirituality recognizes that God is telling one story, not two, and the theologies that recognize this truth are rich in spiritual resources. The great Jesuit scientist Pierre Teilhard de Chardin, in works such as *The Phenomenon of Man* (1959) and *The Divine Milieu* (1960), tried valiantly to reconcile the Christian doctrine of creation with the scientific theory of evolution, seeing Christ (cf. Eph. 1:10) as the "Omega point" of the universe, drawing all things forward to himself. Sympathetic to his task, but critical of some aspects of his "process" thinking, Protestant theologians such as Jürgen Moltmann and Colin Gunton argue in different ways for a deeply Trinitarian understanding of the essential unity of creation and redemption. In so doing, they draw on the richly sacramental tradition of Eastern Orthodox thought, represented by contemporary thinkers such as John Zizioulas and Alexander Schmemann.

Finally, an important consequence of a recovered *Christian* spirituality with reference to creation is the growing recognition that we humans have an obligation to care for it. Christians, like all people, have been helped in this regard by the vivid images of the earth from space, which have become a powerful symbol of what a good and fragile gift the earth is. The new ecological awareness that such photos dramatize is accompanied by unavoidable evidence of the degradation of the good creation through human activity. Although eschatologies that see the earth headed for immediate destruction (whether motivated by a particular brand of exegesis or by environmental doom-saying) continue to have an influence, growing numbers of Christians recognize that in Christ, the "new Adam," our gardener's task is restored, and creation has a hope and a future. Christian camps and conference centers, long located in places of great natural beauty as a way of directing people to worship the Creator God, are more and more using those ecologically significant locations to help people understand that the Christian gospel is good news for "all things," including creatures of the earth, not just humans. This new awareness is embodied in organizations such as the Evangelical Environmental Network, with its widely circulated Evangelical Declaration on the Care of Creation and A Rocha International (whose remarkable story of the inclusion of creation in the missionary task is told in two books by Peter Harris, *Under the Bright Wings* [2000] and *Kingfisher's Fire* [2008].

Both of Harris's books take their title from the poetry of Gerard Manley Hopkins, who believed that "The world is charged with the grandeur of God." Poets and artists often lead the way into a Christian spirituality of creation. Awareness of the Spirit of God, whose word has gone out through creation to "the ends of the earth," continues to draw people to God. The challenge to Christians is to connect such experience of God in creation with our experience of God in Christ Jesus, "through whom all things hold together."

Sources Cited

Berry, W. *Sex, Economy, Freedom and Community* (1993).

Gunton, C. *The Triune Creator* (1998).

Moltmann, J. *God in Creation* (1985).

Schmemann, A. *For the Life of the World* (1973).

Wright, C. *God's People in God's Land* (1990).

Wright, N. T. *Surprised by Hope* (2008).
Zizioulas, J. *Being as Communion* (1985).

For Further Reading

Bouma-Prediger, S. *For the Beauty of the Earth* (2010).
Collins, F. *The Language of God* (2007).
Dillard, A. *Pilgrim at Tinker Creek* (1974).
Gunton, C. *The Triune Creator* (1998).
Levertov, D. *The Stream and the Sapphire* (1998).
Wilkinson, L., and M. R. Wilkinson. *Caring for Creation in Your Own Backyard* (1992).
Wilson, E. O. *The Creation* (2006).

CHAPTER 29

CONTEXTUAL SPIRITUALITY

ROBERT M. SOLOMON

Christian spirituality has both a catholicity (universality) and a locality (particularity) — catholicity because its source and focus is the triune God: Father, Son, and Holy Spirit, and locality because it is expressed in different persons, cultures, and social contexts, and at different periods of history, and therefore has to be contextual.

The Bible does speak about an underlying and essential unity in spirituality that stretches across cultures and different contexts. Hence, though we are many and varied in our backgrounds and life situations, we have "one body and one Spirit ... one hope ... one Lord, one faith, one baptism; one God and Father of all, who is over all and through all and in all" (Eph. 4:4 – 6). Because there is one triune God working in and through all cultures and social contexts, there is a foundational unity in all authentic forms of Christian spirituality that is derived from the life and mission of this one triune God. At the same time, diversity in expressions of spirituality is to be expected according to context. This article deals with the contextualized diversities in the expression of Christian spirituality, recognizing that such discussions must be based on an underlying unity of all authentic Christian spiritualities derived from the Trinitarian life and mission, and the canonical Scriptures and historical traditions of the Christian faith.

Much has been written about contextualization (and related terms, such as *indigenization*, *localization*, and *inculturation*) and the need to contextualize the Bible, theology, the presentation of the gospel, and expressions of church. Christian spirituality, too, needs to be contextualized because it has to be located and expressed in a particular sociocultural context in an appropriate and relevant way. We are chosen by the Father to be obedient to Jesus through the sanctifying work of the Holy Spirit (1 Peter 1:2 – 3) — this is a common reality for all Christians. At the same time, we recognize that Jesus, who was incarnated in a particular time, place, and culture continues to express his life in Christians living across time and space through the creative work of the Holy Spirit. In this sense, the universality of the life of the risen Jesus continues to be expressed in the particularities in which his disciples live, in whom his life is found, and through whom it is expressed. This principle is demonstrated in Acts 15 when the early church faced the challenge of determining what form of Christian spirituality was to be expected of Gentile Christians. The key church leaders decided that Gentile Christians were free to express their life in Christ without having to be unnecessarily burdened with Jewish forms of spirituality that had a greater affinity and continuity among Jewish Christians.

To say it differently, the text of Christian spirituality is Christlikeness — Christians are called to become like Christ, and this text has to be expressed in different contexts. It is helpful to explore three such contextual aspects: personality and life stages, culture, and society.

Personality, Life Stages, and Spirituality

James Houston has helpfully pointed out the differences between the terms *temperament, personality*, and *character* by defining them differently. Temperament is connected with the biological makeup of the person—one is born with a temperament, and it does not change, even after one becomes a Christian. Personality is the result of early interactions with significant others, while character has to do with habits: virtues and vices. The most interesting idea in this regard is the possibility that different temperaments and personalities may express Christian spirituality in different ways—all equally biblical and authentic.

In his discussion of Christian spiritual formation, Robert Mulholland uses the Myers Briggs Types to illustrate the relationship between personality and piety and the diversity of spiritualities that can be found among Christians because of differences in personality. Not everyone would find journal keeping or early morning quiet times useful or interesting. Others have identified forms of spirituality, such as Augustinian, Franciscan, Thomistic, and Ignatian, that are personality related. People are drawn to any one of these because of congruencies with their personalities. The point to note is that Christian spirituality can be expressed in different ways by different people simply because of differences in personality. The implication is to avoid the danger of imposing any one personality-related form of spirituality on all; for example, when a church leader insists that church members must adopt spiritual patterns that are more attuned to his or her personality. Not all will be drawn to a deeply contemplative life or a busy and active ministry among crowds. Paul made this point, though not for exactly the same reasons, when he asked rhetorically whether all spoke in tongues or all prophesied, or all preferred administration or any of the other spiritual gifts (1 Cor. 12:29–30). Likewise, Richard Foster has identified six historical streams of Christian spirituality: the contemplative, virtuous, charismatic, prophetic (socially active), evangelical (Word-centered), and sacramental (incarnational).

Some personality types seem to be more dominant in certain cultures. For example, studies have shown that American clergy tend to be more extroverted while British clergy are more introverted. The differences manifest themselves in how pastoral ministry is done and how pastoral spirituality and church life are expressed.

Spirituality takes different shapes or receives different foci at different stages of life's journey. Hence, the pattern of spirituality in adolescence would be different from that in middle or old age. Erik Erikson pioneered in exploring life stages and the psycho-spiritual quest in each stage, while Donald Capps has used Erikson's framework to explore Christian resources, such as the Beatitudes, biblical stories, and John Bunyan's portrayal of the Christian journey, to show the varying spiritual focus as human life progresses in its journey—in terms of one's struggles with sin, growth in virtue, and formation of the self.

Culture and Spirituality

The question whether cultures have their own "personality" has been explored by anthropologists. This has been used by missiologists to explore evangelism and discipleship in various cultures. For instance, Western and Eastern cultures have been contrasted and the implications for cross-cultural missions explored. Sherwood Lingenfelter and Marvin Mayers show the tensions that exist in terms of how time, crisis, values, and judgment are experienced. Western cultures are said to be more task-oriented while non-Western cultures tend to be more relationship-oriented. While such characterization may be too simplistic, and globalization and cross-migration blur such cultural differences, they are still relevant in many areas—including expressions of Christian discipleship.

In the areas of spiritual formation and pastoral care, David Augsburger has argued that in Western, Asian, and African cultures, guilt, shame, and anxiety respectively play a significantly overt role in the cultural psyche of the people. If this is true, it implies that the shape of spirituality may vary from culture to culture, and that there is much more work that needs to be done in developing non-Western spiritualities in a global Christianity that is dominated by theologies and spiritualities developed in Western Christian literature. For example, shame is a concept and experience that is yet to be explored deeply in terms of its connection with human depravity and the alienation and fractures in relationships. The existence of shame points to the importance of communal and relational dimensions in Christian discipleship. The experience of sin as a shameful illness or condition, and of salvation as a deeply therapeutic and restorative process, remains to be explored more deeply in cultures where shame, disgrace, face, and dignity are important features.

Different expressions of Christianity in terms of liturgy, ministry, spirituality, and emphases seem to find their own niches in various cultures, according to Peter Brierley. He shows, using denominational growth patterns worldwide, that Anglicans, Presbyterians, and Pentecostals seem to have grown especially well in Africa, East Asia, and Latin America respectively. Could this be due to the way each of these denominations has found resonance in its particular host culture?

Christian values and habits, while they may be universally understood in similar ways up to a certain point, nevertheless, often find different expressions in different cultures. For example, the fruit of the Spirit listed by Paul can take on different incarnations in different contexts. How does one experience or display patience? In one context, it may mean spending half a day in the post office for a transaction that might take only fifteen minutes elsewhere. In another context, it may mean being willing to wait at the airline counter for an extra ten minutes. Kindness is something that is universally recognized, but it also has strong cultural coloring. In a culture that values privacy or is anxious about imposing one's ideas and plans on another, adequate personal space must be given. Christian kindness may be in the form of making one's help discreetly available; anything more would amount to being insensitive and overbearing. In another culture this may be seen as a cold and inadequate expression of kindness. Similarly, ideas of self-control, perseverance, and so on would differ from culture to culture, not to mention within cultures, between the old and the young. In a culture that has idealized rugged individualism and independence, an ethos of harmony and conformity may be seen negatively, and any Christian spirituality derived from the latter culture may be accused of being a culture of conformity, contrary to the countercultural teachings of Scripture. On the other hand, a different culture that celebrates individual expressiveness may be perceived by others as promoting a spirituality of rebellion. Issues such as Christian obedience, prophetic resistance against sinful aspects of the status quo, and so on may be understood and applied differently in different cultural milieus.

Central to Christian spirituality are relationships: the relationship of Christians with God, one another, and others. The biblical command to love God and neighbor expresses well this relational core in Christian living. How relationships are expressed depends very much on cultural notions and standards. In some cultures, maintaining smooth interpersonal relationships is of utmost importance, to the extent of denying tensions in a relationship and bending truth to service the relationship. In other cultures, this would be seen as a dangerous compromise and inauthentic. How does one learn to speak the truth in love? There are as many answers as there are cultures, as Bernard Adeney has shown.

Francis Fukuyama has shown that trust, an important component in relationships, varies from culture to culture. He identifies the differences between high-trust and low-trust cultures and how societies and businesses are organized. People doing business across cultures have to negotiate between these differences if they are to avoid disasters and embarrassments. Some cultures place their trust more on processes and procedures, documents and laws, rules and technical competence, while others may rely more on their knowledge of and relationship with the persons with whom they are dealing. With such differences, values such as kindness, punctuality, graciousness, truthfulness, and so on may be ranked differently, in terms of importance, in different cultures.

Social Contexts and Spirituality

Christians are deeply shaped by the social contexts in which they exist and live, cope and manage, thrive and prosper. Christians living in a war-torn country may have a different concept and experience than Christians living in a peaceful and prosperous nation. Their aspirations, concerns, anxieties, and temptations would be shaped differently. The experience of Christians living in a place where their faith is a minority or where they may be persecuted would differ from that of those who live in a place where Christianity is a majority religion.

In the history of Christianity, the first few centuries were characterized by periods of intense persecution. In such a situation, martyrdom was a common enough feature of Christian life and was seen by many as a sign of Christian commitment and maturity. Some sought martyrdom as a goal of spiritual formation. When Christianity became the official religion of the Roman Empire and was transformed from being a persecuted minority to a Christendom, monasticism replaced martyrdom as the new ideal of Christian spirituality. With the exploration of new worlds by Western powers at the beginning of the modern period, missionary endeavor became the new ideal of Christian spiri-

tuality. The actual situations, of course, were more complex and colored by many historical streams and challenges.

In the contemporary scene, many Christians in developed and fast-developing nations are struggling with the rise of modern technology and consumerism, with consequent social trends, such as rampant individualism and self-absorption. Social values are rapidly changing amid which the teaching and modeling of Christian values, such as obedience, submission, and self-giving love, have become increasingly challenging. On the other hand, technical innovations, such as the Internet, have made it easier for Christians to study the Bible, listen to sermons, connect with other Christians, and be well-informed. Knowledge explosion, however, does not guarantee spiritual maturity; in fact, there is now a greater need to discern between good information and useless information.

The rise and dominance of technology in modern societies has significant effects on how Christian spirituality is conceived of and experienced. David Noble has argued that the first Christian millennium tended to see technology and salvation (and perfection) in opposition and as antithetical. This is characterized by how Augustine understood the relationship between grace and perfection—the focus was on divine grace. According to Noble, it was different during the second Christian millennium where technology and salvation/perfection were seen together synergistically rather than in opposition (Noble, 12). This may explain, in part, trends in modern spiritualities that resemble a "do-it yourself" approach and that have created a marketplace of spiritual methods, tools, and techniques.

The rise of postmodernism has changed the emphases of much of contemporary spirituality: Christian doctrine and institutions do not hold the kind of attraction and importance they once had in the earlier modern sociocultural environment. The emphasis on stories, image over word, community, openness to other perspectives as against settled positions, and an egalitarianism over hierarchies has been seen both negatively and positively, as can be evidenced in debates on emerging churches and new postmodern Christian spiritualities.

Consumerism is a big challenge in Christian spirituality today, and it affects the shape and life of churches. The rise of megachurches and other emerging forms of churches are changing the experience of attending church, where it feels more like a religious mall, where Christians can put together their own spiritualities from a buffet of spiritual choices, according to their own tastes. Moreover, living in a marketplace of increasing choices, the level of long-term and faithful Christian commitment is also being seriously challenged. It is in this light that denying self and taking up the cross to follow Jesus in a consumerist world is being increasingly addressed by concerned Christian pastors and thinkers who have pointed out the rising trend of a spirituality of gratification.

The same call to Christian discipleship in a place dominated by hunger, war, poverty, and other deprivations is addressed differently. In such contexts, trusting God for daily provisions and survival, handling persecution, or learning how to live with people of other faiths who may be abusive or prejudiced may take central stage.

Similarly, there are differences in approaches to Christian discipleship between those living in rural settings and those who live in highly urban environments. The former would relate to God through natural cycles, the natural environment, the needs and concerns of farmers, and the reality of close-knit communities. The latter would be driven by highly stressful urban living, the need to find small communities amid anonymous urban jungles, competitiveness, and consumerist pursuits. The Bible provides both rural and urban settings—where farming, sheep and cattle, seasons, and natural elements are the focus on the one hand, and cities, walls, business practices, and royal palaces are the concern in other settings. For many Christians living today in highly urban environments, many of the biblical images and metaphors may be found to be remote and strange—such as shepherds and sheep and the cultivation of the spiritual life (seed, water, rain, growth, harvest). Likewise, spiritualities developed by urbanized Christians may cut little ice with the millions still living in rural communities. The transfer of knowledge through printed word and other forms of modern technology, the predominant use of classroom methods in spiritual formation, the adoption of management and psychological paradigms in spiritual formation, the highly individualistic forms of spirituality may all seem foreign and inappropriate when teaching spirituality among rural Christians who may respond better to more oral, communal, and narrative methods.

The Multifaceted Relationship between Christian Spirituality and Its Contexts

Much has been discussed about how Christianity should relate to its cultural and social context. Richard Niebuhr's classical list of the many forms of relationships, using various christological models, is still helpful today. In reality, Christian spirituality relates to its context in a complex spectrum of ways. In the first place, it has to be incarnated in its own context—the word or text is always incarnated in a context. There is no such thing as a Christian spirituality without a particular context. This also means that any form of Christian spirituality developed in a specific context cannot be assumed to be readily relevant or fitting in another context. Sadhu Sundar Singh's comment that the gospel must be brought into India in an "Indian cup" rather than a Western cup is as true today as it was in his day. This brings into question the globalized forms of tools for Christian spirituality (usually developed in the West) that are uncritically used globally through marketing and ready funding. There needs to be developed local expressions of Christian spirituality that are more authentic and relevant in any given context.

At the same time, Christian spirituality stands against every context in a prophetic stance. All contexts are tainted by sin and injustice, and Christians, if they are to be faithful to Christ, must be countercultural. In a racially prejudiced society, they must practice inclusive love for the other; in a materialistic world, they must live generously and simply; in a corrupt society, integrity is called for. In this process, what Christians proclaim and practice may be seen as irrelevant, but they are most relevant in this apparent irrelevance.

In being grounded in and yet challenging its contexts, Christian spirituality will produce transformation of those contexts. In this way, not only are Christians redeemed, but their communities and contexts are also redeemed by the grace of God through the gospel of Christ. It is in this sense that we understand more clearly the biblical teachings that we are in the world but not of the world, and that we are sent into the world by the triune God to fulfill his mission to redeem every context in this world.

Sources Cited

Adeney, B. *Strange Virtues* (1995).

Augsburger, D. *Pastoral Counseling across Cultures* (1986).

Brierley, P. *Future Church* (1998).

Capps, D. *Deadly Sins and Saving Virtues* (1987).

————. *The Decades of Life* (2008).

Erikson, E. *Identity and the Life Cycle* (1980).

Foster, R. *Streams of Living Water* (1998).

Fukuyama, F. *Trust* (1995).

Houston, J., "Principles of Spiritual Direction," Lectures at Prinsep Street Presbyterian Church, Singapore (1992).

Lingenfelter, S., and M. Mayers. *Ministering Cross-Culturally* (2003).

Mulholland, M. R., Jr. *Invitation to a Journey* (1993).

Niebuhr, H. R. *Christ and Culture* (1951).

Noble, D. *The Religion of Technology* (1997).

For Further Reading

Bevans, S. *Models of Contextual Theology* (2002).

Bloesch, D. *Spirituality Old and New* (2007).

Costa, R. *One Faith, Many Cultures* (1988).

Dyrness, W. *Learning about Theology from the Third World* (1990).

Flemming, D. *Contextualization in the New Testament* (2005).

Groody, D. *Globalization, Spirituality, and Justice* (2007).

Hesselgrave, D., and E. Rommen. *Contextualization* (2003).

Kavanaugh, J. *Following Christ in a Consumer Society* (2006).

Lyon, D. *Jesus in Disneyland* (2000).

Taylor, B. *Entertainment Theology* (2008).

Twitchell, J. *Shopping for God* (2007).

CHAPTER 30

CHRISTIAN SPIRITUALITY IN INTERFAITH ENCOUNTER

TERRY C. MUCK

If Christian spirituality is living all of life before God, through Christ, in the transforming and empowering presence of the Holy Spirit, then interreligious encounters with people belonging to other religions traditions have a spirituality component to them. Such encounters are increasingly a part of the life of Christians around the world. It may very well be that at one time Christians lived in religiously homogeneous cultures where meeting a person of another religious tradition was rare. Such is no longer the case. Many, if not most, cultures in the world today are de facto religiously plural, and meeting Hindus, Buddhists, Muslims, and others is increasingly common. Each meeting has spiritual dimensions—and spiritual consequences.

Since this is an increasingly common event for world Christians, we should have a way of evaluating how we do when we relate to non-Christians. That is, how do we know when an interfaith encounter has been sufficiently Christian? From a Christian spirituality point of view, we have two guidelines, a personal one (growing in Christlikeness) and a vocational one (participating in the larger purposes of God). An interfaith encounter that meets biblical criteria of faithfulness in the realm of spirituality answers at least these two questions:

1. Did I grow in Christlikeness during and as a result of this encounter?
2. Can I say that my participation in this encounter was consistent with the larger purposes of God?

One of the biggest mistakes in talking about interfaith encounters is to assume that there is a single way a Christian relates to people of other religious traditions. Making this assumption leads to endless debates about whether a Christian should relate to people of other religions evangelistically or dialogically or in friendship or as if we are confronting enemies. These debates are endless and fruitless because there is no single way a Christian relates to people of other religious traditions—there are many ways Christians relate to people of other religious traditions. Many, if not most, of them are valid. Indeed, many are required by biblical mandate. The context of the encounter usually determines which mode of interaction takes place.

So to talk about spiritual practice in the context of interreligious encounter means to talk about many spirituality issues, some of them common to all interfaith encounters, some of them specific to unique modes of interaction. Below are six of the most common modes of interaction with people of other religions—debate, dialogue, partnership, advocacy, friendship, growth—along with descriptions of both the mode of interaction and the spirituality issues most commonly associated with that mode.

Debate

There can be no question that one inevitable mode of interaction between people of different religious traditions will be debate. The religions of the world are quite different from one another, each envisioning a certain way the world is structured and each recommending a different way of dealing with such a world. As I often tell students in my world religions course, if at the end of the semester you think that all religions are the same, you have not been paying attention.

Furthermore, people do not hold the truths of their religions lightly. They believe in them because they are important and because they have shown themselves to satisfactorily address life's major questions—Who am I? What am I doing here? Where am I going when I die? When confronted with a religion that answers these questions differently, many, if not most, people want to talk about the differences, and such talk often leads to debate, with each person championing the truth and effectiveness of the way their religion answers the key questions of life.

How does one exhibit Christlikeness in an encounter where disagreement is the primary mode of interaction? Christian spirituality is especially important here. There is a saying common among veterans of interfaith encounter: doctrine divides, practice unites. That is, discussions about competing religious beliefs, incompatible in many respects, almost always leads to debate, and sometimes acrimonious debate, as each side tries to produce a winning argument.

One way to mitigate the negative feelings often associated with such debates is to at some point inject an element into the discussion that answers the question: How does this particular doctrine express itself in my spiritual practice? All of a sudden, the tone of the conversation changes. Common ground—mutual experiences of faith—pulls people together. The differences by no means disappear. But Christlikeness appears in the form of identification with the other person as a child of God, created in God's image, trying to relate to "God" in the best way he or she knows how.

This is indeed part of God's plan of reconciliation of the whole world. People will not be reconciled to God and each other until they can have respectful disagreements about important issues. Reflection on Acts 17 can reveal how such an interfaith doctrinal conversation can take place.

Dialogue

When people of two different religious worldviews begin speaking to one another, they often experience what philosophers are fond of calling incommensurability. By incommensurability, philosophers are referring to an inability to communicate on any meaningful level. One person talks about the grace of God as if everyone understands what the grace of God means, and another person talks about the laws of karma as if even children can comprehend, when in reality neither concept can be comprehended by the other person and efforts to communicate what is meant also fail.

In such situations of incommensurability, the preferred conversational form required is called a dialogue. A dialogue is a conversation in search of a conversation. A religious dialogue is a mutually agreed upon discussion that is an attempt to create the ground whereby a meaningful conversation about spiritual matters can take place. It is like the meeting prior to the start of a baseball game between the umpires and the two managers of the teams held at home plate to discuss the ground rules under which the game will be played. That is what a dialogue is—a discussion of religious warrants and authorities, in short, the ground rules for having a conversation.

Once the ground rules have been established, the conversation often morphs into something other than a dialogue—debate, partnership, friendship, self-advocacy, and growth. But it is very important not to allow that movement to take place too soon, before incommensurability is overcome. And that is where spiritual practice is important, because to have a dialogue means you *want* to have a dialogue. And that means you must see the other person as someone who has worthy things to say. Even though you probably disagree with some of the religious things the other person believes, you still want to talk meaningfully to them, expecting to find things about God in their experience and beliefs that you would not otherwise know. Jesus models this type of interaction with the Samaritan woman in John 4. Contrary to the social conventions of the day, he takes time to talk to her, actually listens to her, and takes her comments seriously. Only after trust and mutual respect have been established does he offer guidance.

Part of God's plan is that all things of this world, including all religious things, will come together under the lordship of Christ. Some things will be found compatible with God's reign, some things not. The Holy Spirit will help us sift the wheat from the chaff. But without being able to talk about wheat and chaff, such discernment cannot take place. Dialogue helps us have those conversations.

Partnership

People of different religions can maintain their differences and still cooperate on a host of problems having to do with human flourishing: poverty relief, justice debates, disease elimination, job creation, and so on. Such cooperation is needed in a world where the culture creating functions once performed by governments and business alliances are more often culture destroying than culture creating. We live in a world where nation-states are reduced to police forces and armies, and corporations are interested in only their bottom line. Although not universally applicable, there is a great deal of truth to the statement that the religions of the world are the only group still interested in the kind of values that lead to true human flourishing.

Of course, partnership cannot extend to everything, and knowing when to draw the line is one of the functions of Christian spirituality. A bad partnership (a partnership with someone on a project that will neither foster Christlikeness nor enhance God's overall plan) does little good. Whatever the end of the project, the means of doing it must conform to the shaping influences of Christian spirituality for the Christian to be involved. Similarly, a good partnership could involve Christians and Muslims working together to reduce world terrorism, Buddhists and Christians working toward civic stability in Sri Lanka, Hindus and Christians finding the keys to religious liberty in India—all

involve worthy goals and, if done in a Christlike way, can be both faithful and effective.

Of course, the other person(s) in the partnership will bring to it their own spirituality issues. As we have learned from recent public debates regarding the Muslim's founding figure, the prophet Muhammad, Muslims will not participate in partnerships with people of other religions unless they respect the person of Muhammad. When that respect is lacking (as with the cartoons published in a Danish newspaper), Muslims are wary of partnership projects.

Perhaps the most spiritually challenging dimension of the partnership mode of relating to people of other religions is choosing partners. If this were purely a business transaction, we would choose partners based on profit potential and workplace effectiveness. In the spiritual realm the choice factors shift a bit. We ask questions such as, Will this partner be able to respect my faith in Jesus? And will I be able to respect his or her faith in X? Will this partnership bring glory to God? Or will it be something I constantly will have to be apologizing for? In a partnership between a Christian and a non-Christian, the project is the occasion for the relationship, and both must honor God.

Self-Advocacy

Many contacts with people of other religious traditions are evangelistic in nature. That is, they are self-conscious attempts on the part of Christians to present the gospel story to non-Christians in such a way that they will be attracted to it—enough so that hopefully at some point the Holy Spirit works in their lives to bring about conversion.

Although many, if not most, Christians agree in principle with the idea of Christian witness, there is growing disagreement about the way witness is done. Three *P* words characterize the disagreements: *proselytizing, persuading,* and *proclaiming. Proselytizing* is witness with the idea of trying to make the other person in our own image. In religious terms, it means we see our Christian ideas in both transcendent terms and cultural terms—and only one cultural form can carry the transcendent properly. *Persuading* is witness with the idea that somehow the other person will want to be seen as a person made in God's image. In religious terms, it means we acknowledge the other person's agency and the province of conversion as belonging to the Holy Spirit, not the mission worker. *Proclaiming* is witness with the idea of converting the other person to an ideal. The ideal may be religious (Protestant, Catholic, Jew), a religious mode (fundamentalist, liberal, radical), or secular (peace, justice, the American way).

In terms of Christian spirituality, it seems evident that the mode of self-advocacy most in sync with the fruit of the Spirit—love, joy, peace, patience, kindness, goodness, faithfulness, gentleness, self-control—is persuasion. "Since we live by the Spirit, let us keep in step with the Spirit" (Gal. 5:22–25). One way to practice Christian spirituality in this mode is to compare and contrast. When talking religion with non-Christians, one finds both similarities and contrasts between Christianity and the other person's religious tradition. Mistakes in perception and relational responses are most often made when we overemphasize one or the other: either we see similarities between our religion and theirs, to the exclusion of the differences, or we see differences so profoundly that we miss the similarities. Thus, we end up either seeing the "other" as so different as to be inhuman, or so similar that one religion becomes as good as another. Neither position leads to either Christlikeness or to harmony with God's plans.

Friendship

One thing that draws people of different religious traditions together is the appeal of the "other's" spiritual practices. Once we learn something about how others practice their religion, we often find ourselves attracted to both the practice and the practitioner. We are attracted to the Jewish seder and kosher eating; we are intrigued by Buddhist meditation techniques; the Five Pillars of Islam seem like such a good way to live the religious life. I suppose we could cynically admit that some of this

attraction, at least, is a result of the grass is always greener syndrome. But even if one allows that a certain portion of this attraction can be accounted for in that way, it still leaves a great deal of genuine curiosity about the other's spiritual practices.

It is this attraction and the resulting curiosity, more than anything else, that draws us into friendships with people of other religions—doctrine divides, spirituality unites. While what a person believes may still appear nonsensical to us, the way they do it shows so much sincerity, goodwill, and good fruit that we cannot help our attraction. In what way is friendship, attraction, or love a spiritual practice?

Discernment is necessary here also. The Bible details both good and bad attractions to people of other religions and their practices. In the Old Testament the young men of Israel were sometimes attracted to the fertility cults and practices of Baal worship. This was an example of a bad attraction to another religion's spiritual practice. Yet other spiritual practices are drawn into the orbit of Christian practice seamlessly—the use of proverbs to succinctly capture wisdom, the form of a baptismal practice using water, the observations of the stars, the star of Bethlehem to announce Christ's coming, and many others.

Ephesians 1 says that God's great plan is that all things be made one (be reconciled) under the lordship of Christ. It is difficult to imagine this kind of unity taking place among people who display nothing but enmity toward one another. Friendship with people of other religions, and genuine appreciation for the Christ-honoring parts of their religions is an indispensable part of Christian spirituality when it comes to people of other religions.

Growth

Of course, respectful friendships are not just strategic in terms of bringing others to Christ. They also contribute to our own spiritual growth. We learn from the ways God's common grace is evident in the lives, practices, and religions of non-Christians. As Christians we can always expect personal spiritual growth to occur if we are open to the surprising ways God works in all people's lives, even people of non-Christian religions.

This truth seems incontrovertible but is not simple to practice. It can create awkward moments perhaps best typified by the apostle Paul's cautions to his charges at Corinth regarding eating meat offered to idols. In this teaching, Paul seems to balance three seemingly contradictory truths: the meat itself is not evil or tainted, immature believers might somehow think it is, and the witness of Christians eating offerings to false gods might negatively influence the growth of God's kingdom. Paul's way of seeing the thread throughout all three truths is to say that one factor one must consider in relationships with people and practices of other religions is that witness is important and there is a difference between mature and immature Christian believers in understanding this dynamic.

Translate this to a modern issue—for example, to whether the Hindu spiritual practice called yoga can be faithfully used by Christians for both spiritual and physical health. Paul would probably tell us that there is nothing inherently wrong with the part of yoga (the "meat") that has to do with physical stretching and breathing. But for Christians to practice it might raise questions with immature Christians and observing nonbelievers. And the unknown part is what actually takes place in a Hindu person's spiritual life as he or she practices this ancient discipline. Perhaps it is necessary, Paul might say, for something explicitly Christian to be injected into yogic practice for it to become something that would foster Christlikeness in a Christian and contribute to God's overall plan for the world. Similar issues current in the Christian world are the Christian's use of centering prayer, which relies on some spiritual techniques common in Buddhism; sweat lodges, which use a Native American practice as a spiritual tool; or Christian seders, the adaptation of the Jewish practice found in the Old Testament.

Christian spirituality as it relates to interfaith relationships seems, then, to have three primary dimensions. First, there is Christian spirituality *in* interfaith encounter. It is incumbent upon Christians to behave in the presence of, and in conversation with, non-Christians in a way that reveals something of the Christian understanding of God's grace. Such encounters must be characterized by that grace, or they fail in their spiritual dimension. Second, there is Christian spirituality *as* interfaith encounter. One can say that the friendships and relationships one develops with people of other religious traditions are a Christian spiritual practice in and of themselves. And third, there is Christian spirituality *because of* interfaith encounter. We must be open to the possibility that through encounters with non-Christians and through their spiritual practices, we may experience understandings and spiritual growth that would not otherwise occur. God is everywhere present, and we dare not miss the signs of his presence and the message he sends to us through such life events.

For Further Reading

Griffiths, P. *Christianity through Non-Christian Eyes* (1990).

King, U. *The Search for Spirituality* (2009).

Mouw, R. *Uncommon Decency* (1992).

Muck, T., and F. Adeney. *Christians Encounter the World's Religions* (2009).

Netland, H. *Encountering Religious Pluralism* (2001).

Newbigin, L. *The Gospel in a Pluralist Society* (1989).

Seager, R. *The World's Parliament of Religions* (1995).

Thomas, O. C. *Attitudes toward Other Religions* (1969).

CHAPTER 31

SPIRITUALITY AND TRANSFORMATION

M. ROBERT MULHOLLAND JR.

Identity is the basic issue in transformation. Our character, our way of being in the world, our way of relating to others, our way of responding to the issues and circumstances of our lives all flow from our understanding of our identity. Our identity provides the foundation on which rests our worldview, our value system, and our behavior patterns.

We Were Created in God's Image (Gen. 1:26–27)

Paul says, "All have sinned and are falling short of the glory of God" (Rom. 3:23 — translations are the author's unless otherwise noted). His clear implication is that we are intended to be in the "glory" of God. Peter confirms this: "His divine power, having given to us all things for life and godliness through the experience of knowing the one who *called us to his own glory* and goodness, has given to us through these things precious and exceedingly great promises, in order that through these you might become *partakers of the divine nature*" (2 Peter 1:3–4). Numerous other passages make this amazing assertion as well (cf. Rom. 15:7; 2 Thess. 2:14; Heb. 2:10; 1 Peter 5:1, 10).

One aspect of the Greek word *doxa* (glory) designates the essence of a person, that which makes a person who he or she is. To speak of God's glory is to speak of God's very being, the essence of God's nature (Kittel and von Rad). Jesus conjoins the human and the divine aspects of glory in his prayer for his followers: "The glory you have given

me I have given to them" (John 17:22). The "glory" God gave to Jesus is the "glory" Jesus had with God "before the world existed" (John 17:5), the "glory" of the Word who was God (John 1:1), the Word who became flesh manifesting the "glory" (John 1:14). The concept of Jesus having the "glory" of God is not too problematic, especially in light of Jesus' statements, "I and the Father are one" (John 10:30), and "the one who has seen me has seen the Father" (John 14:9). Paul seconds this: "God ... who has shone in our hearts for the revelation of the knowledge of the glory of God in the person of the Messiah" (2 Cor. 4:6).

The most significant aspect of Jesus' prayer, however, is his statement that he has given this "glory" to us. He seems to be indicating he has made it possible for us to be restored to the glory of God for which we were created and from which we have fallen short. In other words, it is now possible for us to experience transformation from our false identity rooted in things other than God to our true identity "hidden with Christ in God" (Col. 3:3).

This transformation is inseparable from being restored in a relationship of loving union with God. Preceding Jesus' statement about giving us the "glory," he prays concerning those who believe in him, that "all of them may be one, Father, just as you are in me and I am in you" (John 17:21). Jesus is praying that we might be in the same relationship of loving union with God as he is. This is confirmed by Jesus' statement, which concludes his assertion that he has given us the glory that God gave to him, "in order that they may be one as we are one" (John 17:22). To be restored to the glory for which we were created is inseparable from being restored to a relationship of loving union with God.

Paul characterizes this restoration by describing its goal: "Until we all attain: (1) the unity of the faith and (the unity) of the knowledge of the Son of God; (2) complete personhood; (3) the degree of maturity of the fullness of the Messiah" (Eph. 4:13). Paul structured this sentence to indicate that the unity of the faith = complete personhood = the degree of maturity of the fullness of the Messiah. The apostle's intent is clear in the structure of the Greek text: Until we all reach (1) *eis* (unto) the unity of the faith, (2) *eis* (unto) complete personhood, and (3) *eis* (unto) the degree of maturity of the fullness of the Messiah. In other words, it is in a relationship of loving union with God ("the unity of the faith") that we find our true identity ("complete personhood"), which is restoration to the image of God or Christlikeness ("the degree of maturity of the fullness of the Messiah"). Note especially that "the unity of the faith" is also "(the unity) of knowledge of the son of God." The term for "knowledge" here indicates an experiential knowledge as contrasted with cognitive knowledge (Paul generally uses *gnosis* for cognitive knowledge [cf. 1 Cor. 8:1, 7, 10; 13:2, 8] and *epignosis* for experiential knowledge [cf. 1 Cor. 13:12; Eph. 1:17, 4:13; Phil. 1:9; Col. 1:9, 10; 2:2; 3:10]).

This is a significant issue. The difference between knowing about God cognitively and knowing God through a deep, intimate, personal relationship of loving union is like the difference between reading about skiing and actually skiing. Paul is indicating "the unity of the faith" is a deep, intimate, personal relationship of loving union with the Son of God. We are nurtured into our true identity in the image of God through this relationship.

Paul articulates this understanding when he tells the Colossians they have divested themselves of their old identity ("the old self") and have entered into a new identity ("the new self"), "which is being renewed in knowledge according to the image of the one who created it" (Col. 3:9–10). Paul is here again speaking of experiential knowledge and indicates this new identity is developed in the experience of becoming increasingly restored to the image of God for which it was created.

The restoration to the image or glory of God has from the earliest days been stressed in the Eastern Orthodox tradition. Perhaps the boldest affirmation is found in Athanasius, who, referring to Christ, wrote: "He, indeed, assumed humanity that we might become God" (sec. 54). For Athanasius, and much of the Orthodox tradition, "deification" or "theosis" (being restored to the image/glory of God) entailed not simply cosmetic changes to fallen human nature, but a restoration of that nature to God's original purpose. The Catholic tradition has not been devoid of this understanding of transformation, either. Teresa of Avila asserted, "One can say no more—insofar as can be understood—than that the soul, I mean the spirit, is made one with God" (Teresa of Avila, 178). Thomas Merton put it like this: "This Spirit of God, dwelling in us, given to us, to be as it were our own Spirit, enables us to know and experience, in a mysterious manner, the reality and presence of the divine mercy in ourselves. So the Holy Spirit is intimately united to our own inmost self, and His presence in us makes our 'I' the 'I' of God" (Merton, 46).

On the Protestant side, Calvin believed the Holy Spirit united the soul to God in a spiritual marriage (Calvin, 3.1.3. The same insight infused his successors as well; "Of the reality of the union between Christ and the believer . . . the Puritans had no doubt" (Wakefield, 441). In the Wesleyan traditions, *sanctification* is the term regularly employed to describe restoration in the image of God: "What is it to be sanctified? To be renewed in the image of God, in righteousness and true holiness" (Outler, 140). Another phrase employed by Wesley and his descendent traditions is "Christian perfection," which is defined as perfection in love; loving God with all one's heart, soul, mind, and strength and one's neighbor as oneself. Wesley said, "Herein is our love made perfect … because as he is, so are we in this world.… In this world, they (those perfected in love) are as their Master" (Outler, 270). Once again the purpose of transformation is to become Christlike in a relationship of loving union with God.

We Are Being Transformed into God's Image

Christian spirituality then involves a process of transformation, of being nurtured and restored to wholeness in the image of God through a growing relationship of loving union with God in Christ through the Holy Spirit.

It is essential to recognize that this process is the restoring action of God in us through the Holy Spirit and not a result of our own efforts. Paul indicates this: "All of us, beholding the glory of the Lord without masks, are *being* transformed into the same likeness from glory into glory, just as by means of the Lord, the Spirit" (2 Cor. 3:18). When Paul says, "from glory into glory," he indicates that the process of transformation takes us from glory (the essence of our false identity) to glory (the essence of our true identity in the image of God). In addition to being transformed (cf. Rom. 12:2), Paul also speaks of this transformation as "*being* renewed" (2 Cor. 4:16; Col. 3:10), and "*being* saved" (1 Cor. 1:18; 15:2; 2 Cor. 2:15; cf. also "*will be* saved," Rom. 5:9–10; 9:27; 10:9, 13; 11:26; 1 Cor. 3:15; 1 Tim. 2:15; "*were* saved," Rom. 8:24; "*might be* saved," 1 Cor. 5:5; 10:33; 1 Thess. 2:16; "*have been* saved," Eph. 2:5, 8; "*being* rooted and grounded in love," Eph. 3:17; all passive voice).

The expression "being saved" raises questions about the nature of "salvation." Many would say "salvation" is what happens when a person responds to God's cruciform love in Christ and accepts Christ as Savior and Lord. They then have "been saved." Paul, however, speaks of believers in a process of "being saved." Peter expresses the same idea: "As newborn babies, eagerly desire the pure spiritual milk in order that you might *grow into salvation*" (1 Peter 2:2). Peter and Paul both indicate that "salvation" is neither a starting nor ending point but a process that has a beginning (cf. "newborn babies," 1 Peter 2:2; "born again," 1 Peter 1:3, 23; and "born of God," 1 John 3:9; 4:7; 5:1; Jesus also discusses with Nicodemus the necessity of being "born anew," John 3:1–9) and the goal of which is maturity into Christlikeness, the image of God.

Essential to this process of transformation is "being rooted and grounded in love" (Eph. 3:17). We have already noted that we were created in the image of God for a relationship of loving union. "God spoke us forth in himself before the foundation of the world to be holy and blameless in his presence in love" (Eph. 1:4; *en auto* is usually translated "in him," referring to Christ in Ephesians 1:3, but can also be translated "in himself," referring to God. The term *exelaxato*, usually translated "chose," literally means "spoke forth" and, in conjunction with "before the foundation of the world," indicates something God "spoke forth" before he spoke forth creation in Genesis 1, namely, "us"). When Adam and Eve turned away from this relationship of loving union, they became self-referenced beings, "false selves," separated from the relationship with God in which their true identity was to be found. Instead of being pervasively God-referenced beings, humanity became pervasively self-referenced, creating an insurmountable problem.

Any effort self-referenced beings make to restore the relationship with God is, by its very nature, a self-referenced effort that only serves to highlight and deepen the separation, not overcome it. God, however, in cruciform love, entered into the depths of that separation, maintaining the relationship of loving union from God's side. God indwells the heart of human deadness to restore life, plumbs the depths of human darkness to bring light, enters the nadir of human brokenness to re-create wholeness, goes to the center of human woundedness to heal, and is at the core of human bondages to liberate.

To put it simply, God, in Christ, in the mystery of grace, in cruciform love, indwells humanity's sinful state in order that human beings might be restored in a relationship of loving union and be transformed into Christlikeness, the image of God. Paul conveys this reality starkly: "God made to be sin him who knew no sin in order that we might become the righteousness of God" (2 Cor. 5:21).

The issue of such transformation, however, has a dark history. Since the goal of spiritual transformation is Christlikeness, or the image of God, all too often the virtues of Christlikeness have become "rules" for Christian living that ecclesiastical authority and/or communal ethos impose upon followers. In such instances, the Christian life becomes a facade of virtues, keeping a list of dos and don'ts, an outward show with little inner transformation. This is not to say that virtues have no place in transformation or in the Christian life; they are essential. But "virtues" that are merely window dressing result in "whitewashed tombs" — outwardly beautiful but dead within (Matt. 23:27). When virtues become rules, relationship with God is construed as a contract by which believers "please" God, and God provides in turn a heavenly home or even earthly prosperity and well-being right now. Such a relationship is much easier than losing oneself for his sake, denying one's false identity, and entrusting oneself to God in loving abandon. It is only from such abandonment to God that genuine virtues emerge as dispositional manifestations of love offered to God for the well-being of others.

How Transformation Comes About

God has done everything necessary to make possible our being transformed into God's image. In a very real sense, the ball is now in our court. Will we allow God to nurture and restore us into that for which we were created — the image of God? To put it more bluntly, will we be crucified with Christ?

If we are to be transformed into Christlikeness,

our false selves must be abandoned, our false identities forsaken. Transformation in the spiritual life is not a matter of a few repairs or a new coat of paint on the old structures of our lives. Paul says: "You have discarded the old self with its deeds" (Col. 3:9); "Our old self has been crucified with him" (Rom. 6:6); "Those who belong to the Messiah Jesus have crucified the flesh with its passions and lusts" (Gal. 5:24); Paul uses the terms *flesh* or *life according to the flesh*, to refer to the self-referenced way of being. Paul knows only two modes of existence for humans, "life according to the flesh," or "life according to the Spirit" (cf. Rom. 8:4–7); "We who have died to sin, how will we still live in it?" (Rom. 6:2); "we have died with Christ" (Rom. 6:8; cf. Col. 2:20; 3:3).

Jesus mandates: "If any wish to come after me, let them deny themselves, take up their cross daily and follow me. For whoever wishes to save their life will lose it; but whoever loses their life on account of me will save it" (Luke 9:23–24). The false self is consistently engaged in a persistent effort to preserve its self-referenced structure of being. When it becomes "religious," it brings God into the structure of its false identity but on its own terms. God becomes yet another means to preserve its self-referential nature. Jesus calls us to deny this pervasive structure of self-referenced being. This is not a call to divest oneself of a few bad behavior patterns, to eliminate a few vices, to polish up a few "rough edges," add a few virtues. It is a call to a radical abandonment of the entire self-referenced structure of being. Jesus' call to "take up our cross," clarifies what it means to deny ourselves. In the Roman world, the cross was the symbol of complete marginalization, of utter dehumanization. On the cross one's entire structure of being became meaningless; one's identity was reduced to nothing. This total loss of our self-referencedness is essential if transformation into our true selves, the "life hidden with Christ in God" (Col. 3:3), is to be actualized.

One of the most dangerous and difficult aspects of transformation is how a self-referenced being divests itself of its false self without the action being self-referenced. The answer is found in Jesus' question to Peter, "Do you love me more than these?" (John 21:15). Even in the original Greek text, the identity of "these" is ambiguous. Jesus was not asking Peter if he loved him more than he loved the other apostles, his boat, his fishing equipment, and the 153 large fish he has just caught, all of which formed something of Peter's identity. Since we have been created to find our true identity in a relationship of loving union with God, whenever we love something more than we love God, we engender a false identity, an identity rooted in and nurtured by those things we love more than we love God.

The love Jesus speaks of here is agape love, a pervasively other-referenced orientation, a relationship unstained by any vestiges of self-referencedness. The only safe way to abandon our false selves is to love God for himself alone. To love God for what we receive from God is still a self-referenced act. The essence of all genuine spiritual disciplines in the process of transformation is the offering of some aspect of our false identities to God in loving abandonment. Spiritual disciplines are not a means of transforming ourselves by our own efforts. Nor are they a means to gain and maintain God's favor. True spiritual disciplines, through which we offer ourselves to God in love, become means of grace by which God works to transform us to wholeness in his image and restore us to his glory. Attachment to God in love is the only sure way to be detached from those things that have formed our false identities and held us in bondage to our self-referenced way of being. Through this deepening attachment to God in love, our lives are increasingly liberated from the destructive and dehumanizing worldviews that misshape human life, from the false values that warp and distort human activities and relationships, and from the perverted behavior patterns that cripple individuals and poison communities. Through the regenerating work of the Holy Spirit as we are transformed into the image of God, our lives are increasingly shaped by a kingdom worldview, our values become kingdom values, and our behavior patterns become Christlike.

Transformation Is for the Sake of the World

Christlikeness is not a privatized possession that insures us an eternity in heaven. In our pervasively privatized and individualistic Western culture, we almost automatically think of spirituality and transformation to wholeness in the image of Christ as something between an individual and God. Christlikeness, however, is a life of loving union with God poured out for the sake of others. Christlikeness is characterized by compassion, kindness, lowliness, meekness, and longsuffering in its relationships with others (Col. 3:12). It is a life radically other-referenced for the well-being of the other (Phil. 2:3–4). Genuine spirituality and transformation unite our relationship with God and our relationships with others in a symbiotic reality. The nature of our relationship with God manifests itself in the nature of our relationships with others (cf. Matt. 25:31–46, where Jesus is unmistakably clear that the way we treat others reveals our relationship with God). This is why Jesus reduces the entire Torah to a single, two-sided mode of being: totally other-referenced love (*agape*) for God and completely other-referenced love (*agape*) for others. In this tripartite conjunction between us, God, and the other, we discover our true identity as a self that we can love (*agape*) in a totally un-self-referenced way. This is the goal of genuine spirituality and transformation.

Because a deepening union with God in love necessarily engages us with the world, persons being restored in the image of God challenge the destructive and dehumanizing worldviews that misshape human life. They confront false values that warp and distort human activities and relationships. They question the perverted behavior patterns that cripple individuals and poison communities. Transformation into the image of Christ sets us against entrenched political, economic, and social structures that demean and marginalize persons, structures that hold persons in bondage to the prevailing powers of the culture, structures that abuse the world and its resources for material gain and personal pleasure. Given this reality, it is more comfortable to restrict spirituality to an individual, privatized "hobby" and transformation to the superficial smoothing out of a few rough places in our lives and character, a cosmetic adjustment that enables us to be in the world for God. This being in the world for God means that we maintain control of both our relationship with God and our lives in the world. However, the transformational dynamic of Christian spirituality is an ongoing process through which we are enabled to be in God for the world. God is in control of our relationship with God and our lives in the world, so just "as he is, so are we in this world" (1 John 4:17 KJV). This is our true identity for which we were created.

Conclusion

Transformation is for the spiritual life what growth and development are for the physical life. Both begin with a birth (in Christian terms, "redemption" or "regeneration") that initiates a process of maturation (in Christian terms, "transformation" or "sanctification") that, when healthy, results in wholeness as a mature person (in Christian terms, "Christlikeness"). This analogy is flawed, however, in that the Christian life begins in a context of unlikeness to Christ, a state of having fallen short of the glory of God (Rom. 3:23). Thus, transformation in the spiritual life is the process of growth from a false identity as a pervasively self-referenced being to the true identity of a pervasively God-referenced being.

Sources Cited

Athanasius. *On the Incarnation.* Trans. a religious of C.S.M.V. (1944).

Calvin, J. *Institutes of the Christian Religion*, 2 vols. Trans. J. McNeill (1960).

Kittel, G., and G. von Rad. S.v. "*Doxa.*" In *TDNT*, 2:232–35.

Merton, T. *The Inner Experience* (2003).

Outler, A., ed. *John Wesley* (1964).

Teresa of Avila: Interior Castle, CWS (1979).

Wakefield, G. "The Puritans." In *The Study of Spirituality*, ed. C. Jones et al. (1986), 437–45.

For Further Reading

Collins, K., ed. *Exploring Christian Spirituality* (2000).

Haase, A. *Coming Home to Your True Self* (2008).

Kelley, T. *A Testament of Devotion* (1992).

Leech, K. *Experiencing God* (1985).

Merton, T. *Contemplation in a World of Action* (1998).

———. *The New Man* (1961).

Mulholland, M. R., Jr. *The Deeper Journey* (2006).

Nouwen, H. *In the Name of Jesus* (1992).

Squire, A. *Asking the Fathers* (1976).

CHAPTER 32

GRACE AND SPIRITUAL DISCIPLINES

GORDON T. SMITH

Few questions are more central to understanding the fundamental character of Christian spirituality and how Christian growth is fostered or nurtured than the proper role of spiritual disciplines and practice. What place does discipline, through specific spiritual practices, have in the Christian life? And what is the relation between grace, which is the work or provision of God, and these practices, which involve human initiative and effort?

These have always been thorny theological questions. In her history, the church has recognized that it is possible to overstate one side of this equation—the relationship between grace and human discipline—or, at least, if not to overstate, to describe one side in a way that improperly discounts the other. There have been many movements in the history of Christianity that have discounted human effort completely and insisted that the Christian should be entirely passive; encouraged men and women to "let go and let God"; and maintained that all spiritual growth is the work of God and God alone, and therefore that there should be no urgent call to specific human practices.

On the other hand, the church has sometimes entertained the opinion that the reformation of the Christian is chiefly the responsibility of the Christian, and that through determined personal effort and persistence, his or her life can genuinely be changed. Indeed, it is maintained, there can be no change without the assumption of personal responsibility for it, so that there is virtually a one-to-one correlation between human effort and spiritual advance.

One can and must be sympathetic to both sides of this tension and appreciative of the challenge of articulating the relationship between them. Christians of different traditions or denominations will without doubt nuance this relationship differently. And yet there are two fundamental axioms that can help them navigate these waters. The first is that the Christian life is one of complete dependence on the grace of God; it is not a self-construction project. And the second axiom is its counterpart: that indeed the Christian can and must take responsibility for his or her actions and reactions, and that the grace of God becomes housed or experienced when divine grace is intentionally appropriated.

The Primacy of Grace

When we speak of the primacy of grace, we do no more than affirm the primacy of God. We are insisting that God is the source of life, that human persons are creatures and thus entirely dependent on their Creator. And thus all that exists necessarily came through, and is now dependent on, God. The New Testament witnesses to the unique mediating role of Christ Jesus, the second person of the Trinity, through whom all things have been created and, in similar fashion, through whom all things have been redeemed and are being made whole. And just as this grace, the life of God, is mediated through the Son, it is realized in the world through the Spirit, who, in the language of the Nicene Creed, is the Lord and giver of life.

The church has consistently witnessed to a two-fold expression of the grace of God within individual Christians and the church. First, grace is the fundamental expression of the love of God: to speak of grace is to affirm the favor or goodness of God that is offered as a gift, as God's essential way of being toward all creation. To live in or under the grace of God, then, is to receive or accept this grace as gift; it is to dwell in the love of God that is freely given even though it is unmerited. God cannot be other than gracious, for it is in the very nature of God to love unconditionally. And there is no other way fully to know the love of God than to live in this grace.

Second, grace includes strength and empowerment; it is the life of God sustaining the life of the creature. The Christian recognizes that one cannot live self-dependent (e.g., as "god"), but only in dependence on God who is the source of life. The defining mark of sin is autonomy, which is to live, as the apostle Paul puts it, in the "flesh." But in fact, one truly lives only as one lives as a *creature*— that is, as one dependent on the Creator.

The Trinitarian character of the grace of God is crucial here; the grace of God the Creator is mediated through the Son and effectual in the life of the Christian by the Spirit. Gordon Fee suggests there is no more profound Pauline statement than the benediction of 2 Corinthians 13:14: "The grace of the Lord Jesus Christ, and the love of God, and the fellowship of the Holy Spirit be with you all" (Fee, 363). The church has always recognized that Christ Jesus is the quintessential demonstration of the grace of God; even more, the very embodiment of this grace. Further, the church has affirmed that the life of Christ sustains the life of the individual Christian and of the church. Thus, the call of John 15 is to the faith community: to the church and the individual person insofar as they dwell and remain in Christ. The life of Christ Jesus is the meat and drink of the church.

The Spirit is the means by which the grace of God in Christ becomes known; by the Spirit the love of God is not merely recognized but actually known and experienced (Rom. 5:5); and this same Spirit becomes the source and deliverer of divine strength (Fee, 840). So the Christian and the church live by conscious and intentional response to the Spirit. One either lives "in the flesh," meaning in spiritual independence or autonomy, or one lives in radical dependence on God. Thus, the New Testament calls believers to "walk in the Spirit."

Reformed Christians have also consistently affirmed that the grace of God is communicated to the world—and is evident in the life of the Christian and of the church—through "Word and Spirit"—an indissoluble unity of truth and power. This acknowledges the intimate relationship between Christ Jesus as the divine Logos, the Word incarnate, and the Scriptures as the written or inscripturated Word. The Scriptures are the continuing revelation of God who is first and foremost revealed in Christ; as such, the Scriptures are the abiding witness to Christ. Thus, one can live in intimate communion with Christ only insofar as one is deeply attentive to the Scriptures.

But we can speak of this Word only with a parallel reference to the Spirit. Only by the Spirit can the Bible be effective as the revelation of Christ to the Christian and the church. The Spirit is the originating author of the ancient text and the one who utilizes the reading and proclamation of this text to illumine minds, rekindle hearts, and strengthen wills. The Scriptures become a gracious force only through the anointing and power of the Spirit.

Thus, in the end what sustains the Christian's life is the Word and Spirit. This is the grace of God, the life and strength of God, and the revelation of God's love and mercy. The Christian life is not self-constructed; rather, it is transformed by this grace from beyond itself. The church lives not by strategic planning, but by Word and Spirit. The church lives by this grace of God—specifically the grace that is known by Word and Spirit. And this grace of Word and Spirit is also mediated to believers through the sacramental acts given the church — baptism and the Lord's Supper.

The church has continually testified to this grace in its hymnody, most notably by its testimony to the wonder and sufficiency of this grace. The church sings about "amazing grace" or the "wonderful grace of Jesus," which is both "amazing" and "greater than all my sin." In this same vein, Charles Wesley's magisterial "And Can It Be That I Should Gain?" includes the recurring chorus: "Amazing love! how can it be, that Thou, my God, shouldst die for me." In the same hymn, Wesley speaks of this grace as "so free, so infinite" that it has the power to liberate sin-imprisoned spirits.

The Call to Intentional Spiritual Discipline

God's grace is always primary; but it is equally axiomatic in Scripture (e.g., Luke 9:23; 2 Tim. 2:3–7) that spiritual discipline is essential to growth in grace. The importance of the work of the Spirit in the life of the Christian and the church cannot be overstated. And yet it is *mis*stated whenever this affirmation of the priority of grace erases any call to spiritual practice, by which we mean the intentional and focused appropriation of God's grace.

The grace of God transforms; it purifies and makes all things new. Through it one can experience forgiveness. The whole of the Christian life flows from this headwater. Atonement and forgiveness cannot be earned or merited. They are gracious acts of God to be received. And yet the grace of God is not only about forgiveness. The grace God offers is not merely the gift of a status change in God's eyes, but the gift of God's own self. Grace then has a remarkable content, substance, and purpose; it is the actual life of the triune God provided for the renewal of human beings. And thus the church and the Christian want nothing more than to know this transforming grace, to know the power of God, in Christ, by which the Spirit renews and restores the creation. Yet what is clear from the Scriptures and affirmed historically by the church is that the appropriation of the grace of God calls for human responsibility and action. Grace is never earned, but the only acceptable responses to its reception are obedience and disciplined intent. While all is of grace — even the desire and will to appropriate this grace are God's gifts — there is a persistent call in Scripture to the simple and disciplined acts of the Christian, and of the church, in receiving this gift.

A disciple or follower of Jesus is one who accepts a particular call, represented in baptism: to die to self and live for Christ, to submit to the way or the authority of Christ. At conversion a person is made alive in Christ through the grace of the Spirit. This experience of the justifying and renewing grace of God is one wherein a seed of the life of God is planted, so to speak; and the Christian is called to nurture and cultivate this seed, to grow up in the grace of God that has been planted in the human heart (1 Peter 1:22–2:3). While affirming the priority of grace, the Scriptures also recognize that we "work out [our] salvation with fear and trembling" (Phil. 2:12), and that we grow up into Christ Jesus, the living head of the church "as each part [of the church] does its work" (Eph. 4:16). Dallas Willard has ably popularized the theological foundations for spiritual discipline, insisting that participation in the kingdom and companionship with Christ are only experienced through the disciplines of the spiritual life (Willard, 26). But, as he rightly notes, we will only appreciate this if we recognize that salvation is not just forgiveness but truly a whole new order of life (32).

Two helpful images, perhaps, are those of the doctor and the farmer. A doctor knows that there is no healing per se through her own wisdom or skill; rather, the body heals itself — or better, the body is healed by processes built right into the fabric of creation — and the doctor simply takes prudent steps to facilitate and encourage this healing dynamic. Similarly, a farmer knows that he is not the grower. He cultivates the soil, plants, and waters, and prays for enough sunshine to bring the seeds to life. But all the growth comes from dynamics embedded by the Creator; the farmer is but an agent of God whose practices allow God to do what only God can do.

When we speak of spiritual discipline or practices, we recognize that conversion or initiation into the grace of God is but that—an initiation. It is only the beginning, the launch into a journey of growing in the grace of God, of maturing in the faith and seeking the holiness that is, in essence, the life of God. The new Christian recognizes the call of Christ to follow, to be a disciple, and joins fellow Christians who share their commitment and purpose. And this journey is framed and nurtured by discipline, by specific practices through which one is able to appropriate the grace of God.

Some Christian traditions, including those influenced by revivalism, have suggested that conversion is so deep and powerful that a person is already and fully *transformed* by the initiatory experience. There is an element of truth here; conversion is an experience of the transforming grace of God. Along with experiencing the justifying grace of God, forgiveness, and divine adoption, the believer has also been changed at the very core of his or her being. Yet the better part of wisdom recognizes that at best the transformation in view is one of deep reorientation and realignment. Having been reconciled to God, the believer is ready to begin a Christ-ward journey in the Spirit. At this point such a journey has only just begun. Thus, the church has always recognized that Christian converts are thereby initiated into a journey of faith in the company of others, and that deeper transformation into Christ's likeness will come incrementally as they embrace the practices that facilitate growth in grace (2 Peter 3:18).

Donald Bloesch rightly speaks of baptism as a confirmation of the electing grace of God and also as a demonstration of God's power to foster genuine righteousness in the believer. This doesn't happen instantaneously, but rather through a lifetime of "the obedience of faith and works of love" (Bloesch, 329). As Bloesch notes, speaking very intentionally from within the Reformed theological tradition, we cannot discount the vital place of human action or response to the grace of God. The insistence on human responsibility for spiritual growth and development does not discount or diminish the priority of grace; to the contrary, it is but a way by which the church insists that the Christian is not entirely passive in the face of the grace of God (Bloesch, 332–33). This grace must be appropriated and lived.

Discipline in the Christian life speaks of intentionality, of firmly purposing to live by the grace of God. In so doing, one anchors one's life in the justifying grace of God—the deepening assurance that one is loved, accepted, and forgiven—but also in the sanctifying grace of God—that grace by which, as Thomas Oden notes, one is gradually transformed toward loving God and resisting evil (Oden, 212). One embraces or "practices" those actions or routines that foster the capacity to appropriate and receive this "sanctifying" grace. Oden captures the wisdom of millennia of Christian writings in observing that "the fullness of sanctifying grace is not ordinarily received immediately at the beginning of conversion but grows through an extended developmental process" (Oden, 214). The practices, then, by which one appropriates this grace are indicators of a new way of being. As a Christian, one now identifies with the in-breaking of the reign of Christ. The challenge is that this kingdom is only evident, as often as not, to the eyes of faith; it is easy for Christians to be sucked into the mores of "the world"—into imitating how cultures and societies that are fundamentally materialistic or secular do life. The Christian has to move ahead against the grain. One must not choose the easy default mode, but rather the way of doing life that is consistent with the reign of Christ. And this requires discipline because the inertia of one's own former life, and of the surrounding culture, encourages autonomy, secularity, and moral capitulation rather than radical dependence on God. What the Christian seeks is not merely to receive the grace of God but also to allow that grace to become *habituated* in oneself (Oden, 219) or, as Willard stresses, in one's *body* (Willard, 75ff.). And yet it is still all of grace, for "this habituation is enabled by the Spirit through Word and Sacrament" (Oden, 220).

Baptism and the Lord's Supper are also important rites by which the church appropriates the justifying and sanctifying grace of God. But then with these fundamental markers, prayer and the study of Scripture are the central means by which grace is habituated in Christians' lives. Thus, the faith community joins in regular, typically weekly, gatherings for worship—gatherings in which space is created for the prayers of the people and the proclamation of the Word. Also, Christians have consistently recognized the vital place of private daily devotions—once again, for prayer and the study of Scripture. This twofold practice is foundational to the whole of the Christian life and to the life of the church since together they constitute the essential way by which a person or a community appropriates the grace of God.

Then also, as complements to these, there are a number of spiritual practices that are either encouraged by the Scriptures or commended to Christians by the spiritual masters of the church. Each is a practice that either fosters the capacity to pray and attend to the Scriptures or fosters the capacity to live in the world consistent with the grace received in prayer and the study of the Scriptures. For example, solitude and silence are the settings in which one attends, in prayer, to the voice of God received through the Scriptures; and service becomes the habitual practice flowing out of prayer and the study of the Scriptures.

We can also speak of Sabbath observance, fasting, and simplicity. Work is good, but one day in seven we set aside our work to cultivate our relationship with God and allow grace to more deeply infuse our lives. Food and sex are good, but through fasting and abstinence we affirm that while good in themselves, they can be set aside so that we can renew our sense of dependence on God. Money is good in itself, but given that the love of money is the root of much evil, many Christians actively choose to live simply, not only within their means, but also even below their means, so that they can be more generous in their gifts to the poor and other worthy causes, and can more easily resist the materialistic pull of a consuming economy.

Twenty-first-century Christians are also rediscovering some of the ancient practices of the church—disciplines or practices that may have been more typical of a Christian community that sought to live faithfully in a pagan environment. When the surrounding culture becomes increasingly secular, or even anti-Christian, believers are wise to ramp up their focus on spiritual practice. They cannot lean on the host culture to reinforce their faith in God or foster their soul transformation. In a secular society, for example, there are no Sunday laws; thus the Christian observance of Sabbath will cut against the grain and markedly so. And there are other ancient practices being rediscovered by Christians in pre-Christian or secularized post-Christendom societies. These include pilgrimage, which can become a metaphor for the spiritual life; spiritual direction and friendship; and daily routines of formal prayers, things typically practiced in monastic communities but now often followed by Christians in mainstream settings.

Spiritual disciplines or practices are to be encouraged for each person (and allowing for diversity of temperaments and differences in need) as they cultivate their own relationship with God and their personal vocation for serving him in the world. But these personal spiritual practices are always but the complement of the practices of the faith community. Indeed, one of the key dynamics of spiritual growth is to be found, precisely, in the interplay between the practices of the individual and those of the community. Personal devotions are the counterpart of the worship of the church. But there are also practices wherein, for example, the individual draws on the strengths of the community. John Wesley, like many others, insisted that those who were part of Methodist communities should regularly participate in small groups for mutual encouragement. Spiritual direction and spiritual friendship are vital practices that draw the individual into the riches of the spiritual heritage and foster genuine accountability to God through the community. All of this, of course, is to be done to the same end: that the Christian and the faith community would grow in faith, hope, and love.

Sources Cited

Bloesch, D. *The Holy Spirit* (2000).
Fee, G. *God's Empowering Presence* (1994).
Oden, T. *Life in the Spirit* (1992).
Willard, D. *The Spirit of the Disciplines* (1988).

For Further Reading

Chan, S. *Spiritual Theology* (1998).
deSilva, D. *Sacramental Life* (2008).
Dykstra, C. *Growing in the Life of Faith* (2005).

CHAPTER 33

MISSION AND MINISTRY

DENNIS P. HOLLINGER

It is quite common to think of mission and ministry as the "active life" in which we do the will of God within the church and the world. Spirituality then is perceived as the "inner life" that enables mission and ministry to be accomplished. In contrast to this perception, it is far better to understand mission and ministry as part and parcel of the spiritual life. The inner life and the outer life are not separate spheres of the Christian life, for the inner self and the outer self can never be fully divided. One is not merely a means to the other, for inward spirituality and mission/ministry, while not the same, are always in tandem in God's economy. Both are callings of God and both are integral to our spiritual journey in Christ as whole beings. While we carry out ministry and mission through our external bodies, body and soul are connected in that "the soul constitutes itself through the body. It is not just that we have a body, or that we use a body, but also that we are bodies" (Howard, 83).

It is also quite common to think of mission and ministry as our individual work on behalf of God. In reality it is God's mission and ministry in which we participate, not just as individuals, but also as Christ's community, the church. Our individualistic cultural ethos frequently hinders our ability to grasp that God's work is always in relationship to his body, the church. In this work he uses individual gifts to accomplish the mission and ministries of the church. Thus, mission, ministry, and the whole of spiritual formation always involve our individual gifts and journeys as well as our corporate belongings and identities.

The Church Gathered and Scattered

Mission and ministry are expressions of God's work through his people in the church and the world. One way of describing these expressions is that part of the church's task is evident when the church gathers for worship, *koinonia* (fellowship), and preaching/teaching. These are ministries ordained by God to enable believers and the corporate body to be the church and "to equip his people for works of service, so that the body of Christ may be built up until we all reach unity in the faith and in the knowledge of the Son of God" (Eph. 4:12 – 13 TNIV). The other dimension of the church's task is when it is scattered in mission to the world in word and deed. This is both the *missio Dei* (God's mission in the world) and the church's mission to the world. Hence mission and ministry incorporate divine realities and human realities, for God chooses to do his work in the world through frail humans, broken vessels (2 Cor. 4:7).

There is no one descriptive text that explicitly brings these two dimensions (the church gathered and scattered) and the five tasks of the church together (three when gathered and two when scattered), but they are clearly implied throughout the whole of the New Testament. Moreover, they are embodied in the early church as evidenced in Acts 2:42–47 (TNIV):

> They devoted themselves to the apostles' teaching and to fellowship, to the breaking of bread and to prayer. Everyone was filled with awe at the many wonders and signs performed by the apostles. All the believers were together and had everything in common. They sold property and possessions to give to anyone who had need. Every day they continued to meet together in the temple courts. They broke bread in their homes and ate together with glad and sincere hearts, praising God and enjoying the favor of all the people. And the Lord added to their number daily those who were being saved.

Implicit in this text and evidenced throughout the book of Acts is the shape of Christian mission and ministry, incorporating a rhythm of gathering and scattering, living together as believers and living in the world among unbelievers. While this rhythm includes specific acts of inward spiritual formation, it is itself the very fabric of a holistic spiritual life. At the heart of spiritual life is everyday life guided by the Spirit in relation to both the body of Christ (the church gathered) and the world (the church scattered).

The Church Gathered

As demonstrated in Acts 2, the church gathered for three primary purposes: worship, *koinonia*, and preaching/teaching. While each of these ministries could be viewed as a means to an end (i.e., faithful witness in the world or spiritual maturity), it is far better to view each as an embodiment of what the church and individual believers are called to be and do in their faithfulness to Christ and his body.

The ministry of worship is a continual reminder that the Christian life begins and ends with the triune God. While we utilize human and cultural forms and expressions in our worship, both the object of worship and the enablement to worship are divine. In Acts 2 this ministry is evident in the following phrases: "the breaking of bread and … prayer" (v. 42); "They broke bread … together" (v. 46); and "praising God" (v. 47). Worship is God-centered in that individual believers gather as the corporate body to confess, proclaim, experience, and reenact divine reality. Just as the Ten Commandments begin with the vertical dimensions that orient life to God before moving to the horizontal realities of life in the world, so worship orients life to God, the fountain of our being and doing.

While worship does bring enablement to individuals and the church for life in the world, worship is first and foremost a response of honor and adoration to God, and thus a vital part of Christian spirituality. For the early church, it incorporated songs and hymns, prayers of praise and petition, the reading and preaching of Holy Scripture, and the Eucharist, the Lord's Supper (i.e. "the breaking of bread"). The Lord's Supper incorporates the whole person and all of one's senses to bring us into the very presence of Christ. In the Lord's Supper, Christ is present and nourishes the life of the believer and the corporate life of the church. At the same time, the Eucharist is a thanksgiving to God for the central act making possible the church — the death and resurrection of Christ.

A second purpose for the church gathered is *koinonia*, or fellowship. It means, literally, to share in common, and the body of Christ gathers to share in common its life in Christ through the work of Christ as enabled by the Holy Spirit. In Acts 2 "they devoted themselves to … fellowship" (v. 42); "all the believers were together and had everything in common" (v. 44); "everyday they continued to meet together"; and "[they] ate together with glad and sincere hearts" (v. 46). *Koinonia* can take on many forms of expression: small groups, prayer groups, accountability partners, and simply being together as brothers and sisters in Christ — expressions that can be understood as spiritual disciplines.

Again, this ministry may appear to be a means to an end (i.e., strength for mission in the world), and that is indeed a result of *koinonia*. But at its heart, fellowship is an embodiment of the very nature of the church, a community of believers who share together in encouragement, love, prayer, and by these the very source of its existence — Christ himself. Thus, Christian spirituality and the ministry of *koinonia* are intricately related. Moreover, fellowship reflects the unity of the church, a oneness that itself is a reflection of the triune Godhead (John 17:11, 21). Such oneness in *koinonia* is not merely a sign of the church gathered, for Jesus said that through such unity "the world will know that you sent me and have loved them even as you have loved me" (John 17:23 TNIV). Thus, the ministries of the church gathered are always tied to mission in the world.

The third ministry of the church gathered is preaching and teaching God's Word. In Acts 2:42, "They devoted themselves to the apostles' teaching." The apostles' teaching at this point included the oral teachings of Christ, the Old Testament and apostolic teachings that would eventually become the corpus of the New Testament. The significance of the teaching ministry of the church is evidenced in the fact that Jesus' great commission includes it: "Teaching them to obey everything I have commanded you" (Matt. 28:20).

The church is the community of the Word. The Word is both the final source of its beliefs and actions, but also a life-giving enablement for those beliefs and actions. And as Paul wrote to Timothy, "All Scripture is God-breathed and is useful for teaching, rebuking, correcting and training in righteousness, so that all God's people may be thoroughly equipped for every good work" (2 Tim. 3:16–17 TNIV). It is in and through the Word, along with the gift of the Holy Spirit, that the church is connected to God and his purposes. The preaching and teaching of God's Word nurtures and builds the body, but it is also a sign that the church is not merely a human gathering. It is God's gathering, anchored in the Word, reflecting the Word, and empowered to live that Word.

The preaching ministry of the church is closely tied to its worship ministry, for in both dimensions the Word is central and in both God's presence, guidance, and empowerment are evident. A central element in early Christian worship was also the reading of the Word, a practice too frequently minimized in contemporary evangelical churches.

The Church Scattered

The church is not only the church when it gathers for ministries of worship, fellowship, and preaching/teaching. This very body is also sent into the world, scattered as Christ's church, to carry out his mission. Of course, part of the mission to the world can and does take place inside the gathered community, as evidenced by the fact that evangelism frequently takes place when a church gathers. But the mission of God is to be demonstrated primarily by the church as it carries the gospel message and actions to the world. To that end, the mission of the church scattered includes both word (verbal proclamation) and deed (acts of mercy and justice). Charles Van Engen defines the mission of the church this way:

> Mission is the people of God intentionally crossing barriers from church to nonchurch, faith to nonfaith, to proclaim by word and deed the coming of the kingdom of God in Jesus Christ; this task is achieved by means of the church's participation in God's mission of reconciling people to God, to themselves, to each other, and to the world, and gathering them into the church through repentance and faith in Jesus Christ by the work of the Holy Spirit with a view to the transformation of the world as a sign of the coming of the kingdom in Jesus Christ. (Van Engen, 26–27)

Evangelism (the fourth task) is a clear mandate of the church of Jesus Christ and one that he honors. In Acts 2 "The Lord added to their number daily those who were being saved" (v. 47). Throughout the book of Acts, the apostles carried out Jesus' mandate given just before he ascended to heaven, "You will receive power when the Holy Spirit comes on you; and you will be my witnesses in Jerusalem, and in all Judea and Samaria, and to the ends of the earth" (Acts 1:8). Wherever they went, the apostles and other followers of Christ continually proclaimed the gospel, the good news of Christ, inviting men and women to repent, believe, and follow Christ.

The great missionary statesman Leslie Newbigin pointed out that "there has been a long tradition which sees the mission of the Church primarily as obedience to a command.... [This] tends to make mission a burden rather than a joy, to make it part of the law rather than part of the gospel" (Newbigin, 116). Rather, we should see evangelism flowing from a life of worship and the joy experienced in God's grace. This is clearly evidenced in the Great Commission of Matthew 28, for before Jesus gave the commission we read, "Then the eleven disciples went to Galilee, to the mountain where Jesus had told them to go. When they saw him, they worshiped him" (vv. 16–17). Following the worship service on the mountain (in Matthew always a place of significant encounter), Jesus gave the mission mandate, "Therefore go and make disciples of all nations, baptizing them in the name of the Father and of the Son and of the Holy Spirit, and teaching them to obey everything I have commanded you. And surely I am with you always, to the very end of the age" (vv. 19–20). Worship and mission, while not identical, are always intimately related and part of spirituality in which our total lives are lived in and through the transforming presence of the Spirit.

It is clear in Jesus' great commission that the task of the church is not just to make converts, for the only imperative in the text is "make disciples," those who would be true followers of Christ. That is the reason Jesus gives the guidance as to how true disciples are formed: baptizing believers as the outward sign of God's work of grace, and teaching the newfound disciples what it means to truly follow Christ in every sphere of life. Evangelism is the work of the whole church, though clearly some have special gifts in this area. It is at the heart of the church's mission because it flows from the heart of the biblical narrative: creation, fall, redemption, and consummation. Though God created a good and beautiful world for humans to steward, the fall wreaked havoc in every dimension of life and above all in our relationship with God. Redemption in Christ is the solution to the fall and human sin, and evangelism is the means by which the church calls alienated, fallen sinners to repent, believe the gospel, and follow Christ. As in all dimensions of mission and ministry, this is God's work, using fallen but redeemed humans as his instruments.

The second part of the church's mission (and the church's fifth task overall) is deed, acts of mercy and justice, in which the gospel is evidenced in the actions of the church. This too is part of evangelism but is not necessarily tied to specific acts of evangelism, nor is it a means to evangelism. Our actions of love, justice, and Christian virtues flow from the very presence of God in our lives into a hurting world. In Acts 2 the actions of mercy and justice are seen primarily in relation to the social and physical needs of believers, but throughout Scripture it is clear that this is a mandate rooted in the Creation mandate of Genesis 1–2, in which humans are called to be caretakers of this world for its inhabitants' good. This social dimension of mission is buttressed by the Pentateuch and the prophets' call to care for the poor and downtrodden, and is mandated by Jesus' call to be salt and light in the world (Matt. 5:13–16). In Acts 2 it is evidenced in the believers' abundant generosity, "They sold property and possessions to give to anyone who had need" (v. 45 TNIV).

At times throughout history, evangelism and social responsibility, or word and deed, have been pitted against each other. While Christian proclamation and Christian presence in deed are not the same, they are both integral parts of the church's mission to the world. "The missional community which Jesus intended and which the apostles formed and taught was to testify to the gospel in every dimension of its existence. Its message was never understood as simply a verbal communication.... The gospel of Jesus Christ defines a new reality" (Guder, 137). Binding up the wounds of the broken, calling the culture to justice and righteousness, and embodying newness of life in every sphere of existence are part of what the church is called to do in the world. This means, in the words of Simon Chan, that "the essential nature of mission is for the church to be the body of Christ.... The church's primary mission, then, is to be itself, which is to be Christ for the world" (Chan, 39–40).

A Holistic Approach: Bringing Head, Heart, and Hands Together

Throughout the history of the Christian church, the inner life and the outer life have frequently been segmented from each other, and the mission and ministry tasks of the church have been separated from each other and from spirituality. One way of viewing the history of Christian expression is through the lens of head, heart, and hands (Hollinger). For some believers, the mind, or thinking, is the core element of Christian faith, with the head being the central dimension of our lives. For others the heart (i.e., will, affections, inner patterns) is viewed as the most salient dimension of life, and the primary locus of Christian growth. For still others the hands or actions have been viewed as the primary essence of Christian experience, for we are what we do, whether that be evangelism or social compassion.

In contrast to this segmented life in which theology, spirituality, and mission are distinct from one another, we must view both the human self and the Christian life from a holistic perspective. Dallas Willard describes it this way, "What we have before us in our study of spiritual formation is the whole person, and the various basic dimensions of the human self are not separate parts. They are aspects thoroughly intermingled with each other in their natures and actions" (Willard, 34). All this means that our ministry, mission, and theology are integrally related to each other, and all are forms of our spirituality. One is not merely a means to the others, for all are central expressions of our calling in Christ. This flows from a theological anthropology that accentuates the wholeness of the human self in which the body, mind, soul, and heart are all part of one human whole.

The ministries of the church gathered and the mission of the church scattered cannot be done without strong biblical and theological foundations to guide, or without Spirit-filled dynamics to nurture and empower. Similarly, Christian understanding (the realm of the mind) is facilitated by a spirituality of the heart and an active life of the hands, which help the mind to truly understand God's truth. Moreover, a spirituality of the heart, without theological guidance and active mission, is easily led captive by the varied false spiritualities that abound in our time. "The head, heart and hands need each other in the sense that they nurture each other, and each is integral to the expression of the others" (Hollinger, 33).

Jesus' own life reflected the kind of rhythm we need as we seek to carry out ministry and mission today. That rhythm incorporated actions of word, deed, and withdrawal for prayer and meditation. The early church followed the same pattern. The early followers of Christ could not imagine spirituality without ministry and mission, and could not imagine ministry and mission without divine presence and empowerment. They intersected in every dimension of life and were all part of the "spiritual life," the calling of God for individuals and for the church.

In our postmodern, fragmented world, there has been what some have called a collapse of time and space, which makes difficult the achievement of a balanced life incorporating spiritual disciplines and mission. Traditional places of significance and traditional times for significant acts and celebrations have been lost in a cyber world with its instantaneous information and its boundaryless modes of interaction. In such a context, Paul Jensen calls for a subversive spirituality that stands against the temper of our times. He believes "that empowered inward spirituality—expressed in creating time and space for God through solitary and communal spiritual practices—correlates with transforming outward mission—expressed in word and deed" (Jensen, 4). Jensen's subversive spirituality is compatible with an understanding that Christian spirituality is the domain of lived Christian experience. It is about living *all of life* before God, through Christ, in the transforming and empowering presence of the Holy Spirit.

Above all, what is needed is for believers to follow the example of Christ. In Mark 1, after a fast-paced schedule of ministry and mission in which he calls disciples, teaches the people, confronts evil, and heals the sick, "very early in the morning, while it was still dark, Jesus got up, left the house and went off to a solitary place, where he prayed" (v. 35). It is precisely this rhythm of holistic spirituality that Christians so desperately need today.

Sources Cited

Chan, S. *Liturgical Theology* (2006).
Guder, D. *The Continuing Conversion of the Church* (2000).
Hollinger, D. *Head, Heart and Hands* (2005).
Howard, E. *The Brazos Introduction to Spirituality* (2008).
Jensen, L. P. *Subversive Spirituality* (2009).
Newbigin, L. *The Gospel in a Pluralist Society* (1989).
Van Engen, C. *Mission on the Way* (1996).
Willard, D. *Renovation of the Heart* (2002).

For Further Reading

Cullen, B. *Authentic Spirituality* (2001).
Foster, R. *Streams of Living Water* (1998).
Lovelace, R. *Dynamics of Spiritual Life* (1979).
MacLaren, D. *Mission Implausible* (2004).
McKnight, S. *A Community Called Atonement* (2007).
Nouwen, H. *Creative Ministry* (1971).

CHAPTER 34

THE FUTURE OF CHRISTIAN SPIRITUALITY

JAMES M. HOUSTON

Perhaps there can be no greater ambiguity than with the word *spirituality*, for it can refer either to God's Spirit or to the diverse domain of the human spirit. The two are not the same. For example, Christians may claim that their actions are guided by God's Holy Spirit, when in fact they are driven by a great deal of self-ignorance and even self-deception. For the very name of the Holy Spirit implies that he is "Other" than ourselves. Yet, paradoxically, our privilege as Christians is to experience how intimately personal he can be within us. Christian spirituality claims to express the lived faith of the believer in personal experience with Christ. Concerning the future of Christian spirituality, therefore, we can only venture some expectations about its human expressions. As expressive of the divine, Jesus reminded Nicodemus, the Spirit of God is like the wind, unpredictable in his movements. And "so it is with everyone born of the Spirit" (John 3:8).

The Limits of Prediction

Five things can be considered predictable. The first is that because of the increasing power of humanity to produce technology, the ambiguities of the contest between good and evil will intensify. The second is that with globalization we should anticipate demographic shifts that will relocate the center of Christian influences within the Southern Hemisphere, and with this an attendant eclipse of North American expressions of Christianity. The third prediction is based on changing demographics with the rapidly aging population in the West. The fourth is that as church denominations remain with distinct identities often reflective of historical reactions no longer relevant or now distorted further by exaggerations, reforms will be needed to bring renewal by what is transparent and truthful.

While they are all significant, these four predictions tend to interpret history from a merely human perspective. The fifth form of prediction, "the prophetic," is the most profound, since it is based on the historicity of the Christian faith itself, by which I mean the active presence of God in human affairs throughout human time, together with an ever-deepening need to be indwelt by the Holy Spirit's "spiritual discernment" of the Word of God, to "test the spirits" against error and heresy.

1. Ambiguous Advance of Technology

First, deepening ambiguity will occur within technical society. Why do we anticipate this? In the postwar years, Jacques Ellul saw Western society becoming increasingly squeezed in the grip of technology (Goddard). He recognized that the essence of *techné* lies in the indefinite generation and extension of technical motivations and skills. From this observation, he could make a prediction for the future; namely, that it would be characterized by the intensification of ambiguities between good and evil. If Charles Dickens interpreted his Victorian society to be living in "the best of times and the worst of times," how much more we shall see ambiguity intensifying ahead of us. However, we venture our predictions in the light of the apostle Paul's assurance to the Roman Christians: "Where sin increased, grace increased all the more" (Rom. 5:20). Christ has defeated Satan, so evil is not boundless, terrible as the genocides of the 20th century have been. The Christian life is a progressive life, renewed under progressive revelation, until eventually it will be fully transformed into the likeness of Christ. The element of hope is stronger and more virile than ever, so that the Christian can be freed to be "plain-speaking." As Paul assures the Corinthians, "Since we have such a hope, we are very bold" (2 Cor. 3:12).

In contrast, the secular cultural historian Jacques Barzun could only recognize our contemporary postmodern culture becoming an age of decadence. By "decadence" he meant literally "a falling off," as a wave breaks on a shore, where its power appears futile and restless, with no clear lines for advance (Barzun, xvi). It is the age of cults, fads, and unbelief; boredom is its malaise. It is the age of mass culture, turned into pop culture, which appears like an impending new Dark Age. It seems to require small minorities like the desert fathers and mothers, or like the founding Benedictine monks, or like Luther to light candles once more in tiny cells.

The American dream of "bigness," even of mass campaigns, is no longer conducive to such spiritual renewal. This moral decadence is described as "postmodern," not because it is an advance on the "modern," but because of its disenchantment with many things "modern." Once God is no longer on the horizon, all horizons seem to be forfeited and to leave us with only a yawn. Now the electronic revolution is making cyberspace a replacement for social space and historical connectedness. The social cohorts of youth are being distinguished by the successive electronic inventions they fashionably adopt, each dividing one narrowly sliced chronological group from another. This robs youth of social skills and constitutes a formidable challenge for church fellowships to cohere between age groups.

Yet for most Christians today, there is still little knowledge of the rich traditions we have inherited in Christian spirituality. Christian thinkers, both theologians and more popular writers, often display deficiency by not being well grounded in the history of the Christian church. Consequently, they have no yardstick by which to measure contemporary movements or to weight the strengths and weaknesses of previous movements of Christian spirituality. As an unfortunate result, even Christians can have too few defenses to prevent themselves from being shaped by the contemporary host culture. Today's religious descendants of the evangelical revival of the 18th century, or the Pentecostal movement of the early 20th century, are often ill equipped historically to understand and appreciate the rich resources of the spiritual movements of earlier centuries.

2. Geographic Shift of Global Christianity

Second, globalization will reorientate the locale of Christian influence. We no longer think of British colonialism as the center of Christian influence, though at one time it was. That center has shifted to the United States as the world's superpower. Yet American influence may already be in decline. We all live in one sphere, where action at one point on the earth's surface produces reaction elsewhere. The expanding scale of globalization points also to the increasing complexity of present and future ways of life.

The awareness since the 1960s of environmental deterioration, and now of climate warming, is intensifying the contemporary sense of unpredictability. Compared with the confident "futurist" ideas of the 1970s, we are now far less certain about our future. Likewise, the nature of spirituality—humanist or Christian—is not static, but a dynamic, ongoing series of experiments, challenging us to keep looking forward to the future. Certainly when the scale changes, prospects will also change. So we ask two questions: First, is the demise of American influence within sight? And will the Southern Hemisphere lead the future of Christianity? The answer to both must be yes. If, then, the norms of Anglo-Saxon colonial missionary Christianity no longer hold, and are regarded as belonging to the 19th century, will we say the same of American expressions of Christian spirituality for the remainder of the 21st century?

Our response lies in a series of questions. Will we be as financially endowed for our "ministries"? Will there be as much youthful volunteering in the emerging and more decadent culture of narcissism? Will we become more disenchanted ecclesiastically with the breakup of mainline denominations and their apostasy? Are new missions from the Southern Hemisphere already beginning to missionize those in the Northern Hemisphere? If popular expressions of Christianity become more political, will they lose credibility? With aging populations, will the youth of the churches in the Northern Hemisphere become increasingly more disenchanted with conservative forms of Christianity? These issues already face us.

If the church was challenged by science and evolution in the 19th century, its credibility today is much more over issues of moral character. Protestants need to follow the lead of the Roman Catholic Church, which, since the Second Vatican Council, has recognized that its highest priority should not be the amount of its budget or the size of a congregation, but the quality of Christian living experienced within the church fellowship and a renewed call to holiness.

The newer interest in retreats, spiritual direction, instruction in prayer, and spiritual formation, and in the links between holiness of life and charitable acts are all signs of this change. But the American instinct to organize programs for spiritual formation is doomed to fail. Hopefully, *being* a Christian is beginning to take precedence over *doing* many things. Mary, not Martha, still needs to be recognized as having done "the better part."

Politically and culturally in retreat, Christians can only remain resilient by being grounded in the lived life our Lord has set before us: "Let us not love with words or tongue but with actions and in truth" (1 John 3:18 TNIV). There can be no substitute for simple consistency of belief and action.

A growing literature indicates demographically that the future numerical strength of Christianity is swinging to the Southern Hemisphere. Mission initiatives once taken by the North are now being made more indigenously from the South. New issues are arising in the context of globalization. Mark Noll has raised three questions in this context: How close is the world of spirits to our own everyday world and consciousness? Does conversion always have to be of individuals alone, when in other societies whole communities have become Christian? And can the Bible be read legitimately in different ways, or with emphasis on different books of the Bible? (Noll, 33–37).

Various forms of Pentecostalism that emphasize "power encounters" will continue to dominate wherever indigenous cultures live in fear of evil spirits or are characterized by a porous form of the psyche, where other spirits are invasive of their own identity. Already the challenge for thoughtful Christian leaders in Asia, Africa, and Latin America is how Christian charismatic movements can be safeguarded doctrinally from the cultural underground of pagan spiritism. At the same time, it must be determined whether Western Christians need to be more open to the supernatural and to believe in the possibilities of miraculous healings, exorcisms, and more mystical forms of experience.

There is also the challenge to reconsider whether individual conversion has been, and will be, the norm of evangelical faith. What are we to make of the mass conversions of the Celtic missionaries in the 6th century or of the Untouchable caste of the poorest Indians in the 21st century? What of the large number of ethnic minorities converted en masse in the underground churches of southwest China today? Are their intense experiences of crying for a week or more needed for their change of life to be lasting and transformational? Perhaps such phenomena call in question the role compunction had in the early church, but which is almost unknown in our modern world. Should Protestants revise their nonpractice of confession and, like medieval Christians, recover a stronger penitential role in their practice of the faith? It might restore some credibility to being a Christian, for after all, we are truthfully described in Scripture as sinners.

3. Aging of Western Populations

The third change is what has been described as "the demographic tsunami" facing us within the next decades — the aging population and the prospect of half our Western population becoming over sixty-five years of age. Already baby boomers face retirement, and the increasing challenge of caring for aged parents, perhaps half of whom are entering dementia, Alzheimer's and other mental diseases. Escalating costs to health and welfare systems of governance will force Western cultures to change to become more caring of their seniors and to face human mortality more realistically than the contemporary cultural denial of death allows. The intensification of professionalism since the postwar years and the "functional identities" forced on us now imply that to be "retired" is to lose a sense of identity as the condemnation of the aged. Few if any seminaries have courses in geriatric pastoral care, so the culture within the church is no different from the secular culture. Therefore, it could be that secular cultural change in this regard may lead the churches, ironically, to follow suit in far more relational concerns for the aged and disabled. It is realistic to project that the aging of the population may be the trigger for a relational reformation of the Christian churches.

4. Disenchantment with Institutions

The fourth change relates to cultural disaffection with institutions, including the status quo of denominations. One reaction is to affirm that one is "a more authentic Christian" by not going to church at all! Another is the growing popularity of the emerging church movement, which identifies with the culture of postmodernism without always understanding the doctrinal consequences.

Root System of a Prophetic Spirituality

Unlike contemporary secular culture, which can only ascribe the evaluation "decadent" by subjective judgment, the Christian faith has a biblical and historical foundation and a prospective future — both of which are prophetic. For Scripture proclaims that God is the Alpha and Omega and that human cause and effect are always set within a larger framework of divine providence. This gives meaning to the past and provides hope and predictive confidence when anticipating the future. The loss of both biblical and historical consciousness is therefore a very serious threat today. For their atrophy blinds us to both the promise and the judgment of God.

Ours is a historic faith of God's intervention in time, providing a covenant with his chosen people Israel, speaking through his prophets and apostles in his Word, and now uniquely revealed by Jesus Christ himself, through the Holy Spirit. Likewise, when we become cut off from the communion of saints and have little benefit from the rich resources of various Christian devotional traditions and are living with contemporary consciousness alone, our religion quickly becomes as secularized as our culture.

Implicit in this prophetic awareness is that the Christian past can never be forgotten in its future. Increasingly it will help the church gain perspective as time moves forward. Whatever gives us cognition of the eternal, the glory of God, the love and truth of God, unites us within the worshiping community of God's people. Then the memory of the Lord's Supper, the sacramental meaning of baptism, and indeed the continuance of the church as the living community of the apostolic tradition become resources for its future development.

Robert Wilken has winsomely exemplified that an effective Christian teacher is necessarily also a historical theologian. As such, he or she will never isolate biblical scholarship as though it were mere textual study. Rather, such study will be treated for what it is, namely, a commentary from the centuries, rich in trained insights into and wise applications of the Scriptures. Thus, Christopher Hall, converted in the Jesus movement of the early 1970s, admits as a scholar of the church fathers that his "individualistic, evangelical bent has been tempered by a historical, theological and spiritual lengthening of memory" (Hall, 6).

I rejoice to see this historical rediscovery, although it implies that we also need to become more spiritually discerning of all the past follies of the church. This need was well summarized by an old friend, Richard Halverson, chaplain to the United States Senate, who used to say: "Christianity was birthed in Palestine soil to become relational; then it developed in the Greek lands to become philosophical; in the Roman world it expanded to become institutional; then in the Anglo-Saxon world it became cultural; and now, in the American economy it has become an enterprise!"

In writing his *Institutes*, John Calvin was aware that truthful continuity with the early fathers of the church was essential for defending the orthodoxy of his reforming friends a thousand years later. Surely no account of Christianity is adequate that cannot trace its historical continuity from its beginnings with Jesus Christ, then with his apostles, and beyond with the writings of the early fathers, to our contemporary status quo. It is this that gives support to projections of the future of the church, and indeed of its spirituality. Its past resources have brought Christianity to its present form. Past and future must be held in balance to have a genuinely Christian perspective on what God has done and will do for his people. But when we remember the past church reforms in pursuit of truth — perhaps

with their own eccentricities — we can also dare to hope for a biblically faithful future, uncompromised by acquiescence to cultural pressures.

Likewise today, we can only critique, and thus anticipate the reforms needed to address the weaknesses of, contemporary Christianity when we know something of its modern history. For example, it was the French Revolution, in conjunction with the American Revolution, that triggered a new phase of the human spirit's quest of "freedom." At its best, it sponsored the liberation of slaves, through champions like the English Christian politician William Wilberforce. At its geographic extremity, on a new continent, it experimented with what French observer Alexis de Tocqueville saw in North America to be "the rise of the Individual." Half a century later, John Weiss observed the absurdity that "America is an opportunity to make a Religion out of the sacredness of the individual." As Leigh Eric Schmidt suggested, American cultural religion has gradually narrowed to little more than "a frame of reference for the self" (Schmidt, 4).

Much of our own modern awareness of spirituality has arisen only since the 1960s, as a concomitant of the rise of postmodernism. When the Cuban missile crisis threatened us with a nuclear holocaust in 1962, we became afraid of our own technical inventions. Our youth rebelled against the effects of rationalism, institutional bureaucracy, sexual inhibition, and other things they perceived as "repressive" of the human spirit. "Postmodern" then became a signifier of disenchantment with what had been previously esteemed as "modern."

However, much of the secular content of what now appears to be postmodern still adheres to metaphysical materialism. What is genuinely postmodern is the way of thinking that gives primacy to "spirit" rather than to the "material," which has given vogue to "spirituality" as expressive even of renewed forms of paganism. On the other hand, postmodernism's positive effect on the Christian life has been to unite spirituality and dogma, seeing truth as holistic, theology as the grammar of faith, and religious knowledge as personal participation in the scripturally informed knowledge of God. To have such knowledge of God means that we will also fear, obey, and love him. Yet we are only beginning to conceive and to practice how theological scholarship in particular, and Christian teaching in general, can become less abstract and more personal in daily life. "Spiritual theology" is no longer just a branch of the science of theology, but the way theology takes the initiative with us, and is then lived out in us personally.

Attentiveness to Word and Spirit

A welcome new trend is to reconsider the challenge of Bible reading, not just as a scholarly hermeneutical skill, but also as a way of living. We should not just ask, "What do the Scriptures mean?" and assume without question the old Enlightenment conception of this fundamental epistemic task. Rather, we need in the future to be reconnected with all of the history of the church. Then we shall enquire this way instead: "How does the Scripture transform its readers into becoming the body of Christ?" William Abraham seeks this in his seminal work, *Canon and Criterion in Christian Theology* (1998). Then reading Holy Scripture again becomes a process of sanctification, as the medieval practice of *lectio divina* was originally meant to be.

In his inaugural lecture at Oxford University, John Webster asked if there is such a thing as "Holy Scripture." The answer cannot be a literary definition, but rather one drawn from dogmatics. Indeed, it must be a robustly Trinitarian one, in which God's self-presence is discovered through both Word and Spirit. Then, as Webster states it, "Reading Scripture is inescapably bound to regeneration.... Through the Spirit of the crucified and risen Christ we are given the capacity to set mind and will on the truth of the Gospel and so to read as those who have been reconciled to God" (Webster, 89).

The Scriptures themselves provide a new spiritual attentiveness, that is, a receptive and humble disposition to live out the faith from what has been given. In other words, the future of Christian spirituality must lie within the reawakening of the Bible as the source of the triune revelation of God, the communicative, fellowship-establishing relatedness of God as Father, Son, and Holy Spirit.

In his critically important guide for the exegesis of Scripture as key to the Christian way of living, Augustine of Hippo said: "There are two things on which all interpretation of Scripture depends: the process of discovering what we need to learn, and the process of presenting what we have learnt" (Augustine, 8). He continued:

> It is therefore necessary above all else to be moved by the fear of God towards learning his will: what it is that he instructs us to seek or avoid.... After that it is necessary, through holiness [or piety], to become docile, and not contract holy Scripture—whether we understand it (as when it hits at some of our vices) or fail to understand it (as when we feel we could by ourselves gain better knowledge or give better instruction)—but rather ponder and believe that what is written there, even if obscure, is better and truer than any insights that we can gain by our own efforts. (33–34)

No less now than in the 16th century, the church of the future needs another biblical reformation. So Augustine would teach us that far from seeking mastery over the text of Scripture, we should allow it to have mastery over us. For it is love of God, not self-love, and in its practical expression, the love of neighbor, that frees us to read, to know, and to respond to his Word. Then we will be given spiritual discernment, which is freedom from self-love to love God with God's own love. This alone allows us to anticipate the future of Christian spirituality. It must be a revival of true Bible readers for a deepening of Christian spirituality. As Jesus prayed for his disciples in the upper room, "They have obeyed your word.... I have given them your word.... Sanctify them by the truth; your word is truth" (John 17:6, 14, 17).

Sources Cited

Augustine. *On Christian Teaching.* Trans. R. P. H. Green (1997).

Barzun, J. *From Dawn to Decadence* (2000).

Goddard, A. *Living the Word, Resisting the World* (2002).

Hall, C. *Worship with the Church Fathers* (2009).

Noll, M. *The New Shape of World Christianity* (2009).

Schmidt, L. E. *Restless Souls* (2005).

Webster, J. *Holy Scripture* (2003).

Wilken, R. *Remembering the Christian Past* (1995).

For Further Reading

Fiddes, P. *Participating in God* (2000).

Foster, R., and G. Beebe. *Longing for God* (2009).

Houston, J. *Joyous Exiles* (2006).

Houston, J., and M. Parker. *Seniors in the Church* (2010).

Lubac, H. de. *Scripture in the Tradition.* Trans. L. O'Neill (1968).

McIntosh, M. *Christology from Within* (2000).

Packer, J. I. *Rediscovering Holiness* (2009).

Scorgie, G. *A Little Guide to Christian Spirituality* (2007).

Swinton, J. et al. *Living Well and Dying Faithfully* (2009).

PART TWO

DICTIONARY ENTRIES

A

Abandonment
See **Surrender.**

Accedia
See **Sloth.**

Accountability

Accountability refers to the obligation to answer to another for choices, decisions, and actions in light of their consequences and outcomes. For an individual to be accountable implies a singular responsibility, which cannot be off-loaded to another, to answer for one's own actions, and receive praise or blame and, when appropriate, reward or punishment. Also central to the meaning of accountability, especially with respect to spirituality, is the idea that we are answerable to *someone.*

Scripture is replete with references to accountability. Israel was accountable to God, individually and collectively, for keeping his commandments (Lev. 5:17; 7:18; 19:8) while their leaders were accountable to God for the care of his people (Ezek. 34:2–10). Individuals are also accountable to God for the wicked, "to dissuade him from his ways" (Ezek. 33:7–8). Through the incarnation, the Son made himself accountable to the Father for humanity's salvation and welfare. Jesus taught his disciples that they too were answerable to God (Matt. 12:36; Luke 12:48) for their individual lives, and also for whether they loved others as he loved (John 13:34–35). This involves confronting and restoring sinners (Matt. 18:15–18), and even caring for the wicked (Matt. 5:43–48). The apostle Paul also frequently wrote of believers' accountabil-ity to God (Rom. 14:12; 1 Cor. 3:1–23) as well as to and for one another (Rom. 13:8; 1 Cor. 5:1–3; Gal. 6:2). Like its Savior, the church must see itself as accountable for its efforts toward the salvation and welfare of humanity.

Legitimate evangelical spirituality, by necessity, involves an interpersonal, relational dynamic experienced within the context of a community of faith. Scripture makes it clear that accountability relationships within such a community are essential for its growth and development. All members are accountable to God for their individual behavior and the welfare of others. They are to provide for one another's needs, as well as hold each other accountable for living righteously. Leaders are particularly accountable for the spiritual care and well-being of those whom they have been called to serve. The failure to acknowledge this responsibility has resulted in far too many shameful cases of abusive leadership within the church. The biblical principle of accountability (1 Peter 5:2–4) should foster a properly sobered leadership culture of humility and prayer.

See also Responsibility; Small Groups.

For Further Reading: S. Hauerwas, *A Community of Character* (1981); G. McKenny, "Responsibility," in *The Oxford Handbook of Theological Ethics*, ed. G. Meilaender and W. Werpehowski (2005); L. Richards, "Accountability," in *A Practical Theology of Spirituality* (1987), 85–96; D. Watson, *Covenant Discipleship* (1991).

John R. Lillis

Active Life and Contemplative Life

The *active* life has been distinguished from the *contemplative* life in Catholic spiritual tradition.

The active life refers to the outer life of a Christian in which one loves the neighbor in practical ways. The contemplative life, on the other hand, is the inner life of gazing on God, of prayer, meditation, and contemplation. The spiritual life, based on love, includes both, as indicated by the two chief commandments identified by Jesus: love to God and love to the neighbor (Luke 10:27).

Origen was the first to identify Martha as the biblical model of the active life and her sister Mary the model of the contemplative. Jesus praises Mary in the story (Luke 10:38–42), yet it is obvious that the life of discipleship Jesus calls his followers to includes both listening to him and serving the neighbor (Luke 10:25–37), as the parable of the good Samaritan makes clear. The prophet Anna (Luke 2:36–37) may be seen as an example of the contemplative life. "She never left the temple but worshiped night and day, fasting and praying." Yet we are warned not to love only in thought but in action (1 John 3:17–18).

There is a spectrum of emphasis on one form of life or the other, and this became clear institutionally in the religious orders of the Roman Catholic Church. The distinction is used by Gregory the Great and Thomas Aquinas. The Benedictine tradition put emphasis on enclosure, reciting psalms, *lectio divina*, and manual labor. The main emphasis was on personal growth rather than service in the world. The Franciscans and Dominicans of the 13th century put more emphasis on that service, including helping the poor and sick, and preaching in cities. Nevertheless, some Benedictines teach in the world, and the Franciscans and Dominicans have regular hours of prayer. In general, Protestants have rejected the concept of a totally contemplative life, and Americans in particular have been activist Christians. American evangelicals have sometimes emphasized the need for evangelism and social reform without a similar emphasis on the inner life.

In the 20th century, Thomas Merton brought together the active and contemplative lives by first going deeply into contemplation in a Cistercian abbey, then coming to the realization on a busy street corner that he was not different from all the people around him. He said that he loved all these people, though he did not know them. Thus, his contemplation resulted in an awareness of his common humanity, which then led him to engage with the problems of the world in a form of action appropriate to him: he was a writer.

The Christian spiritual life necessarily includes both the active and the contemplative lives, and they must not be separated. It may be necessary to emphasize one or the other temporarily; some persons will find one or the other more congruent with their personality type and vocation; some stages of life may call for one more than the other. Yet it is important to recognize how each is dynamically connected to the other and neither must exclude the other in principle but both become a unity.

See also Retreats.

For Further Reading: *Into the Great Silence*, directed by P. Gröning (2005); T. Merton, *Conjectures of a Guilty Bystander* (1966); idem, *Contemplation in a World of Action* (1973); P. Palmer, *The Active Life* (1999).

Bradley P. Holt

Addictions and Recovery

Addiction is a physical, psychological, and behavioral dependence, obsession, or compulsion to use substances or engage in various forms of activities. Most commonly, the term refers to an addiction to a substance (e.g., alcohol, drugs, nicotine), but it can also include references to other substances and behavior—food, gambling, sex, money, crime, pornography, the Internet, television, etc.

The most difficult problem for most people to understand is that addictions are a disease. Although the American Medical Association classified addictions (especially to alcohol and drugs) as a disease in the mid-20th century, many people consider addictions as a sign of moral failure or the result of individual choice. Addictions are a chronic, progressive, often fatal, incurable, and yet treatable disease. Addictions are like allergies: the afflicted person will always be affected by the addictive substance or behavior. The only treatment is total abstinence, just as lack of exposure to an allergen is the best treatment for an allergy sufferer. The disease is physical, psychological, and spiritual. It affects the body in many ways—most notably in altering brain functions, but also in causing cancers, respiratory illnesses, neurological problems, etc. Psychologically, it is both caused by and aggravates various psychological illnesses, especially depression and bipolar disease. Spiritually, addictions affect individuals and their relationships with family, friends, colleagues, and what is often called their "Higher Power," or what many people call God. About two-thirds of addictions seem to be rooted in genetic factors, although separating these from social influences is difficult, if not impossible.

In spite of their manifold causes and widespread and devastating effects, addictions can be treated, but not cured, in a variety of ways. Healing can occur, but a cure is not possible. For example, an alcoholic cannot "drink normally," and so the healing from alcoholism involves total abstinence. Medication can often mitigate or even remove the physical and psychological dependence. Various forms of therapy have been successful. In general, these fail to deal adequately with what addicts often describe as "the hole in the soul," the deep and desperate spiritual hunger and loneliness associated with all forms of addiction. To address this need, the Twelve-Step program of Alcoholics Anonymous and the movements it has spawned consistently address addictions as a spiritual problem for which only a spiritual answer is sufficient. The goal for the addict is "a spiritual awakening," usually a gradual process of finding a new relationship with oneself, with others, and with "the God of my understanding." Individuals recognize that they are utterly trapped by their addiction and

that only by depending on God—a power greater than themselves—can they find freedom from their addictive thinking and behavior. Working the Twelve Steps is, in effect, a spiritual discipline in which people replace one form of destructive behavior with a constructive form of life based on healthy relationships with themselves, others, and God.

See also Twelve-Step Programs.

For Further Reading: AA Services, *Alcoholics Anonymous* (2001); idem, *Twelve Steps and Twelve Traditions* (1981/2002); E. Kurtz and K. Ketcham, *The Spirituality of Imperfection* (1992).

John M. Mulder

Adolescent Spirituality

Adolescence is a culturally conditioned life stage between childhood and adulthood that varies in length and experience in developed societies. Many traditional societies have no such phenomenon. Adolescence emerged in Western countries by the early 1900s, and recently its length has been increasing. Theorists now conceive of adolescence roughly in three phases: *early*—ages ten to thirteen; *mid*—fourteen to eighteen; and *late*—eighteen to the mid- to late twenties and beyond. Some prefer the term *emerging adulthood* to late adolescence. Adolescent spirituality refers to youths' lived experience of God that spans these years.

In the Christian tradition, the spirituality of youth has contributed to significant developments and movements. Jesus' mother, Mary, Origen, and Catherine of Sienna made formative spiritual decisions in their teen years, and Francis of Assisi and William Wilberforce did the same in their twenties. In the West, the age cohort now passing through adolescence is Generation Y, also called the millennials (born 1981–1995 in the United Kingdom and Australia, and 1981–2000 in the United States). Sociological studies on millennials' spirituality in Western societies have found a widespread interest in spiritual phenomena but a relatively small percentage that are seriously seeking or practicing historic Christian spirituality. A nationally representative American study of mid-adolescents by Smith and Denton (2005) showed that though religion and prayer were important to them, their faith was consumer-oriented, self-absorbed, and moralistic, and they viewed God as distant except in crisis. Moral therapeutic deism has been coined to describe this faith that has little to do with theological notions such as sin and salvation typical of historic faith traditions.

Offering another perspective, developmental theorists underscore the importance during late adolescence of dealing effectively with uncertainty and ambiguity to form ethical and spiritual commitments. In Erik Erikson's eight-stage model, identity formation is a prime developmental task for midadolescents who begin differentiating their spirituality from that of their parents in the teen years. Yet identity (and virtue) is seldom formed only individually, but also communally and through role models. As mentored pathways into adulthood have disappeared and communal rites of passage into adulthood have declined, adolescents often struggle becoming adults. Thus, many observers have called for adults and families to plug the mentoring deficit in the spiritual and identity formation of adolescents.

In this milieu, adolescent Christian spirituality has taken shape along trajectories involving various mentor roles. First, with the West's erosion of family and ethical foundations, self-giving love expressed within the triune God is emerging as a formational center for adolescents whose spirituality has become communal, even tribal. For them, personal connection within a Christian community that mentors them with Trinitarian love is essential.

Second, important efforts are under way to make the family an integral part of youth ministry, rather than an appendage, by helping the home (whether blended, single parent, or intact) be a venue for spiritual transformation and guidance.

Third, charitable foundations, education councils, and seminaries have responded to Western biblical illiteracy by addressing the spiritual formation of Christians in secondary schools and institutions of higher education. The Lilly Foundation has funded programs of theological study, worship, and community for U.S. high school students at forty-nine schools of theology and funded extensive research on adolescent spirituality and how it is impacted during the college years.

Fourth, many adolescents are attracted to spiritual guides from Christian history. Following Jesus and others, they pray in solitude and community, go on retreat, read Scripture, and engage in contemplative practices such as *lectio divina*, the Jesus Prayer, and Ignatian meditation. They also involve themselves in social justice and compassion. Sustaining such practices is challenging in their time-compressed lives, but help is coming from student ministers and other mentors.

Fifth, adolescents have long been immersed in an image-saturated media, which has functioned in many instances as a default mentor. Their spirituality is likewise rich in images. Drawing on web-based resources and social networks, they readily employ Christian art, icons, and participatory liturgy in their formation.

Finally, scholars of adolescent spirituality have contributed to spiritual formation literature. Notable works include Mark Yaconelli's *Contemplative Youth Ministry* (2006) and Kenda Creasy Dean's *Practicing Passion* (2004), an important work in spiritual theology, in which she argues that only contemplation of Jesus' death and resurrection can supply youth with passion to live in joyful abandon to him, even, if necessary, at the cost of life itself. The crucified and risen Jesus still has mysterious power to breathe life and hope into adolescents so often experiencing pain and bleak prospects.

See also Children; Family Life; Human Development; Parenting.

For Further Reading: D. Bass and D. Richter, *Way to Live* (2002); C. Clark, *Hurt* (2004); S.

Collins-Mayo et al., *Making Sense of Generation Y* (2006); K. C. Dean and R. Foster, *The Godbearing Life* (1998); L. P. Jensen, *Subversive Spirituality* (2009); S. D. Parks, *Big Questions, Worthy Dreams* (2000); S. Savage et al., *The Spirit of Generation Y* (2008); C. Smith and M. L. Denton, *Soul Searching* (2005); C. Smith and P. Snell, *Souls in Transition* (2009).

L. Paul Jensen

Adoration

Adoration is the Godward gaze of grateful delight that melts self-will and purifies the soul. Originally the word *adoration* represented homage paid to one highly esteemed, as in worship; a feeling of profound love and admiration; and the veneration of religious objects. More than just an inward feeling, adoration also generates physical expressions, such as bowing the head (Ex. 34:8), raising the hands (1 Tim. 2:8), kneeling (1 Kings 8:54), and falling prostrate (Gen. 17:3; Rev. 1:17).

Old Testament words for adoration involved sound and related mostly to public worship. Some have felt this should continue to be true exclusively, while others — from C. S. Lewis to A. W. Tozer, and well beyond their circles — have felt that adoration also allows silent, private expression.

Biblically, adoration was variously expressed: in public (Ps. 35:18), through proclamation (Ps. 9:14), in shouts of joy (Ps. 71:23), with music (Ps. 92:1), through spoken word (Ps. 34:1), and in song (Ps. 33:1). Even though adoration and praise are closely related, they can be meaningfully differentiated. Adoration conveys the nuances of delighted fascination and love; there is a heart orientation and strongly affective aspect to it. Yet even when feelings may lag, adoration as an act of the devout will is still fitting. Many Christians appreciate the fact that adoration also has profound moral implications — through the imitative principle operating in all worship, we become like who or what we adore. Adoration reflects and trains desire.

The early church believed that adoration was reserved for God alone; directing adoration toward anyone or anything other than God was idolatry. However, controversies arose distinguishing adoration (*latreia*), which was reserved for God alone, from veneration (*duleia*), which was accorded to the saints from the time of Augustine. The Second Council of Nicea, in AD 787, concluded that adoration was for the worship of God alone, and ruled that the practice was not to be applied to earthly rulers, angels, or saints, all of whom could be venerated but not adored.

For evangelicals, the focus of adoration is most commonly Jesus Christ. The two most often reprinted hymns in 175 Protestant hymnals are "All Hail the Power of Jesus' Name" and "Jesus, Lover of My Soul" — both hymns of Scripture-based, Jesus-centered adoration.

See also Celebration; Praise; Worship.

For Further Reading: G. Beale, *We Become What We Worship* (2008); D. Eastman, *A Celebration of Praise* (1984); M. Kilpatrick, *Adoration* (1999); R. Mouw and M. Noll, *Wonderful Words of Life* (2004); R. Myers, *Thirty-one Days of Praise* (1994); M. Noll and R. Thiemann, eds., *Where Shall My Wond'ring Soul Begin?* (2000).

Dan R. Crawford

Aelred of Rievaulx (1109 – 1167)

English Cistercian authority on spiritual friendship. He was an abbot and writer, and, by his extraordinary leadership gifts and insights into relationships, a builder of Christian communities. He advocated pure Christian love for others in his life and his writings, especially in *The Mirror of Charity* (1142) and *Spiritual Friendship* (1167).

He was born in Hexham, Northumbria, and raised in an educated Christian family that included three generations of married priests living along the English-Scottish border. Reflecting a feudal custom of nobility educating promising youth of respected families, Aelred was sent to the Scottish court of King David I (1124–1153) at age fifteen, where he became a notable success.

Meanwhile, privately he was in distress, believing that his true Christian vocation had eluded him. He had been deeply affected by reading Cicero's *Dialogue on Friendship*, even though its deficiencies in biblical truth were evident to him. In this state of mind, he traveled to York on legal business of the court. On that journey, two life-changing encounters occurred. He met Bernard of Clairvaux, who saw in him great promise of faith and intellect and encouraged him to write. He also visited the newly founded monastery at Rievaulx. Without returning to the court, he entered the monastery at age twenty-six. Within six more years, he was its master of novices, and eventually its abbot, when he returned in 1147 from an initial appointment as abbot of Revesby.

As abbot of Rievaulx, he began the major written work of his life, *Spiritual Friendship*; it took him twenty years to complete it. He drew profound significance from Jesus declaring his disciples to be his friends (John 15:15). For Aelred, friendship was a means of growing in spiritual perfection. God is friendship, he maintained, citing 1 John 4:16, and cultivating friendship is a means of growth toward spiritual perfection.

During the final decade of his life, which was characterized by poor health, Aelred continued to instruct monks pastorally on the value of loving God by loving one's neighbor (Matt. 22:39). Some detractors have misconstrued Aelred's flowery romantic prose, stylish at the time, as suggestive of a violation of Christian purity and propriety, but there is no evidence that such allegations were ever credible. Almost a thousand years later, Aelred of Rievaulx remains one of the leading advocates of the value of Christian friendship.

See also Friendship, Spiritual.

For Further Reading: W. Daniel, *Life of Ailred of Rievaulx*, trans. F. M. Powicke (1950); A. Squire, *Aelred of Rievaulx* (1969).

Pamela Baker Powell

Affections

The apostle Paul wrote, "Those who live according to the sinful nature have their minds set on what that nature desires; but those who live in accordance with the Spirit have their minds set on what the Spirit desires" (Rom. 8:5). Christian affections are dispositions and character traits that are grown in believers' hearts as they move toward being like Jesus Christ. The Christian's affections are to be built on the values, beliefs, and teachings of the faith.

The idea of affections grew out of the word *affect* and its connotation of change. Philosophers have regarded affections as changes to a person's mind, heart, or body, which are related to, or even equated with, emotions. However, *affections* as a theological term has come to mean a more general set of specific qualities that a Christian is to pursue, and which go beyond simple emotions. As affections are rooted in our values and beliefs, we are to cultivate them with mind and will, as well as heart. To grow religious affections, the mind and will work deliberately to develop and change the whole person so that the emotions, actions, and reactions naturally reflect the character of Christ in the situations and trials they encounter.

Our thinking, evaluations, and judgments inform our emotional patterns, habits, and motivations. Learning to think Christianly results in the growth of a believer's affections; it produces specifically Christian emotional patterns, habits, and motivations. Therefore, it makes sense for Scripture to exhort believers to fill their minds with the thoughts, laws, and stories of God (Deut. 6:4–9). This setting of the mind on God's Word and its application produces the great Christian affections as God's truth becomes part of the heart. The resulting affections are central to Christian morality, character, and actions — love of God and neighbor, joy in the Lord, peace, hope, and a hatred of evil, among others.

The nonbeliever, according to the NT, is characterized by another set of affections. Envy, pride, love of money, and hatred of others become the natural inclinations of those not being transformed into the likeness of Christ (2 Tim. 3:2–6).

One's dominant affections, good or bad, are the natural outflowing of beliefs and values; recognizing this enables greater insight into the state of one's own heart. Cultivating godly affections becomes one of the primary goals of sanctification and Christian growth. One can choose a life of sacrifice and love for God and neighbor or one of selfishness. Affections, as primary motivation for actions, play a massive role in how people make choices and live out their lives. As Jesus taught, "Good people bring good things out of the good stored up in their heart, and evil people bring evil things out of the evil stored up in their heart" (Luke 6:45 TNIV).

See also Emotions.

For Further Reading: D. Carson, *The Difficult Doctrine of the Love of God* (2000); J. Edwards, *Religious Affections*, ed. J. Houston (1984); M. Elliott, *Feel: The Power of Listening to Your Heart* (2008); D. Willard, *Renovation of the Heart* (2002).
Matthew A. Elliott

African-American Christian Spirituality

African-American Christian spirituality begins with the experience of Africans suffering enslavement and dehumanization in North America while the gospel was being preached to them. The capture, forced migration, and enslavement of millions of Africans brought about centuries of extreme suffering for the ancestors of modern-day African-Americans. Throughout the American South, these enslaved Africans were evangelized by Christian slaveholders and plantation missionaries. Although they were told to love Jesus, they were mainly taught one text from the Bible: "Slaves, obey your masters." They were not allowed to read the Bible for themselves. In many states,

slaves were denied literacy and religious freedom by law to prevent them from educating and organizing themselves for rebellion. Under these conditions, at secret gatherings held late at night deep in the woods, the slaves sang and prayed and danced a religion of faith and hope in a God who would deliver them from bondage. Their own preachers spoke prophetic words affirming their humanity and their desire to be free. Their dances, prayers, songs, and other spiritual practices reflected the rich ancestral heritage of the traditional religions of Africa. Negro spirituals are the best-known legacy of this period of black suffering and spiritual struggle. In songs such as "Go Down, Moses," "Swing Low, Sweet Chariot," and "Were You There When They Crucified My Lord?" the spiritual longings of these underground faith communities come to voice with lyrics invoking biblical narratives of salvation and deliverance.

The prophetic witness for justice, equality, and freedom has endured among African-Americans from slavery times to the present century. During the civil rights movement, Martin Luther King Jr. arose as a preacher and theologian who felt called by God to confront the social, political, and economic injustices experienced by his people in the segregated South. At the 1963 March on Washington, his repeated refrain was, "I have a dream." However, the same speech began with a serious critique of the nightmare of injustice and racism in America. King used the prophetic words of Amos 5:24 to give divine sanction to his discourse of discontent and also to his poignant embrace of the American dream, saying, "No, no, we are not satisfied, and we will not be satisfied until justice rolls down like waters, and righteousness like a mighty stream" (cf. Amos 5:24).

While the formative experiences of the enslaved Christians in the 19th century and the triumphant witness of the twentieth-century civil rights movement remain the key markers of the spirituality of African-American Christians, the fuller picture requires other approaches and practices to be taken into account. Robert Franklin, an ethicist who is also a minister in the Church of God in Christ, has identified six traditions of African-American spirituality (Sanders, 136–38).

The *contemplative tradition* lifts up the praxis of prayer and meditation as the central virtue and value in Christian formation. Howard Thurman, a mystic, activist, and campus pastor who pioneered integrated Christian worship in the 1950s is a noteworthy exemplar of this tradition.

The *holiness tradition* seeks to achieve purity of life and thought by means of practices such as fasting, prayer, and renunciation of worldly influences. Pioneers of this tradition include Charles Price Jones of the Church of Christ Holiness, U.S.A., and C. H. Mason, founder of the Church of God in Christ.

The *Pentecostal/charismatic tradition* emphasizes personal empowerment through the Spirit by tarrying in worship. William J. Seymour was the pastor of the 1906 Azusa Street revival that launched Pentecostalism as a global Christian witness.

The *social justice tradition* pursues public righteousness and the protection of the poor. Its praxis is public activism, protest, and community-based ministry. King is the best-known exemplar of this tradition, but there are numerous others, including Adam Clayton Powell Jr., Vernon Johns, Jesse Jackson, and Willie Barrow.

The *Afrocentric tradition* highlights the cultural distinctiveness and aesthetics of African people through the recovery of African modes of worship, such as drumming and dancing. John Bryant initiated a neo-Pentecostal movement in the African Methodist Episcopal Church that embraces African liturgical practices and symbols with enthusiasm.

The *evangelical tradition* emphasizes knowledge and study of God's Word via the disciplines of proclamation and teaching. Prominent among the contemporary exemplars of this tradition are religious broadcasters Frederick K. Price and T. D. Jakes.

These various approaches to African-American Christian spirituality all converge in celebration of God's compassion for human suffering, and all find expression in preaching and praise. The sermons of this tradition are preached with prophetic fire and fervor, and are sometimes sung or intoned, always intending full engagement of the hopes and dreams of the hearers. And the distinctive melodies and rhythms of gospel music, drawn freely from the spirituals, the blues, jazz, and other streams of African-American artistry and performance, continue to offer healing and hope to the world.

See also Allen, Richard; Exodus; King, Martin Luther Jr.; Liberation Spirituality; Spirituals; Truth, Sojourner.

For Further Reading: M. L. King Jr., *Stride toward Freedom* (1964); P. Paris, *The Spirituality of African Peoples* (1994); A. Raboteau, *Slave Religion* (1978); C. Sanders, *Empowerment Ethics* (1995); H. Thurman, *Jesus and the Disinherited* (1996); J. Washington, ed., *Conversations with God* (1995).

Cheryl J. Sanders

African Christian Spirituality

African Christian spirituality today is a vast river, fed by countless streams from almost two millennia of the gospel's continuous presence in Africa. Notably, African indigenous languages lack an equivalent term for "spirituality" or "spiritual life," since African tradition understands all of life to be lived in relation to transcendence and/or the spiritual realm. For the present purpose, African Christian spirituality may be defined as the lived experience of African believers in their relationship with God, in Christ, through the Spirit, and in relation to others in the human community and to the cosmos. Given the diversity of African peoples and of Christian traditions across the continent, it is more accurate to use the plural—African Christian *spiritualities*. Nonetheless, there is sufficient commonality to warrant the singular form as an overarching term.

One major tributary has its sources in early Christianity from North Africa, with its confluence of Semitic, Greek, Latin, and indigenous African traditions. Certainly the experience of persecution and martyrdom forms an undercurrent for many of these emergent spiritualities. The Alexandrian school produced such towering figures as Clement, Origen, Athanasius, and Cyril, whose writings were seminal to the development of Christian spirituality. With the eremitic and coenobitic spiritualities founded by Antony of Egypt and Pachomius, respectively, desert monasticism from African soil shaped later centuries of monasticism worldwide, with its call to sacrifice, radical discipleship, poverty, celibacy, obedience, and daily ordering of the life of prayer, study, and work.

The Coptic Church, shaped significantly by Alexandrian Christianity and later flowing into Abyssinia (Ethiopia) and Nubia (Sudan), takes on distinctive expressions of spirituality through its vernacular translations of the gospel message into Coptic languages. Such Coptic traditions of spirituality continue to this day. From the western regions of North Africa, two streams of spirituality arose: one ascetic, typified by the Donatists, and the other pneumatic, typified by the Montanists. Through the writings of leading theologians like Tertullian and Augustine, African Christians forged new streams that have shaped Western Christian spirituality to the present.

A second major tributary of African Christian spiritualities includes the mission-initiated spiritualities derived from Western missionaries to Africa since the 15th century. Hence, many streams of Euro-American spiritualities have nurtured African believers: Iberian and Roman Catholic, Lutheran, Reformed, Anglican, Presbyterian, Methodist, Anabaptist, and Quaker, among others. In particular, the Pietist and evangelical movements have significantly shaped the faith experience of large numbers of African Christians, with their emphases on the centrality of Christ's death on the cross for salvation, the need for personal conversion or "new birth," Bible reading and prayer, and the coming kingdom with its consequent call for fervent evangelism and social activism. Two examples suffice to illustrate the outworking of these spiritualities on African soil: (1) the evangelical abolitionists' mission to resettle freed African slaves in Sierra Leone and Liberia in the late eighteenth and early 19th centuries, that witnessed leaders like Samuel Ajayi Crowther; and (2) the Keswick piety of evangelical perfectionism, advocating total surrender to Christ and triumph over the power of sin, which fueled the dramatic rise in faith missions across the continent and found powerful expression in Andrew Murray in South Africa.

A third major stream is African initiated Christian spiritualities, which seek to cultivate authentic faith experience that is meaningful and relevant to African Christians in accordance with their worldviews and practices. Often these arise in reaction to the Western missionaries' tendency to promote excessive individualism; focus on the "interior" life and future reward in heaven; emphasize faith as intellectual assent to theological propositions; create dichotomies between the sacred and profane; denigrate African culture; and in certain colonial contexts, to be complicit in dehumanizing African peoples. In contrast to Enlightenment Christianity's stress on rationality in religious faith and expression, African Christians, shaped through longstanding oral tradition, incline toward spiritualities conveyed in myth, proverb, narrative, prayer, symbol, ritual, song, and dance.

Emergent African Christian spiritualities generally exhibit the following interrelated characteristics. First, they hold a cardinal view of faith as the aspiration for fullness of life in Christ, summed up in John 10:10: "I have come that they may have life, and have it to the full." Second, this spirituality of life must be manifest in the everyday, concrete realities of existence where Christ is triumphant over any forces that diminish life, whether physically, emotionally, or spiritually. This liberative aspect is highlighted particularly in those contexts, whether of colonialism, neo-colonialism, or globalization, in which Africans suffer injustice and oppression, and it is especially forceful in its articulation by female Christians. Third, it is deeply communal, a living-in-relationship based on biblical teaching and quintessential African understanding that "a person is a person through other people." Moreover, this communal orientation is inclusive, extending hospitality and care to the most vulnerable and marginalized in society, and encompassing the living, the departed, and the unborn. Fourth, it is ecological, in that the mystery of life incorporates the entire cosmos. Fifth, it is dynamic, understanding the human person in the process of becoming, as illustrated in creative Christian initiation rites. Sixth, it is an integral spirituality that promotes a holistic approach to life, rejecting false dichotomies between sacred and profane or material and immaterial. Finally, it is a joyful, celebratory spirituality that sings and dances even in the midst of adversity. While these features characterize many expressions of African Christian spirituality, one prime example is Desmond Tutu's spirituality of justice, peace, and reconciliation.

A fourth tributary of African Christian spiritualities is formed by the confluence of pneumatic, Pentecostal, charismatic, and neo-Pentecostal spiritualities over the past century. Like subterranean springs, these spiritualities rise forcefully across sub-Saharan Africa and greatly swell the numbers of African converts to Christianity. With worldviews shaped by primal religions that assume the reality and power of the spiritual realm, Africans often resonate deeply with spiritualities that highlight the experience of the Holy Spirit. These spiritualities share core emphases, including personal salvation in Christ through the transforming work of the Spirit; ritual symbolism, for example using holy water and oil; and pneumatic phenomena such as speaking in tongues, prophecies, dreams and visions, exorcisms, and miracles including healing. Indigenous prophets, such as William Wade Harris of Liberia, Garrick Braide of the Niger Delta, Isa-iah Shembe of South Africa, and Simon Kimbangu of the Congo, have together evangelized millions of Africans and left their indelible mark on African Christian spirituality. Likewise, renowned African Pentecostal preachers and church planters, such as Kenyan Joseph Kayo (Deliverance Church); Nigerians Enoch Adeboye (Redeemed Christian Church of God), Matthew Ashimolowo (Kingsway International Christian Centre), and David Oyedepo (Winners Chapel); and Ghanaian Mensa Otabil (International Central Gospel Church) serve as fountainheads of neo-Pentecostal spirituality across Africa and beyond. Together with parallel developments in other continents, their international ministries feed the contemporary cascade of Pentecostal/charismatic Christianity worldwide.

See also Harris, William Wade.

For Further Reading: A. Anderson, *African Reformation* (2001); J. Asamoah-Gyadu, *African Charismatics* (2005); N. Finneran, *The Archaeology of Christianity in Africa* (2002); O. Kalu, ed., *African Christianity* (2005); L. Magesa, *Anatomy of Inculturation* (2004); J. Pobee, *Toward an African Theology* (1979); A. Shorter, ed., *African Christian Spirituality* (1978).

Diane B. Stinton

African Indigenous Spirituality

African indigenous (traditional) religions have different and sometimes competing ideas of spirituality. These stem from the unique histories, religious experiences, and cultures of the diverse ethnic groups that constitute Africa. Therefore, while it is possible to speak of "African indigenous spirituality" as a unified reality on the ground of what the ethnic groups share in common, it is important to exercise caution when generalizing to avoid undermining the distinctive understandings of spirituality by each of these ethnic groups.

In African indigenous religions, spirituality is a complex phenomenon that is rooted in the belief in a symbiotic relationship between the spiritual and human worlds. Spirituality does not signify entering into a nonhuman arena, in this case the sphere of spirits, but rather the embracing of the interrelatedness of the spheres of humans and spirits. Describing the major features of African indigenous notions of spirituality will be helpful.

The first is holism. In African indigenous thought, spirituality is construed as permeating all aspects of human life. There is no dualistic contrast or mind-set in the indigenous cosmologies, because the worlds of spirits and human beings intersect and mutually interact. Also, African indigenous spirituality is not confined to the arena of morality and ethics. It permeates every nook and cranny of human existence. Thus, anyone who seeks the locus of African indigenous spirituality must be ready to study the indigenous economy, politics, culture, religious traditions and taboos, and social structures — the relationship between human beings and spiritual beings, and human beings and non-human beings, such as trees.

The second feature is communality. African indigenous cosmologies consider relationship sacred and spiritual. Human beings negotiate their identities and can attain their full potentials only in the context of communion with the members of their community. In indigenous thought, therefore, human community includes the living, dead, living-dead (or ancestors), lesser gods, and Supreme Being. The rites of passage from those of the unborn to burial rites represent this all-encompassing communality.

A casual observer may assume that in this relationship the ancestors are the sole arbiters of authentic relationship. This is, however, a misunderstanding of the complexity that underlies the negations, dialogues, and dialectics that inform the interactions between spiritual and human beings. For example, while human beings are to remember and uphold the traditions of the land in order not to incur the wrath of gods and ancestors, these spirit beings also must provide, guide, and pro-

tect human beings if they want to be obeyed and remembered. This perception of human–spiritual being relations is evident in the persistent quest by many Africans to know what spiritual beings expect from them. Many will consult diviners and other religious leaders for this reason, particularly on the issues that significantly affect their daily lives, such as illness, poor harvest, barrenness, etc. This mind-set influenced many African Christian grassroots theologies of spirituality.

The third feature is usage of sacred objects. Adherents to the indigenous religions use sacred objects as symbols of humans' localization of the presence of spiritual beings. The uninformed observer may take these sacred objects at face value and mistake them for the spiritual beings themselves. Even when people offer prayers, perform rituals, and offer sacrifices in the presence of the objects, they are not to be understood as worshiping the objects. The sacred objects function as windows upon the mystery of divine presence and also demonstrate the worshipers' inadequate, but useful, attempts to appropriate divine presence. Sacred objects can be found in family shrines and community shrines. They vary in form and represent different divinities, although in West Africa ancestral objects are predominant.

The fourth and final feature is dynamism. African religious traditions are not static but actively developing. This state of affairs affects spirituality as well. Although African indigenous religions do not promote conversion of people from other religions, they are open to other religious ideas. Historically, Christianity and Islam have influenced the changes that are occurring in the indigenous religions. Therefore, it is hard and perhaps impossible to reconstruct some pre-Christian and pre-Islamic religious traditions of Africa. A study of African indigenous spirituality should also examine what has been borrowed from foreign religions and also the exchange of ideas between African indigenous religions and other religions such as Christianity. For example, a careful study of the practice of exorcism and spiritual warfare in the majority of African Christian churches reveals a close affinity with the traditional perception of the necessity of warding off and controlling the activities of evil spirits in human affairs.

See also Primal Religions, Spirituality of.

For Further Reading: A. Ephirim-Dinkor, *African Spirituality* (1997); P. Kalilombe, "Spirituality in the African Perspective," in *Paths of African Theology*, ed. R. Gibellini (1994), 115–35; J. Olupona, ed., *African Spirituality* (2000); P. Paris, *The Spirituality of African Peoples* (1995); A. Shorter, *African Christian Spirituality* (1978).

Victor I. Ezigbo

Afterlife

The biblical understanding of the afterlife is one that emerges over time and includes everything from texts that seem to operate without a well-defined understanding of a possible afterlife to those that contain hints that such a possibility exists, to those in which a well-defined idea of the afterlife is clearly envisioned. Significantly, each such view of the afterlife appears to have clear implications for Christian spirituality. Underdeveloped views of the afterlife, as reflected in Ecclesiastes, contribute to an understanding of life as self-contained within one's own experiences here and now, which leads to a valuation of earthly existence as meaningless, one best comprised of eating, drinking, and merriment. Conversely, even a rudimentary conception of an afterlife, like that reflected in Job's introspection (19:25–27), results in resilient faithfulness in the face of despair and suffering.

A Christian worldview that includes a robust belief in the afterlife redefines life in a way that is not confined to the immediate experiences of this life. Rather, it broadens the horizon against which the believer conceives of existence enabling him or her to live in a way that is not dependent upon nor controlled by instance gratification, but one that is enlivened and authenticated by the ultimate reality that lies beyond the immediate horizon of this life. As such, a belief in the afterlife reinforces the believer's accountability for this life in several respects. First, such an orientation results in attention to preparation for the end of this life and the continuation of existence beyond death. This preparation is active in nature and includes, among other things, being full of the oil of God's Spirit in anticipation of the return of the Son of God (Matt. 25:1–13). Second, a worldview that includes an understanding of the afterlife results in a life in which a person uses his or her divinely given talents and gifts to the fullest in order to be pleasing to the God who is the judge of all things (Matt. 25:14–30). Third, a belief in the afterlife encourages the believer's relationships with the vulnerable and marginalized to reflect values and investments not controlled by the mores of society but informed and shaped by the knowledge that how one lives this life becomes the basis for how one experiences life after death (Matt. 25:31–46). Finally, a belief in the afterlife orients one's pursuit of God in this life in such a way that the ultimate goal of seeing the face of God and experiencing him in a direct and unmediated fashion is facilitated (Rev. 21–22).

See also Heaven; Hell; Resurrection.

For Further Reading: M. Kelsey, *Afterlife* (1982); W. Martindale, *Beyond the Shadowlands* (2005); A. R. van de Walle, *From Darkness to the Dawn* (1985).

John Christopher Thomas

Aging

Human aging involves physical, cognitive, and psychological changes on the path of life. The Bible affords special status to those who are aging, from the command to "honor your father and your mother" (Ex. 20:12) to NT instructions to appoint mature church leaders and care for the elderly.

Human aging engages us in the perennial question of genetic versus environmental influence, and our personal role in adjusting to these forces. For most people, the word *aging* invokes a sense of loss and decline rather than gain and growth. The reality of diminished capacities and opportunities as one grows older is usually met with apprehension. To disregard these impending changes may lead to missed or diminished opportunities for psychological growth and spiritual development. Aging does pose a developmental task; to age healthily, one must find a way to compensate for inevitable losses and to actually discover the gains that aging may offer.

The apostle Paul, quite familiar with weakness and losses, wrote, "Though outwardly we are wasting away, yet inwardly we are being renewed day by day. For our light and momentary troubles are achieving for us an eternal glory that far outweighs them all" (2 Cor. 4:16 – 17). This speaks of a potential to grow, though it may call for a shift in focus on one's existence and life course.

Gene Cohen, a prominent gerontologist, introduced the concept of *developmental intelligence* "expressed in deepening wisdom, judgment, perspective, and vision," an optimal integration of our capacities and experiences. Cohen found that the advantage of older brains is their more complex neural architecture, an increased ability to have more balanced emotional responses, the plasticity of the brain, and the increased capacity to process information by using both sides of the brain. These abilities, paired with a positive outlook on aging, may lead to new creativity and engagement with life. God's design is marvelous. Even our brains can be renewed if we continue to challenge them.

However, for most humans, the creaturely fears of decline and death are not easily overcome by reassurances of the possibility of intellectual regeneration. To deal with those fears, the spirit must also be addressed. As Paul Tournier suggested, we should enjoy the creative adventure of living while attaching ourselves to transcendent values and to accepting the human condition in faith and trust. The Scriptures invite us to strive for holy living, embrace soul crafting, and acquire the virtues that lead to peace and gratitude (Col. 3).

Since aging may potentially widen rather than narrow our experience, the task of living is to glorify God with a positive embrace of aging and a growing attachment to him, so that, as the apostle Paul suggests, "his life may be revealed in our mortal body" (2 Cor. 4:11).

See also Body; Death and Dying; Human Development.

For Further Reading: G. Cohen, *The Mature Mind* (2005); J. G. Harris, *Biblical Perspectives on Aging* (2008); P. Tournier, *The Adventure of Living*, trans. E. Hudson (1965); idem, *Learn to Grow Old*, trans. E. Hudson (1972).

Linde J. Getahun

Alfred the Great (849 – 899)

Warrior-king of the West-Saxons. Alfred was born in Wantage, Berkshire, England, and became king in 871, ascending the throne amid conflict with the Danes, who were threatening to overtake Wessex. After several years of war, Alfred successfully defeated them at the battle of Ethandún; their leader, Guthrum, acquiesced to terms of peace and submitted to baptism. While marching to war, Alfred gathered many new forces under his command, so that subsequently Wessex became a rallying point for the Saxons. By freeing the country of the invaders, Alfred unified England and established the foundation for the eventual sovereignty of his successors.

Alfred's achievements were not limited to uniting England and driving out invading kingdoms. He codified and promulgated the old English laws of which he approved, and he spent much of his later life restoring what had been devastated during the war with the Danes. Moreover, he not only encouraged learning but also became educated himself. He translated several early medieval texts into Anglo-Saxon, including Boëthius's *Consolation of Philosophy* and Gregory the Great's *Pastoral Rule* and *Dialogues*. Alfred's great contribution to spirituality was his defense of the Christian heritage in England in the face of pagan advances, as well as his preservation of Christianity's written resources. His legacy is that of a man who established a unified England in which both learning and genuine commitment to the Christian faith could flourish.

For Further Reading: T. Taaffe, "Alfred the Great," in *CE*.

Joshua Dean

Alienation

Alienation is one way of describing fallen human experience. As such, alienation can be discussed in terms of the divine-human relationship, interpersonal and human-environment relationships, and intrapersonal relationships. Rich metaphorical language is used in Scripture to describe the alienation experienced in these relational systems. In Genesis 3, for example, after having sinned, man and woman cover themselves (v. 7) and hide from the presence of God (v. 8), and are then banished by God from their original and hospitable home in the garden of Eden (v. 23). Experiences of intimacy, harmony, peace, unity, and fulfillment were replaced with distance, displacement, shame, fear, pain, and toil. The resultant and paradigmatic human relational condition of alienation is similarly depicted in Ephesians 2 as "hostility" (v. 16) and being "excluded ... without God ... far away" (vv. 12–13).

One way of elaborating on alienation draws on recent advances in psychology-theology dialogue that seeks to integrate attachment theory, family systems theories, and relational models of the self. From such perspectives, alienation refers to the experience of insecurity, emotional distance, a lack of interpersonal contact and reciprocity, and

both inter- and intrapersonal conflict. Maintained by internal and social processes, often linked to self-protection, awareness of alienation is usually extremely difficult. Equally difficult is the challenge of increasing a person's awareness of the possibility of actualizing a richer, more fulfilling alternative experience. Miroslav Volf has described multiple normative alienating strategies that persons experience at the hands of others and/or personally employ to manage interpersonal injuries and to construct a coherent identity in the face of injustice and amid many competing voices. Likewise, attachment and systems theorists describe normative avoidance and distancing relational patterns that persons engage in to manage anxiety, distress, shame, despair, and hurt. Intrapersonally, internalized relational experiences, and particularly those that are traumatic and painful, are often isolated from each other and not brought into contact, thereby preventing change that could lead to improved functioning and fuller experience.

Volf, along with Stanley Hauerwas and John Howard Yoder, symbolically make use of the cross as a solution to alienation. The experience of God's just love embodied in the cross can reconcile estranged parties by putting to death the enmity and division that previously existed between them (Eph. 2:16). The biblical language used to describe the transforming experience of God's love further illuminates the process of change and its outcomes. Transformed relationships are described as being "brought near" (v. 13), destroying the previous barrier and "dividing wall of hostility" (v. 14), and making the persons "fellow citizens" (v. 19). In addition, the imagery of *dwelling* is used — dwelling in peace with God and each other (vv. 19–22), and by extension with oneself and all of creation (Col. 1:20). In fact, peace is the defining outcome of such transformed relationships. The experience of God's embracing love for his enemies (Rom. 5:10) then becomes a model for living the Christian life that can transform each relational system.

Transformation is not a one-time experience, nor does it occur in isolation from the other relational systems. Ongoing awareness of oneself-in-relation, monitoring and regulating security-insecurity and closeness-distance in each relational system is required, as are continued experiences of reassurance, being cared for, belonging, and safety with God and others. Inherent and learned self-alienation and persistent contextual forces that move the developing self toward separation, enmity, isolation, and division will remain. Thus, Christian formation is perhaps best understood as a developmental and therefore dialectical process that involves repeatedly resting in the embracing love of God and others and extending that to others, while also engaging in self, other, and God exploration; that is, countering alienating forces by coming close and venturing out without being swept too far away.

For Further Reading: J. Berkman and M. Cartwright, eds., *The Hauerwas Reader* (2002); L. Shults and S. Sandage, *Transforming Spirituality* (2006); M. Volf, *Exclusion and Embrace* (1996); J. H. Yoder, *He Came Preaching Peace* (1985).

Peter J. Jankowski

Allegorical Exegesis

Allegorical exegesis involves the search for hidden meanings in Scripture. It is often contrasted with a more literal or historical-grammatical approach. There are both potential benefits and clear dangers associated with allegorical exegesis—depending entirely on where and how it is practiced. The primary attraction and driving force behind allegorical exegesis is the intuitive sense that there is often a deeper, richer, fuller meaning in Scripture than one finds in the surface story line. Disciplines such as meditating on Scripture and theological reflection, as well as an awareness of the obvious interconnections within Scripture, all fuel this search for deeper insights. Biblical statements such as "It is the glory of God to conceal a matter; to search out

a matter is the glory of kings" (Prov. 25:2) suggest that complexity may be built into Scripture so that people will seek out hidden truths as they would buried treasure (Prov. 2:4).

At the same time, allegorical exegesis can become speculative. Obvious examples of speculative excess are occasionally found in church history. Allegorical exegesis emerged early in the history of biblical interpretation with such Alexandrian commentators as Philo and Origen. Augustine cemented the value of this approach as one of several approved avenues of biblical interpretation for the next thousand years. The Protestant Reformation was, in part, associated with correcting the abuses of allegorical interpretation and the return to a more textually tethered approach to interpretation.

One of the key insights of modern hermeneutics has been the importance of authorial intent. If an author, such as John Bunyan in his *Pilgrim's Progress*, wrote an allegory in which he intended each person and event to have an obvious symbolic meaning, then the only appropriate approach to understanding this work is to interpret it allegorically. On the other hand, if someone communicates something he or she intends to be taken literally, then any effort at explaining away this message in a more figurative or allegorical manner is faulty and inappropriate.

The key to interpreting Scripture, and the related question of the legitimacy of allegorical exegesis, is careful discernment of how both the human author and the ultimate Divine Author intended a given passage of Scripture to be taken. Thus, the appropriateness of allegorical exegesis of a given text stands or falls with whether the original authors of Scripture (both human and divine) intended a deeper or hidden meaning. Unfortunately, there are few simple answers here, and Christians have often been divided in how they interpret various passages. Ultimately this topic should stimulate even more careful study of Scripture so that readers can discern the properly intended meaning of each passage and ascribe to it a more figurative or allegorical interpretation only when that is appropriate. The historical pervasiveness of allegorical interpretation highlights at the very least a persistent felt need for soul-nourishing engagement with Scripture as a medium of transforming truth and the living voice of God.

See also Bede; Symbol.

For Further Reading: G. Bray, "Allegory," in *Dictionary for Theological Interpretation of the Bible*, ed. K. Vanhoozer (2005); E. Johnson, "Author's Intention and Biblical Interpretation," *Hermeneutics, Inerrancy and the Bible*, ed. Earl D. Radmacher et al. (1984), 407–30; M. Silva, *Has the Church Misread the Bible?* (1987), republished in *Foundations of Contemporary Interpretation* (1996).

Brian C. Labosier

Allen, Richard (1760–1831)

Founder and first bishop of the African Methodist Episcopal (AME) Church. Allen was born into slavery in Philadelphia and raised near Dover, Delaware. He was spiritually awakened around the age of twenty. As a result, he began to exhort his friends and to experience doubts and temptations; and finally he had an emotional crisis—all these things reflecting the prevailing pattern of evangelical conversion. Having been influenced by Methodist preaching, he joined a Methodist society. He manifested a vibrant religious life, spending many hours in prayer and meditation, and often launching into prayer or preaching immediately upon waking from sleep.

Allen was allowed to buy his freedom after his owner was convicted by a Freeborn Garrettson sermon. From 1783 he spent several years in itinerant preaching that led to many people being awakened. In 1786 he returned to Philadelphia where he began preaching four or five times daily and started prayer meetings and religious society meetings. He and other Africans attended St. George's Methodist Episcopal Church where they endured intensifying harassment from white church leaders. Many of these African-Americans eventually left St. George's and established the Free African Society and their own church (Bethel), which was dedicated by Francis Asbury in 1794. In 1816 Allen called together other African churches in the mid-Atlantic region for a conference at Philadelphia in which the African Methodist Episcopal Church was founded and he was elected bishop, having previously (1799) been ordained a deacon by Asbury. *The Life and Gospel Labors of the Rt. Rev. Richard Allen* (1833), Allen's short autobiography with appended treatises, was published after his death. It provides insight into his Methodist spirituality, revealing his preference for plain doctrine, good discipline, and extempore preaching, and his strong emphasis on charitable works in imitation of Christ. An important aspect of Allen's legacy is the independent ecclesiastical space he created in which African-Americans could have their dignity validated, use their spiritual gifts, and develop their leadership potential.

See also African-American Christian Spirituality.

Geordan Hammond

Alline, Henry (1748–1784)

Mystic revivalist of the Great Awakening in Nova Scotia. Born in Rhode Island, Alline moved northward with his farming parents to Nova Scotia in 1760. Fifteen years later, on the eve of the American Revolution, he experienced a profoundly emotional conversion that altered the course of his remaining years. Though relatively uneducated, and initially suspect for that reason, he soon began preaching the new birth throughout Nova Scotia and New Brunswick with powerful effect. His own conversion had a strikingly ecstatic and mystical aspect; in the effusive language of his *Journal* (1806), "Attracted by the love and beauty I saw in his divine perfections; my whole soul was inexpressibly ravished with the blessed Redeemer.... My whole soul seemed filled with the divine being."

The goal of his highly emotional revival preaching was to see his own ecstatic experience replicated in his adherents. His conversion narrative was remarkable enough later to be studied in William James's *Varieties of Religious Experience* (1916). He was the beneficiary of various spiritual influences through his eclectic reading—including William Law, mystic Jacob Boehme, and the charismatic Methodist Joseph Fletcher.

The itinerating Alline cultivated among the rural population of Nova Scotia and New Brunswick a decidedly otherworldly outlook and sense of special destiny as a peculiar people highly favored of God. These convictions in turn inclined the Yankees there to stay aloof from the political revolution under way in the colonies to the south. Indirectly, then, this otherworldly evangelist contributed to the preservation of a British North America and to the founding of Canada, into which it eventually evolved.

Alline was a strident opponent of most things Calvinistic, favoring rather the heart, the emotions, extemporaneity, and direct appeals to the will, all in the manner typical of the New Light preachers of that era. He left an exceptional legacy through his many original hymns and spiritual songs, his *Journal*, and an idiosyncratic theological treatise with the self-deprecating title *Two Mites* (1781). Though already in failing health by his midthirties, he attempted a final preaching tour of his native New England in 1783 and died soon afterward of tuberculosis.

See also Revival.

For Further Reading: J. Beverley and B. Moody, eds., *The Life and Journal of the Rev. Mr. Henry Alline* (1982); J. Bumstead, *Henry Alline* (1971); *Henry Alline: Selected Writings*, SAS (1987); G. Rawlyk, *Ravished by the Spirit* (1984); idem, ed., *New Light Letters and Songs* (1983).

Glen G. Scorgie

Ambrose of Milan (c. 340–397)

Early Christian bishop, preacher, and theologian. Born in Trier, the son of the Praetorian Prefect of Gaul, Ambrose became a lawyer and political official in northern Italy. Under pressure he was consecrated bishop of Milan in 374 at the death of the Arian bishop Auxentius. Then an unbaptized Catholic believer, Ambrose was baptized, ordained, and appointed bishop in one week. A gifted communicator, he staunchly defended orthodox theology against paganism and Arianism. He also confronted immorality and crime, even excommunicating Emperor Theodosius for a massacre at Thessalonica, declaring: "The emperor is within the church, not above the church."

Ambrose authored numerous exegetical and theological works, notably *On the Duties of the Clergy* (ethics adapted from Latin moralist Cicero's *On Duties*), and *On the Sacraments* (his Greek also advancing Eastern influence in the West). His teachings on asceticism, with those of Augustine (himself converted and baptized under Ambrose), did much to establish the monastic clerical model. Ambrose incorporated hymns into liturgical worship (authoring "O Splendor of God's Glory Bright" and others) and introduced antiphonal chanting from the East. Such breadth of interests has led some falsely to ascribe the "Te Deum" and Athanasian Creed to him. After Ambrose's death in 397, his venerated remains were placed with those of martyrs Gervase and Protase, and may still be viewed (with his mosaic portrait) at the Basilica of St. Ambrose in Milan.

For Further Reading: F. Homes Dudden, *The Life and Times of St. Ambrose* (1935); A. Paredi, *St. Ambrose* (1964); B. Ramsey, *Ambrose* (1997).

David Morris

Anabaptist Spirituality

Sixteenth-century Anabaptists were the largest group of Radical Reformers. Direct descendants include Mennonites, Amish, and Hutterites. In later centuries, others, including the Church of the Brethren, Brethren in Christ, and the Bruderhof, also called themselves Anabaptist.

"Anabaptist" means "rebaptizer," originally a disparaging term for radicals who insisted on baptizing adult believers, even those who were previously baptized as children. Anabaptists were restitutionist, trying to become as pure as they understood the early, apostolic, pre-third-century church to be. Anabaptists were suspicious of clericalism—insisting that the Holy Spirit empowered all believers, not just priests—and of rites and rituals that might be regarded mechanistically. They rejected ostentation and many aspects of Roman Catholic worship: masses, candles, fasting, requiem masses, images, and pilgrimages.

Anabaptists had the distinction of being the only group persecuted by both Roman Catholics and Protestants, a legacy of suffering remembered in the monumental seventeenth-century martyrology, *The Martyrs Mirror*. Persecution is one reason why Anabaptists migrated often. Originally a largely urban movement, because of persecution, central European Anabaptists soon became rural, the "quiet in the land."

The Radical Reformation did not spring forth fully formed; neither did it simply return to the earliest centuries. This renewal movement grew from and built upon prior dissent. It had affinities for and likely was influenced by previous medieval movements, including monasticism, mysticism, asceticism, charismatic apocalypticism, and "pure church" movements such as the Waldensians and Lollards.

Early Swiss leaders included Conrad Grebel, Felix Mantz, and Michael Sattler; most died as martyrs. South German luminaries included Hans Denck, Hans Hut, Pilgram Marpek, and Jacob Hutter. North German/Dutch leaders included Melchior Hoffman, Dirk Philips, David Joris, and Menno Simons.

We know little about how Anabaptists worshiped or prayed. Their gatherings, because of persecution, were often secret (in barns, woods, boats, caves); few records were kept. Austere settings reinforced simple worship. Leadership was widely shared because of informal worship contexts and theological convictions that the Spirit could inspire anyone. Moreover, leaders were often imprisoned or executed, necessitating regular emergence of new leaders.

They did not often produce detailed systematic theological works. They were usually Trinitarian and subscribed to the Apostles' Creed, but faithful obedience was often prioritized over careful doctrinal formulation, deeds as the necessary validation of creeds. Often their theology is known through hymns, for example, the *Ausbund*, a sixteenth-century hymnal still prized and employed by the Amish.

Anabaptists did not divide life into religious and secular. Faithful living and discipleship were intrinsically connected to prayer; they led to and reinforced each other. Hans Denck is still often quoted: "No one can truly know Christ unless one follows him in life; and no one may follow Christ unless one has first known him."

Seven key themes in historic Anabaptist spirituality may be noted. First, baptism of regenerated believers is a sign of both new life and membership in the visible body of Christ, the church. With believers, "where two or three are gathered," one experiences the actual presence of Jesus Christ. Some spoke of three baptisms—Spirit, water, blood: first regeneration, then baptism by water, possibly followed by martyrdom.

The second is the giving and receiving of counsel from church members and celebrating the Lord's Supper only in the context of a reconciled community. Their strict view of the rule of Christ (Matt. 18) often led to stern, even harsh, church discipline (banning, shunning). While such practices now seem problematic, they contrasted with how other sixteenth-century Christians practiced discipline (imprisonment, torture, execution, war).

Third, there is lively reliance on the ongoing, regenerating power, presence, and activity of God through the Spirit and consequently fervent witnessing, inviting others to faithfulness.

Fourth, each believer is responsible to be familiar with—and obedient to—the Bible. They memorized extensive Bible passages. Believers were expected to exercise personal spiritual devotion. Imprisoned Anabaptists and those facing execution often evidenced fervent prayer.

The fifth is following Jesus as model and teacher in one's behavior, especially as commended in the Sermon on the Mount (simplicity, nonconformity, nonviolence, truth-telling, refusal to take oaths). Other Reformers criticized the ascetic, penitential, and simple lifestyles, arguing that they inappropriately imposed monastic ideals on all and risked works righteousness.

The sixth theme is economic sharing, mutual aid, and service on behalf of those in need, offered in the community of believers but to the wider world as well.

In the seventh and final place is yieldedness (*gelassenheit*) to God and openness to and even expectation of suffering, especially as nonconformist dissent would lead to persecution and worse. Even violence was to be met with nonresistance.

What comprises Anabaptist spirituality today? It is less common for Mennonite individuals, families, or congregations to have common traditional spiritual disciplines (morning/evening devotions, family worship, Bible study). Mainstream North American Mennonites are affected—and to some degree sundered—by many influences: conservative/evangelical, charismatic, relational/therapeutic, feminist/liberationist, and contemplative/liturgical. Anabaptism is growing most quickly in the global south, where its character is evangelical and charismatic.

In recent decades, Anabaptism has influenced many (e.g., Will Campbell, Stanley Hauerwas, Richard Hays, Clarence Jordan and the Koinonia community, James McClendon, New Monasticism, *Sojourners*, Glen Stassen, Will Willimon). Such authors admire the Anabaptist willingness to follow the costly way of Jesus, imitating his revelation of God as self-giving, powerless, cross-bearing, and servant. They contend that Anabaptism is particularly relevant for post-Christian contexts and our violent world, given its separation of church and state, wisdom for sustaining faith as "resident aliens" in hostile or apathetic cultures, voluntary relinquishment of power, priority of peacemaking and social justice, and commitment to service.

See also Bruderhof; Peacemaking.

For Further Reading: C. Dyck, *Spiritual Life in Anabaptism* (1995); *Early Anabaptist Spirituality: Selected Writings*, CWS (1994); T. Finger, *A Contemporary Anabaptist Theology* (2004); R. Friedmann, *Mennonite Piety through the Centuries* (1949); W. Klaassen, *Anabaptism: Neither Catholic Nor Protestant* (2001); J. Rempel, *The Lord's Supper in Anabaptism* (1994); A. Snyder, *Following in the Footsteps of Christ* (2004).

Arthur Paul Boers

Analogy, Analogical

Analogy is a comparison based on a resemblance between things that are otherwise unlike. It implies that both things are grounded in, and belong to, a greater and common whole. As a vision, analogy projects a language of harmony and wholeness based on similarities-in-difference. Unlike metaphors and similes, which are figures of speech, analogy is a more comprehensive, reasoned, and systematic comparison between beings, objects, or events.

The analogical use of language in relation to God posits that the God who is infinite is, nevertheless, not altogether unknowable, even if finite humans cannot define or know him fully. By means of analogy, one can conceive of God and describe him truly (that is, realistically, and not merely as an imaginative projection), though never comprehensively. In this way, analogy is able to hold together apophatic and kataphatic insights into speech about God. Analogy draws from a creational grounding when it assumes God's immanence (Ps. 19; Rom. 1:19). But God's transcendence is also maintained, since such language is believed to be creaturely and never sufficient to capture the fullness of God's reality (Isa. 55:9).

With respect to traditions of theology and spirituality, the analogy of being—the assumption of likeness between finite and infinite being—has been associated particularly with Thomism, especially its proofs of God's existence. Protestants, however, are generally warier of this approach, which grounds its theological arguments on a perceived likeness between the creature/creation and the Creator. Instead, Protestants focus on the primacy of scriptural revelation and affirm the biblical interpretation methodology of the "analogy of faith" (cf. Rom. 12:6)—that is, comparing Scripture with Scripture.

Analogy, then, may be seen as the basis of religious speech or as a process of (logical) reasoning that helps define the limits of God-talk. But there is more. The different construals of analogy suggest different "speeches" about God, born of different religious imaginations and traditions. Indeed, one could argue that underlying the different construals of analogy and languages for God are particular religious imaginations and traditions to which one is socialized and enculturated. The use of analogical language for God is consistent with a religious outlook that emphasizes continuity, the sacramental and the visual, as in the Roman Catholic and Eastern Orthodox traditions. The alternative (dialectical) language more typical of Protestant traditions stresses discontinuity, disruption, and proclamation of the Christ-event.

What can we say to this apparent divide in religious orientations and, by extension, Christian spiritualities? The Scripture portrays Jesus Christ as both *Logos* and *Kerygma*. If this is so, then both the sacramental/ritual element (which attests to Christ's continuing presence in the world) and the proclamation dimension of Christian faith (which points to Christ's message in the Bible) need to be held together and affirmed in Christ's community. Word as disruption

and as continuing presence should complement each other, even if manifestation through symbols and rituals need to be qualified by the priority of scriptural revelation in the community.

See also Apophatic and Kataphatic Ways.

For Further Reading: H. U. von Balthasar, *The Theology of Karl Barth* (1972); F. W. Dillistone, *Christianity and Symbolism* (1955); L. Dupré, *The Other Dimension* (1979); T. D. Gener, "The Catholic Imagination and Popular Religion in Lowland Philippines," *Mission Studies* 22, no. 1 (2005): 25–57; A. F. Kimel Jr., ed., *Speaking the Christian God* (1992); E. L. Mascall, *Existence and Analogy* (1967); S. McFague, *Metaphorical Theology* (1982); D. Tracy, *The Analogical Imagination* (1991).

Timoteo D. Gener

Anchorites
See **Hermits and Anchorites.**

Ancient Christianity
See **Chapter 13.**

Andrewes, Lancelot (1555–1626)

Well-known preacher, gifted scholar, and influential leader in the Church of England during the reigns of Elizabeth I, James I, and (briefly) Charles I. He was educated at Cambridge University, where he later served as master of Pembroke College. Ordained in 1580, he caught the attention of Queen Elizabeth, who made him dean of Westminster Abbey in 1601. King James successively appointed him as bishop of Chichester (1605), Ely (1609), and Winchester (1619). Known to be fluent in fifteen languages, he was one of the scholars who prepared a new authorized translation of the Bible, published in 1611 and commonly referred to as the King James Version.

During his life, Andrewes's fame rested primarily on his preaching. He preached the funeral sermon for Queen Elizabeth at Westminster and many feast day sermons at the court of King James. His sermons were highly learned, complex, and witty—a style often called "metaphysical." The modern poet T. S. Eliot described Andrewes's preaching in these words: "Andrewes takes a word and derives the world from it; squeezing and squeezing the word until it yields a full juice of meaning which we would never have supposed any word to possess."

Andrewes made a deep and lasting impact on Christian spirituality in three important ways. First, he was a principal architect of the Anglican *via media* (the "middle way" between Roman Catholicism and Puritan Calvinism), building on the work of Richard Hooker and John Jewel, which looked to Holy Scripture, human reason, and church tradition for authority. Second, he was an admirable example of personal prayer, spending five hours per day in private meditation and prayer. His *Preces Privitae* (Private Devotions, written in Greek, Hebrew, and Latin), first translated and published shortly after his death, has been read and appreciated by many up to the present. Third, he was an influential translator of the English Bible, leading the team that prepared Genesis through 2 Kings in the King James Version. Because English-speaking Christianity since the Reformation has been so deeply shaped by this translation of the Bible, Andrewes's greatest long-term impact is undoubtedly in this area.

See also Caroline Divines.

For Further Reading: L. Andrewes, *Private Devotions*, trans. J. H. Newman (1840); A. Nicholson, *God's Secretaries* (2003); G. Rowell, ed., *The English Religious Tradition and the Genius of Anglicanism* (1992); R. Schmidt, *Glorious Companions* (2002).

David Montzingo

Angela of Foligno (c. 1248 – 1309)

Mystic and Franciscan tertiary. Born to a wealthy family in Umbria, Angela married and reared three sons. At thirty-seven she repented of her worldly lifestyle and underwent a dramatic conversion. When her mother, husband, and sons died suddenly around 1288, she donated her possessions to the poor, joined the Franciscan Third Order, and gave herself fully to seeking Christ. Disrobing completely before a cross, she offered her bodily members in purity to God (Rom. 6:13). Like Francis, Angela's devotion perennially focused on the cross of Christ and Holy Communion. She served the poor, tended lepers, and served as spiritual mother to many during her lifetime. She was beatified in 1671.

Angela's *Book* contains two parts: "Instructions" on the spiritual life and a "Memorial"—her spiritual autobiography transcribed and edited by her relative and confessor, "Brother A." Organized into thirty steps, Angela's "Memorial" recounts her conversion, enjoyment of divine presence, intimacy with Christ, apophatic darkness, and ineffable union with God. While containing more stages than others, Angela's spiritual itinerary parallels various medieval schemas and was circulated widely, especially in sixteenth-century Spain.

Angela's life and writing offer readers encouragement and insight regarding their progress toward spiritual maturity. Although her asceticism was extreme, Angela's experiences of divine sweetness, spontaneous shouts, and frequent ecstasies will resonate with Pentecostal and charismatic Christians. All will appreciate her obvious love for Christ, her deep humility, and her sacrificial service to those in need.

For Further Reading: *Angela of Foligno: Selected Writings,* CWS (1993); P. Lachance, *The Spiritual Journey of the Blessed Angela of Foligno* (1984); C. Mazzoni, ed., *Angela of Foligno's Memorial* (1999).

Glenn E. Myers

Angels

Angels are heavenly beings that serve God and humanity. The Greek term *angelos* literally means "messenger." Angels frequently assume human form to communicate God's messages to humanity (e.g., 2 Kings 1:3; Acts 10:3–4) and assist humanity in offering their prayers to God (e.g., Rev. 5:8; 8:3–4). Additionally angels rejoice when people repent of their sins and turn to God (Luke 15:10). Jesus was strengthened throughout his ministry through angels, especially during his temptation in the desert (Matt. 4:11) and in his prayers in the garden of Gethsemane (Luke 22:43). An angel also removed the stone from his burial tomb (Matt. 28:2). Angels unceasingly worship God (Rev. 5:11–13; 7:11–12). Gabriel (e.g., Luke 1:19, 26) and Michael (e.g., Jude 9) are the only named angels in canonical Scripture. However, there are various divisions of angels, including archangels, cherubim, and seraphim. Pseudo-Dionysius posited in his influential sixth-century *Celestial Hierarchy* that there are nine ranks of angels.

Angelic praise serves as a pattern for all humanity in worshiping God. Worship should not be directed toward angels since they are created beings and their ministry is always directed toward God and Jesus whom they joyfully serve (Luke 15:10). Angels play a more prominent role in the Orthodox Church, are honored each Monday in their liturgy, and frequently appear in their icons. Their praise has inspired the Trisagion hymn (i.e., "Holy God, holy mighty, holy immortal, have mercy on us") in the Divine Liturgy of John Chrysostom. Further, the Sanctus drawn from Isaiah 6:3 is common in Roman Catholic, Orthodox, and Protestant worship. Likewise, the Gloria of Luke 2:14 has inspired some of the greatest compositions of choral music.

Over the centuries, many prominent theologians from both the Western and Eastern churches have written about angels. Origen, while not the first, studied them more expansively and emphasized the role of guardian angels (cf. Matt. 18:10; Acts 12:15). Other writers who contributed to the church's understanding include Gregory of Nazianzus, John Chrysostom, Augustine, Gregory the Great, Pseudo-Dionysius, Hugh of St. Victor, and

Thomas Aquinas. The Puritans also examined the role and importance of angels. Illustrative of this is Isaac Ambrose's *Communion with Angels* (1662), in which he explores how the ministry of angels varies across the stages of a person's life and how a person might become more aware of their significant ministry. Other Protestants have addressed this subject, perhaps most notably Karl Barth.

A proper spirituality of angels reminds Christians of the spiritual realm that includes both those who are faithful to God as well as the powers of evil and darkness.

Angels are God's agents of protection and provision for humanity and reinforce the importance of a biblical sense of mystery as an integral component of faith. Angels teach contemporary Christians that while they gaze upon the face of God in pure contemplation, they are also always active in God's ministry to those on earth.

See also Warfare, Spiritual.

For Further Reading: *Angelic Spirituality*, CWS (2002); K. Barth, *Church Dogmatics* III/3 (1960), sec. 51; S. Chase, *Angelic Spirituality* (2002); J. Danielou, *The Angels and Their Mission* (1957); D. Garrett, *Angels and the New Spirituality* (1995); B. J. Oropeza, *99 Answers to Questions about Angels, Demons and Spiritual Warfare* (1997).

Tom Schwanda

Angelus Silesius (1624–1677)

Mystical Polish poet. Named Johann Scheffler at birth, Silesius was born to a landholding Lutheran dissident in Breslau, Silesia. After the death of both parents, Silesius enjoyed a privileged education. Beginning at the humanist Elisabeth gymnasium and continuing on to Strasbourg and Padua, Silesius earned his doctorate in medicine and philosophy in 1648. During his years as a student, he spent time in Holland where he first encountered the mystical writings of Jakob Boehme, which would influence him greatly.

Working as the private physician of Count Sylvius Nimrod of Wuerttenberg-Oels, Silesius experienced rocky relationships with the Lutherans at court. After meeting with censorship from the court chaplain when attempting to publish a collection of mystical writings, Silesius converted to Roman Catholicism. He adopted the name Johann Angelus and published his mystical writings under the name Angelus Silesius.

The Cherubinic Wanderer (1674), Silesius's remarkable collection of poems, favors almost exclusively the epigrammatic couplet. These epigrams, which are examples of structural excellence, yield brief explosions of insight and reflect Silesius's distilled spiritual observations. The collection of poems focuses on humanity's oneness with God, ponders scriptural paradoxes, and, in accord with the apophatic mystical approach, reflects on the impossibility of rationally comprehending God. His work has sometimes been mistakenly interpreted as pantheistic. Prior to his death in 1677, Silesius became increasingly provocative, writing acerbic anti-Protestant pamphlets and becoming a staunch supporter of the Counter-Reformation.

Sarah G. Scorgie

Anger

Anger is perhaps the most pervasive of the seven "deadly sins." Evagrius mentions it more than the other principle thoughts that haunt Christians. It not only can destroy self and others, Cassian argues; it can exclude God's Spirit from residing within.

Evagrius describes it as "a boiling and stirring up of wrath against one who has given injury or is *thought* to have done so." Aquinas adds that it combines the pain of injury and the pleasures of vengeance and inflicting injury. Early monastics were particularly concerned that it interferes with praying. Gregory distinguished different types of anger, the worst being that which arises quickly and dissipates slowly, while the "best" is that which arises slowly and dissipates quickly (cf. Prov. 14:29;

Eph. 4:26). The ancients argued that it most often arises from avarice when desire to possess or control is thwarted.

Scripture warns against anger (Job 36:18; Prov. 29:8; Matt. 5:22; Eph. 4:31; Col. 3:8; James 1:19–20). Some insist that there is justifiable or "righteous" anger (see Eph. 4:26; also examples in Ex. 32:19; 2 Sam. 12:5; Neh. 5:6; Matt. 18:34). But Cassian disagreed with Gregory the Great's allowances and forbade all anger (noting "without cause" was a later addition to Matt. 5:22) except that directed against one's own sin. Not only is anger dangerous and easily justified, but all of these mentioned warned of its effects on human judgment, discernment, and discretion. And once unleashed they were concerned that anger is difficult to restrain.

Early monastic writers insisted that the prescription for anger is not venting, a point that has been corroborated by contemporary psychology. Nor is ongoing suppression the answer, particularly when it results in a feigned patience — the "silent treatment" that appears virtuous but inwardly stores up anger.

Early Christian writers suggested strategies toward the cultivation of patience. The first line of defense against anger is a temporary silence and containment that allows one to recall the mercy of others in light of one's own past transgressions, widens the heart to offset the pressure that increases with anger's constriction (cf. the Gr. *arkhein*), and allows a reappraisal (or reframing) of the situation that aroused the anger to consider whether the harm suffered was *really* done out of any forethought or ill will. Second, one should not blame others for one's own inability to exercise the virtue of patience. Third, people should seek the wisdom and exposure community provides. Fourth, they should practice opposite behaviors, such as blessing persecutors and singing psalms. Fifth, they must rebuff the need to be in control or possess. Sixth, they must have self-knowledge and recognize patterns and triggers so as not to be ambushed. Finally, they should confront the injuring party (Matt. 5:23–26).

See also Emotions; Sins, Seven Deadly.

For Further Reading: J. Cassian, *The Institutes*, trans. B. Ramsey (2000); *Evagrius of Pontus*, trans. R. Sinkewicz (2003); D. Okholm, "To Vent or Not to Vent?" in *Care for the Soul*, ed. M. McMinn and T. Phillips (2001), 164–86; Thomas Aquinas, *Summa Theologiae*, 2.2 Q 158.

Dennis Okholm

Anglican Spirituality

The Anglican Communion is an association of national Anglican churches organized as dioceses in 160 countries with a membership of approximately 80 million people. Following the Reformation of the church in England in the 16th century, Catholic and Reformed emphases have been part of Anglicanism. These were initially contained within a common liturgical practice grounded in English culture. However, in recent times, doctrinal, liturgical, and cultural diversity has become more pronounced, and so differing spiritualities live side by side within Anglicanism. Today the Anglican Communion embraces evangelicals and Anglo-Catholics (with liberal and conservative strands in both cases), theological radicals, and demonstrative charismatics, all modified by the ethnic and cultural variety of the Anglican Communion.

Each of these streams within Anglicanism has its own spiritual giants, people who exemplify the distinctive spirituality of their particular heritage. For evangelical Anglicans, the great sixteenth-century Reformers who sought to purify the doctrine of the church by appeal to Scripture have a special place. These include William Tyndale (1494–1536); Archbishop Thomas Cranmer (1489–1556), and Bishop Nicholas Ridley (1500–1555), all of whom were martyred for their Reformed faith. From a later time, Charles Simeon (1759–1836) and John Stott (1921–) are extolled as exemplars of evangelical spirituality. Evangelical spirituality is today very much a Word-centered spirituality in which personal prayer, obedience to biblical teaching, and evangelism are stressed. For Anglo-Catholics, John Henry Newman (1801–1890), John Keble (1792–1866), and Edward Pusey (1800–1882), the founders of what is called the "Catholic Revival," are exemplars of Anglo-Catholic spirituality with its stress on the holiness of the priest, the centrality of the Eucharist, and the apostolic continuity of the church. For later liberal Catholics who wanted to be open to critical biblical scholarship and to see Anglicans involved in the pain and suffering of the world, Bishop Charles Gore (1853–1932) and Archbishop William Temple (1881–1944) are models of this tradition of spirituality. The still later charismatic Anglicans of the post-1970 period often see Michael Harper (1931–) and Terry Fulham (1930–) as exemplars. In charismatic Anglican spirituality, the stress is on the immediate awareness and empowering of the Holy Spirit. Charismatic spirituality has influenced Anglicans very widely by introducing new expressive music and a sense of joy in worship. Finally, Richard Hooker (1554–1600) must be mentioned. He is widely taken to exemplify the spirituality of mainstream Anglicanism where the study of Scripture so central to evangelical spirituality and the sacramental life of the church so central to Catholic spirituality are brought together.

Faced with the reality of these four very different expressions of Anglican spirituality, each with variants within, pinpointing what is generic is challenging. As a way forward, I outline what I believe most Anglicans would recognize and accept as characteristic of Anglican spirituality. In taking this path, I am implying that each position mentioned above takes us to the perimeter at different points, yet there remains a large common center where most Anglicans can be found.

First, Anglican spirituality embraces a wider vision of the church than the local congregation. Anglicans believe that while each parish is truly church, it is only a local expression of the whole church. This larger vision of the church for Anglicans is first of all realized in the diocese and national church, and then most fully in the worldwide Anglican Communion, without forgetting for a moment that the whole church, the church universal, is more than any one denomination. From this it follows that Anglican spirituality has a "high" view of the church.

Second, this wider vision of the church is reflected in the Anglican view of ordained ministry. The bishop unites and oversees the parishes in his or her diocese (in 2009 there were twenty-four female bishops), yet each ordained minister is recognized in every Anglican diocese worldwide. Still, permission from the diocesan bishop to officiate is always demanded for ministry outside of one's parish. Anglicans thus also have a "high" view of ordination. Consequently, almost universally Anglican spirituality values clerical ministry while at the same time emphasizing the ministry of every believer.

Third, Anglicans give equal place to Word and sacraments. One should not eclipse the other. Anglican liturgies have not less than two Bible readings, often having three or four. Holy Communion is celebrated solemnly and reverently, usually each Sunday. Prayerfulness is encouraged both at a corporate and at an individual level. Because Anglicans greatly value set liturgies, Anglican spirituality characteristically has a liturgical element.

Fourth, alongside the emphasis on corporate and personal devotion, Anglicans believe they are to be involved in the world with all its injustice, poverty, and pain. Anglican spirituality shows itself in practical service for those in need and in social action.

Fifth, in matters of doctrine, Anglicans agree that Scripture is to be given first importance and authority. Nevertheless, the contribution of both tradition and reason are acknowledged. Thus, Anglicans believe that the meaning of Scripture in new and different circumstances calls for prayer and careful and reasoned reflection in the light of the tradition of the church. From this mainstream view of the theological enterprise, it follows that Anglican spirituality tends to be particularly appreciative of prayerful and thoughtful responses to difficult issues facing the church.

Sixth, Alan Bartlett's description of Anglican spirituality as "a passionate balance" between extremes captures well the essence of Anglicanism. Anglican spirituality gives equal weight to both the corporate and individual aspects of the Christian life; to clerical and lay leadership; to Word and sacrament; to Scripture, tradition, and reason; and to worship in the Spirit in the church and Christlike service in the world.

See also Cambridge Platonists; Caroline Divines; Oxford Movement.

For Further Reading: A. Bartlett, *A Passionate Balance* (2007); B. Kaye, *An Introduction to World Anglicanism* (2008); S. Platten, ed., *Anglicanism and the Western Christian Tradition* (2003).

Kevin Giles

Animals

Our relationship to animals and their role in Christian spirituality must be understood in the context of God's purposes for creation. Animals were created first for his good pleasure and to reveal his glory (Gen. 1:24–25; Rev. 4:11), demonstrating their intrinsic, not merely instrumental value. Our subsequent dominion (Gen. 1:26–28) consists of delegated rule and stewardship, not ownership. God's concern for his creation did not end with the fall (Gen. 9:8–17; Ex. 23:10–11; Ps. 24:1–2), nor did humankind's accountability as stewards (e.g., 2 Chron. 36:21). Caring for animals reveals the image of God in us and cultivates virtues such as compassion, humility, gentleness, and responsibility.

This was understood by even the earliest Christians, who viewed the animal world as a source of natural revelation about God, revealing his glory and providing a living witness of his attributes. Animals were not just sources of food and income; they were symbols, metaphors, and object lessons—even sources of mystery and awe. The power of lions, wolves, and lambs as symbols has been seen for millennia in the words of the OT prophets (Isa. 11:6; 53:7) and Jesus (John 10), medieval and renaissance art, and works such as C. S. Lewis's Chronicles of Narnia. From the 2nd century through medieval times, bestiaries—books describing the moral and spiritual significance of various animals—were among the most popular types of literature. This reflected the view that nature was God's book for revealing moral and spiritual truth to humankind.

More recently, views of our proper relationship to animals have diverged along several different lines. Some view animals as oppressed and objectified, deserving of liberation and empowerment much like the poor in liberation theology. Others fear that any concern for animal welfare can only come at the expense of human welfare and will blur our distinctiveness as image-bearers of God. Grounding our views in a biblical theology of creation will help to avoid these extremes. Dominion and stewardship represent two complementary aspects of our responsibility toward creation and should not be placed in opposition to one another. Stewardship entails ensuring that God's purposes for creation continue to be realized until redemption is complete (Rom. 8:18–21). Our lives will be enriched if we renew our appreciation for God's animal creation and the role animals can play in Christian spirituality. It represents a return to a theme that has been prevalent throughout Christian history.

See also Creation-Centered Spirituality; Francis of Assisi; Franciscan Spirituality.

For Further Reading: R. Berry, ed., *The Care of Creation* (2000); R. Grant, *Early Christians and Animals* (1999); A. Linzey, *Animal Theology* (1995); R. Wennberg, *God, Humans, and Animals* (2003).

Bruce Rideout

Anselm of Canterbury (c. 1033–1109)

Medieval monk, theologian, and bishop. Anselm was born into Burgundian nobility to a pious mother and a father who rebuffed religious interests. After a period of undisciplined living, in 1059 he entered the monastic school at Bec under countryman Lanfranc. Benedictine vows (1060) and appointment as a prior (1063) soon followed. His initial writings were letters and especially prayers; however, his elevation to abbot of Bec (1078), and thus also to prior of its school, encouraged him to pursue philosophical studies, and eventually to produce related writings that have become classics.

Anselm's *credo ut intelligam*, "I believe that I may understand," inspired the closely argued *Monologion* and *Proslogion* (1078–1079), explorations of how God's being is evidenced in truth, goodness, and vision. The *Proslogion*'s systematic ontological argument for God's existence is still debated. Respecting Scripture and traditional authorities, his use of intellectual reasoning to defend and detail the Christian faith anticipated later Scholastic thinkers.

Having visited England and his mentor Lanfranc (Archbishop of Canterbury since 1070), Anselm reluctantly was consecrated (1093) to that office. In a spirit of dependence on divine grace, he wrote *De Incarnatione Verbi* (1095), which anticipated his classic *Cur Deus Homo* (1098). Exploring "why God became human," he combined a feudal sense of how our dishonoring of God necessitated Christ's substitutionary sacrifice with a theological sense of how God's honor also occasioned a generous forgiveness more than sufficient for humanity's flawed nature and unfulfilled duties. This objective view of the atonement powerfully informed Christian orthodoxy, being warmly embraced in the "cross-centered" evangelical tradition. Anselm's reflections remind all that the Eucharist is a celebration of these divine realities.

Widely revered, Anselm was a new kind of

saint: reasoning more than recounting, winsome more than inspiring wonder. Centuries later, Karl Barth found in his *fides quaerens intellectum* an inspiration for his own renewed orthodoxy.

For Further Reading: B. Davies, ed., *Cambridge Companion to Anselm* (2004); G. Evans, *Anselm and Talking about God* (1978); R. Southern, *St. Anselm: A Portrait in Landscape* (1990); G. Williams, *Anselm: Communion and Atonement* (1960).

James D. Smith III

Antony of Egypt (251 – 356)

Pioneer Egyptian monastic. He is often (though incorrectly) called the first monk and founder of monasticism: he himself imitated a tradition of "holy solitaries" — men who lived ascetic lives at the edges of Egyptian towns. His innovation was that when he heard the word of the Gospels preached — "Sell all you have, give to the poor, and come, follow me" — he sold his belongings, gave away the proceeds, and moved out into the desert to live as a hermit. This he did decades before Constantine's legalization of Christianity — so spiritual declension of the church under state sponsorship was not the initial impetus for Christian monasticism. Athanasius's *Life of Antony* is our only source on the Egyptian monk's life, aside from a few "sayings" and a small set of letters. Athanasius's book paints a prototypical holy man. During an initial period of some two decades of desert solitude, Antony lived a life of severe asceticism and battled (physically as well as psychologically) with demons. But for the remainder of his long life (he died at 105), his holiness proved a magnet for pilgrims of all sorts, and he was repeatedly called back from the remote desert. On these trips, he guided communities of monks in the desert's fringe (Athanasius portrays him as the spark that lit a monastic exodus to the desert), where he also prophesied and did miracles of healing. During the Great Persecution under Diocletian (303 – 313), he returned to the city to stand in the Roman courts in solidarity with Christians destined for martyrdom — miraculously, without himself being martyred. When confronted by pagans and Arians, he confounded them with Spirit-led wisdom. He even presided in courtrooms, where he solved difficult cases and healed relational breaches. After his death, the *Life* became the genre model for all saints' lives that followed. It was instrumental in the conversion of Augustine of Hippo, and to this day it is used as a touchstone for monastic reform movements. In short, Antony's life illustrates the paradox of monasticism: by isolation from mainstream society, the monk gains spiritual authority and power to heal society.

See also Asceticism; Desert Fathers and Mothers; *Fuga Mundi;* Hermits and Anchorites; Monasticism.

For Further Reading: P. Brown, *Society and the Holy in Late Antiquity* (1982); D. Chitty, *The Desert a City* (1966); B. Ward, ed., *The Sayings of the Desert Fathers* (1987); R. Williams, *Where God Happens* (2007).

Chris R. Armstrong

Anxiety

Anxiety is excessive worry about events or circumstances; it manifests itself in symptoms such as impaired concentration, sleep disturbance, irritability, fatigue, physical tension, and restlessness. The individual experience of these symptoms may vary from mild and occasional to more frequent and severe. Higher levels of anxiety may cause distress and impair the person's functioning in interpersonal relationships (e.g., couple relations, parenting, and family interaction) and employment settings. Some individuals may manifest particular anxiety disorders as noted in the *Diagnostic and Statistical Manual of Mental Disorders* (4th ed., 2000), such as panic attacks, agoraphobia, social phobia and other specific phobias, obsessive-compulsive disorder, or generalized anxiety disorder.

Cognitive behavioral therapy is the most

common psychological intervention for anxiety that has demonstrated effectiveness. Cognitive interventions attempt to alter distorted beliefs, self-appraisals, and situational judgments that produce anxiety. Behavioral interventions include systematic exposure to situations that evoke anxiety and relaxation techniques to reduce the experience of anxiety. Combined, these interventions help individuals to learn how to think and behave in ways that are more adaptive and less anxiety producing.

Spirituality can be helpful in dealing with anxiety. One example of distorted perceptions that resulted in anxiety is found in the account of the twelve spies sent into the land of Canaan by Moses (Num. 13–14). When they returned, ten spies reported that the people there were giants and that they felt comparatively like grasshoppers in their own eyes. Anxiety often enlarges our perception of feared circumstances and decreases our sense of self-efficacy. The remaining two spies felt it was possible to proceed because "the Lord is with us." An anxious-ambivalent relationship with God may create more opportunity for anxiety. In the Sermon on the Mount (Matt. 6:25–34), Jesus told us that pursuit of the kingdom of God includes recognition that our heavenly Father knows what we need and that he values us and provides for us. Similarly, Paul (Phil. 4:6–7) encourages us to recognize that God is always nearby, so we may avoid anxiety by presenting requests to God in prayer and finding peace in God. A sense of God's presence and openness to God's perspective on life challenges can help individuals avoid cognitive distortions and find biblical beliefs that promote internal peace.

See also Depression; Joy; Peace.

For Further Reading: A. Hart, *The Anxiety Cure* (2001).

Mark Stanton

Apatheia

Apatheia, a Greek transliteration, denotes in its literal sense the absence of passions. Originating as a concept in Stoic philosophy, it is commonly translated as dispassion. Stoics celebrated the ability to prevail over passions or unnatural impulses, viewing them as disordered emotions. In the early centuries of the Christian church, this philosophical concept found its way into ascetic practices and became a characteristic often attributed to God. The doctrine of divine impassibility arose from the appropriation of this philosophical category and so asserted that God, in his divine nature, cannot be acted upon by something created so as to experience pain or suffering.

Early Christian ascetics began employing this philosophy in an attempt to conform themselves to God's image. These ascetics understood unbridled passions as limiting factors in this attempt and sought methods by which to control them. Slowly, Stoic distinctions associated with the practice began to erode. The process of redirecting, or properly ordering passions superseded the original Stoic concept of eliminating them altogether. Passions, many Christians believe, enable one to better love both God and neighbor, but only when they are properly ordered and controlled (Gal. 5:22). Through efforts physical, mental, and often spiritual, the practice of *apatheia* has become a core discipline in Christian spirituality, aimed at conforming one's thoughts, words, and deeds to the image of God.

See also Emotions; Purity of Heart; Self-Control.

For Further Reading: R. Bondi, *To Love as God Loves* (1987); R. Sorabji, *Emotion and Peace of Mind* (2002).

Joshua L. Hickok

Apocalyptic Spirituality

In the popular imagination, the word *apocalyptic* elicits images of cosmic-scale judgment and the end of the world. In today's evangelical community, the term is often associated with debates over the tribulation, the rapture, the millennium, or the nature of the resurrected life. Does *apocalyptic spirituality* refer, then, to a religious mind-set that focuses on divine retributive justice or that probes the mysterious details of God's end-time scenario?

When we consider the Bible and the Christian tradition as a whole, such an understanding proves inadequate. The term *apocalyptic* describes books, passages, and events that "unveil" mysteries—mysteries that have to do not only with the future, but also with the divinely superintended past, and with unseen realms, either holy or demonic. And Christian "spirituality" refers not only to a visionary imagination or a desire to experience the mysterious, but to how God's Holy Spirit nourishes the human spirit, fires the imagination, informs the mind, and transforms even our physical dimension. Christian identity matures by grasping God's involvement in our past and future and his sovereign rule over the whole cosmos. Spirituality influenced by the apocalyptic sees this world as interconnected with beings and worlds unseen and the present time as linked with both salvation history (even primordial prehistory) and the future of which we have been given glimpses of hope (or warnings). So the faithful worship in Spirit and in truth.

To have a robust Christian apocalyptic spirituality is to discern, with Elisha (who saw the angelic hosts and chariots), with Job (who exchanged facile interpretations of his fate for the vision of God), and with Paul (who knew our fight is "not with flesh and blood") that more is going on than appears to be going on! It is to see, by the Holy Spirit, above, beneath, behind, and before the surface, to recognize that our lives are entirely significant because they are caught up with what God has done and will do, and with the rebellion or the homage of unseen beings of whom we are only occasionally aware. Christians recognize these deeper realities with awe and gratitude, not with idle curiosity or hysteria. For at the center of mystery is the greatest unveiling of God: Jesus, the incarnate Lord, whose presence sanctified our world, whose appearing interprets the unseen God, and whose will is to reconcile all things to himself, whether in heaven or on earth.

See also Crisis; Mystery.

For Further Reading: J. Collins, *The Apocalyptic Imagination* (1998); P. Reardon, *The Trial of Job* (2005); M. Wilcock, *The Message of Revelation* (1975).

Edith M. Humphrey

Apophatic and Kataphatic Ways

Apophatic and *kataphatic* describe two classical ways of knowing God. *Apophatic* ("without images") is a way of knowing God by negation. Advocates of this way aver that the divine Reality, dwelling in a world beyond human understanding and thus ineffable and inexpressible, cannot be known by ideas, images, and language. To say, for example, that God is Father or love is to fall infinitely short of divine realities. One must enter "the cloud of unknowing" and immediately experience him in the union of negation. No name from Scripture or Christian tradition adequately describes him. Rather, God is known in the darkness by detachment, prayerful silence, and contemplation. Proponents appeal to Moses approaching God in "thick darkness" (Ex. 20:21) and a "cloud" (Ex. 24:15).

A strong apophatic emphasis is found in Gregory of Nyssa, Pseudo-Dionysius, Meister Eckhart, *The Cloud of Unknowing,* John of the Cross, and the Eastern Orthodox Church. In his *Mystical Theology,* Pseudo-Dionysius wrote: "One is supremely united by a completely unknowing inactivity of all knowledge, and knows beyond the mind by knowing nothing." Apophatic themes are prevalent in Christian mysticism and monasticism and appear occasionally in contemporary postmodernism.

Kataphatic ("with images") is a way of knowing God by affirmation, namely, through his self-revelation mediated by the intellect and senses. Applying the human mind to created realities (e.g., fatherhood, goodness, justice) analogously yields truths about the Almighty. Likewise do the teachings of Scripture, the sacraments, and the symbols of the faith. Although through general and special revelation the human mind comprehends aspects of the Divine Being, it does not grasp the fullness of his reality.

Kataphatic spirituality is dominant in Augustine; Luther; Calvin; the spiritual exercises of Ignatius; and the teachings, liturgy and art forms of the Catholic and Protestant traditions. Catholicism, however, values more highly the apophatic way than does Protestantism. Both apophatic and kataphatic ways (as affirmed by writers such as John of Damascus) direct the seeker to God. The living God, often hidden in mysterious darkness, cannot be fully known by the human mind. But what humans need to know about God, who also is light, is revealed via analogies from the creation and in the truth-bearing language of Scripture.

See also Analogy; Images; Silence; Symbol.

For Further Reading: V. Lossky, *The Mystical Theology of the Eastern Church* (1957); B. McGinn, *The Foundations of Mysticism*, vol. 1 (1991); D. Turner, *The Darkness of God: Negativity in Christian Mysticism* (1995).

Bruce A. Demarest

Apostolic Fathers

The apostolic fathers were the earliest Christian authors after the NT. The term has been in vogue since 1672 when it was used by the French scholar J. B. Cotelier in the title of a two-volume work on these authors. He identified the *Letter of Barnabas*, two works ascribed to Clement of Rome (fl. 96), *The Shepherd of Hermas*, the letters of Ignatius of Antioch, a letter of Polycarp of Smyrna (c. 69 – c. 155), and an account of his martyrdom as having been written by "holy fathers who were active in apostolic times." *The Letter to Diognetus* (last quarter of the 2nd century), and the fragments

of Papias (fl. 100) and Quadratus (fl. 120) were added to this corpus in the following century. The *Didache* (1st century) was included after its discovery in 1873.

Modern scholarship has often levied too harsh a judgment on the piety of these authors and writings. The Scottish theologian T. F. Torrance judged them deficient, for, in his perspective, they failed to build on the solid foundation of the NT's monergistic soteriology. Instead, under the degrading influence of Hellenism and Judaism, they were riddled with moralism and legalism. The matter, though, is more complex than this analysis allows. There are undoubtedly moralistic elements in the apostolic fathers—for example, the assertion by *2 Clement*, a sermon by someone other than the author of *1 Clement*, that almsgiving is as good as repentance, and is, in fact, better than both fasting and prayer (16.4). But there are also passages such as the prayer of *1 Clement* 59–61 that is constructed around the author's reverence for and submission to a sovereign God, and *Diognetus* 9.2–5 that contains one of the richest expressions of Pauline soteriology in the literature of the ante-Nicene period.

The earliest of these writings is probably the *Didache*, made up of teaching on the way of life and the way of death (the *Letter of Barnabas* also has "two ways" material), instructions about food, baptism, fasting, prayer, the Eucharist, and leadership, as well as a brief apocalyptic section. The corporate experience of worship is clearly something treasured, though participation in the Eucharist is limited to those who have been baptized.

First Clement was written at the close of the 1st century to the church at Corinth to persuade the Corinthian believers to find a solution to a schism they had experienced. At the heart of the appeal is a call to repentance, humility, and the recovery of the harmony and proper order of the church. Encouragement to practice humility is found by looking at Christ's death for sinners. The author also draws explicitly on the letter to the Hebrews to establish the Christian life on a profound christological foundation.

The other writing attributed to Clement, *2 Clement*, is definitely a sermon, but one whose provenance and author are unknown. J. B. Lightfoot regarded it as "confused in thought," which recent scholarship has not disputed. Yet through the medium of an "exhortation" (*enteuxis*), the preacher is seeking to encourage faithfulness in the midst of the challenges of living in a pagan culture.

In common with the rest of the apostolic fathers, the piety displayed in Ignatius's seven genuine letters is one that is nourished by the church and devoted to orthodoxy. Moreover, the letters set forth a nascent spirituality of martyrdom, one that is more fully developed in the account of Polycarp's martyrdom. Confronted with choosing between the traditional piety of the Roman Imperium, which involved doing reverence to the "genius" or spirit of the emperor, and continuing as Christ's faithful disciple and being executed, Polycarp chose the latter and so reaffirmed the cost of discipleship for Christian readers. A clear distinction is made between the martyrs and Christ: the latter is worshiped as "the Sinless One [who died] for sinners," while the former are loved as "disciples and imitators of the Lord."

The *Letter of Barnabas*, which hovered about the fringes of the NT canon until the late 4th century, is composed of exegetical reflections on the OT and an exposition of the two ways. Although some of the letter's interpretations may seem odd to the modern reader, it reveals the second-century church's fierce determination to hold on to the OT as part of its scriptural and spiritual heritage.

The Letter to Diognetus is an apologetic piece, written to a figure, otherwise unknown, who has had prolonged contact with a Christian community but needs some penetrating questions answered. The answers given reveal a high Christology, a conviction that knowing Christ is a matter of divine revelation rather than human discovery, and a cross-centered spirituality. There is a great emphasis on the Christian community, for true spirituality is a spirituality of love binding men and women together in a love of God and neighbor.

See also Ignatius of Antioch; *Shepherd of Hermas.*

For Further Reading: P. Foster, ed., *The Writings of the Apostolic Fathers* (2007); M. Holmes, ed. and trans., *The Apostolic Fathers* (2007); C. N. Jefford, *Reading the Apostolic Fathers* (1996).

Michael A. G. Haykin

Aquinas

See **Thomas Aquinas**.

Arndt, Johann (1555 – 1621)

German Lutheran mystic and influential post-Reformation thinker. After studying theology at four universities, Arndt, the son of a small-town pastor in Anhalt (central Germany), returned to Anhalt where he was ordained in 1583. He pastored a church in Badeborn but came into conflict with his Calvinist-oriented prince and was ousted in 1590. He then occupied pulpits in nearby Lutheran areas — Quedlinburg, Braunschweig (Brunswick), and Eisleben; in 1611 the Duke of Braunschweig-Lüneburg appointed him as general superintendent in Celle.

A prolific writer, Arndt had a wide readership in Protestant Europe. Strongly influenced by late medieval mysticism (Eckhart, Tauler, and Thomas à Kempis) and contemporary spiritualism (Paracelsus and Valentin Weigel), he produced his major work, *Four Books Concerning True Christianity*, in 1605 – 1610. He argued that humankind, created in the divine image, was intended to serve as God's partner. Humans lost this status in the fall but can be restored to their original position. People are not divine in any way, but God can possess persons who have repented and turned to Christ. The true Christian is one who has died to the world and in whom Christ lives. Christ brings spiritual healing and restores the divine image within the person, who now lives joyfully with the hope of eternal life. God places his kingdom in the human heart as an inner light for the soul. The true Christian turns away from the world and allows the light of this new nature in Christ to stream out of one's being. Nature itself mirrors the divine greatness, sovereignty, and love, and as Genesis 1 shows, light is the distinctive feature of the divine sphere.

Arndt essentially introduced the medieval mystical tradition into Lutheranism. It drew from natural theology's creation belief—the progression that humans experience is not chiefly one of sin to grace but of nature to grace. He refuted his critics by claiming this was in harmony with the Lutheran confessions. His emphasis on an inclusive and ecumenical faith marked by personal piety, in contrast to the narrow, exclusive polemics of Lutheran orthodoxy, laid the groundwork for Pietism. Two other significant works were a prayer book, *A Little Garden of Paradise* (1612), and a collection of evangelical sermons, *Postilla* (1616).

See also Pietism.

For Further Reading: *Johann Arndt, True Christianity,* CWS (1978); C. Lindberg, ed., *The Pietist Theologians* (2005); E. Lund, *Johann Arndt and the Development of a Lutheran Spiritual Tradition* (1979).

Richard V. Pierard

Arts, The

See Chapter 26.

Ascent, Stages of Spiritual

The "ascent of the soul" has become part and parcel of the Christian tradition, despite its Hellenistic origination (beginning with Pythagoras and climaxing with Plato and Plotinus). This Hellenistic typology, however, was not repugnant to early Christian theologians whose Lord had ascended into the heavens to be the "firstborn" of many brothers (Rom. 8:29). Not only had Jewish apocalypticism paved the way (focusing on the "ascended" figures of Enoch and Daniel), but also present were the OT psalms of ascent, sung by devout Jews who traveled seasonally up to the temple in Jerusalem where God's presence dwelt. Thus, the apostle Paul could speak rapturously of being "caught up to the third heaven" (2 Cor. 12:2), and even today, Christians worldwide participate in Origen's liturgical *sursum corda*—"Lift up your hearts!"

Generally, this ascent is presented as consisting of a three-staged ladder, roughly corresponding to the threefold way of purgation, illumination, and union. Early Christians baptized this Platonic template as they described progress in the Christian life, though they were not always attentive to its dangers. For underlying Platonic ascent is escape: contemplation of the higher world of ideas promises salvation from the present "world of appearances" of which ignorance, not sin, is the basic human predicament. For this reason, Protestants have tended to follow Luther in his negative evaluation of ascent, deeming God's descent to us to be the decisive moment for Christian theology. While this is true, ascent has proved an invaluable category for theologians articulating the process of sanctification and union with Christ, the final "return" of all things to communion with their Creator, and participation in Christ, the one who has ascended to the Father.

While Origen was the first Christian to develop a formal, three-step theology of ascent (properly locating "ascent" within the body of Christ, the church), it was Augustine who had greater success in breaking free from its Platonizing tendencies. While one of his earliest Christian works outlines a seven-step schematization of the soul's ascent to God (*De quantitate animae*), Augustine later abandoned this project after writing his commentary on Romans. However, this seven-step pattern remains an important literary device in the Christian tradition (quoted even by Calvin). Perhaps Augustine's greatest legacy to spiritual literature, though, is his *Confessions*, which narrates his personal and geographic descent (away from God, the church, and his Christian mother) and the corresponding return or ascent of his soul back to God. It is here that ascent takes a sharp turn inward (following Plotinus), for Augustine discovered that while he sought for God "outside," all the while God was "within"—for "God is closer to me than I am to myself" (*interior intimo meo*). It is this interiorized version of the soul's ascent that held sway throughout the Middle Ages, accruing to itself elitist and creation-denying tendencies.

As a result, Anders Nygren can summarize the religious temper of the Middle Ages by the phrase "the upward tendency." Those who inherited Augustine's seven-grade ascent are many (Gregory the Great's *Seven Steps to Spiritual Perfection*, Bonaventure's *The Mind's Ascent to God*, Jan van Ruysbroeck's *Seven Steps on the Ladder of Spiritual Love*, Teresa of Avila's *The Interior Castle* with its seven mansions, John of the Cross's *Ascent to Mount Carmel* with its seven stages of love), and its other colorful variations similarly bear the mark of Augustinian desire and inwardness (Guigo's *Ladder of Monks*, Richard of St. Victor's *De gradibus caritatis*, Walter of Hilton's *Scale of Perfection*, Jean Gerson's three-step *Mountain of Contemplation*, and even the twelfth-century Cistercian monastery entitled *Scala Dei*—"God's ladder").

By the time of the Reformation, Luther was determined to do away with all such ladders, perceiving them to be "ladders of merit" and a repetition of the original sin of ambition. He emphasized the Christian's status as one "simultaneously justified *and* a sinner," instructing Christians instead to follow their Lord in making the "downward turn" to those in need. However, Luther's rejection of ascent (and the medieval "spiritual disciplines" associated with it) led to ambivalence about how—if at all—one could pursue Christian growth. Less than a century after Luther, the Pietist Johann Arndt wrote his famous treatise *True Christianity*, which attempted, once again, to build into German Protestantism a language appropriate to describe a Christian's progress in Christ.

Calvin, on the other hand, embraced both descent and ascent, not as the paradigm of the individual soul, but as the summary of salvation: God has come as human to stand in for us (descent), and yet as human he also leads us back to the Father (ascent). Borrowing Plato's image of the ladder, Calvin argued that the ladder is Christ. Ascent is not *to* union with Christ, but is affected only *by* union with Christ, whereby the Christian ascends by participation in him, to the Father, by the Spirit. There is no technique or set of stages, simply a call to deeper relationship. So, then, he declared in a sermon on Acts 1, "It is not all to have entered, but we must follow further, until we are fully united to Jesus Christ." In gentle response to the Platonic threefold way, Calvin emphasized that "Christ is the beginning, middle, and end," though he could also call worship and the Lord's Supper "ladders."

In evangelical spirituality, the emphasis on personal (and often climactic) conversion led to an ambivalent stance toward progress, which was rarely described in ascending terms. More appropriate was a typological description of the threefold way as exodus (conversion), wilderness (testing), and the Promised Land (union with Christ). John Bunyan's *Grace Abounding* is an autobiographical account that follows much the same pattern: conviction, then "sweet discoveries of blessed grace" in Christ alone, and then union with Christ. Yet despite John Wesley's famed emphasis on instant sanctification, he still describes perfection in stages. But the emphasis would remain on the soul's ability to receive, surrender, and "passively" obey by making oneself more available to the working of God. In the 20th century, these emphases found their way into the Holiness, Keswick, and charismatic movements, all of which strive for a deeper surrender to God and — in the words of the hymn — "Just a Closer Walk with Thee."

See also Climacus, John; Threefold Way.

For Further Reading: É. Bertaud and A. Rayez, "Échelle Spirituelle," in *Dictionnaire de Spiritualité* 4 (1961); J. Canlis, *Calvin's Ladder* (2010); B. Demarest, *Seasons of the Soul* (2009); B. Hindmarsh, "End of Faith as Its Beginning," *Spiritus* 10 (2010): 1–21; A. Louth, *Origins of the Christian Mystical Tradition* (1981); D. Steinmetz, "Luther and the Ascent of Jacob's Ladder," *Church History* 55 (1986): 179–92; F. Van Fleteren, "The Ascent of the Soul in the Augustinian Tradition," in *Paradigms in Medieval Thought*, ed. N. Van Deusen (1990), 93–110.

Julie Canlis

Asceticism

The word *asceticism* comes from the Greek *askēsis* and literally means exercise, practice, or training. In earliest Christianity, *askēsis* could refer to the study of the Scriptures or bodily discipline, or be used as a technical term for the monastic life. The most common use of the word was in reference to an austere or disciplined life. Such bodily discipline is not unique to Christianity, since it was also characteristic of early Buddhism and ancient Judaism. The OT is greatly concerned with bodily actions, observing ascetical practices as diverse as fasting, abstaining permanently from certain foods, not touching a woman during her menses, requiring that a person perform purification rites after sexual intercourse, adopting sexual continence, and wearing coarse garments. Furthermore, the Essenes, a Jewish communal group, were rooted in the teachings of the Hebrew Bible and committed to fulfilling its precepts by incorporating many ascetic practices into their way of life. These practices included celibacy, a simple life free of material possessions, temperance in food and drink, simplicity of dress, reserve in speech, desert separatism, and strict rules of ritual purity.

Ancient Greek and Roman philosophy also advocated asceticism. The Stoics are the most well-known of the ancient schools of philosophy for adopting ascetic tendencies. They believed that humankind was perfectible in its earthly existence, thus creating the need to live ascetically. The task of human beings, for Stoics, was to cultivate their own soul so that they could achieve complete harmony between what they desired and sought after and what right reason set down. In his *Meditations*, Marcus Aurelius wrote,

> By remembering, then, that I am a part of such a whole, I shall be content with everything that happens. And inasmuch as I am in a manner intimately related to the parts which are of the same kind with myself, I shall do nothing unsocial, but I shall rather direct myself to the things which are of the same kind with myself, and I shall turn my efforts to the common interest, and divert them from the contrary. Now, if these things are done so, life must flow on happily.

The goal, therefore, of Stoicism is *apatheia*, that is, moving beyond those powers (such as anger) that affect one's behavior and disposition. In part, this was accomplished through various types of asceticism.

From its earliest history, Christianity also practiced a number of forms of asceticism, due, at least in part, to its Judaic heritage and the influence of Greek and Roman philosophy. Already in the NT literature a paradigm for asceticism is presented in the person of John the Baptist, who lived in the wilderness, wore camel's hair clothing, ate locusts and honey, and fasted with his disciples (Mark 1:6; 2:18). Jesus himself established a firm foundation for the ascetical lifestyle when he admonished his followers to deny themselves, take up their cross, and follow him (Mark 8:34). As well, Jesus often fasted and seemed to care little for accumulating material possessions.

Soon after Jesus' earthly ministry, there was a dispute between those Jews converted to Christianity and the Hellenized Christians. The core of this dispute centered on the need for non-Jews to receive circumcision, on whether to observe the rules of clean or unclean foods, and on food sacrificed to idols (cf. Acts 15:1–21). Though the apostle Paul urged that all food may legitimately be eaten by Christians, he also fasted (Acts 14:23) and advocated, for some, celibacy (1 Cor. 7:25–40), together with a "spiritual marriage," a term for the practice of female Christian ascetics who lived with men, lay and ordained, where both parties took a vow of celibacy. In the Greek-speaking church of the Christian East, the participants of this practice were termed "beloved," and in the Latin-speaking Western church, the participants were known as "virgins secretly introduced." The earliest nonbiblical reference to the practice is from the 1st century, and there are numerous references to the practice from the 2nd century onward. Both orthodox and heterodox ecclesiastical authors, as well as secular emperors, were familiar with the practice that had spread to most church provinces in ancient Christianity by the 4th century. Although references to the practice are scarce in comparison to other ancient ascetic phenomena, it is certain that celibate men and women lived together in a chaste relationship for mutual support and encouragement. This arrangement was necessary since they were unable to obtain such support and encouragement outside of marriage in the prevailing Roman culture. Some scholars have argued convincingly that the apostle Paul introduces this practice in 1 Corinthians 7:36–38, arguing also for its presence in Philo's *On the Contemplative Life*, as well as in the *Shepherd of Hermas*. That said, it appears that in addition to "normative" ascetical practices, such as fasting, celibacy, and avoidance of material possessions, perhaps as early as the 1st century, the Christian churches were institutionalizing practices of asceticism.

See also Desert Fathers and Mothers; Detachment; Monasticism.

For Further Reading: S. Fraade, "Ascetical Aspects of Ancient Judaism," in *Jewish Spirituality*, ed. A. Green (1986), 253–88; C. Stewart, "Pre-Monastic Asceticism," in *The Historical Atlas of Eastern and Western Christian Monasticism*, ed. J. Laboa (2003), 32–35; V. Wimbush and R. Valantasis, eds., *Asceticism* (1995).

Greg Peters

Asian Christian Spirituality

Speaking about "Asian" Christian spirituality is a complex venture. With almost four billion people and hosting approximately 60 percent of the human population, Asia is the world's largest and most populous continent. Although in the popular imagination the term *Asian* typically refers to people of the far eastern, southeastern, and perhaps the southern regions of the continent, Asia is actually divided into six different areas (east, west, north, south, southeast, and central), each with its huge range of different histories, cultures, and languages. The fact that Asia encompasses forty-seven separate nationalities, with some countries like India and Indonesia having upwards of six hundred to over eight hundred languages that are natively spoken, is a reminder of the risks of generalization.

Contrary to common misunderstanding, Christian spirituality is not new or even recent to Asia, since Christianity was born in the eastern Mediterranean, which is an area in western Asia. Christianity spread to Armenia, Georgia, and according to tradition, also the Parthian Empire (Iran) and India as early as the 1st century through the preaching of Jesus' own apostles. Nestorian Christianity was introduced to Tang China and Mongolia in the 7th century, although by the late 14th century most forms of Christianity were struggling for survival. Although Roman Catholicism began to take root in India, China, Japan, Philippines, and Vietnam in the 16th century, Protestant forms of spirituality did not take root until much later during the 19th century. By 2008 it was estimated that there were approximately 335 million Christians living in Asia and constituting 9.1 percent of the total population.

The distinctive feature of Christian spirituality in Asia is its historic and continuous encounters with the diverse faces of indigenous religiosity. As the cradle of most of the major world religions, Asia is a continent rich with religious symbols, practices, and rituals. Islam is a significant presence in Pakistan, Indonesia, and elsewhere. India is the birthplace of Hinduism, Buddhism, Jainism, and Sikhism, with its spirituality highlighting the illusory nature of the cosmos (*maya*) and the negation of human desire. Indigenous Indian religiosity emphasizes detachment from material and sensual pleasures through yoga, meditation, knowledge, and devotion. In contrast, the Chinese spirituality tends to be world-affirming and pragmatic. As the birthplace of both Taoism and Confucianism, the cosmo-anthropocentric nature of Chinese religiosity highlights the importance of harmony (*dao*) with nature and in social relationships. Polytheism, shamanism, and animism also provide the context of folk spiritualities in many regions of Asia.

That Asian Christians usually live as minority communities has important spiritual implications. They are often compelled to function without the advantages of cultural power and influence, and sometimes in the face of persecution and suffering. In addition, they have often felt the need to express their spirituality in correlation to the already existing forms of religiosity. Although in the past most missionaries tended to be pessimistic about the spiritual values of Asian religions, some of the early Jesuit missionaries attempted to develop Christian spirituality in dialogue with different aspects of Asian cultures. In more recent times, some Christians, especially in the Catholic tradition, have attempted to more radically incorporate indigenous religiosities. In India, for example, some have attempted to combine Christian spirituality with the Hindu tradition of metaphysical advaita (nondualism) and techniques of yoga. In Japan, zen

meditation has been incorporated into Christian meditation and prayer. In China and other countries influenced by its religious traditions, attempts have been made to combine the mysticism of Daoism and the Confucian ritual of ancestor veneration into Christian spirituality.

The most vibrant expressions of Christian spirituality in Asia are the more conservative and evangelical ones, which Protestant missionaries have introduced since the 19th century. Bible-centered, cross-centered, conversion oriented, and evangelistically active, Asian evangelical spirituality highlights the uniqueness of Christ as the Son of God and crucified Savior. This conviction serves as a clear boundary marker separating these evangelical believers from nonbelievers. In much of East, South, and Southeast Asia where pluralism and polytheism are the norms, the notion that the path to truth and salvation comes exclusively through Jesus Christ represents a novel and radical idea. The unique aspect of this spirituality is also related to the importance placed on the Bible as a single source that defines the core of Christian spirituality. Although many Asian religious traditions have sacred Scriptures and classics, evangelical spirituality is characterized by greater focus on a single text as God's inspired and authoritative revelation.

In much of Asia, the evangelical form of spirituality cannot be easily distinguished from Pentecostalism, the world's fastest-growing spiritual movement. Highly influenced by the revivalist tradition of the Protestant missionaries, Asian evangelical churches are often characterized by fervent prayers, confessions of faith, enthusiastic preaching, and joyful singing. The Theology Committee of the National Council of Churches in Korea has noted the common characteristic of the worship practices of the Korean church is freedom from liturgical forms "due to the influence of the Pentecostal movement." In many parts of Asia, furthermore, most Christian spirituality reflects a much stronger awareness of the supernatural than is characteristic in the West. For example, many evangelical believers in Asia could recount first-hand contacts with an angel or a demon. Furthermore, many of the supernatural events in Scripture are considered normal, including miracles, healing, exorcism, and speaking in tongues.

The activist impulse in Asian Christian spirituality has manifested itself in two main ways. First, it has expressed itself in participation in struggles for justice and freedom from various forms of oppression and poverty. Spirituality of this kind has two seminal moments: openness to all humans, especially the poor, and a willingness to respond to the hearkening call of God's Spirit. The Minjung theology of Korea and the Dalit theology of India are both expressions of this form of spirituality. Second, the activist spiritual impulse may be discerned in the cross-cultural missionary movements among Asian Christians. In 2007, for example, more than fifteen thousand Korean Protestants were active in intercultural missionary service, making it the largest missionary-sending nation after the United States. In China, the Back to Jerusalem movement represents an eschatological and missionary spirituality of carrying the gospel into the Muslim world and eventually to Jerusalem. Once that happens, it is believed that the gospel will have been proclaimed to the entire world and the second coming of Jesus Christ will occur.

See also Korean Christian Spirituality.

For Further Reading: D. Aikman, *Jesus in Beijing* (2006); D. Baker, *Korean Spirituality* (2008); S. Chan, *Spiritual Theology* (1998); S. Moffett, *A History of Christianity in Asia*, 2 vols. (1998–2005); S. Rayan, "The Search for an Asian Spirituality of Liberation," in *Asian Christian Spirituality*, ed. V. Fabella et al. (1992), 11–30.

David S. Nah

Assessment of Spirituality

Spirituality signifies a strong relationship to God, lived out with others in the transforming and empowering presence of the Holy Spirit. In general terms, assessment is about measuring, gauging, or evaluating a particular entity. The assessment of spirituality is an undertaking mandated by Scripture (Ps. 139:23–24; 1 Cor. 11:28; 2 Cor. 13:5) and further legitimized by the fact that an intentional and broadly measured plan for input/understanding, analysis, and integration can assist the spiritual growth process.

It is, of course, much easier to take note of outward behaviors than to assess one's values or the internal state of a person's heart. Historically, spiritual assessment most often was itself relational, facilitated by a priest or pastor, spiritual director, or "soul friend." A vital question today is: How can assessment of spirituality be reliable? At the very least, reliable assessment must involve holistic examination—that is, it will not oversimplify, but will take into account the complex variables involved in an individual's spirituality as it is lived out in relationship to God and others.

The assessment of spirituality takes many forms, and the results obtained by such instruments will vary in importance. Every assessment strategy must first identify the particular variables it will attempt to measure—in other words, it must determine at the outset the key indicators of spiritual life that it will probe. Such a list of indicators will always be significantly conditioned by the historical, disciplinary, and theological assumptions of the assessors. At various points in history, such variables as humility, subjection to authority, radical self-sacrifice, a mastery of "the flesh," or manifestations of the supernatural have been regarded as the sine qua non of true spirituality. On a parallel track, the imitation of Christ has implied many different ideals to believers through the centuries. Today transdisciplinary spiritual assessment is just as likely to prioritize variables such as openness to difference, empathy, a passion for justice, and appropriate boundary maintenance. The ongoing challenge is to craft criteria that conserve biblical ideals and also reflect contextual needs.

Assessors need to be clear about the nature and limits of their particular approach to taking "biopsies" of the spiritual life. They must also resist the temptation to focus on variables for which relatively reliable assessment instruments conveniently exist, and perhaps pass over other more difficult to measure criteria that are actually more crucial to Christian spirituality per se. Once the subjective and contextual nature of assessment priorities is humbly acknowledged, the results can become helpful (though tentative) feedback in constructing a reliable profile of one's spiritual life. For example, holistic assessment of spirituality will naturally include an evaluation of the quality and tenor of one's relationships. How does one approach relationships? What do people know of themselves and their ability to make and grow friendships, resolve conflict, have empathy for and appreciation of others? How have their experiences in life contributed to the ways in which they engage in relationship? There is a variety of instruments that provide facets of the psychological and sociological makeup of persons and contribute to an integrative evaluation.

Obtaining a reliable assessment of spirituality will depend on the breadth of the assessments, the validity of the tools (e.g., acknowledging the limits of self-reportage), and one's ability to confirm the assessment and process of spiritual growth within interpersonal relationships. Each individual assessment tool is, after all, a way of taking a small snapshot into the entirety of a person's growth and life. A solid ethic of assessment will place it appropriately within the whole of each individual life, institution, and community. Ongoing assessment of spirituality, motivated by a desire for continued growth in Christlikeness, must include multiple angles of examination and involvement to give a comprehensive and reliable picture of how we are living life "in the Spirit." Ultimately, spiritual assessment cannot safely be handed off to technicians; in the end the spiritually mature must also be involved, as the ones best attuned to recognize the life of the Spirit in another, or the lack thereof (1 Cor. 2:5; 14:37; Gal. 6:1).

For Further Reading: J. Fee and J. Ingram, "Correlation of the Holy Spirit Questionnaire with the Spiritual Well-Being Scale and the Spiritual Assessment Inventory," *Journal of Psychology and Theology* 32, no. 2 (2004): 104–14; R. Foster, "Spiritual Formation Agenda," *Christianity Today*, January 2009, 29–33; T. Hall and K. Edwards, "The Spiritual Assessment Inventory," *Journal for the Scientific Study of Religion* 41, no. 2 (2002): 341–57; S. Sandage et al., "Relational Spirituality and Transformation," *Journal of Spiritual Formation and Soul Care* 1, no. 2 (2008): 182–206; L. VandeCreek et al., "Using INSPIRIT to Conduct Spiritual Assessments," *Journal of Pastoral Care* 49, no. 4 (Spring 1995): 83–89.

Mary E. Sanders and Glen G. Scorgie

Assurance

Historically this doctrine deals with the question of whether certainty with regard to salvation is possible prior to death. The NT assumes it is a part of normal Christian experience. It speaks of being saved in the past tense (Eph. 2:8) and of Christians knowing that they have passed from death to life (1 John 3:14). In the face of all that might conceivably separate a Christian from God, Paul is confident that nothing can do this (Rom. 8:38–39). The NT even defines saving faith as the confidence believers have that their hope of eternal life will be realized (Heb. 11:1). Yet the NT also recognizes that there can be saving faith without assurance (1 John 5:13). And the warning passages in the NT indicate that there can be smug presumption (1 Cor. 10:12; 2 Cor. 13:5; Heb. 2:1–4; 3:12). The bases for Christian assurance are God's faithfulness (2 Cor. 1:18–20; 2 Tim. 2:13), the death and resurrection of Christ (Rom. 8:31–34; Heb. 10:21–22), and the indwelling Holy Spirit, who is the foretaste of future glory (Rom. 8:16; 2 Cor. 1:21–22; 5:5;

Eph. 1:13–14; 4:30; 1 John 3:24; 4:13). The first two of these bases are ones from which Christians infer their status as children of God. The final one entails what John Calvin called the Spirit's inner witness, which is direct and supernatural, although the Spirit can also use means—such as the Word of God and the Lord's Supper—to give the believer assurance of salvation.

During the medieval era, Thomas Aquinas bracketed the experience of the NT church as extraordinary and argued that only a special revelation from God could give assurance. The matter became deeply controversial during the Reformation when Martin Luther, Ulrich Zwingli, and John Calvin sought to return to the position of the NT and maintain that assurance is a blessed dimension and privilege of authentic Christian experience. Calvin, for example, knew of the reality of doubt but was convinced that true faith is aware of its status, and this through the work of the Holy Spirit, who unites the believer with Christ. Union with Christ is thus the ground of the believer's assurance.

It has been argued that the heirs of the Reformers, particularly the Puritans, moved away from this robust conviction about the normativity of assurance. The Westminster Confession of Faith (1647), for instance, concedes that faith and assurance can be separated. Discontinuity between the Reformers and the Puritans about assurance has been variously traced to the Puritan emphasis on predestination or on particular redemption. The issue, though, is more complex than has been allowed. The Reformers were responding to the lack of assurance in medieval thought, and their theological formulations also reshaped the pastoral landscape, thereby introducing new issues. The Puritans, on the other hand, were ministering in a context where all who were members of the English state theoretically belonged to the Protestant Church of England, and thus they were concerned about the dangers of nominal Christianity. The emergent cultural impact of modernity in the 17th century with its stress on the individual also played a part in the different emphases of the Reformers and their heirs.

It is noteworthy that the Roman Catholic Council of Trent was adamant in its anathematization of the doctrine of assurance. The ferocity of their reaction to the Reformers was, in part, due to the loss of ecclesial privilege the Church of Rome had in the process of assurance. It was also based, however, on the fear that the assurance being promoted by the Reformers would erode the incentive to live a holy life and would issue in immoral lawlessness. This anathematization raised a question that is still a vital issue in Christian spirituality: does assurance, by intensifying confidence and gratitude, foster a more mature Christian spirituality, or does it actually foster relative indifference to spiritual formation? While this should be an ever-present concern, a careful reading of the NT compels a stance similar to that of the Reformers: assurance of salvation is indeed normative for the Christian life and should intensify, rather than diminish, the believer's grateful resolve to grow in grace.

See also Confirmation.

For Further Reading: J. R. Beeke, *Assurance of Faith* (1991); M. Eaton, *No Condemnation* (1995); T. Schreiner and A. B. Caneday, *The Race Set before Us* (2001); A. S. Yates, *The Doctrine of Assurance* (1952).

Michael A. G. Haykin

Athanasius (c. 296 – 373)

Archbishop of Alexandria. One of the early church fathers recognized as highly influential in the development of the doctrine of the incarnation. Apparently born and raised in Alexandria, Athanasius was a Christian from an early age. He received a classical education and was adviser to the current archbishop (whom he succeeded) while attending the Council at Nicea (325). It was the resulting Nicene Creed that he fiercely defended from attacks by Arius, and his arguments resulted in some of his most important contributions to the development of Christian doctrine. Jesus was said by the Arians to be the perfect example of a godly human and therefore rewarded by God with elevation to sonship. In other words, Jesus was of a *similar* substance to the Father (*homoi-ousios*) but was not the *same* essence (*homo-ousios*). Indeed, Arius went so far as to claim that Christ must have been created if he was son to the Father. The Arians' ringing battle cry was "There was a time when he [Jesus] was not."

In his central work, *On the Incarnation of the Divine Word*, and in other writings from 339 to 359, Athanasius refuted this. He insisted that a perfect human could not save: only God can save. Therefore, if Christ saves as the Scriptures tell us, then indeed he must be God incarnate. Athanasius argued that even in churches that supported Arianism, Christ was worshiped. Yet only God is worthy of worship, so the followers of Arius have doubly condemned themselves by worshiping a created being whom they call Christ, but they have also blasphemed the holy God incarnate in Christ by calling him a created being. Whatever is said of the Father may also be attributed to the Son.

The existential reality for Athanasius was that Jesus *was* God, the second person of the Trinity, who chose to be incarnated as a human: intentionality of the divinity to enter into humanity was central. The incarnation formed his spirituality in the statement "God became man so that man might become God." The incarnation changed everything. Using 2 Peter 1:4 and 1 John, Athanasius claimed that this incarnational presence of Christ is available to all who accept him, which enabled anyone to access the Father through Christ at anytime. What some traditions call glorification or sanctification, Athanasius called deification, recognizing that we will only be completely restored when we are with him in glory.

The battle for the doctrine of the incarnation

continued to rage for decades, and while Nicea triumphed at Chalcedon in 451, it often appeared as though all would be lost. He would be exiled on five different occasions, and at those times he often went to the desert to live with the fathers and mothers to pray, study, and write. It was there he made the acquaintance of Antony, the first and greatest of the desert fathers: the subject of his biography *The Life of Antony*. It became one of the most influential books of the early church, a classic of Christian spirituality.

See also Antony of Egypt; Deification.

For Further Reading: J. Ernest, *The Bible in Athanasius of Alexandria* (2004); S. Finlan, *Theosis* (2006); T. Weinandy, *Athanasius* (2007).

Kelby Cotton

Atonement, Theories of

Atonement refers to God's act of "reconciling the world to himself" in the cross (2 Cor. 5:19). The implications in the atonement for spirituality are thus based on an event apart from all human accomplishments but still involving those who receive God's abundant mercy by grace through faith.

In relating the atonement to the spiritual life, Scripture lifts up a number of metaphors, such as sacrifice, substitution, and ransom. The sacrificial system of OT worship implied that a mediator is required between sinful humanity and a holy God. The sacrifices typified a perfect sacrifice (Christ) that carries away the sins of humanity (Isa. 53:3–4; Heb. 9–10). Christ died "for our sins" (1 Cor. 15:3), bearing "our sins in his body on the tree, so that we might die to sins and live for righteousness" (1 Peter 2:24). Christ's bearing our sins as our substitute is therefore inseparably tied to a spiritual life oriented toward others, a dying to self and a rising up in righteousness (Rom. 6:3–4). Jesus also informed his disciples that he was to offer his life as a ransom to redeem us from slavery to sin and death (Mark 10:45), something that his disciples were to follow by grace in serving others in Christ's name.

Atonement theory and its implications for the spiritual life are currently an area of considerable discussion. Prevalent in the West has been Anselm's satisfaction theory of atonement, which stressed the act of Jesus as the God-man in satisfying the Father by restoring proper honor due the Father as the Lord who has been offended by human sin. Rejecting the medieval idea that a ransom should be paid to Satan, Anselm stressed the role of Jesus as the God-man in repaying the debt of human honor to God. As divine, Jesus had the power to restore honor to God, and as human, he could do so on our behalf in fulfillment of the human obligation to God. The value of Anselm's satisfaction theory of atonement (and the penal substitution theory, which developed as a more refined variant of it) for the spiritual life is in the seriousness with which it took sin as the ultimate human rejection of God's lordship and the helplessness of sinful mortals to provide satisfaction. The grace that infuses the spiritual life is not dependent on human piety but on the event by which God fulfills justice for us in the cross (Rom. 3:25–26). Evangelical spirituality has thus responded to the terror of sin and judgment by clinging to the cross as the only possible refuge. Abelard's "moral" theory of atonement (by which God's love is exemplified in the cross) has had value in evangelical spirituality, but only as a consequence of the deeper satisfaction won by Christ.

Anselm's theory, however, has been criticized recently, even among evangelicals, mainly because it is thought to distort the conception of the divine-human relationship that frames the spiritual life. It has been noted that "satisfaction" is not a biblical concept. Ransom, which is a biblical concept, shifts the weight of atonement theory from the image of a wrathful God whose honor is restored to a loving God who is honored by fulfilling justice through mercy. Moreover, the idea that God's honor is restored through the unjust slaughter of God's Son on the cross seems disturbing to many; for example, as a legitimizing of violence or of patriarchal "child abuse." Though satisfaction and its implications for spirituality are not totally to be discounted, it must be conceded that God the Father in Anselm's theory does play a relatively passive role as a distant patriarch to whom proper honor must be restored. As a remedy, greater stress has been placed on the Father's suffering in handing over the Son to the cross (Rom. 8:32), while the Son bore the suffering of offering himself up to the cross by the eternal Spirit (Heb. 9:14). The triune God embraced us in suffering love so that we could extend this embrace to others. Shattering all systems of exchange, the cross releases an abundant outpouring of divine love into our hearts by the divine Spirit, so that Christ's death becomes a seed that spawns many seeds. The spiritual life is thus not only a clinging to Christ for an escape from wrath but also a following of Christ in suffering love for others. The spiritual life integrates a clinging to the crucified Christ alone in finding a merciful God and a life of seeking to be transformed into the image of Christ as the one who manifests God's costly grace and love to others.

See also Anselm of Canterbury; Cross.

For Further Reading: G. Aulén, *Christus Victor* (1931); J. Green and M. Baker, *Recovering the Scandal of the Cross* (2000); F. Keshgegian, "The Scandal of the Cross," *Anglican Theological Review* 82, no. 3 (Summer 2000): 475–92; K. Kitamori, *Theology of the Pain of God* (1965); J. Moltmann, *The Crucified God* (1974).

Frank D. Macchia

Attentiveness

The Christian practice of attentiveness involves the habitual cultivation of a way of being that frees one to be fully, lovingly present to God—and in turn, oneself and neighbor—in the rounds of daily life. In the Bible, the Gospels reveal Jesus Christ as the full embodiment of the truly attentive life as summed up in his declaration: "The Son can do nothing by himself; he can do only what he sees his Father doing" (John 5:19). Jesus' own prayerful rhythm of life fixed his gaze upon loving attentiveness to the Father and yieldedness to the work of the Holy Spirit as exemplified when he prays during his baptism (Luke 3:21) and, full of the Spirit, is led into the Judean desert for forty days and nights to be tempted; he returns in the power of the Spirit (Luke 4:1–14); he prays all night before choosing the Twelve (Luke 6:12–16) and into the fourth watch after feeding the five thousand (Matt. 14:22–25); and he rises early (Mark 1:35) and regularly withdraws to "lonely places" to listen and pray (Luke 5:16).

Through the centuries, Christians with a desire to obediently attend to and cooperate with the movement of God's Spirit in every dimension of life have developed the requisite capacities for prayerful listening, noticing, and discerning by engaging in spiritual practices that require an intentional, unhurried inner and outer posture. The desert fathers and mothers of Egypt, Syria, and Palestine (3rd–4th centuries) embraced an ascetical life in the wilderness to be purified and set apart for God's purposes by attending to the work of the Spirit during extended periods of solitude, silence, listening prayer, spiritual warfare, and Scripture meditation. Those following Benedict's Rule (6th century) continue to integrate prayer and work (*ora et labora*) in acknowledgment that all of life is sacred and designed to be lived in reverent awareness of God's abiding presence. Cistercian abbot Bernard of Clairvaux (twelfth century) taught that only through divine gifting can the soul completely "attend to God," yet through worship, meditation, reading, prayer, and obedience one can choose to refocus attention and enter into "sweet familiarity" with God. The *Spiritual Exercises* of Ignatius of Loyola (16th century) emphasize the examen, in which the prayer of consciousness and con-

science—of God's active presence and one's own sinfulness—lays a foundation for attending to God. Brother Lawrence, a lay member of the Discalced (barefoot) Carmelites (17th century) learned to maintain "an habitual sense of God's presence" in the midst of his busy kitchen duties by directing his thoughts always toward God; his insights were posthumously published in *The Practice of the Presence of God*. In the Eastern Orthodox Hesychast tradition, the Jesus Prayer, or the Prayer of the Heart, "Lord Jesus Christ, Son of God, have mercy on me, a sinner," was popularized in the Russian classic *The Way of a Pilgrim* (19th century).

At the core, attentiveness means being present to God's presence. To this end, many contemporary Christians engage in practices based on the life of Christ and his followers. Spiritual disciplines, such as solitude, silence, listening prayer and discernment, examen, the Jesus Prayer, meditation on Scripture, extended retreats, uniting prayer, service, and sacrifice nurture the capacity to become more awake to the reality of the Lord's presence in order to faithfully serve God.

See also Contemplation; Presence of God; Silence.

For Further Reading: E. de Waal, *Lost in Wonder* (2003); L. Ford, *The Attentive Life* (2009).

Natalie Hendrickson

Augustine of Hippo (354–430)

Early Christian bishop and theologian. Apart from the scriptural authors, no other figure had a greater impact on Christian spirituality down to the Reformation than Augustine. The main details of his early life are well known, since they are recorded in his spiritual classic, the *Confessions* (397–401). After his early years and education as a rhetorician in the Roman province of Numidia, North Africa, he moved to Italy in 383, where he first taught in Rome and then later in Milan. He had been raised by a Christian mother, Monica, but had long rejected Christian truth claims. At first he was attracted to Manicheism, a neo-Gnostic cult, but the move to Milan in 384 ended this attraction. Conversion to Christianity came in the summer of 386 in a garden in Milan after he had resumed going to church to hear the preaching of Ambrose, the Milanese bishop. The critical moment came through the reading of a Pauline text, Romans 13:13 – 14, by means of which, he later wrote in his *Confessions*, "the light of confidence flooded into my heart and all the darkness of doubt was dispelled." His conversion, though, was also an embrace of a celibate, monastic lifestyle, for figuring in his turning to Christ was the story of Antony, the father of Egyptian monasticism. Baptism followed in 387, and then a move back to North Africa the next year.

After three years in a semimonastic environment in his hometown of Thagaste, a visit to the coastal town of Hippo Regius led to his being forcibly ordained presbyter by the church there. In 395 he was elected bishop of Hippo, where he would remain till his death. Two years into his episcopate, studies in Romans 9:10 – 29 and Pauline theology led him to abandon belief in the freedom of the will, and to declare, "the grace of God had the upper hand." This conviction and emphasis on divine grace permeates his *Confessions* and anticipates later struggles against Pelagian emphases on self-effort as sufficient to attain a righteous life.

His *Confessions* is a spiritual masterpiece. As the classic account of conversion in the ancient church, the *Confessions* helped to make conversion a central theme in Western spiritual thought. It depicts God as primarily seeker rather than sought. Over against this seeking love of God is sinful humanity's refusal to be found and delight in sin. Release from sin's bondage comes through the mediator Christ Jesus as God woos humanity through Christ. This Christ-centered focus of his spirituality is well seen in another text where he asks, "Where are we going? To Christ. How do we get there? Through Christ."

Such Christocentricity, though, does not sideline the Trinity. Augustine's *On the Trinity* (399 – 422) is one of the most profound theological reflections in the patristic era on the nature of the Godhead. Although the Arian controversy had been officially addressed at the Council of Constantinople (381), Arianism was still very much alive in the Latin-speaking Western Roman Empire. *On the Trinity* is thus both a response to the ongoing Arian crisis and a rich work of scriptural meditation and spirituality. Central to his purpose in the book is determining how the persons of the Trinity are to be distinguished. Augustine demonstrates, on the basis of 1 John 4, that the Holy Spirit's hypostatic individuality is found in his being the bond of love between the Father and the Son. This point has significant practical implications, for Augustine is drawing on an argument previously made in the anti-Pelagian tracts. If, as he argued there from Romans 5:5, the summit of the Spirit's extra-Trinitarian activities is to inflame the hearts of men and women with love for God, then this must be a sure indication of the Spirit's inner-Trinitarian relations with the Father and the Son.

Augustine also found himself constrained to relate Christian spirituality to a major societal crisis in late antiquity. The Western Roman Empire was in a state of political and military collapse during the final thirty years of his life. Augustine's *On the City of God* (413 – 27) is his comprehensive, albeit rambling, response to this situation. He refused to see the so-called Christian Roman Empire as the eschatological goal of history, as some fourth-century Christian authors had. Rather, he stressed that while Christians are members of an earthly community, they are also involved in a pilgrimage toward an eternal home. Those on this journey are part of a holy community, "a city" that lives by faith, hope, and self-denying love and is marked by humble obedience to God. Due to their involvement in earthly communities, however, Christians should be good citizens and be involved redemptively in secular culture.

When Augustine died in Hippo in 430, he did so reading four of the penitential psalms of David that he had had copied out and pasted onto the walls of his bedroom. This reveals a final key area of his piety: a constant interaction with the Scriptures that nourished his thought as no other words could.

See also Pelagianism.

For Further Reading: *Augustine of Hippo, Selected Writings*, CWS (1984); P. Bright, ed., *Augustine and the Bible* (1999); P. Brown, *Augustine of Hippo* (2000); H. Chadwick, *Augustine* (2001); A. Fitzgerald, ed., *Augustine through the Ages* (1999); J. O'Donnell, *Augustine* (2005); B. Studer, *The Grace of Christ and the Grace of God in Augustine of Hippo*, trans. M. O'Connell (1997).

Michael A. G. Haykin

Authority

Power (*dunamis*) is the strength and ability to influence or control events or people. Authority (*exousia*) is the freedom or prerogative to act, the right to exercise power due to one's office or credentials. Authority legitimates the expression of power and designates the proper limits within which power is exercised.

The Trinitarian God possesses supreme authority and corresponding power to rule over creation, including the sovereign right to act in human history and rule nations (Acts 1:7; Dan. 2:21). All human authority originates with God, including that of civil institutions (Rom. 13:1–7). God delegates his authority to Jesus to establish his rule on earth (Matt. 28:18) and judge humanity (John 5:27). Jesus' authority derives from his obedient sonship (John 5:19–20) and sacrificial work (Phil. 2:5–11). He exercises authority over the spiritual realm (Eph. 1:21; 1 Peter 3:22) and manifests the power to rescue humans from Satan's rule by forgiving sins, subjugating demons, and dying for the sins of the world (Mark 2:10; Luke 4:36; John 10:18).

Jesus delegates his authority to the church to act on behalf of his global mission (Matt. 28:18–20). He authorized and empowered his disciples to heal, cast out demons, and proclaim the good news (Luke 9:1). Believers possess authority to live as God's children (John 1:12) and participate in his redemptive work by building up his church (2 Cor. 13:10) and furthering the gospel. Personal and collective spiritual authority is derived from a living relationship with the risen Christ made manifest by the Holy Spirit. It functions properly only where Jesus reigns as Lord (Matt. 18:20).

Submission to authority is necessary for communal harmony. Believers are urged to submit to leaders (1 Cor. 16:16; 1 Thess. 5:12–13; Heb. 13:17) and to one another out of reverence for Christ (Eph. 5:21; Phil. 2:3; 1 Peter 5:5). The abuse of authority is a demonic temptation to idolatry. The devil tempted Jesus to submit to his authority, not God's, and to use his power in an illegitimate manner (Luke 4:1–13). Jesus' delegated authority is expressed not as coercion, but as the power of a servant.

For Further Reading: R. Bauckham, *God and the Crisis of Freedom* (2002).

Mark W. McCloskey

Autobiography, Spiritual

From Augustine's *Confessions* to Julian of Norwich's *Revelations* to John Bunyan's *Grace Abounding*, the impulse to reflect on spiritual experience in first-person narrative has been perennial for Christians. I (*autos*) reflect upon my past experience (life, or *bios*) and represent this afresh in a form of words (*graphe*). My motivation for doing so may be doxological, as a monument of praise to God; it may be apologetic, to defend and explain my present spiritual condition; or it may be inspirational, to encourage others to share in a similar experience. But the principle by which a person selects, arranges, and highlights the events of his/her narrative will invariably be governed by theological conviction. Whereas the classical ideal saw the genre reserved for the mighty deeds of public men, the Christian tradition has fostered a much more egalitarian ideal in which each human life is potentially a theater for the divine drama of redemption. Because the "lives of the saints" display effectively how divine revelation is meant to terminate not in propositions but in the transformed lives of men and women, autobiography is a genre especially associated with spirituality. Spiritual autobiography was given new impetus with the vernacular mysticism of the late Middle Ages, and in the modern period it flourished, along with hymn singing, as one of the most distinctive forms of evangelical spirituality, given the evangelical emphasis on conversion and the personalizing of faith. For over three centuries, from the *Journal* of John Wesley to Charles Colson's *Born Again*, evangelical experience has been expressed in a variety of autobiographical forms. *The Diaries of John Sung*, Chinese evangelist, illustrate the continuing importance of this genre in the global spread of evangelical Christianity.

See also Biographies; Testimony.

For Further Reading: D. B. Hindmarsh, *The Evangelical Conversion Narrative* (2005); A. Mandelker and E. Powers, eds., *Pilgrim Souls* (1999); P. Ricoeur, "Life: A Story in Search of a Narrator," in *Facts and Values*, ed. M. Doeser and J. Kraay (1986), 121 – 32.

D. Bruce Hindmarsh

Awe

See **Fear of the Lord.**

B

Bach, Johann Sebastian (1685 – 1750)

German composer and organist. Born into an extended family of Lutheran church musicians, he attended the choir school at St. Michael's Church in Lüneburg. From 1703 until 1707, he worked as a church organist in Arnstadt then accepted a similar position in Mühlhausen, but soon resigned, claiming he had not been able to achieve his vocational goal of producing a "well-regulated church music." In 1708 he became chapel organist for Duke Wilhelm Ernst August in Weimar. Eventually falling out of favor with his employer, he accepted an offer in 1717 to become music director for the Prince of Anhalt-Cöthen. Because the court was Calvinist, Bach's duties were now largely confined to instrumental music.

From 1723 until his death, Bach worked in Leipzig as cantor of St. Thomas Church and city music director. His primary duties included overseeing the music education of the boys at the Thomasschule and providing music for Leipzig's four main churches. He composed weekly cantatas, rehearsing and performing them alternately in the Churches of St. Thomas and St. Nicholas, while furnishing music for weddings, funerals, and civic occasions as needed. Major vocal works from this time include the *Magnificat*, the *St. John Passion*, the *St. Matthew Passion*, the *Christmas Oratorio*, and the *Mass in B Minor*.

Bach reportedly composed five liturgical cantata cycles, of which nearly two hundred individual pieces survive. These represent the core of his life work. Though his production slowed in the late 1720s (due perhaps to discouragement with his work environment), he continued to rehearse and perform cantatas regularly for the rest of his life. Placed between the gospel reading and the sermon, cantatas served as musical exegesis of the day's scriptural theme(s), and Bach's profound treatments of the text establish him as an authoritative expositor of Scripture.

Bach's interest in biblical themes and his identity as a committed believer are confirmed by the contents of his library, which included two complete editions of Luther's writings, Abraham Calov's *Bible Commentary* (with marginalia in his own hand, highlighting, for example, passages encouraging believers to persevere in their divinely appointed vocations), and scores of other works by both Pietist and Orthodox writers—as well as by the Christian symbolism he often incorporated in his pieces. Furthermore, he demonstrated a keen interest in the Lutheran chorale, basing many of his organ and vocal works on traditional tunes and texts.

After Felix Mendelssohn resurrected the *St. Matthew Passion* in 1830, an event credited with launching the so-called Bach awakening, Bach's status as a composer rose to unparalleled heights, while his work became for many an enduring legacy of Christian devotion.

For Further Reading: H. David and A. Mendel, eds., *The New Bach Reader*, rev. C. Wolff (1998); J. Pelikan, *Bach among the Theologians* (1986); M. Unger, *Handbook to Bach's Sacred Cantata Texts* (1996); C. Wolff, *Johann Sebastian Bach: The Learned Musician* (2000).

Melvin P. Unger

Baillie, John (1886–1960)

Renowned Scottish theologian and ecumenist. Reared in the evangelical Calvinism of a Free Church manse and educated in Scotland and Germany, Baillie taught theology in Canada and America before returning to New College, Edinburgh, in 1934. His thought channeled the conservative piety of his upbringing and the liberal theology of his education into nuanced examinations of the human response to the divine initiative. The presence of God, encountered in Scripture and sacrament, history and the religious consciousness, is comprehended through faith, reason, and experience; it evokes grateful worship, prayer, and self-reflection leading to righteous action. Baillie's interest in the diverse human answer to the divine Word presumed a more generous scope to revelation than that allowed by the exclusivist Word-centered theology of Karl Barth then dominant in Reformed circles. As such, in alliance with his brother, Donald, his mediating theology offered a critical but genuine appreciation for the phenomenon of religion that fostered a truly catholic spirituality. This so-called liberal evangelicalism is beautifully expressed in *A Diary of Private Prayer*—a spiritual companion for tens of thousands of Protestant ministers and laypersons since its 1936 publication. A devoted churchman, Baillie was also prominent in the formation and incipient leadership of the World Council of Churches.

For Further Reading: D. Fergusson, ed., *Christ, Church and Society: Essays on John Baillie and Donald Baillie* (1993).

Todd Statham

Balthasar, Hans Urs von (1905–1988)

Swiss theologian of aesthetics. Author of over a thousand books and articles, Balthasar was one of the most culturally proficient and prolific of Roman Catholic theologians. For many years a Jesuit (1929–1950), he was also among the first Roman Catholics to take Karl Barth seriously. They became fast friends in Basel, where Balthasar, twenty years Barth's junior, was a university chaplain. Barth approved of the young man's interpretation of his writing, and Balthasar, like Barth, became rigorously Christ-centered in his theology.

Balthasar is not easily categorized because of the breadth of his scholarship. He is distinctive in emphasizing the importance of beauty in God and in the Christian life. His huge scholarly work *The Glory of the Lord* (1982–1991), written in multiple volumes, has the subtitle *A Theological Aesthetics*. Perhaps no modern theologian since Jonathan Edwards has given such attention to the aesthetic perspective. For him, the beauty of God is manifest in the divine glory. Balthasar focused in a distinctive way on the saving events in the life of Christ of the cross, the descent into hell, and the resurrection. His *Mysterium Paschale* (Mystery of Easter; 2000) delineates the profound love of God in which Jesus goes even to hell to save to the uttermost.

Like his contemporary Karl Rahner, Balthasar wrote about spirituality as well as theology. His book *Prayer* (1961) asserts, "Prayer is communication, in which God's word has the initiative and we, at first, are simply listeners." For Balthasar, then, the gospel must always be the norm and critique of all spirituality in the church. His other spiritual writings include *Engagement with God* (1975).

See also Beauty.

For Further Reading: E. Oakes and D. Moss, eds., *The Cambridge Companion to Hans Urs von Balthasar* (2004).

Bradley P. Holt

Baptism

Christian spirituality is fundamentally a baptismal spirituality. To be a Christian is to be a baptized one (Matt. 28:18; Acts 2:38; Rom. 6:3–4). The meaning of baptism is, in many respects, the meaning of the Christian life. Baptism is an act of union with Christ. The Christian is marked by radical identification with the cross of Christ; indeed, baptism suggests that one's primary identity is now completely in Christ. This identification speaks of both death and life and becomes the central fact of one's existence. In baptism one is buried with Christ (Col. 2:12) and then made alive in and through him. This suggests that baptism is also a political act, for in baptism one essentially declares that ultimate allegiance is owed only to Christ—not to family or clan, denomination or nation, but only to the one who is Lord of all.

Acts 2:38–42 fleshes out the full meaning of baptism and thus of a baptismal spirituality: "Repent and be baptized, every one of you, in the name of Jesus Christ for the forgiveness of your sins. And you will receive the gift of the Holy Spirit.... They devoted themselves to the apostles' teaching and to the fellowship, to the breaking of bread and to prayer." We note, then, that baptism speaks of the forgiveness of sins: the washing away of guilt and the purification of conscience (1 Peter 3:21). A baptized person is a forgiven person, and to live as a baptized person is to live under God's mercy in deep awareness of the amazing grace by which one is saved from sin and death.

Baptism also speaks of the gift of the Spirit. Many Christians, especially those in Eastern traditions, see a link between Acts 2:38 and the experience of Jesus when he was baptized by John the Baptist. They have viewed the baptism of Jesus as the model or example that gives meaning to the Christian baptism, suggesting that in similar fashion one's baptism speaks of the grace of the Spirit given to each Christian as he or she comes to faith in Christ.

And then also, baptism speaks of one's identity within the faith community, the church. Baptism is a rite of initiation into Christian fellowship and thus to one's participation in the body of Christ. Thus, baptism is an ecumenical act; there is one baptism (Eph. 4:5) and by this act one is incorporated into a people whose fundamental identity is not race or language or gender but rather a common faith in Christ.

See also Conversion; Sacrament; Water.

For Further Reading: G. Beasley-Murray, *Baptism in the New Testament* (1962); D. Bridge and D. Phypers, *The Waters That Divide* (1977); O. Brooks, *The Drama of Decision: Baptism in the New Testament* (1987); K. Roy, *Baptism, Reconciliation and Unity* (1997).

Gordon T. Smith

Baptism of the Holy Spirit

Interestingly, the proclamation that Jesus is the one "who will baptize with the Holy Spirit" (John 1:33) is attributed to John the Baptist in all four canonical Gospels (cf. Matt. 3:11; Mark 1:8; Luke 3:16)—interesting for its unanimity there, and equally for its relative absence in the rest of the gospel material and the NT as a whole.

While the explicit imagery of baptism in or with the Spirit is lacking elsewhere in Scripture, it is likely that Luke intends his readers to understand Pentecost as the fulfillment of John the Baptist's prophecy. In his inaugural Christian sermon on the day of Pentecost, Peter preaches that God had promised through the prophet Joel to "pour out my Spirit on all people" (Acts 2:17) and that the resurrected Jesus, having "received from the Father the promised Holy Spirit . . . has poured out what you now see and hear" (2:33). The language of "outpouring" readily bespeaks baptism; here it is Jesus who is the paradigmatic recipient of the promised Spirit of the God of Israel, and who in turn pours out the Spirit on the fledgling church. Similarly, the gospel of John narrates that the resurrected Jesus appears among his beleaguered disciples, and, blessing them with divine shalom, breathes on them and says, "Receive the Holy Spirit" (John 20:19–22). In these stories, then, the baptism, presence, and power of the Spirit are all tied closely to the person of Jesus, the Anointed of the Spirit (cf. Acts 10:38).

The majority tradition in the history of Christian thought has understood the baptism of the Spirit, then, to be associated with the creation of the church and, derivatively, with the initiation of individual believers into the Christian community with its faith and practices. In this regard, the baptism of the Spirit has been closely linked to water baptism and regeneration.

Probably the most glaring exception to this majority interpretation arose in the eschatological expectations of the visionary twelfth-century thinker Joachim of Fiore, who anticipated a revolutionary Age of the Spirit to commence in 1260. By placing the Spirit's reality largely in the future, Joachim tended to dissociate the presence and activity of the Spirit from church history up to and including his own time; for him, the "baptism of the Spirit" most properly named an era yet to come. This association of the Spirit with a radically eschatological future has drawn the guarded admiration of contemporary Protestant theologian Jürgen Moltmann, but created its own set of problems by its tendency to sever the Spirit's presence and activity from the historical figure of Jesus Christ and the *ekklesia* he established.

In the centuries after Joachim, a considerable number of Christian movements made comparable claims regarding the Spirit. The Puritan, Methodist, and nineteenth-century Holiness movements, for example, all tended in their own ways to distinguish between Christian conversion as faith in Christ and a subsequent experience of the Spirit, often (though not always) described as Spirit baptism. For Puritans, this second experience was identified as assurance of one's election; for John Wesley and his Methodists, it was identified as Christian perfection or entire sanctification—the pure love of God expelling all sin.

The Pentecostal movement, which traces its recent beginnings to the Azusa Street revival in early twentieth-century Los Angeles, offered an interpretation of Spirit baptism that was at least partially dependent on these earlier traditions. Thus, Pentecostals generally have insisted that the baptism of the Spirit is a work of God in the Christian believer that occurs subsequent to conversion. While this Spirit baptism may be understood to purify the believer of the effects and power of original sin, or to fill the believer with divine love, the emphasis usually has fallen on the notion of empowerment for service (especially of bearing Christian witness). This interpretation draws heavily upon the Lukan tradition, in which Jesus instructs his disciples to "stay in the city [Jerusalem] until you have been clothed with power from on high" (Luke 24:49; cf. Acts 1:8). This anticipation of an outpouring of the Spirit's power found fulfillment at Pentecost; further, since the disciples there "were filled with the Holy Spirit and began to speak in other tongues as the Spirit enabled them" (Acts 2:4), Christians in the Pentecostal movement largely have understood the Spirit baptism of a Christian believer to be properly (and, generally speaking, inevitably) evidenced by the gift of tongues.

The charismatic renewal movement, beginning roughly in the late 1960s, has tended not to insist on the gift of tongues as the evidence of Spirit baptism, seeing it instead as but one of the Spirit's many possible gifts to Christian believers.

The very phrase "baptism of the Holy Spirit" itself seems to imply a decisive and dramatic experience of some kind. It has thus found its most extensive usage in Christian communities that place a higher premium on individual experience of the Spirit's presence and power. Such an emphasis may at times foster an overdependence on dramatic experiences and lead to extreme subjectivism; this danger has been acknowledged in Pentecostal, charismatic, and American Holiness circles alike.

The most effective, and most theologically astute, corrective to such radical subjectivism is to acknowledge that the Spirit—and so also the baptism of the Spirit—is inevitably and closely linked to Jesus Christ throughout the NT writings. An experience of the Spirit is, fundamentally, an experience of the Christ witnessed to in the Scriptures. So, for example, Paul wrote that the Spirit whom God sends into our hearts is "the Spirit of his Son"—and that it is precisely this Spirit of God's Son who cries "Abba, Father!" Paul's description of this rather dramatic experience, then, likely needs to be understood in relation to the cry of Jesus in the garden of Gethsemane (Mark 14:36).

Outside the Pentecostal, charismatic, and American Holiness movements, both Roman Catholic and Protestant interpreters have tended largely to call attention to the early church's association of Spirit baptism with water baptism, without simply equating the two. The result has been a renewed emphasis on the idea that the Spirit gives regenerating life to new believers as they are initiated into the Christian community.

See also Fire; Pentecostal Spirituality; Puritan Spirituality.

For Further Reading: J. Dunn, *Baptism in the Holy Spirit* (1970); K. McDonnell and G. Montague, *Christian Initiation and Baptism in the Holy Spirit* (1991); J. Moltmann, *The Spirit of Life* (1992); C. Pinnock, *Flame of Love* (1996); R. Staples, *Outward Sign and Inward Grace* (1991).

Michael Lodahl

Baptist Spirituality

Baptist spirituality derived its initial features from Puritanism in England in the early 17th century when Baptists originated, but it has undergone significant modifications over the four centuries of Baptist history, particularly in America. In its Puritan beginnings, Baptist spirituality is best characterized as a contemplative spirituality, for the Puritans, though they looked to John Calvin for their theology, deliberately revived many features of late-medieval monastic piety. As John Bunyan, the chief architect of Baptist spirituality, depicted it in his spiritual autobiography, *Grace Abounding*, and in *The Pilgrim's Progress*, Puritan/Baptist devotion revolved around intense meditation on Scriptures and extemporaneous prayer reminiscent of *lectio divina*. Bunyan said that he was "never out of the Scriptures." Like other Puritans, Baptists also used the Psalms in corporate worship and in their homes.

They diverged from other Puritans, however, in their application of the voluntary principle in religion. Resisting the efforts of James I (1603–1625) and Charles I (1625–1649) to impose the *Book of Common Prayer*, Bunyan opposed recitation not only of set prayers from the prayer book but even the Lord's Prayer. Prayer must come from the heart under inspiration of the Spirit in accordance with Scriptures. Although this outlook tended to push them toward the individualist end of the faith spectrum, Baptists also valued intimate local gatherings where they admonished and encouraged one another through preaching and praying together.

Baptist spirituality shifted from a contemplative to a conversionist mode during the Great Awakening (c. 1720–1750), which accentuated the experience of conversion. Baptists now meditated on Scriptures and prayed, whether individually or corporately, not so much for their impact on their entire spiritual lives as on the front end of them—conversion, whether one's own experience or the conversion experiences of others. In effect they focused on the pilgrim's *beginning* rather than the pilgrim's *progress*. When business burgeoned during the 19th century in America, where 80 percent of Baptists reside today, Baptist spirituality absorbed much of the pragmatism that characterized it. As in other businesses, spirituality involved negotiating with God the terms of their covenant. The faithful prayed to achieve the objectives of the corporation—winning converts, building new edifices, improving finances, and the rest.

A traumatic 20th century produced a wide array of spiritualities from which Baptists, like other Christians, have opted to choose: contemplative, conversionist, holiness, charismatic, social justice, incarnational, evangelical, secular, oriental or quasi-oriental, diverse Roman Catholic (Benedictine, Cistercian, Franciscan, Dominican, Carmelite, Ignatian, et al.), or other religious traditions (Orthodox, Reformed, Quaker, Methodist, et al.). Because of their commitment to individual liberty and group autonomy, one will find a Baptist or two attracted to one or more of these options, which are not mutually exclusive. A large number are seeking to return to their contemplative roots. An intense zeal for missions and evangelism tilts the spirituality of most persons in the Southern Baptist Convention toward a conversionist approach.

The quest for holiness characterizes some Primitive Baptist groups, while North American (German) and Baptist General Conference (Swedish) Baptists still reflect, to some extent, their heritage of European Pietism. The modern charismatic movement has drawn a number of Baptists, including some churches, into it. Social justice has appealed to large numbers of Baptists, particularly African-Americans and persons sympathetic with their cause. Many Baptists have felt a pull toward the liturgical and incarnational spirituality of the Church of England. A large number of Baptists in the southern United States would identify themselves as evangelicals, who stress the Bible and doctrine as keys to the spiritual life. Secular spirituality exerted a potent pull for many Baptists during the 1960s. Similarly, New Age and oriental, or quasi-oriental, spiritualities have attracted Baptists.

So, too, have offerings of other Christian traditions. It is not surprising to see Baptists retreat to Roman Catholic monasteries or obtain spiritual direction from a priest, monk, or nun. Some serious Baptist seekers find real spiritual help in a particular Catholic contemplative tradition, such as the Ignatian, Benedictine, Cistercian, or Carmelite, and sometimes identify with a special figure in such traditions, such as Francis de Sales or Thomas Merton.

Others have felt drawn toward Eastern Orthodoxy, the Church of England, or other Protestant church traditions in much the same way. As Western culture reverses the shift from an iconic and tactual to a more typographic mode on the eve of the Reformation of the 16th century, many Baptists are discovering icons not simply on their computer screens but in Orthodox churches. They have also rediscovered the deeply biblical liturgy of the Church of England they once spurned. In an increasingly noisy world, others have reappraised the Quaker emphasis on silence. The critical challenge for Baptist spirituality today is to hold on to what is of the essence of its own tradition while sampling such a bewildering array of spiritualities.

See also Anabaptist Spirituality; Puritan Spirituality.

For Further Reading: E. G. Hinson, "Baptist and Quaker Spirituality," in *Christian Spirituality: Post-Reformation and Modern*, ed. L. Dupré and D. Saliers (1989), 324–37; idem, "Baptist Approaches to Spirituality," *Baptist History and Heritage* 37, no. 2 (2002): 6–31.

E. Glenn Hinson

Barth, Karl (1886–1968)

Reformed theologian and pastor. Born in Basel, Switzerland, Barth became one of the most influential and extensively published Christian thinkers of the modern era. His theological education, which took him to the German universities of Berne, Berlin, and Marburg, abruptly ended in 1909; thereafter he served as pastor in the Swiss village of Safenwil (1911–1921).

Barth's academic career began in 1921 when he accepted the chair in Reformed theology at the University of Göttingen. That opportunity came as the result of a commentary he had published on Romans in 1918, one that made clear how passionately concerned with Holy Scripture Barth was. This constituted a very different sort of theology for his time. Barth's Word-centered theology found detailed expression in his thirteen-volume *Church Dogmatics* (1931–1968).

For Barth, the human encounters divine revelation as reality first and possibility second. By *possibility* Barth meant the reflective ability to "tell ourselves" what God has already told us about himself. This reiterative knowing and speaking of God is roughly equivalent to what is commonly called *experience* of God; it is existential knowledge. Whatever we come to think and speak reflectively of God, in fact, however we do these things, is given positive shape and critical delimitation by our prior encounter with God's Word. Our thinking and speaking are thus a repetition of God's own.

Consequently, people should never regard their existence as an adequate basis on which to construct a genuine spirituality. There are no experiential criteria (such as feelings of dependence, beatific visions, or peculiar senses of comfort) by which to validate the reality of God's revelation and our genuine engagement with it. That would be, in effect, to establish the reality of God after our possibility—to mediate God's revelation according to some class of assumed human qualities.

Barth did not intend to invalidate human experience per se, but rather to set it in its proper relation to God's act. Consistent with his Reformed heritage, he simply wanted to allow God to remain the free and living God in our experience; free, that is, to constitute each moment of his real contact with human life. God takes up entirely human attributes in his revelation but does not leave them "as they are." Rather, he assumes flesh and language in a way that they become adequate to him: as Lord he lives in the unfettered power to continually relate himself to that which he is not, and which even stands against him.

To illustrate Barth's critical attitude toward the spiritual life as a human possession on the one side, together with his positive portrayal of that life when and where it is the ongoing experience of God's act on the other, it is instructive to consider Barth's well-known critique of Pietism. While Barth's criticisms softened over time, his basic reservations about Pietism remained in effect: like mysticism, Pietism attempted to locate a privileged way to God. The Pietists at least appreciated the extent of human sin and thus passionately embraced the way of sacrifice and negation. But for them it still was a *way* of negation. For Barth, by contrast, self-sacrifice and personal asceticism cannot be prescribed as means to an end, for such means are already corrupted by our human sin and limitations. God's negation of our humanity is so total that we cannot take even our self-denial for granted as being the way of life in God's Spirit.

After Christ, we certainly do live in the disposition of humility and obedience to God

(Phil. 2). In describing the spiritual life, however, we dare not imagine innate knowledge capacities within the human spirit, or look to meditative routines as channels of the divine, or turn to sacred practices as tapping into the deep recesses of our soul. We might do such things, too, but never as given means. Rather, we confess the obedience of Christ as, in fact, our own, to the extent that God continually places us in him.

In other words, the secondary possibility of reflectively experiencing God is not a human but a divine possibility. For Barth, God *is* as he is known in Christ Jesus. Yet this knowledge, again, is not as a construct, feeling, or datum we natively have and build upon. It is rather a realm-structuring, kingdom-advancing, existential event continually brought about by the Holy Spirit. The Spirit-filled life is thus the continuing event of faith created and sustained by God as we are constituted in the life of Christ. Barth's is a holistic spirituality: perceiving moment by moment in our human operations what we humanly cannot—namely, *God's* truth. As the Spirit places God before us and sets us before him in the witness to Christ, which is to say, as God himself continually elects the reality of Scripture as the condition of every possibility, so we are.

See also Reformed (Calvinist) Spirituality.

For Further Reading: E. Busch, *Karl Barth and the Pietists*, trans. D. Bloesch (2004); E. Jüngel, *God as the Mystery of the World*, trans. D. Guder (1983); W. Krötke, "The Humanity of the Human Person in Karl Barth's Anthropology," trans. P. Ziegler, in *The Cambridge Companion to Karl Barth*, ed. J. Webster (2000), 159–76; A. Lewis, *Between Cross and Resurrection* (2001); J. Mangina, *Karl Barth on the Christian Life* (2001); J. Webster, *Barth's Moral Theology* (1998).

Aaron T. Smith

Basil of Caesarea (330–379)

Bishop of Caesarea, liturgist, and theologian. Although raised in a wealthy Christian family and educated at the highest levels in Constantinople and Athens, Basil did not come to Christian faith until his conversion at age thirty. Of this conversion he wrote: "I opened my eyes to the wonderful life of the evangelical truth." He and his younger brother, Gregory of Nyssa, and his best friend, Gregory of Nazianzus, comprise the Cappadocian fathers. For a time, he lived the monastic life, writing a rule that is still used today in Orthodox coenobitic monasteries. Eventually his spiritual insights, administrative gifts, and theological brilliance led to his ordination and then election as bishop of Caesarea.

Basil stood firm for the truth of the Nicene Creed against the continuing attacks of the Arians who denied the divinity of Jesus and the Holy Spirit. His two major writings in this battle are *Against Eunomius* and *On the Holy Spirit*. In the first, he argued persuasively not only for the unbegottenness of the Son, but also for the eternal, ineffable generation of the Son. Hence the Son proceeds from the Father and has done and will continue to do so eternally.

On the Holy Spirit was written to defend against direct attacks of the Spirit's divinity by the aptly named *pneumatomachi* (fighters against the Spirit). Basil was the first to truly claim equality for the Spirit within the Godhead. He thus developed a vocabulary for speaking of the "three in one/one in three" that is still in use today in both the East and West. His unwillingness to deny the Spirit equal power and presence means that in later Eastern Orthodox spirituality, the Holy Spirit is more obviously central in liturgy, prayer, and even polity than is readily apparent in the Western church. Indeed, Basil's desire for equality of the Godhead is still crucially important. In the 6th century, the Nicene-Constantinopolitan Creed of 381 was translated to Latin for the Western church. In doing so, one phrase was altered to say the Holy Spirit proceeds "from the Father *and from the Son.*" The Eastern church fathers declared that this addition of the "filioque" ("from the Son") was a reduction of the fullness of the Godhead and a change they had not approved. The difference between Eastern and Western creeds remains to this day.

Basil believed that the Scriptures should be read and studied in order not only to live eternally with God, but also to show God's love for his people here and now. In famine and sickness, Basil made sure the church organized care for the poor, a ministry in which he personally assisted. He also transformed the liturgy of the church, encouraging all to attend and claiming that worship was the heart of true theology. Basil died at the age of forty-nine, leaving behind more than 350 letters and a tremendous legacy in both East and West.

See also Cappadocians.

For Further Reading: G. Barrios, trans. and ed., *The Fathers Speak* (1986); L. Bouyer, *A History of Spirituality* 1 (1982): 335–43; S. Hildebrand, *The Trinitarian Theology of Basil of Caesarea* (2007); V. Lossky, *In the Image and Likeness of God* (1985).

Kelby Cotton

Baxter, Richard (1615–1691)

Puritan pastor and prolific theologian. Ordained in 1638, though sickly and lacking a university degree, he effectively discipled Kidderminster, a town of two thousand adults, during the Interregnum. With over seventeen hundred other clergy, he left the Anglican ministry in 1662, refusing the terms of ministerial continuance in the restorationist Act of Uniformity, and became a full-time writer. At Kidderminster he produced three outstanding books, the massive *Saints' Everlasting Rest*, the electrifying *Reformed Pastor*, and the piercing *Call to the Unconverted*. Later masterworks were the compendious *Christian Directory* and *Life of Faith*, and *The Divine Life*, on knowing, walking with, and meditating on God. Despite his acceptance of the Anglican articles, the Canons of Dort, and the Westminster standards, his "political" spin on the doctrines of atonement and justification, plus his overall irenic eclecticism, set him apart from other Puritans and led to his being called a "Baxterian," the only one of his kind. Yet his pastoral presentations of the gospel, conversion to Christ, Christian obedience, and whole-souled communion with God were purely Puritan and classic of their kind.

Baxter developed four Puritan emphases distinctively.

First, *rationality*. Stressing the intrinsic reasonableness of Christianity and the unreasonableness of infidelity, Baxter rationally analyzed all theology and taught analytical discursive meditation as the way to know the power and pleasure of revealed divine realities. Thus, explicitly, he evoked heart love to the lovely Creator God of nature who is the loving Redeemer God of Scripture. Involving imagination in analogizing from the seen to the unseen was for him integral to this process.

Second, *duty*. Both as human beings and as converted believers, Christians must seek ever to keep God's law, and where the law enunciates nothing directly, they must labor by casuistical analysis to discern and do what will please God most. Important, therefore, are educating conscience, cultivating virtuous habits, mortifying vicious ones, and maintaining humility and self-distrust in the face of the deceitful sinfulness of our hearts. Conscious embrace of the lordship of Christ must be central throughout.

Third, *hope*. Baxter directed Christians to meditate for at least half an hour daily on their hope of heaven, thus energizing themselves and being energized by God for consecrated living. His own self-discipline here helps to explain his seemingly limitless energy in ministry.

Fourth, *discipleship*. "The primitive, pure, simple Christianity consisted in the daily serious use of … the Creed, Lord's Prayer, and Ten Commandments." This is the true path for all. "Do thus, and thou wilt be like those examples of the succeeding church, in uprightness, purity, simplicity, charity, peaceableness, and holy communion with God." In this dimension of historic churchliness, Baxter's vision and heart found their abiding anchorage.

See also Puritan Spirituality.

For Further Reading: R. Baxter, *Practical Works*, 4 vols. (1990); T. Beougher, *Richard Baxter and Conversion* (2007); N. H. Keeble and G. F. Nuttall, *Calendar of the Correspondence of Richard Baxter*, 2 vols. (1991); J. I. Packer, *The Redemption and Restoration of Man in the Thought of Richard Baxter* (2003).

J. I. Packer

Beatitudes

Beatitudes are promises in Scripture guaranteeing God's blessings in terms of supernatural benefits and provisions. The use of the passive voice ("blessed is," "blessed are") is a reminder that God is the one who graciously blesses his people with gifts.

Some beatitudes are found in the OT; for example, at the very outset of the Psalms, "Blessed are those . . ." (Ps. 1:1 – 2 TNIV). But the best-known beatitudes are the nine listed in the opening verses of Jesus' Sermon on the Mount (Matt. 5:3 – 12). These beatitudes include positive character qualities to emulate (poverty of spirit, meekness, mercy, purity of heart) or describe various activities to be undertaken (mourning, hungering and thirsting for righteousness). On the side opposite these promised blessings, and directed toward others, are warnings of coming judgment. For example, Jesus pronounced God's judgment ("Woe to you . . .") seven times on the teachers of the law and Pharisees in Matthew 23:13 – 36, following each pronouncement with a specific explanation for it.

Those who desire to experience God's blessing, and avoid his judgment, will naturally be inclined to align their lives accordingly. Yet it is important to see that these are not legalistic means of earning or deserving God's blessings. Being pure in heart or genuinely hungering and thirsting after righteousness never take place simply through human effort. Implicitly there is an element of God's antecedent grace and goodness in all the beatitudes. Yet at the same time there is also a crucial role for human choice and involvement in experiencing the blessings of these beatitudes. These blessings do not come indiscriminately or automatically upon everyone; rather, they are calls for action. They are designed to motivate and help prepare people for God's blessings by prompting them to seek out God who alone can meet all of their needs. The beatitudes should serve as catalysts for changed lives by highlighting the dispositions and behaviors that are particularly pleasing to a holy and righteous God.

See also Kingdom of God; Lord's Prayer; Mercy; Social Justice.

For Further Reading: D. Garland, "Blessing and Woe," *Dictionary of Jesus and the Gospels*, ed. J. Green et al. (1992); R. Guelich, *The Sermon on the Mount* (1982); T. Johnson, *When Grace Transforms* (2002); P. Yancey, *The Jesus I Never Knew* (1995).

Brian C. Labosier

Beauty

Beauty has often played Cinderella at the theological ball. Her two sisters, truth and goodness, have enjoyed more attention and respect, while she has languished, unwanted in the highest levels of theological reflection. As a result of such theological disenfranchisement, beauty is everywhere trivialized, sentimentalized, and commodified. The pagan ancients saw it as a reality coequal with truth and goodness, and they revered and even worshiped it. Our own century has seen it nearly emptied of meaning in the twisting it has undergone in commercial "beauty" culture. The fine arts also seem at times far from beauty's precincts, and the viewer is often bewildered by its absence in the gallery. There even seems to be a deliberate attack staged against beauty in much contemporary art. How do we understand or receive beauty? What is its proper place in the spiritual life, and how is it to be defined?

The classical starting point for arriving at a definition of beauty is the human body. Its proportions, face and form, graceful movement, and athletic power—all are seen as admirable in themselves, apart from their usefulness. Physical beauty compels our appreciation, even when we decry its overemphasis in society. Moral virtue and wisdom are ranked higher in Scripture, but thankfully comparisons are seldom invited. Simply put, beauty needs no justification but is gratuitous and everywhere present in God's creation. The millions of varieties of flowers, bird plumage, and everything from ice crystals to nebulae are all without explicit pragmatic value but yet still beautiful in themselves. It is as though God has said, "People do not live by bread alone, but require beauty as much as physical sustenance."

Hunger for beauty is manifest everywhere. Yet Christians sometimes question its importance and are even vaguely suspicious of it—as though it might be a distraction from holiness. This is the result of confusion over its trivialized state and loss of true essence. What passes for beautiful is often an abased notion more like "prettiness" than a fully developed sense of the beautiful. Indeed, mere prettiness can be corrosive in relationships, in self-image, even in aesthetics and the arts. The demand that our own bodies conform to fashions of prettiness can lead to extreme self-treatment and even self-hatred, with serious potential for mental and emotional illness. But in the Psalms, for example, genuine beauty is always connected with God's creation and is thought to reflect and manifest God's "glory" (*kabod* or *shekinah*). The reality of this glory is transcendent and awe-inspiring and probably better translated as *sublime beauty*.

The category of the sublime was hotly debated in eighteenth- and early-nineteenth-century Europe and addressed in Edmund Burke's *On the Sublime* (1756). In this magisterial essay, Burke elucidated a theory of beauty and the sublime that opposes these two—associating beauty with pleasure and relaxed joy, while connecting the sublime with awe, terror, and trembling. But the biblical vision of God's glory combines beauty and the sublime in one profound reality—*shekinah*.

Beauty at its most real is embedded with truth, goodness, and majesty in God's character and being. The fact that the creation is radiating this glory in a reflected manner is a clue that beauty and sublimity are at the heart of both God's general and special revelation. The pillar of cloud and fire, the burning bush, the stormy manifestations throughout the OT, and most perfectly in the revelation of God's mystery in Christ—all these point to the vision of sublime beauty contained in the Bible.

Exodus 28–31 outlines specific instructions on how the Tent of Meeting and the priestly accoutrements were to be fashioned—and beauty is specifically yoked to glory in the very beginning of these passages. Not only this, but the fact that these instructions are God-breathed is driven home when the artists Bezalel and Oholiab are described as "filled with the Spirit of God in wisdom, in understanding, in knowledge, and in all kinds of artistic craftsmanship." Beauty is everywhere enshrined in the Tent of Meeting.

So at the meeting place between God and human beings beauty and glory are joined as the fitting evocation of the most profound mystery: the divine joining with the human, as the apostle Paul says it, "Christ in you, the hope of glory." This can be seen as the divine underwriting of the human enterprise of art—that is, of beauty-making. Over all of this hovers the deepest and most beautiful mystery of all, the incarnation—God taking on the *human* measure of beauty, the body, and upturning it through his *kenosis* (Isa. 53).

In our practices of Christian spirituality, there will always be a place for the contemplation of the beautiful—both in God's creation and more directly in the character and reality of God's own being. Beauty is at the heart of our Creator, and our love of God leads us inexorably to celebrate God's sublime beauty as coequal with God's truth and goodness.

See also Balthasar, Hans Urs von.

For Further Reading: H. U. von Balthasar, *Seeing the Form*, trans. E. Leiva-Merikakis (1982); H. G. Gadamer, *The Relevance of the Beautiful*, trans. R. Bernasconi (1987); E. Gilson, *The Arts of the Beautiful* (1965); B. Herman, "Wounds and Beauty," in *The Beauty of God*, ed. D. Trier (2006), 110 – 20.

Bruce Herman

Bede (The Venerable Bede) (c. 672 – 735)

Early English biblical scholar and church historian. Bede was born near Durham, England, entered Benedictine monastic life at age seven, becoming a deacon at nineteen and a priest at thirty. At the time, his monastery at Wearmouth-Jarrow had one of the largest libraries in the Western world, and also received many visitors who expanded the monk's awareness of the larger world. Bede absorbed this learning, blended it with Celtic Christian traditions of piety and evangelism, and put it to work in the service of the church. Altogether he wrote more than sixty books, including theological treatises, expositions of Scripture, translations, natural history, and even hymns.

Bede is best known for his five-volume *Ecclesiastical History of the English People*, which chronicles the history of England from Caesar's invasion in 55 BC to the events of Bede's own day. These books provide extensive insights into how English Christianity, culture, and society developed. Bede's use of multiple sources and attention to detail makes this work an important source for the self-understanding of the English; it is one of the greatest works of history of the early Middle Ages.

For Bede the writing of history was a spiritual discipline. He personally modeled the integration of intellect with love of Christ for the service of the church. He closed his own last book, which contains most of the limited information available about him, with a short prayer that captures his understanding of the role of intellect in Christian spirituality: "And I pray thee, loving Jesus, that as Thou hast graciously given me to drink in with delight the words of Thy knowledge, so Thou wouldst mercifully grant me to attain one day to Thee, the fountain of all wisdom and to appear forever before Thy face."

For Further Reading: G. H. Brown, *Bede the Venerable* (1987); D. H. Farmer, ed., *The Age of Bede* (1983); B. Ward, *The Venerable Bede* (1998).

Christopher Morton

Beguines

Laywomen who founded Christian communities beginning in the late twelfth century were part of a widespread spiritual renewal in which tens of thousands of women encountered a personal relationship with Jesus. Viewing themselves as brides of Christ, middle-class women in the emerging towns of northern Europe pooled their resources to establish houses where they could pursue Christ, share vibrant fellowship, and serve the needy. Eventually known as Beguines, many of the first women came from well-to-do burgher families. Initially including women who lived at home, the Beguines were predominantly widows and single maids who formed communities across Belgium, Germany, the Netherlands, and northern France. Their first households were small, but after receiving endowments from Countess Johanna of Flanders and other nobility in the 1230s, scores of large Beguine complexes (*beguinages* or *Begijnhoven*) were established in Belgium, each housing several hundred women. Strasbourg boasted a thousand Beguines, and Cologne two thousand.

Beguine communities provided a safe domicile with opportunity for spiritual formation where older women mentored younger sisters and all heard Scripture read daily. Because Bibles were few, those desiring to learn God's Word joined such a community. Committing themselves to chastity and obedience, Beguines lived a semimonastic life but were always free to leave the *beguinage*. Most Beguines supported themselves by working in the textile industry, teaching children, serving as maids, or ministering to the sick and dying. Income beyond what was required for their subsistence was given to the poor.

Many women possessed a basic education and were able to read and write in the vernacular. Several thirteenth-century Beguines wrote devotional works, poetry, and Christian formation manuals—some of the first literature in Europe's vernacular languages—providing spiritual reading to other Beguines and laypeople. Hadewijch of Brabant, the most skilled Beguine author, employed the genre of courtly love poetry to express the inner sweetness we experience with Jesus, as well as the heartache we endure as we mature beyond the blush of first love. Mechthild of Magdeburg penned a handbook for spiritual formation entitled *Flowing Light of the Godhead*, inviting believers into bridal intimacy with Jesus. Educated by the Beguines, Beatrice of Nazareth wrote her booklet, *Seven Manners of Holy Love*, exploring various ways that we experience our love relationship with God. Marguerite Porete's work, *Mirror of Simple Annihilated Souls*, called believers to die to self; however, Marguerite bordered on heterodoxy and was burned at the stake in 1310 for persisting with her questionable teaching. Available in English translation, all of these writings emphasize the role of suffering in our spiritual formation and describe the wilderness of the soul that we experience as we mature in our faith.

While the Beguine movement flourished in the 13th century and revived during the sixteenth, it faded over the ensuing generations, and only a few Beguines now continue the tradition. More than one dozen large *beguinages* are preserved today in Belgium and can be visited by tourists and pilgrims. This remarkable movement offers contemporary laypersons a model of Christian initiative, vibrant community, selfless service, thirst for God's Word, and intimacy with Christ.

See also Women.

For Further Reading: F. Bowie, ed. *Beguine Spirituality* (1990); H. Grundmann, *Religious Movements of the Middle Ages* (1995); *Hadewijch: The Complete Works,* CWS (1980); S. Murk-Jansen, *Brides in the Desert: The Spirituality of the Beguines* (2004); G. Myers, *Seeking Spiritual Intimacy: Journeying Deeper with Medieval Women of Faith* (2011); W. Simons, *Cities of Ladies* (2001).

Glenn E. Myers

Benedictine Spirituality

Benedictine spirituality involves a fifteen-hundred-year tradition that began with Benedict of Nursia and his monastic rule in the 6th century. It dominated medieval Western Europe. Its purpose is to seek God and live out gospel precepts by God's grace in communal life (the "school for training in the Lord's service"). Benedict insisted that Scripture was the ultimate guide for our lives, and his rule was simply an aid for us to live by the Scriptures and apply the monastic tradition to local circumstances. Since he represents the tradition of *cenobitic* monasticism, common life (*koinos bios*) is essential to the transformation of the person into Christlikeness. In this community, or *schola*, one becomes an apprentice, learning with others who share a common purpose the skill of living as a disciple. Among others, notable representatives of this tradition include Gregory the Great, Bernard of Clairvaux, Hildegard of Bingen, Anselm, Jean Leclercq, and Thomas Merton.

Benedictine spirituality begins with listening. Indeed, the first words of Benedict's Rule are: "Listen carefully, my son, to the master's instructions, and attend to them with the ear of your heart." In this way, one is in a posture to hear God's call to the individual on this particular day. This requires a relative degree of silence—the cessation of inner noise.

As a training school, the community requires discipline and regulation. Toward that end, Benedictines make three vows: stability, obedience, and *conversatio morum*. The first involves commitment to the same community and way of life, believing that we can only change into the likeness of Christ if we remain on course with the same people over a long period of time; this is over against the wandering *gyrovagues* of Benedict's time who went from monastery to monastery, somewhat like church-hopping today. The second involves obedience to a superior (the abbot who exercises charitable and wise leadership) as well as mutual obedience (which, again, requires listening to the other); ultimately this objectifies divine providence and counters our need to be in control. The third can be loosely translated "conversion of life" (or "fidelity to monastic life") — the promise never to be satisfied with where one is in one's relation with God but to be constantly open to God's transforming work.

Central to Benedictine life is balance and moderation. This is evident in the way that Benedict divided the day into periods of work, study, and prayer, along with rest and meals. Work was typically but not exclusively in the form of manual labor. It is not an end in itself but serves the purposes of self-subsistence, discipline, and charity. To guard against overwork, which may lead to pride, self-justification, and inattention to God, study and prayer are interspersed. Study of Scripture and spiritual readings (often as *lectio divina*) was not for scholarship, though the tradition has made outstanding contributions, but for transformation. Prayer — especially the recitation of Psalms — is the *opus Dei* (work of God) and is distributed throughout the day (the "liturgy of the hours" which was originally eight communal observances of the "daily office"), setting a healthy rhythm to the day that sustains all other activities and makes one constantly aware of God's presence in all of life. The Benedictine's concern is for a balance between body, mind, and soul. Benedict's is no disincarnate spirituality; it is aimed at the conversion of the whole person. Everything, even tools, is part of God's gracious regime in the salvation of his people.

Moderation requires discernment in every aspect of each individual's life. Benedictine spirituality is not after religious heroes or spiritual gold medalists, and its approach to the Christian life is not "one size fits all." For the monastery, Benedict did not regulate *everything* in his rule. He recog-nized the infinite variety, complexity, and individuality of human beings, so that the abbot bears the heaviest responsibility of exercising charitable discretion in each circumstance with each individual for whom he must give an account to God. Still, despite the moderation, austerity is a characteristic of Benedictine spirituality; but even the note of austerity is blended with a chord of temperance to avoid extremes that might lead to pride, presumption, and individualism.

The Benedictine concept of poverty (one of the typical monastic "evangelical vows" that is implicit in the three mentioned above) differs from the Franciscan ideal of divestment. Instead, the emphasis is on common ownership that involves stewardship, trusteeship, and temperance, so that one experiences freedom from attachment and enjoyment of God's good gifts.

Two noteworthy characteristics are humility and hospitality. The former was emphasized by Benedict, particularly in chapter 7 of the Rule of St. Benedict. In essence, humility involves accurate and truthful self-knowledge. Hospitality was emphasized in the rule by its insistence that all guests were to be received as Christ, though there is to be care that worldliness and disruption of routine not infect the community's life.

See also Benedict of Nursia; Monasticism; Religious Life; Rule of St. Benedict.

For Further Reading: *The Benedictine Handbook* (2003); E. de Waal, *Seeking God* (2001); T. Kardong, *The Benedictines* (1988); K. Norris, *The Cloister Walk* (1997); D. Okholm, *Monk Habits for Everyday People* (2008); B. Taylor, *Spirituality for Everyday Living* (1989).

Dennis Okholm

Benediction/Blessing

A benediction is a pronouncement, by the authority of God's Word, of divine favor on others, including or implying a prayer or wish for God's further grace on the recipient(s), and sometimes containing a doxology. Though this word is not used in the Bible, the concept of benediction is closely linked with the scriptural terms *blessing*, *bless*, and *blessed*.

Blessing, in the broad sense, is the continuous working of God to bring about good in the lives of people. More specifically, blessing may involve making or pronouncing holy by a spoken formula or sign; favoring, making happy, or giving to; calling God's favor upon; praising, glorifying, or calling holy. God may bless us directly, we may bless God directly, or we may bless one another in the Lord's name. Some blessings that may flow from God to us include food, water, housing, community, grace, peace, justice, and above all, eternal life in Christ.

The terms *benediction* and *blessing* are often used interchangeably, benediction being the Latinized form of the English *blessing*. Although they cover much the same range of meaning, *benediction* has a more formal or ceremonial sense to it. Biblical examples of these prayerful pronouncements include Jacob blessing his sons (Gen. 49:1 – 28), Jesus blessing the children (Mark 10:16), and Jesus blessing the disciples before he ascended (Luke 24:50 – 51). Paul and other NT writers often introduced their letters with benedictions (Eph. 1:2; 2 Peter 1:2; 2 John 3) and wrote other benedictions in the latter portions of their letters (1 Thess. 5:23 – 24; Heb. 13:20 – 21; Jude 24 – 25).

Two biblical benedictions are widely recognized and used. The "Aaronic" or "priestly" benediction is an act of blessing in which God puts his name on his people (Num. 6:22 – 27). The "apostolic benediction" is a well-known Trinitarian blessing often used at the end of worship services: "May the grace of the Lord Jesus Christ, and the love of God, and the fellowship of the Holy Spirit be with you all" (2 Cor. 13:14).

Benedictions and blessings may be spoken or written, formal or informal. Formal instances may include the pronouncement at the end of a worship service and the blessing at a marriage ceremony. Less ceremonial instances may include prayers at meal-times, at the arrival and departure of friends or relatives, and when praying for one in need. Those (not necessarily ordained ministers) giving the benediction or blessing sometimes raise their hand or hands (Lev. 9:22; Luke 24:50) or place one hand on the forehead or shoulder of the recipient (Gen. 48:14; Mark 10:16). These ministries of devoted believers convey symbolically the power and favor of God to all who receive by faith God's marvelous gifts.

For Further Reading: R. Banks, "Blessing," in *The Complete Book of Everyday Christianity*, ed. R. Banks and P. Stevens (1997); P. O'Brien, "Benediction, Blessing, Doxology, Thanksgiving," in *Dictionary of Paul and His Letters*, ed. G. Hawthorne et al. (1993); C. Westermann, *Blessing in the Bible and the Life of the Church*, trans. K. Crim (1978); J. L. Wu, "Liturgical Elements," in *Dictionary of the Later New Testament*, ed. R. Martin and P. Davids (1997).

Robert V. Rakestraw

Benedict of Nursia (480 – 547)

The "father of Western monasticism." He was born in 480 in the mountainous Umbrian province of Nursia to an upper-class family. Early in his life, he went to Rome to study the liberal arts, but after a year and a religious conversion, he abandoned his studies and left the worldly city. He spent two years forty miles northeast of Rome with a group of ascetics in Affile (then called Enfide), where, according to Gregory the Great (his hagiographer), he performed his first miracle. He was probably twenty years old when he went five miles farther to Subiaco, where he lived alone for three years on a hillside in a cave, being ministered to by a neighboring monk (and later by some shepherds) who brought him bread and clothing.

As his notoriety grew, he was persuaded by the monks of a monastery (that tradition identifies as Vicavaro) and against his better judgment to come out of solitude to replace their lost abbot. Gregory tells us they tried to poison Benedict's drink after they found his demands too burdensome, but the poison was detected when Benedict blessed what they were about to drink and the pitcher cracked, exposing the plot. Benedict graciously left unharmed and alive.

He returned to Subiaco where many gathered around him to become his disciples. Eventually he established twelve monasteries, each with twelve monks overseen by a dean or prior, and Benedict in charge of it all.

After some twenty-five years, when Benedict was about fifty years old, he founded the monastery at Monte Cassino (about eighty miles south of Rome) with a small band of monks. It was here that he spent the rest of his life, and it was here that he composed the famous Rule of St. Benedict. Though he meant the rule to apply only to Monte Cassino, it became the most influential monastic rule in the West and still provides definitive guidance for Benedictine monasteries today. The rule commends its practitioners to go further with Basil and Cassian, both having influenced Benedict's own spiritual development.

He met with his sister Scholastica, a nun, once each year, the last meeting of which was prolonged by a miraculous thunderstorm (according to Gregory's account) so that his sister could spend more time with her brother shortly before she died. Tradition fixes his death on March 21, 547. His feast day is July 11.

The *Dialogues* of Gregory the Great (a Benedictine and pope in the late 6th century) is the only account we have of Benedict's life, and one has to sift through legend to discern some of the facts. But, along with the Rule of St. Benedict (the only writing of Benedict we have), we get a good stylistic portrait of the man.

See also Benedictine Spirituality; Monasticism; Rule of St. Benedict.

For Further Reading: T. Kardong, *The Life of St. Benedict by Gregory the Great* (2009); T. Fry, ed., *RB 1980: The Rule of St. Benedict in Latin and English with Notes* (1981).

Dennis Okholm

Bennett, Dennis Joseph (1917 – 1991)

Charismatic Episcopal priest. Born in England and reared in the United States, Bennett received his education at San Jose State University and Chicago Theological Seminary. Following a brief ordination in the Congregational Church (1949), he was ordained an Episcopal priest (1952) and became rector in Van Nuys, California (1953). In a pivotal turn, he experienced Spirit baptism and speaking in tongues, which led to opposition and subsequent resignation of his parish. Bennett became vicar of St. Luke's Episcopal Church in Seattle, Washington, and consequently became a pioneer in the emerging charismatic movement; he turned this struggling congregation into a beacon for charismatic renewal among mainline churches. Following the death of his first wife, Elberta, in 1961, he married Rita Marie Reed (1934 –) in 1966. He and Rita cofounded Christian Renewal Association (1968) and helped launch Episcopal Renewal Ministries (1973; now Acts 29 Ministries). They embarked upon proclamation of the renewal via services and workshops in churches, seminaries, and university campuses in the United States and around the world. Upon resignation from St. Luke's in 1981, he and Rita began to concentrate on full-time writing and speaking engagements. In his best-known work, *Nine O'Clock in the Morning* (1970), Bennett not only tells his story as part of the larger charismatic movement, but encourages contemporary pursuit of Spirit baptism.

See also Charismatic Spirituality.

Martin Mittelstadt

Bernadette of Lourdes (1844 – 1879)

French Catholic mystic. Bernadette is remembered for her visions of a young woman later identified as the Virgin Mary. The daughter of an impoverished miller in the village of Lourdes in southern France, she began at age fourteen seeing apparitions of a "small young woman" decked in a white veil and rosary of pearls, inviting her to return daily to hear words of spiritual wisdom and orders to go to the priest asking that a chapel be built so that processions of pilgrims might come.

Some neighbors questioned Bernadette's sanity, but reports of miracles soon squelched the doubts. Springwater miraculously poured from the once dry spot where the apparitions appeared. Witnesses verified other miracles, but the most spectacular moment occurred when Bernadette asked the woman who she was. The answer finally came: "I am the Immaculate Conception." Was it coincidence, some wondered, that this answer came a mere four years after Pope Pius IX had declared the dogma of the immaculate conception?

In her early twenties, Bernadette entered the seclusion of a convent while her fame soared. Churches were constructed in honor of the Virgin, including the massive Sanctuary of Our Lady of Lourdes. Bernadette was canonized a saint in 1933.

Lourdes is today one of the most popular Catholic shrines in Europe, with some five million visitors a year. Pilgrims come to be healed from physical maladies by praying or bathing in the springwater or drinking it straight. Such signs of the sacred are offset by brazen commercialization. Hawkers are everywhere selling their wares; shops are filled with novelties, from "Mother of God" bottle openers to bottled Lourdes holy water and T-shirts.

See also Marian Devotion; Extraordinary Phenomenon.

For Further Reading: S. K. Kaufman, *Consuming Visions: Mass Culture and the Lourdes Shrine* (2005); H. E. Pauli, *Bernadette: Our Lady's Little Servant* (1999).

Ruth A. Tucker

Bernard of Clairvaux (1090 – 1153)

Monastic reformer, theologian, persuasive preacher, and spiritual director. He was born into a pious, aristocratic home, the third of seven children. Provided with a classical education, at age twenty-two he renounced social and monetary privileges and entered the monastery at Citeaux, near Dijon, affiliated with the rigorous Cistercian order. Three years later he became the founding abbot of what would become the famous Cistercian monastery at Clairvaux — a foundation that attracted many members, including thirty of his extended family. Bernard served the monastery at Clairvaux for thirty-eight years until his death. During his lifetime, Bernard's monastery founded some sixty-five Cistercian communities in various parts of Europe that drew thousands into their ranks.

Bernard suffered physically and emotionally throughout his life. He experienced a serious depressive illness at the death of his mother and a life-threatening sickness at age twenty-eight. His physical constitution was weakened as a result of the relentless demands of ministry and the rigors of an ascetic lifestyle that he believed was required for achieving virtue. Although his ministry style at times was confrontational, he nevertheless was a man of holiness, humility, and Christ-centered devotion and service. He was thus both tender and tough.

Bernard immersed himself in the Scriptures and the church fathers, particularly Origen, other early Eastern fathers, Augustine, and Gregory the Great. His principal writings include eighty-six sermons on the Song of Songs (which he interpreted as a mystical allegory of the soul's relation to God), the treatises *On Grace and Free Will* and *On the Love of God*, and several hundred extant letters of spiritual counsel. He also wrote hymns well known in worship today, such as "Jesus, Thou Joy of Loving Hearts," "Jesus, the Very Thought of Thee," and "O Sacred Head, Now Wounded" — with lyrics excerpted from much longer meditative poems. Bernard's writings are Scripture-based, Christ-centered, and warmly affective. Jesus Christ was everything to him: truth, love, beauty, and eternal salvation. His stated purpose in expounding the Scriptures was more to move hearts than to exegete subtleties. A rhetorical genius, his writings have been described as "prose poised at the brink of poetry."

Highly engaged in both ecclesiastical and political affairs, Bernard served as unofficial counselor of prelates and princes. He mediated many disputes both within his Cistercian order and in the wider church, including the papal schism of 1130. He also interceded to make peace between factious civil rulers. Pope Eugene III commissioned Bernard to preach the address that launched the Second Crusade in 1146 to free the Holy Land from the Turks. Bernard believed that the crusade was willed by God, although the venture ended in a resounding defeat. One of the most influential figures in Europe during his lifetime and one of the foremost spiritual authorities of all time, Bernard was canonized by Pope Alexander III in 1174 and declared a doctor of the church in 1830 by Pope Pius VIII.

Bernard's chief theological emphases include the following. All humans, as images of God, possess a longing for and capacity to know God. Sin creates emptiness of heart that is filled only by relationship with the living Lord. Grace alone draws pre-Christians savingly to God. Consistent with Roman dogma, he believed that Mary, mother of Jesus, is a vital intercessor and spiritual refuge for Christians. Bernard exercised a strong influence on Luther, Calvin, and the Puritans. Luther described Bernard as "the greatest preacher in church history," and Calvin characterized him as "a Reformer four hundred years before the Reformation." The latter appealed to Bernard's writings second only to those of Augustine.

The leading theological controversy of the period pitted Bernard against Peter Abelard (1079 – 1142), the period's dominant philosopher and theologian. Bernard, who believed that truth was secured by Scripture, faith, and spiritual experience, vigorously opposed the latter's scholastic subtleties, rigorous use of reason and philosophy,

and certain questionable beliefs. In connection with the debate, Bernard wrote the treatise *The Errors of Peter Abelard*, which he delivered to the pope. The controversy between the two leading figures of the period essentially was a struggle between the confessional mystic and the Christian rationalist.

Tradition records that Bernard performed miracles of healing. He also carried on an extensive ministry of spiritual guidance, both in person and by correspondence. His soul care ministry was highly attentive and directive, more like that of Jesus than Carl Rogers. He listened prayerfully to directees' life stories, asked open-ended questions, told biblical stories to make a point, urged directees to be honest with God and with themselves, and encouraged accountability relationships in community. In his direction ministry, he boldly cited biblical warnings and threats. Although at times gentle and tender, he was not averse to rebuking and chastising persons for their sins. He was prepared to offend errant souls in the name of the gospel. Bernard also urged obedience to what he perceived as rightful ecclesiastical authority.

See also Cistercian Spirituality.

For Further Reading: *Bernard of Clairvaux: Selected Writings,* CWS (1987); E. Gilson, *The Mystical Theology of Saint Bernard* (1955); B. S. James, *St. Bernard of Clairvaux Seen through His Letters* (1953); A. J. Luddy, *Life and Teaching of St. Bernard* (1950); J. R. Sommerfeldt, *Bernard of Clairvaux* (2004); D. E. Tamburello, ed., *Bernard of Clairvaux: Essential Writings* (2000).

Bruce A. Demarest

Bible, Reading the

The first relevance of the Bible to spirituality stems from the fact that Christianity is one of the revealed religions of the world. This means that the Christian faith rests on a book that Christians believe to be a revelation from God — a book of supernatural origin that is authoritative for belief and conduct. As a sphere of thought and practice, spirituality has a permanent inclination to elevate subjective experience, and one aspect of this subjectivity is that throughout the history of spirituality, individuals and movements have been able to attract a following by simply hanging out their shingle. Acceptance of the Bible as a divine authority for belief and practice at once sets parameters to what is viewed as normative for true spirituality. The revelatory nature of the Bible is thus the foundation for Christian spirituality.

The Bible sets a norm for legitimate spiritual experience in two ways. Positively, it instructs us by both precept and example. The precepts are usually phrased as commands: "Remember the Sabbath day by keeping it holy" (Ex. 20:8); "Worship the Lord your God and serve him only" (Luke 4:8). More often, though, the Bible gives us pictures and examples to be emulated—pictures of people building altars and going on pilgrimages to worship in Jerusalem, narrative accounts of people praying or quotations of actual prayers, proverbs that express insights into the spiritual life, or poems that express the motions of the soul toward God.

This positive thrust is balanced by warnings in the Bible against aberrant spirituality. Idolatry is the most pervasive enemy to true spirituality in the Bible, but there are others as well: magic in myriad forms, setting up one's own forms of worship (e.g., Judg. 17), chanting interminable prayers (Matt. 6:7), being religiously moved but not toward God (1 Cor. 12:2), multiplying humanly concocted religious rituals (Col. 2:16–23).

First, then, as a revelation the Bible stands as a guidebook by which Christians differentiate between true and false spiritual experiences. Second Timothy 3:16 provides a brief list of what the Bible contributes to the practice of the spiritual life: it teaches, rebukes, corrects, and trains.

Second, the Bible is a book that Christians read as a source of spiritual nurture. The metaphors by which the Bible itself expresses the assimilation of its words hint at this. The most evocative is perhaps that of God's Word as food that is eaten and digested (Ezek. 3:3; 1 Peter 2:2; Rev. 10:9–10).

In regard to the Bible as a source of spiritual nurture, we need to note something that is obvious but that can be overlooked: the Bible consists of words. Here, too, the metaphors that we find within the Bible itself are very instructive. The most customary way in which biblical writers and speakers within the pages of the Bible refer to the content of the Bible is the designations *word* or *words* of God. It is also referred to in the NT as a book and scroll. Mainstream Christian spirituality is practiced by people of the Book, something that is not true of all types of spirituality.

Of course the effects of the Bible are not automatic. Merely reading or reciting the words does not constitute spiritual nurture. Again, we can gain insight by noting the words and metaphors by which biblical writers themselves conceive of the Bible: the Bible is a book that people hide in their hearts (Ps. 119:11), that abides in believers (John 5:38), that believers abide in (John 8:31), and that people meditate on (Ps. 1:2 and many other passages).

That these things are even possible is a tribute to the power of the Word itself, and here, too, biblical metaphors encapsulate what we need to say on the subject. The Bible is a lamp that illuminates (Ps. 119:105; 2 Peter 1:19), a sharp sword that pierces (Heb. 4:12), a mirror in which people see themselves (James 1:22–25), and something so durable that it lasts forever (1 Peter 1:25). Jeremiah 23:29 describes the word of the Lord as a fire and a hammer that strikes a rock in pieces; Hebrew 4:12 calls God's Word living and active. A lesser book would not have assumed the central role that the Bible has assumed in Christian spirituality.

What kind of reading produces the best spiritual effects? Answers include these: when we obey it (Luke 11:28), believe it (John 2:22), keep it (2 Chron. 34:21), receive it (2 Thess. 2:13), and "accept the word planted" (James 1:21). All of these appropriations of God's Word name a certain stance that the spiritual seeker displays toward the Bible.

But the spiritual impact of the Bible also rests on reading and studying it in keeping with its literary nature. The Bible is a literary anthology, and readers will get more out of it if they read it in keeping with its literary nature and intentions. The first trait of literature is that its subject is human experience, rendered concretely rather than abstractly. Instead of discoursing about virtue, literature portrays characters engaged in virtuous actions. Instead of telling us that God's provision is sufficient, the poet in Psalm 23 takes us on the round of a shepherd's routine on a typical day. Literature "shows" rather than "tells" and as a result gives us the voice of authentic human experience. This is perhaps chiefly how reading it becomes a spiritual experience.

Literature also has an aesthetic dimension to it, a dimension that through the ages has often been called beauty. This beauty — this proficiency of form — is an important part of the total experience of reading the Bible as literature. It heightens the impact of what a biblical passage conveys, but beyond that it is one of the reasons that reading the Bible can "set the affections in right tune" (as John Milton said about poetry). A work of literature is not a delivery system for an idea but rather a house in which readers take up residence and out of which they look at life. Any aspect of a biblical text that enables a reader to take up residence in it makes possible the spiritual effect of reading and meditating on the Bible.

See also Spiritual Reading.

For Further Reading: B. Bowe, *Biblical Foundations of Spirituality* (2003); E. Peterson, *Eat This Book* (2006); L. Ryken, *How to Read the Bible as Literature* (1984); L. Ryken et al., eds., *Dictionary of Biblical Imagery* (1998); D. Whitney, *Spiritual Disciplines for the Christian Life* (1991), chaps. 2–3.

Leland Ryken

Bible Memorization

See **Memorization, Bible.**

Biblical Spirituality

See **Chapters 3 and 4.**

Biographies and Spiritual Formation

Biographies and memoirs have had a profound impact on spiritual formation since the early centuries of Christianity. Such works, which include the more specialized categories of autobiography and hagiography, give flesh and bone to the matter of Christian spirituality. The father of spiritual memoir is Augustine, whose work *Confessions* (397) has influenced countless Christians and prompted them to tell their own stories of faith. Augustine's deeply self-reflective memoir is written in the form of a prayer, with candid acknowledgments of envy and pride and lust and illicit sex (though only prior to his conversion and commitment to Christ).

Augustine himself was influenced not only by reading Scripture but also by an earlier spiritual biography, the *Life of Antony* by Athanasius. Like other volumes of hagiography the book is filled with incredible miracle stories. Even earlier spiritual biographies, such as *The Passion of Perpetua and Felicitas*, sought to give martyrs recognition for their sacrifice. An important spiritual biography of the 6th century was *The Life of St. Benedict* by Pope Gregory the Great. The volume features miracles and spiritual formation but also focuses on pastoral care and theological issues.

Spiritual biographies sometimes appeared in anthologies. A bestseller in the 13th century was Jacobus de Voragine's *The Golden Legend*, a collection of hagiographies credited for transforming countless lives; tales of miracles associated with relics figure prominently in it. Women were particularly notable among the spiritual memoirists of late medieval times. Julian of Norwich, for example, is known through *Showings*, a narrative of her successive visions of Christ while she was an anchoress living in a small cell attached to a church. She was a celebrated English mystic even in her own day and was visited on one occasion by Margery Kempe (1373–1438) who also wrote a spiritual memoir, *The Book of Margery Kempe* (c. 1437).

The Reformation is not particularly known for its spiritual biographies, with the exception of John Foxe's *Book of Martyrs* (1563), which featured martyrs from NT times onward. Its major focus, however, was on Christians executed by Catholics as heretics, including Jan Hus and John Wycliffe. The volume served as a spiritual guide (and shaper of a polemical disposition) for Protestants for generations.

One of the great spiritual memoirs of all times is John Bunyan's *Grace Abounding* (1666). Less well known than his *Pilgrim's Progress* (1678), Bunyan's autobiography has stood the test of time and is still widely cited today. Another spiritual classic is Jonathan Edwards's *Life and Diary of David Brainerd* (1749). Brainerd, a missionary to Native Americans, kept a diary of his setbacks and spiritual difficulties. Many readers ever since have been encouraged through the realization that their own struggles are not unique.

Missionaries have frequently been the authors or subjects of spiritual biographies, especially within evangelicalism. Indeed, such works have come to be *the* characteristically evangelical version of the larger genre. One classic is *Hudson Taylor's Spiritual Secret*, a memoir that recounts his striving against sin until he found the secret—that of resting in the Lord. A more recent spiritual biography is Elizabeth Elliot's *A Chance to Die* (1987), recounting the spiritual pilgrimage of Amy Carmichael, an earlier missionary to India. Therein Elliot wrote: "To Amy Carmichael I owe what C. S. Lewis said he owed George MacDonald: as great a debt as one can owe another.... Amy became for me what some now call a role model. She was far

more than that. She was my first spiritual mother. She showed me the shape of godliness." In the early 1950s, Elliot's husband, Jim, along with four other young pioneer missionaries, were killed by native tribesmen in Ecuador. The widowed Elisabeth Elliot wrote *Through Gates of Splendor* (1957) and *Shadow of the Almighty* (1958), bestsellers based on these events and her martyred husband's daily journals. The latter volume, which made famous Jim Elliot's dictum that "he is no fool who gives what he cannot keep to gain that which he cannot lose," has inspired a generation of evangelicals to deeper faith and missionary involvement. James and Marti Hefley's *By Their Blood: Christian Martyrs of the Twentieth Century* (1979) is the modern Foxe's *Book of Martyrs*; it has inspired many to dedicate themselves to God and become more deeply involved in missionary work.

A goldmine for spiritual biography can also be found among nineteenth-century African-Americans, both slave and free. Jarena Lee, born free in 1783, became an itinerant Methodist preacher and recorded her spiritual journey in *Religious Experience and Journal of Mrs. Jarena Lee* (1849). Another similar nineteenth-century narrative was entitled *The Story of the Lord's Dealings with Mrs. Amanda Smith the Colored Evangelist* (1893).

Twentieth-century spiritual memoirs also abound. *Surprised by Joy* (1955) by C. S. Lewis recounts with characteristic wit his now familiar conversion story: "In the Trinity Term of 1929 I gave in, and admitted that God was God, and knelt and prayed: perhaps, that night, the most dejected and reluctant convert in all England." Henri Nouwen, professor, Catholic priest, and writer known for his work *Wounded Healer* (1979) among others, also wrote *Genesee Diary* (1981), *The Road to Daybreak* (1990), and other forthright reflections on his spiritual pilgrimage.

Also open and honest with her spiritual struggles is Kathleen Norris in her many books, including *Dakota: A Spiritual Geography* (2001), which tells the story of returning to South Dakota and allowing its people and land to draw her back to spiritual roots and to new ways of finding God. One of the most widely discussed spiritual memoirs of the 21st century is Mother Teresa's *Come Be My Light* (2009), a volume that discusses in frank terms her doubts and despair. Spiritual biography and memoir have changed over the centuries; no longer stories of supersaints, they reveal authentic struggles with which the reader can easily identify. Biography and memoir are exceptionally engaging forms of spiritual writing. Less directly instructive than some other genres, they are often quietly yet profoundly formational.

See also Autobiography, Spiritual; Hagiography; Journal, Spiritual.

Ruth A. Tucker

Birgitta of Sweden (1303–1373)

Catholic mystic and reformer. Birgitta was the founder of the Birgittines (also known as the Order of the Holy Savior); she was canonized by the Council of Constance in 1415. Born into wealth to a mother with royal lineage and a father with lands and political prestige, Birgitta married young and gave birth to four sons and four daughters. But the center of her life was religious devotion, spurred by visions and manifested through humanitarian outreach.

In her *Celestial Revelations*, she recorded her visions, including one of Mary giving birth to Jesus and the "glorious infant" lying naked on the ground. Mary, recognizable with typically Swedish blonde hair, influenced European art for generations. But Birgitta was far more than a visionary mystic. She denounced the corruption of the papacy, particularly under Pope Urban V and Pope Gregory XI, prophesying Urban's death if he returned the papacy to Avignon—a prophecy unfulfilled. Her prayers were published in the popular medieval *Book of Hours*—prayers that promised among other things the release of relatives from purgatory. While many clerics scoffed,

ordinary laity prayed her prayers, relieved that purgatory could be emptied without paying a heavy price.

One of Birgitta's daughters succeeded her as the head of the Birgittine order and became venerated as St. Catherine of Sweden, recognized for her protection against miscarriages and abortion.

For Further Reading: *Birgitta of Sweden: Life and Selected Writings*, CWS (1989); B. Morris, *St. Birgitta of Sweden* (1999).

Ruth A. Tucker

Blood of Christ

Blood has a rich cultic tradition. In the ancient Near East, blood is the bearer of life and life force. In fact, blood and life are considered virtual synonyms. This concept forms the basis of two divine prohibitions in the covenant with Noah: the prohibition to eat flesh with its blood and the prohibition to shed human blood in Genesis 9. In cultic usage, the blood of animals was used in the sacrificial rites as having the power for atonement, purification, and consecration. This practice somewhat echoes the Passover narrative whereby blood smeared on the doorsteps and the lintel of homes protected the firstborn from death (Ex. 12:7, 13).

The NT continues in the tradition of the OT, for, here too, "without the shedding of blood there is no forgiveness" (Heb. 9:22). However, for the NT, Jesus Christ is at the same time the High Priest and the sacrificial lamb whose blood is shed (Heb. 9:12–14, 22; 10:22; 13:11–12). As in the OT, the blood of Christ has the power to atone for and purify from sin and to sanctify by setting believers apart for a reconciled life of communion with God and with one another (Eph. 2:13, 18; Heb. 10:19; 13:12).

Christian spirituality is drenched in the blood of Christ. The death of Christ not only constitutes "the hub of apostolic preaching"; it is also at the center of the church liturgy, as can be seen in the celebration of the Eucharist. A long tradition in the church consists in seeking a "richer and fuller relation with God" by visualizing, contemplating, singing, or invoking the blood of Christ. This practice centers on a number of motifs, the chief of which are the love motif, the merit motif, and the power motif (power to cleanse, heal, transform, protect, overcome, or deliver).

See also Atonement Theories; Lord's Supper.

For Further Reading: L. Morris, *The Cross of Jesus* (1988); B. Pugh, "A Brief History of the Blood," *Evangelical Review of Theology* 31, no. 3 (2007): 239 – 55; G. Tomlin, *The Power of the Cross* (1999).

Mabiala Justin-Robert Kenzo

Bloom, Anthony (1914 – 2003)

Also known as Metropolitan Anthony of Sorouzh, Anthony Bloom was a prolific Russian Orthodox bishop, monk, and writer who served in England and for all Western Europe. He was instrumental in introducing Orthodoxy to Europe and England and was a well-known authority on Russian religious history and prayer.

Bloom's spirituality centered on authentic personal experience of the church and prayer. He was instrumental in advancing the ecumenical movement in the latter part of the 20th century by stressing the spiritual unity of the church. Nevertheless, Bloom was averse to an ecumenism that neglected the great tradition of the church. The Orthodox Church in England grew rapidly under his leadership without encouraging the proselytizing of others. He became a prominent member of the ecumenical Fellowship of St. Alban and St. Serge, which is dedicated to unity between Eastern Orthodoxy and the Christian West. Bloom was seen as a living link to the Orthodox spirit of Russia in Western Europe.

Bloom is best known for his works on prayer, including *Living Prayer* (1966), *Beginning to Pray* (1970), *God and Man* (1971), *Meditations on a Theme* (1972), *Courage to Pray* (1973), and *The Essence of Prayer* (1986). Bloom's understanding of prayer was strongly oriented to Russian Orthodox mysticism. He stressed the value of praying with icons, silence (hesychasm), contemplation, and repetition of the Jesus Prayer. His overarching concern was to integrate the physical and spiritual dimensions of prayer into a holistic experience of union with God.

See also Russian Spirituality.

For Further Reading: G. Crow, *This Holy Man* (2005).

Ian Smith

Blumhardt, Johann Christoph (1802 – 1880), and Christoph Blumhardt (1842 – 1919)

Johann Christoph Blumhardt and his son, Christoph Blumhardt, are two of the most religiously influential yet least well-known figures of the 19th and 20th centuries. Johann Christoph Blumhardt became famous in Germany because of sensational events that unfolded in the small village of Möttlingen where he was the parish pastor. According to various reports, for the better part of two years (1842 – 1843), Blumhardt found himself dealing with a purported case of demonic possession. Gottlieben Dittus, a parishioner, approached him complaining of strange events happening in the night. Through Dittus, Blumhardt would be drawn into a struggle, the dramatic crescendo and denouement of which came with the shriek of the demonic power that "Jesus is Victor!" This phrase would become the spiritual watchword and theological thematic for both Blumhardts in their respective ministries.

Blumhardt reflected on this episode in dialogue with Scripture and the tradition of Württemberg Pietism in sermons, letters and a popular circular, the *Blätter aus Bad Boll*. In these, the phrase "Jesus is Victor" became shorthand for the inbreaking power of the kingdom of God to liberate humanity from spiritual and physical bondage. Though the elder Blumhardt would increasingly emphasize the social dimensions of the kingdom, it was his son Christoph who would develop this aspect most fully. Christoph came to the conviction that though his father had recovered a hope for the kingdom of God as made concrete in real physical transformation, he had not seen that the full expression of this hope included the transformation of the social conditions of humanity. While for the elder Blumhardt, "Jesus is Victor" had implied the *healing of the body*, for Christoph it implied the *healing of the body politic*. In contradistinction to his father, he began to envision the struggle with the powers and principalities in explicitly social and political terms. The powers against which Jesus struggled, and over which he would triumph, were now those structures that oppressed humanity and curtailed human flourishing.

These insights led the younger Blumhardt into the Social Democratic Party, which he would eventually represent in the regional legislature (1900–1906). In socialism, Blumhardt believed that he discerned a hope for a transformed world that was remarkably similar to the hope that the kingdom of God represented, and because the established church had consistently aligned itself with the status quo, Blumhardt argued that the atheist socialists were more Christian than the Christians. However, after only two years of work, he began to have serious doubts, not about the ideals of socialism, but rather about the practical platform and turbulent party politics he experienced. Though he would remain committed to socialism until his death in 1919, Blumhardt became less sanguine about human attempts to bring the kingdom into the world: though they were an imperative, they were nonetheless flawed, awaiting the coming of Jesus to bring their hopes to fulfillment.

The Blumhardts' peculiar form of spirituality focused on the second petition of the Lord's Prayer, "Thy kingdom come." This petition captured the basic form and content of individual and communal Christian life, which was described as "waiting and hastening" toward the kingdom of God. The task of the Christian is both to wait on God and to hasten toward God's coming. The Christian community prays for and expects the living God to break into the world in the form either of penultimate signs or of the final appearing of the kingdom of God on earth. At the same time, the community lives in the light of the promise of the coming kingdom by striving for justice, peace, and reconciliation, which in turn can become signs or parables of the kingdom.

Through the biographical work of Friedrich Zündel and the Blumhardts' letters, hymns, sermons, and other devotional writings, the Blumhardts have provided inspiration to widely divergent movements. From Pentecostalism to liberation theology, from dialectical theology and Karl Barth to the nineteenth-century faith-healing movement, they have proven to be figures with an extraordinary spiritual depth and theological flexibility and fecundity.

See also Devil, Demons, and the Demonic; Health and Healing; Kingdom of God; Social Justice.

For Further Reading: C. Blumhardt, *Action in Waiting* (1998); V. Eller, ed., *Thy Kingdom Come* (1980); D. Ising, *Johann Christoph Blumhardt* (2009); F. Macchia, *Spirituality and Social Liberation* (1993).

Christian T. Collins Winn

Body

Scripture testifies that not only is the material world good (and remains so, even though now fallen), but also that earthly human existence is inherently embodied and that our bodies matter to God. According to the Genesis account, humans were first given life as embodied creatures. Throughout the Scriptures, soul and body are linked, with each needing the other to constitute a true human being. In fact, the body comes first, created by God before the breathing into it of the life-giving spirit that animates the human self. It is in this embodied form that human beings are originally called "very good" by God himself. True human life is lived out, and God is worshiped, through the body. Likewise, the consequences of sin are not only spiritual, in the sense that they involve loss of the original close relationship with God, but are also physical, including pain in childbirth and a disordered relationship with nature (Gen. 3). Death, sin's final penalty, is seen throughout the OT as the dissolution of that most precious gift of the human body, with its return to the very dust from which it was formed.

The NT brings the ultimate testimony of the importance of the human body, as the Word of God takes on true human flesh, a real body that is fully human, in order to redeem not only human souls (if that were even possible), but human bodies as well. The gospel writers make quite clear that Jesus' body had all the normal limitations of human physicality. The resurrection of Jesus was not an immaterial phenomenon; he appeared in a renewed but real physicality. In 1 Corinthians 15 Paul gives careful attention to our Christ-grounded hope of a similar resurrected embodiment for all eternity. Such hope of continued existence as embodied souls is an essential part of the good news of Jesus Christ. In Revelation 20 – 22, John reminds us that our future is an embodied one, when human beings will be what they were meant to be, worshiping and glorifying God for eternity.

One of the greatest threats to early Christianity was Gnosticism; and ever since then variant forms of this early heresy have continued to challenge a proper Christian view of the body. This gnostic trajectory espouses a generally negative assessment of the physical, material world, seeing it as a hindrance to the spirit, and regarding the body (as "the flesh" taken literally) as the primary place the human disposition toward sinfulness resides.

While Scripture acknowledges that our physical bodies can pose obstacles to spiritual growth and therefore require discipline (1 Cor. 9:24 – 27), it goes well beyond Scripture to treat the body as the principal root of sinfulness.

Christian spirituality therefore must be careful to factor the body into the call to become a Christian. Actions performed through the body do not and cannot leave the interior life unaffected, for the body is more than a detached and nonchalantly worn "earth suit." Nor is the body necessarily (though it can be) a distracting impediment to worshiping God, but rather an essential instrument of worship in heartfelt emotion, word, and deed. The body receives perhaps its greatest dignity as a "temple" — a sacred residence — for the living reality and presence of God's Holy Spirit (1 Cor. 6:19 – 20, 2 Cor. 6:16). Against all persistent tendencies to the contrary, Christian spirituality therefore properly emphasizes the care and stewardship of the body, while also respecting and appreciating the effects of the body (health and illness, injury and recovery, addictions and cosmetic surgery, fatigue and rest, nourishment and deprivation, intellectual ability and chemical balances) on one's integrated spiritual condition.

See also Holistic Spirituality; Sexuality; Soul.

For Further Reading: R. S. Anderson, *On Being Human* (1991); G. Carey, *I Believe in Man* (1975); M. Jeeves and W. Brown, *Neuroscience, Psychology, and Religion* (2009); M. Miles, *Augustine on the Body* (1979); idem, *The Word Made Flesh* (2005); N. Murphy, *Bodies and Souls, or Spirited Bodies?* (2006); H. W. Wolff, *Anthropology of the Old Testament* (1974).

Christopher Morton

Boehme, Jacob (1575 – 1624)

German Lutheran mystic and philosopher. Born in Alt-Seidenberg, Saxony, son of a farmer, he received only a minimal education and learned the cobbler's trade. He then settled in nearby Goerlitz where he spent the remainder of his life, first operating a shoemaker's shop and then a modest commercial enterprise that involved extensive travel. This enabled him to come into contact with like-minded thinkers, enhancing his reputation as a shoemaker-philosopher.

Boehme's thought is confusing and at times contradictory. Although unlearned, Boehme had a keen mind and brought together in his literary works the devotional strains of medieval piety with nature theories of the Renaissance. After a profound religious awakening in 1600 where he experienced the inner birth of the deity, he gained the knowledge that in Yes and No all things consist. This was a cosmological struggle between good and evil that had its cause in the two aspects of God himself. He then spoke of God in profoundly mystical terms, emphasizing the Trinity in both its spiritual and natural aspects, and showed that the roots of all life were to be found in the metaphysical-psychological symbols of the living God. His first book, *Aurora: The Beginning of Dawn* (1612), actually a mishmash of ideas, gained the attention of a Lutheran orthodox hard-liner who persuaded the town council to forbid Boehme from any further writing.

For the next six years, Boehme adhered to the ban, but finally he yielded to the wishes of his growing circle of admirers and turned out some twenty-four works over the next five years, many of which were published after his death. During the silent years, he expanded his reading to encompass books by Paracelsus, Valentin Weigel, and various alchemists and chiliasts. His works exhibited a mixture of gnostic, Neoplatonic, kabbalist, and pansophist spirituality, and, as a result, he had an important influence on later romanticism, idealism, and even existentialism.

On the other hand, Boehme remained close to the Lutheran tradition, and Christian elements pervaded such important volumes as *Mysterium Magnum* (1620) and *On the Election of Grace* (1623). He coordinated his philosophical understanding of the qualities in nature with his ideas about God and believed the kingdom of God achieved a harmony between the spiritual and material worlds. He said humans must die to self and live on the higher plane, thus making the true Christian life a mystical imitation of Christ's suffering and ultimate triumph. Several of his emphases appealed to later Pietists: the necessity for Christ to live in believers, that the regeneration of the individual person contributes to the regeneration of fallen humanity, that the Bible is the living Word of God, and that true faith demands Christian social responsibility. Also appealing to Pietists were his criticisms of bibliolatry (too much weight placed on the literal words of Scripture), the doctrine of election, and contemporary Protestantism's (defective) view of heaven as a place of eternal bliss and idleness.

See also Pietism.

For Further Reading: *Jacob Boehme: The Way of Christ,* CWS (1978); J. J. Stoudt, *Jacob Boehme* (1957); D. Walsh, *The Mysticism of Innerworldly Fulfillment* (1983); R. Waterfield, ed., *Jacob Boehme* (2001).

Richard V. Pierard

Bonar, Horatius (1808 – 1889)

Scottish pastor, author, and hymn writer. He came from a long line of clergymen and was brother to the equally famous Andrew Bonar (1810 – 1892), with whom he is sometimes confused. Born in Edinburgh and educated there under Thomas Chalmers, he ministered at Kelso, Scotland, for twenty-nine years before returning to Edinburgh in 1866 to serve the Chalmers Memorial Church until his death. Bonar and his evangelical congregation joined the Free Church of Scotland during the Disruption of 1843. He was a prolific author, publishing his sermons, including the *52 Family Sermons* and *Light and Truth,* a five-volume cycle of sermons from Genesis to Revelation; devotional works, such as *The Night of Weeping, God's Way of Peace*, and *The Everlasting Righteousness*; and biographies of other Scottish clergy.

Bonar was a decided Calvinist and outspoken premillennialist, but also a promoter of international panevangelical cooperation. This is seen in his editing the popular journal *Christian Treasury* for two decades, and especially in his public defense of D. L. Moody's evangelistic campaigns, which John Kennedy of Dingwall condemned as "hyper-evangelism." Bonar's voluminous writings are of a consistently high quality, characterized by a Romantic spirit, great forcefulness of expression, and pastoral application. His fluency with the core doctrines of Reformed Protestantism gave him a wide range for experiential and emotional piety. The combination can be seen in his many hymns, some of which (notably "I Heard the Voice of Jesus Say" and "Come, Ye Sinners, Poor and Wretched") have enjoyed wide usage. He published three volumes of *Hymns of Faith and Hope*.

See also Reformed (Calvinist) Spirituality.

Fred Sanders

Bonaventure (1217–1274)

Franciscan spiritual theologian. He established a synthesis between Francis of Assisi's simple faith and scholastic theology, offering Christians an exceptional model of uniting head and heart.

Reared in Bagnoregio, Italy, as Giovanni, he matriculated at the University of Paris at seventeen and in 1243 assumed the name Bonaventure as he joined the Franciscan order. He accepted the Franciscan chair of theology in Paris in 1253 and taught beside Aquinas. In 1257 he was elected as the seventh minister general of the Franciscan order, a post he held for seventeen years, navigating the young order through troubled waters stirred by the so-called Spiritual Franciscans and ensuring its spiritual legacy. The final year of his life, he served as cardinal bishop of Albano. Entitled the "Seraphic Doctor," Bonaventure was canonized in

1482 and declared doctor of the universal church in 1588.

As mystagogue Bonaventure wed kataphatic meditation with pseudo-Dionysian apophatic contemplation. While moderating the absolute poverty purported by Francis and the Spirituals, Bonaventure presented the Poverello of Assisi as a model for spiritual formation in his *Life of St. Francis: The Triple Way*, which expounds the classic stages of spiritual growth: purgation, illumination, and perfection.

Most valuable to evangelical believers are Bonaventure's reflections on Christ's life and God's order in creation as avenues for spiritual growth. In his *Tree of Life*, Bonaventure offers forty-eight meditations on our Lord's life, passion, and glorification to kindle our affection for Jesus. *The Journey of the Soul [Mind] into God* invites us as his readers into God's holy presence. Stirred by desire, we ascend Jacob's ladder as we progress through six stages of contemplation, represented by the fiery seraphim's six wings. In the first two steps, we focus outward, employing our senses and imagination to meditate on creation as well as the principles inherent in the universe. As we turn inward on the next two rungs, we apprehend God's glory by considering the complexities of the *imago Dei* in the human soul—memory, intellect, and desire—and reflecting upon our restoration through Christ our exemplar. In steps five and six, we gaze upward, contemplating God's oneness in being and goodness in Trinity, where charity flows among the persons of the Godhead because it is of necessity self-giving. Finally, our minds find rest as we pass beyond cognitive faculties into the seventh stage, experiencing God's presence purely by love.

See also Franciscan Spirituality.

For Further Reading: *Bonaventure*, CWS (1978); I. Delio, *Simply Bonaventure* (2001); Franciscan Institute, ed., *Works of St. Bonaventure*, 15 vols. (1960–); Z. Hayes, *The Hidden Center: Spirituality and Speculative Christology in St. Bonaventure* (1992).

Glenn E. Myers

Bonhoeffer, Dietrich (1906–1945)

German pastor and theologian, Bonhoeffer was raised in Berlin, where his father taught psychiatry and neurology at the University of Berlin. Bonhoeffer studied first at Tübingen and then at Berlin, where he worked under the guidance of Reinhold Seeburg. During his student years, he was impacted by Karl Barth and would combine the influences of his liberal Berlin education with Barth's emphasis on revelation into a life of reflective action in the midst of the rise and fall of Nazism.

Bonhoeffer combined vigorous theological thinking with deep pastoral concerns. During the years of his academic development and his time lecturing at the University of Berlin (1931–1933), Bonhoeffer was engaged in various forms of church ministry, from leading youth ministries and writing catechisms for children to his involvement in the ecumenical movement. His involvement in ecumenism, as well as his time as a guest lecturer at Union Theological Seminary in New York City (1930–1931), gave Bonhoeffer a vision of a church transcending nationalistic boundaries and living out the vision of the Sermon on the Mount. His reflection on the sermon would come to fruition in his book *Discipleship*, written during his time as the director of one of the Confessing Church's preachers' seminaries. Here Bonhoeffer brought together a group of young seminarians who ate, worshiped, studied, and ministered together. His vision of Christian spirituality and the importance of the church community is captured by his other book from this period, *Life Together*.

Following the closing of the seminary by the Gestapo, Bonhoeffer started writing *Ethics*. In this uncompleted book, Bonhoeffer laid out a vision of Christian ethics built on Jesus Christ and not on philosophical foundations, for Bonhoeffer believed that traditional Western and philosophical concepts of morality no longer held. The ethical question is not a question of the right thing to do; instead, the true ethical question concerns the will of God. Following from this, Bonhoeffer wrote that Christian ethics is based on following Christ's own self-giving, conceived of as his "vicarious representative action" on behalf of all humanity. To live ethically, in other words, is not to adopt a set of principles, but to follow the living Christ by giving oneself for others, even if that means taking on guilt. Bonhoeffer's role in the plot to assassinate Adolf Hitler can only be understood in light of *Ethics*.

Bonhoeffer was arrested in 1943 and spent the last two years of his life in prison. From his cell, Bonhoeffer wrote letters to his best friend, Eberhard Bethge, that include nascent ideas regarding the future of Christianity. These ideas, which included such notions as "religionless Christianity," "living life before God without God," and "the polyphony of life," have worked on the imaginations of countless people in the years following Bonhoeffer's death, on April 9, 1945, in a concentration camp at Flossenbürg. These letters provide a partial but vibrant vision of following Christ in a new context.

For Further Reading: E. Bethge, *Dietrich Bonhoeffer* (2000); G. Kelly and F. B. Nelson, *The Cost of Moral Leadership* (2003); J. Lawrence, *Bonhoeffer: A Guide for the Perplexed* (2010); S. Plant, *Bonhoeffer* (2004).

Joel Lawrence

Book of Common Prayer

The *Book of Common Prayer* (BCP) is actually a family of books, descended from the first English Prayer Book of 1549, containing both the words of and instructions for services conducted in Anglican churches throughout the world. The purposes of the BCP are participation of the whole congregation in the church's worship, edification of the laity in biblical truth and Christian practice, and unification of the church through common words and patterns of worship.

The first BCP was prepared as part of the English Reformation, during the reign of King Edward

VI (1547–1553), who ordered all the churches of his realm to cease using the Latin Mass and begin using this new English Prayer Book. Its original title, *The Book of Common Prayer and Administration of the Sacraments and Other Rites and Ceremonies of the Church after the Use of the Church of England*, indicates the comprehensive nature of its contents: daily services for morning and evening, a lengthy litany, a weekly service of Holy Communion, as well as services for baptism, confirmation, marriage, praying for the sick, and burial of the dead. The principal architect of the prayer book was Thomas Cranmer, archbishop of Canterbury from 1533 to 1556, whose aim, according to R. T. Beckwith, was to produce a book for public worship in which "biblical teaching is incorporated throughout, all that is misleading or meaningless is excluded, words are audible, actions are visible, and congregational participation in speaking, singing, and reception of the Sacrament is encouraged."

The BCP has been revised several times since its original publication, starting in 1552 with a more radical version and culminating in 1662 with the edition that is still the official prayer book for the Church of England. The first version outside England was the Scottish Prayer Book of 1637, followed by an American version in 1789. Today the Episcopal Church in the United States uses its own version of the BCP officially approved in 1979, incorporating contemporary English language, insights from liturgical scholarship in the 20th century, and practices from the Catholic revival of the 19th century. Other versions of the BCP are used by churches in more than fifty countries, especially in those that were once part of the British Empire (e.g., Australia, Canada, Ireland, Kenya, New Zealand, Nigeria, South Africa, et al.).

The BCP has been and continues to be one of the most influential books in shaping the spiritual life of cultures, churches, and individuals since the Reformation of the 16th century, particularly in the English-speaking world. Combining Protestant doctrine with Catholic worship, it has produced a rich stream of piety that continues to be both biblical and historical, both evangelical and sacramental. Its first impact was on the national life of England in the 16th and 17th centuries, where it helped develop a Christian culture defined by worship according to the Prayer Book. Even dissenting English Christians of that time (Baptists, Congregationalists, Presbyterians, and Quakers) could not escape its influence, structuring their beliefs and worship in reaction to the Prayer Book. Then, as the British Empire expanded around the world, the BCP, along with the King James Bible, traveled with leaders, chaplains, and missionaries, so that new churches begun outside England often used it. This is why the Anglican Communion today, with its eighty million members, is the third largest Christian family in the world.

But the BCP has also shaped personal and familial spiritual life, following the principle of *lex orandi, lex credendi* (the law of praying is the law of believing). Although it has never been fully realized, the original Prayer Book vision of people worshiping together daily in a uniform service, hearing the Bible read and expounded in their own language, receiving Holy Communion frequently, and observing the calendar of the church year has tended to produce Christians who are regular churchgoers, biblically literate, appreciative of Christian tradition, and very practical in their daily piety. Those who use the BCP usually appreciate beauty and order in worship, sometimes elevating them over orthodox beliefs and emotional expression, and limiting mystical experiences to the private sphere. Although intended for public worship, the Prayer Book has also been used for regular family worship and individual daily devotions, both by clergy and laity. It has been a major vehicle for a simplified daily cycle of Benedictine monastic worship to become part of the lives of ordinary people.

See also Anglican Spirituality.

For Further Reading: R. T. Beckwith, "Thomas Cranmer and the Prayer Book," in *The Study of Liturgy*, ed. C. Jones et al. (1992), 70–74; D. deSilva,

Sacramental Life (2008); M. Hatchett, *Commentary on the American Prayer Book* (1981); C. Hefling and C. Shattuck, eds., *The Oxford Guide to the Book of Common Prayer* (2006); C. Price and L. Weil, *Liturgy for Living* (1979).

David Montzingo

Booth, William (1829–1912), and Catherine Booth (1829–1890)

Cofounders of the Salvation Army. Providentially born in England the same year. Catherine Mumford, daughter of a Wesleyan pastor, a very articulate girl who grew up painfully shy but ended up becoming a bold writer and preacher, was expelled from her local church for being overenthusiastic spiritually. She joined a group led by the gifted William Booth. William, who grew up poor, had a special passion for the poor and oppressed. Catherine shared his passion and extended it to include explicit efforts toward the equality of women. In 1855 the two married. Together they resolved to wage war against poverty and sin. In Catherine's words, "If we are to better the future, we must disturb the present." By 1865 they established a rescue mission that in 1878 was renamed the Salvation Army. The Booths were such evangelists that they unabashedly regarded impoverished drunken people as precious lost souls for whom Christ died. They reached out in terms that made sense to the urban poor by marching through the streets as a band, preaching the gospel and singing hymns that had the tunes of drinking songs. They helped the honest poor and criminal poor alike. They worked tirelessly for the destitute, the oppressed, the aged, the lazy, the homeless, the prostitutes, the chronically sick, the unemployed, and anybody else who was unsaved. They withstood violence from non-Christians who threw rocks, tragedy at home from infant death, and scorn from mainline Christians who disapproved of their lack of observance of the sacraments. Because the Salvation Army's converts were rejected by the churches, the converts were enlisted strategically into the Army's ranks. By 1881, partly due to William's unusual ability to network and organize effectively, the Army had become international. In 1890 (with the help of journalist W. T. Stead) the widowed General Booth cast his vision for the Army in a book, *In Darkest England and the Way Out*—which galvanized the movement considerably more. William eventually was so respected that he attended the coronation of King Edward VII (1902) and received an honorary doctorate from Oxford University (1907).

See also Holiness Movement; Social Justice.

For Further Reading: C. B. Booth, *Catherine Booth* (1970); R. Collier, *The General Next to God* (1965); T. Yaxley, *William and Catherine: The Life and Legacy of the Booths* (2003).

Sarah Sumner

Bossuet, Jacques-Benigne (1627–1704)

French bishop and theologian, known primarily as a gifted orator and vernacular stylist. Born to a prosperous family in Dijon, Bossuet studied theology in Paris and became a priest in 1652. His intellectual skill served him well in Metz, Paris, as tutor to the dauphin and as bishop of Meaux. Throughout his career, he was a vocal opponent of French Protestants and free thinkers of all kinds, arguing that from the beginning they were hopelessly varied and confused; hence, that they should return to the Roman Catholic truth.

Bossuet's spirituality is marked by his critique of the minimization of human activity described in the Quietism of Madame Guyon. He particularly condemned the idea of one of Guyon's most famous disciples, François Fénelon, that a sort of "pure love" can be the highest spiritual goal. However, his *Funeral Orations* (eulogies of famous Roman Catholics from 1656–1687) were considered classic spiritual literature already in their time. These sermons were very powerful, for he was able to capture spiritual emotion in a precise and poetic manner. Most important was his ability to explain and apply grand themes, such as providence, eloquently and in ways that stimulated spiritual life.

See also Quietism.

For Further Reading: *Bossuet: A Prose Anthology,* ed. J. Standring (1962); O. Chadwick, *From Bossuet to Newman* (1987); R. Costigan, "Bossuet and the Consensus of the Church," *Theological Studies* 54, no. 4 (1995): 652 – 72; M. Sluhovsky, *Believe Not Every Spirit* (2007).

Jason Zuidema

Bounds, E(dward) M(cKendree) (1835 – 1913)

Civil war prisoner, Holiness theologian, and champion of intercessory prayer. At age twenty-four, this native Missourian gave up a promising legal career to become a pastor in the Southern Methodist Church, only to be imprisoned and see his church property confiscated by the federal government at the onset of the war. After a year in jail, he became a Confederate chaplain and laid many of those to whom he ministered in their graves. Postwar he pastored a number of churches, including one in war-torn Franklin, Tennessee, and another in an affluent section of St. Louis. He spent his prime professional years writing for denominational newspapers, using them as platforms to speak for holiness and against burgeoning Methodist liberalism. Meanwhile, in one five-year stretch, he experienced the death of his first wife and his first two sons. In an act of considerable sacrifice, he walked away from his longstanding Methodist affiliation on principle. Without a salary, and having relinquished his pension, he lived his remaining years modestly. He spent three morning hours every day in prayer, waking his household for 4:00 a.m. worship services. He preached to the few congregations that appreciated his sublime and otherworldly messages, and in relative seclusion, he wrote a number of works (most of which was published posthumously). He wrote primarily on prayer, but also on the primacy of Scripture and on the call to entire sanctification made possible through the Holy Spirit. He repudiated worldly power, money, and status, particularly among pastors, and called people into lives as pilgrims and sojourners on earth.

Bounds lived to witness the release of just two books: *Preacher and Prayer* (1902), which was later repackaged as *Power through Prayer* (1907), and *The Resurrection* (1907). After his death, one of his disciples diligently circulated these books and edited and published nine others, seven of them on prayer. These prayer books are widely available separately and in *The Complete Works of E. M. Bounds on Prayer* (1990).

For Further Reading: L. Dorsett, *E. M. Bounds* (1991).

T. C. Porter

Bradstreet, Anne (c. 1612 – 1672)

British-American Puritan poet. Bradstreet lived in England until she traveled to Massachusetts with her husband and her parents in 1630. She is best known for her poetry that was published without her knowledge in England by her brother-in-law. While it was unfashionable for women to express themselves, Bradstreet became the first British-American woman to publish poetry and America's first published poet. Following the broader scope of Puritan meditation, poetry was often classified as "occasional," written because of a specific occasion, or "formal," a regular practice at set times. Most of Bradstreet's poetry is representative of the occasional style, addressing the daily events common to many of her time. Puritan piety was shaped by the daily events of life, including affliction, and Bradstreet often wrote of her losses: her husband's frequent absences due to his political responsibilities, the burying of three of her grandchildren, and the destruction of her home by fire. Her poetry also soars in gratitude to God and rejoices in the gifts and blessings of life. Her longer poem,

"Contemplation," provides a good illustration of the Puritan practice of meditation on creation or "spiritualizing" the creature. Bradstreet's personal faith reflected in her poetry is a spirituality that understands Jesus as the bridegroom of the soul, following the tradition of Song of Songs. She modeled the importance of a spirituality of daily life and God's sustaining mercy and growth amid the afflictions of life.

See also Poetry and Poetics; Puritan Spirituality.

For Further Reading: *Early New England Meditative Poetry*, SAS (1988); R. Rosenmeier, *Anne Bradstreet Revisited* (1991); and E. White, *Anne Bradstreet* (1971).

Tom Schwanda

Brainerd, David (1718–1747)

Puritan missionary to Native Americans. David Brainerd was born in Haddam, Connecticut, orphaned at fourteen, converted at twenty-one, and then drawn to missionary work. Physically and temperamentally, Brainerd was an unlikely candidate for missionary service, yet his life and brief career of four years, as preserved in his diary, have inspired numerous persons to adopt missionary service.

Brainerd struggled greatly in coming to faith in Christ. Extremely scrupulous and overwhelmed in his lost spiritual state, his conversion account depicts a moving experience of eventual encounter with "Divine glory." Equally intense was his probing the spiritual condition of fellow students at Yale, including Samuel Hopkins, who was led to faith in Christ. Mentored in a Puritan ethos, Brainerd was devoted to sacrificial piety, persistent labor, and a feeling of deep obligation to bring the gospel to the unconverted. His intense personality was also given to melancholy and despondency as well as, at times, a judgmental disposition. Brainerd was an example of genuine spirituality encased in a clay jar. During Brainerd's Yale days, a student overheard Brainerd describe a tutor as having "no more grace than this chair." When this was reported, Brainerd was expelled. Grieved by the experience but undeterred in his love for God and desire for service, he continued his preparation for ministry, was licensed to preach in 1742, and soon after began his ministry with Native Americans in New York, Pennsylvania, and New Jersey. His final days were spent battling tuberculosis in the home of Jonathan Edwards, where Edwards's daughter Jerusha became his nurse (and possibly his fiancée) until his death on October 9, 1747. Following Brainerd's death, Edwards edited Brainerd's diaries and published *An Account of the Life of David Brainerd*, believing that "true religion and virtue" were superbly modeled in Brainerd's life.

See also Puritan Spirituality.

For Further Reading: J. Edwards, *The Life and Diary of David Brainerd* (1749); G. Marsden, *Jonathan Edwards: A Life* (2003).

Wayne S. Hansen

Breath Prayer

Breath prayer, an intimate form of unceasing prayer, connects attention of the heart turned toward God to the rhythm of respiration. The earliest reference to breath prayer appears in *Ladder of Paradise* by John Climacus, who wrote in step twenty-seven: "Let the remembrance of Jesus be present with your every breath." In the late 13th century, Nicephorus the Hesychast of Mount Athos, in his *On Watchfulness and the Guarding of the Heart*, described breath control as an aid to practicing the Jesus Prayer. *Hesychia* (Gr. for "quiet" or "silence") is the goal of attending to the rhythm of respiration so that the prayer of the intellect is found in the heart.

In the modern West, breath prayer has been embraced as an aid to the practice of the presence of God. He is as near to each individual as one's breath; dependence upon him is as essential to life as breathing is to the human body. Awareness of God, the giver of breath and life (Gen. 2:7; Ezek. 37:1–14; Acts 17:25), increases when the believer, whose heart is turned toward God, internally gives attention to the rhythmic, subconscious act of respiration.

As accessible to us as respiration, breath prayer may be practiced anytime and anyplace. Because it quiets the mind and heart, breath prayer serves to stay one's mind on what is true, noble, and right (Phil. 4:8–9) and against internal distraction and temptation that draw one away from God.

This form of contemplative prayer assigns words or desires to the inhalation and exhalation of breath, such as a name of God ("Savior," "Comforter/Come"), a brief Scripture ("Majesty/Praise," Ps. 8; "Come, Lord, help me," Ps. 70:1; "Peace," Phil. 4:7), or a classic prayer (Jesus Prayer, Paschal Prayer). Or one may inhale "Christ" and exhale fear or any condition inhibiting a believer from Christlike living.

See also Centering Prayer; Jesus Prayer; Prayer of the Heart.

For Further Reading: A. Calhoun, *Spiritual Disciplines Handbook* (2005); R. DelBene, *Breath Prayer* (1981); M. Thompson, *Soul Feast* (1995).

Nancy R. Buschart

Brethren of the Common Life

The Brethren of the Common Life were the driving force of the medieval renewal movement, the *Devotio Moderna* (Modern Devotion) founded by Gerhard Groote (1340–1384) in the Netherlands. The movement's early leaders established houses for women, Sisters of the Common Life, and then men—with the Brothers the smaller but more influential of the two groups. The movement spread to Belgium, Germany, and Switzerland. Its greatest legacy is the spiritual classic, *The Imitation of Christ*, which is universally attributed to Thomas à Kempis (c. 1380–1471).

The movement made the experience of imitating Christ accessible to the working classes beyond the confines of rural monasteries of the day. Members lived in cities, sharing their possessions in common like the early church (Acts 2:44). They earned income for their houses by copying and selling sacred texts or producing goods for the textile industry rather than taking a vow of poverty and begging for alms as did the mendicant orders like the Franciscans and Dominicans. The Brethren did not take rigid monastic vows, but made voluntary resolutions that were flexibly applied to individuals and houses. They functioned under civil not canon law—a "middle way" between parish life and religious orders.

The Brethren operated dormitories and schools for youth, one of them attended by Martin Luther during 1497 and 1498 at Magdeburg. From their business activity, they donated house profits to the poor. They did evangelism at weekly meetings known as collations, in which the brothers gave spiritual teaching in the common language of the people. Collations drew strong opposition from the Dominicans and parish priests who saw these as invading their domains. The brothers attracted women, youth, laity, and clergy to meditation practices conducted in the vernacular of the masses.

The Brethren, comprised mostly of laymen and some priests, also spawned a reformed monastic community—the Augustinian Canons Regular at Windesheim. Because the congregation functioned under canon law for religious orders, not civil authority, it enjoyed protection from intense opposition to "middle way" gatherings. And some like Thomas à Kempis and entire houses found it easier to join the Windesheim congregation. Even with its monastic rule, the congregation was still able to maintain much of the flexible spirit typical of the Brethren of the Common Life by adapting monastic patterns around each house's unique character and needs of its members.

By the mid-16th century, the emergence of the printing press and the Protestant Reformation effectively ended all three branches of the *Devotio Moderna*. Printing gradually replaced copying of texts, which had been the houses' area of expertise and chief source of income. Moreover, many houses converted en masse to Protestantism with its rejection of celibacy and emphasis on the family as the primary locus of spiritual formation. Though a few houses did survive into the late 1600s, not much of the movement remained.

Scholars agree that the Brethren left a considerable legacy in both Catholic and Protestant understanding and practice of sanctification, most notably among Jesuits and Puritans. Some scholars in the early 20th century held that Modern Devotion beliefs also had a strong affinity to the Protestant doctrine of justification—a view that has been undermined by more recent studies that have shown little continuity with this Protestant doctrine. It is now generally recognized that the movement's heart meditation on Jesus' life and death and imitation of his virtues constituted its greatest continuity with Protestantism.

See also *Devotio Moderna*.

For Further Reading: *Devotio Moderna: Basic Writings*, CWS (1988); A. Hyma, *The Christian Renaissance: A History of the "Devotio Moderna"* (1924); W. Landeen, "Martin Luther's Intervention in Behalf of the Brethren of the Common Life in Herford," *Andrews University Seminary Studies* 22 (1984): 81–97; R. Post, *The Modern Devotion* (1968).

L. Paul Jensen

Brother Lawrence (1611–1691)

Carmelite laybrother and spiritual adviser, also known as Lawrence of the Resurrection. Brother Lawrence was a member of the Discalced ("barefoot") Carmelites. Apart from the fact that he was born Nicholas Herman in Lorraine, France, there is no reliable information on his early life. He served in the French army for a portion of the Thirty Years' War, during which he was wounded, and subsequently as an aide to William de Fuibert, treasurer of the French government. He took the name Lawrence of the Resurrection upon becoming a lay brother (c. 1661).

Brother Lawrence is best known through the book titled *The Practice of the Presence of God* (1693), first published shortly after his death. While he is usually identified as the author, the book in fact consists of a memoir of four conversations with Lawrence written by Joseph de Beaufort, a senior churchman in the Diocese of Paris, and a collection of some of Lawrence's letters of spiritual counsel, written to a variety of inquirers, most of whom were women. These conversations and letters contain very little information about Lawrence himself but offer important insights into Christian spiritual life. In some editions, a series of spiritual maxims by Lawrence are also included.

Both the conversations and the letters provide a window into a spirituality of serene submission and humble simplicity for which he was, and is, known. Shortly after entering a Carmelite monastery, Brother Lawrence was assigned duties in the kitchen. For several years, he labored with considerable frustration and resentment. Then, for reasons not fully known, he had a life-altering encounter with the reality of the presence of God—indeed, with God himself—in the kitchen. Often described by others as mystical, the resulting spirituality was not one of method or program but a way of life, an ongoing "practice." It is a way of life that is, before all else, life *coram deo*, before God, and all work—whether in the kitchen or the cobbler shop, to which he was later assigned—is done "for the love of God."

See also Presence of God; Unceasing Prayer.

For Further Reading: W. Johnston, *Christian Mysticism Today* (1984); M. Pennington, "The Practice of the Presence of God," in *Christian Spirituality*, ed. F. Magill and I. McGreal (1988), 336–39.

W. David Buschart

Bruderhof (Society of Brothers)

The Bruderhof, now known as Church Communities, is a small international Christian communal movement of families and singles that originated in Germany in 1920. Inspired by the Sermon on the Mount, the early Christian church as described in Acts 2:42 – 47 and 4:32 – 35, and the sixteenth-century Anabaptists, as well as the kingdom theology of the Blumhardts and founder Eberhard Arnold (1883 – 1935), members seek to live in such a way that all are of one heart and soul, claim no possessions as their own, hold all things in common, and testify in word and deed that love, justice, truth, and peace are the will of God for all people.

The church is not understood as a religious institution but as God's redemptive community in the world. This means that members live simply and honestly, renounce all worldly goods, and devote themselves entirely to an integrated life in the service of Jesus Christ and his kingdom that includes work, worship, apostolic mission, education, and family life. This is made possible on the basis of repentance, conversion, and faith in a total surrender of everything to Christ and his church. Members take lifetime vows of obedience, service, and poverty. While respecting the state and its calling, members affirm the sanctity of all human life and thus refuse to engage in war or any other form of violence.

True, honest, and open relationships are highly valued in the community and depend on the following: sexual purity and fidelity between one man and one woman in marriage; humility, whereby gifts and talents are exercised on the basis of service, not preference or performance or position; straight speaking in love and rejection of all forms of gossip; mutual admonition wherein sin and selfishness are confronted in a spirit of humility; and church discipline, wherein opportunities of silence and solitude are given to those who seek reconciliation with Christ. Important decisions are made together in unanimity; spiritual leadership is provided by brothers and sisters entrusted to do so. Membership is open to all who are called to serve Christ and neighbor in the vocation of church community.

See also Anabaptist Spirituality.

For Further Reading: E. Arnold, *God's Revolution* (1984); idem, *A Joyful Pilgrimage* (1999); J. H. Arnold, *Discipleship* (1994); M. Baum, *Against the Wind* (1998).

Christian T. Collins Winn

Buber, Martin (1878 – 1965)

Jewish sociologist and philosopher mainly known for his "I-Thou" thesis. Buber was born in central Europe, and from his midtwenties to early thirties, he focused his attention on the Hasidism (a form of Jewish faith) of his family's heritage. There he was taught the concept of "hallowing the everyday." Part of this hallowing includes interacting with each person you meet during the day as if he or she is truly a whole person, and such interactions will help to transform yourself in the process.

After moving to Jerusalem in the 1930s to teach sociology at Hebrew University he developed this thesis more and eventually published his thoughts in the book *I and Thou* (1922). This book, which would influence a number of Christian thinkers, most notably Karl Barth and Dietrich Bonhoeffer, was written in the 1920s but took longer to influence English speakers because of the delayed translation (1937). Drawing upon the ideas of Hasidism, *I and Thou* places renewed emphasis on the role of relationship in one's own human development and on the understanding of the life of the self not as a separate concept but as one rooted in relationships.

Relationships that seek to protect the "I" by relating only to others as an "it" will never fully form and will not enable either person to become his or her whole human self. Instead, by engaging with "the other" as a fully valuable person (in the German, the word *Thou* carries with it a sense of deep familiarity), one's "I" grows because of that encounter. Even of more importance, when we engage with the "other" in a personal and caring manner, we meet the ultimate "other," God, in the life of faith. Buber's influence on Christian spirituality, especially on the role of spiritual friendships and on the necessity of community for a fully formed spiritual life, continues today as many in the Christian community who are focused on the life of the triune God draw upon the insight of Buber's "I-Thou" thesis.

See also Friendship, Spiritual.

For Further Reading: R. G. Smith, *Martin Buber* (1967).

Christopher Morton

Buddhist Spirituality

The heart of Buddhist spirituality is meditative practice. This is not to deny the importance of Hindu devotionalism (*bhakti*), residues of which still endure in Buddhist spiritual practice, such as hymn singing (*ragas*), sacrifice, and *puja* (worship). Nor is it to deny the scores of spiritual practices resident in cultural Buddhism around the world (including the West), practices such as *dana* (gift-giving, central to Engaged Buddhism) and working for world peace (central to Soka Gakkai in the West). In Buddhism all these practices, what one might call the Lesser Spirituality, are considered skillful means (*upaya*) that help one on the spiritual path.

The essence of Buddhist spiritual practice, however, is meditation, what one might call the Greater Spirituality. Buddhist meditation is spiritual practice aimed at "cleansing the mind of impurities and disturbances." This goal is universal, yet the actual methods of meditation vary from Buddhist school to Buddhist school, from country to country, and from continent to continent. In the welter of all this variety, however, three main roots of meditative practice can be discerned: *vipassana* meditation, *zen* meditation, and *tantric* meditation.

Vipassana meditation is usually translated as insight meditation. The vipassana meditator, after establishing physical calm through posture and breath control, focuses his or her mind on a meditative topic. The *Visuddhimagga*, the key meditative text of vipassana meditation, lists forty main meditative topics. A person's spiritual guide chooses the topic most appropriate to the personality of the meditator. The purpose of this focus on a meditative topic is to show the suffering and temporariness of all existence. These "insights" then lead to the realization of the nonexistence of an enduring human self or soul. These acknowledgments of suffering, impermanence, and no-self then open the mind to true reality, a nondiscursive awareness of present reality, the oneness of all being, or more precisely, nonbeing. Realization of this emptiness (*sunyata*) of all being is called enlightenment and leads the meditator to a totalized nothingness called *nirvana*.

Zen meditation, the meditative practice that became common in so-called Northern Buddhism or Mahayana Buddhism, differs not at all in the preparations used for vipassana meditation, using similar posture and breath-control techniques. And it similarly describes the nondiscursive understandings of reality that are the goal of meditation practice (emptiness and nirvana). Where it differs markedly is in the method of meditation itself. It specifically attempts not to use discursive methods that produce spiritual insights that help the meditator along on the path to Enlightenment. According to zen practitioners, it is the very process of rational thought that produces insights that prevent the meditator from seeing the emptiness of reality clearly. So zen encourages practices that attempt to break down rational thought. The principle meditative practice is to fill the mind with a *koan*, a short saying, usually in the form of a question, that has no rational answer: "What is the sound of one-hand clapping?" is a familiar *koan*, one of thousands in the zen traditions.

Tantric meditative practice attempts to broaden the meditative experience beyond the shaping of the mind, using either rational or nonrational techniques, common to vipassana and zen practices. Tantrics resort to the three *M*s of *tantric* meditative practice: *mudras*, *mantras*, and *mandalas*. *Mudras* are postures of the hands, each posture representing a spiritual practice seen as efficacious: teaching, protecting, calming, respecting. *Mantras* are Sanskrit sayings that bring spiritual calm and insight not only by the meaning of their content, but by the physical intonation of the words that produce vocal vibrations that are in tune with the deepest rhythms of the universe—one writer called this sonic theology. *Mandalas* are intricate circles of geometric design; some have literal pictures mixed in the geometrical layout. The circular geometric design draws the eye from the peripheral circles (each of which teaches a lesson) to a single-pointed, nondual center, a point representing both the oneness and emptiness of all being. Tantric meditators, most common in the Tibetan Buddhist tradition, draw attention to the breadth of their practice, encompassing the mind (using mandalas), speech (using mantras), and the body (using mudras).

As far as techniques go, there are many similarities between Buddhist spiritual practices, especially meditation, and Christian spiritual practices. The cultivation of the spiritual life (*bhavana*) finds resonances in both traditions. Some of the more obvious examples: the importance of physical postures (kneeling as a sign of submission), the use of mantras (the Jesus Prayer), mudras (hands raised in worship), koans (some of Jesus' parables), and so on. But two important differences stand out. First, the goal of Buddhist spirituality, no matter what the school, is to gain an understanding of the absence of any enduring human self or soul. This is not compatible with Christianity's spiritual goal of union (not identification) of the enduring human soul with God—the restoration of the relationship humans had with God in Eden. Second, there is the relationship of salvation (or emptiness) with spiritual practice. As a Christian spiritual practice tends to follow the salvation we enjoy as a gift from God, spiritual practice is a form of sanctification. In Buddhism, spiritual practice is that very process of salvation, not an evidence of it. Imagine the process of sanctification without the necessity of salvation and you have a picture of the function of meditation in Buddhism as distinct from Christianity.

Still, these differences should not forestall the great advantages both Buddhists and Christians can gain from understanding one another's approaches to spirituality. Because they do have so many overlapping features, spirituality is a fruitful area of common ground that can lead to spiritually satisfying conversations and mutual learnings.

See also Zen.

For Further Reading: W. Rahula, *What the Buddha Taught* (1974); S. Shaw, *Buddhist Meditation* (2008); T. Yoshinori, ed., *Buddhist Spirituality*, 2 vols., WSEH (1993 – 1999).

Terry C. Muck

Buechner, Frederick (1926 –)

American writer and preacher. Buechner is one of the most prolific, varied, and honored spiritual writers alive today. He was a young novelist in New York who felt called to the ministry through the preaching of George Buttrick, attended Union Seminary in New York, and became a Presbyterian minister. His early charge was as a chaplain at the Phillips Exeter Academy, where he faced the yawning disinterest and unbelief of boys who saw no value in faith or the Bible. He brought the Bible to life by avoiding platitudes and noticing details and by being imaginatively creative and completely honest.

This approach may be seen in *Wishful Thinking* (1973), *Telling the Truth* (1977), and *Beyond Words* (2004), among other works. He intends to be a kind of evangelist in his writing, as the audience he has in mind is not in the first place the regular churchgoer, but rather the skeptic, the one who doubts, the one for whom the freshness of the gospel has not yet bloomed. He accomplishes this by honesty, by admitting his own doubts and struggles in the faith. Yet his thought is clearly rooted in Scripture. His literary skill carries his insights right into the specifics of modern life.

Buechner has written many novels, among them a tetrology entitled *The Book of Bebb* (1979) and two others about medieval saints, *Brenden* (of eighth-century Ireland) and *Godric* (of tenth-century England). These novels illustrate his concepts of the spiritual life: it is not about sanctimonious words or sentimental feelings, but is found rather in the passions and struggles of daily life.

Sermons are another frequent genre for Buechner, as indicated by *The Magnificent Defeat* (1966) and *Secrets in the Dark* (2006). One of his best-known quotations has influenced college programs concerning vocation all across the country: "The place God calls you to is where your deep gladness and the world's deep hunger meet."

Buechner's memoirs, in several stages, reflect one of the major themes of his spirituality: listen to your life. His own reflections, which are often wry observations on the grace of God, give examples of this spiritual practice and provide the title for yet another work, *Listening to Your Life* (1992). Among his memoirs are *The Sacred Journey* (1982), *Now and Then* (1983), *Telling Secrets* (1991), and *The Eyes of the Heart* (1999).

For Further Reading: V. Allen, *Listening to Life* (2002); D. Brown, *The Book of Buechner* (2006); F. Buechner, "The Longing for Home," in *The Longing for Home*, ed. L. Rouner (1996), 63 – 78.

Bradley P. Holt

Bunyan, John (1628 – 1688)

British Nonconformist pastor and author of *The Pilgrim's Progress*. Bunyan lived during some of the most turbulent decades of the 17th century for Nonconformists. He came from a modest background that provided little formal education. Two significant influences that awakened an interest, though they did not actually lead to his conversion, were the Puritan classics by Arthur Dent, *The Plain Man's Pathway to Heaven* (1601), and Lewis Bayly, *The Practice of Piety* (1612) — both brought to his marriage by his first wife. Similar to Luther and John Wesley, Bunyan suffered from lengthy struggles with spiritual turmoil and doubt, and

eventually found peace and assurance through reading Luther's *Commentary on Galatians*. This internal anguish of his soul was later replaced by the external suffering of imprisonment, twice due to his refusal to adhere to the Church of England's conditions for authorized preaching. The first occasion lasted almost twelve years and became one of his most prolific periods of writing. Bunyan often found himself drawn into theological controversies; he attacked the formality of the Church of England and what he regarded as an unbalanced Quaker tendency to distort the role of the Spirit in relation to Scripture. His theology was Calvinistic though blended with a strong evangelical spirit.

Bunyan produced more than sixty works; the two most popular are his spiritual autobiography, *Grace Abounding to the Chief of Sinners* (1666), and *Pilgrim's Progress* (1678), both written in prison. Part 2 of *Pilgrim's Progress* (1684) focused on Christian's wife and children and emphasized the more communal nature of sanctification. *Holy War* (1682) utilized military imagery he gained while serving in the parliamentary army. Additionally, Bunyan penned *I Will Pray with the Spirit* (1663), based on 1 Corinthians 14:15; it emphasized the guiding power of the Holy Spirit in prayer while attacking the *Book of Common Prayer*, which he believed denied the vitality of the Spirit's role in prayer. Though Bunyan was well acquainted with the theological issues of his time, he typically downplayed his education and insisted that the Bible and Foxe's *Book of Martyrs*, the only works available to him in prison, were his primary reference works.

John Owen was deeply impressed by the heartfelt depth of Bunyan's preaching. Beyond the 17th century, Bunyan's legacy has been most firmly established by *Pilgrim's Progress*, which has been translated into over two hundred languages and is the most popular devotional book in English next to the Bible. Its enduring freshness can be traced to Bunyan's imaginative use of biblical metaphors and allegorical interpretations of life. He also draws upon the bridal language of Song of Songs to reinforce the mutual desire for intimacy between Jesus and individual believers. Some of Bunyan's recurring themes transcend time and stress that the Christian life as a journey, conversion as a process, the emptiness of formal or external religion, the necessity of perseverance in the face of struggle and temptation, the value of supportive relationships of others, and Christ's intercessory prayers for the church. While the temptation in the present century is often to lose sight of heaven, Bunyan constantly challenges readers with the importance of meditating on heaven, where Christ is waiting for those who seek him.

See also Baptist Spirituality; Journey, Spiritual; Pilgrimage; Puritan Spirituality.

For Further Reading: R. Greaves, *John Bunyan* (1969); M. Mullett, *John Bunyan in Context* (1996); I. Rivers, *Reason, Grace, and Sentiment* (1991), 89–163; W. Tindall, *John Bunyan Mechanick Preacher* (1964); and G. Wakefield, *John Bunyan the Christian* (1992).

Tom Schwanda

Bushnell, Horace (1802–1876)

Urbane New England pulpit theologian. After a false-start secular career, Bushnell trained for the Congregationalist ministry at Yale then settled into a long Hartford pastorate where his erudite, eloquent sermons and publications garnered attention for their fresh take on the stale theological debates then current in New England. It was his enthusiastic reception of romantic thought that enabled such a critical handling and creative reworking of evangelical Calvinism. In *Christian Nurture* (1847), he countered evangelical insistence on an "anxious bench" conversion by endorsing the gradual growth of faith through the nurturing Christian family and community. Despite Bushnell's intent to defend the higher truth of the orthodox position on Christ's divinity and death against Unitarian attacks, conservatives were unsettled by the claim in *God in Christ* (1849) that religious words—biblical and doctrinal—are only figurative of an ineffable reality, as well as *The Vicarious Sacrifice* (1866) for its emphasis on the cross's evocative influence. Bushnell is little read today but remains significant inasmuch as his path to liberal orthodoxy traversed the fault lines of traditional evangelical piety, particularly between personal conversion and churchly catechesis, the systematic mind and the sentimental heart in appropriating divine truth, and the objectivity of revelation and its subjective use for devotion and doctrine.

For Further Reading: R. Edwards, *Of Singular Genius, of Singular Grace: A Biography of Horace Bushnell* (1992); *Horace Bushnell: Sermons,* SAS (1986).

Todd Statham

Byzantium and the East (600–1700)

See **Chapter 14.**

C

Call to the Ministry

The call to the Christian ministry is that summons by the living God to a particular vocation—namely, a consecrated life of pastoral care, congregational leadership, and ministry of Word and sacrament. The language of call and calling (Gr. *kaleo, klesis*) is widespread in Scripture, especially the Pauline literature, and underscores the fact that people are invited to enter into reconciled relationship with God and then go out in service for him. The Christian's calling has two vectors—the first coming in and the second going out. Each believer has the twofold privilege of a relationship with God and a ministry for God. Yet within this encompassing framework there is a specific vocation of pastoral ministry to which some believers are called.

The offices of church leadership bring heightened opportunity to accomplish good or inflict harm, so wise churches will be cautious, careful, and discerning in the matter of appointments to these positions of special influence (1 Tim. 3). This discernment process, which normally culminates in ordination, weighs evidence of the candidate's personal wholeness, virtue, godliness, and competence. It also necessarily seeks to discern the evidence of an antecedent divine call to the ministry. Ultimately, it is this call that confers ministerial authority, protects against the tyranny of people pleasing, and sustains the minister with resolve during times of difficulty and doubt. It is cause for considerable encouragement and gratitude that God never abandons those who are called (1 Thess. 5:24).

This so-called "call to the Christian ministry" should not be conceptualized as superior to other Christian callings, or as the only one that involves ministry and service to others. Nevertheless, it warrants careful attention because of its strategic impact on the welfare of the entire church. While it does not demand a superior spirituality, it does require that biblical ideals for all believers will be exemplified in their leaders. A solid measure of self-understanding, and especially an awareness of the inner motives that drive one's actions, are critical to "the long obedience" of a lifetime of pastoral ministry. Humility, sensitivity to the seductive draw of power, and personal appropriation of the motif of cross-bearing are critically important as well. The pastoral ministry allows for many personalities and temperaments, but it is difficult to fulfill it without a genuine love for people, Christ's church, and the essential pastoral tasks of preaching, teaching, and healing.

Healthy churches, led by gifted ministers, are the contexts in which the initial stirrings of a call to the ministry are most likely to be felt by others. Such stirring by the Spirit may be prompted by countless factors, including a growing inner restlessness with the status quo, a face-to-face encounter with the pain of another, a simple invitation to share in an exciting ministry, or a powerful impression from reading a biblical text. Yet the discernment of a call to the Christian ministry is too important to be left to an individual alone. A candidate's inward conviction of calling must be confirmed—ideally, sooner rather than later—by a resonant affirmation from the discerning community of faith (Acts 13:2). Ultimately, the discernment of calling is communal, not merely private.

It is also reasonable to assume that a person called to the ministry will demonstrate suitability and aptitudes for it. Nevertheless, such promise is often latent rather than developed, and in any event, the call remains an "unfettered choice by God not influenced by human preconditions" (as the selection of King David from among the sons of Jesse famously illustrated). For those so called, the pastoral ministry is a life, not merely a living, and a great privilege.

See also Vocation.

For Further Reading: B. Gordon, *Calvin* (2009); E. B. Holifield, *God's Ambassadors: A History of the Christian Clergy in America* (2007); B. Johnson, *Hearing God's Call* (2002).

John P. Powell

Calvin, John (Jean Cauvin, 1509–1564)

Theologian and magisterial church Reformer. Calvin studied law in various places, including Paris. As far as theology is concerned, he was self-taught. Little is known about his conversion in 1533–1534, partly because he preferred not to speak about himself. What he did say was that his so-called conversion was unexpected (*subita*). Even more significant is the fact that he probably did not even mean a conversion from unbelief to belief, but rather a change in terms of moving to a "purer doctrine." Calvin was thus already a believer before he had what can be called a church conversion.

He sought to live his life in the fear of the Lord—that is, with respect, like that which children have for their parents, and in Calvin's case especially for his father. But in Calvin this fear also has an element of anxiety—not the neurotic anxiety described by twentieth-century psychologists and read back into Luther and Calvin, but the anxiety of a person keenly aware of his or her guilt before God. It involves both the torment of the conscience caused by awareness of being a sinner and having to appear before a righteous and wrathful God, and also the heavenly rest of the conscience when it finally experiences forgiveness and renewal.

When Calvin was forced to flee France due to the persecution of Protestants, he ended up in Geneva, a city that had recently joined the Reformation in 1536. Staying and working there was not his own choice, but he saw the claim that his fatherly pastor, Guillaume Farel, put upon him as a call from God that he had to obey. This attitude was central to Calvin's spirituality. In Geneva Calvin became a preacher and eventually a pastor. He was forced to leave there when a dispute rose up between him and the city council concerning the independence of the church. From 1538 to 1541, he served as preacher of the French-speaking refugee congregation of Strasbourg. When the city council of Geneva urgently pleaded with him to return to that city, Calvin did so, despite having said that "it would be better to die at once than to suffer repeatedly on that torture rack." He went back because he feared to put his own desires ahead of God's will. On this occasion, Calvin designed his own

seal, depicting a hand, and in that hand a heart. Especially revealing were the words he wrote on it. Calvin wanted to give his entire heart to God *prompte et sincere* (willingly and honestly). And these two characteristics were evident throughout his life: the *prompte* in his persistent diligence and the *sincere* in his transparency and candor.

In Geneva Calvin continued to preach, teach, and pastor until his death. During that time, the city was flooded with refugees, especially from France. In his work, Calvin continually kept the entire European church situation in mind, and, especially in his letter-writing, tried to attain unity among all those who confessed Christ. He participated in discussions between the Protestant and Catholic camps, maintaining an ecumenical attitude. He also sought unity with Lutherans and Anabaptists, although he did not avoid polemics with these groups either.

Calvin's life was marked by many disappointments and difficulties. His child died shortly after birth, and his wife died after eight years of marriage. Calvin also experienced extremely ill health that caused him constant pain and fatigue. In Geneva, Calvin never had the position of leadership that is often ascribed to him. Although he was the most important preacher, city regulations were not made by him but by the civil authorities. When Michael Servetus was arrested and condemned to be burned at the stake in accordance with the imperial right, Calvin tried in vain to bring him to repentance.

Among Calvin's works, his *Institutes of the Christian Religion* receives the most attention. The success of the *Institutes* (final edition in 1559) as the most important systematic work in the history of Reformed Protestantism can be attributed to both its form and content. As a second-generation Reformer, Calvin made use of the work of Luther, Melanchthon, Zwingli, and Bucer, in addition to dealing directly with the Bible and the writings of the church fathers. The style is humanistic, and the text itself is filled with short but clear formulations.

Calvin intended this work as a guide for his students, who would thereby be better equipped to follow the lectures in which the Reformer explained the Bible text by text.

Calvin's commentaries, characterized by careful exegesis, are far more extensive. He also published many smaller theological works, catechisms, and church orders. In his teaching about the church, the preaching of the gospel was crucial. His most significant contributions to the reformation of liturgy include congregational singing and rhymed psalms.

Calvin's spirituality is centered on the honor of God and the salvation of humanity. This is reflected in the beginning of the *Institutes*, where Calvin states that "Our wisdom . . . consists almost entirely of two things: the knowledge of God and of ourselves." Knowledge of God not only underlines our own sinfulness and inadequacy, but implies knowledge of God the Redeemer. True knowledge of God therefore leads directly to true piety. "By piety," Calvin wrote, "I mean that union of reverence and love to God which the knowledge of his benefits inspires." This reverence for the majesty of God results in a dynamic balance in which Calvin stresses the fatherhood of God and his endless love and mercy, as well as the terror of the holy and righteous God in his wrath and punishment. People were created to bring honor to God; in order to facilitate that after the fall into sin, God came to humanity with his redemption. The doctrine of predestination is not the central point of Calvin's theology. He does teach election, but on this point as well, it is about God's honor and humanity's salvation. Because God elects sinful people to salvation, all honor is due him for that eternal salvation.

But it also means that people can be certain of that salvation, because it does not depend on them in the least. For Calvin, providence and election are not just doctrines to teach, but truths to experience. Calvin found all of this brought into practice in the Psalms. In his opinion, both the kindness of God and the encouragement to thank him were never better expressed than in this OT book. For him the Psalms served as "an anatomy of all feelings of the soul." Every heart-felt emotion could be found there, and anyone who desired to make progress in the school of God needed them.

Union with Christ was an essential idea for Calvin. It also involved immediate union with the body of Christ, through the work of the Holy Spirit, who gives and sustains faith. Calvin defined faith as "a firm and certain knowledge of God's benevolence towards us." This close union with Christ leads to a life of prayer, and it is no wonder that by far the largest chapter of the *Institutes* is on prayer. Through preaching and sacraments, the church is both a means to and a visible form of that union with Christ. Therefore, he gives much attention to sanctification—both of the church and of the individual believer—as the self-evident consequence of justification.

Calvin's doctrine of God's overall providence certainly does not make him stoic. He assumes a large role for emotions. Living under God's providence brings rest without taking away all unrest. Such unrest is part of the life of a pilgrim; as Calvin put it, "We are always on the road." This phrase expressed his general view of life and unconsciously summed up his personal story. Believers are "on the road" because heaven has become their new home country; only when they arrive there will their journey finally end. Christians are "just sojourners on this earth, so that with hope and patience they strive toward a better life." If heaven is one's home country, on earth one will feel at home both everywhere and nowhere at the same time.

See also Puritan Spirituality; Reformed (Calvinist) Spirituality.

For Further Reading: I. Hesselink, *Calvin's First Catechism* (1997); *John Calvin: Writings on Pastoral Piety*, CWS (2001); H. Selderhuis, *Calvin's Theology of the Psalms* (2007); idem, ed., *Calvin Handbook* (2009).

Herman Selderhuis

Calvinist

See **Reformed (Calvinist) Spirituality.**

Camaldolese Spirituality

An approach to Christian spirituality that cultivates inner growth by silence, fasting, contemplative prayer, and meditation on Scripture through *lectio divina*. Similar to Carthusians, Camaldolese believers unite solitude with community: younger monks/nuns live corporately in the monastery, while more mature members inhabit nearby hermitages.

Romuald of Ravenna (c. 950 – 1027) founded the monastery of Camaldoli near Arezzo, Italy, seeking to return medieval monasticism to the Rule of St. Benedict and the eremitic model of solitude as the locus of personal transformation and spiritual warfare. Disillusioned with monastic mediocrity, Romuald purported the "threefold good" — solitude, community, and mission — emphasizing gòdly lifestyle and affection for Jesus. Among key leaders, Peter Damian (1007 – 1072) underscored solitude and ascetic discipline in his works on the spiritual life, including his *Rule for Hermits*, *On the Eremitical Order*, and the *Life of Romuald*. Rudolf, fourth prior of Camaldoli, penned their *Constitutions*, and Bruno-Boniface of Querfurt depicted early developments of Camaldoli in *The Life of the Five Brothers*. All but one of the several Camaldolese congregations (networks) remain as Benedictines.

By their example, the Camaldolese believers invite contemporary Christians to nurture solitude in their pursuit of an intimate relationship with Christ. Romuald welcomes believers to a transforming encounter with God: "Sit in your cell as in paradise.... Realize above all that you are in God's presence.... [Die to] yourself completely and sit waiting, content with the grace of God."

See also Benedictine Spirituality; Griffiths, Bede; Solitude.

For Further Reading: P. Belisle, ed., *The Privilege of Love: Camaldolese Benedictine Spirituality* (2002); P. Damian, *Selected Writings on the Spiritual Life*, trans. P. McNulty (1959); T. Merton, *The Silent Life* (1957).

Glenn E. Myers

Câmara, Hélder (1909 – 1999)

Hélder Pessoa Câmara, Roman Catholic archbishop of Olinda and Recife, Brazil. He was integral to the development of liberation theology, nonviolently mobilizing his native Brazil and all of Latin America for social justice for decades.

Born into a large lower-middle-class family, he developed a keen sense of Christian spirituality as a young boy. At twenty-two, having studied philosophy and theology, he was granted a special authorization to be ordained prior to the minimum age of twenty-four. Dom Hélder was profoundly influenced by at least two themes of Vatican II: that there should be more lay participation in the liturgy and greater access to versions of the Bible in the "mother tongue" of the faithful. He also believed that true followers of Jesus and the communities they formed would "feed the hungry, clothe the naked ... and seek justice." His beliefs demanded a response to the widespread poverty and social injustice he saw around him, and led him to stand for what he believed, even during periods of Catholic opposition, and at a high cost to his career.

Dom Hélder was auxiliary bishop for twenty-eight years in Rio de Janeiro and became internationally known as the "bishop of the slums" for denouncing social and racial divisions and fostering the cause of the poor. Dom Hélder was appointed archbishop of Olinda and Recife at age fifty-five and served in that capacity for twenty years until retirement. During those years, and despite persecution and threats to his life, he became a leader against the authoritarianism and human rights abuses perpetrated by a repressive military dictatorship.

He wrote an antiviolence tract, *Spiral of Violence* (1971), and authored several books, translated into many languages, including the devotional guide *Sister Earth* (1987/2008). He started organizations and cooperatives and launched national campaigns to fight poverty. He received numerous awards and decorations from religious, educational, and civil institutions, and he was nominated for the Nobel Peace Prize in 1973. He died from a heart attack at age ninety.

See also Latin America; Liberation Spirituality.

For Further Reading: H. Câmara, *Essential Writings*, MSMS (2009).

Minoa Chang

Cambridge Platonists

The Christian church after the time of Christianity's legalization in AD 312 has repeatedly sought to return to a pristine form, to a time when it was primitive (meaning basic, pure, and simple). During the 17th century, England saw the birth of the Cambridge Platonists, one of the less usual of these movements, as this one was rooted in philosophical high learning rather than in the rejection of learning and philosophy often associated with other primitive church movements.

Seeking a pure Christianity, scholars known as the Cambridge Platonists, and led by such noted writers as Benjamin Whichcote (1609–1683), Henry More (1614–1687), Ralph Cudworth, (1617–1688) and John Smith (1618–1652), reacted against much of the Western tradition that underlay the theologies of their day. First, they rejected Aristotle, who was the great philosopher of the medieval period, especially as he was interpreted by Thomas Aquinas, and whose influence was still strong in Protestant Scholasticism at the time of their writings. They replaced Aristotle with the philosophy of Plato, Plotinus, the Neoplatonists, and other like-minded thinkers from the Greek-speaking world.

Another essential feature of the Cambridge Platonists was their favoring of the Greek church fathers as opposed to the Latin fathers who provided the foundation for Western theology. They shelved Tertullian and Augustine and put in their place the Greek fathers, especially Origen, whose theology was viewed as an anathema to many Catholic and Protestant theologians of that time (and of ours). As for the great leaders of the Protestant Reformation, Luther and Calvin, the Cambridge Platonists merely ignored them, treating them with silence as they sought to go even further in their efforts to reform the Christian faith more thoroughly than the Westernized and Latinized Reformers had managed.

The Cambridge Platonists, who were well versed in both theology and philosophy, sought to bring the two disciplines together. In this their movement was seen to counter the Puritan writers, whom the Cambridge Platonists saw as antirationalists. For the Cambridge Platonists, reason was "the candle of the Lord," and thus reason and God's love, another emphasis of Greek theology, became essential to developing and understanding the doctrine of God and an ethical system. This helped lead to a more moderate and tolerant theology than that of some of the other Reformers, as well as encouraging intellectual engagement by the Christian.

Christian spirituality sometimes struggles with the tension between a faith of the heart and a faith of the intellect. The Cambridge Platonists provide a model for Christian spirituality that takes seriously the challenges of philosophy as well as a tolerant spirit in the outworking of the Christian faith, giving space for believers to live in community while also living the life of faith as reason leads them.

See also Anglican Spirituality; Caroline Divines; Oxford Movement.

For Further Reading: *Cambridge Platonist Spirituality*, CWS (2004); C. A. Patrides, *The Cambridge Platonists* (1969).

Christopher Morton

Camps and Camping

Christian camping moves participants from the comfortable security of everyday life to a new environment, typically outdoors, in order to deepen their understanding of God and further their spirituality. Although to "go apart" from the world in order to grow closer to God is an ancient and honored practice, current models of organized Christian camping originated in North America in the late 19th century. These early Christian camping efforts themselves grew out of the evangelistic camp meetings that originated during the late 18th and early 19th centuries on the American frontier. Like these revival meetings, early Christian camping involved basic facilities, such as wagons and makeshift tents that enabled those of even the most limited economic means to participate. Having evolved and spread throughout the world, evangelical Christian camping is now more sophisticated and organized internationally as an alliance of national and regional associations under the auspices of Christian Camping International.

Camping provides a unique opportunity to develop the relational, transformational, and vocational dimensions of spirituality. Jesus, the living Word, walked with his closest disciples for an extended period of time, and allowed them to learn experientially what it meant to know God, to love, and to minister the gospel. Camping provides similar opportunity for today's disciples to "walk" with the Word in a more intense, comprehensive, and "round the clock" manner. Formative programs can last for longer periods of time than the brief weekly meetings of most church education, and thus allow for learning experiences more conducive to transformation. These experiences also occur as a break from the normal flow of events, providing a retreat from the stresses and distractions of everyday life. The context naturally provides learning experiences similar to the effective informal teaching of Jesus as he walked with his disciples.

Most organized camping allows Christians to experience the interdependence of living as the family of God by practicing the relational dynamics of community. Although practiced most frequently through age-segregated youth groups, family camps can introduce an intergenerational aspect through which participants experience the church as "extended family." Activities designed to build a climate of trust, as well as interdependence and commitment, can enhance the individual and corporate spirituality of the body of Christ.

Formation occurring in the outdoor context provides a deeper understanding of God as creator as well as a greater appreciation for his creation. This context also gives occasion for reflection and discussion concerning the "earth-keeping" responsibilities that Christians have as stewards. Beholding the beauty of God's creation in a camping context evokes a response of awe, wonder, worship, and praise not experienced in most Western Christians' daily, urban environments.

See also Retreats.

For Further Reading: W. Graendorf and L. Mattson, *An Introduction to Christian Camping* (1984); L. Mattson, *Christian Camping Today* (1998); S. Venable and D. Joy, *How to Use Christian Camping Experiences in Religious Education* (1998).

John R. Lillis

Canaan Hymns

Xiao Min, a peasant woman and a house-church Christian, has composed more than thirteen hundred indigenous Chinese hymns. Often considered the "official hymnal" of the house churches in China, these songs are collectively known as the Canaan hymns and are also used in many Three-Self churches and throughout the Chinese diaspora.

The Canaan hymns are pentatonic and have the musical flavor of Chinese folksongs. Through use of imagery and themes that resonate in the Chinese worldview, the songs reflect a spiritual intimacy with God not possible through foreign hymns. One house-church member describes the Canaan hymns in this way: "When we sing the

Canaan hymns, we feel that God is entering into our very beings."

The three dynamics of Christian spirituality highlighted in this volume are all represented in the Canaan hymns. The sample hymn below (#270) contains themes of relation with nature, God, and the body of Christ; having a transformed attitude; and participation in God's purposes:

> The small grass never resent the barrenness of the soil.
> They are able to take deep root wherever they go.
> The stream never resents the height of many mountains,
> Flowing and bending, rushing to moisten the soil....
> May we love one another.
> This is truth and not emptiness.
> Let not things of the past crush our spirits.
> Let us have broadened hearts.
> From the corner of the sea to the shore of the sky,
> From the shore of the sky to the corner of the sea
> We labor together,
> For one person cannot complete the Great Commission.

The grass and stream represent believers related in a community. As the grass cannot grow apart from the stream, Christians cannot survive in isolation. They must labor together to accomplish God's purposes while having their attitudes transformed into those of Christ.

The Canaan hymns adapt the traditional Confucian emphasis on relationship. Fundamental to the ancient Chinese worldview, relationships connect one individual to another in devotion (*qing*) and loyalty (*zhong*). These virtues are emphasized as one Christian submits to another and as the whole body submits to Christ the head.

See also Asian Christian Spirituality; Worship.

For Further Reading: I. Sun, "Songs of Canaan," *Studia Liturgica* 37, no. 1 (2007): 98–116; http://www.canaanhymns.org.

Paul L. Neeley

Cappadocians, The

Leading fourth-century proponents of the Council of Nicea from central Asia Minor. Most prominent are Basil of Caesarea, Gregory of Nazianzus, and Gregory of Nyssa. Their efforts were central to normalizing the explicit profession of the full Godhead of the Son and the Holy Spirit, a profession that came from lives of prayer, worship, and devotion to the Scriptures.

Important influences include the great teacher Origen of Alexandria, whose contributions to the faith were vast, yet at times suspect. To preserve his best work, particularly his exegetical theory, Basil and Gregory of Nazianzus compiled selections into the *Philokalia* (of Origen). The national saint of Cappadocia was himself a disciple of Origen. Gregory Thaumaturgos (the "Wonder-Worker") (213–270) was a pioneering evangelist and missionary bishop in Cappadocia and renowned for performing miracles, healings, and exorcisms. Among his disciples was the grandmother of Basil and Gregory of Nyssa. Thus, also influential were women, especially Nonna (mother of Gregory of Nazianzus) and Macrina (Basil and Gregory of Nyssa's older sister). The latter was a prominent teacher and monastic leader, eulogized by Gregory of Nyssa in the *Life of Macrina*. Together they embodied a compelling multigenerational family spirituality.

The passion of Jesus Christ is central to Cappadocian reflection. That God is known from the cross—life in death, light in darkness, power in weakness—led them to emphasize the incarnation as the revelation of the life of God, so that all Scripture is seen to speak of the incarnate Word, doing so in a twofold manner, either of his divinity (the human who is God) or humanity (the God who is human). Moreover, this led them to highlight the total difference between the Creator and creation. Now, all inherent links were severed between God and creation, so that the God revealed on the cross was recognized as totally unknowable to the soul apart from God's initiative. This knowledge of God was beyond knowledge of created things, known only in the darkness of unknowing—the revelation that the uncreated is not created, since the uncreated became created, demonstrating both. So knowledge of God comes foremost in receiving God's grace in worship, prayer, and holiness, not by the rationalism of their opponents, Aetius and Eunomius, who taught knowledge of divine things through logical syllogisms. In contradistinction, the Cappadocians taught that divine knowledge comes through illumination and that reason is feeble apart from receiving fullness in the faith.

The Cappadocian commitment to the incarnation also saw them emphasize social concern for slaves and the poor—because now all human flesh has been honored. Moreover, monasticism was integral to their Christianity. While Gregory of Nazianzus sought a scholarly asceticism, Basil's involved greater physical exertion. It was Basil's monastic rule, the *Asceticon*, that would become the dominant rule in the Greek communion.

See also Basic of Caesarea; Gregory of Nyssa; Gregory Nazianzus; Vision of God.

For Further Reading: J. Behr, *The Nicene Faith* (2004); A. Louth, *The Origins of the Christian Mystical Tradition: From Plato to Denys* (2006); J. McGuckin, *St. Gregory of Nazianzus: An Intellectual Biography* (2001); A. Meredith, *The Cappadocians* (1995).

Timothy J. Becker

Cardenal, Ernesto (1925–)

Nicaraguan poet, revolutionary, and mystic. Cardenal began writing poetry at age seven. His university studies were in Mexico City and New York. After European travels, resistance work against Anastasio Somoza, and several years at Trappist and Benedictine monasteries, he was ordained a Roman Catholic priest in Managua in 1965. *Salmos* (1964) and *Oración por Marilyn Monroe* (1965) date from this period. Among his primary influences are Ezra Pound and Thomas Merton. In all his writings, Cardenal reflects a spirituality, and indeed an ontology, of love. As he wrote in *Vida en el Amor* (1979), "Everything that is not love is fundamentally impossible." His simple language and narrative style make his poetry accessible. The extensive *Canto Cósmico* (1989) combines epic, testimonial, and mystical language with images from the Bible, quantum physics, and everyday life.

El Evangelio en Solentiname (1979), influential for liberation theology, was a result of exploring the radical implications of the gospel with the islanders of Solentiname. From 1979–1987 Cardenal was Nicaragua's Sandinista minister of culture. He believed that the Sandinista revolution was a creative synthesis that overcame the contradiction between Marxism and Christianity. In 1983 he was chastised publicly by Pope John Paul II for that involvement. He later distanced himself from the Sandinista Front, criticizing its authoritarian streak, though he did not renounce his revolutionary ideals.

See also Latin America; Liberation Spirituality.

Nancy E. Bedford

Care of Souls

The care of souls, or "soul care" as it has come to be described, has a long history. It can be traced back to Jewish sages and wise guides of Israel, ancient Greek philosophers who were regarded as "physicians of souls," Jesus' counsel and teaching in the NT, and desert fathers and mothers who offered spiritual guidance and direction to multitudes. It was present in the patristic era when discipline and consolation were common practices, in the medieval church whose ministers were sometimes called "curates," and now in the contemporary pastoral theology movement with its focus on care and counseling.

Today the care of souls is classified within the broad context of pastoral ministry. In fact, the pastoral theology and pastoral care movements reflect efforts to recover and preserve the primary role of ministers as providers of soul care. The ministry of healing was once regarded almost exclusively as the mission and mandate of the church. This was before it evolved into a more collaborative and sometimes overlapping task between religious ministers and psychotherapists. Charles Holman, author of one of the earliest works on the subject of the cure of souls, insisted that the minister, more than anyone else, ought to be the most interested and competent in such a field. Carl Jung echoed the same sentiment: "We cannot expect the doctor to have anything to say about the ultimate questions of the soul. It is from the clergyman, not from the doctor, that the sufferer should expect such help." Indeed, for much of church history the care and cure of souls was treated above all as a spiritual undertaking—a perspective that ministers today need to reclaim despite the avalanche of new modes of caring dispensed by modern psychologies as added resources for the church.

Within the broad field of pastoral theology, the acknowledged ministerial tasks are primarily healing, sustaining, and guiding (although others in the field add *reconciling* as well). Seward Hiltner of the Meninger Clinic, the birthplace of Clinical Pastoral Education (CPE), said that *healing* has to do with the restoration of functional wholeness; *sustaining* involves comforting via upholding or standing by and with a sufferer; and *guiding* refers to the shepherding aspect of providing spiritual direction to people. He viewed the three together as a unified task, one that encompasses all the dimensions of shepherding.

Integrating them into his own applied understanding, Henri Nouwen, in his book *The Living Reminder* (1977), recast these three shepherding functions into the overlapping roles of a *pastor* (one who heals the wounds of the past), a *priest* (one who sustains life in the present), and a *prophet* (one who guides others into the future). In his unique ministry of soul care, Nouwen, as a pastoral theologian himself, wore all three hats, so to speak, in ways that seemed almost indistinguishable.

Ironically, according to pastoral theologian Thomas Oden, the contemporary practice of pastoral care has become removed from the classical tradition to which it owes its identity. Oden has lamented the fact that pastoral care today generally suffers from amnesia. As a corrective, he has documented this pastoral tradition, pointing out that it includes, for example, the writings of Cyprian on patience, jealousy, and envy; Tertullian concerning the soul; Chrysostom about the priesthood; Ambrose on the responsibilities of the clergy; and many helpful texts of Augustine dealing with the soul, happiness, patience, and grief. He singled out Gregory the Great's *Pastoral Care* as the prime example of classic pastoral counseling, a book regarded as indispensable in the field for more than a millennium. This magnificent work was followed by Bonaventure on the right ordering of the soul; Aquinas's treatment of subjects such as happiness, fear, anger, the emotions, the dispositions, love, and desire in his *Summa Theologica*; and Hugh St. Victor on preparing for confession, anointing the sick, and caring for the dying. Additionally, Oden has acknowledged the pastoral care contribution of the Reformation tradition, highlighting Luther's letters and table talk, Zwingli on the pastor, Calvin's letters, Martin Bucer on visiting the sick and the poor, George Herbert's *Country Parson*, Jeremy Taylor's spiritual exercises, Richard Baxter's reflections on self-acquaintance, and many eighteenth-century writers like Nicolas von Zinzendorf, Jonathan Edwards, and John Wesley, who all showed enormous interest in caring for individuals as well as communities.

Needless to mention, caring was paramount in the way ministry was carried out by the aforementioned exemplars. Their emphases coincided with the main thrust of the classic tradition of soul care. In fact, the Latin term *cura animarum* ("cure of souls") carried even more the sense of care than the idea of cure or healing. Just the same, both components figure in the history and art of Christian soul care. As David Benner has observed, "The response to the need of a remedy for sin and assistance in spiritual growth" involves the combined essence of "nurture and support as well as healing and restoration" of souls. Soul care has as its overarching goal the spiritual formation of the Christian's character. In essence, soul care is spiritual care aimed at the totality of humans as spiritual and bodily beings made in the image of God.

At the present time, the ever-expanding discipline of Christian soul care encompasses many intersecting approaches to spiritual formation and cuts across the fields of professional counseling, lay caregiving, and pastoral counseling, while drawing from the combined constructive wisdom of psychiatry and psychotherapy. Moreover, the field significantly includes varied styles of spiritual companioning (spiritual friendship, spiritual guidance, spiritual mentoring, and spiritual direction). Of the four companioning approaches mentioned, spiritual direction is the most venerable and the one most closely associated with the long established history of the cure of souls. Accordingly, Gary Moon and David Benner have suggested, its modern-day rediscovery represents "the recovery of the lost jewel in the crown of Christian soul care."

See also Counseling; Direction, Spiritual; Inner Healing; Mentoring, Spiritual.

For Further Reading: D. Benner, *Care of Souls* (1998); W. Clebsch and C. Jaekle, *Pastoral Care in Historical Perspective* (1964); S. Hiltner, *Preface to Pastoral Theology* (1954); C. Holman, *Cure of Souls* (1932); C. Jung, *Modern Man in Search of a Soul* (1939); C. Kemp, *Physicians of the Soul* (1947); J. T. McNeill, *A History of the Cure of Souls* (1951); G. Moon and D. Benner, *Spiritual Direction and the Care of Souls* (2004); T. Oden, *Care of Souls in the Classic Tradition* (1984).

Wil Hernandez

Carmelite Spirituality

Carmelite spirituality has its roots in the establishment of the Order of Our Lady of Mount Carmel in the late twelfth century. The Rule of St. Albert, which serves as the foundation of the order's spirituality, was given to the community between 1206 and 1214 and has remained generally unchanged. The rule states that Carmelites are to strive for a life of solitude, retirement in one's cell, silence, renunciation, and penance. Penance includes severe poverty, manual labor, abstinence from meat, fasting for the greater part of a year, and, most important, a life of prayer.

The Carmelite is to practice constant communion with Christ through unceasing prayer. Whenever distractions enter the mind, the Carmelite is simply to recollect his or her thoughts and return to the work of prayer. Contemplation is the womb that gives birth to works of faith. This relationship between the active and contemplative dimensions essentially defines the delicate balance of Carmelite spirituality: the weight of the active life against its necessary root, the contemplative one. Solitude, silence, and self-denial are further practices that are designed to support this balance and cultivate the Carmelite goal of the soul's union with God through a life of unceasing contemplative prayer.

The contributions of the Carmelites to Christian spirituality have been especially meaningful in the Roman Catholic tradition. They emphasize devotion to Mary as the mother of God, and Joseph, whom they call father. They were also the first to practice the daily celebration of the Eucharist, a tradition that has since become widespread in Catholic worship. The Carmelites were advocates of the doctrine of the immaculate conception of Mary even before its formal definition at Vatican I in 1869. Modern ecumenical practices of contemplative prayer stem from the prayer practices of the Carmelites. No other order has produced so many writers on mysticism; these include Teresa of Avila, John of the Cross, Edith Stein, and Thérèse of Lisieux, whose "Little Way," a simplified approach to God emphasizing his merciful love, continues to impact Christian spirituality. The teachings of John of the Cross were particularly influential for the late Pope John Paul II.

See also Dark Night; John of the Cross; Mendicant; Teresa of Avila.

For Further Reading: *The Collected Works of St. John of the Cross*, trans. K. Kavanaugh and O. Rodriguez (1991); Teresa of Avila, *The Way of Perfection*, ed. H. Carrigan Jr. (2000).

Cynthia Cheshire

Carmichael, Amy (1867–1951)

Writer and missionary to India. Carmichael was the founder of Dohnavur Fellowship and the author of more than thirty books relating to her orphanage work in India, particularly as it related to spiritual formation. Born in Northern Ireland of Presbyterian parents, she was strong-minded and independent, shunning any association and collaboration with other missionaries. Her closest ties were with the Keswick Convention, whose director, Robert Wilson, had adopted her after the death of her parents. The focus of her ministry was rescuing girls — orphans, child widows, and temple prostitutes.

Carmichael was committed to celibacy and expected those who worked with her to make the same commitment. As a young woman while briefly ministering in Japan, she testified that while she was meditating and praying in a cave, God spoke to her, assuring her that he would meet all her needs — especially her struggles with loneliness — as a single woman. In India she formed the Sisters of the Common Life — a Protestant religious order for single women who were forced to leave the ministry if they married. Many who joined the ministry had grown up at Dohnavur.

Carmichael was very critical of other missionaries in India and was concerned that Dohnavur might become contaminated with the outside world. "O to be delivered from half-hearted missionaries!" she wrote. "Don't come if you haven't made up your mind to live for *one thing* — the winning of souls." She held a tight rein over her work, convinced that she was divinely directed by God — sometimes through Jesus, other times through angels or visions. She died at Dohnavur after fifty-five years of ministry at the age of eighty-three.

For Further Reading: D. Bingham, *The Wild-Bird Child: A Life of Amy Carmichael* (2004); E. Elliot, *A Chance to Die: The Life and Legacy of Amy Carmichael* (1987); S. Wellman, *Amy Carmichael* (1998).

Ruth A. Tucker

Caroline Divines

These were a loosely connected group of clergy in the Church of England during the 17th century who collectively developed a distinctly Anglican approach to Christian faith and practice through their preaching, writing, poetry, and ministry. Lancelot Andrewes was the spiritual father of this group, which also included William Laud, John Cosin, George Herbert, Jeremy Taylor, Nicholas Ferrar, Herbert Thorndike, Thomas Ken, Simon Patrick, and many others (see More and Cross for more). Building on the sixteenth-century work of John Jewel and Richard Hooker, they pursued a *via media* (middle way) between Roman Catholicism and Puritan Calvinism, based on Holy Scripture and church tradition as understood by human reason. They were loyal to the monarchy, believing in the divine right of kings even in a time of revolution, and to the worship and theology of the *Book of Common Prayer*, adhering to a set liturgy even when it was banned during the Commonwealth.

The English term *Caroline* comes from the Latin word for Charles, *Carolus*. Strictly speaking, the Caroline period refers to the reign of Charles I (1625–1649) and Charles II (1662–1685) in England. Practically, this period began in 1594 with the publication of Hooker's *Of the Laws of Ecclesiastical Polity* (books 1–4), and ended with the first two decades of the 18th century. During this period, the King James Version of the Bible was produced (1611), the first English colonies in America were established (Jamestown in 1607, Plymouth in 1620), and the edition of the *Book of Common Prayer* that became the standard for all other prayer books was developed (1662). One of the Caroline divines, George Herbert, wrote some of the finest English poetry, while another, Jeremy Taylor, wrote two books of practical Christian living (*Holy Living* and *Holy Dying*) that deeply influenced several generations of Anglican Christians. A third, Nicholas Ferrar, established and led the Christian community of Little Gidding, recalled by T. S. Eliot in the last of his *Four Quartets*.

Taken as a whole, the Caroline divines developed a form of Anglicanism with the following characteristics. First, they had a high view of Episcopal ministry, believing that bishops were in apostolic succession dating back to the 1st century. Second, they celebrated an essentially catholic liturgy, combining ordered beauty with scholarly preaching. Third, they practiced a sacramental piety, placing great emphasis on the efficacy of the Eucharist and baptism. Fourth, they followed an Arminian theology, believing that while God wills all to be saved, humans have the free will to accept or reject that salvation. Fifth, they taught a practical spirituality that stressed right behavior as a sign of God's grace operating in a person's life. Sixth, they led a church life that depended on ordained ministry rather than laity, resulting in rather limited congregational involvement. These characteristics laid the foundation for the "high church" party within the Church of England and deeply influenced the Oxford Movement of the 19th century.

See also Andrewes, Lancelot; Anglican Spirituality; Caroline Poets; Oxford Movement.

For Further Reading: P. More and F. Cross, *Anglicanism* (1957); G. Rowell et al., eds., *Love's Redeeming Work* (2001); J. Taylor, *Holy Living and Dying* (2007); J. Wall, *George Herbert* (1981).

David Montzingo

Caroline Poets

Caroline devotional poetry, composed during and sometimes between the reigns of Charles I and II, is often described as metaphysical. Though John Dryden and others censured the esoteric thought and excessive wit of metaphysical verse, poets of the period used philosophical learning, startling metaphors, and ingenious wordplay for sacred ends to portray the complex, often unstable, relationship between fallen humans and the perfect, inscrutable God with whom they longed to commune. As with Shakespeare's Hamlet, Caroline devotional poets often pondered, "What should such fellows as I do crawling between earth and heaven?" only to recognize that a "special providence" governed the unfolding of their lives and the operation of the universe.

The Welsh priest and poet George Herbert (1593–1633) wrote on the cusp of the Caroline age, but his posthumously published collection of religious verse, *The Temple* (1633), was issued well into the reign of Charles I. *The Temple* was composed when the ecclesiastical *via media* or "middle way" of Elizabeth I was under siege. Herbert's priestly commitment to a moderate Church of England is most evident in "The British Church," in which he joyfully viewed the "perfect lineaments, and hue" of a church that is "neither too mean, nor yet too gay," neither "outlandish" nor "undrest." *The Temple* conveys a sense of temporal and spatial order, and thus physical and spiritual security, because it is embedded in and shaped in part by the church calendar as well as by the architecture of the church and the spaces, objects, and ceremonies within it. Yet despite an overarching sense of sacred order and harmony in the collection, the speaker in many of the poems is spiritually out of tune. Herbert neither minimized sinful nature nor concealed spiritual scuffles with God. However, the moments in which the feeble speaker is overcome with grief, fear, discontent, disorder, or desperation are considerably offset by those in which he hears the voice of a tender and forgiving Lord, who calls to and comforts him, gently guiding him toward spiritual assurance.

The Temple was a major influence on seventeenth-century devotional poets because its dramatic, dialogic, and devout sacred idiom resonated with the spirituality of Christians across the confessional spectrum. The Welsh poet and translator Henry Vaughan (1621–1695) described himself in the preface to *Silex Scintillans* (1650, 1655), his two-part volume of devotional poetry, as a "pious convert" of Herbert. Vaughan viewed *The Temple* as "holy writing," habitually importing Herbert's words and images into his lyrics. However, these allusions are often recontextualized in poems that speak of spatial, temporal, and spiritual disorientation. By the time Vaughan, a royalist Anglican, published *Silex Scintillans*, England had endured civil war, Charles I had been executed, Oliver Cromwell ruled as Lord Protector, and the church was governed by Puritans. Therefore, a number of Vaughan's poems envision a poisoned and tattered church ruled by men who seek personal glory rather than the public good. Cut off from the "true church," Vaughan spiritually reoriented himself in his lyrics by turning to biblical, alchemical, and hermetic discourses that helped him uncover evidence of the Creator in the world of nature where he found the spiritual steadfastness that humanity lacks. So, too, he nostalgically dwelt on the past, both on the pristine early days of humanity as recorded in Genesis, and on the "harmless age" of childhood (in his poem "Childhood"). These partial revelations of God spiritually sustain the speaker of *Silex Scintillans* as he awaits the second coming of Christ.

The devotional writings of the English priest, chaplain, and poet Thomas Traherne (c. 1637–1674) are often studied alongside those of Vaughan, because both poets were drawn to the subjects of nature and childhood, which they associated with innocence and light. Though granted a clerical post during the Interregnum, Traherne was ordained in the Episcopal Church of England at the Restoration, and the spiritual optimism of his works reflects changing political circumstances as well as his personal temperament. His poems do acknowledge the sinful habits of humanity; yet they register far less spiritual angst than those of Herbert or Vaughan, as Traherne eagerly gestured toward wonder, beauty, delight, felicity, and bliss, themes that surface time and again in his lyrics. Drawing on an eclectic range of sources, from the biblical, mystical, and hermetic to the scholastic, humanist, and Neoplatonic, Traherne constituted the Christian in his works as an active, if morally imperfect, agent who can freely choose, through grace, to experience with childlike wonder and delight the world God created and intended.

See also Caroline Divines.

For Further Reading: P. Cheney et al., eds., *Early Modern English Poetry* (2006); D. Inge, ed., *Happiness and Holiness: Thomas Traherne and His Writings* (2008); J. Post, *English Lyric Poetry* (1999); A. Rudrum, *Henry Vaughan* (1981); H. Wilcox, "George Herbert," in *The Cambridge Companion to English Poetry: Donne to Marvell*, ed. T. N. Corns (1993); R. Young, *Doctrine and Devotion in Seventeenth-Century Poetry* (2000).

Holly Faith Nelson

Carthusian Spirituality

Carthusian spirituality nurtures intimacy with God through solitude in the context of a small community. Practicing silence, ascetic disciplines, and utter simplicity, these monks relish God's presence as they study, read Scripture, eat, and labor alone in their gardens and workshops. Relinquishing active ministry, Carthusians dwell "hidden with Christ in God" (Col. 3:3) and commit their lives to contemplative prayer. Their lifestyle calls Christians of all denominations to cultivate solitude and profound affection for Christ.

Living originally in groups of twelve monks plus a prior, Carthusian charter houses provide members with separate cells (four-room hermitages) arranged on three sides of a common area. The fourth side accommodates the chapel, chapter house, infirmary, and refectory where meals are celebrated together on feast days. They gather corporately in the chapel for morning Eucharist, vespers, and matins; the other liturgical hours are said alone in their cells. Once each week they set aside silence to enjoy conversation during a three-hour walk together. Carthusian monks are ordained, and the *conversi*—lay brothers who handle the practical affairs of the compound—live a balance of the active and contemplative life. A few female communities exist.

Initiated in 1084 by Bruno (c. 1030 – 1101), the Carthusian order was one of several new movements reviving desert spirituality in the 11th century. The first charter house was founded in the Chartreuse Mountains north of Grenoble, France, and the new order was approved by Pope Innocent II in 1133. It called its first general council in 1141 and boasted 195 priories at its peak. Carthusians follow guidelines from Guigo I, fifth prior of the Grand Chartreuse, recorded in his *Customs*, a simple instruction with ample freedom. In his *Letter to the Brothers at Mont-Dieu* (*Golden Epistle*), William of St. Thierry lauded Carthusian piety as the highest model of Christian spirituality.

Though few in number, Carthusians have made a remarkable imprint on Christian devotion over the centuries through their translation and printing of spiritual classics. Carthusians preach through the written page. Their authors include Adam Scott, Denis the Carthusian, and Guigo II, who's *Ladder of Monks* encapsulates monastic devotion in the four steps of *lectio divina*. Ludolf of Saxony's *Life of Christ* impacted generations and inspired Ignatius of Loyola's spiritual exercises. Through writing and example, Carthusian spirituality offers all believers a model of ascetic rigor and singular devotion in the pursuit of union with God through eremitic solitude and contemplation.

See also Monasticism; Sacred Heart; Solitude.

For Further Reading: A Carthusian, *The Way of Silent Love*, trans. an English solitary (1993); *Carthusian Spirituality*, CWS (1997); *Guigo II: Ladder of Monks and Twelve Meditations*, trans. E.

Colledge and J. Walsh (1981); R. Lockhart, *Halfway to Heaven* (1999).

Glenn E. Myers

Cassian, John (c. 360 – 432)

Early spiritual theologian. Cassian was originally a monk in Bethlehem who traveled throughout Egypt, learning monastic theology from the monks of the desert. He explicated the spirituality that he learned in two works, both written in Latin: *The Conferences* and *The Institutes*. These works were written many years after Cassian had moved from Egypt to Gaul (Marseilles) after a lengthy sojourn in Constantinople with John Chrysostom. In Gaul, at the bishop's request, Cassian founded two monasteries, one for men and one for women. Apart from his two monastic treatises, Cassian also authored *On the Incarnation of the Lord* in an attempt to address the heresy of Nestorianism, and engaged in a debate with Augustine of Hippo regarding Pelagianism.

Cassian's spirituality is thoroughly monastic. *The Institutes* are directed toward assisting monks in overcoming the eight principal vices, and consist of twelve books. The first four books discuss monastic clothing, the canonical hours of prayer, and the virtues. The remaining eight books each discuss one of the principal vices (gluttony, fornication, avarice, anger, sadness, acedia, vainglory, and pride). *The Conferences* comprise twenty-four books, detailing the monastic theology of fifteen Egyptian monks. In the work, Cassian constructs a unified spirituality where the monk's *telos* (final end) is the kingdom of God or beatitude and his *skopos* (this-worldly end) is purity of heart. For Cassian, humility makes it possible for the monk to discern between the truly good and lesser goods, and such discretion leads to purity of heart. Purity of heart prepares one teleologically for the fullness of God's kingdom but makes contemplation of God in the present life possible also. Cassian believes that contemplation in this life anticipates and is a participation in heavenly contemplation. Purity of heart, for Cassian, progresses over the course of one's life. It consists of differing degrees and has three main characteristics: ascetical practice, growth in love, and tranquility of heart. Regarding asceticism, Cassian states that though ascetical practices can help one toward purity of heart, they are not the goal but rather a means toward the greater ends (*telos* and *skopos*). Therefore, the monk's bodily mortifications must always remain balanced, giving Cassian's spirituality a healthy perspective on God's creation (including the human body) that is lacking in much early Christian monastic literature.

See also Monasticism.

For Further Reading: T. Merton, *Cassian and the Fathers* (2005); C. Stewart, *Cassian the Monk* (1998).

Greg Peters

Catechumenate

For two millennia now, the church has been confronted with the daunting task of helping new believers become mature disciples. Early on in its history, the catechumenate was developed to accomplish this purpose. The root Greek word, from which *catechesis*, *catechumen*, and *catechism* also come, means to "sound downward," as a sonar does, or to "echo." Using oral instruction and strict discipline, many church fathers treated the catechumenate like athletic training. Doctrinal instruction was only part of it; its purpose was more comprehensive preparation for baptism and first Communion, which were deferred until new believers were considered ready.

The catechumenate emerged in the 2nd century and for at least two reasons. First, the church began attracting larger numbers of people who, coming from pagan backgrounds, knew little about the story of salvation and Christian belief. Second, the threat of persecution made conversion a weighty decision. Such high cost demanded high commitment, which in turn required careful and serious training. Thus, the precedent of Philip's *immediate* baptism of the converted Ethiopian eunuch (Acts 8) gave way to a judiciously longer period of baptismal preparation.

However varied in the particulars, the ancient catechumenate had certain features that won widespread acceptance by the 3rd century. Ordinary believers shared their faith with friends, neighbors, and coworkers, drawing them into the orbit of house churches, most of which were located in urban areas. At some point, these seekers would request enrollment in the catechumenate. Church leaders would examine them to see if they were ready and willing to submit to the regimen of training, and "sponsors" (most likely Christian friends) would testify to their readiness. Then church leaders would train the catechumens in the biblical story, Christian doctrine, and Christian living, always with a view toward transformation, while their sponsors served as mentors. At the end of this period, catechumens would be examined once more to assess their readiness. If so, they would undergo a highly choreographed set of rituals—exorcisms, vigils, fastings, anointings, and prayers—which culminated on Easter morning in baptism, confirmation or chrismation, and their first Eucharist. During Easter week the "neophytes," as they were called, would receive further instruction, mostly on the sacraments.

The catechumenate was shortened by the late 4th century, largely due to the flood of new believers clamoring to enter the church. Eventually it faded away almost entirely—but not quite. Abbas in the desert, and abbots in the monasteries that came later on, continued the practice of training "athletes for God"—though over time the practice tended, unfortunately, to create a perception of the "religious" as spiritual elite. Centuries later the Reformers rediscovered the importance of the catechumenate, by then known as confirmation, as a means of preparing baptized believers for their first Communion. They wrote catechisms too, usually in a question-and-answer form, as instructional aids. Luther believed that the home was the best place for such instruction and therefore urged parents to catechize their children. Over time, however, pastors and teachers assumed the major responsibility for that endeavor. The evangelical movement developed a different strategy for catechizing new believers. Far more rigorous than most small groups today, these "colleges of piety" (Pietists), "bands" (Moravians), or "class meetings" (Wesleyans) guided believers through a process of doctrinal training and spiritual discipline.

Today various parachurch movements, such as Bible Study Fellowship and Navigators, as well as churches that stress discipleship, represent the latest iterations of the catechumenate, which now, as always, provides instruction in basic Christian beliefs and practices. If there is a difference today, at least in evangelical churches, it is that approaches to "the catechumenate" are typically less cohesive, integrative, rigorous, or connected to the administration of the sacraments and less focused on the spiritual formation of the catechumen. Nonetheless, the original vision, to some extent at least, carries on — to help believers, both new and old, in very intentional ways to become mature in Christ.

See also Conversion; Formation, Spiritual.

For Further Reading: M. Johnson, *The Rites of Christian Initiation* (2007); J. Van Engen, ed., *Educating People of Faith* (2004); J. Westerhoff III and O. C. Edwards Jr., eds., *A Faithful Church: Issues in the History of Catechesis* (1981); E. Yarnold, *The Awe-Inspiring Rites of Initiation* (2001).

Gerald L. Sittser

Catharism

Catharism (from Gr. *katharoi*, "pure ones"), a sect that emerged during the Middle Ages, and widely regarded as heretical, is most prominently defined by its dualistic belief in equal and opposing creative forces. Though the full origin of Catharism is debated, most agree that Gnostic dualism, and more specifically Manichaeism, had significant influence. The Cathars or Cathari (as adherents of Catharism are called) probably also appropriated the dualistic teachings of Bogomil, a Bulgarian priest during the mid-10th century.

The central belief of Catharism is of two opposing and creative principles — one good (which formed positive spirit) and one evil (which formed negative matter) — that are at war with each other. This dualistic belief system caused Cathars to pursue a life of asceticism and flee from physical and material desires, seeing all material creation as evil. As in earlier Manichaean communities, the practicalities of these beliefs varied among Cathars and caused two classes to develop: the elite "perfects" and the less rigorous "believers." "Perfects" adhered to a strict lifestyle that condemned marriage and abstained from any animal products. "Believers" lived less rigid lives but sought to receive a sacrament when in danger of death. The work of Jesus was minimally significant to Cathars; they acknowledged that he had preached good doctrine, but they saw no value in his suffering, death, or resurrection.

Catharism began in Western Europe but found less hostility in Eastern Europe, though a significant number of Cathars remained in southern France. The Christian church in Europe was no stranger to heresy and judged Cathari believers to be such. Dominic and Bishop Diego made significant spiritual contributions to the church in the 12th and 13th centuries by responding to Catharism with a call for orthodox teaching among Christians in southern France and a more disciplined lifestyle.

Though their initial success was varied, Bishop Diego's and Dominic's efforts had lasting effects on Christianity's response to heresy in France and throughout Europe. Unlike some of his contemporaries, Dominic had no part in the violent and repressive measures that the Christian church adopted against the Cathars, but rather saw lasting improvement in the spiritual and moral life of clergy as the proper response and solution to heresy. Like many other instances of heresy throughout Christianity's history, Catharism exposed areas of weakness in the church's practice and theology and caused clergy to reevaluate their teaching and lifestyle.

For Further Reading: E. Ladurie, *Montaillou* (1978); G. Shriver, "Images of Catharism and the Historian's Task," in *Contemporary Reflections on the Medieval Christian Tradition*, ed. G. Shriver (1974), 67 – 80; P. Vaux-de-Cernay, "A Description of Cathars and Waldenses," in *Heresies of the High Middle Ages*, ed. W. Wakefield and A. Evans (1991), 235 – 41.

Julie Oostra

Catherine of Genoa (1447 – 1510)

Italian mystic and humanitarian. Catherine selflessly served the sick and dying in Genoa and later became the hospital's director. The youngest of five children born into a leading noble family with close papal connections, her parents arranged her marriage at sixteen to a nobleman. Having wished to join a convent, she now found herself in a violent, abusive, and childless marriage.

In her midtwenties, she experienced a mystical union with God, and later her husband had a similar conversion experience and joined with the Franciscans. With no connections to a religious order, she sought God in private devotion and in serving the needy, particularly during the late fifteenth-century plague that wreaked havoc on Genoa, killing some 80 percent of the population.

Catherine is best known through her writings: *Dialogues of the Soul and Body* and *Treatise on Purgatory*. The former volume is a cleverly written conversation — sometimes argument — between her spiritual inclinations and physical desires. The latter describes purgatory very differently than was typically portrayed by mystics; it was a not a pit of sulfur populated by suffering sinners, but rather a pleasant place to prepare for eternal glory.

Before she died, she gave to her goddaughter this blessing: "Jesus in your heart! Eternity in your mind! The will of God in all your actions! But above all, love, God's love, entire love!" She was canonized in 1737.

For Further Reading: C. Balfour and H. Irvine, *Saint Catherine of Genoa* (2008); Catherine of Genoa, *The Life and Doctrine of Saint Catherine of Genoa* (2009); *Catherine of Genoa*, CWS (1986).

Ruth A. Tucker

Catherine of Siena (1347 – 1380)

Mystical writer of the Dominican order. Born the twenty-fourth child in her family, Catherine Benincasa demonstrated a distinct sensitivity to God. At age six, while walking home from the church of Saint Dominic, she experienced a vision of Christ blessing her as he would a priest. Thereafter, her growing spirituality and devotion to God informed her choices and defined her relationships. Despite family efforts toward a traditional marriage, Catherine defiantly pursued her call, joining the Third Order of Saint Dominic at age sixteen. After living in solitude for three years — a time of profound dialogue and experiential living with Christ — Catherine began a varied public ministry within a turbluent society and the Catholic Church.

Her ministry embraced the dying masses victimized by the bubonic plague, or Black Death — the most devastating pandemic in human history. The plague's severity worsened social upheaval and focused her attention on injustice, especially the needs of the marginalized. One prisoner requested she be by his side as he faced execution. Later she told her confessor, Raymond of Capua, "My heart cannot grasp it.... I received his head into my hands.... [I was] so aware of the fragrance.... I could not remove the blood." A contemplative awareness of God's love for her moved Catherine to an outpouring of love for others in word and action. Increasingly attracting followers, she humbly valued spiritual discourse and accountability with Raymond, as well as with her Dominican sisters.

Catherine steadfastly served Christ, not personal agendas, yet inevitably repositioned views of women's roles in ministry. Defying convention, her convictions led her to bold confrontations with Pope Gregory XI, commanding him to leave Avignon, where the papacy had become a French puppet, and return to Rome. In 1970 Pope Paul VI affirmed her "charism of exhortation" when he named Catherine a doctor of the church. Her holy boldness with papal authorities was only part of Catherine's extensive correspondence. Nearly four hundred of her letters survive, signifying her widespread influence and engagement with others from the destitute to the powerful.

Catherine's most famous work, *The Dialogue* (1378), focuses on her life's central theme: a ministry made possible by her ever-deepening dialogue with God. In *The Dialogue*, she records the Lord's conversations with her: "Your love should be sincere: You should love your neighbors with the same love with which you love me." Catherine's mother, previously thwarting her daughter's attempts to live unconventionally, joined the Dominican Third Order after widowed and worked closely with her. In the chaos of Catherine's own "dark ages"— fraught with plague, schism, and poverty—she offered a voice of clarity and compassion.

See also Dominican Spirituality.

For Further Reading: A. Curtayne, *Saint Catherine of Siena* (1980); Raymond of Capua, *The Life of St. Catherine of Siena*, trans. G. Lamb (2003).

Kimberly Dawsey-Richardson

Caussade, Jean-Pierre de

See de Caussade, Jean-Pierre.

Celebration

Celebration carries a number of related meanings. Fundamentally, it is an action or event that marks a special occasion or affirms something important or good. Usually it is communal, and normally implicit in it is a sense of rejoicing. Christians have much to celebrate in the grace and goodness of God, their salvation in Christ, and the empowering presence of the Holy Spirit. Yet historically, in their worship, personal devotion, and lifestyle, evangelicals may not easily be associated with celebration, as their theology has tended to view the world quite negatively. Following the Puritans, their worship has tended to be stripped of much ceremony and drama, and their devotional practices are usually centered on the study of Scripture and the practice of extempore prayer, in each case with a considerable emphasis on the obeying of divine commands. A common word has been "observance" rather than "celebration." They have "observed" the Lord's Supper rather than "celebrated" the Eucharist, and the language of "divine ordinance" has characterized their spirituality, with its emphasis on obedience to God's will as communicated through Scripture, rather than celebrating human creativity. So the Puritans rejected any written words in worship that they perceived to be of human invention and allowed only those practices that they could understand as being either commanded or exemplified in Scripture. This has tended to make their worship, and that of their evangelical heirs, quite cerebral and lacking in joyful emotion.

Yet there has been joy and rejoicing. While it can be found in some of the Puritan writings, it became more communal and public when the evolving hymnody moved beyond metrical psalms and their limiting meters in the 18th century. Hymns began to express the joy of God's saving grace, and the outpouring of joyful, as well as penitent, emotion in times of revival encouraged the development of more exuberant expressions of worship. This has become apparent as the

Christian community has become more ethnically diverse, and is particularly evident in the worship of charismatic renewal, which has influenced many mainstream denominations, especially those with large evangelical constituencies. Such has been the change in worship ethos that the beginning of the 21st century sees some worship specialists arguing for a correcting move away from services that are wholly celebratory, to ones in which there is shadow as well as light, confession of sins as well as the celebrating of God's goodness. A greater engagement in issues of justice and peace has also tempered the note of celebration and has led many evangelicals to respond in their worship to the brokenness of the world in their worship, as well as in practical acts of service and prophetic witness. Nonetheless, the closing decades of the 20th century saw a theological shift in which evangelical lifestyle affirmed contemporary culture in worship and daily living. There are differing views as to whether this is an accommodation to the spirit of the age or a life-affirming celebration of human creativity as a gift of God.

See also Eucharistic Spirituality; Joy; Thanksgiving; Worship.

For Further Reading: C. Ellis, *Gathering: A Theology and Spirituality of Worship in Free Church Tradition* (2004); R. Foster, *Celebration of Discipline* (1978); J. White, *Protestant Worship* (1989).

Christopher J. Ellis

Celibacy

Choosing to remain unmarried and abstaining from sexual activity for spiritual reasons is recorded early in church history when the ascetic lifestyle gained popularity during the first three centuries. Like martyrdom, the celibate life grew in popularity among Christians seeking purgation and spiritual maturation through intense physical discipline. Thus, celibacy became associated with the physical and spiritual rigors of monastic life and eventually became mandatory for priests in the Roman Catholic Church, though not the Eastern Church. The Protestant church initially rejected the constraints of celibacy during the Reformation and even went so far as to elevate the position of married clergy above that of celibate clergy. Recently this Protestant view is being replaced by growing regard for the spiritual and ministerial benefits of the voluntary celibate life.

Celibacy was more than just a physical fast as celibate individuals seek to satisfy all desires with the pleasure of intimate spiritual union with God. By abstaining from the physical pleasures of sex, one's mind and soul were more able to understand the spiritual fulfillment that comes only from God—and not from another person. Early on celibacy was also a means of Christian female empowerment, since the submissiveness and restrictions associated with patriarchal marriage were thereby avoided.

Motivation for celibacy often came in the belief that it was a more perfect lifestyle, as Jesus himself was celibate and presented the benefits of this way of life to his disciples in Matthew 19:10–13. Jesus' explanation here makes it clear that only some individuals, who are able to accept this teaching and to "whom it has been given," are expected to maintain celibate lives.

Given that "at the resurrection people will neither marry nor be given in marriage," celibacy is often motivated by an eschatological desire for the world to come (Matt. 22:30). Celibacy is also seen as freeing one from the logical obligations that come with marriage and children. Paul insisted that it was good for a man not to marry, and offered an important rationale for singlehood, but conceded that one should marry as a means to avoid sexual immorality (1 Cor. 7). Further, Paul did not allow for divorce as a way to establish celibacy, but encouraged married individuals to fulfill their marital duties.

See also Body; Chastity; Monasticism; Sexuality.

For Further Reading: D. Cozzens, *Freeing Celibacy* (2006); John Paul II, *The Theology of the Body* (1997); I. Kauffmann, *Follow Me* (2009).

Julie Oostra

Celtic Spirituality

Celtic spirituality refers to the distinctive traditions of life, prayer, and worship rooted in the early Christian cultures on the fringes of the British Isles, particularly Ireland, Wales, and the highlands and islands of Scotland. Christianity came to Britain under the protection of the Roman Empire, but it spread beyond Roman territory and flourished after Rome withdrew, so that Ireland, in the dark centuries after the fall of Rome, was probably the brightest light of Christian culture in all of Western Europe. From Ireland, Columba, in the 6th century established a center on Iona, from which much of Scotland and northern England were Christianized, leading to the establishment (under Aidan) of another monastic center at Lindisfarne (Holy Island). Wandering Celtic monks evangelized much of northern and central Europe in an arc reaching (with Columbanus) as far as Austria. Today Iona and Lindisfarne remain important centers of spirituality, both generic and Christian.

Though eventually this isolated branch of British Christianity was reunited with Roman Catholicism, its distinctive character has continued to exert a powerful, though sometimes ambivalent, influence on Christian spirituality. It has often been tempting for Christians to read into Celtic Christianity what they see missing in their own time. Thus, there have been many revivals and discoveries of "Celtic spirituality" over the centuries, which usually reveal, as Ian Bradley has sensitively demonstrated, more about the needs of their own time than about the early centuries of Irish and British Christianity.

Nevertheless, the spiritual legacy of Celtic Christianity is important, not so much because it is *Celtic*, but because it has enabled Christians to recover and reaffirm often-neglected aspects of "mere Christianity," which turn out to be "mere humanity," redeemed and set on its true course: the importance of creation, of physicality, of human connectedness to a particular place and to other creatures, of rituals and rhythms in life, and, most important, the presence of God in our daily activities.

All of these characteristics are aspects of rural paganism as well, a fact that has made some Christians suspicious of all things "Celtic." On the other hand, contemporary "neo-pagans" are often bemused to find that the high points of Celtic culture turn out to be Celtic *Christian* culture. These apparent contradictions are the result of the fact that Christianity in these Celtic lands was initiated by a Roman culture that withdrew before it left a permanent mark on the native culture. The result is a kind of redeemed, Christianized paganism. Since *pagan* in its original meaning meant not "anti-Christian" but rather something like "rooted in a place," the traditions of Celtic Christianity are particularly attractive to our largely urban culture.

Some of these attractive features of Celtic Christianity are caught in potent visual symbols, such as the Celtic cross—the circle, which pictures creation, centered on and upheld by the self-giving love of God, pictured by the cross. Likewise, the great illuminated gospels, particularly the *Book of Kells* (produced on Iona) and *The Lindisfarne Gospels*, gloriously reflect an awareness of the interpenetrating Word and Spirit of God, which bind creation together and give it life.

It is the Celtic tradition of prayer that has been most inspiring to recent Christians. Some of this is caught in ancient hymns like "St. Patrick's Breastplate" ("I bind unto myself today the strong name of the Trinity"), with its very popular verse:

Christ as a light
Illumine and guide me.
Christ as a shield
O'ershadow me.
Christ under me;

Christ over me;
Christ beside me
On my left and my right.
This day be within and
Without me.

But the greatest source for Celtic prayer is the collection of "hymns and incantations" called the *Carmina Gadelica*, gathered from the oral traditions of the highlands and islands of Scotland at the end of the 19th century. These prayers and blessings invoke and recognize God's presence in the most mundane experiences of life: rowing a boat, building a fire, or milking a cow. Though the activities themselves may be foreign to most contemporary Christians, the recognition of the daily immanence and intimacy of God is deeply attractive. Another feature of this tradition is its vivid Trinitarianism, evident in this invocation from a typical personal prayer:

I am placing my soul and my body
In Thy safe keeping this night, O God,
In Thy safe keeping, O Jesus Christ,
In Thy safe keeping, O Spirit of Perfect Truth.
The Three who would defend my cause
Be keeping me this night from harm.

These splendid and intimate prayers invoking the triune God into every aspect of daily life have entered many anthologies, prayer books, and liturgies. They have also been the model for a revived tradition of prayer (available in many anthologies of the contemporary work of David Adams, long-time minister of the church on Lindisfarne) and the hymns and songs of John Bell of the Iona community. In particular, the text and spirit of this vital remnant of an old tradition informs *Celtic Daily Prayer*, an influential book of prayers and readings published by the Northumbrian Community. The dispersed Northumbrian community itself, centered on Lindisfarne but with an influence around the world, is one of the best examples of the happy contemporary merging of Celtic and evangelical spirituality.

See also Patrick of Ireland.

For Further Reading: I. Bradley, *Celtic Christianity* (1999); T. Cahill, *How the Irish Saved Civilization* (1995); O. Davies and F. Boyd, eds., *Celtic Christian Spirituality* (1995); E. De Waal, ed., *The Celtic Vision: Selections from the Carmina Gadelica* (1988).

Loren Wilkinson

Centering Prayer

Centering prayer is a specific form of contemplative prayer (also known as mental prayer, monastic prayer, or simply meditation). Centering prayer takes its name from the practice of quieting oneself and focusing on a word, repeated most often silently to oneself, as a way of focusing on God and "centering" one's life around this encounter with God. For example, one might repeat the word "Savior" slowly and quietly, often in rhythm with your breathing. As your breathing slows and you enter into a quieter and more contemplative state, you would stop repeating the word and simply rest with your mind centered on God. When distractions occur, you may repeat this word again to return to this still, quiet place. You may or may not repeat your word to transition back to your active daily life. Variations may include using icons to focus one's vision, rather than having one's eyes closed. The amount of time one spends in centering prayer depends on how proficient one is in such forms of still prayer and how easily one is able to stay attentive to God without being distracted or fading into sleep.

The purposes of centering prayer are many. It establishes a pattern for finding a time and quiet space in the midst of one's busy life. It refreshes and recharges the body and mind, as well as the spirit. It creates a space for a person to listen to oneself and one's body. Most important, though, it creates a regular opportunity for one to listen to the voice of God in one's life, simply being still and opening oneself up to God's Spirit.

The tradition of Christian contemplative prayer in general can be traced back to the Greek influence on pre-Christian Judaism and was reinforced through the conversion of Gentiles from the late 1st century on. This philosophical approach reached its apex in the works of Plotinus and his famous phrase that the goal of the spiritual life is the "flight of the alone to the One." This understanding of finding God by focusing on one's interior life influenced spirituality East and West though Pseudo-Dionysius and Augustine. This tradition of prayer was definitively chronicled and hence popularized by Bede Frost in the early 20th century. Later in the century, Thomas Merton would make the concept of contemplative prayer accessible to laypeople, and later his fellow Trappists Thomas Keating and Basil Pennington would promote Merton's insights through numerous books and workshops and the establishment of Contemplative Outreach, an organization promoting contemplative prayer.

See also Breath Prayer; Hesychasm; Jesus Prayer; Prayer of the Heart.

For Further Reading: B. Frost, *The Art of Mental Prayer* (1930); A. Louth, *The Origins of the Christian Mystical Tradition* (1981); T. Merton, *New Seeds of Contemplation* (1962).

Todd E. Johnson

Chambers, Oswald (1874–1917), and Gertrude Chambers (1883–1966)

Coauthors of the bestselling daily devotional *My Utmost for His Highest* (1927). Oswald Chambers was a late–Victorian era British Protestant preacher, educator, and evangelist whose influence was vastly extended following his death through the literary efforts of his spouse Gertrude (née Hobbs), also known as "B," "Beloved Disciple," and "Biddy." Millions have been influenced by their famous daily devotional, which has been continuously in print, in many languages, since its original publication.

Both were born into British Baptist homes deeply affected by the Holiness movement and subsequently operated within Pentecostal, Methodist, and other transdenominational settings. Oswald's call to Christian ministry came to him at Scotland's Dunoon Training College and followed a five-year "dark night of the soul." Subsequent involvement in the Pentecostal League of Prayer and mission journeys to the United States and Japan resulted in his conviction that success on the mission field required training and a life surrendered to God: "broken bread and poured out wine."

This innovative communicator married a skilled stenographer. Chambers told her "God will use us as one." The Bible Training College they founded in 1911 on the outskirts of London emphasized elements known today as spiritual formation. In an era that often overlooked women, many students were female. A sense of divine call to offer spiritual first-aid among soldiers of the Great War led them, with their young daughter, Kathleen, to labor three years in chaplaincy work at Zeitoun military camp in Egypt with the Young Men's Christian Association (YMCA). When Oswald died at age forty-three from complications following an emergency appendectomy, Gertrude relayed the news back to Britain as "Oswald in His presence." Until her death, Biddy drew on her notes of Oswald's words to publish them as articles and books. They shared a remarkable story of trust and obedience, looking to God's provision for purpose, direction, and finances.

See also Devotions, Personal.

For Further Reading: D. McCasland, *Oswald Chambers* (1993).

Kim Olstad

Charismatic Spirituality

Charismatic spirituality gives particular emphasis to the person and work of the Holy Spirit in the life of the church, especially through the use of "spiritual gifts." Throughout its history, the church has had figures and movements that encapsulate this form of spirituality. It can be seen in the NT church, especially in the Acts of the Apostles and at Corinth, but also has antecedents in relation to OT figures: the prophets, priests, and kings of Israel. A central motif in this spirituality has always been a personal encounter with the Holy Spirit, who then works within the person bestowing gifts and graces, especially the gifts of love, power, revelation, and wisdom. Encounters with the Holy Spirit have resulted in an empowerment for the individual concerned, both in terms of personal piety and intimacy with God, but also in terms of energy to "go out" in order to be a witness in and to the world. Over the course of history there have been a number of movements associated with this spirituality, such as Montanism in the 3rd century, the Cathars in the 11th century, and the Alumbrados of the 16th century. Each movement has contextualized this spirituality somewhat differently because it always exists alongside other theological traditions. This is obviously seen in the modern era of the church, with the rise of global Pentecostalism. In the United States, this form of spirituality was aligned with the Holiness movement of the 19th century and emerged as a force at the beginning of the 20th century. It is often regarded as the epitome of the charismatic tradition in the modern period. In the latter part of the 20th century, it connected with other forms of Christianity in the Protestant and Roman Catholic traditions and became what is now called the charismatic renewal movement. To be sure, attention was still given to the person and work of the Holy Spirit, but it looked and felt very different when contextualized alongside other Christian traditions. Therefore, charismatic spirituality has what has been called a "plug and play" quality to it: bringing life and vitality to more institutional forms of Christianity but always in concert with these other traditions. It is a spirituality that travels well.

Alongside this attention to the Holy Spirit, there are specific areas of practice that have either been characteristic of charismatic spirituality or have been given a particular charismatic expression. Four areas stand out.

First, charismatic spirituality is expressed in specific forms of praise and worship. Worship services often have an informal atmosphere with contemporary music led by bands rather than traditional accompaniment. Often charismatic songs are short and can easily be memorized, allowing worshipers the freedom to clap, raise, and wave their hands in the air, as well as dance and move in time to the beat of the music. Songs from this spirituality have been classified as praise, love and commitment, intercession, ministry (that is, during times when people are being prayed over), and awe and glory. Second, there is inspired speech. Often this is linked to the narrative of Pentecost (Acts 2), when the Holy Spirit fell upon the disciples and they spoke in tongues and declared the wonders of God. Peter interprets the event as a fulfillment of Joel's prophecy (2:28–30): that the Spirit of prophecy has been poured out on all flesh. This is understood within charismatic spirituality to mean that the Holy Spirit is able to communicate directly through various forms of inspired speech, such as: prayer, speaking and singing in tongues, prophecy, messages of wisdom and knowledge, discernment, preaching, and testimony. Third, there is a strong holiness feature to charismatic spirituality, although its expression has varied according to the context in which the spirituality finds itself. Early Pentecostals had a strong connection to the Wesleyan Holiness tradition, and this can still be seen today in some denominations. Holiness codes often mean that the spirituality can appear sectarian and world-denying. There is a clear recognition of the reality of sin and a belief that godliness is a pre- and corequisite for the intimate presence of the Spirit to remain. Fourth, there is an emphasis on spiritual power, which has its roots in the promise of Acts 1:8: "You will receive power when the Holy Spirit comes on you." This power of the

Spirit is the anointing that was on the Messiah, Jesus Christ, during his earthly ministry, and it is now on the church. The church is to continue in the ministry of Jesus until he returns at the end of the age. The Holy Spirit gives the church power to witness to the kingdom of God here and now in signs and wonders. Very often healing is a focal point of charismatic power, often understood in terms of physical, emotional, or spiritual healing. The kingdom of God was inaugurated at the first advent of Christ and will be consummated at the second advent of Christ (although precise eschatological schemes vary). In the meantime, in the now and not yet of the kingdom, the church witnesses to the glory of God in the power of the Holy Spirit. It is this direct experience of God's very presence in the weakness of humanity that is understood to empower believers in their Christian lives.

See also Gifts; Glossalalia; Pentecostal Spirituality.

For Further Reading: M. Bonnington, *Patterns in Charismatic Spirituality* (2007); M. J. Cartledge, *Encountering the Spirit* (2007); J. Goldingay, "Charismatic Spirituality: Some Theological Reflections," *Theology* 99 (1996): 178–87.

Mark J. Cartledge

Chastity

To be chaste (from Latin *castus*, meaning pure) involves abstaining from all sordid or unlawful sexual behavior. It is holiness in the domain of human sexuality, its importance stemming from the intricate body-soul unity of human persons. Among other things, it implies complete abstinence from sexual activity prior to or outside of one's marriage. To be chaste in the fullest sense also encompasses a complementary purity of heart, mind, and inward disposition; it has interior as well as outward dimensions. Stated positively, a chaste spirit is a faithful spirit, one that is focused and steady in its allegiance. To be chaste is a binding moral imperative upon every Christian regardless of his or her sexual past; virgins and non-virgins alike are called to be chaste (1 Cor. 6:9–11). The inclusive scope of this invitation displays the gracious possibility of new beginnings for all.

Yet, to be chaste in today's world constitutes a formidable challenge, given the normalization of sexual indulgence, the ubiquity of sexualized messages and images, and the addictive potential of sexual appetite. Nonetheless, a chaste lifestyle remains possible through the power of the indwelling Spirit. As with all revealed moral imperatives, its observance ensures that lives will be lived well and protected from the inevitably deleterious consequences of transgression.

To be chaste is a fitting reflection (Matt. 5:48) and necessary condition (Matt. 5:8) of Christian spiritual maturity. Obedience to the revealed will of God is critical to enjoying relational intimacy with God (John 15:10) and communion with the Holy Spirit (Eph. 4:30); this instance is no exception. Sexual expression is treated as "sacramental" in Scripture—as a sign and seal of an antecedent, lifelong covenant between persons. Consequently, to indulge in sexual expression outside of such a covenantal union fosters disordered relationships and disconnections within the self. Such outcomes sabotage the personal holism and relational health that comprise the *telos* of Christian spiritual formation. The regulation and restriction of one's physical behaviors and mental reflections can deepen the grooves of habituated disposition (that is, of virtue) and serve as a kind of strength conditioning for successful spiritual combat in other dimensions of life. Through the proper ordering of desire, one's taste for the beauty of holiness can also increase. Moreover, the sustained discipline of being chaste deepens faith in God, inasmuch as it requires the Christian to trust that the obedient life is more fulfilling than one of moral compromise and fleshly indulgence.

Typically, though not uniformly, the cognate term *chastity* has referred more narrowly to either a specific monastic vow or to sexual abstinence *prior to* marriage. The vow of chastity denotes a monk's solemn commitment to chaste living within the framework of lifelong celibacy. Chastity in the other narrower sense—that is, sexual abstinence *before* marriage—is the way single persons can obey the biblical mandate that sexual activity is only permitted between one man and one woman, united in marriage as "one flesh" (Gen. 2:24).

At times in Christian history, Gnostic and Neoplatonic influences have nurtured an undue regard for a life of sexual abstinence (and its quintessential expression, perpetual virginity) as spiritually superior. While the unmarried status of Jesus himself as well as some biblical passages (e.g., 1 Cor. 7:8–9) can be artificially construed to support this, the overarching message of Scripture is that marriage is honorable and the bed undefiled (Heb. 13:4). Yet, even after alien philosophical influences have been removed from play, premarital chastity remains a Christian virtuous ideal. It is especially challenging in a sex-saturated culture in which couples now marry later in life. But as with every act of necessary relinquishment, the chastening discipline of chastity forms the self and intensifies the savor and satisfaction of communion with God.

See also Sexuality.

For Further Reading: D. Knight, *Chastity* (1985); P. Riley, *Civilizing Sex: On Chastity and the Common Good* (2000); L. Winner, *Real Sex: The Naked Truth about Chastity* (2005).

Glen G. Scorgie and Julie Oostra

Chesterton, G(ilbert) K(eith) (1874–1936)

English writer of essays, poetry, fiction, and biographies. Brought up Unitarian, G. K. Chesterton became an Anglican (1908) and finally a Catholic (1922). He was a prominent and persuasive apologist for orthodox Christianity, debating publicly with major figures such as George Bernard Shaw. In his greatest apologetic work, *The Everlasting Man*

(1925), he argues as a Christian humanist for Christ's incarnation as being the fulfillment of the ideals of justice of the Hebrew people, but equally fulfilling the ideals of beauty and order that he saw as underlying classical Greek and Roman cultures. His great importance to the defense of the faith in his own generation was extended through the influence he had on several of the Inklings, especially C. S. Lewis, who credited G. K. Chesterton's writings with having much to do with his coming to faith.

Chesterton's legendary corpulence, his robust appreciation for the good things of life, and his immense joie de vivre reflected a Franciscan type of spirituality, profoundly rooted in the physicality of the incarnation and deeply earthly. Chesterton saw the world around him as bearing ample daily evidence of a loving and personal God to whom the only reasonable response is love and worship. To the modern era, Chesterton became an exemplar of the *via positiva*—the way of celebration and abundance entered in by way of self-renunciation and repentance, but thereafter enjoyed with feasting and laughter. Despite his impressive intellect, Chesterton saw that the great news of the gospel was granted only to those who were willing to enjoy life with childlike wonder and exuberance. His many writings include *Orthodoxy* (1908), *St. Francis of Assisi* (1923), and *Autobiography* (1936). Chesterton is bracing reading for any evangelical who is weary of familiar rhetoric and wants the challenge of meeting a great intellect on the way to childlike prayer.

See also Literature and Christian Spirituality.

For Further Reading: A. S. Dale, *The Outline of Sanity: A Biography of G. K. Chesterton* (1982); C. Hollis, *The Mind of Chesterton* (1970); C. S. Lewis, *Surprised by Joy* (1984).

Maxine Hancock

Childlikeness, Spirituality of

Christians have sometimes defined spirituality, the spiritual life, Christian faith and life, piety, or one's relationship to God as "childlike." Given the Bible's many references to children and its stunning array of child-related terms and metaphors, biblical perspectives on "childlikeness" or being "like a child" vary widely. "Childlike" can refer to children as well as adults and to immature as well as exemplary attitudes or behaviors. The notion of "childlike" as immature is expressed, for example, in 1 Corinthians. Here Paul characterizes the Corinthians as "people of the flesh, as infants in Christ" in contrast to "spiritual people" (3:1 NRSV). He has fed them "with milk, not solid food" (3:2) and speaks about them as "my beloved children" (4:14). He also admonishes them to be "adults" rather than "children" in their "thinking" (14:20).

Yet the Bible also includes passages in which becoming "like a child" is expressed in positive or exemplary terms. For example, all three Synoptic Gospels include accounts of Jesus blessing children and telling his disciples, "Let the little children come to me; do not stop them; for it is to such as these that the kingdom of God belongs. Truly I tell you, whoever does not receive the kingdom of God as a little child will never enter it" (Mark 10:14–15 NRSV; see also Matt. 19:13–15; Luke 18:15–17). In Matthew, Jesus links "becoming like" a child to humility and true greatness: "Whoever takes a humble place—becoming like this child—is the greatest in the kingdom of heaven. And whoever welcomes one such child in my name welcomes me" (Matt. 18:1–5 TNIV).

Building on these and other child-related biblical passages, Christians over the centuries have reflected on the spiritual significance of childhood, variously interpreted the meaning of a "childlike" faith, and cultivated spiritual practices aimed at helping adults become "like children." For example, Moravian leader Nicholas von Zinzendorf encouraged an intimate relationship with Jesus and a "religion of the heart," in part, by emphasizing the believer's status as child. In his *A Celebration of Christmas: A Conversation* (1806), German theologian Friedrich Schleierm-

acher (1768–1834) spoke about childlikeness as an ability to be present in the moment. Theologians have linked many other qualities to a "childlike" faith, such as dependence, purity, humility, trust, acceptance, innocence, openness, wonder, tenderness, an ability to forgive, or playfulness. Coupled with discussions of "childlike" qualities of faith, some Christian thinkers have also spoken about children's own spiritual perspectives, insights, questions, and experiences and how adults might not only "become as little children" but also learn from children themselves.

See also Faith; Fatherhood of God; Humility.

For Further Reading: R. Aasgaard, "Paul as a Child," *Journal of Biblical Literature* 126 (2007): 129–59; M. Bunge, ed., *The Child in Christian Thought* (2001); M. Bunge et al., eds., *The Child in the Bible* (2008).

Marcia J. Bunge

Children and Spirituality

At the foundation of a Christian view of children is the conviction that each human being bears the image of God and that Jesus entered this state through the incarnation. In the Gospels, his valuing of children as messengers of the kingdom is prophetic. Nonetheless, from the period of the early church to the 16th century, concern within the church for children's spiritual development was often incidental. Definitions of spirituality were framed by adult concerns for holy living and spiritual perfection and expressed in practices such as self-denial, prayers, and cognitive understanding of the Scriptures.

Some in the early church viewed children as basically void of the *logos* (in Greek philosophy the faculty enabling truly human functioning) and consequently unable to relate to God. Others, like John Chrysostom, defended their importance. The early practice of infant baptism demonstrates popular concern for the child's spiritual condition.

In Greek philosophy the *logos* was the reasoning and speech center of human functioning. Augustine's formulation of "original sin" cast children as noninnocent, saved only by the grace of baptism. Thomas Aquinas declared that only baptized children were prone to spiritual awareness. In the later Middle Ages, with the sacrament of confirmation more prevalent, the formalizing of catechetical instruction for children is noted. Around 1400, Jean Gerson's *Drawing the Little Ones to Christ* evidenced this concern. The Protestant redefinition of family as a sphere in which significant commitment to Christ could be expressed also raised new possibilities. John Locke's concept of *tabula rasa*, which described children as passive recipients of their experiences, accentuated their potential and the importance of spiritual formation. Jean Jacques Rousseau described children as "noble savages, born free and yet in chains." In sum, society at large and generations within the church vacillated between seeing children as innocent or incomplete, prophetic or pathetic, offering hosannas or to be "seen but not heard."

The late 19th and early 20th centuries saw a major shift in thinking on children and spirituality. The shift was due to the increase in psychoanalytic and sociocultural studies in child development and some reconciliation between Christian theology and human development theories. Two approaches to theologizing on children's spirituality are the "theology of childhood" and "child theology." The former emphasizes the status of children before God. This approach informed a 2004 study by Scripture Union, which concluded that children are recipients of the common grace that begins at childhood and are fully able to relate to God because their status is nested in covenant relationship and Jesus' invitation into God's kingdom (Matt. 19:14; Mark 10:14; Luke 18:15 – 17). Child theology, on the other hand, focuses on kingdom living as exemplified by children and childhood, taking Matthew 18:1 – 14, wherein Jesus sets a child in the midst as focus for theological contemplation, as its seminal text.

A contemporary Christian view of children and spirituality can be founded on three key bases. The first is biblical statements indicating the status of children in God's kingdom: (a) Children are made in the image of God, and as such they inherit the essence needed for relationship with their Creator (Gen. 1:26; 5:1 – 2; Ps. 22:9 – 10). (b) Children and childhood as metaphors of God's kingdom exemplify kingdom qualities and characteristics of discipleship (Matt. 18:3 – 5; Mark 9:36 – 37; 10:13 – 16; Luke 18:15 – 17). (c) Children have a place in God's ministry and can be agents of change (1 Sam. 3:1 – 21; 16:8 – 13; Matt. 1:23). (d) Children are gifts of God (Ps. 113:9; 127:3 – 5; Isa. 8:18). (e) Children are active participants of the faith and ordained for worship (Deut. 12:8 – 12; Ps. 8:2; Matt. 21:12 – 16).

The second basis is the action of the Creator Spirit in children. Children, and not just adults, are subjected to the work of the Creator Spirit because they too have the *imago Dei*. Thus, children can become spiritually aware through the sensitizing work of God's Spirit in them.

The third basis is the concept of covenant, espoused by both Roman Catholic and evangelical scholars (e.g., H. U. von Balthasar, R. Buckland, K. Rahner, S. Cavalletti, J. Moltmann, R. Nye, J. Mercer, B. Miller-McLemore, and C. Stonehouse). These agree that children's relationship to the Creator God is based on the covenant promise that unites every created being with the Creator. Hence, life before God for children is not defined by tasks, but rather by their status as heirs of the kingdom and by an invitation of the highest order; and Jesus' action of welcoming children is an expression of the God-child relationship.

When children's spirituality is defined as relational awareness to God (as in Nye), child functioning has to be taken into consideration. Children express their spirituality in developmentally appropriate ways as they derive representations of God images, make meaning of their God-child encounters, and connect their experiences to daily living. Representations of God images are temporal identities of the transcendent until cognitive maturity leads the child to differ. A main tool to help children make meaning of their spiritual encounters is language; and Berryman has developed an approach termed "godly play" for this purpose. When children are able to make meaning of their experiences with God and connect them to their daily functions, they are actually showing signs of spiritual growth.

See also Adolescent Spirituality; Children's Literature; Family Life; Human Development; Parenting.

For Further Reading: J. Berryman, *Godly Play* (1991); M. Bunge, ed., *The Child in Christian Thought* (2001); R. Coles, *The Spiritual Life of Children* (1990); G. Cupit, *Perspectives on Children and Spirituality* (2006); D. Hay and R. Nye, *Education, Spirituality and the Whole Child* (1998); B. Hyde, *Children and Spirituality* (2008); B. Miller-McLemore, *Let the Children Come unto Me* (2003); C. Stonehouse, *Joining Children on the Spiritual Journey* (2005).

Rosalind Lim Tan

Children's Literature

Word and story are basic to being human. Through stories, children live many lives, see many places, go through many of the vicissitudes of life, and therefore learn much about how to live. They learn how to understand and communicate with others, how to interpret and use words well, and how to recognize that they and their lives are part of a larger story.

That larger story, as Northrop Frye clarifies in his book *The Great Code*, is most clearly seen in the Bible. The ultimate end of a "story" understanding of life is, as Tolkien says, a "Eucatastrophe"—an unexpected good ending. Perhaps no other characteristic need be truer of literature for children,

therefore, than that its stories end with hope. The "great code" of Scripture reveals the full richness and significance of the themes, archetypes, and images that permeate the world's great literature.

Literature also gives children what George MacDonald called "moral imagination." In their vicarious experience of others' lives through stories, children learn to envision the effects of their actions, the "story" they are living.

Children should read Bible stories, certainly. For very young children, stories such as "The Good Shepherd" and Psalm 23 can also be dramatized in "godly play." For older children, in order to understand fully the working of God in life, the *whole* story must be told—something we often shy away from. In telling the Joseph story, for instance, we always include his "coat of many colors," but we leave out the arrogance of his dreams and his coat, which leads to the downward spiral of his life. And we almost always omit the seamy story of his brother Judah who nevertheless is the character who learns and changes the most. Teens, especially, need to hear that God's good ending works out through our difficulties and failings, as it did for both Joseph and Judah.

Historical fiction gives children knowledge of the past and therefore perspective on their own lives—awareness that their forerunners in history shared their struggles. As Rosemary Sutcliff, a writer of historical fiction, says, such stories show "that doing the right/kind/brave/honest thing doesn't have to result in any concrete reward … and that this doesn't matter; the reward lies in … having kept faith with one's own integrity—and probably in being given a more difficult thing to do next time."

Fairy tales and fantasy, as C. S. Lewis adamantly affirmed, convey truth far more accurately than many "true-to-life" stories. "If you really read fairy tales," asserted G. K. Chesterton, "you will observe that one idea runs from one end of them to the other—the idea that peace and happiness can only exist on some condition." And, as Gandalf says about dark woods to Bilbo in *The Hobbit*, if you want to get to the other side, "you must either go through or give up your quest."

Some Christians have trouble seeing fairy tales and fantasy as worthwhile — even though such stories point us, with greater accuracy than almost any other literature, to the larger story — and to God. G. K. Chesterton credited the start of his conversion to the magic of fairy stories: "I had always believed that the world involved magic: now I thought that perhaps it involved a magician." Such stories help children (and adults) see their way through the murkiness of everyday reality to rock-bottom spiritual truths.

Parents need to read the books their children are reading. Banning certain books is not nearly as constructive as telling children what we don't like and listening to what they like. Rather than building a case against books that children are going to read anyway, such discussion leads to both literary and spiritual insight, thus giving children tools for a wise "reading" of both literature and life.

Finally, parents need to read aloud to their children — and not just when they are preschoolers. Cocoa and popcorn can keep this up as a family tradition even through the teen years. Reading aloud gives children time to "clothe" characters and circumstances with their imagination and thereby to work through their own hopes and fears. These books sink deeply into the subconscious of children and become touchstones for discerning good literature — which helps them to see their lives as part of the good story that God continues to tell through them.

For Further Reading: G. K. Chesterton, "The Ethics of Elfland," *Orthodoxy* (1995); N. Frye, *The Educated Imagination* (1967); I. and P. Opie, "Introduction," in *The Classic Fairy Tales* (1974); K. Paterson, *The Invisible Child* (2001); R. Sutcliff, "History Is People," in *Children and Literature,* ed. V. Haviland (1973), 305–13; J. R. R. Tolkien, "On Fairy-Stories," in *The Tolkien Reader* (1966);

H. Wilkinson-Teel and M. R. Wilkinson, *A Time to Read* (2004).

Mary Ruth K. Wilkinson

Chittister, Joan D(augherty) (1936 –)

Benedictine nun and writer. Chittister evidenced from childhood a passion for inclusivity that cut a wider swath than official Roman Catholic doctrine. Her father died when she was three. When her mother remarried a Protestant, the theologically reflective child was immersed in the uncommon world of an interfaith marriage. She entered the Benedictine Sisters of Erie, Pennsylvania, in 1952, and within weeks contracted polio. Her four-year struggle with the disease left her with a deep understanding of suffering. She taught school from 1955 to 1974, and in 1971 she became the first Benedictine nun to earn a Ph.D. (Communications). Since 1974 she has worked internationally in the fields of education, religious life, and public service. In 1990 she became the executive director of Benetvision, an organization rooted in her writings and activities, which seeks to provide spiritual resources for Christian engagement with contemporary issues.

Chittister has received numerous honorary doctorates, as well as awards for her civic, church, international, and interfaith contributions. Her more than three dozen published writings emphasize justice, peace, and equality. Speaking with frankness but without cynicism, she urges her readers to avoid embracing a false distinction between sacred and secular and to make their voice heard as the life of God in the world.

Her award-winning autobiography, *Called to Question: A Spiritual Memoir* (2004), welcomes readers into her wisdom of years. *In Search of Belief* (1999), which roots itself in the Apostles' Creed, may interest readers looking for a fresh engagement with their theological heritage.

Diane S. George Ayer

Cho, David Yonggi (1936–)

Pastor of the world's largest church—Yoido Full Gospel Church in Seoul, Korea, with seven hundred thousand members. Raised a Buddhist, Cho became a Christian at age eighteen when he was healed of tuberculosis. After graduating from Full Gospel Bible Institute, he joined a tent church in 1958 in a slum area of Seoul initiated by his future mother-in-law. In 1961 he started a second church, Full Gospel Revival Center, and by 1964 the membership had increased to three thousand through a combination of Cho's preaching a Pentecostal faith, emphasizing the baptism of the Holy Spirit, physically evidenced initially by tongues-speaking, as well as supernatural signs and divine healing, ardent prayer, and street evangelism.

In 1964 bad health because of overwork led Cho to develop home cell groups, which have since become a trademark of the church. Cho organized these groups to great effect, and by appointing women to be trained as leaders, he greatly elevated their status. Cells are places for learning God's Word, praying, and practicing a fruitful Christian life; and cell groups are encouraged to multiply and form new cells, contributing to conversion growth.

As a Pentecostal, Cho's spirituality emphasizes experience expressed through narratives such as testimony, prayer to solve human problems, and a belief in divine healing as well as material blessing. Cho's doctrine of a threefold blessing based on 3 John 2 breaks down the dualism between the physical and spiritual, emphasizing that God's blessings apply to all aspects of life. While theological imprecision has led to misunderstanding and criticism, his success could be attributed to contextualized theology and praxis.

See also Korean Christian Spirituality; Pentecostal Spirituality.

For Further Reading: W. Ma, *David Yonggi Cho* (2004).

Kiem-Kiok Kwa

Choral Music

The essence of the choral art is to sing with one voice. Disciplined choral performance achieves a level of communal utterance unparalleled in beauty and power—a true blending of voices and spirits, in a medium that combines the intellectual and expressive power of stirring texts with the evocative potential of rhythm, melody, and harmony. For this reason, the choral art is admirably suited to elevated expressions of Christian unity, serving as an auditory aesthetic in the worship and spiritual formation of believers. Choral music cannot be replaced by solo music or by congregational singing.

For many centuries the history of Western choral music was more or less synonymous with the history of music in the church. Sacred music was a functional, vocal art, serving the liturgy. Until about 1430, choirs of male singers sang chant in unison, as it had become standardized and then been preserved in manuscripts dating back to about AD 900. With the flourishing of choral polyphony in the 1500s came growing concerns about secularization and textual intelligibility—a matter addressed ultimately by the Council of Trent. Among Protestants, an emphasis on congregational participation in the vernacular supported a flourishing choral tradition, particularly among Lutherans and Anglicans, who developed the church cantata and anthem, respectively.

Under the influence of the Enlightenment, amateur choral singing for convivial purposes became widespread. With the founding of singing societies, performances moved more and more to the concert hall. Programs still included sacred repertoire, however; especially influential were the oratorios of G. F. Handel, which remained popular after his death—*The Messiah* being a particular favorite. Bach's works, too, received renewed attention after 1830.

During the 19th century, women began appearing in church choirs. The secularization of church music, represented by increasingly grandiose, concert-oriented works, gave rise to the Cecilian movement, which sought to restore chant and unaccompanied polyphony to the Catholic liturgy.

In the 1960s, a desire for simplicity and accessibility led to a widespread decline in the artistic, literary, and theological merit of choral music in the church among both Protestants and Catholics. Nevertheless, college and university choirs continued to perform sacred repertoire of enduring quality, albeit mostly in concert settings.

Throughout its history, sacred choral music has struggled with questions of function, secularization, and artistic worth. Despite historical changes in style and taste, these issues remain relevant.

See also Beauty; Worship.

Melvin P. Unger

Christian Science

Christian Science is the faith-based healing system founded by Mary Baker Eddy (1821 – 1910) and associated with the First Church of Christ, Scientist in Boston. Eddy was born in New Hampshire and raised in the Congregational Church. She was attracted to esoteric religion in her adult years. She credited the birth of Christian Science to her own miraculous healing after a fall in Lynn, Massachusetts, in February 1866. Her public teaching began in 1870, and her *Science and Health with Key to the Scriptures* was first issued in 1875. She founded the Church of Christ, Scientist in 1879.

Christian Science healing involves firm commitment to the extreme version of idealism advocated by Mrs. Eddy. Trust in God demands denial of the reality of matter, disease, and death. Her *Science and Health* text states, "There is no life, truth, intelligence, nor substance in matter. All is infinite Mind and its infinite manifestation, for God is All-in-all." Hence, "sin, sickness, and death will seem real (even as the experiences of the sleeping dream seem real) until the Science of man's eternal harmony breaks their illusion with the unbroken reality of scientific being."

The life of the Christian Scientist revolves around the Bible as understood through Mrs. Eddy. She remains the pastor emeritus, and her writings are sacrosanct. Healing is sought through prayer and through the help of trained practitioners and Christian Science nurses. Relying on traditional medicine is discouraged except in the case of the use of glasses and the setting of bones. Christian Scientists look to the mother church in Boston for spiritual nurture. Sunday worship services are broadcast live through radio and the Internet, and literature is available through reading rooms. As well, the church employs forty-eight lecturers worldwide. *The Christian Science Monitor* is the most visible expression of the church, though explicit teaching is confined to one article.

Christian Science's genteel spirituality belies the controversy that has always surrounded its founder and her theories. Mrs. Eddy was the object of scorn and ridicule through the last four decades of her life though her followers idolized her. More important, her views about the unreality of sickness and death remain bitterly contested, especially when this involves the death of children under the care of Christian Science.

For Further Reading: A. Dickey, *Memoirs of Mary Baker Eddy* (1929); C. Fraser, *God's Perfect Child* (1999); G. Gill, *Mary Baker Eddy* (1998); R. D. Thomas, *With Bleeding Footsteps* (1994).

James A. Beverley

Chrysostom, John (c. 344 – 407)

Preacher, exegete, and bishop of Constantinople. He was one of the most eloquent preachers and influential exegetes of the early church, which earned him the appellation "Chrysostom" (The Golden Mouth) after his death. Born in Antioch to wealthy parents, his father died, leaving his mother to raise the child. He received the best possible education for a career in rhetoric, but after baptism in his late twenties, he became deeply committed to the Christian life, studying theology and Bible instead. He also began practicing extreme asceticism while living as a hermit. Even though he later became an active teacher and church leader, he honored time alone with God, ever yearning for the life of study and prayer.

Ordained as a priest, the church in Antioch soon recognized that John Chrysostom was homiletically gifted, and he became famous for the power and conviction of his preaching. In 397 he was called against his will to be the bishop of Constantinople. His fiery oratory was expected, but his reforms of the local clergy, his education of the laity, and his unwillingness to compromise confronted the wealth and power of the church hierarchy. His lifestyle was also an affront to many, for he lived simply, giving away most of his wealth not only to the poor but also to build hospitals. This all led finally to his exile to Armenia by the court of Empress Eudoxia in 403 and, after great suffering, a premature death.

John Chrysostom's fame rests not only on his magnificent delivery. His writings and teaching helped created a school of exegesis that was rooted in a hermeneutic based on application of the biblical text only, as opposed to the excessively allegorical approach of those who followed Origen and the Alexandrian school. This resulted in scholarship, spiritual discernment, and practical application that worked together not only to inform the hearers, but to transform their lives in practical ways. Some of his 236 letters are classic pieces of spiritual direction, while others show why he alienated and aggravated people of power. The majority of his many sermons continue to be widely read. Within many Orthodox churches, the St. John Chrysostom Liturgy is still the weekly worship service and was set to music by Peter Ilich Tchaikovsky and Sergei Rachmaninoff.

For Further Reading: D. Attwater, *St. John Chrysostom* (1939); F. C. Baur, *John Chrysostom and His Time,* 2 vols. (1960); J. N. D. Kelly, *Golden Mouth* (1995); R. Krupp, *Shepherding the Flock of God: The Pastoral Theology of John Chrysostom* (1991).

Kelby Cotton

Church

The church as the newly configured, Spirit-empowered people of God emerged immediately following Pentecost and from the first was characterized by devotion to apostolic teaching, fellowship, breaking of bread together, and prayer. According to Luke's portrait, it was a community acquainted with supernatural manifestations, radical in its familial generosity, buoyed by a spirit of praise, and circumspect in its reverence for the holy nature and demands of the God who was among them by his Spirit (Acts 2:42–47; 5:1–11).

Later the apostle Paul (in epistles written to *churches*) developed important images of the society of believers, and none more central than the church as the body (and embodiment) of Christ in the world (1 Cor. 12–14). The divine presence within the church gives the community of believers its identity and vitality. While God is everywhere present and also indwells individual believers, he is present in a special way in the midst of the saints (Matt. 18:20). Believers are to contribute to the church in such a way that it becomes ever more a "temple"—a locale where the Spirit of God is profoundly present and manifest (Eph. 2:22). Thus, from the first the apostles discerned the crucial importance of sustained connection with this inward presence, and as their first priority, in the face of various distractions, to give their attention to the spiritual disciplines of prayer and the ministry of the word (Acts 6:4).

The church as the body (or embodiment) of Christ also means that it is the instrumental means by which Christ acts in the world. It is an *agency* with a significant role to play in bringing salvation and healing to the world. The church is called to *do* the will of God as well as *be* the people of God.

The word of Christ is not only received but also sent. God sent Christ to the world as both expression and expresser, and he now sends the church to continue the transforming mission of God.

The church also exists for the benefit of its members. Led by the Spirit, Christians pool their gifts, strengths, and abilities, and in so doing build up one another. The church is to provide an ecological environment in which all of its members can flourish and grow — and not least in the spiritual dimension of their lives. When this occurs, the church is not only a *vehicle* of salvation; it is also an *embodiment* of that salvation itself. It becomes a city set on a hill (Matt. 5:14), a shining manifestation of a singular sociology — an alternate way of doing life together. And as God is Trinity — unity in the midst of diversity — so the church is to live as a model of unity in diversity.

The quality of congregational life is a key determinant of personal and corporate flourishing. Formation occurs through formal and informal associations with a congregation, its culture, and its story over time. The existence of the church is a persistent reminder that life lived before God always has a corporate dimension to it. Love for God and love for one's neighbor are two vectors from the same Spirit-enlivened matrix. At their best, relationships within the church can be genuine spiritual friendships. Participation in all-too-imperfect community can also function as a crucible of soul crafting, as one grows in capacity for empathy, ability to recognize the presence of Christ in others, and willingness to open wide one's heart to others nonetheless. Moreover, the Christian's calling is never to "do it all," but rather to contribute what one can to the larger pool of giftedness. This way of seeing vocation can be a source of profound personal freedom, contentment, and fulfillment.

The forms of the church necessarily change over time. During intense transitions and upheaval, the interior ethos of the church may feel odd and even disillusioning. Under such circumstances, believers have options. First, they can resolve to *endure* the imperfections and frustrations of a particular church for Christ's sake and their own maturation. A second option is to *explore* more life-giving, alternative fellowships, for there come times when it is no longer helpful for oneself or others to remain in a particular congregation. A third possibility is to *invent*. Sometimes Christianity has needed pioneering figures to reinvent church. Monks, friars, Anabaptist communities, and mission organizations are just some of the many who have pioneered new ways of being church.

See also Chapter 9.

For Further Reading: T. Bolsinger, *It Takes a Church to Raise a Christian* (2004); D. Guder, *The Missional Church* (1998); S. Johnson, *Christian Spiritual Formation in the Church and Classroom* (1989); H. Küng, *The Church* (1967); H. Snyder, *The Community of the King* (1977); J. Wilhoit, *Spiritual Formation as if the Church Mattered* (2008).

Evan B. Howard and Glen G. Scorgie

Cistercian Spirituality

Robert of Molesme (d. 1111), a Benedictine abbot, founded the Cistercians (Lat. *Cistercium*) in 1098 in Cîteaux, France. His efforts of monastic reform based on the Rule of St. Benedict sought to recover the themes of poverty, simplicity, and solitude that had been lost over the centuries of increasing monastic wealth and power. Jesus' example of simplicity, living among the poor, was a major influence for the Cistercians. The order experienced substantial growth under Bernard of Clairvaux, who emphasized a Christ-centered mysticism based on the humanity of Jesus and devotion to the Virgin Mary that combined both the intellect and affections, and contemplation and action. Some of his most significant writings include his sermons on the *Song of Songs* and *On Loving God*. The Cistercians continued their expansion to about 1250, then experienced a period of decline due to the plague, and in particular, the external interference by church hierarchy that appointed absentee abbots and led to their eventual termination in 1791 by the French Revolution. The movement experienced revival during the 19th century, and their presence spread throughout the world. Women found greater opportunities to associate with the order during this period. Already in the late 16th century a division arose between the Order of Cîteaux and the larger Cistercian Order of Strict Observance or Trappists. Thomas Merton is representative of the latter group.

In addition to Bernard, other early noteworthy Cistercians include William of St. Thierry, author of the influential *On Contemplating God* and the *Golden Epistle*, and Aelred of Rievaulx, best known for his still popular *Spiritual Friendship*. For generations, the predominantly male order did little to encourage Cistercian nuns, though Beatrice of Nazareth (1200–1268), author of *The Seven Stages of the Love of God*, was an exception. While technically Hildegard of Bingen remained a member of the Benedictines, Bernard played a vital role in endorsing her writings.

Theologically the Cistercians are indebted to Augustine and stress the reality of sin, the necessity of grace, and spiritual growth motivated by desire and love for God. This foundation inspired the early members to see themselves as a school of love. The desert fathers and mothers and Gregory the Great also reinforced or extended these themes. In turn, the Cistercians influenced Roman Catholics and Protestants alike. Martin Luther and John Calvin, the Puritans and Dutch Pietists, and later evangelicals including Charles Spurgeon were particularly fond of Bernard. This appeal was often due to the strong reliance on the Song of Songs and emphasis on love and contemplation of God that anchored Cistercian spirituality.

The Cistercians, who at their peak in the early 13th century numbered about seven hundred fifty monasteries and today claim approximately three hundred monasteries, provide wisdom toward the development of a balanced contemporary evangelical Christian spirituality. Their comprehensive foundation in the union with God in Christ, the primacy of Scripture as witnessed through community prayer grounded in praying the Psalms, the personal and group use of *lectio divina*, the integration of the head and heart, and the cultivation of an experiential knowledge through the contemplative attitude of love and devotion to God that bears witness to Jesus Christ through action in the world are all worthy goals of integration.

See also Benedictine; Bernard of Clairvaux; Camaldolese Spirituality; Trappists.

For Further Reading: L. Bouyer, *The Cistercian Heritage* (1958); E. de Waal, *The Way of Simplicity* (1998); L. Lekai, *The Cistercians* (1977); A. Louf, *The Cistercian Way* (1983); B. McGinn, *The Growth of Mysticism* (1994); B. Pennington, *The Cistercians* (1992); S. Tobin, *The Cistercians* (1995).

Tom Schwanda

Clare of Assisi (1194–1253)

Prominent female associate of Francis of Assisi. Clare Offreduccio was born to a wealthy family in Assisi, Italy. There, at age eighteen, she came into contact with Francis and his teaching, most likely through hearing one of his sermons. Francis's preaching so impressed her that she chose to identify personally with a lifestyle of radical poverty. This decision put her at odds with her parents, who had hoped that through marriage she would advance the family fortunes. One night in 1212, Clare secretly left her parents' home with two companions and met Francis and his disciples. There he had her cut her hair and replace the clothing provided to her by her wealthy family with a simple tunic and veil.

Francis then placed Clare temporarily in a Benedictine convent while he tried to determine the most appropriate permanent place for her. Her family, enraged at what she had done, tried to persuade her to come home and eventually attempted, unsuccessfully, to drag her from the convent by force. Eventually Clare became the abbess of a religious house founded by Francis in 1215, and his lifelong friend and confidant.

The way of life at the house was quite ascetic. The women slept on the ground, abstained from eating meat, wore only sandals on their feet, and refrained from any unnecessary speech. From this house a women's order emerged to parallel the Franciscan order; its members are called the Poor Clares. The order took a vow of strict poverty, taking in nothing but what the Franciscans could procure for them through begging, despite attempts by Pope Gregory IX to persuade them to accept a few basic necessities.

Clare lived on several decades after Francis and served as the most significant champion of his cherished standards of poverty and rejection of property ownership. She also remains significant for the way in which she embodied for women the spirituality of Francis. From 1225 until her death, Clare was reportedly sick, likely the result of her extreme ascetic practices. She was declared a saint in 1255 by Pope Alexander IV.

See also Francis of Assisi; Franciscan Spirituality.

For Further Reading: R. Armstrong, ed. and trans., *Clare of Assisi: Early Documents* (1993); M. Bartoli, *Clare of Assisi*, trans. F. Teresa (1993); *Francis and Clare: The Complete Works*, CWS (1982); C. Ledoux and C. Dees, *Clare of Assisi* (2002).

Mary M. Veeneman

Clement of Alexandria (c. 150 – 215)

Prominent early representative of Alexandrian Christianity. A well-educated Greek, versed in the philosophies of his time, and also aware of "barbaric" (Celtic, Indian, Scythian, Egyptian) wisdom traditions, Clement was a masterful biblical exegete, drawing on the best of Alexandrian Judaism, and

a theologian intimately acquainted with a broad spectrum of early Christian traditions and practices. While passing on the teachings of "the elders" — charismatic Christian teachers of an earlier generation — he remained curious and open-minded in his investigation of sundry doctrines, irrespective of their orthodoxy, and quite dismissive of the dislike of philosophy espoused by some fellow Christians.

Like Irenaeus of Lyon, Clement understood the Christian life as progressing from conversion to "deification" not only on earth but also beyond death. His theology centers around the transformative revelation of the divine Logos that leads humanity from *exhortation* to ethical *training* and then to doctrinal *instruction*. Ultimately, the Logos became human in order to show how humans can be deified. Thus, a Christian studies "to be a god," aiming to become a "true gnostic" — that is, a human being who "lives as an angel on earth, already luminous and resplendent like the sun," a "God-bearer" moved directly by the Lord, even "a god going about in the flesh."

Clement reworks an older theory (ascribed to the elders) that posited an ontological transformation of humans into angels, of angels into archangels, and of archangels into "first created angels" at the end of every millennium. The millennial cycles and the transformative ascent on the cosmic ladder are internalized as descriptions of an interior phenomenon, for which the perfect shorthand is, indeed, "deification." This view, rooted in the apocalypticism of the Second Temple era, occupied early Christianity's theological mainstream and remained central in fourth-century Cappadocian and later Byzantine monastic spirituality.

See also Deification.

For Further Reading: B. Bucur, *Angelomorphic Pneumatology* (2009); J. Kovacs, "Divine Pedagogy and the Gnostic Teacher according to Clement of Alexandria," *Journal of Early Christian Studies* 9 (2001): 3 – 25; E. Osborn, *Clement of Alexandria* (2005).

Bogdan G. Bucur

Climacus, John (c. 579–649)

Byzantine theologian of ascent. Monk of St. Catherine's Monastery in Sinai from the age of sixteen until his death. At thirty-five years old, John became a hermit at one of St. Catherine's eremitical retreats for forty years. At seventy-five he was elected hegumenos (i.e., abbot) of the larger, cenobitic community at St. Catherine's. John earned the epithet "Climacus" ("ladder") by being the author of the extremely influential *Ladder of Divine Ascent*, though he is also known in Greek as "John the Scholastic."

The *Ladder of Divine Ascent* is a spiritual treatise for monks, structured into thirty steps, one for each year of Christ's life. Collectively, they present John's spirituality: the monk's break with the world (steps 1–3), the active life (steps 4–26), and the contemplative life (steps 27–30). Beginning with the practical, ascetical steps of the spiritual life, the monk who ascends to the top of John's ladder achieves a state of stillness and prayer, achieves dispassion (*apatheia*), and possesses the theological virtues of faith, hope, and love. Regarding monasticism, John states that there are three forms of monastic life: (1) living in solitude, (2) living a "life of stillness" with one or two others ("the royal way"), and (3) living in community. John's spirituality and theology of monasticism were widely influential in the Byzantine era and continue to influence Eastern Orthodox Christianity.

See also Ascent, Stages of Spiritual.

For Further Reading: J. Chryssavgis, *John Climacus* (2004).

Greg Peters

Cloud of Unknowing, The

The Cloud of Unknowing is one of the most widely read works of Christian spirituality and mysticism. Written in the 14th century by an anonymous author to an unnamed individual, it has been one of the most influential treatises on prayer in the second Christian millennium. Although the author is unnamed, there are other texts written by the same author, often compiled in modern volumes of *The Cloud*. These treatises include *The Epistle of Privy Counsel* and *The Epistle of Prayer*, all part of a tradition known as the English Mystics. The *Cloud* is a contemporary of other English spiritual works, such as those by Richard Rolle, Julian of Norwich, and Walter Hilton. In spite of the differences between these authors, each wrote from the perspective of a solitary life, and each was influenced by Neoplatonism.

Although the *Cloud* is a treatise of practical spiritual instruction, it is rooted in a thoroughgoing and highly developed Neoplatonic worldview. In particular, the author is strongly influenced by the ancient Eastern writer known as Pseudo-Dionysius the Aeropagite. The author insists that in our mortal existence, no one may ever fully comprehend God with our intellect. Instead, there is always a "cloud of unknowing" between humanity and God, one that can be penetrated only by "darts of love" sent by God toward us. Still, God is the fitting object of our desires and our wills, and though God will remain outside of our grasp in our lifetime, directing our lives in such a Godward direction ensures our greatest fulfillment. To do this, all Christians are advised to set aside time in their lives to focus on contemplation and communion with God, though only a few are called to a contemplative vocation. This communion is not an intellectual "knowing" but is one that requires faith to believe in the divine presence that exists behind the cloud of unknowing. By focusing our attention on God and forgetting all else, we will find ourselves with a deep experience of God's presence.

The Cloud is not a linear or clearly organized treatise. Rather, it is cyclical and repetitious. It is firm in tone, offering a corrective to an impulsive and easily distracted young man. It is a treatise that insists on conversion: conversion from sin to love; conversion from love of the world to love of God; conversion from intellectual certainty to faithful encounter. In the end, *The Cloud* is a textbook presentation of the *via negativa*, or a spirituality of apophatic prayer. It is a sustained reminder that God is always beyond our full understanding; God is always more than we can imagine or articulate; and most important, God is always greater than what God has created and can never be contained by it.

See also English Mystics.

For Further Reading: *The Cloud of Unknowing*, CWS (1981); B. Pennington, *Centering Prayer* (1980); *The Pursuit of Wisdom and Other Works by the Author of The Cloud of Unknowing*, CWS (1988).

Todd E. Johnson

Columbanus (c. 543 – 615)

Well-educated Celtic missionary and abbot; also known as Columna and Columban. Born in Ireland, he should not be confused with Columba of Iona (521 – 597). His legacy was formed in his travels throughout Western Europe preaching the gospel, allegedly performing miracles that resulted in the conversion of many pagans to Christianity, and founding Christian communities. The abbeys Columbanus founded in Luxueil, France, and Bobbio, Italy, housed two of the finest libraries of the medieval period. Sixty-three of his disciples from Luxueil brought the gospel and Columbanus's monastic rule to France, Germany, Switzerland, and Italy and are credited with founding more than a hundred monasteries.

Several of Columbanus's works have survived: *Seventeen Short Sermons*; *Six Epistles*; *Latin Poems*; and his two most influential works, his *Monastic Rule* and *Penitencial*. His rule stressed obedience, silence, fasting, poverty, humility, and chastity and was approved by the Council of Macôn in 627 before being superseded by the similar Rule of St. Benedict before the end of that same century. His *Penitencial* helped spread the Celtic practice of repeatable, private penance; this was a movement away from the singular, collective, and public penance of the early church and one that dominated the Western understanding of penance until the Second Vatican Council (1962 – 1965). Thus, Columbanus's contribution to Christian spirituality is twofold: his involvement in the understanding and practice of penance influenced the church for over a millennium, while his example of Christian outreach and missionary activity has endured to the present day.

See also Celtic Spirituality; Penitence.

For Further Reading: M. Earle and S. Maddox, *Holy Companions* (2004); T. Fiaich, *Columbanus in His Own Words* (1974).

Cynthia Cheshire

Comenius, John Amos (1592 – 1670)

Pietistic educational reformer. Comenius is known today as "the father of modern education." He was an educator, writer, ecumenist, and from 1632 to the end of his life, bishop of an old pietistic evangelical communion called the Unitas Fratrum, or "Unity of the Brethren," with roots among the followers of Jan Hus. He lived through the religious strife of the Thirty Years' War (1618 – 1648), in which some members of his Brethren church (forebears of today's Moravian Church) were slaughtered and the rest exiled from their homelands of Bohemia and Moravia. His allegory *The Labyrinth of the World and the Paradise of the Heart* (1623), treasured as a jewel of Czech culture, tells of a young pilgrim traveling through the world seeking truth. He discovers the sinfulness shot through every vocation (his portrayal of the academic world is particularly incisive) and every walk of life (evangelicals will squirm at his negative portrayal of family life). Near despair, the pilgrim finally discovers the "paradise" of heart devotion to Jesus Christ in the company of the redeemed — portrayed as a small, ragged remnant. Comenius dedicated his life to ecumenical brotherhood and international peace. To those ends, he pioneered a truly liberal mode of public schooling grounded in Baconian empiricism and biblical morality, aided by the innovation of illustrated textbooks and accessible equally to boys and girls (a radical idea at the time). An Enlightenment man, Comenius worked throughout his life on a Christian "pansophy" — that is, an encyclopedic summary of all knowledge. His vision of an international "College of Light" helped inspire the founding of the British Royal Society.

See also Moravian.

Chris R. Armstrong

Communion of Saints

Originally, the phrase "communion of saints" (Lat. *communio sanctorum*) may have referred to the communal nature of the sacraments of baptism and Eucharist. Now it identifies the church as a community of the righteous, including those on earth as well as those in heaven. It appears first in the Apostles' Creed as a reflection of Hebrews 12.1: "We are surrounded by such a great cloud of witnesses." The term encompasses the church militant (on earth) and the church triumphant (in heaven) — and, for Roman Catholics, the church penitent (those undergoing purification in purgatory).

The theological underpinning of the doctrine is belief in the unity of the body of Christ in heaven and on earth through the mediation of the resurrected Lord. Baptism is the door of entrance into the body of Christ, the church, and that which brings new believers into communion with the entire church, both in heaven and on earth. Liturgical communities (especially Catholic, Anglican, and Orthodox) emphasize the role of specific saints in the wider context of the Christian community. The church on earth and the saints in heaven form one continuous community, and it is this that makes their intercession for specific needs possible.

In the Orthodox tradition, the saints are especially bound together through mutual love and prayer. Christians are thus free to ask for prayer from any church member, such as a departed father or mother, whether they are officially saints or not. The less liturgical Protestant traditions, however, interpret the communion of saints as a "community" of saints that is focused primarily on the character and quality of relational life among Christians within their local churches, but which is also appreciative of the long historic procession and inspiring example of the faithful who came before. Nonetheless, evangelical Christians generally forbid directing prayerful petitions toward those who have departed this life.

See also Martyrdom; Pauline.

For Further Reading: M. Garijo-Guembe, *Communion of the Saints* (1994); E. Lamirande, *Communion of the Saints* (1962); J. Pelikan, *The Christian Tradition* (1985); K. Ware, " One Body in Christ," *Sobornost* 4, no. 2 (1982): 179–91.

Ian Smith

Community

See **Chapter 9.**

Community, Experiments in

Born on the day of Pentecost, the church has been a worshiping, praying, serving, and witnessing community whose vocation is to point the world to Christ. According to Acts 2:42–47, the early Christian community enjoyed "the favor of all the people" because of the generous, healing, prayerful, and joyous character of their community. The quality of their community evangelized their neighbors. The apostle Paul describes the church as a body with many members, each of whom is necessary (1 Cor. 12:1–31). To be a Christian is to be part of a community.

The first monastic communities arose within a few years of the Emperor Constantine's legalization of Christianity in the early 4th century. From the beginning, monasticism was lay led and was a prophetic witness against the secularization of the church. Organized by Pachomius, the first communities had a common rule of life or spiritual practices by which they lived their faith.

During the Dark Ages, Benedict of Nursia founded a network of communities around Subiaco in the mountains east of Rome. Later on, from his base at Monte Cassino, he emerged as the father of Western monasticism. The Benedictines continue today, known for their disciplined balance of work, prayer, and study. Their rule of life is widely embraced beyond Benedictine communities by Protestants as well as Catholics because of its wisdom and moderation. Many other officially sanctioned monastic orders emerged in the centuries that followed, up into our own day, some of which still follow the Benedictine Rule.

By the twelfth century, in what is now Belgium, a new kind of intentional community began among laypeople, the Beguines and Beghards. Unlike official monastic orders, which had become cloistered and often aligned with the interests of Christendom (the collaboration of the church with secular power), these communities were formed by ordinary men and women who sought to live in holy community among the poor. Members of each household established their own customized rule of life. There were no permanent vows of membership. Beguines and Beghards were self-supporting and were located among the poor, where they ministered to their neighbors through teaching, healing, and other forms of service. The Brethren of the Common Life began in the 14th century with Gerhard Groote and was a powerful semimonastic lay movement that focused on living in community and serving in educational ministry among the poor.

During the 19th century, many utopian Christian communities formed in North America, including the Shakers, the Oneida Community, and Amana Colonies. Most of these experienced persecution from the dominant church, and the majority failed for various reasons.

With the decline of Christendom in the West, a new kind of monasticism is on the rise. Koinonia Farm, the birthplace of Habitat for Humanity, is a notable example. The new monasticism is lay driven and ecumenical, with adherents choosing intentional community, especially in "abandoned places of empire." Many follow a rule of life. As has always been the case, new expressions of Christian community flourish whenever the dominant church becomes mired in the world.

See also Monasticism

For Further Reading: Benedict, *The Rule of Saint Benedict*, ed. T. Fry (1998); W. Harmless, *Desert Christians* (2004); W. Simons, *Cities of Ladies* (2001); J. Wilson-Hartgrove, *New Monasticism* (2008).

Elaine A. Heath

Compassion

Compassion is suffering with, or sharing solidarity with, those who suffer, leading to a desire to relieve that suffering. Sometimes synonymous with mercy, compassion can be distinguished in that it motivates merciful action.

God's nature is compassionate and merciful (James 5:11), and he is compassionate to those whom he chooses to be (Ex. 33:19; Rom. 9:15). Compassion leads God to gather his people and restore their fortunes (Deut. 30:3). The prophets were deeply aware of God's mercy and compassion to sinful humanity (Isa. 30:18–19), which led him to bless them and withhold judgment. Yet judgment will be meted out without compassion on those who reject God (Jer. 15:6). Jesus had compassion on the crowds who were like sheep without a shepherd (Matt. 9:36) and was moved to heal their sick and feed them (Matt. 14:14–20). In the parable, the Good Samaritan's feelings of compassion for the injured Jew led him to take action by binding his wounds and incurring expense at the inn (Luke 10:25–36).

Christians should be clothed with compassion (Col. 3:12). Moreover, unity with Christ, in tenderness and compassion, should motivate Christians to imitate Christ's attitude of humility (Phil. 2:1–7). In the Christian tradition, compassion was a locus and way of contemplation in orders like the Franciscans, and a motivating force in liberation spirituality. These are not merely personal characteristics but should also be the posture of the body of Christ, since compassion is not merely private sentimentality but also has a public dimension. Philosopher Arthur Schopenhauer introduced it as a motivating factor for ethics, and E. F. Schumacher regarded it as crucial in economics and use of technology.

Other world religions, such as Buddhism and Islam, also teach compassion, though the motivation and purpose are different. Christians, motivated by compassion, may find that they can join hands with people of other faiths in acts of mercy. The distinguishing mark for Christians is that they are following the example of God in Jesus Christ.

See also *Kenosis; Love; Mercy.*

Kiem-Kiok Kwa

Cone, James (1938–)

Architect of black theology. Raised in "separate but equal" Bearden, Arkansas, and the African Methodist Episcopal Church, James Cone rose to prominence one year after the assassination of Martin Luther King Jr. with the publication of *Black Theology and Black Power* (1969). This theological trope, written with a distinctive holy anger, represents both in theory and method an approach to Christian spirituality from an unapologetically militant black perspective of the 1960s. Theoretically, Cone's black theology of spirituality attempts to reconcile the Christian gospel with the Black Power movement of the time so that freedom from oppression becomes the primary foci of any relevant life in God. In fact, blackness, under Cone's theology, is no longer considered a sin but a badge of honor, symbolic of where the presence of God is in overturning systematic socioeconomic and political oppression. For Cone, in this sense, even Jesus was black.

Methodologically, Cone's spiritual theology is a contextual theology: black diasporic sources and norms are recovered to offset (white) Eurocentric/American hegemonic ones that do not genuinely reflect the cultural uniqueness of African-American Christianity. To this end, Cone's hermeneutic lens unabashedly includes spirituals, blues, biblical passages, and thinkers like Malcolm X to affirm black agency and black self-dignity in God, which the legacy of racism constantly challenges.

Besides teaching at Union Theological Seminary since 1970 and producing countless scholars under his tutelage, Cone's enduring influence is as a public intellectual in dialogue with other liberationists, an activist engaged in historical projects that support "nonpersons" regardless of race, and a Christian who maintains an abiding celebration of the God of the oppressed. His impact is also traceable, more than forty years later, on the current wave of black theology with its suspicion of otherworldly eschatologies, cheap grace, nonrevolutionary consciousness, and avoidance of race-class-gender analysis in spiritual theologies. His writings include *Black Theology and Black Power* (1969), *God of the Oppressed* (1975), and *Martin and Malcolm and America* (1992).

See also African-American Christian Spirituality; Liberation Spirituality.

For Further Reading: E. Antonio, "Black Theology," in *Liberation Theology*, ed. C. Rowland (2007), 79–104.

Roy Whitaker

Confirmation

Confirmation is the rite by which ministers invoke the Holy Spirit on already baptized and properly catechized believers. In the Roman Catholic and Eastern Orthodox churches, confirmation (or chrismation, as the Orthodox call it) is a sacrament.

In some Protestant churches, however, the rite is still performed, but it is not elevated to the level of a sacrament. The Anglican and Episcopal churches regard confirmation as a ritual commonly believed to be a sacrament but not ordained by Christ himself. The rite entails a bishop, priest, or pastor anointing the candidate with a special ointment consisting of oil and balsam from a chrism, which in the Orthodox and Catholic traditions must be blessed by a bishop. As the celebrant anoints the candidate, he or she calls down the Holy Spirit.

One interesting development is how the Roman Catholic Rite for the Christian Initiation of Adults (RCIA) has incorporated confirmation into a fuller baptismal rite, demonstrating the close connection between water baptism and the gift of the Spirit. And surely one of the critical questions for the church today is how congregations can ritually articulate this essential dimension of initiation into Christian faith. Many have concluded that the rite of water baptism does need a parallel and twin rite of "confirmation" or "chrismation"—a rite that signals that the gift of the Spirit is integral to the Christian life.

Evidence of the rite's origins is abundant in the NT and early church writings, although development occurred with respect to its external form. Yet there is an assumed connection between the sending of the Holy Spirit on Pentecost and the subsequent gift of the Spirit to converts. Confirmation is a "making fast or sure" of one's baptismal faith, and it furthers the work of grace begun in the recipient through baptism. The rite symbolizes God's continuing work both in the individual Christian and the church community, and it testifies to the distinctly Trinitarian nature of conversion by connecting the process of salvation not only to the work of the Father and the Son, but also to the Holy Spirit.

See also Assurance; Sacrament.

For Further Reading: A. Kavanagh, *Confirmation* (1992); T. Scannell, "Confirmation," in *CE*; T. Ware, *The Orthodox Church* (1997).

Joshua Dean

Confucian Spirituality

Confucianism is one of the schools of classical Chinese philosophy. It emphasizes the mind as an instrument capable of making moral judgments—but one that is morally neutral in its own intrinsic nature. By way of analogy, human eyes can distinguish color, but eyesight itself is devoid of color. We cannot describe one's eyesight as red or yellow, for eyesight is a power that transcends color. And so is the mind with respect to right and wrong.

The mind-in-itself can distinguish goodness from evil, which is the substance of morality. Neo-Confucian Wang Yang-Ming (1472–1529) called it *liang-zhi,* an innate ability found in all men and women. If one follows the path of *liang-zhi*, he or she may eventually come to know the way of the sage. The mind is the ultimate good. However, this does not mean that the mind is the perfection of good, but that the mind is the root or origin of good.

In this sense, Yang-Ming regards *liang-zhi* as the way to sagehood, which follows the inner urge of the human heart and its desire for the good. *Zhi liang-zhi* is the formula that Yang-Ming proposed for the extension or realization of the knowledge of good. The term *liang-zhi* actually comes from the *Book of Mencius*, which also refers to the "inborn capacity to know the good" as mentioned above. *Liang-zhi* also implies the "inborn ability to do good," or *liang-neng*, which enables persons to act according to their original good nature by the practice of virtue, leading to complete self-transcendence.

According to Mencius (371–289 BC), the most important Confucian philosopher after Confucius himself, the starting point of the mind is good. The feeling of alarm caused by seeing a child who is about to fall into a well proves that people have the ability to recognize and to do what is right. However, this ability is like a tiny spark that needs to be fanned into flame. Mencius pointed out that anyone with the initial sensibilities of the Four Beginnings (that is, commiseration as the beginning of humanity, shame and dislike as the beginning of righteousness, deference and compliance as the beginning of propriety, and a sense of right and wrong as the beginning of wisdom) will also know how to develop them to the fullest extent, and the result will be like a fire beginning to burn.

Once these four abilities are fully developed, they will be sufficient to make one a sage who will know how to protect people in the world. Confucian perfectionism begins with the cultivation of the human self but culminates in a total transformation of the world. Mencius assumed that human nature is the necessary and sufficient ground for perfection. Perfection cannot be imputed from without but must be cultivated through inner self-effort.

This is the way for a sage in Chinese philosophy. The cultivation of *liang-zhi* (conscience) is *nei-sheng* (the ability to do good), while the protection of all people within the world is *wai-wang* (kingship or leadership). To be a sage in Chinese tradition involves more than just cultivating one's internal personality; it also requires one to behave properly in society. A sage, therefore, should contribute to the world by objectifying his or her innate morality. However, this is where the real problem of Chinese philosophy lies. Mencius taught a lot on how to be a good king, but he rarely taught on how to establish a good system of government.

How to apply the in-side morality to an outside world is always the problem of Confucian spirituality. Modern Confucians usually maintain that the challenge to self-realization does not come from the external world, but from self-ignorance and egoism. The Confucian way, which suggests an unceasing process of self-transformation as a communal act, is therefore an attempt to show that knowledge, properly understood as a humanist value, can ultimately free us from the constrictions of the privatized ego.

Confucius identified the principle of the cosmos with the innate moral instincts of human beings. Christians, by contrast, believe that God is the ultimate truth of the universe. The cosmic principle is silent, but God is speaking. The way of Confucian spirituality is introspective meditation, while that of Christian spirituality, while allowing for such attentiveness to the heart, is preeminently transformation through listening.

See also Buddhist; Zen.

For Further Reading: J. Ching, *Chinese Religions* (1993); W. T. Chan, *A Source Book in Chinese Philosophy* (1973); J. Yeung, *New Horizon of Chinese Culture* (2005).

Hing-Kau (Jason) Yeung

Conscience

Conscience is the ability to discern the moral dimensions of human life. The formation of conscience requires obtaining knowledge and wisdom, learning to make distinctions between right and wrong, and the resolved commitment and capability to act according to one's ethical convictions. Conscience involves a holistic integration of reason, affections, and volition in order to make deliberate and conscientious decisions about what should or should not be done (Callahan, 14). From a theological perspective, conscience is an aspect of the *imago Dei*. Humans bear the image of God in our varying abilities to distinguish between good and evil and to act more or less in moral or immoral ways. While all humans possess a conscience, they have varying aptitudes for understanding right from wrong due to the effects of sin (Rom. 1:12–16) and other factors. The possession of a conscience does not guarantee ethical behavior. It is the educating, nurturance, and use of conscience that fosters moral and spiritual growth and enables greater integrity between belief and behavior.

Conscience has two dimensions. First, conscience may act as a source of conviction after we have made a decision or engaged in morally questionable behavior. These pangs of conscience elicit guilt, shame, regret, judgment, or fear of punishment for doing what ought not to have been done or failing to do what one should have done. A second more formative dimension is "antecedent conscience" (Curran). The use of conscience comes before one acts by providing moral guidance for decisions and actions. It enables us to think, reflect, and discern what should be done before a decision is made or an action occurs.

In order for conscience to guide us prior to any act or decision, it must be continually educated, cultivated, and developed, since it has important human and spiritual dimensions, as well as interior and external qualities. In Christian faith, conscience is nurtured and fed by the Scriptures, Christian tradition and community, and the ongoing work of the Holy Spirit, as well as through practices that enable persons to take deliberate steps in acting according to conscience. The Scriptures aid in the ongoing formation of conscience in many ways by the moral guidance they offer. Conscience is educated through such things as biblical laws, narratives, wisdom, prophetic material, the teachings of Jesus, parables, and concrete guidance provided in the Epistles for attitudes and behaviors. Scripture provides important content for conscience, inculcates a desire for what is good and right (Phil. 4:8–9), and orients us toward God's intended purposes for the world.

The various streams of Christian tradition also provide sources of moral wisdom necessary for developing conscience. The stories of Christians in the past, with their legacies and teachings, provide valuable perspectives for the nurturing of conscience. Sources from Christian history and tradition can provide positive and negative models for attitudes and behavior. There are positive examples for moral behavior as well as dubious ones that should not be emulated. Participation in Christian community is also a crucial means by which conscience is nurtured through the preaching, teaching, and embodying of Scripture, educational experiences, participation in the sacraments, service to others, and relationships that offer moral wisdom and guidance. Christian community affords a context for moral discourse, deliberation, and discernment with wise mentors important for gaining knowledge, heightening moral awareness, and forming conscience.

Conscience is also formed through the work of the Holy Spirit. The Holy Spirit aids in the formation of conscience by convicting persons of guilt (John 16:9), through the process of sanctification, and by helping persons discern the voice of God (1 John 4:1–6). Spiritual growth involves the development of virtues, or moral attributes such as goodness, kindness, love, mercy, faithfulness, wisdom, and self-control (Gal. 5:22–26; 2 Peter 1:3–11). Conscience also requires the virtue of courage. The acquiring of knowledge and spiritual growth are important but so is taking steps to act according to what we know and what we believe. This requires courage to act according to one's convictions, especially in difficult circumstances. The development of conscience involves a practiced determination to live and act according to our moral convictions. We learn to do the right things by exercising conscience in doing right things.

It is important to attend to and use the sources of conscience in a balanced and integrated manner. For example, one source, such as Scripture, may correct perspectives from tradition. Likewise, the Holy Spirit cultivates the internal moral dispositions necessary for conscience while Christian practices remind us that conscience has visible dimensions. Wisdom from mentors can help us discern competing voices and to better recognize ways of thinking and living more consonant with Christian faith. The formation of conscience requires willful determination to know, learn, and understand, a reliance on the wisdom of others, and openness to the Spirit who desires to form us so that we live and act according to what we believe.

See also Conversion; Conviction.

For Further Reading: M. Augsburger, *The Christ Shaped-Conscience* (1990); S. Callahan, *In Good Conscience* (1991); C. Curran, "Conscience in Light of the Catholic Moral Tradition," in *Conscience*, ed. C. Curran (2004), 3–24; R. Gula, *Moral Discernment* (1997); A. Verhey, *Remembering Jesus* (2002).

Wyndy Corbin Reuschling

Consecration

Consecration is the solemn action of setting something or someone apart for the service of God. All Christian acts of consecration find both their source and their highest example in the life and self-sacrificial work of Jesus Christ.

Acts of consecration are found throughout Scripture. In the OT, they are found in God's selection of Israel as his particular people (Ex. 24), of the priesthood to his service (Ex. 29; Lev. 8), of prophets to the delivery of his message (Isa. 6), and of ritualistic objects to his worship. In the NT, they are seen most particularly in the baptism of Jesus (Mark 1; Matt. 3; Luke 3; 4; cf. John 10:36), the designation of Paul and Barnabas to a particular ministry (Acts 13:2), and to the calling out of the church as the people of God and as a "royal priesthood" (Rom. 8:28; 1 Peter 2:9).

In liturgically higher churches, specific acts of consecration are seen in four particular instances: the dedication of the communal elements of the Eucharist or Mass, the inauguration of a bishop (Episcopal ordination), the dedication of altars, and the dedication of church buildings. In addition, within the Roman Catholic Church, there are those who have publicly vowed to live the "consecrated life," a lifestyle characterized by a more rigorous form of discipleship including such disciplines as chastity and poverty.

In evangelical circles there is less agreement about the timing and means of consecration. It has been associated variously with regeneration, baptism, sanctification, and Spirit baptism. It is commonly understood, however, as a decisive step of voluntary, complete, and final surrender of oneself and, conversely, the dedication of oneself to the pursuit of God, personal holiness, and ministry for the purpose of glorifying him and expanding his kingdom.

See also Detachment; Holiness; Sanctification; Surrender.

Bernie Van De Walle

Consolation and Desolation

While the language of consolation and desolation can be found as far back as the writings of Origen, it gained greater currency in the 16th century, notably in the *Spiritual Exercises* of Ignatius Loyola, where questions of consolation or desolation are the crucial matter in hand when it comes to the "rules of discernment." To discern, for Ignatius, is to attend to the movements of the heart — notably consolation that speaks of peace and joy and an interior life that is growing in faith, hope, and love. Desolation is the counterpart — feelings of anger, sorrow, fear, or simply tepidness, emptiness of soul, and little desire for God.

Desolation is not necessarily wrong in itself; indeed, the cause of sorrow or fear or anger may be quite understandable; and even tepidness or emptiness of soul may quite simply be part of the ebbs and flows of the spiritual life. And yet the Christian is wise to be alert to the presence of desolation and consider its cause or source — whether it be neglect of spiritual discipline or some exterior factor.

And consolation is not necessarily "good." It may be nothing more than good feelings caused by misguided motives or aspirations. For Ignatius, the Spirit guides and counsels in consolation; but consolation itself must be tested to confirm that this peace or joy arises from the good, the noble, and the worthy of praise, the peace that only Jesus gives (John 14:27).

See also Ignatian; Lament.

For Further Reading: T. H. Green, *Weeds among the Wheat* (1984); G. Smith, *The Voice of Jesus* (2003).

Gordon T. Smith

Consumerism

In the ethos of consumerism the consumption of goods and services becomes the central definition of the self, a definition at odds with the biblical understanding of personhood. People have always had basic material needs for food, clothing, and shelter. In the past these items were usually made by the family or the local community and were life necessities. With the success of the Industrial Revolution, so many products were manufactured at such a fast rate that new markets were needed. Since production exceeded need and demand, advertising campaigns were launched to create perceived needs.

These new "manufactured" needs undermine our sense of self. We are told that a change of hair color or new car will change our lives, that a new scent will bring romance. The right labels convey status and define our place in society, and we become the sum of the products we consume. One Internet company warns those who don't use their service, "It's as though you don't even exist." A consumer society is made up of isolated individuals competing for the best goods and services—who are, in the words of Ivan Illich, "the prisoners of addiction and the prisoners of envy." If our core identity is that of consumer, we may view even other people as commodities—replaceable and interchangeable, like the many other products in our lives.

Ironically, consumerism is a materialism that denigrates the created world. For example, "fast food" has been degraded and denatured, attractively packaged, and aggressively marketed. Large portions and nutritional deficits contribute to obesity and other health problems of consumers, who then buy pills from pharmaceutical companies who aggressively market their products.

Years of consumption, waste, and resulting pollution have taken a great toll on the planet. We have been consuming non-renewable resources and are reaching our limits. "Consumer Society" is unsustainable, and humanity needs a new model for the future.

Christian spirituality offers an antidote to such trivialization of the self and degradation of nature. In a life that is lived before God, the believer's identity will be based on a deep understanding of the Creator's delight in their uniqueness. Grounded in this understanding of personhood, they can develop alternative responses to others and the world, such as caring, wonder, delight, and contentment.

As a reductionist, materialistic understanding of life, consumerism is at cross-purposes with the Christian message that people, their neighbors, and the whole created order have meaning because they were brought into being by a loving God, to be encountered and cared for rather than used and exploited.

Dictionaries list a secondary definition of "consumerism" as groups working together for the common good against the abuses of consumer society. Christians have much to offer this kind of work. The antidotes to consumerism include simplicity, gratitude, generosity, and community—virtues from the Spirit, which the church can model for a watching world.

Further Reading: W. Berry, *Sex, Economy, Freedom and Community* (1992); C. Blomberg, *Neither Poverty nor Riches* (1999).

Sharon Gallagher

Contemplation

Contemplation is sometimes used interchangeably with meditation, and though there is overlap and interaction between them, they are two distinct forms of spiritual practice. The ancient method of praying Scripture or *lectio divina* indicates that meditation is the second movement and contemplation the culminating fourth movement. Meditation is more mental and cognitive reflection while contemplation is more affective and attentive gratitude. Meditation requires study, rumination, and explanation, using the mind, while contemplation depends on savoring, enjoying, and experiences of the heart. Richard of St. Victor (1111–1173) observed that "meditation investigates, contemplation wonders." Thomas White, an English Puritan, drew a similar distinction using the bridal language of Song of Songs: "Meditation is like the kindling of fire and contemplation more like the flaming of it when fully kindled. The one is like the spouse seeking Christ, and the other like the spouse's enjoying of Christ."

Richard Foster, in his *Streams of Living Water*, summarized the essence of the contemplative life this way: It is "the steady gaze of the soul upon the God who loves us."

Foster's definition reveals that contemplation is both a specific type of prayer and an attitude of life. Applied to Christian spirituality, the common link that unites these various definitions is that contemplation is a loving and sustained gaze upon God's presence in creation and God's mighty acts. Contemplation may also produce mystical experiences with God that assists a Christian in living in deeper union and communion with Christ, also known as spiritual marriage.

Contemplation requires openness and sensitivity to the Holy Spirit, but that subjectivity has been misused at times throughout the history of the church. Karl Barth was one prominent theologian who rejected contemplation based on his misunderstanding that it did not focus on God and lacked a biblical foundation. Contemplation can be misdirected to the self rather than God and therefore requires discernment. But Barth missed the instances of contemplation in Scripture itself (e.g., Pss. 27:4; 63:1–5; 73:25; Luke 2:19; 10:39, 42; 2 Cor. 12:2–4; et al.). Many recognize Jesus as a model of the contemplative life, pointing to John 14–17, which reveals the oneness and intimacy of love he shares with God, his Father. Jesus also demonstrates that a balanced spiritual life will consist of both action and contemplation, or better, contemplative action.

Many of the most respected leaders of the church have written on or practiced some form of contemplation. The list includes Augustine, the Cappadocian fathers, John Chrysostom, Gregory the Great, Bernard of Clairvaux, Symeon the New Theologian, Ignatius of Loyola, and Teresa of Avila. While neither Luther nor Calvin would normally be considered contemplative, contemplative themes and images are present in their writings. The Puritans and Dutch and German Pietists also represent a rich expression of Protestant contemplation. Surprisingly to some, Jonathan Edwards's *Personal Narrative* reflects a robust expression of contemplation. Contemplation is equally present in the evangelical hymnody of Charles Wesley, Philip Doddridge, and Fanny Crosby. Many popular contemporary evangelicals have embraced contemplation, including Bruce Demarest, Richard Foster, James Houston, Eugene Peterson, the late Robert Webber, and Dallas Willard.

There is no guarantee, of course, that if a person prays in a certain way it will produce a contemplative experience. Nonetheless, praying Scripture through *lectio divina*, singing meditative music of Taize and other forms of contemporary Christian praise music, centering prayer, and the Eastern Orthodox Jesus Prayer can nurture a more sensitive contemplation and stimulate deeper communion with God. The benefits of contemplation may include increased love and knowledge of God, greater consciousness of one's sins and rebellion, increased awareness of God's presence, greater sensitivity to those who are oppressed or in need, and peace and greater assurance of God's promises.

See also Attentiveness; Meditation.

For Further Reading: H. U. von Balthasar, *Prayer* (1961); B. Demarest, *Satisfy Your Soul* (1999); R. Foster, *Prayer* (1992); idem, *Streams of Living Water* (1998); T. Merton, *New Seeds of Contemplation* (1961); T. Schwanda, "Gazing at God," *Reformed Review* 56, no. 2 (2002/2003): 101–21; R. Webber, *Divine Embrace* (2006); T. White, *Method of Divine Meditation* (1655); G. Zinn, ed., *Richard of St. Victor*, CWS (1979).

Tom Schwanda

Contemplative Life

See **Active Life and Contemplative Life.**

Contemporary Alternative Spiritualities

It is now fashionable to deplore religion and celebrate spirituality. Thus, even traditional religious views are often packaged as alternative spiritualities. Three examples illustrate this reality. First, Tibetan Buddhism, one of the most rigorous religious paths, has gained popularity through the attractive spirituality of the Dalai Lama, known as "His Holiness." Likewise, New Age beliefs have gained new ground through the gentle teachings of Eckhart Tolle, a German mystic now based in Vancouver and promoted by Oprah Winfrey. Third, the biblical message of Jesus has been recast in the emergent church movement through the voices of Brian McLaren, Andrew Jones (Internet name: Tall Skinny Kiwi), Karen Ward, and other Christians attuned to a postmodern age.

The astounding popularity of the Dalai Lama, author of *Freedom in Exile* (1990) and many other bestselling works, is a perfect case of how contemporary spirituality is subject to the media. What else can explain the allure of this Tibetan leader and his brand of Buddhism? He is a media darling and has learned the art of adapting the Buddhist message to the masses. His foibles are overlooked and even his pluralistic outlook is used as proof of the truth of the Buddhist path. No one in the history of Buddhism has introduced more people to the Middle Way. What makes this achievement especially noteworthy are the politics surrounding the Dalai Lama and the international persecution he faces from Communist China.

A pluralistic vision is also central to Eckhart Tolle. His writings *The Power of Now* (2004) and *A New Earth* (2008) quote Jesus frequently, but Tolle also cites Buddha often and uses Hindu advaitist philosophy as the underlying ideology for spiritual growth. Tolle also says that his theories are consistent with the highest forms of Islam. Tolle was born in Germany in 1948. He was raised in a dysfunctional home and claims a spiritual breakthrough just after his twenty-ninth birthday. He was involved in British academia for a while but moved to Vancouver in 1993 to advance his New Age practice. Oprah promoted him in 2008, and he gained instant fame as a spiritual teacher.

While emergent leaders have not known intense media promotion like the Dalai Lama or Tolle, Brian McLaren, author of *A Generous Orthodoxy* (2004) and numerous other works, has been voted one of the twenty-five leading evangelicals by *Time* magazine. The emergent movement is best understood as the postmodern face of a new generation of evangelicals, including Dan Kimball, Sally Morgenthaler, Erwin McManus, Doug Pagitt, and Tony Jones. Spurning both rationalistic and pragmatic forms of evangelicalism, emergent leaders decry outdated epistemology and a consumer model of church life. McLaren and other emergents understand postmodern angst but want to meet it with the radical narrative of Jesus and his relational and communal solution to the human dilemma.

Of course, even leaders in alternative spiritualities are subject to the power of the older and larger religious traditions. For example, Brian McLaren is attacked regularly by fundamentalist Christians for alleged departures from doctrine. The emergent leader Tony Jones was targeted for his endorsement of homosexuality. Other emergent leaders are viewed with suspicion for their appreciation of Catholic mystics or even ancient church liturgies. There is even growing internal dissent over boundaries of doctrine, since some emergents are worried whether the postmodern friendliness has gone too far.

On the Buddhist front, the Dalai Lama has received intense criticism from other Tibetan Buddhist groups, especially over his rejection of the worship of a controversial protector deity named

Dorje Shugden. This controversy led to international protests against His Holiness. While New Age leaders seldom receive internal criticism, Eckhart Tolle has been critiqued for his mystifying sentences. Of more significance, Oprah was the object of scorn for her endorsement of *The Secret* (2006), the New Age book from Rhonda Byrne. Critics within the New Age movement said it was far too materialistic to be treated as a valid spiritual tool.

Alternative spiritualities depend on freedom for their existence. The Internet has provided one such venue for minority and alternative voices. This is especially significant in the case of Muslims who tire of orthodoxy and/or repressive Muslim regimes. Progressive versions of Islam are noted in Gary Bunt's *iMuslims: Rewiring the House of Islam* (2009) and in the media reports from Mona Eltahawy, an Egyptian journalist and social analyst. On a more mundane level, social media technology is changing the face of religion and spirituality. Twitter and Facebook serve as spiritual portals in a wired age, both for alternative and traditional spiritualities.

Alternative spiritualities are seldom new. Rather, traditional paradigms and practices are cast in new language and style or are fine-tuned to add new insights and address concerns of contemporary society. Thus, the Dalai Lama, Tolle, and emergent leaders express traditional teaching in fresh vocabulary but also add concerns about ecology and the environment to their spiritual vision. In their own particular way, each of these alternative spiritualities also pays serious attention to the presence of evil in the world. This is especially significant in the case of Tolle, because New Age teachers usually deny or understate the reality of evil.

It is important for those interested in spiritual paths not to be too overly impressed by rhetoric against religion and for spirituality. After all, contemporary alternative spiritualities will usually look much like the larger religions from which they originate. As well, false spiritualities can be advanced simply on the appeal of the claim that what is being offered is not religion. That is no guarantee of virtue or truth. One ancient and famous source of spirituality warned of the need to test the spirits (1 John 4:1).

For Further Reading: T. Miller, *America's Alternative Religions* (1995).

James A. Beverley

Contentment

The satisfied heart. The restful soul. The grateful spirit. The uncoveting joy of those who own the word "enough" no matter how much or little they have. These qualities mark the experience called contentment. Christian contentment, in Jeremiah Burroughs's insightful definition, "is that sweet, inward, quiet, gracious frame of spirit, which freely submits to and delights in God's wise and fatherly disposal in every condition."

Images of those joyfully free of materialistic dependencies and hunger for prestige, such as Francis of Assisi or Mother Teresa, are invoked as we consider this wonderful quality of spirituality. Or one may picture Jesus, calm and unworried (even sleeping!) amid the Galilean sea storm (Luke 8:22–25), or Paul, who had "learned to be content whatever the circumstances ... whether well fed or hungry, whether living in plenty or in want" (Phil. 4:11–12).

This Pauline text about "the secret of being content" (Phil. 4:12) can be considered a biblical watchword. For Paul, contentment is "learned" as an aspect of spiritual formation; it has to do with one's response to circumstances. Though the original word he employed meant "self-sufficient" and connoted a frame of heart in which one is fully satisfied within irrespective of his or her situation, it is clear in the context that for the Christian disciple this is a grace imparted through God's strength and his riches in Christ (4:13, 19). This radical dependence on God's providence displays a grace of self-sufficiency rooted in God-sufficiency by which Paul can describe himself as "having nothing, and yet possessing everything" (2 Cor. 6:10). The same line of thought is present in 1 Timothy 6:6–8, where despite the "nothing" we both brought into the world and take out of it, we have "great gain" if we have "godliness with contentment"; so "food and clothing" suffice.

One resource from contemplative tradition that can help evangelicals and other Christians to live this mystery is what Ignatius of Loyola, in his *Spiritual Exercises*, called the Principle and Foundation. Two key terms used in the statement are *disinterest* and *detachment*: he says we can only fulfill our purpose as humans (to praise, reverence, and serve God our Lord) by a spirit of disinterestedness in all created things — not wanting long life rather than short, plenty rather than little, and so on — because we are detached from them due to a stronger attachment, namely, to God and his will for us. Just so, we find contentment.

See also Detachment; Simplicity.

For Further Reading: J. Burroughs, *Rare Jewel of Christian Contentment* (2009); W. Samson and S. Claiborne, *Enough* (2009).

David L. Rowe

Contextual Spirituality

See **Chapter 29.**

Conversion

The language of Christian conversion describes both the initial response to the message of God's grace and an ongoing process of renewal and reform. The primary use of the term refers to the genesis of spiritual experience. For the Christian spiritual tradition, this of course means the first step or steps in which a person comes to faith in Christ and accepts the call to be a child of God and a member of his church.

Evangelicals — notably those influenced by revivalism — have often viewed conversion as a punctiliar experience: the experience of a person who chooses to become a Christian, perhaps in response to preaching or the witness of a Christian, and from one moment to the next is considered to be a Christian believer. But in fact, for most individuals, conversion is a complex experience of being drawn to Christ by the gracious witness of the Spirit who illumines the mind, moves the heart, and strengthens the will; and this process will likely involve a number of human witnesses and often takes place over an extended period of time. In other words, conversion still speaks of a beginning — the initiation into Christian faith — but it is not so much one moment or event as a series of events and experiences that collectively form the point of departure for a lifetime of spiritual growth and transformation.

Furthermore, the language of Acts 2:38 ("Repent and be baptized ... for the forgiveness of your sins. And you will receive the gift of the Holy Spirit") suggests that a Christian conversion has both an internal and external dimension: a personal subjective experience of faith, of which repentance is the crucial expression; and the sacramental church-mediated experience of baptism, the necessary complement to repentance. Both dimensions testify to the most crucial element of all — the presence of the Spirit of Christ who now indwells and empowers the new Christian to grow in faith, hope, and love.

Best understood, conversion is not an "end" but a beginning — ideally a good beginning, a good foundation for a life in Christ and in Christian community. In coming to faith in Christ, one joins a community of Christians who together seek to mature in faith and together witness to the reign and mission of Christ in the world. Thus, while conversion is personal and subjective, it is also distinctly communal; it is an initiation into Christ and the life of the Spirit and at the same time an initiation into the life of the church.

See also Baptism; Conviction; Faith; Penitence; Regeneration.

For Further Reading: B. Kallenberg, *Live to Tell* (2002); A. Krieder, *The Change of Conversion and the Origin of Christendom* (1999); G. T. Smith, *Transforming Conversion* (2010).

Gordon T. Smith

Conviction

Two discrete meanings of conviction are addressed here: "conviction of sin," and deeply held belief. Conviction of sin has been a recurring theme in evangelical explanations of the process whereby a person becomes a Christian. This has theological, experiential, and pastoral (or evangelistic) dimensions. Theologically, the notion is rooted in this analysis of the human condition: "All have sinned and fall short of the glory of God" (Rom. 3.23). Such a view of human nature has been embraced both by Calvinists, such as Jonathan Edwards and George Whitefield, and by Arminians, such as John Wesley and his followers.

Yet the notion of conviction also carries an experiential meaning; it refers to a psychological state in which, through the work of the Holy Spirit, a person becomes convinced of his or her own sinfulness and, consequently, his or her need of repentance and faith in the atoning work of Christ. The preaching of the cross is a pastoral response to what can be an overwhelming sense of personal sinfulness. "How can I be saved?" is an existential cry that can be expanded to the more reflective question, "How can a sinner be reconciled to a God who, though loving and merciful, is awesome and holy?"

In revivalism, evangelists often underscore the sinfulness of their hearers, because they are persuaded that a deep conviction of this fact is a necessary prelude to repentance and saving faith. Often conversion has been seen as a process that begins with conviction of personal sin and leads through repentance and "the sinner's prayer" to faith, regeneration, and fellowship with God. While there is logic to such a view, it is a mistake to assume a rigidly organized series of steps. Evangelical preaching in the 21st century has to deal with a Western culture in which the notion of sinfulness has often been replaced by therapeutic or relational concepts, such as guilt feelings or shame. This is where Scripture and doctrine need to orient pastoral and evangelistic pragmatics. The conviction of sin can also be seen as a continuing theme in the way some evangelicals construe the Christian life, insisting that believers continue to examine themselves and their sinfulness prayerfully, so that they may continue to repent, seek God's forgiveness, and receive divine grace and the assurance of salvation anew.

Pastoral care needs to respond both to the theological reality of sin and the experiences of brokenness and alienation that often mar human lives. The doctrine of grace provides a context in which human sinfulness can be named and owned realistically and a means whereby hope and love can encourage the opening of the heart to God's forgiving love. Such a response may be provided to individuals through counseling and spiritual direction or through the offering of prayers of confession in worship. While evangelicals have resisted the notion of absolution, they have consistently preached the forgiveness of sins and celebrated the experience of such forgiveness in their hymnody and testimonies.

The term *conviction* may also refer to a deeply held belief. Many evangelicals belong to so-called believers churches, in which membership is dependent on a clear set of beliefs and through which clear boundaries are drawn between those inside and those outside the community of faith. While typically resisting the liturgical use of creeds, they have often used confessions of faith as a means of declaring their convictions. While different denominations will explain the nature of the church in different ways, evangelicals are united in seeing the church as a convictional community.

See also Conscience; Conversion.

For Further Reading: J. Edwards, *Works*, 2 vols., ed. E. Hickman (1974); D. Gillett, *Trust and Obey* (1993); J. W. McClendon and J. Smith, *Convictions* (1975).

Christopher J. Ellis

Coptic Spirituality

The Coptic Orthodox Church is an ancient Egyptian tradition that traces its origin to the evangelist Mark in the 1st century (c. AD 41–44). Confessionally non-Chalcedonian (Miaphysite), the Copts are in communion with the other Oriental Orthodox churches—Syrian, Armenian, Indian, and Ethiopian—and thus distinct from the smaller Chalcedonian Orthodox church in Egypt. The Copts have rejected the Council of Chalcedon (451) out of concerns that it mitigated the ineffable union of divinity and humanity expressed in Cyril of Alexandria's phrase, "one nature (*mia physis*) of the incarnate Word of God." This precision reflects a commitment to the paradox of salvation: God really became human without ceasing to be God; salvation is received in the mystery of worship; the body and blood of Christ really are life-giving, uniting the worshiper to God. Despite centuries of separation, reconciliation over Chalcedon with the Roman Catholics and Eastern Orthodox has begun to occur, with partial agreements reached in 1989 and 1991.

Being Egyptian is very important for the Copts. Thus, the flight of the holy family into Egypt plays an important role in Coptic devotion. Also important are its founder, Mark the Evangelist, and its fathers, particularly the patriarchs Athanasius and Cyril, and monks Antony, Pachomius, and Shenuda (350–466). The patriarchate is regarded as an unbroken chain that begins with Mark and spans the 1st to the 21th centuries, witnessing to the importance for the Copts of continuity and mediation—that apostolic charism is passed down through relationships. The monastic life is also vital to Coptic piety and forms another link between the modern and ancient faith. Contemporary monasticism continues to draw its forms from Antony (the hermit) and Pachomius (the community), and it remains central for the spiritual guidance of the church.

With the rise of Islam in the 7th century, the Copts began their long history as a minority people in Egypt, eventually leading to cultural and spiritual decline. In the last century, however, renewal has followed the pontificates of popes Cyril VI and Shenuda III. Of particular importance, the Coptic Sunday school movement of the 1940s–1950s contributed to the strengthening of monasteries and seminaries.

Coptic piety is also marked by commitment to saints, relics, healings, exorcisms, and mystical phenomena, such as resisting death or miraculous icons that may heal, weep, bleed, or emit light. Moreover, Coptic piety can also be seen in the traditions of having distinctly Christian names and tattoos of the Coptic cross on the inside of the right wrist.

See also Cyril of Alexandria; Desert Fathers and Mothers.

For Further Reading: H. Badr, ed., *Christianity: A History in the Middle East* (2005); O. Meinardus, *Two Thousand Years of Coptic Christianity* (1999).

Timothy J. Becker

Counseling

Counseling encompasses both professional and informal help given to people in need. Licensed professional counselors are trained to assess, diagnose, and intervene with treatment plans to mitigate and solve the presenting problems. Legislation and codes of ethics guide and regulate these counseling professions. There are differences in opinion among Christian counselors about the sufficiency of the Scriptures to meet all psychological needs. Proponents of "biblical counseling," such as Jay Adams, believe that the Bible is the only valid resource available to solve human problems and dilemmas. Conversely, those who embrace the Augustinian declaration that all truth is God's truth believe that there is room for the integration of theology and psychology. The American Association of Christian Counselors, which has the world's largest membership of Christian counselors, is a good example of the latter. Informal counseling has been practiced in the church since biblical times. It ranges from contemplative helping, such as soul care, spiritual formation, prayer counseling, and inner healing, to active guidance, such as pastoral care and counseling, lay counseling, and Stephen Ministries.

The words *counsel* and *counselor*, and their cognates, are used about 150 times in the Bible. Isaiah listed one of the names of the messianic child as the "Wonderful Counselor" (9:6), who will implement God's purposes for humankind. Jesus promised the Holy Spirit as the *paraclete* (John 14:26; 15:26; 16:7) — that is, one who comes alongside others to advocate, comfort, and support. *Paraclete* is an apt description of counselors as well. Studies have shown the importance of the therapeutic relationship in predicting the success of counseling. Christian counselors create sacred and safe spaces where people in need are able to share their pains and be restored to health and wellness. In addition to being competent, counselors need to attend vigilantly to their own personal and spiritual formation (John 15:3–8). It is imperative for counselors to spend time praying and seeking divine guidance for their counselees. Those who seek counseling help may or may not profess the Christian faith. In the therapeutic encounter, counselors embody the compassionate presence of Jesus and minister to the people in need through the power of the Holy Spirit. Christian counselors are "wounded healers," nudging both Christians and non-Christians alike toward wholeness that ultimately is found in Jesus Christ alone.

See also Care of Souls.

For Further Reading: J. Adams, *The Christian Counselor's Manual* (1973); M. McMinn, *Psychology, Theology, and Spirituality in Christian Counseling* (1996); T. Oden, *Care of Souls in the Classic Tradition* (1983).

Ben K. Lim

Courage

Courage is a biblical imperative throughout Scripture (e.g., Josh. 1:8; 1 Cor. 16:13). It is essential to Christian spirituality because life is full of danger and suffering. And seeking God is risky, not only because God is all-powerful and just, but also because God is often experienced as absent. Almost all the virtues require at least a modicum of courage. Without courage we will not dare to love the unlovely, hope when all is dark, or keep faith in the face of cynicism. Wisdom needs courage to face unpleasant truths. Justice needs courage to choose what is right rather than what is safe. Temperance needs courage to deny the domination of legitimate desires.

This does not mean that the virtues are one, as Plato thought. Perhaps ideal courage is necessarily wise, just, and temperate. However, the "unity of the virtues" is neither self-evident nor proved by experience. Someone who is lacking in one virtue is not thereby deprived of all the rest. If courage is used in seeking an unworthy end — for example, robbing a house or cheating on the stock exchange — we might admire the thief's daring but not call it the virtue of courage. However, if a rash boy with little prudence and less self-control risks his life to save a friend, we can still praise him for his courage.

Aristotle explained courage as the proper balance, or mean, between daring and cowardice in seeking what is good. A properly courageous person will not throw away her life needlessly, nor flee when it is appropriate to take a stand. The virtue of courage is neither reckless (an excess of daring), nor overly timid, which is a deficiency. Rather, courage is the appropriate disposition needed to bring about the noblest outcome in a situation of danger. The actions demanded by courage depend on the details of the situation. In some cases, it may take more courage to run away and save your family, rather than to die in a hopeless cause.

In the early church, martyrdom was the primary context for thinking about courage. The stories of the martyrs were primary texts for teaching ethics. Gruesome death without betraying Christ was the highest honor. Positively, courage is the ability to act in a desperate situation without being overcome with fear. Courage is needed to do almost anything that entails risk of harm. Negatively, fortitude is the ability to endure suffering without compromising integrity. We all need courage, because in the end we all must face death.

See also Virtues; Will, Human.

For Further Reading: Aristotle, *Nicomachean Ethics* (1957, many eds.); P. Geach, *The Virtues* (1977); S. Hauerwas, *The Peaceable Kingdom* (1981).

Bernard Adeney-Risakotta

Covenant

A covenant is a solemn pledge to engage in or refrain from some future conduct. It is a concept of crucial importance in the Bible and the history of Christian spirituality. In the OT, covenants are "cut" because they are often made by sacrifice. Even though a covenant normally requires two or more participants in order to be established, the responsibility for fulfilling its obligations can rest with only one. Covenantal relationships differ from legal ones, for they are based on the integrity of those partners making the pledge and not on the judge presiding.

While the Bible records certain humans making covenants and the practice was well-known in the ancient Near East, the most important covenants for biblical spirituality are those made by God with his people. Indeed, God "cuts" covenants with individuals and his people, promising protection and blessing if they do his will (most notably in his Law). Although there are a number of covenants made between God and his people, the OT speaks of them in generally unitive terms. The covenant or covenants of the OT are contrasted with or fulfilled by the new covenant (or testament), which NT writers argue is accomplished by Jesus Christ. This new covenant is seen to transform spiritual life in God's promise of the interiorization of his law in his people (see Jer. 31 and Heb. 8).

Although covenant concepts are prevalent throughout Christian history, they were most intensely developed in the so-called "covenant theology" of the post-Reformation Protestant theologians. One example is to be found in the New England Puritans whose covenant theology explicitly influenced their Christian life. Covenant theology was an organizing key for scriptural revelation, but covenants, more generally, were the basis of church and community life. Although many of the spiritual descendants of the Puritans have reduced their use of the covenant concept in speaking of society as a whole, it continues to be a powerful concept in speaking of the relationships, particularly between the Christian and God and in Christian marriages.

For Further Reading: D. Holwerda, *Jesus and Israel* (1995); M. Kline, *The Treaty of the Great King* (1963); D. McCarthy, *Treaty and Covenant* (1978); P. Miller, *Errand into the Wilderness* (1956).

Jason Zuidema

Cowman, Mrs. Charles E. (1870–1960)

Name under which Lettie Burd Cowman published the influential devotional book *Streams in the Desert.* Charles and Lettie Cowman were career missionaries to Japan, founding the Oriental Missionary Society and returning to the United States only when Charles's health collapsed. His terminal illness caused much physical pain for Charles and forced both of them into six years of retirement. For their mutual comfort and encouragement, Lettie spent her mornings gathering poems and quotations from her wide range of devotional reading. She circulated these readings privately and finally published them in 1925, after Charles's death.

The spirituality of *Streams* is focused on consolation during difficulty. A typical page consists of a brief Scripture passage, a longer quotation from a Christian author, and a poem. Lettie's pattern of citation is uneven, and many quotations are only marked as "selected." The identified authors, however, include leading lights of the missionary, Holiness, and Keswick movements: A. C. Dixon, A. T. Pierson, F. B. Meyer, Andrew Murray, A. B. Simpson, and others. The result is a devotional classic, always in print and still widely used, which has kept these otherwise forgotten voices of classic nineteenth-century evangelical spirituality alive.

See also Devotions, Personal.

Fred Sanders

Cowper, William (1731–1800)

Poet and hymnist. Troubles in Cowper's life began at an early age when his mother died. As an adult, he endured a series of failed romances and suffered several bouts of severe depression to the point of being institutionalized. It was during one of his periods of depression that Cowper received some counsel leading him to embrace an evangelical Christian faith strongly colored by Calvinism. Eventually he found a home with the Unwin family and remained supportive of Mary Unwin after her husband died. Mary Unwin cared for Cowper until her own death, which was a devastating loss for him.

Cowper and Mary Unwin settled in the town of Olney, where John Newton, noted for writing the classic hymn "Amazing Grace," was a pastor. Newton and Cowper developed a close friendship, and Newton involved Cowper in some of his work, including home visitation. The prayers of Cowper were reported to be deeply thoughtful and comforting to those he visited. Newton also recognized Cowper's poetic skill and engaged his assistance in collecting verses for a hymn collection. That collection became the *Olney Hymns* of 1779. At Cowper's funeral, Newton eulogized him as a friend with whom he had "so great an intimacy."

William Cowper was the most popular poet of his day, inspiring Samuel Taylor Coleridge to refer to him as "the best modern poet." His translation

of *Homer* and his extended poem, *The Task*, remain as epic reminders of his work. Considered a pre-Romantic, Cowper included stories of everyday life and English scenery in his work.

Though plagued by periodic bouts of depression, he gave himself to poetic expression of his faith. He contributed sixty-eight hymns to the *Olney Hymns* collection. Listed under categorical headings, the first lines of his most well-known hymns from that collection are "God Moves in a Mysterious Way," "Oh! For a Closer Walk with God," and "There Is a Fountain Filled with Blood."

See also Hymns.

For Further Reading: L. Risk, *A Portrait of William Cowper* (2004).

Edwin M. Willmington

Creation

See **Chapter 28.**

Creation-Centered Spirituality

This religious system of Matthew Fox incorporates ideas from various religions, environmental concerns, the arts, science, philosophy, the Bible, and Christian tradition. Creation-centered spirituality is said to be a return to the true spirituality of the world's common people before the modern age. Since many of its concepts are vague and abstract, creation-centered spirituality is hard to define. Fox offers four spiritual paths as components of creation-centered spirituality: (1) *Via positiva* (positive way), in which we embrace all creation and all beings as manifestations of the divine, and humans as blessings of creation. (2) *Via negativa* (negative way), in which we affirm suffering and emptiness and seek detachment and "letting go." (3) *Via creativa* (creative way), in which the creativity of humans is released and we become cocreators with God. The creation itself is viewed as inherently creative and fertile. (4) *Via transformativa* (transforming way), in which we go out into the world to "befriend creation," relieve suffering, struggle for justice, heal the earth, seek balance and wholeness, and celebrate in worship, art, and dance.

Creation-centered spirituality emphasizes certain themes: a view of creation as a living, unified whole, including even God—what Fox calls panentheism; the merger of world religions, which Fox calls "deep ecumenism"; healing of the rift between science and spirituality; concern for the earth and ecological degradation; recovery of sensuality in ourselves and in nature; the rejection of all dualisms—even that between God and creation; a rejection of all forms of hierarchy and a move toward universal egalitarianism; an emphasis on mysticism; the notion that all is in process and change, including God; and a critique of modern culture. Jesus Christ is reinterpreted as the "Cosmic Christ," which seems to be a kind of paradigm of oneness and harmony with time, space, and "Mother Earth." The ultimate goal of creation-centered spirituality seems to be to embrace and join with all things and God as a unified whole.

Creation-centered spirituality offers some good ideas, such as gratitude for the creation and affirmation of its value. However, although Fox claims to be Christian, creation-centered spirituality is clearly a distinctive religious approach. It incorporates some Christian ideas but employs many other sources, including Matthew Fox's fertile imagination. Creation-centered spirituality seems to be largely a reaction against what Fox perceives as the ills of modern religion and society, and looks toward a new age of peace, harmony, and celebration. Fox's writings include *Creation Spirituality* (1991), *A New Reformation* (2006), and *Original Blessing* (1983).

See also Ecological Spirituality; Feminist Spirituality; Liberation Spirituality.

For Further Reading: R. Bauckham, "The New Age Theology of Matthew Fox," *Anvil* 13, no. 2 (1996): 125–26.

John Mustol

Creativity

Creativity is the ability to bring about the new and to actualize the possible. As such, creativity and spirituality are closely linked. Both invoke a powerful force of transcendence that moves one beyond oneself, the status quo, and what already *is*. Creativity finds its source in God, the creative God. Indeed, God is not only Creator, but also the originating cause of creativity itself. In Gordon Kaufmann's writings, creativity defines God in such an essential way that his concept of God loses all personality as it morphs into "serendipitous creativity." Since evangelical theology is committed to a personal and therefore relational God, the idea of God as an impersonal creative force is unacceptable. Evangelicals are equally convinced that God alone is Creator in an absolute sense. To emphasize this point, medieval theologian Thomas Aquinas denied that humans have any ability to create in the proper sense of the term; they create only in a relative and derivative manner.

If God is creative because God is Creator, human beings are creative because that is how God made them. As created beings, they partake in the nature of their Creator, who, out of bountiful generosity, invites them to share in the divine creative delight. To be sure, throughout their participation in divine creativity, human beings remain human, the other of the divine. The triune God is the source and the ground of creativity, while human creativity is only creativity through participation. This explains the essentially "craftsperson" nature of human creativity. Yet even here to create is to image God, the Creator. Thus, to deny humans opportunities to be creative (e.g., in an efficiency-driven or micromanaged workplace) is to crush the human spirit itself.

Human creativity and spirituality are manifestations of the mystery at the core of human existence. The exercise of creativity, which finds its resources in God's threefold gift of being, language, and power, is not only a way of living and joyfully participating in this mystery. Nor is it simply an actualization of our true identities as God-imaging humans. It is also a quest for meaning. It is an expression of longing for what is "other" and what is beyond. It is no wonder, then, that the text of Ecclesiastes 3:11 is often quoted in connection with artistic creativity: "He has made everything beautiful in its time. He has also set eternity in the human heart" (TNIV).

See also Image of God; Imagination.

For Further Reading: J. Begbie, *Beholding the Glory* (2000); W. Dyrness, *Visual Faith* (2001); G. Kaufman, *In the Beginning … Creativity* (1989); P. Tillich, *Systematic Theology* (1973).

Mabiala Justin-Robert Kenzo

Crisis

Crisis (Gr. *krisis*) is that decisive moment when, due to altered circumstances and/or diminished ability to cope, the status quo is no longer sustainable and something must change. Circumstances can build incrementally toward such a point, but the crisis itself precipitates disjuncture. Out of crisis something new must and will *emerge* — hence the common association of crisis with *emergency*. Stress can intensify over the unanticipated onset of a crisis, uncertain outcome, the difficulty of the choices involved, and the magnitude of their implications. The trajectory of an entire life is often determined by how a relatively few crisis moments are navigated; such intense junctures (also known as "tipping points") are pregnant with promise and peril.

The Christian life is a journey characterized by long periods of relative constancy and incremental development, and then by brief, punctuating episodes of crisis. Christian spirituality is attuned to both dimensions and has much to say about the latter. Repeatedly throughout the OT, the people of God, their devotion dulled by routine or assailed by temptations, wander toward the precipice of ruin. But then, in their desperation — in their *crisis* — they repent and cry for mercy, and God delivers them. Job epitomizes the personal crisis of faith in times of mysterious suffering and extremity — when the choice is whether to curse God and die raging or to submit to the inscrutable wisdom of the God who is in every way above us. The novelist Victor Hugo, in *Les Misérables* (1862), uses imagery from the watery fate of the prophet Jonah to describe his character Jean Val Jean's fall into despair. As circumstances begin to drown Jean, "he drinks in bitterness … [and] it is all liquid hatred to him" — but at the nadir of his crisis, grace surprisingly appears in the form of a bishop who covers his sin. In the NT the revelation of the gospel precipitates the quintessential crisis: whether to reject or acknowledge Jesus as the Messiah, whether to hold out in defiance of his offer or to repent and be converted. Eternal life and eternal death stand in the balance.

Some forms of recent Christian spirituality have highlighted the *punctiliar* (that is, it happens in an instant) nature of crisis and the profound urgency of choice. Søren Kierkegaard, the Danish father of modern existentialism, is best known for his haunting interpretation of the enigmatic biblical story of Abraham offering his beloved only son Isaac as a human sacrifice. According to *Fear and Trembling* (1843), the divine command to kill made no sense to Abraham and seemed to contradict every shard of moral sensibility; yet in that moment, hung suspended in eternity, the man of faith inexplicably chose to obey. He had said "yes" to God. The murder was averted and the crisis passed, but the father would never be the same again.

Building on an existentialist foundation, twentieth-century theologians like Karl Barth developed what was called a theology of crisis. Unlike the immanent God of liberal Protestantism, Barth's God is altogether transcendent, touching humanity at tiny points of intersection (rather like the pinprick dot between a circle and a tangent), such that the divine reality from on high can never hang around for long or be domesticated or incorporated into anything human (e.g., such as a sacred text or a religious sentiment). Accordingly, God arrives out of nowhere, topples us off our chairs with a glancing touch, and then disappears. But we know that it was God, and we are forever changed.

According to British historian David Bebbington, the evangelical tradition has always been conversion-centered. The life-transforming religious experiences of seventeenth-century Pietists and Puritans, as well as those that characterized the Great Awakening of the 18th century and subsequent revivalism, all centered around the crisis moment of "salvation" in which disillusionment with alternatives, conviction of sin, and fear of judgment intensified until they exploded in the massive joy and relieved assurance of grace and eternal life. Given this historical legacy, it was only natural that the Christian life would often be conceptualized by subsequent evangelicals as a *series of crises*, beyond conversion itself, through which important added dimensions of a "deeper," "higher," or more empowered and Spirit-filled Christian life could be appropriated.

Inevitably the spiritual journey involves crises, though not necessarily a normative set. With these in view, the Scriptures encourage vigilant readiness, the virtues of courage and resilience when everything is on the line, and hope in God who makes all things new. Happy are those for whom the old is gone and the new has come (2 Cor. 5:17).

See also Kierkegaard, Søren.

For Further Reading: S. Kierkegaard, *Either/Or* (1992); J. Loder, *The Transforming Moment* (1989).
Glen G. Scorgie

eyes, Fanny became one of the most prolific poets of the 19th century. Her indomitable spirit allowed her never to regret the malady. In fact, she believed that her blindness was the providence of God, and it allowed her to praise him in her poetry without being distracted by the beautiful things around her.

Crosby attended, and later taught at, the New York School for the Blind. As a result, she became an advocate for blind education and related causes. Her stature as a poet afforded her audiences with presidents and other dignitaries. Fanny's poems number more than eight thousand. Her prolific writing style made it necessary for her to use more than one hundred pseudonyms, since publishers would not publish so many poems from a single author.

While Fanny had books of secular poetry published, her reputation and popularity came from her creation of sacred poetry. Poems such as "Blessed Assurance," "Near the Cross," "Safe in the Arms of Jesus," "Praise Him! Praise Him!" and "To God Be the Glory" are often found in modern hymnals. Her writing incorporated various lyrical styles, but her best-known works fit squarely in the revivalist gospel song genre. The content of her poems aligns with her Methodist roots and tends to reflect and express personal experiences of faith. These poems were set to music by some of the finest musicians of her time. Musicians such as William Bradbury and William H. Doane often created tunes specifically to express Fanny's lyrics. These poems set to music became popularized throughout the world through their association with the revivals of D. L. Moody and his evangelistic partner, musician Ira Sankey.

See also Hymns; Poetry and Poetics.

For Further Reading: E. Blumhofer, *Her Heart Can See: The Life and Hymns of Fanny J. Crosby* (2005).

Edwin M. Willmington

Crosby, Frances Jane (Fanny) (1820–1915)

Poet and song lyricist. Blinded at an early age due to the improper treatment of an infection in her

Cross, The

The cross (Lat. *crux*) is the preeminent symbol of the Christian faith. Its presence is ubiquitous — on tombstones, jewelry, heraldry, and church steeples; and more controversially, tattoos, national flags, medieval armaments, and contemporary war memorials. It has been incorporated into centuries of Christian art and the architectural design of classic Christian worship spaces. Even Christian traditions opposed to visual representations of sacred matters will often make an exception for the cross, and allow it (and it alone) to be prominently featured in their assemblies. Countless believers make "the sign of the cross," thereby offering a prayer of Trinitarian devotion and celebrating the crucified Jesus as the human face of God. From formal exorcism rituals to the whimsical practices of pop culture, the sign of the cross is evoked for protection from evil.

It is ironic that what was originally a symbol of gruesome criminal execution during Roman times has become a recognized signifier of a world religion characterized by high moral ideals and offering through Christ salvation, eternal life, empowerment, hope, and love to the world. This in itself is a revealing indicator that Christianity is a faith rooted in inversion, reversal, paradox, and surprise. As Frederick Buechner observed, "The symbol of Christianity is an instrument of death. It suggests, at the very least, hope."

The cross is so much more than Christianity's trademark logo; it is "thick" with meaning and powerfully evocative. At its baseline, it represents the suffering and death of Jesus on a hill outside of Jerusalem. Christians believe that this moment of execution was simultaneously the ultimate indictment of humanity (destroying God's Son), the quintessential expression and assurance of the Father and Son's love for humanity (John 3:16; 15:13), and the dramatic means by which estranged and dying people can be reconciled to God and experience eternal life. When this outlook prevails, Christians sing their grateful intent to "cling to the old rugged cross" and "cherish" it (with the resurrection) as the basis of their hope. Inevitably the two timbers of the cross, one vertical and the other horizontal, have been taken to represent costly reconciliation with God and relational fellowship among believers. Intuitively, as well as for solid theological reasons, Christians have recognized the *centrality* of the cross to their faith. This recognition is echoed in Western languages, in which the *crux* of something is its heart or center, a point that English theologian P. T. Forsyth rather cleverly underscored in *The Cruciality of the Cross* (1948). As nineteenth-century evangelical James Atkinson observed, "It was the Cross on the Hill rather than the Sermon on the Mount which produced the impact of Christianity upon the world."

One point of contention among Christians who treasure what it represents is whether Christ should be depicted on it. Traditionally, the occupied cross (the crucifix) has been an object of devotion and meditation on Christ's vicarious sacrifice. An empty cross is preferred in the Protestant tradition, and especially its evangelical wing, given suspicion of visual representation generally, and a desire to "move on" to the triumphant *telos* of the empty tomb and resurrection.

Consistent with its paradoxical and enigmatic character, the cross has two chief meanings, not one. It represents what God in Christ has done *for* believers (as a substitute); it also represents what God intends should be replicated *in* believers (as something with which we identify). The first evokes gratitude, relief, and love; the second calls for consecration, submission, and trusting embrace. The one is positional and the other mystical. It is true that Christ died *for* the ungodly (Rom. 5:6), and that by his wounds we are healed (Isa. 53:5); yet it is equally true that believers are to deny themselves, take up *their* crosses, and follow Christ (Matt. 16:24), and so "fill up" what is still lacking in his suffering (Col. 1:24). The Lausanne Covenant declares, "A church that preaches the cross must itself be marked by the cross." Christian spirituality that embraces the principle and spirit of the cross must never be construed to legitimize injustice or masochistic suffering. The image of the cross, however, can be a powerful mechanism for reframing some kinds of suffering (both the unavoidable and voluntary varieties) as God-honoring, purposive, constructive, and redemptive—and therefore also meaningful and endurable. Christian spirituality is not suffering-avoidant, since Jesus Christ himself did not run from his cross but with a view to the future scorned the shame associated with it (Heb. 12:2). Thus, Indian Christian Chandran Devanesen can pray, "O Tree of Calvary, send your roots deep down into my heart."

See also Atonement Theories; Cross, Experience of the; Imitation of Christ; Incarnation; Passion of Christ.

For Further Reading: E. Dreyer, *The Cross in Christian Tradition* (2000); J. Moltmann, *The Way of Jesus Christ* (1995); J. Stott, *The Cross of Christ* (1986).

Glen G. Scorgie

Cross, Experience of the

Much of Protestant theology is concerned chiefly with the substitutionary nature of the cross; though within the missionary and Holiness movements of evangelical spirituality there exists the ideal of the "crucified life," drawing on Paul's words in Romans 6:6 that we have been crucified with Christ. That verse serves as the center of gravity for Watchman Nee's influential *The Normal Christian Life* (1958), for example. L. E. Maxwell's *Born Crucified* (1944), which depicts the radical consecration of a Christian life, also reflects this stream within evangelical piety. These are but two of the countless manifestations of the disciple's mystical identification with, participation in, and recapitulation of the experience of the cross.

The NT reflects on the cross in rich and varied ways. In Galatians 6:14 the cross of Christ becomes that by which "the world is crucified to me and I to the world." Romans 6:1–4 describes baptism as a dying with Christ so that we might be raised to walk in newness of life. In Philippi-

ans 2:5–8 Paul urges his readers to be of the same mind as Christ who endured death on a cross. Colossians (1:24) speaks of entering into the sufferings of Christ, completing that which is lacking in Christ's afflictions for the sake of his body, the church. In the Synoptic Gospels Jesus tells his disciples to deny themselves, take up their cross, and follow him (Matt. 16:24; Mark 8:34; Luke 9:23). In Acts (7:59–60), as Stephen is being martyred, his words echo those of the dying Jesus as given in Luke 23:34, 46.

These words of Scripture have come alive in many ways over the centuries. This entry explores three categories of the experience of the cross: martyrdom, contemplative experience, and suffering for righteousness' sake.

For those who underwent persecution and death on account of their Christian faith, the experience of the cross was an event that was replicated in their own bodily suffering. The early martyr Felicitas shows how martyrs identified with the crucified Christ. When enduring severe labor pains in prison just before her martyrdom, a prison guard scoffed that if she was in such pain now, what would she do when thrown to the beasts? She replied that she bore her labor pains alone, but when facing the ferocious heifer in the arena, another would be inside of her who would suffer on her behalf, just as she would be suffering for his sake. On the day of their martyrdom, when the enraged crowd called for the company of confessors to be scourged before facing death, the martyrs rejoiced and gave thanks that they were to attain a share of Christ's sufferings.

In the 16th century, early Anabaptists, who were frequently killed at the hands of other Christians, echoed the experience of the cross of the ancient church: martyrdom was often the cost of Christian discipleship.

Spiritual or mystical participation in the experience of Christ's cross is found in many writers, particularly in the later Middle Ages. Francis of Assisi himself typifies this spirituality, most profoundly in his receiving the stigmata or wounds of Christ during a vision of a winged seraph in the form of the Crucified One. Most of Francis's followers of course did not experience the physical stigmata, but embracing and participating in the passion of Christ continued to be a central element of Franciscan piety.

For Bonaventure, the foremost theologian of Franciscan spirituality, Francis is the exemplar of evangelical perfection, a model for the contemplative ascent that he outlines by stages in *The Soul's Journey into God*, which is an extended meditation on Francis's vision of the crucified seraph. Christians can aspire to appropriate the mystery of the cross through contemplative practice. Because divine love emptied itself on the cross, meditation on the cross, entering into the wounds of Christ, is the path to divine love that can bestow contemplative, inexpressible union with Christ, in love, knowledge, and ecstasy. Similarly, the Franciscan Angela of Foligno found that meditation on the cross led her to an experience of the cross from within and a joyful participation in the total self-emptying of the crucified Christ.

Yet the Franciscans are not alone in articulating a relationship between meditation on and inward imitation and recapitulation of the passion, on the one hand, and apophatic kenosis, or ineffable emptying and annihilation of the self, on the other. Such themes reverberate in the writings of the Beguine Mechthild of Magdeburg, the Dominican Johannes Tauler, and others.

Christian devotion to social justice is yet another expression of the experience of the cross. Martin Luther King Jr. spoke of his imprisonment for nonviolent disobedience during the civil rights era as bearing the cross for his people. Like other liberation theologians, Jon Sobrino offers a spirituality that sees Christ crucified in the suffering of the poor and seeks union with them. By taking risks in prophetic lives, this suffering in love and solidarity with those who bear the burdens of injustice can mirror the martyrs' identification with Christ's passion. Tragically, as witnessed in the courageous lives and brutal deaths of countless believers past and present, it can lead to martyrdom itself.

The categories of this essay therefore are not fixed but are often transcended. Colonial American Quaker John Woolman, for example, dedicated his ministerial labors to social justice, particularly to the causes of the poor, the enslaved, and Native Americans. In his autobiography, he recounts a visionary experience, in which he saw "a mass of matter of a dull gloomy colour ... and was informed that this mass was human beings in as great misery as they could be and live, and that I was mixed in with them and henceforth might not consider myself as a distinct or separate being." An angel announces his death, which perplexes him. "At length I felt divine power prepare my mouth that I could speak, and then I said: 'I am crucified with Christ, nevertheless I live; yet not I, but Christ that liveth in me, and the life I now live in the flesh is by faith in the Son of God, who loved me and gave himself for me.'" His account echoes Paul in Galatians 2, the spiritual participation in Christ's passion of the medieval mystics, and the cross-bearing of Christian social reformers.

In sum, the history of Christian spirituality offers myriad ways of experiencing the cross and beckons contemporary Christians to live a costly discipleship, to seek among the socially disinherited those who are now fulfilling that which remains of the sufferings of Christ, and to embrace meditative modes of prayer that can open the door to spiritual participation in the mystery of the cross.

See also Passion of Christ; Suffering.

For Further Reading: Angela of Foligno, *Complete Works*, trans. P. Lachance (1993); Bonaventure, CWS (1978); M. L. King Jr., *A Testament of Hope*, ed. J. Washington (1990); H. Mursurillo, *The Acts of the Christian Martyrs* (1972); J. Woolman, *The Journal and Major Essays of John Woolman*, ed. P. Moulton (1972).

Michael Birkel

Cyprian (c. 210–258)

North African bishop of Carthage. A trained pagan rhetorician and civil servant, he converted to the Christian faith c. 246. An avid student of Scripture (and Tertullian) with notable administrative gifts, he was elected bishop two years later, and in that role he demonstrated a profound love for the church and a consensus style of leadership on pastoral issues. His treatise *On Prayer* is supremely practical.

The Decian persecution (249–250) created *lapsi*, that is, persons who denied the faith and others who secured *libelli* papers claiming imperial sacrifice. Afterward Cyprian countered those who forbade church readmission for those who had compromised their testimony under duress. On the other hand, he also opposed those who offered such lapsed Christians easy reconciliation; instead, he arranged a *via media*—suitable penance. Another debate emerged in 255, as he declared that those who had been baptized by heretics or schismatics needed rebaptism. He opposed the Roman prelate, Stephen, preferring two councils of African bishops. Several letters among the eighty-one in Cyprian's literary corpus illustrate their debate—which went unresolved when both were martyred under Emperor Valerius.

Cyprian's work *On the Unity of the Catholic Church* (251) is well known for declaring, "One is not able to have God as Father who has not the Church as mother." His influence ranges from Eastern Orthodox advocacy of independent episcopal churches to Vatican II's *Lumen Gentium*, embracing the whole people of God.

For Further Reading: O. Davies, ed., *Born to New Life: Cyprian of Carthage* (1992); M. Sage, *Cyprian* (1975); *St. Cyprian of Carthage: Selected Treatises*, ed. A. Brent (2007).

James D. Smith III

Cyril of Alexandria (c. 376–444)

Bishop of Alexandria. Cyril fully embraced church and state, proving his brilliance in both theology and politics. Succeeding his uncle Theodosius as bishop, he showed the ferocity and canniness needed to retain control in an age of instability. His willingness to employ bribery, violence, and political favors—and his treatment of Jews, heretics and political opponents—has rightly been questioned.

Yet Cyril's contributions as a theologian and apologist are crucial for our current understanding of the incarnation. He argued against the model of a bifurcated Christ where the human and divine natures were kept so distinct that even particular sayings or miracles were being assigned to one or the other nature. Cyril agreed there were indeed two natures in Christ, but these were fully integrated and formed a single entity: the incarnate Logos. Only when the fully divine absolutely embraces the death of fallen humanity can the saving way of resurrection become available to all. "Now the life-giving power of God is the Word, the only Son.... He, though he is Life by nature, took a body subject to decay in order to destroy in it the power of death and transform it into life." The nature of Christ was ultimately decided in Cyril's favor at Chalcedon after his death.

Cyril remains one of the more biblically grounded theologians of the church. His verse-by-verse exegesis of both OT and NT books is extensive and yields real spiritual insight if patiently studied. It is this deep biblical hermeneutic along with the centrality and theological fullness of Cyril's Christology that has led to his place among the early fathers of the church.

For Further Reading: W. Burghardt, *The Image of God in Man according to Cyril of Alexandria* (1957); O. Clement, *The Roots of Christian Mysticism* (1993); J. McGuckin, *St. Cyril of Alexandria* (1994); H. van Loon, *Diophysite Christology of Clement of Alexandria* (2009).

Kelby Cotton

D

Dance

"David danced before the LORD with all his might; David was girded with a linen ephod. So David and all the house of Israel brought up the ark of the LORD with shouting, and with the sound of the trumpet" (2 Sam. 6:14–15 NRSV). Although it has been said that the church has danced its liturgy for centuries, in actuality, Christianity has far less dancing than other religions. In the earliest centuries, Christians would dance in the church and at the tombs of saints and martyrs on their feast days, celebrating their eternal reward. Later, dancing was found at Easter and Christmas celebrations. Much of the evidence we have for a negative view of dance comes from a condemnation for "obscene movements" and "vulgar songs" deemed unfit for Christian piety. However, as Christianity matured and became a more global religion, the indigenous dances of newly converted peoples began to creep into the worship and piety of the newly formed churches.

Liturgical dance, or dance specifically for worship, is a form of prayer in which the body is used as a vehicle for expression and communication. Sometimes dance can be done by one or a few dancers for the larger gathering. Other times, all people who are able to move are invited — and expected — to participate. Some dances are simple, such as procession dances that involve many people, often in a gathering or entrance rite. Other dances, which proclaim or celebrate the gospel or take the form of an embodied prayer within a worship service, may include a select group of people dancing for the entire group. Meditation dances are often performed by one dancer or a few dancers for the rest of the congregation, who prayerfully reflect on the dance.

Many communities are uncomfortable with dance, and especially an expectation that the entire gathering would be invited to dance. The charismatic and Pentecostal movements have been on the forefront of North American traditions to include dance and bodily movement in worship. Even more, many churches in Africa have almost completely integrated their culture of dance into their worship. The Scriptures appear to speak favorably of David's offering of dance, which raises the question of whether the issues concerning dance are more cultural than biblical or theological.

See also Body; Celebration; Joy; Worship.

For Further Reading: J. Davies, *Liturgical Dance* (1984); R. Gagne et al., *Introducing Dance to Christian Worship* (2000); T. Kane, *The Dancing Church* (DVD) (2004).

Todd E. Johnson

Dante Alighieri (1265–1321)

Medieval poet. He has inspired millions with his epic poem the *Commedia* ("Comedy"; later commentators appended the adjective "Divine"), comprising the *Inferno*, *Purgatorio*, and *Paradiso*. One of the world's great poems, the *Commedia* was aptly described by Dante translator Dorothy Sayers as "the drama of the soul's choice." In it, Dante himself journeys through hell, purgatory, and heaven, seeing the eternal results of the choices made by hundreds of historical figures (and a few mythical ones) — all in graphic physical detail. The poem draws from Augustine and Thomas Aquinas as well as classical literature to address important spiritual themes. These include salvation (Dante's own and the reader's), ecumenism and dialectic theology (opposing theologians appear in harmony in

Dante's "circle of the sun"), theology and the arts (the poem contains apologia for poetry, sculpture, and other arts in the service of the faith), philosophy (excurses especially in the *Paradiso* explain the nature of the cosmos), leadership (especially bad leadership: at least one pope shows up in hell!), and romantic love not as an end in itself (the illicit love of Paulo and Francesca land them in hell) but as a means to salvation (Dante's beloved, Beatrice, sends him on his redemptive voyage and guides and disciplines him at crucial junctures). It is well worth getting beyond the gruesome *Inferno* to read the other two books.

See also Poetry and Poetics.

Chris R. Armstrong

Daoist Spirituality

Daoist spirituality is the center of a life that flows in sync with *Dao*, often translated as "road" or "way." *Dao* is found in several schools of Chinese tradition, such as Confucianism that emphasizes *Dao* in terms of moral truth. But within Daoism, the word is nonmoral and above any human value system—*Dao* is the mother of creation and the path of all things. Daoist scriptures refer to it apophatically as being unfathomable, unnamable, impersonal, and without purpose. Yet this *Dao* is said to be the ideal basis for all governments, societies, and people. Alignment with *Dao* brings harmony and well-being to the individual and the cosmos.

In English, *Daoism* refers to two Chinese terms, *Daojia* ("philosophical Daoism") and *Daojiao* ("religious Daoism"). While there has been much scholarly debate around how best to understand the relationship among the strands of Daoism, suffice it to say, the various forms have played important roles in shaping China's spiritual profile.

Philosophical Daoism focuses on two texts, *Laozi* (or *Daodejing*) and *Zhuangzi*, both bearing the names of their supposed authors. This tradition begins with an understanding that humanity has a primordial simplicity known as *pu*. Poetically translated as "uncarved block," the original state is untainted by experiences and definitions of right and wrong. The Daoist sage interacts with the world through *wuwei* ("nonaction"), a yielding disposition that responds to the natural flow of things. Zhuangzi explains how true happiness and freedom come from forgetting the distinctions between oneself and the universe. This is achieved through *xu* ("self-emptying") and *zuowang* ("seated meditation"), techniques later influential in Chan (or Zen) Buddhism and Neo-Confucianism. The quietism of philosophical Daoism enables the sage to relinquish all illusions and return to the true, primordial nature where one is in complete peace and contentment. Only when the Daoist is able to see the world with deference can he or she be in a mystical union with *Dao*.

For religious Daoism, the means of unity with *Dao* is immortality. It envisions the world as having an underlying *qi*, the "cosmic energy" or "force" of *Dao*, with alternating phases of *yin* and *yang*. Much of religious Daoism is focused on bringing balance to *qi* in the individual and the world. Various methods are employed, ranging from meditation, breathing exercises, special diets, and Chinese medicine. For the Daoist, this results in healing illnesses, improving longevity, and ultimately achieving immortality. Through refinement of one's *qi* and shedding all desires and illusions of selfhood, the individual undergoes a spiritual rebirth. An immortal is one who has returned to his or her true nature and has the postmortem potential of uniting with *Dao*.

The gospel of John in the Chinese Bible opens with the words, "In the beginning was the *Dao*." Like *Logos* in Greek thought, *Dao* in Daoism is an *impersonal* source and sustainer of all creation. The Daoist is told to empty oneself from all pretense and return to the primordial condition. The Christian is told to renew the mind, be filled with the Spirit, and be a steward of a redeemed life, uniquely designed by the Creator of the cosmos. In contrast with Daoist spirituality, Christian spirituality is at the center of a life that walks in step with a *personal* God.

For Further Reading: J. Ching, *Chinese Religions* (1993); H. Creel, *What Is Taoism?* (1970); W. de Bary and I. Bloom, eds., *Sources of Chinese Tradition*, vol. 1 (1999); L. Kohn, *Daoism and Chinese Culture* (2004).

Alexander Chow

Dark Night

Dark nights of the soul are those seasons and times in the spiritual life in which God initiates a profound work of purging or purifying the human spirit of sins and vices of the heart that hinder union with God and the Spirit's characterological filling of the believer. The experience is of the felt absence of God (desolation) in contrast to the felt presence of God (consolation). Whereas consolation is intended by God to encourage the believer with the experience of God's presence and direct the heart to God through the spiritual disciplines, desolation is intended by God to be a mirror revealing what is in the heart of the believer.

God is always relationally present to the believer (1 Cor. 6:17) so that nothing, not even sin, can separate one from the love of God (Rom. 8:31–39). Thus, the dark nights of the soul or the seasons of desolations are not God's withdrawing his presence from the believer but only the felt consolation in order to draw near to the believer in truth. Thus, the believer's experience of dryness and aridity in doing spiritual disciplines may be a gift from God in dark nights to reveal those parts of the heart that are filled with the self and not the Spirit, places of the heart that do not love God and neighbor but are attached unhealthily to finite idols of the heart. These are difficult yet meaningful times of God drawing near to love the believer in the truth, to open an experience of God in faith and darkness and not sight, and to prepare the believer to know the fullness of God's love and presence in union,

which begins in this life and is brought to its fullness in the next (Eph. 3:13–19).

These experiences of spiritual trials, darkness, and desolation have been discussed throughout church history, from church fathers Gregory of Nyssa and Gregory Nazianzus, to Bernard of Clairvaux and Aquinas, to Protestants such as Voetius and Hoornbeeck. This tradition reaches its profoundest expression in John of the Cross (*Dark Night of the Soul*), in which two kinds of dark nights—of the senses and of the spirit—are central to his developmental spirituality, as times in which God purges (1) the believer's beginning dependence on consolation as a way to measure the presence of God, (2) the various vices of the heart, and (3) dependence on virtues that were developed in the power of human autonomy. This developmental approach to growth in the Spirit became popularly understood as purgation (dark nights), illumination, and union.

These seasons of desolation became associated with a variety of phenomena in the Scriptures—for example, the putting off of the "old self" (Eph. 4:22), the struggle of faith evident in spiritual young adults in contrast to spiritual children and older ones in the faith (1 John 2:12–14), the lament psalms (Pss. 77, 88; 22:1, "My God, my God, why have you forsaken me?"), and spiritual "thorns in the flesh"—that open the believer to greater humility to find power and dependence on God in human weakness (2 Cor. 12:9–11).

Though dark nights are very meaningful times for the formation of the believer, they can also be very confusing, particularly in understanding the work of God in prayer. The time-worn advice of the church is for a spiritual director to assist the believer in opening to the work and presence of the indwelling Spirit by faith and love amid what seem to be darkness and dryness.

See also Carmelite; John of the Cross; Lament; Light; Teresa of Avila.

For Further Reading: J. Coe, "Musings on the Dark Night of the Soul," *Journal of Psychology and*

Theology 28, no. 4 (2000): 293–307; T. Dubay, *Fire Within: St. Teresa of Avila, St. John of the Cross* (1989); K. Kavanaugh, *John of the Cross*; idem, trans., *The Collected Works of John of the Cross* (1991); T. Merton, *The Ascent to Truth* (1951); G. Voetius and J. Hoornbeek, *Spiritual Desertion*, trans. J. Vriend, CRS (2003).

John H. Coe

Day, Dorothy (1897–1980)

Journalist and social activist. Dorothy Day is best known as the founder of the Catholic Worker Movement and for her work with poor immigrant communities on the Lower East Side of Manhattan, New York. As a young journalist, she worked for a socialist newspaper and led a bohemian lifestyle in Greenwich Village in the company of fellow writers and artists. The birth of a child awakened her spiritual aspirations, and eventually she was baptized, along with her daughter, into the Roman Catholic Church. She described her journey to faith in *The Long Loneliness* (1992).

Her deep concern for the poor and homeless first led her down the Communist path; but she came home to faith and to the church, and discovered there a Lord who genuinely cared for the poor. Though she was always disappointed with the church in this regard, for her, there was no avoiding the fact that the Christ she served called her and the church to be on the side of the poor. In time this advocacy for the poor was matched by her ardent pacifism and her active protest against the arms movement and the proliferation of nuclear weapons. Her mentor was Peter Maurin, a French peasant immigrant, of whom she said: "His ideas and vision would dominate the rest of my life."

While Day was thoroughly Roman Catholic, she remains an abiding witness to all Christians in her devotion to Christ, her advocacy of, and service to, the poor, and her capacity to be simultaneously a critic and a loyal member of her church.

See also Social Justice.

For Further Reading: R. Coles, *Dorothy Day* (1989); *Entertaining Angels: The Dorothy Day Story*, movie directed by R. Rhodes (1996).

Gordon T. Smith

Death and Dying

The contemplation of death is the spiritual discipline of regularly reminding oneself of one's mortality by means of Scriptures, rituals, images, or symbols. Pondering one's death offers perspective to many of the enticements and temptations faced in the struggle with sin. While it seems like a morbid and sobering thing, contemplating mortality can lead to freedom from the three great enemies of the flesh: lust, greed, and misguided pride. The Rule of St. Benedict included it in the list of good works to be cultivated in the Christian life. Along with loving God and one's neighbor, visiting the sick, clothing the naked, and guarding one's tongue, stands the admonition "to keep death before one's eyes daily." Contemplating death invariably happens at funeral services, or when walking through a cemetery. Reminders of life's approaching end can be associated with ticking clocks, calendars, or fading flowers, or by turning one's thoughts to one of the numerous biblical references to the brevity of life and its impending end. The psalmist pleads, "Teach us to number our days aright, that we may gain a heart of wisdom" (90:12). In other words, coming to grips with one's finality is a sure remedy for unreflective, foolish living. The book of Ecclesiastes offers an extended meditation on the temporal nature of human life. And as an ancient Jewish proverb in Ecclesiasticus states, "In all you do, remember the end of your life, and then you will never sin" (7:36).

Along with the contemplation of death, Christian spirituality is concerned with dying well. A body of Christian literature developed from the 15th century onward around the "art of dying," offering practical guidance for those who were dying as well as their caregivers. Some of the core themes include the need to consider God's judgment, the urgency of seeking and offering forgiveness, taking leave of family and friends, observing the Lord's Supper, and surrendering oneself to God's providence and mercy. Roman Catholics as well as Protestant Reformers offered instructions on how to die well within a broader framework of the "art of living." Jeremy Taylor authored two complementary books, *Holy Living* and *Holy Dying*. One of the themes he developed was "remedies against the fear of death."

See also Afterlife; Health and Healing.

For Further Reading: N. Beaty, *The Craft of Dying* (1970); J. Taylor, *The Rule and Exercises of Holy Dying* (1651/2008).

Allan Effa

de Caussade, Jean-Pierre (1675–1751)

French Jesuit spiritual adviser. He is best known for a work attributed to him that evidences a passive spiritual perspective with Quietist leanings. Having entered the Company of Jesus in 1693 and being ordained priest in 1704, de Caussade was employed by several Jesuit colleges but passed most of his life as a spiritual director in various religious communities. He is normally associated with the posthumously published letters of instruction for the Nuns of the Visitation at Nancy, where he was spiritual director from 1733–1740. Although the letters had been read by some in manuscript form in the meantime, the printed book, entitled *Abandonment to Divine Providence*, was officially published only in 1861 and in an edited form that protected it from charges of Quietism. Whether or not de Caussade is the actual author, the letters represent an important addition to French spirituality in the 18th century.

In *Abandonment to Divine Providence*, we find a spirituality that is profoundly interior. The book argues that the present moment is a "sacrament" from God and that self-abandonment to it is a holy state. Further, the self is passive before the divine: "When God lives in the soul, it has nothing left of self, but only that which the spirit which actuates it imparts to it at each moment." Yet beside this radical passivity that seems much like Quietism, the author still does argue that there is some personal activity or cooperation with the divine when the divine requires it. Whatever its relation to Quietism, the self-abandonment and passivity argued here are not the defeat of the soul, but when devoted to God through humility, are its victory.

The book had a profound impact on Roman Catholic spirituality in the decades after its official publication. It has also impacted many others seeking counsel on more profound and vibrant spiritual life.

See also Quietism.

For Further Reading: M. Giles, "The Poetics of Detachment: A Reflection of John of the Cross and Jean-Pierre de Caussade," *Studia Mystica* 18 (1997): 164–71.

Jason Zuidema

Decision Making

The Christian spiritual tradition affirms that to be an adult is to take responsibility, before God, for the choices that one makes. The human person has a volitional center and is thus created with the capacity to make real choices and, by implication, to live with the consequence of these choices. Yet a Christian spirituality also insists that decision making is an act of response to the call and initiative of God. Human beings only choose well when their primary reference is the will and call of God. Further, the Scriptures affirm that in their choosing they are not alone, but that God, through Christ and by the grace of the Spirit, fosters their capacity to choose well.

When it comes to decision making and the will of God, Christians generally fall into one of the following "camps." Some believe that God's will has been preordained for them as a kind of "blueprint." They say that decision making is a matter of determining God's perfect plan for their lives. Others, often in marked or sharp contrast to this first view, insist that God's purposes should not be so narrowly construed; rather, God expects people to take responsibility for their lives and, as they grow in wisdom, similarly grow in their capacity to choose and choose wisely. Still others, reflecting a longer and more central stream of Christian spirituality, affirm that indeed the human person must choose, but that this choosing comes in response to the movement of the Spirit in the world and in the human heart. We choose, but we choose "in the Spirit." Thus, decision making is but part of a process of discernment.

Regardless of where a person comes down in this discussion, some things are axiomatic for Christian spirituality. First, spiritual maturity requires that the Christian learn to choose and take adult responsibility for one's life in response to the grace and call of God. Second, the Christian only chooses well when he or she makes a commitment to grow in wisdom and thus to choose wisely. Third, choosing well requires a critical and honest assessment of one's circumstances, options, and obstacles. And fourth, the Christian does not choose alone; the Spirit of Christ who dwells within the Christian's heart inspires, moves, and encourages and thus fosters his or her capacity to choose well.

See also Discernment; Will, Human.

For Further Reading: D. Huffman, ed., *How Then Should We Choose? Three Views* (2009); G. Smith, *Listening to God in Times of Choice* (1997).

Gordon T. Smith

De Foucauld, Charles Eugene (1858–1916)

French Roman Catholic hermit. He lived a life of solitude, seeking to model the life of the gospel to the communities around him. At first de Foucald was attached to the Cistercian Trappist order, but he soon left to lead a solitary life of prayer. After a brief journey to Palestine, he lived in various regions of Algeria, principally among the Tuareg tribespeople. He learned their customs and language, producing a four-volume dictionary and grammar.

De Foucald's spirituality was marked by his desire to imitate the humble life of Jesus and be a living presence for him in this non-Christian country. His mission was not to impose his message on the local population, but to live with them, show respect, and gradually witness to them. Tragically, on December 1, 1916, he was shot to death outside his compound by passing jihadists connected with the Senussi Bedouin. In the final years of his life, he had begun to ponder founding a new religious order, but only after his death did this become a reality in communities like the Little Brothers of Jesus. Because of his modern eremitical life, his mission of presence, and his untimely death, many consider de Foucauld to be a martyr.

See also Hermits and Anchorites.

For Further Reading: F. Fleming, *The Sword and the Cross* (2003); *Spiritual Autobiography of Charles of Foucauld*, ed. J. F. Six (1964).

Jason Zuidema

Deification

Deification, also known as *theosis*, is the term used to describe the spiritual journey of believers from their baptism/initiation into the Christian tradition to a state of greater holiness in union with God, where they become in their personhood like God. Principally, the theology of deification is rooted in the biblical teaching that humankind has been created in the image and likeness of God. That humanity is made in God's image makes it possible for all postfall humans to return to their pre-fall state of being like God. The term itself comes from the Latin terms *facere* ("to make") and *Deus* ("God"). While deification, if taken literally, suggests the idea of "being made God," orthodox theologians have always taken it to signify "being made *like* God." Most often associated with the Eastern Orthodox tradition, the theology of deification has also been adopted, or selectively appropriated, by Christians in other traditions, including Anglican A. M. Allchin, Lutheran Tuomo Mannermaa, and evangelical Robert Rakestraw. However, the Eastern Orthodox understanding remains by far the most prevalent view.

The theology of deification is, at least in the Eastern Orthodox articulation, dependent on a distinction between God's essence (his nature or inner being) and God's uncreated energies (his operation or acts of power). In this view, God's essence concerns his transcendence, whereas his energies concern God's immanence or omnipresence. Biblical support for a distinction between essence and energies is gleaned from such texts as Habakkuk 3:3–4: "God came from Teman, the Holy One from Mount Paran. His glory covered the heavens and his praise filled the earth. His splendor was like the sunrise; rays flashed from his hand, where his power was hidden"; and Jeremiah 23:24: " 'Who can hide in secret places so that I cannot see them?' declares the LORD. 'Do not I fill heaven and earth?' declares the LORD" (TNIV). In the Habakkuk passage, God's glory would be a reference to God's essence, whereas his praise, which fills the earth, would be a reference to God's energies. In the latter passage, theologians of deification would view the reference to God filling heaven as his essence and his filling the earth as his energies.

Patristic support for the essence and energy distinction is found in Basil of Caesarea, Gregory Nazianzus, Gregory of Nyssa, and Pseudo-Dionysus. Basil, writing to Amphilochius, made a particularly clear statement: "[God's] energies descend down to us while His essence remains inaccessible." Yet, it was not until Gregory of Palamas, and several Constantinopolitan councils in the 14th century, that the doctrine of the essence and the energies of God came to be firmly established as the "received" theology of the Eastern Orthodox tradition. Gregory unequivocally says that the "superessential essence of God is thus not to be identified with the energies."

With this distinction between God's essence and energies established, Eastern Orthodox theologians have argued that deification, then, is a person's conformity or union with God's energies, *not* his essence. That the Trinity's essence is unknowable and unapproachable is taken for granted. Therefore, one is only able to be united with God in his uncreated energies. For some Eastern Orthodox theologians, these energies seem to be another way of speaking about the Holy Spirit. Thus, by becoming united to God's energies, one is ultimately being Spirit-ualized; that is, being imbued to a great degree with God the Holy Spirit. In this manner of speaking, deification is ultimately a pneumatological reality and experience. The biblical support cited for this union is 2 Peter 1:4: "Through these he has given us his very great and precious promises, so that through them you may participate in the divine nature, having escaped the corruption in the world caused by evil desires"; and 2 Corinthians 3:18: "And we all, who with unveiled faces contemplate the Lord's glory, are being transformed into his image with ever-increasing glory, which comes from the Lord, who is the Spirit" (TNIV). Again, this participation in the divine nature is a participation in God's energies, not his essence. Early Christian theologians, such as Athanasius of Alexandria, appear to have espoused the doctrine that is now labeled deification. For example, Athanasius, in *On the Incarnation*, wrote that "[Jesus Christ], indeed, assumed humanity that we might become God." Such thinking was based largely on an exegesis of Psalm 82:6: "I said, 'You are "gods"; you are all sons of the Most High.' " Commenting on this text, Pseudo-Dionysius wrote, "God's word gives the title of 'gods' not only to those heavenly beings who are our superiors but also to those sacred people among us who are distinguished for their love of God."

See also Image of God.

For Further Reading: A. M. Allchin, *Participation in God* (1988); M. Christensen and J. Wittung, eds., *Partakers of the Divine Nature* (2007); S. Finlan and V. Kharlamov, eds., *Theosis* (2006); G. Maloney, *A Theology of Uncreated Energies* (1978); T. Mannermaa, *Christ Present in Faith* (2005); R. Rakestraw, "Becoming Like God: An Evangelical Doctrine of Theosis," *Journal of the Evangelical Theological Society* 40 (1997): 257–69; N. Russell, *The Doctrine of Deification in the Greek Patristic Tradition* (2004).

Greg Peters

Depression

Depression is the experience of a sad and dejected mood and diminished interest in activities that are normally found pleasurable. Mild depression may be a reaction to life circumstances or situational stressors, while major depressive episodes, as noted in the *Diagnostic and Statistical Manual of Mental Disorders* (4th ed., 2000), are more pervasive and may include persistent symptoms of sadness, decreased pleasure, appetite and weight change, sleep pattern change, fatigue, decreased concentration, feelings of worthlessness or guilt, and frequent thoughts of death or suicide. Major depressive episodes cause distress and impair the individual's ability to function in relationships and employment settings. Some individuals experience a less severe but more persistent form of depression termed dysthymia, with moderate symptoms on most days for at least two years. Depression is distinguished from the normal sadness that occurs in bereavement or other losses unless the latter persists and becomes severe.

Depression is caused by some combination of psychological, biological, and interpersonal risk factors. Family history of depression increases the risk of depression, possibly due to genetics. Significant life events, illness, losses, medical conditions (e.g., thyroid problems), and substance abuse may be related to the onset of depression. Depression is commonly associated with brain chemistry and the malfunctioning of the electrochemical transmission process in the brain. The combination of factors is distinct for each person.

Common interventions for depression include psychotherapy and antidepressant medication. Psychotherapy is aimed at understanding the origins of the depression and initiating interventions to alter cognitions and cope more effectively with life circumstances. Cognitive behavioral therapy seeks to change distorted beliefs, problematic or deprecating self-appraisals, and pessimistic situational assessments that underlie and perpetuate depression. Couples therapy for depression addresses relationship dynamics. Antidepressant medication seeks over time to restore the appropriate functioning of neurotransmitters in brain activity. Evidence suggests it is most effective to combine psychotherapy with medication for severe depression.

Depression has sometimes been understood in Christian circles as primarily a spiritual problem or a "dark night of the soul." Conditions that parallel some aspects of modern depression have been noted throughout church history (*see* Sloth). Writers such as Martyn Lloyd-Jones have provided solid insight into possible spiritual aspects of depression (e.g., the idea that "vain regrets" may cause depression because the person is focused on past failures or lost opportunities), but unfortunately also have created the impression that all depression is spiritual and that depressed Christians are a contradiction in terms. Others, such as Archibald Hart, have attempted to balance the spiritual and psychological aspects of depression, recognizing the potential salience of both to understanding and treating depression in Christians. Prescribed spiritual solutions for depression have included Scripture reading and prayer, but caution is warranted when encouraging people with severe depression to read the Bible in isolation, because they find and distort verses that make them feel guiltier and exacerbate their condition or reinforce suicidal ideation. Spiritual exercises (e.g., writing a spiritual autobiography, participating in guided visualization, or completing a Bible study designed to alleviate depressive thoughts) that are experienced in a caring community of believers or overseen by a competent pastoral caregiver or Christian psychotherapist may be most helpful to the individual.

See also Anxiety; Happiness; Joy.

For Further Reading: A. Hart, *Coping with Depression in the Ministry and Other Helping Professions* (1984).

Mark Stanton

De Sales, Francis

See **Francis de Sales.**

Desert

Desert (Heb. *midbar*, Gr. *eremos*) is synonymous with wilderness. The primary scriptural usage of the word implies geological descriptions (dryness, heat, desolate places) but also refers to humankind's individual and communal experiences of solitude, abandonment, and death. Throughout Scripture the desert is both a metaphor and physical place for spiritual testing and refinement, and ultimately divine encounter. While the primary use of the term *desert* in Scripture is in relation to Israel's exodus experience, its implied meaning is also vividly seen in the theme of creation. The Genesis account contrasts the formless and void earth with the creation of Eden. Later uses of the desert motif throughout Scripture mirror this account. Desert experiences expose Israel's dependence on God to return to an Eden-like state. The Azazel rite, part of Yom Kippur, recaptures this theme in the act of releasing a sin bearer into the wilderness (Lev. 16:10–26).

The physical characteristics of a desert correspond with the intended spiritual implications. The desert is a place of struggle, hardship, and demons (Deut. 8:15; Matt. 12:43). Entering the desert therefore, becomes allegorically and actually an entrance into death. The desert demands a dependence on God to sustain life. It acts as a purifying agent on God's people to teach them trust, dependency, and adherence to his commands. It becomes a place and an imploring image to put to death through repentance the revolution against the will of God initiated in Eden.

The NT picks up on the desert theme, recapitulating the Exodus account in Jesus' temptation (Matt. 4:1–11; Mark 1:12–13; Luke 4:1–13). Jesus emerges from the wilderness temptation victorious through his trust, dependence, and unwavering adherence to the commands of God. The early church made use of this theme, establishing a tradition of monastic spirituality in the desert. Their established tradition has given rise to an understanding that the desert is not always a physical place; often it is a spiritual experience. The desert means being baptized with hardship and putting to death one's own self-sufficiency so that the high cost of the grace given by God in Jesus Christ might be fully realized.

See also Asceticism; Monasticism.

For Further Reading: J. Chryssavgis, *In the Heart of the Desert* (2003); B. Nassif, *The Desert Fathers and Mothers* (2010); H. Nouwen, *The Way of the Heart* (1981).

Joshua L. Hickok

Desert Fathers and Mothers

This was a third- and fourth-century movement of Egyptian and Syrian Christians who left cities and villages to live in the desert. They were inspired by the wilderness formation of such biblical exemplars as Moses, John the Baptist, and Jesus, and also of contemporaries such as Antony, whose fame helped spread this populist movement. While some individuals were drawn to self-glorification through excesses in self-denial, most participated in shared mentoring and worship, and some joined nascent monastic communities.

The movement was partly a reaction to the perceived decadence of the age and the moral laxness of the church after becoming the religion of the Roman Empire. Their response was a radical (from Lat. *radix*, meaning "root") call for a return to the core fundamentals of Christian faith: repentance, prayer, fasting, silence, and compassion. In going to the desert, many felt they followed Christ's command to "go, sell everything you have and give to the poor.... Then come, follow me" (Mark 10:21).

The appeal of this austere countercultural movement swept across all levels of society, attracting men and women, rich and poor alike, scholars and illiterate, young and old. By AD 346 there were choices in the desert: one might opt for the eremitic life (to live alone as a hermit) or the cenobitic life (to live in community). The vast majority of the desert fathers and mothers were laity, not clergy. Living in caves or simple handmade huts, they soon attracted others, like John Cassian from Scythia, who observed the lives of the desert teachers and their disciples and wrote of their experience. This resulted in a new literary genre: the Sayings of the Desert Fathers (*Apophthegmata Patrum*) and the Lives of the Desert Fathers (*Vitae Patrum*). While sections of the *Vitae Patrum* are hagiographical, the *Apophthegmata Patrum* are probably very close to the actual wisdom of the desert as shared at the time—simple aphorisms and stories that have retained a freshness and wisdom throughout the centuries.

The movement may appear similar in its practices to Eastern religions like Hinduism and Buddhism, in which disciples gathered for spiritual guidance at the feet of a guru or Zen master. Yet it is not entirely so. While these Christian disciples would approach an *abba* (old man) or *amma* (old woman) to ask for "a word," there was never any hidden, esoteric teaching imparted to a chosen few. Often the healing ministry of Christ was continued as the hungry, the poor, and the possessed came to the desert for help and intercessory prayer. Sometimes scholars might approach an illiterate monk for "a word," or the sick reach out for a healing touch; a mayor might approach a woman of poverty for "a word," and so on. The characteristic dynamic was one person seeking God's presence, speaking to another person seeking the same.

The movement cohered in a shared commitment to the discipline and purity of leaving all to follow Jesus, rather than around any one elaborate doctrinal system. Nevertheless, the movement was thoroughly Nicene in its beliefs, the great Antony himself on occasion leaving solitude to publicly defend orthodoxy. It was a lean spirituality of the one thing; asceticism helped strip away all that was superficial without sacrificing orthodoxy itself.

Hesychia (silence) was practiced in order to hear God's voice, in the spirit of the biblical exhortation to "be still, and know that I am God" (Ps. 46:10). This was not to be simply a stubborn clamping shut of one's lips, but rather expectant waiting and humble watching. As John Chryssavgis has explained, such "silence is fullness, not emptiness; it is not an absence, but the awareness of a presence." Sleeplessness also helped one watch for Jesus. Fasting allowed one to be fed by every word that proceeds from God. Prayer was not scheduled activity, but continual striving toward God. Like the spiritual journey itself, it was that toward which one should always strive; though not always easy, it was always worth the sacrifice. As Amma Syncletica noted, "In the beginning, there is struggle and a lot of work for those who come near to God. But after that, there is indescribable joy. It is just like building a fire: at first it's smoky and your eyes water, but later you get the desired result." Yet common sense was the byword, preventing pride in one's own accomplishments: "If you see a young monk by his own will climbing up to heaven, take him by the foot, and throw him to the ground, because what he is doing is not good for him" (Chryssavgis).

The desert fathers and mothers recognized the natural ebb and flow of the spiritual life. There is a social dimension, a time for mentoring and guidance, but there is a necessary time for solitude and discipline too. The Sayings show the teachers conferring among themselves, growing through dialogue and discussion, and then withdrawing into solitude and silence. The metaphor of withdrawing "into the desert" to be with Jesus has been crucial in the history of spiritual formation. The sayings and lives of the Fathers show how these Christians tried to live the Christian life with integrity and radical simplicity without being compromised by their culture, nor forgetting their commitment to care for one another. They continue to influence many diverse writers, from Roman Catholics Thomas Merton and Henri Nouwen to Orthodox John Chryssavgis to evangelical Shane Claiborne.

See also Asceticism; Antony of Egypt; Coptic Spirituality; Syrian Spirituality.

For Further Reading: D. Chitty, *The Desert a City* (1966); J. Chryssavgis, *In the Heart of the Desert* (2003); T. Merton, *The Wisdom of the Desert* (1970); Y. Nomura and H. Nouwen, *Desert Wisdom* (2000); B. Ward, *The Lives of the Desert Fathers* (1981); idem, *The Sayings of the Desert Fathers* (1975).

Kelby Cotton

Desire

Desire has to do with longing or yearning for, or being attached to or drawn toward, something beyond the self. It is to *want*. In the rich metaphorical language of Scripture, it is to hunger and thirst. The reality of desire creates a ceaseless human quest for satisfaction and is an implicit testimony to humanity's incompleteness. Desire is also a matter of paramount concern, because the focus of desire determines the course and contours of a life. The Christian spiritual tradition does not commend the suppression of human desires, but rather the proper ordering of them. In the Christian view, whether a longing is good or bad is determined by the lawfulness and worthiness of its object.

The fatal moment in the garden of Eden came when the forbidden fruit was perceived to be *desirable* (Gen. 3:6), and since that time humans have been victims of the corruption "caused by evil desires" (2 Peter 1:4). Exhortations to eschew bad desire occur throughout the Bible (for example: lust, love of money, arrogance, vengeance—Matthew 5:27–30; Mark 4:19; 1 Timothy 6:10, 17; 1 John 2:15–17). By contrast, the Christian notion of good desire, as Daniel Akin has articulated it, is "putting the desire for God's will first. When the Lord is our greatest desire, all other desires find their proper expression." Similarly, Ignatius of Loyola believed the experience of salvation means "desiring and choosing only what helps us praise, reverence, and serve God" and thus living in Christ's "loving presence and wisdom." In our theodicy-critical age, many Christian disciples understandably experience tension between what one needs for such an intimate trust level and what one experiences as suffering and evil forces despite the loving presence and wisdom of the sovereign Christ. This tension notwithstanding, the redeemed heart, deep down (beneath any trust-storms) craves God's will.

A signpost of this heart-craving is the psalmist's statement: "Take delight in the LORD and he will give you the desires of your heart" (37:4). Craving or longing for God's will flows from a delightful personal relationship with God, in the context of which he gifts us (or graces us) with his own desires: he implants his own will in our heart. And whoever does God's will lives forever, unlike the fallen world with its desires, which pass away (1 John 2:17).

Another rediscovery in evangelical spirituality has been the connection between the enduring heart desire for God and the lived Christian experience of joy. John Piper, in his *Desiring God: Confessions of a Christian Hedonist* (1986), claims that people were created to enjoy God—and through him everything he created—and that our very enjoyment becomes the glorifying of God that fulfills our "chief end" (in Piper's recrafting of the Westminster Shorter Catechism). In his autobiographical *Surprised by Joy* (1955), C. S. Lewis reflected on *sehnsucht* (Ger., "intense desire"), the familiar experience of inconsolable longing for something unattainable in this world, like a longing for an unknown country that is actually one's true home. Very occasionally people have a flashing apprehension of this destiny and experience true joy, but the moment passes so quickly that it must be relished in wistful retrospect rather than savored in the present. For Lewis such moments are fleeting signs of God and heaven ahead, yet for now still out of reach. The Christian mystical tradition testifies consistently to the paradox that the closer one approaches God, the more soul hunger and thirst intensify. As Bernard of Clairvaux wrote, and many Christians sing, "From the best bliss that earth imparts, we turn unfilled to Thee again."

Some recent writers, such as James K. A. Smith, have pointed out the powerful potential of Christian worship to form the heart and order its desires. Indeed, this is one of worship's principal purposes. Through it worshipers are led to gaze in the right direction—to "fix their eyes on Jesus." In the practices and disciplines of effective worship, hearts are shaped to look like God's and moved increasingly to love what he loves. To summarize, all who know God in Christ may have their godly longings fulfilled, now and forever, both to God's glory and their own enjoyment.

See also Emotions; Will, Human.

For Further Reading: D. Akin, "Desire," in *Baker's Evangelical Dictionary of Biblical Theology*, ed. W. Elwell (1996); J. Houston, *The Heart's Desire* (1992); D. Saliers et al., *Liturgy and the Moral Self* (1998); J. Smith, *Desiring the Kingdom*, Cultural Liturgies, vol. 1 (2009); J. Wakefield, *Sacred Listening: Discovering the Spiritual Exercises of Ignatius Loyola* (2006).

David L. Rowe

Detachment

The aim of detachment is to free oneself from anything to which one could become inordinately attached so that one may better discern God's will and devote oneself totally to God. This is amply illustrated in Ignatius Loyola's *Spiritual Exercises*. The concept of detachment is traceable to the OT idea of holy persons or things taken from their ordinary usage and devoted to God, such was the Nazirite or "holy one" (Num. 6:1–21; cf. Lev. 27). In the NT, Jesus' teachings on discipleship have played a critical role in the practice of detachment. His challenge to a rich young man—"If you want to be perfect, go, sell your possessions and give to the poor, and you will have treasure in heaven" (Matt. 19:21)—has been a source of inspiration for many, including Francis of Assisi. His teaching concerning self-denial and carrying one's cross led to the belief that martyrdom, the act of giving up one's life, was the supreme act of detachment. The Pauline teachings on putting off the old self in order to be reclothed with the new self (Col. 3:5), on baptism as dying with Christ and rising with him to new life (Rom. 6:3–8), have contributed to the idea of detachment as a process of stripping off, renunciation, and abnegation of self.

Within the schema of the Threefold Way to spiritual growth, detachment is usually associated with the purgative way. In popular devotions, detachment takes a variety of forms. For example, Francis de Sales, in his *Introduction to the Devout Life* (1609), warns against excessive attachment to friendships other than friendship based on "acts of charity, devotion and true Christian perfection." In Protestantism the practice of separation is more pronounced in the Free Church tradition. Detachment is more than an attitude; it is a visible separation. Anabaptists refused to carry a sword or take oaths. Quakers broke social conventions by refusing to tip their hats as a sign of respect to members of a higher social class. English Baptists removed themselves from the established church. In the nineteenth-century Holiness tradition, detachment involves separating from specific things, places, and activities that are not intrinsically evil but potentially detrimental, such as the movie theater, smoking, drinking, and dancing. The underlying rationale is to create a contrast community.

Discussions on detachment have seen a discernible shift. In the past, anything less than optimal tended to be viewed as a potential danger, as seen in the above example from the Holiness tradition, whereas in modern discussions what is not obviously sinful is potentially good. The latter approach is exemplified in the Vatican II document *Gaudium et Spes*.

See also Asceticism; Eckhart, Meister; Monasticism.

For Further Reading: K. Ware, "The Way of the Ascetics: Negative or Affirmative?" in *Asceticism*, ed. V. Wimbush and R. Valantasis (1998), 3–15.
Simon Chan

Devil, Demons, and the Demonic

These are descriptive labels used in the Bible and throughout church history to refer to evil spirits. For Christians, the devil is the supreme leader of all demonic spirits. The term *devil* is derived from the Greek term *diabolos*, which refers to one who engages in slander. In Scripture this is the same supreme supernatural force known as Satan, a term meaning "adversary" or "opponent." This being is also called Belial, Beelzebul, the evil one, the prince of this world, besides other functional titles.

In the ancient Greek-speaking world, a "demon" (*daimōn*) was not necessarily an evil supernatural being, but could be used to refer to a deity. Most often it was used to refer to semidivine beings that were inferior to the gods. Throughout the NT, however, the term is consistently used to speak of evil spirits who are associated with the devil and who oppose God and his people.

The Scripture is silent about the origin of the devil and demons. Some interpreters have discerned in the prophecies in Isaiah 14 (against the king of Babylon) and Ezekiel 28 (against the king of Tyre) convincing evidence of a transcendent evil spiritual power standing behind the two kings. If this is the case, then one could infer that the devil rebelled against God before the creation of the world and led a vast number of angels into rebellion with him. Although this appears to be a reasonable interpretation of these texts, not all scholars are agreed on this and, ultimately, there is a great deal Scripture does not reveal about this question.

It is important to note that Jesus did not dismiss belief in evil spirits as superstition, but affirmed it and taught his disciples how to stand up against their malicious influence. It has only been since the time of the Enlightenment that widespread skepticism about the demonic has gripped Western society. Belief in the reality of the demonic is integral to a biblical worldview and essential to a genuinely Christian approach to spiritual formation.

Understanding how demons exert their influence and how they can be counteracted is vital to spiritual growth and ministry. They work in concert with "the flesh" to tempt believers to disobey God (e.g., Matt. 4:3; 1 Thess. 3:5); they exert a deceiving influence and inspire false and misleading teachings (e.g., Col. 2:8); and they can even cause physical illnesses (e.g., Luke 13:11; 2 Cor. 12:7). Christians need to be cautious, however, about overattributing various symptoms and maladies to demonic spirits. There are a variety of chemical, neurological, and psychological disorders that can easily be mistaken for demonic influence. Dissociative identity disorder (DID; formerly known as multiple personality disorder) is a relevant case in point.

For many Christians, the notion of demonic spirits plotting, lurking, and attacking elicits a great deal of fear. There should, in fact, be a healthy respect for these supernaturally powerful entities, especially since Scripture portrays Satan as similar to a prowling lion that is ready to exploit the vulnerabilities of believers (1 Peter 5:8). Nevertheless, believers should have a deep and settled assurance that God is infinitely more powerful than the adversary. By virtue of union with Christ in his resurrection and exaltation (see Eph. 2:5–6), Christians share in Christ's power and authority over this realm (see Col. 2:9–10). The apostle John expresses this well when he says, "Greater is he that is in you, than he that is in the world" (1 John 4:4 KJV).

It is vitally important to realize that there is no ultimate dualism between God and the devil. Scripture makes it clear that the work of Satan and his demons will be brought to a decisive end when Christ returns and brings history to a conclusion (Matt. 25:41; Rev. 20:10).

See also Occult.

For Further Reading: C. Arnold, *Powers of Darkness* (1992); S. Page, *Powers of Evil* (1995); K. van der Toorn et al., eds., *Dictionary of Deities and Demons in the Bible* (1999).

Clinton E. Arnold

Devotio Moderna

The *Devotio Moderna* refers to a form of spirituality popular in the Netherlands and Germany in the 14th and 15th centuries. Around 1420 the phrase was used by Henry Pomerius to identify Gerhard Groote (1340–1384) as the originator of the "new devotion (*devotio moderna*) found today." The designation has stuck to this day.

Groote (or Grote, or Geert) experienced a profound conversion in 1374; he left his house to a group of devout women and retired to a Carthusian monastery, though he eventually returned to public life as an itinerant preacher. After his death, a few of Groote's followers, under the leadership of Florens Radewijns (1350–1400), formed a community of "devout," dedicated to fostering the life of Christ among themselves and others. They pooled their property, supported themselves by copying books, and kept monastic hours of prayer. They honored the vows of poverty, chastity, and obedience, yet they did not apply for official recognition. The loose organization of communities, as they expanded, became known as the Brothers and Sisters of the Common Life. Later some reorganized as a reforming chapter (the Windesheim Chapter) of the Canons Regular. Others (mostly women) associated with the Third Order of Franciscans.

The women's houses were populated by laypersons, while the men's houses inclined toward the spirit of the order of the regular canons, training clergy who served the local parishioners. The devout supported educational reform and established hostels and regular "collations" (sermon discussions) to foster student life. Groote wrote a book of liturgical hours in Middle Dutch for use among his followers, and the devout advanced the development of vernacular devotions. Many copied their favorite devotional texts into personal collections for frequent reference (called *rapiarium*). A number of devotional manuals and other spiritual literature flowed from the pens of the devout, the most well-known being Thomas à Kempis's *The Imitation of Christ* (1471).

A few themes are characteristic of the spirituality of the *Devotio Moderna*. It tended to express contempt for certain aspects of "the world"; for example, its adherents cautioned against academic pursuits, which they thought distracted from the simple knowledge of God through love. The devout also emphasized the passion of Christ and developed aids for meditation that foreshadowed those of Ignatius of Loyola's *Spiritual Exercises*. They reminded clergy and religious laypeople of the need for serious intention in their lives. Humility was another of their emphases. As Christ was the exemplar of the humble life, so followers of Christ were to live humbly, content with simple means and little formal regard. But their central theme was always the imitation of Christ—following Christ in attitude and action toward others. Though this movement anticipated some features of the Protestant Reformation, the communities themselves did not survive the chaos of the following century. By 1600 nearly all the houses of the Common Life were abandoned, though their writings remain to encourage and challenge Christians today.

See also Brethren of the Common Life.

For Further Reading: B. Coldrey, *The Devotio Moderna and the Brethren of the Common Life, 1380–1521* (2002); *Devotio Moderna: Basic Writings*, CWS (1988); R. Fuller, *The Brotherhood of the Common Life and Its Influence* (1995); J. Van Engen, *Sisters and Brothers of the Common Life* (2008).

Evan B. Howard

Devotions, Personal

Personal devotions are the individual and private exercises practiced to enhance the spiritual life by focusing the mind and senses in reverence toward God. Based on the conviction that every believer is meant to experience and enjoy the presence of God, personal devotions or "quiet times" have taken on a special significance within evangelical piety. Following evangelicalism's general focus on the Bible, personal devotions are centered on individual reading and study of the Bible as a principal means of spiritual growth. However, this study is not intended just for the pursuit of knowledge, but has as its primary purpose the forging of a more vital relationship with God. These devotional exercises also include significant time devoted to prayer. Typically, a regular time is set aside each day for this expression of intentional devotion and union with God.

The disciplined life and practice of Jesus provide the pattern followed by evangelicals in their pursuit of the presence of God through personal devotions. In addition to Bible study and prayer, Jesus engaged in other disciplines, such as meditation, solitude, and silence, which are regularly employed in devotional practices. Being alone with God in solitude provides a context for the contemporary believer wherein it is possible to shut out the world's distractions and be silent before him in order to hear his "still, small voice." Bible study is enhanced as one meditates on a portion of that which has been studied.

A schedule of Bible readings is helpful in maintaining faithful personal devotions. Classic devotional books, such as Oswald Chambers's *My Utmost for His Highest* (1951) or Charles Spurgeon's *Morning and Evening* (1866/2005), have provided useful guidance for Bible reading over the years. Contemporary devotional booklets, such as *Our Daily Bread*, have also been a mainstay for the personal devotions of millions throughout the world. Jim and Kaye Johns's *Prayers for the Moment* (2006) and Richard Foster's *Prayer* (1992) have proven helpful in structuring meaningful prayer experiences.

Throughout its history, leaders of the evangelical movement have enthusiastically endorsed personal devotions as a key to spiritual growth and maturity. Noted Christian abolitionist William Wilberforce often spoke of their value and demonstrated it by routinely spending the first two hours of every day in Bible study and prayer, in spite of his hectic schedule as a British parliamentarian. During a particularly strenuous time of sustained demands that forced him to limit his morning devotions to a mere half hour, he expressed the feelings of many when he wrote, "Surely it is the experience of all good [people] that without a due measure of private devotions the soul grows lean."

See also Bible, Reading the; Formation, Spiritual; Spiritual Reading.

For Further Reading: L. Allen, "A Brief History of Christian Devotion," *Faith and Mission* 7, no. 2 (1990): 3–17; K. Boa, *Conformed to His Image* (2001); S. Eyre, *Drawing Close to God* (1995); O. Hallesby, *Prayer* (1975).

John R. Lillis

Dickinson, Emily Elizabeth (1830–1886)

American poet. Born in Amherst, Massachusetts, she was educated at Amherst College and Mount

Holyoke Female Seminary but subsequently remained at her parental home in seclusion for most of her life, a caregiver for her chronically ill mother and a devoted companion to the rest of her family.

Her family was influential in finance, law, and education, entertaining many renowned visitors who included editors, politicians, and clergy leaders. Dickinson's intellectual and spiritual formation continued under the mentorship of family, friends, and the extensive family library. Her literary influences included the Bible, Shakespeare, Wordsworth, Emerson, Longfellow, and particularly Charlotte Brontë's novel *Jane Eyre*. Often seen by readers as an enigmatic eccentric, she was a complex, gifted thinker whose more than eighteen hundred short poems were published only in an authoritative edition (1960) by T. H. Johnson, who also edited her letters (1958). Her poems captivate the attention of readers who have identified her strong interests in science and the natural world. Much of her corpus, preoccupied by death and eternity, has been highly regarded by twentieth-century scholars, some of whom, like Roger Lundin, see in them her Trinitarian beliefs reinterpreted through her probing intelligence and her struggles with the deaths of numerous family members and friends. Her most famous poems include "Because I could not stop for Death" and "Tell all the Truth but tell it slant." They illustrate her profoundly religious imagination and remarkably unique style employing literary innovations not commonly seen until the century beyond her own.

See also Poetry and Poetics.

For Further Reading: G. Grabher et al., eds., *The Emily Dickinson Handbook* (2005); R. Lundin, *Emily Dickinson* (2004); W. Martin, *The Cambridge Companion to Emily Dickinson* (2002).

Lynn R. Szabo

Direction, Spiritual

Spiritual direction is a discipline of soul care and formation that involves a process of discernment. In it a *directee* enlists a *director* to listen together to God's voice in pursuit of a deepening relationship with God and increasing reflection of Jesus in his or her life choices. Although spiritual direction is often one-to-one, it may also transpire within a spiritual direction group.

This process of growth, guidance, and authentic transformation, is a communal activity achieved through the work of the Spirit, the yielded will (of the directee), and the body of Christ (represented by the director). It is achieved through prayerful interaction with God in the presence of another, as they discern God's voice and direct each other's focus to Jesus. The opportunity for the directee is to have a spiritual companion in moving through resistance, recognizing obedience, or embracing spiritual gifts and vocation. By attending to one's own desires and developing the ability to listen to Jesus' voice, the one seeking spiritual direction learns to recognize what may be humanistic yearning and comes to a deeper understanding of what it means to live one's life as an image-bearer of God.

Since the ultimate director in the process of spiritual direction is the Holy Spirit, the task of the human director is to be attentive to the Spirit, the directee's heart, and his or her own heart as well. Spiritual direction has rightly been described as "holy listening" or "the midwifery of the soul"; thus, the director becomes a fellow traveler who acts as mentor, inquirer, accountability partner, or guide as appropriate. Rather than "mediating" access to God, a spiritual director assists a directee in discerning God's voice, actions, and will, the goal being that in this communal effort directees will experience their relationship with God in a new way.

Some speak of a "rediscovery" of spiritual direction, since the concept and practice have been unknown to many contemporary Christians, especially those in evangelical settings. Yet the essence of spiritual direction is present in biblical history, notably when Samuel consults Eli as he puzzles over hearing from God (1 Sam. 3:8 – 9), as Elizabeth affirms Mary's faithful response to the angelic visit (Luke 1:45), and as Jesus questions Nicodemus about his understanding of heavenly things (John 3:12). Paul, in the earliest days of the Christian church, acted as a spiritual director to Timothy, Titus, and others (Eph. 1:17–19; Col. 3:15–17) as he spoke of his desire that "the eyes of your heart may be enlightened." In each age, the church has needed spiritual direction to continually reexamine its call and address its failings. The writings of John Cassian, Ignatius of Loyola, and Teresa of Avila witness that spiritual direction has long offered its gifts to the church.

Eastern Orthodox, Roman Catholic, and Anglican traditions have formally practiced spiritual direction for hundreds of years. Contemporary ecclesiastical traditions vary in how they envision the director's role, offering choices regarding the exercise of power and authority (low to high) as well as various styles for conducting their time together. There is agreement through all these traditions that true spiritual growth requires the presence of another (Rom. 10:14).

Spiritual direction is distinctly different from pastoral counseling and psychotherapy. Prompted by soul hunger rather than crisis or disorder, spiritual direction pursues holistic transformation by bringing one's thoughts, feelings, and actions before God. Rather than focusing on problem-solving or therapeutic techniques, the focus is on discernment, prayer, and listening to God, and may utilize Scripture, poetry, journaling, music, or silence, to list just a few possible options. The understanding of the role of the spiritual director continues to develop as this profession matures. Participation in formal supervision groups is a common expectation for spiritual directors; these are particularly helpful in processing the interior responses of directors in relation to their directees. Training conferences, journals, and associations now offer a growing body of information and advice for Christian as well as non-Christian forms of spiritual direction.

See also Discernment; Discipline; Formation, Spiritual; Mentors, Spiritual.

For Further Reading: J. Bakke, *Holy Invitations* (2000); S. Chan, *Spiritual Theology* (1998); M. Guenther, *Holy Listening* (1992); G. Moon and D. Benner, *Spiritual Direction and the Care of Souls* (2004).

Kim Olstad

Disability

Disability has had an ambiguous history in Christian spirituality. On the one hand, given selective reference to biblical traditions, people with disabilities have been shunned for various reasons. Some conditions such as deafness-dumbness or epileptic seizures have been associated with demonic activity, while other conditions have been understood to be the result of previous sin, whether of the disabled person or of his or her ancestors. Even quite apart from these etiological perspectives, the Levitical law also excluded certain classes of people with disabilities from the priestly vocation or at least from certain priestly activities, and this in turn has translated into the assumption of such people as being no more than second-class citizens among the people of God.

On the other hand, portions of the biblical witness have led to more positive, albeit no less ambiguous, views regarding disabilities. Thus, the physical afflictions suffered by Job, a righteous man, and the Pauline emphases on being strong precisely amid weakness have combined to challenge — too often burden — people with disabilities with having to become models of patience, suffering, and perseverance. Disabilities in this perspective are divine tests of human faithfulness. Even in the best-case scenario, the disabled have often been seen as means to an end, as objects of charity through whom the nondisabled can aid with meritorious acts of kindness. The inevitable result has been an instrumentalization of disability and a reduction of the identities of people with disabilities to their disabling features and characteristics.

With the advent of the civil rights movement, however, people with disabilities have fought for a full recognition not only of their rights but also of their humanity. Medical models of disabilities have been challenged by social constructivist approaches to illuminate the various ways in which stigmatization against various types of handicaps and impairments are socially perpetuated. The result has been a disability critique against all forms of ableism, normalism, and ageism as being politically, economically, and socially discriminatory toward people with differing capacities, including the aged. More recent studies have also highlighted the affective and embodied dimensions of human knowing, thereby calling into question the predominantly cognitivist epistemologies and evaluative norms that marginalize people with intellectual disabilities. Overall, there is a real sense in which nondisability is better understood in terms of temporary able-bodiedness, and human life subsists in interdependent relationality, felt most palpably at the beginning and end of life, albeit more or less present throughout the life span.

In this environment, a disability hermeneutic has retrieved biblical traditions in the search for new theological perspectives. The creation narratives testify to God's celebration of diversity, including that across the spectrum of differently abled bodies and minds. Further, without denying the role of healing, other biblical accounts show that people with disabilities were accepted quite apart from being cured. Perhaps most important, from a christological point of view, that the impairments Jesus suffered in his hands, feet, and side marked his resurrection body suggests that the eschatological alleviation of all tears involves not necessarily the erasure of present bodily impairments but indicates that there are means beyond our comprehension for the final redemption of disabilities within the communion of saints to the glory of the triune God.

There is arguably a preferential option not only for the poor, but also for the weak and the marginalized, which would include people with disabilities. This is not to minimize the bodily suffering that attends to certain forms of physical impairments, but it is a call to discern socially construed forms of suffering and to mobilize at least the Christian community to be more intentionally inclusive regarding people with disabilities than it generally has been. In the body of Christ, which signals the new creation, the reversals of the weak and the strong and the elevation to a place of honor of those who are conventionally despised means that the fellowship of the Spirit is not divided between the "us" and "them," but that each is recognized as contributing in his or her own particular way to the edification of other members. This kind of egalitarianism of the differently abled, modeled after the friendship of Christ who descended to our level in the incarnation, takes time and is even inconvenient. But such a more inclusive vision of the redemptive work of God allows the temporarily able-bodied to welcome Christ in the faces and bodies of people with disabilities, even as people with disabilities also bear witness to the wondrous works of God by the power of the Holy Spirit.

See also Body; Health and Healing; Suffering.

For Further Reading: H. Avalos et al., eds., *This Abled Body* (2007); N. Eiesland, *The Disabled God* (1994); H. Reinders, *Receiving the Gift of Friendship* (2008); T. Reynolds, *Vulnerable Communion* (2008); A. Yong, *Theology and Down Syndrome* (2007); F. Young, ed., *Encounter with Mystery* (1998).

Amos Yong

Discernment

The call to discernment arises from the recognition that the created order is permeated not only with the fundamental goodness of God but also with evil. Such evil consists not only of the consequences of sin but also of evil as a personal force, the "devils" that, in the words of Luther's hymn, "threaten to undo us." Obviously, the Christian and the church long to respond to the Word and will of God, to worship and serve Christ — not just any "Christ," not a pretender, but the Christ of the cross who now lives and reigns with the Father. The Christian and the church long to respond to the Spirit and turn from those "spirits" that would deceive them. The Christian spiritual tradition witnesses to evil's subtlety and the extraordinary capacity of the human heart to self-deceive. And yet, while evil is powerful, through intentional dependence on the Spirit, one can "to some extent" (Ignatius, *Spiritual Exercises*, no. 13) discern God's will in the midst of the ambiguities of life.

And this is the heart of the matter: Can the Christian and can the church discern the movement and call of the Spirit even though we "see but a poor reflection as in a mirror" (1 Cor. 13:12)? The Scriptures provide the foundational principles of the practice; and the church's focused teaching on this topic goes back at least to Origen. Students of this topic recognize, as well, the relevance of Jonathan Edwards' *Religious Affections* and John Wesley's sermons on the witness of the Spirit. Indeed, a host of other voices inform this conversation. But the master of this topic is surely Ignatius Loyola, who in his *Spiritual Exercises* condensed the wisdom of previous generations in a way that was accessible to subsequent generations and to other spiritual traditions. Though his "rules of discernment" are found in an appendix to the *Spiritual Exercises*, one cannot pray under the guidance of his *Exercises* without recognizing their vital place in the prayer and life of the Christian.

Two things are axiomatic to the practice of discernment. First, the inner witness of the Spirit will never contradict the written witness; indeed, to discern is to consider how the Scriptures are to be lived in a particular time and place, to discover how the Spirit applies the truth to a specific person or people. And second, to know the witness of the Spirit, one must be in community. This does not mean that the witness of the Spirit is the same as the voice or will of the community; rather, it is a recognition that those who attend to the Spirit are resolved to live in mutual submission within the body of Christ.

With these two caveats, then, the rules of discernment found in the *Spiritual Exercises* are a supremely helpful guide to discerning well and deciding wisely in times of choice. The working assumption of the rules is not so much a question of good and evil but of good and good. Behind this assumption is the premise that the good is the enemy of the best and that the call of the Christian is not merely to choose the good but to choose the good to which one is called. Both singleness and marriage are good, for example; but what is the good to which this specific person at a specific time is called?

Then, in addition, we can speak of the fundamental working principles for discernment. The first rule is that we are never to choose in desolation. While desolation is not necessarily wrong in itself, it is not the emotional soil in which a person can confidently know that he or she is acting in the Spirit. The Spirit's witness or call will always be in peace. And thus we are wise to determine the cause of the desolation and respond appropriately; if it is fear, to cast our cares upon God; if it is anger, to direct our anger into the presence of God rather than seek vengeance. The Spirit leads in peace, and so we act only when we have peace.

The second rule is the necessary counterpart of the first: our consolation, peace of heart, must be tested. We cannot assume that if we have consolation we know the will of God. We are too capable of self-deception and rationalization. Thus, discernment is both a matter of attending to the witness of the Spirit and of allowing the light of Scripture to shine on our own hearts to test and confirm that indeed the movement of our hearts is the witness of the Spirit.

Thus, that discernment is a learned exercise:

upon reflecting we may see that our choices were governed by the longing for wealth or honor or power rather than the greater glory of Christ. And we may become aware of our own propensities, our own points of vulnerability. Yet, while the learning may be slow, it is fruitful. We grow in wisdom, and a capacity for discernment is vital to such growth. In addition, the Christian grows ever closer to Christ himself, for the witness of the Spirit is nothing other than the voice of Jesus.

See also Decision Making.

For Further Reading: K. Bockmuehl, *Listening to the God Who Speaks* (1990); J. English, *Spiritual Freedom* (1995); T. Green, *Weeds among the Wheat* (1984); G. Smith, *The Voice of Jesus* (2003).

Gordon T. Smith

Discipleship

Although the word *discipleship* is not actually used in the NT, the concept is derived from the experience of being a *disciple* of Jesus ("disciple" is used more than 250 times in the Gospels and Acts). A disciple is a *learner* (from the Greek word *mathētēs*). So to understand the nature of discipleship, it is necessary to explore what it meant to be a disciple in the first-century world.

Disciples were common then. Jewish rabbis had disciples (*talmidim*), literally students of the law. Greek philosophers had disciples, as did the Pharisees (Matt. 22:15–16), as well as John the Baptist (Mark 2:18; John 1:35). The Jews, on occasion, referred to themselves as disciples of Moses (John 9:27–28). Disciples were understood to be followers (students, apprentices, pupils) who were committed to a particular person so as to learn that person's philosophy, teaching, or way of life and then to follow a particular pattern of life, whether by living in a certain way, passing on the teaching to others, or engaging in political or religious activities. Jesus and his disciples shared this common understanding of the relationship between teacher and disciple.

Thus, to follow Jesus meant to do what Jesus did (replicate his ministry, e.g., Mark 6:7–13, 30; Luke 10:1–20) and to believe what Jesus taught (obey his word, e.g., John 8:31–32; 17:6).

Jesus himself described what it means to be his disciple: "If any want to become my followers, let them deny themselves and take up their cross and follow me" (Mark 8:34 NRSV). Self-denial, as Best explains, is commonly confused with "the denial of things to the self, i.e., with asceticism or self-discipline." In fact, it means "the denial of the self itself," that is, renouncing the self that is in rebellion against God. Paul speaks of this process as putting off the old self (the old self is denied) and putting on the new self (found in Christ) (Eph. 4:22–24). Self-denial coupled with cross-bearing (being willing to make any sacrifice for Christ) describes a demanding calling for those who would follow Jesus. This image stands in stark contrast to the contemporary picture of following Jesus in order to be happy, healthy, and wealthy.

In the second half of the 20th century, while churches grew, many questioned the depth of commitment on the part of the new disciples. In part, the resurgence of interest by the evangelical church in classic spirituality has to do with a longing for a new depth of relationship with Jesus. Perhaps our paradigm for the process of growth needs to expand from discipleship training (Bible study, intercessory prayer, and witness) to spiritual formation (the practice of spiritual disciplines). The classic concept of purgation as the first step in the spiritual journey is also helpful. Converts need to wrestle with temptation and choose the virtues over the vices and thus develop a way of living in accord with Jesus' commands.

In the end, it is good to remember that Christian discipleship is all about a relationship with Jesus. It is not primarily about following a set of rules, engaging in ascetical practices, or affirming certain doctrines. It is about becoming ever more conformed to the image of Jesus (Gal. 4:19), and this new reality flows out of an ongoing, unfolding, dynamic association with Jesus. This is a life-long process that involves opening ourselves to the work of the Holy Spirit, via the medium of the spiritual disciplines, in the context of a Christian community so as to be able to love God and love others as our Lord calls us to do.

See also Imitation of Christ; Martyrdom.

For Further Reading: E. Best, *Disciples and Discipleship* (1986); idem, *Following Jesus* (1981); D. Bonhoeffer, *The Cost of Discipleship* (1959); M. Wilkins, *Following the Master* (1992).

Richard V. Peace

Discipline, Divine

A discipline is an activity undertaken to appropriate more fully the loving presence of Christ in the believer's life, which in turn brings about greater conformity to the image of Christ. Typically we think of disciplines as practices initiated by believers, but God himself also initiates discipline. For example, a believer may discipline herself by intentionally moving into solitude as a means of drawing near to God. Alternatively, God may discipline her by allowing, intensifying, or directly causing a set of circumstances that makes solitude more or less inevitable (e.g., getting laid up in bed with an illness). It is interesting to note that the Spirit "drove" Jesus into the wilderness (Mark 1:12 ESV), which suggests a rather forceful initiative by the Spirit. We know that Jesus "learned obedience through what he suffered" (Heb. 5:8 ESV), so we should also expect difficult circumstances to arise in our spiritual training (e.g., James 1:2 – 4). The writer of Hebrews makes clear that God the Father disciplines his children in ways that may seem painful at the time for the sake of their progress in holiness (Heb. 12:7 – 11; cf. Prov. 3:11 – 12; John 15:2).

Typically these occasions of discipline are unwanted, but they do not have to be in order to count as discipline. The apostle Paul came to a place where he was "content" with his adversities

and yet still able to profit from them (2 Cor. 12:10). The key characteristic of divine discipline is that it is a trying or challenging experience meant by God to be instructive or corrective. This is why being disciplined is not easy. God disciplines his children in ways that touch areas in need of transformation. So discipline always seems painful, though it does not always involve adverse circumstances. For instance, in the OT, a firm, verbal correction by God (or a prophet) is considered a form of discipline (e.g., Isa. 8:11), and in the NT, Scripture itself has a disciplinary function (2 Tim. 3:16). It might be helpful to think of how human parents regularly train or discipline their children through verbal instruction without the infliction of any sort of corporal pain.

But because God's discipline at times involves adverse circumstances, it is important to clarify three issues. First, there is a distinction between divine discipline and divine punishment (cf. 1 Cor. 11:32). God's punishment inflicts rightful penalties on guilty persons as means of retributive justice and may or may not lead to their reformation. But for those who are "in Christ" there is now "no condemnation" (Rom. 8:1). The penalty for sin has been paid, and the righteousness of Christ has been applied such that there is no punishment remaining for such persons. Instead, God views them as his beloved children. His discipline is never motivated by wrath or condemnation; instead, he lovingly moves toward his children with rebuke and instruction out of a desire to see them flourish (cf. Rev. 3:19).

Second, the reality of divine discipline does not mean that every negative event in life is directly caused by God or intended by him as discipline. The world, the flesh, and the devil are real sources of human misery, and while God is providentially sovereign over all that occurs, he is not the direct cause of all that occurs. Jesus teaches his disciples to pray that God's will be done on earth as it is in heaven because there is still much that occurs on earth that is not his will. Moreover, when God does allow traumatic events to occur, there are often explanations for these events other than discipline. Disciples must be careful to avoid viewing every life difficulty as orchestrated by God as an occasion of discipline.

Third, understanding God's discipline as the infliction or allowance of pain in response to sinful behavior in order to discourage that behavior is far too simplistic. Such a view suggests that God is primarily interested in changing outward behavior through bringing about adverse circumstances when it is quite clear in Scripture that God desires to transform the inward dimensions of the human person through his loving and strengthening presence (e.g., Mark 7:20–23; John 15:1–11). This is why it is important to primarily view God's discipline as circumstances that God causes or allows in order to draw the human person more closely to himself and thereby make them more like himself.

See also Formation, Spiritual.

For Further Reading: T. D. Beck, "The Divine Dis-Comforter: The Holy Spirit's Role in Transformative Suffering," in *Journal of Spiritual Formation and Soul Care* 2, no. 2 (2009): 199–218; W. Lane, "Discipline," in *The International Standard Bible Encyclopedia*, ed. G. Bromiley (1979); C. S. Lewis, *The Problem of Pain* (1940); N. T. Wright, *Hebrews for Everyone* (2004).

Steve L. Porter

Disciplines, Spiritual
See Chapter 32.

Distractions in Prayer

Distractions are one of the most common hindrances to extended prayer. This may be one of the reasons Jesus taught his disciples to go into a room and close the door when praying (Matt. 6:6). Jesus sought to avoid distractions in his prayer sessions by praying at night or in the wilderness, where solitude and silence were abundant.

The challenge of keeping one's focus during prayer is addressed by many spiritual writers. Even William Shakespeare aptly described the challenge in *Hamlet*, through the mouth of King Claudius, who lamented, "My words fly up, my thoughts remain below. Words without thoughts never to heaven go." Some of the writers employ metaphors like "monkeys jumping around in banana trees" and "a swarm of mosquitoes buzzing in all directions" to describe the distractions that arise while praying.

Great men and women of prayer have offered numerous suggestions for dealing with these distractions. Along with making sure one's physical environment is uncluttered and nondistracting, Teresa of Avila recommended that prayer times begin by settling down in order to enjoy the presence of God, reminding oneself that one is entering a quiet place alone with Jesus. Writing one's prayers in a journal or on the computer, or praying prayers aloud are other ways to keep the mind focused on what is being communicated. Variations in posture, or walking or running while praying, can help the mind stay alert rather than lapse into sleepiness. When distractions arise, as inevitably they do, spiritual writers advise Christians simply to brush them away as if they were annoying flies or gnats, and then return to the work of prayer. Another practice is to take a distracting thought and incorporate it into one's prayer. Thoughts or concerns that recur repeatedly may be indicative of something that needs to be dealt with in greater length and may be God's way of bringing the matter to closer examination, so that it can become the focus of prayer. Most importantly, one should realize that distractions in prayer are part of everyone's experience in prayer and that, through the discipline of dealing with them, they can become less of a hindrance to true prayer.

See also Centering Prayer; Prayer of the Heart.

For Further Reading: V. Seelaus, *Distractions in Prayer* (2005); Teresa of Avila and D. Billy, *Interior Castle: The Classic Text with a Spiritual Commentary* (2007).

Allan Effa

Doddridge, Philip (1702–1751)

English Nonconformist minister and devotional writer. Born in London, Doddridge spent most of his pastoral ministry at Northampton. He devoted the afternoons to visiting and catechizing his congregation. His sermons were characterized by a combination of strong affectivity that was common to the seventeenth-century Puritans but also included an appreciation of the growing importance of reason. The influence of Richard Baxter is clearly evident, and Doddridge's theology reflects a moderate Baxterian Calvinism. His irenic spirit sought compromise and worked toward unity among Nonconformists, and his circle of friends included John Wesley, James Hervey, George Whitefield, the Countess of Huntingdon, Count Zinzendorf, and Isaac Watts. Doddridge played an active role in the evangelical revival of the 18th century and encouraged efforts in evangelism, mission, and assorted works of charity. He is equally remembered for the academy he created for training Nonconformist students, many who entered the ministry. He pioneered lectures in English rather than the traditional Latin and was recognized for his contribution to the study of mathematics. Watts encouraged Doddridge to write *The Rise and Progress of Religion in the Soul* (1745), for which he is best known. This devotional classic of spiritual maturity was instrumental in the conversion of William Wilberforce. It represents the best of experimental piety of earlier Puritans, and its wise and practical guidance can encourage contemporary readers to deepen their lives in Christ. Doddridge also produced the six-volume *Family Expositor* (1739–1756), which provided a biblical commentary for the laity. This indicates the importance he attached to family spirituality. He also encouraged the development of small groups for young men to further their spiritual growth. Monthly celebration of the Lord's Supper as well as hymns composed by Doddridge based on his sermon texts were central to his practice of public worship. Among the more popular hymns are "Hark, the Glad Sound! The Savior Comes," and "O Happy Day That Fixed My Choice."

See also Puritan Spirituality.

For Further Reading: M. Deacon, *Philip Doddridge of Northampton* (1980); G. F. Nuttall, ed. *Philip Doddridge* (1951); and I. Rivers, *Reason, Grace, and Sentiment*, vol. 1 (1991), 164–204.

Tom Schwanda

Dominican Spirituality

Dominican spirituality is the legacy of the followers of Dominic, founder of the Order of Preachers. While no simple formula can reproduce the creative diversity of Dominican life, the words of Pope Honorius III in his approval of the order (and reproduced in the first paragraph of the order's "fundamental constitutions") offer a helpful perspective. Honorius affirms that God "has inspired you to embrace a life of poverty and regular observance and to devote yourself to preaching the Word of God." This blend of the monastic and apostolic lives is what characterizes Dominican spirituality.

Excellent leaders and brilliant scholars explored the ideals of their founder in the centuries after Dominic's death. From the handful of followers at its inception, the order grew by thirteen hundred to around ten thousand friars. Men like Jordan of Saxony (d. 1237) and Humbert of Romans (1200–1277) attracted quality recruits and consolidated the order around fundamental values. Within their 1st century, one of their members was elected pope. As study was essential to the preaching vocation, early Dominicans were pioneers in theology. Dominicans founded the first religious college in Paris. Albert the Great (d. 1280) and Thomas Aquinas wrote their influential works as Dominican friars. While wars and pestilence plagued Europe in the 14th century, the Dominicans gave themselves to ministry and prayer. Dominicans played a central role in caring for numerous women's communities. Meister Eckhart, Heinrich Suso, Johannes Tauler,

Catherine of Siena, and many other mystics and spiritual writers identified with the Dominican tradition as they lived and expressed their relationship with God. As the New World opened up to exploration, Dominican preaching followed. Bartolomé de Las Casas (1484–1566) was an ardent advocate for the just treatment of native populations. His work *The Only Way to Draw All People to a Living Faith* (1534) is a masterpiece of sensitive missionary reflection. Dominican scholars were at the center of many debates of the early modern period. Thomas de Vio Cajetan (1469–1534) urged religious reforms at the Lateran Council of 1512 and argued with Martin Luther in 1518. Later, Dominicans were defenders of the Thomist position in the disputes with the Jesuits regarding Jansenism.

Dominicans in the modern centuries often expressed relationship with God in a spirit of restoration. Rose de Lima (1586–1617) poured herself out in prayer and service to the poor. After the French Revolution, Henri Dominique Lacordaire (1802–1861) drew huge crowds to Notre Dame Cathedral, inaugurated a new evangelization, and reestablished the Dominican Order on French soil. More recent examples of Dominican spirituality might include the open spiritual theology of Reginald Garrigou-Lagrange (1877–1964) or the ecumenical theology of Georges-Yves Congar (1904–1995). Dominican spirituality is lived especially in the communities of men and women who form the First and Second Orders of Preachers, along with the various forms of Third Order Dominicans and other associations and individuals who identify with the Dominican vision of life.

A few traits characterize Dominican spirituality. The most obvious trait is apostolic preaching. In a context where the religious were cloistered in monasteries, the clergy were tied to the service of a single church, and the populous were falling under the spell of heresy, the need was for apostolic proclamation. Dominican spirituality has its contemplative dimension, but it aims to share the fruits of this contemplation with others. Consequently, Dominican spirituality tends to be conscious of the presence of the world, sensitive to the seeker. Artists such as Fra Angelica (1400–1455) have often made use of a variety of media as vehicles for preaching, just as theologians like Lacordaire have taken pains to communicate the Christian message in the language and thought-world of the people.

If the outward thrust of preaching is the first characteristic of Dominican spirituality, the inward impulse of the community in prayer and study is the second. The Order of Preachers was not a missionary society. It was a *religious* order. Like the Canons Regular that form the roots of Dominican spirituality, their form of life was a community of clergy living under the guidance of a rule of life. Dominicans live in a common house. They gather periodically throughout the day (and night) to recite the prayers of the Divine Office, though they may be dispensed from prayers if preaching necessitates. Time for private prayer is scheduled. Dominic himself was known for his passionate and fully embodied prayers. The work of study is particularly cultivated, virtually replacing the role of manual labor found in other monastic communities.

A third characteristic of Dominican spirituality is its functional organization. Whereas its sister order, the Franciscans, might approach poverty from an ideological perspective, Dominicans have often seen their commitment to poverty as a form of identification with their audience or as a means of clearing themselves of unnecessary distractions to ministry. The Order of Preachers is also one of the most democratic of religious communities, flexible in its application of their regulations for the mission of the community.

The strengths of Dominican spirituality are also their weaknesses. An eagerness to incorporate the questions and ideas of the world has periodically led some near the boundaries of orthodoxy. And while for some an interest in study or in prayer may result in a narrow scholasticism or privatized mysticism, the flexibility of life and interaction with secular society has tempted others toward laxity. Dominican spirituality is lived best when each element has place to correct another.

See also Dominic de Guzman; Mendicant.

For Further Reading: B. Ashley, *The Dominicans* (1990); E. Borgman, *Dominican Spirituality* (2000); *Early Dominicans: Select Writings*, CWS (1982); W. Hinnebusch, *The History of the Dominicans*, vol. 1 (1966), vol. 2 (1973); P. Zagano and T. McGonigle, *The Dominican Tradition* (2006).

Evan B. Howard

Dominic de Guzman (c. 1171–1221)

Founder of the Order of Friars Preachers (O.P., the Dominicans), Dominic de Guzman was born in Caleruega, Spain. Around fourteen, Dominic went to Palencia where he studied liberal arts and theology. When famine struck, Dominic sold his possessions, distributing the proceeds to the suffering. After cathedral school, he served as canon regular in his native diocese of Osma.

In 1203 and 1205, Dominic accompanied Bishop Diego d'Acebes and witnessed firsthand the heresies in Italy and France. Albigenses had influenced many with their dualist faith, penetrating critique, and penitential lifestyle. Diego and Dominic, burdened by this situation, chose a strategy of incarnation; traveling on foot and begging their food, they preached the gospel from city to city. Dominic organized a community of women converts at Prouille. From 1207 until 1214, Dominic, under the direct commission of the church, preached throughout southern France. Though often the object of ridicule, Dominic's passion, austerities, and prayerful devotion impressed many.

In time, Dominic developed a formal religious order. In April of 1215, two men made a profession of formal commitment to Dominic, and soon thereafter he secured official approval for the Order of Preachers. Dominic's proposal was novel. His was to be a mobile monasticism, given to the work of preaching — linked to the church in doctrinal orthodoxy, clerical status, and religious observance, yet identified with the populous in voluntary poverty and open ministry. The Order of Preachers used the Rule of Augustine and adapted constitutions from the Premonstratensian canons as their foundational documents.

Dominic sent his followers throughout Europe to preach and establish communities of friars. Dominic devoted himself to visitation and official duties in Rome. He founded separate orders for women and for laity (the Second and Third Orders). In 1220 Dominic called the first general chapter of the order, which, along with the second in 1221, outlined a way of life that has been respected by religious observers for centuries. Dominic led a mission of brethren from a number of orders and died on August 6, 1221.

Outside of a single letter to a community of nuns, no writings of Dominic are known. Dominic's life has been a model of missionary zeal informed by prayerful study and austere living. His vision of an Order of Preachers birthed a missionary community that is active and undivided today.

See also Dominican Spirituality.

For Further Reading: W. Hinnebusch, *The History of the Dominican Order*, vol. 1 (1966); B. Jarrett, *Life of St. Dominic* (1964); F. C. Lehner, *Saint Dominic: Biographical Documents* (1964); S. Tugwell, ed. *The Nine Ways of Prayer of St. Dominic* (1978).

Evan B. Howard

Donne, John (1572–1631)

English poet, Anglican priest, and polemicist. Born in London into a staunchly Catholic family, Donne studied at Oxford University before training in the law at the Inns of Court. While working as a clerk to Sir Thomas Egerton, Lord Keeper of the Great Seal, the trajectory of Donne's life forever altered when he eloped with Egerton's teenage niece, Ann More (1601). Donne and his growing family spent many impoverished years on the social margins, triggering in Donne episodes of psychospiritual despair, to which his letters and work on suicide attest. Though the date of Donne's conversion from the Roman to the Reformed faith is not known, by 1610 he was composing antipapist polemic in support of the Oath of Allegiance, which required English Catholics to swear allegiance and obedience to James I rather than to the pope. In 1615 Donne agreed, with some hesitation, to take up employment in the Church of England, spending the remainder of his life as a priest, royal chaplain, reader in divinity, and eventually dean of St. Paul's.

Donne's religious writings, which include sonnets, hymns, sermons, essays, and devotions, reveal an ecumenical and synthesizing spiritual perspective. Donne adeptly weaves into these works elements of the Catholic and Protestant faith as well as dimensions of the sacred and the profane. It is certainly possible to unravel individual threads in Donne's religious poetry and prose, as many scholars have done in this century and the last. These efforts have at times proven profitable at tracing structures of thought and modes of discourse that inform Donne's spiritual vision. The impact, for example, of liturgical services, patristic principles, sacramental rituals, Catholic meditative methods, Calvinist theology, and mystical language on Donne's spiritual aesthetic have been examined in a series of studies. However, any orderly disentanglement and cataloging of influences runs counter to Donne's conception of the spiritual landscape he inhabits, in which the ideal church is figured as a promiscuous spouse, God a violent ravisher, a priest a hallowed hermaphrodite, and a deceased young girl a heavenly queen.

For all the dazzling wit, vigorous passion, and moral wisdom displayed in his richly textured religious texts, Donne often expresses an intense spiritual anxiety, especially in the face of death. He is all too aware of forces from within and without that threaten to undo the individual and the universe, the microcosm and the macrocosm. Donne is deeply conscious of his corrupt nature that entices him away from the divine will, just as he is acutely sensitive to the fragility of the fallen world with which he often associates infection, disease, fragmentation, dispersal, and decay. Nevertheless, spiritual angst is offset in Donne's writings by a deeply felt sense of divine sovereignty that guarantees ultimate coherence and meaning in this world and the next. This spiritual optimism is perhaps most evident in Donne's sermons, not surprising given his conception of the preacher as one who must "bring man to heaven, and heaven again to man."

See also Anglican Spirituality; Poetry and Poetics.

For Further Reading: T. DiPasquale, *Literature and Sacrament: The Sacred and the Secular in John Donne* (1999); *John Donne,* CWS (1990); J. Johnson, *The Theology of John Donne* (2001); A. Low, "Absence in Donne's Holy Sonnets: Between Catholic and Calvinist," *John Donne Journal* 23 (2004): 95 – 115.

Holly Faith Nelson

Dostoevsky, Fyodor (1821 – 1881)

Russian Orthodox novelist. A sociocultural prophet known for profound analyses of human psychological complexities and self-contradictions, Dostoevsky built on Christian gospel foundations from the universal human predicament of sin and evil to the mysterious transforming merciful power of God revealed supremely in the death and resurrection of the incarnate God-man, Jesus Christ. A pious Orthodox upbringing was temporarily supplanted by Enlightenment atheism, resulting in a traumatic mock execution, four years of prison camp, study of the NT, return to Christian faith, partial identification with organized Russian Orthodoxy, and a mature life exploring possibilities of genuine grace-initiated spirituality of repentance, humility, forgiving love and hope amid despairing doubts and evils of a changing world. In novels such as *Crime and Punishment, The Idiot,* and *The Brothers Karamazov,* Dostoevsky's subtle dialogical style forces readers to probe their own souls for the evils within and offers glimpses of transforming grace that enables freedom to repent and change. Method and content result in complexities of interpretation and explain Dostoevsky's impact on Nietzsche, existentialism, and spirituality in the Christian tradition represented by Dorothy Day and Karl Barth.

See also Russian Spirituality.

For Further Reading: P. Brazier, *Barth and Dostoevsky* (2007); M. Jones, *Dostoevsky and the Dynamics of Religious Experience* (2005); G. Pattison and D. Thompson, eds., *Dostoevsky and the Christian Tradition* (2001); R. Williams, *Dostoevsky* (2008).

Richard F. Kantzer

Doxology

The word *doxology* comes from two Greek terms, *doxa*, meaning glory, and *logos* meaning utterance or word. A doxology is a prayer of praise and affirmation offered to God. The Hebrew term most closely associated with doxology is *kabod*, which like *doxa* is most frequently translated into English as "glory." In the Hebrew, though, *kabod* can mean "weighty" or "of great value," referring to the worth of one's possessions. It can also have an interior or subjective meaning referring to an individual's authority or honor. When either *kabod* or *doxa* were used in reference to God, they conveyed a quality of holiness that was not implied when applied to human beings.

Kabod in the Hebrew Scriptures and *doxa* in the Septuagint were terms used to describe the response to the appearance of Yahweh in the theophanies of the OT. Whether it was Moses' response to God's self-revelation or the presence of God in the tabernacle or temple, the response given was doxology: praise to God for his holiness, justice, beauty, and awesome power. In the NT, Jesus was considered to be the perfect manifestation of God's glory. From Jesus' baptism by John, to his transfiguration, and ultimately in his resurrection and ascension, God's glory was evident in the face of Jesus Christ (2 Cor. 4:6). Empowered

by the Holy Spirit, we offer our doxology to God not only for Christ but *through* Christ who intercedes for us on behalf of the Father and who has already entered into his glory (Heb. 7:25; 13:15). This Trinitarian understanding is found in some of the earliest Christian prayers, such as the doxology that was attached to the Lord's Prayer in later versions of the gospel of Matthew and continues to be recited by Christians today.

The NT is full of doxological statements and prayers from the Canticles of Mary (Luke 1:46–56) and Simeon (Luke 2:29–32) to the doxological summaries and conclusions used by Paul in his epistles (cf. Rom. 8:38–39; 11:33–36; 16:25–27). It appears that their use of the biblical doxologies later grew into doxologies that were regularly part of Christian worship, both in daily prayer and in the liturgy of Word and Table on the Lord's Day. Notable among these are the *Gloria Patri* and the *Gloria in Excelsis*, which continue to have wide use to this day even in churches with little or no liturgical tradition. More important than their history is the theology they embody: that God alone is holy and reveals his holiness and glory in acts of justice and love. For this we give God alone thanks and praise.

See also Celebration; Lord's Prayer; Praise; Worship.

For Further Reading: N. Ayo, *Gloria Patri* (2007); G. Wainwright, *Doxology* (1980).

Todd E. Johnson

Dreams and Visions

Visionary experiences, whether occurring in a waking or a dream state, play a contested role in the history of Christian spirituality. Dreams are an important mode of divine communication in Genesis, figuring in the stories of Abraham (Gen. 15; 20), Jacob (Gen. 28; 46) and especially Joseph (Gen. 37; 40–41); indeed, Joseph not only received a sense of personal destiny through dreams but was also presented as a gifted interpreter of dreams (Gen. 40:8). The story of Moses, however, appears to offer a new approach to divine communication. With this great leader of Israel, dreams and visions were apparently unnecessary: "The LORD would speak to Moses face to face, as one speaks to a friend" (Ex. 33:11 TNIV).

This may provide something of a pattern. Matthew's gospel early recaptures the dreaminess of Genesis; Mary's fiancée, Joseph, like Joseph of old, received guidance in three distinct dreams (1:20; 2:13; 2:19), and even the pagan magi were warned about Herod in a dream (2:12). But Jesus—perhaps reminiscent, and clearly fulfillment, of Moses—presumably did not require divine communication through dreams. As Immanuel, "God with us" (1:23), Jesus himself *is* the divine communication (11:25–30). Even so, there is some gospel evidence of Jesus' own visionary experiences (Luke 10:18; John 1:47–50).

Since "in [Christ] the whole fullness of deity dwells bodily" (Col. 2:9 NRSV), suspicion of overreliance on visionary experiences is understandable; Colossians warns against people who, "puffed up without cause," insist upon "dwelling on visions" rather than "holding fast to the head" of the church, Jesus Christ (2:18–19 NRSV). Nonetheless, dreams and visions have figured largely in some Christian writings, particularly among those whose theological voices were otherwise discouraged or entirely silenced by ecclesiastical hierarchy. Thus, female mystics of medieval Christianity, most notably Julian of Norwich and Catherine of Siena, relied to some extent on claims of divine revelation through dreams and visions to substantiate their rich theological insights. At the same time, the degree to which such extraordinary experiences have historically functioned as validating criteria for holy people must be qualified. Usually visionary experiences alone have been insufficient to establish the credentials of people like Julian and Catherine. The medieval church was generally careful not to regard such experiences as, by themselves, signs of higher spirituality or a definitive form of authentication.

The Reformation's emphasis on the proclaimed Word and the Enlightenment's celebration of reason both undoubtedly discouraged religious reliance on dreams and visions, given their intuitive and radically subjective nature. However, in the last century, dreams and visions, embedded as they are in the Joel 2:28 prophecy fulfilled at Pentecost, have been important in Pentecostal and charismatic spirituality, where there is a relatively heightened expectation that they will function as conduits of important divine communication. With the rise of psychological analysis (including interpretation of dreams) in influential figures such as Sigmund Freud and Carl Jung, in the late 20th century there arose a broader, renewed appreciation for the spiritual potential in "dream work." This is instantiated in such writers as John Sanford, Urban T. Holmes III, and G. Scott Sparrow.

See also Mystery.

For Further Reading: K. Armstrong, *Visions of God* (1994); Julian of Norwich, *Showings*; A. Poulain, *Graces of Interior Prayer*, trans. L. Yorke Smith (1912); J. Sanford, *Dreams: God's Forgotten Language* (1989); P. Wiebe, *Visions of Jesus* (1998).

Michael Lodahl

Drummond, Henry (1851 – 1897)

Victorian polymath and one of the most popular religious figures of his era. Drummond combined a professorship in natural science at Glasgow Free Church College and research excursions to the American frontier, the South Pacific, and eastern Africa with itinerant evangelism to the working and upper classes, influential student missions at British and American universities, and enthusiastic involvement in children's ministry. *Natural Law in the Spiritual World* (1883) made him famous, although its attempt to reconcile evolution to Christianity by arguing that a single law of development pervades both the natural and spiritual spheres appeared to critics as spiritually problematic and scientifically dubious. Drummond's legacy rests chiefly on a bestselling devotional exposition of 1 Corinthians 13, *The Greatest Thing in the World* (1889). Its earnest tone, focus on Jesus as the embodiment of the

Father's love for humankind, and emphasis on practical Christianity perfectly suited the sentimental, non-doctrinal temper of late Victorian evangelicalism. But its winsome sincerity—his good friend Dwight Moody remarked that whereas some occasionally visited this biblical chapter, Drummond seemed to permanently dwell there—and attractive interpretation of the fruit of the Spirit as above all love, illustrated with concrete examples from Jesus' life and teaching, has kept it perennially popular.

See also Love.

For Further Reading: T. Corts, ed., *Henry Drummond* (1999).

Todd Statham

Dualism

Generally speaking, dualism is any system that identifies two modalities as ultimate and distinct. The complicating factor is that the term can denote a number of quite different binary distinctions. Two forms of dualism are particularly significant—the metaphysical and the anthropological. In metaphysical dualism, *all reality* involves two differentiated entities or beings. In anthropological dualism, *humans* consist of immaterial (mind, soul, or spirit) and material (body) aspects.

Both forms of dualism have implications for Christian spirituality. First, consider the fact that Christian spirituality is life *with* God. The very affirmation of such a divine-human *relationship* already implies a certain (valid) kind of metaphysical dualism. God really *is there* as one to whom humans must relate. He is not merely a projection of human imagination or ideals, but an irreducibly differentiated other. Humans stand in relation to this God and can become more like him in character and disposition but can never be absorbed into or become God. God exists in categorical distinction to all that is not God—that is, to everything and everyone else. For Christian spirituality, this inoculates believers against all forms of idolatry (because nothing else is worthy of worship because nothing else is God), and also fosters proper reverence and humility as people who have come to recognize and accept their own subordinate place in the universe.

While certain forms of metaphysical dualism (e.g., Daoism and ancient Manicheanism) see two ultimate realties as coequal, Christian theology emphasizes God's ultimacy and sovereignty. No other beings, and certainly not the powers of evil, are ever coequal with God. The universe is thus characterized by a definitive God-evil power *asymmetry* that unfortunately has not always been adequately appreciated by Christians, including some engaged in "spiritual warfare." The power imbalance in the cosmic conflict between God and Satan, good and evil, is the underlying rationale for Christian hope and the exultation that "God did not give us a spirit of timidity, but a spirit of power, of love and of self-discipline" (2 Tim. 1:7).

In the second place, there is anthropological dualism. Classically, philosophers defined "mind" as entirely immaterial and "body" as completely material. But then they struggled properly to reconnect these two aspects of human personhood. More biblically oriented thinkers see spirit and body as distinct, yet in tight relation. They are different realities, but they stand in a complex, dynamic, and profoundly interdependent relation. Anthropological materialists (mind-body monists), by contrast, reduce consciousness (and related spiritual experience) to a complicated, neurological brain state. Such a "brain-state" model of consciousness implies that all conscious experience can be predicted from physical variables and controlled by physical interventions. But by such an accounting of things a problem remains: What is responsible for the robust, unified, and perpetual *experience* of consciousness? Materialists struggle to offer a satisfactory account.

Anthropological dualists claim that a unity of consciousness and spiritual experience requires a spirit or mind. (They also say that an immaterial spirit unifies a person's identity. When a body dies and God resurrects the body, God does not create a new person. God gives a new body to "the same" person who continued to exist while the first body was dead.) This person, this spirit, relates to God. This personal relation of human spirit to divine Spirit, not just one's own inner consciousness, stands at the core of Christian spirituality.

Anthropological dualism helpfully preempts material determinism and keeps human transcendence alive. On the other hand, it can be vulnerable to disparaging the embodied dimension of reality, minimizing the holistic nature of spiritual life, and even trivializing the resurrection. If Christian spirituality is the human spirit connecting to the divine Spirit, it requires a carefully nuanced form of anthropological dualism. And if Christian spirituality is a real relationship with God, and not just an internal brain state or subjective spiritual experience, it demands the theological underpinning of a properly qualified metaphysical dualism.

See also Body; Incarnation.

For Further Reading: W. Hasker, *The Emergent Self* (1999); C. Taliaferro, *Consciousness and the Mind of God* (2005); D. Willard, *Knowing Christ Today* (2009).

David K. Clark

Dunnam, Maxie (1934 –)

United Methodist church planter, pastor, leader, author, and educator. Educated at the University of Southern Mississippi (B.S.) and Emory University (M.Th.), Dunnam started churches in Mississippi, Georgia, and California. He began writing devotionals for *The Upper Room* in 1973; later he was instrumental in the formulation of The Walk to Emmaus, a spiritual retreat and fellowship experience patterned after the Roman Catholic Cursillo movement. Dunnam returned to the pastorate for twelve years at Christ United Methodist Church in Memphis, Tennessee. In 1994 he helped to found the Confessing Movement within the United Methodist Church. That year he was named president of Asbury Theological Seminary in Wilmore, Kentucky; in 2004 he became chancellor.

Dunnam's most widely published book is *The Workbook of Living Prayer* (1974), in which he defined the goal of prayer as communion and friendship with God, and invited movement from specific prayer time to a life of prayer in which everything is related to God. The book, organized into six weeks of daily reading and interaction, was innovative in the way it incorporated private daily reflection with weekly group interaction. He followed with *The Workbook on Spiritual Disciplines* (1984), devised to lead the reader through the process of Christian growth. That *Workbook* is in ideological harmony with Richard Foster's *Celebration of Discipline*, published six years earlier. Lest anyone think spirituality is a matter of personal striving, *Alive in Christ* (1982) and *The Workbook on Becoming Alive in Christ* (1998) assert that fullness of being is the result of Christ dwelling in believers, and spiritual formation is the process of receiving that union. His writings also include the autobiographical *Dancing at My Funeral* (1973); coauthored *Mastering Personal Growth* (1992), on pastoral life; and *Irresistible Invitation* (2008), his latest workbook on spirituality.

T. C. Porter

Dunstan (c. 909 – 988)

One of medieval England's foremost religious and political reformers. Dunstan was born near Glastonbury into a wealthy and influential Anglo-Saxon family. He was educated by Celtic monks at the ruined Glastonbury Abbey and earned a reputation for piety, artistic ability, and scholarship. As a young man, he first served under his uncle Aethelm, archbishop of Canterbury, then in the court of King Aethelstan, where his ability and piety made him a target of intrigue and envy.

Dunstan made his profession as a Benedictine monk and was ordained priest c. 940. He was appointed abbot of Glastonbury in 943, where he rebuilt the abbey and restored monastic life. After a two-year exile in Flanders, he was recalled to England by King Edgar of Mercia and Northumbria. He was made bishop of Worchester and London in 957, then archbishop of Canterbury in 960, where he served until his death in 988.

Dunstan is remembered for three significant contributions to English church and society. First, he revived the monasteries in England, rebuilding their physical structures, establishing clergy education, and insisting on strict adherence to the Rule of St. Benedict. Second, he beautified the worship in churches, standardizing liturgy, writing music, and making ornaments. He himself was noted for casting bells and other metal objects for worship. Third, he influenced the politics of his time, serving as adviser and critic of several kings. He worked to bring about close ties between church and state, even writing much of the coronation liturgy still used for the English monarch.

For Further Reading: D. Dales, *Dunstan* (1988).

David Montzingo

Du Plessis, David (1905 – 1987)

South African Pentecostal/charismatic ecumenist. He was reared in the Apostolic Faith Mission of South Africa where he received Spirit baptism (1918), his first ordination (1928), and his ecumenical vision.

According to a prophecy from Smith Wigglesworth, Du Plessis would endure opposition and serve as a primary spokesperson for Pentecostal experience between establishment Pentecostals and mainline traditions (1936). Du Plessis moved to the United States in 1948, transferred to the Assemblies of God, and began a tumultuous ecclesial journey where ecumenical foresight led first to removal (1962) and eventual reinstatement (1980) of his credentials. Dubbed "Mr. Pentecost," he sought unity not only among fellow Pentecostals through service as inaugural organizing secretary for the Pentecostal World Conference (1949 – 1958), but also across traditional lines as a Pentecostal observer at the World Council of Churches (1948 – 1983), an ambassador at large at the Second Vatican Council, and the first cochair of the (International) Roman Catholic – Pentecostal Dialogue founded in 1972. Such efforts persuaded Pope John Paul II to confer upon him the prestigious Benemerenti Medal for exceptional service to the Catholic Church (1983). Du Plessis embodied Jesus' prayer for unity and proclaimed the "ecumenicity of the Holy Spirit" across long-established lines. In *The Spirit Bade Me Go* (1961) and *A Man Called Mr. Pentecost* (1977), Du Plessis situated his story among the historical currents of his day.

See also Pentecostal Spirituality.

Martin Mittelstadt

E

Eastern Orthodox Spirituality

See Chapter 19.

Eckhart von Hochheim, Meister (c. 1260 – c. 1329)

German Dominican priest, theologian, philosopher, and mystic. He was born near Erfurt in Thuringia and entered the Dominican order around age fifteen. He studied at the University of Paris and also in Cologne, and earned the degree of *meister*, meaning doctor of theology. He held many prestigious administrative and academic posts, including chair of theology at the University of Paris. Later he spent ten years in Strasbourg practicing the heart of his vocation, preaching. He also gave spiritual direction to Dominican nuns and to lay communities of Beguines, deeply devout women who lived together but took no formal vows. The Beguines were suspect by the church, and some were accused of heresy. Strasbourg was a center of Beguine activity, and Eckhart took inspiration from them and supported them.

Although he was an immensely popular preacher and enjoyed high status for most of his life, three years before his death he came under attack when the archbishop of Cologne accused him of heresy. He was tried, defended himself ably, but died before Pope John XXII (later tried for heresy himself) pronounced a verdict of condemnation on twenty-eight of his propositions. Nevertheless, his writings were preserved and continued to circulate widely among his many disciples, notably, Johannes Tauler and Heinrich Suso. Many of Eckhart's ideas form the basis of the anonymous *Theologia Germanica*. Tauler defended Eckhart in his sermons with the discerning observation that "their master" was misunderstood, because "he spoke from eternity . . . they took it as referring to time."

Eckhart is one of the most influential Christian mystics — and one of the most controversial. He attempted to express the highest metaphysical ideas of divine union in a daring way to simple laypersons, a primary reason the church censured his teachings. In his sermons, written in vernacular German, rather than Latin, he used bold and provocative language to deliberately startle his listeners and awaken them from their spiritual slumbers.

Eckhart described the spiritual journey in three primary ways: detaching, letting the soul become a "desert," an emptiness to make space for God; birthing, the "birth of the Word in the soul" (his favorite image); and breaking through, the "flowing-back" into the divine ground. He used the Neoplatonic scheme of procession and return, inherited from his Dominican teachers, Albert the Great and Thomas Aquinas, to develop what has been described as a "metaphysics of flow" — that all things flow from God in creation and flow back to God into the divine ground.

His theology of the "divine ground" and the "uncreated spark of the soul" are the most controversial aspects of his teaching. It is easy to see why some interpreters claim he so emphasizes unity with God that he obliterates the distinction between Creator and creature, leading to pantheism, such as when he writes, "The eye with which I see God is the same eye as God sees me." However, others claim he stands well within authentic Christian orthodoxy. But Eckhart's mysticism undoubtedly moves beyond the more traditional understanding of union with God as a loving union of two spirits (*unitas spiritus*) to a nondual mystical identity — "God's ground and the soul's ground is one ground." And to realize that transcendent union, he dared to say, in his audacious style of paradox and hyperbole, we must become detached even from God, "and so I ask God to rid me of God," that is, God as object, as cognition, as possession. Eckhart takes the apophatic to its highest degree, insisting we must break through into the "God beyond God."

In spite of his highly speculative, often abstract language, much of his teaching is focused on the concrete, real world of humble, ordinary people. By "detachment" or "spiritual poverty," he did not mean a withdrawal from the world; but finding God in all activities, "to be everywhere at home," which leads to compassionate service: "Even if a man were in a rapture like St. Paul, and knew a sick man who needed some soup from him, I should think it far better if you abandoned rapture for love."

Detachment is related to his idea of *sunder warumbe*, the heart of Ekhart's ethics: "living without a why," free from attachments, fears, constraints. He also writes of *jubilatio*, the joy of those who live in God and see God in all things. Typical of his sermons, which apply the metaphysical to the real, is this concluding appeal: "I say yet more, do not be startled, for this joy is near you and is in you. There is no one of you so crude, or so small in understanding or so removed, that he cannot joyfully and intelligently find this joy within him in the truth in which it exists, even before you leave this church today or before I finish this sermon today. He can as truly find it and live it and possess it within him as God is God and I am a man."

See also Detachment; *Theologia Germanica;* Union with God.

For Further Reading: O. Davies, ed., *Meister Eckhart: Selected Writings* (1994); A. Hollywood, *The Soul as Virgin Wife* (2001); B. McGinn, *The Mystical Theology of Meister Eckhart* (2001); B. McGinn and F. Tobin, *Meister Eckhart* (1986); *Meister Eckhart: Teacher and Preacher,* CWS (1984); *Meister Eckhart: The Essential Sermons, Commentaries, Treatises and Defense,* CWS (1981).

Carole Dale Spencer

Ecological Spirituality

Ecological spirituality covers an array of religious approaches that focus on the relationships between humans, the cosmos, the earth, and other living things. Interest in ecological spirituality has blossomed in recent decades in response to the ecological difficulties the world faces and the problematic nature of human behavior toward the natural world. A desire to reconnect with nature and a search for an ecological ethic has spawned a wide variety of ideas and beliefs. Broadly speaking, ecological spirituality includes such movements as Deep Ecology, Creation Spirituality, Gaia, the revival of ancient pagan beliefs and aboriginal religions, Eastern religions, mixtures of these, and much more.

Within the Christian tradition, an ecological spirituality has developed that respects Scripture and aligns with orthodoxy. This is a holistic approach that takes seriously God as Creator of all things and views the whole of human life as existing within the physical systems and biological communities of planet Earth. It accepts conventional paradigms of Christian spirituality but locates them in the context of our relationships with the earth and its creatures. It denies distinctions between "physical" and "spiritual," seeing *all of life* as comprising Christian spirituality. To put it concretely, things like cars, food, airplanes, bank accounts, buildings, animals, plants, and ecosystems are as much a part of human spirituality as prayer and worship. Therefore, connecting with nature and living in an ecologically sensitive and responsible way are seen as part of normal Christian spirituality. The remainder of this entry will address this "Christian" ecological spirituality.

Ecology concerns the relationships among living things and their environment. Ecological spirituality embraces these relationships, in addition to our relationships with God and other humans, as integral to daily spiritual life. Whatever view of human constitution we hold, we can see that humans *are* ecological beings. We are connected to, embedded in, and dependent upon the ecosystems of God's earth. For example, the oxygen we breathe and the food we eat come from other living things, and ultimately from the soil, from which even our bodies have been formed (Gen. 2:7).

Humans are made in the image of God (Gen. 1:27). Ecological spirituality suggests that, among other things, this means that humans represent God vis-à-vis the rest of creation. We are God's appointed caretakers of earthly creation (Gen. 2:15). This is our stewardship role from which grows an ethic of "creation care." Thus, vocationally Christian spirituality includes sensitivity to and care for God's creation and his creatures.

Ecological spirituality holds that human sin resulted in broken relationships, including the relationship between humans and the creation. The human-caused ecological degradation occurring in the world today is evidence of this. The reconciliation and healing afforded by the redemption of Jesus Christ includes the reconciliation and healing of our relationship with the nonhuman creation. Thus, a rekindling of our spiritual links with nature and changes in our ecological behavior that concretely demonstrate creation care are integral to the transformational aspect of Christian spirituality.

Evangelicals are careful to emphasize that ecological spirituality distinguishes between God and creation. God is worshiped, not creation or its creatures. Ecological spirituality is "theocentric." That is, it is centered on God. Our connection with nature connects us with God and motivates us to love God and neighbor (Matt. 22:37–40) by respecting and cherishing what God has made (Gen. 1:1) and belongs to him (Ps. 24:1). To love and enjoy God is to love and enjoy his creation.

Christologically, ecological spirituality sees Jesus as Lord of all of life, including our ecological life. Not only was he involved in creation (John 1:3), but he became flesh and dwelt within his creation (John 1:14). He became an "earth creature" as it were. Jesus' life exhibited ecological virtues such as simplicity and self-limitation. His death redeems not only humans but all things (Col. 1:20). The redemption of nature is connected to the redemption of humans (Rom. 8:19), so our eschatological vision is one of an embodied existence within a renewed creation (Rev. 21:1). Practically this means Christian spirituality embraces our physical existence and our connections with nature and anticipates the final healing of the whole world when Jesus comes again and establishes his kingdom on earth.

Christian ecological spirituality generally includes certain themes: (1) grateful embrace of the inherent goodness and value of the earth and its creatures (Gen. 1:31); (2) joy and wonder at the beauty and complexity of God's creation as exemplified by such Christians as Francis of Assisi; (3) a regard for nature as a vehicle of spiritual instruction and grace; (4) acknowledgment of the limits of humanity's place within the created order; (5) cultivation of ecological virtues such as humility, self-restraint, frugality, serenity, honesty, and hope; (6)

a "sabbath principle" that involves a slower pace of life, rest for people as well as animals and the land, and the just distribution of resources; (7) recognition that our own welfare and that of our descendants depends on the health of the earth; and (8) a responsibility to share resources with other people in the world.

Ecological spirituality holds that to be truly human is to be ecological, thus Christian spirituality is inherently physical and ecological. God's creation is a wonderful home. Generally, the effects of encounter with God include growing in Christlikeness and participating in the larger purposes of God. The larger purposes of God include our connection with and faithful care of his earth and his creatures.

See also Creation-Centered Spirituality; Liberation Spirituality.

For Further Reading: S. Bouma-Prediger, *For the Beauty of the Earth* (2010); W. Granberg-Michaelson, *A Worldly Spirituality* (1984); W. Jenkins, *Ecologies of Grace* (2008).

John Mustol

Ecstasy

In some traditions, ecstasy is a holy madness that channels divine energy for an experience that would be impossible through rationality. Religious anthropologists have traced the human experience of ecstasy common to enthusiastic movements in various religions, including Christianity, and seen this as a phenomenon that may be discerned even in the ancient prophetic texts of the OT. In this article, we will take our cue from Paul's words "The spirits of the prophets are subject to the prophets," and not elaborate on the anthropological dimensions of such experiences. Instead, we will consider Christian ecstasy in terms of being "directed toward the other" and as patterned for the church by the triune God himself. After all, true communion is possible only for those who "stand outside" themselves (*ecstasy* is from the Latin *ek-stasis,* "standing outside"). This dynamic is revealed in the human-directed love of God, who became flesh in Jesus and who poured out his Spirit on the church. As Irenaeus remarked in *Against Heresies,* the Son and the Holy Spirit are God's two hands, reaching out to embrace humanity. Intimacy with this holy God is possible because God is love, sharing intimacy within the persons of the Trinity, and because God delights to move out to us — to "stand outside" the Godhead ecstatically.

Such an ecstasy does not bypass the mind or the will, but comes out of an integrity and security that are the gifts of God. In John 1:1 the Son faces *pros ton theon*: "with" or "toward" God the Father. Out of the fullness of Father, Son, and Holy Spirit comes all human ability to "go out" toward others, including human others. Paul encourages his Corinthian friends: "Our heart is wide open. You are not restricted by us, but you are restricted in your own affections. In return (I speak as to children) widen your hearts also" (2 Cor. 6:11 – 13 ESV). Human ecstasy does not, then, come "naturally" to us, for we have been wounded by the fall, and we are complicit in the enmity that has arisen among human beings.

In God's economy, ecstatic action forges our healing. Though the fallen condition has caused a break between one human being and another and has put a brake on our confidence to go out to each other, we still desire communion. In Augustine's words, "You have made us for yourself, and our hearts are restless until they find their rest in you." Hampered by fear and hard-heartedness, humans rely wholly on God to make the way. And so in the incarnation, God identifies wholly with humanity, bringing us to him when we could not find the way. The sacrificial nature of ecstasy is revealed at the cross, where the suffering Savior addresses the needs of his mother, his disciples, and the stranger beside him. In response, his followers can say: "For to me, to live is Christ" (Phil. 1:21).

See also Charismatic Spirituality; Pentecostal Spirituality.

For Further Reading: A. Greeley, *Ecstasy* (1974); E. Humphrey, *Ecstasy and Intimacy* (2005); A. Schmemann, *For the Life of the World* (1973); M. Volf, *Exclusion and Embrace* (1996).

Edith M. Humphrey

Education

See **Chapter 33.**

Edwards, Jonathan (1703 – 1758)

Influential American Puritan theologian. He received his B.A. and M.A. at Connecticut's College/Yale; pastored churches in New York, Northampton (1724 – 1750), and Stockbridge (1751 – 1758) Massachusetts; led two revivals in the first Great Awakening (1734 – 1735 and 1740 – 1741); and became president of Princeton in 1758, but died shortly afterward of a botched smallpox inoculation.

Through his pastoral tenures and prodigious literary output, Edwards gained enduring status as one of America's premier theologians and shapers of evangelical Christianity. In sermons like "God Glorified in Man's Dependence" and the treatise *Freedom of the Will,* he presented rigorous and sophisticated defenses of Calvinism that continue to inspire evangelicals. His defense of Calvinism stood in contrast to the emerging Arminianism, which he believed undermined authentic religion by placing too much emphasis on human freedom and human potential for moral reform. Although he lacked the stage presence of George Whitefield, his treatises on revival (e.g., *A Faithful Narrative of the Surprising Work of God* [1737] and *Distinguishing Marks of the Work of the Spirit of God* [1741]) and genuine spirituality (e.g., *Religious Affections* [1746]) helped define central theological contours of American evangelicalism — revivalism, conversionism, and evangelism. Although he considered revival ultimately a supernatural work, he nonetheless encouraged the aggressive promotion of revivals by using emotional appeal as a homiletic strategy (e.g., the famous Enfield sermon, "Sinners in the Hands of an Angry God"). Central to his influence was the portability and adaptability of his theology. In Edwards's time, John Wesley utilized several of his works (e.g., *Affections*), with the most strident Calvinism edited out, and later, during the Second Great Awakening, nineteenth-century revivalists, such as Charles G. Finney, drew on him to inspire their use of "new measures," even though their methods may have departed from his Calvinist theology. Edwards's revival preaching confronted audiences with a gestalt of threat of immanent death and judgment before a holy and wrathful God, faith in Christ as the only escape from hell, and the need to forsake the world and yearn for heaven. He called for stringent spiritual standards, presaging the later Holiness movement, and focused and saw the greatest results among young people. Though he supported significant emotional manifestations, he maintained that the essence of authentic spirituality resides in "gracious affections" that spring from the Holy Spirit and that are most evident in sanctified living. His theology of the nature of religious experience became a source for the crisis-conversionist spirituality that arose in the Great Awakening and became the hallmark of the subsequent evangelical tradition and replaced the more introspective-conversion spirituality of Puritanism. Through the *Life of David Brainerd* (1749), which showcased Brainerd's missionary efforts among the Indians of the New England frontier, he produced a lasting archetype of unrestrained self-sacrifice and suffering for the sake of preaching the gospel that became the heartbeat of evangelical missions and evangelism.

Less familiar, but a vital contribution to contemporary spirituality, is Edwards's Trinitarian vision of redemption, which sees the Holy Spirit as the centerpiece of Christian spirituality. Drawing believers into the fellowship of the Father and the Son and the community of the saints, the Spirit transforms believers in the deepest dimension of their being, or what Edwards called the "soul's disposition." Edwards's phrase "principle of divine love" best captures the nature of the Spirit's transformative work. The Spirit's transformation of the soul's disposition bears the Spirit's personal identity. As the Spirit is the divine person who facilitates the loving fellowship between the Father and the Son, so the Spirit fires in the believer both love for Christ, the Father, and the neighbor. Christian spirituality is also Christlike. Since the Spirit unites the believer to Christ and the Father, all expressions of the Spirit's transformation will be consistent with the life and teachings of Christ. On the most practical level, many saw this in Jonathan Edwards' marriage to Sarah.

See also Affections; Reformed (Calvinist) Spirituality; Revival.

For Further Reading: C. Cherry, *The Theology of Jonathan Edwards* (1974); G. Marsden, *Jonathan Edwards* (2003); G. McDermott, ed., *Understanding Jonathan Edwards* (2009); S. J. Stein, ed., *The Cambridge Companion to Jonathan Edwards* (2007); idem, ed., *The Works of Jonathan Edwards* (1957–).

Steven M. Studebaker

Eliot, T(homas) S(tearns) (1888–1965)

Poet and literary critic. Raised in a prominent Unitarian family in St. Louis, Missouri, he moved to England after completing his studies at Harvard. In some of his early poems, such as "The Love Song of J. Alfred Prufrock" (1917) and "The Waste Land" (1922), Eliot showed himself to be, in the words of Harold Bloom, the master of "the mode of fictive hallucination and lyric derangement ... perfectly expressive of his age." His conversion to Christianity, culminating in his reception into the Church of England (1927), created a sharp divide in his work and its reception. The Bloomsbury group who had published and acclaimed his earlier work quickly distanced themselves. However, after his conversion, T. S. Eliot wrote some of his greatest works, including the play *Murder in the Cathedral* (1935) and the poems that are his culminating achievement, *The Four Quartets* (1939–1942).

According to biographer Lyndall Gordon, Eliot's spiritual pilgrimage began with a vision of transcendent beauty and harmony glimpsed during adolescence in a momentary transformation of an ordinary street in Boston; his quest through the mystics and catechetical instruction brought him to the realization that what humans can access by way of visionary experience "are only hints and guesses, / Hints followed by guesses; and the rest / Is prayer, observance, discipline, thought and action" (from his "Dry Salvages"). Eliot's critical essays brought renewed attention to previously marginalized seventeenth-century devotional poets and preachers, especially John Donne, George Herbert, and Lancelot Andrewes, writers who influenced both his style and his spiritual understanding. While Eliot's exceedingly troubled first marriage and his overt anti-Semitism (expressed in early poems and later renounced, but perhaps not as urgently as one would wish) remain as problems for the Christian reader, there is no doubt that Eliot's postconversion poetry as truly sounds the timbre of faith as his earlier poetry had captured the nuances of despair, rendering him a spiritual mentor to many readers who approach his work as marking out the path of a spiritual journey.

See also Poetry and Poetics.

For Further Reading: H. Bloom, *T. S. Eliot* (1985); J. X. Cooper, *The Cambridge Introduction to T. S. Eliot* (2006); T. S. Eliot, *The Complete Poems and Plays* (1969); H. Gardner, *The Art of T. S. Eliot* (1949); L. Gordon, *T. S. Eliot* (1998).

Maxine Hancock

Elliot, Elisabeth (1926–)

Writer, preacher, radio and conference speaker, missionary. Elizabeth Howard (sister of evangel-ical-turned-Catholic writer Thomas Howard and great-niece of Charles E. Trumbull, editor of the *Sunday School Times*, a "Victorious Life" holiness advocate who was particularly influential in the fundamentalist movement of the 1930s) was born to missionary parents in Belgium but raised in Philadelphia and New Jersey. Elisabeth studied classical Greek at Wheaton College where she met her first husband, Jim Elliot. After Jim and four others were speared to death in 1956 by an unreached jungle tribe in Ecuador, Elisabeth told the story of their martyrdom in her bestselling book, *Through Gates of Splendor* (1957). The book both reflected and stimulated the evangelical ideal of inspirational missionary heroism, ultimate sacrifice, and eternal reward.

Though her fundamentalist theology calls for the prohibition of women in ministry leadership, Elisabeth herself nonetheless served freely as a missionary leader among the Auca Indians who killed her husband. Given her family history, her tragic widowhood, her giftedness and discipline, she emerged as a major voice among conservative evangelicals and fundamentalists. She preached in many venues (even on Sunday mornings) and wrote more than twenty books, sharing her testimony and deep meditations on Scripture. In 1969 she married Addison Leitch, professor of Gordon-Conwell Seminary (d. 1973). In 1977 she married Lars Gren. Her writings include *These Strange Ashes* (1975), *Let Me Be a Woman* (1976), *The Mark of a Man* (1981), *Passion and Purity* (1984), and a biography of Amy Carmichael entitled *A Chance to Die* (1987). Her daily radio show, *Gateway to Joy*, aired from 1988 to 2001. She and Lars retired in 2005.

Sarah Sumner

Ellul, Jacques (1912–1994)

French theologian and critic of technological society. Jacques Ellul had a wide and diverse life, serving in capacities from French Resistance leader during World War II (in which role he worked to save many Jews and was awarded the title Righteous among the Nations) to law professor and sociologist, and finally to Christian writer and theologian. After being a student of Marxism, he came to faith in Christ at age twenty-two. Although a member of the small Reformed Church of France, he rejected Calvinism largely because of the limitations he felt this placed on the freedom of both God and humans. However, Ellul also rejected the influences of philosophical idealism, romanticism, and natural theology. For this reason, many include him in the camp of the neoorthodoxy movement of the mid-20th century.

Ellul is most well known for his writings on the subject of technology and its relationship to faith and to humanity. Ellul uses the term *technique* as a word that encompasses all the modernizing, nonpersonal forces that manifest themselves in society. Technique has as its highest value efficiency, and efficiency brings with it the various systems that work to dehumanize, even as the hand of human beings operate these systems. Thus, for Ellul technology and technique are not good or even neutral; they are demonic powers, creating world systems that destroy human life, human relations, and human freedom. Ellul sees these world systems encapsulated in the idea of the city, which he sees biblically as the height of rebellion against God, going so far as to say, "The city is the direct consequence of Cain's murderous act and his refusal to accept God's protection."

Ellul's theology has implications for how Christian spirituality is lived out in a technological and metropolitan world. Embracing technology and efficiency without reflection on their implications for our humanity and the humanity of our neighbor, can be not only dangerous but also evil. The city, with its depersonalizing forces and technology, seeks to replace our neighbor with objects that empower us. The spiritual challenge for those who inhabit cities and use technology is not to allow the quest for efficiency to replace relationships or make us unwilling to love God and neighbor in self-sacrificing ways. Ellul's many writings include *The Presence of the Kingdom* (1948).

See also Technology and Spirituality; Urban Spirituality.

For Further Reading: D. J. Fasching, *The Thought of Jacques Ellul* (1981); C. Ringma, *Resist the Powers with Jacques Ellul* (1994).

Christopher Morton

Emotions

Emotions are a universal language of the heart that reflect our judgments and evaluations of objects and situations. They are often manifested in our nervous systems and expressed through our bodies as "feelings." Emotions fill almost every page of Scripture. Not only do we hear from the lips of Jesus that loving God and others are the greatest commandments, but we also see the agony and ecstasy of the Psalms, we hear of the love of and delight in his children felt by God the Father, and in many passages in Paul's epistles we feel his emotional pleas. These are simple facts; our question is how to interpret and judge the relevance of the emotions portrayed throughout Scripture.

Our understanding of what role emotion should play in our spiritual formation hinges on how we relate emotions to our minds and thinking. A rationalistic tradition, following a long line of philosophers including Plato, Descartes, William James, and Darwin, has argued that emotion and reason are two very separate systems. In simplified terms, the higher, better person is controlled by reason and logic. Emotions, in this view, are, at best, distractions, and, at worst, animal passions that wage war against our better nature.

Many theologians and Christian philosophers from the church fathers onward have followed this philosophical viewpoint. This has contributed to a downplaying or denial of God's emotion (God's emotions in the text are treated as anthropomorphisms); defining love, joy, and hope as theological constructs rather than emotions we are meant to feel and pursue; the ideas that faith is based on fact not feeling and that ethics are primarily about what we do (Kant); and the general downplaying of emotion in the text of Scripture. In this view, spiritual formation is primarily about what we know about God — having right theology — and how we behave. Emotions are likely to be seen as confusing or a sign of weakness in many situations.

There is, however, mounting evidence to support a different approach. Studies in logic are showing us that emotion is actually based on thinking and judgments and cannot be classified as a system separate from reason. Neurology is finding that a person who loses emotional function also loses reason and logical decision-making abilities. Psychological studies are showing that emotions are high brain functions that give us windows to see thoughts and ideas; they are not lower impulses or mere reflex reactions. In biblical studies, we need to be very careful about going beyond the simple meaning of the text. Is there anything in the text itself that allows us to think, for example, that love for neighbor is a theological concept or command of action that can in any way be divorced from feelings?

Philosophers in this tradition take their lead from Aristotle, who argued that how an individual feels is an important part of his or her ethics and morality. Important Christian theologians, including Thomas Aquinas, Jonathan Edwards, and John Wesley, agreed, making the cultivation of particular emotions central to the process of sanctification and spiritual formation. Emotional tendencies and dispositions are seen as an accurate gauge of spiritual growth, so that to grow more like Christ is to actually feel more love for God and love for neighbor as the years pass. The believer's emotions will change with both his or her situation and growth in Christ. For example, the mature Christian is to weep with those who weep in times of tragedy; to feel another's pain as his or her own is a part of being in God's family.

This is not, in any sense, a view that downplays study, theology, or the role of Scripture. Rather, we learn that emotional tendencies, being built on and flowing out of our values, beliefs, and thinking, must be formed and molded by drilling deep for ourselves into the knowledge and wisdom of God. Both emotional and spiritual maturity are built when stated beliefs and theological constructs become heart-held truth in the tradition of the Bible's ideas of heart-knowledge and wisdom. It is only in doing this that we can keep the greatest of God's commands that will give us life — commands like "love your enemies" (Matt. 5:43) and "rejoice in the Lord always" (Phil. 4:4).

See also Affections.

For Further Reading: G. Clapper, *John Wesley on Religious Affections* (1989); M. Elliott, *Faithful Feelings* (2006); W. Lyons, *Emotion* (1980); M. Nussbaum, *Upheavals of Thought* (2001); R. Roberts, *Spiritual Emotions* (2007); Thomas Aquinas, *Summa Theologiae*, vol. 19, trans. E. D'Arcy (1967).

Matthew A. Elliott

Endo, Shusaku (1923 – 1996)

Renowned twentieth-century postwar novelist and most popular and widely read Christian writer in Japan. Rather than simplistically sermonizing, Endo has his characters work through the uncomfortable challenges of faith that present no easy solutions. Endo provides a penetrating analysis of the conflict that arises within the beautiful and monstrous duality of the human person living at the mercy of forces beyond control. Endo's Christian message is one of radical grace. His protagonists are weak, powerless, duplicitous, conflicted apostates and moral outsiders who encounter God's grace. Endo points to the two founders of the Christian church: Peter, who denied Jesus three times, and Paul, who persecuted the church. Jesus has no words of resentment to those who desert and betray him but instead prays for their salvation. In *A Life of Jesus* (1978), Endo adapts the Christian message to Japanese culture by representing Jesus rather as the Suffering Servant than the more Western emblem of power and majesty. He emphasizes the mother-love of God, which he finds more appealing to the Japanese psyche that inordinately centers on failure and shame. Provocatively, Jesus became "a miserable dog" in order to fulfill the deepest primordial longing of our hearts for someone who will never leave us or betray us.

See also Asian Christian Spirituality.

For Further Reading: E. Mase-Hasegawa, *Christ in Japanese Culture: Theological Themes in Shusaku Endo's Literary Works* (2008); M. Williams, *Endo Shusaku: A Literature of Reconciliation* (1999).

André Ong

English Mystics

The five-hundred-year period between 1000 and 1500 in England is marked by a tremendous output of mystical writings and treatises on spiritual direction; many of these are still read today as resources for the spiritual life. Within this period of prolific output, there was a stretch when some of the greatest spiritual writings of all time were written, and not simply British writings. Between 1300 and 1500, texts were written by Richard Rolle; the author of the anonymous *Cloud of Unknowing* and related works; Walter Hilton, who wrote the classic *The Scale of Perfection*; and Julian of Norwich, who wrote the first book written in English by a woman. It is often these last four that are referred to as the English mystics, though in some cases the entire five-hundred-year output is referred to.

These four authors shared very little in common except their attempt to make sense of their faith while living in very difficult times. From 1337 to 1453, England and France were waging the Hundred Years' War, leaving scores dead in Britain. Famine and disease were more common than adequacy and health, and political and religious scandals were com-

mon. Most notable were the Peasants Revolt of 1381 and the two rounds of the Black Plague between 1348 and 1361 that some estimate killed half of the population. These authors each in their own way offered spiritual counsel to help the people maintain their faith in God in these challenging times.

Although their context was similar, their theologies were divergent, often writing criticisms of their predecessors, such as Hilton's critique of Rolle. Yet there are enough similarities to group these writers and writings together. First and foremost, they are unique among spiritual writings, inasmuch as they are all written to other individuals by authors who were living in solitude. Second, they all wrote in the vernacular (English). Although both Rolle and Hilton knew Latin, they all chose to write in English, as it would give their writings a broader audience among the common folk. Third, all of them write from their experience in testimonial style, offering personal and accessible spiritual advice. Last, they all address the basics of the spiritual life with directness and practicality. Theirs were neither metaphysical nor theological treatises primarily—though they were not without their highly developed concepts and beliefs—but were personal introductions to the spiritual life against the backdrop of the realities of our fallen world. For this reason Christians continue to turn to them for spiritual guidance.

See also *Cloud of Unknowing, The;* Julian of Norwich; Rolle, Richard.

For Further Reading: O. Davies, *God Within* (1988); J. Gatta, *Three Spiritual Directors for Our Time* (1987).

Todd E. Johnson

Enlightenment

The Enlightenment is an era, roughly the 18th century, in which the transition from premodernity to modernity reached critical mass among the cultured elites in Western societies. Central to this transition were major shifts in epistemology, anthropology, and theology, along with changes in attitudes toward authority and toward social institutions (especially church and monarchy).

Before the Enlightenment, many in Europe looked to tradition for truth about God, personal life, and human society. Beginning with the intelligentsia in the Renaissance, people in Western societies gradually turned to reason, rather than tradition, to guide their thinking.

Enlightenment thinkers began their story of Western civilization by glorifying the cultural brilliance of the ancient pagans. Then Christian culture of the medieval period—the "Dark Ages"—extinguished this brilliant light. Revealed theology, rooted in divinely inspired sacred texts, prevented new thinking and inhibited verifiable scientific knowledge. These forces caused cultural darkness and blocked social progress.

Against this backdrop, proponents of the Enlightenment reclaimed pagan sources to promote a new era of natural reason, human goodness, individual freedom, scientific truth, cultural progress, and social optimism. This does not mean that the Enlightenment was entirely antireligious. Rather, for many, natural religion replaced revealed religion. Defenders of natural religion embraced science. They believed in a Creator who designed the universe. But the Creator was not active in the lives of devoted believers. Enlightenment thinkers marginalized traditional belief and practice. They disbelieved in an active, living, spiritual being named God. They largely interpreted religion and spirituality in ethical terms.

Christians reacted against the Enlightenment in several ways. Some took refuge in anti-intellectualism. They focused on literal approaches to the Bible and traditional practices, such as prayer and church attendance. Others accommodated the modern spirit. They argued that religious apologetics, for example, could demonstrate the truths of revealed religion according to the high standards of evidence required by Enlightenment thinkers.

Neither response effectively surmounted the negative impact of the Enlightenment on spirituality.

By the end of the 19th century, Enlightenment perspectives permeated the religious climate among the influencers of culture in the West. In the centers of intellectual, political, or social influence, few believed that one could enjoy a vital spiritual connection with a living and active God. The low ebb of historical Protestant spirituality came in the early 20th century when those holding mainline perspectives marginalized traditional believers. Fortunately, the last two generations have witnessed a renewal of historic faith, as seen in the explosive global growth of the evangelical movement, which has gradually begun reversing the stifling effects of the Enlightenment on Christian spirituality.

See also Extraordinary Phenomena; Modernity; Secularization.

For Further Reading: G. Craig, *Reason and Authority in the 18th century* (1964); B. Young, *Religion and Enlightenment in Eighteenth Century England* (1998).

David K. Clark

Envy

Envy is one of the seven "deadly sins" defined as sorrow for another's good that is perceived as one's own evil (Aquinas). It is the pain we feel when we perceive another individual possesses some object, quality, prosperity, praise, or status that we desire but do not possess, *and* we begrudge it to the one who has it. Though often used as a synonym, envy is different from jealousy, which occurs when one worries about *being* dispossessed of something or someone valued. It differs from greed, which does not necessarily seek to dispossess the other of what is desired. It also differs from the positive act of emulation with which we applaud another for something we would like to be or have.

Scripture warns against envy (Job 5:2; Prov. 3:31; 23:17; 24:1; 27:4; Rom. 1:29; 1 Peter 2:1). It has been linked with the first homicide in the Bible (Gen. 4:2–8), Saul's pursuit of David (1 Sam. 18:7–9), the motives of those who delivered Jesus to Pontius Pilate (Matt. 27:18), and the major cause for international conflicts, civil strife, and interpersonal conflicts (1 Tim. 6:3–5; Titus 3:3; James 3:16). It is disapproved of in all the major religious and philosophical traditions.

Envy involves an unfavorable comparison of ourselves with another who is like us in talent, time, place, rank, and the like. It is sinful, because we grieve over what should make us rejoice — namely, our neighbor's good. This also makes it a despicable vice so that we hide it until it manifests itself in injurious ways. It causes more unnecessary pain to the envier than to the envied. Ultimately, it reproaches God who sovereignly bestows good gifts to whom he wills.

Of all the "deadly sins," Cassian observes that envy is the most difficult to cure because we hide envy from view out of shame and we envy the one whose insight and wisdom we need to cure us of envy. Those who are aware of and admit their envy should then understand how ridiculous envy is in that it hurts them without improving their situation; reassess their values and what makes for human worth; consider that what they envy in others may be due to hard work or God's gifting; and develop countermeasures, such as training themselves to look for and celebrate the positive in others. In the end, practicing Philippians 2:3 is the ultimate prescription.

See also Sins, Seven Deadly.

For Further Reading: J. Cassian, *The Institutes*, trans. B. Ramsey (2000); D. Okholm, "Envy: The Silent Killer," in *The American Benedictine Review* 59, no. 2 (2008): 121–40; Thomas Aquinas, *Summa Theologiae*, 2.2 Q 36.

Dennis Okholm

Ephrem the Syrian (c. 306–373)

Influential and prolific Syrian hymnologist. Few facts are certain, but we do know Ephrem was born and raised in the Mesopotamian city of Nisibis. His family members were Christians during the time of Constantine and embraced the Nicene Creed, yet in 361 they were forced to flee persecution to Edessa. Later biographies mistakenly portrayed him as an ascetic monk shunning society as he composed hymns for worship. In fact, he served the church and community by teaching theology and leading several choirs; and like Joseph in Egypt, he protected the entire community from famine by wise counsel and political leadership. He ultimately died as a result of caring for plague victims in Edessa.

His legacy includes biblical commentaries, prose essays on theological topics, and most important, poetry and hymns of exquisite beauty. Ephrem composed in Syriac (similar to Aramaic), yet during his lifetime his works were translated into many languages, both Eastern and Western. Jerome lauded the beauty and theological soundness of his work, and Ephrem's influence continued into the Middle Ages and beyond. His hymns are still sung today in the Syrian Orthodox Church.

While many ascribed their own verse to Ephrem, we have numerous hymn cycles that are authentic. Their structure is unique, the language is powerful and creative, and the theology is both sacramental and incarnational, seeing God's presence in all the vagaries of this world. Those who yearn for symbolism that is yet rooted in biblical truth will find Ephrem a trustworthy guide. He did not want "to impose his own ideas of the Christian message … but rather to give birth in God's creatures to that true worship of the Creator of all" (Matthews). It was said his hymns acted as sheepdogs, guarding God's flock from heresies (Acts 20:29).

See also Hymns; Syrian Spirituality.

For Further Reading: S. Brock, *Luminous Eye: The Spiritual World Vision of Saint Ephrem* (1992); *Ephrem the Syrian: Hymns*, CWS (1989); E. Matthews Jr., "St. Ephrem: Madrasê on Faith," in *St. Vladimir's Theological Quarterly* 38, no. 1 (1994): 45–72.

Kelby Cotton

Epistemology of Spirituality

Christian spirituality is the condition or state of living *all* of life before God, through Christ, in the transforming power of the Holy Spirit. It can include special mystical experience of the presence or voice of God, but it also includes more familiar experiences of practices, such as prayer, reading of Scripture, worship, repentance, moral renewal, service, and Christian witness. The epistemology of spirituality concerns the ways of knowing or rationally believing or having appropriate (even if uncertain) faith that arises out of Christian spirituality so understood.

We will begin by considering some ways of classifying our belief-forming practices more generally and then applying that classification to the epistemology of Christian spirituality. Notice, first, that some of our beliefs are formed by inference (from other beliefs) while others are noninferential. For example, if you walk into your kitchen and see bits of jam and bread on the counter, you infer from your beliefs about the mess on the counter that a family member has recently had a jam sandwich. But when you believe you have a throbbing headache, this belief is noninferential (i.e., not inferred from other beliefs); instead, it is based solely on the experience of pain you feel in your head. Second, we can see that although our noninferential beliefs are based on our experiences (and not inferred from our other beliefs), there are many different kinds of experience on which they can be based. Perceptual beliefs are based only on sensory experiences, whereas introspective beliefs about how one feels can be based on experiences of pain or pleasure or emotions. Memory beliefs are based on "memory seemings" — that is, experiences of seeming to you that you recently did this or that; and simple logical or mathematical beliefs are based on "logical/mathematical seemings" — that is, experiences of seeming to you that some simple logical or mathematical claim is true (e.g., that $2 + 2$ must be 4, that a proposition can't be both true and false).

Beliefs produced in the process of living all of life before God can be similarly classified. Some are noninferential and others are inferred; and those that are noninferential can be based on experiences of different kinds. Using this classification, we can identify three ways in which beliefs arise out of Christian spirituality: two noninferential ways (that differ from each other in the kind of experience on which the belief is based) and one inferential way.

The first way is for noninferential beliefs to be based on special mystical experiences of the presence or voice of God. In these cases, God seems to be presented to one's consciousness through an awe-inspiring mystical experience as convincingly as physical objects seem to be presented to one's consciousness through sensory experiences. Beliefs formed in this way are typically about God's qualities (e.g., that God is loving or terrifying or overwhelmingly holy) or about what God is currently doing vis-à-vis the person holding the belief (e.g., comforting, guiding, strengthening).

The second way depends on the more familiar experiences involved in living all of one's life before God. The experiences on which these noninferential beliefs about God are based are more like the "seemings" on which we base our memory beliefs or our simple mathematical or logical beliefs. There are many different triggers for these religious seemings. A feeling of guilt might trigger the seeming that God is displeased with you, and on the basis of that seeming you might believe that God is displeased with you. Likewise, upon repentance, you might have a sense of relief that triggers the seeming (and belief) that God has forgiven you. In countless other ways, living one's life before God can trigger religious seemings that form the experiential basis for a multitude of beliefs about God — beliefs that God is present in corporate worship or the Eucharist or private prayer, beliefs that God is speaking to one through the Scriptures or church tradition or the words of a friend or a sermon, beliefs that God wants one to take some specific course of action, beliefs that God has been guiding one's life in specific ways or that God will work things out for the best. These religious seemings can be firm and compelling or merely subtle hints that don't give rise to strongly held beliefs.

The third way for beliefs to arise out of Christian spirituality is inferential. Here one starts with beliefs about the religious experiences people have reported (experiences like the ones mentioned above) and considers various explanations of these reported experiences, including Freudian and other nontheistic explanations as well as traditional religious explanations.

Upon careful consideration of these options, one then judges that some traditional religious explanation is the best explanation (determining which is best by appeal to the standard explanatory virtues) and infers that the religious explanation, with all it says about God and his dealings with us, is true. This is, in effect, to employ an argument from religious experience.

Philosophers writing on the epistemology of religious belief have critically reflected at great length on each of the above three ways in which beliefs can arise out of the experience of living all of one's life before God. For most of the 20th century, discussion of these matters has focused on the third way having to do with arguments from religious experience (e.g., Swinburne). But recently — and partly because of the concern that it is far from obvious whether a theistic or a nontheistic explanation of religious experience is best — the discussion has shifted to the two noninferential ways mentioned above of forming religious beliefs on the basis of experiences arising out of Christian spirituality. Because these noninferential religious beliefs are explicitly based on experiences (either special mystical experiences or more ordinary religious seemings), they are often viewed as too subjective and arbitrary to provide objectively good evidence for such beliefs. Critics have also objected that religious experiences (whether mystical or more ordinary) are without evidential value for any particular religious tradition, such as Christianity, given that they can be found in support of many different and incompatible religious traditions. But prominent philosophers have argued that, despite the concerns highlighted in these objections, beliefs based on special mystical experiences can be formed and made rational in much the same way that ordinary perceptual beliefs are (Alston) and that beliefs based on religious seemings can be as rational as beliefs based on memory seemings or logical/mathematical seemings (Plantinga).

See also Faith.

For Further Reading: W. Alston, *Perceiving God* (1991); A. Plantinga, *Warranted Christian Belief* (2000); R. Swinburne, *The Existence of God* (1979).

Michael Bergmann

Erasmus, Desiderius (c. 1466 – 1536)

Christian humanist. Erasmus was the best known and arguably the most influential of the Christian humanists active during the period of the Protestant Reformation. A man of great intelligence and sharp wit, he desired to use his varied skills to serve the cause of Christ. Living much of the time in England, though traveling to Europe and especially to Italy to meet with other humanists, he wrote extensively on philosophy and theology. He is considered by many to be the first person to make a living solely through writing, which was made possible by his prolific writing and the advent of the printing press.

The humanists of Erasmus's era sought to strip away accretions to early church practice and the overly philosophical veneer of Christian theology. Instead, they wanted to return to a pure faith with an emphasis on good rhetoric and sound practice. Erasmus tried to reclaim the spirituality of the earliest Christians by reading the Scriptures for their plain meaning, praying simple prayers, and seeking to embody a life of faith that all Christians could practice. For him it was not so much the philosophy of Aristotle that mattered, as it had during the Middle Ages, but "the philosophy of Christ."

Many consider his most important work to be his edition of the Greek NT and his translation of that text back into the Latin of the scholarly community. This text was used extensively by the Reformers. Erasmus longed to see the church of his day reformed, as did many humanists, because of its excesses that took the Christian faith away from its roots, or what he called "primitive Christianity." In this he initially found an ally in Martin Luther, but he broke with Luther after their Leipzig debate of 1519, and instead sought to reform the Roman Catholic Church from within. The question of free will in particular divided Erasmus from Luther, with Erasmus defending the concept of freedom. Erasmus's focus on using scholarship to nurture a faithful living out of primitive (that is, NT) Christianity continues to inform many Christians today. He brought together the ideals of loving God with one's whole heart and one's whole mind.

See also Humanism; Will, Human.

For Further Reading: R. Bainton, *Erasmus of Christendom* (1969); R. DeMolen, *The Spirituality of Erasmus of Rotterdam* (1987); J. Huizinga, *Erasmus and the Age of Reformation* (1957).

Christopher Morton

Eriugena, John Scotus (c. 810–877)

Philosopher and theologian who laid a foundation for the widespread apophatic spirituality of the later Middle Ages through his translation of the Pseudo-Dionysian corpus and several works of Maximus the Confessor and Gregory of Nyssa, as well as his commentary on Dionysius's *Celestial Hierarchy*. Following these Greek fathers, Eriugena maintained that God is superessential and that our direct knowledge of the divine is limited: we understand God best by knowing what he is not. He coined the Latin terms from which we derive *kataphatic* and *apophatic*.

Born in Ireland, Eriugena was made head of the palace school of Charles the Bald. In his summa, *Periphyseon,* or *The Division of Nature*, Eriugena sought to harmonize the biblical doctrine of creation with Neoplatonic emanation, asserting that all things exist in God through their "idea" form (see Eph. 1:4) and then manifest in physical existence through the Word. All of creation is a theophany, revealing God's goodness and glory (Rom. 1:20). Ultimately everything will return to God, multiplicity will flow into divine unity, and we will be made godly (deified) by grace. Such a return is possible only through the Word incarnate, as Christ unites created substance with uncreated being.

Quite complex, Eriugena's thought has been misunderstood by many. His great contribution is his impact on later spiritual writers, including the Victorines, Bonaventure, Thomas Aquinas, the Rhenish mystics, the author of *The Cloud of Unknowing*, Nicholas of Cusa, and John of the Cross.

See also Apophatic and Kataphatic Ways; Pseudo-Dionysius.

For Further Reading: D. Carabine, *John Scottus Eriugena* (2000); *Eriugena's Commentary on the Dionysian Celestial Hierarchy*, trans. P. Rorem (2005); B. McGinn, *The Growth of Mysticism* (1994).

Glenn E. Myers

Eschatology

See Chapter 11.

Ethics and Morality

Ethics and *morality* are terms used synonymously to describe standards of goodness and prescribe codes of conduct. Morality encompasses values and commitments that are descriptive of what one believes about what is good, just, virtuous, and right.

Ethics provides the tools and resources by which one thinks about moral beliefs and raises questions pertinent to particular issues. Ethics involves deliberating over options and possible outcomes and putting moral obligations into practice by prescribing attitudes and behavior based on what one believes about what one should do.

Ethics and morality have important theoretical and practical dimensions in that what one believes about what is good ought to translate into attitudes and practices that reflect one's moral commitments. Three main theories of ethics are deontology, teleology, and virtue ethics. Deontology is the study of duty or obligation that grounds ethical behavior in rules to obey. Teleology stresses outcomes, consequences, and ends of decisions and actions, seeking to minimize harm and facilitate greater good for more people. Virtue ethics stresses the character formation of persons and the development of moral attributes that will guide decisions and behavior.

These theories, while helpful for organizing various aspects of morality and assisting in ethical deliberation, do not fully reflect the spiritual, theological, and communal dimensions of Christian ethics. For persons of faith, an important source of morality and ethical conduct is belief in God. This is true for Christians who rely on the particular claims and sources of Christian tradition to guide how they live. Belief in the Trinitarian God of Christian faith provides the authority for and gives shape to the moral life (Hollinger). God the Father is the source of moral goodness and excellence (2 Peter 1:3–4). God is perfectly just, righteous, holy, merciful, loving, and compassionate. God is pure in motives and purposeful in superintending the creation to fulfill God's intentions for the world. God possesses moral qualities that establish the standards to which humans should aspire. Jesus Christ is the example and norm of moral goodness. As the "image of the invisible God" (Col. 1:15), Christ reveals the character of God to humankind by demonstrating compassion, mercy, forgiveness, grace, courage, and justice. Jesus fulfilled the moral requirements of God's law in his exemplary life. Jesus' service to humankind provides a model for attitudes and behaviors that attend to the needs of others. The teachings of Jesus, for example, those contained in the Sermon on the Mount (Matt. 5–7) indicate the high moral standards expected of those who profess Christ as Lord. Jesus' death on the cross is the ultimate example of loving sacrifice for the benefit of others. Christ's life and death extend to humans salvation from sin and a new life with the accompanying expectations of good works befitting the purposes of God and the example of Jesus' life (Eph. 2:8–10; Phil. 2:1–11). The Holy Spirit is the agent of spiritual growth and provides power to do the good works of God. The Holy Spirit facilitates growth in Christlikeness and in virtues such as love, patience, kindness, goodness, gentleness and self-control (Gal. 5:22–25). The Holy Spirit provides wisdom and understanding necessary for living rightly in the world. The Holy Spirit empowers the Christian's witness, providing courage and boldness to proclaim the gospel of Christ in both word and deed. The Holy Spirit shapes the affections of those who desire the life of God above all things and who are committed to integrity, marked by a growing consistency between what one believes to be good, true, noble, and worthy of praise and how one actually lives.

A Trinitarian conception of Christian ethics provides the framework for understanding duties and obligations, God's purposes for the world, and the formation of virtues. Christian ethics and morality does involve duties, outcomes, and virtues in various ways while relying on sources important in Christian faith. Scripture is one such source. While Scripture contains rules for conduct and obligations, it provides moral guidance in a multiplicity of ways through prophetic and didactic materials, narratives, and principles. Christian ethics is informed by the ends God desires and by this moral vision for human life and all of creation. This moral vision involves growth in wholeness and holiness in order for God's restoring justice and reconciling peace to be realized between God, humans, and creation. Humans are invited to participate in the working out of God's intentions by being formed more and more into the likeness of Christ and by serving Christ in the world.

When grounded in the character and actions of God, one's commitment to a life of moral goodness is a response to God and a product of one's relationship with God. Spirituality and morality intersect in that one's desire to reflect the goodness of God will be informed by how well one is growing in the knowledge of God in an intimate and dynamic relationship. Growth in the knowledge of God's own glory and goodness is the starting point for acquiring virtues or moral qualities such as faith, goodness, self-control, perseverance, godliness, kindness, and ultimately love (2 Peter 1:3–8). Virtues have both intrinsic and extrinsic dimensions. They are moral characteristics that reflect one's deepest desires and character that are shaped by the Holy Spirit. However, these moral dispositions are not just interior qualities of personal piety. Virtues are profoundly social and concretely manifested. They are formed in the context of relationships with God and practiced with others. Virtues have important social components in that it is good for others when persons grow in wisdom, compassion, kindness, self-control, mercy, and justice. Virtues provide an important link between spiritual and moral growth. They flow from one's relationship with God (the spiritual) while guiding attitudes, decisions, and behaviors (the moral).

The desire to please God by living a moral life is motivated by a growing love for God. This desire is a mark of spiritual maturity in that the pursuit of God and the desire to live out the moral dimensions of faith are intrinsically good for Christians to pursue.

See also Discipline; Formation, Spiritual.

For Further Reading: D. Hollinger, *Choosing the Good* (2002); R. Lovin, *Christian Ethics* (2000); M. O'Keefe, *Becoming Good, Becoming Holy* (1995); W. Corbin Reuschling, *Reviving Evangelical Ethics* (2008); R. Roberts, *Spiritual Emotions* (2007); F. S. Spencer, *What Did Jesus Do?* (2003).

Wyndy Corbin Reuschling

Eucharistic Spirituality

Eucharistic spirituality is a spirituality centered in the feast. Eating is not only a physical act, but a spiritual one. In the Bible, worship is inseparable from sacrifice, and sacrifice is inseparable from eating. The Greek word *Eucharist* means "thanksgiving" and was the prayer at sacred meals. Communion with God is not only a spiritual reality, but also a physical reality where God and humanity gather together around sacred nourishment.

The five great sacrifices described in Leviticus 1–7, though different and with different purposes, have this in common: they all involve food made sacred by ritual. Worshipers would bring costly animals and fine grain offerings, the very best of their earthly goods, to the feast. God participated by sacred flame, the smoke of which was a "soothing aroma." The priests would get their portions, and the people joined in as well in the peace offering (7:15–16). This feast was a prayer acted out, a symbolic action in which, as de Vaux has said, "the gift made to God is accepted, union with God is achieved, and the guilt of man is taken away."

In the NT, Jesus himself is described as the sacrifice. He not only provides atonement for sin, but, like the OT sacrifices, provides sacred food. Early Christians brought bread and wine that symbolized their very lives and laid them on the table. God receives these very common but precious gifts by uniting his Son with them. Sacrifice meets sacrifice on a common altar. However we might understand the pronouncements "This is my body" and "This is my blood" (Matt. 26:26–28), they parallel Christ's baptismal declaration, "This is my Son, whom I love" (Matt. 3:17). Therefore, the radical implications of the incarnation parallel the radical nature of the Eucharist, a concept developed in John 6:55 where Christ presents himself as a sacrifice that must be eaten so as to nourish our whole being, both physical and spiritual. In a very profound sense, we really do become what we eat. Moreover, the Eucharistic elements are not only the very locus of deep union between God and the worshiper, but also among the worshipers themselves communally. Union with God means union with one another, but this cannot happen if there is lingering enmity (Matt. 5:23 – 24).

Eucharistic spirituality is a prayer acted out, paralleling the Passover, in which the participants were to "remember" the great saving act of God. "Remembering" (Gr. *anamnesis*) was not understood as mere reflection, but an actual participation in the historic event itself through time. Not only are all believers transported back to the cross, but also forward to the marriage supper of the Lamb. The feast is therefore joyful but deadly serious, where the unexamined life risks grave danger (1 Cor. 11:29).

Evangelical spirituality is centered on the written Word and subjective experience of Christ through personal encounter. These are essential. They are not, however, in necessary conflict with the objective experience of the Eucharistic feast, the communal act that draws us into intimate union with God and our neighbor. In fact, both are essential for a holistic Christian spirituality.

See also Celebration; Worship.

For Further Reading: B. Childs, *Memory and Tradition in Israel* (1962); J. O'Connor, *The Hidden Manna* (2005); A. Schmemann, *The Eucharist*, trans. P. Kachur (2003); R. de Vaux, *Ancient Israel*, vol. 2 (1965); G. Wenham, *The Book of Leviticus* (1979).

John E. Worgul

Europe (1700 – Present)

See **Chapter 17.**

European Reformation and Colonial Expansion (1450 – 1700)

See **Chapter 16.**

Evagrius of Pontus (c. 346 – 399)

Early and influential theologian of monasticism. Born into a Christian family, Evagrius served as deacon under Gregory Nazianzus in Constantinople, but then, following a regretted indiscretion, moved to Jerusalem where he stayed with the monastic leaders Melania and Rufinus on the Mount of Olives. Next, he traveled to the Nitrian desert in Egypt, becoming a disciple of Macarius the Great. Labeled an "Origenist" heretic by some, Evagrius's works survived total destruction by being transmitted under the name Nilus of Sinai.

Evagrius's concept of the spiritual life is summarized in his well-known maxim from his treatise *On Prayer*: "If you are a theologian you truly pray. If you truly pray you are a theologian." Behind this statement stands Evagrius's tripartite division of the spiritual life: *praktike* (i.e., practice), contemplation of the physical world, and contemplation of God. This division is summarized most clearly in his three works: *Praktikos, Gnostikos,* and *Kephalaia Gnostica.* In the initial stage of *praktike*, one eradicates evil through the acquisition of virtues via grace and discipline. Evagrius had an intellectual disposition and was psychologically shrewd. Thus, his writings on these moral and ascetical matters were among his clearest and proved the most influential in subsequent Eastern as well as Western monasticism. Within the next stage of his schema, the contemplation of the physical world, one begins by contemplating the "earthly" creation and then moves up to a contemplation of the "heavenly" creation. From here one may finally transition to the third stage — contemplation of the Holy Trinity. Evagrius's contemplative theology has five major foci: that which is corporeal, that which is incorporeal, God's judgment, God's providence, and the Holy Trinity. Thus, Evagrius's understanding of spirituality consists in seeing a person's spiritual life as a movement through three stages, culminating in one's final contemplation of the Holy Trinity in prayer. Evagrius is also credited with providing early Christian spirituality with its original list of the eight (later reduced by others to seven) principal sins or vices: gluttony, fornication, avarice, anger, sadness, acedia, vainglory, and pride.

See also Ascent, Stages of Spiritual.

For Further Reading: J. Driscoll, *Steps of Spiritual Perfection: Studies on Spiritual Progress in Evagrius Ponticus* (2005); L. Dysinger, *Psalmody and Prayer in the Writings of Evagrius Ponticus* (2005); R. Sinkewicz, *Evagrius of Pontus: The Greek Ascetic Corpus* (2003).

Greg Peters

Evangelical Spirituality

See **Chapter 20.**

Evangelism

The English word *evangelism* comes from the Greek verb *euaggelizo*, the core meaning of which is "to proclaim the good news" that the kingdom (reign) of God has come near in the person and work of Jesus, the response to which is repentance and faith (Mark 1:15). This message came to be known as *to euaggelion*, the good news (or *gospel*). In Luke 4:16 – 21, quoting a passage from Isaiah, Jesus describes the good news as coming to the poor and bringing release to the captives, sight to the blind, and freedom to the oppressed. He identified himself as the one anointed to bring this good news. In 1 Corinthians 15:1 – 11, Paul says that Jesus himself is the good news. In particular the good news focuses on his death (for sins), burial, and (especially) resurrection from the dead. Right from the beginning the church has been called to communicate a particular message (the gospel) about a particular person (Jesus) in a particular context (the redeeming, reconciling, restoring work of God in the world).

In the 20th century, the evangelical church in particular focused on the task of evangelism. Billy Graham and his crusades brought new credibility to evangelism as well as drawing large numbers of men and women to faith in Jesus. Furthermore, new methods of outreach were developed with an emphasis on finding ways to make it easy for people to come to faith. Commitment to Jesus became a matter of affirming belief in a few core doctrines and asking Jesus into one's life. Unfortunately, an unintended consequence of this simplification was that while many converts were produced, far fewer disciples were made. (The word *convert* is being used for those who profess some allegiance to Jesus, while a *disciple* is a person who actively seeks to follow the way of Jesus.)

It can be argued that the unlinking of evangelism from spiritual formation in the 20th century resulted in a church with little depth. In the 21st century, new attention has been given to evangelism that contains a call to discipleship. For example, so-called contemplative evangelism invites seekers to join in such activities as spiritual direction, silent retreats, contemplative prayer, and spiritual journaling so as to open the possibility of an encounter with the God who is calling them to faith. Such outreach is done in the context of a community that understands that all people are on a spiritual journey, because this is how God made us, and thus welcomes people to belong even before they come to believe. And, indeed, the community of faith seeks to incorporate and guide men and women to a holistic faith in Jesus — one that is faithful to Jesus' Great Commandment to love God and to love others, engaging in both spiritual pursuits and active ministry to others (especially the poor). Furthermore, those who are called to be evangelists in this new context need to be nurtured for this task in the silence of the retreat center and not just, as in the past, in the bustle and entrepreneurship of the marketplace. It is their own deep relationship with Jesus that gives authenticity to the gospel they proclaim.

See also Conversion; Revival; Testimony; Witnessing.

For Further Reading: W. Abraham, *The Logic of Evangelism* (1989); J. Finney, *Emerging Evangelism*

(2004); M. Green, *Evangelism in the Early Church* (2003); R. Peace, *Conversion in the New Testament* (1999).

Richard V. Peace

Examen

Examen is regular self-examination before God to discern one's faithfulness in following Christ in daily activity. Ignatius of Loyola, a pioneer of this discipline, considered it of such value that those following his *Spiritual Exercises* in retreat settings were given the tool near the outset. More recently, with encouragement from Vatican II, there has been renewed interest in the practice within the Roman Catholic Church and beyond. Instrumentally, examen facilitates greater self-awareness, but the deeper motivation for practicing it is the believer's desire to know God's immanent presence, and to dwell in and serve others through God's immense love in every moment of the day.

At the end of the day or, for Ignatius, at daily intervals, one pauses to examine *consciousness*, asking how one has been present to God; and also to examine *conscience*, asking how one has faithfully served God. This latter assessment of conscience is less concerned about good and bad actions and more with the impulses that underlie them. And here the dangers of unhealthy or excessive introspection are best preempted by making examen an openness to the searchlight of the Spirit, rather than an independent, private probing of one's own inner life.

The first three movements of the examen are gratitude for the gifts of God's love throughout the day; petition for discernment as one continues the prayer; and review of the day, watching for stirrings of the heart and mind. Stirrings that brought life, joy, peace, and energy to one's soul are called consolations. The experiences that created confusion, doubt, and un-Christlike thoughts or behavior are called desolations. Continuing on, the fourth movement is seeking forgiveness for failures in Christlike living; and the fifth and final is renewal of God-given purpose and energy to walk faithfully with God in the next day's activities. Both consolations and desolations point believers to seek God's will. On the one hand, they should do more of what gives life. On the other, desolations profitably point to attitudes, beliefs, and expectations that are contrary to God's design and therefore to be avoided.

The psalmist often prays an examen. "In your anger do not sin; when you are on your beds, search your hearts and be silent" (Ps. 4:4); "Test me, O LORD, and try me, examine my heart and my mind" (Ps. 26:2–3); "Why are you downcast, O my soul? Why so disturbed within me?" (Ps. 42:5); and "Search me, O God, and know my heart; test me" (Ps. 139:23–24). Jesus expressed the fruits of a form of examen when he told his disciples, "My soul is overwhelmed with sorrow" (Matt. 26:38).

Possible examen questions include: For what moment today am I most grateful or least grateful? When today did I give and receive love? When did I have critical, unloving thoughts? Have I noticed God's presence in any of this? Is there some part of my life still untouched by Jesus Christ?

See also Conscience; Forgiveness; Ignatian Spirituality; Penitence.

For Further Reading: T. Gallagher, *The Examen Prayer* (2006); *Ignatius of Loyola: Spiritual Exercises and Selected Works*, CWS (1991).

Nancy R. Buschart

Exercise, Physical Fitness

The spiritual rationale for understanding exercise is grounded in the apostle Paul's words to the Corinthian Christians. He tells them, "Do you not know that your bodies are temples of the Holy Spirit, who is in you. . . . Therefore honor God with your bodies" (1 Cor. 6:19–20 TNIV). Temples are sacred places, so the body should be honored as a sacred vessel of God's Spirit. Furthermore, God became human in order to save humanity from its sinfulness. The body is not the inferior part of humanity. Hence, to honor God is the rationale for physical exercise, which ideally is teamed with spiritual and mental exercise. Physical fitness is an important part of a holistic relationship with God.

Generally, there are five aspects that deal with physical fitness. The first is cardiovascular health, which focuses on the heart, lungs, and circulatory system. One of humanity's God-given tasks is to be stewards and, in part, this means stewards of our body. Moderate aerobic exercise is recommended to take care of our heart and lungs. The second aspect of physical fitness deals with muscular strength. There is no way to build strength without exercising the various muscles. Muscle strength enables the person to function in normal daily life. The third aspect, muscular endurance, is related to strength. Clearly, the issue here is the ability to sustain activity, which can range from actually doing something to being able to cope with something like an emergency. The next aspect concerns flexibility. Exercise develops flexibility, and that enables the person to be able to do more and different things. And the fifth and final aspect of physical fitness focuses on body composition. Basically, this aspect is a comparison of body fat with lean body mass, that is, muscle, bone, etc.

Physical fitness enhances health, wellness, and self-esteem. An image some early church fathers used to describe Christians was "athletes of the Spirit." The only way such an athlete can perform is by practice — by developing physical fitness. Anything less constitutes malpractice. And malpractice dishonors God. To become physically fit requires that the person exercise regularly. It is no different than prayer. The exercise should be reasonable and fitting for the person. Older people cannot do what teenagers do. People with disease or injury, or even the aged, benefit from physical therapy. Beginners should start slowly. Physical fitness takes time. Finally, build variety into the regimen. Becoming physically fit can be accomplished communally, as well as solitarily. Exercising with a group can be motivational, sustaining, and fun.

See also Body; Holistic Spirituality; Leisure and Play; Sport and Spirituality.

For Further Reading: M. Finck, *Stretch and Pray* (2005); A. Jackson et al., *Physical Activity for Health and Fitness* (2004); T. Ryan, *Reclaiming the Body in Christian Spirituality* (2004); idem, *Wellness, Spirituality and Sports* (1986).

Alan Kolp

Exodus

The historic exodus from Egyptian bondage remains the pivotal event of Jewish faith and history. The biblical book of Exodus narrates a number of matters relevant to Christian spirituality: God's action for his people (chaps. 7–15), God's conversation with them (chaps. 19–24), and God's instruction for their worship of him (chaps. 25–31).

The divine deliverance and liberation of the Israelite people was holistic. It produced internal changes while also affecting the external conditions of life. God heard the cry of the Israelites and sent them a deliverer. God also guided them and nourished them through daily provisions. The part of the Lord's Prayer regarding daily "bread" (Matt. 6:11; Luke 11:3), for example, can be traced back to the provision of daily manna that started in the exodus event. The focus of Exodus is on deliverance from bondage and persecution into freedom. The exodus event is normally perceived by the biblical writers as a salvific activity of God; however, God's action was also directed against Egypt's gods (12:12; 15:11; 18:11), and the people could trust in such a protective and powerful God.

The conversation of God with his people expresses his heart's desire that they become a kingdom of priests and a holy nation. The awesomeness of God is felt by the people of God, demonstrating that mystical communion between God and his people is a legitimate form of Christian spiritual experience. Just as God spoke the "Ten Words" of the Decalogue on Mount Sinai, his purpose remains that his people will understand his thoughts and ways and align themselves more closely with him.

The worship theme is addressed twice in Exodus — when God gives instruction, and when the people obey it by building the tabernacle. While some interpreters become preoccupied with deciphering the symbolism of the tabernacle, it is better to dwell on how the artistic God who designed this meeting place still seeks pure worship from his people — the kind that is rooted in sincere, right attitudes toward him.

The exodus event became in the NT a paradigm of Christ-centered salvation (see, e.g., Hebrews) and has remained a powerful, recurring metaphor in Christian consciousness ever since. It has been, for example, a motif for God's work of liberation when applied to African-American social oppression, and in the Holiness movement for the journey of the soul, from initial "salvation" through the wilderness wanderings and eventually to Canaan, the promised land of the higher/ deeper life. Whenever the motif of exodus is used, the hope of believers is that the God who acted in history before will intervene again.

See also African-American Christian Spirituality; Liberation Spirituality.

For Further Reading: T. Longman III, *How to Read Exodus* (2009); J. Shao, "Spirituality in the Prophetic Traditions: An Asian Perspective," in *Perjuangan Menatang Zaman*, ed. H. Mulia (2000), 125 – 50; V. Wimbush, ed., *African-Americans and the Bible* (2000).

Joseph Shao

Experience

See **Chapter 24.**

Extraordinary Phenomena

Extraordinary phenomena refer to occurrences or experiences that are not anticipated in traditional Christian worldviews nor readily explained by current scientific theories. In attempting to understand them, reductionistic explanations are best avoided. Extraordinary phenomena should not be attributed always, solely and directly, to supernatural agents, whether divine or diabolical, or reduced to the purely psychical. The increasing recognition of the paranormal realm has meant that not all of them are to be explained in terms of supernatural causes. Psychic phenomena are often natural phenomena even if current scientific theories are unable to explain them satisfactorily. But the fact that they are natural does not mean that they could not be related in *any* way to either a divine or diabolical source. The problem of relating the two would be similar to the problem of explaining the nature of divine actions: how could a natural event be said to be also an act of God?

Theologically, the issue of extraordinary phenomena is inevitable in view of two considerations. First, an irreducible supernatural element is found at the heart of the Christian faith, namely, the miracle of the resurrection, which makes participation in the divine life possible. Second, extraordinary phenomena are seen as a way of establishing a messenger's credentials. The identity of Jesus as the Messiah is closely linked to his works of miracles and healings (Luke 7:18 – 23). Paul refers to miracles as signs of his apostleship (2 Cor. 12:12).

Discussions on the relationship between extraordinary phenomena and spirituality have usually turned on the latter issue. In modern charismatic circles, there is a tendency to make a direct correlation between holiness and supernatural manifestations. The Christian tradition, however, has consistently maintained that while "signs and wonders" may validate gospel witness in cross-cultural settings, the mere occurrence of an extraordinary phenomenon tells us little about one's sanctity. For example, experiences very similar to glossolalia and being "slain in the Spirit" are described in Teresa of Avila in connection with the higher levels of contemplative prayer. But such experiences also occur among immature Christians (cf. 1 Cor. 12–14). Miracles happened quite spontaneously in a holy man like Sadhu Sundar Singh, but false prophets also performed them (cf. Matt. 7:15–23). Jonathan Edwards would consider them as "uncertain signs" of true religion. Their ambiguity calls for the discerning of spirits.

Extraordinary phenomena have been assessed differently due to different criteria for discernment. Catholicism is open to a wider range of phenomena, including some not found in Scripture, such as the stigmata (Francis of Assisi), flame of love (Philip Neri), Marian apparitions, levitation, and bilocation, whereas Protestantism, governed by the *sola scriptura* principle, tends to discount phenomena not explicitly found in Scripture.

For Further Reading: J. Edwards, *Religious Affections*, in *The Works of Jonathan Edwards*, vol. 2, ed. J. Smith (1959); B. Groeschel, *A Still, Small Voice* (1993); Teresa of Avila, *The Collected Works of St. Teresa of Avila*, 2 vols., trans. K. Kavanaugh and O. Rodriguez (1976).

Simon Chan

F

Faber, Frederick W. (1814–1863)

Poet and hymn writer of the Oxford Movement. Of Huguenot ancestry and Calvinist upbringing, Faber came under John Henry Newman's influence at Oxford, was ordained an Anglican priest in 1839, and converted to Roman Catholicism in 1845. Faber embraced an elaborate and ornate form of Catholicism, similar in style to Italian devotion. He is best remembered today for his hymns, including "Faith of Our Fathers" and "There's a Wideness in God's Mercy," which he wrote in an attempt to bring English Catholic hymn singing up to higher standards at a time when Catholics did not emphasize congregational singing. The hymns have now crossed over into Protestant use as well. Faber also wrote many volumes of spiritual theology, all of high quality. Faber's *Spiritual Conferences* provide pointed pastoral guidance for the Christian life, while his meditations on doctrinal topics (such as *Bethlehem*, *The Foot of the Cross*, and *The Creator and the Creature*), though based on extensive research in scholastic theology, are not dry presentations of doctrine, but evocative explorations of the mysteries of the faith. Writing in a florid style, Faber perfected this genre of the poetic essay on spiritual subjects.

See also Oxford Movement.

Fred Sanders

Faith

Saving faith is the divinely enabled human response of belief and trust in God or Christ. As expressed by the author of Hebrews, "Now faith is being sure of what we hope for and certain of what we do not see" (11:1). As the heart and core of the gospel, faith arises from hearing God's Word (John 20:31) under the influence of the Holy Spirit (1 Cor. 12:3). In the OT, faith typically is expressed by a verb, most often the hiphil form of *'aman*, "believe in" (Gen. 15:6; Ex. 14:31; Isa. 53:1) and signifying depending on and trusting God and his promises. The NT commonly employs the noun *pistis*, "faith," "belief" (Mark 10:52; Acts 20:21; Rom. 1:17), and the verb *pisteuein*, "believe" (see below). Repentance (turning from sin) together with faith (turning to Christ) constitute the two sides of spiritual conversion.

Foundational to genuine faith is intellectual knowledge of the gospel, in Greek often expressed by *pisteuein hoti* ("to believe that"). Knowing essential truths of the gospel (cf. John 2:22; 2 Thess. 2:12; Heb. 11:6) is necessary but not sufficient for salvation. James wrote, "You believe that there is one God. Good! Even the demons believe that— and shudder" (James 2:19). In addition to assent to essential truths, faith's second dimension is trust in and commitment to Jesus Christ and the gospel, often expressed by *pisteuein en*, "to believe in" (Mark 1:15; John 3:15) and *pisteuein eis*, "to believe into" (John 1:12; Acts 10:43; 1 John 5:10). In his *Institutes* (1559) Calvin asserted that faith "is more of the heart than of the brain, and more of the disposition than of the understanding." Failure to commit to Jesus Christ as Lord and Master (cf. Rom. 10:9, 12) constitutes the "cheap grace" vigorously opposed by the German theologian and martyr Dietrich Bonhoeffer, in his classic work *The Cost of Discipleship* (1937). Scripture depicts faith as a gift and enablement of God (Rom. 12:3; Eph. 2:8) that requires our intentional response.

Neoorthodox theologians such as Emil Brunner understand faith as a nonpropositional encounter with the living God. Søren Kierkegaard regarded faith primarily as a matter of passionate commitment. Roman Catholic theology principally interprets faith as intellectual assent to church teachings. Some Catholics emphasize so-called implicit faith, understood as an unconscious orientation to God or the transcendent apart from hearing the gospel and trusting Jesus Christ. Scripture, as evident from the above, certifies informed or explicit faith in Christ but not implicit faith.

In addition to the faith that initiates salvation, Scripture upholds the necessity of ongoing faith, exercised throughout life's journey. As Christians receive Jesus Christ by faith, so we must live our entire lives by faith (Col. 2:6–7; cf. 2 Cor. 5:7). Continual faith involves looking to Jesus, holding fast to the gospel, and trusting God amid life's hardships and trials. Faith, unlike regeneration or justification, admits of degrees—God directing faith to grow (2 Cor. 10:15; 2 Thess. 1:3).

Properly exercised, faith yields rich spiritual formational outcomes, the chief being love of God and others. As expressed by Paul, "The only thing that counts is faith expressing itself through love" (Gal. 5:6; cf. 1 Peter 1:8). Genuine faith issues in a life of obedience that is pleasing to God (Rom. 1:5; 16:26). A multitude of virtues flow from faith, including goodness, knowledge, self-control, perseverance, godliness, and mutual affection (2 Peter 1:5–7), as well as joy, peace, and hope (Rom. 15:13).

Faith opens the door to numerous spiritual graces, including confident access to God (Eph. 3:12), Christ's indwelling through the Spirit (Eph. 3:16–17), effectual prayer (Matt. 21:22), and sincere worship of God (Ex. 4:29–31). Faith empowers believers to resist the assaults of Satan (Eph. 6:16; 1 Peter 5:9), enables perseverance amid trials (James 1:2–3; 1 Peter 1:6–7), and results in bearing abundant spiritual fruit. Whereas salvation is by faith, not works, good works follow, providing certain evidence of genuine faith (1 Thess. 1:3; James 2:14–26). Continual exercise of faith yields growth in holiness (Acts 15:9) or progressive conformity to Jesus Christ (Rom. 8:29). In sum, faith—even the faith that overcomes the world (1 John 5:4–5)—is a sine qua non of an authentic spirituality.

Christians must deal constructively with inevitable assaults of doubt, understood as uncertainty regarding God and his ways. Doubt may be intellectual in nature, questioning difficult doctrines such as the eternal fate of those who never heard the gospel. Doubt also may be emotional, wrestling with why an all-loving and omnipotent God would permit his innocent children to suffer harshly. Christians deal constructively with doubts by searching the Scriptures concerning God's ways, praying over doubts, and reflecting on the writings of Christians who have similarly struggled, such as Augustine and C. S. Lewis. Honestly engaging doubts often results in more settled convictions about Christian verities.

See also Conversion; Good Works.

For Further Reading: H. Bavinck, *The Certainty of Faith* (1980); O. Guinness, *God in the Dark* (1996); J. MacArthur, *True Faith* (1989); A. McGrath, *The Sunnier Side of Doubt* (1990); A. Murray, *How to Strengthen Your Faith* (1997); C. Nelson, *How Faith Matures* (1989).

Bruce A. Demarest

Family Life, Spirituality of

Family life was not the focus of Christian spirituality in its formative years. The bonds of the new Christian family were contrasted in Scripture with family of origin, and the identification of Christians as sisters and brothers recognizing the fatherhood of God was encouraged (Matt.10:34–38; Luke 12:51–53). Illustrative of this is the *Martyrdoms of Perpetua and Felicity,* an early third-century passion narrative about a Roman matron and a slave woman who chose baptism into the illicit new religion and thus certain death over their young children and family ties. Gradually in the early medieval world, ascetic practice or "white martyrdom," which included celibacy, shaped the tradition's spiritual orientation. According to church fathers such as Jerome (*Letter XXII to Eustochium*), family was a hindrance to spiritual practice. During the High Middle Ages, monasticism was the most influential Christian institution, and the "evangelical counsels" of poverty, chastity, and obedience associated with the "life of perfection" were assumed prerequisites for an authentic spiritual life. Priestly orders were shaped according to this ideal. In sum, for at least twelve centuries, marriage and family life were not considered states conducive to spiritual attainment.

Nevertheless, the medieval church defined marriage as a sacrament, thus creating a potential link between spirituality and family. While medieval conceptions of marriage focused more on its necessity for procreation and the avoidance of sin, the implications of the marital sacrament developed. In the late medieval period in the West, with political stability and the growth of an urban merchant class, laypeople began to take spiritual practice more seriously. Motivated by the desire to return to a more apostolic, gospel-inspired life, varieties of lay movements like the Beguines and the Modern Devotion (*Devotio Moderna*) emerged. And mendicant orders, such as the Franciscans and Dominicans, sponsored "third orders" by which laity were provided spiritual formation. With some modification, however, these lay groups were still derivative of the ascetic ideal.

It was during the reform movements of the 16th century, both Protestant and Catholic, that the idea of a spirituality native to, not in spite of or in opposition to, marriage and family gained currency. Martin Luther and most magisterial Reformers, rejecting the monastic ideal, emphasized that marriage was pleasing to God. In Luther's view, family was the arena in which Christian ideals of love, sacrifice, and trust in God were cultivated (*The Estate of Marriage*). While mainline Protestantism did not validate the idea of marriage as a sacrament, it was seen as a covenantal association for the sake of the entire community. Calvin and his successors emphasized the family's responsibility to influence society, thus making it the center of spiritual formation. The Puritan tradition emphasized the idea of the father-husband as spiritual head of the home, charged with the well-being of his flock and, by extension, society. Spiritual practices such as journaling grew out of this tradition.

Anabaptist traditions, in contrast, while embracing family life as the norm, cultivated an ascetic sensibility and tended to see radical discipleship, not family life, as the spiritual ideal. On the Catholic side of the confessional barriers, Francis de Sales's *Introduction to the Devout Life* popularized the idea that marriage facilitated the mutual sanctification of the couple, and that true devotion was not only possible in family life but essential. In his view, spiritual practices could be interiorized and modified for different states of life. More broadly, Catholic devotion to the holy family of Jesus, Mary, and Joseph, the "earthly trinity," was encouraged, which underscored the family's spiritual importance.

In recent years, the idea that family life is spiritually significant has gained momentum. Within evangelical Christian groups, traditionally conceived patriarchal family roles are seen as God-ordained and their fulfillment as spiritual advancement. Roman Catholic teaching stresses the complementarity of the married couple, that the family is a "school of love," and that it has a social function to care for the vulnerable. At the same time, Catholicism retains the ideal of an unmarried priesthood and values the spiritual path of consecrated celibacy. Mainline Protestantism, continuing to assume that family is essential to a godly society, has invested in family focused social services. Christian education for children is emphasized. Concern for the stability of families has thus been a contemporary pastoral focus across denominational divides and the motivation for organizations like Focus on the Family. Recently, changing family structures and new views of gender and gender relations have impacted Christian thinking. The spiritual tasks of blended, extended, adoptive, divorced, remarried, childless, and same-sex families are being developed at the same time that more traditional family forms are seen as the norm.

See also Adolescent Spirituality; Children and Spirituality; Marriage; Parenting.

For Further Reading: E. Boyer Jr., *Finding God at Home* (1988); D. Browning and I. Evinson, eds., *The Family, Religion and Culture* (1996); D. Garland, *Sacred Stories of Ordinary Families* (2003); D. Leckey, *The Ordinary Way* (1982); B. Miller-McLemore, *In the Midst of Chaos* (2006); J. Hanlon Rubio, *A Christian Theology of Marriage and Family* (2003); W. Wright, *Sacred Dwelling* (2007); idem, *Seasons of a Family's Life* (2003).

Wendy M. Wright

Fasting

To fast is to abstain from something, often food. Christian fasting is the voluntary denial of something for a specific time, for a spiritual purpose, by an individual, family, community, or nation. Fasting played a role in more than two dozen incidents in the Bible, and a handful of passages in the Bible discuss fasting. Fasting was a common practice throughout most of church history. In Western countries, it fell into disuse for much of the 20th century but is being practiced more frequently in the 21st century.

Many world religions encourage fasting. In recent decades, fasting has played a role in political protests, in weight-loss programs, and in alternative medicine. In Christian practice, fasting is closely linked to intimacy with God and concern for God's priorities.

Five incidents in the OT link fasting with mourning. For example, David and his men fasted at the news of the deaths of Saul and Jonathan (2 Sam. 1:12). Five other OT incidents illustrate the connection between fasting and repentance, for example, when the people of Israel in the time of Nehemiah read God's Law, then fasted to repent for their sin (Neh. 9:1–2). The yearly Day of Atonement, with its emphasis on repentance, involved fasting (Lev. 16:29–30). Numerous incidents in the Old and New Testaments illustrate the connection between fasting and intercessory prayer. Esther and the people of Israel in Susa fasted to plead with God for their lives (Est. 4:16), and the early Christians in Asia Minor fasted and prayed when they commissioned new elders (Acts 14:23). Moses, Elijah, and Jesus engaged in forty-day fasts.

In addition to its connection with prayer, Christian fasting involves a concern for justice. In Isaiah 58 fasting as an excuse for self-justification is condemned. Fasting, God says, is meaningless unless it relates to a concern for God's priorities: "Is not this the kind of fasting I have chosen: to loose the chains of injustice and untie the cords of the yoke, to set the oppressed free and break every yoke? Is it not to share your food with the hungry and to provide the poor wanderer with shelter—when you see the naked, to clothe them, and not to turn away from your own flesh and blood?" (vv. 6–7).

In the early church, fasting was frequently practiced as a way to free up food and money to give to the poor. In recent decades, Christian relief and development agencies have promoted fasting as a way to learn to pray for the poor with energy and compassion and to release resources to give to the poor. World Vision, for example, promotes a thirty- or forty-hour voluntary "famine" to raise money for development and to encourage prayer and solidarity with the hungry.

Fasting in the Bible involves abstaining from food and sometimes from water as well, although in many cases the details about the fasts are not clear. Throughout Christian history, fasting from food has taken many forms. In some cases, Christians have abstained from all food. In other cases, fasting has taken the form of eating a simpler diet. A "Daniel fast," modeled after the account in Daniel 1, involves eating only vegetables and is common in some parts of Africa. Eastern Orthodox Christians fast frequently, and when they fast, they abstain from meat, fish, dairy, eggs, oil, and alcohol.

Today Christians fast from food and also from consumer items and everyday practices, such as shopping, lattes, Internet or cell phone use, news media, entertainment, and music. These forms of fasting free up time for prayer, Bible reading, and reflection. In some cases, fasting from consumer items or everyday activities also frees up money to give to people in need. People with a history of eating disorders should not fast from food in any form, and people on some medications or who have certain medical conditions need to fast from food very carefully, so these alternative forms of fasting provide options for fasting that can work for anyone.

In much of the two-thirds world, fasting is encouraged as a communal activity. Weekly or monthly congregational fast days are announced, with specific prayer requests to accompany the fast. Increasingly in Western countries, families, small groups, and congregations are fasting together. The fast day, with prayer requests, is announced, and people can choose the form of fasting that works best for them.

Many people who fast report that the act seems to add power to their prayers. For this reason, fasting before praying for healing is a common practice. In affluent consumer cultures, all forms of fasting help participants step back from the powerful voices that encourage excess. Fasting nurtures prayer, makes space for God, and helps Christians experience their need for God.

See also Body; Discipline, Spiritual; Gluttony.

For Further Reading: L. Baab, *Fasting* (2006); R. Foster, *Celebration of Discipline* (1978); T. Jones, *The Sacred Way* (2005); C. Rogers, *Fasting* (2004); T. Ryan, *The Sacred Art of Fasting* (2005); L. Winner, *Mudhouse Sabbath* (2003).

Lynne M. Baab

Fatherhood of God

Biblically, God's fatherhood is understood in two main ways. First, it refers to his being the Creator of all things (Eph. 3:14). This is acknowledged in the Apostles' Creed where God is called "the Father, almighty, maker of heaven and earth." Second, it is the term Jesus used most frequently to address God. It suggests close personal relationship within a familial setting, which for Christians means not only being accepted in spite of our rebellion (like the Prodigal Son), but also loving and redemptive discipline (Heb. 12:7–11). Jesus' unique relationship with the Father constituted the beginning of what eventually would become the Christian doctrine of the Trinity.

Jesus himself teaches that the one he calls Father is also the Father of all who follow him. Thus, he taught his disciples to begin their prayers with "Our Father." After his resurrection he tells his disciples: "I am returning to my Father and your Father" (John 20:17). Calling God "Father" reveals a distinctively Christian understanding, for to recognize God as Father is to be united with one who introduces him to us as his Father.

In the major Christian traditions, the fatherhood of God implies a Trinitarian relationship that goes beyond pure mutuality. There is an irreversible order in the Father's sending the Son and the Spirit to the church. This Trinitarian order is designated by the phrase "monarchy of the Father." The Father is the single principle (*monē archē*) from whom come the Son and the Spirit.

The fatherhood of God carries important implications for spirituality. God as Creator is the basis of the Christian affirmation of the goodness of all created things and a spirituality involving their right use, for example, the practice of temperance as one of the cardinal virtues. Because the world is God's handiwork, it reveals his glory (Ps. 19:1–6) just as a great work of art reveals the greatness of the artist. God as Creator has set his footprints in the world (*vestigia Dei*). Out of this understanding has evolved the ancient Christian practice of meditating on God's creation. But creation reveals God's glory in a deeper sense in that it is the very medium of special revelation that culminates in God becoming man. The idea that God works in and through nature gives rise to a sacramental theology, which has played a central role in the spirituality of the church. In some Christian traditions, the Eucharist, which is called "the sacrament of sacraments," is the ordering principle of personal and corporate spiritual life.

The fatherhood of God understood in the Trinitarian context is the basis for a liturgical spirituality. God sent his Spirit to indwell believers so that they could call God *"Abba*, Father" (Gal. 4:6). The church recognizes this term of address as expressing the most basic and irreducible relationship in the Trinity and between the Trinity and the church, and regularizes it in its liturgy in which prayers are addressed to the Father through Jesus Christ ("in Jesus' name") and in the "unity of the Spirit." It is for this reason that orthodox Christians in all traditions have resisted revisionist attempts, especially from feminism, to rename God in functional terms.

The monarchy of the Father entails its own unique spirituality. The order of the Trinity is reflected in the liturgical order and thus reveals another dimension of interpersonal relationship that is missed in a purely egalitarian concept.

See also Childlikeness; God, Perceptions of; Motherhood of God.

For Further Reading: P. T. Forsyth, *God the Holy Father* (1987); T. Smail, *The Forgotten Father* (1996); J. Zizioulas, *Communion and Otherness* (2006).

Simon Chan

Fear of the Lord

The NT uses several different Greek words for "religion," the most common of which is *threskeia* (e.g., James 1:27). In the ancient Near East, however, no single word expressed that idea. For Egyptians, Babylonians, and others, the idea of "religion" was encapsulated in the phrase "fear of God/the gods." The first reference to "fear of God" in the OT is Genesis 20:11, where the Mesopotamian Abraham complains that there is no "fear of God" in Philistia.

It is against this backdrop that "fear of God" (*yir'at 'elohim*), "fear of the Lord" (*yir'at yhwh/'adonay*), and "fear of the Almighty" (*yir'at shadday*) are to be understood throughout the OT itself. Indeed, *yir'ah* alone is sometimes used in the sense of "piety" (Job 4:6; 15:4; 22:4) or "reverence" (Neh. 5:15; Ps. 5:7). And as is well known, in the OT fearing God more often connoted "reverence/awe" (cf. Deut. 17:19) than "terror/dread."

The double-edged nature of the fear of the Lord has been given classic expression by Rudolf Otto, *The Idea of the Holy* (1917). He coined the

term *numinous*, meaning "aware[ness] of the holy."
He referred to the *mysterium tremendum*, in which
mysterium meant "that which is hidden," "the
Wholly Other"—and *tremendum* meant "shud-
dering; the daunting and repelling moment of the
numinous." He also spoke of the (*mysterium*) *fascinans*, meaning "fascinating; the attracting and
alluring moment of the numinous." Otto's insights
nicely combine these two aspects of the meaning of
"fear" in "fear of God/the Lord." In what follows,
both nuances of *yir'ah* (and its verbal root *yr'*) may
often be seen in the passages cited.

"The fear of the Lord is the beginning [basis]
of wisdom/knowledge" (Ps. 111:10; Prov. 1:7; 9:10;
cf. 1:29; 2:5; Isa. 33:6). Wisdom (the learned ability
to cope) and knowledge (the result of tested experience) share true *yir'ah* as their mutual foundation.
In fact, wisdom and the fear of the Lord virtually
equal each other (Job 28:28).

A similarly close relationship also exists
between *yir'ah* and God's Torah (Ps. 19:7–9; cf.
34:11; 119:63; Eccl. 12:13). To fear God is to obey
him humbly (Prov. 15:33; 22:4), "faithfully and
wholeheartedly" (2 Chron. 19:9; cf. Ps. 2:11).

An additional function of fearing God is to
keep people from sinning (Ex. 20:20; cf. Neh. 5:9,
15; Job 6:14; Ps. 36:1; Prov. 8:13; 23:17). Indeed,
yir'ah is frequently linked to *sur mera'*, "shunning evil" (Job 1:1, 8; 2:3; 28:28; Prov. 14:16;
16:6; cf. Isa. 59:15). Fearing the Lord leads to life
(Prov. 10:27; 14:27; 19:23; 22:4) and is better than
wealth (Prov. 15:16). So intimately is the fear of
God related to wisdom that OT wisdom books
utilize it at crucial places in their literary structures
(Job 1:1, 9; 4:6; 6:14–15; 28:28; 37:24; Prov. 1:7;
9:10; 31:30; Eccl. 5:7; 8:12–13; 12:13).

How is the fear of the Lord in the OT related to
the Spirit of the Lord? David son of Jesse, anointed
by God, asserts that the Spirit spoke through him
and told him to be sure to rule "in the fear of God"
(2 Sam. 23:1–3). And Isaiah said of the ultimate
Anointed One that "a shoot will come up from the
stump of Jesse" and that "the Spirit of the Lord

will rest on him—the Spirit of wisdom and of
understanding . . . the Spirit of knowledge and of
the fear of the Lord" (Isa. 11:1–2; cf. also Acts
9:31).

In the NT, "fear of God/the Lord" (*phobos
theou/tou kyriou*) complements and supplements
several OT texts. In Romans 3:18 Paul echoes
David's plaint concerning universal sin: "There is
no fear of God before their eyes" (Ps. 36:1; cf. Luke
18:2). Believers alone know how to fear the Lord
(Luke 1:50; 2 Cor. 5:11; 1 Peter 2:17). A holy God
is to be feared (Luke 23:40; Rev. 11:18; 15:4), worshiped (Rev. 14:7), praised and served (Rev. 19:5).

In Acts 2:5 Luke refers to diaspora Jews who
worshiped the Lord with godly fear. He also mentions "God-fearing" Greeks (17:4, 17) and other
Gentiles (10:2, 22, 35; 13:16, 26, 50)—non-Jews
who did not follow every detail of Jewish custom
but nevertheless attended synagogue and believed
in the God the Jews worshiped. In so doing, they
joined the train of those who truly fear the Wholly
Other, those whose expectant spirits respond in
joyful abandon to the uncreated Spirit.

For centuries of Christian history, as even a
casual survey of the *Philokalia*, for example, demonstrates, the fear of the Lord was still regarded as
the appropriate response to the triune God with
whom relationship had been restored through
Christ. By the early 17th century, however, Johann
Arndt in his *True Christianity* (1605–1610) warned
that the children of the Reformation no longer
felt appropriate fear of a holy God, before whom
Luther had fallen down as dead, but instead were
claiming their justification with a casual sense of
entitlement, which, by severing the link between
grace and gratitude, was proving deadly to spiritual
life.

Except during awakenings and revivals, sustaining healthy fear of the Lord has often been
challenging for Protestants. Without it, however,
the centrality of the cross is logically unsustainable,
obedience becomes optional, and respect is almost
impossible. C. S. Lewis called modern Christians

to recovery of reverence for God — who, in the now-famous Chronicles of Narnia image of the lion Aslan, is depicted as good but not safe. Likewise, evangelical mystic A. W. Tozer complained in the early 1960s that "in the majority of our meetings, there is scarcely a trace of reverent thought ... little sense of the divine Presence, no moment of stillness, no solemnity, no wonder, no holy fear. But always there is a dull or a breezy song leader full of awkward jokes."

Nineteenth-century liberalism tragically assumed that the fatherhood of God rendered the fear of God obsolete; the same assumption has virtually triumphed in evangelical circles as well. In Hebrews 12, salvation through Christ is contrasted to the terrifying experience of Israel before God's presence at Sinai. Nevertheless, the chapter ends with an exhortation to worship him with reverence and awe, "for *our* God is [still] a consuming fire" (v. 29). The ancients properly perceived the fear of the Lord, as an encompassing way of life rather than a slim silo of sentiment, to be the essence of true religion. It is *how* to live all of life before God. In the words of James Houston, the good news is that "such fear brings blessing in every sphere of life."

See also Presence of God; Wonder.

For Further Reading: "*yr'...*," *TDOT* 6:290–315; E. Peterson, *Christ Plays in Ten Thousand Places* (2005); R. Pfeiffer, "The Fear of God," *Israel Exploration Journal* 5, no. 1 (1955): 41–48; B. Waltke, "The Fear of the Lord," in *Alive to God*, ed. J. I. Packer and L. Wilkinson (1992), 17–33; L. Wilson, "The Book of Job and the Fear of God," *Tyndale Bulletin* 46, no. 1 (1995): 59–79; J. S. Yuille, *Puritan Spirituality: The Fear of God in the Affective Theology of George Swinnock* (2007).

Ronald F. Youngblood and Glen G. Scorgie

Feminist Spirituality

Feminist spirituality can be understood broadly as the experience and praxis of that which contributes to the well-being and flourishing of women and, by extension, to that of all of humanity and indeed of all life on earth. By definition, this thriving does not refer only to interiority, but to embodied reality, so that it works against body-mind or body-spirit dualisms and involves a flourishing in wholeness that always has a material or bodily dimension as well as ecological implications.

From a specifically Christian perspective, this is sharpened by the conviction that spirituality cannot be divorced from the Spirit of God. The Holy Spirit's work of creating and sustaining the earth, of "greening" the world (Hildegard of Bingen) and renewing all things, is therefore understood in connection to the concrete contours of women's lives: where the Spirit is, there should be freedom for women to live abundantly in all of their manifold particularities. Given the relative poverty of pneumatology in much of Christian tradition, especially in its Western manifestations, Christian feminist spirituality can be understood as a struggle to bring the transformative work of the Spirit, sometimes closely identified with Wisdom, to the forefront of Christian praxis and theology. Such spirituality has a strong communal dimension.

Several influences come together in Christian feminist spirituality. In the first place, it involves the retrieval and celebration of female Christian mysticism, as manifested in women such as Macrina, Ebba, Hildegard of Bingen, Marguerite Porete, and Teresa of Avila. A second influence is that of intellectually path-breaking women of faith who envisioned new possibilities for women in church and society, such as Christine de Pizan, Sor Juana Inés de la Cruz, or Antonia of Württemberg. A third strand of influence is the history of female activists, leaders, preachers, and teachers who dedicated their lives to the pursuit of justice, such as Sojourner Truth, Frances Willard, Antoinette Brown, or Ida B. Wells. A fourth element is the influence of global women's movements, with their push against gender injustice and their capacity to link grassroots organizations with networks of women all over the world, who may profess different religions or no religious faith at all, but who are committed to finding paths to justice and greater flourishing for women. This sort of work, which brings together women of many different walks of life and cultures, has pushed practitioners of Christian feminist spirituality to learn to recognize the work of the Spirit of life in unexpected places and has also allowed space for conversation about life-giving approaches to Scripture practiced by women in different cultural settings.

Christian feminist spirituality is manifested in many ways: in the writing of liturgies and hymns that go beyond merely masculine language for God; in the coming together of women for worship and action; in the uncovering of the inconsistency between the life abundant promised by Jesus and the way women are often treated in the Christian church; in the promoting of the leadership and the gifts of girls and women in the community of faith; in the developing of healthy ways of interpreting the Bible and tradition; in the struggle for the health and reproductive rights of women and against gendered violence; in the promoting of literacy, education, and strong voices for women; in the rediscovering of forms of women's spirituality through the centuries; in eco-feminism and the defense of creation; in the unmasking of injustice; in the raising of consciousness about how racism and classism work together with sexism in reimaging work and the workplace; in the celebrating of the different phases of the lives of women; and in the empowering of women and men to live together in greater justice and peace. Above all, feminist spirituality is cultivated by resisting concrete manifestations of injustice and by encouraging the flourishing of life abundant for all in the Spirit of the God of life.

See also Gender; Masculine Spirituality; *Mujerista* Spirituality; Womanist Spirituality.

For Further Reading: K. Baker-Fletcher, *Dancing with God* (2006); M. Grey, *Sacred Longings* (2003); E. Johnson, *Quest for the Living God* (2007); M. Kanyoro, ed., *In Search of a Round Table* (1997);

P. L. Kwok, *Postcolonial Imagination and Feminist Theology* (2005).

Nancy E. Bedford

Fénelon, François (1651–1715)

Gifted French theologian, preacher, and spiritual writer. He was born into an aristocratic family and privately tutored in classical literature, philosophy, and theology. In 1675 he was ordained to the Roman Catholic priesthood and joined the Sulpician order. In 1678 Fénelon was appointed by the archbishop of Paris to head a community of women converts from Protestantism. After revocation of the Edict of Nantes, he was conscripted by King Louis XIV in 1686 to labor for three years in regions of France seeking the reconversion of Huguenot Protestants to the Catholic faith. Thereafter he became private tutor and mentor for the king's young grandson, the Duke of Burgundy. In 1695 he was appointed archbishop of the prestigious see of Cambrai.

Drawn to the contemplative piety of Madame Guyon, Fénelon became involved in the controversy over Quietism. He defended the former from charges of heresy, arguing that her mystical passivity was consistent with classical Catholic spirituality. When the Inquisition condemned Guyon's views, Fénelon reluctantly accepted the church's decree, although losing his influential position in the royal court. As archbishop he was an outspoken opponent of the Jansenist revival in France, writing several tracts against the movement. Fénelon's later years were invested in monastic life at Cambrai: writing, laboring in the formation of priests, and offering spiritual direction both in person and through numerous letters to a wide range of people. A carriage accident weakened his frame and led to his death at age sixty-five.

Fénelon's letters and writings in the areas of literature, philosophy, theology, and spirituality were published in 1830 in thirty-three volumes. Gentle and approachable in demeanor, his spiritual writings are characterized by abandonment of self-interest, love of God above all else, and submission of the human will to the divine will. His writings bear affinity to themes enunciated by Francis de Sales and Brother Lawrence. His many letters are laden with practical guidelines for faithful Christian living, reflected in titles such as "On Freedom from Self," "False Notions of Spiritual Progress," and "When We Feel Abandoned by God." He insisted that ordinary lay folk could live God-honoring and spiritually fulfilling lives in their ordinary callings in the world. Fénelon's spiritual writings enjoy revived interest today among both Catholics and Protestants.

See also Guyon, Madame; Quietism.

For Further Reading: *Fénelon: Selected Writings*, CWS (2006); F. Fénelon, *Christian Perfection* (1947); idem, *The Royal Way of the Cross* (1982); idem, *Talking with God* (1997).

Bruce A. Demarest

Finney, Charles Grandison (1792 – 1875)

American revivalist and theologian, founder of Oberlin theology. Called "America's greatest revivalist," Finney was the leading figure of the Second Great Awakening. Originally trained in law, he turned his attention to ministry immediately following his own dramatic conversion in 1821. He first served as a missionary to the expanding American frontier, seeing thousands turn or return to God under his ministry. After serving two significant pastorates in New York City, Finney finally moved to Oberlin, Ohio, to pastor First Congregational Church, to serve as professor of theology at Oberlin College and, eventually, to become its president.

Finney's theology matched the optimism of antebellum America. He insisted on the relative goodness and indispensability of human involvement in the saving work of God. He rejected Old School Presbyterian's pessimism about human potency in regard to regeneration and, rather, asserted the ongoing human ability to freely choose for Christ and to pursue a life of holiness. What keeps humanity from Christ and following him is its lack of willingness, not its lack of ability. To be saved, humanity simply has to choose Christ and follow him.

Further, Finney asserted that revivals, which to that time had been understood as "surprising works of God," are not solely miraculous happenings. Instead, revivals occur whenever humanity rightly employs the means that God has ordained for that purpose. Among these providential means, or "new measures," are (1) encouraging women to pray in public meetings; (2) the use of the "anxious bench," an area near the front of the assembly where those unsure of their spiritual state would receive greater attention; (3) protracted meetings; (4) the use of informal and emotionally charged language in preaching; and (5) the quick admission of new members into the church.

Finney's theology of sanctification followed a similar pattern. He asserted that "entire sanctification" or "the baptism of the Holy Ghost" was a synergistic work of God and humanity, which humanity entered by an act of faith subsequent to conversion. It was the privilege of all believers and empowered them for both holy living and effective ministry. The sanctified, therefore, ought to make a difference in this world. This "Oberlin theology" led to Oberlin College's deep involvement in such social issues as abolition, suffrage, and temperance.

See also Evangelism; Revival; Will, Human.

For Further Reading: J. Gresham, *Charles G. Finney's Doctrine of the Baptism of the Holy Spirit* (1987); C. Hambrick-Stowe, *Charles G. Finney and the Spirit of American Evangelicalism* (1996); G. Rosell and R. Dupuis, eds., *Original Memoirs of Charles G. Finney* (2002).

Bernie Van De Walle

Fire

While never an object of veneration in itself, fire with its rich biblical and cultural associations has been incorporated into Christian spiritual practice for centuries. Symbolically, fire in the OT is especially associated with God's presence (e.g., Ex. 3:1–6; 13:21), and also with God's purifying and refining of the covenant people (Prov. 17:3), God's acceptance of offered sacrifices (Lev. 1), the prayers of God's people as carried upward by incense (Ps. 141:2), and God's final judgment of the wicked (Isa. 66:15). In the NT, God's purifying, illumining, and empowering presence is associated specifically with the Holy Spirit (Matt. 3:11–12; cf. Acts 2:3). Final judgment, whether of the church (1 Cor. 3:10–15) or of the unbelieving world (2 Peter 3:7), is pictured as fiery, in continuity with OT symbolism. Under both covenants, believers are encouraged to live their lives in awe-filled reverence before God who "is a consuming fire" (Deut. 4:24; cf. Heb. 12:28–29).

Liturgically, candles and incense have been used in Christian worship from at least the 4th century. While the formal use of these elements was rejected by some Puritan and Nonconformist Protestants, the ancient connections continue to be expressed, often transmuted into metaphor: the heart burns with love for God (cf. John Wesley's heart "strangely warmed"); prayer is "the motion of a hidden fire that trembles in the breast" (Montgomery). In popular North American religious experience, campfires have often served as the place of conversion or confession. The metaphor of the "family altar" to describe worship within the family domesticates the biblical symbolism of fire and locates it within the Christian home. The charismatic renewal of the latter part of the 20th century was often spoken of figuratively in terms of fire.

Influenced by the recovery of earlier Christian traditions and also by a reengagement with the traditions of Judaism, many evangelical Christians now light candles as an aid to focusing their thoughts for prayer or to mark the beginning of Sabbath. Candles are also often used in corporate worship, especially at special celebratory times.

See also Baptism of the Holy Spirit; Holiness; Pentecostal Spirituality.

For Further Reading: D. Bass, *Receiving the Day* (2000); C. Hummel, *Fire in the Fireplace* (1978); J. Montgomery, *Methodist Hymn and Tune Book* (1917); M. Ross, *The Fountain and the Furnace: The Way of Tears and Fire* (1987); M. Zimmerman, *Celebrating Biblical Feasts* (2004).

Maxine Hancock

Food

Food is ubiquitous in Scripture. It sustains and nourishes life and also brings joy. At creation and thereafter God provided food, in the form of plants and fruit, for all his sensate creatures (Gen. 1:29), a point not lost on either the psalmist (Ps. 104) or the apostle Paul (Acts 14:17). During the exodus and Israel's subsequent wilderness wandering, God supernaturally provided manna—food from heaven—to sustain them in otherwise deadly conditions (Ex. 16). Frequently in Scripture, bread serves as a synecdoche for food and in this sense becomes ultimately a metaphor for Christ himself—the Bread of Life who also came down from heaven, but who can completely satisfy the hunger of the world (John 6).

Humanity must ingest food regularly to stay alive. This fact underscores the fragility of mortal existence and humanity's radical dependence on God. Such dependence is etched in Christian consciousness by the phrase embedded in the Lord's Prayer—"Give us today our daily bread" (Matt. 6:11), where bread almost certainly represents more, though not less, than people's daily food requirements.

The divine satisfaction of our need for food should evoke gratitude. Originally during *Sukkok* (the Feast of Tabernacles), one of Judaism's great festivals, worshipers gathered in Jerusalem to celebrate the historic wilderness provision and also to give thanks for their own annual harvest ingathering of food. Jesus himself set an example of pausing first to give God thanks for food, something long perpetuated in the Christian practice of giving thanks or "saying [thanks for] grace" prior to daily meals. In this way food consumption becomes a physical trigger for sustaining a properly grateful and God-conscious tone to one's days.

On the other hand, an inordinate desire for food can become a temptation and ground for compromise, as biblical figures like Eve and Esau ruefully discovered. Part of the discipline of fasting is to ensure that our need for physical food remains properly ordered. Nor is there any place for gluttony (excessive consumption) in the spiritual life.

Food is also used metaphorically in Scripture. Jesus informed his disciples, following his encounter with the Samaritan woman, that his "food" was to do the will of his Father in heaven (John 4:34). To participate in the larger purposes of God was for Christ a soul-nourishing and energizing experience—living in that flow made him more fully alive.

Food enhances both fellowship and celebration. In the first place, eating with others is a transcultural sign of social acceptance and a way of cultivating human friendship and fellowship; there is a mysteriously uniting dynamic to being at table together. And second, banquets are a timeless way to gather in celebration. Not incidentally, one of the earliest recorded practices of the NT church was breaking bread together joyfully (Acts 2:46). Both of these dynamics are presupposed in the Christian eschatological vision of a great marriage supper of the Lamb (Rev. 19).

But the greatest convergence of food and Christian spirituality is found in the ongoing observance of the Lord's Supper, wherein Christ becomes "bread" for his people and "real food" (John 6:55), infusing them, as they feed on him in their hearts, with the supernatural life needed to sustain and renew their own. With this in view, the Lord's Supper becomes also a time of thanksgiving (hence Eucharist) for what has been provided, of reconciled table fellowship with others, and of collective anticipation of a greater banquet still ahead.

See also Body; Consumerism; Fasting; Gluttony.

Glen G. Scorgie

Foot Washing

The Christian practice of foot washing was instituted in the words and actions of Jesus (John 13:1–20). In the shadow of the cross, Jesus rose from the dinner, laid aside his garments, poured water into a foot basin, washed the feet of his disciples, and then dried them with the towel he was wearing. In his concurrent dialogue with Peter, Jesus revealed that this foot washing was no mere offer of hospitality, as Peter presumed, but an act that would be understood fully only "after these things" (that is, after the resurrection). When Peter initially refused the washing, Jesus revealed that it had soteriological significance—Peter's future destiny was dependent upon it.

In response to Peter's attempt to dictate which washings were most needful, Jesus revealed its purpose and meaning: "A person who has had a bath needs only to wash his feet; his whole body is clean." In these words of Jesus, the common practices of bathing at home and providing water for washing the dirt off the feet of guests were transformed into a sacramental sign, wherein those who had undergone the bath of baptism had no need of additional washing, except for the feet.

Foot washing was to function as a sign of the continual cleansing from sin available to the believer after conversion and baptism. Jesus' expectation that the practice of foot washing should continue is made clear in his instructions concerning it (John 13:14–17). Thus, when believers offer and receive foot washing, they follow the Lord's example and command. They also become both ministers and recipients of the grace of God to each other, through this act of humble service that signifies the ongoing forgiveness of sin available to them all.

New Testament evidence suggesting that such foot washing continued on as a distinctively Christian practice includes 1 Timothy 5:10. The practice can also be documented in every century of the history of the Christian church from Tertullian to Augustine, Bernard of Clairvaux to Martin Bucer, and Anabaptists to Seventh-day Adventists and Pentecostals.

Though foot washing continues to be practiced in a variety of Christian traditions, including Roman Catholic, Orthodox, Anglican, and certain other denominations and groups, the practice is absent among many Protestant and evangelical groups. The historical roots of this omission lie partly in Luther and Calvin's rejection of foot washing as a papal practice. Evangelical communities influenced by this negative assessment of the practice tend to disregard the cleansing language of John 13 and instead to treat Jesus' conduct as an example of the humble service believers should show to one another.

See also Forgiveness; Humility.

For Further Reading: J. C. Thomas, *Footwashing in John 13 and the Johannine Community* (1991); idem, "Footwashing," in *Religion Past and Present*, ed. H. Betz et al. (2007); J. Vanier, *The Scandal of Service* (1996).

John Christopher Thomas

Forgetting

See **Remembering and Forgetting.**

Forgiveness

Forgiveness is at the heart of the Christian gospel. Through Jesus all people can come to God the Father as forgiven, fully accepted as God's beloved children. Thus, the message of forgiveness is all good news. The problem is that God calls on us to practice forgiveness toward one another (e.g., Matt. 6:12). And this human-to-human forgiveness is fraught with complexity and struggle. It is one thing to joyfully accept God's forgiveness of our failings; it is quite another to forgive another person for having harmed us. Our difficulty in offering forgiveness stems from a normal and also necessary aspect of human nature. God created us

to experience anger and outrage when humans hurt each other. We need to have a keen sense of evil and harm in order to know when things are amiss and should be addressed. We would not want to live in a world where people were not disturbed when humans hurt one another.

The crux of the matter is: How do we respond to person-to-person injury? Some Christians are prone to quoting Scripture to wounded persons, expecting them to immediately and completely forgive their perpetrator. However, deeply wounded persons are not likely to be motivated to forgive on the basis of biblical commands alone. Such an approach is likely to actually short-circuit the forgiveness process, leaving the wounded person feeling abandoned, misunderstood, and alienated.

Forgiveness is a process; it is a journey along what may be a long and convoluted road. Forgiveness needs to begin with affirmation of and compassion for the wounded one. Hurting persons must share their story with others who will receive the complete story with concern and kindness. The damage done and the pain the person is suffering need to be validated. This embracing of the hurting person and his or her story and pain is a crucial component of the forgiveness process and must take place in order for the individual to reach a place of readiness to offer forgiveness. The church community serves a vital function in this regard.

Having received the comfort of divine and human love, the wounded person can now contemplate releasing anger and resentment toward the offender and offering forgiveness. This involves handing over to God the Father all rights to exact revenge for what has happened. It is a profound act of faith and trust in God to believe that he loves us deeply, cares very much about the wrong and hurt inflicted on us, and takes seriously the effect on us. As we offer our right to exact revenge to our wise heavenly Father, we experience the release and freedom of forgiveness. We may still experience pain and ongoing consequences from how we were wounded, but we no longer carry the burden of anger and vengefulness that could render us embittered and diminished in spirit. Entrusting judgment to God through forgiveness frees God to do something redemptive and healing not only in our own lives but also in the life of the offender.

See also Examen; Penitence; Reconciliation.

For Further Reading: D. Kraybill et al., *Amish Grace: How Forgiveness Transcended Tragedy* (2007); D. Morris, *Forgiving the Dead Man Walking* (1999); M. Seibold, "When the Wounding Runs Deep," in *Care for the Soul*, ed. M. McMinn and T. Phillips, (2001), 295–308; D. Tutu, *No Future without Forgiveness* (1999).

Myrla Seibold

Formation, Spiritual

Spiritual formation and the related terms *spirituality* and *spiritual growth* have become popular. While their contemporary usage transcends any single tradition, our focus here is on the Christian context, wherein their expanded usage signals the recovery of neglected but important themes. *Christian spirituality*, the broadest term, is the sum total of a person's lived experience in the transforming presence of God. It encompasses every dimension of life, both personal and public. *Spiritual formation* is a more refined term connoting a particular dynamic within Christian spirituality. Jeffrey Greenman has noted that it involves "our continuing response to the reality of God's grace shaping us into the likeness of Jesus Christ, through the work of the Holy Spirit, in the community of faith for the sake of others." Some differentiate formation (of an unformed object) from transformation (that requires the remaking of something), while others see a difference between formation as human effort, and transformation as God's refining and integration of those human efforts. Nonetheless most who use the term *spiritual formation* are aware of both the human and divine sides of the process.

Spiritual growth is an equally valid depiction of the mysterious process by which the life of the Christian comes into ever more resonant alignment with the pattern and character of Jesus Christ (2 Peter 3:18). Being an organic image, spiritual *growth* underscores how it is the impulses of divine life that actually propel things ahead ("God made it grow," 1 Cor. 3:6). The growth metaphor also highlights parallels to human growth generally and thus allows for spurts of transformation in response to crises, as well as ostensibly uneventful seasons of gradual movement toward maturity in Christ.

Formation is always occurring because shaping influences are ubiquitous and unrelenting. However, such formation may actually be negative and deformative, shaping a person in ways that are at odds with the gospel. Therefore, the proper question is not *whether* one is being formed, but *how* and *in what direction*. It is critically important that believers are conscious of the dynamics affecting their lives and are then very intentional about pursuing their formational goals.

This is reinforced by a consideration of some primary biblical passages that employ *morphe*, the root word of *formation*. Jesus' transfiguration (Matt. 17:5; cf. Mark 9:7; Luke 9:35) reveals how being in God's presence through prayer can transform a person. The apostle Paul illumined the goal even more by declaring that God's plan is for us "to be conformed to the likeness of his Son" (Rom. 8:29). Paul also recognized the importance of countering the pervasive formative nature of the world by being transformed through the renewing of our minds (Rom. 12:2). However, this formative process in Christ is not limited to the mind alone, as Paul employs the birthing metaphor of a midwife and declares the more expansive nature of maturing in Christ: "My dear children, for whom I am again in the pains of childbirth until Christ is formed in you" (Gal. 4:19). Further, this transformation is a continuous process guided by the Holy Spirit (2 Cor. 3:18).

Historically, *spiritual formation* was first employed by the Roman Catholic Church to describe the process of formation for priests. This formation of the spiritual life complemented the academic pursuit of knowledge. Beginning in the 1960s, Protestant seminaries began to incorporate a similar emphasis, integrating the classroom with the chapel. The United Methodist Church broadened this focus to include the church at large through their ministry of the Upper Room. However, it would be a mistake to limit the Protestant interest in spiritual formation to the latter half of the 20th century. Calvin's usage of the term *piety* in the 16th century already indicated an awareness of the importance of spiritual formation. The intentional usage of spiritual practices, especially in their communal form, united with a dependency on the Holy Spirit's gift of grace, encouraged growth toward spiritual maturity. Further evidence that the principles of spiritual formation are not alien to the evangelical tradition can be found in the Puritans and Pietists of the 17th century and the evangelical awakenings of the 18th century. During these periods, the focus of spiritual formation was expressed in the language of growing in godliness, devotion, or walking with God.

The previous definition reveals the complexity and multilayered nature of spiritual formation. While formation should be taken seriously, Christians need to resist the temptation to place excessive emphasis on personal performance and external measurements of achievement. This lifelong process combines an intentional and continuing human response, including various time-honored strategies and disciplined approaches to God's prior initiative of grace. Therefore, Christ's presence within the human heart inspires the imitation of Christ. Grace promotes a disciplined effort that is motivated by love and gratitude to God. Central to this process is a dynamic shaping of the soul into conformity to the likeness of Jesus Christ. Luke 2:52 describes the totality of this formation that is not limited to isolated or compartmentalized aspects of life; it follows Jesus' pattern who "grew in wisdom and stature, and in favor with God and [humanity]." This is impossible without the Holy Spirit who generously applies grace to transform human lives. The Holy Spirit is the foundation for all true *Spirit*-ual formation. While each person must respond to the impulses of God's life-giving Spirit, no one travels this journey in isolation from others, who together provide support, accountability, and connection with the long tradition of the communion of saints. Supportive relationships governed by grace can also prevent an unhealthy and self-critical preoccupation with personal progress that ignores God's desired involvement. Further, spiritual formation properly understood is not for personal gain or self-improvement but rather for God's glory and the sake of the world. It is just as likely to flourish during times of critical struggle as during periods of tranquillity and success. The missional outlook of this term reinforces that spiritual formation involves both loving God and loving one's neighbor.

See also Direction, Spiritual; Discipleship; Journey, Spiritual.

For Further Reading: K. Collins, ed., *Exploring Christian Spirituality* (2000); L. Cunningham and K. Egan, *Christian Spirituality* (1996); B. Demarest, *Satisfy Your Soul* (1999); R. Foster, *Celebration of Discipline* (1988); J. Greenman and G. Kalantzis, eds., *Life in the Spirit* (2010); E. Howard, *Brazos Introduction to Christian Spirituality* (2008), 267 – 97; R. Mulholland Jr., *Invitation to a Journey* (1993); M. Thompson, *Soul Feast* (1995); D. Whitney, *Ten Questions to Diagnose Your Spiritual Health* (2001); J. Wilhoit, *Spiritual Formation as if the Church Mattered* (2008); D. Willard, *Renovation of the Heart* (2002).

Tom Schwanda

Fosdick, Harry Emerson (1878 – 1969)

American Baptist minister of the liberal tradition. He pastored churches in New Jersey and New York, and taught homiletics at Union Theological Seminary. While ordained to the Baptist ministry, he also served as "guest minister" at First Presbyterian Church in New York City (1918–1925). Educated at Colgate and Union Theological Seminary, he was influenced by William Newton Clarke and the writings of Walter Rauschenbusch.

A turning point in his career came in 1922 when he preached his most famous sermon, "Shall the Fundamentalists Win?" While attempting greater tolerance between fundamentalists and liberals, Fosdick's sermon was perceived as an attack on key theological issues and ignited the fundamentalist-modernist controversy. Pressure from both conservative Baptists and Presbyterians ensued, which led to severing his relationship with First Presbyterian Church. John D. Rockefeller Jr., a friend of Fosdick, offered him the position of pastor at Park Avenue Baptist Church in 1925, which became the renowned Riverside Church in 1930. He remained as minister of the congregation until 1946.

As a polished pulpiteer and skillful writer, Fosdick forged an influential ministry. His person-centered gospel connected with the needs of individuals and made him the most recognized Protestant preacher in the country. His successful *Christian Living* (1937); *Faith for Tough Times* (1941); *On Being a Real Person* (1943); sermons; and familiar hymn, "God of Grace and God of Glory" (1930), spoke powerfully to millions of people who were struggling with real-life issues, and some even referred to him as a "pastoral psychologist." Always possessing high Christian standards for living, he made his "evangelical liberal" version of Christianity both relevant and appealing, though in later life his theological understanding became more conservative. His other writings include *The Meaning of Prayer* (1915), *The Modern Use of the Bible* (1924), and an autobiography, *The Living of these Days* (1956).

Wayne S. Hansen

through serious Scripture study, strengthened through Dietrich Bonhoeffer's writings on costly discipleship, and purified through the refining fire of unanswered prayer, as his mother suffered and eventually succumbed to the ravages of multiple sclerosis.

After college he earned a doctorate in pastoral theology from Fuller Seminary (1970). A recorded minister of the Friends Church, Foster's first pastorate drew his focus to soul growth; he and his congregation (which included Dallas Willard) pursued intimacy with God by experimenting with spiritual habits documented in the Bible and the Christian classics. As they explored such practices as Scripture meditation, prayer, solitude, fasting, and sacrifice within the context of daily life, Christian spiritual formation emerged as the central theme of Foster's calling.

Foster discerningly reacquainted contemporary evangelicals with the ecumenical wisdom of the historical church in his influential writing, teaching, and Renovaré renewal ministries. Through the pen of this award-winning Quaker—in such groundbreaking books as *Celebration of Discipline* (1978), *The Freedom of Simplicity* (1981), *Prayer* (1992), *Streams of Living Water* (1998), and numerous articles and editorial works, including *Devotional Classics* (coedited 1995) and *The Renovaré Spiritual Formation Bible* (lead Renovaré editor 2005)—evangelicals have learned how to live out what Renovaré terms the "with-God life" by following their covenant, which calls for "utter dependence" on Jesus as "ever-living Savior, Teacher, Lord, and Friend." Teaching Christians the transformational value of embracing the spiritual disciplines, many of which were practiced by Jesus himself, and then imitated by his followers for centuries, is one of Foster's most enduring gifts to the contemporary church.

Natalie Hendrickson

Foster, Richard J. (1942–)

Influential evangelical Quaker author. As a youth, Foster's personal life with Jesus was established

Foucauld, Charles Eugene de

See **De Foucauld, Charles Eugene.**

Fox, George (1624 – 1691)

Principal founder and organizer of the Quakers, later called the Religious Society of Friends. He was born in Drayton-in-the-Clay, Leicestershire, England, son of a Puritan weaver. He had little formal education, was apprenticed to a shoemaker, and spent some time as a shepherd. He came of age during the English Civil War and went through a period of intense wandering, spiritual seeking, and deep disillusionment with established religion as well as with the dissenters and sectarians. In 1647, at the moment of his deepest despair, he heard a voice within saying, "There is one, even Christ Jesus, that can speak to thy condition." He reported, "When I heard it, my heart did leap for joy." More "openings" followed, in which he experienced the infinite love of God. He recalled, "I saw also, that there was an ocean of darkness and death; but an infinite ocean of light and love, which flowed over the ocean of darkness."

These experiences prompted him to begin preaching a radical message of empowerment by turning to the light of Christ within, without the mediation of church, priest, or sacrament. His *Journal*, heavily edited by Thomas Elwood and published posthumously in 1694, describes his spiritual journey and the rise of the Quaker movement in language and experiences that sometimes echo the book of Acts. In 1652, upon his release from a year in Derby prison for illegal preaching, he journeyed north, and at a place called Firbank Fell, he met up with another group of radicals called the Westmoreland Seekers. So many of this group, including its leaders, joined with Fox that Firbank Fell came to be regarded as the birthplace of the Quaker movement. But more likely, it was a manor house in Northwest England, Swarthmore Hall, home of Margaret Fell and her husband, Thomas Fell, a judge. The support of the Fells became a turning point in the nascent Quaker movement. Margaret became a key leader and author of numerous writings, including a biblical defense of women's right to preach, and Swarthmore Hall became the head-

quarters of the movement. In 1669, eleven years after her husband's death, Margaret Fell married George Fox. They spent the rest of their life (though rarely together) shaping a new kind of Christianity that was biblical, contemplative, and prophetic but considered unorthodox by their coreligionists.

Fox was attacked fiercely for his view of Scripture. Although Scripture shaped his entire worldview, and he accepted its authority, he invited intense hostility when he elevated the Holy Spirit above Scripture. He claimed that while the Bible was God's written revelation, neither the power nor the truths of the written words could be understood rightly without directly experiencing the Spirit.

Fox spent most of his time, when not imprisoned, in missionary travels to Ireland, Europe, the West Indies, and the American colonies, gathering followers, planting new meetings, and creating a democratic organizational structure he called "gospel order." Fox supported the controversial move to allow women to have their own meetings, giving them a measure of independence and authority revolutionary for its time. Quaker development was immeasurably aided by Fox's ability to attract influential and educated leaders, such as William Penn and Robert Barclay, to provide theological formulation to what was essentially a grassroots experience-based social-religious movement. Fox taught his followers to reject war and the use of violence, to refuse to pay tithes, and to resist conventional gender and social distinctions.

See also Quaker Spirituality.

For Further Reading: D. Gwyn, *Apocalypse of the Word: The Life and Message of George Fox* (1986); L. Ingle, *George Fox and the Creation of Quakerism* (1966); G. Nuttall, *Studies in Christian Enthusiasm* (1948); A. Roberts, *Through Flaming Sword: The Life and Legacy of George Fox* (2008).

Carole Dale Spencer

Fox, Matthew (1940 –)

A leading contemporary New Age religionist and promoter of what he calls "creation spirituality." In the 1960s and 1970s, as a Roman Catholic Dominican priest, Matthew Fox slowly developed and began to promote his ideas. In 1984 he founded Friends of Creation Spirituality, which publishes a journal and supports his work. Because of Fox's unorthodox teachings, the Roman Catholic Church silenced him, and eventually he left it in 1993. He was ordained a priest in the American Episcopal Church the following year. In 1996 he founded the University of Creation Spirituality in Oakland, California, which became Wisdom University in 2005. Here he seeks to bring business, art, science, religion, and spirituality together. Fox is a gifted, creative, and charismatic leader, speaker, and writer. He has written some twenty-eight books to date along with numerous other works. He travels and speaks widely, promoting his ideas. Fox's approach emphasizes ecological connections and is widely interreligious, embracing diverse religious perspectives. More recently Fox has dubbed his movement a "New Reformation" and started what he calls the Ancestral Wisdom Education (AWE) Project to reform education of children and teens. He continues to explore and promote new ideas.

See also Creation-Centered Spirituality.

For Further Reading: M. Fox, *Confessions* (1996); www.matthewfox.org.

John Mustol

Franciscan Spirituality

Many Christians, including some Protestant evangelicals, practice Franciscan spirituality, but professed Franciscans are the official keepers of the tradition. These followers include three branches of the first order, the Friars Minor (1209), the Friars Minor Conventuals (1517), and the Friars Minor Capuchins (1619); the second order, the Poor Clares; and the Third Order, which includes both laypersons who practice a spiritual discipline and the many later Catholic Franciscan orders. There are also Anglican, Lutheran, and ecumenical Franciscan orders.

Franciscan spirituality includes distinctive emphases on poverty, joy, prayer, reform, missions, preaching, and the creation. All of these go back directly to Francis of Assisi (1182–1226) who lived a passionate life of imitation of his Lord Jesus Christ. In the Franciscan Rule, officially approved by Pope Honorius III in 1223, Francis's simple list of Bible passages from 1209 is expanded to include rules concerning novices, education, and carrying out the business affairs of the order. But his spirit of encouragement suffuses the hard rules of poverty, chastity, and obedience.

One distinctive theme of Franciscan spirituality is voluntary poverty. Francis insisted that his brothers should not only avoid any contact with money on a personal basis, but that the order itself should remain without property or money. At a minimum, Franciscan spirituality calls for a rejection of a materialist or consumerist lifestyle, and therefore the practice of simplicity.

Francis's joy is not only from his freedom from worldly possessions, but his delight in instant obedience to his Lord. Francis was a literalist in his hearing of the gospel, and put it into practice however he could, with no quibbles. Francis's reliance on God to supply his needs reminds one of Matthew 6:25–34 ("Therefore I tell you, do not worry about your life ..."). Francis took the Scriptures very seriously, as is indicated by his informal rule of 1209, consisting of the list of Bible passages he thought most pertinent to following the Savior.

Franciscan spirituality certainly puts prayer at its center, as Francis and his friends devoted themselves to daily prayer and to worship in the churches wherever they happened to be. The rule calls on brothers to pray the Our Father many times a day. Francis often went on retreat for extended prayer. The Poor Clares exemplify the Franciscan focus on prayer in a life devoted entirely to contemplation.

One of the themes often overlooked is the Franciscan desire for reform in the church. Francis's early call from Christ at San Damiano indicated the need for such reform, and his attendance at the Fourth Lateran Council (1215) stimulated his thinking about what was needed. Francis's life can be seen as a call for reformation before the time of the Protestant Reformation. He was totally loyal to the church, avoiding all the heresies that were flourishing in his day, but he was also aware of the many faults of the church, which he sought to repair.

International missions have been an important part of the Franciscan legacy. The names of familiar cities in California come from Franciscan missions: among them Los Angeles (from the church near Assisi where the earliest Franciscans gathered), and supremely San Francisco, the name of the saint himself. Much can be criticized about Franciscan missions in the Americas in the 16th century, but the order has changed its ways since then, and missions remain an important part of Franciscan spirituality.

Franciscan spirituality has a special place for the humanity of Jesus and for the Holy Land. Francis's staging of the Christmas Mass at Greccio led to our present-day crèches. But far more, it renewed the awareness that Jesus was really a human being. It was to the Franciscan order that Pope Clement VI granted custody of the holy pilgrimage sites all across the Middle East in 1342.

Franciscan spirituality today often recalls Francis's special relationship to the creatures and his desire for peace. Given our concern about the vanishing of species and global climate change, his care for creation is a theme very much appreciated. He was also a reconciler of opponents in the factious world of Italian city-states and therefore provides a model of Jesus' words "Blessed are the peacemakers."

Franciscan spirituality cannot be reduced to a sentimental love of pets or a statue in the garden, but the ecological theme in Francis is a distinctive contribution. Further, Francis is not simply about the creation, but also the redemption: he calls all who will listen to become disciples of the Lord Jesus Christ and renewers of the church.

See also Ecological Spirituality; Francis of Assisi.

For Further Reading: M. Crosby, *Finding Francis, Following Christ* (2007); I. Delio et al., *Care for Creation* (2008); *Francis of Assisi: Early Documents*, ed. R. Armstrong et al., 3 vols. (1999 – 2001); B. Ramon, *Franciscan Spirituality* (2009); W. Short, *Poverty and Joy* (1999).

Bradley P. Holt

Francis de Sales (1567 – 1622)

Early modern Roman Catholic bishop, spiritual guide, author, preacher, and cofounder (with Jane de Chantal) of the Visitation of Holy Mary. Born in Savoy into an aristocratic family and schooled by the Jesuits as a youth, de Sales early decided to dedicate his life to the spiritual revitalization of the Catholic faith. After studying civil and canon law at the University of Padua, he convinced his parents to allow him to enter the priesthood. He became coadjutor to the bishop of Geneva (in exile in Savoy as Geneva was a Protestant city) and was sent on a mission to reclaim the Chablais region for the Catholic faith. In 1602 he was raised to the episcopal office. His main efforts as bishop were directed toward reform and spiritual renewal. He took seriously the directives from the Council of Trent that required bishops to be true shepherds in their dioceses. He preached regularly, introduced diocesan catechetical training, strove to reform religious orders, and provided spiritual guidance for scores of people as well as participated in diplomatic activity on behalf of the Duke of Savoy. His teaching has been characterized as "devout humanism."

De Sales was in contact with and influenced the leading lights of the spiritual renewal sweeping the French-speaking world, such as Pierre de Bérulle, Madame Acarie, and Vincent de Paul. He was viewed as a gifted preacher who, contrary to the practice of the day, preached "heart to heart," using vivid imagery to communicate his love of God to his listeners. He was also a sought-after spiritual director instrumental in shaping that pastoral ministry. Among those who sought his spiritual guidance were many laywomen. In 1609 he published his most popular book, *Introduction to the Devout Life*, which was based on the letters written to Madame de Charmoisy, one of his correspondents. This guide to a deepened spirituality practiced in the midst of an ordinary life was an immediate success, even across confessional barriers. Although the Catholic reform had reaffirmed the value of religious life and the celibate priesthood, de Sales gave voice to the spiritual longings of laypersons. The book affirmed the value of marriage as a spiritual calling and taught that spiritual practices must be adapted to the duties of one's "state in life."

Central to de Sales's pastoral vision was the idea that God was raising up devout individuals in all walks of life to leaven the loaf of Christendom. Hence, the Savoyard encouraged spiritual engagement for persons in all walks of life. Chief among his teachings was the practice of the "little virtues," such as gentleness, humility, patience, simplicity, and cordiality that are realized in relational contexts. He looked to the Jesus of Matthew 11:28–30, who invited all to come "and learn from me, for I am gentle and humble in heart" as a model.

De Sales's other major work, *Treatise on the Love of God* (1616), explores "the story of the origin, progress, decay, operation, properties, advantages and excellence of divine love." It contains his fullest theological vision expressed in the poetic language of image and example at which he excelled. At the core of the *Treatise*, as indeed all his writing, is the bishop's vision of an interconnected world of human and divine hearts. Although in essence beyond description, God may metaphorically be said to have a heart that is the source of all love. Trinitarian, the heart of God is imagined as relational and dynamic—as pulsing, breathing, and beating. In its fullness, the heart of God overflows, creating the world and especially the human heart that is

designed to beat in rhythm with its divine counterpart. But, through sin, human hearts do not always align themselves with God. The human-divine heart of the gentle, humble Jesus is thus needed and, if allowed to "live" in human hearts, may align them with the heart of the Creator. In de Sales's mind, transformation of heart takes place both vertically and horizontally—in the intimate communication of prayer and sacramental participation, as well as in human communication. Thus, preaching, teaching, family and marriage, friendship, spiritual guidance, and the like are seen as relational avenues through which heart can speak to heart.

In 1610, with widowed Jane Frances Frémyot, Baroness de Chantal, de Sales cofounded the Visitation of Holy Mary, an innovative congregation for women. Madame de Chantal was the first superior. The Visitation emphasized external simplicity and moderation and focused on the interior asceticism of living the little virtues. While originally conceived as a diocesan congregation without formal vows and enclosure, as the directives of the Council of Trent were implemented, the Visitation became a formal, enclosed order.

Nineteenth-century France saw a revival of interest in promulgating the Salesian spirit, and a number of religious orders and lay associations were founded to appropriate and promote de Sales's vision. These include the Salesians of Don Bosco, Daughters of Mary Help of Christians, the Salesian Cooperators, the Oblates of St. Francis de Sales, the Oblate Sisters of St. Francis de Sales, the Missionaries of St. Francis de Sales, and the Daughters of St. Francis de Sales.

See also Jane Frances de Chantal.

For Further Reading: *Francis de Sales and Jane de Chantal: Letters of Spiritual Direction*, CWS (1988); A. Ravier, *Francis de Sales*, trans. J. Bowler (1988); W. Wright, *Heart Speaks to Heart* (2004); idem, "That Is What They Are Made For," in *Spiritualities of the Heart*, ed. A. Callahan (1990), 143–58.

Wendy M. Wright

Francis of Assisi (1182–1226)

Founder of Franciscan Orders. Of all the saints, Francis is reputed to be the person most like Jesus. He has been chosen as one of the ten most influential persons of the second millennium, an influence due not mainly to his writings but to his life. The son of an upwardly mobile cloth merchant, Pietro Bernadone, the young Francis was a carefree party boy. But he was changed by a series of conversions into a carefree preacher of the gospel. He spent a year in a fetid dungeon, was summoned by Jesus himself in the Church of San Damiano to repair his broken-down church, and came to embrace lepers. Most dramatically, he stripped the very clothes off his back—which were a sign of his wealth and social rank—and returned them to his father, saying that henceforth he would acknowledge only "our Father who art in heaven." He remained free from any possessions for the remainder of his short life, embracing "Lady Poverty" over any other woman.

Francis took the instructions of Jesus in Matthew 10:9 literally, choosing to go without money, extra clothes, and even sandals. His lifestyle attracted followers who lived by working and begging, seeking to help the poor and lepers; and his little band worshiped together and lived wherever they could find a place.

Francis wanted to preach and therefore saw the need for papal permission for his little band of brothers. He was given an audience with Pope Innocent III in 1209. After walking to Rome, Francis's band presented their unsophisticated plan, mainly consisting of Bible verses, for the pope's approval. To the surprise of many, they succeeded, though a more substantive "rule" had to be approved later, in 1223. Rejoicing in their new status as an approved order, the Friars Minor, or "little brothers," decided to serve their Lord by both contemplation and action. They aimed not to be monks, but a new form of religious order, more flexible and poorer, so as to imitate their Master, the poor Jesus, and be free to serve everyone without "baggage." Later the order came to resemble other Catholic orders.

Among the significant events in Francis's life were his preaching to the birds to praise their Creator and preaching to a sultan. His biographers tell us that he had an extraordinary relationship with many animals. His preaching to the birds has defined Francis for some, including designers of medieval frescoes and modern garden pottery. In 1219 he traveled to Egypt with the soldiers of the Fifth Crusade and was dismayed by their behavior. He managed to cross the battle lines and appear before Sultan Melek-el-Kamel. He found the sultan to be amazingly courteous, for Francis expected to become a martyr for preaching the gospel to a Muslim. Rather, it appears that they came to regard each other with respect.

On his return, his order had grown dramatically, from his eleven companions originally to now thousands of men in many countries. Francis differed from many of them by insisting on absolute poverty for the order, and not just for individuals. He resigned as head of the order in 1220. One of his most significant innovations was the Christmas Eve Mass in Greccio, in which he used a live ox and ass to emphasize the humanness of Jesus' birth. Our Christmas crèches developed from this event.

In 1224 at a mountain called La Verna, Francis fasted on a forty-day retreat and had a vision of a seraph that was also Jesus on the cross. It is alleged that the five wounds of the Crucified began to form on his hands, feet, and side. These wounds later were understood by Franciscans to be the divine stamp of identification between the Lord and his devoted disciple. When death was near in 1226, Francis lay in the convent at San Damiano and dictated his most famous song and prayer, the "Canticle of the Creatures," or "Canticle of the Sun." This poem is unquestionably of Francis's composition. (The widely known prayer, "Lord make me an instrument of your peace...," though it clearly represents the spirit of Francis, was first composed in the 20th century.) His legacy includes the example of a joyful life in poverty, his orders, a distinctive attitude to the created order, the Christmas crèche, and his canticle of praise. He wrote very little and regretted late in life that he had abused his body through a too strict asceticism. In 1979 Pope John Paul II named Francis the patron saint of ecology.

See also Franciscan Spirituality.

For Further Reading: R. Armstrong et al., eds., *Francis of Assisi: Early Documents,* vol. 1 (1999); G. K. Chesterton, *St. Francis of Assisi* (2008); L. Cunningham, *Francis of Assisi* (2004); M. Galli, *Francis of Assisi and His World* (2003); P. Moses, *The Saint and the Sultan* (2009).

Bradley P. Holt

Francke, August Hermann (1663–1727)

Foremost second-generation German Lutheran Pietist. Francke grew up in Gotha (Thuringia) where his father, a devout lawyer, had moved in 1666 to serve as a counselor to the local duke. He studied theology at Keil and Hebrew in Hamburg. Then he continued his education in Leipzig, where he lived in the home of Philip Spener's son-in-law. In 1685 he completed a master's degree in Hebrew grammar, which allowed him the right to give lectures on the Bible. The following year, he and a friend formed the *Collegium Philobiblicum,* a group that concentrated on Bible study, a neglected area in the theological curriculum. In 1687, while doing additional work in biblical exegesis, he underwent a profound conversion experience that liberated him from all doubt. He returned to Leipzig full of zeal and in his lectures expounded a new understanding of the Bible, which had a life-changing impact on the students. Although he was supported by Spener, his enthusiasm for the new birth angered the orthodox clergy and university faculty. They turned against the "Pietists," as they labeled the group, and after some violent incidents, the study group was shut down and Francke was expelled from the city.

He briefly served a church in Erfurt where he became embroiled in Pietist reform issues. The Brandenburg elector had decided to found a new university in Halle to compete with the Saxon and orthodox Leipzig University. Over the objections of the orthodox clergy, Spener arranged for Francke to pastor St. George's Church in suburban Glaucha and to teach Greek and oriental languages at the university. Transferring to the theology faculty in 1698, he promoted biblical and practical education along the lines of Spener's *Pia Desideria* (1675) and oriented the faculty in a Pietist direction.

Serving a poverty-stricken parish, he discovered that children, many of whom were orphans, were receiving no education at all. In 1695 he started a school in his home and soon required larger facilities. Three years later he established an orphanage and began construction on what became a large complex of buildings. His enterprise transformed the sleepy town on the Saale River into the international center of Pietism. Gifted with boundless energy and enthusiasm, organizational ability, and a flair for public relations and fund-raising, Francke built his foundation into a small city of nearly three thousand people. At the center was the orphanage (*Waisenhaus)* that provided housing for poor youth and the schools that offered quality education for people at various levels of society. University students served as teachers, reflecting his conviction that they should live as well as study the Christian faith. A teacher training institute prepared good teachers and theologians to spread his ideas regarding godly education.

The Francke Foundation was a beehive of philanthropic activities. It trained and sent Protestant foreign missionaries; Halle students went to India, America, the Russian Baltic lands, and beyond. A dispensary marketed medicines throughout Europe, and a hospital was the first in Germany to give medical students clinical instruction. Other enterprises included a retail book store, a library open to the general public, and a printing plant that produced Bibles and religious literature. The resulting Canstein Bible Society became the foremost distributor of the Scriptures in eighteenth-century Europe. Also, Francke maintained extensive ecumenical ties that enabled his reform ideas to be spread widely. No one better than he exemplified Pietism's distinctive character of turning inward to establish a direct relationship with God through faith in Jesus Christ and then outward to relate to the larger society and do God's work there.

See also Pietism.

For Further Reading: E. Griffin and P. Erb, eds., *The Pietists: Selected Writings* (2006); C. Lindberg, ed., *The Pietist Theologians* (2005); G. Sattler, *God's Glory, Neighbor's Good* (1982); W. R. Ward, *Early Evangelicalism* (2006).

Richard V. Pierard

Freedom of Choice

Freedom of choice, which stands against the ancient fates and biological and theological determinisms, is rooted in the covenant concept of Judaism and Christianity. According to the Scriptures, God took initiative to enter into a covenant with the Hebrew people first through Abraham (Gen. 12:1 – 3) and then through Moses (Ex. 20). In the Christian view, God effected the new covenant envisioned by Jeremiah (Jer. 31:31 – 34) in and through Jesus as Israel's Messiah (Matt. 26:28; Mark 14:24; Luke 22:20; 1 Cor. 11:25; Heb. 9:15). The covenant does not signify a master-slave relationship — God as a tyrant, making harsh and absolute demands, and the people of God as obsequious and obedient servants groveling at the tyrant's feet. Far from it, it entails rather a parent-child relationship. As Jesus portrayed the covenant from the divine perspective in his matchless parable, God is the compassionate, loving parent who lays aside all oriental dignity and races down the road to embrace the errant prodigal and take him

back as a son, the patient parent who goes out to conciliate the pouty elder brother and to absorb his rage (Luke 15:11 – 32). Looked at from the human side, as the apostle Paul made clear to the Romans, the covenant means we have not received "a spirit of slavery" but "a spirit of adoption" in which we cry, "Abba! Father!" (Rom. 8:15 NRSV). Like children who know they are loved, we approach God in freedom, "the glorious freedom of the children of God" (Rom. 8:21). Freedom, however, as Paul reminded the Galatians, does not give us a license to do whatever we want. Actually, it places a still weightier responsibility on us. It requires serving others through love (Gal. 5:13). As our loving parent, God has a right to expect us to emulate and imitate what God is disclosing to us in Jesus Christ and what the Holy Spirit inspires and directs. But no more than a wise human parent does God lay down hard and fast rules and stand by with a club to see that we do them. We do not live under law but under grace. Grace is more than God smiling on people. It involves God's personal presence, the Holy Spirit. The gift of the Spirit does not take away personal responsibility. Instead, the Spirit liberates believers from bondage to sin (John 8:32 – 36) and supplies them with the motive and the ability to do what pleases God (Phil. 2:13). Martin Luther once summed up this concept of freedom: "By virtue of faith the Christian is the most free lord of all and subject to none; by virtue of love he [or she] is slave of all and subject to everyone."

See also Image of God; Obedience; Simplicity; Social Justice; Will, Human.

For Further Reading: "*Eleutheros...*" in *TDNT*, 2:487 – 502; M. Luther, *The Liberty of the Christian* (1520), many eds.

E. Glenn Hinson

French (School of) Spirituality

Movement of seventeenth-century Roman Catholic spirituality that became a principal devotional influence in Roman Catholicism in the modern period. Developing out of the Catholic Reformation, it focused the spiritual life of the Catholic laity on the experience of the passion of Jesus and the pursuit of individual holiness. Its beginnings are most associated with the thought of Cardinal Pierre de Bérulle (1575–1629) whose writings emphasized the experience of the incarnation and humiliation of Jesus.

Bérulle's significance is in the emphasis he put on the entire mystery of the incarnation, in Christ's greatness and abasement. No doubt, Bérulle did emphasize the grandeur and absolute perfection of God in general, but he focused his vision on these themes in Christ. Because of Christ's original magnificence, his acceptance of humanity represented for Bérulle a deep self-surrender, a renunciation, a humiliation—all themes that would characterize French School thinking. Some have noted that this degrades Christ's humanity more than the early church councils had intended, but it was nonetheless very important for Bérulle. For him the renunciation and humiliation of Christ's humanity should characterize all humanity. All should take on an attitude of radical servitude to Christ—a total abasement (Fr. *anéantissement*). This renunciation pushes out the self but also seeks to reproduce the "states" of Christ during his earthly life. Indeed, Bérulle's teaching about the imitation of Christ's experience, including Christ's love of his mother, Mary, constitutes the practical center of his spirituality.

Besides his literary and pastoral activities, Bérulle became superior of the Oratory of Divine Love, work that was taken over by Charles de Condren (1588–1641) after Bérulle's death. Although de Condren's literary corpus was not as important as that of his predecessor, he was a very important spiritual adviser in Parisian society in his time. De Condren put special emphasis on Christ's passion, sacrifice, and the state of victimhood.

Bérulle's thought was refined and popularized by other disciples as well. A first example is that of Jean Eudes (1601–1680), founder and inspirer of various religious communities, particularly the Congregation of Jesus and Mary (the Eudists). Eudes's writings provided one of the most accessible resources for understanding and promoting the French School's spirituality. He argued that Christian meditation should continue and fulfill the life of Jesus Christ. Eudes was particularly motivated to share this message at missions throughout France—a mission vision shared by his later disciples.

Indeed, this apostolic or missionary desire was another central pillar of the French School. This was equally seen in the thought of another follower of Bérulle, Jean-Jacques Olier (1608–1657). Olier studied under the Jesuits but received his most significant spiritual stimulus from Vincent de Paul and de Condren. From de Condren he was particularly impressed by the idea that the renewal of religion lay in the formation of zealous new priests dedicated to the incarnate Christ and a renunciation of selfish desire. Olier embodied this desire in the formation of the Society of Saint-Sulpice, a society that devoted its energy to the training of diocesan priests. These priests were not just to be formed intellectually, but to have deep interior spiritual experience characterized by the contemplation of Jesus. The concern for the holiness and formation of priests underlined but also promoted their dignity.

Yet it was not only these main contributors who sculpted the French School's particular spirituality. An underestimated yet incredibly important contribution was made by women. Though it may be difficult to recognize specific accents of the French School in the thought of some of them, there is no doubt that they drew inspiration from its members. Although many other examples of aspects of women's spiritual contributions could be mentioned, a particularly important one was the devotion to the heart of Christ. In the 1670s, Marguerite Alacoque (1647–1690), a Visitadine nun, claimed to have received visions of Jesus' heart, visions that prompted her to promote the devotion to the "Sacred Heart" in its modern form. In such devotion, Jesus' physical heart is said to represent the divine love for humanity and is meant to stimulate deep mystical experience.

The French School of spirituality deeply influenced French Roman Catholicism, but also worldwide Catholicism in the centuries following. Indeed, it was a main staple of Catholic spirituality until well into the 20th century. Its foci on deep spiritual life, the training of priests, and methods of prayer and devotion, which were well-adapted for lay participation, made it easily transplantable around the world.

The impact on Protestant spirituality is difficult to assess. Negatively, it is this form of Roman Catholicism that which most troubled Protestants in the modern era. Rather than seeing the Christocentrism of the French School in a positive light, most Protestants saw it as a replacing of Christ by counterfeit religious devotion, a religion of works in the place of Christ. Nonetheless, it is intriguing that this revival of a sort of heart religion in Roman Catholicism in which regular Catholics were encouraged to have a personal and intimate relationship with the incarnate Christ was paralleled in the Pietist revivals in Germany and elsewhere, which often had very similar concerns.

See also Jansen, Cornelius.

For Further Reading: R. Deville, *The French School of Spirituality: An Introduction and Reader* (1994); E. Howells, "Relationality and Difference in the Mysticism of Pierre de Bérulle," *Harvard Theological Review* 102, no. 2 (2009): 225–43; A. Milton, "Pierre de Bérulle: The Search for Unity," in *Spirituality of Western Christendom*, vol. 2 (1984): 105–23; W. Thompson, ed., *Bérulle and the French School: Selected Writings*, (1989); M. V. Woodgate, *Charles de Condren* (1949); A. D. Wright, "Bérulle and Olier: Christ and the Blessed Virgin Mary," in *The Church and Mary*, ed. R. N. Swanson, Studies in Church History 39 (2004), 271–79.

Jason Zuidema

Freud, Sigmund

See **Psychoanalysis.**

Friendship, Spiritual

Friendship is a unique category of human relationship in which affection and regard of one person for another is manifested for good in an enduring relational bond. It is rooted in general likemindedness, trust, loyalty, and commitment to the good of the other. Available to all of humanity, friendship is not subject to the boundaries of age, class, race, gender, marital status, education, intelligence, socioeconomic level, nationality, or religious affiliation.

Friendship has a spiritual aspect when it is open to the manifestation of God's love (agapē) through the Holy Spirit, evidenced transformatively in personal human relationship. Christian spiritual friendship is an experience of three-way companionship: with oneself, one's friend, and Christ. Spiritual friendship differs from two other important relationships, spiritual direction and spiritual mentoring, by reason of its comfortable intimacy, unstructured egalitarian dynamics, and the absence of role differentials.

While some have perceived personal friendship as exclusive, preferential, and antithetical to the nature of the church and the teaching that we are all one in Christ (Gal. 3:28), an examination of the biblical witness gives evidence of multiple friendships among the faithful. Jesus himself chose twelve disciples (Mark 3:13–14), whom he called "friends" (John 15:15); three whom he especially favored for companionship (Luke 9:28); and one whom he particularly loved (John 13:23). In practice, Jesus clearly differentiated among relationships. This mitigates against the assertion that Christians should exclude themselves from appropriate intimacy in personal friendship.

Some of the greatest philosophers and Christian theologians in history have reflected on the nature of friendship. For the ancients, friendship was a high and cherished relationship. The Greek philosopher Aristotle claimed that without friends no one would choose to live. In his *Nicomachean Ethics*, he classified friendship into three types: the useful, the pleasant, and the good. "Useful and pleasant friendships, which have value, though transient, will dissolve as usefulness or pleasantness diminishes or disappears. It is only in the good that [people] in mutual affection and regard can establish a permanent and trustworthy relationship that manifests itself by unselfishly and genuinely seeking the other's best."

Cicero, Roman philosopher, writer, orator, and politician, defined friendship as perfect "accord in all things human and divine, conjoined with mutual goodwill and affection." He also maintained that "no one can be a friend, unless [he] is a good [man]."

Cicero's writings significantly influenced the development of the most thorough and lasting theology of Christian friendship, *Spiritual Friendship* (c. 1167), written by the twelfth-century Cisterian monk and abbot, Aelred of Rievaulx. Aelred took much of Cicero's dialogical format and basic relational truths and injected into them his own keen social intelligence as well as his insight drawn from biblical theology.

Aelred defined Christian friendship as two people together with Christ as their bond. Highlighting the biblical witness of Jesus' declaration to his disciples: "I no longer call you servants.... Instead, I have called you friends" (John 15:15), and paraphrasing 1 John 4:16 as "The one who dwells in friendship, dwells in God," Aelred boldly asserted that God is friendship.

Whereas human friendship is the personal association of those who in goodness share like-mindedness and mutual heartfelt affection and love, trust in the other, and welcome the other in an enduring relationship of loyalty and true hospitality of heart, spiritual friendship takes this friendship love deeper so that it becomes an experience of three-way companionship: oneself, the other, and the Holy Spirit. In the midst of this three-way dynamic, God's love motivates and gradually transforms each heart into a purer love for the other and for God.

Christian spiritual friendship is an expression of the relationship of love in Christ and is focused on the good, true, honorable, and virtuous. It calls friends to a process of development in human relationships into which the Holy Spirit is invited. Gradually, in the midst of agape love, the Spirit is able to increasingly modify and mold friends more closely into the image of Christ (John 15:12). Over time, as God is glorified in the friendship, the friendship itself becomes part of the result of the redeeming work of Christ on the cross. Aelred of Rievaulx has maintained that Christian friendship begins in Christ, continues in Christ, and is perfected in Christ. Thus, spiritual friendship has not only the potential to be a lifelong relationship, but also an eternal relationship in the communion of saints.

See also Aelred of Rievaulx; Buber, Martin.

For Further Reading: D. Benner, *Sacred Companions* (2002); L. Carmichael, *Friendship* (2004); J. Chittister, *Friendship of Women* (2006); K. Leech, *Soul Friend*, 1977; C. S. Lewis, *The Four Loves* (1960); G. Meilaender, *Friendship* (1981).

Pamela Baker Powell

Fruit of the Spirit

According to the apostle Paul, "the fruit of the Spirit is love, joy, peace, patience, kindness, goodness, faithfulness, gentleness and self-control. Against such things there is no law" (Gal. 5:22–23). This is not an exhaustive list but rather illustrates the qualities of someone who "walks by the Spirit." Elsewhere Paul cites faith, hope, and love as three vital dispositions also granted by the Spirit. Evidently, walking in the Spirit can bear many different kinds of "fruit."

The fruit of the Spirit are universally applicable virtuous ideals, while the gifts of the Spirit are individual talents or skills that enable one to contribute to the well-being of others. Another distinction between the two categories is that gifts are distributed selectively to different people (1 Cor. 12), while the fruit of the Spirit are meant for all believers. Some have tried (unsuccessfully) to make further rigid distinctions between gifts and fruit of the Spirit. Gifts, for example, have been conceptualized as natural talents or learned skills, while fruit have been viewed as divine in origin and solely given by grace. In Aquinas, gifts are natural (developed), while fruit are supernatural (infused). Such speculations create an unnecessary dichotomy between natural and supernatural. The truth is that both "fruit" and "gifts" are metaphors for the work of God in a person's life. A person is not a tree, but the metaphor of fruit emphasizes that these characteristics grow out of a deep relationship with God, rather than from our own efforts. However, there are natural human qualities in all the fruit, even though their perfection may only come from the Holy Spirit; and the same is true of gifts.

The foundation of Christian spirituality is grace. By the grace of God, we are freed from sin and given the ability to live in freedom as children of God (Gal. 5:1). The apostle Paul argued that "the entire law is summed up in a single command: 'Love your neighbor as yourself'" (Gal. 5:14). However, the Great Commandment is not a new law to replace the old one. Rather, the key is to live by the Spirit and not be controlled by the lusts of the flesh. Those who are led by the Spirit are not under the law (an external restraint), and the works of the flesh will not be part of their behavior (Gal. 5:19–21). Instead, they will experience the fruit of the Spirit. Where the Spirit of God is, there is liberty; and believers will be changing by the Spirit into the image of the Son (2 Cor. 3:17–18).

See also Joy; Love; Peace; Self-Control.

For Further Reading: T. Keating, *The Fruits and Gifts of the Spirit* (2007); P. Kenneson, *Life on the Vine* (1999).

Bernard Adeney-Risakotta

Fuga Mundi

Latin words meaning "flight from the world." A critical attitude toward the world had some roots in Judaism, in the teaching of Jesus, and in apostolic writings, but "flight from the world" originated during the long era up to the time of Constantine when becoming Christian put people at great risk. Tertullian, the first Latin theologian, in his exhortation *To the Martyrs*, written during the persecution under Septimius Severus at the outset of the 3rd century, painted a picture of the world sufficiently gloomy to make martyrdom look like a rather happy alternative. Separation from the world should not distress a Christian. The world is full of darkness. It contains the worst impurities. Thence the martyrs should think of "flight from the world" as transition to a better place. Neither Tertullian nor Origen, a half-century later, looked favorably on flight from persecution. It is not surprising, then, to see "flight from the world" gain full currency among those who considered themselves the martyrs' successors—the monks. They literally fled the world and went into the desert. The widespread dualism—the belief that matter is evil and the spirit alone good—undoubtedly influenced some, but most went in the hope that they might attain what Jesus' beatitude promised: "Blessed are the pure in heart, for they will see God" (Matt. 5:8). They could not demonstrate the faithfulness of the martyrs in the world; they had to retreat from it just as Jesus had done when he spent forty days and nights in the desert.

See also Asceticism; Desert Fathers and Mothers; Detachment; World.

For Further Reading: D. Chitty, *The Desert a City* (1966).

E. Glenn Hinson

Fuller, Andrew (1754–1815)

Baptist pastor-theologian. Fuller was born in Wicken, a village in Cambridgeshire, England, where his parents rented a dairy farm. In 1761 his parents moved a short distance to Soham, where his family began to regularly attend the local Calvinistic Baptist church, and where Fuller was converted in November 1769. Baptized the following spring, he joined the church, and in 1774 he was called to be the pastor of the work. He stayed until 1782, when he accepted the pastorate of the Calvinistic Baptist congregation in Kettering, Northamptonshire, where he ministered till his death.

Fuller's time in Soham was decisive in the development of his theology and piety. Here he began a lifelong study of the Scriptures and the works of Jonathan Edwards (1703–1758), which led to his becoming the most able Baptist theologian and apologist of his day. Among his early works was the epoch-making *The Gospel Worthy of All Acceptation* (1784) that championed fervent evangelistic preaching. This work proved to be a decisive refutation of Hyper-Calvinism, which had been a key reason for the spiritual stagnation of many Baptist churches in England and Wales. This book also opened the way for the formation of the Baptist Missionary Society (1792), which he served as secretary until his death. Extensive involvement in this society gave his piety a strong missional flavor. He once wrote, "True churches of Jesus Christ travail in birth for the salvation of men."

Also noteworthy is Fuller's *Memoirs of the Rev. Samuel Pearce* (1800), which went through at least five editions and innumerable reprintings in the 19th century. Modeled after Jonathan Edwards's life of David Brainerd, it recounted the life of Samuel Pearce (1766–1799) of Birmingham and presented his "holy love" as a model of evangelical spirituality.

See also Baptist Spirituality.

For Further Reading: M. Haykin, *One Heart and One Soul* (1994); P. Morden, *Offering Christ to the World: Andrew Fuller (1754–1815) and the Revival of Eighteenth Century Particular Baptist Life* (2003).

Michael A. G. Haykin

Fullness of the Spirit

The Scriptures speak of the fullness (*plerōma*) of the Spirit in the life of the Christian, and also of fullness for specific tasks of ministries. Both are instances of the Spirit's transforming and empowering presence in the life of the believer. The Christian spiritual tradition affirms that Christ came so that the love of God would be poured into our hearts (Rom. 5:5), our joy might be made complete (John 15:11), and we would know a peace that surpasses understanding (Phil. 4:7). The genius of Christian spirituality is precisely that love, joy, and peace are not commodities, but each is specifically the fruit of God's very self. Thus, the Scriptures speak of the indwelling of God in the believer; more specially, of the indwelling of the third person of the Trinity, the Holy Spirit. The ultimate gift of God, then, is God's very self: baptizing, purifying, empowering, and filling the church and thus individual Christians also. In this initiatory instance, the language of *filling* may reflect an allusion to the original human creation imagery of receiving the breath (or Spirit) of God (Gen. 2:7), which in Christian initiation once again "fills the lungs" and reanimates with new life (1 Cor. 15:45).

This indwelling or fullness is not incidental of the Christian life; Christ came that believers might be filled with the Spirit. Neither is this "fullness" of the Spirit the prerogative of a few super-saints or elite Christians. Rather, all who come to Christ in faith and repentance and are baptized receive the gift of the Spirit (Acts 2:38); indeed, this is the most crucial element of a Christian conversion. The full expression of this experience of God's grace, the grace of the Spirit, does not come at one's initiation into Christian faith; it grows and matures over time, and indeed, many have had what for them was an experience of Spirit-filling sometime after their conversion. The goal is to become more fully animated, through and through, with the Holy Spirit's controlling, purifying, and empowering presence. And yet it is essential that we speak of this gift as both promised and anticipated in their conversion to Christ. Further, the experience of this fullness is not static; rather, the Scriptures call Christians to be filled with the Spirit as an ongoing dynamic of the spiritual life (Eph. 5:18).

Donald Bloesch and other theologians have rightly stressed that our understanding of the fullness of the Spirit needs to be governed by three critical parameters: Christ Jesus, the Scriptures, and the church. When we speak of the fullness of the Spirit, we speak specifically of the fullness of the Spirit of Christ. Christ dwells in the Christian and in the church through the Spirit. Thus, we speak of pneumatological Christology: if we do not have the Spirit, we do not have Christ (Rom. 8:9). But we must also speak of a christological pneumatology: the Spirit who fills us is the Spirit of the incarnate, crucified, risen, and ascended Christ. Nor is there inherent tension between Spirit and Word in Christian spirituality. The indwelling of the Spirit is governed and grounded by the Scriptures; we are born again of Word and Spirit; we cannot hope for the indwelling of the Spirit if we are not at one and the same time indwelt by the Word (Col. 3:16). Indeed, the assumption of Ephesians 5 is that in being filled with the Spirit we will be filled with wisdom. And then also, the church is the fellowship of the Spirit. Thus, while we can speak of the fullness of the Spirit in the life of the individual Christian, there is a powerful interplay between this "fullness" and the experience of the grace of the Spirit in the church. We cannot hope to know the fullness of the Spirit if we are not in fellowship with the people of God (the household or temple in which God dwells by his Spirit; Eph. 2:21 – 22; 3:19).

What is the evidence of this fullness? Thomas Oden helpfully speaks of Paul's references to the fruit of the Spirit: love, joy, peace, patience, kindness, goodness, faithfulness, gentleness, and self-control; but then, also, he speaks of the theological virtues of faith, hope, and love (see Rom. 8:14; Gal. 5:16, 25). And the point is that each of these arises in the life, work, and relationships of the Christian through the gracious initiative of the Spirit. Thus, to speak of fullness is to speak of the Spirit who purifies, equips, and sustains the Christian believer in the life of Christ. But the Christian is not entirely passive in this relationship with the Spirit. Rather, the Scriptures speak of the active responsibility of the Christian to, first, be filled with the Spirit (Eph. 5:18), then set one's mind on the Spirit (Rom. 8:5 – 6), and then be guided by the Spirit (Gal. 5:25) — that is, to live in conscious and intentional response to the presence and initiative of the Spirit in the heart and mind of the Christian.

Can and should the Christian ask to be filled with the Spirit? While certainly appropriate for Christian initiation — we note that in conversion one can be filled with the Spirit (see Acts 9:17) — a good case could be made that following conversion one is simply called to live in a manner that is consistent with this fullness, this divine indwelling. As Andreas Kostenberger suggests, the "believers' major efforts should be directed toward manifesting the Spirit's presence in ever-increasing measure, both individually and corporately."

Then also, as noted above, the Scriptures speak of the fullness of the Spirit for specific callings and responsibilities; for example, John the Baptist was filled with the Spirit in his mother's womb (Luke 1:15 – 17), and Paul was filled with the Spirit before he spoke to a magician (Acts 13:9). This suggests it is both appropriate that Christian believers, while certainly filled with the Spirit for their life and work, can and should seek a special measure of this filling when faced with extraordinary responsibilities or challenges. In so doing, we recognize our deep dependence on the grace and power of the Spirit. Thus, whether for the daily routines of life or for the special challenges and opportunities that emerge, we walk in the Spirit in radical dependence on the grace of the Holy Spirit. We sing, in the words of the nineteenth-century hymn: "Breathe on me, breath of God; fill me with life anew, that I may love what Thou dost love and do what Thou wouldst do."

For Further Reading: D. Bloesch, *The Holy Spirit* (2000); J. Dunn, *Baptism in the Holy Spirit* (1970); G. Fee, *God's Empowering Presence* (1994); A. Kostenberger, "What Does It Mean to Be Filled with the Spirit?" *Journal of the Evangelical Theological Society* 40, no. 2 (1997): 229–40; T. Oden, *Life in the Spirit* (1992); J. Stott, *Baptism and Fullness* (1975).

Gordon T. Smith

Fundamentalist Spirituality

Fundamentalism is "militantly anti-modernist Protestant evangelicalism," in George Marsden's term. Thus, its spirituality has mostly the same content as classic evangelical spirituality of the kind exhibited in the age of Dwight Moody. But fundamentalism took on a sharper edge in the institutional and ideological conflicts of its formative period in the early 20th century. Fundamentalism was a protest movement, a denominational renewal strategy, and a coalition of cobelligerents against liberalism. But as a spiritual tradition, it has had a few key commitments: truth, authority, and purity.

Fundamentalists lead with truth claims and consider the best test of authentic Christianity to be whether a person affirms true, biblical doctrine. Furthermore, the believer is under obligation not just to believe the truth, but also to "contend earnestly for the faith." R. A. Torrey, whom Marsden called "one of the chief architects of fundamentalist

thought," frequently made the point that "Christ and His disciples attacked error."

Closely related is the claim of authority. Fundamentalists emphasize submission to the absolute authority of the Bible as God's Word. The literalism with which fundamentalism approaches the Bible entails that God's will is generally so plain in the words of Scripture that any deviation is best explained as willful disobedience to God.

Following from these two commitments is the fundamentalist emphasis on purity. The church is to be composed of orthodox believers (that is, those who hold to a set of fundamental, or central, truths) with lifestyles of personal holiness rather than worldliness (that is, those who submit to the authority of God's revealed will). The quest for purity has frequently led to multiple divisions within the churches, beginning with the attempt to drive the liberals from the old denominations, but usually ending up as an exodus of the fundamentalists from those bodies. Some fundamentalists insist on multiple degrees of separation, not only remaining visibly separate from liberals, but also maintaining separation from those who fail to separate.

Some elements of the fundamentalist spiritual temperament are related to the fortunes of the movement through the middle of the 20th century, as it lost most of its chosen battles within the denominations and the wider culture, especially in America. After the symbolic public discrediting of creationism in the 1925 Scopes trial, fundamentalists were increasingly excluded from traditional centers of prestige and influence. Since they already held that the church's primary mission involves the spiritual tasks of evangelizing and making disciples, most fundamentalists found it natural to disengage from their cultures. Thus, the "militantly antimodern" leading edge of the movement has tended to reinforce a leaning toward privatizing and personalizing spirituality. However, because fundamentalism is a submovement within the larger stream of evangelical Protestantism, these distinguishing features only count for a small portion of fundamentalism's spirituality. The bulk of the sermons, books, and magazines produced by fundamentalists are devoted to the standard topics of classic evangelical spirituality: conversion, prayer, Bible study, Christian fellowship, personal holiness, revival, and trust in God.

See also Modernity.

For Further Reading: G. Marsden, *Fundamentalism and American Culture* (1980).

Fred Sanders

Future of Christian Spirituality

See **Chapter 34.**

G

Gandhi, Mohandas Karamchand (1869–1948)

Considered by the people of India to be the father of their nation. Mahatma ("Great Soul") Gandhi or Bapu (Father) is chiefly celebrated and revered for leading the *ahimsa* (nonviolent struggle) for independence from the British colonizers. He was assassinated by a member of a Hindu political party who disagreed with his political strategies and religious philosophy.

E. Stanley Jones, a profound Christian thinker and missionary and a good friend of Gandhi, once asked him: "How can we make Christianity naturalized in India, not a foreign thing?" Gandhi responded, "First, I would suggest that all of you Christians, missionaries and all, must begin to live more like Jesus. Second, practice your religion without adulterating it or toning it down. Third, emphasize love and make it your working force, for love is central in Christianity. Fourth, study the non-Christian religions more sympathetically to find the good that is within them, in order to have a more sympathetic approach to the people."

These four points sum up Gandhi's thought on Christianity and Christian spirituality—that the central theme should be Jesus and his teaching. The "nuclear" teaching of Jesus, according to Gan-

dhi, can be found in the Sermon on the Mount. The pinnacle of the message of Christ, he insisted, is seen on the cross. Gandhi wrote: "Christ died on the cross with a crown of thorns on his head, defying the might of a whole empire." This was the impetus for Gandhi's *ahimsa* movement. Jesus' *ahimsa*, according to Gandhi, was active *ahimsa*. It was not passive nonviolence. This is why Gandhi deeply appreciated that "with [Jesus'] dying breath on the cross, he is reported to have said: 'Father forgive them, for they know not what they do.'"

Gandhi was of the opinion that the Western church had historically misunderstood Jesus' approach to social spirituality. Jesus' mission was not passive and weak, but active, bold and robust; and as such it constitutes an enduring and inspirational example for all. Among other writings, Gandhi left an autobiography, *The Story of My Experiments with Truth* (1948).

For Further Reading: *Gandhi: Selected Writings*, ed. R. Duncan (1971); E. S. Jones, *Gandhi* (1948).

R. Boaz Johnson

Gender and Spirituality

Gender refers to socially constructed expectations of what masculinity and femininity ought to look like—the roles and attitudes that men and women should embrace, and the ways they each should behave. Such assumptions have affected and continue to affect the spiritual experience of Christian men and women.

According to Scripture, God created humans as sexually differentiated beings—"male and female he created them" (Gen. 1:27). Moreover, the Scriptures affirm that males and females are not to allow their sexual differences to alienate them from one another. Rather, they are to come together in enriching partnerships characterized by interdependence and mutuality, for only through such relationships can they experience their intended likeness to God. But in distinction from sexuality, which is biological and physiological, gender denotes evolving social assumptions about how sexually differentiated human beings ought to conduct themselves toward one another and in relation to the larger world.

To observe human life is to note its diversity. The research of Lawrence Kohlberg and Carol Gilligan, for example, has demonstrated that men and women tend to approach moral reasoning somewhat differently. It remains to be seen whether these differences in approach stem from biological differences or reflect gender socialization, but parallel differences may emerge in the domain of spirituality as well. For example, it appears that male physiology may predispose men more strongly than women toward pornography and the objectification of the opposite sex, thereby creating unique challenges to men's spiritual health. At the same time, as numerous feminist theologians have observed, the relational priorities of many women may tempt some to compromise their convictions or acquiesce to trivialization and the underdevelopment of the self.

The temptation to make sweeping, speculative pronouncements about the *essence* of being a male or the complementary *essence* of being a female, however, should be resisted. These remain fascinating mysteries of life, best glimpsed when men and women are allowed to interact with one another in free, spiritually informed and mutually respectful environments. In the resulting paired "dance" of diversity-in-unity a glimmer can sometimes be apprehended of the exhilarating dynamic of the interior life of the Trinity itself. There one experiences neither the homogenization of difference nor the polarization of parties, but rather a celebration of the ongoing, graceful swirl of life together.

For awhile at least, the first humans got along as they were supposed to—without male supremacy, female subjugation, or differentials of power. Tragically, Adam and Eve used their God-given freedom to rebel, and thereby unleashed the corrupting power of sin on themselves and their descendants. Among sin's countless tragic effects was the mutation of original, divinely appointed human relationships into pathological ones of reciprocal blaming, interpersonal alienation, and gender oppression. Authentic Christian spirituality is attuned to the heart of God and is therefore outraged by abuse and oppression in whatever forms they manifest themselves. Spiritual persons perceive what socially constructed gender norms often disguise or distort—the fundamental equality of men and women in the eyes of God (Gal. 3:28). When expressed in the covenant of marriage, the apostle Peter advised Christian husbands, "Live with your wives in an insightful way, showing respect to them as less empowered ones who are actually *equal heirs* with you of the gracious gift of life" (1 Peter 3:7 AT). Godly men living in a patriarchal society were challenged to view women through different eyes and to choose to live ahead of the curve of the coming kingdom. Peter noted, significantly, that how one responded to this challenge would affect his prayer life.

From early on, church leadership structures have been typically patriarchal (e.g., the church *fathers*), with the priesthood and foremost educational opportunities accessible only to men. The domain of spiritual life, by contrast, has been surprisingly gender symmetrical. One has only to think of Benedict and Scholastica, Francis of Assisi and Clare, Teresa of Avila and John of the Cross, Francis de Sales and Jane de Chantel, to recognize how consistently this pattern has played out. Obviously the spiritual life was pursued on gender-differentiated lines, but more to bracket the complicating dynamic of sexuality and to accommodate prevailing social norms than because the capacities of men and women for the rigors of the pursuit of God were thought to be much different.

In some ways the religious life was especially empowering for women, whose choice of the celibate cloister liberated them from marital submission and the strictures of ordinary life. The bracketing of sexuality among the religious leveled the playing field to some extent, allowing "holy women" like Catherine of Siena and Hildegard of Bingen to reprove corrupt authorities and speak reason to popes. The spirituality of women in Christian history reflected their ability to make the most of their limited opportunities. Relatively restricted socially and sometimes confined to close quarters, women like Julian of Norwich chose to excel in the mystical life. Prevented from preaching and leading, many women simply channeled their irrepressibly creative energies into spiritually enriching poetry, literature, hymnody, and ministries of compassion. One might assume that men are generally favored in the distribution of the more assertive and "apostolic" gifts of the Spirit, except that intrepid women have greatly outnumbered men among the effective foot soldiers of the modern missionary movement. In his binding encyclical *Mulieris Dignitatem: On the Dignity and Vocation of Women* (1987), Pope John Paul II affirmed the fundamental equality of women and men, even in the distribution of giftedness.

Expressions of Christian spirituality, however, continue to be accommodated to shifting gender expectations. Despite the dominance of men in church leadership, the larger proportion of faithful adherents consists of women, even while some observers complain that the faith itself is becoming "feminized." Today the dominant cultural notion of maleness involves strength, capacity for retributive violence, and a certain civilization-defying wildness of heart. This has not always been the case. Before the emergence of "muscular Christianity" in the 19th century, there were the iconic ideals of the Christian gentleman and lady—themselves fusions of earlier medieval desiderata of gallantry, Renaissance ideas of refined courtesy, and English ideals of gentility. Significantly, all of these emphasized the restrained focus of otherwise undisciplined passion, not its cathartic expression. Historical perspective can help Christians transcend fads in gender and avoid treating them as normative paradigms for male and female identity. Some truths, though, remain constant: How we relate to others affects our relationship with God; and spirituality flourishes best when gendered relationships are characterized by Christlike friendship, regard, and collaboration.

See also Feminist Spirituality; Masculine Spirituality; Womanist Spirituality.

For Further Reading: K. Giles, *The Trinity and Subordinationism* (2002); C. Gilligan, *In a Different Voice* (1982); B. MacHaffie, *Her Story: Women in Christian Tradition* (2006); R. Pierce and R. Groothius, eds., *Discovering Biblical Equality* (2005); R. Radford Ruether, *Women and Redemption* (1998); G. Scorgie, *The Journey Back to Eden* (2005).

Kevin Giles and Glen G. Scorgie

Geography, Spiritual

Spiritual geography is a field of interdisciplinary interest that considers the interplay of nature and the numinous in human experience. The term came into popular use with Kathleen Norris, *Dakota: A Spiritual Geography* (1993), and Belden C. Lane, especially *The Solace of Fierce Landscapes* (1998). Spiritual geography develops themes shared by biblical and spiritual theology with human geography, literature (place in fiction and non-fiction, including memoir, adventure, and travel narratives), art and art history (landscape), social criticism and philosophy, and environmentalism.

The interests of spiritual geography are rooted in the Bible, where the connection between God's covenant people and the land is explicit, and where both events and metaphors are specific to place. They also draw on the medieval concept of "the Book of Nature" as God's second and complementary self-disclosure. Spiritual geography considers how our physical surroundings condition and contextualize our reading of the Bible; how doctrines of creation and incarnation inform our understanding of ourselves as earth creatures living in specific places; and how place functions to concretize and clothe the human experience of the transcendent with specificity and immediacy. It considers the nature of "holy places" (privately, as places where we have experienced God's presence; or corporately, as in places of worship, shrines, or sacred sites) and how such places, visited or remembered, may function to renew or focus our spiritual lives. Spiritual geography is interested in the whole range of human experience of place. The ascetic, parched space in which the distinctive spirituality of the desert fathers developed may represent one pole; pastoral scenes or the cozy interiority of domestic space another; and the vastness of prairie, ocean, or mountains with evocations of "the sublime" yet another. While attentiveness to place and landscape creates a rather natural kinship to romanticism, agrarianism, and regional ecological writing, spiritual geography is not interested only in the love of nature nor only in nostalgia for the real or imagined pastoral; nor is it concerned only with contemporary environmentalism, all of which it takes into account as representing aspects of human experience of place. It considers the development of a biblical earth-consciousness and asks what kind of natural and built environments might nurture a fully human life.

Spiritual geography explores a cluster of inter-related questions relevant to Christian spirituality. It asks about the affective bond that rightly exists between humans and the particular place where one is "at home," and considers what differentiates place from space. Matters of imaginative framing are considered. Aesthetic issues are of interest, as the relative values of such elements as familiarity and estrangement, exposure, and refuge are explored. The historical privileging of models of itinerancy ("pilgrims and strangers" or "apostles" as heroic figures) over equally biblical images of "settling" and "dwelling" as pictures of God's blessing (Ps. 37:3; Jer. 29:5 – 10) may well have inhibited the development of a robust theology of place, as historical valuing of "rural" over "urban" landscapes may have contributed to the rise of suburban life in America. Ethical concerns within spiritual geography include asking how we might resolve — or live with — the tensions between preserving wilderness and harvesting food or other materials, between care for the earth and care for the humans who inhabit it. Spiritual geography is also concerned with how we might create cities that are humane and livable and that encourage the life of the spirit. Overall, spiritual geography is concerned not only to describe the human relationship to a physical environment and the impact of that on Christian spirituality, but also to ask how might wellness of the Christian spirit in rooted congregations affect the aesthetic, productive, and affective aspects of particular places?

A robust theology of place grounds spiritual geography in the following three ways: (1) *By particularizing place.* Specific named or described places ground most events in the Scriptures from creation forward. Place is not incidental to God's dialogue with his people, nor should it be to us. The monastic vow of stability bound monks to a particular place. In North America, the profound restlessness and rootlessness that derive from being both immigrant peoples and frontier oriented have fostered forms of religious expression with little connection to any particular place. Spiritual geography encourages a consideration of what is lost spiritually when place is not particularized. (2) *By recognizing the sanctity of place*. Both by creation and incarnation, place is sanctified (or, in some understandings, sacramentalized). Whether one sees earth as sacrament (as in Eastern Orthodox thought, cf. A. Schmemann, *For the Life of the World*, 1970) or, following Calvin, as "the elegant structure of the world serving us as a kind of mirror, in which we may behold God, though otherwise invisible" (*Institutes*, 1.5), the earth is clearly blessed by being created and sustained by the Word of God, and then by having been inhabited by the Living Word (see John 1:1 – 18; Heb. 1:1 – 3). Place in the sense of a particular geography with all of its overlay of geology, terrain, collective memory, and contemporary community is "holy ground." (3) *By relativizing the value of place* within a larger picture of obedience. As important as place is and should be in the life of the Christian, it is nonetheless a relative value (as are all good things) and is secondary to obedience to the call of God. So, God calls Abraham and Sarah out of Ur of the Chaldees — not because it was not a good place, but because God had a specific task and calling for them that required them to live "portably," with a tent and an altar.

    See also Sacred Space.

For Further Reading: J. Appleton, *The Experience of Landscape* (1975); W. Berry, *The Unsettling of America* (1977); W. Brueggemann, *The Land* (2002); A. Dillard, *Holy the Firm* (1977); A. Durning, *This Place on Earth* (1996); J. Ellul, *The Meaning of the City* (1970); C. Gunton, *Christ in Creation* (1992); Y. F. Tuan, *Topophilia* (1990).

Maxine Hancock

Gerson, Jean (1363 – 1429)

French theologian and church leader. Gerson lived during the stormy period of the Great Schism (1378 – 1417) when two popes (and, for a time, three) vied for the power over the Roman Church. He sought to purify the church as well as reform the University of Paris where he was chancellor, though many of his goals were not reached. Gerson participated in the Council of Constance (1414 – 1418), which ultimately resolved the Great Schism, though he failed to recognize the necessity of the more radical reforms advocated by John Hus, who was condemned to death at Constance in 1415. He favored church council over the pope in matters of authority. This reduced his popularity when in 1870 the doctrine of papal infallibility was introduced. However, since the 1960s he has reclaimed his appropriate stature as one of the most significant theologians of the medieval period. Gerson was equally effective in addressing theological students at the university and guiding young children in the principles of the Christian faith. He stressed the importance of combining the intellect and affect — reflective of Bernard, one of his favorite theologians — and wrote over five hundred works. *Mountain of Contemplation* (1400) was written for his own sisters as well as others who lacked formal education. Later Gerson expanded these themes for theologians in his *Mystical Theology*, which first appeared as *Speculative Treatise* (1402 – 1403) and *Practical Treatise* (1407). Topics of his writings included various aspects of purity, the hearing of confessions, and the testing of mystical experiences. The depth of his works later earned him the title of "consoling doctor." His contemplative spirituality influenced not only Roman Catholics such as the Brethren of the Common Life and Francis de Sales, but also Richard Baxter and other seventeenth-century Protestants. Gerson's legacy stresses the availability of the spiritual life for all people, regardless of their training or background.

For Further Reading: *Jean Gerson: Early Works*, CWS (1998); B. McGuire, ed., *A Companion to Jean Gerson* (2006); idem, *Jean Gerson and the Last Medieval Reformation* (2005).

Tom Schwanda

Gertrude the Great (of Helfta, 1266 – c. 1302)

German mystic. Born in Thuringia, she entered the Benedictine Helfta monastery (influenced by Cistercian reforms) near Eisleben as an orphan at the age of five. Helfta was an important center for education and mysticism at the time, and the gifted Gertrude received extensive academic and spiritual training from Gertrude of Hackeborn, Mechthild of Hackeborn, and Mechthild of Magdeburg. During her training in 1281, Gertrude experienced a life-changing vision of Christ. This mystical experience had a lasting impact on Gertrude's life and theology, and she turned to focus her attention to studying Scripture and the church fathers. Gertrude served as a spiritual director and counselor and was extremely popular. Feeling urged by God, Gertrude wrote down her spiritual experiences and insights to encourage others.

A significant amount of Gertrude's works have survived, all written in Latin though not all written by her own hand. Her works are called *The Herald of Divine Love* (*Legatus divinae pietatis*) and are divided into five books. Gertrude's mysticism draws primarily from Scripture passages and is deeply embedded within the liturgical context of her monastic life. Her writings influenced the Friends of God movement in Germany (an informal and widely spread mystical and communal movement among laypersons and clergy that focused on the development and growth of the interior life in the context of spiritual friendships) and contributed significantly to the Devotion to the Sacred Heart of Jesus movement, becoming popular especially in the Spanish-speaking world.

Gertrude's mystical and practical theology is strongly Christocentric and seeks union with God. Influenced by bridal mysticism, she focuses on the love and suffering of Jesus with the heart of Christ as a central focus of her devotion and yearning. Fully captured by Christ's tender love and grace, Gertrude emphasizes the role of repentance, humble submission to the will of God, praise, suffering, spiritual exercises, and the Eucharist for spiritual formation.

Gisela H. Kreglinger

Gifts of the Spirit

The gifts of the Holy Spirit are ministries and powers exercised in the church by God's grace in service to others. The classic text of Scripture used in discussions on spiritual gifts is 1 Corinthians 12 – 14. Paul enumerates various means of blessing others through ministries and powers, such as wisdom, knowledge, healing, prophecy, discernment of spirits, speaking in tongues, interpretation of tongues, administration, apostleship, and teaching (1 Cor. 12:8 – 10, 28). These gifts are interactive, since wisdom guides knowledge, discernment evaluates prophecy, and the interpretation of tongues explains the message implied in tongues. The vision here is of an interactive fellowship that builds itself up in love (Eph. 4:16).

Paul used the term *charismata* (from the root *charis* or *grace*) for these gifts in order to stress that they are gracious bestowals of divine favor from person to person (or person to congregation) in the power of the Holy Spirit. Indeed, Paul stressed early on in 1 Corinthians that everything one possesses is received from the Lord so that no one is superior to anyone else: "For who makes you different from anyone else? What do you have that you did not receive? And if you did receive it, why do you boast as though you did not?" (4:7). Paul then applies this principle to the powerful manifestations of the Spirit's gracious help through the spiritual gifts. No one can boast of any accomplishments, for these gifts are given in the Spirit, by the Lord, and from the heavenly Father (12:4 – 6). Our competence is from God (2 Cor. 3:5), leading us to sober-minded judgment concerning our abilities (Rom. 12:3). The gifts are meant to highlight Christ's lordship in all things (1 Cor. 12:3) and to edify (build up) the congregation in a way that is consistent with the love of God revealed in Christ (13:1 – 13;

14:26). These gifts must also be exercised in a way that is orderly or sensitive to congregational mores (11:5 – 16; 14:26 – 40), to a diversity of gifted expressions, and to congregational discernment of their value (14:23, 29 – 32), especially in the light of apostolic instruction (14:36 – 38). The goal is a differentiated unity among Christians in which a diversity of gifted expressions is cherished: "If the whole body were an eye, where would the sense of hearing be?" (12:17). Speaking the truth in love, the whole body of Christ grows toward the fullness of Christ from the contributions of every part (Eph. 4:15 – 16).

Considerable discussion has surrounded the entire topic of spiritual gifts and their role in the spiritual life. First, the NT resists a separation of the natural from the supernatural. There are passages in the NT that speak of ministry gifts (*doreas*) (Eph. 4:7 – 16) or graces (Rom. 12:3 – 7). These ministries, like apostleship, evangelism, giving, and administration, seem more explicitly inclusive of natural talents and established functions than the powers of the Spirit listed in 1 Corinthians 12:8 – 10, such as healing. The difficulty is that these lists of ministries and powers are not so neatly separated as such. Prophecy is mentioned in all of the lists (Rom. 12:6; 1 Cor. 12:10; Eph. 4:11). Such gifts as apostleship and administration are mentioned right alongside the gifts of healing and prophecy in 1 Corinthians 12:28. In the light of this complexity, some prefer to speak of a spectrum of spiritually gifted forms of service that spans established ministries and spiritual powers. Thus, the accent on the supernatural nature of spiritual gifts is qualified by insight into the natural human capacities that are enhanced by the work of the Spirit. Divine healing, for example, may utilize and magnify the body's natural healing potential. A spirituality that accents these gifts need not so stress the supernatural that natural capacities in reaching for God's supernatural work are neglected in the process. Second, though we are to desire spiritual gifts, we do so while following the way of love as the supreme goal (1 Cor. 14:1), for love is the only thing that lasts for eternity (1 Cor. 13). We are thus not to seek "rashly" after spiritual gifts as an end in themselves.

In recent decades, a number of Christians have reported that greater charismatic awareness has become part of a rich spiritual renewal. Such awareness has caused life to become more purposeful, oriented more consciously toward the empowerment of lay Christians to serve others. The thought that all Christians bear the Spirit and have been commissioned toward some form of ministry can also spiritually enrich the church, changing it from an audience attentive to a preacher to a community of spiritually gifted Christians who seek under the guidance of those who exercise oversight to speak the truth of Christ to one another in love (Eph. 4:15 – 16; 5:18 – 21). Spirituality moves from self-preoccupation toward the goals of the kingdom of God as we become increasingly sensitive to the gifted nature of the spiritual life. The grace by which we serve others can also lead to greater humility as we wonder at the strength of the Spirit at work through human flesh.

See also Baptism of the Holy Spirit; Charismatic Spirituality.

For Further Reading: A. Bittlinger, *Gifts and Graces* (1968); J. Koenig, *Charismata* (1978); D. Lim, *Spiritual Gifts* (1979); S. Schatzmann, *A Pauline Theology of Charismata* (1987); M. Turner, *The Holy Spirit and Spiritual Gifts* (1998).

Frank D. Macchia

Gilbert of Sempringham (1083 – 1189)

Founder of the Gilbertines, Gilbert established the only English monastic order of the Middle Ages. Part of the vast twelfth-century spiritual renewal that spawned numerous new orders, the Gilbertines welcomed hundreds into Christian community to learn Scripture, cultivate prayer, and nurture spiritual growth.

Son of Jocelin, Norman Lord of Sempringham, Gilbert studied in France and was ordained by Bishop Alexander of Lincoln. Unable to establish a monastic foundation for men, Gilbert donated his family inheritance to found a cloister for seven young women of his parish in 1131. In time, lay sisters joined the convent to attend the nuns, and lay brothers cultivated the fields. When the Cistercian order declined to accept oversight of the convent, Gilbert added Augustinian canons to provide spiritual direction and pastoral care. Similar to Fontevrault and Prémontré, the Gilbertines maintained double houses, with a wall dividing the chapel to separate men and women for propriety. Nuns followed the Cistercian interpretation of Benedict's Rule, canons kept the Augustinian Rule, and all were to emulate the example of Christ.

Living more than one hundred years, Gilbert died in 1189 and was canonized thirteen years later. The Gilbertine order grew to twenty-six houses but declined because of the Black Death and was disbanded by Henry VIII during the Reformation. Gilbert's legacy to Christian spirituality is his care for the women of his parish, willingness to experiment with the structure of double houses, and careful establishment of a movement that endured for centuries.

For Further Reading: R. Foreville and G. Kier, eds., *The Book of St. Gilbert* (1987); B. Golding, *Gilbert of Sempringham and the Gilbertine Order* (1995).

Glenn E. Myers

Global Christianity (1700 – Present)

See **Chapter 18.**

Glory of God, The

Glory is an essential characteristic of God and is the fundamental reason Christians respond by glorifying him. God's majesty is expressed in all of his names, but the word *glory* expresses it most succinctly. "Glory" in Hebrew (much of the OT) is *kabod*, from a root signifying "weight"; in Greek (in the Septuagint and the NT) the word is *doxa*, which originally meant a "reputation." God's glory represents the imposing majesty and splendor that are characteristic of him and that he radiates when he reveals himself.

God's glory is a main theme of Scripture. The OT associates God's glory, the sheer magnificence of God's presence, with his creation, theophanies, acts of salvation, and judgment. The glory is a devouring fire, shrouded with clouds on Mount Sinai. In clouds and fire, God's glory accompanied Israel through the wilderness and filled the tabernacle and temple. God's glory gave his people victory, but it also accompanied his judgment. There is a clear connection in the OT between God's glory and other attributes, such as holiness, power, greatness, and majesty. God's glory makes him unapproachable by humans, but it also reveals his nearness and an eschatological hope. Indeed, the NT testifies that God's glory is revealed in the incarnation. Jesus reveals God's glory in his teaching but also in his death and resurrection. The NT writers testify that Christ's people, the church, reveal God's glory and should continue to glorify him. It is the full appearance of God's glory that is the people of God's eschatological hope.

God's glory is also a central theme throughout the history of Christian spirituality. An early example of one whose spirituality was particularly inspired by this concept is Gregory of Nyssa. For Gregory, God's glory was not something to be comprehended analytically, but contemplated spiritually. Indeed, God's glory and essence are beyond human comprehension. In this we see that Gregory is one of the earliest Christian theologians significantly impacted by Neoplatonic philosophy. Further, he is thereby also a major figure in the history of *apophatic* theology and spirituality.

Safeguarding God's glory was also a key in the

thought of the sixteenth-century Reformers. An important example is that of John Calvin whose constant and underlying theme was the glory of God. This informs his critique of Roman Catholicism, for his fundamental disagreement was that its theology and practice robbed God of glory that was rightly due him. Indeed, for Calvin the great bone of contention in the 16th century was how God's glory may be kept safe. Calvin argued that even though Roman Catholic conceptions of free will, merit, preparations, and so on might not seem to be of central importance beside the great doctrines of the Trinity or the incarnation, any robbing of God's glory denies the fundamental principle that all glory should be his alone. This fundamental doctrinal position translated into Calvin's spirituality, in which he sought purity and holiness in all things. Calvin's interest in this devotion was classically formulated in the first answer of the Westminster Shorter Catechism: "Man's chief end is to glorify God, and to enjoy him for ever."

Calvin and the Reformed theologians were not alone in the 16th century in this quest for God's glory. Ignatius of Loyola, principal founder of the Society of Jesus (the Jesuits), formulated the society's motto as *ad maiorem Dei gloriam* (for the greater glory of God). The Jesuits had a considerably different theological basis and spirituality than Calvin, but as Calvin's influenced the Reformed tradition, so Loyola's significantly informed and formed the spirituality of the Counter-Reformation.

The modern period saw many of these same themes continue to be further expounded and experienced. Often a deeper understanding of God's glory came because of a challenge to it in this period. Rationalist philosophers claimed that with the advances of science and reason, God's glory was increasingly irrelevant to understanding human life. Christians responded in a variety of ways — some promoted an anti-intellectual emotional revivalism or mysticism, others sought to show the unity of good critical science with the Christian faith, and still others lowered their gaze from a seemingly far-off heaven to look within the human spirit for glimpses of the divine. These are not the only responses to the challenges to God's glory in this era, yet they persist in showing that conceptions of and responses to God's glory continue to preoccupy the various branches of Christianity.

A final remark: God's glory has been most memorably expressed by Christians in poetry and song. Often, a Latin "gloria" or an American "glory, glory, hallelujah" has profoundly influenced the experience and embodiment of a particular Christian's spiritual experience. Further, the giving of glory in worship is called *doxology* — often the most moving point of any liturgy. It is not without reason that Johann Sebastian Bach appended the initials SDG (*soli Deo gloria* — "to God alone the glory") to the end of each of his cantata scores.

See also Beauty; Holiness; Wonder; Worship.

For Further Reading: H. U. von Balthasar, *The Glory of the Lord* (1983 – 1991); J. R. Beeke, *Living for God's Glory: An Introduction to Calvinism* (2008); G. Kittel, "Doxa," in *TDNT*, 2:232 – 55; R. Stark, *For the Glory of God* (2003).

Jason Zuidema

Glossolalia

Glossolalia refers to Spirit-inspired speech delivered in a human or heavenly language unknown to the speaker. The compound Greek term consists of *glossa* (tongue) and *lalein* (to speak) with more than half of thirty-five NT references in 1 Corinthians 14. Here Paul addresses the misdirected enthusiasm of the Corinthians by calling for intelligibility during public worship; it is only through interpreted tongues or prophecy that both believers and unbelievers receive edification (vv. 2, 23). Paul refutes those out of control and calls for silence if there is no one to interpret (vv. 27 – 28). But Paul also encourages glossolalic prayer for personal edification; in the proper context, individuals pray in private tongues addressed to God, for they "do not speak to other people but to God. Indeed, no one understands them" (v. 2 TNIV).

Turning to the day of Pentecost in Acts 2, Luke tells of bystanders who hear followers of Jesus speaking in their own languages (v. 11). The diversity of tongues appears as symbolic representation of Luke's interest in Spirit-initiated inclusivity, the gospel for people of all tongues. When Peter crosses the Gentile barrier and proclaims Jesus to the household of Cornelius, listeners begin "speaking in tongues and praising God" (Acts 10:46), and when Paul encounters Ephesians familiar with only John's baptism, these people also "spoke in tongues and prophesied" (Acts 19:6). Luke narrates the respective glossolalic activity in conjunction with the geographic and ethnic spread of the gospel from Jews in Jerusalem to Caesarean Gentiles on Jewish soil and to Gentiles in Greek territory.

In contrast to the relative frequency of tongues in the NT, reports of glossolalia occur sporadically throughout church history until an exponential burst in the twentieth-century Pentecostal and charismatic movements. Classical Pentecostals typically identify speaking in tongues as evidence for Spirit-baptism, which they see as a postconversion personal experience for the purpose of power in witness (Acts 1:8). Current theologies highlight sacramental impulses, such as spontaneous and playful encounter with God, egalitarian impulses that challenge social privilege so often bound up with public discourse, and eschatological experience as a foretaste of future intimacy with the living Jesus. Though dispensationalists continue to advance the cessation of tongues, as well as other gifts of the Spirit, with the end of the apostolic age, the practice of glossolalia continues to grow so as to become a normative practice for an increasing percentage of Christians.

See also Charismatic Spirituality; Ecstasy; Pentecostal Spirituality.

For Further Reading: M. Cartledge, ed. *Speaking in Tongues: Multi-Disciplinary Perspectives* (2006); G. Fee, *The First Epistle to the Corinthians* (1987); K. McDonnell, *Charismatic Renewal and the Churches* (1976); W. Samarin, *Tongues of Men and Angels* (1972).

Martin Mittelstadt

Gluttony

Gluttony is first on the list of the cardinal, or "deadly," sins. According to early monastics (such as Evagrius, Cassian, and Gregory the Great) who came up with the list, this is the first to be defeated: if one cannot conquer a deadly thought or passion that has to do with the body, then one is not likely to conquer a more insidious enemy that attacks in the spiritual arena. At the same time, because we are embodied beings that require food, we are never completely rid of gluttonous thoughts.

The Bible does not say much about gluttony (see Deut. 21:20; Prov. 23:20–21; 28:7; Matt. 11:19 and parallels; Titus 1:12). Furthermore, in Christianity no foods are off limits as they are in other religions such as Judaism, Islam, and Hinduism. People are not to make gods of their bellies nor to be overly concerned about food (Matt. 4:4; 6:25; Rom. 14:2–3; 1 Cor. 8:8; Phil. 3:19; Col. 2:20–23; 1 Tim. 4:1–5). Interestingly, food plays an important role in the biblical narrative—in the fall, the exodus, Jesus' wilderness temptation, his first miracle at Cana, the Last Supper, the Eucharist, and the eschatological banquet.

Gluttony has to do with the way we desire and consume our food, particularly in the context of the communities in which we find ourselves. Ultimately it refers to a desire or a longing that seeks to be filled inordinately (in the wrong way). Thus, it does not just refer to overeating; a person who has an eating disorder, such as anorexia, may actually be gluttonous given the six aspects of gluttony that early Christians identified: (1) eating too much; (2) eating at the wrong time, such as not waiting for the community; (3) anticipating eating with preoccupied and eager longing; (4) eating expensively, especially when others have too little; (5) seeking delicacies or being fussy about food; and (6) paying too much attention to food, such as when we are overscrupulous about the food we eat or too concerned with the way our bodies look. As one can see from this list, gluttony has much to do with preoccupation of thoughts about food. Further, in many of these cases, the glutton neglects his or her relationship to others. Disordered eating reflects disordered relationships—with ourselves, others, the earth, and God.

Temperance (the right ordering of our appetites) is the countervailing virtue to be cultivated primarily through the practice of fasting, which is different from dieting, which puts the focus back on self. Fasting includes meditation on Scripture, the support of the community, moderation, and individual tailoring.

See also Body; Fasting; Food; Sins, Seven Deadly.

For Further Reading: M. Bringle, *The God of Thinness* (1992); J. Cassian, *The Institutes*, trans. B. Ramsey (2000); D. Okholm, "Being Stuffed and Being Fulfilled," in *Limning the Psyche*, ed. R. Roberts and M. Talbot (1997), 317–38.

Dennis Okholm

Gnosticism

Gnosticism was an early heretical perspective on the Christian life. Scholars disagree on the exact historical context that formed the matrix of Gnosticism, but by the 2nd century it had become a major threat to Christian thought and teaching, as seen in the fact that key Christian authors, from Ignatius of Antioch to Irenaeus of Lyons, responded to it at length.

Common to nearly all forms of Gnosticism was a radical cosmological dualism: the created realm was deemed inherently evil and opposed to the realm of the spirit, which was considered essentially good. Trapped within the bodies of certain human beings, namely, the elect, were divine substances, which were their souls or real selves. In the words of the Gnostic *Gospel of Philip*, "The soul ... is a precious thing and has gotten into a despised body." The goal of life was thus defined in terms of escape from the material realm.

Escape or salvation entailed recognition of this divine element within one's being, and thus salvation was primarily self-enlightenment. For most, though not all, Gnostics, this enlightenment was the work of Jesus. The Gnostic Jesus, though, is quite a different person from the Jesus of the NT. Christ's incarnation and his death and resurrection were downplayed, often rejected, and emphasis was placed on Jesus as a teacher.

Finally, Gnostics had a great interest in freedom. There was, for instance, a stress on freedom from biblical morality, which resulted in either strict asceticism or libertine indulgence. In the *Acts of Thomas*, for example, marriage is described as "filthy intercourse," which, when it is abandoned, makes one a "holy temple, pure and free from afflictions and pains." It is also noteworthy that Gnostics generally had no qualms about avoiding martyrdom for their beliefs. They reasoned that since Christ never really suffered in the flesh and died, it was unlikely that he would work through the flesh now.

Supporting their views were various writings that Gnostics seem to have regarded as canonical. They rejected, in turn, the entirety of the OT as authoritative Scripture as well as parts of the NT, which forced the church to begin to think through what constituted Scripture. By the 4th century, however, Gnosticism had largely ceased to be a threat to the church. In recent years, largely because of the discovery of a cache of Gnostic writings at Nag Hammadi in Egypt, there has been renewed interest in Gnosticism as an alternative form of early Christianity.

See also Augustine of Hippo; New Age Spirituality.

For Further Reading: W. Foerster, ed., *Gnosis: A Selection of Gnostic Texts*, 2 vols., trans. R. McL. Wilson (1972); K. King, *What Is Gnosticism?* (2003); B. Pearson, *Ancient Gnosticism* (2007).

Michael A. G. Haykin

God, Perceptions of

The importance of one's perceptions of God is often overlooked but cannot be overstated. After all, we serve the God we imagine, and we introduce others to that God as well. This is not to say that humans somehow invent God. But the ability to apprehend accurately the fullness of God's being, character, and ways is always limited by human fallibility. It is easy, and sometimes tempting, to confuse one's perceptions of God with the reality of God.

These perceptions of God are initially shaped by early experiences of attachment to and trustworthiness of important caregivers. Faith development theorists suggest that the character and behavior of one's early caregivers form a template for one's implicit ideas about God. Psychoanalyst Ana-Maria Rizzuto calls perceptions of God that are based on experience "God images." If we experience our caregivers as safe, responsive, and loving, we initially assume that God is also safe, responsive, and loving. This makes possible what developmental psychologists call a "secure attachment" to God. If, however, we experience our caregivers as distracted, unreliable, or terrifying, we may initially believe that God is the same—or we may invent an opposite, wishful image of God in order to moderate the emotional distress we suffer in that important but untrustworthy relationship with the caregiver. These perceptions may lead us to relate to God in either avoidant or overly clingy ways and to experience insecurity in our relationship with God.

We also develop perceptions of God that are based on our cognitions; Rizzuto calls these "God concepts." The learning about God that is acquired through teaching, preaching, study, and conversation also shapes one's perceptions of God and God's character and ways of being in relationship with humans. Unfortunately, these cognitions are sometimes no more accurate than the flawed conclusions based on experiences. The unexamined and only partially accurate God images and God concepts of those who teach us about God, both formally and informally, become part of our belief system, our God images and God concepts. We perceive God as being a particular way, and when something is perceived as real, it becomes real in its consequences. Thus, our interpretations of our ongoing experiences of God support our existing perceptions, whether they are accurate or not.

Holding one's God images and God concepts up for the Spirit's illumination and correction is an essential part of one's spiritual journey. Spiritual formation is at least partly about increasing the congruence of one's experiential and cognitive perceptions of God with the reality of God as portrayed in Scripture. Clearly, it becomes necessary to bring a reflective, self-aware approach to reading Scripture so that one becomes aware of a tendency to read one's prior assumptions about God into the text rather than allowing the text to challenge and change those assumptions.

This intentional opening of one's perceptions of God to examination and refinement is most helpfully done in community. Allowing others to probe and question is more likely to reveal taken-for-granted perspectives than is study in isolation. Since perceptions of God are shaped in relationship, perhaps it is only logical that they will be reshaped in relationship as well.

A word about anxiety is in order. Because perceptions of God are fundamental to a sense of universal order and coherence, and because they are at least initially implicit and therefore comprise unexamined beliefs on which we act with confidence, the formative process of making them explicit can leave us with a temporary sense of disorder and anomie. It becomes important, both as individuals and as communities of faith, to trust that the One who desires to be perceived rightly and who invites humans into confident, authentic relationship is also One who will protect, guide, and bless as those humans submit their perceptions to the Spirit's wisdom and correction.

See also *Kenosis.*

For Further Reading: J. Balswick et al., *The Reciprocating Self* (2005); J. Fowler, *Stages of Faith* (1995); J. Hagberg and R. Guelich, *The Critical Journey* (2004); J. Loder, *The Logic of the Spirit* (1998); A. M. Rizzuto, *The Birth of the Living God* (1981); M. Thompson, *Family: The Forming Center* (1997).

Carla M. Dahl

Good Works

Good works can be understood in general terms as acts of benevolence that one undertakes in favor of others based on religious convictions. In other words, they denote acts that are morally honorable, pleasing to God, and beneficial to others.

Since at least the 16th century, the place and the role of good works in Christian experience have constituted a point of contention between Protestants and Roman Catholics. In recent years, however, one can observe, particularly in the context of ecumenical dialogue, a movement toward mutual understanding whereby justification is seen as both forensic and intrinsic. It is forensic in that it refers to the gracious act of God, who, on account of Christ's work, declares one just (Rom. 4:3–5; Gal. 3:6). As such, justification relates to one's outward position before God, not one's inward life. It is justly called "imputed righteousness." Yet righteousness is also intrinsic in that it inaugurates a way of being, a life of righteousness, made possible by one's faith in Christ. It is this reality that some Christian traditions refer to as "infused righteousness." It is righteousness that manifests itself in good works (James 2:18–23). In the words of John Tyson, echoing John Wesley, "The faith that justifies is a lively faith that is manifested in actual righteousness and good works."

The place of good works is not only debated in connection with faith and justification; it is also rather problematic in Christian spirituality that too often favors practices such as silence, solitude, contemplation, and centeredness. Yet the reality is that true spirituality is inseparable from good works. Good works flow from an intimate relationship with the living Christ, in whom believers, who are God's workmanship, are created to do the very good works that God prepared beforehand for them to do (Eph. 2:10). Hence, as Thomas Oden put it, "The heart of the Gospel is God's good work for us. What we do in response is a story every believer lives out. It is the story of faith becoming active in love."

See also Faith; Grace.

For Further Reading: T. Oden, ed., *The Good Works Reader* (2007); P. Palmer, *The Active Life* (1990); J. Tyson, ed., *Invitation to Christian Spirituality* (1999).

Mabiala Justin-Robert Kenzo

Gospel Songs

Revivals connected to the Second Great Awakening of the early 19th century ushered in musical song with spontaneous characteristics. The "Singing Pilgrim" Philip Phillips is believed to have first associated the term *gospel* with these songs, and the revivals of Charles Finney offered the first published revival songbook of them. Revival music has been widely published, from the six-volume *Gospel Hymns* of Philip Bliss and Ira Sankey to the multiple volumes of *Favorites* songbooks edited by twentieth-century gospel songwriter John W. Peterson.

The musical style of the gospel song closely follows the Sunday school songs of William Bradbury—catchy melodies, simple harmony and rhythm, and repeated refrains. Sometimes called "experience hymns," these songs include lyrical content that expresses the personal testimony of a changed life through personal salvation. In addition, they have been used to persuade and exhort people to experience their own personal salvation. Writers who established the foundation for this expression were poets such as Fanny Crosby ("Blessed Assurance," "He Hideth My Soul," "Jesus Is Tenderly Calling You Home"), poet-musician Philip Bliss ("Almost Persuaded," "Whosoever

Will," "Hold the Fort"), and Ira Sankey, who composed the music for several poets of the era ("The Ninety and Nine," "Faith Is the Victory").

Revivalism in the 19th century involved a strong liaison between revival preachers and musicians. The role of the musician rose to equal that of the preacher as musicians gained popularity. Revival teams such as Moody-Sankey, Chapman-Alexander, Sunday-Rodeheaver, and Graham-Barrows-Shea maintained the team concept throughout the 19th and 20th centuries. This elevated role of the musician eventually had an attendant impact on the regard for musicians in the local church. Subsequently, the liturgical structure of revival services impacted church worship, with the tripartite music-preaching-decision model becoming normative for church worship in evangelical settings. The gospel song also laid a foundation for the shorter worship songs of the 1960s, followed by the "praise and worship" style of Christian music. Popular subgenres of the gospel song include contemporary gospel, urban gospel, and Southern gospel.

The gospel song has not been without its controversies. Serious musicians and hymnists have long decried this style of musical expression as excessively personal and exclusive, musically trite and simplistic, and frequently deficient in doctrinal content. The *Harvard Dictionary of Music* notes ruefully that the influence of gospel songs "extended beyond the confines of the revival meetings into the regular services of the church." However, for many on the evangelical side of the worship spectrum, the genre has provided a meaningful tool for expressing personal faith.

See also Revival; Testimony.

For Further Reading: D. Hustad, *Jubilate II: Church Music in Worship and Renewal* (1993).

Edwin M. Willmington

Grace

The wellspring of grace is the eternal divine disposition. Grace first comes to people as the undeserved favor and blessings that God bestows on all of his creation. Grace is the foundation stone of Christian theology. It expresses God's one-sided love in his deep relationship with his creation, and awakens and animates believers to respond appropriately to his endlessly benevolent ways. Grace expresses the divine initiative that creates, establishes a generous relationship with what is created, proactively sets in motion a costly reconciliation plan even without being asked to do so, and patiently persuades a willfully lost creation to receive divine reconciliation. All that is perfect and good in Christian experience can be attributed to "the God of all grace" (1 Peter 5:10). In response, Christians are to express thankfulness, celebrate God's graciousness toward them in worship, humbly ask for this disposition to continue toward others and themselves, and seek to mirror such amazing grace in their own relationships with others.

Extrinsically, grace is expressed in God's relationship with creation. Common grace is the expression of divine grace that underlies every good thing that exists and occurs in the world. No good received, possessed, or accomplished is possible without this grace. Special grace, on the other hand, is the unmerited favor shown to sinners, the action of God on behalf of undeserving people, Christ's gift of his own being as the supreme revelation of God's favor, God's method of saving, God's power working in persons, the new state of existence entered through faith, and a synonym for the gospel.

In Reformed theology the concept of grace has often been made subordinate to the more dominant doctrine of justification. However, it can be argued that the reverse is true: that justification is both a judicial explanation of how grace is effectuated in the redemptive work of Christ and a means of securing the fullness of grace in the lives of the redeemed. In other words, grace enables justification, and justification points to grace. An emerging view among Pauline scholars is that the center of Paul's thought does not lie with justification by faith but with grace, where justification is one of many ways to describe this grace.

Christian anthropology teaches that even in our sinful nature we are predisposed for grace. The gospel of grace uniquely fulfills the dimly apprehended longings of our hearts, longings that are reawakened by Grace personified. Something deep in our nature, of which we have but an obscure awareness, can only be fulfilled by God's grace. The axiom that "grace does not destroy nature but perfects it" rings true; grace transforms a possibility inherent within human nature into an actuality. Since human nature cannot even exist without grace, we are graced creatures made in the image of God who are open to his grace only by grace. Although sin wounds, diminishes, and disorders our soul's readiness for grace, sin cannot completely destroy this ontological structural need and desire for grace. In addition, it is specifically through the special and saving grace of Christ that God redeems, restores, fulfills, and perfects us toward finding our deepest satisfaction and fullness in God.

The message of the gospel of grace in Christ radically challenges both religious moralism and worldly efforts at self-salvation or self-aggrandizement — tendencies that exist in all religious and philosophical systems. Jesus did not depict two alternative ways of salvation: the world's way and his way, but rather three alternatives — the world's way, the religious way, and his way of grace, as portrayed in the parable of the prodigal son, with God being the initiator of grace who runs to people. They come to their senses when they realize two things simultaneously: that they are more lost and wicked than they ever thought possible, and also that they are more loved and desired than they could ever imagine. Grace leads to spiritual and psychological liberation and rest. Knowing that they are already lovingly accepted enables them finally to stop running and hiding and to admit their brokenness. Attempting to change one's life through religious self-effort will lead either to pride (in the case of perceived success) or to self-condemnation (in the case of failure). However, life change through grace leads to humble confidence by receiving the divine initiative and accepting the offer in Christ, allowing him to transform the heart from the inside out. Thus, change begins in the interior and moves outwardly, as opposed to being violently imposed from the outside. Furthermore, it is this kind of grace that genuinely refuses to submit to ungodliness (Titus 2:11 – 12), and it drove Paul to spend his life "working harder" than all the other apostles so that he burned on without burning out (1 Cor. 15:10). Receiving grace is first and foremost receiving Christ, and then the different expressions of his graciousness as well. It is through the exercise of the instrument of faith that believers are enabled to receive and appropriate the fullness of God's grace.

The gospel of grace has been the defining impulse of the evangelical tradition, even while various aspects of grace have been made central, subordinated, or expressed differently. This impulse is best celebrated by the most popular evangelical hymn in the world, "Amazing Grace." The power, beauty, and simplicity of "Amazing Grace" lie in its candid portrayal of humanity's sinful reality, and a deep desire for continual grace, restoration, and unconditional love — conditions and intrinsic desires to which Christians and non-Christians can personally and existentially relate. Its composer, John Newton, best summed up the gospel of grace in the final days of his life, "My memory is nearly gone, but I remember two things: That I am a great sinner and that Christ is a great Savior."

See also Faith; Good Works.

For Further Reading: K. Barth, *God Here and Now* (2003); C. Braaten and R. Jenson, eds., *Union with Christ* (1998); D. Coffey, *Deus Trinitas* (1999); B. Demarest, *The Cross and Salvation* (1997); T. Keller, *The Prodigal God* (2008); A. McGrath, *Iustitia Dei* (2005).

André Ong

Graham, Billy (1918 –)

American mass evangelist and evangelical ecumenist. Perhaps no single person personifies twentieth-century evangelicalism worldwide better than Billy Graham. After the fundamentalist-modernist struggles of the early 20th century, conservative Christianity was increasingly marginalized. Out of this experience emerged a number of leaders with conservative theological convictions and a desire to engage the larger culture; Billy Graham became the most prominent among them.

Graham was converted to the Christian faith in 1934 at a revival meeting. This started him on a course that took him to several colleges, finally graduating from Wheaton College. During this period he struggled with legalism, which he ultimately rejected, and the authority of the Scriptures, which he finally embraced as the infallible Word of God and central to his faith. This latter theme (epitomized in Graham's own signature phrase "The Bible says . . .") became one of the hallmarks of the evangelical movement he was to lead.

Graham became an evangelist for Youth for Christ International, one of the many new organizations formed out the evangelical movement, and in this capacity began to preach all over the United States and Europe following World War II. In 1949 he preached in Los Angeles at a series of tent meetings that launched him into the headlines of America and to the forefront of evangelicalism; and the next year he founded the Billy Graham Association. In the years that followed, he also played prominent roles in the founding of a leading evangelical magazine, *Christianity Today*, and the Lausanne Movement for World Evangelization, uniting Christians from numerous denominations around the advancement of the gospel. He preached to millions both in stadiums and through radio and television all over the world. Graham's dedication has always been to proclaim the historic message of the Christian faith to nonbelievers. An important part of this ministry was the inclusion of follow-up, utilizing both parachurch organizations (e.g., the Navigators) and local churches, to ensure that the new life into which he invited people was nurtured.

Graham's ministry has been marked by an emphasis on biblical preaching. He has always preached basic Christianity and the availability of a personal relationship with Jesus Christ. One of his earliest books captured this emphasis in its title *Peace with God* (1953). He also helped to advance the experience of the new birth through his book *How to Be Born Again* (1977) and *Decision* magazine.

Through his years of ministry, Graham has helped to bring to mainstream culture the basic concepts of forgiveness of sins, a personal relationship with Jesus Christ, the authority and faithfulness of the Bible, and the new life that comes through the Holy Spirit. These ideas, which Graham would call the historic faith, are now considered foundations of evangelical Christian spirituality. His personal spirituality has been reflected in a lifelong and faithful marriage partnership with Ruth Bell Graham (who died in 2007), financial integrity, healthy organizational teamwork, respect for local churches, and support for civil rights. He has written an autobiography titled *Just as I Am* (2007).

See also Evangelism; Revival.

For Further Reading: W. Martin, *A Prophet with Honor: The Billy Grahm Story* (1991); J. C. Pollock, *The Billy Graham Story* (2003).

Christopher Morton

Gratitude

See **Thanksgiving.**

Greed

Greed is the inordinate love of material things and, by extension, of power, position, and anything else that can be obtained. It is not the "having" or "wanting" that is always wrong, but the selfish or hedonistic motives, unjust means, and misplaced trust that make such pursuits wrong. Synonyms are insatiableness, avarice, and covetousness (cf. Gr. *pleonexia*, from *pleon*, "more," and *echo,* "have"). Prototypes of greed in Scripture have included Gehazi, Judas, and Ananias and Sapphira. The "deadly sin" of greed often leads to social injustice, oppression, and crime, as the prophets often pointed out (Jer. 22:13 – 17; Ezek. 22:27; Hab. 2:6 – 9). Jesus taught that we cannot serve two masters — wealth and God (Matt. 6:24; Luke 16:13). Paul called the "love of money" the "root of all kinds of evil" (1 Tim. 6:6 – 10) and linked greed with idolatry (Eph. 5:5; Col. 3:5). Greed can manifest itself in different ways; even frugal persons can hide the vice in a cloak of virtue if their frugality is an attempt to alleviate anxiety about future security.

John Cassian pinpointed its origins primarily in a lukewarm and halfhearted commitment to God, something of which both the rich and the poor are susceptible (the poor lacking the opportunity but not the will or disposition for greed). Then "reasonable excuses" are found to make the case for avarice; for example, our terms "having it all," "the good life," "financial success," and "economic security."

To overcome greed, one must first recognize and name it, but in our capitalist culture, we are often socialized by business and advertising to treat it as a virtue; few would perceive it as undesirable until it leads to criminal behavior. One must also realize that it often leads to the opposite of what it promises; in fact, it can be accompanied by anxiety and depression (Eccl. 5:10 – 17; Luke 12:13 – 34). So it is to be avoided at all costs, and it is not to be fed, since to feed it only inflames it. Instead, values must be reoriented (Matt. 6:33; Rom. 8:5), realizing that material possessions do not of themselves confer knowledge, skill, courage, or any other meaningful human quality. Reducing wants also counteracts greed. Cultivating virtues of charity and justice helps us diffuse the power of "mammon" and appreciate the effect that inordinate levels of consumption have on others.

See also Consumerism; Marketplace Spirituality; Poverty; Simplicity; Sins, Seven Deadly.

For Further Reading: J. Cassian, *The Institutes,* trans. B. Ramsey (2000); R. Foster, *Money, Sex and Power* (1999); J. Kavanaugh, *Following Christ in a Consumer Society* (1991).

Dennis Okholm

Gregory Nazianzus (329 – 389)

A Cappadocian father and bishop of Constantinople. Born into a wealthy family, son of the bishop of Nazianzus, Gregory was highly educated. He learned of the monastic life from Basil of Caesarea and acquired a lifelong desire for the secluded life of prayer and study, which would be continually interrupted by his loving obedience to family and church.

In 362 he responded to his aging father's request for assistance in the management of the bishopric. Reluctantly ordained, Gregory served there until his father's death in 374. He then spent several years in prayer and study on the family estate until called by Basil, now bishop, to Constantinople to help in the battle against the Arian heresy. The controversy was not restricted to civil theological debate. Gregory described in a letter how the Arians invaded their little chapel where he was pastor and disrupted a baptismal service: "They have desecrated the altars, profaned the mysteries. As we stood between those to be baptized and those who were throwing stones at us, we had no recourse against the stoning except prayer." A series of brilliant parish homilies against Arianism, which were later published as *Five Theological Orations,* were so powerful and influential on the entire city that he was appointed bishop of Constantinople in 381. However, he stayed in the see less than twelve months, resigning and retiring to Nazianzus for prayer and study.

Theological reflection was never divorced from pastoral presence for Gregory; hence, the core of his spirituality can be discerned in the corpus of his sermons, letters, and poetry. Indeed, Gregory the Great was influenced by this theme in Gregory

Nazianzus's work when he wrote his own classic *Regula Pastoralis* (*On Pastoral Practice*). The eloquence and beauty of his work is not diminished by its theological and scriptural integrity as he calls each believer to the imitation of Christ. The deeper one grows in Christ, he explained, the more prayer-filled and contemplative one becomes. At times one feels as though Gregory's prayer is Christ's and, ultimately, also echoes one's own: "Everything that exists prays to thee / And to thee every creature that can read thy universe / Sends up a hymn of silence. / In thee alone all things dwell." Gregory's spirituality embraced mystery and paradox as much as rational, theological analysis, and he used Scripture to support his entire theological system. In particular he affirmed the divinity, equality, and activity of the Holy Spirit. This is reflected in the Spirit's presence and guidance in each Christian's ever-deepening life of prayer and subsequent growth in Christlikeness.

See also Cappadocians.

For Further Reading: G. Barrios, ed., *The Fathers Speak* (1986); L. Bouyer, *History of Christian Spirituality*, vol. 1, trans. M. Ryan (1963); O. Clement, *The Roots of Christian Mysticism* (1993).

Kelby Cotton

Gregory of Nyssa (c. 335 – c. 395)

Fourth-century Cappadocian father. He was the first to develop a Christian apophatic theology in which we know God through "unknowing." Gregory was born into a saintly aristocratic family in Asia Minor. He was probably educated at home, receiving the finest teaching in Greek philosophy. He was encouraged in the spiritual life by his sister Macrina. He married and taught rhetoric until he was persuaded by his brother Basil the Great to become a (married) priest. Later Basil made him bishop of Nyssa, though he was never well suited to administrative tasks. He was deposed and exiled by the Arians in 376 but was able to return two years later. For years Gregory was overshadowed

by Basil, but after his brother's death in 379, Gregory established himself as a leading theologian of the Christian East. He played an important role in defending Nicene orthodoxy at the Council of Constantinople in 381.

Gregory's corpus consists of doctrinal, ascetical, and mystical writings. His masterpieces of the spiritual life are *Life of Moses* and the commentaries *On the Song of Songs* and *On the Beatitudes*. Only Gregory's doctrinal work, *On the Making of Man*, was translated into Latin and had some influence in the medieval West. Gregory's mystical theology, now considered among the most profound and original patristic writings, while long revered in the East, received limited attention by the Western church until the 20th century. Renewed interest in his spiritual writings came primarily through the work of Hans Urs von Balthasar and Jean Daniélou (1905 – 1974).

Gregory combined his apophaticism with the concept of *epektasis*, the endless pursuit of the inexhaustible love of God. This most distinctive Nyssen theme appears constantly in both *Life of Moses* and *Homilies on the Song of Songs*. In both works Gregory reads Scripture allegorically and contemplatively in the Alexandrian way, going beyond the literal sense (*historia*) to the mystical sense (*theoria*), where he finds the deepest spiritual meaning of Scripture. Thus, in *Life of Moses* every event in Moses' life is symbolic of the Christian's spiritual journey. Moses becomes the paradigm of the soul's journey when he first encounters God in the light of the burning bush, but light yields to darkness as he climbs Mount Sinai and enters the cloud and sees God in the "dazzling darkness." This moving from the light of knowledge to the mystery of darkness is Gregory's paradoxical "seeing that consists in not seeing." Knowing through comprehension is transcended, and knowing through love draws us into an insatiable communion with God. In his *Homilies on the Song of Songs*, Gregory describes spiritual growth as dynamic, unending ascent: "At each instant what is grasped is much greater than what had been grasped before, but since what we are seeking is unlimited, the end of each discovery becomes the starting point for the discovery of something higher, and the ascent continues.... We go from beginning to beginning by way of beginnings without end."

Gregory's apophatic spirituality reminds us that the images of God we construct are not the reality of God, and perfection is perpetual becoming; we can never reach a terminus; there is always something more to be discovered about ourselves and about God.

See also Cappadocians.

For Further Reading: H. U. von Balthasar, *From Glory to Glory: Texts from Gregory of Nyssa's Mystical Writings*, ed. and trans. H. Musurillo (1961); idem, *Presence and Thought: An Essay on the Religious Philosophy of Gregory of Nyssa* (1995); P. Gregorios, *Cosmic Man* (1988); J. Smith, *Passion and Paradise* (2004).

Carole Dale Spencer

Gregory the Great (c. 540–604)

Pivotal medieval pope. "The Great" is the customary honorific for Pope Gregory, the first practicing monk to be elected to the papacy (590–604). Roman Catholics designate him doctor of the church and one of six Latin fathers. Born of noble blood and ascending to the secular prefecture of Rome before entering the monastery, he became pope at a time of barbarian invasion, plague, drought, famine, and the abdication of responsibility by the old Roman senatorial class. He filled the leadership void, negotiating peace with the invaders, draining the coffers of the church on behalf of the suffering, and leading penitential parades beseeching God to turn back the plague. His leadership in Rome is considered a key moment in the rise of the papacy to Western power both ecclesiastical and secular. However, appalled by claims of the patriarch John of Constantinople to be "ecumenical patriarch," Gregory styled himself "servant of the servants of God" (though still assuming the Western primacy of the Roman bishop).

Gregory's extant writings include the *Pastoral Care*, which throughout the Middle Ages was given to every new Western bishop at consecration; the *Dialogues*, a hagiographic account of Italian saints, including the only contemporary biography of Benedict of Nursia; the very long *Commentary on Job* (*Magna Moralia*); sermons on the Gospels, Ezekiel, and the Song of Songs; and more than eight hundred administrative letters.

Gregory sent Augustine of Canterbury and a group of other monks to missionize England for the Roman Church; they encountered a lively Celtic church and remnants of earlier Gaulish missions, and they established the episcopal see at Canterbury and refounded the ancient See of York. Under his culturally sensitive guidance, that mission cleansed and repurposed, rather than destroying, pagan places of worship and adapted, rather than completely supplanting, customs of the Celtic church.

A great spiritual as well as administrative leader, Gregory elaborated a spirituality both supernatural and earthy, hybridizing the prior work of Augustine of Hippo and John Cassian. His lively sense of the sacramental presence of God in creation can often look like credulous supernaturalism (as in the *Dialogues*), but he also insisted that Christians foster and practice *discretio* (discernment) to judge accurately where God is talking in their experience of the world. He treated suffering as an instance of God's sanctifying speech to us; even our sins, he counseled, God transforms into stages of growth. He made the emotional virtue of *compunctio* (compunction) a central value in Western spirituality; this is a kind of godly sorrow for sin, mixed with both a fear and a joyful desire for God, whose etymological root refers to the "piercing" of Peter's hearers recorded in Acts 2:37. For this reason Dom Jean Leclercq called him "Doctor of Desire." Gregory was perhaps as much "father of medieval Western spirituality" as Augustine was father of medieval Western theology.

See also Care of Souls.

For Further Reading: R. Markus, *Gregory the Great and His World* (1997); J. Moorhead, *Gregory the Great* (2005); T. Oden, *Care of Souls in the Classic Tradition* (1984); C. Straw, *Gregory the Great* (1988).

Chris L. Armstrong

Grief

Grief is the profound human experience that accompanies major loss. It entails cognitive, emotional, and spiritual processing. While much has been said about the course of grief (e.g., Kübler-Ross's well-known stages of grief: denial, anger, bargaining, depression, acceptance), for most people grief is a convoluted and complicated process that waxes and wanes. Despite the fact that each individual has a unique journey through the valley of grief, there are common aspects of grief that nearly everyone experiences.

Grief is an awareness of the pain of having lost someone or something significant in one's life. It can manifest on an emotional level as sadness/depression, emotional numbness, mood fluctuations, anger, resentment, guilt, hopelessness, or loneliness. The individual may be flooded with recollections or attempt to quash all memories. He or she may experience cognitive impairment in concentration and memory. Relationships may be disturbed. Physically, disruptions of everyday functioning in sleeping, eating, and sexual activity are typical. Fatigue/lethargy or somatic symptoms, such as headaches or digestive disturbances, may occur. Spiritual manifestations include anguished questioning of God, anger at God, and/or deep longings for which words are inadequate. A grieving person may feel a need to cry out to God almost constantly or, conversely, feel that his or her prayer life has dried up completely. The pervasive way that grief affects all levels of functioning can lead to a sense of disorganization, inducing fear that the pain and other symptoms may render the individual completely nonfunctional.

Grief is a necessary emotional response to loss, a healthy and normal healing process that parallels the healing process the body goes through in reaction to physiological damage. Some people attempt to circumvent the pain of loss by avoiding embracing grief, but this only serves to foster psychological and spiritual dysfunction. Grief is one of those necessary pains that M. Scott Peck discusses in the classic *The Road Less Traveled*, and attempting to bypass grief will only prolong and complicate the pain. Grief must have its day. Moreover, the grief process takes however long it takes, which is to say, we should never inflict on others or ourselves an expectation of when someone should be finished with grieving.

Social support, attention to one's spirituality, and consistent self-care facilitate the grief process. Resolution of grief occurs when one has been able to accept and express all the feelings the loss generated and to move on into a "new normal" life. Spiritually, people often discover that navigating through a profound grief experience strengthens their faith and fosters spiritual growth.

See also Lament.

For Further Reading: E. Kübler-Ross, *On Death and Dying* (1969); C. S. Lewis, *A Grief Observed* (1961); G. Sittser, *A Grace Disguised* (2004).

Myrla Seibold

Griffiths, Bede (1906–1993)

Camaldolese Benedictine mystic and an early Christian interpreter of Hinduism. Born Allan Griffiths in England, he studied in Oxford and credits C. S. Lewis, who became a lifelong friend, with influencing him to become a Christian. He grew up with a love for poetry and nature, but it was his deep intellectual searching that eventually led him to join the Roman Catholic Church in 1936. He was a monk of Prinknash Abbey for fifteen years and then appointed prior of Farnborough Abbey. During this period, the rhythm of reading, study, and work in the fields were deeply formed in him. Since childhood he had felt a kinship with India, and when the opportunity came, he went there in 1955.

Critical of Western Christianity's attempts to impose its structures and symbols, Griffiths developed his Saccidananda Ashram (Hermitage of the Holy Trinity) as a place for contemplative life, inculturation, and interreligious dialogue. Monks in his ashram wore the saffron-colored robes of Hindu holy men; the liturgy used English, Sanskrit, and Tamil, with readings from the holy books of the various religions, and ended with the *arati*, a Hindu way of worship by waving lights before a shrine. A stroke in 1990, while weakening Griffiths physically, was a psychological breakthrough that renewed him and allowed for a more profound experience of self and God, which he called a "feminine" spiritual approach.

For Further Reading: S. Du Boulay, *Beyond the Darkness* (1999).

Kiem-Kiok Kwa

Groote, Gerhard

See *Devotio Moderna;* **Brethren of the Common Life.**

Growth, Spiritual

See **Formation, Spiritual.**

Gutiérrez, Gustavo (1928–)

Dominican priest generally regarded as the father of Latin American liberation theology. Born in Lima, Peru, of Quechua descent, he received his doctorate in religious studies from the Catholic University of Lyon. He is professor at the Pontifical Catholic University in Lima, John Cardinal O'Hara professor of theology at Notre Dame University, and a visiting professor at various universi-

ties in Europe and North America. He is a member of the Peruvian Academy of Language and holds honorary degrees from some twenty universities around the world. In 1993 the French government awarded him the Legion of Honor for his work on behalf of the oppressed.

Gutiérrez's major work, *A Theology of Liberation* (1971), originally published in Spanish in Lima, was translated into many languages and remains a classic of liberation theology (most recent English revision in 1988). Living and working among the poor, he felt that the most pressing question that the Latin American historical context poses to Christians is how to speak about God as a God of love to people regarded as nonpersons. From this starting point, he claimed that the task of theologians is to read the Bible from the perspective of the poor and to show that the God revealed in Jesus Christ is a God of justice who acts to liberate people from every form of oppression.

During the last four decades, Gutiérrez has developed this seminal theme in several books and many articles. He developed it in depth from the perspective of spirituality in *We Drink from Our Own Well: The Spiritual Journey of a People*, originally published in Spanish in 1983 (Eng. trans. 1984/2003), which promises to become a classical work on the subject. In it he presents spirituality as the following of Jesus that starts with an encounter with the Lord brought forth by the Spirit, and which then leads people into a collective liberating venture—an all-embracing community journey involving a style of life that reveals their acceptance of God's gift of adoption as sons and daughters, which God bestows on them.

In 1983 Gutiérrez's "new way of doing theology" was officially condemned by the Vatican through the Congregation for the Doctrine of the Faith, led by Cardinal Ratzinger (now Pope Benedict XVI). It was viewed as placing orthopraxis above orthodoxy and as fostering (under Marxist influence) class conflict. The fact remains, however, that this theological method has become part and parcel of liberation theology not only in Latin America but also around the world.

See also Latin America; Liberation Spirituality.

For Further Reading: R. M. Brown, *Gustavo Gutiérrez* (1980); A. Nava, *The Mystical and Prophetic Thought of Simone Weil and Gustavo Gutiérrez* (2001).

C. René Padilla

Guyon, Madame Jeanne-Marie (1648–1717)

Catholic evangelist and mystic. Jeanne-Marie Guyon traveled through the French countryside and beyond seeking to bring renewal among Christians whose spiritual senses were dulled. Born into a wealthy family in Montargis, she was a sickly child who spent her early years in a convent. She wanted to become a nun, but when she was sixteen, her parents arranged a marriage to a much older wealthy aristocrat. Life under the cruelty of her mother-in-law was relieved when she was widowed at twenty-eight, allowing her to more fully explore the solace she had found through mystical ecstasy.

Influenced by Père Lacombe, a Barnabite monk, she embraced Quietism, a passive spirituality of finding perfection by losing oneself in God. Convinced that God was leading her to spread her newfound faith, she began traveling as an evangelist, leaving her two young children behind. Catholic clerics were not impressed with her message, and her audacious style was deemed improper for a woman. When she was ordered out of one town, she moved on to another. She reported that wherever she went, she found a hunger for a deeper sense of God. She preached in private homes and in town markets, her ministry reaching across the social spectrum from washerwomen to physicians. Young girls were particularly keen to hear her message. Nuns and monks welcomed her into their monasteries. Paris socialites, including two duchesses and a countess, formed a group that met with her regularly.

While promoting a passive Quietism, Guyon actively sought holiness through various forms of asceticism. She rolled in stinging nettles, sucked bitter herbs, walked with sharp stones in her shoes, and pulled out healthy teeth, convinced she was enhancing her oneness with God.

Guyon ignored the threats of church and government authorities and was finally arrested by officials of Louis XIV. She was confined a second time in the Bastille for seven years, the last two years in solitary confinement. After she was released, she lived with her son and discontinued her preaching. Her devotional writings and memoirs were banned by the Catholic Church.

Her influence went far beyond Catholicism. John Wesley was one of her admirers. Of her he said: "How few such instances do we find of exalted love to God, and our neighbor; of genuine humility; of invincible meekness and unbounded resignation."

See also Fénelon, François; Quietism.

For Further Reading: Madame Guyon, *Autobiography of Madame Guyon* (2009); J. Johnson, *Madame Guyon* (1999).

Ruth A. Tucker

H

Hadewijch

See **Beguines.**

Hagiography

There are four major meanings of this term, which

is formed from the two Greek words for "holy" (*hagios*) and "writing" (*graphē*). The first meaning—which we will discuss below—refers to legendary accounts of saints dating from the ancient and medieval periods. Second, hagiography can refer to any biography of a saint, even in modern times. Third, the academic discipline that studies documents concerning saints may be called the field of hagiography. Finally, a biography of any person that is too uncritical, too full of praise, is sometimes criticized as "hagiography."

The premodern accounts of saints' lives, with which we are mainly concerned here, had their beginnings in accounts of the lives of martyrs of the first three centuries. Later, the lives of monks, nuns, bishops, and other holy persons appeared. Among the most well known and best written of these is the *Life of Antony* by Athanasius. This account of the desert father became a model for other lives of the saints.

In the Middle Ages, these accounts became more and more stereotyped. Conventions about the characteristics of a holy martyr, holy virgin, or a holy monk became fixed, so that their individuality was less important than their common virtues, self-denial, and miracles. The purpose of these accounts was not to give accurate biographical information, but to edify the reader and to increase the saint's reputation for holiness. In some cases, this would serve to aid in the canonization of the saint; that is, to enter his or her name on the roll of saints celebrated on given days of the year. The assumption was that people needed models of holiness for their own Christian lives, and that holiness itself led to benefits for those who invoked the name of the saint in prayer. An example of such a text that is still popular today is the *Little Flowers of St. Francis*.

Since the 19th century, when modern historiography was developed, biographies have been distinguished from hagiographies. A biography must conform to the standards of history writing, with evidence, no miracles, and careful attention to factualness. On the other hand, the medieval stories are often full of miracles that are not told with the sobriety and purposefulness of the NT miracles, but lavishly and indiscriminately coated as frosting on the life story of the saint. Many of these miracles concern the power of the corpses and relics of the holy persons. Thus, their value for history is to show the ideals people held for holiness when they wrote the accounts. Apart from the questionable miracles, however, the hagiographies that tell of self-sacrifice, care for those in need, and heroic witness to Christ still have power to inspire us today.

See also Biographies and Formation Spiritual.

For Further Reading: L. Coon, *Sacred Fictions* (1997); T. Head, ed., *Medieval Hagiography* (2001).
Bradley P. Holt

Hammarskjöld, Dag (1905–1961)

Swedish diplomat and private Christian. Hammarskjöld was born to a father with a family background of civil service and a mother with an ancestry of academics and clergy. The trajectory of Hammarskjöld's own life would marry these spheres of political engagement and religious devotion. He was an excellent student at Uppsala University, after which he held several teaching positions before becoming an esteemed economist and chairman of the National Bank of Sweden. Finally, in 1953, he was appointed secretary general of the United Nations.

Although he was presumed to be agnostic, Hammarskjöld was, in reality, a fervent believer. He kept a spiritual diary throughout his life, which he referred to as "a White Book concerning my negotiations with myself—and with God." This manuscript, discovered and published after his death as *Markings* (1964), bears no record of his worldly life as an international civil servant. Similarly, Hammarskjöld's outward life held few clues to his hard-wrought faith; he did not engage in any communal aspect of Christianity, including any liturgical or sacramental experiences. Rather than participate in the traditions of institutional religion, he wrote about his desire to "build up a personal belief in the light of experience." One of the creeds Hammarskjöld established was that, in the troubled modern era, "the road to holiness necessarily passes through the world of action." His U.N. peacekeeping operations certainly exemplified this belief; he was awarded the Nobel Peace Prize posthumously in 1961. A man of ethics and action until the end, Hammarskjöld died in an airplane crash en route to a peacekeeping mission in the Congo.

Sarah G. Scorgie

Handel, George Frideric (1685 – 1759)

Music composer. Handel composed music in several idioms, from instrumental to vocal. His musical work began in Germany where he was born. He later relocated to Italy and became known for his well-formed Italian operas. However, the most productive and best-known part of his work took place in England, where he spent most of his adult life.

Though a Lutheran, Handel did not show any particular fervency in his religious views.

There is, however, some evidence that he had an enlarged spiritual awareness later in life, particularly related to his composition of *Messiah*. Handel composed not only for his own church, but also for Anglican, Calvinistic, and Catholic churches. His move into writing oratorios seems to have been driven by artistic changes, economics, and the waning appeal of his operas. Since the oratorio form was quite akin to opera, but without the complications of staging, it was more accessible to a larger and less professional populous — both for performers and audiences.

Handel is credited with the development of the oratorio form. While he is most remembered for his sacred oratorios, and especially his *Messiah*, not all of his oratorio works were in the sacred category.

Still, in addition to *Messiah*, he also composed oratorios from other biblical accounts — *Esther, Saul, Israel in Egypt, Judas Maccabeus, Samson,* and *Jephtha*. In all, he composed twenty-nine oratorios.

Originally *Messiah* had been commissioned by the Lord Lieutenant of Dublin to be a sacred oratorio that would crown a series of other performances in 1742. Charles Jennens wrote the libretto, taking it from the Old and New Testaments of the King James Bible. The first London performance was in 1750 as a benefit for the Foundling Hospital, of which Handel was a director. The work had immediate success and has become a standard piece of choral literature in both sacred and secular contexts.

See also Choral Music.

For Further Reading: P. H. Lang, *George Frideric Handel* (1996).

Edwin M. Willmington

Happiness

Although in contemporary usage *happiness* denotes a feeling of satisfaction or pleasure, it is classically understood as a sustained sense of well-being and flourishing. Aristotle identified happiness (*eudaimonia*) as the highest human good, "doing and living well," something sought for its own sake and nothing else. Pascal wrote: "All men seek happiness. This is without exception. Whatever different means they employ, they all tend to this end." For Christians, God is the ultimate source of happiness. In his *Institutes*, Calvin clarified, "If God contains the fullness of all good things in himself like an inexhaustible fountain, nothing beyond him is to be sought by those who strive after the highest good and all the elements of happiness." Similarly, Teresa of Avila, in her *Exclamations*, noted that "God is happy, since He knows and loves and rejoices in Himself without the possibility of doing otherwise. . . . Thou wilt not enter into thy rest, my soul, until thou becomest inwardly one with this Highest Good."

Shalom may be the OT term most closely aligned with this classical meaning, signifying well-being, wholeness, fulfillment, prosperity, and absence of strife; and translated in the Septuagint as *sōzō* ("save"), *eirēnē* ("peace") and *teleios* ("complete"). The *Theological Wordbook of the Old Testament* suggests that shalom "was influential in broadening the Greek idea of *eirēnē* to include the Semitic ideas of growth and prosperity." Blessed are those receiving God's shalom (Num. 6:24–27; cf. Luke 2:14). Messiah is called the "Prince of Shalom" (Isa. 9:6; cf. Eph. 2:14: Jesus "is our peace").

In the NT, *makarios* ("blessed") may be translated as "happy" (e.g., Rom. 14:22 NASB), as can be *chara* or *chairō* ("joy, rejoice," e.g., Matt. 18:13; 25:21; 2 Cor. 7:9). Jesus Christ offers his people abundant eternal life (John 10:10) through the Holy Spirit (John 7:38–39), whose fruit is joy (Gal. 5:23; cf. Luke 10:21). Paul wrote, "The kingdom of God is … peace and joy in the Holy Spirit" (Rom. 14:17). Complete, everlasting happiness will be the believers' eschatological experience when God dwells among his people (Rev. 21:3), and they "will see his face" (Rev. 22:4), the beatific vision of God, which is not yet possible (1 Tim. 6:16, cf. Ex. 33:20). Pascal encapsulates the matter in his *Pensées*: "Happiness is neither without us or within us. It is in God, both without us and within us."

See also Anxiety; Depression; Joy.

For Further Reading: J. Houston, *In Pursuit of Happiness* (1996); D. Naugle, *Reordered Love* (2008); T. Oden, *The Living God* (1987); L. Rouner, ed., *In Pursuit of Happiness* (1995).

Klaus Issler

Harris, William Wade (c. 1860–1929)

African prophet and evangelist. Popularly known as Prophet Harris, he was an itinerant charismatic prophet in the tradition of African Indigenous (or Independent) Churches (AICs). Born in Liberia of the Grebo ethnic group, he exerted enormous spiritual influence on both his contemporaries and those who have come to know about him. He considered himself called by God to reconcile the peoples of Africa in the presence of Western colonization and exploitation.

Prophet Harris's spirituality should be understood in the contexts of his own religious experience, the indigenous religious traditions and realities of Africa, and his vision for the spiritual renewal of Africa. After a revelatory experience while in prison in 1912, he declared himself a prophet with a message of renewal for Africans. With boldness, he condemned fetish practices and idol worship and beckoned African peoples to burn their idols and to turn to God for solutions to their existential needs. He saw himself as God's messenger whose message had the capacity to address the sociopolitical, economic, and spiritual needs of Africans. African indigenous understandings of the interrelatedness of the spiritual and human worlds were central to his message. He required his followers to worship the true God in Jesus Christ, for there was no aspect of their daily lives and experiences that God could not touch. This is what is distinctive about his message vis-à-vis the message of the mission churches in Ivory Coast, Liberia, and other African countries he visited. For example, when Harris suffered a paralytic stroke in 1925, the missionaries of the Methodist Episcopal Mission saw it as "God's judgment for his living in polygamy, preaching polygamy, and baptizing polygamists." They presented the Christian gospel message in ways that lacked constructive engagement with African indigenous religious spirituality. But Harris's message for Africans was contextual: he sought to express the Christian message from within the experiences of his African contemporaries.

See also African Christian Spirituality; Revival.

For Further Reading: G. Haliburton, *The Prophet Harris* (1971); J. Pritchard, "The Prophet Harris and Ivory Coast," *Journal of Religion in Africa* 5 (1973); D. Shank, *Prophet Harris* (1994).

Victor I. Ezigbo

Havergal, Frances Ridley (1836 – 1879)

Hymn writer, devotional writer, and poet. Born in Astley, England, and influenced by her father, William Havergal, an Anglican clergyman, hymnist, and composer, Frances herself wrote hymns, the most famous of which is "Take My Life and Let It Be." Her best-known work, *Kept for the Master's Use* (1879), is basically a commentary on that song. In her childhood, Frances was gripped by conscious spiritual struggles, poor physical health, and the pain of losing her mother to early death. She experienced deep loss again when her older sister, her personal tutor, left and married. In her unasked-for extended times of aloneness, Frances developed her great intellectual abilities and also her capacity for seeking God. She wrote books, tracts, essays, leaflets, and small gift cards, and also works for children — all with the assumption, as she put it, that "a great deal of living must go into very little writing." Of her seventy hymns, "I Gave My Life for Thee" and "Like a River Glorious" are especially loved. Collections of her poems can be found in *The Ministry of Song, Under the Surface,* and *Under the Shadow.* Having declined the opportunity to marry, she devoted herself to learning languages (Latin, Greek, Hebrew, German, French) and music. She steeped herself in Scripture, memorizing whole books of the Bible, such as Isaiah and Psalms. As her frail health permitted, she was also active in Christian service.

See also Hymns.

Sarah Sumner

Health and Healing

For Christians, health can be understood as the state of being in which all the domains of one's life — mind, body, spirit, relationships, emotions, finances, connection to the created world — are congruent with God's intended purposes. It is helpful to conceptualize this state of being as *degree of* congruence rather than as a dichotomous, either-or condition of health or lack thereof. At any given time, an individual may experience a greater degree of health in one area of life than in another. Impediments to optimum health include consequences of one's own choices and behavior, the impact of decisions and behaviors of others, and the general brokenness of the fallen world that results in illness, accident, and catastrophe.

As health is multidimensional, so is healing. All healing comes from God, no matter what the avenue. Prayer, proper nutrition, exercise, counseling, devotional reading, medication, Bible study, preaching, surgical intervention, journaling, meditation, sufficient sleep, trustworthy relational experiences — all of these can be *means* of healing, but the *source* of healing is God, who says, "I am the LORD, who heals you" (Ex. 15:26).

Complete healing of all ills will not come in earthly time. Yet creaturely finitude is a human reality and, in its own way, a blessing. For example, limited healing and difficulties during the healing process, according to Scripture, serve to sensitize us to the pain of others (2 Cor. 1:3 – 6). They may also serve to further God's work in developing spiritual maturity. As even Ernest Hemingway wrote, in *A Farewell to Arms,* "The world breaks everyone, and afterward many are strong at the broken places."

Although some Christians believe Scripture provides guarantees of physical healing — in James 5, for example — it is interesting to note that the adjacent passage also exhorts believers to patience in suffering. Suffering is an integral part of formation and remains part of individual and communal narratives even after the painful events have passed. It appears that healing and suffering are paradoxical companions, not mutually exclusive experiences.

The common question, "Why are some healed in ways they desire and some are not?" is not answerable by humans, even though we might be able to make some linkages to choices and consequences or to unexpected gifts and blessings that have come as a result of our ills (see, e.g., Paul's experience of a "thorn in the flesh" [2 Cor. 12:7–10] and Job's authentic encounter of God [Job 42:1–6]). Attempts to explain definitively the presence or absence of healing perhaps represent natural human desires to make meaning of life.

Although health and healing are sometimes seen as individual constructs, it is important to acknowledge two communal aspects. First, communities also demonstrate varying degrees of congruence with God's intended purposes. God spoke through kings and prophets against oppressive social structures, institutional injustice, and communal immorality and conveyed God's promise that humility and repentance would bring healing (see, e.g., 2 Chron. 7:14; Isa. 58). Second, Jesus included the community in some of his miracles of healing. "Jesus told them to give her something to eat" (Luke 8:55); "Take off the grave clothes and let him go" (John 11:44) — these invitations recognize the importance of supportive community in the healing process.

See also Aging; Death and Dying; Disability; Inner Healing.

For Further Reading: F. MacNutt, *Healing* (1999); S. Seamands, *Wounds That Heal* (2003); J. Shuman and B. Volck, *Reclaiming the Body* (2006).

Carla M. Dahl

Heart

Of all the psychological terms used for the person in the Bible, perhaps the "heart" (Heb. *leb*, Gr. *kardia*) is most central for understanding the person. The heart is used for the core of human personality and is the nexus of human will, affect, and intellect (Prov. 23:7–8; 27:19). The heart is what drives a person and dictates the direction of one's life (Prov. 4:23; Eccl. 10:2). With the heart, humans think, feel, doubt, believe, remember, and act. The heart is revealed in what one desires and acts on. It also becomes evident in actions taken against one's better judgment or contrary to what one really wants to do. Jesus said that where one's treasure is, that is where one's heart will be. The heart indicates what one really loves. The goal is to love God with the whole heart (Mark 12:30), to trust in God with all the heart (Prov. 3:5), and to love from a pure heart (1 Tim. 1:5). The believer is to have a clean heart (Ps. 51:6, 10) and a heart of integrity, speaking truth from the heart (Ps. 15:1–2). However, fallen human nature distorts the functions of the heart.

What makes the heart so complex is that there is a hidden dimension to it that we may not be aware of, layers to it that lie below the surface. The fallen human heart can become hidden to itself, able to deceive itself so that it is no longer fathomable or transparent to itself. It can become proud (Prov. 16:5) and fat or unresponsive to the Word (Ps. 119:70). As such, the heart can harden itself to God (Zech. 7:12) and become incurably deceived and deceiving (Jer. 17:9–10). This can include both the simple self-deception of repressing painful experiences into the hidden heart ("Even in laughter the heart may be in pain, and the end of joy may be grief" [Prov. 14:13 NASB]), as well as more malevolent forms of self-deception resulting from deeper motives of sin and hiding from guilt and shame. In these cases, various levels in the heart result from repressing parts of unwanted experiences into the recesses of the heart.

Most serious is the conscious intention in persons since the fall to not want to experience the truth of one's sinfulness and guilt before God. Though God designed the heart to have integrity and to be transparent in truth, he also allowed since the fall a strange capacity for the heart to deceive itself, to become opaque to the truth of its own state and other realities that might be painful or excessively revealing. The extent of self-deception can be so extreme, according to Jeremiah, that sometimes the heart cannot even be known by the self, but only by God (Jer. 17:10). Even the believer does not always know what is going on in the deep, but can trust that the Lord sees into the motives better than oneself (Prov. 16:2). Similarly, the psalmist prayed, "Examine me, O LORD, and try me; test my mind and my heart" (Ps. 26:2 NASB). He asked God to search and try the heart, to see if there was any "offensive way" in him (Ps. 139:23 – 24). This resulting "hidden heart" becomes the repository of a host of painful, false, and sinful beliefs and desires that become part of the memory and character of a person, of which one may be more or less aware.

Though the preconverted conscious sins of the heart may no longer be reflected in the believer's conscious beliefs and desires, they may remain implicit in the dynamics of the habituated vices of the heart. Thus, a person may have two sets of warring beliefs and desires—one set related to truth and goodness, the other to falseness or sin. The deep "fleshy" beliefs and desires, if strongly habituated, can continue to drive the person against his or her will and conscious good desires and beliefs. No quick rational correction of these beliefs will suffice to change them.

Though some change of the unbeliever's heart is possible through loving relationships, cognitive retraining, and behavior change, only the process of conversion and the love of the Spirit can ultimately provide an experience strong enough to penetrate into the heart and resolve the self's deep attachment to sin and negative beliefs and desires. This is the promise of the new covenant (Jer. 31:31 – 34; Ezek. 36:26). Being loved in truth by fellow believers (Eph. 4:15) and having the heart retrained by spiritual disciplines (meditation on the Word, prayer, obedience) are legitimate means of grace that help unearth or "put off" these deep beliefs and desires and reinforce the putting on of healthy virtues in Christ by opening the heart to the ministry of the Spirit of truth, who alone is the true agent of change in the heart of the believer (Gal. 5:16 – 23; 1 Thess. 5:23; 1 Peter 1:2). The Lord will also use trials and spiritual dark nights to unearth the heart. Ultimately, God alone at the judgment will "bring to light the things hidden in the darkness and disclose the motive of men's hearts" (1 Cor. 4:5 NASB).

See also Affections; Holiness; Methodist Spirituality; Pietism; Will, Human.

For Further Reading: J. Coe and T. Hall, *Psychology in the Spirit* (2010); E. Johnson, *Foundations for Soul Care* (2007); H. Nouwen, *The Way of the Heart,* (1981); R. Saucy, *Transforming Your Heart and Life* (2010); D. Willard, *Renovation of the Heart* (2002); H. Wolff, *Anthropology of the Old Testament* (1981).

John H. Coe

Heaven

The term is used in the Bible in two overlapping senses: the dwelling place of God and the destination of his people. Traditionally Jews distinguished three heavens. The first was the sky; the second was the sphere of the sun, moon, and stars; and the third, the so-called "third heaven" (2 Cor. 12:2 – 4), in which God and his angels are present. Although God is present everywhere, he is present in a special way in heaven. Thus, Christians are taught to pray to "our Father in heaven" (Matt. 6:9). Likewise, Jesus "came down from heaven" to conduct his earthly ministry (John 6:51), and after his resurrection ascended back "into heaven" (Acts 1:11). At times heaven is so closely identified with God that the term becomes synonymous with God himself (Luke 15:21).

The Bible reflects a progressive understanding of the afterlife. Initially the OT pictured it as an underworld location or abyss called Sheol (Hebrew) or Hades (Greek), which was far removed from God's presence. By NT times the current abode of deceased believers was identified as God's presence; they were thus "in heaven." At death believers depart to be with Christ (Phil. 1:23) while they await his return to earth (1 Thess. 4:14 – 17). New Testament believers are properly challenged to store up treasures in heaven (Matt. 6:20) because their citizenship is there (Phil. 3:20).

Yet the ultimate hope of believers involves another step in this progression: the end-time creation of a new heaven and a new earth. Although heaven is often used in Scripture to refer to the present abode of God and the present dwelling place of deceased believers (2 Cor. 5:1–4), the promise of bodily resurrection points ahead to more than floating about in ethereal outer space. Resurrected believers will inhabit a new earth for all eternity (Rev. 21–22). At the end of time, the dwelling place of God and the destiny of believers will be combined in a re-created world where "God himself will be with them" (Rev. 21:3). Rather than fostering earthly indolence, the prospect of heaven properly encourages believers to serve faithfully and to persevere. At the same time, it ensures that the horizon of Christian consciousness extends beyond this life and this world.

See also Afterlife; Hell.

For Further Reading: R. Alcorn, *Heaven* (2004); K. Boa and R. Bowman Jr., *Sense and Nonsense about Heaven and Hell* (2007); B. Milne, *Message of Heaven and Hell* (2003); S. Oliphint and S. Ferguson, *If I Should Die before I Wake* (2005); J. Russell, *A History of Heaven* (1997).

Brian C. Labosier

Heiler, Friedrich (1892–1967)

German theologian of ecumenism and religion. Born and raised a Roman Catholic, he entered an evangelical fellowship after receiving Lutheran communion and thereafter called himself an evangelical Catholic. Critical of the dialectical school of theology, he believed that God had revealed himself in many ways, including nature, human conscience, and other world faiths.

Heiler theorized a series of concentric circles to aid authentic dialogue among religions and cultures. The outer rim represented the diverse visible features of religions; moving inward, the next ring marked the conceptual discourse of theological and philosophical formation; the next one toward the center stood for religious experience; and finally, the dynamic center itself was the intuitively apprehended and ultimate divine reality. Though he conceptualized the mystic unities of divine reality and sacrificial love as the same in all religions, he believed Christianity was superior because Christ has made the way possible for humanity to have direct access to God.

Heiler's own personal worship remained Christian, and Heiler was a champion of the high church movement in Germany. Viewing the church as a mystical body in union with Christ, this movement sought a stronger emphasis on the sacraments (especially the Eucharist), a moderate recession of the sermon, and a richer liturgical form of worship. Thus, for many years Heiler led a small church fellowship at Marburg, where he taught, dedicated to these ends.

Kiem-Kiok Kwa

Hell

The biblical view of hell is based on a composite of terms and concepts, which together convey the idea of an ultimate place of punishment and abandonment by God. These terms include the Abyss, an underworld place of torment that includes the realm of the dead and their place of punishment (Luke 8:31; Rom. 10:7; Rev. 9:1–2, 11; 11:7; 17:8; 20:1, 3); Hades, the temporary place of abode for the dead (Matt. 11:23; 16:18; Luke 10:15; 16:23; Acts 2:27, 31; Rev. 1:18; 6:8; 20:13–14); Gehenna, a fiery place of eternal punishment for those who reject God (Matt. 5:22, 29–30; 10:28; 18:9); and the Lake of Fire, the final place of punishment, torment, and eternal death for the triumvirate of evil (the great red dragon, the Beast, and the False Prophet), as well as those whose names are not found written in the Lamb's Book of Life (Rev. 19:20; 20:10, 14, 15; 21:8). This is the second death from which believers are exempt (Rev. 20:14–15). Many speculative notions of hell have been seared into Western consciousness through the enduring influence of the medieval poet Dante's depictions of hell in the *Inferno* portion in his epic poem, *The Divine Comedy.*

The church in the modern era has been under a great deal of pressure to espouse a kinder and gentler damnation. Nonetheless, the reality behind the sobering biblical images of hell impacts the believer's spirituality in at least three ways. First, it acts as a warning of the eternal death that awaits those who do not maintain a proper relationship with God. Second, it helps to spur missional, evangelistic activity motivated by compassion for the eternal welfare of others. Third, it assures believers that the injustices often witnessed and experienced in this life will not go unpunished, because God is a just judge who will punish unrepentant evildoers.

See also Afterlife; Heaven.

For Further Reading: W. Crockett, ed., *Four Views on Hell* (1992); D. Powys, *"Hell": A Hard Look at a Hard Question* (1997).

John Christopher Thomas

Herbert, George

See **Caroline Poets.**

Hermits and Anchorites

These are contemplatives, whether men or women, living alone. The word *anchorite* derives from a composite Greek word *ana-choros*, which means "without place" or solitary. Antony has often been singled out as the originator of this form of monasticism, but when he decided to take up this vocation, he sought out another hermit for guidance. The fact is, early Christian hermits could invoke biblical precedents; for instance, the prophet Elijah hiding from Ahab in the Wadi Cherith and later moving to Zarephath (1 King 17), and Jesus' forty-day retreat as he clarified his calling after his baptism (Luke 4:1–13).

Evidence suggests that hermits began to appear during a long era of peace that extended from the reign of Emperor Gallienus (260–268) to the last great persecution under Diocletian (304–311). Antony took up his call to the desert around 271. As Christian discipline deteriorated further when Constantine tilted imperial power toward the church, a trickle turned into a steady stream. Hermits, both men and women, could and did turn up in almost any remote area, but Egypt, Sinai, and Syria attracted the largest numbers. In Egypt Antony drew many imitators and had constantly to relocate to conserve his solitude. In Sinai the hope of seeing God as Moses had seen God lured large numbers. In Syria a more rigorous type of hermitism developed possibly at about the same time as it grew in Egypt and Sinai. It distinguished itself by its severity, primitivism, mortification, and individualism.

A number of different types of hermits or anchorites developed in the early centuries, partly under dualist influence. *Dendrites* (Gr. *dendron* equals "tree") lived in trees. *Catenati* (Lat. *catena* equals "chain") loaded themselves down with huge chains to demonstrate triumph of spirit over body. *Stylites* lived on pillars so as to separate themselves as much as they could from the earth. Syria's most famous monk, Simeon Stylites (c. 390–459), lived atop his pillar laden with chains for more than thirty years. Benedict of Nursia favored the communal type of monasticism developed in Egypt by Pachomius because it guarded against extremes and was less rigorous. He spoke disparagingly of two other types. *Sarabaites*, he accused, "live up to the practice of the world" without any rule to guide them; *Gyrovagi* spent their time wandering from place to place. Hermitism did not come to an end in the early period of Christian history, however. In both East and West, cenobite monastic orders permitted selected monks who felt called to the solitary life to live as hermits. Essentially hermitic orders such as the Carthusians also appeared during the Middle Ages. In the 14th century, Richard

Rolle chose to abandon the life of a scholar and live as a hermit and served as a spiritual guide for nuns at Hampole in England. By this time, religious authorities took care to distinguish anchorites from hermits. Anchorites were confined to cells, while hermits could move about freely. To become an anchorite, one had to go through a rigorous examination and live sealed into a "cell," usually attached to the back of a church, under a rule. Noted anchoresses included Julian of Norwich.

See also Monasticism.

For Further Reading: D. Chitty, *The Desert a City* (1966); T. Merton, "The Case for Eremitism," in *Contemplation in a World of Action* (1971); *Anchorite Spirituality: Ancrene Wisse and Associated Works*, CWS (1991).

E. Glenn Hinson

Hesychasm

Hesychasm is the Eastern Orthodox Church's spiritual practice of *stillness*. The Greek term *hesychia* literally means "silence, quiet, or tranquillity," though it also came, in the early Christian church, to refer to a solitary monk. The church historian Sozomen spoke of "the monks in the desert" who loved "tranquility," and in his *Foundations of the Monastic Life*, Evagrius of Pontus referred to the solitary monastic life as "the way of stillness." The so-called "hesychastic method of prayer," primarily based on the invocation of the name of Jesus (e.g., the Jesus Prayer), is aimed toward the goal of deification, including the pray-er's ontological transformation through his or her experience with the energies of God. This form of hesychastic prayer is constructed on the continuous utterance of "Lord Jesus Christ, Son of God, have mercy on me a sinner" and came to full fruition in the late Byzantine period, especially in the writings of Nicephorus the Hesychast, Pseudo-Symeon the New Theologian, Gregory of Sinai and Gregory Palamas, and in nineteenth-century Russia, particularly evidenced by the publication of *The Pilgrim's Tale*, also known as *The Way of a Pilgrim*.

As with Byzantine monasticism in general, hesychastic theology was founded on a renunciation of one's family and worldly goods, complete surrender to the will of God, and a life of absolute single-minded devotion toward God. Evagrius admonished monks in his *Foundations of the Monastic Life* to remain "seated in your cell, gather together your mind, give heed to the day of your death, and then look at the dying of your body. Consider the situation, accept the suffering, condemn the vanity that is in this world, and show no weakness in virtue and zeal so that you can abide always in the same purpose of practicing stillness." Likewise, Gregory of Nyssa, in his *Life of Moses*, said that the result of Moses' forty-year exile in the wilderness was his achieving a state of *hesychia*. Since at least the 4th century, then, *hesychia* has been a technical theological term designating the silence and/or tranquillity of heart a monk achieves, having gained victory over the passions and moving toward a full contemplation of the Trinity. The foundation of hesychastic practice is the *via negativa*, a realization that human conceptions of God fail to adequately describe the true essence of God. Therefore, a hesychast enters into silence, foregoing the words that ultimately fail to express God fully. Though a theology of hesychasm is found in early Christian spirituality, its fullest flowering was reached only in the 14th century and later.

For Gregory Palamas—fourteenth-century monk, archbishop of Thessaloniki and one of the outstanding promoters of hesychasm—*hesychia* was the climax of all Christian practice and prayer, so much so that he prescribed a particular posture and breathing technique during prayer to facilitate the recitation of the Jesus Prayer and the attainment of stillness. This led Palamas's detractor, Barlaam the Calabrian, to label Palamas and his followers *omphalopsychoi* ("navel-gazers"). For Palamas, however, a particular posture and breathing rhythm facilitated one's liberation from the passions and one's will so that he or she could achieve a state of pure hesychastic prayer. Palamas had learned such hesychastic discipline from his own spiritual father, Gregory of Sinai (d. 1346). In his *On Commandments and Doctrines*, Gregory of Sinai described a typical day and night for the hesychast. During the day, a hesychast is to devote himself to the remembrance of God by alternating between prayer, reading, and the chanting of psalms. An hour is spent in each activity, and this pattern is repeated four times during the day, accounting for twelve hours of the hesychast's waking hours. During the night, the Sinaite monk said, a beginning hesychast was to sleep half the night, keeping vigil the other half. A hesychast midway on the path to perfection should keep vigil for one or two hours, sleep for four hours, and then rise to chant psalms and pray for four hours before sunrise. Finally, a "perfect" hesychast is to stand and keep vigil without interruption throughout the entire night. Due to the favorable decisions of three Constantinopolitan synods (in 1341, 1347, and 1351), Palamite, hesychastic theology became the "official" spiritual theology during the remaining years of the Byzantine Empire and beyond.

With the destruction of the Byzantine Empire in 1453, the spiritual heart of Eastern Orthodox Christianity shifted to Russia, though Mount Athos in Greece always remained the titular center of Eastern Orthodox spirituality. The theology of hesychasm moved there too, propounded most fully in *The Pilgrim's Tale*. In this spiritual story, a "homeless pilgrim," after hearing the apostle Paul's admonition to the Thessalonians to "pray without ceasing," begins to wander from "place to place for a long time." His goal: to find out how one can pray without ceasing. He encounters monks, priests, and educated laymen who have all discovered that such a task is possible only when one engages in a continual, hesychastic recitation of the Jesus Prayer. Near the end of the text, the pilgrim concludes, "Contemplative hesychasts are like pillars supporting the piety of the church with their mystic and unceasing prayers." For the pilgrim, and in the hesychastic tradition generally, to pray is to practice *hesychia*.

See also Jesus Prayer; Russian Spirituality; Silence.

For Further Reading: J. Meyendorff, *A Study of Gregory Palamas* (1998); A. Smith, trans., *The Pilgrim's Tale* (1999); M. Toti, "The Hesychast Method of Prayer," *International Journal for the Study of the Christian Church* 8, no. 1 (2008): 17 – 32.

Greg Peters

Hilary of Poitiers (312 – c. 368)

Bishop of Poitiers and chief Western defender of the Nicene Creed. Around 350 he was elevated to the episcopacy, a position that exposed him to the complex of issues surrounding the later "Arian" debates in the West. He participated in a council of like-minded bishops in Roman Gaul that disfellowshiped an archbishop accused of denying the full deity of the Son. Shortly thereafter, however, Hilary was himself banished to the Greek East — yet without being deposed as bishop. Over the next several years, the exiled Latin bishop rubbed shoulders with Greek peers involved in continuing debates over the divine nature of Christ. This exposed him to Greek arguments on the deity of Christ, the writings of Origen of Alexandria, and even Greek hymnody — all of which shaped his ministry from then on. Upon the death of the emperor who banished him, Hilary was able to return home as a champion of the full deity of Jesus Christ.

Hilary is best known for his writings on Holy Scripture; arguably, what today we call the Bible constituted the core of his spirituality. Of these the best known is his *On the Trinity*, an apologetic tome of scriptural exegesis focused on the relationships between the persons of the Trinity. On the surface, the book is polemical against various Trinitarian heresies of his day. In it, however, Hilary not only defended orthodox Christology, but also was at pains to articulate a theology of Scripture and scriptural exegesis, one that was radically non-, even antirationalist. Informing this was his conviction that God's nature is uncreated, eternal, and infinite, and one in which believers are called to participate (2 Peter 1:4). Therefore, the reader must approach the words of Scripture as the very revelation of God, with a humility that allows the Scriptures to speak paradoxes to the mind that challenge and reshape the soul, conforming the life of the mortal human mind to the greater life and reason of the immortal and eternal God. The test of any authentically Christian reading of Scripture, then, is whether it allows the latent power of Scripture to work this transformation.

Besides his apologetic ministry and scriptural exegesis, Hilary is secondarily known for furthering the exposure of the Latin West to the hymnody of the Greek East, and for his own creative hymn writing, some vestiges of which survive to this day.

For Further Reading: M. Barnes and D. Williams, eds., *Arianism after Arius* (1993); C. Beckwith, *Hilary of Poitiers on the Trinity* (2008); T. Torrance, "Transition to the West: The Interpretation of Biblical and Theological Statements according to Hilary of Poitiers," in *Divine Meaning* (1995).

Matthew Bell

Hildegard of Bingen (1098–1179)

German Benedictine abbess, visionary mystic, poet, composer, and more. She has been recognized in recent years as one of the most remarkable women in Christian history. Her writings on theology, medicine, and natural science drew extraordinary respect at a time when few women had a public voice. She was accorded greater authority than perhaps any woman up to that time. She advised kings and emperors, bishops and popes, yet she described herself as merely "a feather on the breath of God."

Hildegard was born into a noble family and placed in a convent at age eight to be trained under an anchorite named Jutta. When Jutta died, Hildegard became the abbess of Disibodenberg monastery. Later she founded a monastery of her own at Rupertsberg, near Bingen, plus several daughter houses.

In her poetry she described the visions she experienced from childhood. In 1141 she had a vision that changed the course of her life when God commanded her to write down everything she would observe in her visions. And so she wrote: "When I was forty-two years and seven months old, the heavens were opened and a blinding light of exceptional brilliance flowed through my entire brain. And so it kindled my whole heart and breast like a flame, not burning but warming ... and suddenly I understood the meaning of expositions of the books."

Though she herself never doubted their divine origins, she needed her visions to be sanctioned by the church. She wrote to Bernard of Clairvaux, the most powerful man of her time, seeking his affirmation. With his influence, she was brought to the attention of Pope Eugenius (1145–1153), who gave papal imprimatur on her first visionary work *Scivias*, and her fame began to spread through Germany and beyond. As a visionary mystic, she served a prophetic role rather than as a teacher of contemplation. Her apocalyptic visions and her preaching were closely connected with her program for reform of the church. In 1158 she began the first of her four preaching tours. She received approval for this "apostolic ministry" from the pope.

She wrote prolifically on a broad range of topics: biblical commentary, moral and spiritual teaching, dogmatic instruction, theology, natural science, and herbal medicine. Her three major theological works are *Scivias (Know the Ways of the Lord)*, *The Book of the Life of Merits*, and *The Book of Divine Works*. Light is a key image in her writings—the divine light in the human heart, and the light of God that shines through all creation. She saw the world as marvelously structured and dazzling in its beauty. A joyful exuberance pervaded her spirituality.

Music was another one of Hildegard's great gifts. She composed seventy-seven songs, among the finest and most distinctive music written in the Middle Ages. Hildegard is also known for the illuminations that illustrate her writings. They were probably created by nuns under her direction, with the designs and images based on her visions. Like her music, they show startling originality and uniqueness for their time. With the breadth of her talents, Hildegard was able to express her visions in word, symbol, color, and tone. In recent years she has become a figure of great interest to feminist scholars and is highly regarded by the contemporary New Age movement.

See also Feminist Spirituality; Women.

For Further Reading: S. Flanagan, *Hildegard of Bingen* (1989); M. Fox, *Illuminations of Hildegard of Bingen* (1985); *Hildegard of Bingen: Selected Writings,* trans. M. Atherton (2001); B. Newman, *Sister of Wisdom* (1987).

Carole Dale Spencer

Hilton, Walter (1340–1396)

Late medieval English Augustinian canon. He was educated in the arts and civil law at Cambridge and later in canon law. It is likely that Hilton lived for some time as a solitary religious but appears to have joined the Augustinian canons around 1386. Since the priory was authorized to arrest, examine, and imprison heretics, it is assumed that upon entering the priory Hilton entered into the religious controversies of his day. He may be the author of a work entitled *Conclusions Concerning Images*, which was a response to Lollards who called for the destruction of religious images.

Hilton is the author of spiritual works in both English and Latin: *The Scale of Perfection, Mixed Life*, and *On the Image of Sin*. Book 1 of *The Scale* is a defense of the contemplative life, which, Hilton believed, is the special domain of those vowed to the religious life. Book 2 of *The Scale*, written sometime later, expands book 1, frequently takes up points made in book 1, and expands upon them in greater detail. Book 2 affirms that contemplation is something to which all Christians should aspire. *Mixed Life* is addressed to a layman with a family, upon whom Hilton impresses that those not living a vowed religious life should not try to copy the habits and patterns of the religious life but should instead engage in contemplative activity appropriate to one's state and commitments. *On the Image of Sin* expresses Hilton's dissatisfaction with his life as a solitary. He felt that he was of little practical service to God and the church. This work assists in understanding why Hilton became an Augustinian canon. In addition to these texts, Hilton may be the translator of *The Prickynge of Love*, an English translation of *Stimulus Amoris* by the thirteenth-century Franciscan James of Milan.

For Hilton, there are three parts of the contemplative life: knowledge of God by reason; affection, without understanding of spiritual things; and knowing and loving God perfectly. Full contemplation is a special gift of God and is not common. One passes through four stages of the spiritual life: (1) calling from worldly vanity; (2) correcting; (3) magnifying, when the soul is partly reformed and is given the gift of perfection and the grace of contemplation; and (4) glorifying, when the soul is fully reformed in the bliss of heaven. Though all Christians are encouraged to engage the contemplative life, Hilton held the vowed religious life in highest esteem.

See also English Mystics.

For Further Reading: J. Clark and R. Dorward, "Introduction," in *Walter Hilton: The Scale of Perfection* (1991); J. Milosh, *The Scale of Perfection and the English Mystical Tradition* (1966).

Greg Peters

Hindu Spirituality

It has become almost axiomatic in the scholarly religious studies literature on Hinduism that there is no single Hinduism in India (and by extension throughout the world), but many "Hinduisms." That means that many approaches to spirituality exist in Hinduism, corresponding at least in part to the variant strains of Hinduism itself.

To be sure, some commonalities run throughout them all. Since the goal of all "Hinduisms" is the eventual rejoining of the self with the all-encompassing Braham (*braham-atman*) after many, many rebirths (*samsara*) according to the laws of reward and demerit (*karma*), spiritual practice serves to move one closer and closer to the goal of release (*moksha*) by prescribing practices that increase the likelihood of positive rebirths. However, this goal can be reached by several different paths (*maggas*), theoretically each as good as the others. Here we consider three of the many different types of Hinduism—classical, caste, and the modern Hindutva—and their preferred modes of spirituality.

Classic Hinduism is the type of Hinduism that emerged, in what is now India, during the first five centuries AD, a time of political and economic unification of what had previously been simply a loosely affiliated assortment of kingdoms ruled by maharajas. Political unification is often followed by ideological uniformity, sometimes an unconscious result of groupthink, sometimes a very conscious use of ideology for political purposes. Most of what is termed Hinduism in modern religious studies textbooks (see previous paragraph) coalesced about this time.

This understanding of the religious life privileges the "religious" person who devotes energies to an ascetic lifestyle occupied with meditative practice, physical austerities, temple rituals and rites, and efficacious pleadings with the gods for various divine favors. The religious virtuoso in such a system came to be known as the *sannyasin* or holy man. One's life was spent first with study, then family, then retirement, and finally ascetic homelessness, the four stages of an ideal life. Entire systems of practical wisdom and philosophy, such as the yogic system, emerged to instruct devotees in the proper and efficacious ways of living one's life so as to honor the gods.

Parallel to this life, and coexistent with it, was caste Hinduism with its own set of expectations on what a spiritually in-tune Hindu's life should look like. Caste Hinduism charges its devotees to live formatted lives prescribed by their birth status. Each caste and subcaste had its own rule of life to follow (*dharmashastras*) that told them how to marry, what to work at, whom to associate with, and how to worship. Spirituality, then, is following the well-articulated duties one assumes as a member of a particular caste group. The result of this type of spirituality provides transcendent rewards (a better rebirth) for living according to one's duty (*dharma*).

This understanding of duty as spirituality can seem confusing to Westerners and Christians used to understanding spirituality in once for all, transcendently mandated morality. Caste, for example, can mandate a willingness to fight in wars (if one is in one of the Ksatriya caste groupings). An implicit mandate to be willing to use force as a requirement of one's spirituality seems strange to religions that advocate a more absolute understanding of peacemaking, for example. Put another way, each caste grouping has its own set of "ten commandments," lists that may seem to conflict with other groups' listings of moral guidelines.

Or consider a third group of Hindus that has become extremely important to understand in modern, postindependence India. These are Hindus most influenced by an understanding of Hindutva or "Hindu-ness." Hindutva is a largely political movement in India that uses religious teachings as a way of confirming Hindu nationalism. It embraces teaching related to the uniqueness of the modern nation state called India, and at times to geographical India, ethnic Indians, and the common languages of India, particularly the importance of Sanskrit. In this case, Hindu spirituality refers to a very public commitment to an ideology of nationalism.

How Hindutva plays out in relation to spirituality varies somewhat, but it certainly all relates to a rejection of foreign religions such as Christianity and Islam. It embraces certain sectarian religions that have their roots in Indian soil—Jainism, Buddhism, Sikhism—by bringing them all under the Hindutva umbrella. But it rejects conversion away from Hinduism as not just being a religious choice but a kind of treasonous act against Indian-ness. This understanding of spirituality comes very close to what many would call faithful citizenship; the values of national loyalty, patriotism, and ethnocentrism become extremely important spiritual values.

In all this complexity, one longs for some kind of central and universal understanding of Hindu spirituality, but this may be wishful thinking. However, reading a very popular Hindu text called the *Bhagavad Gita* gives one a flavor of what Hindu spirituality is all about. The *Bhagavad Gita* is actually a short text taken from a larger Hindu epic called the *Mahabharata* and tells the story of a man named Arjuna who finds himself in the midst of a midlife spiritual crisis. The way he attempts to resolve it, with the help of an incarnation of the god Vishhu, reveals much about what it means today to be Indian and spiritual.

See also Yoga.

For Further Reading: K. Sivaraman et al., eds., *Hindu Spirituality*, vols., WSEH (1997).

Terry C. Muck

History of Christian Spirituality
See Chapter 12. See also Chapters 13–18.

Holiness

Holiness describes the complete otherness of God's nature, which elicits both fear and attraction from humans in their aspiration to and appropriation of this divine characteristic. Many other themes of Scripture represent an action of God toward people. While the atonement refers to God's work of satisfying the cost of human sin, mercy represents God's patience with offense, and justice engages God in dealing with disparity, holiness is innate to the nature of God. Deep consciousness of this ineffable divinity at once motivates and fulfills the human longing for wholeness. In all of God's dealings with creation—human and otherwise—holiness becomes evident as a result of divine presence.

Two basic emphases accompany discussions: the condition of being holy (holiness) and the process of becoming holy (sanctification). Whether stated or implicit, holiness drives any pursuit of spirituality in remediating the deficiency that is evident in humanity because of estrangement from God. Holiness is often narrowly represented as purity. Although pure motive and pure living are significant parts of a proper understanding of holiness, they are not a complete description. Holiness also has the following features.

First, it is proximate. God's presence is evident in each case where holiness is described. God's nature never fails to affect that which is in proximity. In this way, God's holiness sustains all that is created. Willful sin causes estrangement with the resulting absence of holiness. By a decision of the will, humans may also experience proximity to God through Jesus with the resulting transformation into being holy as God is holy.

Second, it is relational. The pursuit of holiness is not behavioral or propositional only. Some have attempted to codify holiness in rules or doctrines. This effort is inconsistent with the relational nature that proceeds from the character of God in love. Further, the transcendence and mystery of God's nature leaves the constraint of doctrines wanting. While holiness results in behavior that is different from a life that is not reconciled to God, behaviors are not the object of pursuit but the evidence.

Third, it is transformational. God is wholly

other. The deep longing of every person to be holy is met with fear in the presence of such otherness. The effect of God's presence is to transform people, places, or objects in becoming other than their natural state or condition. God makes all things that are in relationship with him to be other as well. They are transformed and thus become separate or sanctified in the likeness of God and for God's purposes.

Fourth, it is engaged. Though by nature holiness is separate or other, it also is engaged with what is not holy. Motivated by love, God's nature compels engagement in redemptive efforts. Anything in proximity to God that is transformed to reflect his nature and purposes will also be engaged in God's restorative priority.

Fifth, it is (re)integrative. God's nature appropriated by the Holy Spirit to the life of a willing person transforms it wholly—not merely the spiritual dimension, or the social, but also the psychological, physical, and intellectual dimensions; not absolute perfection, but a purposeful perfecting of God's original image in a person. It is God who makes one holy by influencing the life of a person expressing faith in Christ to be made whole again in healing the sickness that disintegrated or marred the image once imprinted upon humanity.

Allowing God to be near, by surrendering selfish independence, results in our natures being transformed to become holy as God is holy and our priorities being reordered to become God's priorities. Personal nature flows into social responsibility that reflects both the nature of Christ and the salvific priority of God in the world. Conversely, social relationships form the personal nature of an individual, thereby framing the assertion by John Wesley that there is no personal holiness without social holiness.

The archetype of this restored condition is the person of Jesus Christ. Hence the essence of holiness is Christlikeness, and the pursuit of holiness is reflecting Christ.

See also Baptism of the Holy Spirit; Sanctification.

For Further Reading: M. Lodahl and T. Oord, *Relational Holiness* (2005); K. Mannoia and D. Thorsen, *The Holiness Manifesto* (2008); J. Webster, *Holiness* (2003).

Kevin W. Mannoia

Holiness Movement

The Holiness movement describes a spiritual current within the nineteenth- and early twentieth-century church emphasizing the work of the Holy Spirit in the experience of sanctification as well as social engagement. Attaining heart purity and the filling of the Holy Spirit were prominent themes within the movement. Influence from a variety of sources includes the Protestant Reformation with its emphasis on individual faith, seventeenth-century Pietism, the Roman Catholic emphasis on community faith, and a unique Wesleyan interpretation of the Eastern Orthodox concept of theosis.

The most direct influence resulted from the eighteenth-century Methodist revival. John Wesley's publication of *A Plain Account of Christian Perfection* (1777) represents a standard reference point for the Holiness movement. Terms such as *entire sanctification*, *Christian perfection*, *holiness*, and *infilling of the Spirit* became common in the movement as adherents sought a deeper, inner work of purification in living the holy life.

The Holiness movement became clearly defined within the broader church spectrum during the revivalism of the Second Great Awakening with its emphasis on the work of the Holy Spirit and entire sanctification. It represented a strong ecumenical dimension in early years. Although largely driven by American Methodists, many non-Methodists contributed to the Holiness movement. Presbyterian William Boardman promoted holiness through his evangelistic campaigns and book *The Higher Christian Life* (1858). Asa Mahan of Oberlin College and evangelist Charles Finney also promoted holiness as a result of their own personal experiences. Mahan testified to a baptism of the Holy Spirit in which he was cleansed from the inclination to sin—a phrase reminiscent of Charles Wesley's "bent to sinning."

An early reference point for the Holiness movement is the Tuesday Meeting for the Promotion of Holiness begun in New York City by Sarah Lankford and her sister Phoebe Palmer in 1836. The emphasis focused on being wholly devoted to God and experiencing a subsequent inner transformation by eradication of the carnal nature. Phoebe Palmer published *The Way of Holiness* (1854), which became a foundational book for the Holiness movement by providing an experiential description of how to live a life free from sin and have entire sanctification.

The early emphasis on inner cleansing through the filling of the Spirit was integrated with social concern during the social upheavals of the 19th century. This integration of social and personal transformation gave the movement a prophetic dimension especially related to national issues as well as freedom of worship, heart purity, and sanctification.

The perceived narrowness of early twentieth-century voices championing *sola scriptura* served as a contrasting force motivating the Holiness movement to emphasize right living as well as right belief. The resulting effect placed it at odds with fundamentalism in appealing to multiple sources of truth, embracing a broad diversity of views on eschatology, and believing that the church could make a difference in society before the return of Christ. This motivated active social engagement on behalf of the poor as well as aggressive missionary efforts.

Late in the 19th century, a Pentecostal emphasis became noticeable in camp meetings where people were invited to come out of worldliness in living a holy life. The first of these convened in 1867, led by Methodist ministers. The second camp meeting was called a Pentecost. Later, Holiness preacher William Seymour emphasized this Pentecostal experience in his Los Angeles church.

A revival there in 1906 drew other Holiness preachers like C. H. Mason. Though criticized for its emphasis on demonstrable gifts, this largely interracial revival, known as the Azusa Street revival, birthed the Pentecostal movement, which quickly splintered along racial lines as well as leaving the Holiness movement with Pentecostal and Revivalist branches. The Pentecostal movement, with its heavy emphasis on gifts, especially tongues as a confirmation of the gift of the Holy Spirit, quickly became more isolated from the Revivalist branch. The historic Holiness groups expelled or distanced themselves from the Pentecostals as too extreme and without substance and order.

The Holiness movement was characterized by salvation through grace, instantaneous sanctification and infilling of the Holy Spirit, revivalism, and the living of holy lives. These emphases became codified in behavioral expectations of the many denominations birthed in the late 19th century. Disputes arose regarding the nature of sanctification. Specifically, the question of sanctification as an instantaneous attainment as a second work of grace subsequent to regeneration, or an ongoing process of appropriating grace has fueled continuing debates. Consistent with the roots of the movement, early support for civil rights in the mid-20th century continued, although sometimes such support was more rhetorical than real.

The Holiness movement was forged on basic commitments to heart purity, social concern, women's ordination, creation care, racial equity, economic relief, and liberal arts education. These remain central concerns for the churches and organizations that the movement spawned.

Churches birthed in the Holiness movement and the subsequent rise of Pentecostalism represent significant impact on global Christianity and continue to represent fast-growing segments of the church worldwide.

See also Methodist Spirituality.

For Further Reading: M. Dieter, *The Holiness Revival of the Nineteenth Century* (2006);

W. Kostlevy, *Historical Dictionary of the Holiness Movement* (2001).

Kevin W. Mannoia

Holistic Spirituality

Life in God includes all dimensions of human experience. Holistic spirituality acknowledges the entirety of our life — the mundane and the profound, the quotidian and the sublime — and suggests that no element is untouched by or unimportant to that life in God. Holistic spirituality challenges the common dichotomy between what is secular and what is sacred. All things are from God; all things are offered to God.

The classic spiritual direction question — "Where is God in this?" — is one that belongs to a holistic spirituality. The assumption that God is indeed present in all things, at all times, invites one to unexpected encounters with the divine in the midst of any human activity. The Order of St. Benedict provides a fifteen-hundred-year-old model of holistic spirituality. The Benedictine exhortation to "pray and work" represents a commitment to see all of life, whether in the chapel or the kitchen or the garden, as interconnected and, perhaps more importantly, as worship.

In holistic spirituality, therefore, spiritual practices can emerge organically out of any dimension of life. Beyond the familiar disciplines of Bible study, devotional reading, and prayer, holistic spirituality recognizes the forming potential of time spent in nature, with friends, in the workplace, or even in home maintenance. This awareness can provide encouragement to persons who find themselves in a spiritually dry place on the journey. The advice of spiritual director Dom John Chapman, "Pray as you can, not as you can't," becomes a way of nurturing the ongoing relationship with God in the dailiness of life, including periods when spiritual energy ebbs.

One hallmark of holistic spirituality is integration — not merely the intellectual exercise of bringing together discrete disciplines or concepts, however, but the embodied practice of living in increasing wholeness. One's cognitions, emotions, values, and commitments become less compartmentalized from one another. Individual and communal responses to God's call to wholeness and holiness are informed through reflection on the biblical and theological foundations of faith, the theoretical and practical dimensions of praxis, and personal experiences of God in the past and present. This reflection serves as the basis for the ongoing process of integration that is essential for Christian maturity in the whole of life.

See also Body; Exercise, Physical Fitness; Leisure and Play; Work

For Further Reading: R. Foster, *Streams of Living Water* (2001); R. Rolheiser, *The Holy Longing* (1999); J. B. Smith, *The Good and Beautiful Life* (2010).

Carla M. Dahl

Holmes, Urban Tigner, III (1930 – 1981)

Episcopal professor and dean. Known to his familiars simply as Terry, Urban Tigner Holmes III was professor of pastoral theology at Nashotah House in Wisconsin before becoming the dean of the (Episcopal) School of Theology at Sewanee, Tennessee. He believed that without thorough theological training, the church ran the risk of dangerous sentimentality. Without the freedom of the mind that comes with an ongoing education, he believed, the very facets of historic religion itself can become a form of idolatry. In Holmes's view, the theologian was specifically poised to lend a critical perspective to the church.

Holmes believed that the gospel must be applicable to modern humanity in a way that would be understood through real-life experience. He incorporated creative methods of expression — for example, storytelling and art — into his seminary classes, believing self-expression to be a vital part of a spiritual journey.

Influenced by Carl Jung's search for meaning and well versed in history, theology, and social anthropology, Holmes intensified the focus on spirituality in the School of Theology, instituting a class on the phenomenology of religion and ascetical theology. He also wrote a small library of books, including *Ministry and Imagination* (1976), *Spirituality for Ministry* (1982), and an analytical *History of Christian Spirituality* (1980), in which his intellectual formalism led him to disdain Pietism.

Sarah G. Scorgie

Holy Spirit

See **Chapter 7.**

Holy War

The gospel of Luke tells a story of Jesus and his disciples being refused hospitality by Samaritan villagers "because [Jesus'] face was set toward Jerusalem" (Luke 9:53 NRSV). The disciples James and John, presumably on the strength of stories of holy warriors like Joshua and David in their Scriptures, prodded Jesus, "Lord, do you want us to call fire down from heaven to destroy them?" (Luke 9:54). Jesus' rebuke speaks volumes about a Christian theology of holy war (that is, war to advance or protect God's interests).

The idea of holy war in Israel's Scriptures, with Yahweh the God of Israel as the Divine Warrior, was predicated upon the conviction that Israel was God's elect and holy people. Old Testament narratives offer several interrelated rationales for the necessity of divine warfare, including: (1) the greater glory of God and recognition that Yahweh is supreme, (2) the vindication of Israel as God's elect people, (3) the hardness of heart of Israel's enemies, and (4) the threat of pagan peoples' idolatry infecting the purity of Israel's faith and worship.

It is all the more striking, then, that Jesus entirely rejected a theology of holy war or divine violence in his own ministry, explicitly teaching his followers to "love your enemies [and] do good to those who hate you" (Luke 6:27). Nonetheless, some Christians have been reluctant to assume that Christ's example altogether supersedes the aforementioned OT practices and perspectives, and also cite from the NT that Christ brings not peace but the sword (Matt. 10:34), the ongoing legitimacy of the state's use of force (Rom. 13:4), and the final apocalyptic battle of Revelation. Thus, for example, the twelfth-century saint and mystic Bernard of Clairvaux could write movingly of Jesus' nonviolent response to the violence of the Roman state, "O Sacred Head now wounded, with grief and shame weighed down," but could also serve as the church's primary preacher of the Second Crusade.

Perhaps most troubling, however, in any sanction of holy war, is the thinly veiled presence of human sinfulness, ready to exploit the opportunity for abuse of power, vengeance, anger, cruelty, and egregious self-interest. In a world increasingly destabilized by sectarian jihads, the way forward for courageous Christians is to apply biblical warfare motifs to the real but often invisible conflict against the principalities and powers (Eph. 6). While at times requiring confronting of evil in its materialized forms, this battle prioritizes spiritual weaponry and may extend even to one's own inner struggle with sin.

See also Violence; Warfare, Spiritual.

For Further Reading: K. Armstrong, *Holy War* (1988); S. Baron and G. Wise, *Violence and Defense in the Jewish Experience* (1977); S. Gundry, ed., *Show Them No Mercy: Four Views on God and Canaanite Genocide* (2003); J. Williams, *The Bible, Violence, and the Sacred* (1991).

Michael Lodahl

Hope

See **Chapter 11.**

Hopkins, Gerard Manley (1844–1889)

English Jesuit priest and poet. Hopkins was born into a comfortable Anglican family and from boyhood onward displayed both sensitivity to natural beauty and hunger for a deeper relationship to God. At Oxford he was at first deeply influenced by the Oxford Movement, the attempt to revitalize the Church of England by taking it back to its medieval Catholic roots. Eventually he determined that approach to be superficial and converted to Catholicism. Shortly afterward he entered the Jesuit order. During his rigorous years of training, he discovered the medieval theologian Duns Scotus, whose understanding of creation gave a central place both to the incarnation and to the uniqueness of each created thing. When Hopkins entered the Jesuit order, he gave up poetry as inconsistent with his vocation, but he returned to it with "The Wreck of the Deutschland," a long and difficult poem occasioned by the shipwreck of five exiled nuns, which explored how God, "ground of being and granite of it," works his will in creatures. It is widely acknowledged as the greatest devotional poem in the English language. Hopkins died in middle age after years of difficult assignments as parish priest or teacher. None of the poems that later made him famous were published for thirty years.

His relatively small number of poems, accompanied by the nuanced insights in his letters, journals, and devotional writings, became a major influence on twentieth-century literature and, more recently, on Christian spirituality. Most famous are a series of poems that celebrate God's closeness to creation, reflected in lines like "The world is charg'd with the grandeur of God" and "Christ plays in ten thousand places, / Lovely in eyes and lovely in limbs not his / To the father through the features of men's faces." Many have also found great comfort in the "Terrible Sonnets," a series of prayers written out of depression that rival the darkest psalms, both in the fierceness of their argument with God and in the tenacity of their faith. Though Hopkins often felt his life a failure, one of his last poems, "Comfort of the Resurrection," affirms comfort in the face of death:

> World's wildfire leave but ash:
> In a flash, at a trumpet crash,
> I am all at once what Christ is, since he was
>   what I am and
> This Jack, joke, poor potsherd, patch, match-
>   wood, immortal diamond,
> Is immortal diamond.

Such eloquent faith continues to comfort and challenge all readers of Hopkins's poetry.

See also Ecological Spirituality; Poetry and Poetics.

For Further Reading: R. Hansen, *Exiles* (2008); P. Mariani, *Gerard Manley Hopkins* (2008); B. Waterman Ward, *World as Word: Philisopical Theology in Gerard Manley Hopkins* (2002).

Loren Wilkinson

Hospitality

Hospitality is a religious practice with roots deep into antiquity. It is encouraged not only as a moral virtue (Job 31:32; Isa. 58:6–7), but also a sacred duty (Lev. 19:33–34). Christians draw upon a rich Hebrew tradition, such as Abraham and Lot in Genesis 18:1–8 and 19:1–11 and Rahab in Joshua 2. Scriptural injunctions link God's provisions as host of Israel to Israel's care as host to aliens and strangers (Lev. 25:23; Ps. 39:12).

By the 1st century, an elaborate travel network gave rise to a burgeoning hospitality industry (Luke 2:7; 10:34–35). Since the early expansion of Christianity benefited from enhanced mobility, the NT abounds with references to hospitality. The itinerant Jesus received hospitality (Matt 26:6; Mark 1:29; Luke 14:1; John 12:1–2). Christians treasure Lukan stories like Mary and Martha's entertainment of Jesus (Luke 10:38–42), Jesus as the guest of Zacchaeus (Luke 19:1–10), and Jesus' dinner with Emmaus's disciples (Luke 24:13–32).

Ironically, whereas both Hebrew and Greco-Roman hospitality creates a noble opportunity for the host, Jesus' presence creates a role reversal. Jesus the guest becomes Jesus the host and transforms outsiders to insiders.

Early Christians shared goods and services (Acts 2:46), thereby creating and sustaining gospel partnerships. Like Jesus, Peter (Acts 10:6, 48) and Paul (Acts 16:15; 18:7; 21:4, 8, 16; 28:7) relied on hospitable contacts. Moreover, NT writers entreat Christians to practice hospitality (Rom. 12:13; 1 Tim. 3:2; 5:10; and Titus 1:8; Heb. 13:2; 1 Peter 4:9). Finally, numerous references equate God's eschatological kingdom as unending hospitality (Luke 14:15–24; 22:18–30; Rev. 19:7–9).

As a Christian practice, hospitality cultivates community, creates space for the stranger, advances the gospel, and fosters gratitude. For contemporary examples, see L'Arche, The Catholic Worker Movement, and The Simple Way.

See also Benedictine Spirituality; Food; Love Feast.

For Further Reading: J. Koenig, *New Testament Hospitality* (1985); C. Pohl, *Making Room* (1999).

Martin Mittelstadt

Houston, James M. (1922–)

Spiritual theologian and mentor. Born in Scotland to Brethren missionary parents, Houston studied at Edinburgh and Oxford (D.Phil.), where he became a published scholar and university lecturer in geography (1947–1971). There he met regularly with a wide circle of Christian intellectuals, including C. S. Lewis, to reflect Christianly on the widest range of human interests and concerns. Houston left his professional career at Oxford in 1970 to become the founding principal of Regent College in Vancouver, Canada, an international graduate school with a unique focus on lay theological education. In 1976 he also co-founded the C. S. Lewis Institute in Washington, DC, to bring Christian thinking to the domains of personal and public life in America's capital.

In 1991 Regent College created for him a professorship devoted to spiritual theology—a prescient and pioneering initiative. As a spiritual theologian Houston has developed fresh, big-picture insights by creatively integrating an unusual breadth of reading. He has spoken prophetically to the secularization and depersonalization of human life in Western culture and the church, and he has awakened many to a neglected ecumenical heritage of Christian spirituality. His imagination has been baptized into Scripture and the doctrine of the Trinity, and his disposition shaped by numerous literary and classic spiritual writers, including Kierkegaard, Pascal, and Bernard of Clairvaux. At the personal level, tutoring skills Houston cultivated at Oxford grew into a remarkable lifelong practice of spiritual direction. With the active support of his wife, Rita, his guidance has been characterized by generosity of spirit, profound empathy, and a sometimes startling gift of discernment.

His most influential writings include the trilogy of *The Transforming Friendship* (1989), *In Search of Happiness* (1990), and *The Heart's Desire* (1992). *The Mentored Life* (2002) describes the relational conditions of the restorative journey from individualism to personhood. *Joyful Exiles* (2006) is filled with autobiographical insights, while *The Psalms as Christian Worship* (2010), co-authored with Bruce Waltke, reclaims a vital biblical resource for Christian spirituality.

For Further Reading: J. I. Packer and L. Wilkinson, eds., *Alive to God: Studies in Spirituality Presented to James Houston* (1993); A. D. Thomas, "James M. Houston," *Crux* 29, no. 3 (1993): 2–10, and *Crux* 29, no. 4 (1993): 17–27.

Glen G. Scorgie

Hsi, Pastor (Xi Shengmo) (1835–1896)

Chinese evangelist, pastor, and founder of opium refuges. Born Xi Liaozhih in a family of medical doctors, he grew up familiar with traditional Chinese medicine. After winning an essay competition organized by British missionaries, he became their assistant, writing tracts and helping to translate the NT. He changed his name to Xi Shengmo ("overcomer of demons") when he converted to Christianity.

Xi grew in the Christian faith by studying Scripture, praying, fasting, and experiencing the power of the Holy Spirit to protect, heal, and cast out demons in everyday circumstances. His obvious gifts in evangelism led him to start worshiping groups in twenty-seven villages and set up fifty opium refuges, which also established churches. He trained reformed addicts to be evangelists and assistant refuge keepers, and his transformed spirit of gentleness was a deep influence on others. For Xi, Christianity was lived out and real in all aspects of life. Thus, he established a utopian community with farming and animal husbandry based on Christian principles. He agreed to be the village elder on the condition that worship should cease at the local temple. The parish council reluctantly agreed, and the village prospered. He nevertheless declined a second term of office.

See also Asian Christian Spirituality.

For Further Reading: G. Taylor, *Pastor Hsi: A Struggle for Chinese Christianity* (1977).

Kiem-Kiok Kwa

Hugh of St. Victor

See **Victorine Spirituality.**

Human Development

Human beings are not static, but change and develop over time; and Scripture itself is replete with developmental narrative. Throughout Scripture children and youth were endued with value and a purpose: growth toward godly maturity. Spiritual formation was therefore a sacred commission (Deut. 4:9; Prov. 22:6), with consequences

for those who hindered or sabotaged it (Matt. 18:6). But spiritual development was also expected to continue throughout the life cycle, as numerous Scripture texts attest (e.g., 1 Cor. 14:20; Eph. 4:14–15; 2 Peter 3:18).

Developmental psychology involves the study of human beings across the life span—from conception to death. By reason of its insights into how humans develop, it can contribute in significant ways to the process and goal of Christian spiritual maturity. In the past, psychology's recognition of spirituality as a fundamental component of human development was somewhat tenuous. More recently, however, and partly because of more generic meanings ascribed to the term, spirituality has begun to occupy a more central role in scholarly understanding of what it means to be a human being. For example, in 1991 the United Nations Convention on the Rights of the Child concluded that spirituality was a distinct component of human development worthy of universal rights and protection. This document was significant in that it differentiated spiritual development from cognitive, moral, or social development and established its importance as a formative structure in children's lives. Other research has suggested an implicit awareness of spirituality as a component of human experience. In a recent UCLA study (funded by the Templeton Foundation) of over 100,000 students representing 236 colleges and universities in the United States, 77 percent of respondents agreed that "we are all spiritual beings."

While the Christian community has focused largely on faith formation, spirituality in the field of developmental psychology has been approached from a more inclusive and existential perspective. The most widely referenced work on spiritual development is James Fowler's Six Stages of Faith Development. In the 1970s, Fowler conducted interviews with 359 people across a range of ages (3.5–84 years). Relying heavily on Piaget's stages of cognitive development, Kolhberg's stages of moral development, and Erikson's stages of identity development, Fowler explored various ways human beings conceptualize and relate to God (or a transcendent being) across the life span, and the influence of the transcendent on personal beliefs, values, and behavior. In stage 1, *intuitive-projective faith* (ages 2–7), children's thinking is egocentric and focused on issues of safety and well-being. Belief tends to be imaginative and imitative, situated primarily in narrative differentiations of good and evil. Stage 2, *mythic-literal faith* (ages 8–adolescence), involves a linear, concrete conceptualization of moral conduct, and the practices, symbols, and traditions associated with the faith community with which a child is associated. Authority is viewed as external, represented through dominant figures and rules. The adolescent stage, *synthetic-conventional faith*, is characterized by an emotionally laden adherence to persons, symbols, beliefs, and values associated with a faith orientation, often generating intense meaning and loyalty. *Individuative-reflective faith*, stage 4, involves reexamining and testing the concordance of external belief statements with the emerging, authentic self. Belief ideals are internalized and integrated into one's identity. Stage 5, *conjunctive faith*, is characterized by the ability to embrace paradoxical realities, such as recognizing in humans both good and evil, and by behaviors reflecting inclusion and service. *Universalizing faith*, stage 6, involves sacrificial commitment to love, care, and justice, which Fowler describes as both freeing and threatening. Though Fowler conceptualized faith development as a series of progressive stages, he concurred with Kohlberg's view that placement within stages reflected complexity of belief and resultant action rather than chronological age.

While other stage-based theories have been proposed, they seem to share common attributes. These include (1) developing a knowledge base about a belief system (e.g., Scriptures, liturgies, teachings); (2) internalizing a set of core beliefs and values that provide meaning, coherence, and belonging; (3) acting in accordance with the belief system; and (4) experiencing transformation or transcendence reflective of the belief system. The most predominant use of stage theories has been to provide structure for faith formation activities, especially with reference to teaching children.

Recently there has been a movement away from stage theories to a more relational conception of spiritual development. This blending of developmental psychology and theology is founded on the premise that human beings were created for relationship with God and others, and that humans are born of relationship and into relationship that profoundly shapes self-perception and belief, often maintaining stability across the life span. For example, H. Richard Niebuhr and Ana-Maria Rizzuto proposed that a child's first conceptualizations of God are derived from relationships experienced with primary caregivers early in life. Other researchers frame children's spirituality as more present-focused, infused with imagination and wonder, and centered on goodness, characteristics that can generate a heightened sense of interrelationship and mystery. In accordance with Lev Vygotsky's concept of zone of proximal development, Christian education has emphasized the role of parents, youth workers, and religious educators in the process of faith formation of youth and adolescents. The role of spirituality in vocational choice and mate selection has been examined in early adult development literature; and nurturing, parenting, and caring for others, along with a heightened sense of social responsibility, have been related to spirituality in adulthood (Palmer).

Ecological theories of human development (e.g., Urie Bronfenbrenner) situate development within a specific historical and geographical context, and stress the dynamic interaction of family, community, tradition, and culture, including religion, on personal formation. Changes in influential persons, environmental conditions, or religiocultural ideologies across time can alter or even transform belief, values, attitudes, and behaviors. Spirituality has historically had a robust association with various developmental markers and life transitions, such as child dedication, baptism, confirmation and initiation ceremonies, Communion, marriage vows, and end-of-life rites. In addition, common themes such as formation and transformation, vocation and recreation, calling and becoming, and childlikeness and maturity intersect both human development and spirituality.

Development implies growth; and spiritual development has been portrayed as a path or a journey to becoming. Though the starting points for both are clearly evident, the end point or goal has been more ambiguous. What is generally agreed on is that between the beginnings and the endings is the call to live with courage and authenticity, increasingly embracing and integrating action and contemplation, simplicity and complexity, certainty and wonder.

See Chapter 27. *See also* Adolescent Spirituality; Aging; Children and Spirituality; Midlife Transition.

For Further Reading: J. Balswick et al., *The Reciprocating Self* (2005); P. Benson and E. Roehlkepartain, "Spiritual Development," in *New Directions for Youth Development* 118 (2008): 13 – 28; J. Fowler, *Stages of Faith* (1981); P. Palmer, *The Active Life* (1990); E. Roehlkepartain et al., eds., *The Handbook of Spiritual Development in Childhood and Adolescence* (2006).

Kate Scorgie

Humanism

As summarized in the aphorism of English poet Alexander Pope, "presume not God to scan / The proper study of mankind is man," humanism refers to a turning of scholarly attention away from theological to specifically human concerns, with the ethical goal of improving the quality of human life. Whether or not modified by the adjective *secular*, humanism is now often seen as an enemy of Christianity. However, Christianity and humanism have not historically been antithetical, despite the claims of such eminent writers as Francis A. Schaeffer that the Renaissance with its "humanistic elements" was directly opposed by the Reformation and "scriptural Christianity." The early Renaissance recovery of classical Greek and Latin texts led to strenuous Christian scholarship, producing, as Douglas Bush puts it, "that union of religious faith and classical culture which is called Christian humanism." Great Christian humanists of the later Renaissance include Erasmus and John Milton.

During the 19th century, the term *humanism* came to be used increasingly as standing over against Christian orthodoxy as a term denoting human autonomy. During the 20th century, the promulgation by the American Humanist Association of Humanist Manifesto I (1933) and II (1973); and "Humanism and Its Aspirations," or Humanist Manifesto III (2000), established humanism as superseding existing religions and as explicitly antisupernaturalist. Christianity, however, continues to be as it has always been, profoundly concerned with what constitutes the truly human life. The real philosophic enemies of Christianity are not humanism, but skeptical and naturalistic doctrines, which lead to the prideful assertion that science can tell us all that can be known about what it is to be human.

A renewed Christian humanism includes a rapprochement between evangelical Christianity and the arts and also the renewal of rigorous evangelical scholarship in all disciplines. A renewed understanding of the meaning of *imago Dei* as the source of the dignity and worth of every human person, and fresh examination of the implications of the doctrine of the incarnation, with an emphasis on the full humanity of Christ without compromising belief in his full deity, grounds this renewed Christian humanism.

All forms of humanism are, meanwhile, about to be challenged by charges of speciesism (i.e., the affording of special privileges to humans over other life forms), and by posthumanism. Common cause between humanists, whether secular or Christian, may well yet be made to resist the erosion of the ancient understanding of the significance and centrality of humans as the living creatures who have the power to reflect and make choices, including moral choices. Christian humanism will continue to affirm on the basis of an ever fuller exploration of both Scripture and human learning, that to be fully human is to live in loving relationship with both our creator God and the created order.

See also Enlightenment; Image of God.

For Further Reading: M. C. D'Arcy, *Humanism and Christianity* (1970); D. Bush, *The Renaissance and English Humanism* (1939); L. Oser, *The Return of Christian Humanism* (2007); S. Ozment, *The Age of Reform: 1250–1550* (1980); J. I. Packer and T. Howard, *Christianity: The True Humanism* (1985); A. Pope, *An Essay on Man* (1733); F. A. Schaeffer, *How Should We Then Live?* (1976).

Maxine Hancock

Human Personhood
See **Chapter 8.**

Humility

Humility is a proper human disposition grounded in bracingly clear self-assessment — including awareness of one's creaturely status, limitations, and sinfulness in relation to the Creator's sovereign power and holiness (Prov. 22:4). Humility, which is compatible with human dignity and self-esteem, has long been considered a core Christian virtue and a necessary counter to the fundamental human pathology of overreaching pride. It has also been an ideal of the monastic movement since at least the 6th century; Benedict of Nursia considered it foundational to his famous rule. For Benedict, humility involved not only reverence to God and obedience to his will, but also choosing contentment and appropriate obedience to others.

Such self-denial is counterintuitive for ego-centric humanity. Humility is neither instantly nor easily attained; Calvin described humanity as fearing and loathing humility, seeking to avoid it at all costs. As such, it is not an easy decision but occurs in response to hearing God (2 Kings 22:19). Humility is a habit acquired through repeatedly putting aside one's sin nature — selfish ambition and vain conceit (Phil. 2:3). As imperfect beings, obtaining and abiding in God's grace occurs only by humbling oneself (Luke 18:14; James 4:6). When actively expressed in relationship with God, humility assures one of divine forgiveness and healing (2 Chron. 7:14). Christ is the definitive model of this virtue; he humbled himself, choosing to take on human form and being obedient to the point of death on a cross (Phil. 2:8). One can choose humility only by taking on Christ's gentle and humble nature (Matt. 11:29). The more that Christlikeness is pursued in humility, the more the wisdom of God is reflected in one's life (James 3:13). Thus, humility distinguishes God's people in a divisive, self-gratifying world (Mic. 6:8). Humility is also actively expressed in relationships with others (Gal. 5:13). However, humility does not mean abject self-abasement; it is choosing others before self-gratification (Rom. 8:3). As Dallas Willard points out, this self-denial breaks the iron grip of sin, enabling a fuller restoration of goodness to the soul. Humility is a paradox; by following Christ's sacrificial example, one's humanity is further restored (Eph. 4:32–5:1). Rather than crippling one before God and others, humility enables one to progress from strength to strength (Ps. 84:7). Thus, humility becomes a conduit for God's healing transformation of humanity.

See also Pride; Sins, Seven Deadly.

For Further Reading: Bernard of Clairvaux, *The Steps of Humility and Pride*, CFS (1989); J. Calvin, *Golden Booklet of the True Christian Life* (1952); D. Willard with D. Simpson, *Revolution of Character* (2005); E. Worthington, *Humility* (2007).

Johanna Knutson Vignol

Humor

Exhortations in the Bible toward sobriety, taming of the tongue, and holy living (Eph. 4:17 – 5:20) have long been interpreted in the Christian tradition as a general disapproval of joking and humor. Nevertheless, the antihumor strain present in many Christian subcultures has always been counterbalanced by humor in the Bible itself, in the writings and practices of ordinary Christians, and—some would argue—in the nature of the universe. Conrad Hyers sums up this broad perspective: "The panorama of creation, revelation, and redemption witnesses to what might justly be called the humor of God." The grand Christian narrative, in which a fallen creation is redeemed, suggests a comic rather than tragic shaping of history.

Moreover, the Bible witnesses throughout that God works in ways that could be termed comedic: surprising reversals, unlikely heroes, and stinging ironies. For example, God chooses an obscure group of nomads to be his people, promising Abraham and Sarah a son in their old age—a son who is named "laughter." Reading biblical stories with an eye for humor also reveals comedic details: David defeats Goliath (an unlikely hero and a comic reversal), but the story also includes the boy David standing helplessly in armor far too large for him. In the NT, Jesus uses humor and exaggeration in his teaching, remarking about logs in people's eyes and offering a nagging widow as a model for prayer. Literary humor in the Bible as well as the comedic contours of the redemption story suggest, then, that humor is an aspect of God's nature given to the human species as part of our *imago Dei*.

Humor ought to be neither cheap, nor cruel, nor ignorant. Instead, humor in the Christian life should signal spiritual health. It is a sign of trust when we are able to see the mirth and delight in the world, and a sign of humility when we are able to laugh at ourselves. Creaturely humor, including about our humblest creaturely nature, has a long history in the Christian tradition. Prophetic humor also has an important place. Prophetic humor slips behind our defenses to flash its blade of critique. This can serve several redemptive purposes: enabling a distressed group to speak truth to power, deflating self-righteousness and pomposity, and exposing follies.

Past and contemporary Christian writers who have used various kinds of humor include G. K. Chesterton, C. S. Lewis, Flannery O'Connor, Anne Lamott, the editors of the satire magazine *The Wittenburg Door*, and the editors of larknews.com.

See also Joy.

For Further Reading: F. Buechner, *Telling the Truth* (1977); C. Hyers, *And God Created Laughter* (1987).

Debra Rienstra

Hurnard, Hannah (1905 – 1990)

Writer, missionary. Author of the celebrated allegory *Hinds' Feet on High Places* (1955) and its sequel, *Mountains of Spices* (1977). Born into a wealthy Quaker family in Colchester, England, and trained for two years at Ridgelands Bible College, Hannah Hurnard adapted the idea for her two bestselling books from John Bunyan's *The Pilgrim's Progress*. So fearful was she in her youth that she stuttered severely. She recovered at age nineteen sometime after attending a Keswick Conference. Her spirituality reflected a tragic blend of extraordinary insight into the Christian journey and profound vulnerability to grave theological error. In stark contrast to *Hinds' Feet* (her first-rate story of repenting from fear), *Eagles' Wings to the Higher Places* (1981) promotes pantheism and other New Age beliefs. From book to book, Hurnard's characters progress from the "high places" of Christianity to the "higher places" of anti-Christianity. In the context of being a missionary in Israel unsupported by any agency for fifty years (residential from 1932 to 1948, and moving back and forth to England from 1949 to 1972), she drifted theologically. She was traumatized by certain experiences, such as that of seeing a Muslim woman "not more than twenty years old" die upon arrival at the Mission Hospital one perilous night in Palestine without ever having heard the gospel. Though critics accuse Hurnard of denying the reality of hell (having called it "temporary"), in *The Unveiled Glory* (1956) she writes, "Hell must surely be the terrible experience of being allowed to reap the full harvest of sin." She died of untreated cancer.

Sarah Sumner

Hus, John (c. 1372–1415)

Bohemian pastor and reformer. Hus preached at Prague's Bethlehem Chapel, center of the Bohemian reform movement, addressing the corruption of the church and its leaders and the urgency for renewed spiritual zeal. He consistently asserted that truth was found in Scripture rather than in the words of the pope, church councils, or tradition. His writings, including *On Simony* and separate *Expositions* on the Apostles' Creed, the Decalogue, and the Lord's Prayer, addressed both moral and educational needs. He also wrote *The Daughter*, a devotional work for a group of pious women.

His most mature and influential work, *The Church*, reflects a Pauline understanding that the church is comprised of those predestined in heaven and earth who believe by faith in Jesus Christ and not in some organization governed by the pope or councils. It was this doctrine that branded him a heretic. Hus agreed to attend the Council of Constance (1414–1418) when promised the opportunity to defend his position. However, he was silenced, convicted, and burned at the stake on July 6, 1415, singing a hymn of praise to God.

Hus recognized the importance of corporate Christian formation and made important worship reforms in preaching in the vernacular, introducing and expanding congregational participation, and producing hymns in Czech. Hus was a significant reformer before the Protestant Reformation, and he inspired Luther, though the theological gap between them was broader than Luther realized. While Hus asserted the authority of Scripture and encouraged the laity to receive both the bread and chalice in the Lord's Supper, he affirmed transubstantiation, proper veneration of the Virgin Mary, purgatory, and special masses for departed souls. Nonetheless, he provides a model of contending for biblical truth as the foundation of the spiritual life and the significance of purity for church leaders. Further, Hus's teachings inspired the later *Unitas Fratrum* or Moravian Church.

For Further Reading: T. Fudge, "'Ansellus dei' and the Bethlehem Chapel in Prague," *Communio Viatorum* 35, no. 2 (1993): 127–61; M. Spinka, *John Hus* (1968); idem, *John Hus at the Council of Constance* (1965).

Tom Schwanda

Hyde, John ("Praying Hyde") (1865–1912)

Missionary and prayer intercessor. He graduated from Carthage College, Illinois, and immediately joined the faculty there. However, believing he had heard God's call to the Punjab people of India, he soon resigned that position and entered McCormick (Presbyterian) Theological Seminary in Chicago. Upon graduation in 1892, he sailed for India where he spent the remaining twenty years of his life ministering to and praying for Indians and Pakistanis.

Known by many as "Praying Hyde," Hyde often spent long vigils in prayer, from thirty-six hours on his knees in intercession by some accounts, to thirty consecutive days and nights by others. In 1896, after visiting many villages in the state of Punjab, he observed that there had been no conversions that year. His response was to plead with the Lord. He became known for his urgent prayer, "Oh God, give me souls or I die!"

In 1904 Hyde attended the Sialkot Convention and helped to start the Punjab Prayer Union that encouraged missionaries and native Christian workers to covenant to pray until God sent revival to India. At the Sialkot Convention in 1908, Hyde dared to ask God for a soul to be saved every day that year—and by the time of the convention the following year, four hundred salvations were reported.

Suffering a weak heart, Hyde was forced to return to America in 1911. Passing through Wales on the way, he met G. Campbell Morgan who said it was Hyde who taught him what real prayer was. Many intercessors today continue to be inspired by Hyde's passionate and persevering prayer.

See also Intercession.

For Further Reading: E. Carré, ed., *Praying Hyde* (1982).

Cynthia Hyle Bezek

Hymns

Hymns are songs of worship that express praise and thanksgiving toward God. They may be distinguished from praise songs by their formal structure and content: hymns are essentially sacred poetry set to music. Hymns can be distinguished from choral music because their central function is congregational participation in worship. Twice the NT urges the use of "psalms, hymns and spiritual songs" in Christian worship (Eph. 5:19; Col. 3:16).

Hymns play several significant roles in Christian spirituality; principally they enable a congregation to praise God in song. The corporate nature of hymn singing helps congregations to experience and express their oneness in Christ. Since hymns resonate with affective as well as cognitive dimensions of human personality, hymns can communicate emotion as well as doctrine. They are as capable of inducing experience as of describing it. Hence, in describing praise, thanksgiving, or new birth, hymns create a mood and a context in which those Christian experiences can be evoked and realized. Hymns also teach and instruct, and many

Christian traditions view their hymnology as a sort of catechism in song. The marriage of text with music makes the lyrics both more memorable and more evocative. Due to their ability to communicate information and induce experience, hymns play a vital role in spiritual formation. Hymns are also used as prayers because they give people the words to express their own deep feelings; to borrow Brian Wren's phrase, singing a hymn is like "praying twice."

The standardization of church music, which began with Pope Gregory the Great, led to a movement away from congregational song, but one of the great developments of the Protestant Reformation (as an acted parable of Martin Luther's doctrine of the priesthood of all believers) was the return to an emphasis on congregational song through the use of Christian hymns. Some were developed from earlier medieval resources, like Bernard's poem "O Sacred Head, Now Wounded." Luther himself created over one hundred hymns, the most famous of which is "A Mighty Fortress Is Our God." Those in the Reformed tradition preferred to sing metrical versions of the Psalms because they were esteemed to be of divine origin. Isaac Watts is viewed as the father of English hymnody because his *Hymns and Spiritual Songs* (1707) signaled a decisive movement away from the exclusive use of psalm singing in Protestant worship. The hymns of Watts and William Cowper were particularly popular among English evangelicals. The prodigious hymn production of John and Charles Wesley wed popular hymnody to the task of the Great Awakening. The connection between hymnody and revivalism made hymn singing a particularly important and enduring feature of evangelical worship.

The productive marriage between hymns and transforming corporate worship continued in North America. Initially Americans used hymns of European origin, but soon America developed its own homegrown hymn writers, such as Fanny Crosby and D. L. Moody's associate Ira Sankey (1840–1908), who created evocative hymns to use in evangelistic services. In nineteenth-century America, a distinction developed between "hymns," which were composed by the founders of the various Christian traditions, and the newer "gospel songs," which were an invention and communication of the camp meeting experience. The late 20th and early 21th centuries have seen a "worship war" develop between partisan advocates of, respectively, traditional hymns, gospel songs, and even newer praise music (the latter often consist-ing of brief Scripture texts attuned to the strains of contemporary music and performed by bands).

See also Praise Music; Spirituals; Worship.

For Further Reading: A. Bailey, *The Gospel in Hymns* (1950); T. Berger, *Theology in Hymns* (1995); R. Brown, *How Hymns Shape Our Lives* (2001); M. Noll and R. Thiemann, eds., *Where Shall My Wond'ring Soul Begin?* (2000); B. Wren, *Praying Twice* (2000).

John Tyson

I

Icons

Icons are windows to heaven representing Christ, the saints, and salvation history. While worship or adoration belongs to God alone, icons in the Eastern Orthodox tradition are due relative veneration or honor. Icons are a consequence of the incarnation of the infinite, invisible God as a finite, visible human being, since Jesus was fully the "image (*eikōn*) of the invisible God" (Col. 1:15). If the cosmos, OT theophanies, and the church are iconic, more so is humankind an icon, being created in the image of the Supreme Iconographer. Hence, filled with the Spirit, saints themselves are depicted as images (that is, as imagers) of Christ.

Icons were largely unchallenged from earliest symbolic representations (fish, shepherd) until the 8th and 9th centuries, when iconoclasm ("icon smashing") opposed them for five reasons: (1) OT prohibition of idolatry, (2) gnostic incompatibility between matter and spirit, (3) denial of the hypostatic union of Christ's two natures, (4) accusation of late innovation, and (5) Islamic influence. John Damascene, the Seventh Ecumenical Council, Theodore Studite, and many martyrs responded to these accusations. The Decalogue forbade idols, but not all images: the tabernacle was patterned after heavenly things and adorned with cherubim (Ex. 25–26). The image mediates the presence of the person depicted but, unlike idols, is not that person. As Basil of Caesarea wrote, the honor passes from type to prototype. Later theology would add that icons are presences of God who penetrates the material through his uncreated grace, overcoming the distance between type and prototype. Christians do not worship matter, but its Creator; they are saved not *from* matter, but *through* matter, since the Son assumed matter. Icons do not present Jesus' human or divine natures separately, but their hypostatic union, his person. Last, iconophiles (Gr. for "friends of icons") invoked witnesses that placed iconography in NT times.

While Calvin rejected icons, Luther allowed them for instructional and aesthetic purposes. Icons are today increasingly popular among Protestants, widespread in Roman Catholicism, and a distinctive mark of Orthodoxy. Among evangelicals, the use of icons is not common; if they are utilized, it is normally in the context of private devotions rather than public worship.

Iconographers exercise their universal priesthood by offering matter back to God and by teaching a theology in color, a gospel in images. While addressing people within their culture (clothing, architecture), icons present a realized eschatology through their nonnaturalistic perspective. Uncreated light comes from all directions, suggesting God's omnipresence in a transfigured cosmos. Successive events are presented simultaneously in a transcendence of time and space. Elongated bodies, wings, and mountains represented below knee height indicate the heavenly life of earthly beings.

Iconic spirituality is both active and contemplative. Actively, Christ is encountered in his living icons, the poor, and in the purification of the image of God in us. Contemplation involves bodily senses: hearing words and hymns, seeing icons. One joins the heavenly banquet, sitting at the open side of Abraham's table in Rublev's depiction of "the Trinity" (Gen. 18). One enters the darkness of supra-luminous unknowing of God by venerating the icon of the transfiguration, where a "bright cloud" (Matt. 17:5) surrounds Jesus. Icons are transcended in the final stage of prayer, that of silent, wordless, and imageless adoration.

See also Imagery; Images; Russian Spirituality.

For Further Reading: John of Damascus, *Three Treatises on the Divine Images*, trans. A. Louth (2003); L. Ouspensky and V. Lossky, *The Meaning of Icons*, trans. G. Palmer (1982); E. Sendler, *The Icon*, trans. S. Bigham (1993); Theodore the Studite, *On the Holy Icons*, trans. C. Roth (1981).

Radu Bordeianu

Ignatian Spirituality

The *Spiritual Exercises* serve as the essential expression of the spirituality of Ignatius Loyola. This guide to prayer reflects both his vision of the spiritual life and the vital place of mental prayer and spiritual direction for Christians who are genuinely engaged with the world.

The influences that shaped the theology of Ignatius include his own historical, linguistic, and cultural setting. He was a Spanish Basque, raised in an aristocratic setting that was inexorably part of sixteenth-century Roman Catholicism. He was also impressed with the lives of St. Dominic and St. Francis, notably their unreserved devotion to Christ. Also, few sources were so influential as the *Imitation of Christ*, his constant companion at key points in his early adult life. Yet, Ignatius Loyola is not a "child" of the *Imitation* and the movement out of which it arose, the *Devotio Moderna*. There are similarities between the *Imitation* and Ignatian spirituality, but there is also a significant difference, notably in the Ignatian insistence on apostolic service in the world. As significant as any source for the spirituality of Ignatius is his own experience—the vision of Christ and the Holy Trinity that animated his life and his theology during his sojourn in Manresa, in eastern Spain, along with a second in La Storta, Italy, following his university studies.

There are three fundamental contours to the spirituality of Ignatius Loyola. He had a theocentric view of creation, affirming in his *Spiritual Exercises* that "man was created to praise, reverence and serve God our Lord"; his basic assumption was that all things were created to the greater glory of God. The counterpart to this was the Ignatian principle of humility, which stands at the core of his spirituality: holiness is found in the rejection of self-sufficiency and in unqualified dependence on God. A key element or mark of this perspective is captured by the Ignatian principle of "seeking God in all things." Another dimension of this deep theocentric vision of the Christian life is that since God is the source of life and of goodness, the only possible response to God is thanksgiving and joy in the world—and this gratitude is the central dynamic of the *Spiritual Exercises*.

Second, Ignatius's spirituality, while Trinitarian, is thoroughly Christocentric. The earthly life of Christ is the ideal for the Christian life; and the living risen and ascended Christ is the reality that determines the history and personal situation of every believer. Christ is King, and history unfolds as an ongoing conflict between Christ and evil. The Christian is called to continual realignment with the purposes of Christ. In the *Exercises*, the attention of the pray-er is always on Christ—the life of Christ, especially his humility; the mission and purposes of Christ in the world; and the cross of Christ that marks the life of the pray-er.

And third, Ignatius's spirituality is anthropocentric; for Ignatius, true humility is seeing oneself in truth, surrendering oneself to the purposes of Christ; the *Spiritual Exercises* are in many respects a journey in self-knowledge, self-possession, and self-emptying in response to the mystery of God in Jesus Christ and in his cross. It is not, then, a spirituality that discounts the self; on the contrary it is a spirituality of deep personal engagement with Christ and thus of self-awareness. For Ignatius there is only one spirituality for each person: that which is lived in this body, in this life, in response to the personal call of God.

These three elements or contours of Ignatian spirituality are not unique, but what makes them distinct is the way in which Ignatius configured each element toward a mysticism of service, of apostolic engagement with the world. This left an indelible impact on the development of spirituality in Western Christianity. The church had always affirmed that the Christian is called to both prayer and service. But the consistent testimony of spiritual writers was that prayer and contemplation are the higher calling. Thomas Aquinas insisted that in service the Christian shares the fruits of contemplation. Yet contemplation is still the higher calling. But for Ignatius, God is found in all things, in both the contemplative and the active life. And his spirituality is distinctly that of a "contemplative in action." The Christian is called to discern the purposes of God in the world and in personal experience, and then to embrace that call and serve with joy and generosity. Ignatian spirituality, then, is very much the spirituality of the active life. Neither prayer nor service is secondary; the Christian is called to both. The dynamic of an authentic Christian life is found in the interplay of prayer and service, a relationship that is reciprocal. One's prayers are informed by apostolic work; and work is informed and sustained by prayer.

This meant, then, that Ignatius was not impressed with prayer in itself; longer prayers were not necessarily better or more effective. Rather, prayer was effective if it led to a genuine encounter with Christ, fostered humility, and sustained the demands of apostolic work and obedience in the world. Thus, Christians of other traditions have found a rich trove in Ignatian spirituality, particularly those who value its apostolic or active orientation marked by flexibility and adaptability, its radical Christocentric character (while Trinitarian), and the call to be contemplatives in action.

One of Ignatius's greatest gifts to the church is the small section of the *Spiritual Exercises* known as the Rules of Discernment. These "rules" are a classic distillation of ancient wisdom that has particular relevance to the process of decision making. The rules speak of desolation—those times in which it is wise not to choose, for one should only make decisions in consolation—and consolation that must be tested to confirm that it is truly from God.

Some have understandably shied away from the military motifs in Ignatian spirituality, reflecting not so much the gospel as Ignatius's feudal social environment. The downside of this is that this is a spirituality that has perhaps not sufficiently developed the passive dimensions of a full Christian spirituality. So one will find that spiritual directors, even those within the Ignatian tradition (Jesuits), will draw on other sources, such as John of the Cross and his emphasis on the dark night.

Nevertheless, Ignatian spirituality provides Christians today with a masterful articulation of the medieval spiritual life: to know, love, and serve Christ. And this is a spirituality from which Christians of all traditions can learn with much benefit.

See also Consolation and Desolation; Ignatius of Loyola; Sulpician Spirituality.

For Further Reading: J. English, *Spiritual Freedom* (1995); *Ignatius of Loyola: Spiritual Exercises and Selected Works,* CWS (1991); G. Traub, *An Ignatian Spirituality Reader* (2008).

Gordon T. Smith

Ignatius of Antioch (c. 35 – 110)

Bishop of Antioch and one of the most revered martyrs in the early church, author of seven epistles composed during his journey to martyrdom in Rome. What may be singled out as the main "components" of Ignatius's spirituality — martyrdom, Christology, hierarchy, the Eucharist, and spiritual pedagogy — are in fact intimately linked and inseparable. Ignatius sets forth an anti-Docetic spirituality, radically patterned on Christ's incarnation, death, and resurrection, and shaped by concern for the ecclesial community and by principles of spiritual pedagogy. The event of Christ's descent to earth and ascent after the resurrection — both simultaneously awesome and mysterious — dwarf any "heavenly mysteries" trumpeted by the various apocalyptic visionaries. In reaction to his opponents' claim to charismatic experiences, Ignatius states that interest in heavenly realities is not what makes one a Christian, and that such knowledge (to which he implicitly lays claim) is in any case not to be disclosed carelessly.

Overall, for Ignatius, spiritual experience must be shaped and validated by prior commitment to orthodox Christology, and by the sacramental and communitarian context of the hierarchical apostolic church. Far from opposing charisma and institution, Ignatius viewed the threefold order of ministry — in other words, the "institution" — as itself a spiritual reality. It is only in unity with the bishop that Christian believers will become, as he says, "God-bearers and temple-bearers and Christ-bearers." Of crucial importance is Ignatius's understanding of martyrdom as the beginning of true Christian discipleship, the fulfillment of his episcopal ministry, and, generally, the royal avenue toward Christlikeness. A line from his *Epistle to the Romans* remains indelible in Christian conscience: "I am the wheat of God, and I am ground by the teeth of wild beasts that I may be found pure bread."

See also Apostolic Fathers; Martyrdom.

For Further Reading: R. G. Hall, "Astonishment in the Firmament," in *The Jewish Roots of Christological Monotheism*, ed. C. Newman et al. (1999), 148 – 55; A. O. Mellink, *Death as Eschaton: A Study of Ignatius of Antioch's Desire for Death* (2000); W. Schoedel, *Ignatius of Antioch* (1985); R. D. Young, *In Procession before the World: Martyrdom as Public Liturgy in Early Christianity* (2001).

Bogdan G. Bucur

Ignatius of Loyola (1491 – 1556)

Founder of the Jesuits. Born Inigo Lopes de Loyola, Ignatius was raised a member of a ruling Basque family, loyal to the crown of Castille. As a young man, he served as a page to the king's court and there developed the sensibilities of sixteenth-century Spanish aristocracy, including themes that would be central to his life and writings: chivalry, knighthood, and discipline. Later, during the battle of Pamplona, his leg was injured, and when it was later rebroken and reset, he had to endure a prolonged period of recuperation.

During this time of convalescence, he experienced a profound conversion, influenced largely by his reading in *Life of Christ*, by Ludolph of Saxony, and *The Golden Legend* (on the lives of the saints). His resolve to follow in the ways of the saints led him to Montserrat, in eastern Spain, where he came under the influence of Benedictine monks, and from there to Manresa, not far from Montserrat, where he had a profound mystical experience of the Trinity and of the grace of God.

Following a visit to the Holy Land, Ignatius spent ten years in university studies, first in Spain and then in Paris; and while pursuing his studies, he formed a "society": a core group of fellow students who agreed to live a life of poverty, chastity, and apostolic service. Eventually this group agreed to call themselves the Company of Jesus, and in time they received papal approval for the formation of a new order (in September of 1540), the Society of Jesus (Jesuits). Ignatius became the first superior general.

Ignatius was the principle drafter of the Jesuit Constitutions, which were formally adopted in 1540. They emphasized the importance of discipline and self-denial, obedience to the pope and to one's superiors, and most of all, as their abiding theme, the central motif of the order: *ad majorem Dei gloriam*—"for the greater glory of God."

The impact of the order was felt on multiple fronts. Many Protestants assume that the primary work of the Jesuits was to counter the rise of Protestantism. But while they were certainly key players in that effort on behalf of the papacy, the primary impact of the order founded by Ignatius was felt in mission and education. Ignatius sent his colleagues and new recruits on missions around the world: the most famous being Francis Xavier (1506–1552), missionary to South and East Asia, and Matteo Ricci (1552–1610), who went to China. In addition, the order was influential in establishing schools and colleges. Indeed, the emphasis on education as a means of Christian mission is a Jesuit hallmark. Within a decade of their founding, over a dozen schools had been started; by 1626 there were more than four hundred Jesuit colleges, and by 1729 there were more than eight hundred. In the 17th and 18th centuries, a high percentage of educated people in Roman Catholic Europe studied in schools run by Jesuits.

And yet the greatest impact of Ignatius Loyola was through his particular understanding of Christian spirituality and how the spiritual life is sustained or cultivated. Jesuits were encouraged to cultivate an interior spirituality through meditation on the Scriptures and Ignatius's own *Spiritual Exercises*. This manual or guide to directed formal prayer reflects Ignatius's personal experience of contemplation and his conviction that the apostolic life in the world must be informed by a life of intimate consecration to Christ. Originally designed as a four-week retreat for Jesuit novices, the *Exercises* have been adapted for many settings, for both clergy and lay spiritual formation. The meditations and instructions are structured around four "weeks": the first week focuses on self-knowledge and sin; the second week on Christ as King and Lord; the third week on the passion; and the fourth week on the risen life of Christ. The *Exercises* draw on the imagination; strengthen the will; and integrate intellect and affect to foster self-knowledge, consecration to Christ, and joy in the world. It is then no surprise that many Christians, not only Roman Catholics, find them to be an invaluable guide to prayer.

Ignatius Loyola would no doubt say of himself that he was first and foremost a spiritual director. While as a young man he was not very effective as a spiritual guide, he recognized that he needed more theological training, and in time he truly became a premier mentor of the spiritual life—to guide and direct and, through wise counsel, form faithful and generous servants of the living Christ.

See also Consolation and Desolation; Ignatian Spiituality.

For Further Reading: *The Autobiography of St. Ignatius Loyola,* ed. J. Olin (1992); C. de Dalmases, *Ignatius of Loyola* (1985); *Ignatius of Loyola: Spiritual Exercises and Selected Works,* CWS (1991); J. O'Malley, *The First Jesuits* (1993).

Gordon T. Smith

Illumination of Scripture

Christian tradition generally has insisted that both a proper understanding of and appropriate response to the words of Scripture rely squarely on the guidance and illumination of the Holy Spirit, the ultimate author of Scripture (Matt. 22:43; Heb. 10:15). The study of Scripture should therefore always be undertaken in a spirit of prayerful dependence rather than with an air of self-sufficiency.

The dynamic of illumination is evident in Luke's gospel story of the resurrected Jesus and the two forlorn disciples on the Emmaus road (Luke 24:13–32). The unrecognized Christ "explained to them what was said in all the Scriptures concerning himself" (v. 27), such that their "hearts [were] burning within" them as he was "open[ing] the Scriptures" to them (v. 32). Similarly, the apostle Paul wrote that a veil shrouds human minds, preventing a proper reading of the Scriptures (2 Cor. 3:14–15). This "veil is taken away" "whenever anyone turns to the Lord"; further, "the Lord is the Spirit, and where the Spirit of the Lord is, there is freedom" (3:16–17)—including, presumably, the freedom to interpret Scripture christologically (4:3–6). This is corroborated in the gospel of John, where Jesus promises the coming of "the Spirit of truth," who "will bring glory to me by taking from what is mine and making it known to you" (John 16:13–14). Thus, the early church was warned to "test the spirits to see whether they are from God," and the criterion for testing is that "the Spirit of God ... acknowledges that Jesus Christ has come in the flesh" (1 John 4:1–2).

The notion of the illumination of Scripture, accordingly, relies on a confidence that God's Spirit reveals the reality of Jesus Christ to the believer within the context of the church. This assuredly need not lead to a unanimous interpretation. Augustine, for example, was confident that this christological hermeneutic, enlivened by the Spirit, allowed for differing interpretations of biblical texts—as long as "a reader believes what you, the Light of all truthful minds, show him to be the true meaning"—even though, surprisingly enough, "it may not even be the meaning the writer had in mind." The fundamental criterion for legitimate interpretation was the upbuilding of love for God and neighbor. Augustine's principle relies on Jesus' own insistence that all of the Jewish Scriptures "hang" on the Torah commandments to love God and neighbor (Matt. 22:36–40). We may be confident, taught Augustine, that the Spirit labors to illuminate our readings toward greater love.

More than a millennium later, that profoundly Augustinian thinker John Calvin also placed profound emphasis on the need for the Spirit's illumination of Scripture—an emphasis sustained in subsequent Protestant giants like John Wesley, Jonathan Edwards, and Abraham Kuyper. Though these leading thinkers all had a healthy appreciation for the critical place of the church in a Spirit-illuminated reading of Holy Writ, the more than occasional temptation among their followers—particularly those of a more mystical bent—has been to rely almost entirely on one's "individual experience" as the fundamental criterion for understanding Scripture. The Pietist tradition has been vulnerable to this temptation, although in its wisest moments it has insisted on the importance of reading the Scriptures with the help of the church's history and traditions of interpretation and application.

Recognizing the necessity of the church as the historical community of interpretation of the Scriptures need not and should not be positioned in a contrasting or competitive relation with the Spirit's illumination of the Word. If we believe Paul's characterization of the Corinthian congregation as "God's temple," the very dwelling place of God (1 Cor. 3:16), then we may be confident that the Spirit guides the church through history toward "the truth that is in Jesus" (Eph. 4:21).

See also Bible, Reading the; Light; Spiritual Reading.

For Further Reading: Augustine, *Confessions*, bk. 12; J. Calvin, *Institutes of the Christian Religion*, 1.7; A. Heron, *The Holy Spirit* (1983); A. Kuyper, *The Work of the Holy Spirit* (1900); B. Ramm, *The Witness of the Spirit* (1959).

Michael Lodahl

Image of God (imago Dei)

At the very outset, the Bible declares that humans — men and women equally so — are uniquely made in the image and likeness of God (Gen. 1:26–27). Many have observed that *likeness* modifies *image* here, underlining our similarity rather than absolute equivalency with God. Early in Christian history, Irenaeus suggested that image and likeness here should be differentiated. Thinking christocentrically, he identified the divine *image* especially with human understanding reflecting the Logos, while divine *likeness* denoted holiness or obedient moral conformity to the same Logos — incarnate in Jesus Christ, the Savior. Many subsequent interpreters (including Aquinas) affirmed the distinction, but with a significant twist. Being more philosophically focused than the earlier tradition had been, they taught that in the fall humanity lost its moral likeness to God but retained its *rational* nature in more or less pristine condition. This view emphasized a common structural element — rationality — as *the* way humans image God. Given this perspective and cultural views identifying emotions with weakness, many have unduly privileged intellect over affections (and other aspects of a fully embodied spirituality) when pursuing a God-intended humanity.

The *imago Dei* adheres to the essence of each human being, regardless of his or her level of competence (Gen. 9:6). It makes human life sacred and gives each person great dignity and worth. This is foundational to human rights; it has influenced the vision of Western civilization, and in the face of oppression it has been a dagger to the conscience and a goad to action. It has informed the efforts of Christians like William Wilberforce and Martin Luther King Jr. on behalf of victims of slavery and racial injustice; of Mother Teresa for the poor and destitute; and of Jean Vanier and Henri Nouwen in solidarity with persons with severe disabilities. This way of seeing should profoundly affect the spiritual consciousness of believers in their interactions with others, so that such relations are never exploitative or merely transactional, but have a tone of respect, grace, and gentleness, and are pervaded by awe of the capacity for eternity in others. To encounter another human being is always to encounter transcendence; this is a spiritually attuned consciousness that transforms all human meeting.

The image of God has more than one dimension. To begin, God is triune — experiencing within himself an eternal communion of the persons of the Godhead. So the image of God is a *social* likeness. It indicates an ability to reflect in our relations something of the interactive, loving mutuality within the Trinity.

God is also holy and glorious in his essence and powers. As image-bearers, humans also have the capacity to reflect this holiness and glory, for God has crowned humans "with glory and honor" (Ps. 8:5) and equipped them with qualities and powers that mirror his own, including conscience, virtue, reason, recollection, creativity, and authentic choice-making. God's human creatures are called to be holy and whole as he is.

And finally, God is a God who *acts* — who does things (like creating, sustaining, and redeeming). God's image in humans therefore has a *functional* side as well. It involves the capacity for creative work, responsible sovereignty over the rest of creation, and participation in God's own kingdom-building project on earth.

The spiritual journey toward the restoration of the tarnished (defaced but not erased) image of God begins with regeneration but subsequently involves numerous relational (connecting), moral (becoming), and functional (doing) transformations. The ideals of the fully restored image are embedded in human consciousness and reflected in our perennial yearnings, and expressed more definitively in the text of revealed Scripture. But the fully restored image of God is still discovered supremely, as it was once historically embodied, in Jesus Christ — who was simultaneously the fullest revelation of God's nature (Col. 1:15; Heb. 1:3) *and* the definitive paradigm for our own restored humanity (1 Cor.

15:45). Relationally, he was in full communion with the Father and in consistently self-giving associations with others; morally, he was able to resist sin in the power of the Spirit (Luke 4; Heb. 4:15); and functionally, his "food" was to align his life's efforts with the purposes of his heavenly Father (John 4:34; 5:19). In these ways, Christ revealed what it means to be fully human.

Normally it takes time for this Christlike pattern to be replicated in the lives of Christians. We hear the call to die to our selfish selves in many ways (Mark 8:34; Rom. 12:1; 2 Cor. 4:10; Eph. 5:1). As we practice this, we are transformed by the renewing of our minds to be more like Christ (Rom. 12:2; Col. 3:10). The Spirit uses other believers (Gal. 4:19) and Scripture (2 Tim. 3:16–17) to form the mind of Christ within us (1 Cor. 2). Though believers will not experience the fullness of this until the resurrection (Phil. 3:20–21; 1 John 3:2), they are sustained by the assurance that they are predestined to be conformed to the image of Jesus (Rom. 8:29). The *image of God* implies that humanity finds its identity, no less than its fulfillment, only in relationship to God.

See also Deification; Icons; Imagery; Images.

For Further Reading: H. Blocher, "Anthropology, Theological," in *Global Dictionary of Theology* (2008), 42–45; D. S. Cairns, *The Image of God in Man* (1953); D. Hall, *Imaging God* (1986); V. Harrison, *God's Many-Splendored Image* (2010); A. Hoekema, *Created in God's Image* (1986).

James L. Wakefield and Glen G. Scorgie

Imagery

Imagery, as it relates to the Christian faith, can refer to two distinct ideas: (1) figurative language and (2) mental images.

(1) Imagery, in the sense of figurative language, is very common throughout the Bible. For example, Psalm 29 uses the imagery of a storm to portray the power of God, and Jeremiah describes a potter working with clay as an aid to understanding God's role with the nation of Israel (Jer. 18:1–11). Shepherds with their sheep (Ps. 23; Ezek. 34; John 10:1–18) and vines with their branches (John 15:1–11) are used to depict God's relationship with humans. The imagery of city and garden recurs frequently from the beginning to the end of the Bible. New Testament writers use many different kinds of figurative language to describe Jesus, including the Lamb of God, the Stone rejected by builders, the Light of the World, and the Bread of Life.

Scholars disagree whether the masculine language for God, including the designation of God as Father, is figurative language or whether it reflects something inherent in the nature of God. Feminine and maternal language for God (Deut. 32:18; Isa. 46:3–4; Matt. 23:37) is often cited to argue that "Father" is only one way to view God.

Scholars have described the figurative language in the Bible using the overlapping concepts of metaphor, symbol, analogy, vision, and image. In addition to the biblical literature, these forms of imagery are common throughout history in many kinds of Christian writing. The use of figurative language communicates that God's power, love, and grace can be understood best by making multiple comparisons to aspects of human experience, with the understanding that none of them individually fully conveys a complete understanding of God's nature or power. In addition, the use of verbal imagery in writing about God and the Christian faith conveys the reality that God works in ways beyond our ability to describe logically.

(2) Imagery, in the sense of mental images, plays a significant role in many kinds of prayer. Christians often use the figurative language of the Bible to create a mental image that guides and enhances their prayers. In the ancient prayer form called Ignatian prayer, a mental picture of a biblical scene is used as a gateway to imagine one's participation in the story. Guided meditations, often used in retreat settings, rely on mental images. Typically, a guided meditation invites the listener or reader to

create a mental image of a scene from Scripture or a setting from nature or everyday life in order to have an inner encounter with Jesus. Another prayer form that relies on mental images is inner healing prayer; participants are usually asked to remember an incident from earlier in their lives and then invited to imagine Jesus entering into that incident, bringing healing, compassion, truth, and insight.

Because imagination, which is required for prayer using imagery, can lead people astray (Isa. 65:2; 66:18; Ezek. 13:2, 17), Christian practitioners who engage in guided imagery and inner healing prayer often pray for the guidance of the Holy Spirit and for God's protection against evil before leading a group or individual into prayer. Many individuals report significant encounters with God and profound healing through the use of guided imagery in prayer.

See also Icons; Image of God; Images.

For Further Reading: N. Frye, "Theory of Archetypal Meaning: Apocalyptic and Demonic Imagery," in *The Bible in Its Literary Milieu*, ed. J. Maier and V. Tollers (1979), 57–66; D. Jeffrey, *People of the Book* (1996); P. McCulloch, *Touching Jesus* (2001).

Lynne M. Baab

Images

Images are visual representations of people, animals, or objects. Images have played a significant role in Christian worship and faith development throughout most of Christian history. In preliterate times, images were viewed as powerful aids to memory, helping Christians remember biblical stories and principles. They were also viewed as a way to help Christians engage with the faith journey of biblical characters and saints, a means of participating in a pilgrimage without a physical journey. In the Eastern Orthodox churches, images of Jesus and the saints, called icons, have held a significant place in prayer and worship.

The second commandment forbids the creation and worship of images (Ex. 20:4–6). Generally, Christians have stressed that idolatry was the central point of the command. However, opposition to the use of images in worship and the devotional life, called iconoclasm, has erupted numerous times in Christian history. At the end of the medieval period, when the use of images had proliferated, iconoclastic voices were particularly strong. Many of the Reformers limited the use of images in worship and stressed the preaching of the Word, believing that the use of images without faith in Jesus Christ and an understanding of grace becomes superstition, idolatry, or magical thinking. John Calvin, for example, believed that images needed to be removed entirely from worship spaces.

As a result, many Protestant denominations have emphasized words and music, instead of images, in worship. A significant shift in recent decades toward a reaffirmation of the value of images in prayer and worship has resulted from numerous factors. More Protestant Christians have adopted devotional practices based in Roman Catholicism and Eastern Orthodoxy, both of which have a rich visual heritage, using images to nurture prayer, worship, and commitment. Christians are increasingly interested in exploring the significance of artistic gifts in the light of humanity's creation in the image of a creative God. Globalization and connections with the world church have enabled Western Christians to experience vibrant and culturally diverse expressions of faith in stories and images from around the world.

Trends in the wider culture have also encouraged a new emphasis on visual images. Visual artists, in company with all artists, are increasingly viewed as spiritual guides who have insight and wisdom to offer. Visual images have proliferated in the many new communication technologies of the late 20th and early 21st centuries. As a result of all these forces, Protestant Christians today are engaging with visual images, the visual arts, and visual artists in unprecedented ways.

The concerns of the Reformers and other iconoclastic voices from church history are still relevant. Because images—more so than words—can have multiple meanings, words and the Word are still deeply significant in making known the gospel of Jesus Christ. Biblical sensitivity and the willingness to learn from the Christian historical tradition can inform the wise and Spirit-led use of images in worship, prayer, and congregational communication.

See also Icons; Image of God; Imagery.

For Further Reading: W. Dyrness, *Reformed Theology and Visual Culture* (2004); idem, *Visual Faith* (2001); D. Freedberg, *The Power of Images* (1989); D. Morgan, *The Sacred Gaze* (2005).

Lynne M. Baab

Imagination

Modern conceptions of the imagination can be traced back to Romantic aesthetic theory of the early 19th century. This suggests from the start that whatever we say about imagination and spirituality, the discussion will necessarily include a consideration of the role of the arts in spirituality. Additionally, it is helpful to be aware that imagination has two important aspects: (1) it is a mental faculty that we all possess; (2) it provides certain materials (such as works of art) that can foster the spiritual life.

Embedded in the word *imagination* is the word *image*, and this is foundational for any understanding of imagination. Imagination is a mental faculty by which we "image forth" truth, and by which we experience life. Immanuel Kant expressed the essential idea when he wrote that "we have a faculty … by which we judge forms without the aid of concepts." The imagination complements the rational intellect, which is adept at processing abstractions and propositions. In terms of modern "brain theory," the imagination is "right brain" discourse.

To illustrate this point, the sixth commandment of the Decalogue tells us propositionally, "You shall not murder." The story of Cain's murder of Abel (Gen. 4:1–16) embodies that same truth in the concrete form of characters performing a set of actions, with no propositional statement or command attached. Psalm 19:1 asserts a proposition about nature when the poet tells us that "the heavens declare the glory of God." We experience that same truth in a sensory or "imaged" form when we go for a walk on a beautiful day.

Here, then, is one dimension of the imagination in regard to spirituality; we possess spiritual knowledge through concrete experiences and mental images as well as through rational concepts and intellectual constructs. We live by a world *picture* as well as a world *view*. Spiritual experience consists not only of theological concepts, such as God's attributes and the commands asserted in the Bible, but also of images like light and darkness and of stories such as Ruth and Boaz and Mary and Martha. The imagination gives us spiritual knowledge in the form of "right seeing." When asked to define *neighbor*, Jesus did not provide a "left brain" definition but instead told a parable in which we see neighborly behavior in action.

Another look at the word *imagination* reveals the word *imagine*. To imagine is to call into being something that did not exist up to that point, and/or that does not exist at all in the empirical world around us. The imagination opens up a world of alternate possibilities to the familiar world. At this point, a fruitful analogy between the mental faculty of imagination and the religious concept of faith emerges. Both imagination and faith enable us to experience and embrace a reality that transcends the physical world around us. Of course, analogy is not the same as identity; we cannot baptize every act of imagination as being a manifestation of Christian faith. Still, we can discern the potential of our imagination to become the avenue by which we cultivate faith in unseen spiritual realities.

Most Christian traditions of meditation incorporate the imagination in some form. The first of three steps in medieval contemplative traditions was to "compose the scene" — that is, imagine oneself present at an event narrated in the Gospels. Richard Baxter's Puritan classic devotional book *The Saints' Everlasting Rest* (1650) is partly an exercise in imagining what heaven is like.

In addition to being a faculty of perception and a way of knowing, the imagination produces the arts and enables us to assimilate them. The imagination enables people to experience beauty, whether in works of art or in nature. In turn, the link between beauty and a sense of the numinous has nearly always been an important part of spiritual experience (see, e.g., Phil. 4:8).

If we extend this, for the past two centuries, scholars who theorize about the arts have enthroned the imagination as the human faculty that produces works of art, literature, and music. Applied to the spiritual life, the arts provide the materials for spiritual experience. While artistic experience is not automatically spiritually laden, it can always become such when a person makes devotional use of the arts and offers them to God in a spirit of worship. This is especially true when the subject matter of artistic works is explicitly Christian.

The Bible itself is a work of imagination by virtue of its literary nature. The characteristic way in which biblical writers express truth and beauty is not the theological abstraction or intellectual proposition but the literary embodiment of human experience in an artistic form. This is most immediately seen in the prevailing genres that make up the Bible. There is, of course, some expository writing in the Bible in the form of historical chronicles, treatises, and discourse material. But approximately 80 percent of the Bible is made up of distinct literary genres, such as story, poem, vision, epistle, proverb, and oratory. The Bible consistently "images" experience and truth, and whenever people use the Bible as part of spiritual experience, the imagination plays a key role.

The imagination did not escape the effects of the fall. It carries the same permanent possibility of expressing what is untrue and perverse that the rea-

son, emotions, and will possess. Whether we translate Genesis 6:5 as "imagination of the thoughts" (KJV) or simply "inclination of the thoughts" makes no difference to the meaning of the verse: the thought life of fallen humans can be evil as well as good. Yet the abuse of something that God created good does not cancel out its goodness in principle and in potential.

See also Beauty; Creativity.

For Further Reading: C. S. Lewis, "The Language of Religion," in *Christian Reflections* (1967); L. Ryken, *The Liberated Imagination* (1989); idem, ed., *The Christian Imagination* (2002); M. Warnock, *Imagination* (1976); W. Wiersbe, *Preaching and Teaching with Imagination* (1994).

Leland Ryken

Imago Dei

See **Image of God.**

Imitation of Christ

Virtuous leaders inspire others to emulate them; so, too, Jesus and Paul inspired early Christians to be like themselves. "You became imitators of us and of the Lord," Paul wrote (1 Thess. 1:6–7), while exhorting believers to be imitators of God and to emulate Christ's self-giving love (Eph. 5:1–2). Imitation was not to be limited to external behavior; it was also to embody the same mind, heart, and humility that Christ displayed in his incarnation and crucifixion (Phil. 2:5–11). In authentic worship, a powerful incentive toward imitation is to catch a vision of God's holiness and to find oneself drawn toward it in self-forgetful adoration. Paul echoed this connection by comparing believers' worship of Christ with Moses encountering God on the mountain. Like Moses, we descend the mountain where communion has occurred with our faces radiating a reflected glory (2 Cor. 3:17–18). Followers of Christ have always practiced imitation in many historically and culturally conditioned ways. Learning various nuances of the paradigm can help us gain distance from our own biases and learn from imitation practiced in other traditions and eras.

When the twelve apostles were confronted by Jesus' invitation to follow him, they left their vocations in first-century Palestine and followed him in a mission that initially they profoundly misunderstood. For the Twelve, becoming like Jesus was intermittent and incremental, though they lived with him in continuous apprenticeship — a requirement of the Jewish disciple-teacher relationship. But Jesus was physically unavailable to the apostolic churches, which experienced instead the Spirit's presence in ways unknown before Jesus' death. These differences, and the sharp distinction made by liberal scholars between the Christ of faith and the Jesus of history, prompted a twentieth-century German school to argue that imitating Christ and following Jesus were radically separate realities. More recent scholarship has argued for substantial continuity between the two, noting that the language of following Jesus in the Gospels became that of imitating Christ in the Epistles.

In his letters to churches, Paul described believers as being "in Christ" — a term that implied an obligation to imitate Christ's example and teaching *as well as* to participate in his life. Jesus' teaching in John's gospel, particularly the vine metaphor, also denoted imitation and participation. The branches (Jesus' disciples) participate in the True Vine (Jesus), *and* they stay joined to the Vine through abiding and prayer in the same way that Jesus stayed in communion with his Father — doing and saying only what he saw and heard his Father doing and saying (John 5:17; 12:49; 15:1 – 8). In the Sermon on the Mount, Jesus taught that his disciples were to be perfect like their heavenly Father (Matt. 5:48). Essential to such imitation is prayer, by which the virtues Jesus commended flow from the Father to the disciples who are given the heart righteousness asked of them. As Peter later wrote, "He has given

us very great and precious promises, so ... you may participate in the divine nature" (2 Peter 1:4).

In the patristic age, martyrdom became *the* preeminent way to imitate Christ. Early Christians expected that following Jesus would end in martyrdom, and many gave their lives rather than sacrifice to Caesar. Yet some renounced Christ and betrayed fellow believers. Debate ensued over whether such ones could repent or be restored to fellowship. From AD 150 on, a system of merit and penance emerged that allowed for genuine repentance to be demonstrated while denying assurance of salvation in the present (1 John 5:11 – 13). Such confidence was suspended until after death — when ample virtue had been attained. This theological structure undergirded all subsequent forms of imitation until the Protestant Reformation. As persecution faded, the focus changed to imitating Christ's virtues and eradicating the seven deadly sins — which became a preoccupation of the desert fathers and mothers. The monastic tradition inspired by the desert tradition preserved this form of imitation, as did the ascetic branch of spiritual theology.

Fascination with Christ's humanity in the medieval era gave rise to meditation on specific incidents in Jesus' life and imitation of particular details, such as Jesus' poverty, homelessness, celibacy, and preaching — these in reaction to the church's accumulation of wealth and power and lack of spiritual vitality. Francis of Assisi took a literal approach to imitating Christ: adopting his first-century dress, experiencing the stigmata, and wanting to be buried naked. Later both the Protestant and Catholic Reformations adopted less literal and more inward patterns of imitation drawn from the *Devotio Moderna*. This late medieval movement stressed heart humility fostered by affective meditation on the cross in devotional practices made accessible to the working masses. It also produced Thomas à Kempis's *The Imitation of Christ* (c. 1450), which has gone through thousands of editions and greatly influenced Catholics and Protestants — especially Jesuits and Puritans.

Yet the Protestant tradition developed a different theological foundation for imitation. God's acceptance of sinners at the moment of repentance and faith in Christ's merits destroyed the idea of human merit and penance and restored the assurance of salvation. Luther held that imitation did not bring about adoption; rather, becoming a child of God made imitation possible. Still, a sanctification (i.e., imitation) gap has plagued Protestantism, one to which many have tried to respond, including Charles Sheldon in his popular book *In His Steps* (1896). But Sheldon's question, "What would Jesus do?" has been criticized as fruitless if not coupled with the question "*How* would Jesus do it?" Dallas Willard thinks Sheldon's question is reductionist and short-circuits imitation without the question of means, which leads to imitating Jesus' communion with his Father and realizing this communion as if Jesus occupied believers' roles today.

Imitating Christ, then, is not solely a matter of copying his virtues or his behaviors, and it is certainly not about mimicking every incidental cultural detail of his life. The capacity to imitate derives from God's multifaceted grace—divine initiative, power, and embrace—that enfolds believers into the communion of the triune God. Believers access this grace by looking to Jesus—back to his earthly life, now to his risen life, and ahead to his physical appearing when "we shall be like him, for we shall see him as he is" (1 John 3:2). Imitation is the eschatological goal and simultaneously the gracious means by which believers are being transformed into Christ's image.

See also Cross, Experience of the; Discipleship; Suffering.

For Further Reading: G. K. Beale, *We Become What We Worship* (2008); M. Bockmuehl, *This Jesus* (1996); J. Johnson, *Invitation to the Jesus Life* (2008); E. Peterson, *The Jesus Way* (2009); P. Sheldrake, *A Spirituality and History* (1992); E. J. Tinsley, *The Imitation of God in Christ* (1960); N. T. Wright, *After You Believe* (2010).

L. Paul Jensen

Incarnation

The word *incarnation* derives from the Latin translation of John 1:14, "The Word became flesh." In an act of supreme condescension, the second person of the Trinity who is beyond space and time left heaven's glory and, entering our world, assumed a sinless human nature through the virgin birth. Concerning the incarnation, the apostle Paul wrote that God sent "his own Son in the likeness of sinful humanity to be a sin offering" (Rom. 8:3 TNIV). John attested to Christ's coming in human flesh to expiate sins and destroy the devil's work (1 John 3:5, 8; 4:14). As expressed by Calvin, "God's natural Son fashioned for himself a body from our body, flesh from our flesh, bones from our bones, that he might be one with us." In the narrow sense, the incarnation refers to Christ's entry into the world at his first advent. In the broader sense, it pertains to the Son's entire life and ministry on earth, from his virgin birth to his ascension to heaven with his divine, human nature.

The Western tradition stresses Christ's sacrifice on the cross for sins. The Eastern tradition stresses the humanity of the incarnate and risen Christ as the way to God. Thus, the Word incarnate potentially brought humanity into union with the divine, transfiguring the race into the new humanity. As expressed by Athanasius in his *The Incarnation of the Word of God*, "The Word became man that we might become god." Adopting a functional view of the incarnation, liberal theology claims that Jesus was a mere man indwelt by the Logos, who served as an inspired teacher and ethical prophet. On this showing, Jesus was not the God-man, but God-in-man. Liberation theology teaches that Christ became incarnate to engage oppressive human institutions and powers and to free the poor and marginalized from exploitation and injustice in what amounts to a social spirituality.

Since Christ took on human flesh in time and space, the incarnation demonstrates that God values highly the material creation. Physical reality is not inherently evil as claimed by Greek metaphysical dualism. Rather, God is found in everyday realities: in the painting of an artist, the care of a physician, and the compassionate act of a friend. By virtue of the incarnation, suggested William Temple. Christianity in a manner is the most materialist of the world's religions. The incarnation, moreover, establishes that all persons, as images of God, possess high dignity and significance. In terms of human destiny, the Word made flesh imparts everlasting spiritual life to all who believe (John 5:24; 10:10). The incarnation, furthermore, furnishes the highest motive for evangelism and mission. Even as the Father sent his Son into the world to recover the lost, so Jesus summons his followers to publicize abroad the good news of salvation (John 17:18).

From the incarnation derive important features of Christian spirituality. The fact that God in Christ left the galaxies to dwell on planet Earth enables us to know and experience his great love (John 16:27; 1 John 4:9–10). The Son who clothed himself with human flesh makes his home with believers (John 14:23), as does the triune God (1 John 4:12, 15–16), resulting in intimate communion. Believers, moreover, know experientially the comfort and power of the Spirit sent by the incarnate and risen Son (John 14:26; 15:26). By virtue of the Son's intimate relation with the Father, the prayers of his servants are heard and answered (John 14:13; 16:23). To deepen spiritual life and bear lasting fruit, believers abide in Jesus, drawing spiritual sustenance from him (John 15:4–7). Following Jesus' example, believers live in the world while not identifying with the world's system (cf. John 17:11–15). Like the Master, disciples serve God's kingdom purposes while rejecting the world's values and vices (1 John 2:15–17). The incarnate Lord, furthermore, serves as a model that his servants imitate for spiritual authenticity (Eph. 5:1–2). Finally, since the Word made flesh displays the Father's glory, believers experience a legitimate Christian mysticism defined as an intimate, transforming encounter with the invisible God that transcends full rational comprehension and verbal articulation. Through the eyes of faith, disciples "see" the Father (John 14:9) and the glory of the preincarnate Christ (John 17:24). Mysticism requires a body to fulfill its destiny (Underhill).

The incarnation of the Son, then, is a reality of supreme importance to Christian identity and spirituality. According to John, anyone who denies Christ's coming to earth in human flesh is a "deceiver," a "liar," and "the antichrist" (1 John 2:22; 4:3; 2 John 7). Remove the incarnation, argued C. S. Lewis, and there is nothing Christian left.

See also Body; Cross, *The Kenosis;* Resurrection.

For Further Reading: D. Baillie, *God Was in Christ* (1948); M. Erickson, *The Word Became Flesh* (1991); M. Green, ed., *The Truth of God Incarnate* (1977); M. Lucado, *God Came Near* (1987); J. Orr, *The Christian View of God and the World* (1948).

Bruce A. Demarest

Indifference

See *Apatheia;* Contentment.

Inge, William Ralph (1860–1954)

Provocative English Anglican dean. Inge was born in Crayke, Yorkshire, to an ecclesiastical family. His father was an Anglican curate and Oxford provost, and his maternal grandfather was an archdeacon in northeast England. After an illustrious educational career, Inge eventually became dean of St. Paul's Cathedral, London, in 1911. During this time, Inge earned his nickname "the gloomy dean" for his darkly witty social criticisms, which he voiced as a regular columnist for the *Evening Standard*. He expressed caustic views about the health of democracy in the modern world, and he supported the arts and animal rights. He believed that humane treatment of "our distant cousins in fur and feathers" had fallen far short of the divine intention, and he strove to reconcile religion with evolutionary progression.

Outspoken and theologically liberal, Inge was a prolific writer, producing influential works in the areas of Christianity, contemporary ethics, and Platonism. One of his most important theological contributions was his work *Christian Mysticism* (1899), which helped to reignite a Western interest in its theme. Inge approached mysticism from an academic perspective, attempting to deduce its true nature by examining the experience of religion in various cultures, over time. Inge is also remembered for his attempts to reconcile Christianity and Platonism, having twice given appreciative Gifford lectures on the philosophy of Plotinus. In some ways his work echoes themes and sensibilities of earlier seventeenth-century Cambridge Platonists. His other writings include *Personal Religion and the Life of Devotion* (1924).

For Further Reading: A. Fox, *Dean Inge* (1960).

Sarah G. Scorgie

Inner Healing

Inner healing is a form of prayer counseling practiced in many Christian denominations. Its founder is Agnes Sanford, and prominent practitioners include Dennis and Rita Bennett, Francis and Judith McNutt, Leanne Payne, John and Paula Sandford, David Seamands, Ruth Carter Stapleton, and more recently, Ed Smith of Theophostic Prayer Ministry.

There are some commonalities in inner healing practices. A prerequisite is that the counselees must be believers of Jesus Christ. Inner healing is based on the psychodynamic belief that present psychological and relational dysfunctions are rooted in past traumas and wounds. Counselees are asked to recall the most painful memories of the past. Then they are encouraged to invite either Jesus or the Holy Spirit to go to the past memories (or distorted lies) to heal these pains. Some practitioners,

such as Ed Smith, take demonization seriously, and the McNutts consider renunciation of past occultic involvement central to the success of inner healing.

The practitioners of inner healing are not required to receive formal education and do not claim to be mental health professionals. Most have some informal training, and some are certified to preserve the integrity of their programs. Although mental health laws and code of ethics do not apply to inner healing practitioners, there is an assumption that practitioners will adhere to the moral standards of Scriptures. Inner healing utilizes basic listening skills in making assessments of problems. Some practitioners actively lead counselees to renounce the occult or seek forgiveness. Counselees are encouraged to use visualization to see Jesus ministering to them in their past traumas. The inner healers facilitate the process, and the counselees describe their experience with Jesus. Others, such as Theophostic counselors, use prayer by asking Jesus to speak the truth to distorted lies about the past.

Opponents of inner healing criticize this mode of healing for its faulty theology and practices. Some see inner healing as hypnotic induction, psycho-heresy, occultic, memory abusive, and New Age. Significant controversial issues include teachings on repressed and false memories related to childhood abuse, soul ties, in utero regression, and dialogue with spirits.

On the other hand, many believers have testified to the effectiveness of inner healing, claiming release from their psychological traumas and experiencing a closer and growing relationship with Jesus and his people. Inner healing, like all healing, is ultimately God's prerogative. When practiced within the confines of Scriptures, it may be an aspect of God's redemptive and healing work with his people (James 5:13–16).

See also Care of Souls; Counseling; Health and Healing.

For Further Reading: A. Sanford, *The Healing Light* (1983); D. Seamands, *Healing for Damaged*

Emotions (2004); E. Smith, *Healing Life's Hurts through Theophostic Prayer* (2005).

Ben K. Lim

Intercession

Intercession is prayer in which praying people mediate between people in need and God who can answer their needs. Moses provides a classic biblical example of intercession. After God's people turned from him to worship the golden calf, God intended to destroy them. But Moses pleaded, "Turn from your fierce anger; relent and do not bring disaster on your people" (Ex. 32:12). And the Lord answered Moses' prayer.

In his high priestly prayer in John 17, Jesus offered an example of intercession in which he prays not only for his friends, but also for future generations "who will believe in me through their message" (v. 20). Intercession is the privilege and responsibility of every believer. In 1 Timothy 2:1, Paul urged that "requests, prayers, intercession and thanksgiving be made for everyone" (cf. Eph. 6:18) and set the example by interceding for various churches. Intercessors today often use his prayers (e.g., Eph. 3:14–20; Phil. 1:9–11; Col. 1:9–17) as models for their own. Intercession can be offered for large-scale matters such as evangelization or revival. Reformer John Knox is famous for pleading, "Give me Scotland or I die!" The eighteenth-century Moravian church is noted for its one hundred years of nonstop intercession for global evangelization. The Moravians' example inspired the intercession that preceded later revivals in America and England, which in turn led American evangelist D. L. Moody to conclude that "every work of God can be traced to some kneeling form."

However, noted theologians have made it clear that intercession for individuals is also crucial. Eighteenth-century British Anglican William Law believed that praying for individuals cultivates the intercessor's heart: "There is nothing that makes us love a [person] so much as praying for him." And during the Nazi occupation of his nation, Norwegian Ole Hallesby observed, "Our prayer for a spiritual awakening will without question be most effective if we take up the work of interceding for certain individuals in particular."

When believers make intercession, they join the fellowship of Jesus, who "lives to intercede" for his own (Heb. 7:25), and the Holy Spirit, who "intercedes for the saints" (Rom. 8:27). Intercession is so important to God that he graciously provides an alternative when believers don't know how to pray. In such instances, as the apostle Paul explained, "the Spirit himself intercedes for us" (Rom. 8:26). Intercession, patterned after the mediating work of Christ, provides a remarkable opportunity to transcend self-interest and participate in the good purposes of the sovereign God for others. An unintended outcome is that by enlarging an intercessor's own heart, persistent intercession can also be personally transformative.

See also Petition.

For Further Reading: J. Dawson, *Intercession, Thrilling and Fulfilling* (1997); W. Duewel, *Mighty, Prevailing Prayer* (1990); D. Eastman, *Love on Its Knees* (1989); A. Murray, *The Ministry of Intercession* (1898); D. Sheets, *Intercessory Prayer* (1996).

Cynthia Hyle Bezek

Interfaith Encounter
See **Chapter 30.**

Internet

The Internet describes a category of digital networked technologies, such as email, the World Wide Web, and social networking software. It is the "network of networks" that allows people to share information and interact with others in ways that eliminate previous constraints of time and geography. Since the 1980s, the Internet has also become a space where religion and spirituality are discussed and engaged.

A variety of expressions of religion can be found online, from cyberchurches to online Bible study resources to Christian social networking sites. From these different forms, several dominant narratives of use have surfaced. First, the Internet may be seen as a spiritual medium, facilitating spiritual experience for individuals and communities, and so it is utilized as a *spiritual network* or a place where spiritual encounters are made and activities performed. The Internet may also be seen as a sacramental space that can be set aside for religious ritual or activities, so that the Internet becomes a *worship space*. For some the Internet is primarily used as a tool for promoting a specific religion or set of beliefs, and so the Internet becomes a *missionary tool* for making disciples or converts. The Internet can be viewed as a technology to be used for affirming one's religious community, background, or theology; here the Internet can be seen as helping an individual build and maintain a particular *religious identity* by connecting into a global, networked community of believers. Finally, for some, the Internet is viewed as a *functional technology*, used to support the social practices or work-related tasks valuable to the religious community.

Similar to the debates emerging around technology in general, there have been a range of critiques as well as calls for embrace of the Internet by Christian groups. Some warn of how the Internet might be a threat to moral purity and child safety, as well as genuine Christian community, communication, and reciprocity. Conversely, others advocate the Internet's potential to reinvigorate religious communication and make faith relevant to contemporary society. Many of the concerns raised by Christian leaders are related to fears that Internet use will call churchgoers to "plug in, log on, and drop out" of face-to-face religious participation. However, research on religious use of the Internet does not support these assumptions.

Many studies have found that practices and beliefs of Internet Christianity are closely connected to offline Christianity and its related communities. As the Internet becomes increasingly embedded in our everyday lives, it offers new opportunities to transform the performance of spiritual disciplines of prayer, study, and the sacraments. It also raises the question of whether the Internet is shaping our spiritual consciousness and how we live our lives, or whether our relatively intact spirituality is infusing the Internet.

For Further Reading: H. Campbell, *Exploring Religious Community Online* (2005); idem, "Spiritualising the Internet: Uncovering Discourse and Narrative of Religious Internet Usage," *Heidelberg Journal of Religion on the Internet* 1, no. 1 (2005), online; Q. Schultze, *Habits of the High-Tech Heart* (2002); A. Zukowski and P. Babin, *The Gospel in Cyberspace* (2002).

See also Technology and Spirituality.

Heidi Campbell

Iona Abbey

Iona Abbey is an ancient cloister church emblematic of Celtic Christianity. In 563 the Irish monk Columba planted a monastic community on Iona, a small island off the southwest coast of Scotland. A succession of talented abbots made Iona Abbey the center of a monastic network dispersed around the Celtic regions of western Britain and Ireland, distinguished for its piety, learning, and zeal for the evangelization of pagan Scotland and Northumbria. But as the papacy extended its political and religious reach into Britain, Iona's influence waned before Roman insistence upon liturgical and doctrinal conformity, especially after the landmark Synod of Whitby (664). During the Middle Ages, the abbey was taken over by the Benedictines. It fell derelict during the Reformation and remained so until 1938, when a Scottish minister, George MacLeod, realized his vision of a spiritual retreat center out of the ruins. The historical fog enveloping Celtic Christianity that frustrates clear-sighted reconstructions of its essence and form has made Iona a symbol pliable to theological yearnings that may or may not reflect the actual spiritual habits of the Celts of old. Post-Reformation Scots looked back at Iona as an evangelical and non-Episcopalian forerunner of their own Presbyterian state church. The ecumenical Iona Community founded by MacLeod claims to embody the holistic spirituality of Celtic Christianity through its commitment to social justice, care of creation, and life in community. In the tradition of monastic hospitality, pilgrims seeking rest and rejuvenation are still welcomed to the restored abbey. Through the widespread dissemination of the community's liturgies, songs, and devotional resources, Iona once again serves as the spiritual center of the Celtic dispersion — now reaching far beyond the original pale.

See also Celtic Spirituality.

Todd Statham

Irenaeus (c. 130 – 200)

Bishop, apologist for orthodoxy, biblical theologian. Born in Asia Minor, Irenaeus moved to Lugdunum in southern Gaul, where he was appointed bishop in 177. Two written works survive: *Against Heresies* expounded and criticized Gnostic theology, and *Demonstration of the Apostolic Preaching* was a brief catechetical work.

Against the Gnostics, Irenaeus developed a comprehensive biblical theology and defended an unbroken tradition of teaching, which he deemed guaranteed by the apostolic succession of bishops and summed up in the "canon of truth." Irenaeus's opposition to Gnosticism derived from his belief that it threatened apostolic faith, not from a negative spirit. Thus, he was tolerant of, and even attracted to, Montanism, and he urged the bishop of Rome to tolerate those who celebrated Easter according to the date of the Passover, even though Irenaeus personally disagreed with them.

Anthropology was fundamental to Irenaeus's spirituality. He taught that Adam was created by God from real material earth, in the image and likeness of God, and animated by the breath of life. He was relatively perfect but was still morally, spiritually, and intellectually a child, with a long way to go to reach the resemblance of his Maker. That process of development was interrupted by the fall, which disordered Adam's whole nature and that of the human race who fell with him. Fallen humans can neither reform themselves nor attain salvation, which was accomplished by the Son of God.

The fall that occurred in the first Adam is remedied through "recapitulation" by the second Adam. Through the economy of salvation, God accustomed his people to live as strangers in the world and to follow his Word, but the climax of the economy of salvation was achieved in the incarnation, by which humans are enabled to see and to participate in God, while God is accustomed to live in humans. At every point of Christ's life, he reverses the disobedience of Adam so that those who are gathered up in Christ regain what was lost in Adam, becoming the likeness and image of God. Although perfection comes only after resurrection, union with the incarnate Son and with his Spirit is experienced in this life through the operation of faith and love through the sacraments.

Irenaeus gives us a grand vision of humans as created good but immature, of the Word incarnate as making gloriously visible what we are designed to be, of the manner in which the Word recapitulated every stage of human life, so that those who participate in him are transformed into the very likeness of God, the creatures in whom God's own glory is most fully manifested. From the perspective of Irenaeus, "the glory of God is a living man and the life of man is the vision of God."

See also Incarnation; Gnosticism.

For Further Reading: R. M. Grant, *Irenaeus of Lyons* (1997); E. Osborn, *Irenaeus of Lyons* (2001).

Terrance L. Tiessen

Irving, Edward (1792–1834)

Enigmatic Scottish divine. Irving shot to fame in the 1820s from the pulpit of the Scots' Church, London, drawing the curious and the critical alike to hear a thundering message of the imminent return of Christ to judge an apostate generation and divided church. Under suspicion for promoting prophecy and tongues in worship as well as seeking the restoration of the apostolic church's fivefold office (Eph. 4:11), the Church of Scotland defrocked him in 1833 for teaching that the Son of God took on *sinful* human nature at the incarnation. He died in 1834, exhausted and already marginalized within the Catholic Apostolic Church, which was born out of his ministry. Irving's deep impact is markedly disparate. His controversial and easily misunderstood teaching on the humanity of Christ is now reassessed as a significant contribution to Christology, motivated in part by a spiritual concern to assure troubled souls of God's saving love for the whole of humanity to the uttermost depths of its plight. His premillennialism left an apocalyptic trace on subsequent evangelicalism even as his high sacramental and liturgical piety inspired discontent with the oracular austerity of traditional evangelical and Reformed worship. All the while, Pentecostal historiography honors him as a church father of the charismatic movement.

See also Charismatic Spirituality.

For Further Reading: G. W. P. McFarlane, ed., *Edward Irving* (1996); H. C. Whitley, *Blinded Eagle* (1955).

Todd Statham

J

Jacopone da Todi (1230–1306)

Franciscan mystic. Jocopo Benedetti, nicknamed Jacopone ("Big Jim") by common folk who thought him eccentric, was, next to Dante, the greatest poet of his time. Born to an affluent family of Todi, Jacopo was highly educated and became a successful lawyer. He married a beautiful noblewoman whose tragic death at a party jolted him out of his vanity, and he became a penitent. As such, he acted out bizarre behavior to make a moral point, such as putting a packsaddle on his naked body and a bit in his mouth and going about on all fours imitating an ass in the town square. He was uninhibitedly countercultural, and many people considered him mad.

After ten years, Jacopone joined the Franciscans. As he became prominent in the order, he came into conflict with the majority of brothers who no longer embraced poverty. Eventually he suffered five years of solitary confinement at the hands of his nemesis, Pope Boniface VIII. In prison he underwent deep spiritual refinement and wrote a famous poem describing his experience, *"Que farai, fra Iacovone?"* ("What will you do, Fr. Jacopone?"). His poems, written in the Lauda genre of the time, though spiritually sophisticated, were simple and easily sung among the general populous, and thus remembered for generations. Jacopone's "madness" is best attributed to a heart overflowing with love and contemplative ecstasy, and he is deeply revered in mystical literature.

See also Franciscan Spirituality; Poverty.

For Further Reading: L. Oliger, "Jacopone da Todi," in *CE*; G. T. Peck, *Fool of God* (1980); *Jaco-*

pone da Todi: Lauds, CWS (1981); E. Underhill, Jacopone da Todi (1919).

John E. Worgul

James, Book of

James's spirituality is anchored in an understanding of God as Creator, the Father of the heavenly lights (1:17). According to James, the Creator God is the source of all wisdom (1:5), holds in special regard those the world has not rewarded (2:5), yearns for our friendship (4:5 – 6), and will be our final Judge (4:12; 5:9). James knows God's will from the Scriptures (our OT) and from the teachings of Jesus. He writes with the purpose of persuading his readers to live single-mindedly as friends of God (2:23; 4:4), assuming that, as God's friends, they will receive God's perfect gifts to enable life (1:17): wisdom from above (1:5; 3:17 – 18), the word of truth (1:17 – 18), the implanted word (1:21), grace (4:6), and exaltation (4:10). However, James is certain that belief in God will always result in actions that demonstrate that the believer shares God's point of view; these actions could be considered spiritual practices, but they include all the habits of our daily living. James calls such unity of belief and action "perfection" (1:4, 22 – 25; 2:14 – 26); we might now call it a life of integrity or personal authenticity. He is confident that this perfection is readily available from God if believers will but ask (1:5 – 8; 5:13 – 18). James knows that integrity of life must be actively pursued — the book is full of commands — and that pursuing the things of God also means avoiding the pursuits of those who do not love God (1:27; 4:1 – 10). In particular, friendship with God will be demonstrated in two important ways: the use of one's money and the careful control of one's words. These two are important because their abuse destroys the community, which James is particularly concerned to preserve. James speaks strongly against envying or showing partiality to the rich (1:9 – 11; 2:1 – 17; 5:1 – 6), and

for caring for the poor, especially the widow and orphan (1:27). He warns of the destruction done by words of anger (1:19 – 21), and calls for caution in speaking and teaching (1:26 – 27; 3:1 – 12; 4:11 – 12; 5:12). James anticipates that anyone who pursues friendship with God will encounter trials and temptations, and even false wisdom (1:2 – 4, 12 – 16; 3:15 – 16; 5:13 – 18). He reminds his readers that these obstacles do not come from God but are to be endured on the path toward God. Friends of God hope for fullness of life with God, for themselves (the crown of life, 1:12) and for the world (2:5; 5:7 – 11). And they will be rewarded if they draw those who wander from the truth back to God (5:19 – 20), the very task James himself has attempted in this brief letter.

See also Good Works.

For Further Reading: P. Davids, "Controlling the Tongue and the Wallet," in *Patterns of Discipleship in the New Testament*, ed. R. Longenecker (1996), 225 – 47; P. Hartin, *Spirituality of Perfection* (1999); L. Johnson, *Brother of Jesus, Friend of God* (2004); E. Tamez, *The Scandalous Message of James*, trans. J. Eagleson (2002).

Jo-Ann Badley

James, William (1842 – 1910)

American psychologist and philosopher. Born in New York, the son of Henry James, a Swedenborgian theologian, he earned a medical degree from Harvard, teaching anatomy there before turning to psychology. His work *The Principles of Psychology* (1890) was foundational for the development of laboratory psychology in the United States. He later shifted his attention to philosophy and became one of the most influential American philosophers of his time, developing and popularizing pragmatism as a distinctly American philosophy.

In addition to empirical science, religion was also one of James's main interests, and the tension between the two greatly influenced his philosophy.

Two of his major books, *The Will to Believe* (1897) and *The Varieties of Religious Experience* (1902), vigorously supported the vitality and validity of religious experience in the lives of devotees against what he called the limited perspective of empirical science. One of the major themes in *Pragmatism* (1907) was the empirical support this philosophy could provide for religious experience.

James tended to discount the issues that occupied philosophical theologians and focused more on the experiential realities, the doubts and aspirations of living individuals. Though not developed in a precise fashion, James theorized a finite, pantheistic, immanent God, belief in whom meets humans' most basic needs. He argued that such belief provides an essential basis for meaning that leads the truly faithful into the "fruits of genuine religion" or "saintliness." Using Matthew 7:20, James insisted that the authenticity of religious life should be evaluated according to its "moral helpfulness," as evidenced by the "the best things history has to show" in the lives and actions of the saintly.

James's work has left an indelible mark on the psychology of religion and continues to influence the study of moral development. Students of Christian spirituality can benefit from James's work and his rigorous defense of humanity's right to believe, as well as the empirical support he offered for the legitimacy of religious experiences. His concern for the life experiences, including doubts, of genuinely religious people can be a source of encouragement to those struggling in their spirituality. There is also great benefit in the rich variety of theological perspectives and religious traditions represented in James's studies.

For Further Reading: R. Burgt, *The Religious Philosophy of William James* (1981); J. Carette, ed., *William James and the Varieties of Religious Experience* (2005); B. Perry, *The Thought and Character of William James* (1948); C. Taylor, *The Varieties of Religion Today* (2002).

John R. Lillis

Jane Frances de Chantal (1572 – 1641)

Cofounder (with Francis de Sales) of the early modern Catholic women's congregation the Visitation of Holy Mary. Born in Dijon, in the wake of the French Wars of Religion, the second child of a provincial magistrate, Jane received an education preparing her for marriage. At the age of twenty, she wed Baron Christophe de Rabutin de Chantal and happily took up the responsibilities of that position. Following the birth of their youngest child, her husband was mortality wounded in a hunting accident, leaving the young widow desolate. Despite her family's expectations that she remarry, Jane began to conceptualize her life anew, desiring to serve God in a radical way. In 1604 she met Francis de Sales, the charismatic bishop of Geneva, and began a spiritual direction relationship with him that gradually ripened into a remarkable spiritual friendship and collaboration.

Although her guide first counseled her not to strain beyond her widowed circumstances, they eventually conceived an innovative religious congregation designed for women such as Jane. After making provisions for her surviving children, in 1610 the two cofounded the Visitation of Holy Mary in the town of Annecy in Francis's diocese. In contrast to the austere reformed orders of the day, the Visitation emphasized external simplicity and moderation and focused on interior asceticism in the gentle Salesian spirit. "Live Jesus!" was the congregation's motto. It attracted women with a deep love of God who, because they were widows, frail of health, or handicapped, would not be admitted to other religious orders. The Visitation took its inspiration from the scriptural story of Mary's visit to her cousin Elizabeth (Luke 1:39 – 56).

Mother de Chantal (as she was called) was noted for her wise and gentle style of spiritual guidance through which she sought to "win hearts" for the love of God and neighbor. After her mentor's death in 1622, she became the chief architect of their burgeoning community, establishing practical rules to realize the spiritual vision they shared. In the process, she gifted the tradition with her own spirit. Unlike her friend, Jane de Chantal did not write for publication yet left a voluminous correspondence that gives insight into early modern Catholicism as well as the foundational years of the Visitation.

See also Francies de Sales.

For Further Reading: E. Stopp, *Hidden in God* (1999); idem, *Madame de Chantal* (2002); W. Wright, *Bond of Perfection* (2001); idem, "Jane de Chantal's Guidance of Women," in *Modern Christian Spirituality*, ed. B. Hanson (1990), 113–38.

Wendy M. Wright

Jansen, Cornelius (1585–1638)

Roman Catholic bishop of Ypres, Belgium, and father of Jansenism. At the Catholic University of Leuven, Jansen was confronted with what he felt was a conflict between the Pelagian tendencies of the Jesuit theologians and those more explicitly of Augustinian heritage, choosing to associate himself with the latter. In his writings, especially in his posthumously published book simply entitled *Augustine* (1640), Jansen was particularly impressed by Augustine's understanding of the radical nature of human depravity and the necessity of divine grace and predestination. Although he was a critic of Jesuit theology and held closely to Augustinian versions of sin and grace, he was not any closer ecclesially to the Protestants. Practically, this focus on radical sin and the divine grace of predestination, which he believed echoed Augustine's, led him to promote a spirituality that condemned the moral laxity in some parts of the Catholic Church and encouraged greater attentiveness to purity before God.

His opponents in the Catholic Church, however, conflated his teaching with that of the sixteenth-century Protestants, which led to a formal condemnation of some of his teaching by the papacy. In France his followers, most notably those in the Port-Royal monastery, were forced to sign a form confessing their error. Among other effects, this requirement led Blaise Pascal, a supporter with links to Port-Royal, to write the famous *Provincial Letters* (1657), in which he harshly attacked the Jesuits for their immoral ethical casuistry. Further, Pascal and others argued effectively that the Jesuit attack was not so much on Jansen as it was on Augustine, something no theologian would ever contemplate.

Despite the formal condemnation by the Roman Catholic magisterium, his books and those of his followers continued to have a wide readership. Further, some of those who were excommunicated by the Roman Catholic Church constituted their own denomination, the Old Catholic Church, which continues to exist to our day.

See also Augustine of Hippo; Pascal, Blaise; Will, Human.

For Further Reading: W. Doyle, *Jansenism* (2000); L. Kolakowski, *God Owes Us Nothing* (1995); A. Sedgwick, *Jansenism in Seventeenth-Century France* (1977).

Jason Zuidema

Jerome (342–420)

Patristic ascetic and biblical translator. Born into a wealthy Christian family as Sophronius Eusebius Hieronymus, Jerome was afforded the opportunity to study extensively in Rome. Afterward he traveled broadly, exploring myriad Christian communities and important Christian sites. During a three-year stay with a community of hermits, Jerome developed an enduring interest in Christian asceticism that shaped his later life.

In AD 382 Jerome was appointed to a secretarial position under Pope Damasus, who commissioned him to rework and synthesize the varying Latin translations of the Bible under close textual scrutiny to the original Greek. Beginning with the Gospels, Jerome launched an arduous translation task that would continue for the rest of his life. In the process, Jerome learned Hebrew and translated from the Hebrew OT, not the Greek Septuagint as was customary. This translation of the sacred text known as the *Latin Vulgate* is his most lasting legacy. After the death of Damasus in 385, Jerome traveled to the Holy Land and established two monasteries near Bethlehem.

Heading the monastery dedicated to men, Jerome began writing prolifically. He composed monastic rules for both monasteries and tenaciously worked through biblical commentaries on nearly every book of the Bible. His commentaries employed a variety of exegetical methods, ranging from a very literal Antiochian process to the typological and allegorical method practiced by the Alexandrian school. Jerome also wrote extensively as a polemicist defending orthodox interpretations of Scripture and beliefs. Amid these defenses Jerome advocated a strict form of asceticism and fiercely condemned spiritual abuses. Jerome emphasized practices of renunciation and encouraged rigorous principles of study and prayer. Jerome's judicious textual criticism and implementation of biblical principles in ascetic life established a credibility that propelled his many works and methods into common use throughout the rest of Christian church history.

See also Asceticism.

For Further Reading: S. Rebenich, *Jerome* (2002); M. Williams, *The Monk and the Book* (2006).

Joshua L. Hickok

Jesus, Name of

In Scripture the name stands for the person (Acts 5:40, 41; 3 John 7). This association carries varied significances. Since Jesus sustains a special relationship to the Father, believers who act in Jesus' name act as representatives of Jesus and have the same access to God (Eph. 2:18). This is the significance of praying in the name of Jesus (John 16:23–24). At baptism the name of Jesus is invoked on the one baptized (James 2:7), implying that he or she now belongs to Jesus (Acts 2:38). The name of Jesus is also closely associated with healing and miracles (Acts 3:6, 16); it brings salvation (Acts 4:12) and elicits humble adoration (Phil. 2:9–10). From this association a whole tradition of devotion to the name of Jesus has developed.

Given the power associated with the exalted name of Jesus, it is not surprising that a certain mystique quickly developed around the name itself. Also, whenever Christians begin to emphasize "heart religion," a prominent place is given to personal devotion to Jesus. This tendency develops naturally from the fact that only the second person of the Trinity takes on a form to which humans could readily relate. Thus, devotion to the name of Jesus is spread across many different Christian traditions, e.g., in the medieval "affective" mysticism of Bernard of Clairvaux and Thomas à Kempis. It became formalized in Bernardine of Siena (1380–1444), "the Apostle of the Holy Name."

Similar trends can be found in Protestant Pietist movements since the 17th century. A strong Jesus-centric piety, which gave special prominence to the name of Jesus, could be seen in many segments of evangelical Christianity in the 19th century, for example, in A. B. Simpson and E. W. Kenyon. This emphasis on Jesus' name became a central feature of the Oneness Pentecostals in the early 20th century.

Devotion to the name of Jesus takes many forms. A simple form is to repeat the name of Jesus affectively or to sing songs of passionate devotion addressing Jesus directly, both of which induce deep feelings of devotion. Many such songs were written by holiness and Pentecostal songwriters in the 19th and early 20th centuries, such as A. B. Simpson's "Himself" and the Oneness preacher G. T. Haywood's "Jesus, the Son of God." In hesychasm, one of the key elements is the use of the Jesus Prayer ("Lord Jesus Christ, Son of God, have mercy on me, a sinner"), which is repeated over and over again, not to evoke feelings but as a means to dispel discursive thought and achieve "stillness" in preparation for mental prayer. An outgrowth of Jesus devotion is the practice of "deliverance" commonly found among Pentecostals and charismatics, in which one suspected of being demon possessed is asked to say, "Jesus is Lord" (cf. 1 Cor. 12:3).

See also Authority.

For Further Reading: I. Hausherr, *The Name of Jesus* (1978); D. Reed, *"In Jesus' Name": The History and Beliefs of Oneness Pentecostals* (2008); *The Way of a Pilgrim*, trans. H. Bacovcin (1992).

Simon Chan

Jesus Christ
See **Chapter 6.**

Jesus Prayer

The Jesus Prayer, also called the Prayer of the Heart, is one of the oldest extrabiblical prayers and an example of a formal "arrow" prayer directed heavenward. It is adapted from the cry of the two blind men in Matthew 20:30–31 (cf. Luke 18:38) and the tax collector's prayer in Luke 18:13. It was introduced into Christian worship by the Eastern branch of the church as early as the 4th or 5th century. The classic version of the Jesus Prayer reads, "Lord Jesus Christ, Son of God, have mercy on me, a sinner." The prayer often is abbreviated to "Lord Jesus have mercy on me" or simply "Lord have mercy." To a lesser degree, the Jesus Prayer has been employed in Roman Catholic devotion, frequently as, "Lord, make haste to help me. Lord, make speed to save me."

Orthodox churches in particular believe that those who recite the prayer, either silently or aloud, fulfill Paul's injunction in 1 Thessalonians 5:17 to "pray continually" or "pray without ceasing" (NRSV). Beyond invoking the name of Jesus and confessing the essence of the gospel, the Jesus Prayer is said to facilitate inward peace, purity of thought, and remembrance of God. Continual recital of the prayer leads to internalizing its message such that one's life becomes the prayer. The Jesus Prayer is commended as a transformational exercise not only for monks, but also for ordinary believers. Against critics that decry repetition of formal sentences, advocates of the prayer cite Psalm 136 where the sentence, "His love endures forever," occurs twenty-six times.

The Eastern church father John Chrysostom advises, "Whether eating, drinking, sitting, serving, traveling, or doing anything, to unceasingly cry: 'Lord Jesus Christ, Son of God, have mercy on me,' that the name of the Lord Jesus Christ, descending into the depths of the heart, may subdue the pernicious serpent and save and quicken the soul." In the nineteenth-century spiritual classic, *The Way of a Pilgrim*, an anonymous Russian peasant journeyed across his vast homeland reciting the prayer learned from a spiritual director of an Orthodox monastery. In Orthodox monastic practice, the prayer is spoken rhythmically and repeatedly, often accompanied by a prayer rope and prostrations before the cross.

In the last hundred years, the Jesus Prayer has become increasingly popular among Christians of many denominations. As a classical spiritual exercise, the Jesus Prayer has been associated with the silent contemplation involved in hesychasm, although avoiding some of the latter's mystical excesses.

See also Breath Prayer; Centering Prayer; Hesychasm; Russian Spirituality.

For Further Reading: L. Gillet, *On the Invocation of the Name of Jesus* (1985); J. Talbot, *The Way of the Mystics* (2005), 185–97; *The Way of a Pilgrim*, trans. H. Bacovcin (1992).

Bruce A. Demarest

Jewish Spirituality

Biblical religion and classical Judaism had their own unique mix of organized religious practices and individual spiritual experience; and though some recent interpreters have tended to force Jewish spirituality away from Jewish religious practice toward mystical experiences, classical or modern, we are on safer ground to find the roots of Jewish spirituality in its religious forms.

Attempts to define Jewish spirituality often fail to discover anything particularly Jewish. So, for example, in the introduction to *Jewish Spirituality* (1986), edited by Arthur Green, spirituality is "striving for life in the presence of God." A more explicitly Jewish approach might look either to Jewish concepts like "holiness" (Heb. *qedušah*), "righteousness" (Heb. *ṣedeqah*), "covenant love" (Heb. *ḥesed*), "faithfulness, truth" (Heb. *'emunah*), "repairing the world" (Heb. *tikkun 'olam*), or even to Jewish practices such as a kosher lifestyle. In other words, Jewish spirituality, to be authentically Jewish, will overlap with Jewish religiosity, admitting that the latter spans a wide range, from Orthodox piety to modern secular identification with parts of one's Jewish heritage. Despite recent attempts, like that of Eliezer Diamond, to ground Jewish spirituality in an ascetic tradition, and a long history of Jewish mystical life, it is probably safe to say that the dominant traditions of Judaism through the ages would ground spirituality in the divine presence in this world, and thus find spiritual expression in a life lived well here and now, as opposed to a focus either on the afterlife or an escape from life.

By any reckoning, Jewish spiritual life has its roots in the Hebrew Scriptures (*tanak*), particularly the Torah, or first five books of Moses. Basic are belief in the one God of the Shema (Deut. 6:4) and observation of the Ten Commandments, or more broadly, the concept of *halakhah* (the "way"), best thought of as a collection of norms of conduct, drawn from both the written (*Torah*) and oral law. *Halakhah* is often illustrated but never supplemented by narratives known collectively as *Haggadah*, in which aspects of *halakhic* behavior are expounded or illustrated by experiences of life.

These were given systematic form in the Talmud, a collection of rabbinic interpretations that defined much of Judaism for the first millennium of the Christian era and beyond, often mediated by the central communal figure of the local rabbi, who was in turn hugely influenced by the great teacher-rabbis whose thinking dominated European Judaism from medieval times to the present. Even Kabbalah, the dominant Jewish mystical tradition that came to focus with publication of the *Zohar* in the 13th century, was in its original forms widely used to interpret *Torah* and *Talmud* in relation to its esoteric views of God and creation.

Alongside the kind of Jewish spirituality that finds its roots in Pharisaic Judaism and the rabbinic traditions outlined above, there have from biblical times been Jews, and Jewish movements, committed to a less literal interpretation of Torah. New Testament readers are familiar with Sadducees, a "reformed" tendency within the Judaism of the day. By the 17th and 18th centuries, Jewish thinkers like Benedict Spinoza and Moses Mendelssohn were wrestling with questions of reason and revelation, and these would become important parts of a discussion that far transcended, and often offended, more Orthodox Judaism. As in what would become liberal Protestantism, the spirituality of these groups often appealed to the prophetic tradition of social justice, not infrequently seeing this as an ethical but less legalistic approach to life in the presence of God. Although not accepted in many of the rabbinic centers of European Jewry, a merely ethical Judaism in the "prophetic" tradition (Mic. 6:8: "act justly and . . . love mercy") has been immensely formative within Western Jewish circles from the Renaissance to the present. If there has been a downside, it has been the alienation of these "ethical (and sometimes fairly secular) Jews" from traditional synagogue life. Reformed Judaism has only partially taken up the slack, while many modern Jews have sought spiritual guidance from sources far removed from traditional Jewish life.

In addition to the enormous challenge of the

European Renaissance and later Enlightenment, Judaism has faced the challenge of assimilation into the dominant Western Christian culture. Although Jews once were also a prominent minority in many Muslim lands, assimilation was never really an option as it was for Jews in post-Enlightenment Europe, where Jewish intellectual life became part of the mainstream.

For much of Judaism, both orthodox and secular, the defining moment in modern history came with Adolf Hitler's attempt to eliminate the Jews as a people. A strong belief in God and divine protection for his ancient people had always been fundamental to Jewish life and practice, but with the slaughter of six million Jews in the most enlightened society of Europe, these beliefs were profoundly shaken. Even traditional orthodox Jews found themselves wondering whether Jewish life and spirituality would need to find their way in a world where God, at least in traditional forms, was dead. Dealing with this has become the great challenge to Jewish spiritual and intellectual life in the post – World War II world.

Just as the Holocaust (*Shoah*) has challenged the deepest beliefs about God and the world, so the establishment of a Jewish state has provided continued hope. While only a small percentage of worldwide Jewry has made *"aliyah"* (a return) to live in Israel, the very existence of "the Land" has been a rallying point for Jewish spiritual life. If the land exists, the people continue, and for many it is but a short step to affirm that God is still active. Thus, Israel and the Holocaust have become twin pivots for virtually all Jewish spiritual movements and aspirations in the modern world, a vivid reminder that Jewish spirituality has always been primarily communal.

See also Covenant; Suffering.

For Further Reading: E. Diamond, "The Way of Torah as Askesis," *Cross Currents* 57, no. 4 (2008): 563 – 77; L. Greenspoon and R. Simkins, eds., *Spiritual Dimensions of Judaism*, Studies in Jewish Civilization 13 (2003); "Judaism," *Encyclopedia of Judaism*, ed. J. Neusner et al. (2000); L. Kushner, *Jewish Spirituality* (2001); Y. Lachower and I. Tishby, *The Wisdom of the Zohar* (1989); B. Raskas, *Jewish Spirituality* (2004); R. Sands et al., "Spirituality and Religiousness among American Jews," *International Journal for the Psychology of Religion* 18, no. 3 (2008): 238 – 55; G. Scholem, *Kabbalah* (1974); idem, *The Messianic Idea in Judaism and Other Essays on Jewish Spirituality* (1995).

Carl E. Armerding

Joachim of Fiore (1135 – 1202)

Apocalyptic spiritual writer, called for reform in the church and promulgated a threefold interpretation of history that influenced the Middle Ages and captured the imagination of generations since. Born in Calabria, Italy, Joachim took vows around 1171 at the monastery in Corazzo, where he was elected abbot and led the monastery into the Cistercian order. Soon he withdrew to a hermitage, encouraged by Pope Lucius III to record his apocalyptic notions. By 1191 Joachim left the Cistercians to establish the monastery of San Giovanni in Fiore. Although aspects of his teaching were eventually condemned, Joachim counseled kings and popes and founded the Florensian Order, recognized as one of the four pillars of the church by Lateran IV.

In his letters and three major works, the *Book of Concordance*, the *Exposition of the Apocalypse*, and the *Ten-Stringed Psaltery*, Joachim summoned the church to repentance as he warned of imminent judgment, sketching diagrams of the impending tribulation by Saladin and the eventual papal Antichrist. Believing that the interpretation of the book of Revelation had been revealed to him, Joachim viewed John's apocalypse as the key to the past, present, and future. Seeking to unlock mysteries regarding end times, uncover numeric symbolism, and elucidate the harmony of biblical themes, he saw all of history configured in three overlapping dispensations reflecting the Trinity. The age of the Father corresponded to the OT, belonging to married people. Beginning with King Josiah, the age of the Son incorporated the NT, emphasized grace, and continued to Joachim's day, centered on the clergy. The age of the Spirit, predicted to commence around 1260, would remain rooted in Scripture and would be characterized by freedom of the Spirit. This final *status* would be inaugurated by a new monastic order of traveling preachers and another of contemplative monks interceding for the world. Within a decade of Joachim's death, two orders of mendicant friars emerged, the Dominicans and Franciscans, spreading revival across Europe. Over the centuries, various movements identified themselves as Joachim's new spiritual men; however, some of these groups, such as the Spiritual Franciscans, became elitist and schismatic.

Joachim makes fascinating reading for contemporary Christians. While guarding against divisiveness and recognizing the limitation of end-times schemas, many will resonate with Joachim's apocalyptic fervor. All will recognize his emphasis on repentance, God's sovereignty over history, and the Holy Spirit's empowerment for worldwide evangelization.

See also Apocalyptic Spirituality; Second Coming.

For Further Reading: *Apocalyptic Spirituality*, trans. B. McGinn (1979); B. McGinn, *The Calabrian Abbot* (1985); M. Reeves, *The Influence of Prophecy in the Later Middle Ages: A Study of Joachimism* (1969); idem, *Joachim of Fiore and the Prophetic Future* (1999).

Glenn E. Myers

Johannine Spirituality

John's remarkable attention to the Spirit in his gospel signals his interest in the spiritual formation of his readers. And yet to grasp John's interests, we need to read his gospel, understanding that it was written not simply to describe conversations in antiquity, but it was written with us in mind. John anticipates that we will be reading him. He provides prompts that help us along (6:1) and even translations (1:41) for those who are not bilingual. And as a narrator, he departs from his story to explain things to us (2:20–22). So when we read a text such as 4:24, "God is spirit, and his worshipers must worship in spirit and in truth," we need to realize that this is a message not simply for a Samaritan woman, but for the reader John knows will be studying his gospel. This shift in hermeneutical perspective is essential if we are to distill the deeper meanings in John's narrative.

Therefore, when we talk about John's notion of spirituality, we are right to distill it from the narratives in his gospel. John provides many direct teachings from Jesus about the Holy Spirit, particularly in his farewell (14:17, 26; 15:26; 16:13–15). He provides stories about personal rebirth (3:1–21), worship (4:7–26), Spirit-baptism (1:33), and the mystical consumption of Christ (6:52–63). He also explains how the release of the Spirit must await Jesus' glorification (7:39), and in his death and resurrection we have hints that the Spirit is suddenly active (19:30; 20:22).

John also underscores the seriousness of spiritual formation because he understands the dramatic difference between this world and the life of God. John has what we call a *dualistic* framework. Darkness and light, falsehood and truth, above and below—such twinned concepts remind us that despite God's profound love for this world (3:16), the world itself has succumbed to sin and is antagonistic to God's rule. And therefore we must choose. Adopting a spiritual life that loves God and his Son does not simply mean joining an addendum to one's life. *It is a reorientation, a reformation of thinking and living.* Battle lines have been drawn. Followers of Jesus embrace the light, flee the darkness, love the truth, and recognize that life in this world will indeed involve a struggle with forces that will either wish to sabotage Christ and his people (10:10) or cynically subvert the truth (recall Pilate's query: "What is truth?" [18:38]).

However, it is within John's wider narrative of people's engagement with Christ that we learn the broad concepts of spiritual encounter and formation as John would have them. Two concepts shape John's understanding. First, disciples must have a personal encounter with Christ that leads to faith; and second, this faith must be wed to an understanding of what is believed.

These themes are modeled almost as a template in the first disciples in the gospel (1:35–51). In Judea Jesus meets a potential disciple named Andrew. His posture is important: Andrew is "seeking" Jesus, "following" Jesus, is eager to "remain" with Jesus; and when he meets Jesus, he is told to "come and see." Andrew then finds his brother Peter, who then is told to do the same: he, too, must come and see Jesus. Next, in Galilee Jesus meets Philip, who also sees Jesus, "follows," and then finds his friend Nathanael, who is told to "come and see." This is the vocabulary of spiritual encounter for John. Disciples must come, see, follow, and remain with Jesus, and this language is threaded throughout the gospel (cf. Jesus' encounter with the Greeks in 12:20–26). Of course, more could be said of this encounter. Disciples who have this encounter must realize the intimate knowledge Jesus has of them (1:50) and how it is an encounter that will transform (3:3; 14:23–24).

But John also thinks that spirituality without knowledge presents another sort of danger. Likely the heresy that is addressed in John's first letter took root in a community that had deep spiritual experiences (1 John 2:20) but had little theological understanding (1 John 4:1–2). Therefore, John's stories of encounter and transformation always include symbols of knowledge. In his opening chapter, one key sign of discipleship includes a comprehensive catalog of titles for Jesus (Rabbi, 1:38; Messiah, 1:41; Son of God, 1:49; et al.) telling us that followers of Christ must know whom they follow. What you believe is as important as belief itself, which explains why John also offers us such explicit theology in his gospel.

These twin motifs—encounter and knowledge—run through the gospel consistently, and they form John's answer to spirituality. The Samaritan woman's story has all the marks of spiritual formation. Ominously, the Nicodemus story does not. For John, Christian faith and discipleship are not simply driven by spiritual experience. John urges that spirituality *must* be accompanied by a thoughtful, intellectually sound understanding of the content of belief. But the reverse is also true. A spirituality that is merely cognitive will miss the mystical features of Christian life. In a word, Johannine spirituality weds ecstasy ("The wind blows wherever it pleases.... So it is with everyone born of the Spirit" [3:8]) with theology ("Don't you believe that I am in the Father, and that the Father is in me?" [14:10]). It is for this reason that the Spirit is called "the Spirit of truth." Spirit (twenty-four times) and truth (twenty-five times) appear throughout John's gospel like a plumb line: we must experience Jesus in the Spirit, and we must know the truth. To miss either is to succumb to some of the classic difficulties the church has seen throughout its history.

See also Knowledge of God.

For Further Reading: M. Coloe, *Dwelling in the Household of God* (2007).

Gary M. Burge

John XXIII (1881–1963)

Convener of the Second Vatican Council. Angelo Giuseppe Roncalli was born to a large family in Italy. In 1892 he entered seminary and began the practices of keeping a spiritual journal and of receiving spiritual direction. In 1896 he was admitted to the Secular (meaning that the members live their lives in the world) Franciscan order and took vows in 1897. Subsequently, Roncalli served as a chaplain and a bishop and eventually represented the Vatican as a member of an apostolic delegation. In 1953 he was made a cardinal, which made him able to vote for, and eligible to be elected, the next pope. Upon the death of Pius XII in 1958, Roncalli was elected pope and took the name John XXIII.

Although his pontificate lasted less than five years, it was made memorable by his calling of the Second Vatican Council (1962 – 1965). That event led to significant changes in the worship and lived experience of the Roman Catholic Church. In 2000 John XXIII was beatified, which is the first step in the process of being made a saint, by the Catholic Church.

Pope John XXIII's pontificate was marked by visiting the imprisoned and the sick and contributing to Catholic social teaching with *Mater et Magistra* and *Pacem in Terris*, which reflect both his concern over the Cold War and his openness to the larger world. His contribution to Christian spirituality includes his stress on, teaching about, and personal attentiveness to compassionate ethical engagement with the social needs and perils faced by humanity. Moreover, his confident and winsome encouragement of greater Catholic involvement in the larger world context reminded the church that authentic Christian spirituality can thrive within human culture rather than necessarily be removed from it. At a personal level, his legacy includes *Journey of a Soul* (1999), an autobiography distilled from his lifelong discipline of recording his spiritual reflections.

See also Vatican II.

For Further Reading: Pope John XXIII, *Essential Writings* (2008); idem, "Mater et Magistra," *Catholic Social Thought* (1992); idem, "Pacem in Terris," *Catholic Social Thought* (1992).

Mary M. Veeneman

John of Damascus (c. 655 – c. 750)

Byzantine monk, theologian, apologist, and hymnographer, who wrote under Arabic rule at the Mar Sabba monastery near Jerusalem. John of Damascus embodied the inseparability of doctrine, asceticism, and divine worship in the Eastern Christian understanding of theology. He was the author of the *Fount of Knowledge*, a three-part compendium of philosophy, heresiology (including a treatment of Islam as Christian heresy), and doctrine. The doctrinal treatise, entitled *The Exact Exposition of the Orthodox Faith*, offers a clear and systematic presentation of patristic theology, synthesizing the main lines of Eastern tradition: the Creed of Nicea and Constantinople, the asymmetric Christology of Chalcedon, and the distinction between divine *ousia* and divine *energy* implied by the Sixth Ecumenical Council; an optimistic anthropology in which the distinction between "image" and "likeness" in the Genesis narrative offers the beginning and the ultimate goal of humanity's journey toward deification; an acute awareness of the postfall brokenness of humanity, leading to the understanding of Christian existence as ascetic struggle for gradual purification, illumination, and union with God; the Pseudo-Dionysian apophatic and kataphatic theologies; and the firm belief that the expected transfiguration of matter at the eschaton is anticipated by the sacraments of the church, verified in the lives of the saints, and visually represented in the icons.

John of Damascus's spirituality is perhaps most evident in his hymnography, much of which is still currently used in Eastern Orthodox churches, and in his *Three Apologies* in defense of the icons. In his defense of the icons — for which John was condemned and vindicated posthumously at the iconoclastic council of 753 and the Seventh Ecumenical Council (787), respectively — John of Damascus demonstrates that by revering the icons, believers worship the one represented in the icons. Moreover, he insists that matter is a suitable vehicle for God's active presence (*energies*). Reverence for the icons thus becomes a test case for one's commitment to the reality of the incarnation and to the horizon of deification. In the Damascene's famous words, "I do not worship matter; I worship the God of matter, who became matter for my sake and deigned to inhabit matter, who worked out my salvation through matter."

See also Icons.

For Further Reading: S. Griffith, "John of Damascus and the Church in Syria in the Umayyad Era," *Hugoye: Journal of Syriac Studies* 11 (2008), online; A. Louth, *St. John Damascene* (2002); D. Sahas, *John of Damascus on Islam* (1972).

Bogdan G. Bucur

John of the Cross (1542–1591)

Influential Spanish mystic. Born in relative obscurity, John of the Cross became leader of the Discalced ("barefoot") Carmelite friars and provided some of the most profound reflections in spiritual theology of how God transforms the believer's soul through love developmentally over time and how the believer can cooperate with these varying movements of the Spirit's love. Born Juan ye Depes in a small town near Avila, Spain, into a noble but poor family, John was raised by his widowed mother, attended Jesuit college, was received into the Carmelite order, and attended the Carmelite College of San Andres in Salamanca. There he studied the theological and spiritual traditions of the Carmelites and was ordained in 1567. He continued his studies at the University of Salamanca, one of the great centers of Thomistic study at that time. He was persuaded by Teresa of Avila, then in her fifties, to join the Discalced Carmelites, a reform movement within the Carmelites, and it was at this time that he changed his name from John of St. Matthias to *Juan de la Cruz* (John of the Cross). In 1571 he founded a house of studies for friars preparing for ordination. From 1572 to 1577 he assisted Teresa in being spiritual director to her and the nuns at the motherhouse of Teresa's reform. During this period, John was imprisoned by the Calced ("shoed") Carmelite friars, which began an ongoing controversy over the nature of monastic reform and the spiritual life. During the next decades, John would write some profound spiritual poetry and in-depth commentaries on the spiritual life. He died in 1591, having been banished to the remote monastery in the province of Andalusia, Spain.

John's greatest contributions to the church are his poetic expressions of the spiritual life and experience of God, along with rigorous and thoughtful commentaries on these poems and the spiritual life (spiritual theology), which were fueled by his intense training in the thought of Thomas Aquinas and the Carmelite tradition. His efforts in "spiritual theology" attempt to integrate a biblical-Thomistic theology of spirituality with (1) empirical reflections on the ministry of the Spirit indwelling the human spirit, (2) the various ways the Spirit works developmentally through time in the believer's life, and (3) the psychological dynamics that hinder the believer's cooperation with the Spirit — with an aim to helping others better discern and cooperate with the Spirit's work. His *Ascent of Mount Carmel* and *Dark Night of the Soul* form parts of a work intended to assist the believer in the spiritual life, from the "beginner" stage when God provides consolation to encourage faith and efforts in spiritual disciplines, to "dark nights of the soul" in which God withdraws consolation in order to draw nearer to the soul with truth and love, to stages of "illumination" in which the Spirit is experienced as present by faith and love, to full "union" in which the believer in this life and the next experiences the full extent of the love of God, being filled up with the fullness of his presence (Eph. 3:16–19). In particular, *The Ascent of Mount Carmel* articulates the tension between the new self in Christ and the unhealthy passions and attachments of the former manner of life, and sketches out a program to shed the old self and put on Christ. The path of detachment or *nada* (nothing) is the process of the human soul letting go of its various idols of the heart in order to attach to God in love.

If the *Ascent* represents the believer's part in transformation, the *Dark Night of the Soul* portrays the Spirit's work, particularly during "dark nights" or those seasons in the spiritual life when God initiates a profound work of purging or purifying the human spirit of various sins and vices of the heart to open the heart for the filling of the Spirit and union with

God. Whereas seasons of consolation or the felt presence of God are intended by God to encourage the believer in directing the heart to God through the spiritual disciplines, dark nights or desolation, times of spiritual dryness or the felt absence of God, are intended by God to be a mirror revealing what is in the heart of the believer. God is not withdrawing his presence from the believer during times of desolation, but only the felt consolation in order to draw near to love the believer in the truth of the sins of the heart to fill one with God's presence. While the *Ascent* encourages how the believer is to cooperate with the Spirit in the dark nights (the "active nights"), the *Dark Night of the Soul* provides an understanding of the Spirit's work during these times (the "passive nights"). The culmination of John's reflections on Christian mysticism and the soul's preparation for knowing the fullness of the love of God and indwelling presence in union can be found in his *The Spiritual Canticles* and *The Living Flame of Love*.

In 1926 John of the Cross was declared to be a doctor of spiritual theology by the Roman Catholic Church. His influence has grown in the 20th century with the increased attention to spiritual formation within Catholicism and Protestantism, including evangelicalism.

See also Carmelite Spirituality; Dark Night; Teresa of Avila.

For Further Reading: J. Coe, "Musings on the Dark Night of the Soul," *Journal of Psychology and Theology* 28, no. 4 (2000): 293–307; T. Dubay, *Fire Within* (1989); E. Howells, *John of the Cross and Teresa of Avila* (2002); K. Kavanaugh, *John of the Cross* (1999); idem, trans., *The Collected Works of John of the Cross* (1991); T. Merton, *The Ascent to Truth* (1951).

John H. Coe

John Paul II (1920–2005)

Occupant of one of the longest and first truly global pontificates in history. Before becoming pope, he was a playwright, actor, poet, and professor of ethics who became convinced that the horrors of twentieth-century life were the result of a crisis of ideas, especially ideas concerning the human person. Probing and understanding the notion of the human person became the central theme of his pastorate and vocation. His prepapal work, *The Acting Person* (1969), was devoted to uncovering the metaphysical sense and mystery of personhood, while his *Lectures from Lublin* (2005) attempted to reconstruct the foundations of the moral life. In *Love and Responsibility* (1981), he carefully analyzed the different dimensions of love that culminate in the giving of oneself to others. In his first encyclical, *The Redeemer of Man* (1979), he announced Christian anthropology as the great theme of his pontificate. From his monastic level of mysticism to his relentless world evangelism, to his final days of suffering during which he compassionately shared the dignity of the sick and dying, John Paul II demonstrated that it was possible to be fully human and a disciple of Christ living excellently in all spheres of existence.

For Further Reading: G. Weigel, *Witness to Hope: The Biography of Pope John Paul II* (2005).

André Ong

Johnson, James Weldon (1871–1938)

Preserver of African-American spiritual traditions. Shaped by the buoyancy of Reconstruction, the flowering of the Harlem Renaissance, and the intractableness of Jim/Jane Crow America, Johnson reflected as poet-activist the Afrocentric strand in African-American Christianity and recouped the aesthetic images and imaginativeness of African-American religion.

In the early 1900s, Johnson and his brother composed a song titled "Lift Every Voice and Sing" to honor Abraham Lincoln's birthday. Adopted by the NAACP in 1919 as the "Negro National Anthem," this song models a theocentric ode that ties God's graciousness with tragic, weary souls; it moves beyond traditional theodical discourse — justifying God in a world of pain — to stress a meditative disposition toward a providential and good God who is obeyed in spite of the unjust realities of the world. Although Johnson became the first African-American to pass the Florida bar, it is his literary output in collections such as *The Book of American Negro Spirituals* (1925), *The Second Book of American Negro Spirituals* (1926), and *God's Trombones: Seven Negro Sermons in Verse* (1927) that aptly captures the character of black spirituality and underscores how a life lived before God is always a culturally mediated phenomenon.

On the whole, Johnson's ecclesiology exhibits a prophetic temperament that incorporates social commitment into spirituality as is evident in his condemnation of what he considered irrelevant forms of the church that divided the energies of the "Negro Church" in worshiping God. Decades after his accidental automobile death, Johnson's impact is unquestioned in the black community, yet his legacy remains essentially unknown in the public square.

See also African-American Christian Spirituality.

For Further Reading: R. Byrd, ed., *The Essential Writings of James Weldon Johnson* (2008); J. Johnson, *Along This Way: The Autobiography of James Weldon Johnson* (1933); E. Levy, *James Weldon Johnson* (1973); S. Wilson, ed., *The Selected Writings of James Weldon Johnson*, vol. 2 (1995).

Roy Whitaker

Johnson, Samuel (1709–1784)

England's most famous eighteenth-century literary critic, essayist, and biographer. Best known for compiling the great *Dictionary of the English Language* (1755), Johnson was also a devout Christian. His diaries serve as a sporadic life record and as a repository of his prayers. His letters often included a prayer for the recipient or a request for prayer for himself. Johnson gathered many of his prayers and entrusted them to a friend, George Strahan, who gathered additional prayers of Johnson's from other sources and published them posthumously as *Prayers and Meditations* (1785).

While Johnson's prayers are extemporaneous, touching on matters ranging from asking for blessing on a new publishing project to expressions of grief at his wife's death, they are stylistically influenced by the *Book of Common Prayer*. Although he seems regularly to have failed to achieve the kind of orderly practice of the faith to which he aspired, his diaries and *Annals* describe his resolutions (especially on or near his birthday, at New Year's, or during Lent) to establish a rule of life in the form of spiritual and personal disciplines, ranging from "to study the Scriptures in the original Languages" to "to rise early" and "to take good care of my health." Lacking assurance of acceptance with God, he at one point turns to Richard Baxter's autobiography in an attempt to resolve his doubts. Despite his long struggle for an assured faith, he repeatedly and earnestly entrusts his life and eternal salvation to Christ as Savior. His final written prayer, dated December 5, 1784, shows him at last to be at peace.

Johnson's prayers and diaries afford a window into a rigorous Anglican devotion in the 18th century. While devoid of the consolatory affective religious experience of the revivalists of the same period, Johnson had a devotional practice that served both to center his profound intellect and to provide spiritual discipline to counter his erratic habits of life. Although his spiritual life has been ignored or downplayed by many of his biographers, Samuel Johnson can scarcely be known apart from his prayers.

See also Anglican Spirituality.

For Further Reading: S. Johnson, *Works, Vol. I: Diaries, Prayers, and Annals*, ed. E. L. McAdam Jr. with D. and M. Hyde (1958); J. Wain, *Samuel Johnson* (1974).

Maxine Hancock

Jones, E(li) Stanley (1884–1973)

Methodist missionary and evangelist in India. Jones believed that he experienced two conversions, a horizontal change on the outside at fifteen years, and two years later a vertical change when he was radically and enduringly changed on the inside as well. In 1907 he sailed for India as a missionary with the Methodist Episcopal Church and was appointed pastor of a church in Lucknow. In 1928, having declined to be appointed bishop, he embarked on a ministry of evangelism through roundtable discussions with Hindus and Muslims and writing; in this way, he blended spiritual life with deep intellectual discussions on Christ.

For Jones, religion was humanity's response to a personal God when God's thoughts, will, and purposes become one's own. Evangelism has to be integrated, appealing to the whole person — mind, body, and spirit — and should also have a social outcome, such as in church unity; and he put this in practice in his roundtable discussions. Spirituality, *bhakti*, was absolute dependence and self-abandonment to God. Keen to make Christianity less Western and alien to Indians, he developed an indigenized Christ of the Indian road, since Jesus came to fulfill all truth everywhere. Jones also started a Christian ashram movement in which Indians and foreigners could live together for a time, as equals, to reflect on the verities of life. The ashram was important for the Indianization of the church as he blended Indian characteristics of simplicity of life and intense spiritual quest in a disciplined setting. His autobiography, *A Song of Ascents* (1968), provides further illumination.

See also Asian Christian Spirituality.

Kiem-Kiok Kwa

Jones, Rufus Matthew (1863–1948)

Prolific author, educator, and Quaker leader. He is best known for his scholarship on mysticism and for his relief work that led to the creation of the American Friends Service Committee. Born into a devout Quaker family in South China, Maine, and educated at Haverford College and Harvard University, he taught philosophy at Haverford from 1893–1934. He wrote fifty-six books and countless journal articles, and lectured widely. He became the leading voice for modernist Quakers in the 20th century but also worked tirelessly to build bridges between all branches of Friends.

One of Jones's life goals was to create a fresh, new historical interpretation of the Quaker movement. He believed the clue to understanding Quakerism was found in its mystical roots, which he called "affirmative mysticism," and its core belief, which he termed the "inner light," defined as "something Divine, 'something of God' in the human soul." He understood mysticism as a direct, unmediated experience of God. He was strongly influenced by William James's theories on religious experience. He helped shape the spirituality of numerous theologians in the 20th century, among them Harry Emerson Fosdick and Howard Thurman. Among his best-known works are *Social Law in the Spiritual World* (1904), *Spiritual Reformers in the Sixteenth and Seventeenth Centuries* (1914), *The Church's Debt to Heretics* (1924), and *New Studies in Mystical Religion* (1927).

See also Quaker Spirituality.

For Further Reading: E. Vining, *Friend of Life: The Biography of Rufus M. Jones* (1958).

Carole Dale Spencer

Journaling, Spiritual

Journals have existed in many forms through the centuries. They have been used to record the exploits of explorers like Richard Burton, the experiences of missionaries like David Livingstone, the struggles of diplomats like Dag Hammarskjöld, and the conversions of future saints like Augustine. Reading journals by spiritual pioneers like John Wesley, Blaise Pascal, and Henri Nouwen brings insight, encouragement, and faith as we walk our own spiritual journey.

Christians have long used personal journals as a tool for spiritual growth. The most common use is the recording of one's life as it unfolds so as to be able to say yes and no to the influences that bear upon that life in accord with the admonition to pay attention to our lives (1 Tim. 4:16). Over time such journals give one the ability to construct a spiritual autobiography to describe the unfolding interaction of God in one's life. In addition, spiritual journals enable believers to engage with their own lives by helping them process the past, engage seminal figures in their present, work with their dreams, and discern God's future for them.

Journals are also used in conjunction with other spiritual disciplines. For example, Ignatius of Loyola commended a written review of prayer at the conclusion of one's daily prayer, whereby one seeks to discern and record what God may have been saying, how one felt (as a way of discerning God's intention), and the nature of the whole prayer experience. Or when Christians engage in the discipline of spiritual reading, the journal is a great place to record key insights. As another example, if we engage in the discipline of fasting, not only can the journal record our struggles and successes, but it also provides a convenient place to record food intake. Or we can record our struggles with materialism (a buyer's diary) as we seek to practice the discipline of simplicity. Journals, as aids to focused reflection and remembering, can be powerful tools for spiritual formation.

See also Examen; Remembering and Forgetting.

For Further Reading: H. Cepero, *Journaling as a Spiritual Practice* (2008); R. Klug, *How to Keep a Spiritual Journal* (2002); R. Peace, *Spiritual Journaling* and *Spiritual Autobiography* (1998); I. Progoff, *At a Journal Workshop* (1975).

Richard V. Peace

Journey, Spiritual

The image of spiritual journey is a core reality of historic Christian experience, beginning with Abraham's journey from known, comfortable Haran to an unknown land that God would show him (Gen. 12:1). Israel's journey from slavery in Egypt to the freedom of the Promised Land required forty years of wandering in the wilderness. Both journeys proved rewarding, but neither was an entirely pleasant excursion.

The Christian spiritual journey is predicated upon five foundational realities. First, we were created in the image of God (Gen. 1:26), which, second, is inseparable from a relationship of loving union with God. Third, we have turned away from this relationship. Fourth, God desires to restore us to fullness of life in loving union and wholeness in God's image. Fifth, God's cruciform love, in Christ, has established the relationship of loving union on God's part. The Christian spiritual journey is the process through which God, in Christ, through the Holy Spirit, regenerates us in the image of God and draws us into loving union.

A love relationship always leaves the beloved free to say no. God's cruciform love, manifested in Christ, reveals that God will never say no to the relationship. Our spiritual journey depends on our willingness to respond to God's cruciform love by the loving abandonment of ourselves to God by losing our lives for his sake (Mark 8:35).

Having rejected God as the source of our being and the center of our identity, we have developed, as Thomas Merton observed, substitutes that form a false identity that finds its meaning, value, and purpose in things other than God. This pervasive structure of self-referenced being misshapes all our perspectives, warps all our values, distorts all our relationships, and perverts our lifestyle. This "false self" must constantly be abandoned if God is to draw us back into loving union and renew us in God's image. Insights into the nature of this journey—which moves from bondage to the false self toward wholeness in vital union with God—are captured in John Bunyan's *Pilgrim's Progress*.

The journey of abandonment is a daily practice in every relationship and every situation. Jesus illustrated the nature of this practice when he asked Peter, "Do you truly love me more than these?" (John 21:15). "These" is ambiguous, even in the original Greek. Was Jesus referring to the other disciples? Peter's boat? His nets? The large catch of fish? All of these would have been part of Peter's identity as a fisherman. Jesus was asking Peter (and us) whether we love him more than all those things that have previously (mis)shaped our identity. Is our identity "hidden with Christ in God" (Col. 3:3) in the relationships, circumstances, and situations of our life, or are we continuing to find our identity in those things that have formed our false self? The Christian spiritual journey is a daily, loving abandonment of our false self to God in love.

See also Conversion; Formation, Spiritual; Threefold Way.

For Further Reading: A. Haase, *Coming Home to Your True Self* (2008); K. Leech, *Experiencing God* (1985); T. Merton, *The Inner Experience* (2003); M. R. Mulholland Jr., *The Deeper Journey* (2006).

M. Robert Mulholland Jr.

Joy

Joy (Gr. *chara*) is a prominent fruit of the Spirit (Gal. 5:22) and a defining characteristic of the Christian life. Literally hundreds of references to joy pervade both testaments of the Scriptures. It is the root of important cognate actions like *rejoice* and *enjoy*. Yet for all this it is infrequently mentioned in reference works and curiously challenging to define. At least this much seems clear: joy is a buoyant sense of well-being, intense satisfaction, and exultant delight that naturally expresses itself in laughter, song, gratitude, largeheartedness, and generosity. And it is obviously highly desirable.

Often joy and happiness are treated as synonyms. When they are differentiated, it is usually by regarding joy as the deeper and more durable of the two—more a basic disposition than a fleeting emotion, and more characteristically grounded in broad perspective rather than in passing circumstances.

Joy can be experienced in response to a wide range of positive life events—the birth of a child, a wedding, a successful harvest, finding a job, or scoring a winning goal. It may be a more sustained disposition in response to longer-term circumstances—the gift of a good marriage, for example, or a meaningful career. And there are also degrees or gradations of joy, culminating at the top end in *great* joy and *fullness* of joy.

The Christian spiritual tradition locates the ultimate source of joy in God (Ps. 16:11), and presupposes that it is God's desire for his creatures to experience this joy themselves. Jesus' goal was that his joy might be in his disciples and that their joy might thereby be "complete" (John 15:11). The joy on which the Scriptures focus is exultant response to grace experienced or anticipated. According to Don Saliers, it is a disposition grounded ultimately in a deep and sustained attunement to what God has done, and promised to do, in Christ.

Jesus' reference to "his joy" is a reminder that Christian joy is not merely a Christian's own calculated response to positive or promising circumstances, but is also an expression of the supernatural life of God within. It is, in other words, a characteristic manifestation of the Spirit's own nature and indwelling presence. Thus, the apostle Paul writes: "The kingdom of God is not a matter of eating and drinking, but of righteousness, peace and joy in the Holy Spirit" (Rom. 14:17).

A significant consequence of joy that gives buoyancy to the human spirit is resilience. As the prophet Nehemiah famously observed, "The joy of the LORD is your strength" (Neh. 8:10). Christian joy is focused on the end ahead and gets its "lift" from what God has promised—it is, in other words, "joyful in hope" (Rom. 12:12; cf. 1 Peter 1:8). But though such joy comes from the Spirit, it requires willing alignment with it in order to experience it fully. Thus, the Scriptures reiterate the imperative, "Rejoice!" And part of the power of corporate praise times are that they can winsomely compel those who might otherwise remain cynical individuals to grow together into joyful persons. The worship liturgy can become a compelling instrument for crafting joyful dispositions. It helps that joy is one of the most contagious of all the human emotions.

Joy surfaces memorably in such classics as Pascal's testimony ("Joy, joy, joy, tears of joy"), Bernard's "Jesus, Joy of Man's Desiring," and the Westminster Shorter Catechism's acknowledgment that man's chief end is to love God and *enjoy him* forever. Oscillations in subjective states (including joy and sorrow, delight and discouragement) are inevitable, and the low points assail even the great — perhaps especially the greatest souls. But sorrow and experiences of the "dark night" are exceptions rather than the rule, temporary periods that do not dislodge joy as the characteristic spirit and underlying ethos of Christian experience. Christian joy is perennially expressed in music, poetry, dance, celebration, humor, and laughter. And on that note, we end with Patrick Kavanagh's exhilarating image of the resurrection: "A laugh freed forever and for ever."

See also Fruit of the Spirit; Happiness; Love.

For Further Reading: C. S. Lewis, *Surprised by Joy* (1955); M. Lloyd-Jones, *Joy Unspeakable* (1984); W. Morrice, *Joy in the New Testament* (1984); D. Rienstra, *So Much More* (2005); S. Wirt, *Jesus, Man of Joy* (1991).

Glen G. Scorgie

Julian of Norwich (1342/1343 – after 1416)

Medieval English mystic. Julian of Norwich was thirty years old when, in 1373, she received sixteen revelations or showings that became a profound focal point in her own life, forever transformed the face of English devotional literature, and deepened the tradition of Trinitarian-incarnational theology she had inherited. Some twenty years later,

she became an anchorite. To become such a recluse required a vocation, which her showings provided. In Julian's case, she entered a cell that was part of St Julian's Church, Norwich, and perhaps had already written the first of two accounts of her revelations. She was spurred on in her reflections by two subsidiary visions (in 1388 and 1393).

Julian had been on the verge of death when she received her initial visions, having been granted "the gift" of a bodily sickness for which she had asked God since her youth. She had also prayed for more feeling "in the passion of Christ," imagining that she would have this experience in solidarity with Mary Magdalene and others of Christ's lovers. At this point, Julian may have been a Benedictine nun, but evidence of the details of her life is scant. In becoming an anchorite, Julian probably had a symbolic experience of death: there is evidence of the office of the dead being performed by the bishop while anchorites were walled in. Julian may have taken her name from her church. Though symbolically dead to the world, Julian would not have been entirely cut off. She received visitors, provided counsel, and had a role of spiritual authority; she had servants who formed part of her "household"; she prayed for the souls of others; to all in the community she exemplified the life of holiness, of being set apart for God; and she received supportive gifts and bequests. Yet one should not downplay the unique discipline of the solitary life. Under its rigors she produced a heavily revised and much longer version of her revelations.

The long text of Julian's *A Revelation of Divine Love* (this modern title reflecting her observation that all the revelations are grounded and unified in the first one) is regarded as a work without precedent in the subgenres of spiritual prose, though Julian worked carefully with the more typical short text when preparing it. Her rhetoric stands in the tradition of *lectio divina*. She engages contemporary discourses in a way that subverts the pretensions of linear speech and instrumental reasoning, preserving the tension involved in "speaking the incomprehensible God," as one theologian has recently put it, the tension of "reconciling" the apophatic and kataphatic traditions. Her theology is profoundly incarnational-Trinitarian and joyful: "Sodeinly the trinity fulfilled my hart most of joy.... The trinity is our maker, the trinity is our keper, the trinity is our everlasting lover, the trinity is our endlesse joy and our blisse, by our lord Jesu Christ and in our lord Jesu Christ. And this was shewed in the first sight and in all. For wher Jhesu appireth the blessed trinity is understand, as to my sight." In the astonishingly compressed, homely, and affirming image of "a little thing the quantity of an haselnot," she relates how "it is all that is made" and that "it lasteth and ever shall, for God loveth it. And so hath all thing being by the love of God." Such an affirmation, along with such stylistic features as borrowings from the local geography of East Anglia, have made Julian a worthy, theologically fortified spokesperson for our belated ecological movement. The self likewise has its being by the love of God: "And I sawe no difference betwen God and oure substance, but as it were all God." Julian strikingly and consistently emphasized the fact that God is love and her book the showing of his love: "Who shewed it the? Love. What shewid he the? Love." This provides the basis for one of the best-known and best-loved summaries within her theology, the assurance that "alle shalle be wele, and alle maner of thing shalle be wele." In the 17th century, complete copies of her long text were preserved by French Recusant nuns. Otherwise, very few early manuscripts of either work (and only one medieval one) are known to exist. Yet Julian's writings have survived to become, at least recently, a very rich and widely appropriated resource for many people, "evenchristen" and otherwise, hungering for a spirituality that enables them to live joyful and purposeful embodied lives.

See also English Mystics; Rolle, Richard; Women.

For Further Reading: D. Aers and L. Staley, *The*

Powers of the Holy (1996); D. Baker, *Julian of Norwich's* Showings (1994); V. Gillespie and M. Ross, "With mekeness aske perseverantly," *Mystics Quarterly* 30 (2004): 125 – 40; L. Herbert McAvoy, ed., *A Companion to Julian of Norwich* (2008); J. Shickler, "The Cross and the Citadel," *Studia Mystica* 21 (2000): 95 – 125; *The Writings of Julian of Norwich*, ed. N. Watson and J. Jenkins (2006).

Norm Klassen

Jung, Carl G. (1875 – 1961)

Swiss psychiatrist and psychotherapist, prolific writer, and founder of analytical (Jungian) psychology. Many consider him the father of psychospirituality for his distinct contribution to the psychology of religion. He was born Karle Gustav II Jung in a small town in Switzerland, the only surviving child of Paul Achilles Jung, a rural pastor of the Swiss Reformed Church, and Emilie Preiswerk. Jung was married (1903 – 1955) to Emma Rauschenbach until her death, and together they had five children.

Jung was influenced by the great philosophers Plato, Immanuel Kant, and Arthur Schopenhauer, as well as by his travels abroad and the world religions he studied extensively. In his early years, he was mentored by psychiatrist Eugen Bleuler (1857 – 1939), and later, by psychiatrist/neurologist/psychoanalyst Sigmund Freud (1856 – 1939).

The close friendship Jung had with Freud for many years did not survive their ideological differences. Among other things, Jung disagreed with Freud's emphasis on sexuality as a prime source of motivation, his disdain for religion and the belief that it was a neurosis to be cured, and his theory of the unconscious.

Jung continuously wrestled with core concepts of Christianity, believing that life has a spiritual purpose beyond the material world, and that the heart of all religions is the journey of individual transformation (individuation). Yet to him the institution of religion distorted and obstructed true spirituality and healing, while the absence of religion was a main cause of psychological disorders. To this day, Jung influences psychology, the wider society, and Christianity with his theory of personality types and his concept of archetypes (universally recognizable symbols of personality).

Others of his famous concepts include the collective unconscious (versus the personal unconscious), the meaning and interpretation of dreams, the meaning and use of symbols and rituals, and the shadow (repressed weaknesses and instinct of the unconscious mind). He believed that if the shadow is not consciously acknowledged and integrated, it will become darker and impede healing and transformation. Jung paved the way for many different schools of psychology and psychotherapy, and created an indelible bridge between psychology and spirituality that still influences us today.

See also Dreams and Visions; Psychoanalysis.

For Further Reading: D. Bair, *Jung* (2003); J. Dourley, *The Illnesses That We Are* (1989); R. Hopcke, *A Guided Tour of the Collected Works of C. G. Jung* (1999); C. Jung, *Memories, Dreams, Reflections*, ed. A. Jaffé, trans. R. and A. Winston (1989); R. Moore, *Carl Jung and Christian Spirituality* (1988).

Minoa Chang

Justin Martyr (c. 100 – c. 165)

Second-century apologist for the full truth of the gospel. Justin was born in Syria to Gentile parents. In search of God, he pursued human philosophies, contemplating immaterial ideas until told of the Hebrew and Christian Scriptures and urged to pray for divine light. "Straightway a flame was kindled in my soul; and a love of the prophets, and of those men who are friends of Christ, possessed me," he wrote. So converted he began his vocation as a Christian philosopher, combining evangelism with apologetics by expounding the prophets and Jesus in accord with the apostolic tradition until he was martyred in Rome for refusing to offer sacrifices. Extant are three genuine writings: *First Apology* (argues Christians are not atheists but, agreeing with the highest human reasoning, hold to the revealed truth of the invisible and immutable God whom they obey even to death); *Second Apology* (appeals for mercy to Christians in face of persecution); and *Dialogue with Trypho* (maintains that Israel's covenant and ceremonial laws predicted and were superseded by the Christ who came as Jesus, teacher of truth and dying but risen Savior, whose words "filled with the Spirit of God, and big with power, and flourishing with grace" also "possess a terrible power in themselves"). Justin should probably be seen more as a bridge figure portraying and handing down early, mainly orthodox Christianity than as a direct influence on the medieval development of spirituality. Modern studies often (incorrectly) focus on ambiguities of Justin's language about the universal Logos from which he derives his theory relating Christian revelation to universally accessible truths, hints of an absolutely transcendent Father God, which weakens God's direct involvement in salvation and threatens a second-rank eternal Son, and an overly intellectualist understanding of sin and salvation through knowledge of truth. A generous yet faithful reading of Justin's texts attests to his theology being Scripture-based and his premodern exegesis always apostolically bound and Christ-centered. He affirms the divine identity of Jesus and the saving power of Jesus' blood and words that lead to repentance and transformed lives of believers, nurtured by the real presence of Christ in the Eucharist and spiritual gifts, longing for resurrection bodies at Christ's second advent, and ready to face death with fellow believers under persecution.

See also Martyrdom.

For Further Reading: L. Barnard, *Justin Martyr* (1973); J. Morgan-Wynne, "The Holy Spirit and Christian Experience in Justin Martyr," in *Vigiliae Christianae* 38 (1984): 172 – 77; E. Osborn, *Justin Martyr* (1967); M. Root, "Images of Liberation: Justin, Jesus, and the Jews," in *The Thomist* 48 (1984): 512 – 34.

Richard F. Kantzer

K

Kagawa, Toyohiko (1888–1960)

Japanese minister to the poor, evangelist, and prolific writer. Kagawa was the illegitimate son of a philandering businessman and a geisha. Both parents died when he was four. His foster mother, his father's wife, was violent. Kagawa wound up at his rich uncle's home and was schooled at a Buddhist monastery. But he was disowned for his allegiance to Jesus Christ, introduced to him by an American missionary. From that point, poverty was his lot. While at Kobe Seminary, he developed distaste for doctrine at the expense of action. During and after seminary, he spent five years in the slums preaching and tending to the sick and addicted. He slept with the poor and fed them on his meager income. Then he voyaged to the United States to study at Princeton University and Seminary. He became convinced that charity alone was not enough, that the systemic causes of poverty must be attacked. He returned to Japan for a life of activism and writing. In the 1920s he was arrested twice on charges related to labor activism. He wrote novels in jail. Upon release he founded various humanitarian organizations and then focused on evangelism. Japanese military police arrested him in 1940 for peace propaganda and for apologizing to China on Japan's behalf. He lectured around that time in both Europe and the United States, where (with E. Stanley Jones) he lobbied in vain against impending war. His many books (over 150 published) include *Behold the Man* (1941), *Brotherhood Economics* (1936), and *The Cosmic Teleology* (1957).

Kagawa's spirituality was deeply rooted in the redeeming love of God manifested in Jesus Christ. His call to individuals and nations was to ascend toward God through prayer and abiding in him. The result is an integration of the inner and outer life, evidenced in such fruit as love, global peace, simplicity, collaboration, ecological harmony, justice, and equality.

See also Asian Christian Spirituality.

For Further Reading: R. Schildgen, *Toyohiko Kagawa* (1988).

T. C. Porter

Kataphatic

See **Apophatic and Kataphatic Ways.**

Keating, Thomas (1923–)

Pioneer of centering prayer. Thomas Keating was born in New York in 1923. He had a religious awakening during his freshman year at Yale University at age seventeen, where he discovered the catholic nature of the church and, for the first time, that God desired to have a personal relationship with each person. Keating took this to heart and began a regular practice of personal prayer and Scripture reading. He transferred to Fordham University and graduated in two years. At age twenty Keating entered into the Cistercian order (Trappists), and at age twenty-five he was ordained a Roman Catholic priest; he later became an abbot of a Cistercian monastery.

Keating is most famous for promoting the work of fellow Cistercian Thomas Merton and his writings on contemplative prayer or centering prayer. In the 1970s Keating, with fellow monk Basil Pennington, began promoting contemplative prayer among the Trappists and later to those outside the religious community. In 1984 Keating founded Contemplative Outreach, an ecumenical and interfaith organization to teach the practices of contemplative prayer. Beyond his retreats and workshops, Keating has promoted contemplative prayer through numerous books and articles. Like Merton before him, he is actively engaged in inter-religious dialogue among monks and nuns around the world. His works include *Open Mind, Open Heart* (1986) and *Intimacy with God* (1994).

See also Centering Prayer; Contemplation; Merton, Thomas; Trappists.

Todd E. Johnson

Kelly, Thomas Raymond (1893 – 1941)

Quaker educator and spiritual writer. He attended Wilmington and Haverford Colleges and received his Ph.D. from Hartford Theological Seminary. He taught at Wilmington and Earlham Colleges, the University of Hawaii, and Haverford College until his early death by heart attack. His failure to earn a second Ph.D. at Harvard led to a spiritual crisis and then to a mystical encounter with the divine presence that reoriented his life. He captures the power of such an experience in these words: "It is an overwhelming experience to fall into the hands of the living God, to be invaded to the depths of one's being by His presence, to be, without warning, wholly uprooted from all earth-born securities and assurances, and to be blown by a tempest of unbelievable power which leaves one's old proud self utterly, utterly defenseless."

The last three years of his life he spoke and wrote frequently about the spiritual life. These writings were collected and published posthumously as *A Testament of Devotion* in 1941 by his friend and colleague Douglas Steere. *A Testament of Devotion* mines the writings of the Christian mystics, integrating their thought with traditional Quaker spirituality. The book gained a huge following far beyond his original Quaker audience and has since become a Christian devotional classic. See also his posthumous *The Eternal Promise* (1966).

See also Quaker Spirituality.

For Further Reading: R. Kelly, *Thomas Kelly* (1966).

Carole Dale Spencer

Kelsey, Morton T. (1917 – 2001)

Episcopal priest, retreat leader, marriage and family counselor, and educator. Kelsey, a professor of theology at Notre Dame and San Francisco Theological Seminary, authored more than forty books on the integration of theology, depth psychology, and spiritual formation. Having studied with Carl Jung in Switzerland, he wove Jungian personality theory into many of his writings. Kelsey's writings have influenced many charismatic renewal leaders, both Protestant and Catholic, including Agnes Sanford and John Wimber.

Chief emphases in Kelsey's works include the integration of spirituality and psychology (*Christo-Psychology* [1984]), silence and meditation that properly diminish the human ego (*The Other Side of Silence* [1976]), contemplation using guided imagery (*Myth, History and Faith* [1974]), dream analysis to access the unconscious world (*Dreams* [1978] and *God, Dreams, and Revelation* [1973]), journaling (*Adventure Inward* [1980]), and spiritual direction (*Companions on the Inner Way* [1983]). He also examined and appraised the phenomenon of tongues speaking in *Tongue Speaking: An Experiment in Spiritual Experience* (1964) and a sequel, *Tongue Speaking: The History and Meaning of Charismatic Experience* (1981).

Kelsey pursued the *via positiva*, employing imagination to insert readers into the ancient biblical narratives. His writings are substantive, life related, eclectic, and in places controversial. Concerning the latter, he incorporated Eastern forms of meditation into formational protocols, emphasized myth as the way humans engage spiritual reality, and approved the normalization of homosexuality, which he perceived to be a basic personality orientation over which persons have little control and therefore should not be changed or punished (*Sacrament of Sexuality* [1986]).

See also Charismatic Spirituality; Jung, Carl.

Bruce A. Demarest

Kenosis

Kenosis, from the Greek verb *kenoō* ("empty," "make of no effect") in Philippians 2:7, affirms that God's Son in an act of supreme self-renunciation divested himself of heavenly glory, adding humanity to his deity in order to serve God's redemptive purposes on earth. The early Christian hymn reflected in Philippians 2:6–11 affirms Christ's eternally preexistent condition ("being in very nature God," v. 6a) and his willingness to surrender temporarily his essential equality with God (v. 6b). Obedient to the Father's will, the Son took "the very nature of a servant" (v. 7b) and being "made in human likeness" (v. 7c) was perfectly fitted to die for humanity on a cross (v. 8).

The verb *ptocheuō* ("reduced to poverty") in 2 Corinthians 8:9 likewise teaches the Son's self-renunciation. On earth Jesus Christ drew upon his incommunicable qualities laid aside at his *kenosis* (e.g., omnipotence, omniscience) to perform supernatural works of miraculous healings, excising demons, and raising the dead.

Following Christ's example (1 Peter 2:21) of humiliation, yet without demeaning personal self-worth, the Lord's disciples abandon privileges, ambitions, and desires—characteristics of the false self. Followers of the Master lay down their lives in other-centered service empowered by the Holy Spirit. In Pauline language the kenotic life involves "sharing in [Christ's] sufferings, becoming like him in his death" (Phil. 3:10). It is characterized by self-forgetfulness, obedience to the Father, humility, and generosity—or realization of the true self. Following obediently the Word who relinquished heavenly glory will involve personal sacrifice, rejection, and suffering, divinely enabled by the joy of future resurrection. The kenotic principle estab-

lished by our Lord represents the foundation and core of Christian discipleship.

See also Compassion; God, Perceptions of; Humility; Incarnation.

For Further Reading: D. Dawe, *The Form of a Servant* (1963); D. Power, *Love without Calculation* (2005); O. Zijlstra, *Letting Go* (2002).

Bruce A. Demarest

Keswick Movement

Building on the momentum of the spectacularly successful 1873–1874 Moody-Sankey evangelistic campaign in Great Britain, the Keswick Movement began in 1875 in the small town of Keswick in England's Lake District when Canon T. D. Harford-Battersby, vicar of St. John's Anglican Church (Keswick), and his Quaker friend Robert Wilson brought together six hundred clergy and laypeople for three days of meetings dedicated to the "promotion of practical holiness." From that initial gathering a rather loosely connected association of similar conventions has developed and continues to gather in various locations around the world.

Initially Keswick relied heavily on the devotional writings and teaching of William Boardman, Robert Pearsall Smith, and the latter's more famous wife Hannah Whitall Smith, author of *The Christian's Secret of a Happy Life* (1875). The goal of Keswick gatherings has always been the transformation of ordinary Christians into effective members of the body of Christ. From its early days, Keswick teaching has posited sanctification both as crisis—as a personal surrender to the fullness of the Holy Spirit—and as process, in the form of ongoing growth in holiness. Far from advocating the eradication of the sinful nature, Keswick teachers have instead emphasized the "counteracting" power of the Holy Spirit to enable Christians to live in victorious daily dependence on the indwelling presence of Christ.

Speakers must conform their messages to the teaching on holiness that has been agreed upon by the leadership of the convention. This includes reckoning oneself dead to sin (Rom. 6:11) and surrendering to the fullness of the Spirit.

For many decades, the convention talks followed a set topical sequence: first, the consequences of sin in the life of the believer; second, the cross and resurrection of Christ as God's remedy for sin; third, the full surrender of the cleansed life to God; fourth, the fullness of the Spirit and the indwelling Christ; and fifth, the life of disciplined and sacrificial service. Although it has not followed this sequence as rigidly since the mid-1990s, the Keswick Convention Council has maintained a commitment to the deepening of the spiritual life of individuals and churches through careful exposition and application of Scripture, emphasizing the lordship of Christ, personal and corporate transformation, evangelism, missions, discipleship, and interdenominational unity.

Keswick's stress on unity in diversity can be seen from the wording on a banner strung at every Keswick gathering: "All One in Christ Jesus." The Baptist, Presbyterian, Anglican, Brethren, Methodist, Reformed, and charismatic wings of evangelicalism have all been represented among Keswick's speakers. They have included Bishop H. C. G. Moule, F. B. Meyer, Andrew Murray, W. H. Griffith Thomas, Donald Grey Barnhouse, G. Campbell Morgan, and more recently Billy Graham and John Stott.

Some who embrace a Holiness position, such as A. M. Mills, have indicted Keswick teaching for substituting obedience or the avoidance of conscious sins for true holiness, that is, the cleansing of the heart. Other critics on the Reformed side, such as B. B. Warfield, have dismissed it as a form of perfectionism. Nevertheless, and despite its humble origins, the Keswick Movement has consistently offered a rich experience of teaching to all ages. Its influence spans the globe, with a continued strong emphasis on missions.

See also Holiness; Perfection; Regeneration.

For Further Reading: S. Barabas, *So Great Salvation* (1952); J. B. Figgis, *Keswick from Within* (1985); J. R. McQuilkin, "The Keswick Perspective," in *Five Views on Sanctification*, M. Dieter et al., ed. S. Gundry (1987), 151–83; J. C. Pollock, *The Keswick Story* (1964); C. Price and I. Randall, *Transforming Keswick* (2000).

William R. McAlpine

Kierkegaard, Søren (1813–1855)

Danish philosopher and theologian. He critiqued both rationalistic Lutheran orthodoxy and speculative, objective philosophy, arguing for the importance of subjective appropriation of Christian truth and the strenuous nature of the God relationship. Kierkegaard acquired a strong religious sensibility through the influence of his pietistic father, who introduced him to Moravian spirituality. He studied philosophy and theology at the University of Copenhagen, writing his thesis on the concept of irony in Socrates. He became an opponent of the burgeoning influence of Hegelian philosophy on theology in Denmark. Kierkegaard aspired to the parish ministry but resigned himself to an author's vocation, living off his father's inheritance. His literary output was staggering, amounting to more than thirty books and numerous volumes of journals.

Kierkegaard directed prophetic critiques toward the Lutheran state church, which he called *Christendom*. He was convinced that the lifestyles and preaching of its clerics were far beneath the NT ideal. Acknowledging that he also fell short, Kierkegaard claimed that all he sought was an admission from church authorities that genuine Christianity no longer existed in Denmark.

Kierkegaard considered his diverse authorship to have a unifying purpose: the reintroduction of true NT Christianity into *Christendom*. In doing so, he regularly made use of pseudonyms — fictional "authors" whose narrative perspective corresponded to one of three stages, or spheres, of life. The aesthetic was characterized by immediate gratification and the pleasures of sensuality. The ethical was represented by commitment and moral rigor. The religious sphere comprised two further divisions. Religiousness A, or the Socratic stage, included a genuine but general belief in God. The movement to Religiousness B occurred through a transforming encounter with Christ, the *Absolute Paradox*. The border between A and B was the choice to have faith in Christ or to be offended by the paradox. While one can and must choose, the choice is made possible only through the divine gift of grace.

Transition to Religiousness B required, for Kierkegaard, acknowledgment of sin, human finitude, and the necessity of divine revelation. While affirming the traditional Lutheran doctrine of *inherited* sin, Kierkegaard described it in relational terms in his books *The Concept of Anxiety* and *Sickness unto Death*. Sin is the *misrelation* of the self to God, to others, and to oneself. Despair constituted the breakdown of the self's potential as an authentic human being yet was a necessary prelude to transforming faith.

Kierkegaard was deeply affected by mystical writers in the Christian tradition. An impulse for the imitation of Christ, which he developed in part through engaging Thomas à Kempis's classic work, ran through his writings. For Kierkegaard, true Christianity is not defined by the correctness of doctrinal or propositional belief; it is a relationship to Jesus and the attempt to follow him as *pattern*. Essential Christianity is marked by the individual's inward appropriation of Christian truth and authentic relationship to God. Kierkegaard's great contribution to Christian spirituality is the reminder that because Christianity is inwardly appropriated, the authenticity of spirituality cannot be analyzed or judged objectively or by reference to external manifestations.

See also Crisis; Will, Human.

For Further Reading: C. Evans, *Kierkegaard* (2009); D. Gouwens, *Kierkegaard as Religious Thinker* (1996); S. Walsh, *Living Christianly* (2005).
Kyle A. Roberts

King, Martin Luther, Jr. (1929–1968)

Renowned African-American leader. Before King's spiritual legacy became nationally and globally cemented, his early Christian formation was influenced by a combination of factors: coming from a line of Baptist clergy; being reared in a loving, middle-class home in Atlanta; and confronting the nightmarish reality of a racialized American South riddled with socioeconomic and political inequality. After graduating from Morehouse College (1948), Crozier Theological Seminary (1951), and Boston University (1955), where he wrote his dissertation on comparative views of God, and in championing the civil rights movement (1955–1968), King's spiritual theology finally became crystallized: the Christian faith at its best is a lived experience in God at the nexus of contemplation and action. For King, spirituality is a way of life in which one constantly reflects on biblical teachings and relies on divine sovereignty while taking personal responsibility for states of injustice and striving to make the world a "beloved community."

King's socially conscious brand of spirituality within African-American Christianity was a unique blend of four distinct traditions: the black church, liberal Christianity, Gandhian nonviolent ethics, and American civil religion. King was nurtured in a black church ethos that recognized that the biblical God is on the side of justice, and those who work for justice are on the side of God. King embraced this theocentric outlook and moral conviction during his multiple challenges to and arrests for breaking "unjust laws." Moreover, King's self-definition as an "evangelical liberal" is reflective of his Euro-American education, which stressed the ties between the reality of a personal God, the goodness of humanity, and criticism of ideologies of oppression. King's spiritual theology also merged Jesus' life and teaching of love with Gandhi's nonviolent resistance methodology, not just to change laws, but also to transform people.

King read the *imago Dei* (image of God) onto all persons as equal inheritors of a deserved human dignity — despite race and class — in the eyes of God. He invoked the divine and prophetic rhetoric alongside U.S. founding documents like the Constitution to demonstrate the fissure between what America preached and what it practiced. For King, the spiritual life, especially for a supposed Christian nation, requires heartfelt consistency.

King's impact is indelibly stamped on the American and global consciousness as a Christian leader who collapsed the church-world paradigm. Religion is life. Next to his leading of the March on Washington (August 28, 1963) and his nationally celebrated birthday (January 15), King's "I have a dream" speech and "Letter from Birmingham Jail" also remain national treasures and spiritual resources for the ages. Desiring to be remembered solely as a "drum major" for justice or a servant of humanity based on Mark 10:35 – 45, King (who was assassinated by a gunman on April 4, 1968) also models an incarnational theology with a strong Americanized prophetic sensibility: living an authentically spiritual life enabled by faith in the triune God presupposes a risky embodiment of the gospel — a *Kierkegaardian-esque* "leap of faith" — where one is working in Christ for others and by others in the social arena.

See also African-American Christian Spirituality; Social Justice.

For Further Reading: L. Baldwin, *Never to Leave Us Alone: The Prayer Life of Martin Luther King Jr.* (2010); C. Carson, ed., *The Autobiography of Martin Luther King Jr.* (1998); M. Dyson, *April 4, 1968: Martin Luther King Jr.'s Death and How It Changed America* (2008); J. Washington, ed., *A Testament of Hope: The Essential Writings and Speeches of Martin Luther King Jr.* (1986); C. West, "Prophetic Christian as Organic Intellectual: Martin Luther King Jr.," in *The Cornel West Reader*, ed. C. West (1999), 425 – 34.

Roy Whitaker

Kingdom of God

In the gospel of Mark, Jesus begins preaching the gospel by saying, "The time is fulfilled, and the kingdom of God has come near; repent, and believe in the good news" (1:14 – 15 NRSV). In the gospel of Matthew, Jesus begins, in the language of Jewish reserve that Matthew preferred, with, "Repent, for the kingdom of heaven has come near" (4:17 NRSV). In the gospel of Luke (4:18 – 21), Jesus' first sermon was based on Isaiah 61, wherein God's Anointed One brings good news for the poor, release to the captives, recovering of sight to the blind, and liberty for those who are oppressed; and he concluded with, "Today this scripture has been fulfilled in your hearing" (NRSV). Furthermore, many of Jesus' parables are parables of the kingdom, and the Sermon on the Mount begins with an announcement concerning the poor; namely, that "theirs is the kingdom of heaven."

Laypeople and scholars alike agree that the kingdom of God was at the heart of Jesus' good news. But the problem is that we are often vague about what it means. If we do not know what its characteristics are, how can we notice when mustard seeds of the kingdom of God sprout in the midst of our lives, and give God thanks? Clues to the term's meaning are in the prophet Isaiah.

Every time Jesus proclaimed the coming of the kingdom of God, he used words that came from the Aramaic translation of the prophet Isaiah. Aramaic scholars like Bruce Chilton see this most clearly, but the indebtedness to Isaiah is evident even in English translations. Jesus' beatitudes are a paraphrase of Isaiah 61, Jesus' first sermon in Luke 4:18 – 21 is based on Isaiah, and he quoted Isaiah far more than any other book of the Bible. The Dead Sea Scrolls and the NT indicate that Isaiah was the book read most often in Jesus' time. So the place to look for the context and meaning of the kingdom of God in people's understanding, then, is the sixteen passages in Isaiah that proclaim that God is coming to bring us deliverance. These are the passages Jesus pointed to when he prophesied that the kingdom of God is coming: Isaiah 9:1 – 7; 11:1 – 16; 24:14 – 25:12; 26:1 – 21; 31:1 – 32:20; 33:1 – 24; 35:1 – 10; 40:1 – 11; 42:1 – 44:8; 49:1 – 26; 51:1 – 53:12; and chapters 54, 56, 60, 61, and 62. These passages proclaim that God is coming to bring us deliverance, as Jesus said in Luke 4 — good news, release, healing, liberty, and God's presence.

These chapters in Isaiah give clues about the characteristics of the reign of God. Seven themes, seven characteristics of the reign of God, run throughout these chapters: *deliverance* (or redemption and release); *justice* that delivers us from poverty and oppression and restores us to community; *peace* that delivers us from violence and injustice; the *presence of God* as Holy Spirit, Light, and Deliverer; the *joy* of participating in God's deliverance; *healing* of the sick, especially the blind; and *return* from exile — which Jesus interpreted as repentance and return to God. And throughout Isaiah, these seven characteristics of the reign of God come because of God's compassion (Isa. 13:18; 14:1; 27:11; 30:18; 49:10, 13, 15; 54:7, 8, 10; 55:7; 60:10; 63:7, 15).

These are all happenings, gifts of God, things God does. "The zeal of the LORD of hosts will do this" (Isa. 9:7 NRSV). Therefore, most scholars prefer to translate the Greek as "reign of God" rather than "kingdom of God." It is not a place, like the kingdom of Siam, but an action of God, God's reign. We could even translate it "God's deliverance." In this light many themes in Jesus' ministry and teachings shine brightly. Jesus brought deliverance; he fed the poor and confronted the authorities who did injustice to them; he taught peacemaking; he healed the blind; he spoke of joy; he proclaimed and brought God's presence; he called for repentance. And Jesus also taught compassion. And he taught, just as Isaiah did, that God is the Compassionate One who delivers us.

When we understand these themes of the reign of God, we can more readily identify the times when the mustard seeds of God's reign break into our own experience, and we give thanks. Jesus proclaims that now we experience the mustard seeds of the reign of God; the whole mustard bush will come in the future at a time that no one, not even Jesus, knows (Matt. 24:36; Mark 13:32; Acts 1:7). In the meantime, it is not for us to spend our energy speculating about the "when"; Jesus says no one knows. The point, rather, is to give thanks for the mustard seeds in our lives and to live lives that fit the seven characteristics of the reign of God.

This is also what "the kingdom of God is among you" means (Luke 17:21 NRSV). Reflecting the holism of Hebraic spirituality, it is about so much more than an inner feeling, even though there is an important inward dimension to the kingdom. It involves an interior sense of joy and gratitude for God's miraculous, delivering presence. When Jesus teaches us to pray "your kingdom come, your will be done, on earth as it is in heaven," that means real fulfillment of God's will for these seven characteristics of the reign of God on the real earth, not a mere Platonic idea. It means an event of overcoming injustice, or overcoming violence, or overcoming the sense that God is absent, or bringing about repentance and return to God. When your child is healed of serious heart disease and healed of blindness, as my son David was, you cry real tears of thanksgiving for the breakthrough of God's reign in our real lives.

See also Beatitudes; Lord's Prayer; Social Justice.

For Further Reading: B. Chilton, *God in Strength* (1979); G. Stassen, *Living the Sermon on the Mount* (2006).

Glen Harold Stassen

Knowledge of God

According to Christian Scripture and tradition, "knowledge" is not a process, content, or system we can take for granted when its object is *God*. God is neither as we are, nor is he perfectly continuous with other objects we can know. In fact, the Bible teaches that God cannot be perceived by our natural senses (Ex. 33:20; John 1:18), which according to predominant, empirical theories are essential to knowledge in shape and substance. But for rationalist epistemologies, too, God presents a special challenge. For how should finite and fallen operations of knowing be adequate to the infinite and holy (Job 42:3; Isa. 6:5)?

The first thing that must be said about the knowledge of God, therefore, is that when and where it occurs in the human, it remains God's knowledge of himself. We cannot take native functions of the human person for granted as capable of the divine and simply render God according to assumed patterns of thinking, feeling, willing, or any combination thereof. Our knowledge of God is but a repetition of God's self-knowledge, which constitutes its own movement in our intellection, emotion, and volition. We might thus distinguish, as Karl Barth does, between "primary" and "secondary" forms of God's objectivity. That secondary objectivity in which God makes himself known — or that mode of his being in which he accommodates himself to us — is Jesus Christ. It is in Christ as the second triune person that we encounter God's knowledge of himself in truthful human operation. Moreover, it is by perceiving Christ that our own acts of knowing are enabled to partake of God's.

Theologians at least since Augustine have concluded that being the knowledge of God is something proper to Christ as God's Son. At the same time, it is considered proper to the Holy Spirit as the third triune person to exist as the love of God. Both in God's self and in our reiterative experience, therefore, the knowledge and love of God are coordinate modalities. They go together. One does not know God yet relate to him in an attitude of disinterest, since that would be inconsistent with God's revealed existence. Nor does one love God when the object of affection is simply the mysterious abyss of human negation. For knowledge to be

knowledge and love to be love, each must occur in the other; each mode of being must penetrate into the other. With respect to God, knowledge and love are reciprocally defining as they are interpenetrating or "perichoretic."

Knowledge of God is, in other words, inherently relational. To know God is to love him; it is to be wholly invested in his ways and intentions, receiving them as our own (so Ex. 33:13; Jer. 22:16). So as John Calvin famously observed, the knowledge of God necessarily involves truthful knowledge of ourselves. We come to perceive ourselves relative to God, as creatures whose entire being is sourced in, sustained by, and directed toward him. It may thus be helpful to conceive of the knowledge of God as our participation in the divine disposition of love through Christ by the Spirit.

For us to "have" knowledge of God is to *live* in Christ's Spirit. It is to take on the vocal cadences, kinetic motions, and hopeful expectations of Christ by the power of his Spirit, which is to say, by the coincidence of his character with our own (1 Cor. 1:18–2:16). It is to live out the grace and truth of God himself as we are adopted into his genealogy (Rom. 8). That is, our epistemology is structured upon the scaffolding of a more primal ontology: being in the revolution of God's turning outside himself. The spirituality of knowing God is thus not an otherworldly, suprasensible, enraptured state. It is something that completely engages our corporeality even as it is based in, governed by, and aimed an inward toward God.

The Holy Spirit creates a disposition of faith that shapes and defines one's whole person. As he does this, knowledge of God emerges. It comes, as John Wesley stressed, only with human rebirth. Knowledge of God occurs only as our senses are remade by and brought under the tutelage of the Holy Spirit, by whom spiritual things are discerned (John 14:26; 1 Cor. 2:14).

John's gospel is particularly clear that faith and knowledge are mutually conditioning. The consistency of their common occurrence suggests that for John "belief" and "knowledge" form a hendiadys: they are two terms conveying a single idea (see 6:69; 8:31–32; 10:38; 11:42; 14:7–10; 17:8). The idea is that the posture of obedience—prayerfulness, self-discipline, conscious dependency, and ultimately self-sacrificial charity in the name of Christ—such essential temperament is the pulse of the knowledge of God.

See also Wisdom.

For Further Reading: Augustine, *The Trinity*, trans. E. Hill (1991); K. Barth, *Church Dogmatics* II/1, secs. 25–27; "Ginōskō ...," *TDNT*, 1:689–719; J. Calvin, *Institutes of the Christian Religion*, bk. 1; J. Wesley, "The Great Privilege of Those That Are Born of God," in *Sermons on Several Occasions*, vol. 1 (1836).

Aaron T. Smith

Korean Christian Spirituality

In its short history (Roman Catholics finally gained a toehold in 1784, Protestants in 1884), Korean Christianity has produced a unique set of spiritual values and expressions. The major factors in this formative process have been indigenous religiosity, a specific type of conservative and pietistic Christianity introduced by Western missionaries, and rapid sociopolitical changes throughout its history. Although there is risk in generalization, the following values and practices are distinctly characteristic of Korean Christian spirituality.

The first is seen in the various expressions of Christian devotion. During the earlier years of exclusively Catholic presence, and then during the twentieth-century Japanese occupation and the subsequent Korean War years (1950–1953) for both Catholics and Protestants, Korean Christians developed an extremely otherworldly approach to religion, even to the extent of willingly putting their lives and the lives of others at risk for the "glory of God." Under the altered circumstances brought about by socioeconomic develop-

ments since the 1970s, this zealousness now tends to find its expression in cross-cultural missionary endeavors.

The second is prayer practices, which seem to reflect a combination of biblical ideals and indigenous valuation of diligent devotion, as found in Shamanism and Shamanistic Buddhism. Daily dawn prayer meetings have been the norm since the nationally significant Pyungyang revival of 1907. Initially special prayer mountains attracted tens of thousands to revival rallies. Such geographically elevated destinations have since become common to Korean Christian spirituality. And since Korean independence, prayer meetings have mushroomed throughout the country. Since the 1970s, Friday overnight prayer has become another regular feature of local churches, and in large churches, daily overnight prayer is also spreading. It is not only the formal programs that are unique, but also the modes of prayer practices. A loud unison prayer, sometimes involving shouting and wailing, was witnessed in the 1907 revival, and this tradition has been kept in prayer mountains and Pentecostal churches, as well as during annual revival rallies of local churches. Fasting has become another unique expression of one's spiritual commitment, ranging between a series of breakfast prayers to a forty-day fasting prayer. One prayer mountain is particularly known for its strong emphasis on fasting prayer.

Related to the prayer tradition is the strong religious orientation around "experience." Mystical religious experience is part of the indigenous psyche, and as in other religions, Christians have generally expected God's (often miraculous) intervention to meet serious human needs. Even before the introduction of Pentecostalism, the work of the Holy Spirit in a believer's life was a favorite subject of Bible study rallies and revival meetings. Thus, testimonies to healing and miracles are common across Christian denominations. The Korean prayer mountains and other religious gathering places have served as open "marketplaces" where various theologies and experiences are freely shared and disseminated across denominational boundaries.

Equally strong is an emphasis on the Word. Early revival meetings were, in effect, weeks of extended Bible study, bringing many local congregations together in a large place. The Scripture was diligently studied and prayed over. Such study was not seen as an intellectual exercise; the focus was always on practical application of the Scripture to everyday Christian life. In recent years, new forms have emerged, including various discipleship programs and QT (quiet time) guides.

Another feature of Korean Christian spirituality is the importance attributed to a strong local church. Perhaps coupled with a traditional value placed on religious structures, many early Christians found their local churches to be spiritual and social havens, with some Christians identifying with more than one concurrently. Christianity was often branded as a "Western" (that is, foreign) religion, and persecution and marginalization were common experiences. Refusal to participate or continue ancestral family rites (which triggered a massive persecution of early Catholics) has been a thorny issue for many Christians. Church buildings, therefore, have become strong symbols of Christian solidarity. Consequently, Korean Christians tend to give sacrificially toward church building projects.

Last, with increased legitimacy, expanding freedoms, and economic advances, the previous otherworldly emphasis of Korean Christian spirituality is giving way to its opposite—a focus on this world. This shift is having both positive and negative consequences. Positively, Christians are more actively engaged with social issues in their thinking about and endeavors to be faithful to their mission in life. Negatively, however, Christianity has become for some a commodity to be exploited in a consumerlike pursuit of personal gain. Korean Christianity, with its now stagnant growth against a backdrop of increasing religious pluralism, faces a serious challenge to define itself in the new social environment. Its unique spiritual tradition may still be valid, but its expression should be relevant to the changing context.

See also Asian Christian Spirituality.

For Further Reading: V. Fabella et al., *Asian Christian Spirituality* (1992); Y. H. Lee, *The Holy Spirit Movement in Korea* (2009).

Wonsuk Ma

L

Labor, Manual

Work was created for human beings before the fall of Adam and Eve. This fact is important, because work is therefore intended as part of the development of human beings into their ultimate destiny in God's sovereign plan. The impact of the fall, however, was to mix difficulty and challenge into the goodness of work as the labor of human beings was subjected to resistance from creation and to frustration and pain.

In our modern world, more and more people are disconnected from manual labor—the working of one's body in the act of creation, restoration, or some other activity. For most of human history, the norm of human activity was manual labor, with only the elite being spared from the connection of the human body with their daily tasks. Today more and more people are completely disconnected from manual labor and, with that loss, experience a disconnect between their bodies and their contribution to life. While manual labor should not be viewed simplistically as spiritual, since the impact of the fall has made manual labor often dehumanizing and harmful to human life, the role of manual labor in Christian spirituality should not be overlooked.

Historically this connection was best presented in the monastic life. In the Benedictine tradition, the Benedictine rule established a sevenfold pattern for the six days of the week outside of the Sabbath. The activities of the monastic life of course included traditionally "spiritual" activities, such as prayer, worship, and meditation. However, manual labor was included in the rule not merely to ensure that the monastery operated, but because it was seen as part of the essential calling of the human life. This was captured by the common monastic Latin phrase *ora et labora*, which means "pray and work." The two were intertwined and served one another and the spiritual formation of the monk's life.

With modern life more and more disconnected from manual labor for many in the industrialized West, many Christian spirituality movements now involve manual labor, often in the form of mission to the wider world, as part of their program of formation. These movements affirm that human beings were created and intended to work and that this work does not take away from spiritual pursuits but rather affirms the anti-gnostic reality of the gospel, which seeks to bring the whole earth as well as individual lives into submission to the Lord Jesus.

See also Benedictine Spirituality; Work.

For Further Reading: D. R. Sorg, *Holy Work* (2003); M. Volf, *Work in the Spirit* (1991).

Christopher Morton

ize spiritual pilgrimage and aid the inner journey of drawing near to God. Participants walk slowly through the labyrinth while engaging in meditative prayer and reflection. While the labyrinth has pre-Christian origins, it was, like so many other elements of antecedent cultures, claimed and appropriated for Christ's honor and Christian use. A fourth-century basilica was the site of the earliest known Christian labyrinth, yet the most famous is the classical eleven-circuit labyrinth of Chartres Cathedral, built in thirteenth-century France. In it the contours of the cross are clearly highlighted. It was replicated and popularized in the late 20th century through prayer walks at interior and exterior labyrinth installations at Grace Cathedral in San Francisco.

Participants commonly testify that the labyrinth facilitates a deeper sense of aesthetic order and centeredness. Among Christians, including a growing number of evangelicals, a discerning use of permanent and portable labyrinths at special services, retreats, and conferences has become one means of fostering prayer practices that engage one's whole being—not only the heart, mind, and spirit, but the body as well. The aim is to nurture attentiveness to the work of the Holy Spirit that leads ultimately to obedience to God. Although the formally practiced stages of the prayer walk follow the classic movements of purgation, illumination, and union, many simply walk the labyrinth to let go of burdensome distractions in order to become focused and fully present to God.

See also Pilgrimage.

For Further Reading: A. Ahlberg Calhoun, *Spiritual Disciplines Handbook* (2005); L. Artress, *Walking a Sacred Path* (2006).

Natalie Hendrickson

Labyrinth

An ancient curvilinear pathway motif—with only one way in and back out—designed to symbol-

Lament

Lament gives expression to some of the deepest, most personal, and most wrenching of human emotions. Humans have always grieved, and the world's literature and cultures are replete with manifold ways of expressing this, from elaborate rituals and nonverbal forms to penetrating literary compositions and deeply moving musical works.

In the Bible, lament includes many expressions of mourning over death. Periods of mourning varied, from seven days for Joseph and Saul (Gen. 50:10; 1 Sam. 31:13) to thirty days for Moses and Aaron (Num. 20:29; Deut. 34:8) to seventy days for Jacob (perhaps reflecting Egyptian custom: Gen. 50:3). Weeping commonly accompanied such mourning (Num. 20:29; Luke 8:52; John 11:33, 35; Acts 9:39). Practices included fasting and wearing sackcloth (Jonah 3:7–8), sitting in and/or covering oneself with dust and ashes (Job 42:6), removing shoes and eating special foods (Ezek. 24:17), and forgoing washing and anointing with oils (2 Sam. 14:2). Professional female mourners could be called upon to help mourn (Jer. 9:17–18; Amos 5:16).

Lament was not restricted to mourning over death, however. Crises of many sorts—wars, sickness, feelings of alienation from God (or abandonment by him), and consciousness of sin—were likewise occasions for lament. The prophets mourned over the conditions of the people to whom they were sent and even lamented in anticipation of their destruction. Micah, for example, cried out: "Because of this I will weep and wail; I will go about barefoot and naked. I will howl like a jackal and moan like an owl" (1:8). Jeremiah's mourning was perhaps the most passionate and eloquent of all: "Oh, that my head were a spring of water and my eyes a fountain of tears! I would weep day and night for the slain of my people" (9:1). Again, it was Jeremiah who lamented: "Cursed be the day I was born! May the day my mother bore me not be blessed! Cursed be the man who brought my father the news, who made him very glad, saying, 'A child is born to you—a son!'" (20:14–15). Jewish tradition also attributes to Jeremiah the book of Lamentations, which is a series of laments—more properly, dirges—over the destruction of Jerusalem.

The richest source of laments in the Bible is the book of Psalms. More than half of the psalms are laments of one type or another. According to Claus Westermann, the typical pattern of the individual lament is as follows: (1) address to God, (2) complaint, (3) confession of trust/assurance of being heard, (4) petition, and (5) vow to praise/praise. The critical elements are the *complaint*, the *petition*, and the *vow to praise*. In the *complaint*, the psalmist lays out his troubles. In the *petition*, he prays with the goal of persuading God to respond. In the *vow to praise*, the psalmist anticipates the time when he will be able to praise God once again, or else simply breaks into praise.

The psalms of lament offer instruction in proper ways of addressing God in times of distress. In contrast to a carefree and simplistic attitude of "Don't worry, be happy," true biblical spirituality embraces the full range of human emotion, including sadness, despair, even anger. David and other psalmists—as was Job—were secure enough in their relationship with their God that they could challenge him, asking hard questions. What is striking about the many examples of biblical lament is that those lamenting were not atheists. They all clung to their belief in God, even when he seemed to them to be distant and uncaring. They remembered the past, when God *had* met them, and this formed the basis for their confidence that God would once again hear them and respond (Ps. 42:4). The believing community formed a safe place for lamenting. And in the end, the goal was to once again praise God (the vow to praise). The most desperate expression of lament is Psalm 88, where there *is* no vow to praise, where the images are unrelentingly negative. The psalmist sees no hope at hand and simply waits in silence, embracing—if that's the right word—the wait.

There is much to be said about silence and pain. Sometimes we hear God more clearly in our pain. As C. S. Lewis wrote in *The Problem of Pain*, "God whispers to us in our pleasures, speaks in our conscience, but shouts in our pains: it is [God's] megaphone to rouse a deaf world." And God himself helps us in our weakest hours. Paul writes in Romans 8:26: "In the same way, the Spirit helps us in our weakness. We do not know what we ought to pray for, but the Spirit himself intercedes for us with groans that words cannot express."

For many Christians, music can speak in the silence. Some of the most profoundly moving compositions in this regard are *requiems*, written in connection with the Roman Catholic Requiem Mass, which is celebrated for the repose of the dead. Some of the most famous are by Mozart, Berlioz, Verdi, Brahms, and Fauré. The "St. Matthew Passion" by J. S. Bach, while not a requiem, also deserves mention here, for its moving presentation of the depths of Jesus' suffering.

See also Consolation and Desolation; Dark Night; Grief.

For Further Reading: J. Bayly, *The View from a Hearse* (1969); G. L. Carr and G. Carr, *The Fierce Goodbye* (1990); D. Howard, "Psalm 88 and the Rhetoric of Lament," in *"My Words Are Lovely": Studies in the Rhetoric of the Psalms*, ed. R. Foster and D. Howard (2008), 132–46; C. S. Lewis, *A Grief Observed* (1963); C. Westermann, *Praise and Lament in the Psalms*, trans. K. Crim and R. Soulen (1981); N. Wolterstorff, *Lament for a Son* (1987).

David M. Howard Jr.

Latin America, Christian Spirituality in

One of the most significant expressions of Christian spirituality in the Western world is the one that emerged in Spain in the 16th century, during the time of the conquest of what later came to be known as Latin America. Represented by Teresa of Avila and John of the Cross, this spirituality placed Jesus Christ at the center of the Christian experience and left as a legacy several works still counted among the very best written during the golden age of Spanish literature.

Unfortunately, the Christ that the conquistadores brought to the New World was not the living Christ of these Spanish mystics; it was the Christ of the church-state of Spain, whose way was advanced by the sword. And the final result of the belligerent evangelization that was carried out in his name was countries with a veneer of Christian faith but void of Christian substance.

The huge shortage of priests combined with the close association of the Roman Catholic missionary enterprise with the violent conquest brought about by the Spanish Empire provided no basis for the fulfillment of the church's commission to make disciples of Jesus Christ. It is not surprising that the outcome of that enterprise was the beginning of what may be regarded as a Latin American type of Roman Catholic spirituality, generally marked by the deep polarization that exists between the wealthy minority and the poor majority of the population. For the former, Christianity became a religious justification of authoritarian governments and exploitative economic systems; for the latter, it became popular religiosity—a religion that majors on patron saints' celebrations and pilgrimages to holy shrines but relegates church dogmas and rites to a secondary place, and is rather common in the countryside and in urban slums.

These two forms of Roman Catholic spirituality have permeated religious life in Latin America since colonial times and up to the present. To be fair, however, among the protagonists of the first evangelization of this continent there were several commendable exceptions. Such was the case, for instance, of Bartolomé de Las Casas, the sixteenth-century Dominican "Defender of the Indians." Going against the general trend of his day, he saw in the Indians the poor to whom Jesus came to announce good news, and he regarded Jesus' special concern for the poor as the key to Christian theology and spirituality. His spiritual legacy has been preserved by some resilient Roman Catholic Christians who, often in sharp divergence from the church and its official teachings, have struggled to keep the fire of the gospel burning in their personal and community life and mission.

In his outstanding work on *The Other Spanish Christ* (1933), John A. Mackay argued that the kind of spirituality that Latin America desperately needed was the Christian spirituality represented by the sixteenth-century Spanish mystics. He found traces of that spirituality in the writings of several contemporary Spanish and Latin American authors, including the philosopher Miguel de Unamuno — the "prince of modern Christian thinkers," who exercised a profound influence on him.

One suspects that if Mackay had written his classic book years later, he would not have overlooked two developments in the "spiritual history" of Latin America — one negative and the other positive — that have been part and parcel of Christian spirituality on this continent during the last four decades or so.

On the negative side is the emergence of popular Protestant religiosity. Writing from the perspective of his own day, Mackay pointed to the Protestant missionary movement, first from Europe and later from the United States, as the means God was using for the rediscovery of the living Christ. For him, what Protestantism offered to Latin America was not an institutional church but "a personality, one who bears the marks of the Other Spanish Christ" — the living Christ that the missionaries who came with the *conquistadores* failed to bring. Without denying Mackay's basic thesis, it must also be said that the greatest deficiency of the Protestant gospel was its individualism. Strongly influenced by the Enlightenment, this movement did not always take adequate account of the social dimension of human life; it conceived of men and women as free to pursue their own individual happiness and failed to see their interdependence. As a result, it fostered a church movement largely constituted by people more concerned about selfishly enjoying the benefits of salvation, including health and wealth, than about participating in the fulfillment of God's purpose for his entire creation. In

the last two or three decades, this problem has been exacerbated by an amazing increase in the number of neo-Pentecostal megachurches that preach the so-called prosperity gospel.

On the positive side is the contribution that Latin American theology, both Roman Catholic and Protestant, has been making to the rediscovery of a spirituality focused on Jesus Christ and his ministry as the key to understand the practical meaning of living in light of the kingdom of God — a kingdom of justice and peace — in the midst of the kingdoms of the world. Even more encouraging is the way in which an increasing number of churches in Latin America are translating that theology into what is now known as "integral mission," in which word and deed, love and justice, the personal and the social are kept together in terms of signs of the kingdom.

See also Liberation Spirituality; *Mujerista* Spirituality.

For Further Reading: C. Bussmann, *Who Do You Say?* (1985); G. Cook, ed., *New Face of the Church in Latin America* (1994); G. Gutiérrez, *Las Casas* (1993); J. Míguez-Bonino, *Faces of Latin American Protestantism* (1997); C. R. Padilla, *Mission between the Times* (1985).

C. René Padilla

Laubach, Frank C. (1884 – 1970)

American missionary and world literacy champion. Laubach's early ministry in the Philippines was filled with numerous setbacks and heartache, including the death of three of his children to malaria. In 1929 he had a life-changing encounter through which he felt divinely challenged truly to love the Muslim people with whom he lived. Laubach began reading the Christian mystics to cultivate a greater openness to God's presence and guidance to assist him in developing his literacy method known as Each One Teach One. Over a forty-year period, he visited and assisted 103 countries in developing methods to improve their literacy and was responsible for producing literary primers in 315 languages. Laubach recorded many of his spiritual struggles and discoveries. *Letters by a Modern Mystic* (1937) captures some of his life-transforming experiences, and *Game with Minutes* (1953) reveals his early attempts to develop minute-by-minute awareness of God. These two works communicate Laubach's indebtedness to Brother Lawrence's *The Practice of the Presence of God* and assert that God is everywhere present and will lead those who surrender their will and depend on God's guidance. Laubach stressed the importance of prayer, believing it was the strongest power to accomplish God's purposes. Further, he maintained that Christians are often ineffective in serving God because they devote such a small portion of time and awareness to God. Additionally, he wrote a number of books on peace and justice, including *Wake Up or Blow Up* (1951), *The World Is Learning Compassion* (1958), and *War of Amazing Love* (1965). Laubach possessed a deep experiential or practical understanding of the Christian faith. Similar to earlier writers of Christian mysticism, his language sometimes lacks theological precision, yet he maintained his evangelical heritage. Some of Laubach's spiritual writings resemble those of another evangelical mystic of his time, A. W. Tozer. His active life inspired by contemplation demonstrated the importance of integrating prayer with action.

See also Brother Lawrence.

For Further Reading: K. Norton, *Frank C. Laubach* (1990); H. Roberts, *Champion of the Silent Billion: The Story of Frank C. Laubach* (1961).

Tom Schwanda

Law, William (1686–1761)

Anglican theologian and mystic. Law was born in the village of King's Cliffe, Northamptonshire, and went on to graduate from Emmanuel College, Cambridge, with both his B.A. (1708) and M.A. (1712). He was elected to a college fellowship in 1711, the same year as his ordination. When Law declined to take the oath of allegiance to George I upon his accession in 1714, his academic career came to an early close. He later retired to Putney, where he resided in the household of Edward Gibbon, the grandfather of the historian, from 1723–1737. In 1740, he returned to his hometown, where he was to live out the remainder of his life. His final years were ones of chastity, charity, prayer, and intense study. He was seen by many of his contemporaries as a man of quiet introspection and isolation from the dominant spiritual trends of his time. He was deeply impacted by French and German mysticism.

Law is most remembered for *A Serious Call to a Devout and Holy Life* (1729), a devotional work that has become a spiritual classic and that is admired for its lucid prose. Influenced by the writings of Thomas à Kempis, Johannes Tauler, and Jan van Ruysbroeck, it set forth a more decidedly contemplative perspective on spirituality than other contemporary works. It has, though, an ascetic rigidity that fails to appreciate much of human culture and achievement. It achieved great success within his lifetime, earning him a large, enduring audience.

Another of Law's most seminal works is *The Spirit of Love* (1752–1754), which was published in two parts and reveals the profound influence of the German Protestant mystic Jacob Boehme. Penned in an enigmatic tone, which dovetails with its mysticism, it deals with the concerns that dogged his later years, especially the indwelling of Christ. His influence on contemporary religious thought was acknowledged by John Wesley, who was influenced by one of Law's early writings, *Christian Perfection* (1726), which provided the catalyst for Wesley's own spiritual development.

See also Anglican Spirituality.

For Further Reading: A. K. Walker, *William Law* (1973); *William Law*, CWS (1978).

Michael A. G. Haykin

Laypersons and Spirituality

Strictly speaking, there are no Christian "laypersons" in the sense commonly used: second-class, not ordained, and not qualified. Since the ascension of Christ and the outpouring of the Spirit, the whole people of God are clergy in the true meaning of that word — blessed, endowed, and appointed. The Greek word for "laity," *laikos,* is never used by an inspired apostle to describe a Christian person. So Christian spirituality must address the perspectives, experiences, and challenges of the whole people of God — referred to in the NT as the *laos,* or people of God. But that requires forming a Christian spirituality not only for those whose primary engagement is in the church — as with pastors, prelates, and popes; monks, missionaries, and mystics — but also for those who live and work in the world.

The standard "lay" spirituality in the evangelical tradition involves daily Bible reading and prayer, attendance at worship services and sacraments, and witnessing. But this caters to the two-level spirituality whereby pastors, missionaries, and religious specialists are the only ones who spend all their time doing spiritual things, which is not really the case. Ordinary Christians are relegated to experiencing Spirit life only in their discretionary time, after work, sleep, and family responsibilities. Reacting to the two-level spirituality of the church of his day, the higher for the monk and priest and lower for the person in home and workplace, Martin Luther argued that the ordinary person in the midst of everyday life was actually serving God and responding to God's call. To a large extent, Vatican II recovered this integrated approach to everyday spirituality.

In contrast to the aforementioned two-level spirituality, a proper "lay" spirituality makes sense of family, workplace, money, friendship, neighboring, civic responsibilities, the poor, and the spiritual powers at work in the world. Ordinary experiences are evocative of spiritual growth and meaning: speaking, listening, driving, riding a bus, commuting, working, dreaming, being interrupted, growing older, having sexual hunger, questioning, wasting time, seeking to control time, drivenness, laziness, boredom, happiness, discovering identity, having a secret to keep, feeling pain, and loneliness. All the ordinary passages in life are open doors to transcendence: conception, birth, childhood, puberty, menstruation, adolescence, going to college, leaving home, getting married, becoming a parent, experiencing singleness, losing close relatives or friends to death, getting old, retiring, and dying.

There are profound biblical reasons for a lay spirituality: because God became human and matter matters; because the Holy Spirit has been poured out on all of life; because God's desire for us is not that we become religious but fully human; because people are image-bearers built to resemble our relational God; because creation bears the signature of God; and because our ultimate destiny is a fully embodied existence in a garden city where God is everywhere.

Take sleep, for instance. We spend about one-third of our life doing it, and without a spirituality of sleep, we will miss the meaning of it and the opportunity it affords for spiritual formation and faith development. Psalm 127:2 notes that "in vain ... you rise up early and go late to rest, eating the bread of anxious toil; for he gives to his beloved sleep" (RSV). But verse 2 is informed by what precedes it: "Unless the LORD builds the house, those who build it labor in vain. Unless the LORD watches over the city, the watchman stays awake in vain" (v. 1 RSV). To go to sleep is an act of faith, an affirmation that God is God and we are not God. We are not running the world. We can trust God while we sleep (Mark 4:26–29). Choices about sleep constitute an arena of spiritual formation.

The workplace is another area Christian people frequently regard as a spiritual diversion. But work is an ideal context in which to observe ourselves, as Cardinal Wyszynski notes in his classic volume on spirituality and work — namely, that by the sweat of our brow our souls are laid bare. But there is more to it than that. Work, even work in this still somewhat fallen world, becomes a vehicle of spiritual growth, a place where we can tell God we love him, where the Spirit fruit can be nurtured and the vices dealt with.

Friendship is often considered a diversion from the spiritual life, especially in monasteries. But as Aelred of Rievaulx so wisely demonstrated in his classic *Spiritual Friendship*, friendship is a pathway to God. The triune God is a relational God. Human beings made in God's image are relational beings. And we experience God and grow spiritually mainly through relationships. Our relational history is often our spiritual history. The last judgment, if Jesus is to be believed, is in terms of our relationships.

Far from taking us away from the world and everyday life, Christian spirituality calls us to find God and be found by God right where we are, in the center of life rather than at its periphery. And that, after all, is what God did himself when he wanted to reveal himself. He went through a complete human life from conception to resurrection.

See also Vocation.

For Further Reading: R. Banks and R. P. Stevens, *The Complete Book of Everyday Christianity* (1997); E. Dreyer, *Earth Crammed with Heaven* (1994); Brother Lawrence, *The Practice of the Presence of God*, ed. J. J. Delaney (1977); P. Parker, *The Active Life* (1990); E. Peterson, *Leap over a Wall* (1997); A. Schmemann, *For the Life of the World* (1988); R. P. Stevens, *Down-to-Earth Spirituality* (2003); H. Weber and S. Neill, eds. *The Layman in Christian History* (1963).

R. Paul Stevens

Leadership, Spirituality of

Christian spirituality addresses a holistic vision of life lived before God, through Christ, in the transforming and empowering presence of the Holy Spirit. Leadership is a process of social influence in service of group goals. Recent literature frames leadership as a relational endeavor that adheres to high ethical standards and transcends self-interest. Leaders impart hope, sustain morale, and prompt others to contribute willingly and sacrificially to the welfare and progress of the group. Leadership as a personal quality refers to an integrated constellation of virtue-oriented attributes foundational to influencing others and pursuing collective success. A Christian spirituality of leadership speaks to a biblically informed and integrated view of the purpose, character, relationships, and leadership practices of Jesus' followers in the context of a biblical community and its mission in the world. It places supreme value on the glory of God, the cross of Christ, the transforming power of the Holy Spirit, and the moral authority of selfless service.

A spirituality of leadership is governed by metaphors of the leader as disciple, servant, and shepherd. Leaders are first and foremost cross-bearing disciples. The cross is at the heart of discipleship, and discipleship resides at the heart of leadership. Leading is premised on following Jesus and learning from him in an intimate, transforming relationship (Matt. 11:28–30).

Leaders are servants. The NT term *doulos* refers to a common household servant or slave. Jesus took the form of a servant (Phil. 2:7) and demonstrated his servant heart by washing the feet of his disciples (John 13:14–15). Jesus' death on the cross was a radical expression of service (Phil. 2:6–11). Paul viewed himself as a servant of Christ (Rom. 1:1) and considered his apostleship as a call to service for the sake of Jesus, his church, and all people (1 Cor. 9:19; 2 Cor. 4:5). Accordingly, leaders affirm service over self-interest (Matt. 20:26–28).

Leaders are shepherds. Jesus is the Good Shepherd who gathers lost sheep into God's fold (John 10:1–21) by dying for them and rising again (Matt. 26:31–32). He is the Great Shepherd who provides his flock with all they need to do God's will (Heb. 13:20–21). Jesus seeks leaders who share his shepherd's heart. Paul refers to leaders as shepherds (the Greek term for "pastor" means shepherd, Eph. 4:11). The shepherd metaphor is used to describe the leadership of local elders (Acts 20:28–29). Jesus' commission to Peter to "feed my sheep" (John 21:17) is reflected in Peter's admonition to local leaders to act in the character of a good shepherd by providing selfless, watchful, courageous, and caring leadership for the community (1 Peter 5:1–5).

Informed by these metaphors, a spirituality of leadership highlights five interdependent realities of the Christian life and biblical community. First, a spirituality of leadership is inextricably bound to God's purpose to restore humanity from the temporal and eternal consequences of the fall and to sum up all things in Christ (Eph. 1:1–14). Spiritual leaders contribute to this cosmic purpose by building redemptive communities; serving as catalysts for faith, hope, and love; and participating in acts of service and witness.

Second, a spirituality of leadership views leadership as a Christ-centered, Spirit-led process of spiritual transformation. The source of effective leadership is a saving, intimate, transforming relationship with the risen Christ. Through the Spirit, Christ empowers his servants for service and witness. Accordingly, leaders are attentive to the Spirit's voice and cooperate with his transforming work in themselves and the world.

Third, a spirituality of leadership highlights the connection between the quality of the leader's relationship with Jesus and the leader's spiritual influence. The Spirit makes possible the personal virtues that enable the leader to maintain the Christlike relationships necessary for the health of the redemptive community. Spiritual leaders embody faith, hope, and love, and demonstrate these in patterns of caring, humble service, and effective witness. Mature character is a requisite for local leadership (1 Tim. 3:1–12) and provides the basis for practices such as resolving conflict, and demonstrating forgiveness, forbearance, and mutual respect. Consequently, a spirituality of leadership values mature character more highly than factors typically associated with effective leadership, such as charisma and technical competence.

Fourth, a spirituality of leadership embraces an ethos of service. Spiritual power is released in the world through the selfless service of disciples who share Jesus' heart. Leaders employ power to build up the community, and they influence others through loving persuasion. As such, a spirituality of leadership rejects the attitudes and behavior patterns embedded in the prideful ethos of the world system: the perversion of authority, the lust for rank and privilege, and the abuse of power expressed in dictatorial relationships and controlling behavior (Matt. 20:20–28).

Fifth, a spirituality of leadership embraces the priesthood of believers, which affirms that every believer has direct access to God, participates in the transforming power of the Holy Spirit, and is responsible to God to contribute to his work by living and sharing the gospel (Rom. 12:1–8; 1 Peter 2:9). Since all are endowed with spiritual gifts, each is called to contribute regardless of formal or professional role. Consequently, the exercise of spiritual influence is not limited to formal positions such as elder or pastor.

Believers called to public leadership encounter both great opportunity and temptation. Positions of secular power afford the opportunity to glorify God (Matt. 5:14–16) and bring justice to all (Prov. 28:12; 29:2–7). But believers are vulnerable to the corrupting influence of power. Power fuels prideful ambition, feeds narcissism, and presents opportunity to gratify base impulses. In the face of these temptations, believers are called to live exemplary public lives, deserving the respect of contemporaries, including nonbelievers (2 Cor. 8:21; Phil. 2:15; 1 Peter 2:11–12). Accordingly, public leaders must depend on the Spirit to exercise the self-control (temperance) to resist these harmful drives and lead in a Christlike manner.

See also Management; Marketplace Spirituality; Work.

For Further Reading: L. Ford, *Transforming Leadership* (1993); J. Kouzes and B. Posner, eds., *Christian Reflections on the Leadership Challenge* (2006); T. Laniak, *Shepherds after My Own Heart* (2006).

Mark W. McCloskey

Lectio Divina

See **Spiritual Reading.**

Lee, Jarena (1783–after 1849)

African-American itinerant evangelist. Jarena Lee was born in Cape May, New Jersey, to free parents. She moved to Philadelphia in 1804 where she heard Richard Allen, later the founder of the African Methodist Episcopal denomination, preach at the flagship Bethel African Methodist Episcopal Church, and there determined, according to the *Religious Experience and Journal of Mrs. Jarena Lee* (1849), that "this is the people to which my heart unites." She was soon converted; subsequently she struggled with backsliding for several years, until she learned of the Methodist doctrine of sanctification and sought and received this blessing.

Lee was initially rebuffed by Allen when she asked to preach. He told her that the Methodist discipline did not allow female preachers. In 1819, after a six-year marriage to Joseph Lee, a pastor, and a continued struggle with her call to preach, Lee stepped up and preached at Bethel, seizing an opportunity created by the hesitancy of another preacher. From this point, Allen allowed her to preach as an official exhorter, though he was not willing to ordain her. Lee commenced her life of itinerant evangelism primarily in the Middle Atlantic and Northeastern states. Lee's *Journal* contains frequent references to guidance from divine voices and visions. Her spiritual life was driven by her overriding concern for the salvation of souls. She was subsequently regarded as an inspirational and empowering figure for African-American

women desiring to be respected within the church and validated in Christian ministry.

See also African-American Christian Spirituality; Allen, Richard; Feminist Spirituality; Women.

Geordan Hammond

Leisure and Play

The most important principle underlying a Christian view of leisure is expressed in the fourth commandment of the Decalogue: "Six days you shall labor and do all your work.... On [the seventh day] you shall not do any work.... For ... [God] rested on the seventh day" (Ex. 20:9–11). Instead of being antagonists, work and rest are part of a harmonious cycle. God commanded both work and rest; if work is a spiritual calling, so is leisure. An important aspect of the very nature of leisure is also expressed in the quoted verses: leisure draws a boundary around a person's acquisitive urges and clears a space for spiritual exercise and growth.

Definitions of the word *leisure* provide a helpful avenue toward understanding the spirituality of leisure. One derivation (Fr. *leisir*, from Lat. *licere*; Eng. *license*, from the same root) carries the idea of freedom from ordinary obligations. The other derivation (Gr. *skole*, Lat. *schola*; Eng. *school*, from the same root) carries the idea "to halt or cease" and implies time for education of the mind and development of the person. Applied to spirituality, leisure represents time beyond the obligations of physical and economic necessity that can be used as growing time for the human spirit and for spiritual exercises.

Leisure can also be defined by the activities that we perform in our free time. Leisure time can be filled with specifically spiritual activities, such as prayer, meditation, reading, private or public worship, and what the Puritans called "Christian conference" (godly conversation). Nonetheless, an important aspect of leisure is that it needs to be experienced as freely chosen and not done as a required duty; spiritual exercises can fall into the category of either work or leisure, depending on how a person perceives and pursues them.

If leisure can thus be defined in terms of time and activity, it is ultimately a quality of life. Leisure in its highest reaches is a state of being. Josef Pieper calls leisure "a mental and spiritual attitude" that includes as its ingredients "an attitude ... of inward calm, of ... letting things happen," and of celebration.

What, then, of the related concept of play? Under what conditions does it become part of the spiritual life? It does so when people receive it consciously as a gift from God, with gratitude to God who has freed them to play in the Spirit.

The theology of both leisure and play begins with the character and acts of God as portrayed in the Bible. If God is a worker, he is also the God who rests (Gen. 2:1 – 3) and who is refreshed by that rest (Ex. 31:17). Additionally, the extensive OT annual calendar of feasts and appointed festivals had the effect of making religious leisure an essential ingredient in how God's people related to him. In the NT, the life of Jesus as recorded in the Gospels is replete with pictures of retreats from work and attendance at dinner parties, and we find as well Jesus' command to contemplate the lilies of the field (Matt. 6:28).

See also Sabbath; Sports and Spirituality; Work.

For Further Reading: L. Doohan, *Leisure* (1990); P. Heintzman et al., eds., *Christianity and Leisure* (1994); R. Johnston, *The Christian at Play* (1983); H. Lehman, *In Praise of Leisure* (1974); J. Pieper, *Leisure: The Basis of Culture* (2010); L. Ryken, *Redeeming the Time* (1995).

Leland Ryken

Lewis, C(live) S(taples) (1893 – 1963)

The most influential Christian writer of the 20th century. Lewis's works skillfully connect reason (argument and evidence) with imagination (story and metaphor). His theological works, such as

Mere Christianity (1952), use rational, apologetic evidence for the faith, and they stress doctrines common to all Christians. Narrative works, such as the Chronicles of Narnia (1950 – 1956), use imagination to arouse desire for God (*sehnsucht*). In Narnia one *feels* the pervasive presence of an unmanageably great but also immeasurably good King.

Lewis began life in Belfast, Ireland. As a child, he loved Norse myth. At fifteen he rejected God, due in part to human suffering. In 1929 he converted to theism. He realized that his critique of God presumed an ultimate standard of good. Without God, this standard has no ground. Two years later, as he describes in *Surprised by Joy* (1955), he converted to Christ. In 1956, after years as a bachelor professor at Oxford and Cambridge, Lewis joined Joy Davidman Gresham in a civil union just so she could stay in Britain. But surprised by another Joy, he fell deeply in love with his wife in the year after marriage. Lewis and Joy then sought Christian marriage. Tragically, Joy soon contracted cancer and died in 1960, severely testing Lewis's faith and leading to his painfully honest reflection, *A Grief Observed* (1961).

Lewis became a household name with the publication of *Screwtape Letters*. (He made the cover of *Time* on September 8, 1947.) He imagined infernal letters in which a seasoned devil, Screwtape, mentored his nephew, Wormwood, an incompetent tempter. This typifies Lewis's approach to spirituality. *Screwtape Letters* (1942) uses imaginative language and vivid metaphor to disrupt rational objections and awaken spiritual responses, and it uses incisive observation and astonishing insight to reveal to readers the self-serving machinations of sinful human hearts.

Lewis followed traditional spiritual practices. An Anglican, he revered the Eucharist (though he attended church without enthusiasm). He stressed prayer, generosity, humility, and character formation. But perhaps Lewis's greatest contribution to Christian spirituality is his insight into human motivations and character, as seen in books like *The Great Divorce* (1945).

Lewis stresses a spirituality of the routines. In "Weight of Glory," he says ordinary humans matter more than civilizations. Just as there is more to his apologetic than rationalism, there is more to his spirituality than moralism. In the end, both serve the spiritual life, and spiritual life is about desire for God. God made our hearts to long for him. And only God satisfies.

See also Imagination; Literature and Christian Spirituality.

For Further Reading: J. R. Duncan, *The Magic Never Ends* (2005); G. Sayer, *Jack: A Life of C. S. Lewis* (2005).

David K. Clark

Lex Orandi, Lex Credendi

A Latin phrase meaning "the law of worship is the law of belief." Before either creeds or canon were established, the early church created and maintained doctrines and dogma based on the way the church worshiped. In the early church this referred specifically to the prayers and liturgy that constituted church worship before the written tradition and councils defined orthodoxy. In this period, the entirety of the professed faith of the church was contained completely within worship practice and not in formalized text.

In modern times, the understanding of *lex orandi, lex credendi* is used in an interpretive manner and not so much for the constitution of doctrine. For example, when one is seeking to understand or participate in the faith of the church, one can observe that belief within the liturgy of the church. Therefore, an interpretation or example of the belief of the church is present in a substantial way in liturgical practice. The general and specific expressions of the liturgy together frame the content of orthodox belief. This can be seen in all the ancient liturgical services of the church as well as in the later Anglican *Book of Common Prayer*, in which the practice of prayer reveals Anglican theology.

Inversely, Christian liturgy not only reveals the faith, but the faith shapes and informs the liturgy. The prayers of the faithful conform to the professed belief of the church. In the ancient liturgies, for example, prayers that were offered over the bread and wine in Communion were expressed in a way that grows out of the faith and actions contained in the liturgy. One could reverse the dictum and say, "*lex credendi, lex orandi.*" Thus, a reciprocal relationship exists between doctrine and liturgy in the worshiping life of the church.

This means that the prayers of the church are expressions of the corresponding beliefs of the church. The commonly expressed words of worship reveal the commonly held faith of the church. This can be seen most dramatically throughout the 8th and 9th centuries during the great iconoclastic debates. The liturgical practices of the church prior to the 8th century regarding the use of icons in worship provided a significant precedent for establishing them as church dogma in the Seventh Ecumenical Council of AD 787.

See also Rule of Life.

For Further Reading: G. Dix, *The Shape of the Liturgy* (1981); L. Mitchell, *Praying Shapes Believing* (1985); G. Wainwright, *Doxology: The Praise of God in Worship, Doctrine, and Life* (1984); G. Wainwright et al., *The Study of Liturgy* (1992).

Ian Smith

Liberation Spirituality

Liberation spirituality is the distinctive sense of vocation and praxis associated with liberation theology. Liberation theology first came to voice in the 1960s in the writings of Paulo Freire, Gustavo Gutiérrez, and other Catholic theologians in Latin America who promoted a preferential option for the poor. Latin American liberation theology embraced three goals: (1) critique of oppression, (2) advocacy of the rights and humanity of the oppressed, and (3) liberation as spiritual praxis. The word *praxis* refers to the integration of theory and practice made possible with the awareness that God is on the side of the oppressed.

In 1969, one year after the assassination of Martin Luther King Jr., theologian James Cone developed black theology as a radical religious response to the secular black power movement. Cone and the black and womanist theologians following his lead drew heavily upon the Negro spirituals, sermons, and other expressions of African-American spirituality in their analyses of slavery, discrimination, and the suffering of black people.

A key OT paradigm for liberation theology and spirituality is the story of Moses and the exodus, for a basic feature of liberation spirituality is the deep conviction that the presence of God is revealed in the liberation of oppressed people. Moses was called by God to lead the children of Israel from slavery to freedom by bringing a mandate of liberation to their Egyptian oppressors. This commissioning of Moses to prophetic leadership was God's way of responding to the suffering and the prayers of the Hebrew slaves. Moses' work required him to use words, wonders, and symbols to "speak truth to power." His prophetic spirituality empowered him to console the oppressed and confront their oppressors. Moses has great importance as a model for several key aspects of liberation spirituality, namely, prophetic vocation, social awareness, intercessory prayer, and discernment of divine presence in the work of liberation.

Two NT texts are most often cited as benchmarks of liberation spirituality. First and foremost is Luke 4:18, where Jesus stands in the synagogue to read from the book of Isaiah the announcement of his anointing to proclaim good news to the poor and his commission to set the oppressed free. Second is the Matthew 25 parable of the sheep and the goats, where Jesus commends the holistic spiritual praxis of nations and individuals who feed the hungry, give drink to the thirsty, take in the stranger, clothe the naked, and visit the sick and incarcerated, because "whatever you did for one of the least of these brothers and sisters of mine, you did for me" (v. 40 TNIV).

Some churches reject liberation theology because it relies heavily on Marxist social analysis. Others reject it because of instances of treating the lives of the oppressed, rather than Scripture, as its authoritative "text." Nevertheless, its global influence as a force for justice and human equality is undeniable.

See also Feminist Spirituality; Guitérrez, Gustavo; Latin America.

For Further Reading: J. Cone, *God of the Oppressed* (1975); P. Freire, *Pedagogy of the Oppressed* (1970); G. Gutiérrez, *A Theology of Liberation* (1988); A. Hennelly, ed., *Liberation Theology* (1990); T. Runyon, ed., *Sanctification and Liberation* (1981); J. Sobrino, *Spirituality of Liberation* (1988).

Cheryl J. Sanders

Lifestyle

The word *lifestyle* is attributed to Alfred Adler, a psychologist, who coined it in 1929; and by the early 1960s, it was in common usage. It refers to the comprehensive manner in which a person lives, including his or her habits, conduct, language, dress, responses to others, interpersonal relationships, and a host of other factors. It is also a matter of considerable importance in Scripture (e.g., 1 Tim. 4:16) and critical to personal integrity.

For the Christian, lifestyle is a way of living life with Jesus Christ at the center, which is, of course, easier said than done. One cannot do this without denying self, family, and close relations. Jesus issued strong warnings about putting self, family, and others ahead of God. Beyond self, the Christian lifestyle is one that envisions each believer as a brother or sister in Christ and each nonbeliever as created by and for God, in God's image. At least three factors shape a Christian lifestyle: other people (Prov. 27:16), circumstances (Rom. 8:28), and the strength of one's self-discipline and resolve (1 Tim. 4:7).

The Christian lifestyle requires choices. Confronted with multiple options each day, believers must continually be choosing how they will live. Otherwise, they will unintentionally, but inevitably, fall into some other lifestyle—one that reflects the prevailing culture or one that has already been embraced by close associates.

Are there guidelines that constitute a Christian lifestyle? From theologian to theologian, any "lifestyle" list would differ and would consist of various lists of rules and prohibitions, as well as positive promises, found in the Bible. But they would all conclude that a Christian lifestyle is Christ's life, lived out in human style. It will not be Christ's own earthly life exactly replicated, for he was unique. Nor, at the other extreme, can it be a style of living dependent on one's own resources and reflective of secular autonomy from God. Rather, it is a life infused with the indwelling presence of Christ, lived out in a refreshingly individuated but consistent personal lifestyle. It is perhaps best seen in Paul's statement, "I have been crucified with Christ and I no longer live, but Christ lives in me. The life I now live in the body, I live by faith in the Son of God, who loved me and gave himself for me" (Gal. 2:20).

For Further Reading: D. Crawford, *EvangeLife* (1985); C. Koch, *Creating a Christian Lifestyle* (1996); D. Whitney, *Spiritual Disciplines for the Christian Life* (1997).

Dan R. Crawford

Light

Light symbolizes the experience of God's radiant presence that exposes evil, supplies wisdom and guidance, facilitates encounter with him, and stimulates transformation into God's own likeness.

Such luminosity is the antidote to all that darkness represents. Throughout Scripture and the experience of the church, the luminous vision of the Lord, whether perceived with the eyes of the body or of the soul, witnesses to the paradox of Emmanuel—namely, that the transcendent God is nonetheless with his people to save them and make them holy.

Glorious light rested on the tabernacle (Ex. 40:34–38) and the temple in Jerusalem (1 Kings 8:10–11; 2 Chron. 7:1–3). It was a sign that the Lord had chosen to sojourn with Israel, even though the highest heavens are not large enough a dwelling for him (2 Chron. 6:18). He dwelt among the people of Israel in order to lead them, much as he led them in the wilderness, to himself, for his light leads to the place of his dwelling (Ps. 43:3). Among those thus lovingly led were the prophets, initiated into their ministries by the divine light (Isa. 6:1–4; Ezek. 1), and they spoke of this light dawning upon Israel (and making her radiant with reflected glory) in a yet greater way in the day of her redemption (Isa. 60:1–5).

Peter, James, and John beheld this light from the transfigured Jesus (Matt. 17:1–8; Mark 9:2–8; Luke 9:28–35), who claimed to be *the* light of the world (John 8:12; cf. Matt. 4:16). A similar vision, this time of the Lord ascended, initiated Paul into apostolic service (Acts 9:1–5) much as it did the prophets of old—an experience of the light of God that Paul declared to be for the entire church (2 Cor. 3:7–18). The epistle of 2 Peter, too, declares this by setting the apostles' vision of Jesus' transfiguration in tight literary succession with the believer's own transforming participation in the divine nature (2 Peter 1:3–4, 16–18), a transformation that makes them, in a secondary sense, as the rest of the NT teaches, "the light of the world" (Matt. 5:14) and "light in the Lord" (Eph. 5:8–14).

Subsequent generations of Christians, particularly Gregory Palamas and Symeon the New Theologian, speak of God's gracious light in just this way—as an encounter with God in prayer that transforms us, supplying a foretaste of the transfiguration of all creation in light.

See also Dark Night; Illumination.

For Further Reading: E. Humphrey, *Ecstasy and Intimacy* (2006); *Gregory Palamas, The Triads*, CWS (1983); Symeon the New Theologian, *On the Mystical Life*, 3 vols., trans. A. Golitzin (1995–1997).

Matthew Bell

Literature and Christian Spirituality

The conjunction of "literature" and "spirituality" echoes and recalls the relationship between letter and spirit, the biblical and traditional question of allegory. Does literature belong to the realm of the (carnal) letter (that kills) (2 Cor. 3:6)? Does an invocation of spirituality skew a "normal" (or self-contained) understanding of literature? While a discussion of the complex interplay of what Kevin Vanhoozer, in the *Dictionary for Theological Interpretation of the Bible*, refers to as the worlds behind, of, and in front of the text is beyond the scope of this short essay, once we set aside the pursuit of an original or final univocal meaning in a text, we can focus on prudential judgment in our various hermeneutically situated readings without abandoning holism. Allegorical reading, which *combines* letter and spirit within a determinate field of possibilities, involves this acknowledgment. Paradigmatically, we read the letter of the OT (including historical events and literal meanings) christologically. Only when we refuse to read the OT in the light of Christ does it become the mere letter, the letter that kills. What matters most in the study of literature is that it needs theology to provide sufficient reason for our disciplined continued engagement, that reason being the divine revelation of what it means to be human. Karl Barth, in *The Humanity of God*, observes that all culture represents "the attempt of man to be man and thus to hold the good gift of

his humanity in honor and to put it to work." The human is "the being who interests God," to whom he commits himself ineluctably in the incarnation. The incarnation closes the gap between letter and spirit even as it announces the most profound discontinuity, the in-breaking of the other. In considering literature in relation to Christian spirituality, we look primarily to participate in the life that comes from God and is sustained by him; we produce and read words in the revealed Word. The incarnation enables an endless task of rereading, connecting, and applying daily—a task that nevertheless in no way augments the work of Christ. Dante's great insight, Nicholas Boyle has argued, is that "it is only in relation to Christ that human doings are part of history, and only as part of history that human doings become the subject-matter of his poem," making the *Divine Comedy* the paradigmatic Christian poem. Christian readers of history and culture must negotiate Stanley Fish's accusation that they always produce the "same text," an accusation from which we are sheltered only by the incarnation itself.

The Bible has animated the conjunction of literature and Christian spirituality throughout history, from the translation into the vernacular of biblical texts and their dramatic presentation in medieval mystery plays, to the rendering of the fall narrative in *Paradise Lost*, to the muted but still biblically insistent apologetics of The Chronicles of Narnia. Petrarch and his humanist followers read the Bible in terms of its affective power; they took as an implication of being made in the image of God the call to emulate him in creativity and manifested a new commitment to the active life in their spirituality. The contribution of Protestant poetics to the seventeenth-century English lyric rested upon an understanding of the written word as the embodiment of divine truth. Donne, Herbert, Vaughan, Traherne, and Taylor saw in the written formulations of Scripture, models for their own work and used the lyric to analyze the personal life in religious terms. Unfortunately, an exaggerated emphasis on the will, when combined with a nominalistic uncoupling of the relationship between word and thing, would leave humanist, Protestant, and a number of aspects of post-sixteenth-century Roman Catholic poetics vulnerable to skepticism and instrumental reasoning.

The allegorical practices of the church in liturgy have encouraged the current recovery of allegory in theological exegesis. From baptism to Holy Week, in liturgy we place ourselves in the biblical story and make the events real in our ongoing complementary readings. This method unfurls itself in the incorporation of nonsacred texts. Students of liturgy appreciate the role of literature in making biblical and liturgical texts fresh through processes such as defamiliarization and through a mode of knowing unavailable to conceptual rationality, particularly in metaphoricity. Reciprocally, students of literature find themselves challenged by the extent to which authors can be fruitfully read or put their texts into the context of liturgy; it imposes a discipline not unlike that of the sonnet form, say, or the expectation of corporately conditioned engagement and reception. Kathleen Norris has compared liturgical worship to the writing of poetry for the times. She has also noted the listening heart required of both and the unquantifiable joy of discovery that can attend both. Liturgy itself can be highly literary: Thomas Cranmer was one of the great stylists of the English language. The importance of other spiritual writings to the literary corpus of their language (Augustine's *Confessions*, St. John of the Cross's *Dark Night of the Soul*, Julian's *Showing*) gives us pause to consider the relationship between spiritual formation on the one hand and rhetorical discipline and objectives on the other.

A spiritual writer like Dostoevsky makes us conscious of what Rowan Williams, in *Dostoevsky: Language, Faith, and Fiction*, calls an ineradicable solidity in one another, tested and proven through dialogical language and feeling, which in turn depend on theological commitments. Freedom, where Dostoevsky (as well as the influential critic Bakhtin) is concerned, means language—both the ongoing possibility of dialogue and the constraint of needing to be intelligible to another. With Orthodox theology in view, Williams explains that our linguistic freedom and interdependence "resonate with the interdependent life of a universe that is addressed and sustained by a Word from God." T. S. Eliot has commented that the theological work of Hooker and Andrewes prepared the ground for the age of Shakespeare and Jonson. A rich theological study by A. M. Allchin has explored the implications of this remark in terms of participation in God, which holds that humans are only fully themselves and truly fulfill their nature in communion with God, a doctrine similar to that underwriting Dostoevsky's approach to language. Such communion enfolds an exploration of human nature; it is a humanism, accessible only in conjunction with those other profoundly mysterious doctrines of incarnation and Trinity. In literary terms, that exploration proceeds according to and reciprocally questions the shaping influence of genre.

The unthematizable theme of joy attends the spirituality of participation in the reality of God in all three of its relational, transformational, and vocational aspects. Evidence of joy abounds in modern prose of Christian spirituality, in a brimming remark like Annie Dillard's "There is only this everything" and Norman Wirzba's ecological meditation "The dark night of the soil." As a literary theme, joy would bear infinitely more attention by Christians. It marks Australian novelist Kim Scott's *True Country*, which interweaves the Aboriginal (and Thomistic) belief that objects and acts have their value through participation in a transcendent reality, the discovery and recovery of identity by the protagonist, a lapsed Catholic, and the prospect of political reconciliation based on a comfortable Aboriginal welcome. Marilynne Robinson somehow uses the long letter that is *Gilead* to suggest an open-ended dialogue between fathers and sons spanning three generations, while laughter easily misunderstood and never fulsome enough pervades the epistle from the opening page.

See also Imagination; Poetry and Poetics.

For Further Reading: N. Boyle, "The Idea of Christian Poetry," *Who Are We Now?* (1998); V. Brady, "Aboriginal Spirituality," *Literature and Theology* 10 (1996): 242–51; P. Cavill, et al., *Christian Tradition in English Literature* (2007); A. Hass, D. Jasper, and E. Jay, eds., *The Oxford Handbook of English Literature and Theology* (2007); D. Jeffrey, *People of the Book* (1996); B. Lewalski, *Protestant Poetics and the Seventeenth-Century Religious Lyric* (1979); H. de Lubac, *Medieval Exegesis*, 2 vols., trans. M. Sebanc and E. Macierowski (1998–2000).

Norm Klassen

Liturgical Prayer

The word *liturgy* comes from the two Greek terms *laos* ("people") and *ergia* ("work" or "service"). Liturgies in the ancient world were acts of public service done for the people and by the people, hence the "people's work" had two directions to its meaning. An example of an ancient liturgy would be the construction of a public bath, donated by a person or persons of means for the greater community. It was a community service. *Liturgy* was the term chosen by the Christian church to describe its ritual services (e.g., Phil. 2:17). The people's work was to pray for the world, hence a community service. The goal of liturgical prayer, then, was to provide a common prayer for the people to offer together thanks and praise to God as well as intercession and supplications for all of creation and its redemption.

Today liturgical prayer is often understood as rote prayer, prescribed prayer, or formal or empty prayer by those in free church traditions; while those in the liturgical traditions consider their prayers part of their historic connection to the apostolic church. In light of the Roman Catholic Church's reforms in the Second Vatican Council,

there has been a recovery of both early rites and prayers, in particular those found in the (so-called) apostolic tradition of Hippolytus along with the goal of "full, conscious and active participation" of all worshipers, not just the liturgical leaders. Both these texts and these ideals have had an impact on the revisions of mainline Protestant worship books since the 1970s. Along with this has been the growing interest of evangelical and emergent congregations in ancient church prayers and liturgies, a pattern referred to as "ancient-future" worship.

The basics of liturgical prayer are a rota of daily prayer, often prayed more than once a day privately or in community, along with the weekly service on the Lord's Day with the pattern of gathering, sharing liturgy of the Word and liturgy of the table, and dismissing the people to serve in the world. Within these basic structures a regular and predictable pattern of prayer forms, such as the Lord's Prayer, doxologies, creeds, confessions of sin, assurance of pardon, and a fixed eucharistic prayer.

Liturgical prayer often follows the rhythms of the church year. The prayers and confession that would be particular to a specific day or season are considered to be "indexical elements" of the liturgy. Those parts that remain constant regardless of the day or season are called the "canonical" elements. The purpose of liturgical prayer to tell the whole story of God is greatly assisted by the use of the church year, as each year the story of the gospel is told from the anticipation of the first coming of Christ, through the birth and ministry of Jesus Christ, his dying and rising, ascending and sending of the Holy Spirit, and the ministry of the Holy Spirit in and through the church until Christ's second coming. It is within this framework of the story of God that the people pray for their lives and the life of the world. This is a service that benefits the world but is offered to the glory of God.

For Further Reading: P. Bradshaw, *Early Christian Worship* (1996); C. Cherry, *The Worship Architect* (2010); R. Webber, *Ancient-Future Worship* (2008).

Todd E. Johnson

Liturgical Spirituality

See **Chapter 22.**

Liturgical Year

Also known as the Christian year or church year, this is an ancient pattern for ordering time using both the weekly rhythm of Sunday and the seasonal significance of Christ's life. Early Christians drew upon their Jewish roots and quickly converted the seventh day of the week, or Sabbath, to the first day of the week, or Sunday, often called the Lord's Day (Rev. 1:10). During the first three centuries, the church transformed the Jewish observance of Passover into the joyful celebration of the risen Christ at Easter. By the end of the 4th century, Jesus' birth was celebrated on December 25 and his manifestation to the non-Jewish world on Epiphany, January 6. Over the centuries, the liturgical year expanded with the addition of a full spectrum of saints' holy days. Luther removed most of the saints' days while maintaining many of the festivals of Christ; Calvin and later Reformed believers focused almost exclusively on Sunday as the Lord's Day. In the 18th century, John Wesley suggested a modified calendar that reflected many of the seasons of Jesus' life that had been observed previously. The liturgical year was intended to sanctify time as belonging to the Lord and aid remembrance of God's saving acts in history in Jesus Christ through the Holy Spirit. Christopher Kiesling correctly asserts that "the liturgical year is like a giant potter's hand gently shaping our lives daily year after year" more fully in Christ.

A summary of the liturgical year suggests ways that a person can be shaped by Christ. Frequently the year is divided in two cycles, the first of light and the second of life. Advent and the cycle of light begin the Christian year by watching and waiting for Christ's birth and his second coming. Christmas celebrates the fulfillment of God's promises in the incarnation of his Son and his promised return. Epiphany speaks of Jesus' manifestation to the entire world through his ministry. The cycle of life

begins on Ash Wednesday, retracing Jesus' Lenten journey to the cross. This six-week period leads to Triduum, or the three days of Maundy Thursday, Good Friday, and Easter Saturday. Easter celebrates Christ's triumphal victory over death and darkness and extends for forty days until Ascension declares the liberating message that Jesus now stands at the right hand of God to intercede for Christians. Ten days later, Pentecost remembers the outpouring of the Holy Spirit that birthed the church and empowers Christians to continue Christ's mission to the world. Recently the period between Pentecost Sunday and the beginning of Advent has been called ordinary time. It reminds believers that even in one's normal everyday activities God is with us.

The liturgical year can serve as an important spiritual discipline for both individuals and churches to center their lives on the unfolding drama of Christ's life and ministry. Some have misunderstood this method for telling time to be overly rigid and restrictive. More accurately the Christian year provides a highly flexible and creative format to guide Christians in employing the full range of biblical teaching to enrich their remembrance of the life and ministry of Jesus Christ. The principles of the liturgical year can be adapted to any worship style.

See also Time, Sanctification of.

For Further Reading: A. Adam, *The Liturgical Year* (1981); H. Hickman et al., *New Handbook of the Christian Year* (1992); C. Kiesling, "The Formative Influence of Liturgy," *Studies in Formative Spirituality* 3, no. 3 (1982): 377–85; T. Talley, *The Origins of the Liturgical Year* (1991); R. Webber, *Ancient-Future Time* (2004); idem, ed., *The Services of the Christian Year* (1994).

Tom Schwanda

Liturgy of the Hours

This is also known as the Divine Office, daily prayer, or fixed-hour prayer. According to Clement of Alexandria and Origen, Eastern Christians prayed in the morning, noon, and night, while the early Western sources of Tertullian and Cyprian reveal that prayer was said there five times daily. Christians were motivated by the biblical admonition to "always pray and not give up" (Luke 18:1) and "pray continually" (1 Thess. 5:17). In the 6th century, Benedict created a sevenfold pattern of prayer reflecting Psalm 119:164, "Seven times a day I praise you." His motto *ora et labora* ("prayer and work") created a rhythm of monastic spirituality that sought continually to integrate God into all aspects of life. The Psalms were central to these prayers, though other Scriptures and hymns were also included. Various patterns have been used to organize the Psalms and other readings. During Benedict's time, the entire Psalter was prayed through weekly; today most monastic communities take four weeks to cover all the Psalms.

Luther, Calvin, and Thomas Cranmer (1489–1556), who produced the *Book of Common Prayer* (1549), reduced the frequency of prayer to morning and evening, which had always been the primary pillars of prayer, but also expanded its usage to engage all people, not just the clergy. More recently Vatican II has promoted extensive historical research that has inspired the recovery of daily prayer for all God's people. Theologically the liturgy of the hours recognizes it is the result and extension of Jesus' continuous prayer for the church and serves to sanctify time by reminding believers that all time belongs to God. The renewal community of Taizé reflects one popular expression of the contemporary retrieval of fixed-hour prayer.

Daily prayer, though structured, need not inhibit the Holy Spirit from facilitating dialogical interaction between the church at prayer in public worship and individuals at prayer in their personal lives, so that each is renewed by the other. The liturgy of the hours, properly understood, forms Christians to recognize that prayer is not so much an activity used in random times of need; rather, it cultivates an attitude or awareness of God's continued presence in the world.

See also Time, Sanctification of.

For Further Reading: A. Boers, *Rhythm of God's Grace* (2003); *Book of Common Prayer* (1979); *Daily Prayer* (PCUSA, 1987); G. Guiver, *Company of Voices* (2001); R. Taft, *The Liturgy of the Hours in East and West* (1993); P. Tickle, *The Divine Hours*, 4 vols. (2003–2006).

Tom Schwanda

Llull, Ramon (1232–1316)

Contemplative missionary apologist. Llull uniquely demonstrated how contemplative life enables the active life. His daring missionary exploits and prolific vision-inspired writings combined with this-worldly wisdom and realism in persevering penance, adoration, and service of Christ. Born, married, and buried in Majorca, he experienced a Pauline-type conversion at age thirty, then patiently studied the Arabic language and Islamic religion (including Sufi mystical influence) for the next ten years while growing as a contemplative. He then wrote, traveled, taught, preached, and prayed to fulfill his threefold vocation: evangelize Saracens with the aid of rational persuasion from commonalities experienced in faith and knowledge; write against unbelievers' errors; and establish monastic mission schools. As a Franciscan tertiary (that is, as a layperson associated with the Franciscans), he bridged twelfth-century Franciscan Carthusian spirituality and fourteenth-century *Devotio Moderna* (and possibly Spanish mysticism) in a life devoted to knowing and loving God.

For Further Reading: A. Bonner, ed. and trans., *Doctor Illuminatus: A Ramon Llull Reader* (1993); J. Hillgarth, *Ramon Lull and Lullism in Fourteenth-Century France* (1971); A. Vega, *Ramon Llull and the Secret of Life*, trans. J. W. Heisig (2003).

Richard F. Kantzer

Loneliness

Loneliness is a painful experience of relational deprivation. It invades the human soul with effects of sadness, anxiety, and shame due to the absence of meaningful relational contact. It is important, however, also to realize that loneliness is not a single and unified phenomenon with fixed characteristics. It is beneficial to approach it as an ambiguous and deeply personal experience, which takes on diverse qualities and meanings in different social, psychological, and spiritual contexts.

It is useful to differentiate three types of loneliness. *Emotional* loneliness is related to being deprived of "an intimate other." Deep longings for mutuality and affirmation in relationships of love or friendship are not met. *Social* loneliness is related to a lack of belonging to a fellowship. The result is social isolation with deprivation of social empowerment and cultural goods. *Existential* loneliness touches the metaphysical sphere. It denotes a generalized sense of alienation, abandonment, and disconnect from oneself, others, and the world at large. While the first two types of loneliness may be temporary, due to changes in life circumstances, the last one, once entrenched, tends to become a more permanent disposition.

Approaching the phenomenon of loneliness within the Christian framework, the biblical creation narratives offer a basic perspective, namely, that it is not good for a person to be alone (Gen. 2:18). This straightforward observation reveals a basic pattern in the Christian interpretation of human life: as men and women created in the image of a triune God, we are always and everywhere persons-in-relation, connected to one another in webs of mutual belonging. In suffering and sorrow, as well as desire and joy, we are linked to each other. Mutual interaction within communities reveals our basic location in the created order. Consequently, unintentional loneliness reveals a broken order, a deep wound in the sacred web of human life. Loneliness threatens human dignity and self-respect. It is not only a severe burden and health risk for the individual person; it is also a challenge to general social and cultural dynamics within a society. Research reports from the West

suggest that this kind of loneliness might be one of the most widespread forms of human suffering and disease in late-modern societies.

Loneliness should be differentiated from two related concepts, namely, aloneness and solitude. *Aloneness* points to the basic fact that every person comes into this world alone, must live as a separate person, and eventually dies his or her own death. Such aloneness does not necessarily imply loneliness. The wasteland experience of painful loneliness develops only when our aloneness is not transcended through personal interactions and transformed through the fellowship of understanding and being understood. Aloneness can shift in an entirely different direction when it becomes transformed into creative *solitude*. In such a condition of solitude, one can discover that to be alone is actually a deep blessing. One may withdraw for a time into silence, prayerful listening, and gratitude. In short, people can be alone without being lonely. In such nourishing solitude, we touch upon the core experience of becoming present to ourselves and to the living God.

See also Solitude.

For Further Reading: J. Cacioppo and W. Patrick, *Loneliness* (2008); E. Elliot, *The Path of Loneliness* (2007); J. Hartog et al., eds., *The Anatomy of Loneliness* (1980); M. Hojat and R. Crandall, eds., *Loneliness* (1989); E. Jackson, *Understanding Loneliness* (1980); H. Nouwen, *Reaching Out* (1998).

Leif Gunnar Engedal

Lord's Prayer

Jesus prayed often but taught only one prayer. Thus, the Lord's Prayer (also called the "Our Father") is preeminent and prominent. The Gospels report it twice: in the Sermon on the Mount (Matt. 6:9–13) and in response to the disciples' request (Luke 11:2–4).

Some read Luke 11 as being about *how* to pray, but disciples would have known how to pray. Jeremias argues that they wanted—like other religious groups—their own distinct prayer, "a fixed prayer." The Lord's Prayer was the first Christian office. The *Didache* called for three daily recitations—probably during traditional times of office prayer: morning, noon, and night. Ambrose, Caesarius of Arles, and Augustine recommended frequent daily repetition. Its corporate intention is clear because of the absence of first person singular pronouns.

In the first centuries, new believers were instructed in the Lord's Prayer only near the end of their lengthy catechumenate; they did not say it corporately until the first Communion after their baptism. In medieval times, people recited *Paternosters* (Lat. for "Our Fathers") using prayer beads, the forerunner of the rosary.

Origen, Aquinas, Meister Eckhart, Calvin, Zinzendorf, Wesley, and Barth wrote with deep appreciation for this prayer's significance. Tertullian and Cyprian said that it summarized the gospel. Like the Apostles' Creed, it is one of Christianity's primary summarizing texts. Luz claims that "there is scarcely a Christian text that had such a strong effect (a) in piety, (b) in worship, (c) in instruction, and (d) in dogmatics."

Luther asserted: "I am convinced that when a Christian rightly prays the Lord's Prayer at any time ... his praying is more than adequate." Twentieth-century mystic Simone Weil's spiritual life revolved around its attentive recitation. She says: "It is impossible to say it once through, giving the fullest possible attention to each word, without a change, infinitesimal perhaps but real, taking place in the soul." While there is consensus on this prayer's primacy, its interpretation is another matter. Luz notes that there are three primary interpretations: *dogmatic*, theological and doctrinal; *ethical*, guidance on how to live well; and *eschatological*, looking forward to Jesus' return.

Others argue that the prayer functions as a *model* for prayer: beginning with praise of God and longing for God's reign, moving toward physi-

cal ("daily bread") and spiritual (forgiveness and temptation) petitions, and closing with doxological praise. The familiar doxology is not found in the earliest texts, but no scholar believes that such a prayer could have concluded with either "rescue us from the evil one" (Matt. 6:13 NRSV) or "do not bring us to the time of trial" (Luke 11:4 NRSV).

Christian worship often follows the prayer's threefold movement: beginning with praise and directing one's attention to God via invocation, song, and Scripture reading; relating to one's own life, needs, and commitments through sermon, prayer, offering, and Communion ("daily bread"); and concluding with further praise of God.

Not all agree on the prayer's structure. Some argue that it is divided in two, with three petitions about God (name, kingdom, will) and four about our needs (bread, debts, temptation, trial). Others say the first four are about good things (name, kingdom, will, bread) and the last three are matters to avoid (debts, temptation, trial). Still others contend there are three petitions for God's welfare (name, kingdom, will), one for our physical welfare (bread), and three for our spiritual welfare (debts, temptation, trial).

Some Protestants, prioritizing spontaneous extemporaneous prayer, downplay regular use of this prayer. Yet in twentieth-century Canada and the United States, this prayer became a contested "culture wars" agenda item as to whether it should be said in public schools. This is ironic given the fact that the early church reserved it for adult catechized believers. Another controversy revolves around whether addressing God as "Father" is patriarchal and exclusive.

A recent inspirational example of the power of this prayer comes from the Old Order Amish. They pray this at every meal, upon rising and before retiring, at worship, before traveling, and on any occasion calling for prayer. They believe that composing prayers evidences a lack of humility: one could never improve on what Jesus taught. After the horrifying Nickel Mines, Pennsylvania, mass murder of schoolgirls in 2006, local Amish believers astonished watching media by extending forgiveness to the killer and his family. They testified that they had no choice because they were formed by this prayer. They tap ancient traditions: the Rule of Benedict (6th century) commended regular daily repetition of this prayer specifically because the forgiveness petition encouraged monks to live reconciled with each other.

This text deserves pride of place in individual devotions and corporate worship, in our theology, and in how we live.

See also Beatitudes; Kingdom of God; Social Justice.

For Further Reading: K. Barth, *Prayer*, trans. S. Terrien (1985); A. Boers, *Lord, Teach Us to Pray* (1992); J. Jeremias, *The Prayers of Jesus*, trans. J. Bowden et al. (1967); D. Kraybill et al., *Amish Grace* (2007); U. Luz, *Matthew 1–7*, trans. J. Crouch (2007); S. Weil, *Waiting for God*, trans. E. Craufurd (1951).

Arthur Paul Boers

Lord's Supper

The Lord's Supper is a symbolic meal, which Christians normally celebrate in connection with Sunday worship. As a rule, this simple rite of eating bread and drinking wine (or an equivalent) comes as the second half of the service of worship, following the ministry of the Word. Usually it is expected that only Christian believers participate; more recently, in some traditions, children and those who are sincere in their search for Christ are also welcomed.

In this meal, the church looks back in remembrance of the cross of Christ, looks forward in anticipation of the coming reign of Christ, and looks to the present in a dynamic encounter with the risen and ascended Christ. In so doing, the Christian community affirms again the forgiveness of God that is found in Christ and renews its covenant to walk in faithful obedience to Christ and the church. Thus, the Lord's Supper is vital to spiritual growth and ongoing conversion—turning from sin and embracing the righteousness of God.

While the Lord's Supper—its meaning and practice—has, tragically, been a source of division and debate in most of the church's history, the last half-century has witnessed a remarkable endeavor in critical theological reflection on the meaning of the Lord's Supper, and this has fostered a recognition of points of commonality among Christian traditions and has renewed an appreciation for the place of the Lord's Supper in Christian spirituality. Of particular note in this regard is the 1982 publication of *Baptism, Eucharist and Ministry* (by the Faith and Order Commission of the World Council of Churches). This work has been complemented by a growing appreciation, in many circles, of the sacramental character of the Christian life. And several points are emerging from this ongoing conversation regarding the place of the Lord's Supper in Christian spirituality.

In the process, Christians are appreciating how diverse streams in the history of the church have profiled and sustained distinctive emphases on the Lord's Supper and how these have shaped and informed life in the Spirit within these traditions. Evangelicals with their strong emphasis on the memorial aspect of the Lord's Supper have recognized how their own tradition also includes an appreciation of the communal character of this meal—especially as it has been profiled in Plymouth Brethren and Anabaptist practices. Their heritage also includes the strong Puritan emphasis on the Lord's Supper as a time of covenant renewal, specifically the renewal of baptismal vows. All Christians need to be learning from those in other traditions, and increasingly evangelicals are recognizing the need to recover the strong emphasis on joyful hope in the Eucharist, something perhaps more typical of the Orthodox Church; and they are also learning to affirm the emphasis on both forgiveness and spiritual nourishment, themes prominent in the Anglican *Book of Common Prayer*. Through this wonderful cross-pollination, some abiding themes remain — demonstrating the vital place of the Lord's Supper in Christian spirituality.

First, through the Lord's Supper, the church is drawn into the life of the triune God. The focal point is the person of Christ Jesus: Christ is remembered; Christ presides; and the hope of the church, celebrated in this meal, is the triumph of Christ. Yet the celebration, while Christocentric, should be thoroughly Trinitarian: the church celebrates a "Eucharist" — giving thanks to the Creator. And the church calls upon the ministry of the Spirit to anoint and bless and draw the communicants into the presence of Christ. The Lord's Supper, like nothing else, empowers the church to be truly Trinitarian — not merely understanding the Trinity or, better, seeking to understand, but rather actually entering into the triune life of God.

Second, the Lord's Supper is an act of communion with the risen Christ; but it is also an act of intentional communion or fellowship with fellow Christians. The Lord's Supper keeps Christian spirituality from being entirely personal or subjective; rather, through this meal together, each believer is drawn more deeply into the common life in Christ that is shared with other Christians.

Third, the Lord's Supper is an essential complement to preaching and to the ministry of the Word. In this meal, the Word preached is not only heard but also received. Thus, the Lord's Supper should follow the proclamation from Scripture so that having listened to the reading and exposition of Scripture, the Christian and the whole faith community will consciously accept the call to "let the word of Christ dwell richly within you" (Col. 3:16). The Lord's Supper keeps Christian spirituality from being one-sided and cerebral.

And fourth, there is a growing appreciation of the link between the Lord's Supper and the mission of the church in the world. The bread that is broken within the community is a sign of the deep need for both physical bread and the Bread of Life within a broken and fragmented world; and through this meal the church is empowered to fulfill its mission in word and deed.

Frequently evangelical Christians have viewed the Lord's Supper as a meal that can be celebrated occasionally — perhaps monthly — but not necessarily weekly. And yet the testimony of John Calvin and then also John Wesley, and others, is being heard and increasingly appreciated — voices that assumed that this meal would be celebrated weekly, each time Christians gathered for worship. Could it be that the Lord's Supper is, indeed, integral and utterly essential to the Christian spiritual life, so vital and so essential that it should be celebrated more often? Could it be that in the post-Christian secular and pluralistic West it is even more crucial that the church, each time it gathers, affirm and appropriate the very elements that are witnessed to in this meal? But whether or not churches move to a more frequent celebration, there is no avoiding the fact that the Lord's Supper is integral to the Christian life and therefore to the church's growth in faith, hope, and love.

See also Eucharistic Spirituality; Love Feast.

For Further Reading: *Baptism, Eucharist and Ministry*, Faith and Order Paper No. 111 (1982); J. Calvin, *Institutes of the Christian Religion*, 4.17; I. H. Marshall, *Last Supper and Lord's Supper* (1980); A. Schmemann, *For the Life of the World: Sacraments and Orthodoxy* (1973); G. Smith, ed., *The Lord's Supper: Five Views* (2008); L. Vander Zee, *Christ, Baptism and the Lord's Supper: Recovering the Sacraments for Evangelical Worship* (2004).

Gordon T. Smith

Love

Love is a strong, self-giving affection that stands at the heart of Christian spirituality. According to 1 John 4:8, God is love. Out of love, God brought the world into being, sustains it, and directs it toward some ultimately meaningful end. By virtue of that same love, God constantly seeks those whom he has made. Alluding to the hymn in 1 John 4:7–10, Bernard of Clairvaux said, "God both loves more and before we do." For us the spiritual life is therefore a response to God's initiative. We love because God first loved us (1 John 4:19). Upon reflection the logic of divine initiative becomes apparent. Physicists now tell us that our sun is one of millions of suns in our galaxy, the Milky Way; and our galaxy is one of more than 150 billion galaxies. How could we mortals get God's attention unless God chose to enter into communion with us? There's no way. As Catherine of Siena put it, the "Mad Lover" has fallen in love with those he has made and pursues them as Hosea went after the unfaithful Gomer.

In biblical imagery, what God has done is to enter into a covenant relationship with us. Very early on, Jews and then Christians began thinking about their relationship to God as in the analogy of husband and wife in marriage and to use the love tryst of newlyweds in the Song of Songs to interpret the relationship between God and the church or between God and the individual soul. As the deepening of a marriage bond depends on growth in love, so too does the deepening of our relationship with God. We want to do what the first and greatest commandment says, "Love the Lord our God with all your heart and with all your soul and with all your mind and with all your strength" (Mark 12:30; cf. Deut. 6:5). In modern idiom, we might say that we want to fall head over heels in love with God. We can understand pretty well how we may fall more and more deeply in love with a spouse or a friend whom we see, hear, and touch. But how will we fall in love with a Lover whom "no one has ever seen" (John 1:18)?

Brother Lawrence, a prescient seventeenth-century Carmelite laybrother, gave a simple answer. To love God with all your heart, you have to get to know God. But that answer raises another query: How will we get to know God, whom no one has ever seen, enough to love God? Once again, Scrip-

ture reminds us, God, the Eternal One, must and has come to our aid. God, as it were, speaks to us through nature, through history, and through our own lives. As to nature's word, a psalmist reminds us, "The heavens declare the glory of God; the skies proclaim the work of his hands. Day after day they pour forth speech; night after night they display knowledge" (Ps. 19:1–2). If we learn how to see and to listen, we will get to know God through the works of God's hands (Ps. 8:3–5). As much as we may come to know God through nature, however, in the Hebrew view that pales by comparison with what we may learn through God's action in history. That is true of *all* history, but it is especially true of certain special moments in history. For the Jewish people, the moment of God's self-disclosure that transcends all others is the exodus from Egypt: "I carried you on eagles' wings and brought you to myself" (Ex. 19:4). For Christians God's revelation of God's self reached its apogee in Jesus. "No one has ever seen God," John reminds us, "but God the One and Only, who is at the Father's side, has made him known" (John 1:18). The Greek says literally, "He has exegeted God for us." Not surprisingly, through the centuries, Christian meditation has focused on the Gospels above all other Scriptures, for in the Jesus story, we believe we will come the closest that humans can come to knowing God.

Yet there remains the question: How is God known in our own lives? Jesus himself answered that question in the commandment to love one another as he has loved us (John 15:12). The last words of his "high priestly prayer" show how this works: "I have made you known to them, and will continue to make you known in order that the love you have for me may be in them and that I myself may be in them" (John 17:26). In his first letter, John makes sure we won't miss the point: "God is love. Whoever lives in love lives in God, and God in them" (4:16 TNIV). Francis de Sales and Jane de Chantal headed their letters with the exhortation, "Live Jesus!" They meant, "Let Jesus reign in your inmost self, your heart!"

"Living Jesus," or abiding in love, links up closely in Christian spirituality with the second great commandment, "Love your neighbor as yourself" (Lev. 19:18; Mark 12:31). In his letters to the Galatians (5:14) and to the Romans (13:9) the apostle Paul insisted that this commandment "fulfilled" or "summed up" the whole Law. How does it satisfy the commandment to love God with all your heart, soul, mind, and strength? In loving neighbor as yourself, you love as God loves, and you demonstrate thereby that the God of love indwells you. The question Jesus put to the people of his day was whether they construed "neighbor" too narrowly. He challenged them with the parable of the good Samaritan (Luke 10:30–37). In the Sermon on the Mount, Jesus phrased it more dramatically when he insisted that neighbor love requires love even of enemies, exhibiting such love in prayer for those who persecute you (Matt. 5:44). Why does our covenant with God demand so much? So that we may be children of our heavenly Father, who "causes his sun to rise on the evil and the good, and sends rain on the righteous and the unrighteous" (Matt. 5:45).

See also Compassion; Fruit of the Spirit.

For Further Reading: *Bernard of Clairvaux: Selected Works,* CWS (1987); *Francis de Sales, Jane de Chantal, Letters of Spiritual Direction,* CWS (1988); B. Pennington, *A School of Love: The Cistercian Way of Holiness* (2000).

E. Glenn Hinson

Love Feast

This was originally a gathering in early Christianity that included a communal meal. Although the term only occurs explicitly in Jude 12, scholars typically link it to the meal and similar abuses described by Paul in 1 Corinthians 11. However, if the love meal and remembrance meal were connected or one and the same in earliest Christianity, they were distinguished by the 2nd or 3rd century.

The practice was notably revived by Moravian churches and early Methodists who modeled their *love feasts*, meals meant to encourage harmony and mutual goodwill, on this early church practice. In Moravian churches today, the meal, often consisting of a sweetened bun and a hot drink (although regional variation is significant), is served in the context of a church service but is not considered a replacement for Communion. Usually it is accompanied by singing and testimony, which, again, focus on love and harmony. Typically, love feasts are held on special occasions tied to festivals of the church year or anniversary days of the congregation.

Although not always explicitly called "love feasts," many churches in most denominations serve light refreshments or a meal following the Sunday worship services. Many churches note the community-building and also the missional benefits of sharing food together.

See also Hospitality; Lord's Supper.

For Further Reading: D. Eller, "The Recovery of the Love Feast in German Pietism," in *Confessionalism and Pietism*, ed. Lieburg (2006), 11–30; E. Ferguson, "Lord's Supper and Love Feast," *Christian Studies* 21 (2005–2006): 27–38.

Jason Zuidema

Lukan Spirituality

Luke's overall purpose in Luke-Acts is to confirm for his readers that God's great plan of salvation has come to fulfillment in the life, death, resurrection, and ascension of Jesus the Messiah and continues to unfold in the growth and expansion of the church. For Luke, personal and community spirituality are inextricably linked to participation in this salvation-historical plan and especially to the role of the Holy Spirit in its fulfillment. Those who are spiritual (or Spiritual) are filled, empowered, and guided by the Holy Spirit. Their lives are characterized by piety, humility, service, and the expectation that God is accomplishing his purpose in the world and that they have the privilege of joining as humble servants in that work. Mary's simple response to the angel Gabriel's announcement that she will be the mother of the Messiah epitomizes Lukan spirituality: "I am the Lord's servant.... May it be to me as you have said" (Luke 1:38).

Luke's birth narrative (Luke 1–2) introduces his two-volume work by confirming the continuity between the old age of promise and the new age of fulfillment. The Spirit of prophecy—dormant for centuries—is renewed in the life of the birth narrative characters, evidence that God's eschatological salvation is about to arrive. These characters represent the righteous remnant within Israel. Their spirituality is revealed in (1) their faithfulness to God's covenant laws (1:6; 2:22); (2) their joyful anticipation of his eschatological salvation (1:14, 44, 47, 58, 68; 2:20, 29–30, 38); (3) their humble and contrite hearts (1:38, 43, 48); and (4) their openness to be filled, used, and guided by the Holy Spirit (1:15, 41, 67, 80; 2:25–26).

Luke's ultimate paradigm of spirituality is, of course, Jesus himself. Jesus is conceived by that Spirit (1:35) and as a child is filled with wisdom and God's grace (2:40, 52), experiencing unique intimacy with his heavenly Father (2:49). During his public ministry, Jesus' vibrant spiritual life is exhibited in his close communion with the Father by means of his anointing, filling, and empowering by the Holy Spirit. The Spirit comes upon him at his baptism (3:22); enables him to resist temptation (4:1); and anoints him to proclaim the good news, heal the sick, and cast out demons (4:14, 18). Jesus' prayer life "in the Spirit" (10:21) is particularly important for Luke, who records more of Jesus' prayers than the other Gospels. These prayers demonstrate his full dependence on the Father and passionate desire to accomplish his messianic mission (3:21; 5:16; 6:12; 9:18, 28; 11:1; 22:32; 23:34, 46). Jesus' final cry from the cross in Luke's gospel are words of intimacy and dependence: "Father, into your hands I commit my spirit" (23:46).

Just as dependence on the Holy Spirit characterized the Messiah's life and ministry in Luke's gospel, so in Acts the church's spiritual life is dependent on the filling of and guidance by the Holy Spirit. At Pentecost the resurrected and exalted One who bore the Spirit during his earthly ministry now pours out the Spirit on his followers, who are empowered to take the gospel to the ends of the earth (Acts 1:8). The early church's spirituality is epitomized in Luke's summaries of their activities: devotion to the apostles' teaching, fellowship, breaking of bread, prayer, and care for those in need (Acts 2:42–47). These are not legalistic requirements meant to earn salvation, but the joyful response of God's people, who are called to live lives wholly devoted to him and to participate in his redemptive plan of the ages.

For Further Reading: J. Fitzmyer, *The Gospel according to Luke I–IX* (1970), 143–258; M. Turner, *Power from on High* (1996).

Mark L. Strauss

Lust

Lust is one of the first two "deadly" sins, along with gluttony. Because it involves the mind *and* the body, early monastics such as John Cassian insisted that few ever gain complete victory over it. We must distinguish the temptation from the sin. While the sense organs may be the instrument, the source of our lust is the heart. Still, Cassian and Gregory the Great encourage us to take care with our senses, since in our fallen embodied state we are struck with impure thoughts even against our will. When the mind consents to the wrong thought by taking delight in it, then we commit the sin. Like gluttonous thoughts, our sex drive is necessary for our survival, but all such thoughts or passions must be "trained."

Early monastics taught that lust must be battled on two fronts: the body through "fasting" (i.e., flee the sensory temptation; they cite 1 Cor. 9:25–27) and the mind with a contrite spirit (or fear of God) through constant meditation on Scripture, manual labor, and humility (they cite 1 Peter 1:13–16).

At the same time, physical and spiritual disciplines reveal the limits of our ability to overcome lust — willpower is not enough. The ultimate solution is not a result of human effort, but of divine grace (Ps. 16:8) — which, for Cassian, was demonstrated by what goes on in our thoughts during sleep. This is why abstinence is different from chastity, the countervailing virtue against lust.

Abstinence is the result of sheer human determination — discipline for which there should be a place in the Christian's life; however, it is often motivated by fear of an STD or pregnancy, for instance, and it involves, as Stewart puts it, a constant battle to "wrestle lust to a truce." On the other hand, chastity is the result of divine grace, accompanied by discipline, which can cross the border even of our waking and sleeping. Note that the first step to tackling any addiction is to admit that one is not in control. Here the motivation is love of God, others, and self. Chastity, which includes integrity, is a social virtue that spawns human relationships founded on love over against selfish desire and manipulation. It also requires patience and humility (admitting dependence on God).

See also Celibacy; Chastity; Desire; Sins, Seven Deadly.

For Further Reading: J. Cassian, *The Conferences*, trans. B. Ramsey (1997); idem, *The Institutes*, trans. B. Ramsey (2000); C. Stewart, *Cassian the Monk* (1998); Thomas Aquinas, *Summa Theologiea*, 1.2 Q 77 and 2.2 QQ 146 – 48.

Dennis Okholm

Luther, Martin (1483 – 1546)

The first of the Protestant Reformers. For Luther the foundation of Christian discipleship was baptism. It serves as the polestar, guiding the believer through life and death. The proclamation of the Word of God combined with the washing in water joins the baptized to the body of Christ, placing them within the believing community. God declares the recipients to be God's beloved and gives them the Holy Spirit to confirm their faith, empower their discipleship, sustain them in suffering, and bring them to eternal life.

Baptism breaks the bondage of original sin, which, for Luther, is rooted in humanity's ruptured relationship with God. Without even recognizing it, people are unable to love or trust God. Luther described the sinner as *incurvatus in se*, curved in on oneself. This is the concupiscence or lust that Luther deplored, for it makes one's neighbors and even God subservient to one's desires.

Through baptism God changes the relationship with humanity. The Christian emerges from the waters of baptism *simul iustus et peccator*, simultaneously saint and sinner. It is not the case that when there is more of one there is less of the other. Rather, one is wholly both before God in every moment of one's existence, for God sees the believer in completeness: the enemy of God who must be exposed and condemned, and the bride united with Christ the bridegroom in his righteousness and self-giving. Baptism is an enduring sign of God's Word as law and gospel. It forces one to confess the virulence of one's sin and one's desperate need for mercy (law). It also leaves one no doubt as to the boundless generosity of God, teaching one to speak the language of repentance the whole of one's life, daily drowning the old Adam and raising the new (gospel). This is why Luther could write with such joyous abandon: "If you are a preacher of grace, then preach a true and not a fictitious grace; if grace is true, you must bear a true and not a fictitious sin. God does not save people who are only fictitious sinners. Be a sinner and sin boldly, but believe and rejoice in Christ even more boldly, for he is victorious over sin, death, and the world."

The Christian, says Luther, emerges from the waters of baptism priest, bishop, and pope. There is no spiritual hierarchy in the body of Christ. By baptism all are called into the royal priesthood to proclaim the gospel, comfort the troubled, and pray for the world. Some will be set apart for the public responsibilities of preaching and celebrating the sacraments, but they act out of their baptismal calling, not some superior gift of the Spirit given through ordination or personal visions. Others, for example, will be spouses, parents, plumbers, teachers, stockbrokers, musicians, or healthcare workers. These are not just jobs but God-given vocations in which believers take on the new life in Christ.

Luther celebrates the freedom the gospel creates in the lives of the faithful with this paradoxical statement: "A Christian is a perfectly free lord of all, subject to none. A Christian is a perfectly dutiful servant of all, subject to all." The power and constancy of God's grace remain for believers no matter what earthly life may bring. Hence, they are "lords" over all tribulation. Simultaneously they are never above the needs of others. Since nothing can separate them from the saving power of Christ, they need not fear engaging the world on its own terms—politics, law enforcement, education and child welfare, family life, care for the elderly, protection of the poor and vulnerable. This is where Christians make the justice and mercy of God known to the world. Luther is comfortable with sinning boldly for the right purposes, and nothing merits that risk more than care for the neighbor.

Luther believed that all Christians would be subject to *Anfechtung* (temptation, trial) as long as they lived. The core of these attacks is doubt of God's benevolent intentions *pro me* ("for me"). Luther urges the believer to hold to the promise of salvation and new life in Christ. Do not let this misery loosen your grip, he insists, but cry out to God, reminding God that "I have your promise." According to Luther, this terrifying experience of despair proves to be the forecourt to paradise. Here is Luther's theology of the cross. God's grace is hidden in obscure, dishonorable, and dark places. It does not emerge in bold glory but is revealed in loss and suffering and the crushing realization that one deserves God's condemnation. One must be made empty to be filled with the grace of Christ. Baptism and the Lord's Supper, the two sacraments recog-

nized by Luther, are important to the life of faith because they are objective signs given by God to console the believer and to proclaim unequivocally that the gospel is true for this individual. The power of the sacrament is grounded wholly in God's promise. There is no way one can make oneself worthy of it, but then there is no need to. One just comes to the table, hears the proclamation, "This is my body given *for you*," and receives the elements. One claims the promise of salvation in Christ Jesus for one's own simply by trusting it, that is, by faith alone.

The background to Luther's spirituality is a fiercely eschatological, almost apocalyptic, expectation. In Luther's view, his opponents were deliberately seeking to undermine the truth of the gospel, and it was his responsibility to free the Word and defend the unsuspecting faithful from the damning abuses of false worship and teaching. Because Luther thought there was nothing less than eternal salvation at stake, he did not hesitate to denounce his opponents as demonic and unconditionally rejected by God. In this, Luther violated his own best insights regarding the power and determination of Christ to rescue and redeem.

See also Lutheran Spirituality.

For Further Reading: M. Luther, *Devotional Writings*, vols. 42 and 43 in American Edition of *Luther's Works* (1955–1976); idem, hymns 51, 134, 229, 230, 299, 350 in *Lutheran Book of Worship* (1978); idem, *Small and Large Catechisms*, in *The Book of Concord*, ed. R. Kolb and T. Wengert (2000); *Luther's Spirituality*, CWS (2007); D. Ngien, *Luther as a Spiritual Advisor* (2007); J. Strohl, "Luther's Spiritual Journey," in *The Cambridge Companion to Martin Luther*, ed. D. McKim (2003), 149–64.

Jane Strohl

Lutheran Spirituality

Lutheranism began as a reform movement within the Roman Catholic Church in the 16th century.

Although the evangelicals, as they called themselves, did not intend to leave the church, their criticisms of Catholic teaching and practice did not ultimately allow them to remain. Initially Lutheran spirituality was best defined by what it was not or what it was no longer. Proclaiming the evangelical gospel was not just a matter of good preaching. Reforming the practices that shaped the life of piety for the faithful was equally critical.

Justification by grace through faith apart from the works of the law meant that individuals could do nothing to secure or advance their salvation. Indeed, the greatest danger besetting believers was works righteousness, which Luther denounced as the first and last sin. Acts of piety, from monastic vows to the veneration of saints, allegedly advanced believers along the way to salvation. Lutheran practice distinguished itself by rejecting such things. Monasticism, for example, was dismissed as a blasphemous manifestation of human hubris. In contrast, the Lutheran spirit was to be nourished in the tasks of everyday life, meeting the needs of family, friends, and community. This was not meritorious in the eyes of God, but it was most pleasing.

Lutheran spirituality is rooted in the sacraments. Through baptism one is joined to Christ. Daily remembrance of baptism renews that identity so that the believer may drown the old Adam and raise up the new to a life of witness and service. The sacrament of the altar, no longer celebrated as a sacrifice but received as a meal, is foundational to the life of faith. Here, as part of the gathered body of Christ, individuals hear Christ's saving words, "for you," spoken to them.

The hearing of the preached word is at the center of Lutheran religious experience. Faith is not something one accumulates to hold in reserve; it is created anew each time the gospel promise sounds on the ear and breaks through every form of resistance to penetrate the heart. "Lord, I believe. Help thou my unbelief." This is the predicament of the Lutheran spirit, and so one must hear the gospel in word and sacrament over and over again as long as one lives. For this reason, corporate worship has always been the most powerful element in the shaping of Lutheran identity. No private devotional practice can remain healthy apart from it.

Lutheran spirituality emphasizes the discipline of prayer and the study of Scripture. Hymnody also plays an important part in the life of Lutherans. From Luther's "A Mighty Fortress Is Our God" to the contemporary compositions of Herman G. Stuempfle Jr. and Susan Briehl, Lutherans have confessed their faith musically with extraordinary beauty and power. Perhaps the most distinctive practice of this community historically was the ongoing use of Luther's Small Catechism to form the identity of its members. In Luther's day, the heads of households (and here was one place where women were granted authority in the ministry of the community) were responsible to teach all who lived under their roof this summary of the faith. Instruction in the catechism was also part of the school curriculum for both boys and girls. It may have been inculcated with a rigor seemingly at odds with the Christian freedom it confessed. Yet it is also true that the catechism taught people to speak the language of free grace. Lutheran communities recognized the value of having these empowering words at the ready when needed. Memorizing the Small Catechism and being examined by the church council were traditionally part of the preparation for confirmation. In some Lutheran circles, this practice has weakened in recent years.

What kinds of disciples are these spiritual practices intended to nurture? Lutherans are to be people with no illusions about the power of sin in the world and in their lives. Self-righteousness is hardly saving, and there are no self-made saints. At its root, sin for the Lutheran is the ongoing struggle to love the God we have, the God of the cross, rather than the god we want to make in our own image. This is a painful process. Time and again our sources of comfort are torn away so that we may know Christ and him only. Lutherans understand this, but enduring it is a whole different matter. In many ways Lutheran teaching is for people *in extremis*. The bottom has fallen out of their world. These are the people who really understand the vanity of works righteousness, who can break their fall only by clinging to the promise of Christ. There will be life beyond failure and wrongdoing, beyond sorrow and fear, because the God of our Lord Jesus is a God of infinite chances.

This life of faith is grueling, but it is also joyous. Convinced that it is God's mercy and human trust that allow love to flourish, the believer is free to live in the world, doing works of justice and compassion. The bondage is finally broken. I am no longer so curved in on myself, so consumed by my own desires, that the world around me barely registers. Now I am free truly to serve, exhilarated by the realization that this is not all about me. The key question is not, "What shouldn't I do?" but, as one eminent Lutheran theologian put it, "Now that you don't have to do anything, what are you going to do?" Lutheran spirituality at its best is sassy and confident. With the saving grace of Jesus Christ so squarely in our corner, nothing can finally defeat us, not even death itself.

The roots of the Lutheran movement lie in the struggle to proclaim the evangelical gospel. Collective recoil from its experience of false teaching's gravely harmful effects invigorated the tradition. It is not surprising that one of its ongoing concerns is with *reine Lehre*, pure doctrine. This pole has always required the balancing influences of affective faith expression and commitment to active discipleship. Another ongoing concern for Lutherans has been the relationship of justification and justice. We do not earn salvation by our works, but given the world's desperate need, are we not called to immerse ourselves in good works, the danger of works righteousness be damned? These two defining polarities cannot be resolved. Polarities can, however, be managed. It is the movement between one pole and the other that maintains for Lutherans the healthy tension of faith and works.

See also Luther, Martin.

For Further Reading: *Evangelical Lutheran Worship* (hymnal of the Evangelical Lutheran Church in America, 2006); B. Hanson, *A Graceful Life: Lutheran Spirituality for Today* (2000); *Lutheran Book of Worship* (hymnal of the Evangelical Lutheran Church in America, 1978); F. Senn, "Lutheran Spirituality," in *Protestant Spiritual Traditions*, ed. F. Senn (1986), 9–54; K. Stjerna and B. Schramm, eds., *Spirituality: Toward a 21st Century Lutheran Understanding* (2004).

Jane Strohl

M

Macarius

See *Pseudo-Macarian Homilies*.

MacDonald, George (1824–1905)

Scottish Victorian novelist, mystic, and theologian. Born in rural Huntly, Aberdeenshire, Scotland, into a financially struggling family with strong roots in Scottish Reformed Protestantism, he was well educated, and his studies at King's College, Aberdeen, included classical languages (Latin and Greek) and the sciences (math, physics, and chemistry). He taught himself German and read widely in German and English literature. While studying theology in London, he was exposed to the lectures of A. J. Scott, whose passion for theology and literature influenced him in his own development as a writer and theologian. MacDonald's career as a pastor was short-lived, and he turned to writing as a creative way to continue his pastoral vocation, employing primarily story to draw people closer to God.

MacDonald's body of writing is extensive and includes a range of genres, including novels, fairy tales, poetry, sermons, and essays on a wide range of themes (literature, human development, and aesthetics) all from a theological perspective. Influenced by the Western literary tradition and especially the German artistic fairy tale, the Bible, and mysticism, he helped develop a genre that is now known as fantasy. By embedding his theology within fantastic stories (such as *The Princess and Curdie*, *Lilith*, and *Phantastes*), he sought to recover a more mystical and sacramental understanding of the world and the Christian life. His influence on further generations of Christian writers is significant, especially upon such famous Inklings as C. S. Lewis and J. R. R. Tolkien.

See also Imagination; Literature and Christian Spirituality.

For Further Reading: M. Knoepflmacher, introduction to G. MacDonald, *The Complete Fairy Tales* (1999); "George MacDonald," *Christian History and Biography* 86 (2005).

Gisela H. Kreglinger

MacNutt, Francis Scott (1925–)

Catholic priest and faith healer. Following undergraduate studies at Harvard, MacNutt completed an M.F.A. in speech from Catholic University of America. Sensing a call to the priesthood, he completed his Ph.D. at Aquinas Institute of Theology, joined the Dominican Order (1950), and was ordained to the Catholic priesthood (1956). A pivotal turn came in 1967 while attending a charismatic Protestant retreat; MacNutt received the baptism in the Holy Spirit and responded to a prophecy that he would become an instrumental proponent of healing not only among fellow Roman Catholics but also among emerging charismatics.

MacNutt began to conduct successful healing and deliverance services and provide instruction on the restoration of healing to contemporary Christianity. While MacNutt witnessed instantaneous healings, he also emphasized the role of healthy living through medicine and pastoral counseling. Not without controversy, MacNutt married Judith Sewell in 1980 and suffered subsequent excommunication (later overturned) from the Catholic Church. Ironically, during this time his ministry gained popularity among Protestants and classical Pentecostals. MacNutt's published works, particularly *Healing* (1974, rev. 1999), *Power to Heal* (1977), and *Delivered from Evil Spirits* (1990), remain popular due to his straightforward teaching and practical guidance. As founder and director of Christian Healing Ministries, he and his wife maintain a rigorous ministry schedule.

See also Charismatic Spirituality; Health and Healing; Inner Healing.

Martin Mittelstadt

Management, Spirituality of

Management entails working with and through people to accomplish the objectives of both organizations and their members. Leaders who embrace the spirituality of management imbue this definition with special meaning. They recognize that their overall objective is to serve God and that the indwelling of the Holy Spirit is the gift of God to those redeemed through Jesus Christ. Moreover, working with and through God's people also entails working with and through the Holy Spirit. Leaders have both the objective to serve God and the gift of partnering with God as the Holy Spirit is present in others. In this presence, the Holy Spirit is experienced as encounter; and through this encounter, transformed lives culminate in transformed organizations: the workplace is no longer just a physical entity but community.

Themes found in creation, fall, and redemption can help leaders design work that encourages this encounter. In the creation story in Genesis 1 and 2, God gifts his people with the opportunity to contribute to the continuing process of creation. In this cocreation role, people demonstrate creativity in naming animals and perform agricultural work that necessitates competence, both roles requiring personal volition. As it was not good for man to be alone, God designed people to work in community. Because God's creation was good, people are enjoined to do work that is meaningful. Yet the fall in Genesis 3 brings toil; when humans are separated from God, work becomes burdensome or sorrowful. Work loses its meaning, workers' self-interest separates them from others and limits their own self-knowledge. In God's redemption through Jesus Christ, people reclaim their role as cocreators. People are once again gifted with the opportunity to work toward the completion of God's design at creation. Yet work still has limitations in a fallen yet redeemed world; it is no longer perfect and at times can be toilsome.

Using themes from creation, leaders design jobs so that employees experience personal meaning that is congruent with their deeply held values, for example, using teams; decentralizing decision making; allowing employees to work in a way that is personally authentic; valuing employees' sense of calling, including their call to roles outside of the workplace; and creating a positive work culture.

Using themes from the fall, leaders recognize that at times work will be toilsome. They therefore understand the importance of modeling their own spiritual journey in doing difficult work. They strive to act as people of character, emphasizing trust, honesty, moral integrity, and spiritual connection in their work with others. Knowing that evil exists in the workplace as in the world and in themselves, they recognize that part of their calling will be to face the fallen nature of others, disagree with colleagues, make decisions that are painful to all, and sometimes face their own error, sin, and self-deception. In doing so, they recognize their reliance on God; seek his forgiveness; and model gratitude, forgiveness, grace, and humility in their actions. Leaders act in ways that are consistent with their own faith, even when they may encounter personal costs in doing so.

Leaders are called to use their companies as instruments of redemption, providing the goods and services that are needed for human flourishing, minimizing toil, and making a positive difference for their stakeholders and the world. But in this redemptive role, the management by spirituality is also a prophetic call to honor employees. The Holy Spirit is not a supernatural helper who observes from the sideline to bless and multiply the outcroppings of work. Instead, the work of the Holy Spirit is woven into the fabric of community. When leaders, in their anxiety over success or survival, subordinate their employees to the mission of their organization, they tear at that fabric and step away from their partnership with God.

The spirituality of management is risky business. It requires not only bucking current management models, but also taking a longer-term view, making decisions that sometimes incorporate a noneconomic calculus, valuing and investing in people, and recognizing that toil is part and parcel with the good. Leaders cannot do this difficult work alone; as fallen creatures, they must rely on the Holy Spirit to guide their thoughts, heal their relationships, and constantly realign goals that are pulled toward selfishness. But leaders can see these complex and difficult tasks as the gift of partnering with God and relying on the Holy Spirit within themselves, encountered in community to see the work of the kingdom done on earth as it is in heaven.

See also Leadership, Spirituality of.

For Further Reading: E. Colyer, "Thomas F. Torrance on the Holy Spirit," *Word and World* 23, no. 2 (2003): 160 – 67; M. Diddams and D. Daniels, "Good Work with Toil: A Paradigm for Redeemed Work," *Christian Scholars Review* 38, no. 1 (2008): 64 – 82; L. Fry, "Toward a Theory of Spiritual Leadership," *Leadership Quarterly* 14, no. 6 (2003):

693–727; P. Montana and B. Charnov, *Management* (2000).

Margaret Diddams

Manning, Brennan (1936–)

Former Franciscan priest, contemplative, and author. Manning was born in New York City and raised in Brooklyn. He attended St. John's University for two years before enlisting in the Marines and being sent to fight in Korea. In 1956 Manning had a life-changing experience in which he came to understand all of Christianity as an intimate relationship with Jesus. He then completed an undergraduate degree in philosophy at St. Francis College in Pennsylvania; afterward he graduated from St. Francis Seminary (1963) and was ordained into the Roman Catholic priesthood.

Manning became involved in university ministry, serving in numerous academic and ministerial positions at several Catholic institutions. In the late 1960s, he took a two-year sabbatical from the Franciscans, moved to Spain, and joined the Order of the Little Brothers of Jesus of Charles de Foucauld. This order focused on living with the poor and doing manual labor during the day and engaging in contemplation at night. Manning worked as a water carrier, a mason's assistant, a dishwasher, and a voluntary prisoner and spent six months in contemplation in a remote cave in the Zaragoza desert.

He has authored fourteen books, including *Abba's Child* (1994), *Ruthless Trust* (2001), *The Furious Longing of God* (2009), and the bestselling *Ragamuffin Gospel* (1990). He is known for his candid honesty (e.g., he has been open about his battle with alcoholism) and the recurring theme of the unrelenting and unconditional love of God as witnessed to in the life of Jesus Christ. His central message of sinners moving toward self-acceptance has influenced many.

See also Childlikeness; Grace.

Brad D. Strawn

Marian Devotion

A discussion of Mary within the confines of the subject of spirituality must address two intersecting themes: Mary's spirituality and Marian devotion. The former refers to the spiritual life of the mother of Jesus as she is presented to us in the gospel of Luke, while the latter, the subject of this article, denotes a web of devotional practices that focus on Mary as an exemplar and object.

Marian spirituality is a subject foreign to most evangelicals because of evangelicalism's Reformation heritage. Mary in general and Marian devotional practices in particular are often seen to deny key Reformation doctrinal emphases. Where the Reformers said salvation was by grace alone through faith alone in Christ alone, Mary seemed to embody a spirituality in which salvation was the result of grace working in cooperation with human merit and mediated through almost innumerable "created mediators" — the saints — of which Mary stood at the head.

It is therefore worth recalling that the origins of Marian spirituality are ancient. Far from being a medieval corruption of a purer, earlier faith, the origins of Marian devotional practices are so old as to be impossible to date. Contextual analysis of the earliest pieces of evidence — a second-century document, *The Protevangelium of James*, and a third-century hymn, the *Sub Tuum Praesidium* — suggest that these are not aberrations, but rather reflect already long- and well-established patterns of devotion.

The Council of Ephesus (431) granted official approval to such patterns. Convened to resolve a christological debate between Nestorius and Cyril over the nature of the union of the divine and human natures of Jesus Christ, the council dogmatically defined and authorized the title *Theotokos*, the God-bearer or the Mother of God, as christologically appropriate. From the instant of his conception in the womb of Mary, Jesus Christ is the human instantiation of God the Son. She, in turn, is the mother of the man who is God.

Christology was not the only matter decided at Ephesus. As the victory sermon of Cyril of Alexandria makes clear, the approval of *Theotokos* implied the approval of the rich Alexandrian Marian devotion from which it came and with which it was associated. The burgeoning of churches dedicated to Mary from the 5th century onward provide prima facie evidence of the flourishing of Marian piety following the council. Theologians as disparate and far-removed as John Calvin and John Henry Cardinal Newman recognize the dogmatic definition of *Theotokos* as the watershed in the development of Marian devotion, granting it a legitimacy it had not previously enjoyed.

At the Reformation, specific Marian practices were challenged. From 1521 until his death, Martin Luther was increasingly vehement in his denunciation of any pious practice that distracted believers from Christ or distorted their perception of him as the loving Savior. Especially criticized was the piety, found in Bernard of Clairvaux and other medieval writers, that appealed to the mother of mercy over against her Son, the angry Judge. At the same time, however, Luther maintained a deep and almost sentimental devotion to Mary throughout his life and never denied accepted teaching on Mary's perpetual virginity or holiness. John Calvin was decidedly more circumspect, criticizing both piety and doctrine, and the churches of the Reformed tradition generally have followed suit. The Church of England managed to retain some strains of the strong Marian spirituality inherent in pre-Elizabethan English Christianity. As a result, Marian themes and practices coexist sometimes less than peaceably alongside traditional Protestant denunciations of perceived Marian abuses in Anglicanism.

In this space, it is impossible to document the various ways and forms in which Mary is venerated in Roman Catholic and Orthodox faith, but it is possible to group kinds of devotion in different ways. First, Marian devotion can be organized as a series of specific practices. The Rosary, the Angelus, the Salve Regina, the Immaculate Heart of Mary, alongside many other forms of devotion, take Mary as their focal point. Second, Marian devotion can also be associated with specific places where Mary is said to have appeared, such as the Church-approved Lourdes (France) and Guadalupe (Mexico) and the more controversial Medjugorje (Bosnia-Herzegovina).

From 1854 to 1950, a century bookended by the papal definitions of the immaculate conception and bodily assumption as dogma, Marian devotion — especially apparitions — was emphasized in the Roman Catholic Church. Since the Second Vatican Council, however, official church teaching has tended toward tempering Marian devotion by anchoring it more securely in the Bible and the first centuries of Christian faith. Even the strong Marian devotion of John Paul II sought a biblical cast in his encyclical *Redemptoris Mater*. Benedict XVI will likely not depart from this trend toward simplicity.

Given its history of Marian suspicion, it is hard to imagine Marian devotion flourishing within the confines of evangelicalism. Nevertheless, there is room within the movement for Marian devotions that remain true to its central concerns. Evangelicals might begin by turning to the Reformation writers themselves for guidance. Even the sober John Calvin says more about Mary than do many contemporary evangelicals. This is to say nothing of Reformers with more generous understandings of Marian devotion, for example, Luther, Bullinger, and Hooker.

The Reformers did not dismiss Mary or Marian devotion, but sought to anchor it in the Bible. Under their guidance, evangelicals could turn afresh to Luke 1 – 2 and find there rich biblical resources for a genuinely Marian, genuinely evangelical devotion. One thinks here of the regular recitation of the Magnificat, Mary's song of praise to God in Luke 1:46 – 55. Liberated from its Advent and Christmas confines, this song is in fact a précis of the OT that places Mary at the head of a long line of women and men used by God to liberate God's people. There may even be room for attenuated forms of the Rosary that may be used not to pray to Mary but rather to meditate on events of the gospel.

Thus, even if it seems at first blush to be counterintuitive, it is legitimate to ask whether evangelicals may turn to at least some forms of Marian spirituality as means of increasing their devotion to Jesus.

See also Bernadette of Lourdes; Mary.

For Further Reading: W. Abbott, ed., *The Documents of Vatican II* (1966); S. Boss, ed., *Mary* (2007); L. Gambero, *Mary and the Fathers of the Church* (1999); idem, *Mary in the Middle Ages* (2005); E. Johnson, *Truly Our Sister* (2004); J. Pelikan, *Mary through the Centuries* (1998); T. Perry, *Mary for Evangelicals* (2006); idem, ed., *The Legacy of John Paul II* (2007); M. Rubin, *Mother of God* (2009).

Timothy Scott Perry

Marketplace Spirituality

Integrating the words *marketplace* and *spirituality* seems oxymoronic. "It is not possible. That's why I am a monk," said one Eastern recluse. The marketplace is a place where goods, services, and values are exchanged — whether in a rural developing world village or on the Internet. It is a tough place. Powers visible and invisible rage: greed, Mammon, technology, and globalization. But the connection can be made.

Remarkably in the Western world there is renewed interest in taking one's soul to work. People are invited to cultivate transcendence, interdependence, and love in the workplace itself. Directors are spiritual elders of a corporation. The company is a system of being, not just doing. Mission statements incarnate a "higher purpose." Some of this caters to self-actualization and hopes to ramp up flagging motivation by tapping into

a spiritual evolution and global synergy. But the new business spirituality addresses the God-shaped vacuum in the souls of people left unattended both by religious communities and secular humanism.

There are points of convergence and challenge between the "secular" business spirituality and its Christian alternative. The discontinuity arises from the lack of any reference in "secular" business spirituality to a supreme, transcendent, and personal God and its focus on "human transcendence," something that is truly oxymoronic. Mostly the new business spirituality is monistic rather than theistic. The continuity turns on the desire to bring our whole person, including our souls, into the work experience and to grow spiritually in the center of one's work life rather than at the perimeter when it is all over or before it starts. So a Christian marketplace spirituality encourages the experience of God while one works and cooperates with God in the work itself. It further views the workplace as a location for spiritual struggle and an arena of spiritual nurture. There are two ways of approaching this.

The first is to consider spirituality *in* the actual context of marketplace activity. Spiritual disciplines are pathways of responsiveness to the seeking Father. Some, like prayer, may be practiced while at work without becoming distracted or inefficient. Brother Lawrence, in the monastery kitchen, found that the workplace did not divert him from God, because he simply went to God in prayer before, during, and after any task he undertook. Some people keep an object, image, or symbol in their workplace to remind them that God is with them. Hospitality is a spiritual discipline that means making space for others in our hearts. Too often the door of someone's office is open but their heart is closed. Meditation can take place as we look at things, people, and problems familiar to us until they become unfamiliar. In the long tradition of the church, this means combining the contemplative life of Mary and the active life of Martha, thus becoming an active contemplative. But there is more.

Second, there is the potential of spiritual growth *through* marketplace activity itself. The way we work in the marketplace reveals the need of our souls, our Achilles heel, which may be a need to be needed, to control, or to be approved. We grapple with resistance not only as we encounter the visible and invisible powers outside but our flesh as well. The seven deadly sins, described in Scripture as "works of the flesh," are revealed. It is also where the Spirit fruit, traditionally called "virtues," can be nurtured (Gal. 5:16–26). God is there, supporting the workers and the business; he is there in colleagues who bear the image of God and in occasional charismatic events. So, as some wise counselors have suggested to persons wishing to leave business and go into the monastery (or pastoral ministry) to find God and grow spiritually, the solution may be simply to go deeper.

See also Lay Persons; Leadership, Spirituality of; Money; Vocation; Work.

For Further Reading: D. Bakke, *Joy at Work* (2005); J. Costa, *Magnificence at Work* (2005); J. Renesch, ed., *New Traditions in Business* (1992); E. Silvoso, *Anointed for Business* (2002); R. P. Stevens, *Doing God's Business* (2006); R. P. Stevens and A. Ung, *Taking Your Soul to Work* (2010).

R. Paul Stevens

Marriage

Marriage is a spiritual, legal, and social union between a man and a woman. Jesus, when confronted with the Shammai-Hillel divorce controversy, redirected attention to the Torah's narratives regarding the creation of male and female and the original intent of marriage (Gen. 1:27; 2:23–25; Matt. 19:3–6). Later the apostle Paul suggested that marriage is not just a social or legal arrangement, but in fact a "profound mystery" with deep spiritual significance (Eph. 5:21–33). John Calvin, in theologizing marriage as a covenant, described it as an unveiled mystery.

Marriage is a metaphor of the unconditional love of God for the nation of Israel and of Christ for the church. Each time a man and a woman walk down the aisle, they reenact and proclaim the redemptive gospel of Jesus Christ. They do this in the presence of God and his people. Martin Luther's "two kingdoms" concept has been applied to marriage, highlighting its nature as both a secular institution and a divine mystery reflecting the eternal kingdom of God. God sanctions both. According to Luther, marriage on earth is temporal, and during this interim fulfills significant human needs. Marriage is one (though not the only one) of God's solutions to the loneliness of humankind (Gen. 2:18–23). Like singleness, it is a gift for some (1 Cor. 7:7). Marriage provides companionship, sexual pleasure, psychological wholeness, and a safe environment for procreation (Gen. 1:28; 2:24–25). Among other things, longitudinal research by Waite and Gallagher (2001) showed that those who are married are happier, wealthier, healthier, and have children who adjust better in society. The latter is important, for the foundation for a strong family is a strong marriage.

Marriage is indeed a mystery. In his dialogue with the Sadducees, Jesus revealed that in heaven "people will neither marry nor be given in marriage" (Matt. 22:30). In one of his many conversations, Jesus also redefined family (and by implication marriage) to include anyone who "does the will of my Father in heaven" (Matt. 12:50). The church becomes the family of families, in which both those who are married and those who are not are embraced in the kingdom of God. Marriage on earth is a temporary phenomenon, but the marriage relationship between God and the church is eternal. While it is important to emphasize the sanctity of marriage, it is quintessential to view marriage from an eschatological perspective that culminates in the wedding of the Lamb (Rev. 19:7).

See also Family Life; Sexuality.

For Further Reading: G. Bromiley, *God and Marriage* (1980); L. Waite and M. Gallagher, *The Case for Marriage* (2001); J. Witte Jr. and E. Ellison, eds., *Covenant Marriage in Comparative Perspective* (2005).

Ben K. Lim

Marriage, Spiritual

The concept of spiritual marriage has a rich and varied history. At times it has referred to a marital relationship of love without sex. More frequently, especially prior to the Protestant Reformation, it signified a state of virginity and celibacy in which a religious person, male or female, was betrothed to Jesus. This was, admittedly, conceptually awkward for some male Christians, since Jesus married the soul of the person that, regardless of gender, was feminine. The biblical basis for spiritual marriage is greatly indebted to the Song of Songs, but the same language appears in numerous variations elsewhere in Scripture (e.g., Ps. 45; Isa. 54:5–6; 62:4–5; Jer. 2:2; 3:14, 20; Hos. 2:19–20; Matt. 9:15; 22:1–14; 25:1–13; 2 Cor. 11:2; Eph. 5:31–32; Rev. 19:7–9; 21:2; 22:17). There is common agreement throughout these passages that God or Jesus is the husband or bridegroom, and the corporate entity of Israel or the church is the bride.

Origen, in the 3rd century, was first to speak of the individual soul as the bride. Numerous devotional classics have been written on this metaphor of spiritual intimacy, including Bernard of Clairvaux, *Sermons on the Song of Songs*; Jan van Ruysbroeck, *Spiritual Espousals* (also called *Adornment of Spiritual Marriage*); Teresa of Avila, *Interior Castle*, especially the seventh mansion; and John of the Cross, *Spiritual Canticle*.

Closely related is *brautmystic*, the bridal mysticism of certain medieval laywomen known as the Beguines. Hadewijch, for example, and Mechthild of Magdeburg, author of *The Flowing Light of the Godhead*, both wrote extensively on this theme. Gregory of Nyssa's sermons on the Song of Songs reflect Eastern Orthodoxy's frequent use of spiritual marriage imagery to depict transforming union with God.

The Protestant Reformation permitted and encouraged marriage among clergy. Luther, Calvin, and Menno Simons (c. 1496–1561) expanded the usage of spiritual marriage to include all Christians, whether collectively or individually, with Jesus. Among the Puritans, this language reached a height that rivaled the medieval mystics of the Western Catholic Church. Richard Sibbes (1577–1635) and John Owen (1616–1683) represent many Puritans who devoted major works to this topic (also known to them as mystical marriage). Jonathan Edwards, Charles Spurgeon, Hudson Taylor, and Watchman Nee also utilized this language in their preaching. Roman Catholic and Protestant understandings of spiritual marriage both recognize the necessity of God's grace that initiates this relationship. Distinctions arise between Protestants, who associate this with a believer's union with Christ that occurs through justification, and some Roman Catholics, who have understood it as the highest form of contemplative prayer, reserved for those more advanced in the spiritual life.

While the language of spiritual marriage may sound unusual to contemporary ears, it points Christians to the depth of God's desire and love for humanity, and reminds believers of the importance of the intimacy that is available to them through union and communion with Christ.

See also Beguines; Carmelite Spirituality.

For Further Reading: E. Dreyer, "Jesus as Bridegroom and Lover," in *Who Do You Say That I Am?* ed. J. Cavadini and L. Holt (2004), 207–35; J. Leclercq, *Monks on Marriage* (1982); B. McGinn, *Flowering of Mysticism* (1998); G. Peters, "Spiritual Marriage in Early Christianity," *Trinity Journal* 23, no. 2 (2002): 211–24.

Tom Schwanda

Martyrdom

Originally, the Greek *martus* denoted a "witness" to spiritual truth (Acts 1:8, 22). Jesus' teaching and example connected disciples' identity and witness with love (John 13:35), and "laying down one's life" (John 15:13) as its greatest expression. While denying oneself, taking up one's cross, and following Jesus (Mark 8:34) could be metaphorical, the apostles anticipated that the *imitatio Christi* would involve suffering (1 Peter 2:21) and assumed that persecution would attend all who resolved to live godly lives (2 Tim. 3:12).

Earlier Hebrew witnesses experienced miraculous deliverances but also faithfully endured in deprivation, imprisonment, torture, and death (Heb. 11:35–40). Seven executed Maccabeans embodied both spiritual realities (2 Macc. 7). Stephen placed his persecutors, who were preparing to stone him, among ancestors who killed prophets and the Righteous One (Acts 7:51–60). Under Roman persecution, "martyr" increasingly described the "white robed" saints slain for their faithful testimonies to the Word (Rev. 6:9–11).

For Christians, martyrdom is tragic but also redemptive. Jesus promised that whoever lost his or her life for his sake and the sake of the gospel would save it (Mark 8:35). Biblically, the martyr anticipated a "better resurrection" and divine commendation (Heb. 11:35, 39–40). In Stephen's train, one lived miraculously, full of grace and power (Acts 6:8), presenting "the face of an angel" (Acts 6:15), and at death viewed heavenly realities (Acts 7:55–56).

Across generations, believers have found these heroes inspiring their own spiritual journeys. Ignatius of Antioch, eagerly approaching martyrdom, penned inspiring epistles. Perpetua in North Africa, earliest known Christian woman author, witnessed through journaling her captivity and by her death. Polycarp of Smyrna, past his mideighties, left "precious bones" for treasure in a suitable place—anticipating relics. Ambrose and Augustine confirmed incidents of miracles at the gravesites of martyrs and saints. Monasticism expressed a "bloodless martyrdom" of the will. John Foxe's *Book of Martyrs* appeared (1563). In the Roman *liturgy*, after the Virgin Mary and apostles, martyrs rank before other saints. Until 1969 their *venerated* relics were necessary in every consecrated altar. The "greater love" shown by Christian martyrs has rendered them beloved by countless fellow pilgrims.

Today legions following Christ worldwide embrace Auca martyr Jim Elliot's words: "He is no fool who gives what he cannot keep to gain that which he cannot lose." The ancient voice of Tertullian finds refrain in Christian musician Steve Green's song "The Faithful," crowning a Voice of the Martyrs video (1998): "The blood of the martyrs is the seed of the church." Their sacrifices dramatically illustrate both the cost of discipleship and the all-sufficiency of God's grace in this life and into the next.

See also Discipleship; Persecution; Communion of Saints; Suffering.

For Further Reading: E. Elliot, *Shadow of the Almighty* (1958); B. Gregory, *Salvation at Stake* (1999); H. Musurillo, *The Acts of the Christian Martyrs* (1972); D. Veerman, *Foxe: Voices of the Martyrs* (2007).

James D. Smith III

Mary

A discussion of Mary within the confines of the subject of spirituality must address two intersecting themes: Mary's spirituality and Marian devotion. The former, the subject of this article, refers to the spiritual life of the mother of Jesus as she is presented to us in the gospel of Luke, while the latter denotes a web of devotional practices that focus on Mary as an exemplar and object.

In Luke 1:5–38, the author introduces Mary's piety by contrasting it with that of Zechariah and Elizabeth, the parents of John the Baptist. Whereas the couple is presented as old, pious, and barren (thereby echoing the OT theme of righteous yet barren parents), Mary is young, single, and presumably fertile, and her piety is not mentioned. Whereas Zechariah and Elizabeth are exceptional, Mary is not. We may assume, then, that prior to the annunciation, Mary's spirituality was, simply, nondescript.

At the annunciation, however, a deeper faith is disclosed. Zechariah doubts Gabriel's message, but Mary believes. Zechariah refuses to believe the angelic announcement and asks for proof: "How can I be sure of this? I am an old man and my wife is well along in years" (Luke 1:18). He is rendered mute both to judge his unbelief and to give the proof he asked for. During her angelic encounter, Mary asks an apparently similar question: "How will this be, since I am a virgin?" (v. 34). Surface similarity aside, Mary asks *how* God will bring about what he has promised, not for proof that God can or will do so. Where Zechariah doubts, Mary trusts.

Overlaying this foundational trust is the confident obedience embodied in the words, "I am the Lord's servant. May it be to me as you have said" (Luke 1:38). Often mischaracterized as (female) passivity in the face of the (male) deity, such depictions fail to recognize Luke's broad application of the term translated "servant" to men and women, especially in Acts. It is his synonym for "disciple." This mischaracterization also ignores the significant women of the OT (in the Septuagint) who also share the title: Deborah, Jael, Esther, and Judith, liberators of God's people. Rather, the title expresses an obedience that rests in the power of God to exalt the lowly.

Confident obedience is explored more fully in the Magnificat, or Mary's song (Luke 1:46–55). The song itself is an intricately constructed précis of the OT, leading many commentators to wonder whether Mary actually sang it. Three positions are generally taken. The majority hold that the song was composed at a later time and placed by Luke into the mouth of his character. One minority of scholars holds that Mary sang it as a Spirit-inspired utterance at the time and in the way narrated by Luke, while a second suggests that Mary composed it later in life and dictated it to Luke.

Whatever theory of composition is adopted, the song expresses two key themes in Mary's spirituality: a deep knowledge of the biblical story of God's dealings with humanity, and the ability to see one's life as caught up in that story. This is further accentuated in the birth account (2:1–52), where Mary "ponders" and "treasures" all that has happened thus far (2:19, 51). The vocabulary again suggests a deliberate synthesis of specific events into a narratival whole.

To trust, confident obedience, biblical literacy, and applicability is added ambiguity. Luke's presentation of Mary concludes with two temple stories (2:23–40; 41–52). Though they are separated in narrative time by twelve years, their situation side by side in the gospel, their shared setting, and similar conclusions suggest that they are to be read together. In the first, as Mary and Joseph present Jesus at the temple, Simeon warns her that a sword is to pierce her soul (2:35). The nature of that sword is made clear in the subsequent story when Mary is rebuked by Jesus with the words, "Didn't you know I had to be in my Father's house?" (2:49). The sword appears to signify the division between mother and Son brought about by Jesus' growing awareness of his unique identity and mission.

From this point on, Mary ceases to be a character in the gospel, and two subsequent allusions (8:19–21; 11:27–28) only accentuate the ambiguity further. They provoke readers to wonder whether Mary is in fact a disciple and leave that question unresolved. Left unnamed as present at the cross or resurrection, as Luke's gospel ends, it is fair to ask whether Mary is a disciple or not.

This question is finally resolved in Acts 1:14, when Luke names Mary among the disciples awaiting the Holy Spirit. So it is that perseverance completes Luke's description of Mary's spirituality. She is a spiritual exemplar and model disciple not because of the unique experiences that mark the beginning of her journey with the Lord. Tied as they are to the incarnation, these will not be repeated. Rather, what makes her a model is her willingness to ponder God's work and her place therein not simply at one point in time, but throughout her life, marked as it was by both deep spiritual experiences and extended periods of ambiguity.

Often overlooked as a spiritual model or guide in evangelicalism because of the movement's Reformation heritage, Luke's Mary nevertheless presents biblically centered Christians with a model of spiritual practice.

See also Bernadette of Lourdes; Marian Devotion.

For Further Reading: S. Boss, ed., *Mary* (2007); J. Green, *The Gospel of Luke* (1997); E. Johnson, *Truly Our Sister* (2004); T. Perry, *Mary for Evangelicals* (2006); B. Roberts Gaventa, *Mary* (1999).

Timothy Scott Perry

Masculine Spirituality

Part of creation and its goodness, masculinity is established in Genesis 1:27: "God created human beings in his own image ... male and female he created them" (TNIV). Maleness is central to a man's personhood in all that he does, including how he relates to God and others. Masculine spirituality offers a vision of life with God and others that takes into account and affirms the male identity of men.

Though always at least implicit in the Christian tradition, masculine spirituality per se is a relatively recent phenomenon. While sexual differentiation is rooted in creation, gender roles are socially constructed and malleable over time. The Industrial Revolution of the 18th and 19th centuries altered not only the economic order, but also domestic life, and triggered a reappraisal of male and female roles and identities. Out of this Victorian-era flux emerged "muscular Christianity," with its celebrated ideal of a vigorous, strength-conscious masculinity. In such works as Harry Emerson Fosdick's *The Manhood of the Master* (1913), Jesus was regarded as the supreme exemplar of such virtues—as the quintessential *man*. Concurrently an alliance, typified by the YMCA, was forged between Christianity and sports, especially team sports, which has proved particularly enduring within evangelicalism.

Further along, and this time in response to feminism, another men's movement evolved during the 1980s and 1990s that was popularized by Robert Bly's *Iron John* (1990). Authors such as Richard Rohr and James Nelson seek to offer a Christian perspective on masculine spirituality. From an evangelical vantage point, however, caution must be observed toward much of the men's movement because of its expressed New Age underpinnings and frequent embrace of homosexuality.

Masculine spirituality also emerged among more conservative evangelicals with the Promise Keepers (est. 1990) ministry to men. It recognizes that men receive their masculine identity through personal affirmation from their fathers, male role models, and ultimately God the Father. Young men must be initiated into manhood, but this process is proving elusive where the traditional family has disintegrated. As a result, many younger men are seeking mentors and men's groups to provide healthy father figures. Promise Keepers and similar ministries also highlight the Christian man's responsibility to be a disciplined, faithful, monogamous spouse and responsible leader in the home.

Many conservative evangelical men emphasize male proclivity to respond bravely to challenges and calls to action and sacrificial service during their spiritual pilgrimage. Some assume that the complementary role of women is to be nurturing and submissive. Such men readily identify with such heroic archetypes as the adventurer, warrior, lover, king, and prophet. Valiant champions of the faith—from Moses, David, and Elijah in Scripture, to Patrick, Luther, and courageous missionaries throughout the centuries—serve as their exemplars. Masculine spirituality fosters the cultivation of virtues such as courage and faithfulness; so far it has not addressed to the same degree the subtler issues of power that also challenge spiritual growth.

See also Feminist Spirituality; Gender.

For Further Reading: S. Boyd et al., eds., *Redeeming Men* (1996); J. Eldredge, *Fathered by God* (2009); idem, *Wild at Heart* (2001); A. Janssen and L. Weeden, eds., *Seven Promises of a Promise Keeper* (1994); J. Miller, *Biblical Faith and Fathering* (1989).

Glenn E. Myers

Maximus the Confessor (580 – 662)

Heroic champion of orthodoxy. Maximus, called the Confessor, stands as a giant with one foot planted in the East, with its emphasis on the reality of transcendence, and the other foot in the West, with its insistence on the significance of creation. He was born in a village of the Golan and entrusted to a Palestinian monastery when orphaned at the age of nine. Forced from two monasteries by Persian invasions, he eventually settled in Carthage.

Maximus was mentored by Sophronius, a vigorous opponent of monophysitism, a heresy that asserted that Jesus, although God-man, had essentially one nature in that his humanity was absorbed into his divinity. This heresy was predominant in the Eastern portions of the empire, which felt politically disenfranchised and ready to open their doors to Islamic invaders. When Sophronius died, Maximus took up his mentor's mantle as champion of the Chalcedon Creed, which proclaimed both human and divine natures in Christ "unmixed and unconfused."

Constantinople compromised with monothelitism (conceding Christ's two natures but allowing one divine will), but Maximus stood firm, thereby becoming an enemy of the state. He sought backing from Rome, and the Lateran Synod of AD 640 affirmed that Christ willed our salvation through both his human and divine natures. Taken prisoner in AD 653, Maximus endured three trials, was condemned for treason, and was finally exiled to Lazia on the east coast of the Black Sea after scourging, and with his tongue and right hand cut off. Maximus understood that Christology is directly linked to cosmology and that the incarnation affirmed the essential goodness and integrity of the material world against the Eastern impulse to deny its ultimate reality. His teaching was embraced at the Sixth Ecumenical Council in AD 680.

For Further Reading: H. U. von Balthasar, *Cosmic Liturgy: The Universe according to Maximus the Confessor*, trans. B. Daley (2003); O. Clement, *The Roots of Christian Mysticism*, trans. T. Berkeley (1993); *Maximus the Confessor: Selected Writings*, CWS (1985); *The Philokalia*, vol. 2, trans. G. Palmer (1981).

John E. Worgul

M'Cheyne, Robert Murray (1813 – 1843)

Saintly Church of Scotland minister whose tragically short life has cast a long shadow through Andrew Bonar's bestselling *The Memoir and Remains of Robert Murray M'Cheyne* (1844). Deeply affected by his mentor Thomas Chalmer's vision of revitalizing parish ministry to respond to the throes of the industrial revolution in Scotland, M'Cheyne's pastorate in working-class Dundee was characterized by evangelistic preaching, local mission, diligent home visitation, and compassion for the sick and the poor. It was also famously visited by revival in 1839 – 1843. Daily communion with God through the study of Scripture, introspection upon his consciousness of sin and grace, and fervent prayer were the bedrock of a life ground down by frantic work and fragile health. The *Remains'* testimony to M'Cheyne's "absorbing love to the Lord Jesus" — characterized by a piercing awareness of redemption through the cross, a love for the Bible, and an activism of word and deed — has rightly established it as exemplary of evangelical spirituality. Nor to be overlooked is the effect on his contemporaries and posterity of the special burden M'Cheyne carried in his heart for the conversion of the Jews.

See also Reformed (Calvinist) Spirituality.

Todd Statham

Mechthild of Magdeburg (c. 1207 – c. 1282)

German mystic. She was born to a wealthy and respected family; at the age of twelve she had a profound spiritual experience, stirring in her the desire to live a life of poverty and lowliness. Rather than choosing the traditional path of entering a monastery, she chose ascetic homelessness and joined a Beguine community (pious lay women) in Magdeburg to pursue a more devoted religious life in a community. Mechthild received spiritual direction from the Dominican monk Heinrich von Halle. Mechthild spent the last phase of her life (c. 1270 – c. 1282) at the Benedictine Helfta monastery by Eisleben, where she influenced Gertrude the Great.

Mechthild wrote one piece called *The Flowing Light of the Godhead*, completing it over an extended period of time. It is the oldest piece of mystical writing written by a woman in the German language. The Song of Songs, the Gospels, the writings of Bernard of Clairvaux, courtly literature, and other sources resound creatively in her writing. Mechthild's use of poetic language is striking, bursting with vivid and pungent imagery, giving the reader a sense of immediacy and closeness to her accounts and experiences. The great range of genres, themes, and images reminds one of a spectacular fireworks display, seeking to approach the unspeakable beauty of God, and his boundless love for his creation. Her influence upon future German mysticism is considerable.

Fully steeped into the mystery of the Holy Trinity, Mechthild urges her readers toward union with God, holding ascetic practices for those in temptation and spiritual refreshment for the weary in a nuanced balance. With a high but not uncritical regard and love for the church, Mechthild understood herself and the church as the bride of Christ, engaged in an intimate dialogue with God, patiently enduring pain and yearning for the ultimate union with the beloved.

See also Beguines; Women.

Gisela H. Kreglinger

Medieval West (600 – 1450)

See Chapter 15.

Meditation

Meditation is the spiritual practice of focused attentiveness. Christian meditation has traditionally been focused on the Scriptures of the Old and New Testaments, read personally and christocentrically. "Spiritual reading" of works that encourage or instruct in such focused thought is secondary to the private, contemplative focus on Scripture. Meditation is most often silent but can also include oral reading, recitation, singing, chanting, journaling, creative interpretation, or physical movement — all ways through which reverent attention can be offered to the text.

The practice of Christian meditation is rooted in the practice of Jesus himself. From Jesus' use of Scripture, especially in his Emmaus Road discourse (Luke 24:25 – 27), it is clear that meditation on the Hebrew Scriptures constituted an important part of Jesus' devotional practice. After his resurrection and ascension, believers incorporated the remembered words of Jesus and the words of the first apostles into their worship and meditation (Col. 3:16). The rich use of the OT throughout the NT is evidence for and illustrative of early Christian meditative practice, the Hebrew Scriptures read in the light of Christ's life, death, and resurrection.

In the monastic tradition, meditation was an integral aspect of the life of prayer. According to Jean Leclercq, it required the monk not only to think about the Scriptures, but "to practice a thing by thinking of it … to fix it in the memory, to learn it."

In the 12th and 13th centuries, new emphasis was placed on emotional engagement in meditative practice, with the person inserting himself or herself into a visualized reenactment of a biblical event. This "meditation of the historical event" allowed the person to imagine, for example, standing in the place of Mary at the foot of the cross, seeking to feel what she had felt, and so to enter into the inner spiritual meaning of the event. The goal of such meditation was ultimately to experience union with God. The *Spiritual Exercises of St. Ignatius* (1548) combined such visualization with the examination of one's own sinfulness, with a view to deepening repentance and enhancing wonder at God's grace.

After the Reformation, Protestant meditation placed a renewed emphasis on the Bible as God's Word; the printing press, vernacular translations, and widening literacy made the reading and meditation of the Scripture available to rank-and-file Christians. Following John Calvin's insistence that every word of Scripture should be received as spoken directly to the reader by the mouth of God (*Institutes*, 7.1), Puritan meditation was intensely oriented toward the Scriptures, with the intent not merely to memorize and recite the words, but also to apply them to one's own life.

From the 16th century on, there was an outpouring of books instructing the laity in meditative practice; writers like John Bunyan (1628–1688) and Richard Baxter (1615–1691) popularized Puritan methods of meditation. In the Methodist revival of the 18th century, John Wesley taught meditation and spiritual reading as part of Christian practice; Wesleyan hymnody added significantly to the repertoire of meditative texts.

The emphasis on memorizing Scripture that was part of both Puritan and evangelical experience diminished in the 20th century as dominant educational theories rejected rote learning and recitation. A new emphasis on the relational basis of meditation was called for. Robert Boyd Munger's short allegory, *My Heart, Christ's Home* (1954), served to renew an understanding of daily meditation on Scripture as time spent in personal, privileged conversation with Christ.

In recent decades, there have been several developments in Christian meditation. (1) A return to pre-Reformation sources of Christian meditative practice. Silent retreats, often guided by some form of the Ignatian exercises, are part of the spiritual practice of many. (2) A renewed interest in meditative foci other than Scriptural texts. In *Celebration of Discipline* (1978), Richard Foster encouraged focused meditation on some aspect of creation as preparation for learning how to meditate on Scripture (24–25). (3) An increased openness toward some aspects of Eastern meditation seen to be compatible with Christian meditation. Thomas Merton is the primary influence on this turn; the Buddhist practice of mindfulness is seen as a way of becoming attentive to the present moment. (4) A growing awareness of the neurological effects of meditation, with an interest in the therapeutic or cognitive, rather than purely spiritual, benefits it confers, with many therapies incorporating meditative practices.

While these developments may enrich both our understanding and practice of meditation, coming to know God through thoughtful, attentive, and regular reading of Scriptures will continue to ground and distinguish meditation that is Christian. In *Life Together* (1939), Dietrich Bonhoeffer wrote, "Meditation … lets us be alone with the Word.… We ponder the chosen text on the strength of the promise that it has something utterly personal to say to us.… We expose ourselves to the specific word until it addresses us personally." The goal of meditation is first and always to enjoy fellowship with the triune God and the outcome of transformation as the Spirit of God operates through the Word in the "renewing of [our] mind" (Rom. 12:2).

See also Contemplation.

For Further Reading: H. U. von Balthasar, *Christian Meditation*, trans. M. T. Skerry (1989); D. Jeffrey, ed., *English Spirituality in the Age of Wesley* (1987); U. M. Kaufmann, *The Pilgrim's Progress and Traditions in Puritan Meditation* (1966); J. Leclercq, *The Love of Learning and the Desire for God*, trans. C. Misrahi (1982); T. Merton, *Spiritual Direction and Meditation* (1975); J. I. Packer, *A Quest for Godliness* (1990); J. Stott, *God's Book for God's People* (1982).

Maxine Hancock

Memorization, Bible

Bible memorization is the discipline of systematically committing to memory selected verses and passages of Scripture. In preliterate societies, or quasi-literate ones without general access to sacred texts, memorization is essential to devout reflection and meditation on their contents. The Jewish community modeled this practice in its own disciplined attention to the words of the Hebrew Bible, especially the Torah. Both Jews and Christians ever since have been inspired by the psalmist's prayer, "I have hidden your word in my heart that I might not sin against you" (Ps. 119:11), and have discovered that memorization can be a useful way to embed divine words deeply in one's consciousness. For Christians, the validity of this discipline is reinforced by the example of Jesus, who resisted Satan's temptations in wilderness isolation by responding each time with a (presumably memorized) text of Scripture (Luke 4:1–14).

Early church fathers, including Augustine and Peter Chrysologus (380–450), encouraged Scripture memorization as a basis for meditation; and it seems reasonable that their advice was heeded by at least some in the generations that followed them. Nevertheless, for many centuries Bible memorization occurred most often unconsciously as the Scripture-dense liturgies and catechisms of the church were etched in the minds and hearts of observant believers.

By the 1550s, a chapter and verse numbering system was developed that made locating and reviewing specific texts much easier. With the Reformation came a heightened regard for Scripture, which also encouraged memorization. On the other hand, Gutenberg's concurrent printing revolution, by providing near-universal access to Scripture, may actually have made memorization seem less urgent.

The rise in the popularity of Bible memorization among evangelicals appears to be rooted in the Sunday school movement, begun in 1780 by Robert Raikes (1736–1811) of Gloucester, England. Leaders of this movement discovered early on that rote memorization had only very limited effects; it was more formational when the text's meaning and relevance to life were also explained clearly. Thus began a venerable association of Sunday school lessons and weekly assigned Bible verses. From badges and awards ceremonies to prizes and free weeks at summer camp, evangelicals have been creative about incentivizing Bible memory work. The Navigators, founded by Dawson Trotman in 1933, is an international discipleship ministry with a strong emphasis on the discipline of Bible memorization.

Meanwhile the hegemonic status of the Authorized (King James) Version of the Bible began to crumble with the proliferation of alternative English-language Bible translation in the 20th century. An unwitting consequence of this was a decline in the perceived need for precision in Scripture quotation; and this perception seriously undermined the rigor and discipline required to do Bible memorization properly.

Many evangelicals still appreciate the value of Scripture memorization for both personal evangelism and devotional meditation. Speedy recall of intrinsically powerful Scripture texts (Heb. 4:12) is considered highly advantageous during evangelistic encounters, while having it "in one's heart" enables meditation on it "day and night" just about anywhere (Ps. 1).

Even though literacy is the norm today, and Bibles are widely available and relatively inexpensive, Bible memorization remains a profitable spiritual discipline. Especially when the proper interpretation and relevance of memorized texts are also thoroughly explained, the discipline of memorizing the Bible has a powerful formational potency and a unique contribution to the cognitive restructuring so necessary to the renewal of the mind.

See also Spiritual Reading.

For Further Reading: The Navigators, *Topical Memory System* (2006).

Cynthia Hyle Bezek

Mendicant Spirituality

Mendicants served God by divesting earthly wealth and living free of material possessions. Following Christ, mendicants emptied themselves (Phil. 2:7) and raised their own support by soliciting (*mendicare*) donations of food, shelter, and clothing as they proclaimed the gospel, tended the sick, and aided the poor. They sought literally to obey Jesus' instruction to the apostles (and the Seventy-two) to live by the food and lodging offered in each village: "Take nothing for the journey — no staff, no bag, no bread, no money, no extra shirt" (Luke 9:3 – 5 TNIV; cf. 10:3 – 7).

Such a lifestyle of poverty, coupled with itinerant ministry, ignited waves of revival across Europe in the 12th and 13th centuries and was known as the *vita apostolica* — apostolic life. By the thousands, godly monks, clergy, and laypeople traveled two by two about the countryside, begging alms and declaring the gospel to eager crowds. Following Peter Waldo (c. 1140 – 1218), the Waldensians preached to common people and provided portions of Scripture translated into the vernacular, beginning in southern France and northern Italy. Often considered to be the first Protestants, the Waldensians won many to Christ, especially among those led astray by the heretical Cathari/Albigensians. In northern Italy, the *Humiliati* established a similar life of simplicity. Shortly afterward, Francis of Assisi and Dominic Guzman responded to Christ's call to radical poverty. Mendicant friars of the Franciscans and Dominicans crisscrossed Europe and sent missionaries around the world. In contrast to many wealthy bishops of the time, these mendicants incarnated Christ's love to the populace by caring for those in need and preaching in the common language. As well as the friars (brothers), a second order of women and a third order of laypeople emerged among the Franciscans and Dominicans. Other mendicant orders include the Carmelites and Augustinian hermits. Although by the time of the Reformation the mendicant lifestyle was sometimes abused, its initial impulse was exemplary and ushered an untold multitude into vital relationship with Christ.

Some Protestant and Catholic missionary movements have manifested a similar spiritual impulse, with missionaries raising their own funds and living simple lives, although usually still "wealthy" in comparison to those to whom they feel called to witness. The example of the original mendicants is an invitation to all Christians to fundamental detachment and challenges the materialism of the church today, especially in affluent nations.

See also Dominican Spirituality; Franciscan Spirituality.

For Further Reading: G. Audisio, *The Waldensian Dissent: Persecution and Survival* (1999); H. Grundmann, *Religious Movements in the Middle Ages* (1995); C. H. Lawrence, *The Friars* (1994); idem, *Medieval Monasticism* (2001).

Glenn E. Myers

Mentoring, Spiritual

Spiritual mentoring involves passing on formative wisdom about the Christian life from a more spiritually mature Christian to others less developed in the faith—often by sustained example as much as through words. Among the various "sacred companionships" available to Christians, spiritual mentoring differs from spiritual friendship inasmuch as it is not a peer relationship. It differs from spiritual direction by reason of its less structured dynamics and more extensive personal association between the parties involved. By contrast, spiritual direction was and is, in fact, a specialized relationship developed by Ignatius Loyola and the Jesuits, with its own methodological training and professional standards, and designed primarily to facilitate discernment. Spiritual mentoring is a more inclusive and flexible category of relationship. Significantly, it achieves what mere instruction simply cannot. It is always most effective when it occurs in a context of relational trust and on a foundation of shared life experience.

Spiritual mentoring can be observed in Scripture. While for three years Jesus made disciples of the Twelve, he also mentored them into his experience of transforming communion with the Father. Barnabas mentored the apostle Paul and Mark; Paul in turn guided Timothy and urged believers at Philippi to practice what they had learned from him or seen him doing (Phil. 4:9). The *Didache*, an important first-century Christian document, indicates that spiritual mentoring was already in place early on. The *Didache* guides a typical spiritual mentor in the context of a three-year relationship with a new believer. The mentor is to address how the young Christian should respond to persecution, live communally and morally, deal with sin, practice dependence on God, and be nourished through baptism and the Lord's Supper.

Spiritual mentoring is more focused on the life of the soul in relationship to God than is discipleship, as that term has come to be understood. The latter ought to include such mentoring but denotes a more comprehensive process of shaping people into Christians—one that also includes, for example, basic instruction in doctrine, ethics, and daily practices. Spiritual mentoring is legitimized by the biblical principle of "the priesthood of all believers" and remains key to the effective intergenerational transmission of living faith.

See also Direction, Spiritual.

For Further Reading: K. Anderson and R. Reese, *Spiritual Mentoring* (1999); A. Calhoun, *Spiritual Disciplines Handbook* (2005); J. Clinton, *The Mentor Handbook* (1991); M. Ford, *Traditions of the Ancients* (2006); J. Houston, *The Mentored Life* (2002).

Nancy R. Buschart

Mercy

The practice of mercy is the demonstration of compassion and love, especially to those at risk and on the margins. The Christian life is built from beginning (1 Peter 1:3) to end (Jude 21) on the mercy of God. Mercy is so important that God desires it even above sacrifice (Matt. 9:13; 12:7). Jesus considered mercy one of the weightier matters of the law (Matt. 23:23) and indicated that the model of mercy for his followers is his Father in heaven (Luke 6:34). There even appears to be a spiritual gift of showing mercy (Rom. 12:8).

In Scripture there is a close consequential connection between showing mercy and receiving mercy (Matt. 5:7; 18:33; James 2:13). The NT is replete with examples of acts of mercy. One of the most frequent requests for mercy comes to Jesus from those who are infirm or demon possessed (Matt. 9:27; 15:22; 17:15; 20:30–31). Mercy is displayed in the acts of the Good Samaritan (Luke 10:37), who had compassion for one who fell among the robbers, bound up his wounds, transported him to an inn, paid for his provision, and promised to pay for any additional costs incurred. A rich man named Lazarus asked Abraham to have mercy on him by dipping his finger in cold water and placing that drop on his tongue to quench his thirst (Luke 16:24). Mercy is very much the point when Jesus speaks of those who feed the hungry, give drink to the thirsty, welcome the stranger, clothe the naked, and visit the sick and those in prison (Matt. 25:31 – 46). Jude (21 – 23) instructs believers to show mercy to those who doubt and others who have become contaminated by sin. Thus, when believers follow their Lord in preaching the gospel to the poor, praying for the sick, caring for the poor and marginalized, and extending to others the mercy they themselves have received, they identify both with their Lord and with those whom their Lord loves. Latin American theologian Jon Sobrino argues for a direct link between mercy and spiritual transformation; when a person shows mercy toward the poor and oppressed, they themselves become more humanized, or rehumanized. In a sense, the poor become the agents of the transformation or salvation of the very one who is helping in their deliverance and the restoration of their human dignity.

Among Pentecostals, those discerned to have the spiritual gift of showing mercy include Mark Buntain of Calcutta; Margaret Gaines of Aboud, the West Bank; Dario Lopez of Lima, Peru; and Terry Goodin of Gallup, New Mexico.

See also Beatitudes; Compassion.

For Further Reading: M. Gaines, *Of Like Passions* (2000); D. Lopez, *The Liberating Mission of Jesus* (2010); J. Sobrino, *The Principle of Mercy* (1994).

John Christopher Thomas

Merton, Thomas (1915 – 1968)

American Trappist monk. Merton was born in France to Owen Merton, New Zealander, and Ruth Jenkins Merton, American, artists who married while studying in Paris. His early childhood was complicated by his mother's death and his father's nomadic impulses. In 1941 Merton entered monastic life at the Abbey of Gethsemani near Louisville, Kentucky, and remained a monk until his death in 1968. He briefly attended Cambridge University and later engaged in graduate studies on William Blake and Gerard Manley Hopkins at Columbia University. Thoroughly immersed in the lifestyle of the 1920s in New York City, Merton embraced friendships that would last the course of his life with men of letters, including Robert Giroux and Robert Lax, and the artist Ad Reinhardt. His astonishing conversion and subsequent monastic vocation to the Cistercians of the Strict Observance are recorded in his classic spiritual autobiography, *The Seven Storey Mountain* (1948), claimed by some literary critics as the best of its genre in twentieth-century American literature. It has been translated into dozens of languages.

By the time Merton was in his early twenties, he was a published poet and had already written several unpublished novels. His significance as a writer continued throughout his life and extended far beyond Catholic readers into secular society, in nearly one hundred books and collections. His journals, essays, and volumes of poetry have influenced millions of readers who follow his journey as a deeply committed Christian monk. They sought his wisdom on war and peace and race relations in the 1960s, but also for spiritual and contemplative direction before and after that tumultuous decade. Merton was a prolific correspondent, writing more than twenty thousand letters in which he recorded his responses to the world around him.

His dual vocation as a contemplative monk and writer was a paradox that drove him to a profound search for the will of God in his life, daily and eternally, in spite of his human failings — failings he recorded as a testimony to God's grace in his struggles with sin and forgiveness. His concerns for social justice led him to identify with poverty activist Dorothy Day and to write for the *Catholic Worker*. He engaged American presidents and Congressmen, civil rights leader Martin Luther King Jr., and Nobel Prize winners Boris Pasternak and Czeslaw Milosz, along with artists, musicians, and writers of cultural esteem and influence all over the world. He was invited into discussions preceding Vatican II and visited the Dalai Lama in 1968, in a meeting that initiated serious interreligious dialogue between East and West in the modern age.

Merton is sometimes controversial among evangelical Christians who are skeptical of monasticism as a spiritual vocation. Only more recently has the study of the desert fathers and the church traditions of intellectual and spiritual formation made a much wider audience of Christians more interested in Merton. Conversely, Merton was giving conferences in the sixties to students from the Southern Seminary in Louisville who were taken to Gethsemani for educational reasons. Like many others who would follow, they found common ground for people of faith and experienced the foreshadowing effects that Merton's life would have on future generations of seekers after spiritual truth.

See also Trappists.

For Further Reading: G. Kilcourse, *Ace of Freedoms: Thomas Merton's Christ* (1994); R. Labrie, *The Art of Thomas Merton* (1974); J. Montaldo and P. Hart, eds., *The Intimate Merton* (2001); M. Mott, *The Seven Mountains of Thomas Merton* (1984); W. Shannon, *Silent Lamp* (1993); W. Shannon et al., *The Thomas Merton Encyclopedia* (2002); L. Szabo, ed., *In the Dark before Dawn* (2005).

Lynn R. Szabo

Methodist Spirituality

Methodism received its name because of its methodical spiritual practices. Founded by brothers John and Charles Wesley in the early 18th century, Methodism began as a "holy club" for undergraduates on the campus of Oxford University. Members gathered for regular practices of Bible study, theological reflection, prayer, and accountability. Eventually they began to address social injustice as part of their discipline.

Essentially a semimonastic lay movement in the Anglican Church, the backbone of Methodist spirituality was the structure of class, band, and societies, and the General Rules that John Wesley established to guide Methodists. Wesley developed the class and band meetings based on influences from the Moravians and a number of other groups in Europe that practiced various forms of intentional community. This structure provided a systematic way for Methodists to "watch over one another in love," as Wesley put it, so that they could progress in holiness of heart and life. The goal of Methodism was to "spread scriptural holiness across the land" in order to transform society.

Classes were groups of seven to twelve members who met weekly for mutual edification and accountability. Each member would answer the same question: "How does your soul prosper?" These small groups were the means through which persons entered Methodist societies. Originally, people were required to attend a class meeting weekly in order to be part of the Methodist Society.

Band meetings were of a confessional nature, with members meeting in groups of six to share their temptations and sins, and to pray for one another. These were optional and were the most rigorous of the meetings in terms of the degree of transparency required by members.

Society meetings were worship celebrations, with Scripture reading, prayer, and a sermon. All three of these meetings were held to cultivate holiness of heart and life—a spirituality that was deeply grounded in practices of prayer and other spiritual disciplines, and that was actively engaged in healing the wounds of the world.

The three meetings were all guided by Wesley's General Rules, which were inspired by Isaiah 1:16–17. Still found in *The Book of Discipline of the United Methodist Church*, the rules are: (1) Do no harm; (2) Do all the good you can; (3) Attend upon all the ordinances of God. The "ordinances" were the classical Christian spiritual disciplines, including Bible reading, prayer, fasting, corporate worship, and Communion. Underneath each of the three General Rules, Wesley set forth a variety of applications, such as resisting slavery, practicing frugality in one's financial management, and the like. From the beginning, then, Methodist spirituality involved the integration of disciplined practices of spiritual formation, community formation, and social justice, with a goal of holiness of heart and life, for the transformation of the world.

Methodist spirituality has also been marked from the beginning by a robust hymnody. Charles Wesley penned more than five thousand hymns, many of which continue to be sung in churches today. The *United Methodist Hymnal* opens with John Wesley's list of seven admonitions about the correct way to praise God through singing.

As Methodism came to North America and evolved from a primarily lay-led Holiness movement into a denomination, it lost its original emphasis on the threefold structure of class, band, and society meetings. In response to the racial divide in North America, Methodism split between north and south, and new Methodist denominations formed, including the African Methodist Episcopal (AME) Church. The AME Church continued to hold fast to the doctrine and discipline of the Methodist Church, while developing spiritual traditions reflecting the profound struggle for civil and human rights for black Americans.

During the 19th century, a new Holiness movement emerged, led by lay Methodists such as Phoebe Palmer, who called the Methodist church back to its vocation of holiness. Through camp meetings, small groups, publications, and other means, holiness Methodists urged Christians to be sanctified. These holiness leaders, many of whom were women, also led social reform in abolition, temperance, women's rights, child labor laws, the humane treatment of the mentally ill, and more. Their vision of holiness included disciplined spiritual practices and lively, emotionally engaged worship coupled with vigorous social reform. The holiness Methodists were increasingly ostracized by mainstream Methodism, ultimately leading to the formation of many new denominations that reflected Wesleyan theology and holiness commitments. These included the Church of the Nazarene and the Salvation Army. Pentecostalism also emerged from the Holiness movement, with its spirituality focused on the power and gifts of the Holy Spirit.

With the fundamentalist-modernist controversy of the early 20th century, mainstream liberal Methodism moved even further from its origins as a Holiness movement. For much of the 20th century, as a result, liberal Methodist spirituality has been one of strong corporate liturgical practices coupled with liberal social activism. Evangelical Methodist spirituality has tended to focus on individual spiritual practices.

Today a number of reforming emphases are again emerging within Methodism, calling forth a renewed emphasis on holiness of heart and life that integrate personal piety with social justice. Thus, the early holiness emphases of Methodist spirituality continue to shape disciples in Methodist traditions.

See also Moravian Spirituality; Pietism; Wesley, Charles; Wesley, John.

For Further Reading: W. Abraham and J. Kirby, eds., *The Oxford Handbook of Methodist Studies* (2009); E. Heath and S. Kisker, *Longing for Spring* (2010); R. Maddox, *Responsible Grace* (1994); L. Ruth, ed., *Early Methodist Life and Spirituality* (2005); A. Taves, *Fits, Trances, and Visions* (1999); K. Watson, *A Blueprint for Discipleship* (2009).

Elaine A. Heath

Midlife Transition

This describes the passage roughly between the first and second halves of life. For some this transition involves little disequilibrium. For others the transition is a season of distress with one's life, marriage, career path, financial situation, or relationship with God—hence the older term, *midlife crisis*. Authorities identify the midlife transition or crisis as occurring between ages thirty-five and forty (Jung), thirty and sixty (Erikson), thirty-five and forty-five (Levinson and Sheehy), or thirty-five and fifty-five (Conway). Recent research has shown that persons in their forties are the least happy, with age forty-four said to be the unhappiest. A midlife transition, involving painful disorientation, may last for months or years.

Carl Jung, who initially investigated the midlife phenomenon, distinguished between the morning of life orientated to the outer world by developing the ego and the afternoon of life by cultivating one's inner spiritual world. First-half questions include, "What vocation shall I seek?" and "What avocations shall I pursue?" Second-half questions involve adaptation to one's inner world, specifically discovering and nurturing one's true self. Jung envisaged the often turbulent midlife transition as bridging life's two halves.

Existentially, a crisis of identity prompts midlife people to ask, "Who am I?" and "Who do I want to become?" Western culture's preference for youth over maturity tends to foster a sense of worthlessness. Sensing that better years are behind, the midlifer often experiences anxiety at the prospect of his or her mortality, accompanied by fatigue and depression. Physically, this transition involves a decline of energy and potentially distressing psychosomatic symptoms. Relationally, marriage may become conflicted through preoccupation with interpersonal neglect. One or both partners may attempt to recapture the excitement of romance through an extramarital affair.

The midlife transition often involves a vocational crisis in the form of career dislocation. Either unemployed or trapped in their jobs, the person at midlife may pose questions such as, "Have I accomplished what I hoped to accomplish?" and "What is my legacy?" Spiritually, diminished connection and dissatisfaction with God may prompt the midlifer to explore other religious alternatives as potential sources of satisfaction and meaning.

Yet the Christian may discover in a midlife transition the opportunity to work and pray through the summons to healing and transformation rather than flee its challenges. With Habakkuk, one may confidently call upon God to "revive [his] work in the midst of the years" (3:2 KJV). While some biblical characters were called to divine service in their youth, one may find in the accounts of prophets, apostles, and others inspiring narratives of changed life and fresh vocation.

See also Aging; Human Development.

For Further Reading: J. Brewi and A. Brennan, *Mid-Life* (1982); B. Buford, *Half-Time* (1994); E. Erikson, *Childhood and Society* (1950); C. Jung, *Modern Man in Search of a Soul*, trans. W. Dell and C. Baynes (1933); D. Levinson, *The Seasons of a Man's Life* (1978).

Bruce A. Demarest

Military Orders

These began in the 11th century as monastic associations for Christian knights to serve God by tending the sick, defending Christian pilgrims, and eventually guarding Europe from Islamic invasion. As devoted believers, members lived in community, taking vows of chastity, poverty, and obedience. They committed themselves to daily prayer, learning Scripture, fasting, and other spiritual disciplines.

Three orders are of note, each incorporating three classes of members: knights, priests, and brothers. The Knights Hospitallers (Order of St. John of Jerusalem) originated around 1023 in Jerusalem to provide medical care for the sick and pilgrims visiting the Holy Lands. After Christians conquered Jerusalem in 1099 during the First Crusade, Hospitallers offered lodging and an armed guard to numerous pilgrims and were officially recognized as a monastic order in 1113. The Knights Templars were founded in 1119 to protect pilgrims traveling to the Holy Lands. They received their rule in 1128, penned by Bernard of Clairvaux, who also wrote *In Praise of the New Knighthood*, supporting the military monastic orders. Receiving donations from royalty around Europe, the Templars grew to some twenty thousand members and wielded substantial power until their suppression by the papacy in 1312. At the end of the 12th century, the Teutonic Knights were founded to settle the wilderness of Prussia and Christianize its inhabitants. Other military associations emerged, especially in Spain and Portugal. Several remain, most notably the Hospitallers — or Knights of Malta — who focus on social welfare work in our day.

As many present-day Christians consider it necessary to withstand terrorism, medieval soldiers assumed it was their duty to resist militant Islam. While not condoning atrocities committed in war, contemporary readers can recognize the genuine attempt of devoted believers to serve Christ in the age of chivalry.

See also Rules, Religious.

For Further Reading: M. Barber, ed., *The Military Orders* (1994); H. Nicholson, *Templars, Hospitallers, and Teutonic Knights* (1993); M. Walsh, *Warriors of the Lord* (2003).

Glenn E. Myers

Milton, John (1608–1674)

Generally regarded as the greatest English writer after Shakespeare. He is additionally the prototypical Christian poet of the English-speaking world. While the devotional potential of Milton's writing is always just below the surface, even in Milton's many volumes of polemical prose, it is preeminently in his poetry that we find the materials for spiritual nurture.

To understand how Milton contributes to the history of spirituality, we need to understand how poetry achieves its effects. Poets think in images, not abstractions. Additionally, a poem is not a delivery system for an idea but rather a poet's sharing of an affective or reflective experience.

As an entry into Milton and spirituality, one cannot do better than read selected sonnets (such as 7, 9, 14, 18, 19, and 23). Sonnet 19, for example, contains the declaration that "they also serve who stand and wait" — surely one of the most memorable affirmations ever of the disposition of a faithful Christian soul. On one level, we can follow the spiritual movements of the poet's mind and feelings, allowing him to be our representative, saying what we also think and feel. But inasmuch as most of these poems are addressed to people who appear before us as spiritual models, we can further ponder how these exemplary people (three of them women) embody a spirituality that we can emulate.

Milton's major spiritual work is the epic *Paradise Lost* (1667). His main strategy is simple, based on an arrangement by pairs of books. For two books Milton invites us to live with images of Satan, evil, and hell. Then he lifts us imaginatively out of that morass to contemplate images of heaven and paradise (bks. 3–4). Next we live with images of a celestial battle between good and bad angels (bks. 5–6), followed by images of God's creation of the world (bks. 7–8). As we read the story of Adam and Eve's fall (bks. 9–10), our imaginations dwell on images of temptation, evil choice, and consequences of evil. Finally, Milton leads us to contemplate fallen human history, culminating in the redemptive life of Christ (bks. 11–12). Living with the great images of the Christian faith is a spiritual exercise.

Milton's preeminent portrayal of the spiritual life is his story of Adam and Eve's life in paradise in Book 4 of *Paradise Lost*. This is Milton's vision of how God intends human life to be lived. It is a Puritan vision of the spiritual life, with all of life opening upward to God. It is a life of continuous gratitude and worship, of work and leisure in balance, and of harmony with nature and one's fellow humans. His less celebrated follow-up, *Paradise Regained* (1671), reflects imaginatively on Christ's temptation and inspires readers by the second Adam's triumph through endurance (as Adam and Eve should have done).

See also Literature and Spirituality; Puritan Spirituality.

For Further Reading: C. A. Patrides, *Milton and the Christian Tradition* (1966); J. E. Thorpe, *John Milton* (1983).

Leland Ryken

Ministry

See **Chapter 33.**

Miracles

See **Extraordinary Phenomena.**

Mission

See **Chapter 33.**

Modernity

Modernity is an intellectual mind-set or sensibility associated with a historical period in the West that reached its flowering in the 18th century. Its roots go back into the Renaissance; its ending is more ambiguous. Some scholars claim the modern era ended with Nietzsche, others say in the late 20th century, and still others suggest it is not yet over but has merely evolved. But modernity is recognized less for its dates and more for its characteristics and values. Regrettably, these values inhibit profound spiritual life by focusing on reason, science, and human effort as the sources of human flourishing.

Typically, these qualities and values are placed in contrast to those of premodernity and postmodernity. In contrast to moderns, premoderns value the traditions of the past. Where they value reason, they connect it clearly to the great minds of the ancient world. Tradition possesses authority to guide individuals and society toward a stable life.

Moderns, however, feel that tradition restricts personal freedom. They turn their faces to the future and hope to shed tradition. They long to experience freedom and social progress. And moderns look to human reason to guide that progress.

In philosophy, Rene Descartes was an important influence. Frustrated by the continuous religious warfare of the 16th century, Descartes sought to construct a method of resolving disputes in which the truth of a belief could be systematically uncovered. Through his "methodological rationalism," Descartes tried to establish foundational beliefs that could not be doubted. Building on these foundational beliefs, Descartes thought the human mind could deduce belief with certainty. So like modernity more broadly, Descartes did not begin with religious tradition but argued that human reason produces absolute knowledge that leads to social good.

The Industrial Revolution and scientific advances reinforced confidence that human reason could produce social progress. Science produces tangible, verifiable results that not only challenge certain religious traditions but also produce material benefits. Confidence in the human mind's ability to learn through science combined with increasing emphasis on the individual, and this interacted with more positive views of human nature and more optimistic views of human potential. The individual was elevated in importance over the group. Thinkers emphasized human rights. In government, moderns rejected the notion that God designed royal families to rule. Instead, they argued that all persons have a right to participate in their own governance, and this urge propelled the rise of democracy.

A son who grows up in an abusive home must make his peace with his family of origin. Just so, spiritually minded people who grow up with a modern sensibility must make peace with that heritage. Certain values of modernity threatened Christian spirituality. As moderns wrested control of knowledge from traditional authorities, they placed faith in opposition to reason. As they emphasized the rights of individuals, they argued against the hierarchical power structure of the church. (Sinful abuse clearly aided the force of this argument.) As they championed the results of science, moderns gradually came to assume not just that science is a powerful tool of knowledge, but that science is the *only* path to knowledge. Reason, embodied in science, dazzled the world with its accomplishments. Faith, the realm of spirituality, retreated to the margins. Faith became a private experience, not to be confused with the real world of intellect, commerce, or society.

Western Christians had to do something with modernity. Friedrich Schleiermacher sought to rehabilitate Christian thinking and theology by recasting it as the church's reflection, not on Scripture or tradition, but on religious experience. This led to what is broadly classed as liberal theology. In North America, some conservative Christians seek to prove the Christian worldview in the absolute manner required by modernism. What is broadly called fundamentalism sometimes exhibits this strategy.

But other Christians resisted the modern spirit in order to preserve space for spirituality. Karl Barth placed confidence in Christ speaking to the church in an experience of encounter. What became the so-called neoorthodox movement emphasizes the miracle of God speaking through the Word but does not engage in reasoned arguments to prove that miracle. In North America, some conservatives simply choose to trust the Bible. They exhibit an anti-intellectual spirit: they just believe the Bible no matter what the scholars say.

Today modernity is waning. Certainly, much that is of value remains. But Descartes' quest for certainty failed. Technological progress came at the cost of diminishing global resources. Economic opportunism has created horrible injustices. Science, when harnessed by governments, produced horrors like the threat of nuclear warfare.

Consequently, Christians interested in spirituality feel less urgency to engage the values of modernity. Indeed, the spirituality of the exploding Christian movements outside the West largely ignores the empirical, naturalistic, epistemic, and social concerns of modernity. At the same time, the impetus of the scientific method to explore human nature through the social sciences, for example, certainly adds insight that can enrich Christian spiritual experience. Many younger Christians respect these new insights even as they connect them with a renewed interest in ancient traditions, venerable symbols, and time-honored practices.

The characteristics and values of modernity suffocated Christian spirituality for many years. Now, as modernity's flaws become increasingly obvious, there is newfound space for Christian spiritual resurgence. By exploring ancient practices, integrating creative insights from new ways to understand the human self, and emphasizing the unique sacred pathways of each individual believer, Christians are freed up to integrate robust, but properly humble, accounts of Christian truth with soul-satisfying experiences of life with God.

See also Enlightenment; Postmodernity; Secularization.

For Further Reading: P. Berger *The Sacred Canopy* (1967); M. Berman, *All That Is Solid Melts into Air* (1982); A. Cascardi, *The Subject of Modernity* (1992); A. Giddens, *Consequences of Modernity* (1990); G. Pattison, *Art, Modernity, and Faith* (1991).

David K. Clark

Molinos, Miguel de (c. 1628–1697)

Spanish Catholic priest and Quietist writer. After moving to Rome and becoming close to Pope Innocent XI, he wrote *The Spiritual Guide Which Disentangles the Soul, and Brings It by the Inward Way to the Getting of Perfect Contemplation and the Rich Treasure of Internal Peace* (1675). It became the starting point for the movement known as Quietism. It was widely praised and influenced people in Italy, Spain, and France. Other writers associated with this movement are Madam Guyon, François Fénelon, and Jean de Caussade.

Soon, however, the Jesuit order and the French King Louis XIV attacked this teaching, fearing its effect on the spiritual practices of Catholics. They prevailed over the pope's friendship and the high opinion of many by using the Inquisition. Many followers of Molinos were questioned for evidence, and the pope was forced in *Coelestis Pastor* (1687) to judge the book as heretical. Molinos was arrested in 1685; two years later, despite recanting all his errors, he was condemned to prison for the rest of his life.

Perhaps Molinos was falsely condemned, as his critics attributed statements to him not found in his book. The basis of his teaching was that of the Spanish mystics Teresa of Avila and John of the Cross, who were later honored as doctors of the church. Molinos seemed to go beyond them by implying that verbal prayer, meditation, fasting, and particularly confession (penance) were only for beginners; once one had attained to passive contemplation, the need for these spiritual practices was over. He emphasized the state of perfect peace found in the contemplation of God. One can easily imagine followers running to extremes with these ideas.

To put the point more generally, Quietism was the opposite of formalism, the idea that outward performances are the essence of the spiritual life. Molinos taught that attaining perfection in union with God was more important than all the spiritual practices demanded by the church. It is understandable that many Protestants, then and now, have sympathized with Quietism. It must be noted, however, that Molinos taught and practiced the partaking of Communion daily and complete obedience to one's spiritual director, practices not usually associated with Protestantism. What his teaching rescued, however, was the sense of grace as a gift, beyond all striving.

See also Quietism.

For Further Reading: *Miguel de Molinos,* CWS (2010).

Bradley P. Holt

Monasticism

"Monasticism" shares the same root as the English word *monk* (Lat. *monachus,* Gr. *monachos*), meaning "solitary," one who lives alone. By the 4th century, in a letter of Jerome, the term was applied to monks who lived in communities. Accordingly, "monasticism" refers to those who either live alone, in a solitary manner, or to a group of persons who live together in community striving toward a common end and engaged in a shared apostolate (i.e., mission in life). As well, monastics adopted a number of ascetic disciplines, including times of fixed prayer, strict dietary regimens, disciplined periods of manual labor and/or study, and submission to an abbot or abbess.

Consequently, a unique monastic spirituality emerged, characterized primarily by prayer, solitude/silence, and asceticism, evidenced uniquely in vows of poverty, chastity, and obedience. Benedict of Nursia summarized this spirituality as a "conversion of life." For monastics these practices were not legalistic, but the framework through which spiritual growth was moved along. Hence Benedict's insistence that his Rule was merely "for beginners" and was intended to hasten the monk on to perfection. Though the Protestant Reformers largely rejected monasticism, they sought to maintain the essence of its spirituality and commend it to all Christians, especially the pursuit of holiness, sexual discipline, and regular, disciplined prayer and Bible reading.

There is no date to which the beginnings of monasticism can be assigned with any certainty. Some date it to Acts 2:42–47, when the early Christians held everything in common. Yet this is likely a misreading of the historical facts. It is true that poverty, both communal and personal, became a foundation stone of monasticism when it took on a more institutional form in the early 4th century. Others often date the founding of monasticism to the calling of an Egyptian monk named Antony. But the *Life of Antony*, written by Athanasius of Alexandria, states that Antony was able to place his sister in a community of virgins and that Antony himself was able to become a disciple of a local hermit. Consequently, it seems impossible that Antony was the founder of monasticism, though he was surely its most influential pioneer. Some scholars think that the *Shepherd of Hermas* was referring to some form of proto-monasticism when mentioning "virgins" (in Similitude 9.11). If true, it would date the rise of monasticism to the middle of the 2nd century. It is likely that early forms of monasticism also arose in Syria in the 2nd century. All things considered, it seems best to be cautious, concluding that Christian monasticism had its origins in the earliest history of the church.

Concerning forms of monasticism in the early Christian church, Jerome describes three types of monks living in the Egyptian desert: cenobites (those in community), anchorites (those living as solitaries), and those who associated in groups of twos and threes with no rule. The fifth-century monastic theologian John Cassian described four types of monasticism prevalent in his time: cenobites, anchorites, sarabaites (those who live for themselves), and monks of short-lived fervor. Benedict is an important witness, like Cassian, to the shape of early monasticism. In his Rule for Monks, Benedict's first chapter describes four kinds of monks: cenobites, anchorites/hermits, sarabaites, and wanderers. Of these, he considered only cenobites and anchorites legitimate.

Monasticism was not a fringe movement of the Christian church. It was prominent and pervasive, with monasteries in cities, towns, deserts, islands, and caves, and on pillars. Though the number of monks in the earliest centuries is impossible to confirm, it is generally agreed that the largest monasteries were those in the Pachomian federation in Upper Egypt. In *The Institutes*, Cassian described one of these Pachomian monasteries wherein five thousand monks were under the direction of one abbot. Likewise, the historian Palladius stated in the *Lausiac History* that there were monasteries whose population totaled seven thousand men. Not only did Palladius claim that there were hundreds of monks in Upper Egypt, but he also discussed monasteries in Lower Egypt, claiming that those around Alexandria numbered two thousand members while the Nitrian desert was home to five thousand monastics. Despite exaggeration, these figures show that the institution of monasticism was large by the 4th century. Furthermore, monasticism's geographic extent was also vast, stretching from Spain and England in the West to Syria in the East.

By the 5th century, monasteries were found alongside the Christian church. The most prevalent order in the West from the 6th century was monasteries following the Rule of Benedict of Nursia. Though there were other monastic rules, Benedict's gained acceptance, culminating in the Council of Aachen's decree in 817 that all monasteries of the Frankish kingdom were to follow it. Originally written for his own community of Monte Cassino, the Rule of Benedict also came to govern all Cluniac and Cistercian monasteries. Cluny, founded in 910, anchored a reform movement that spread rapidly across Europe. Characterized by a strict adherence to the Rule of Benedict and noted for its long hours of liturgical ceremony, Cluny became the motherhouse for approximately a thousand monasteries. In 1098 Robert of Molesme, deciding that Cluny was not, in fact, observing the Rule of Benedict correctly, set off with companions to found Cîteaux. Rejecting Cluniac liturgical customs and Cluny's acceptance of wealth and pomp, the Cistercians saw themselves as returning to the simplicity of the Rule of Benedict, especially a return to manual labor and strict diet. Like Cluny, the Cistercians grew rapidly, and at their height there were approximately four hundred monasteries. Not nearly as numerous, the Carthusians, founded in 1084 by Bruno of Cologne, was the strictest of the cenobitic Western monastic orders. Following their own rule, the Statutes, a Carthusian spends his days in private prayer and study, joining other members of the community only infrequently for liturgy, eating, and recreation. The other main monastic orders, at least in Western Christianity, tend to follow the so-called Rule of Augustine, which grew out of several authentic letters, sermons, and treatises of Augustine. Adaptable to a greater degree than Benedict's Rule, the Rule of Augustine was often chosen by those orders engaged in both action and contemplation, especially the Canons Regular, such as the Premonstratensians and Victorines.

See also Benedictine Spirituality; Desert; Desert Fathers and Mothers; Rules, Religious.

For Further Reading: *Athanasius: The Life of Antony and Letter to Marcellinus*, CWS (1980); Benedict of Nursia, *The Rule of Benedict*, ed. T. Fry (1981); John Cassian, *The Conferences*, trans. B. Ramsey (1997); idem, *The Institutes*, trans. B. Ramsey (2000); D. Knowles, *Christian Monasticism* (1969); J. Laboa, ed., *The Historical Atlas of Eastern and Western Christian Monasticism* (2003); C. Peifer, *Monastic Spirituality* (1966).

Greg Peters

Money

Important spiritual questions are raised by money. From the beginning of Christian history, church leaders have recognized that economic life is an incarnation of the spiritual life. But the Bible seems to have two voices on money: it is a blessing and a curse.

Jacques Ellul noted that the OT regarded wealth as a blessing (Deut. 30:9) — though the exemplars Abraham, Job, and Solomon depended on God rather than their wealth (Gen. 13:8 – 18; Job 1:21). Money is a sacrament as God is the giver of wealth (1 Sam. 2:7 – 8; Eccl. 5:19). This also produces "the scandal of wealth" whereby God sometimes gives wealth to the wicked (Job 21:7 – 21; Ps. 73:12 – 13).

Money is also a temptation. The pursuit of wealth for its own sake is a vain, destructive thing leading to self-destructive autonomy (Prov. 30:8; Hos. 12:8). Wealth is an *illusionary* security and will not satisfy (Eccl. 5:10). In the NT there are dark warnings: the rich are accursed and riches are the wages of sin and unrighteousness, especially toward the poor, with whom God takes his stand against the rich. Money too easily becomes an alternative god ("Mammon," which means firmness and stability). According to Jesus, "You cannot serve both God and Money" (Matt. 6:24). It is not neutral. It has an ability to inspire devotion sharing many of the characteristics of deity — giving security, freedom, and power. So the "almighty dollar" is a power (Eph. 1:21). Jesus calls it "wicked Mammon" or "worldly wealth" (NIV). And Paul says, "The love of money is a root of all kinds of evil" (1 Tim. 6:10).

Can the two voices of Scripture be heard as one harmonious word from God? Yes, if we seek first the kingdom of God.

First, our handling of money is revelatory of the state of our souls. Are we pinched misers or extravagant givers and grateful stewards, finding prayer and worship around both giving and receiving? Second, our use of money invites dependence on God who is the provider of everything we need. Behind this is the spiritual discipline of relinquishing ownership to God and practicing thanksgiving. Third, by giving we "profane Mammon" (Ellul) and liberate money for sacramental purposes. This happens especially when we give to the poor with no strings attached (2 Cor. 9:7) and generously as the Spirit enables (Rom. 12:8; 2 Cor. 9:6). Fourth, we are invited to practice some form of voluntary impoverishment (Acts 4:35 – 37). And finally, if so directed, we should sell all and follow Jesus.

John Wesley, in a famous sermon on the use of money, offered a simple though not simplistic solution for the ambiguity, spirituality, and ministry of money: "Gain all you can, save all you can, give all you can."

See also Accountability; Consumerism; Greed; Marketplace Spirituality.

For Further Reading: L. Burkett, *Business by the Book* (1990); J. Chrysostanus, *On Wealth and Poverty*, trans. C. Roth (1984); R. P. Stevens, *Disciplines of the Hungry Heart* (1993).

R. Paul Stevens

Montanism

In mid-second-century Asia Minor (Phrygia), a Christian named Montanus began to prophesy, claiming a Holy Spirit infilling that anticipated the second coming of Christ. Among others, two prophetesses, Priscilla (Prisca) and Maximilla, soon joined him in leadership. The movement relativized the early church episcopate's claims to apostolic authority and referenced Philip's daughters (Acts 2:17; 21:8 – 9) in their own defense while summoning believers to prepare righteously for an imminent New Jerusalem.

By the 180s this "new prophecy" reached Rome, Byzantium, and Carthage, drawing converts and critics. Central to its appeal was a compelling exercise of authority, vitality, and discipline. Claiming direct revelations from God, their oracular sayings freshly proclaimed truth for life's challenges. Moreover, these inspirations often came during enthusiastic worship gatherings. Finally, there was a rigorous emphasis on ascetic spiritual discipline. These factors gained for Montanism its foremost convert, Tertullian. His arguments *On the Soul* (c. 207) prioritize Scripture but also cite a Spirited "sister" who prophesied, conversed with angels and the Lord, practiced discernment, and ministered divine healing.

Critics called Montanist ecstasy abnormal, their oracles a threat to scriptural authority, their flamboyance pagan, and their female leaders suspect. But teachers like Irenaeus also saw the greater danger in a powerless gospel and the quenching of the Spirit (1 Thess. 5:19 – 20). In his judgment, sound orthodoxy did not necessitate a somber orthopraxy. Many today affirm this "charismatic"

conviction and regard the Montanists as their own provocative spiritual forebearers.

See also Tertullian.

For Further Reading: Eusebius, *Church History*, 5.16 – 18; C. Robeck, *Prophecy in Carthage: Perpetua, Tertullian, and Cyprian* (1992); C. Trevett, *Montanism* (1996); H. Von Campenhausen, *Ecclesiastical Authority and Spiritual Power in the Church of the First Three Centuries* (1969).

James D. Smith III

Moody, D(wight) L(yman) (1837 – 1899)

American revivalist. He came to fame as "Crazy Moody" for his unconventional but highly effective methods of drawing hundreds of children to his weekly Sabbath school in Chicago, Illinois. His continuing fame, however, came as the 19th century's most famous revivalist. Moody and his song leader, Ira D. Sankey, held extraordinarily successful campaigns on both sides of the Atlantic beginning in 1867 and continuing into the 1890s.

Moody's evangelistic preaching focused on what he called the "3 *Rs*": *ruined* by the fall—everyone is a sinner from birth and consequently absolutely helpless; *redeemed* by the blood—the love of God prompted Jesus Christ to die as humanity's substitute; and *regeneration* by the Spirit—the work of conversion is primarily divine and not an act of human self-reform. In contrast to much revivalistic preaching, Moody's messages focused on God's love for humanity rather than on his impending wrath. In addition, Moody promoted a work of the Spirit, subsequent to regeneration, that equipped believers with power for service, particularly for evangelism.

Consequently, Moody's own spirituality was activistic, leading him to establish a number of ministries, including the Sunday school work, a church, Bible conferences, publishing companies, and three educational institutions for the training of "gap-men"—those who knew the Bible and would make it their business to reach others with the gospel. These schools were the Northfield Seminary for Girls (1879), the Mount Hermon Massachusetts School for Boys (1881), and the Chicago Evangelization Society, later renamed Moody Bible Institute (1887).

The success of Moody's various enterprises, including his revivals, was due, at least in part, to his salesmanship and entrepreneurship. His innovations included the solicitation of support from a broad spectrum of local clergy (including Catholics); the mass advertising of his meetings; the use of large and public venues; the "inquiry room"—a quiet place away from the main hall where those under conviction could respond calmly and privately to the call of God; and the raising of needed funds from a network of wealthy and like-minded philanthropists.

See also Evangelism; Revival.

For Further Reading: L. Dorsett, *A Passion for Souls: The Life of D. L. Moody* (1997); B. J. Evensen, *God's Man for the Gilded Age: D. L. Moody and the Rise of Modern Mass Evangelism* (2003); T. George, ed., *Mr. Moody and the Evangelical Tradition* (2004); S. Gundry, *Love Them In: The Proclamation Theology of D. L. Moody* (1976).

Bernie Van De Walle

Moral Re-Armament

See **Oxford Group.**

Moravian Spirituality

The Moravian Church originated on the estate of Pietist nobleman Nicholas Ludwig von Zinzendorf (1700–1760) in eastern Saxony when Protestant refugees from Moravia founded the community of Herrnhut (1722). Herrnhut soon became a center for Pietists from different parts of Germany and other European countries who modeled their community on the ideals of the early Christian church. After a spiritual revival on August 13, 1727, the inhabitants of Herrnhut believed God had renewed the (Czech) Unity of the Brethren in their midst. Beginning in 1732 overseas missions became one of the Moravians' main objectives.

Influential for Moravian spirituality was Zinzendorf's "theology of the heart," according to which a personal experience of faith was more important than a rational understanding of dogma. Eighteenth-century Moravian piety was Christocentric and focused on the passion of Christ, whose blood and wounds were adored as signs of his suffering and as symbols of salvation. Christ's suffering was often described in graphic terms in sermons as well as in hymns.

Moravian spirituality was aimed at the development of individual faith and a "personal connection with the Savior." Much time was devoted to individual pastoral care. Each person was a member of a so-called choir (choirs were groups organized according to gender, age, and marital status). Moravian missionaries had an aversion to mass conversions but encouraged conversion of individuals—including, perhaps most notably, John Wesley at Aldersgate.

Important to Moravian spirituality was an emphasis on community and fellowship. Moravians founded different types of congregations. In addition to the so-called town congregations where church life was concentrated on Sunday mornings, Moravians also founded congregational settlements—exclusive communities where life was regulated by the church and only church members were allowed to live. These congregational settlements could be found in Germany, Great Britain, the Netherlands, Denmark, Pennsylvania, and North Carolina. In the congregational settlements no distinction was made between religious and secular activities. Each activity was intended to serve the common good of the community and to serve Christ. In the settlements Moravians gathered for daily worship. In addition to Sunday morning sermons there were daily services during the week, including the frequent singing meetings (*Singstunde*), liturgies, prayer meetings, love feasts, Holy Communion (monthly), and foot washing (until the early 19th century).

Moravians considered the singing of hymns an expression of the state of their hearts as well as a means to strengthen fellowship. The daily *Losungen*, or Watchwords, contained scriptural readings for every day that guided private devotions and provided the topics for many of the services. The Moravian aesthetic was an expression of Moravian spirituality. Churches were simple, unadorned spaces; however, they often contained paintings of the suffering Christ. Since Moravians did not distinguish between the religious and the secular, the churches were not considered separate sacred spaces and, before the 19th century, had no altar or pulpit. Choral and instrumental music played an important role in Moravian life. Choirs sang during love feasts, the liturgical services in the evenings, and on holidays. Trombone choirs (later mixed brass) accompanied outdoor events (e.g., Easter morning and funerals).

See also Methodist Spirituality; Pietism; Zinzendorf.

For Further Reading: C. Atwood, *Community of the Cross* (2004); A. Freeman, *An Ecumenical Theology of the Heart* (1998); N. Knouse, ed., *The Music of the Moravian Church in America*, Eastman Studies in Music 49 (2008).

Paul Peucker

More, Hannah (1745–1833)

Evangelical writer and educator. More, a widely heralded literary figure, moved easily among England's high society and political elite of the day, names that included Samuel Johnson, Edmund Burke, Horace Walpole, William Wilberforce, John Newton, William Gladstone, and Thomas Macaulay. Born in a village near Bristol, the daughter of a schoolteacher, she grew up in humble circumstances. As a youth she attended a girls' school headed by her older sister, and at seventeen she began teaching at the school and writing plays for the students.

Her financial fortunes improved after her wealthy fiancé of six years failed to set a date for their marriage. To compensate for the canceled wedding plans and his apparent deception, he paid her a stipend sufficient for her to live on for the remainder of her life, thus allowing her to engage in writing fulltime. In the years that followed, her gradual evangelical conversion set the stage for her shift away from secular topics and her focus on moral values and spirituality.

In addition to plays and poetry, she wrote religious tracts and widely circulated writings supporting the abolitionist cause, including her lengthy poem "Slavery," which influenced the demise of British slave trade. Her signature volume on spirituality was *Practical Piety*. Here she admonished the reader to avoid "all such society, all such amusements as excite tempers" or that "awaken thoughts which ought not to be excited." Also to be avoided were "books which excite the passions." Practical piety above all was "a harmony between our prayers and our practice."

More put piety into practice in her own educational endeavors — the founding of Sunday schools for the poor that offered literacy alongside religious and moral teachings. With her sister, she founded nine schools that served some twenty thousand impoverished youth. Though criticized by Anglican clerics for inciting ideas of equality among the lower classes, she was widely recognized as one of England's leading philanthropists and a supporter of women's rights.

See also Self-Control; Social Justice.

For Further Reading: P. Demers, *The World of Hannah More* (1996); C. H. Ford, *Hannah More: A Critical Biography* (1996); A. Stott, *Hannah More: The First Victorian* (2004).

Ruth A. Tucker

More, Thomas (1478–1535)

English Roman Catholic lawyer, statesman, and writer. More is best known for his book *Utopia* and his refusal to sign the Act of Succession. As a young man, he considered serving as a priest or in a religious order but ultimately decided on a family and a career in law. More won favor with King Henry VIII, who appointed him to a number of civil posts, including Lord Chancellor in 1529. However, More retired the post in 1532, disagreeing with Henry's willingness to break with the pope if he was not granted an annulment of his first marriage. More was imprisoned in 1534 for refusing to sign the Act of Succession, which declared the nullity of Henry's first marriage and the validity of the second, contrary to the pope's judgment. More was condemned for treason and beheaded in 1535.

More's spiritual life was marked by great austerity. He wore a hair shirt and slept on the floor, using a log for a pillow. He also spent Fridays entirely in prayer, and he recited the Little Office of the Blessed Virgin Mary daily. While most of his writings were political or polemical in nature, he also composed a few spiritual works, some written in his final days of imprisonment. Among these are his *Treatise on the Most Blessed Sacrament*, *Treatise on the Passion of Christ*, and *Dialogue of Comfort against Tribulation*. His personal integrity was immortalized in the motion picture *A Man for All Seasons* (1966).

See also Active Life and Contemplative Life.

For Further Reading: J. Monti, *The King's Good Servant But God's First* (1997).

Matthew Kemp

Mormon Spirituality

Latter-day Saints (Mormons) understand spirituality as the strength, experience, and development of personal worthiness. Their motivation in this comes from Jesus' admonition, "If ye love me, keep my commandments" (John 14:15 KJV).

Mormon spirituality is shaped by a worldview that differs significantly from that of evangelicals. They believe they are literally sons and daughters of their heavenly Father. During a premortal existence, they chose to follow Jesus Christ rather than Lucifer. That choice established their initial human worthiness. They were deemed worthy of receiving mortal bodies and were subsequently born into times and places specially chosen for them. Their human families allow them to learn their lessons and do the most good with their individual personalities and talents. By the enabling power of the Holy Spirit, they hope to be faithful in all things, live eternally with their heavenly Father and Jesus Christ, and share in their fullest joy by becoming gods themselves.

Baptized at age eight, Mormons make repeated assessments of their worthiness as they are called to higher levels of faithful living. Those who seek baptism after the age of eight must first be found worthy of it. They must believe in Christ, humble themselves before God, have true sorrow for their sins, fully repent of them, and understand the covenant they are entering. This baptismal covenant sets the standards for their ongoing evaluations of worthiness. In baptism, Mormons covenant to be faithful church members, bear others' burdens, faithfully witness of God, serve God, and keep his commandments. God covenants to forgive their sins, pour out his Spirit in abundance for their guidance and help, and allow them someday to rise in the first resurrection.

All baptized persons are confirmed as members of the LDS Church when they receive the gift of the Holy Spirit through the laying on of hands. Thereafter they must continue to obey God's commands to remain worthy of this gift. This baptismal covenant is renewed weekly as Mormons remember Christ's atonement in his sacrament (Communion, or the Lord's Supper). They are to judge their own worthiness before partaking of the bread and water (not wine); those who partake without repenting of their sins eat and drink damnation to their souls.

Mormons must develop their gifts and talents. They are expected to grow in consistent obedience to all of God's commandments, including loving service to God, family members, and neighbors; keeping the Sabbath holy; fasting for specific purposes; sacrificing for the sake of others; having appropriate work; keeping their bodies pure; practicing charity and honesty; obeying proper authorities; furthering the spread of the gospel; tithing; attending church regularly; and studying the Book of Mormon (the truth of which is subjectively attested by "a burning in the bosom" experience).

To qualify for future exaltation, Mormons must receive their temple endowment and be married (for eternity) in the temple. They must participate in the salvation of past family members through proxy works for the dead. In order to participate in any temple activities, adult members must be found worthy of a temple recommend (permit). They only receive this if they have kept God's commands and their covenants for the previous two years.

Males spend much of their life serving in two priesthoods. Bishops interview males when they reach the age of twelve to determine their worthiness for the Aaronic priesthood. Deacons (ages twelve–thirteen) serve the Lord's sacrament. Teachers (ages fourteen–fifteen) encourage other members to live the gospel, and they prepare bread and water for the sacrament service. Priests (age sixteen and above) may baptize; administer the sacrament; ordain other priests, teachers, and deacons; and even run meetings in the absence of higher authorities. A bishop presides over the members of this Aaronic priesthood and administrates the functions of each ward (i.e., congregation). All who belong to the higher Melchizedek priesthood are thereby elders, with authority to bestow the gift of the Holy Spirit by the laying on of hands, administer to the sick, bless children, and conduct church meetings. High priests serve as bishops, councilors, church administrators, and mission presidents. Apostles administer the church and receive

revelation, and one of the apostles is recognized as prophet and president of the church. All below him serve in their authority under his keys. Mormons believe that all other churches and ministers lack the proper priesthood authority to baptize believers into the one and only true church.

This hierarchical structure and the Mormon understanding of covenantal (contractual) responsibilities shape the experience of Latter-day Saints. This framework allows them to seek and receive God's guidance for almost every area of their lives. Daily prayer functions as the core of their experience. Mormons address God as their heavenly Father and pray with humility and with gratitude that he hears them. It is considered improper to pray to Jesus Christ or to seek a direct and personal relationship with him. They express thankfulness for their heavenly Father's blessings, confess their failures, and ask for forgiveness and strength to be more faithful. Mormons ask for guidance and receive specific impressions from the Holy Ghost about what they should do and say in particular situations. They are unashamed in asking for material abundance and responsible power in their spheres of influence. Mormons who serve in LDS temples report experiencing miracles, healings, and conversations with departed relatives and friends. These experiences are recited as apologetic proofs that Mormon claims are true. Mormon church services focus more on renewing contracts than on adoration of the heavenly Father. Mormons can be certain they will be raised from the dead; however, the quality of their eternal life (exaltation) will depend on how well they have kept their contracts. In 2007 LDS apostle Henry B. Eyring cautioned: "It is hard to know when we have done enough for the Atonement to change our natures and so qualify us for eternal life." Mormons believe that what Christ has done is of great effect. But its application in individual lives depends on the individual's response and faithful performance of contractual duties. Mindful of their need to achieve as much as possible for the kingdom of God, Latter-day Saints strive to be worthy of the greatest opportunities through faithful love and service of God, family, and neighbors.

For Further Reading: Church of Jesus Christ of Latter-day Saints, *Gospel Principles* (2009); *Encyclopedia of Mormonism* (1992, updated online by Brigham Young University); *Joseph Smith: Selected Writings, SAS* (1989).

James L. Wakefield

Motherhood of God

As with other feminine metaphors for God, the notion of God as Mother has often been downplayed in Christian thought and practice. However, a maternal dimension in God is easily gleaned from various strands of Scripture (cf. Gen. 1:2; Deut. 32:18; Isa. 42:14; 49:1; Jer. 31:20; Matt. 23:37; John 3:5) and has been present as a minor yet persistent theme in the theological tradition. In the church fathers, "Mother" is at times identified with the Holy Spirit, as when Gregory of Nazianzus posits Eve as a metaphorical representation of the Spirit in his discussion of Adam-Eve-Seth as a Trinitarian typology. During the Middle Ages, the motherhood of Jesus was explored by theologians as diverse as Julian of Norwich and Anselm of Canterbury. More recently, "Mother" has been used liturgically as an alternative or complementary designation for the first person, as in the expression *Dios Padre y Madre* or "Father and Mother God," often used in Latin American prayers, both Catholic and Protestant. The motherhood of God encompasses all of these dimensions, but "Mother" should not be seen as the name of a given divine person. Admittedly, God's maternity is most often thought of in connection with the Spirit, as when the Spirit is identified in John 3 as the "Mother" who allows a person to be born again, or when the Syriac tradition lifts up the motherly office of the Holy Spirit. However, as in the case of creation, redemption, and sanctification, God's maternal work as a whole is the work of the triune God and not exclusively that of the

Spirit. The motherhood of God should therefore be understood through the lens of Trinitarian doctrine as a reference to the work of fecundity, bringing forth life and cherishing it, that is shared by the Godhead. Given the unease of much of the tradition with female metaphors for God generally and with the maternal work of the Spirit specifically, the motherhood of God has often found expression indirectly, either through the practical elevation of Mary to a quasi-divine status or through the depiction of the church as mother.

See also Fatherhood of God; Feminist Spirituality; God, Perceptions of.

For Further Reading: C. Bynum, *Jesus as Mother* (1982); M. Grey, *Introducing Feminist Images of God* (2001); Julian of Norwich, *Revelations of Divine Love* (1984).

Nancy E. Bedford

Mother Teresa

See **Teresa of Calcutta.**

Movies and Spirituality

In the eyes of some, movies and spirituality are an unlikely duo. Aren't movies about escape and entertainment — too often containing sex, violence, and destructive stereotypes? And isn't spirituality about connecting with the transcendent and being changed by it? Additionally, isn't spirituality first of all about lived experience, not doctrine? Yet most of the discussion concerning religion/theology and film has focused more on thematic content than spiritual experience. Hasn't film been used religiously more as a teaching tool than a spiritual exercise?

But in the experience of a growing number of moviegoers, watching a film has become a form of communion, an engagement with an art form that invites first order experience prior to any second order criticism. Like the novel for those living in earlier centuries, film has become one of contemporary culture's primary means of connecting with our inner lives. Viewers watching a movie enter into the subjective experiences of those on the screen—their longings, failings, self-discoveries, and hopes. Furthermore, as viewers are affected by these screen portrayals, they find themselves reflecting on their own lives and choices vis-à-vis those on the screen. In this open, inquisitive place, some even have eyes to see and ears to hear God.

Herbert Jump, a Congregational minister, wrote "The Spiritual Possibilities of the Motion Picture" in 1910, finding parallels with Jesus' use of parables. Vachel Lindsay, writing in 1915, saw in movies "a higher form of vision-seeing." But such ideas created little traction at the time. Even in the 1960s, when most denominations awoke from their video slumber and published their first books on the conversation between church and cinema, there were few readers. After all, the movies discussed remained stillborn, seldom being available for viewing. But VCRs, DVDs, and Netflix have changed all this. Movies that affect the human spirit are now regularly recommended and seen by others. Consider, for example, *Shawshank Redemption* (1994). It was initially a disappointment at the box office, but later word of mouth concerning the movie's ability to inspire hope as it portrayed the human spirit made it the top film on the Internet Movie Database's 2009 list of 250 all-time favorites. The power of filmic story to affect the human spirit is contagious.

Most persons can identify those particular movies that have spiritually affected them. Thousands, for example, have sought reconciliation with their fathers after seeing *Field of Dreams* (1989). A young Korean woman recently arranged for her congregation to watch *X-Men* (2000) and was stunned by the intergenerational conversation that took place afterward between comic book–reading teens and their elders in the church over how each had felt judged by others in our society for being a "mutant." This writer's call to full-time intentional ministry came while watching *Becket* (1964); for a former seminary student, it came while seeing *March of the Penguins* (2005). For a friend, his faith in Jesus was rekindled through watching *Magnolia* (1999). People both within the church and outside it recognize that movies provide primary stories around which we shape our lives. Presenting aspects of their daily lives both intimate and profound, real and imagined, movies exercise our moral and religious imagination.

Like all experiences of play, movie watching is done "for fun," and yet it proves productive. When viewers watch a movie, most come expectant that the story will captivate and are disappointed if it does not. This personal engagement provides a potential for the shaping of their lives. Through film, meaning is made visible and communion fostered. Movies affect the spirit, letting the viewer even on occasion be "surprised by joy." When C. S. Lewis first used this phrase, he had in mind his early aesthetic experiences with children's literature, Norse mythology, Wagner's music, Greek drama, and science fiction—all of which opened him up to the divine (to "Joy"). Movies in the 1920s and '30s were yet to be appreciated for their spiritual power by many, including Lewis. But film has arguably become the 21st century's primary art form. Americans see on average almost one movie per week. Here is how millions receive the stories and myths by which they make sense of their lives. Here is one significant context in which spirit reaches out to spirit, and where even Spirit is serendipitously experienced.

For Further Reading: C. Barsotti and R. Johnston, *Finding God in the Movies* (2004); G. Higgins, *How Movies Helped Save My Soul* (2003); R. Johnston, *Reel Spirituality* (2006); G. Lynch, "Film and the Subjective Turn," in *Reframing Theology and Film*, ed. R. Johnston (2007), 109–25; C. Marsh, *Cinema and Sentiment* (2004).

Robert K. Johnston and Catherine M. Barsotti

Mujerista Spirituality

An approach to spirituality grounded in the liberative praxis of Mujerista theology—a process of enablement for Latina women that seeks to develop their sense of self and moral agency. Such a theology helps them to understand the multilayer oppression around them, as well as to design and work for their preferred future.

Ada Maria Isasi-Díaz has articulated her understandings of Mujerista spirituality after reflecting on the experiences of Latina women as well as her own. She argues that traditional understandings of spirituality that led her to prayer, meditation, and penance actually made her uncomfortable, because they tend to counterpose body and spirit as if a person could be divided in two. Since, for her, soul and body cannot be separated, to be spiritual means to recognize all of the holistic needs of all human beings, particularly Latina women, and to struggle alongside them by helping them to recognize their oppression and move toward their liberation. Participation in this struggle against oppression and for liberation, Isasi-Díaz argues, is what allows her to become fully the person that God intends her to be, and to experience God more closely. In this sense, getting closer to God and struggling for justice are one and the same thing for her. In light of this, she does not think about herself in terms of "spirituality," but as having a deep relationship with God. This relationship finds expression more in being faithful to who she is and what God wants of her, and by being in active solidarity with the poor, than in kneeling, fasting, mortifying the flesh, or negating herself.

See also Feminist Spirituality; Liberation Spirituality; Womanist Spirituality.

For Further Reading: A. M. Isasi-Díaz, *En la Lucha/In the Struggle* (2004); idem, *Mujerista Theology* (1996).

Nora O. Lozano

Murray, Andrew (1828–1917)

South African religious leader and devotional writer. Murray was educated in Scotland and the Netherlands and served as a minister of the Dutch Reformed Church in South Africa. He blended his Calvinist theology with the Holiness movement and was both a forerunner and supporter of the Keswick Movement.

Murray's healing from a throat condition that was caused by extensive preaching that silenced his voice for two years convinced him of the importance of faith healing. Murray drank deeply from the well of Christian mystical writers, including Bernard of Clairvaux (even naming his home "Clairvaux"), Catherine of Siena, Jan van Ruysbroeck, Teresa of Avila, Madame Guyon, Count von Zinzendorf, and William Law. In turn, he inspired the Scottish Presbyterian Alexander Whyte and Watchman Nee. Murray was a popular devotional writer of nearly 250 books and booklets, often emphasizing the themes of intimacy with Christ and the importance of prayer. *Abide in Christ* (1864, Eng. trans. 1882), based on John 15:4, was his first English publishing venture and perhaps his most popular work. Other significant writings include *With Christ in the School of Prayer* (1885) and *Absolute Surrender* (1895). His writings reflect a popularized expression of evangelical mysticism that is both more accessible and less refined than later writers such as A. W. Tozer. He was also active in promoting evangelistic revivals, ministerial conferences for personal renewal, and missionary work throughout South Africa, England, and America. Though Murray frequently addressed the racial issues of South Africa, his spirituality was more personal than communal and tended to neglect the deeper political needs of his country.

See also Keswick Movement.

For Further Reading: W. Douglas, *Andrew Murray and His Message* (n.d.); J. Du Plessis, *The Life of Andrew Murray of South Africa* (1919).

Tom Schwanda

Music
See **Chapter 26.**

Muslim Spirituality

Muslim spirituality involves striving to experience God but, in keeping with the holism of Islam, includes seeking to live all of life according to his will. The Sufis, who crystallized this spirituality, focused on the former as their goal but developed a path of attitudes and practices involving all of life to attain that end. These mystics in turn have influenced non-Sufi Muslims, who concentrate on the externals of the law, especially since the major theologian al-Ghazali (1059–1111) sought to combine the inward dimensions of Sufism with the outward dimensions of orthodoxy and orthopraxy.

The Qur'an describes pious Muslims as being obedient, humble, and chaste; persevering; giving alms; worshiping; and fasting (33:35). And although later theologians and legal scholars would stress verses about the transcendence of God (e.g., 9:129), the mystics emphasized verses speaking of his nearness (e.g., 50:16) and reciprocal love for believers (e.g., 5:54) — though in the Qur'an God does not love disbelievers (3:31–32).

Originally, Muhammad is seen as a model for spiritual development with his vigils on Mount Hira before his mission and subsequently (Qur'an 73:1–4, 20). But in later popular piety, he became an object of veneration. Jesus in turn was seen by Sufis, as Schimmel has pointed out, not only as a model for such ideals as poverty but also as a source of life-giving breath.

When we look at stages and themes of spiritual formation found in popular Sufi prayer manuals, we see both similarities and contrasts with Christian understandings. The initial condition of humans is rejection. In one manual al-Jilani prays, "Protect us, Oh God, from the evils of ourselves and the illusions of our works, and from the evil of Satan's snares." According to the Qur'an, the rejection involves rebellion against God (72:23), disbelief of his revelation (2:39), and transgression of his will (23:7) as well as the hypocrisy of those who appear righteous (29:11). The Qur'an, however, expresses an optimistic analysis of human nature in which humans are created in a state of natural purity (30:30). Though Shiites have been more aware of the "carnal soul" than Sunnis, the answer to this problem is seen as divine guidance and the developing of the habit of following that guidance, not the necessity of transformation by the Spirit of God.

The first stage in the path to God is seen as repentance. In a manual, Ibn Mu'adh ar-Razi prays, "Wash me from my sins, give me the robe of the redeemed, and in Thy mercy cast me not away from Thy Presence." In the Qur'an, repentance involves turning from sin (5:36) and turning to God (39:54) as well as an attitude of remorse (21:87–88). With respect to the dialectic of divine and human involvement, the Qur'an says God "repents" (turns) toward these who "repent" toward him (5:39).

The second station in the ascent is commonly faith. In another manual, A. Z. al-Abidin affirms: "My God, though my sin has made me fear Thee, yet my confidence in Thee came to my rescue. My God, it is as though I stood before Thee with my sinful soul, and the fullness of my trust in Thee overshadowed it, and Thou didst with me after Thy wont, and covered me with Thy pardon." In the Qur'an, this faith involves trust in God as Lord and Friend (3:56, 83; 67:29). There is a divine involvement in that God gives faith to some (30:56) and could have willed it for everyone (10:99), but by his word some will not exercise it (10:96).

Another theme is submission (the meaning, in fact, of the word *Islam*). After Shiite ritual prayer, M. M. al-Janan required that worshipers recite, "There is no god but God, and we are his surrendered ones [*muslimin*]." Faith and submission (*islam*) express overlapping activities in the Qur'an: "We have faith; witness our submission" (5:111). But submission without faith is inadequate (e.g., 49:14). In the canonical traditions attributed to Muhammad, *islam* is seen as submission to God that is evidenced in particular by practicing the five pillars (confession of faith in God and the prophet identity of Muhammad, ritual prayer, almsgiving, fasting, and pilgrimage). Pious Sufis, however, have tended to internalize these as Jesus internalized the Law in the Sermon on the Mount.

The various stages of spiritual formation for the Sufis lead to love of God and knowledge of God, which for them also involves learning esoteric meanings of religious phenomena. For all Muslims, spiritual formation involves the praise of God. A manual for use in the month of Ramadan includes the words "Thankful praise to God: a praise which brings to the praiser only the reward of pleasing Him." This praise is expressed through Qur'anic recitation, calligraphy, literature, and architecture. Sufis, freed from the common restraints felt by many Muslims, also express their spirituality through elaborate art, music, and dance.

See also Sufism.

For Further Reading: K. Cragg, *Alive to God* (1970); S. H. Nasr, *Islamic Art and Spirituality* (1987); idem, ed., *Islamic Spirituality*, 2 vols. (1987–1991); C. Padwick, *Muslim Devotions* (1961); A. Schimmel, *And Muhammad Is His Messenger* (1985); idem, *Mystical Dimensions of Islam* (1975); M. Smith, *Studies in Early Mysticism in the Near and Middle East* (1995).

J. Dudley Woodberry

Mystery

Mystery (Gr. *mustērion*) is a term that predates the NT by several hundred years. Scholars trace the development of mystery cults dating from the 7th century BC to the 4th century AD but generally agree that the word as it appears in Scripture has no relation to mystery cults. New Testament writers often use the term to describe the gospel, which, though hidden in ages past, is now revealed in the NT era. Accordingly, mystery is the good news of salvation — once concealed; now revealed (cf. Rom. 16:25; 1 Cor. 2:7; Eph. 3:3–5; Col. 1:26).

The central motif of mystery in the biblical sense is *relationship*. According to Louis Bouyer, it is "the revelation of that unequalled divine love to which all previous revelation pointed." The intimacy between Christ and the church, like becoming one flesh in marriage, is a profound mystery (Eph. 5:32). The revelation of this mystery culminates in unmediated communion with Christ, which inspires hope for the ultimate fulfillment of the gospel's promises — it is Christ in us, the hope of glory (Col. 1:27).

Mystery in the postapostolic era expanded to include an assortment of sacred realities, which, in the words of Philip Egan, are "ineffable and inexhaustible, so great that although something can be said, their intelligibility can never be exhausted." Mysteries of the faith include creation, incarnation, resurrection, redemption, grace, church, moral life, spirituality, eschatology, and more. Some theologians caution against invoking mystery prematurely, recommending instead that we go as far as possible with human reasoning before labeling something a mystery. Notwithstanding, whether one's list of mysteries is long or short, mystery thus conceived functions as an epistemological category. What cannot be explained by rational means is called a mystery.

Eastern and Western Christians have taken different paths regarding mystery. Eastern Orthodox Christians tend to be *apophatic*, which is to say they celebrate the indescribability of God and God's truths. Western Christians are characteristically *kataphatic*, seeking to discover and explain all they can of God. Twelfth- and thirteenth-century thinkers Peter Abelard, Anselm of Canterbury, and Thomas Aquinas, for example, sought to demonstrate the rational coherence of revealed truth. During the Enlightenment, church leaders and theologians defended the faith by way of probable reason — and to the extent that epistemological certitude defined the burden of theology, mystery had little to offer.

The post-Enlightenment era has witnessed a

resurgence of interest in mystery. A new generation of spiritual seekers is exploring religious traditions that are rooted in antiquity. Many evangelicals are discovering the spiritual value of the teachings, liturgies, and disciplines of Christian mystics like John of the Cross, Teresa of Avila, Brother Lawrence, Jakob Boehme, and George Fox—who in their own time pursued a biblical vision of mystery, which focused less on explaining the inexplicable and more on experiencing God's unfathomable love and abiding presence.

See also Apocalyptic Spirituality.

For Further Reading: L. Bouyer, *The Christian Mystery*, trans. I. Trethowan (1990); C. Conniry, *Soaring in the Spirit* (2007); M. Cox, *Handbook of Christian Spirituality* (1985); P. A. Egan, *Philosophy and Catholic Theology* (2009); S. Fanning, *Mystics of the Christian Tradition* (2001); B. McGinn, ed., *The Essential Writings of Christian Mysticism* (2006).

Charles J. Conniry Jr.

Mysticism

See **Chapter 25.**

N

Name of Jesus

See **Jesus, Name of.**

Narrative

See **Story.**

Native North American Spirituality

Native North American spirituality refers to a worldview indigenous to North America that understands all of life to be sacred, and those who have this belief endeavor to live in such a way as to respect that sacredness in everyday life. Everything is endowed with some aspect of the spiritual; however, things can become more or less sacred at any given moment. Something may or may not be used at any time by spiritual forces or beings. The goal of Native North American spirituality is to live in harmony with creation and all creatures as well as with the spiritual or spiritual beings.

Native spirituality places a high value on under-standing one's creation story. Creation is of great importance, for by tracing one's ancestry and relation to actual location, one's identity is affirmed as a true human being, connected through ancestors to the "land" or creation. As well, it is through these relationships that one becomes related to the great mystery or to a type of creator.

Native spirituality focuses on harmony in relationships. According to native spirituality, relationships exist between people and people, people and the rest of creation, and people and the spiritual. While these categories may not always be explicit, they show how relationships at all levels of life are key to living a harmonious life. This harmony is not confined to the present but is also aimed at harmony with the past by respecting traditions and ancestors, and with the future by praying or planning for one's grandchildren. For example, it is common among some of the First Nations of Canada that, when thinking about the future, one should think in terms of seven generations ahead. Harmony is highly valued by most Native North American people.

Native North American spirituality acknowledges that there is one supreme entity, and so it reflects aspects of monotheism. At the same time, however, there is also the presence of many intermediaries between the supreme and person or community, and at times these seem to be elevated to the stature of deity, which might account for some early newcomers to North America describing the First Nations as pantheists. Peelman, however, rightly suggests that panentheism is a more helpful term to describe Native American perceptions of the divine. For example, there may be indigenous names translated by the English words *God* or *Great Spirit*, but it is not always clear in the indigenous language whether this God or Great Spirit is regarded as a being or a force, or simply a transcendent mystery. For example, among the Cree of Canada, the "Great Other" or "Mystery" might perhaps have been better translations. People live spiritually attuned lives within a creation located *within* the great mystery—one that also stands over and above the world. Thus, spirituality aims at living in a respectful manner with what is seen and unseen—in short, with the Great Mystery.

Native North American spirituality is not static and cannot be located only in the past, for it continues to develop and grow. In part, this is because Native North American spirituality continues to be a source of identity for peoples who find themselves colonized and in danger of losing their identity. As such, Native North American spirituality aims at maintaining identity as people related to the land.

Native North American spirituality has also influenced Native North American Christians and their spirituality. The visions of Black Elk, who was Lakota and Roman Catholic, are a famous example. Christian expressions of Native North American spirituality also share an affinity with traditional Native concern for harmony of relationships, interpreting these as being with the Christian God, and with his creatures and creation. Both traditional and Christian Native North American spirituality emphasize the spiritual nature of life and the need to live in a holistic manner within the land now referred to as North America.

See also Primal Religions, Spirituality of.

For Further Reading: D. Costello, *Black Elk Colonialism and Lakota Catholicism* (2005); L. Irwin, ed., *Native American Spirituality* (2000); P. Jenkins, *Dream Catchers* (2004); J. Ottman, *First Nations Leadership and Spirituality within the [Canadian Royal] Commission on Aboriginal Peoples* (2002); A. Peelman, *Christ Is a Native American* (1995); M. Wallace, *Finding God in the Singing River* (2005); E. Waugh, *Dissonant World* (1996); R. Woodley, *Living in Color* (2001).

Ray Aldred

Nature Mysticism

Nature mysticism denotes the deep spiritual experience of a person as he or she encounters the natural universe or some part of it. In contrast to Christian mysticism, nature mysticism is nontheistic. The nature mystic focuses on matter, energy, and things, and is not, at least initially, interested in a transcendent personal God beyond and above nature.

Like Christian mysticism, nature mysticism is a diverse phenomenon. Nevertheless, its varied forms have some common features. First, nature mysticism normally involves direct contact with the natural world, by such means as walking in the woods or surfing an ocean wave. But the contact may also be mediated by intellectual activity, as when a scientist studies the laws of nature. Albert Einstein demonstrated a kind of nature mysticism in his deep awe of and admiration for the intelligibility and orderliness of the universe that came out of his scientific study. Or it may be through artistic endeavor, as when a dancer experiences his body in a deeper way, or when an artist comes into intimate contact with the physical elements of her medium and subject. Or it may grow out of ethical concern for the ecological well-being of nature, as in the case of Dave Forman of Earth First! who reported mystical experiences in his contact with nature. Indeed, it may arise in any number of other ways in which humans have intimate experience of natural things.

Second, nature mysticism usually entails a deep sense of connectedness and interrelationality with things, earth, and the cosmos. For example, a mountaineer may experience a unity or "friendship" with the mountain she is climbing. There is often a sense of belonging to a place and to the creatures that inhabit it — of being at home in a particular place within the cosmos. Julia "Butterfly" Hill, who lived in the top of an Oregon redwood tree for two years in order to prevent it from being cut by loggers, had a mystical experience of union with the tree and the hillside on which it was located. Third, nature mysticism tends to affirm sensuality — the feel, sights, sounds, smells, and tastes of things, our bodies, and the world around us. This may be found in a moderate form in the writings of Henry David Thoreau or in Walt Whitman's famous poetry collection *Leaves of Grass*, and in an extreme and perverse form in the use of drugs and ritual sex by some nature cults.

Finally, in some cases, the nature mystic may perceive a universal reality underlying nature. This is usually interpreted not as a personal God, but as a principle, energy, process, or "all in all" that infuses everything — something akin to Jung's collective consciousness, the Brahman of Hinduism, or Spinoza's pantheistic divinity. In any case, the universal reality is generally found in the particular things, places, or processes themselves, not in a transcendent God that is beyond them. The nature mystic immerses herself in physicality, in this world, this cosmos, rather than seeking to go beyond it.

Whereas nature mysticism may lead to belief in a transcendent, personal God, often it does not. Einstein remained agnostic about God until his death. The psalmist wrote that the heavens declare the glory of God (Ps. 19:1), and the apostle Paul wrote that God's invisible qualities are evident in creation (Rom. 1:20). Nature mysticism seems to affirm the idea that human encounters with nature can lead to knowledge of God's attributes — his power, wisdom, and love. It would appear, however, that going on to faith in the Christian God as such requires special revelation (Scripture) and the ministry of the Holy Spirit (John 3:6; 1 Cor. 2:7 – 10).

See also Creation-Centered Spirituality; Transcendentalism, American.

For Further Reading: B. Taylor, "Earth and Nature-Based Spirituality," 2 parts, *Religion* 32, no. 2 (April 2001), and 32, no. 3 (July 2001); R. C. Zaehner, *Mysticism Sacred and Profane* (1957).

John Mustol

Nazianzus

See **Gregory Nazianzus.**

Nee, Watchman (1903 – 1972)

Chinese Bible teacher and founder of the "Little Flock." His theological outlook was initially influenced by the Brethren and Keswick traditions as well as by such spiritual writers as Madame Guyon; but in time he forged his own innovative spiritual theology. This was based on the assumption that a human being consists of three parts (that is, spirit, soul, and body/flesh). In his book *The Spiritual Man* (1968), he said that initially God created a body (*basar*) from the soil and blew the breath of life into it. For Nee, the soul (*nephesh*) is the product of the encounter between the spirit (life) and the body. The spirit is in fact the channel to God and ought to govern one's soul and body.

However, since the fall of humanity, it has been the body that has taken control of the soul and suppressed the spirit. All philosophy, fine art, cultural activities, and the like are viewed as products of the human soul, whose nature is against

God. Christians must therefore give up all worldly pleasures and involvements. The normal Christian life is one that requires sincere repentance for sins and the transformation of one's sinful nature into a Christlike life. To live out the victorious life, the life of Christ, Christians must fully despair of themselves (become broken) and be completely consecrated, in the belief that Christ will take full control of them and then live through them. Not only is Christ the center of the Christian life, but he is also the actual source of Christian works. According to Nee, this is what it means to proclaim, both in words and by deeds, that Christ Jesus is Lord.

Nee was jailed for the final two decades of his life for his efforts to establish and oversee the Little Flock network of Chinese Christians under Communist oppression. The Local Church movement that developed and radicalized from these roots under his successor, Witness Lee, has extended to all parts of the world. Nee denied the validity of all other denominationally affiliated congregations; in addition to such separatist sentiments, his original Little Flock and the larger Local Church movement have manifested highly authoritarian tendencies.

Nonetheless, Watchman Nee's spirituality has greatly influenced Chinese churches well beyond the locus of the Little Flock he helped to birth. Internationally many Christians have been edified by his teachings, most notably through his books *The Normal Christian Life* (1958) and *Sit, Walk, Stand* (1958). Although recently some scholars have questioned his business ethics, his work should be evaluated separately from his personal conduct. However, the fact that his teaching on spirituality has long served as a supporting pillar in the century-long Chinese Christian enterprise is undisputable.

See also Asian Christian Spirituality; Holiness; Keswick Movement.

For Further Reading: W. Lam, *The Spiritual Theology of Watchman Nee* (1985); K. Leung, *Watchman Nee: His Early Life and Thought* (2005).

Hing-Kau [Jason] Yeung

Neo-Pagan Spirituality

Neo-paganism references those movements and practices that embrace duality in the divine (gods and goddesses) in the context of celebrating the rhythms of nature and the gift of sexuality. Contemporary practice of neo-pagan spirituality is singular proof that societies change. From the fifteenth through the 17th centuries, Western European nations were caught in a frenzied and superstitious inquisition against alleged witches. The Burning Times are now past, and modern society manifests a new openness for witchcraft, vampires, druids, and neo-pagan religion.

The rise of neo-pagan spirituality owes most to Gerald Gardner (1884–1964), a British civil servant, who revived "white" witchcraft in the 1950s. Gardner claims to have joined a secret coven in 1939, though it is more likely that he created the movement he would later describe in *High Magic's Aid* (1949) and *Witchcraft Today* (1954). Gardner was influenced by various rites in Freemasonry and other secret societies. He was also impacted by the influential and notorious occult figure Aleister Crowley (1875–1947) and his Magick theory and practice.

Since the 1960s Gardnerian witchcraft has given ground to other forms of neo-paganism. The Church of All Worlds, one of the earliest American-based pagan groups, formed in 1962. Robert Graves explored new forms of deity in *The White Goddess* (1966), and Margot Adler released her influential work *Drawing Down the Moon* in 1979. The emerging New Age movement of the 1980s created space for a neo-pagan alternative, and various neo-pagan leaders took part in the Parliament of the World Religions in Chicago in 1993. Four years later, the award-winning site The Witches' Voice began its Internet presence (www.witchvox.com).

Neo-pagan spirituality is diverse in ritual, but there are common ideological themes across various groups. Devotion is given to an array of gods and goddesses, though most attention is given to the deities of Rome, Greece, Egypt, and old Europe. There is little connection with traditional Judaism, Christianity, or Islam, though Kabbalah has had a significant impact.

Neo-pagans celebrate gender diversity, the feminine, and sexuality. The latter is most famously expressed through sexual motifs in worship or by groups that meet in the nude (skyclad). Neo-paganism values nature, as shown most famously in liturgies built around the seasons of the year and lunar cycles. Of these, the most famous is Halloween, the night when pagans say farewell to the spirits of loved ones who died the previous year.

Neo-paganism has become a significant spiritual alternative for many teens and young adults. The appeal has to do with its pro-feminine, pro-nature, and pro-sexual dimensions but also to the allure of the mysterious and the forbidden in a minority religious tradition. Of course, interest in neo-paganism is also heightened through the dazzling success of J. K. Rowling's Harry Potter series and Stephanie Meyer's Twilight series.

While not all neo-pagans identify with wicca/witchcraft, most neo-pagans have to wrestle with the popular designation of the witch as satanist. This identification is complicated by the fact that some satanists do identity themselves as witches, most notably Anton LaVey (1930–1997), author of *The Satanic Bible* and founder of the Church of Satan. Neo-pagans are also impacted by ancient Christian stereotypes about witches. It is only in the last decade or so that Christian thinkers have engaged neo-pagan leaders on their own terms.

For Further Reading: E. Hopman and L. Bond, *Being a Pagan* (2001); R. Hutton, *The Triumph of the Moon* (1999); P. Johnson and G. diZerega, *Beyond the Burning Times*, ed. J. Morehead (2008); S. Pike, *New Age and Neopagan Religions in America* (2004); S. Rabinovich and J. Lewis, eds. *The Encyclopedia of Modern Witchcraft and Neo-Paganism* (2002).

James A. Beverley

Neri, Philip (1515–1595)

Roman Catholic priest and mystic. Neri was born in Florence, Italy, but spent most of his life in Rome, which earned him the nickname "Apostle of Rome." A layman until 1551, Neri spent his years in Rome visiting hospitals and frequenting many public places in caring for the sick and exhorting all whom he met to serve God. He attracted many people with his preaching and pastoral sensibility, and he encouraged frequent confession and reception of Communion, as well as the development of community among his flock. In 1564 he became religious superior of a community of priests eventually recognized as the Oratorians.

The experiences of divine love that characterized the mysticism of this period were also important in Neri's life. Like that of John of the Cross and Teresa of Avila, his spirituality focused on entering into the mystery of God's love through meditation, prayer, and fasting. In 1544 he had a mystical experience in which a globe of fire entered his mouth and lodged in his chest while he was praying, causing his heart to enlarge. His devotion to prayer and asceticism, culminating in experiences of divine love, stand as the legacy of a person who responded to the political turbulence of the Protestant Reformation by seeking inner peace with God and caring for the spiritually and physically sick.

See also Love; Union with God.

For Further Reading: L. Bordet and L. Ponnelle, *St. Philip Neri* (1932); T. Maynard, *Mystic in Motley* (1946); M. Trevor, *Apostle of Rome* (1966).

Joshua Dean

Neuroscience, Spirituality and

Neuroscience, the study of the nervous system, is a large and rapidly growing field. Areas of research range from the study of individual neurons (cells) to areas such as cognitive neuroscience (study of emotion, memory, motivation, etc.) and neuropsychology (study of the brain and behavior).

Advances in technology have contributed to the rapid growth in neuroscience. Researchers now have the means to image the brain in nonintrusive ways, similar to an X-ray machine. Magnetic resonance imaging (MRI) allows researchers to look at the structure of brain tissue inside the skull of a person. Functional MRIs (fMRI) and positron emission tomography (PET) scans allow researchers to determine what areas of the brain are more metabolically active during various activities or experiences. This allows patterns of brain activity to be observed while participants are engaging in various behaviors, for example, memorizing information, making moral decisions, or even praying.

Recently, neuroscience research has attempted to locate specific areas of the brain that are active during religious experience (e.g., prayer, meditation, ecstatic phenomena, etc.), and some scientists have attempted to make religious truth claims based on these findings. Some have posited, based on this research, that humans are biologically wired for religious experience, while other investigators are more cautious, noting that the brain's metabolic activity during religious experience is not always consistently located. But if humans are indeed embodied creatures (see below), then it should not be surprising that genuine connection with God would have a correlate in the brain. Cautious scientists warn that neuroscientific examination of religious experience cannot confirm or rule out genuine connection with God, and neither can it be used to make truth claims about the validity of God or religion.

With mounting evidence that brain damage, illness (e.g., temporal lobe epilepsy), and some drugs can significantly impact religious experience, questions about the existence of the soul have arisen. What is it that makes humans distinct from other animals and uniquely spiritual? Historically, Christians have answered this question with reference to the soul. For centuries Christians have held to a Cartesian view of the person, positing that humans are made up of two parts, a physical body and a spiritual, immortal, and immaterial soul. It was the soul that was thought to make humans uniquely spiritual and different from other animal species. But if behaviors once ascribed to the soul, such as rationality, moral reasoning, free will, and religious experience, can now be explained as activities of the brain, does Christian anthropology need a soul?

This question is highly debated and has spawned a large amount of writing in recent years by biblical scholars and theologians and Christian neuropsychologists. Many biblical scholars now argue for a monistic perspective on the person (i.e., humans are made up of one substance not two), suggesting that advances in biblical studies do not support a scriptural dualist perspective. This has immediately led some Christians to worry that a monist anthropology will lead to reductionism and determinism in which humans are nothing but biology. They worry that this physicalist position denies anything uniquely spiritual in persons.

Christian neuropsychologists wanting to preserve the monist or physicalist view of the person (non-Cartesian perspective), while avoiding reductionism, have suggested several alternatives. One model, *nonreductive physicalism*, understands humans as embodied, and argues that complex cognitive and social capacities emerge from lower-level brain processes but cannot be reduced to those lower-level operations. In other words, new and sufficiently complex human mental and spiritual capacities emerge from brain processes (e.g., consciousness, moral reasoning, language, relationality, etc.), making persons unique to other organisms. Particularly unique is the human capacity to relate to one another and to God. Again, although these capacities are to be understood as arising from physically embodied humans, they are too complex to be reduced to nothing but underlying brain processes.

A second explanation, the *constitution view* of persons, agrees with nonreductive physicalism in that persons are of one substance not two, but argues that persons and their bodies are not identical. Just as a statue may be made of copper, the statue per se and the copper are not the same thing. This view also maintains physicalism while avoiding reductionism. A third model, *emergent dualism*, treads a middle ground, taking human physicality seriously while maintaining a soul. This position argues that the soul emerges from human biology but is essentially not material—thus preserving an immaterial and immortal soul.

See also Science and Spirituality.

For Further Reading: J. Green, *Body, Soul, and Human Life* (2008); J. Green and S. Palmer, eds., *In Search of the Soul* (2005); M. Jeeves, *From Cells to Souls—and Beyond* (2004); M. Jeeves and W. Brown, *Neuroscience, Psychology, and Religion* (2009); N. Murphy, *Bodies and Souls, or Spirited Bodies?* (2006); N. Murphy et al., *Whatever Happened to the Soul?* (1998).

Brad D. Strawn

New Age Spirituality

The term *New Age* is the popular expression for the multifaceted Western esoteric traditions that serve as a major alternative spirituality to Christianity. Various New Age groups and leaders (Church Universal and Triumphant, Movement of Spiritual Inner Awareness [MSIA], Shirley MacLaine, JZ Knight, James Redfield) became popular in the 1980s and 1990s, though the roots of the New Age go back to earlier movements and figures from the 19th century (Spiritualism, Theosophy, Mary Baker Eddy) and to deeper currents in the long history of esotericism.

Despite remarkable diversity, New Age spirituality coalesces around such major themes as the unity of religions, the divine nature and potential of humanity, and the affirmation of the dawn of a new consciousness for the planet. New Agers usually hold to mild versions of karma and reincarnation and believe that the highest understandings of science confirm esoteric realities. On the latter, Fritjof Capra's *The Tao of Physics* (1975) and Robert Pirsig's *Zen and the Art of Motorcycle Maintenance* (1974) have been influential.

New Agers are open to psychic claims and alternative paths in medicine, including the reading of auras and past life therapy. New Age spirituality is oriented more to retreats, psychic fairs, and seminars than to structured worship and detailed ritual. Morality is also viewed as relative and pluralistic, though there are boundaries. Some New Agers follow specific esoteric Masters (e.g., the ancient warrior Ramtha) or use channeling to consult disembodied spirits. Others gravitate to New Age intellectuals, such as Marilyn Ferguson and Ken Wilber.

The spiritual style of the New Age is open and relaxed, though moments of apocalyptic frenzy have occurred, most notably with predictions of harmonic convergence in August 1987. Likewise, Elizabeth Clare Prophet, head of the Summit Lighthouse, issued doomsday warnings for 1990. Some New Age leaders are now using the Mayan calendar to predict that 2012 will be an epic moment for humanity. Many New Age groups use the language of the biblical Second Coming to describe an imminent turn to peace on planet Earth.

New Agers view Jesus as one among many masters. He was used by the Christ to bring the perennial truths to his time. His life and teachings are best captured in esoteric works like *A Course in Miracles* (1976) or *The Aquarian Gospel of Jesus the Christ* (1908). Western esoteric leaders always hold Jesus in high esteem, though there is no patience for traditional Christology.

See also Creation-Centered Spirituality; Gnosticism; Modernity; Postmodernity.

For Further Reading: C. Albanese, *A Republic of Mind and Spirit* (2006); A. Faivre, *Access to Western Esotericism* (1994); W. J. Hanegraaff, ed., *Dictionary of Gnosis and Western Esotericism* (2005); J. G. Melton, *New Age Encyclopedia* (1990); T. Peters, *The Cosmic Self* (1991).

James A. Beverley

Newman, John Henry (1801–1890)

English controversialist, theologian, and cardinal. Newman is significant to Christian spirituality both for his life story and for his theological and devotional writings. The spiritual odyssey of this English seeker after truth has fascinated Christians of many denominations. Newman's odyssey includes, roughly speaking, a period of nominal Anglicanism, of Calvinist evangelicalism, of rationalist Anglicanism, of the Oxford Movement, and of Roman Catholicism.

Newman's spiritual story began in his Anglican family and came to a turning point at age fifteen in an evangelical conversion. He was deeply influenced by a tutor in the summer of that year and came to Calvinist views thereafter for the next eight years. He went to Oxford, but despite having a brilliant mind, he barely passed his exams. He also struggled with health problems all his life. He was able to join Oriel College as a fellow, however, and rubbed shoulders with the intellectual elite of the university.

Newman was ordained an Anglican priest in 1825 and gradually came to believe in new birth in baptism and in the significance of the Greek fathers for theology. He became vicar of St. Mary's, the university church, preaching sermons that were later published in eight volumes. Although he was not dramatic in his preaching, his intense opposition to the liberal tendencies of the day stirred the hearers. He called for Christians to practice discipline and for the church to remain true to its origins instead of adapting itself to the fashions of the day.

This theme became ever more prominent as he became the editor of Tracts for the Times, a series of ninety short publications (1833 – 1841) occasioned by government control of the Anglican Church. At that time, the Tractarians, as they were called, did not regard evangelicalism as a valid option because it had appeared so recently and reflected the individualism of the Enlightenment rather than the ancient history of the church. The Tractarians later were commonly called the Oxford Movement.

Newman eventually became a Roman Catholic in 1845. That action meant cutting off relationships with his former friends, but for him it also meant coming "home" to the true church, a church that did not compromise its teachings. Yet his journey toward Catholicism was not always clear, and in 1833, during the period when he was unsure how to proceed, he penned a famous hymn while at sea:

> Lead, kindly Light, amid th'encircling gloom,
>   lead Thou me on!
> The night is dark, and I am far from home;
>   lead Thou me on!
> Keep Thou my feet; I do not ask to see
> The distant scene; one step enough for me.

His reception in the Roman Catholic Church was not what he might have expected. His work was frequently frustrated; Catholic authorities blocked his attempts to found a Catholic University in Dublin and a Catholic mission at Oxford University. He became an Oratorian priest and founded the Oratory in Birmingham. Unfortunately, the Catholic hierarchy did not appreciate him until late in his life, when he was made a cardinal in 1879. His later life was comparatively quiet, and he died in 1890.

Newman's writings include a spiritual memoir, *Apologia pro Vita Sua*, a defense of his life path, including his conversion to Roman Catholicism. He made major contributions in *The Idea of a University* to philosophy of education, in *A Grammar of Assent* to philosophy of religion, and in *An Essay on the Development of Doctrine* to the history of Christian doctrine.

Evangelicals can profit from reading Newman for at least three reasons. First, his life story shows a fearless search for truth, whatever the cost. Second, his sermons as an Anglican are full of Scripture and strong appeals to a fervent, disciplined Christian life. And last but not least, evangelicals can profit from Newman's critique of their movement because he had personal knowledge of it but decided to leave. He found evangelicals much too focused on their conversion experience and feelings in general rather than on simple obedience to Christ. In Newman's eyes, they thought themselves justified by feelings and words, which did not change their lives in practice.

The theology of evangelicalism also came under his scrutiny. This theology seemed to him to give all its attention to the cross, and thereby neglected the incarnation, resurrection, assumption, and Pentecost, all of which, with the cross, were aspects of one great act of God to save humanity.

See also Oxford Movement.

For Further Reading: *John Henry Newman: Selected Sermons,* CWS (1994); *John Henry Newman: Prayers, Poems, Meditations* (1990); R. Strange, *Newman 101* (2008).

Bradley P. Holt

New Testament

See **Chapter 4.**

Newton, John (1725 – 1807)

Anglican clergyman, hymn writer, and author. Newton recounted the dramatic story of his evangelical conversion in *An Authentic Narrative* (1764). In March 1748, on a ship in the midst of a life-threatening North Atlantic storm, he cried to God for mercy, after years of unbelief and moral recklessness. He remained a largely isolated believer as he continued his work in the slave trade, becoming captain of his own ship (1750 – 1754). After leaving the sea, he made contact with the leading figures in the evangelical revival in Britain, and his faith became more established. Working as a customs officer at the port of Liverpool, he read widely in theology and was eventually ordained in the Church of England, ministering at Olney in Buckinghamshire (1764 – 1779) and then in London (1779 – 1807). His lasting contribution to Christian spirituality was as a hymn writer and spiritual director through letters. With his friend and poet William Cowper, he published the *Olney Hymns* (1779), which was organized in part to trace "the

rise, progress, changes, and comforts of the spiritual life." Christ-centered and biblical, Newton's hymns made salvation history personal for the singer. His most famous hymn, "Amazing Grace," was written in 1773 to accompany a sermon on the experience of King David. A selection from his vast correspondence was published in *Cardiphonia* (Utterances of the Heart, 1780). A moderate Calvinist, Newton taught that a believer grows in maturity from an initial period of preoccupation with feelings and desire, through testing and temptation, toward a final goal of genuine contemplation. With memorable wit, he offered thoughtful responses to wide-ranging practical questions. He was, as G. R. Balleine wrote, "the St. Francis de Sales of the Evangelical movement, the great spiritual director of souls through the post." A counselor of William Wilberforce, Newton lived long enough to assist in the abolition of the slave trade.

See also Grace; Hymns; Mentoring, Spiritual; Wilberforce, William.

For Further Reading: D. B. Hindmarsh, *John Newton and the English Evangelical Tradition* (1996); J. Newton, *Works* (1808 – 1809).

D. Bruce Hindmarsh

Nicholas of Cusa (1401 – 1464)

German theologian, mystic, and churchman. Niclas Krebs was born in the town of Kues, his name being gradually altered to reflect the place of his birth (Nicolaus de Cusa, Nicolaus Cusanus). In 1416 Nicholas enrolled at the University of Heidelberg and the next year at Paris, where he received his doctorate in canon law in 1423. He was then both student and teacher in Cologne. In 1433 he participated in the Council of Basle and worked for the acceptance of the Hussites into the church. In the same year, he wrote his acclaimed *De concordantia catholica*, a plan for reform of both church and empire. Initially he supported the conciliar movement, but became disillusioned with it, and from

1437 onward aligned himself with Pope Eugenius IV. He served the papacy from 1438 to 1448, being sent, among other places, to Constantinople in the interests of promoting a union between the Eastern and Western churches; in 1448 he was promoted to the position of cardinal.

Nicholas was a man of wide-ranging scholarship, contributing to the fields of physics, geography, mathematics, astronomy, and the reform of the calendar. His most well-known spiritual writings are *On Learned Ignorance* (1440) and *The Vision of God* (1453). The first of these works is a philosophical treatise on the incomprehensibility of God and on negative theology as a means of knowing this God. He employs philosophy, theology, and mathematics to bring the reader to an appreciation of God's ultimate transcendence and of God's nature as "the Essence of all things," an appreciation that brought him under suspicion as a pantheist for a time. *The Vision of God* is a devotional essay guiding the reader, through meditation on an icon of Jesus and reflection on the ever-seeing character of Christ, into "mystical theology," which involves knowledge of God that transcends the ordinary human faculties. Nicholas of Cusa was a complex thinker, a talented statesman, and a forerunner of ecumenical theology.

See also Apophatic and Kataphatic Ways.

For Further Reading: I. K. M. Bocken, ed., *Conflict and Reconciliation: Perspectives on Nicholas of Cusa* (2004); N. Hudson, *Becoming God: The Doctrine of Theosis in Nicholas of Cusa* (2007); T. Izbicki and G. Christianson, *Introducing Nicholas of Cusa* (2004); *Nicholas of Cusa: Selected Spiritual Writings*, CWS (1997).

Evan B. Howard

Niles, D(aniel) T(hambyrajah) (1908–1970)

Asian (Sri Lankan) evangelist, pastor-theologian, ecumenist, and source of the well-loved quote: "Evangelism is one beggar telling another beggar where to get food." Fondly known as "D. T.," he was educated in Bangalore and ordained to the Methodist ministry in 1936. With a growing reputation as a Bible expositor, Niles became executive secretary of the National Christian Council of Ceylon from 1941 to 1945. He spoke at the inaugural meeting of the World Council of Churches (WCC) in 1948, becoming its Department of Evangelism secretary from 1953 to 1959. Regionally, he was instrumental in establishing the East Asia Christian Conference (1957) and compiled the *EACC Hymnal*, which included many Asian hymns he had translated into English.

As intimated in the quotation above, and indeed all his major writings, Niles brought to the fore the spirituality of the evangelist (as well as the evangelizing church) more than simply the quest for right methods or tools for gospel proclamation. He emphasized that the Christian stands alongside (not over against) the non-Christian as a fellow beggar, because the Christian has no bounty of his or her own to offer. The Christian as messenger of the Good News is simply a guest at the Master's table, who then invites others to join with the Lord at his banqueting table. This "being alongside" fellow humans takes place at several levels.

First, the Christian *as* evangelist is a human being just like any other. God designed the Christian life to be lived in the world, which means that every part of life is a frontier of the gospel. Indeed, the gospel must not just be preached to humans, but must also be lived out in relation to all creation, since its ultimate aim is the recovery of the wholeness of creation through Christ (Mark 16:15; Col. 1:23). Second, the Christian visibly represents life in Christ, humbly yet confidently, in and through the church as a missionary community. This community is both an instrument and foretaste of the kingdom, and demonstrates to the world what the gospel of the kingdom can accomplish even now. Finally, the Christian must relate Christ to people of other faiths, humbly yet confidently, in ways that both judge and fulfill the religious status quo. The gospel is put into meaningful language and thought forms (e.g., the Buddhist worldview) familiar to the hearer, not with the intention of grafting into the Christian faith elements of truth in other religions, but simply to restate Christian faith in forms that are meaningful to others. In the process, one's Christian understanding is enriched by the exchange. Niles's writings include *That They May Have Life* (1951), *Upon the Earth* (1962), and *A Testament of Faith* (1972).

See also Asian Christian Spirituality; Evangelism.

For Further Reading: C. Furtado, *The Contribution of Dr. D. T. Niles to the Church Universal and Local* (1978).

Timoteo D. Gener

Nominalism

Nominalism takes the philosophical position that things designated by the same term share nothing but this name. Thus, for example, the nominalist argues that the only thing that trees share in common is the fact that they are called "trees." Nominalism commonly designates the position opposite realism in the late medieval debate over the extra-mental existence of universals. The classical realist argues that universals really exist outside the human mind; the nominalist argues that universals have no extra-mental existence but are merely concepts, or names. The first "nominalist" (predating the late medieval debate) was Boethius (c. 480 – 524). Based on the principle that everything that actually exists must be one in number, Boethius argued that genera and species could not actually exist. Peter Abelard (1079 – c. 1144) argued likewise that universal nouns need not signify actual objects.

But it is William of Ockham who is best known for his formulation of nominalism. In the fourteenth century Ockham argued against the realist position and made his case that no universal existed outside the mind of the knower. What the human mind actually knows is the particular substance — *that* dog or *that* tree — and from those particular objects, the mind creates a generalized concept, which exists only in the mind as a sign. This sign serves to bring images of individuals back into the mind, but no universals actually exist, and thus any notion of universality is created by the mind only.

Nominalism had a wide range of effects, both philosophical and theological. Philosophically, it led some to reject the conception of metaphysics as the science of being. Because there was no universal concept of being, there could be no study of that nonexistent concept. Less well known was nominalism's impact on the history of Christian thought, particularly its influence on the Reformation. This influence was twofold. First, since there is no univocal notion of being — that is, one that is the same for God and humanity — the human knower is not able to understand the divine will. The gap between Creator and creation is thus widened, and as Martin Luther would later explain, God cannot be subjected to or understood through a human's rational analysis. Second, with the shift in focus from universal concepts to particular beings, there was also a move from the corporate (humanity) to the individual (*this* man or *that* woman). This paved the way for a more personal and individualized relationship with God.

See also Modernity; Platonism and Neoplatonism.

For Further Reading: M. Gillespie, *The Theological Origins of Modernity* (2008); J. Gracia, *Individuation in Scholasticism* (1994); W. Ockham, *Philosophical Writings*, ed. and trans. P. Boehner (1990).

Carrie Peffley

Norris, Kathleen (1947 –)

American poet and spiritual writer. Although a Protestant, she is also an oblate (or lay associate) of a Benedictine monastery, Assumption Abbey in North Dakota. Norris, a graduate of Bennington College, was an established poet living a secular lifestyle in New York when she inherited her grandmother's farm in Lemmon, South Dakota, decided to move there, and rediscovered her Presbyterian spiritual roots. She wrote about the effect of place, community, and tradition in her journey back to the Christian faith in *Dakota: A Spiritual Geography* (1993). In *The Cloister Walk* (1996), part journal, part meditation, she further describes her experiences of finding peace and healing through her immersion into the liturgical world of a Benedictine monastery. She plumbs the depths of Benedictine spirituality, meditating on the Psalms, the saints, celibacy, hospitality, and community with the imagination and candor of a twenty-first-century poet and mystic, yet firmly anchored in the real world. In *Amazing Grace: A Vocabulary of Faith* (1998), she writes with frankness and humor of the many religious terms that both attract and repel her. *The Quotidian Mysteries: Laundry, Liturgy and "Women's Work"* (1998) reveals her underlying feminist concerns, and along with *Acedia and Me: A Marriage, Monks and a Writer's Life* (2008), captures an overriding theme in all her writing—overcoming despair and discovering grace in the ordinary and everyday. Her publications also include *Journey* (2000), a collection of poems, and *Virgin of Bennington* (2001).

See also Benedictine Spirituality.

Carole Dale Spencer

North America (1700 – Present)

See **Chapter 17.**

Nouwen, Henri J. M. (1932 – 1996)

Dutch Catholic priest, psychologist, and spiritual writer. By age six, he felt called to the priesthood, celebrating Mass with children at home. Life in World War II Europe revealed parental care and larger human dramas. At age eighteen Nouwen enrolled in "minor seminary," and he was ordained a priest in 1957. He entered the Catholic University at Nijmegen, pursuing doctoral work in psychology; but amid clinical and cerebral studies, he came to prefer the discipline of pastoral counseling, pioneered in America by Anton Boisen and Seward Hiltner. An internship at the Menninger Clinic, integrating religion and psychology, was formative, leading Notre Dame to invite his help in starting their psychology department. His grasp of academic and pastoral disciplines, with a diverse student body, was reflected in *Intimacy* (1969). Lacking his doctorate, however, prospects were limited; and revisiting Holland's theological and academic climate (dissertation unfinished) was frustrating.

Nouwen's supporters included Colin Williams at Yale Divinity School, who recruited him to teach pastoral theology in 1971. During his decade there, books such as *Creative Ministry* (1971), *The Wounded Healer* (1972), and *Reaching Out* (1975) appeared. Articulating fresh approaches to self-understanding and following Christ, they gained him an audience in the arts of pastoral care and spiritual counsel.

Childhood issues, a culturally turbulent era, unease in the academy, and Nouwen's ever-inquiring heart and mind generated a personal restlessness. His mother's death (1978) revealed deep vulnerability and compassion. Four years earlier, he had tasted monasticism at the Abbey of the Genesee. In 1981 he left Yale for Latin America, asking whether this land, long of interest to him, offered a priestly call. In Bolivia and Peru, Nouwen was moved by the poor, and he identified with aspects of Gustavo Gutiérrez's theology of liberation, but he found that his lack of practical skills handicapped his ministry. He would visit Central and South America again, but he realized his greatest gift to the South was the "reverse mission" of speaking and writing of Latino/a spiritual vitality (*Gracias*, 1983), suffering, and the quest for justice for educated audiences in the North.

Two developments were significant in 1982–1983: Nouwen began teaching at Harvard Divinity School and made his first visit to the ecumenical L'Arche community and its founder, Jean Vanier, in Trosly, France. He taught at Harvard spring semesters only, allowing travel and mission. In 1985, even though his Introduction to the Spiritual Life course drew throngs, his busyness, collegial criticisms, and a desire for "downward mobility" motivated a move to L'Arche to serve disabled adults. Nouwen's last decade, as chaplain at the Daybreak community near Toronto, brought reflections on his life's *Road to Daybreak* (1988), revealing it as the road home: vocation fulfilled, vows kept.

Hospitality remains one of the central themes in Nouwen's life and literature. As his fame grew, he remained generous, unaffected, and often child-like in his sense of wonder (his initials J. M. meant "just me"). He respected the diversity of those around him, though less on ideological grounds than through recognizing the great variety of people beloved of God. His writings were typically short—often three points—spiritual reflections inviting readers to see "what's most personal is most universal" and receive the Good News, moving "from the house of fear to the house of love." Abiding in Christ, the *Lifesigns* (1986) of intimacy, fecundity (fruitfulness), and ecstasy (joy), portrayed in John 15, flourished. Serving *In the Name of Jesus* (1990) moved one from "relevance" to prayer, from popularity to ministry, from leading to being led, per Jesus' temptations resisted in Matthew 4:1–11 and Peter's call to shepherd in John 21:15–19. *The Return of the Prodigal Son* (1992) led readers to identify themselves with the younger child, the older child, and ultimately the parent in Rembrandt's masterpiece (Luke 15), and be renewed and reconciled.

Henri Nouwen was the first contemporary Roman Catholic writer so popular among evangelicals—whose passion for the Word inspired him, and to whom he offered historic spirituality and invited the grace and mind of Christ. Some conservative critics have charged him with excessive subjectivism. Nouwen declared in *Bread for the Journey* (1997): "Is everybody finally going to be all right?... Yes and No! Yes, because God wants to bring us home into God's Kingdom. No, because nothing happens without our choosing it. The realization of the Kingdom of God is God's work, but for God to make God's love fully visible in us, we must respond to God's love with our own love. There are two kinds of death: a death leading us into God's Kingdom, and a death leading us to hell.... We must choose God if we want to be with God."

See also Care of Souls; Disability; Health and Healing; Vanier, Jean.

For Further Reading: J. Bengtson and G. Earnshaw, eds., *Turning the Wheel: Henri Nouwen and Our Search for God* (2007); J. Beumer, *Henri Nouwen* (1996); M. Ford, *Wounded Prophet* (1999); M. O'Laughlin, *God's Beloved* (2004); idem, *Henri Nouwen* (2005).

James D. Smith III

O

Obedience

Obedience involves voluntary alignment with the will of another. Obedience to God—hearing, receiving, and responding positively to God's commands—is the way to fullness of life, while disregard or defiance of God's will and ways leads inevitably to death (Deut. 30:11–20). The rationale for such obedience is that the will of the all-knowing and benevolent God will prove good, pleasing, and perfect (Rom. 12:2), and in the end be the best for us. Abraham's test of obedience to God, for example, climaxed when God provided the sacrificial ram and promised that all nations would be blessed through Abraham's offspring, "because you have obeyed me" (Gen. 22:18). In his incarnation and life, Christ willingly and perfectly obeyed the Father (John 4:34; 6:38; 15:10; Phil. 2:8). In his humanity, Jesus "learned obedience" (Heb. 5:8), moving through childhood, ministry, Gethsemane, and the cross; and believers are to imitate the pattern of his obedience (1 Peter 2:21–25).

Obedience to God has its horizontal counterpart in the practice of obedience to certain other qualified persons. For example, the command for children to honor and obey their parents found in the Decalogue (Deut. 5:16), Proverbs (4:1–4), and the NT (Eph. 6:1–2; Col. 3:20) comes with an assurance of consequent blessings.

Obedience was a central tenet of early monasticism. Pachomius formed a monastic community in Egypt based on unquestioning obedience. Likewise, Benedictine communities in Italy required that novices demonstrate obedience to their abbot, who represented Christ. First and foremost, monk and abbot alike practiced vertical obedience to God. The monastic community then practiced obedience to the abbot, who answered to God for any abuse of power. For Benedict, the formational rationale was clear: "The first step of humility is unhesitating obedience which comes naturally to those who cherish Christ above all." Nonetheless, obedience must never be coerced, and it should never override or infringe upon the personal integrity and moral responsibility of the individual believer before God.

Obedience to God is essential to Christian spiritual transformation. Renewed, vibrant, and growing relationship to the Creator, made possible through Christ and his saving work, is to be motivated by love and manifested in obedience, for indeed the two are inseparable. Because God loves his children, he wants them to obey so that relationship with him can increase and their well-being can be ensured. In response to God's love, believers reciprocate with trusting love of their own, and, inevitably then, obedience. Jesus' relationship to the Father is the model for believers. "If you obey my commands, you will remain in my love, just as I have obeyed my Father's commands and remain in his love" (John 15:10). One experiences being loved and so obeys and through such obedience experiences further growth in love and faith. Unless it is motivated by genuine love, obedience will deteriorate into a merely outward and perfunctory obligation. The believer's practice of healthy obedience is enabled by the Spirit, begins in small things, and may become more costly—though ultimately also more rewarding—as the believer follows Jesus (Matt. 10:38–39).

See also Benedictine Spirituality; Rules, Religious; Will, Human.

For Further Reading: D. Bonhoeffer, *The Cost of Discipleship* (1999); W. Brueggemann, "Duty as Delight and Desire," *Journal for Preachers* (Advent 1994): 2–14; J. Chittister, *Wisdom Distilled from the Daily* (1990); F. Huey Jr., *Obedience* (1990); A. Murray, *With Christ in the School of Obedience* (1986).

Nancy R. Buschart

Occult

Occult is a broad term that covers a range of beliefs and practices related to secret knowledge about the supernatural realm and spiritual power. The word is derived from the Latin *occultus*, which means "hidden," "secret," or "private." The term itself never appears in the Bible and was not used by the early church, but that to which it refers is ancient and widespread.

The phenomena closest to this in the world of the Bible were magic, divination, sorcery, astrology, and mystery cult initiation procedures. The latter is especially significant because these rituals were secret (thus warranting the descriptive Greek term *mystērion*, "secret") and offered knowledge and empowering insights into the supernatural realm. In the NT world, the more popular cults with secret initiation rituals included those of Isis, Osiris, Mithras, Dionysus, Demeter and Kore, and Artemis.

Today occultism encompasses the continuing practice of many of these ancient rituals, which recently have experienced some resurgence. Many contemporary Christians categorize such echoes of ancient paganism as occultic, and also include in the category magic; witchcraft; sorcery; divination (including Tarot cards, Ouija boards, seances, and fortune-tellers); shamanism; channeling of spirits; and psychic phenomena, such as extrasensory perception (ESP), telekinesis, telepathy, and psychic healing.

People are often attracted to forms of occultism because they seek increased power in their personal lives, because they are profoundly dissatisfied with a mundane existence, because they want to experience supernatural phenomena, or because they are simply curious. Nevertheless, in continuity with OT Judaism, Christianity rejects occultism as dangerous and something that displeases God. God commanded Israel in the Torah, "Let no one be found among you who sacrifices their son or daughter in the fire, who practices divination or sorcery, interprets omens, engages in witchcraft, or casts spells, or who is a medium or spiritist or who consults the dead" (Deut. 18:10–11 TNIV). Christians believe that the power of Satan and evil spirits stands behind many forms of occultic beliefs and rituals. For a Christian, this is what constitutes the danger in pursuing this form of "secret knowledge." It leads people away from Christ and down a path that Satan potentially could use to hurt them and create an allegiance to him.

See also Devil, Demons, and the Demonic.

For Further Reading: C. Arnold, *Powers of Darkness* (1992); P. Jones, *Spirit Wars* (1997); W. Martin et al., *The Kingdom of the Occult* (2008).

Clinton E. Arnold

O'Connor, Flannery (1925–1964)

Fiction writer and essayist. Born to Roman Catholic parents and raised in Georgia, Flannery O'Connor remained a devout believer throughout her life, which ended prematurely from lupus when she was thirty-nine. Educated at America's most prestigious Creative Writer's Workshop at the University of Iowa, O'Connor explored sin and grace in her stories, whose characters, in the tradition of Southern Gothic fiction, often reside as grotesques and outcasts on the margins of society, bound inwardly and outwardly by their personal failures and limitations. Her concern with the malaise of Catholicism in America during her lifetime led her religious imagination to form a powerful cultural critique. Her theology was orthodox, premised on the atoning death and resurrection of the incarnated Christ; her aesthetics were profoundly sacramental. She authored two novels, *Wise Blood* (1952) and *The Violent Bear It Away* (1960); thirty-two short stories; and a collection of seminal essays on writing and creativity, *Mystery and Manners* (1969). She also had a wide literary correspondence from which more than eight hundred letters are collected in *The Habit of Being* (1988). O'Connor's genius lay in her penetrating intuitions about the motivations of the human heart and the artistic vision that portrays them. Her work is controversial for some Christian readers because it does not sentimentalize or diminish any of the depravity or glory of humanity, illustrating that every individual bears the image and grace of God, however altered by sin and spiritual blindness.

See also Literature and Spirituality.

For Further Reading: J. Baumgartner, *Flannery O'Connor* (1998); H. Bloom, *Flannery O'Connor* (1986); G. Kilcourse Jr., *Flannery O'Connor's Religious Imagination* (2001); R. Labrie, *The Catholic Imagination in American Literature* (1997).

Lynn R. Szabo

Old Testament
See **Chapter 3.**

Ordination

In the Old and New Testaments, God raised leaders for his people, and he expected much of them. God's calling and enabling of these leaders, men and women, is always given primacy, but the human response is never eclipsed. Saul can fail badly, and so can Judas. The leader who is pleasing to God sets an example in prayer, obedience, and godly living. Following Pentecost and the giving of the Spirit on all God's people, all disciples have a ministry (Acts 2:17–18; 1 Cor. 12:7), but not all are leaders. At first the Christian community recognized those God had raised up to lead because their anointing by the Spirit was clearly evident. However, with the passing of time, a way of publicly legitimating Spirit-endowed leaders emerged, the laying on of hands as an act of prayerful commissioning (Acts 6:6; 13:3; 1 Tim. 4:14).

Three significant developments beginning in the early 2nd century gave a more profound meaning to the laying of hands on Christian leaders. First of all, the leadership of a local church was given primarily to one man called an *episcopos* (bishop or overseer). Then the idea developed that the bishop presiding at the Eucharist was offering a gift to God like a priest in the OT. Cyprian (d. 258) was the first to call Eucharist presidents "priests." Believing that Christian communal leaders were priests, a distinct class, greatly enhanced their status. To add to this, Tertullian (d. 225) argued that bishops, presbyters, and deacons were the counterparts of the three Roman aristocratic orders who were set over the plebs, the laity. On this premise, he interpreted the laying of hands on Christian leaders as a social and spiritual reordering (Lat. *ordinatio*) of ordinary believers that elevated them into an elite class. With the passing of time, these three developments coalesced to make the laying of hands on Christian leaders something never envisaged in the NT. To a large degree, the Reformers maintained this "high" view of the laying on of hands, now called ordination, but opposed the idea that the ordained were priests. They depicted the ordained primarily in prophetic terms, as preachers and teachers.

All Christians are called to costly discipleship, a holy life, prayer, and love of neighbor—key elements in Christian spirituality. There can never be two grades of Christians, two strata of Christian spiritualities. However, Christian leaders, especially those who are ordained, must exemplify these virtues. They must do so because by doing so they demonstrate that the church has rightly legitimated their leadership. And conversely, when they fail badly and publicly, they undermine what gives legitimation to their ongoing leadership. Thus, when the ordained fail badly, they hurt not only themselves but also the church and Christian witness to the world.

See also Call to the Ministry; Discernment; Vocation; Vows.

For Further Reading: K. Giles, *Patterns of Ministry among the First Christians* (1985); K. Osborne, *Ministry* (1993); idem, *Priesthood* (1988); M. Volf, *After Our Likeness* (1998).

Kevin Giles

Origen of Alexandria (c. 185–c. 254)

Early contextual theologian. Origen's father was martyred as a Christian when Origen was still young. In the wake of his father's death, a wealthy Christian woman paid for Origen's education to become a teacher of philosophy and the Greek classics. He soon proved himself a polymath, mastering Plato and much of the learning of his age. Considerable numbers of those attracted to Christianity began coming to him for instruction. His was an engagement of Greek philosophy and literary culture that would enlarge the Platonic worldview to embrace and even articulate the mystery of God incarnate for the Greek and Latin worlds.

Origen wrote voluminously, primarily on Scripture, and he practiced many techniques used by biblical scholars today, yet his was not exegesis in the contemporary sense. All his interpretation was aimed to call for soul growth into the image of Christ, an approach Origen and other early fathers termed "allegory." The assumption undergirding such allegory was that layers of meaning deeper than the surface truth of Scripture become accessible to the attentive believer only as she or he advances in holiness and familiarity with the purposes of God in salvation. This involves both ascent into the life of angels and the Trinity above, and flight from the irrationality and darkness of the demons below. In Origen's perspective, the entire order of creation, including the malice of demons (which included, at a personal level, his own father's martyrdom), was mysteriously ordered by God to be part of the epic of salvation. Many later Christians, including Augustine of Hippo, were converted to Christ through initiation into the Scriptures read in this mode of spiritual exegesis.

Although certainly also indebted to models taken from his Greek education, Origen saw his method as commended by the Scriptures themselves, particularly the Wisdom literature attributed to Solomon, and *The Shepherd of Hermas*, which was accepted by many Christians of Origen's day as divinely inspired. In his *On First Principles*, a work of philosophical theology, he derives two interconnected patterns of three from these books. The first triad he saw in Proverbs 22:20, where the Greek text suggested that "counsel and knowledge" exist in a threefold manner; this threefold manner spoke, to Origen's eye, to the life of the body in its historical existence (the "literal" or "bodily" level), to the life of the mind in its discernment of moral truth (the "moral" level), and finally, to the life of the spirit and its sublime awareness of God in Christ (the "allegorical" or "spiritual" level). Origen thus expected the Scriptures to speak to these three aspects of human existence and those audiences in which each aspect is dominant.

Origen detected these three audiences in the *Shepherd*: first, those aware of Christ but unable to call God "Father" or Christ "Husband"; second, those who have advanced to reject the world and the flesh; and finally, those whose mature intimacy with Christ is manifest. This understanding, that there are different audiences to which different levels of Scripture's mysteries are available, finds its corollary in Origen's understanding of the progress of the soul, which he detailed in his *Commentary on the Song of Songs*. There he introduced yet another triad, one he sees in the order of the Wisdom books of the OT. Proverbs speaks to the moral initiation of the would-be Christ follower. Ecclesiastes teaches the now initiated believer the discernment between vanity and verity. Finally, the Song of Songs instructs the discerning, mature disciple in the depths of Christ's personal love for the soul and husbandly affection for the church, thereby giving the mature a language for expressing his or her own thirst for mystic awareness of God.

Origen's aggressive efforts to achieve convergences between the gospel and Greek thought proved controversial in the centuries that followed. His understanding of Scripture's depths of meaning, the soul's ascent, the cosmic epic of salvation, and the relationship between these proved seminal for most, if not all, subsequent Christianity, particularly influencing the development of threefold models of spiritual development. On the other hand, his speculations on what occurred before time (protology) and what would come after (eschatology) have not been embraced. Some two hundred years after his day, some of these more speculative views were formally condemned and masses of Origen's books destroyed. Despite this, he remained an important influence in the Western church through loose Latin translations of some of his more important works, and in the Eastern church through an anthology of his writings preserved by Gregory Nazianzus and Basil of Caesarea. Besides his *On First Principles* and *Commentary on the Song of Songs*, other surviving writings include *An Exhortation to Martyrdom* and a treatise *On Prayer*.

See also Allegorical Exegesis; Ascent, Stages of Spiritual; Platonism and Neoplatonism.

For Further Reading: Eusebius, *Ecclesiastical History*, trans. C. F. Cruse (1990); Origen, *Selected Writings*, CWS (1979); J. Trigg, *Origen* (1998).

Matthew Bell

Orthodox
See Chapter 19.

Otto, Rudolf (1869–1937)

German theologian of religions. Otto grew up in a deeply religious home that instilled in him a profound personal piety. Studies at the universities at Erlangen, a bastion of neo-Lutheranism, and Gottingen, a center for theological liberalism, during a time when religion was under attack by the rationalism of science led to a personal crisis of faith. However, this experience, which Otto called "deconversion," did not result in loss of faith, but to development of his thinking. He had a reconversion through understanding the Bible according to a historical approach and systematic theology. Exposure to religious plurality in England led him to develop an apologetic of religion, not just of Christianity. He eventually taught for the rest of his life at the University of Marburg Divinity School.

While studying the rational side of religion, Otto was confronted with the notion of religious experience and realized the limitation of rationality. He coined the word *numinous* from the Latin *numen*, meaning "holy," to refer to the holy without the moral and rational factors of traditional theologies. In his *Idea of the Holy* (1917, Eng. trans. 1923) and elsewhere, he explained that the numinous was thus a unique aspect of religion; it was inexpressible and could only be understood through experience, not ideas or propositions. He also studied comparative religion, and on a trip to India was struck by new modes of symbolic expressions.

Otto expanded this concept of the numinous to the field of comparative religion by exploring different religious experiences. His philosophical understanding of other religions and a sense of awe before the holy (simultaneously attracting and terrifying) gave him great sensitivity in studying the similarities and differences among religions. All these developed common grounds with people of other faiths. He also translated works on Sufism and Buddhism into German.

See also Fear of the Lord.

Kiem-Kiok Kwa

Oxford Group

The Oxford Group, later Moral Re-Armament, was a Christian renewal movement led by American Frank N. D. Buchman (1878–1961). Originally a Lutheran pastor in Philadelphia, Buchman's ministry was characterized by unusual creativity but marred by conflicts with others. Reflections on the cross of Christ at a 1908 Keswick Conference led him into a profound experience of personal surrender to God and then to writing apology notes to at least six trustees of his church. Subsequent talks in the vicinity of Oxford anticipated his four famous absolutes: honesty, purity, unselfishness, and love.

As YMCA leader at Penn State (1909–1915), Buchman fostered large-scale "house parties" and coined what became trademark phrases (e.g., "quiet times" for "guidance"). While teaching at Hartford Seminary and challenging Ivy League students to join his First-Century Christian Fellowship, he also conducted evangelistic trips to India and China and began to envision Christian renewal on an international scale. Samuel Shoemaker, who joined after meeting Buchman in China in 1918, later hosted the movement's American headquarters at his Calvary Church, New York City, and imparted to Bill Wilson principles that became the spiritual core of Alcoholics Anonymous.

In the late 1920s, South Africans initiated welcoming devotees as the "Oxford Group" (noting many Oxford University graduates among them), and this label was formally adopted as worldwide popularity peaked. Personal spiritual disciplines involved confession of sin to others, surrender to God, restitution to anyone harmed, and listening for God's guidance. "Life changing" meant "five Cs and procedures": winning audience confidence, honest confession, conviction of sin, conversion of life, and continuance through obedience and mentoring. Aspirations toward an international "new world order for Christ the King," however, involved the Oxford Group in political controversies and a militaristic 1938 name change to Moral Re-Armament. Buchman's death completed the drift from a distinctively Christian orientation to a pluralistic "Up with People" agenda.

See also Twelve-Step Programs.

For Further Reading: G. Lean, *Frank Buchman* (1985); A. J. Russell, *For Sinners Only* (1934); *What Is the Oxford Group?* (1933).

James D. Smith III

Oxford Movement

This influential movement within the Church of England sought to revive the catholic theology (and later practices) of the Patristic period and the Caroline Divines (1594–1728), while mitigating the impact of the Reformation on the church. It began in 1833 with John Keble's sermon "National Apostasy," preached at Oxford University in response to Parliament's plan to reduce the number of bishops in the Church of Ireland. In his sermon, Keble argued that the church was a divine institution in continuity with the apostles, not a department of state subject to the decisions of secular leaders. This led to the publication of ninety Tracts for the Times from 1833 to 1841 by various authors on topics such as apostolic succession, the nature of the church, baptismal regeneration, fasting, auricular confession, liturgical changes, and the *via media* (wherein the Church of England was described as a bridge church between Catholics and Protestants).

The principal leaders of the Oxford Movement, often called Tractarians because of their publications, were John Keble, a professor of poetry; John Henry Newman, a fellow of Oriel College; and Edward Bouverie Pusey, the Regius Professor of Hebrew. Although Newman was from an evangelical background, he became the early leader of the movement and wrote many of the tracts, including the last and most famous, *Remarks on Certain Passages in the Thirty-Nine Articles*. He left the Church of England for the Roman Catholic Church in 1845 after becoming convinced that it was the true church descended from the apostles. Pusey then became the acknowledged leader of the movement, which gave rise to what became known as the Catholic Revival and the Anglo-Catholic or "high church" party within the Church of England and throughout the whole Anglican Communion.

Although the leaders of the Oxford Movement from 1833 to 1845 were academic and conservative, their ideas and practices soon produced a deep spiritual renewal throughout the Church of England with the following characteristics. First, it was a spirituality with a great attachment to antiquity, to the life of the first five centuries of the church, in reaction to the growing sense of a modernity that sought to escape the past. Second, it was a spirituality that looked to the authority of church tradition as the true interpreter of the Bible and Christian practice, rather than to human reason or the Scriptures alone. Third, it was a spirituality that valued artistry in both individual and corporate worship, especially poetry, beauty, and pageantry, rather than the dry rationalism and moralism of the previous century.

The impact of the Oxford Movement in Anglican churches can be seen today in the frequent celebration of the Holy Eucharist, the belief in baptismal regeneration, the use of auricular confession, the revival of monastic orders, the sacramental shape of pastoral ministry, and the emphasis on the traditional spiritual disciplines as primary avenues for the growth of personal holiness.

See also Anglican Spirituality; Cambridge Platonists; Caroline Divines.

For Further Reading: O. Chadwick, *The Spirit of the Oxford Movement* (1992); J. Keble, *The Christian Year* (1827); J. H. Newman, *Apologia Pro Vita Sua* (1864); G. Rowell et al., eds., *Love's Redeeming Work* (2001).

David Montzingo

P

Pachomius (c. 292–346)

Early Egyptian monastic leader. Tradition credits Pachomius with establishing the first cenobitic or communal monastery. Like his older contemporary Antony, however, Pachomius was more of a pioneer than a true innovator. Yet by means of his visionary leadership, monastic culture transitioned from individual solitude to a regulated rhythm of shared communal life.

Following his conversion, Pachomius spent seven years as a hermit. He was instructed in a vision to build a monastery in a deserted village of Tabennese on the banks of the Nile, in Upper Egypt. This attracted others, and soon it grew in size, resulting in the creation of nine new monasteries for men and two for women by his death. Pachomius's most significant contribution to Egyptian monasticism was the development of the first monastic rule, which also revealed his organizational genius. Acts 4:32 became foundational to ordering community life, often called *koinonia*, within the network of communal monasteries. Pachomius's rule later influenced Basil in the East and Benedict in the West. The rule actually contains four distinct directives, consisting in turn of lengthy lists to guide communal behavior and regulate worship and prayer. New members were expected to memorize the Psalms and the NT. It is difficult to assess the theological climate of the Pachomian monasteries, since greater emphasis was placed on orthodox practices than orthodox theology (though this does not imply that Pachomius was heterodox). More broadly Pachomius's vision to unite people together with God was advanced by asceticism, combined with love for others and denial of self. The monks' success with agriculture brought increased commercial contact with society—which in turn helped spread Christianity throughout Egypt.

See also Monasticism.

For Further Reading: J. Goehering, *Ascetics, Society, and the Desert* (1999); W. Harmless, *Desert Christians* (2004), 115–57; *Pachomian Koinonia*, trans. A. Veilleux, 3 vols. (1980–82).

Tom Schwanda

Palamas, Gregory (1296–1359)

Hesychastic theologian and apologist. Gregory Palamas was born into an aristocratic family in Constantinople and became well educated in Aristotle's works and Greek philosophy. When he was about twenty, Gregory and his brothers went to Mount Athos to pursue spiritual formation according to the Hesychast (from the Greek word for "silence") tradition, which includes such practices as fasting, sleeplessness, and uninterrupted prayer. Five days a week he spent in isolation; on Saturday and Sunday he participated in liturgy and fellowship with other monks. In the 1330s, Barlaam, a monk philosopher, attacked the Hesychastic method and theology on the grounds that the Hesychast conception of God was too crassly physical. Gregory wrote in response his most important works — *Triads* and the *Hagioretic Tome*. His theology was affirmed as orthodox in three separate councils of the Byzantine Church (1341, 1347, and 1351). He was elected metropolitan of Thessalonica in 1347 and is commemorated by the Eastern Orthodox Church on the second Sunday in Lent.

The Orthodox tradition understands the controversy between Gregory and Barlaam largely as a debate between true theology and secular philosophy, though there is respect for the latter's questions. According to the Hesychastic tradition, by spending long hours in solitude and mental prayer (including the famous Jesus Prayer), monks may gradually become free from attachment to any creatures and other created things. They can finally come to see the uncreated energy of God. They call this the light of Mount Tabor (cf. Matt. 17:1 – 13). This energy is fully divine, but it is different from the unfathomable essence of God. By this distinction, Gregory preserves the absolute transcendence of God while insisting on the possibility of our person-to-person communion with God. Barlaam represents a philosophical approach to God, in which the transcendent God can only be approached speculatively through *via negativa*. For Barlaam, the mystical light seen by the Hesychasts is merely created light and a symbol of divinity. By affirming Gregory as an orthodox theologian, Eastern Orthodoxy affirms theology as primarily an expression of Christian experience. It also confesses that deification involves the whole person (body and soul) in true participation of God.

See also Hesychasm.

For Further Reading: *Gregory Palamas: The Triads*, CWS (1983); G. Papademetriou, *Introduction to St. Gregory Palamas* (2004).

Kin-Yip Louie

Palmer, Phoebe (1807 – 1874)

American Methodist lay theologian. Phoebe Palmer's writings and speaking gave shape to the American Holiness tradition and further influenced the Higher Life movement and Pentecostalism. Beginning in 1836, Palmer and her sister Sarah (both married but sharing a household) held a series of Tuesday Meetings for the Promotion of Holiness in their New York home, which began as prayer meetings for Methodist women but grew to include bishops and pastors as well. In 1837 Palmer had an experience of sanctifying grace that led her to commit herself entirely to the Lord's service in an "altar covenant." This event became the pattern and ideal of her later teaching.

Palmer and her husband had studied John Wesley's theology of Christian perfection attentively and had been struggling over how to attain it. Palmer's breakthrough, "altar theology," combined in one easily accessed package a set of themes that had never previously been synthesized. She linked together entire sanctification, the baptism with the Holy Spirit, the blessing of Pentecost, the enduement with power for service, and entire consecration. Palmer instructed believers to search the Scriptures, become convinced of what God promised in regard to holiness and power, and then claim those promises by faith in the words. No other evidence was necessary beyond the written promises, and the attainment of holiness was instantaneous rather than gradual.

Though the power of holiness was all God's, Palmer's altar theology emphasized the need for believers to offer themselves to God without any reservations and then to take God at his word to sanctify them completely. That moment of entire consecration was what Palmer called "the shorter way of getting into this way of holiness." Palmer's influence was propagated through her 1843 book *The Way of Holiness*, a magazine called *The Guide to Holiness*, and the extensive international ministry travels she and her husband undertook. Palmer's writing style was both conversational and passionate and, though well received in her time, has not remained popular. Palmer opposed women preaching on their own authority, on biblical grounds, but argued for the maximum permissible employment of women in ministry in her book *Tongues of Fire on the Daughters of the Lord*. Phoebe Palmer's books all make it clear that she desired her teaching to be judged by whether it was scriptural, practical, and in line with the broad, main lines of the Christian tradition.

See also Holiness Movement; Methodist Spirituality.

For Further Reading: E. Heath and W. Abraham, *Naked Faith: The Mystical Theology of Phoebe Palmer* (2009); *Phoebe Palmer: Selected Writings*, SAS (1988).

Fred Sanders

Panikkar, Raimon (1918–)

Pioneer of a pluralist theology of religions. Born to an Indian Hindu father and a Spanish Catholic mother, Raimon Panikkar has made interreligious dialogue the work of his life as an ordained Roman Catholic theologian. As an ontological pluralist, he takes religious differences very seriously and understands reality to be the source of such plurality because reality itself is differentiated and plural. True pluralism affirms the irreducibility of all ultimate perspectives. Panikkar updates and modifies the doctrine of the Trinity to account for such divergent religions. This doctrine provides the *form* of a transcendent, personal, and immanent principle and a Trinitarian structure that runs through the different religious systems. As such, pluralism is not possible as a *system* of doctrine and lived belief but only as an *attitude* that respects diversity and meets at the depth of the "Cosmotheandric" intuition. These three horizons—cosmology, anthropology, and God (ontology)—represent the various ascents of the human spirit to the mystery of divinity common to all religions. Panikkar attempts to show in *The Unknown Christ of Hinduism* (1981) that it is therefore possible to make a genuine confession of Christ and simultaneously acknowledge that in some way other religions recognize and acknowledge Christ, or may even elucidate more explicitly the implicit aspects of the Christian doctrine of God.

Panikkar's portrayal of the rich spiritual possibilities common to different religious traditions in *The Experience of God* (2006) attempts to show that the Christian faith does not monopolize spiritual encounter with God, while at the same time going to great lengths to retrieve and modify Christian resources in order to demonstrate the Christian faith's exceptional contribution to spirituality. His pluralist sensibilities understandably want to acknowledge the legitimate experiences of other religious traditions, while minimizing references to Christian exclusivity. As a result of his pluralist epistemology, his resulting affective devotion becomes theocentric and far less Christocentric. Nevertheless, Panikkar's pluralist spirituality allows for critical evangelical appropriation of spiritual expressions of common grace found in other religions.

For Further Reading: J. Komulainen, *An Emerging Cosmotheandric Religion? Raimon Panikkar's Pluralistic Theology of Religions* (2005); J. Prabhu, ed., *The Intercultural Challenge of Raimon Panikkar* (1996).

André Ong

Pannenberg, Wolfhart (1928–)

Future-oriented German theologian. Pannenberg was one of the several theologians who contributed after World War II to a renaissance of Trinitarian thinking. He first came to prominence because of his emphasis on the historical character of divine revelation and because of his powerful commendation of the resurrection of Jesus as a rationally verifiable event in real history—perhaps the strongest such defense to emerge in the 20th century.

Pannenberg's contributions to theology are many; two of his most significant contributions to Christian spirituality are his emphasis on the need for human beings to "risk outwards" toward God and others in order to experience life as God intended it; and his stress on how believers' assured destiny at the end of time should shape how they live in the present.

He recognized that those who seek to control their lives and to protect themselves from hurt inflicted by others or by the way the world works actually close themselves off from what God is seeking to do in their lives. Here Pannenberg built on foundations laid by Martin Buber, a Jewish philosopher, and Karl Barth, a Reformed theologian. Living as we do in a dangerous world, Pannenberg discerned that safety, or at least the offer of safety, is a great temptation to compromise. However, it is only in "risking oneself outwards" toward the world, and ultimately toward God, that human beings find anything meaningful or worth living for. His writings help to frame the promise of Jesus, "Whoever wants to save his life will lose it, but whoever loses his life for me will find it" (Matt. 16:25), in a way that contemporary Christian spirituality can understand and appropriate. This message is especially important for those living in the West with its inclination toward a highly individualized and risk-averse spirituality.

Related to this first emphasis, Pannenberg also attaches great importance to human destiny. Only that which lies at the end of time is ultimately consequential. However, precisely because that is what is ultimately true, it is already becoming true even now; and thus our destiny is meant to determine our present life. Classic perplexing questions, such as how we can be both sinners and at the same time fully justified by God, fade in relative importance as we begin to live out our true destiny—being children of God by the will and love of God—in the present moment. And it is this destiny that provides the security to risk toward the world in love. Christian spirituality, then, is a matter of the living out of what will be true, even though we are aware that it is not yet completely true of us.

Thus, Christians can love outward in the security that who they are is already assured by God's love, the love that is finally triumphant over all. Pannenberg's many publications include *Jesus: God and Man* (1965), *Christian Spirituality* (1983), and his three-volume *Systematic Theology* (1988–1993).

For Further Reading: S. Grenz, *Reason for Hope* (2005); K. M. Wong, *Wolfhart Pannenberg on Human Destiny* (2007).

Christopher Morton

Parenting

Parenting includes all the actions and behaviors provided by a primary caretaker to oversee the development of a child. Parenting does not occur in a vacuum. Following Urie Bronfenbrenner in *The Ecology of Human Development* (1981), family scholars today recognize that child development occurs in dynamic interaction with environments that impact all family members, such as work, school, and media, and that external forces (e.g., school board policies) and larger factors (e.g., culture, socioeconomic status, religion) play a role in family life. Parents must be able to navigate and manage these complex interactions to parent their children effectively (e.g., interface successfully with the child's school teacher or determine how much media exposure is allowed). The ecology of Christian parenting includes strong awareness of the interaction between Christian community, family faith practices, and parenting to bring a child up in the faith.

Parenting is often conceptualized within stages across the family life cycle. Stages begin with major life transitions that require the family to reorganize, such as the birth of a first child or launching the last child into adulthood. In each new stage, parents and children assume new roles or tasks and develop new patterns of communication, problem solving, and interaction. Divorce and remarriage create more complex family patterns and present parenting challenges (e.g., dual residence, different parental values, or different rules at different residences).

Diana Baumrind's research and subsequent explorations of parenting suggest that parents must balance affective support and behavior regulation as they raise their children. Affective support is the provision or nurturance, warmth, and caring that leads a child to know that she or he is loved; behavior regulation is active parenting to promote prosocial and productive behavior and stop inappropriate behavior. Too much or too little of either can distort a child's development and create unrealistic expectations in adulthood. Effective communication facilitates both dimensions. Four styles of parenting are often delineated: authoritative (the preferred style, when parents set clear standards balanced in the context of a nurturing and forgiving relationship), authoritarian (strict rules reinforced by punishment with little warmth), permissive (low expectations of self-control in a context of substantial nurturing), and uninvolved or neglectful (parents are detached, setting few standards and providing little interaction). Many parents demonstrate aspects of more than one style over time, and there may be cultural differences in manifestation of the styles. Authoritative parenting is consistent with Scripture passages such as Ephesians 6:4, which encourage parents to provide correction and tutoring to children in a positive fashion ("nurture") so that the children are not provoked to anger. Jack and Judy Balswick suggest that this type of parenting is consistent with the biblical idea of empowering; it is most effectively provided by parents who themselves have been empowered by God's unconditional love. Balanced or empowering parenting encourages maturity and self-management that prepares the child for adulthood.

Moral and spiritual identity development is an important outcome of parenting. Reimer notes that authoritative parents provide a secure relationship in which a child experiences parental expectations and underlying values and integrates them into self-understanding and self-identity. Attachment theorists suggest that when parents create a secure attachment with their child, they provide an opportunity for the child to experience God as nurturing and empowering because children extend the parent-child experience to their understanding of the God-child relationship.

See also Adolescent Spirituality; Children; Family Life; God, Perceptions of.

For Further Reading: J. O. Balswick and J. K. Balswick, *The Family* (2007); J. O. Balswick et al., *The Reciprocating Self* (2005); K. Reimer, "Moral Identity in the Family," in *Wiley-Blackwell Handbook of Family Psychology*, ed. J. Bray and M. Stanton (2009), 613 – 24.

Mark Stanton

Pascal, Blaise (1623 – 1662)

French scientist and religious philosopher. His contributions to science are significant in their own right, but his religious writings elicit perennial interest among Christians. Pascal had a mystical experience in 1654, when by his own account (found in *Pensées* 913) God burst into his life as fire and then overwhelming joy. Later he would famously remark that "the heart has its reasons, of which reason knows nothing." Thereafter he had a "second conversion," left his work as a scientist, and devoted himself to philosophy and theology. His two most famous works were penned in this period: *Provincial Letters* and *Pensées* (Thoughts). He was significantly interested in Jansenism from the time of his sister's adherence in 1646 until his death.

The *Provincial Letters* (1656 – 1657) is an attack on the ethical method of casuistry, which Pascal explained to be complex reasoning to excuse moral negligence. Pascal advocated that rather than rationalizing their way out of duty, Christians should uphold a high moral integrity and courage. Aside from its religious import, the *Letters* was popular for its rhetorical flair using humor, ridicule, and brutal satire. Of more enduring spiritual significance is Pascal's *Pensées*, first known as a *Defense of the Christian Religion*, but published posthumously in 1670 under the well-known title. In this collection of distinct but related writings, Pascal surveys several philosophical paradoxes, such as infinity and nothing, faith and reason, soul and matter, death and life, and meaning and vanity. He admits that these seeming contradictions used to keep him away from religion but now "have led him soonest to true religion." One is confronted by Pascal's notions of the profound obscurity of the universe and the wretchedness of the human heart. Nonetheless, Pascal appreciates humanity's ability to think about this darkness with humility, pious ignorance, and grace. In conclusion, he advocates that one wager for God's existence, for "if you gain, you gain it all; if you lose, you lose nothing."

The *Pensées* is a classic of French literature and theological contemplation. It is often read to gain a sense of the radical nature of sin and grace and as a tool in Christian apologetics. His penchant for uncertainty and a sort of dialectic has also been seen, justly or unjustly, as a precursor to existentialism. Besides a certain theological discomfort that Pascal experienced, he also endured chronic illness during the entirety of his short adult life, dying at the young age of thirty-nine. His "Prayer Asking God to Use Illness to a Good End" has been helpful to many.

See also Jansen, Cornelius.

For Further Reading: M. O'Connell, *Blaise Pascal* (1997); B. Pascal, *The Mind on Fire: An Anthology*, ed. J. Houston (1989); idem, *Pensées and Other Writings*, trans. H. Levi (1995); J. Van Vliet, "Gambling on Faith: A Holistic Examination of Blaise Pascal's Wager," *WTJ* 62, no. 1 (2000): 33–63.

Jason Zuidema

Passion of Christ

The passion (Gr. *paschō*, "suffering") of Christ refers to the suffering of Jesus in the events lead-

ing up to and including his death by crucifixion. This sense of passion is different from the term's contemporary connotations of zeal or intense desire (e.g., "Her passion is to become a doctor"). What is largely lost in the newer sense, but very present in the older, is the willingness to suffer for a valued cause.

The gospel narratives of the passion of Jesus (e.g., Matt. 26:1–27:61) have long been the focus of Christian devotional meditation, especially during the season of Lent that precedes the annual celebration of Easter. Traditionally the passion begins with the conspiracy to betray Christ, carries through his agony in the garden, his unjust trial, abuse at the hands of soldiers, the crown of thorns, the long Via Dolorosa (Way of Sorrow), the crucifixion itself, and finally his burial.

Meditation on the passion of Christ has traditionally focused on fourteen "stations of the cross," events—many biblical, some traditional—occurring along the Via Dolorosa and culminating in his burial. Observing these stations (or stopping points) is a practice that began with early pilgrims to Jerusalem but coalesced into its present form under the influence of fourteenth-century Franciscans. Such meditation has also traditionally focused on the seven last words (or phrases, really) of Jesus on the cross, beginning with "Father, forgive them" and culminating in "Into your hands I commit my spirit." Some have discerned in these phrases the seminal themes of Jesus' life and redemptive ministry in distilled form.

The arts have long played a compelling role in the commemoration of Christ's suffering. Since the late Middle Ages, passion plays have been popular enactments of the passion of Jesus, the most famous of which is Germany's Oberammergau passion play, which has been faithfully enacted before thousands of observers once every decade since 1634. The Hollywood movie *The Passion of the Christ* (2004) has made these events accessible to a global audience. Some of the church's great music, from "O Sacred Head, Now Wounded" (Bernard of Clairvaux) to the "St. Matthew Passion" (Bach), has commemorated them. In the early 20th century, Pope Pius XI encouraged Roman Catholic devotion to the passion of Jesus as acts of "reparation" for the suffering he had endured.

Protestants are sometimes wary of devotional focus on the passion of Christ, due to the morbidity that is sometimes associated with it, and because it culminates in Good Friday, not Easter, and thus has a penultimate and unsatisfying end point. Strident voices have more recently alleged that collective Christian devotion to the passion of Christ betrays a voyeuristic fascination with pain and torture. Critics suggest that Christianity betrays its pathological character by not only commemorating an event of graphic violence, but also treating it as central to its identity. In response, it is important to understand that the suffering of the passion is not divine sadism, but an inevitable consequence of divine righteousness colliding with resistant human evil. The encounter between the two is always costly.

Reflection on the passion of Christ can serve a number of healthy purposes for Christian spirituality. During Lenten Communion services (when believers remember the body and blood of Jesus), and at other times, it can deepen the believers' apprehension of the seriousness of sin, as well as the depth and extent of divine love. The first evokes remorse, and the second gratitude and loving devotion (1 John 4:19). In the language of Scottish theologian James Denney, "God loves like that!" Moreover, the fortitude of Jesus in the face of daunting suffering can be an inspiration to Christians called to bear up under persecution and difficulties of their own (Heb. 12:2–4; 1 Peter 2:21–23). The third week of Ignatius Loyola's *Spiritual Exercises* is devoted to the passion of Christ and to the purpose of fostering all of these implied meanings.

Significant among the spiritual benefits of reflection on the passion of Jesus is the freedom it gives the guilty consciences of the truly repentant.

"The conscience which is really burdened by sin," said Denney, "does not easily find satisfaction in ... cheap pardon." The assumption of easy forgiveness is out of sync with the deepest needs of the human soul as well as the character of God. The message of forgiveness is insufficient unless there is accompanying assurance that the outstanding moral debt has actually been *paid*. The depth and extent of Christ's vicarious suffering becomes the necessary psychological assurance that the inviolate moral symmetry of the universe has indeed been restored.

See also Cross, Experience of the; Suffering.

For Further Reading: J. Denney, *The Death of Christ* (1951); J. R. Taylor, *God Loves Like That! The Theology of James Denney* (1962).

Glen G. Scorgie

Pastoral Care

See **Care of Souls.**

Patience

See **Fruit of the Spirit; Waiting.**

Patrick of Ireland (c. 390–c. 460)

Pioneering Christian missionary. Patrick is the only Romano-British Christian about whom we have any reliable significant information. Only two of his Latin texts are extant, his *Confession* and a *Letter to the Soldiers of Coroticus*. His Latin style is devoid of learning, of which he speaks regretfully throughout his *Confession*. His date of birth has been a source of debate. R. P. C. Hanson has argued convincingly for placing it at the end of the 4th century. In his *Confession*, written not long before his death, Patrick indicated that he came from a Christian home near Bannavem Taburniae. The exact location of this village in either modern England or Wales, then the Roman province of Britannia, is unknown.

There at age sixteen he was kidnapped by Irish pirates. Taken as a slave to the west coast of Ireland, he was put to work as a shepherd. The trauma of being kidnapped led directly to his conversion to the Christian faith. Six years later he was able to escape and return to Britannia. Shortly afterward he had a dream in which the "voice of the Irish" called him to walk among them again. Dreams played a key role in his life, giving a mystical dimension to his spirituality. It was not until around 432, however, that he was able to return to Ireland.

He was sent there as a missionary by the British church, though some clearly opposed his going. Patrick's mission stands in splendid isolation, for apart from his Irish mission there appears to have been no planned effort in his day to evangelize pagans beyond the frontier of the disintegrating empire. According to both Patrick's witness and archaeological evidence, Christianity spread rapidly throughout the north of Ireland during his time there. In his *Confession*, he said that he baptized thousands, some of whom were leaders of tribal clans. This was the beginning of the Celtic church, whose spirituality preserved key elements of Patrick's own: missionary zeal, Trinitarian conviction, and Bible-centered literacy.

See also Celtic Spirituality.

For Further Reading: P. Freeman, *St. Patrick of Ireland* (2004); R. P. C. Hanson, *Saint Patrick* (1968); M. B. de Paor, *Patrick* (1998).

Michael A. G. Haykin

Pauline Spirituality

The apostle Paul is noted not only for his teaching on Christ and justification, but also for what he said about the life of the Spirit, or life in the Spirit. Casual readers may notice his various listing of the gifts or fruit of the Spirit but miss other references to spirituality because these come in the midst of other topics. In addressing the concerns of the Corinthians, Paul speaks about "those who are spiritual," and in declaring resurrection, he speaks about the "enspirited body" of those who will be raised. Just as the Holy Spirit does not normally call attention to himself, so the life of the Spirit is intertwined with the whole of Christian experience and tends not to attract attention to itself per se.

In Pauline thought (here we consider all letters associated with Paul's name), there is no undefined "spirituality" that is the common property of human beings. Rather, humans are created, like Adam, with a body enlivened by soul (*psychikon soma*, 1 Cor. 15:44–45) and may receive the Holy Spirit as a gift corresponding to their participation in Christ: "Having believed, you were marked in him with a seal, the promised Holy Spirit, who is a deposit (*arrabon*) guaranteeing our inheritance" (Eph. 1:13–14, cf. 2 Cor. 5:5). Christians led by the Spirit must expect, like the anointed Messiah, to suffer (Rom. 8:14–28); the suffering is not empty, but purposeful, for along with the suffering goes the "help" of the Spirit who intercedes and helps us to cry out truthfully, "Father," to God (8:15). It is by the Spirit that we persist in the pattern of Christ, from suffering to glory.

Unlike the philosophers of his day, Paul did not posit a body-spirit: baptism and the Lord's Supper are physical and spiritual mysteries. The spiritual life is interconnected with the physical and has an effect upon all of God's creation, and so Christians pray for its deliverance as well as their own (Rom. 8:21–23.) Again, Paul speaks with one voice about the "Spirit of God" and the concrete life of bodily holiness (1 Cor. 6:7–20): physical habits are not divorced from the spiritual life.

Correcting those who consider that spiritual life is for the elite, Paul affirms it for the entire body of Christ. Unlike old covenant believers, who relied on Moses to speak to God for them, we "with unveiled faces all reflect the Lord's glory [and] are being transformed into his likeness with ever-increasing glory, which comes from the Lord, who is the Spirit" (2 Cor. 3:18). Because he has come into history, we have no need of special spiritual exploits to "bring Christ down" (Rom. 10:6), but know together "the light of the knowledge of the glory of God in the face of Christ" (2 Cor. 4:6). The spiritual life, then, is practical and requires discipline, yet is interconnected with God's mystery—"his incomparably great power," which is "like the working of his mighty strength, which he exerted in Christ when he raised him from the dead and seated him at his right hand in the heavenly realms" (Eph. 1:19–20).

For Further Reading: R. Hays, *Echoes of Scripture in the Letters of Paul* (1989); E. Humphrey, "Why Bring the Word Down?" in *Romans and the People of God*, ed. S. Soderlund and N. T. Wright (1999); F. Watson, *Paul and the Hermeneutics of Faith* (2004); N. T. Wright, *Paul in Fresh Perspective* (2005).

Edith M. Humphrey

Peace

In Christian spirituality, peace designates the experience of a justly reconciled, harmonious relationship between God and humankind, among humans, and between humans and the whole created order. Such peace begins from within, in an assurance given by God, and extends outward from this center. In Pauline expression, God is "the God of peace" (Rom. 15:33; 16:20; Phil. 4:9; 1 Thess. 5:23), "the Lord of peace" (2 Thess. 3:16), or "the God of love and peace" (2 Cor. 13:11). When greeting others with the Hebrew *shalom* or the Greek *eirene*, we do so by acknowledging that it is "from God our Father and the Lord Jesus Christ" (e.g., Rom. 1:7; 1 Cor. 1:3); we do not possess peace in ourselves as an inherent quality. God alone can give peace. Jesus can give God's peace because he is one with the Father, the "I AM." In John's gospel, as he prepared to depart to be with the Father, he assured the disciples that he left them *his* peace, a peace unlike the world's, which would only be cessation of hostilities. Christ's peace is one that touches the heart to calm its anxieties

and fears (John 14:27). Because of our humanness, that would not mean the abolition or elimination of all anxiety and fear; but as Paul reminded the Philippians, God's shalom, which surpasses human comprehension, can "throw a guard around your hearts and minds in Christ Jesus" (Phil. 4:7, my paraphrase). Or seen from another angle, as in 1 John 4:18, "perfect love," which could only mean the love of God, "drives out fear."

Those who experience the peace of the God of peace, however, cannot rest content with what it has done for them. Their experience makes them participants in God's mission—the reconciliation of the world to Godself in and through Jesus Christ. As Paul reminded the Corinthians, God has reconciled the world to Godself through Christ and entrusted to us the continuance of that peacemaking mission (2 Cor. 5:18–19). The whole Christian mission is a grand peacemaking endeavor! The first step in that endeavor is to exhibit the oneness of God's new creation in the body of Christ. The apostle Paul insisted that "though many, [we] are one body in Christ, and individually members one of another" (Rom. 12:5 ESV). Note that he said we "are," not we "will be" or "should be" or "can be." What he intended to imply is that communities of believers have to live up to what we are, a truly reconciled humanity, notwithstanding all of our diversity. How do we do that? Paul seemed to echo the teachings of Jesus in the Sermon on the Mount as he sketched the basics: love with genuine love, strive to outdo one another in honoring one another, be generous and hospitable, bless and do not curse those who persecute you, share joys and sorrows, live in harmony, be humble and not haughty, live peaceably with all if you can, don't try to avenge yourselves, and shame enemies by doing good, overcoming evil with good (Rom. 12:9–21).

In this list the second step already has become manifest—to strive for the reconciliation of humankind with God and with one another. "Blessed are the peacemakers, for they will be called children of God," Jesus said (Matt. 5:9 TNIV). In

Christian perspective, God, the triune God, is the number one peacemaker. Just as Father, Son, and Spirit live in intimate harmony with one another, so have they willed for the whole creation to live in harmony with one another. Through the Son, "the image of the invisible God, the firstborn over all creation," God reconciled everything to God-self, "making peace through his death on the cross, whether things on earth or things in heaven" (Col. 1:15, 20 AT). Observe here that God's peacemaking extends not just to humankind but to the whole creation. Obviously our peacemaking enterprise will aim first at reaching a fractured humanity, for we will find it difficult if not impossible to restore the created order without enlisting fellow human beings. By itself alone, the task of effecting the reconciliation of humankind with God and with one another is an overwhelming one, so daunting that some throw up their hands in despair and abandon any effort. We can persevere only if we keep in mind the conviction that propelled our earliest forebearers, namely, that God is working together with those who love God to achieve this (cf. Rom. 8:28). Just as the apostle Paul, however, we must not pare down God's peacemaking vision to our size. Peacemakers today must address issues such as global warming and depletion of the earth's precious resources that threaten the very survival of humankind. Surely God wants us to be aware that the whole creation is eagerly awaiting the revelation of the children of God (Rom. 8:19).

See also Fruit of the Spirit; Holy War; Reconciliation.

For Further Reading: "Eirēnē in the NT," in *TDNT,* 2:411 – 20; R. McSorley, *New Testament Basis of Peacemaking* (1979); R. Musto, *The Catholic Peace Tradition* (1986); "Shalom in the OT," in *TDNT,* 2:402 – 6.

E. Glenn Hinson

Peacemaking

Jesus' own spirituality was intensely concerned for peacemaking. Jesus wept over Jerusalem because the Jews there did not know the practices that make for peace (Luke 19:41 – 42). He knew that false messiahs were leading rebellions and getting their followers massacred, and anger against Rome was building toward a big rebellion and slaughter. Five times in the canonical Gospels, plus once in the *Gospel of Thomas,* Jesus warned that Jerusalem and the temple were going to be destroyed, which did happen in the years 66 to 70. As the prophets and Jesus had warned, Israel was destroyed and driven into exile. The prophets warned that putting their trust in warhorses, chariots, and military alliances rather than giving their trust to God and doing justice would lead to destruction and exile. They were right. Jesus warned similarly. He was right. His and their warnings are still right.

Jesus himself entered Jerusalem as the Messiah of peace, on the foal of a donkey — not a warhorse — fulfilling Zechariah 9:9 – 10. As he was heading to his own crucifixion, Jesus said, "Daughters of Jerusalem, do not weep for me, but weep for yourselves and for your children. For the days are surely coming when they will say, 'Blessed are the barren, and the wombs that never bore, and the breasts that never nursed'" (Luke 23:28 – 29 NRSV). He told his own followers: When the war comes, do not participate, but flee to the hills (Matt. 24; Mark 13; Luke 21). The Christians fled the rebellion and became the peace party. They conquered Rome, not by making war against it, but by loving their enemy and spreading the gospel. Love was more effective evangelism than violent rebellion.

Jesus' peacemaking was not primarily about what *not* to do. It was about transforming initiatives: go and make peace with your brother and your adversary; go the second mile with your enemy; love your enemies and pray for them; don't judge, but take the log out of your own eye; forgive those who trespass against you; seek first the reign of God and God's delivering justice. The new paradigm of just peacemaking is not so much about what not to do, but about transforming initiatives that work: go and do conflict resolution with your adversary; practice nonviolent direct action; take independent initiatives toward your enemy; don't judge but acknowledge your own responsibility for the conflict and injustice; practice justice, human rights, and international cooperation.

The seventh beatitude may also be translated: *"Joyful* are the peacemakers." They are joyful in part because they experience the breakthrough of the mustard seeds of the reign of God in surprising ways. In Jesus' teaching, the presence, peace, and joy of God accompany God's reign.

See also Anabaptist Spirituality.

For Further Reading: J. Juhnke and C. Hunter, *The Missing Peace* (2001); D. Kodia, *Poverty in Grace* (2005); G. Mortenson, *Three Cups of Tea* (2007); C. Schrock-Shenk, *Making Peace with Conflict* (1999); G. Stassen, *Just Peacemaking* (2008); W. Swartley, *The Covenant of Peace* (2006); J. H. Yoder, *The War of the Lamb* (2009).

Glen Harold Stassen

Peale, Norman Vincent (1898–1993)

American pastor and advocate of positive thinking. Peale was raised in the Methodist tradition but later in life switched to the Dutch Reformed Church. Taking the call to Marble Collegiate Church in Manhattan, he grew the church through the preaching of the power of positive thinking and through his radio show, *The Art of Living*. In 1945 he founded *Guideposts*, a nondenominational magazine, to relay inspirational stories from both ordinary and famous people.

Peale's emphasis on positive thinking brought him many critics, both in psychiatric and Christian circles. Peale had been one of the two founders of the American Foundation for Religion and Psychiatry. However, his cofounder and a large number of psychology practitioners rejected Peale's "positive thinking" orientation as lacking good mental health foundations. Likewise, his positive thinking concept has been attacked by some Christians as encouraging the belief in the "health and prosperity" gospel. Other Christians have argued that belief in the power of positive thinking leads to the view of salvation through works.

Instead of focusing on the challenges of human sin and depravity, Peale focused on joy and opportunities, a strategy that is still embraced by many Christians today, and he continues to inspire people in their Christian spirituality through *Guideposts* and his numerous aphorisms.

Christopher Morton

Peck, M(organ) Scott (1936–2005)

American psychiatrist and author on religion and psychology. Born in New York City, Peck graduated from Friends Seminary (1954), Harvard University (B.A., 1958), and Case Western Reserve University School of Medicine (M.D., 1963). He served in the U.S. Army and worked in medical administrative and clinical positions in the military and private sector. He received professional awards for his work on religion and science, community building, and peacemaking.

Peck's psychological writing has a distinctly religious perspective. His best-known work, *The Road Less Traveled* (1978), which describes the necessary characteristics and habits of a fulfilled person, sold over ten million copies. Though early on he dabbled in Buddhist and Islamic mysticism, in his second book, *People of the Lie* (1983), he wrote that he had made a firm commitment to Christianity as signified by his nondenominational baptism.

In *People of the Lie*, Peck grappled with the religious theme of evil. He described the characteristics of evil people as lacking in empathy, prone to project their evil onto others, and actively resistant to consciousness of their own guilt. He also explored group and spiritual evil, as well as the possibility of demon possession. What made Peck's writing unique was his ability to explore religious themes and ground them in the science of psychology, while not dismissing religion or spirituality. In his later writings, Peck seemed to move away from mainstream Christianity and subsequently received criticism from some conservative evangelical Christians. His other writings include *The Different Drum* (1987), *Further Along the Road Less Traveled* (1993), and *The Road Less Traveled and Beyond* (1997).

See also Devil, Demons, and the Demonic; Sin.
Brad D. Strawn

Penington, Isaac (1616–1679)

Early Quaker theologian and mystic. Socially more privileged than most other early Friends, Penington was a well-educated son of the Lord Mayor of London. Nevertheless, like most other Quakers, he suffered repeated imprisonments for his faith. He wrote many works (four volumes in a modern edition), ranging from essays on civil society and religious rights to theological disputes. Later generations found more sustenance in his letters of spiritual nurture, which are rich in biblical metaphors to describe the intimacy between God and the soul.

Isaac Penington's spiritual counsel, in his *Letters* (1828) and elsewhere, reflects his experiences and theology as a Quaker. He advises his readers to stay focused within. It is there that they meet God, so they should not look to what is outward but rather dwell with the Beloved in the tent that God has pitched for them. He encourages his readers to wait patiently for the guidance of the Seed or Light of Christ. This Light will first bring knowledge of sin, and this inward day of visitation will bring judgment, as all that is of self is searched out and brought under. Thereafter the power of God gives victory over evil and temptation. All things become new. This joyous state is an engrafting into Christ and brings a peace that abstains from worldly, outward violence. A distinctive emphasis is his repeated advice not to look for some great visitation and not to despise the day of small things (cf. Zech. 4:10). He counsels his readers to be humble, to be little, so as not to miss God's presence in unassuming matters.

See also Quaker Spirituality.

For Further Reading: R. Keiser and R. Moore, eds., *Knowing the Mystery of Life Within: Selected Writings of Isaac Penington* (2005).

Michael Birkel

Penitence

Repentance and confession are vital elements of a Christian spirituality — as part of the liturgy or worship of the church and of personal prayer. This penitential dimension of spirituality speaks to the acknowledgment of human responsibility and thus accountability for behavior — or, in the words of the classic liturgies, to having failed God in thought, word, and deed in what we have done or failed to do.

Some contemporary church communities downplay the penitential, thinking that to speak of sin and confession is not "seeker friendly." But this dimension of worship, prayer, and the spiritual life cannot be simply dispensed with as though it were inconvenient or because it may cause discomfort. It is simply too integral to the call of the Scriptures and thus to genuine Christian spirituality.

In the OT, the people of God are called to return to God, to turn from idolatry and to focus afresh on the will of God. To "return to the LORD your God and obey him" is possible because "God is a merciful God" who "will not abandon or destroy you or forget the covenant with your forefathers" (Deut 4:29–31; cf. 30:1–3). Such restoration involves self-examination and repentance. Then obedience.

This turning back to God was recognized as an ongoing need in the life of Israel, so God established the annual Day of Atonement. The high priest, representing the entire community, entered into the Holy of Holies and made atonement for the sin—an act that included a confession of the sins of the people.

We find a distinct emphasis on confession and repentance in the prophetic books. And this prophetic call is complemented throughout the OT with powerful prayers of confession—individual, personal prayers and prayers found in the Psalms and the Prophets that were used in the context of public worship.

In the NT, John the Baptist called the people of God to repentance with the coming of the Messiah, who himself came preaching repentance. For the early church, repentance was an essential component of the gospel cry as they proclaimed Jesus to the world. As in the OT, a rhythm of repentance was to flow from an awareness of God's just and merciful character.

This clear biblical call to repentance finds expression, then, in the evangelical spiritual heritage. During the Protestant Reformation, Martin Luther and John Calvin reacted to the Roman Catholic practice of penance and any suggestion that confession somehow pays the penalty for a person's sin. But they also insisted that true faith in Christ will always be demonstrated in repentance. Calvin spoke of repentance as the necessary fruit of faith, not only when one becomes a Christian, but as a practice that is cultivated during the whole course of our lives.

For the seventeenth-century Puritans, to be a Christian was to be a penitent—one who responded to the mercy of God with a continual practice of confession and repentance, continually turning from sin—a turning enabled by the mercy of God. Eighteenth-century spiritual leaders John and Charles Wesley are well known for their emphasis on the Christian's heartfelt assurance of forgiveness, and they insisted that confession was not a once-and-for-all experience. John Wesley argued that though sin does not "reign" in the Christian believer, it nevertheless "remains" in

the heart of the new Christian, thus necessitating ongoing repentance. The believer is always prone to love the creature more than the Creator and to be "a lover of pleasure rather than a lover of God" (see 2 Tim. 3:4) and therefore needs to be watchful and on guard, purposing to turn from sin and find grace, forgiveness, and healing in the hands of a merciful God.

Though repentance is not the same as conversion, it is so integral to conversion that the Scriptures often speak of conversion by speaking of repentance. And the evangelical spiritual tradition has always maintained that just as there is no conversion without repentance, there is no growth in faith, hope, and love without repentance and confession. This is not demoralizing. Rather, it is a declaration that there is hope in the midst of failure.

We must therefore actively seek to restore the practice of regular confession to our worship and to our individual practice of spiritual discipline, meditation, and prayer. The Christian life is one of continuous repentance and conversion, finding expression in our personal prayers and in our Sunday worship.

We call one another to repentance out of a deep assurance that the God of all grace, mercy, and love is the one who urges us to turn from our sin. The call to repentance is distorted when it is not rooted in the context of the love and acceptance of God. We do not repent in order to "make things right with God." Rather, the act of confession arises out of the confidence that we are loved and accepted. We *are* right with God! That is why we confess our sins. We do not confess our sins lest we take "unworthily" of the Communion table because, in a sense, we are always unworthy. Rather, we come to the Lord's Table as those who live under the mercy of God. We are loved and accepted at the holy meal; and our confession is part of our renewed commitment to walk in love and faith.

Our confession highlights the wonder of the goodness and mercy of God. When we come to confession, we meet not our Judge, but our Healer.

In faith we turn from self-absorption, self-preoccupation, pride, and self-reliance. We joyfully receive the forgiveness of God, by which the Spirit empowers us to turn from sin and to live in the light.

In confession we bring integrity and consistency into our lives. Through the witness of the Spirit, we recognize that our behavior is not congruent with what we believe and know to be true. And through confession, in thought, word, and deed, we are realigned in our walk with God.

For mature Christians, confession becomes less a matter of identifying particular sins or thoughts and more and more a realization that we are "prone to wander," as the hymn writer has put it, prone to become occupied with ourselves, self-reliant rather than dependent on the grace of God.

Finally, through confession our lives are anchored in the joy and peace that are gifts of the Spirit; we live under God's mercy, knowing the joy of abiding in his forgiveness.

See also Examen; Forgiveness.

For Further Reading: M. Boda and G. Smith, ed., *Repentance in Christian Theology* (2006); J. Chryssavgis, *Repentance and Confession* (1990).

Gordon T. Smith

Penn, William (1644 – 1718)

Quaker statesman and theologian. William Penn is best known as the founder of Pennsylvania, established as a "holy experiment" and a haven for religious tolerance, to which Penn invited persecuted Christian minorities, such as his fellow Quakers from England as well as Anabaptists and pacifist Pietists from the European continent. In the realm of spirituality, Penn is best known for several works that bring together complementary dimensions of his own theology and ethics. In *No Cross, No Crown* he took on the role of a religious radical, summoning others to a rigorous ethic that stood in contrast to socially dominant Christendom. He challenged worldly vanities in attire and recreation

as well as unjust customs built on social rank. In the second edition (1682), Penn focused more on the interior motives that bear fruit in exterior virtues, with a tone that was more persuasive than prophetic. The cross must be taken up inwardly, in the heart, through renunciation of self-will and submission to God. Self-denial then leads one to set aside luxury, pride, the pursuit of power, and violence. The second major stream in Penn's thought was that of the rationalist and Christian humanist who seeks wisdom universally. Penn found inspiration not only in Christian sources but also in Socratic philosophy and Stoic virtues. The epigrammatic style of the latter led him to write in the genre of maxims. Here his lasting contribution to Christian spirituality lay in such works as *Some Fruits of Solitude*, with its brief thoughts on such topics as education, discipline, industry, friendship, government, and religion. Of a similar style is *Advice to His Children*, with its succinct counsel on such matters as mercy, humility, justice, generosity, gratitude, and integrity.

See also Quaker Spirituality.

For Further Reading: H. Barbour, *William Penn on Religion and Ethics* (1991).

Michael Birkel

Pennington, M. Basil (Robert John) (1931 – 2005)

Trappist monk and writer. Pennington was a Catholic priest and member of the Cistercian (Trappist) order. He entered the monastery at age twenty, was consecrated a monk at twenty-five, and then was ordained a priest two years later. He later pursued degrees in theology (Pontifical University of St. Thomas Aquinas) and canon law (Pontifical Gregorian University). While a monk at St. Joseph's Abby in Spencer, Massachusetts, in 1975, Pennington, with his abbot Thomas Keating and fellow monk William Meninger, began promoting classical contemplative prayer. Pennington referred to it as "centering prayer," though it was named this by both Keating and fellow Trappist Thomas Merton. Pennington was a friend of Merton's; when Merton died in 1968, Pennington dedicated his life to continuing the work that Merton had done.

Pennington was a prolific writer, completing more than fifty books and a thousand essays. His books include *Centering Prayer* (1980), *A Place Apart* (1983), and *Call to the Center* (1985). He was equally active as lecturer and retreat leader. He, along with Keating, is responsible for the growth of contemplative prayer across denominations and even religious faiths. Pennington's passion was to establish a universal, or "catholic," approach to prayer and spirituality that would bridge East and West, Protestant and Catholic. He was a leader in Catholic interreligious dialogue and a key figure in the Monastic Interreligious Dialogue.

See also Centering Prayer; Contemplation; Merton, Thomas; Trappists.

Todd E. Johnson

Pentecostal Spirituality

Pentecostal spirituality began at the turn of the 20th century with an accent on an experience called the "baptism in the Holy Spirit." The metaphor of Spirit baptism was taken originally from Luke's emphasis on the reception of the Spirit for the expanding and increasingly diverse witness of the churches to Jesus Christ (Luke 3:16; Acts 1:5–8; 2:33). Following Jesus' words in Acts 1:8, "You will receive power when the Holy Spirit comes on you; and you will be my witnesses," the Pentecostals viewed the baptism in the Holy Spirit as connected to a powerful experience of Spirit filling and of empowerment of Christians for witness to Jesus Christ. Implied was a spirituality that was aimed at challenging Christians by energizing the weary or awakening the slothful through a deeper awareness of the indwelling presence of the Holy Spirit in life.

Pentecostals typically point out that this accent on the Spirit's presence and work will cause the church to pay attention to the extraordinary gifts of the Spirit highlighted in the NT (e.g., the book of Acts and 1 Cor. 12–14). The spiritual life was commonly understood as a battle with the dark forces that seek to thwart the purposes of God in the world, so extraordinary or spiritual weapons were thought to be needed. In this battle, not only clergy, but also ordinary Christians were considered gifted in extraordinary ways to witness for Christ and to edify the church. The energizing of the laity through Spirit baptism and spiritual gifts thus became the distinctive hallmark of Pentecostal spirituality globally. The movement has exercised a significant influence on the charismatic movement among Catholics and mainline Protestants as well as on Christianity throughout the two-thirds world.

It is possible to so accent the work of the Spirit that one neglects the anchor of the Spirit's work in the person and work of Jesus Christ. In this light, it is important to note that Pentecostals also highlight the foundational importance of conversion to Jesus Christ. Not so well known is the fact that a significant minority of Pentecostals did come to identify the powerful experience of Spirit baptism with conversion to Christ and identification with him in water baptism. Moreover, Pentecostals who define Spirit baptism as postconversion still tend to see it as in some sense the fulfillment of conversion, for example, as a reception of the already indwelling Spirit within deeper dimensions of the soul or as the Spirit's gushing forth or "release" in life (following John 7:38).

Conversion and Spirit baptism were typically connected for Pentecostals to other aspects of Jesus' ministry as well. Significant as a framework for this larger understanding of the significance of Jesus for the spiritual life was the fourfold gospel of Jesus as Savior, Spirit Baptizer, Healer, and Coming King—adapted from Holiness leader A. B. Simpson's original configuration (in which Jesus' role as Sanctifier was second). The emphasis on Spirit baptism thus not only urged the newly converted to thirst for more of Christ in Spirit baptism and subsequent experiences of Spirit filling or renewal, but also asked them to expect from Christ tangible signs of the Spirit's work in healing and to yearn for the renewal of the world at Christ's coming. In the light of Spirit baptism, the hope for Christ's coming was typically seen as the fulfillment of a former and latter "rain" of the Holy Spirit upon the world. The former rain took place at Pentecost in Acts 2:4, and the latter rain was said to occur in modern-day revival or renewal movements that help to prepare the world for the triumph of Christ's return. As a result, Pentecostal spirituality, with its emphasis on Spirit baptism, implied a certain uneasy relationship with the doom scenarios of dispensationalist eschatology and the alleged failure of this eschatology to view the era of the Spirit as the chief characteristic of the eschatological age foretold in the OT (e.g., Joel 2:18–19). Pentecostal spirituality has thus encouraged a typically evangelical concentration on Christ as Redeemer of the world, but placed the weight of this concentration on the risen Christ alive in the churches today through the powerful presence and gifts of the Spirit.

This accent on the living Christ as saving, Spirit baptizing, and healing has had a significant influence on Pentecostalism globally, serving to inspire a holistic spirituality that emphasizes the deliverance and wholeness of persons in body and soul. Contemporary Pentecostal spirituality has thus emerged especially in the two-thirds world with accents that offer an alternative to the Western preference for the mind or the spirit over the body. Philip Jenkins rightly refers to the characteristic features of spirituality outside the West, where Pentecostalism has a strong presence, as enthusiastic, spontaneous, and supernaturalistic, looking "massively different from those of the older centers in Europe and North America." Pentecostal spirituality in places like Africa, Brazil, and South Korea is not only supernaturalistic but also "material," accenting the healing of the body from disease and evil spirits. The African fear of possession through ancestral spirits is allayed through the infilling of the liberating Spirit of God. Speaking in tongues as a sign of this infilling is often viewed as the groaning of the Holy Spirit from within the human soul for the total liberation of the body that will come at Christ's return. There is also a widespread accent in such places on prosperity through faith, viewing the height of the spiritual life as well-being or shalom.

More recent Pentecostal discussions on spirituality have highlighted the need to mine Pentecostalism's holiness roots so as to deepen the accent on spiritual power with purity of mind and heart. Some have also sought to augment the emphasis on prosperity with a deeper linkage between the work of the Spirit and the way of the cross or of costly discipleship, especially in solidarity with those who suffer. The Pentecostal focus on Spirit baptism can also be fruitfully expanded to involve all aspects of the life of the Spirit. The empowerment of the Spirit is seen here as prophetic in nature, witnessing to the discipleship and justice of the coming kingdom of God.

See also Charismatic Spirituality; Glossolalia.

For Further Reading: A. Anderson, *Moya: The Holy Spirit in an African Context* (1991); S. Chan, *Pentecostal Theology and Christian Spiritual Tradition* (2001); D. Dayton, *Theological Roots of Pentecostalism* (1988); D. Faupel, *The Everlasting Gospel* (1996); P. Jenkins, *The Next Christendom* (2002); S. Land, *Pentecostal Spirituality* (1992); W. Ma and R. Menzies, eds., *Pentecostalism in Context* (2008); F. Macchia, *Baptized in the Spirit* (2006); S. Solivan, *Spirit, Pathos, and Liberation* (1999); A. Yong, *The Spirit Poured Out on All Flesh* (2005).

Frank D. Macchia

Perfection

The terms *perfection* and *perfectionism* generate vigorous debate among theologians and laypeople alike, since they evoke for many the idea of sinless perfection. To be sure, Wesleyans and Calvinists differ in their understanding and articulation of this state. The most fundamental questions with which we are confronted remain: What does perfection entail, and how does one attain it (assuming that it is even attainable in this life)?

A NT verse directly tied to the notion of perfection is Matthew 5:48: "Be perfect, therefore, as your heavenly Father is perfect." The verse has not failed to arouse skeptical responses even from some sincere believers. Does Jesus actually demand this from all his followers? The answer is an unequivocal yes, but it requires that the command be understood in its broader setting. Jesus' call to perfection is located in the middle of his Sermon on the Mount (Matt. 5–7), which has as its immediate context the imperative to love and pray for one's enemies. In essence, if we strive to be like God who "causes his sun to rise on the evil and the good" (Matt. 5:45), we ought to love everyone without any favoritism—our enemies included. Viewed this way, the passage, in reality, is a call to demonstrate perfect love. Luke 6:36 ("Be merciful, just as your Father is merciful") reinforces this rather clearly. As John Stott puts it, we are to "love even our enemies with the merciful, the inclusive love of God." Simply stated, we are to love unconditionally.

In light of this interpretation, perfection then is really all about love and not some impossible moral standard we are to attain. This was how John Wesley, the most popular advocate of this controversial concept, understood its meaning. In the words of Gregory Clapper, it is "nothing more or less than the scriptural injunction to love all, including our enemies." Perfection is about full freedom to love and not necessarily freedom from flaws. On this, Wesley, at least, saw eye to eye with P. T. Forsyth, who insisted in *Christian Perfection* (1899) that love, and not sinlessness, mattered the most insofar as our maturity in the faith was concerned.

The Greek word *teleios*, often translated as "perfection," actually connotes completeness or whole-

ness. This was how the apostle James meant it in his canonical letter, wherein he summoned believers to be perfect, not lacking anything (1:4). James's call to perfection is a call to personal integrity in which there is congruence between faith and works. Evidently, for both James and Matthew, perfection was a reality to be experienced in the here and now. It referred to being in process rather than having already achieved an ambitious end goal. Thus, persons who are growing in love are moving toward completeness, wholeness, and integration—toward that "perfection" in holiness to which they were called.

See also Keswick Movement; Sanctification.

For Further Reading: W. Au and N. Cannon, *Urgings of the Heart* (1995); G. Clapper, *As If the Heart Mattered* (1997); W. Hernandez, *Henri Nouwen* (2006); P. J. Martin, *A Spirituality of Perfection* (1999); J. Stott, *The Message of the Sermon on the Mount* (1978); J. Wesley, *A Plain Account of Christian Perfection* (1952).

Wil Hernandez

Perfectionism

The concept of *perfection* may be understood as the goal of spiritual formation. Perfection indeed has biblical roots with the Greek word *telos*, sometimes translated in English as "maturity." Believers are encouraged to "go on to maturity" (Heb. 6:1) and to be perfect as their heavenly Father is perfect (Matt. 5:48). Yet the concept of achieving perfection has historically sparked controversy, forcing believers to grapple with both its definition and their responsibility to expend effort toward it. In Protestant circles, John Wesley regarded entire sanctification, or Christian perfection, as something achievable in one's lifetime.

Perfectionism, however, often has a negative connotation. As a psychological concept, perfectionism suggests a preoccupation with being perfect. An individual who struggles with pathological perfectionism will believe that anything they do that is not perfect is thereby unacceptable and a direct negative reflection upon themselves. Psychology has illuminated the potential danger of this form of perfectionism, even developing perfectionism scales to measure levels of perfectionism within individuals. Persons with standards that are impossible to live up to may suffer from low self-esteem, depression, personality disorders, and even suicide. Obsessive Compulsive Personality Disorder (OCPD) is a malady of the personality distinct from Obsessive Compulsive Disorder (OCD). OCD primarily involves obsessive thoughts and ritualized behaviors, which are repeatedly enacted to alleviate the anxiety created by the obsessive thoughts. OCPD, on the other hand, involves the entire identity of the person and is hallmarked by preoccupation with orderliness, perfectionism, and control. These individuals may exhibit extreme scrupulousness regarding issues of morality and tend to be both extremely self-critical and demanding and disparaging of others. Perfectionism, seen in this light, can obviously be detrimental to one's mental, spiritual, and relational health.

While spiritual formation of the believer obviously involves a strong intentional component, danger surfaces when perfection is regarded as the *telos* of human effort. If this becomes the case, pathological perfectionism may not be far behind. The pattern of mustering human willpower, failing, and continually repeating is a cycle that may lead to shame and despair. There are several antidotes to this pattern. First, it is important to differentiate *perfection* from *perfectionism*. Perhaps the two translations of the Greek word as either "perfection" or "maturity" suggest that perfection may best be understood not as a final or static state, but rather as an ongoing maturational process of grace. Second, the Scriptures contain assurances of God's unconditional acceptance of believers. "Christ died for the ungodly," and "while we were still sinners, Christ died for us" (Rom. 5:6, 8). God's acceptance is unconditional and prior to any "perfect" work

we might marshal. This leads to the third antidote to perfectionism — imputed righteousness. This concept affirms that the righteousness by which humans are made acceptable to God is a gift from God and cannot be earned. It is not human perfection that facilitates right relationship with God but solely God's great gift in Jesus Christ.

See also Sanctification; Wesley, John.

For Further Reading: M. Anthony and R. Swinson, *When Perfect Isn't Good Enough* (2009); B. Manning, *The Ragamuffin Gospel* (1990); J. Wesley, *A Plain Account of Christian Perfection* (1766); M. Wynkoop, *A Theology of Love* (1972).

Brad D. Strawn

Perpetua (c. 180 – 203)

Early Christian martyr; a young woman of noble rank, executed in Carthage under Emperor Septimius Severus. Vivia Perpetua, the twenty-two-year-old daughter of a pagan father and Christian mother, was among five Christians arrested in 203 for practicing the faith. Her companions, who were also executed, included Felicitas ("Felicity," her then-pregnant servant), Revocatus, Saturninus, and Secundulus. Saturus, a witness who perhaps completed Perpetua's record of their martyrdom, later gave himself up as well. Perpetua and the others were arrested, imprisoned, and wounded first by beasts (a boar, bear, leopard, and wild cow) before an amphitheater of onlookers, then slain by swords. *The Passion of St. Perpetua and St. Felicitas*, detailing the struggles faced and the spiritual triumphs gained before their martyrdom, was immediately treasured and remains the earliest surviving text from a female Christian writer.

Perpetua's testimony (possibly edited by her contemporary Tertullian) epitomizes the courageous faith of the early Christian church. It reveals how she regarded worship and prayer as appropriate Christian responses to oppression, tells about the visions given to her during her captivity, and discloses her "God before family" struggle over leaving her newborn son and embarrassing her pleading father. In one vision she ascended a bronze ladder leading to a heavenly garden, where she was welcomed and fed by a man "white-headed, and in shepherd's clothing." In another she witnessed her deceased brother being rejuvenated with flowing water.

Christians worldwide honor Perpetua and Felicitas each year on March 7, the day of their martyrdom. A basilica in Carthage marks the supposed site of their burial. But their best monument is the text identifying their passion with that of Christ: a willingness to suffer for a cause of surpassing value.

See also Martyrdom; Women.

For Further Reading: C. Robeck, *Prophecy in Carthage: Perpetua, Tertullian, and Cyprian* (1992); G. Streete, *Redeemed Bodies: Woman Martyrs in Early Christianity* (2009).

Rebecca Wilds Smith

Persecution

The Christian faith is seldom allowed to exist uncontested. Wherever they are a minority, or whenever their fortunes ebb and host cultures become inhospitable, believers can be opposed, discriminated against, persecuted, and even martyred. To be persecuted (from Lat. *persecutor,* "to pursue") is to be made to suffer because of one's convictions, to be harassed or punished in a manner designed to injure, grieve, or afflict. Persecution was the common experience of Christians for the first three centuries of the faith and remains the experience of millions of Christians today.

Jesus counseled his followers to anticipate such opposition (Matt. 10:16–39), reminding them that this was the experience of the prophets before them. He also promised that what they endured for his sake would be greatly rewarded in heaven (Matt. 5:12). The epistles of Peter were written to encourage believers facing persecution. The apostle cautioned them never to behave in ways that deserved hostility or warranted retributive reactions from others. But when persecution was truly undeserved, Christians were to be inspired by Jesus' heroic example of courage under fire, to be sustained by the longer view that culminates in glory, and to remember that even in the shorter term, persecution can function positively as a refiner of character.

In parts of the world that are safe and religiously tolerant, the Christian faith is often perceived primarily as a means of personal fulfillment or societal improvement. Where persecution is the norm, however, it is viewed more as a supernatural resource to sustain an alien sojourn and as a basis for hope in the world to come.

Sustained persecution constitutes a serious threat to the long-term survival of the church in any specific context. Christ promised that the church as a whole will survive, but the same guarantee was not extended to the community of faith in specific regions. For example, systemic Islamic persecution through the past thirteen centuries has gradually worn down the church in many regions of the Middle East—such as Egypt, Iraq, and Iran—where it once flourished.

Persecution fosters a spirituality that avoids excessive entanglement in the affairs of this world. It recognizes the importance of solidarity within the Christian community as a bulwark against opposition from outside and attributes special value to the virtues of unshakable faith, resilience, and courage—so that when the dust settles, the persecuted believers will still be found standing (Eph. 6:13).

While properly pursuing justice, perhaps the greatest spiritual challenge facing persecuted Christians is not to retaliate in kind. Jesus' call for his followers to love their enemies and to pray for those who persecute them (Matt. 5:44) is hard enough to comprehend and even harder to obey. It is possible to respond in love rather than hate, however, when the choice to love is framed as witness and as voluntary participation in the ongoing, costly but redemptive mission of Christ in the world.

See also Martyrdom; Suffering.

For Further Reading: P. Jenkins, *The Lost History of Christianity* (2009); S. Rutherford, *Letters* (1891); J. Ton, *Suffering, Martyrdom, and Rewards in Heaven* (1997); R. Wurmbrand, *Tortured for Christ* (2004).

Glen G. Scorgie

Perseverance

In Christian theology and spirituality, "perseverance" can refer to either an element of the doctrine of salvation or a Christian virtue. As a component of Calvinist theology, perseverance (or preservation, eternal security) refers to the belief that once individuals have been reconciled to God through faith in Jesus Christ, they will not and cannot fall from saving grace. God will graciously "keep" them until they die and enter into eternal life in his presence.

The Christian virtue of perseverance consists in continuing to follow and serve Christ despite the challenges of human finiteness and fallenness. In 2 Corinthians, the apostle Paul recounts the sufferings of persecution and then boasts, "When I am weak, then I am strong" (11:23–33, 12:10). Perhaps the best known expression of perseverance outside the Gospels is where Paul writes, "I press on to take hold of that for which Christ Jesus took hold of me.... One thing I do: Forgetting what is behind and straining toward what is ahead, I press on toward the goal to win the prize for which God has called me heavenward in Christ Jesus" (Phil. 3:12–14). Jesus himself provided the most important and profound incarnation of perseverance when he lived an entire lifetime in obedient submission to God the Father, being obedient even to death on the cross (e.g., Mark 14:32–42).

To persevere is not simply to continue. For example, to be stubbornly hard-hearted is not to persevere but rather to persist in rebellion against God. By contrast, to persevere is to continue in and for the good, to continue in and for God. Perseverance is complemented and supported by other Christlike virtues, such as obedience, humility, submission, dependence, self-control, patience, faithfulness, and hope. And as is the case with other virtues, perseverance is possible because of who God is and because of what he does. We can and should remain faithful because he is faithful. While perseverance entails a mysterious combination of human will and divine enabling, ultimately it is realized only by grace and through dependence on God.

As they have at many points in history, in many locations around the world today some Christians remain faithful to Christ in the face of life-threatening persecution. While the Scriptures do not call upon Christians to seek persecution, they do call upon Christ's followers to do as he did — namely, by divine grace and in the power of the Holy Spirit, remain true to the will of God the Father.

See also Reformed (Calvinsit) Spirituality.

For Further Reading: E. Peterson, *A Long Obedience in the Same Direction* (2000).

W. David Buschart

Personality and Temperament

Personality may be defined as an individual's characteristic and relatively stable pattern of thinking, feeling, behaving, and relating to others. While this definition emphasizes the uniqueness of each individual, theorists examine personality from both an idiographic perspective (that which sets a person apart from others) and a nomothetic perspective (that which is common to all humans). Additionally, while there is general consensus about the relative stability of personality traits across the lifespan (with traits being least stable prior to age two and most stable around age fifty), it is important to note that persons remain flexible and responsive to the demands of the situation; in other words, knowing a person's typical pattern of behaviors does not necessarily predict the person's specific behavior in a given situation.

Beyond these general considerations, psychologists greatly differ about the exact nature of personality. Psychologists have varied in considering how freely chosen or determined personality is, and how biological, intrapsychic, interpersonal, and environmental factors contribute to the development and structure of personality. Psychologists have also sought to accurately describe personality, with contemporary trait theorists frequently emphasizing the "Big Five" personality factors of openness, conscientiousness, extraversion, agreeableness, and neuroticism. These five factors have been observed cross-culturally and are relatively stable over the lifespan.

One factor that contributes to personality is temperament. Temperament, which may be defined as one's emotional reactivity, is apparent during infancy, beginning even in the womb, and is thought to be heavily biologically influenced. Temperament is typically understood as having at least three dimensions, including activity level (amount of energy exhibited in behaviors), emotionality (the intensity of one's emotions), and sociability (preference for affiliation or solitude). Research suggests that one's temperament during infancy significantly influences one's later behaviors and personality style. For instance, one's nervous system arousability (related to temperament) may be related to personality traits such as extroversion/introversion or shyness.

It is important to attend to temperaments and personalities when fostering Christian spiritual formation. Just as our unique temperament and personality influences our ways of relating to one another, it also influences how we relate to God. Moreover, just as Scripture reveals that there is both diversity and unity in regard to spiritual gifts (1 Cor. 12), we must also consider the diversity and unity of temperament and personality as they relate to spiritual formation and expression. Historically, various Christian traditions have recognized these differences in spiritual temperament and utilized systems such as the Enneagram, which proposes nine different spiritual temperaments and accompanying primary sins, or the quadrilateral model of Ignatian, Augustinian, Franciscan, and Thomistic personality types, based on the alleged temperaments of those spiritual giants.

Even though temperament and personality are fairly stable during adulthood, they are not necessarily neutral or always good. Like all aspects of our humanity, personality and temperament are fallen and distorted by sin. Even secular psychologists understand that some personalities are maladaptive or "disordered." While we do not choose our personality or temperament, we do exercise some control over some of the factors that can either entrench them or facilitate change over time. Personality qualities and temperament can certainly be examined for the extent to which they are compatible with the biblical picture of Jesus Christ. Scripture clearly indicates that believers are in the process of being renewed in the image of Christ (Col. 3:1–17). Yet such transformation will draw out rather than diminish the believer's uniqueness; indeed, God desires that each person become, more and more, the individual God created him or her to be. An essential task of spiritual formation should be discerning which qualities of one's personality and temperament should simply be accepted as the uniqueness of the individual and which should be submitted to God's refining fire.

Finally, research and common sense confirm that change happens only very slowly and requires patience and long-term persistence. Psychological theories differ in the proposed method for "healing" a personality disorder, but all agree that it is a very slow and arduous process with no guarantees of success. Where psychological theories may reach impasses with regard to the transformation of personality, Christian spirituality remains hopeful because of the transformative power of the Holy Spirit.

For Further Reading: M. Mangis, *Signature Sins* (2008); C. Michael and M. Norrisey, *Prayer and Temperament* (1991); E. Peterson, *A Long Obedience in the Same Direction* (2000), M. V. Rienstra, *Come to the Feast* (1995); R. Rohr and A. Ebert, *The Enneagram* (2001).

Michael Mangis and Brian Post

Personhood

See **Chapter 8.**

Peter of Damascus (or Peter Mansur; fl. 1156 – 1157)

Byzantine monk and spiritual theologian. Peter was a monk at the monastery of Areia in the Greek Peloponnese. Though he shares the family name Mansur with John of Damascus, Peter himself was not from Damascus, and the appellation "of Damascus" is the result of his being confused with John of Damascus. The brother of Leo Antzades, bishop of Nauplia and Argos, Peter is the author of two small texts on the Eucharistic body of Christ and two larger works of spiritual theology. In the *Admonition to His Own Soul* and the *Spiritual Alphabet*, both published in the *Philokalia*, Peter developed a full theology and program of the spiritual life. For Peter, and the Christian tradition in general, each person will ultimately experience either salvation or damnation (i.e., destruction). In Peter's thought, that which leads one toward salvation and away from destruction is a proper spiritual life. Hence, Peter's purpose in the *Admonition* is to explicate a proper spiritual theology. The spiritual life begins when sinful believers use their free choice and the natural knowledge given by God to respond to the voluntary and involuntary trials of life that are meant to be patiently endured. These trials and sufferings bring believers to a place where they must use discrimination to choose either destruction or salvation. Choosing destruction results in the cultivation of the passions (i.e., the vices), whereas choosing salvation results in virtuous living assisted by prayer, spiritual reading, bodily disciplines, and keeping God's commandments. The path of salvation ultimately results in *apatheia* and the contemplation of the triune God himself. Throughout this entire process, Peter writes, believers are assisted by God's grace. The *Spiritual Alphabet* consists of twenty-four discourses, each more or less dedicated to exploring further one of the subjects raised in the *Admonition*, with each discourse beginning with an introductory poetic verse that describes the content of the discourse. Unlike most Byzantine spiritual writers, Peter advocated that his spiritual program was intended not only for monks and nuns but for nonmonastics as well.

For Further Reading: G. Peters, *Peter of Damascus* (2010); idem, "Recovering a Lost Spiritual Theologian," *St. Vladimir's Theological Quarterly* 49 (2005): 437 – 59.

Greg Peters

Peterson, Eugene H. (1932 –)

Spiritual theologian and prophet-pastor. Peterson grew up in Kalispell, Montana, and studied at Seattle Pacific University and Johns Hopkins University. He was the organizing pastor at Christ Our King Presbyterian Church (PCUSA) near Baltimore, Maryland, where he served for twenty-nine years before becoming professor of spiritual theology at Regent College, Vancouver, Canada. In 1998 he became professor emeritus and returned to Montana with his wife, Janice, to write full-time.

His passion for biblically oriented pastoral work and spiritual theology has led to more than thirty-five books, including *Five Smooth Stones for Pastoral Work* (1980), *Working the Angles: The Shape of Pastoral Integrity* (1987), and *Under the Unpredictable Plant: An Exploration in Vocational Holiness* (1992). He is best known for *The Message*

(2002), a decade-long undertaking to transpose the original Hebrew and Greek text of the Bible into the language of today. His five-volume spiritual theology, beginning with *Christ Plays in Ten Thousand Places* (2005), is the harvest of forty years of careful pastoral work and fruitful scholarship.

Peterson's craftsmanship is indigenous to his faith in Christ. His Montana roots were nurtured in spiritual zeal, sensibility, and hard work. He combines three vocations in one: pastor, poet, and prophet. He is skilled in the biblical languages and intent on people hearing the Word of God. With his lyrical voice and lean frame, he has the look and sound of a prophet. His quick sense of humor and his deep regard for people and prayer underscore his primary vocation as a pastor. Peterson is focused on what it means to follow the Lord Jesus in ordinary life, and he is intent on reminding Christians, especially pastors, that the only work worth doing is rooted in the Word of God.

See also Reformed (Calvinist) Spirituality.

Douglas D. Webster

Petition

Among the various forms of Christian prayer, petition is fundamental. Briefly, *petition* refers to a prayer of request to God offered on behalf of oneself (me) or one's community (us), while *intercession* generally refers to a request on behalf of others. Petition is embedded in our very language for prayer. The English term for "prayer" derives from the Latin verb *precari*, meaning to beg or entreat. Likewise, Hebrew and Greek terms for prayer (*hitpallel*, *proseuche*) carry the notion of entreaty.

Petition is prominent in the biblical portrait of prayer. Jacob begged God to keep him safe from his brother (Gen. 32:9–12). Hannah petitioned God for a son (1 Sam. 1:11). Nehemiah requested that his hands might be strengthened (Neh. 6:9). Daniel offered "prayers and petitions" (Dan. 9:17–19). The Lord's Prayer is actually a series of petitions: "May your name be hallowed;" "May your kingdom come," etc. (Matt. 6:10–13). People came to Jesus repeatedly with requests for themselves and others (Matt. 8:2; Mark 5:23; Luke 18:38, 41; John 4:47). Jesus' High Priestly Prayer is a blend of petition and intercession (John 17:1–26). Paul urged that "requests, prayers, intercession and thanksgiving be made for everyone" (1 Tim. 2:1). The penultimate words of the Bible are petition — "Come, Lord Jesus" (Rev. 22:20).

The prayer of petition has also received significant treatment in the history of Christian spirituality; for example, in treatises by such chronologically diffused figures as Tertullian, Thomas Aquinas, and Karl Barth. Prayers of petition (along with those of intercession) have been vital in the history of Protestant evangelical tradition; for example, in Jonathan Edwards's call for an "explicit agreement and visible union of God's people in extraordinary prayer for the revival of religion" (1747), in E. M. Bounds's volumes on prayer in the early 20th century, and in Richard Foster's decision to place "simple prayer" as the first sample of Christian prayer (1992).

Petition is rooted in an understanding that the Creator and Redeemer of the world already offered himself to and for us prior to any petition we make. And it is God who made us to speak, to ask. God made us in relationship, dependent on divine mercies for our life. God commands us to make requests of him (Matt. 7:7; John 16:24; 1 Tim. 2:1; James 5:13). We are weak but he is strong. It is only natural, then, that we should call upon God when we need help. And God is more than willing to help us. The angel Gabriel informed Daniel, "As soon as you began to pray, an answer was given" (Dan. 9:23). "Ask and it will be given to you," Jesus promised (Matt. 7:7). "The prayer of a righteous person is powerful and effective," James assured his readers (James 5:16 TNIV).

Nevertheless, some prayers are *not* answered. Sometimes we perpetuate conditions that hinder our prayers (Ps. 66:18; Prov. 1:28–31; 21:13; James 4:3; 1 Peter 3:7), and sometimes God does not answer our prayers as we wish and no explanation is given

(Ex. 33:18–20; 2 Cor. 12:7–10). Our place is to receive God's promises in their appropriate contexts, to persevere in prayer, to examine ourselves humbly, and to trust. As we learn our way into a life of asking, we will begin to walk into a life of receiving.

See also Intercession.

For Further Reading: K. Barth, *Prayer* (2002); R. Foster, *Prayer* (1992); E. Howard, *Praying the Scriptures* (1999); T. Tiessen, *Prayer and Providence* (2000); S. Tugwell, "A Dominican Theology of Prayer," *Dominican Ashram* 1, no. 3 (1982): 128–44.

Evan B. Howard

Pietism

Pietism signifies a Continental European movement launched in the late 17th century to reclaim the experiential dimension of the Christian faith. It constituted a religion of the heart, where the heart is understood as the controlling and affective center of the self. Originally Pietism was a response to the "barrenness" of Protestant Scholasticism, the brutality of the concurrent religious wars, and the resultant atrophy of spiritual vitality. A longing surfaced to restore the fervency and purity of authentic "heart Christianity." This wistful yearning was expressed early on in Johann Arndt's *True Christianity* (1605–1610), which tapped into neglected late-medieval mysticism to encourage a genuine godliness manifesting itself in active faith.

Philip Jacob Spener was the principal founder of Pietism. In his little classic, *Pia Desideria* (1675), he defined the essence of its message. Spiritual renewal was to be advanced by a "new birth" experience, followed by a commitment to holy living and loving service to others. All this could best be achieved through more diligent study of Scripture, lay empowerment and participation, a charitable spirit under fire, and greater attention to the inner life from which all else issued.

August Hermann Francke helped advance Pietism even further along through his energetic philanthropic work at the University of Halle. He promoted as well as modeled a commitment to evangelism, social outreach, and an experiential approach to learning. The essence of the Pietist movement is captured in a poem written for the funeral service of a young student there: "What is a Pietist? One who studies God's Word, and also leads a holy life according to it.... Piety must first of all nest in the heart."

According to the Pietist vision, a religion that "nests in the heart" is experiential and sincere, holistic in the scope of what it touches, affective no less than cognitive in its lived experience, affectionate in the context of community, and compassionate in its response to human need. The metaphor of "heart" should be understood to connote all these qualities.

The Bible was important to the Pietists because it affirmed and mysteriously stimulated these very qualities of spiritual life. The experiential dimension of Pietist spirituality is epitomized by Francke's conversion experience at Lunenburg, Prussia. There he called upon the God he knew not and became animated with an overwhelming joy, with praises on his tongue. Yet by holding firmly to the authority of the Bible, Francke and his associates kept their experience nourished by and tethered to orthodox Christian belief.

The Pietists also believed that Christian growth could best occur in small, devout Bible study and prayer groups (*collegia pietatis*). The intimacy of these gatherings reflected the close, relational disposition of Pietism, as well as its suspicion of structures of formal power. Laypersons were affirmed, and ministers were admonished to participate humbly as equals. There the spirituality of the heart could express itself as affection, as walls of privilege were dismantled so that familial-like relationships could flourish. The small gatherings Spener organized became known as the "Frankfurt conventicles," while in Sweden similar objectives were achieved through intimate läsare ("[Bible] readers") communities.

This spirituality of the heart also involved an intentional, devout, and holy lifestyle. Francke's essay "Rules for Living," for example, emphasized individual discipline in the areas of work, learning, and health. Likewise, Scandinavian Pietism pursued a combination of conversion, sanctification, and righteous living. The Pietist pulpit emphasized conversion as a crucial beginning but never as an end. Listeners were to examine their hearts, meditate on God's Word, and find their way to heaven.

A religion of the heart also responded to the world's needs with compassion; it was spirituality with a social conscience. Compassion, rather than duty or merit, fueled the Pietists' vigorous endeavors in evangelism, mission, and social service. Francke created an orphanage, homes for widows, facilities for people with disabilities, and educational institutions, and encouraged medical facilities that implemented hygiene reforms. Likewise, George Mueller, a later British Pietist, created an orphanage for the poor in Bristol, England. The Pietist movement was often directed at working-class and new immigrant populations. The social gospel teachings of Walter Rauschenbusch, who had served a church of German Baptist immigrants in New York City, were expressed in *Christianity and the Social Crisis* (1907). He believed that Christians needed to help encourage economic and social justice.

Rather than leave the church, Pietism began as an effort to "leaven" it with experiential Christianity—through, among other ways, a unique Pietist style of sermon and song. True religion started with getting one's heart right with God, and the tests of such belief were service to God and living as Christ followers. Pietism has had a diffuse influence, and among others the Moravian Brethren and their leader, Count von Zinzendorf, have been important developers (through hymnody and missions) and mediators of its distinct charism. At a Moravian meeting in London, John Wesley, the founder of Methodism, found *his* heart strangely warmed, and through the Methodists several Pietist themes were relayed to English-speaking Christianity in Scandinavia and beyond. The Pietist impulse surged again during the nineteenth-century Romantic era; it naturally aligned with the latter's disdain for rationalism and positive emphasis on feelings and the heart. By doing so, it helped significantly to shape the ethos of the transatlantic Second Evangelical Awakening and the larger evangelicalism that grew from it. Pietism's legacy includes attentiveness to Scripture, prioritization of the new birth, nonhierarchical fellowship, and insistence on an inner life that will necessarily manifest itself in righteous living and outward-looking service.

The original Pietist impulse mutated in a myriad of directions, and not all of them were helpful. Where Scripture was abandoned, it devolved into a fluid subjectivity. The liberal theology of Friedrich Schleiermacher, the son of a Pietist minister, is sometimes cited as proof that Pietism can be a slippery slope. In some cases, the Pietist emphasis on feeling has led to anti-intellectualism, its attention to the inner life to privatized faith, and its passion for holy living to unattractive moral fussiness. Yet where it remains tethered to the vitalizing dynamic of Scripture, it continues to embody a fervent, relational, and holistic spirituality that resonates well with the spiritual longings of contemporaries disillusioned with rationalism, formal religion, and the depersonalizing dynamics of modernity.

See also Arndt, Johann; Methodist Spirituality; Moravian Spirituality; Quaker Spirituality.

For Further Reading: A. de Reuver, *Sweet Communion* (2007); E. Griffin and P. Erb, eds., *The Pietists: Selected Writings* (2006); *The Pietists: Selected Writings*, CWS (1983); F. E. Stoeffler, *The Rise of Evangelical Pietism* (1965); C. J. Weborg, "Pietism," *Christian History* 5, no. 2 (April 1986): 17–18, 34–35.

G. William Carlson

Piety

Piety denotes godliness, reverence, dutifulness, and devotion (from Lat. *pietas*, "devoutness"). In

Greek it is *eulabeia*, from *eu* ("good") *lambanō* ("to take hold"). Piety literally means taking hold of the things of God, that is, taking personal responsibility for one's inherent duty to a holy God. In common parlance, the word *piety* is often used loosely as a synonym for spirituality. As there are numerous types of spiritualities, so there are various kinds of piety—some more philosophical or relational even than religious (Platonic piety, aesthetic piety, filial piety, Buddhist piety, Jewish piety, etc.). Piety can be feigned, and often the incentives to do so seem irresistible. Nonetheless, genuine Christian piety has to do with the condition of the heart, the inner person. Calvin defined it as "that reverence joined with love of God which the knowledge of his benefits induces." The seventeenth-century Pietists, for whom piety by some definition was obviously paramount, emphasized the heart and holy living over right doctrine about secondary matters of the faith. In the 18th century, Charles Wesley challenged believers to "unite the two so long disjoined, knowledge and vital piety." In Anglicanism, Catholicism, and Lutheranism, piety (reverence) is seen as one of the "seven gifts of the Holy Spirit." In Christian art, the pieta is a form intended to evoke precisely this response. In the NT, cognates of the word *piety* are in Luke, Acts, 1 Timothy, and Hebrews. In Acts 3:12, Peter proclaimed that the miraculous healing of the lame beggar had nothing to do with Peter's personal piety. By contrast, that God heard Jesus' prayers had everything to do with Jesus' piety (Heb. 5:7). Piety is important, not only at an individual level, but also for intentionally formative communities and institutional cultures.

Sarah Sumner

Pilgrimage

Pilgrimage is religiously motivated travel to experience God or locations where others encountered God, in hopes of being transformed. It is often physical, involving extraordinary expense and exertion.

Ancient Jews made three annual pilgrimages to Jerusalem, during which they sang ascent psalms. Jesus, his disciples, and Paul continued such observances. The magi are sometimes regarded as the first Christian pilgrims.

By the 3rd century, certain believers headed to the wilderness. These desert fathers and mothers bore witness to God's purposes and reign. Early Christian pilgrims visited these exemplary teachers. Desert saints influenced Celtic Christians centuries later: many wandered the earth proclaiming the gospel and trusting God's providence.

By the 4th century, Christians began visiting Palestinian sites associated with Jesus. Most famous were Helena, Constantine's mother, and Egeria, a Spanish nun. Such journeying seems obvious now, but it was a startling innovation. Prior to that, Christians had long avoided Palestine, believing that it was cursed for being the location where Jesus died. In medieval times, the primary pilgrimage destinations were Palestine, Rome, and Santiago de Compostela in Spain. Not everyone could go on such extensive expensive journeys. Labyrinths and Stations of the Cross emerged as local and affordable alternatives. Some religious orders, Franciscans and Dominicans, wandered as a means of missions and evangelism. Itinerant ministry was later embraced by Methodists.

According to Morinis, motivations for Christian pilgrimages include *penitence*, pondering one's sins; *devotional*, encountering God or a shrine associated with the faith; *initiatory*, expecting to be changed; *instrumental*, looking for results, perhaps a healing; *normative*, following a ritual calendar; and *wandering*, having no predetermined goal.

Victor and Edith Turner called pilgrimage "externalized mysticism." Medieval mystics and contemplatives journeyed inward. But pilgrimage was a more accessible way to experience God.

There were always pointed critics, including Gregory of Nyssa (4th century), Wycliffe (14th century), and Erasmus (15th century). Reformers, such as Luther, tapped into long-standing suspicions, legitimately warning against idolizing humans, works righteousness, or confining God to particular places. They denounced a corrupt system of indulgences. Furthermore, some pilgrims were merely escaping duties, responsibilities, and commitments.

After the Reformation, pilgrimage came to be understood less as external experience and more and more metaphorically. Hymns are full of such imagery. Seventeenth-century Puritan John Bunyan titled his classic allegory *The Pilgrim's Progress.*

Yet many Christians now go to the Holy Land to experience places where Bible events happened, to enliven scriptural imagination and understanding. Some tour groups offer baptism-type services in the Jordan River. Christians also visit locations pertinent to their tradition, for example, Geneva, Wittenberg, Canterbury, Aldersgate, or Azusa Street.

Tom Wright shows how evangelicals discarded pilgrimage. He makes a biblical and theological case for reclaiming this practice. Benefits include excellent ways to teach and learn, stimulating prayer, and opportunity for growing in faith and faithfulness.

Pilgrimage often increases as churchgoing diminishes. Europe's six thousand pilgrimage sites draw as many as 100 million people annually. Prominent centers include Medjugorje, Lindisfarne, Iona, and Taizé. Expanding pilgrimage may help reinvent and reinvigorate Christianity.

See also Journey, Spiritual; Labyrinth.

For Further Reading: A. Boers, *The Way Is Made by Walking* (2007); A. Morinis, *Sacred Journeys* (1992); V. Turner and E. Turner, *Image and Pilgrimage in Christian Culture* (1978); N. T. Wright, *The Way of the Lord* (1999).

Arthur Paul Boers

Platonism and Neoplatonism

Platonism and Neoplatonism have provided the intellectual framework for much of Christian the-

ology and spirituality over the past two millennia. To explain the faith, Christians have always, in the words of Dominic O'Meara, "availed themselves of the intellectual means which appeared to be suitable … [and] developed by the philosophical movements of their time." Although Aristotelian logic has taken center stage in Christian theology since the Reformation — and although modern believers are often unaware of, or opposed to, the Platonic conceptualization employed by the church fathers and medieval spiritual writers — the influence of Platonic categories can hardly be overstated.

Platonic thought emphasizes the One from which all else emanates. Rejecting the polytheism of the ancient world, the Greek philosopher Plato described that One as Truth, Being, the Source of all, and especially the Good (in the *Republic*) and the Beautiful (in his *Symposium*). Reality resides in the unseen realm of Ideals, while the material world is a mere reflection, as portrayed in the allegory of the "Cave." According to Plato, our human soul is eternal, while our bodies are part of the corrupt physical world. Awakened by an encounter with Beauty, we must free ourselves from temporal attachments, purify ourselves morally and intellectually, and journey toward a contemplative vision of the Good and union with the One.

Philo, first-century Jewish scholar from Alexandria, wedded Middle Platonism with biblical theology, stepping away from "emanation" terminology by emphasizing *creatio ex nihilo* — creation from nothing — and identifying Plato's One with Yahweh, the personal God of Scripture. Yearning to know God, we embark on a journey of joy in which we seek God for God-self, not for anything he does for us. That search causes us, like Moses, to enter "thick darkness" (Ex. 20:21). Because God is incomprehensible, knowledge of the Holy is possible only through the divine Logos, God's self-revealing Word. "Philo develops an understanding of the Word that sees meditation on Scripture, that is, God's self-disclosure, as central to the soul's search for God," observed Andrew Louth. "This is quite new — and something that the Christian Fathers were to take up and make their own."

In Neoplatonism, the theme of spiritual pilgrimage sharpened with the third-century philosopher Plotinus emphasizing emanation (*proodos*) from the One and eventual return (*epistrophe*) to that One. Renouncing self-focus and contemplating the One/Good/Beautiful, three steps precede ecstatic encounter with the One: detaching from the sensible world, turning within, and gazing upward. Plotinus's pupil Porphyry (d. c. 305) organized his teacher's works into the *Enneads* and closely paralleled Christian thought but ultimately repudiated Christianity. Proclus (d. 485) clarified evil as movement away from the One and conveyed the Neoplatonic framework to the Christian Middle Ages.

While Platonic thought underwent many variations, its essence can be summarized in three movements: all things emanate from the One; they are sustained by that One; eventually fragmentation and multiplicity will cease as all things return to union with the One. A similar threefold pattern is affirmed in the NT as the apostle Paul presents the gospel to the philosophers in Athens (Acts 17:22 – 31) and praises God because all things are "from him and through him and to him" (Rom. 11:36). In threefold movement, the universe is created by God through the Word (John 1:1 – 3); it is sustained by his Word (Heb. 1:3); and all creation will be gathered together in Christ (Eph. 1:10) and presented to God who is all in all (1 Cor. 15:20 – 28). The schema likewise applies soteriologically. As emanation moves away from the One, so our fallen affections wander from God. Through Christ's atoning work on the cross, we turn from our temporal orientation and self-absorption in passionate love toward God (Col. 1:15 – 20). While union with Christ begins at conversion, Christ himself prays for us to become one with him and the Father in the same oneness that they share (John 17:21).

Although Gnostic teachers utilized versions of the Platonic paradigm, early Christian apologists and theologians employed this framework to explain their faith to contemporaries, especially intellectuals who viewed reality through this cosmological lens. Virtually all of the church fathers — from Clement, Origen, and the Cappadocians to Augustine — structured their seamless theology/spirituality along Neoplatonic lines. In particular Pseudo-Dionysius viewed all creation descending from God in ordered hierarchies (see especially his *Divine Names*), and believers ascending back through our kataphatic knowledge of God into an apophatic encounter with the Divine, who is super-essential and beyond being itself (see *Mystical Theology*). Dionysius solidified the Neoplatonic framework in Christian spirituality, and his thought was selectively employed by John Scotus Eriugena, the Victorines, Eckhart, Ruysbroeck, the author of *The Cloud of Unknowing*, Teresa of Avila, John of the Cross, Jean Gerson, Nicholas of Cusa, and others.

In explaining Christian theology, however, Platonic thought has limitations. While humanity bears the *imago Dei*, we are not of uncreated substance nor endowed with a divine spark. Spiritual progress is not an escape from the material world; rather, our bodies are part of God's good creation (Gen. 1) and central to our life on earth as well as our spiritual growth. Although spiritual formation moves toward a greater realization of our union with God, we remain created beings and God remains God. When these distinctions are ignored, Neoplatonism degenerates into works righteousness, panentheism, or a pantheism espoused by gnostic and New Age teachers.

Nevertheless, appreciating Platonic thought is necessary to understand the church fathers and most of the spiritual classics. Evangelicals can affirm many aspects of the Platonic framework. All that exists comes from God who is Spirit (John 4:24), goodness, and truth. In the excessive materialism of contemporary consumer culture, we need a greater focus on interiority and the ultimate realities of the spiritual world. All creation groans to be released from its current futility (Rom. 8:19 – 22).

Although God is beyond comprehension, we can know his unfathomable love (Eph. 3:14–19). Finally, the Christian life was never meant to end with justification, but we are called to spiritual growth that can be depicted as an ascent of love, drawing closer to God as we are transformed from glory to glory into his likeness (2 Cor. 3:18).

See also Plotinus; Pseudo-Dionysius.

For Further Reading: A. Armstrong and R. Markus, *Christian Faith and Greek Philosophy* (1960); H. Blumenthal and R. Markus, eds., *Neoplatonism and Early Christian Thought* (1981); C. Jones et al., eds., *The Study of Spirituality* (1986); A. Louth, *The Origins of the Christian Mystical Tradition* (1981); J. Macquarrie, *Two Worlds Are Ours* (2004); B. McGinn, *The Foundations of Mysticism* (1991); D. O'Meara, ed., *Neoplatonism and Christian Thought* (1982); R. Wallis, *Neoplatonism* (1972).

Glenn E. Myers

Plotinus (c. 205 – c. 270)

Founder of Neoplatonism. Plotinus was born in Egypt and educated in Alexandria under Ammonius Saccas, who also taught Origen. After his education, Plotinus traveled east, intending to study in Persia and India, but settled eventually in Rome. There he began a school of philosophy based on Plato's ideas and wrote his major work, the *Enneads* (six groups of nine treatises), which was compiled by his student Porphyry.

Plotinus developed a hierarchical structure of reality, in which the three primary hypostases are One, Intellect, and Soul. The One is simple and perfect, and emanates into Intellect, or Mind, which in turn emanates into Soul, which generates the physical world. Plotinus had lasting influence on such Christian thinkers as Augustine, Boethius, Gregory of Nyssa, Pseudo-Dionysius, Aquinas, and many of the Protestant Reformers.

It is his first hypostasis—the One—that is most significant for his understanding of spirituality.

The One is the perfect, immutable, and transcendent source of everything; it is completely beyond being and therefore beyond description. Hence, the best way to describe the One is by describing what it is *not*—this is often called apophatic language within Christian theology. Furthermore, according to Plotinus, everything in the world—even matter—comes from the One. Against the Gnostics, Plotinus upgraded the physical world by focusing on the perfection of existence. Since matter exists and comes from the One, matter cannot be evil. Rather, evil is a privation—a lack of the Good, or the One. This privative idea of evil later influenced Augustine's notion of evil. Sin, from a Neoplatonic perspective, is a turning away from perfect, immutable goods to imperfect, mutable goods.

Another significant impact of Neoplatonism on Christian spirituality can be seen by an examination of the concept of Beauty and its place on the ladder of ascent to the divine. In his *Symposium*, Plato had argued that we love beautiful things because they participate in the form of Beauty. Thus, a love of physically beautiful bodies will direct the lover to Beauty itself, as an intelligible form. Plotinus used this to argue that beautiful things in the world draw our souls upward, toward the eternal and immutable. The One draws us to itself by this process. For Neoplatonic Christians, all human souls long to escape the changeable, physical world and return to God.

See also Platonism and Neoplatonism.

For Further Reading: L. Gerson, *Plotinus* (1994); D. O'Meara, *Plotinus: An Introduction to the Enneads* (1993); J. Rist, "Plotinus and Christian Philosophy," in *The Cambridge Companion to Plotinus*, ed. L. Gerson (1996), 386–414.

Carrie Peffley

Poetry and Poetics

Poetry and poetics can heighten our sensitivity to language as a pervasive feature of shared human identity and our prospects for spirituality. The modern elevation of poetry at the expense of prose obscures the fact that certain features that we might associate with poetry have historically been thought to be qualities of language more generally. Where we might be tempted to treat the poetic as a special case, and either revere it unduly or consign it to oblivion, we ought perhaps to allow it to illumine our wider understanding. For instance, we may most readily perceive the role of language in making truth in ways that coordinate with but cannot be reduced to rational argument in poetic lines like the following from George Herbert's "Easter Wings":

> Lord, who createdst man in wealth and store,
> Though foolishly he lost the same
> Decaying more and more,
> Till he became
> Most poor.

We may experience anxiety and physical constriction, including loss of breath, from the fact that, in conjunction with the conceptual content, the lines lose words and rhythm, and the syntax and musicality remain incomplete. The poetry makes us feel the foolishness of our loss (and sin) in our bodies. All language to some degree works in ways beyond conveying information, though it takes a poetic sensibility to help us feel and know things in ways we tend to forget we know them. The power of poetry to make meaning in unexpected ways adds to its potential to disrupt complacency or rationalistic pride, both important dimensions of spirituality. Poetry also reminds us of the complex ways in which language shapes and sustains the communities in which we always already find ourselves. Poetic language can encourage and bear witness to an active and shared spirituality. Bud Osborn, a Christian poet who identifies with the downtrodden of Vancouver's Downtown Eastside, gives a voice to those who have no voice by directly quoting them, inviting us all to see the poetry of their language, its capacity to challenge our patterns of thought, its active power. Such poetry attests and enacts the solidarity of those just trying to survive, and the affirma-tion of language is the affirmation of hope rooted ultimately in the One who gives us all a voice and the church in which to talk. This link with action shelters poetry from those who would enlist it for a bloodless pseudo-contemplative spirituality.

In the 19th century, for people like Matthew Arnold, poetry became synonymous with high culture and with a vague spirituality in its own right, a cluster suitable to replace Christianity, with which secular humanists had become disenchanted. In an influential sermon published as "Learning in Wartime," and citing Arnold specifically, C. S. Lewis offered a two-edged counterclaim: that cultural work becomes spiritual only on the condition of being offered to God; and also, invoking Thomistic reasoning, that it is our nature to participate in culture, that God makes no appetite in vain, and that he exploits natural materials to supernatural ends. Far from accepting a spirituality that took humans as an ultimately self-contained point of reference, Lewis recalled an older world in which God has ordained participation in culture as a means of grace.

A Catholic contemporary of Lewis applied similar thinking specifically to poetry. Between medieval and nineteenth-century thinkers, Galileo and Descartes had inaugurated habits of thinking that privileged quantifiable dimensions as the essence of things. For Jacques Maritain, the poet seeks rather to make visible the relationality within and between things. Two features of poetry in particular, its inner musicality and metaphoricity, suggest complex harmonies and resonances both between things and between knower and known that hint of metaphysical depth. Canadian Christian poet Margaret Avison gives us a wonderful contemporary expression of this immanent transcendence in her poem "The Hid, Here":

> The Milky Way
> end over end like a football
> lobs, towards that still
> unreachable elsewhere
> that is hid within bud and nest-stuff and
>   bright air.

Avison's bizarre metaphor suggests a hiddenness both "out there," beyond the Milky Way, and "here," in a mundane object like a football, a coinherence including bud and nest-stuff, and air as well, all together sustained by the "hid within." And the lines, even without rhyme or obvious metrical pattern, catch and suggest a rhythm in and between objects, implicitly shared by poet and reader too. For the Christian poet, this relationality is grounded ultimately in the triune God who declares himself to be for humanity, and through humanity for all of creation, in the incarnation.

This understanding of activity and the vital connections between things in reality manifests itself paradoxically in an objective attitude toward art on the part of both Lewis and Maritain, with implications for the way we approach spirituality. Both stressed that one has the freedom and the responsibility to pursue beauty for its own sake. It can be difficult for us as Christians, as moderns, to avoid looking for the purpose of things. Yet if we try to make our cultural efforts work out to moral or useful conclusions, we have failed to attend to the reality before us. In the words of Lewis, we in effect "offer the author of truth the unclean sacrifice of a lie," the lie being a failure to attend. Similarly, Maritain argued in his Mellon lectures that the artist must guard against "desertion of the work as master object to which the operative intellect is vowed." Pursuing beauty for its own sake releases us into our humanity experienced as the site of God's gracious, self-giving love. We can in no way divorce that spirituality from all the details of our sheer human being.

At the same time, when we attend to the reality before us and it draws us in so that we recognize its beauty, we recognize simultaneously that it gives more than it has. For Lewis, we can pursue knowledge and beauty "for their own sake, but in a sense which does not exclude their being for God's sake." For Maritain, the awareness of beauty is "the end beyond the end" of poetry. It involves coming into relation with an aspect of reality that could not be known in any other way, certainly beyond functionality. The very condition of appreciating beauty, not looking for a message, is the condition of possibility for its telling us of metaphysical depth. The response of praise and thanksgiving — not to a fact but to a pervasive reality — is natural; the psalter is central to our experience as the deepening of our place in the rhythms and relations of things in God. "Glory be to God," Gerard Manley Hopkins begins one of his poems, instantly assimilating his voice to the discipline and shape of the language of orthodox praise, with which the poem also closes. Then, randomly: ". . . for dappled things." He might have completed the syntactical unit any which way, for, as he goes on to say:

> All things . . .
> He fathers-forth whose beauty is past change:
> Praise him.

Even if we should speak of pain and loss, as inevitably we must, we do so with an expansive resurrection hope of wholeness, harmony, and victory. We return to Herbert's poem:

> With thee
> O let me rise
> As larks, harmoniously,
> And sing this day thy victories:
> Then shall the fall further the flight in me.

Poetic language, in ways we cannot reduce to concepts, reminds us that we participate in a divine reality that we cannot control and that gives us flight.

See also Imagination; Literature and Spirituality.

For Further Reading: D. Barratt et al., eds., *The Discerning Reader* (1995); T. Eagleton, *How to Read a Poem* (2007); M. Edwards, *Towards a Christian Poetics* (1984); D. Jasper, *The Study of Literature and Religion* (1989); S. Prickett, *Words and the Word* (1986); R. Williams, *Grace and Necessity* (2005).

Norm Klassen

Pope John XXIII

See **John XXIII.**

Pope John Paul II

See **John Paul II.**

Porete, Marguerite

See **Beguines.**

Postmodernity

Postmodernity encompasses a broad spectrum of social and cultural perspectives. In architecture the term describes an eclectic combination of many styles in a single structure. Among artists, it designates a movement away from the formal structures of modernist art to forms that celebrate a variety of new and old styles. Postmodern literary deconstructionists claim that readers play a greater role in creating the meaning of a text than the author does. Some philosophers and theologians describe postmodernity in epistemological terms — as the loss of modernity's pursuit of rational certainty in favor of an approach to human knowledge that considers the influences and limitations of contextual factors like culture and language. To experience the world as a constellation of decentralized entities — rather than a static, coherent whole that is united by a single metanarrative — is to experience postmodern consciousness.

Stephen Toulmin offers an insightful account of the modern-postmodern story. He sees two distinct "origins" of modernity. The first was the literary/humanistic phase, which occurred during the late Renaissance (c. 1460 – 1630). It stressed four types of practical knowledge: the oral, particular, local, and timely. Social and political upheaval erupted in the early 17th century. Modernity's second beginning, the philosophical/scientific phase (c. 1630 – 1960), emerged in response to this conflict and was initially conceived as a means to bring together warring factions on a common foundation of rationally adduced facts. This second phase shifted the focus of knowledge away from the practical to the abstract. The oral gave way to the written, the particular to the universal, the local to the general, and the timely to the timeless. According to Toulmin, postmodernity is essentially modernity's coming full circle — a "Re-renaissance" in which the decentralizing themes of modernity's first origin have once again become ascendant.

The postmodern renaissance is more than a recapitulation of the social and ideological conditions that immediately preceded the Age of Reason. It is assimilative, critiquing but still including all things modern. Postmodern identity both depends on and distinguishes itself from modernity. Postmodernity does not abandon the written word; it adapts it to the digital era along with old and new forms of orality. Postmodernity exists among such universalizing forces as national and international conflict, advances in science and medicine, industrial and economic interdependencies, transcontinental air travel, mass media, McDonald's, and the Internet. Yet it rejects utopian notions that the world should be a melting pot that reduces all social and cultural particularities into a single, nondescript amalgam.

Postmoderns live in a world of complexity, brought on by the ubiquity of otherness — sometimes celebrating, sometimes chaffing against ethnic, linguistic, and convictional differences. Postmodernity does not dismiss "the general" but tends instead to focus on both global and local realities together, in mutual complementarity. Our understanding of a given locale, one might say, is keenest when viewed globally. In a word, postmodernity is a *bricolage* of the modern era's two beginnings and all that has transpired since then.

Some people are more imbued with postmodern consciousness than others, but even among those who claim to reject it, postmodernity is having an impact. The new renaissance has proved to be fertile ground for an assortment of spiritualities. Modernity's scientific worldview, which predominated in Western culture since the Enlightenment, has in many circles yielded to reality narratives that take the supernatural for granted. The most significant characteristic of postmodern Christian spirituality is the rejection of modern dualisms, which divided into separate spheres the physical and spiritual, secular and sacred, individual and collective.

Present-day evangelicals are diverse. It is more accurate to speak of evangelical spiritualities than a single postmodern evangelicalism. Theologian Robert Webber identified three primary evangelical groups at the beginning of the 21st century: traditional evangelicals, pragmatic evangelicals, and younger evangelicals. Traditionalists embrace modernity's appeals to science and reason and are committed to the post–World War II ideal of a stable society. Their influence peaked in the 1970s and early 1980s. They are generally resistant to change. Pragmatists came of age during the revolutions of the 1960s and initially reacted against the traditionalism of their predecessors. Eventually they emerged as a fresh religious force, adapting the best practices of business and creating market-driven megachurches. Pragmatist evangelicals, while still influential, appear to have reached their zenith in the mid-1990s.

Young evangelicals, born in the 1980s, 1990s, and early 21st century, are natives of postmodernity. Theirs is a spirituality of symbiotic tensions. They prefer to celebrate paradox rather than resolve it. They prefer "both-ands" to "either-ors." They embrace both mystery and certainty, experience and reason, practice and theory, tradition and innovation, story and proposition, convictional passion and open-minded dialogue, global sensitivity and lively cultural engagement. They are eclectic in their use of ancient and contemporary modes of worship. They are holistic in their use of the disciplines to enact embodied spirituality. They are mystical in their experience of Christ's presence, which transcends knowledge. And they are missional in their efforts to participate in the work of Jesus Christ, who goes before them — into the world he calls them to change.

See also Modernity.

For Further Reading: C. Conniry, *Soaring in the Spirit: Rediscovering Mystery in the Christian Life* (2007); S. Grenz, *A Primer on Postmodernism* (1996); L. Sweet, ed., *The Church in Emerging Culture: Five Perspectives* (2003); S. E. Toulmin, *Cosmopolis: The Hidden Agenda of Modernity* (1992); R. Webber, *The Younger Evangelicals: Facing the Challenges of the New World* (2002).

Charles J. Conniry Jr.

Poverty

The link between poverty and spirituality must be examined in light of the contemporary struggle with poverty and a conception of spirituality as fullness of life before God. The discussion below clarifies the term *poverty*, describes the link between poverty and the pursuit of perfection, redefines poverty as a spiritual value, and affirms the need for Christian spirituality to engage with poverty.

Poverty denotes a condition of material lack experienced by those labeled poor. It is a condition of powerlessness, disempowerment, oppression, and entanglement. The word *poverty*, therefore, is best employed to refer to a "collective phenomenon" and not to individuals being poor. The persistence of the phenomenon has become a global concern; in 2005 the United Nations launched a program to eradicate it. Liberation theologies have emerged to champion the cause of the poor and argue for God's preferential regard for them. Though nations and organizations disagree on the causes, measurement, and methods for alleviating and eradicating poverty, no one disagrees that poverty is an unacceptable phenomenon.

In most religions, material possession is viewed as a hindrance to perfection; hence, a "spiritual" person is one who has taken a vow of poverty. In Asia, priests, monks, and nuns are identified as poor because they possess little and depend on charity. Poverty is regarded as a spiritual value and a way to perfection. In the Christian tradition, radical asceticism and renunciation of possessions dominated the teachings on perfection from the 2nd to the 14th centuries. Religious orders require a vow of poverty for admission. Jesus was the model because he "became poor" to enrich others (2 Cor. 8:9) and he had "no place to lay his head" (Matt. 8:20). The explicit link between poverty and perfection comes from Jesus' challenge to the rich young man to give all to the poor in exchange for heavenly treasures (Matt. 19:21). In 1209 Francis of Assisi heard these words preached and accepted them as a call to live a life of poverty.

A recent study noted by Kenneth Baxter Wolf asks whether Francis of Assisi and others like him should be labeled as poor. The struggles of the forced poor and the voluntarily poor are not the same: the former are under daily pressure to seek deliverance from poverty, while the latter only seek happiness in their faith. Hence, the use of the term *poverty* in connection with the pursuit for perfection has to be redefined lest the destructive nature of poverty is belittled. The Bible does warn of the danger of materialism: material satisfaction may lead to pride and idolatry (Deut. 8:6–20; Prov. 30:8–9), and an inordinate desire for worldly things will destroy the effectiveness of God's Word in one's life (Mark 4:19). However, it is one thing to say that materialism hinders spiritual growth, and it is another to say that poverty contributes to spiritual growth. The poor should not be asked to accept their condition as a means of growth.

The Bible does not teach that material poverty is a spiritual value. Proverbs recognizes that poverty may cause one to steal and so dishonor God (30:9). Deuteronomy has two seemingly contradictory statements on the poor in the same chapter: "There should be no poor among you ... in the land the LORD your God is giving you" (15:4) and "There

will always be poor people in the land" (v. 11). One way to explain the contradiction is in the human failure to practice justice in wealth distribution. The messianic age is one of abundance ("feeding on the wealth of nations"), and its coming is "good news to the poor" (Isa. 61:1–6). The NT emphasizes the need for an inner transformation evident by outward action, which includes helping the poor, for example, Zacchaeus (Luke 19:1–9) and the early church (Acts 4:34–35). Jesus' challenge to the rich young man should be interpreted in the light of the description that he "had great wealth" (Matt. 19:22). Paul's reference to Jesus' "becoming poor" was given in the context of his call to practice generous giving (2 Cor. 8–9). Nevertheless, poverty may still be regarded a spiritual value in a metaphorical sense, the sense present in Jesus' words, "Blessed are the poor in spirit" (Matt. 5:3). The poor with an attitude of dependency on God do have much to teach those who seek perfection.

Christian spirituality requires engagement with the forced poor in the world. As spirituality is about a full life lived before God, Christians must be concerned that those trapped in poverty are given the opportunity to possess such spirituality themselves. As Jesus "impoverished" himself to save humankind, those whose spirituality is defined by and founded on Jesus must likewise have his attitude — that is, to identify with and help those who cannot help themselves. Furthermore, it is the Holy Spirit who enables Christians to act wisely, sacrificially, and generously when encountering the poor.

See also Contentment; Franciscan Spirituality; Greed; Money; Suffering.

For Further Reading: C. Boff and G. Pixleys, *The Bible, the Church, and the Poor*, trans. P. Burns (1989); J. Dixon and D. Macarov, eds., *Poverty: A Persistent Global Reality* (1998); B. Myers, *Walking with the Poor* (1999); G. Stanczak, *Engaged Spirituality* (2006); R. Van Der Hoeven and A. Shorrocks, eds., *Perspectives on Growth and Poverty* (2003); K. B. Wolf, *The Poverty of Riches* (2003).

Sunny Boon Sang Tan

Praise

The biblical understanding of praise encompasses a broad range of dynamic and expressive themes related to the revealed person and work of God. These themes include the recognition and proclamation of esteem, as well as various expressions of honor, heartfelt thanks, and gratitude, particularly as they relate to God's righteousness, faithfulness, saving acts, preservation, and glory (Ex. 15:2; Deut. 32; Isa. 12). There is an interactive relationship between these various themes as they intersect with life circumstances in both predictable and surprising ways.

The Psalms serve as a timeless offering of praise and thanksgiving that trace the many contours of human experience (Pss. 22, 66, 68, 71, 103, 106, 145, 148, 150). A paradigm emerges that defines praise as a responsive and thankful orientation toward God in and through all seasons and circumstances of life. This particular paradigm is displayed admirably in the lives of the apostles (2 Cor. 1:3; 1 Peter 4:16; see also Acts 16:25; 2 Cor. 2:14). Scenes of the heavenly throne room present an overwhelming and eternal declaration of praise centered on the holiness and victory of God (Isa. 6; Ezek. 1–3; Rev. 5:12–13; 7:12; 19:5).

There are two primary domains related to the understanding and practice of praise: form and substance. Forms of praise include private devotional as well as corporate expressions of worship, whether liturgical, traditional, or contemporary. The substance of praise incorporates three interrelated dimensions: the *cognitive or rational* dimension (an understanding of God and his ways), the *affective or emotional* dimension (a personal experience of God and willing expression of gratitude), and the *transcendent or supernatural* dimension (dynamic interaction with the invisible God). These dimensions interact in ways that are personally and holistically transformational as they impact identity, refine purpose, and find expression in lived actions.

A certain transformational progression emerges that is related to this unique dynamic of human and divine interaction. A common catalyst for spiritual transformation is the personal realization of God's unique holiness and splendor. This may lead to a dramatic realization and awareness a person's true condition, now brought to light in God's presence. This moment of epiphany can create a rather disorienting and temporarily debilitating dilemma. There is also a realization of God's comprehensive salvation and redemption in our lives (Eph. 1:1–14; 1 Peter 1:3–9). This leads to a grateful acknowledgment and personal experience of God's grace, accompanied by expressions of delight, deep gratitude, and heartfelt joy.

Cultivating the spiritual practice of praise involves a deliberate attentiveness to the nature, acts, and ways of God. Developing an active awareness of how God is working is a vital aspect of personal spiritual formation. This attentiveness results in well-placed and spontaneous expressions of appreciation leading ultimately to a confessional affirmation of belief and personal commitment in the quest to place oneself more firmly in the center of God's will.

See also Adoration; Celebration; Doxology.

For Further Reading: R. Webber, *Worship Old and New* (1994); N. T. Wright, *For All God's Worth* (1997).

Gino Pasquariello

Praise Music

Contemporary praise and worship music, which sprang to life through Calvary Chapel's Maranatha! Music, the Vineyard Music Group, Integrity Hosanna! Music, and a host of related artists, has grown to national prominence among evangelical Christians. At its core, contemporary praise music is a confessional celebration and proclamation offered by the community of Christians while utilizing popular and culturally relevant musical forms. The movement offers answers to a number of questions: What is the role of the local church in bringing people into God's presence? Does real worship emphasize sensitivity and flexibility or structure and order in its design—or both? What best fosters authentic personal engagement in a worshipful experience?

Exploring the history of corporate evangelical worship reveals a robust expression as congregations gather to proclaim the Word and celebrate covenant. Evangelicals have historically embraced a range of styles, from more to less formal, and including liturgical, traditional, and contemporary expressions. Contemporary praise music emphasizes cultural relevance as one of its top priorities. This is followed closely by the desire to inspire passionate celebration and to foster personal intimacy and interaction with God. To the latter end the immediacy of God's presence is always emphasized.

Congregational praise is to be understood as a response to God's revealed identity (Ps. 22:25–26; 138; 139), as an expression of gratitude (Luke 7:47; 17:11–19), as an attribution of worth (John 20:28; Rev. 4:11; 5:12), and as an opportunity to invite God's power and presence personally and corporately. At their core, such "spiritual songs" constitute a quest for synthesis: a blend of Spirit and truth, of spirituality and doctrine, of expression and knowledge (John 4:19–24). Is creating a service that is musically "relevant" to the prevailing culture thereby "selling out" to that culture? Not necessarily—one of the hallmarks of evangelical practice is the impulse to transcend established forms, including the content and form of traditional corporate music.

Seeking to cultivate a Godward life is also a high priority in praise and worship music. Primary goals include developing openness, vulnerability, receptivity, and dependence, as well as sensitivity to God's presence, and vital reorientation. A certain progression of song selection is typically employed to facilitate this process, beginning with praise and thanksgiving for who God is and what he has done.

Then follow songs emphasizing confession (being open and self-revealing with God) and contemplation (reflecting on the nature, will, and ways of God). Finally, there is a call to exemplify God's character and purposes.

The need for contextualized worship remains as the Christian worldview continues to collide with ever-changing cultures. Addressing a postmodern world requires engagement in a process of reembracing mystery, moving from individualism to community, encouraging holistic participation and involvement, and utilizing more multisensory and aesthetic approaches. Leading God's people into worship requires addressing three indispensable questions of the spiritual journey: Who are the people? Where are they going? And how will they get there? Answering these questions and engaging authentically in this sacred activity involves an ongoing reflection and prayerful discernment of the doctrinal, sociological, and cultural dimensions of music and worship.

See also Hymns.

For Further Reading: J. Frame, *Contemporary Worship Music* (1997); B. Kauflin, *Worship Matters* (2008); R. Webber, *Ancient-Future Worship* (2008).

Gino Pasquariello

Prayer

See **Chapter 23.**

Prayer Meeting

Early Christian believers assembled at the traditional Jewish hours of prayer (Acts 3:1). Ever since, corporate prayer has been central to the life of the church—whether as part of regular Sunday worship services and liturgies, the disciplined rhythms of monastic life (for which Benedict established a healthy balance of prayer and work—*ora et labora*), or the fixed communal prayer practices of lay renewal movements like the Brothers and Sisters of the Common Life.

Prayer meetings per se, however, constitute a distinct form of group prayer—one characterized chiefly by broad participation in extemporaneous petition and intercession. Such prayer meetings have been foundational to the church since its inception as 120 gathered on the day of Pentecost (Acts 1:14–2:41), and later an angel released Peter from prison as the Jerusalem Christians interceded for him (Acts 12:1–17).

And prayer meetings have continued to play a central role in the life of the church. During persecution believers met, and continue to meet, in secret for prayer. The Pietist renewal within Protestantism centered about small groups that congregated for prayer and Bible study, functioning as *ecclesiolae in ecclesia*—little churches within the church. The Moravians established an unbroken prayer chain for over a century, and at a Moravian prayer meeting in London, John Wesley felt his heart "strangely warmed." In turn the Methodist movement built upon local "class meetings" where believers gathered to pray and study Scripture.

In the Great Awakening, Jonathan Edwards identified corporate prayer as a critical prelude to God's bestowing of revival, and in the following century, Charles Finney sent intercessory groups to each city for weeks preceding his crusades. The famous student-led Haystack Prayer Meeting of 1806 is widely regarded as the beginning of the American Protestant missionary movement, and intercessory missionary prayer meetings continue to be key to Christian endeavors in global evangelization (like the Back to Jerusalem movement in China).

The great Prayer Meeting Revival of 1857–1858 blazed across the cities of America and Britain as churches filled daily for prayer. This lay revival witnessed thousands of businesspeople congregate at noon in churches of all denominations, and its flames ignited further renewal around the world. At a Kansas prayer meeting on New Year's Day in 1901, the Pentecostal movement was born.

Large and small, prayer meetings continue to be the locus of spiritual renewal. In many local churches, prayer groups help participants to personalize their faith, and small groups provide accountability and mutual prayer support among believers. Around the globe, concerts of prayer assemble Christians of all denominations to intercede for their cities and world evangelization.

See also Intercession; Petition; Small Groups.

For Further Reading: J. Edwards, *The Works of Jonathan Edwards*, vol. 2 (2004); K. Long, *The Revival of 1857–58* (1998); J. Orr, *The Fervent Prayer: The Worldwide Impact of the Great Awakening of 1858* (1974).

Glenn E. Myers

Prayer of the Heart

An ancient form of prayer whereby the heart and mind of the believer are equally engaged. Its beginnings are found in the Christian writings of the 4th and 5th centuries, yet it became strongly emphasized by the Hesychast authors of the 13th and 14th centuries. This form is founded on the belief that prayer is not simply an intellectual activity. Rather, prayer should involve the whole person, especially the moral and spiritual center of a human being—the heart (Prov. 4:23). God dwells in the human heart, for Jesus revealed that the kingdom of God is found within us (Luke 17:21). As such, the prayer of the heart is the prayer of the Holy Spirit (Rom. 8:17–26). Yet we are fragmented people in a hectic world who need help in finding our hearts, that we may live there in the kingdom of God. The prayer of the heart enables us to make this journey; it seeks to move past all distractions and preoccupations in order to concentrate solely on God. Often, believers will repeat the name of Jesus while bringing heart and mind together before him, in order to center themselves on Christ, "the author and perfecter of our faith" (Heb. 12:2). As Christ is the focus of this form, the prayer of the heart is commonly associated with the Jesus Prayer and centering prayer.

Since the prayer of the heart is the most personal of prayers, it is often the most silent. We are overwhelmed in God's presence and rendered speechless. Yet our wordlessness is prayer, just as the Holy Spirit's intercession is wordless groaning (Rom. 8:26–27). According to Jean-Nicholas Grou, the heart prays, and it is the voice of the heart to which God listens, and it is the heart that he answers. For Richard Foster, the prayer of the heart is a prayer of intimacy, for the heart speaks like a child to God the Father. The prayer of the heart is an act of absolute trust in God's goodness and sovereignty as we offer our torn hearts and minds to God for his healing and comfort. As Henri Nouwen reminds us, when we engage in the prayer of the heart, God's heart becomes one with ours, enabling us fully to love. Thus, it is the prayer of the heart that empowers us to love both God and others with all our being, rendering us full citizens in the kingdom of God (Deut. 6:5; Luke 10:27).

See also Breath Prayer; Hesychasm; Jesus Prayer.

For Further Reading: R. Foster, *Prayer* (1992); J. Grou, *How to Pray*, trans. J. Dalby (1982); H. Nouwen, *The Only Necessary Thing* (1999).

Johanna Knutson Vignol

Prayers for the Dead

Prayer for the dead is the spiritual practice, found mostly in the Roman Catholic, Eastern Orthodox, and Anglican Churches, of praying for those who have died. The practice is tied to the doctrine of the communion of saints, which affirms that the connection the faithful have in Christ is not severed by death. The Roman Catholic tradition further connects the practice to the doctrine of purgatory, which asserts that those who have died must go through purification or expiatory suffering before being united to God. The Eastern Orthodox Church does not hold strictly to a doctrine of purgatory but nevertheless affirms an intermediate state between death and union with God.

There is evidence in the deuterocanonical works to suggest that Jewish people around the time of Jesus prayed for the dead. Scriptural evidence is not definitive; however, several passages in Paul allude to some kind of practice that may have developed into prayer for the dead (1 Cor. 15:29). The earliest archaeological and historical sources attest to the importance of prayers for the dead in the early church, and the subsequent Christian traditions practiced prayer for the dead until the Reformation, after which most of the Protestant churches rejected the practice.

Most Protestants, having rejected the notion of purgatory, are inclined to regard the purposes of such prayers as superfluous. For the church traditions that do practice it, prayer for the dead has spiritual significance. It bolsters belief that through Christ God has overcome the power of death such that the communion that believers have in Christ is maintained even after death. Furthermore, it is a unique way for Christians to express their faith that God will bring those who have died to rest in him until they are resurrected at the judgment day. While such Christian traditions differ on whether the prayers of the faithful are efficacious in helping the dead attain heaven, praying for the dead remains for them a special expression of faith in God's power over death in the midst of grief and pain.

See also Afterlife.

For Further Reading: P. J. Toner, "Prayers for the Dead," in *CE*.

Joshua Dean

Preaching

Preaching is the Spirit-shaped dialogue, grounded in God's Word, between Christ and his church. The apostle Paul's charge to Timothy was emphatic: "In the presence of God and of Christ Jesus.... Preach the Word" (2 Tim. 4:1–2). The preacher's ultimate motivation is not befriending the seeker, convincing the skeptic, or helping the believer; it is to preach the Word in the body of Christ, the church, before the presence of God, the Father, Son, and Holy Spirit. Preaching is used by the Spirit of Christ to call believers out of the small world of their own making and into the large, grace-filled world of God's salvation. The Spirit of Christ shapes the congregation through the proclamation of the Word of God. Through preaching believers hear the Word together.

Preaching in the evangelical tradition emphasizes the good news that through Christ God provides redemption. The curse of sin and death is overcome through unmerited divine grace received through faith in him. Building on the Reformation heritage, evangelicals declare that people are saved by faith in Christ alone, yet they also stress that such saving faith is never alone. Preaching salvation includes deliverance from evil, freedom for righteousness, and devotion to the truth. In the Spirit, preachers preach personal and social reconciliation and transformation through Christ.

Comprehending the fullness of the gospel story is imperative for preaching the Word in the Spirit. If the Bible came to us as lists and lectures, we might be excused for neglecting the overarching gospel story, but instead it has come in a myriad of genres. All Scripture is God-breathed, directed toward Christ, and useful for equipping all God's people for every good work (2 Tim. 3:16; cf. Luke 24:27). The defining elements of spiritual preaching are often assumed to be spontaneity and enthusiasm, but they are actually found in the synergy between the hard work of preparation, heartfelt receptivity to the Spirit's leading, and self-effacing proclamation.

Good preaching draws the people of God into facing honestly the dissonance between the Word of God and the ways of the world. Tension is created by the clash between God's work of redemption and humanity's fallen condition. It generates the Spirit-inspired passion of both preacher and message. Preaching has been defined as truth conveyed through personality. That is to say, the tension evident in the text runs right through the pastor. If the textual tension does not resonate with the preacher so that the preacher is disturbed and delighted, comforted and challenged, the preacher is not ready to preach. If he or she has not experienced the passion of the passage nor understood the dissonance between the Word of God and the human condition, chances are the congregation will not either.

The cultural captivity of the sermon is largely an undiagnosed problem. Jesus accused the religious leaders of his day of possessing the Scriptures but not really hearing the voice of God (John 5:37–40). The scribes were steeped in the Scriptures; they memorized large portions of it and eloquently flattered it. Yet they molded the Bible into their image. Instead of participating in the drama of salvation history, they stood apart from it and ultimately against it.

Spiritual preaching requires hard work and discernment; it requires prayerful, thoughtful attention to God's overarching salvation history, the text itself, and the people to whom one is preaching. Preachers stand on the fault line between the mystery of God and the mess of the human condition. They let the message of Christ first dwell in them deeply (Col. 3:16), the way Jesus, the living Word, enveloped himself in human flesh. Preachers look to the Incarnate One for their communicational model and pedagogical impact (John 1:14). The Word internalized, embodied, and mediated is the dynamic of true preaching.

Good preaching refuses to dumb down the gospel, manipulate emotions, or shrink-wrap the whole counsel of God into a quick snack. Preaching in the Spirit for the sake of Christ and to the glory of the Father is a labor of love that calls for meditation, faithful exposition, and prayer. And all good preachers point people to Christ, not themselves. They cultivate a humility that resists being the center of attention. There is also urgency and immediacy in good preaching that defies a flippant and casual culture. Preachers extend themselves as Jesus did. They lovingly appeal to listeners, call them to reason, and plea for dialogue (Isa. 1:18). Jesus' way of relating to people excludes self-conscious superiority and manipulation. Like him, good preachers proclaim without the presumption of agreement or the cockiness of assured success; in short, they refuse to diminish their listeners.

The apostle Paul would rather have died than allow anyone to deprive him of the right to preach the gospel (1 Cor. 9:16). He felt the power of this imperative in his soul; to preach the gospel was his greatest privilege and his most profound obligation. Freely to obey this imperative is to be both consumed and fulfilled; it is to be both "poured out like a drink offering" (Phil. 2:17; 2 Tim. 4:6) and paraded in "triumphal procession in Christ" (2 Cor. 2:14).

See also Call to the Ministry; Worship.

For Further Reading: W. D. Edgerton, *Speak to Me That I May Speak* (2006); E. Peterson, *Eat This Book* (2006); L. Ryken and T. Wilson, eds., *Preach the Word* (2007); R. Smith, *Doctrine That Dances* (2008).

Douglas D. Webster

Predestination

Central to the biblical understanding of God is his sovereign determination of time and eternity, expressed by the theological terms *predestination* and *election*. More specifically, predestination refers to God's free and unshakable commitment to grant salvation to certain human beings and the precise ordering of the means and events whereby this will take place. The OT root of this teaching is found in God's choice of Israel (Deut. 14:2; Isa. 41:8–9). In the NT the concept is applied to both events (Acts 4:27–28; 1 Cor. 2:7) and individuals (Mark 13:20; John 15:16; Rom. 8:29–30; Eph. 1:5, 11; 2 Tim. 2:10; 1 Peter 1:1–2). The most systematic discussion of the doctrine in the Bible is Romans 9–11.

Out of a desire to avoid the fatalism of Graeco-Roman astrological thought, Stoicism, and Gnosticism, early patristic reflection upon this subject tended to stress human freedom in a way that avoided the radicalism of the biblical position. The first truly predestinarian theologian after the NT era was Augustine, who, over against Pelagius's unbridled exaltation of human freedom, stressed that since the fall, men and women are free only to sin. Ultimately, salvation, freedom from the servitude of sin, is a matter of the divine will. For Augustine, predestination also entailed the reprobation of the nonelect, which caused ongoing controversy after Augustine's death. Initial resolution of this controversy came with the Second Synod of Orange (529) that reaffirmed a mild Augustinianism without the North African's teaching on predestination to perdition.

However, Augustine's teaching on double predestination continued to have its adherents throughout the Middle Ages—for example, Bede and Gottschalk (c. 804–c. 869). It was robustly asserted by all of the leading Reformers and is enshrined in the Reformed Westminster Confession of Faith (1647). It is noteworthy that at roughly the same time as the publication of this confession, Cornelius Jansen, the Roman Catholic bishop of Ypres, was propounding a similar view in his learned *Augustinus* (1640).

The doctrine of predestination is intended to promote reverential awe of God and humility and to provide deep comfort, but in the hands of some proponents it has proven to be spiritually enervating. Emphasis on predestination to the exclusion of human responsibility led some in the 18th and 19th centuries, for instance, to seriously neglect the duty of evangelism and to develop a deeply introspective piety. As the Baptist theologian Andrew Fuller responded, however, the doctrine teaches an unfathomable truth, but not in such a way as to negate the need for passionate evangelism or to clear sinners of their responsibility to respond to God. No wonder, he concluded, the apostle ended his discussion of predestination in Romans 9–11 with a doxology.

See also Will of God.

For Further Reading: P. Jewett, *Election and Predestination* (1985); P. Thuesen, *Predestination* (2009); D. Wallace, *Puritans and Predestination* (1982).

Michael A. G. Haykin

Presence of God

The life-giving presence of God, whether hidden or manifest, is central to the content and practice of Christian faith. As the Rule of Benedict claims, it is by faith that we believe God is everywhere and in all things. Yet he is most actively and benevolently present where he is most welcomed, and especially therefore in the lives and circumstances of those who belong to Jesus Christ. Christian growth brings with it a deepening consciousness and discernment of God's active presence in one's own life, the believing community, and indeed the world. Through Christ men and women can enter their Creator's presence with joy, confidence, and hope, and in that holy presence invariably experience an intensified desire and demand to live holy lives.

The presence of God is depicted in the OT in a variety of ways. God walked in the garden and later allowed Enoch to walk with him. In the life of Joseph, God's presence meant protection in times of trouble and blessings in times of peace. In the book of Exodus, the divine presence was demonstrated in intervention at the Red Sea, then made visible as cloud and fire, and seen again in the radiant glory occupying the tabernacle and later the temple. As a blessing upon their obedience, and employing imagery of Eden's restoration, God covenanted to walk among his people and be their God (Lev. 26:12). In the NT, God is present by his Spirit, and especially so when two or three gather together in Christ's name (Matt. 18:20) or when disciples are willing to take the gospel to the ends of the earth (Matt. 28:19 – 20). Even today the best endorsement any church can receive is when an outsider observes that "God is really among you!" (1 Cor. 14:25; cf. Isa. 45:14).

Throughout the Psalms, and perhaps especially in Psalm 139, God's omnipresence is celebrated. No one can hide from it or escape it, even if he or she wished to do so. The better response, however, lies in the opposite direction — in pursuing an ever-deeper apprehension of the divine presence. The cultivated art of "dwelling" — making one's home — in the presence of God has been famously explored in Brother Lawrence's *The Practice of the Presence of God* (1691). In this widely circulated little classic, Lawrence encourages the people of God to sustain — lovingly, intentionally, and without ceasing — an attentiveness to God's close presence. The believer understands that in this presence, and ultimately nowhere else, is fullness of joy; at God's right hand are the deepest and most enduring pleasures of all (Ps. 16:11). For this very reason, some of the most difficult seasons on the Christian journey are when God seems absent and the believer starkly alone.

Spiritual writers often speak of putting oneself in God's presence, and many, including Ignatius Loyola and Francis de Sales, have offered practical guidance on how best to "locate" oneself there. Such strategies commonly include willingness to relinquish all known sin and live in love, detachment from distractions and preoccupations, contemplation of the person and work of Christ, centering prayer, and active listening for the still, small voice. Above all, such writers — and supremely the mystics among them — have emphasized *intensity of desire* as key to entering and remaining in God's presence, remembering always that above all "it is good to be near God" (Ps. 73:28).

See also Attentiveness; Fear of the Lord; Wonder.

Joseph Shao

Present Moment

The spirituality of the present moment is embodied in the desert fathers' constant exhortation to "pay attention." When inattentive, one is blind to the omnipresent life of God within oneself, the human community, and the created world.

The very existence of spiritual disciplines implies that the Christian must consciously strive to be attentive or present, and that this state of being does not come naturally. In *Awareness* (1992), Anthony de Mello describes our default condition as that of being spiritually "asleep." As we grow in awareness of the state of our heart and the influx of thoughts and emotions, we slowly awake from a life consumed by unconscious fantasies and worries.

Christian mystics have always affirmed that God is equally present in every moment of time and that the ongoing challenge for pilgrims of faith is to appropriate this presence. Similarly, Jean-Pierre de Caussade, in his classic *The Sacrament of the Present Moment* (1741), stresses that there is no "exalted" moment in the future when God will be more present, just as there was no moment in the past when God was not.

According to the Benedictines, who for more than fifteen centuries have been following a rhythm of work and prayer, all time is spent equally in the presence of God, whatever the task. And, as the renowned Carmelite, Brother Lawrence, famously put it in *The Practice of the Presence of God* (1692), "the time of business does not with me differ from the time of prayer." Because every moment is God's moment, the discipline severs all false dichotomies between sacred and secular.

By living in the present moment, one neither naively denies the pain of past wounds nor heads irresponsibly into the future; rather, in an attentive present, one works with the past and plans for the future but does so consciously, in the company of the redeeming Christ.

See also Attentiveness; Brother Lawrence.

For Further Reading: R. Foster, *Prayer* (1992); T. Merton, *Wisdom of the Desert* (1960).

Diane S. George Ayer

Pride

Pride is self-exaltation with correlative depreciation of others and a denial of God's help. It is the essence of sin and the root of all other sins according to Evagrius, Cassian, Gregory the Great, Augustine, Dante, Luther, Calvin, and others. It is related to "vainglory," the difference seeming to be that pride is directed against God, while vainglory is focused on one's relation with others.

With pride it is the comparison that builds up the person. The OT words for pride that derive from the root *allh* convey the sense of scorn or arrogance (see Ps. 10:4; Prov. 3:34). In the NT the word *hubris* is often translated "insolence" (see Rom. 1:30). R. Roberts demonstrates that there is no fixed term for pride in the NT.

Pride is a subtle sin: We are usually unaware of it, and if we are, it is the most difficult to admit, even when pointed out, because we imagine ourselves to be more important than we are, and our culture values self-esteem and fails to appreciate humility (see Schimmel's discussion).

Early monastics warned that pride is difficult to defeat because, unlike other sins that can be opposed with targeted remedies, pride swells when it successfully encounters its spiritual enemies.

Theologically, pride involves the denial of one's finitude, creatureliness, and contingency (see Rom. 1:18 – 28). We end up denying our need even for God. Practically, pride gives rise to moral and social injustice, since it is essentially competitive, springs from self-love, and depreciates others. This can even involve a "collective egotism," manifesting itself as racism, nationalism, class snobbery, and the like (see Prov. 16:18 – 19; Jer. 50:31 – 34; Ezek. 16:49 – 50).

The countervailing virtue to cultivate is humility — acknowledging the truth about oneself. So the "cure" begins with self-awareness. Since this requires healthy introspection, a mentor or spiritual director is helpful. This does not preclude a legitimate self-love that recognizes one's rightful place in relation to others and God. This might help guard against false humility that can actually become a way of being deceitful and proud. Though legitimate expressions of assertiveness, aggressiveness, initiative, self-confidence, and self-esteem are not precluded, Cassian suggested we avoid doing anything for praise as our motive and not be overly bothered with insults or contempt.

See also Humility; Sins, Seven Deadly.

For Further Reading: J. Cassian, *The Institutes*, trans. B. Ramsey (2000); R. Roberts, "The Vice of Pride," *Faith and Philosophy* 26, no. 2 (2009): 119–33; S. Schimmel, *The Seven Deadly Sins* (1992); Thomas Aquinas, *Summa Theologiae*, 2.2 QQ 161–62.

Dennis Okholm

Primal Religions, Spirituality of

The neologism "primal religion" refers to the religious practices of native inhabitants of Asia, Australia, Africa, the Pacific, and the Americas. The advantage that the adjective *primal* has over *traditional* is that it steers away from the suggestion that the religions it designates are frozen in the past; at the same time, it emphasizes their originary nature in relation to global religions such as Judaism, Christianity, Buddhism, and Islam. Despite the distance that separates the regions where they are practiced and despite their irreducible differences, primal religions have some common characteristics. At the risk of being simplistic and or reductionist, three of these characteristics follow.

First, in primal religions there is no firm separation between the profane and the sacred, the natural and the supernatural; consequently, "natural" objects like trees, stones, and mountains may be seen to possess "supernatural" power. The material world is influenced by immaterial forces conceived as gods and spirits. Spirituality pervades all of life, for everything that is participates in the universe's life force. In the words of Thorpe, this "awareness of a holistic unity which prevails when harmony and wellbeing are experienced" constitutes the religious core of any primal group. In the cosmogony that sustains primal religions, a person is, according to Zahan, at once "image, model, and integral part of the world in whose cyclical life he senses himself deeply and necessarily engaged." Among the Bantu in Africa and natives in North America, the land owns the community as much as the community owns the land. Most important, however, is the fact that whatever anyone does within this universe can potentially upset the harmony of the whole.

Second, mediation plays a central role in primal religions. While everything that exists shares in the universe's life force, not everything holds this power to the same degree. There is a hierarchy among existing things, from the Supreme Being to the lesser divinities and the ancestors, all the way down to human beings, animals, trees, and inanimate objects. However, in this order of things, a time, place, object, or individual may embody more power than others. Such times, places, objects, or persons are deemed sacred and serve as contact points with the supernatural for individuals seeking to access a higher power for themselves or their community.

Third, in primal religions, cosmic myths and the rites and rituals that reenact them play a central role in identity formation. Myths form the foundation of life. They validate particular religious practices and explain core beliefs as well as the surrounding natural world. They also provide support and justification for the prevailing social order. As Eliade has pointed out, cosmic myths generally look backward to a time of beginnings, viewed as a sacred time, "a time before the profane world of the present obscured reality and truth." In primal societies, oral traditions ensure the transmission of myths from one generation to another, and dreams serve in their actualization for the present. Rites and rituals are, above all else, means of maintaining harmony or restoring harmony in a primal society. Their role is particularly prominent in those moments of transition that mark the cycle of life (birth, puberty, marriage, and death) or the annual cycles of nature.

The spiritualities of primal religions and Christian faith are both similar and different. In both cases, there is dissatisfaction with what is, a dissatisfaction expressed in a constant quest for deeper and more meaningful relationship with higher forces. The desired goal in both cases is harmony and well-being, which one achieves only through contact with super-sensible realities. Through spiritual exercises, one seeks a transfiguration of one's terrestrial condition.

At the same time, the two spiritualities are opposed on at least two points. To repeat, what stands out in the spirituality of primal religions is its holistic approach, which knows no distinction between the sacred and the profane. Furthermore, the spirituality of primal religions is decidedly anthropocentric. Dealing with African traditional religions, Zahan, who at times overstates his case, says, "It is not to 'please' God or out of love for God that the African 'prays,' implores, or makes sacrifices, but rather to become himself and to realize the order in which he finds himself implicated." The latter point finds support in the often-observed retreat of the divine in primal religions, whereby the Supreme Being may be spoken of as an idle god. This retreat in no way constitutes an impediment for spirituality. In fact, as Zahan puts it, "it could be said that the intensity of religious emotions [in primal religions] is directly proportional to the human soul's feeling of separation from God."

Some scholars are intrigued by the preparatory role that primal religions seemed to have played in the expansion of Christianity in primal societies. Others, including Harvey Cox, are becoming bolder in their assertions of links between primal spirituality and aspects of Christian tradition and practice, most notably in the Pentecostal-charismatic stream.

See also African Indigenous Spirituality; Native North American Spirituality.

For Further Reading: D. Burnett, *World of the Spirits* (2000); H. Cox, *Fire from Heaven* (1995); S. Gill, *Beyond "The Primitive"* (1982); P. Hiebert et al., *Understanding Folk Religion* (1999); J. V. Taylor, *Primal Vision* (1973); S. A. Thorpe, *Primal Religions Worldwide* (1992); H. W. Turner, *Living Tribal Religions* (1971); D. Zahan, *The Religion, Spirituality, and Thought of Traditional Africa*, trans. K. and L. Martin (1979).

Mabiala Justine-Robert Kenzo

Prophet Harris

See **Harris, William Wade.**

Protest

Protest is speaking out against and resisting wrongdoing. As an act of "spiritual defiance" (Foster), protest confronts evil and addresses unjust situations. Protest is an action of hope, guided by faith in God and believing change is possible. Protest is an appropriate response when God's commands have been violated, God's rightful place has been usurped, or harm has been done to others through unjust laws, policies, or practices. Protest brings to public awareness situations of injustice and oppression. When making appeals to God's righteousness, protest is motivated by belief in a transcendent order that should guide public life, laws, and social policies. Protest may have two primary goals. The first is confronting circumstances that are unjust in order to bring about change. The second is maintaining current conditions, believing proposed changes in laws or policies may be detrimental to human beings.

Protest has a rich and troubled history in Christianity. Protestors have often been treated harshly by those, even in the same religious traditions, who desire to maintain the status quo for a variety of reasons. The prophets protested injustices of their time, denounced the complicity of God's people in oppression, and called persons to repent. Jesus spoke against the abuses of the religious elite. Yet

Jesus and the prophets were chastised for disrupting existing religious and social practices. Throughout history, Christians have objected to unjust edicts, tyrants, and abusive power by leaders. Of particular note is the Protestant Reformation, so named because of the protests of Martin Luther against the power of the Roman Catholic Church in the 16th century. However Luther, in turn, suppressed protests of the peasants. The nonviolent protests of civil rights leader and pastor Martin Luther King Jr. were viewed as rebellion by those who believed segregation of the races was ordained by God and ought to be maintained.

Protest in the spirit of Christian faith is not easy. Some may be reluctant to engage in acts of spiritual defiance yet discover that loyalty to Christ propels speaking out and taking action. When motivated by trust in God for the outcome, Christians can experience through faith the peace of Christ that surpasses all understanding, even in situations of conflict and uncertainty.

See also Courage; Social Justice.

For Further Reading: R. Foster, "Radical Prayer," in *Prayer* (1992); M. L. King Jr., *Strength to Love* (1963); T. Smith, *Revivalism and Social Reform* (1957).

Wyndy Corbin Reuschling

Protestantism

See Chapter 19.

Providence

God cares for all that he created; he lovingly sustains it in existence; he established a system of moral governance for it; and he acts within his creation in pursuit of his goals for it, both by ordinary and extraordinary means (often called "miracles"). Of God's creatures, he has a special care for human beings, whom he created in his image with responsibility to steward the rest of creation. God takes particular care of those who are his redeemed people or children.

Our doctrine of providence impacts very strongly the way in which we understand and relate to the world that God cares for and governs. Significantly different models of divine providence are affirmed within the church, including its evangelical wing. While all Christians believe God to be sovereign ruler of the world, they disagree about the extent of the control that God has allotted to himself in creating morally responsible creatures, both angels and humans. Monergists (such as Thomists or Calvinists) believe that God has planned the history of the world in detail so that everything occurs, both good and evil, as the outworking of God's plan, though done in such a way that God is not morally accountable for evil that is done by his creatures. Synergists (such as Arminians or Open Theists), on the other hand, believe that God's plan is more general and that, in willing his moral creatures to act freely, God has limited the extent to which all the details of world history turn out according to his desire. The Eastern Orthodox tradition considers the issue to be one of the mysteries of faith that is hidden from us, but they have been persistently synergistic.

Which model of providence we affirm informs the way we interpret what happens in world history and particularly in our own lives, in the events that we deem good or evil. The approach we take to human suffering, whether our own or that of others, grows out of our understanding of the relative roles of divine and human agency. Monergists, for instance, see the assessment made by Joseph concerning the evil done to him by his brothers as paradigmatic of life in general ("You intended to harm me, but God intended it for good" [Gen. 50:20]). Characteristically, synergists hear Joseph's words as applicable only to events that are significant in the process of God's redemptive program.

It is very important for our spiritual practice to be coherent with our theology. Thus, our prayers of thanksgiving and petition must be offered in light of our understanding of God's action in the past and of what we can reasonably request from him in the future. To thank, praise, or petition God for something that our theology does not attribute to his self-assigned control would create confusion. Either our theological beliefs or our spiritual practice should be revised so that we can live effectively according to God's revelation and expectations.

For Further Reading: T. Flint, *Divine Providence: The Molinist Account* (1998); P. Helm, *The Providence of God* (1994); J. Sanders, *The God Who Risks* (2007); T. Tiessen, *Providence and Prayer* (2000); B. Ware, ed., *Perspectives on the Doctrine of God* (2008).

Terrance L. Tiessen

Psalmody

Psalmody refers to musical settings or arrangements of biblical psalm texts intended for use in worship. The term is also used more broadly to include other, nonmusical ways that psalms are presented in worship.

The poems canonized in the Bible as the book of Psalms were developed over several centuries, especially during the reigns of David and Solomon, for use in the worship of the ancient Hebrews. Jesus' knowledge of the Psalms is evident in the gospel accounts (Matt. 27:46; Mark 12:10), and early Christians adopted psalms for use in Christian worship. In fact, as worship scholar John Witvliet writes, the Psalms have always been "the foundational and paradigmatic prayer book of the Christian church."

While many psalms speak in a first person voice, this "I" is understood to have a communal dimension, so that those praying the Psalms adopt the words as their own while also praying in harmony with the millions of others who have entered the "I" before them. The use of psalms in worship, therefore, teaches individuals the structures, imagery, and postures of biblical prayer while simultaneously enacting the prayers of the gathered body of Christ.

Already in the earliest centuries of the church, verses from psalms were woven into liturgies, and psalms were sung or chanted regularly in worshiping assemblies. Monastic communities of the European Middle Ages developed ambitious patterns of reading aloud or chanting psalms, recording these schemes in psalters, breviaries, and books of the hours. The Reformation brought an explosion of psalmody. Reformers enthusiastically urged ordinary people to pray psalms and especially to sing them in the worshiping congregation; the printing press, vernacular translations, and metrical versions of psalms—such as the sixteenth-century Genevan psalters—made this possible. John Calvin believed that worshipers should sing only the Psalms and other biblical canticles in worship, a practice referred to as "exclusive psalmody" that endures in some branches of the church today. By contrast, Luther advocated the composition of hymns as well, following the exhortation of the Psalms themselves to "sing a new song" as well as the Pauline encouragement to sing "psalms, hymns, and spiritual songs" (Col. 3:16) in community with other Christians.

Hymnody flourished in the 18th and 19th centuries among Protestants, although hymn composers such as Isaac Watts often found their inspiration in the Psalms. In the 20th century, the frequent use of psalms in worship enjoyed a rebirth, thanks to the liturgical renewal movement among Protestants and Vatican II among Roman Catholics. Today Christians continue to practice a wide variety of psalmody: solo and congregational responsive reading, chanting by soloists or choirs, responsive singing by cantors and congregations, congregational singing in traditional and new metrical versions, and the singing of new settings across all musical styles.

See also Emotions; Hymns; Psalms; Worship.

For Further Reading: W. Brueggemann, *The Message of the Psalms* (1984); W. Holladay, *The Psalms through Three Thousand Years* (1993); J. Witvliet, *The Biblical Psalms in Christian Worship* (2007).

Debra Rienstra

Psalms

More than any other, the book of Psalms contains human words *to* and *about* God. As such, the Psalms have been perennial favorites among Jewish and Christian believers. They express human emotions and responses to God in a way not found elsewhere in Scripture. There is ample evidence in both synagogue and church of their use over the centuries in formal, public worship as well as individual, private prayer.

The Psalter is wide-ranging in subject matter, so much so that Martin Luther called it "the little Bible," seeing that it contains expressions of arguably every strand of OT experience and theology. The Psalms also express the full range of human emotion, from the lowest lows of despair and anger to the highest highs of joy in the God of the universe, and everything in between. John Calvin spoke of the Psalter as "'An Anatomy of all the Parts of the Soul'; for there is not an emotion of which any one can be conscious that is not here represented as in a mirror."

The Psalms guide thought, emotion, and will toward God and life. They are profoundly formational, for they provide a faith-informed order to the chaos of human pain and our responses to it. They offer permission to be authentic, yet they are also pedagogical, inasmuch as they align our spirits with the classic response patterns of the people of God. They help move believers from where they are to where they need to be. The Psalms give shape and voice to our shared experiences of life; and in aligning with them, we also deepen our connection to a community that has likewise allowed them to mold the contours of its responses to life.

The early titles given to the book of Psalms present us with hermeneutical clues by which to understand the Psalms. The English title (Psalms) comes from the Greek title, *psalmos*, which refers to a song sung with a stringed instrument. This reveals the Psalms' unique character as compositions to be performed—sung in community as responses to God. The Hebrew title is *tehillim*, meaning "praises," showing us that in the end all of life is to be oriented toward praise. Psalm 72 speaks of "the prayers (*tephillot*) of David" (v. 20), yielding further insight into the nature of these compositions.

For the most part, the Psalms are situated between two poles of human experience: expressions of great joy at one end and expressions of great sorrow or anger at the other. Hymns of praise exalt God in myriad ways for who he is, and they tend to begin with calls to praise, followed by reasons for praise ("Praise the Lord, all you nations.... For great is his love toward us" [Ps. 117]). Psalms of thanksgiving tend to thank God for what he has done: they declare his glory, recount the psalmists' past need, and tell how God has answered ("I love the Lord, for he heard my voice.... The cords of death entangled me.... You, O Lord, have delivered my soul from death" [Ps. 116]). Yet this distinction (who God is/what he has done) is in many ways an artificial one, since we experience God in large measure through what he has done for us; the two cannot be separated. Westermann thus speaks of psalms of *descriptive praise* (hymns of praise, "describing" God's attributes) and *declarative praise* (thanksgiving, "declaring" God's deeds), showing that in the end they are all expressions of praise.

As Brueggemann has suggested, the Psalms can also be considered in terms of life's experiences. From this vantage point, psalms of *orientation* reflect a confident, serene perspective on life, rooted in an ordered outlook on the world. Many hymns of praise are of this type, as are many of the minor categories (e.g., Torah, creation, wisdom, historical, royal/messianic, and kingship of Yahweh psalms). Psalms of *disorientation* reflect the topsy-turvy, disordered, even incoherent experiences of life reflected in the laments. Psalms of *new orienta-*

tion reflect a (re)new(ed) orderedness to life. They have arrived at their new orientation after having passed through the crucible of disorientation, and they include the psalms of thanksgiving and many hymns of praise.

The thanksgiving psalms, in recounting past needs or troubles as well as praising God for answered prayer, serve as a bridge between the psalms of lament and hymns of praise. The laments form the largest single category of psalm types and are some of the most deeply penetrating and transparent modes of expression in all of Scripture. But almost all move from lament to praise in some way.

Over the centuries, individual psalms have spoken in countless ways to believers. The *book* of Psalms, however, has usually been seen as a somewhat random repository, a "holding tank" of sorts, for mostly unrelated psalms. Recent scholarship has helpfully highlighted the coherent message of the Psalter as a *book*, emphasizing Yahweh's divine kingship alongside its human expression through the Davidic line, pointing ahead, ultimately, to Yahweh's eschatological rule over all creation.

Not all psalms reside in the book of Psalms. Elsewhere in the OT we find psalms of Moses (Ex. 15:1–18; Deut. 32), Deborah (Judg. 5), Hannah (1 Sam. 2:1–10), David (2 Sam. 1:19–27; 2 Sam. 22; 1 Chron. 16:7–36), Hezekiah (Isa. 38:9–20), Jonah (Jonah 2), and Habakkuk (Hab. 3), to say nothing of the laments in the book of Lamentations. Most of these embedded psalms celebrate victories or answers to prayer that God has given, though Habakkuk's vision is of God's dramatic appearance in a theophany, and several are eloquent and moving laments (2 Sam. 1:19–27; Lam. 1–5). In the NT, Mary's Magnificat stands out as a signal example (Luke 1:46–55), as does Paul's *kenosis* hymn (Phil. 2:5–11).

See also Psalmody.

For Further Reading: W. Brueggemann, *Spirituality of the Psalms* (2002); H. Donin, *To Pray as a Jew* (2001); W. Holladay, *The Psalms through Three Thousand Years* (1993); D. Mitchell, *The Message of the Psalter* (1997); M. Travers, *Encountering God in the Psalms* (2003); C. Westermann, *Praise and Lament in the Psalms*, trans. K. Crim and R. Soulen (1981); G. Wilson, "The Structure of the Psalter," in *Interpreting the Psalms*, ed. D. Firth and P. Johnston (2005), 229–46; B. Waltke and J. Houston, *The Psalms as Christian Worship* (2010); J. Witvliet, *The Biblical Psalms in Christian Worship* (2007).

David M. Howard Jr.

Pseudo-Dionysius the Areopagite (5th to 6th Century)

Fountainhead of mystical theology. The writings attributed to this anonymous writer were first mentioned by name in a colloquy held in 532 between the Chalcedonians (the Council of Chalcedon confessed that Christ has a divine and a human nature) and a group of monophysite (the belief that the incarnated Christ has one nature only) Severians (followers of Severus of Antioch, d. 538). Hypatius of Ephesus, a Chalcedonian bishop, challenged the authenticity of the Dionysian texts used by his opponents. These writings came allegedly from Dionysius the Areopagite (Acts 17:34). However, the technical theological and Neoplatonic vocabulary of the writings clearly show that these are products of a theological genius of the monophysite tradition living in the late 5th and early 6th centuries. As the identity of Pseudo-Dionysius is shrouded in mystery, so is the original intention of his writings. Was he (Luther's opinion) expounding Neoplatonic philosophy under the pretext of Christian theology? Or was he an orthodox theologian trying to co-opt the best insights of Greek philosophy? Scholars are divided on this fundamental question.

The complete works of Pseudo-Dionysius (the *Corpus Areopagiticum*) comes to fewer than three hundred pages in English translation. The style is condensed and speculative. *The Divine Names*, the longest work, contains philosophical speculations on themes under various headings, such as *being, life, good, beautiful, righteous, omnipotence,* and lastly, *one*. *The Mystical Theology* is a succinct overview of the relationship between affirmative theology and negative theology, and contains his brief but significant discourse on negative theology. *The Celestial Hierarchy* is arguably the single most influential text on angelology in church history. He lays out a theology of *hierarchy* (a word invented by Pseudo-Dionysius) and speculates on the meaning of the nine ranks of heavenly beings as well as the scriptural symbols used to describe angels. *The Ecclesiastical Hierarchy* explains the theological meaning of the ecclesiastical hierarchy and the various rites of the church (baptism, Lord's Supper, consecration of priests, funerals, etc.). There are also ten short letters addressing different issues.

The works of Pseudo-Dionysius reflect a metaphysical framework of remaining, procession, and return. For him, God is the ineffable and unknowable (Gr. *henosis*) one. The essence of God is beyond any human conception. God is the ground of all beings, but God is not a being. In the superabundance of goodness, God gives existence to all beings while remaining absolutely unmoved. All things proceed ontologically from God. All beings also yearn, in their own manner, to return to God. The whole creation is a movement from God to beings and from beings to God. This is also a movement from unity to multiplicity and from multiplicity back to unity.

The metaphysical process is reflected epistemologically in the dialectic of affirmative (or kataphatic) and negative (or apophatic) theology. Since God is the Cause of everything material or immaterial, both material things and mental concepts participate in God and can serve as symbols for God. We can affirm that God is our rock or God is good, while recognizing that God is not identical with a rock or that human goodness is not identical with divine goodness. For Dionysius, to know God truthfully is to participate in God; God is Truth. Since God transcends all beings (including concepts), we have to learn to negate the symbols in our journey back to God. This negation is not simply a rejection of the affirmation (as in logic); it also involves mental effort to transcend the limitation of a positive statement. For example, a rock is hard. When we negate that God is not a rock, we are saying, among other things, that God cannot be confined by the nature of hardness. As we learn to affirm God of more and more exalted symbols, while at the same time negating them, we move closer and closer to knowing God without using any symbols or concepts. Finally, we come to know God in the darkness of unknowing. For Dionysius, this is the true meaning of Moses meeting God in a dense cloud (Ex. 19).

Celestial and ecclesiastical hierarchies serve as the pathway of movement of procession and return. In a hierarchy, one level receives as much divine light as possible from its superior and passes on the light to its inferior. In particular, the ecclesiastical hierarchy contains three levels: the hierarch or bishop, the priests, and the deacons. The hierarch alone can bestow the gift of perfection or union with God; thus he alone can consecrate priests. The priests can bestow illumination, while the deacon can bestow purification. According to Dionysius, the sacraments are different kinds of mystagogy, or means of uplifting us into divine mysteries.

Dionysius provides a theoretical framework and an example for understanding theology as a kind of mystical contemplation, or engaging conceptual speculations as preparation for the final mystical union with God. For the Eastern Orthodox tradition, Dionysius is one among several church fathers, particularly the Cappadocian, who give a Neoplatonic flavor to its mystical theology, with its focus on overcoming the distance between creatures and the Creator. For the Latin church, the negative theology of Dionysius was adopted by Dominicans such as Thomas Aquinas and Meister Eckhart as a form of intellectual mysticism. A conceptless and imageless contemplation of the Ground of Being is regarded as the apex of spiritual life. The medieval work *The Cloud of Unknowing* reinterprets Dionysius by equating the state of unknowing as the ecstasy of love. Postmodernism emphasizes the playfulness of language and the limit of rationality. The Dionysian themes of symbols and super-rational experience of God may yet provide theological recourses for a postmodern Christian spirituality.

See also Platonism and Neoplatonism.

For Further Reading: A. Louth, *Denys the Areopagite* (1989); *Pseudo-Dionysius: The Complete Works*, CWS (1987); P. Rorem, *Pseudo-Dionysius: A Commentary on the Texts and an Introduction to Their Influence* (1993).

Kin-Yip Louie

Pseudo-Macarian Homilies

A series of treatises on the inner life, enormously influential in shaping the spirituality of the Christian East. Written in Greek by an anonymous late-fourth-century Syriac writer, and circulating under the name of Macarius the Great of Egypt, the *Macarian Homilies* were also well-received in Protestant circles interested in a revival of the inner life. John Wesley famously stated, "I have read Macarius and my heart sang." The *Homilies* focus on the transformation of the human being through cooperation with God's grace, so as to experience God "perceptibly and with complete assurance." This typically involves an interior vision of light — the very same experience recorded about biblical prophets and apostles. Thus, the manifestation of divine glory in Ezekiel 1 was not only a real apparition of Christ to the prophet, but also an image of how any Christian soul is to become the Lord's throne of glory. This internalization of the visionary experience is typical of Pseudo-Macarius, for whom "everything is within" — the devil and all the treasures of wickedness, but also God, the angels, the heavenly cities, the treasures of the kingdom.

Experiences such as these call for spiritual discernment, which is the fruit of divine grace assisting one's ascetic labors. Postlapsarian Adam, despite his free will, is incurably sick with disordered and destructive psychosomatic drives, unable to master the evil stirred up within the soul by the devil. Healing comes from Christ, the Divine Physician, but it requires the patient's active cooperation through humility and ascetical life. The latter begins as human endeavor, although it is constantly accompanied by grace, and ends as a divine gift. Baptism and Eucharist offer a foretaste of the Christian's eschatological transformation by fueling an ever-deepening communion with God. However, Pseudo-Macarius insists, without the ascetic life, baptismal grace does not prevent the constant harassment of evil, and the Eucharist does not complete the desired transformation. Briefly put, if the proper way of receiving the sacraments is an ongoing commitment to the ascetical life, the proper context of asceticism is the liturgy of the church.

See also Asceticism.

For Further Reading: A. Golitzin, "Heavenly Mysteries," in *Apocalyptic Themes in Early Christianity*, ed. R. Daly (2009), 174–92; idem, "A Testimony to Christianity as Transfiguration," in *Orthodox and Wesleyan Spirituality*, ed. S. T. Kimbrough (2002), 129–56; M. Plested, *The Macarian Legacy* (2004); *Pseudo-Macarius: The Fifty Spiritual Homilies and the Great Letter*, CWS (1992); C. Stewart, *Working the Earth of the Heart* (1991).

Bogdan G. Bucur

Psychoanalysis

Psychoanalysis, as originally conceptualized by Sigmund Freud, may be understood as both a theory of personality and a theory and practice of psychotherapy. Early Freudian psychoanalysis, often called classical or drive theory, has greatly influenced contemporary thought, introducing such concepts as the unconscious, id, ego, and superego; sexual and aggressive drives; defense mechanisms; and dream analysis.

Freudian theory posits that the personality is largely unconscious. The unconscious is the repository for both the biological psychosexual drives and significant early memories. It is the unconscious that primarily determines behavior in a twofold attempt (1) to protect the conscious mind from awareness of unconscious desires (which creates anxiety and subsequent defense mechanisms) and (2) simultaneously to fulfill them. Psychological symptoms are then understood as compensatory behaviors of the unconscious mind. The goal, therefore, of Freudian psychoanalysis was to make the unconscious conscious so that individuals could make responsible choices regarding their unconscious wishes and drives.

Freud took his understanding of symptom pathology as rigid defenses, symptoms, and rituals designed to manage the seething cauldron of the unconscious, and used it in an attempt to understand religion. For Freud, a male child's desire to own his mother exclusively created conflict between his fear of retaliation from his father and his need of the father for protection from the world. This was the basis of the Oedipal conflict, and Freud psychoanalyzed religion, dismissing it as a kind of cultural Oedipal complex. God served the function of a great parental projection in the sky that humans both needed and feared. Freud theorized that eventually society would outgrow its need for religion in the same manner that a healthy adult outgrows his or her need for a parent.

Following Freud's death, psychoanalytic writers begin to explore religion in more positive ways. This became possible when object relations psychoanalysis took umbrage with Freud's dual instinct model of personality and suggested that the primary human motivation was relational. From this vantage point, connecting with powerful others, even a deity, was not infantile pathology but was the inevitable outgrowth of human relatedness. Relationships were central throughout the life span while the form of relating could mature. Psychoanalysis could now examine the form and function of religious experience (healthy and pathological) without psychological reductionism. In her book *Birth of the Living God* (1979), psychoanalyst Ana-Maria Rizzuto explored the ubiquitous human tendency to formulate inter-

nal God representations. This work has birthed a large literature of empirical research exploring the development and change factors on these images.

Psychoanalysis has always emphasized the human tendency for self-deception. Psychoanalytic psychotherapy, therefore, has been very helpful in assisting people discover what is at work in the hidden parts of themselves. Such self-exploration, when combined with appropriate confession and acceptance, can be extremely helpful in the Christian journey toward authenticity, freedom, and growth. Contemporary psychoanalysis, with its emphasis on self-exploration, centrality of relationship, openness to religion, and the formation of God representations, has had an increasing influence on religious studies, spiritual formation literature, and pastoral counseling.

See also Counseling.

For Further Reading: P. Cooper-White, *Many Voices: Pastoral Psychotherapy in Relational and Theological Perspective* (2007); J. Jones, *Religion and Psychology in Transition* (1996); W. W. Meisnner, *Psychoanalysis and the Religious Experience* (1986); S. Mitchell and M. Black, *Freud and Beyond* (1996); R. Sorenson, *Minding Spirituality* (2004).

Brad D. Strawn

Psychology
See Chapter 27.

Psychology of Prayer

Prayer is central to the practice of Christian faith, with volumes written about its role in spirituality. It is generally accepted that prayer flows from the essence of who we are in body, mind, and soul, yet only recently has there been examination of the interface between psyche and prayer.

A classic contribution to the psychology of prayer is *Primary Speech* (1982) by Ann and Barry Ulanov (1982). Utilizing insights from depth psychology, they posit that the most basic components of our psyche—desire, fantasy, fear, aggression, and sexuality—play a central role in prayer. While some Christians have sought to banish these elements from their awareness and prayer life, the Ulanovs claim that these experiences are foundational to our personhood and therefore must be acknowledged and incorporated into our communication with God. Only as we open ourselves completely to God can we fully know God's love and redemption.

For Christians, prayer involves not only presentation of our entire self to God, but also a surrendering of self, so that the Holy Spirit can fill and guide us. This militates against our natural inclination toward narcissism, characterized by self-focus, self-interest, and self-promotion. The issue of who is in control is of utter importance in the Christian life, and the ability to allow Christ's Spirit to control us springs from the process of prayer. Through prayer we become willing to let Christ be both Savior and Lord of our lives. This willingness is a humble beginning, to be sure, but it is this poverty of spirit that Jesus proclaims as the way to the kingdom of heaven (Matt. 5:3).

Unless we surrender to Jesus in faith, laying aside our desire for control and insistence that things go our way, Jesus can accomplish little in our lives (Mark 6; John 15:1–11). Our difficulty relinquishing control underlies much of our contemporary tendency toward anxiety and exhaustion. Jesus invites us to come to him with our burdens, weariness, and worries, and he promises to help us by yoking himself to us (Matt. 11:28–30). This offering of our will to God does not mean passivity on our part or the annihilation of self; rather, through prayer our life in Christ becomes a partnership whereby we are copilots, steering the ship of our life together with Christ. Amazingly, this surrender of control creates the conditions for God to give us inner peace, fulfillment, and the desires of our heart.

See also Surrender.

For Further Reading: L. B. Brown, *The Human Side of Prayer* (1994); M. McCullough, "Prayer and Health," *Journal of Psychology and Theology* 23, no. 1 (1995): 15–29; A. and B. Ulanov, *Religion and the Unconscious* (1975).

Myrla Seibold

Public Life and Spirituality

Christian presence can be rightfully oriented toward the public square, which includes politics, civil society, and academia. If spirituality is seen primarily as an inward disposition toward God, then engagement in the public realm is considered unnecessary or irrelevant. When Christianity is privatized or secularized, the public character of the gospel is overlooked. With the multifarious issues in the public square, such as the challenge of harmony among religious faiths, ethical issues arising from technology's ongoing development, and environmental care and economic sustainability, the Christian voice is urgently needed. This vision is shared by many devout Christians, including notably, Abraham Vereide (1886—1969), the Norwegian-American founder of the international prayer breakfast movement, which sponsors the annual National Prayer Breakfast customarily attended by U.S. presidents.

The public dimension of the Christian faith is conveyed in God's command to Israel to "seek the peace and prosperity of the city to which I have carried you into exile. Pray to the LORD for it, because if it prospers, you too will prosper" (Jer. 29:7); echoed in Jesus' command to "let your light shine before others, that they may see your good deeds and glorify your Father in heaven" (Matt. 5:16 TNIV); and mirrored in Peter's call to the saints to live good lives among the pagans so that "they may see your good deeds and glorify God" (1 Peter 2:12). Christian engagement in the public realm is part of responsible citizenship. Even though Christians are journeying toward a heavenly city, they presently live in an earthly city. Doing what is good in society is thus an expression and reflection of the holiness and goodness of God in the world.

Developing spirituality that is publicly oriented necessitates being strongly connected in a faith community, which can provide a nurturing place for worship, formation, and support, all of which are essential for robust and mature faith. Such a faith integrates the inner life of contemplation with outward communal life and action in a dynamic rhythm. A Trinitarian framework—with God as Father and sustainer of the world, Jesus Christ as the Savior in whom all things hold together, and the Holy Spirit as the one who empowers disciples and initiates change—provides theological undergirding.

Christians must be firmly grounded in their context so that the issues, concerns, and injustices of that place capture their imagination. Being rooted in a place gives Christians the standing to proclaim the message of justice, truth, and hope found in Jesus Christ. The acts of proclamation, which are the public expression of Christian faith, must also be contextualized. Though the spiritual disciplines and inward posture may be the same for Christians around the world, the style and method of proclaiming the message must be incarnational.

Engagement in the public square should not be merely to identify with or champion a cause; rather, Christians should be led to unmask the prevailing ideologies and to offer better models for understanding the human situation and the plight of the world. When Christians are deeply connected with God, church, and world, they can then present a vision of the hope of the gospel that is authentic and substantial.

See also Holistic Spirituality; Marketplace Spirituality; Secularization.

For Further Reading: C. Mathewes, *A Theology of Public Life* (2007); L. Newbigin, *Truth to Tell* (1991).

Kiem-Kiok Kwa

Puritan Spirituality

Puritanism was a clergy-led Protestant and Reformed holiness and renewal movement, anchored in the Church of England until Parliament abolished Anglicanism in 1645, and thereafter taking Presbyterian and Congregational-Independent (both Baptist and paedobaptist) forms. It sought to glorify God by completing the reformation of English church life, by discipling the nation, and by Christianizing all public life. It was a comprehensive cultural force, pursuing intellectual, ecclesiastical, personal, and civic goals as a means to fulfilling England's manifest destiny, to become a model for the world of true godliness.

The movement's national impact began with Presbyterianizing agitation in the 1560s and was potent for over a hundred years. Eventually, after a quarter-century of persecution under the repressive Clarendon Code, the 1689 Toleration Act decisively marginalized Puritanism by channeling its remnants into now lawful non-Anglican congregations. Those previously called Puritans (a pejorative label given by opponents, implying a holier-than-thou self-image, a perverse pickiness, and real hypocrisy) were henceforth labeled Dissenters, and Puritanism as a national ideology was no more.

Bible-based, Christ-centered, conversionist, and church-oriented, Puritanism was founded on personal and family piety and was nourished by expository evangelical preaching and disciplined prayer. Aristocrats, university teachers, lawyers, merchants, and artisans were involved in the movement. The interregnum under Cromwell aimed at the ideal of Puritan politics, namely, that the saints should rule.

Outstanding Puritan teachers, whose publications won appreciation both in and since their lifetimes, include William Perkins (late 16th century); Richard Sibbes, John Preston, John Owen, Thomas Goodwin, Richard Baxter, William Gurnall, Thomas Manton, Stephen Charnock, John Bunyan, Thomas Watson, George Swinnock, John Flavel (17th century); and John Howe and Matthew Henry, both of whom lived into the 18th century. These and allied writers generated a homogenous, didactic, homiletical popular literature of which

Baxter's *Saints' Everlasting Rest* and *Reformed Pastor* and Bunyan's *Pilgrim's Progress* are perhaps the highlights. From this literature, together with the Westminster Confession, catechisms, and *Directory for Public Worship*, Puritan spirituality may be reliably mapped.

Christian spirituality is shaped fundamentally by what is believed about the self-revealing action of God. The Puritan frame for spiritual life was the mainstream Reformed version of catholic orthodoxy. On God's triunity, sovereignty, and moral perfection (that is, his holy wisdom, goodness, truth, justice, and faithfulness); on the key facts about Christ (his incarnation, mediation, threefold office, bodily resurrection, present reign, and future return as judge); on Anglican anti-Romanism; and on Dort's anti-Arminianism, Puritanism was unremarkable, some eccentrics notwithstanding. Much more remarkable is the depth and thoroughness with which the Puritans explored the realities of conversion and regeneration—the recognition of God's holiness, conviction of sin, the Holy Spirit's changing the desires and direction of one's heart, expression of this change in Godward repentance, faith in Jesus Christ as Savior and Lord, commitment to a totally God-centered way of living by the Spirit's power, and the assurance of salvation through the Spirit's witness. Orthodox in substance, Puritan pneumatology has great richness and landmark quality in its application.

Personal communion with God, as the inner reality of the life of good works, was the central focus of Puritan spirituality, and what Baxter termed "heart-work and heaven-work" (i.e., maintaining pure love to God and neighbor, with strong hope of final glory) is its essence. The disciplines involved in this habit of the regenerate heart were many. Trusting the Father to fulfill all his promises; learning from Christ to be like Christ and doing what he says; obeying the Holy Spirit's teaching in the conscience (moral reason) as to how to please God most fully; continuing to keep on praising, thanking, and rejoicing in all circumstances;

submitting to suffering without discouragement; maintaining spiritual warfare against the temptations of the world, the flesh, and the devil; and practicing the preliminary duties of reflection, self-examination, and resolution as preparation for wholeheartedly fulfilling the major duties listed above. By these means, Puritans cherished and deepened their conscious relationship with God.

Their piety, though intensely individual, was not in itself individualistic, though many sects, under charismatic leaders of an individualistic mind-set, spun off from the mainstream movement at various times. But Puritan Christians were taught to engage earnestly in both the informal fellowship of friends and the established fellowship of church congregations, worshiping and praying together, learning from preachers' sermons and fellow Christians' talk, and bearing their own testimony to spiritual realities in response. In these relationships, all would share a commitment to spiritual advance and growth toward the perfection that God has in store for all believers, and this would bond them together.

The double driving force of Puritan spirituality was thus a longing for God and for holiness, which took the form of a branching out of the converted Christian's desire to know and love and please God into biblically informed and situationally appropriate action across the board. Puritan spirituality entailed an unflagging attention to duty, duty being a divine canopy extending over all life. In society, duty dictated, among other things, that everyone should follow a calling (that is, an occupation practiced for others' good and God's glory). At home, marriage, domestic management, and parenting brought duties in abundance. Home was to be in effect a mini-church, with the man of the house as pastor. Marriage laid on both parties duties of responsible mutual love, and parents were to rear children in knowledge (Bible teaching and doctrinal catechesis) and in virtue (by teaching, modeling, encouraging, and rebuking—all in love), joining prayer with care for them throughout.

This was vital. "A family is the seminary of church and state; and if children be not well principled there, all miscarrieth" (Manton). Protestant Christian home life is a legacy of Puritan spirituality.

The Puritan Christian's final duty was to die well, with affairs in order, a will made, and a heart prepared. Bunyan showed what dying could mean in terms of spiritual conflict and conquest in the crossings of Jordan in both parts of *The Pilgrim's Progress*. Puritan spirituality sanctified not only life, as the beginning of eternity, but also death, as the end of that beginning. Here, surely, is spiritual wisdom for all.

See also Reformed (Calvinist) Spirituality.

For Further Reading: R. Baxter, *A Christian Directory* (1990); J. W. Black, *Reformation Pastors: Richard Baxter and the Idea of the Reformed Pastor* (2004); J. Bunyan, *The Pilgrim's Progress*, 2 pts. (many eds.); P. Lewis, *The Genius of Puritanism* (1979); J. I. Packer, *A Quest for Godliness* (1990); L. Ryken, *Worldly Saints* (1986).

J. I. Packer

Q

Quaker Spirituality

In the midst of a violent civil war in mid-seventeenth-century England, a new religious movement emerged out of the radical Puritan tradition. They called themselves "Children of Light" and "Publishers of Truth" but were derisively called "Quakers" because they trembled when they spoke through the inspiration of the Spirit. Quakers today rarely tremble, and the spirituality of its various contemporary branches has become widely divergent, from evangelical to New Age, from social activist to contemplative, from Universalist to post-Christian.

Quakers today are uniquely divided by two forms of worship. "Unprogrammed" Friends meet in silence, without clergy, music, or visible sacraments; and "programmed," or pastoral, Friends follow a set order of worship, with hymns, Scripture, sermons, and prayers. Early Quaker worship was both contemplative (based in silence and surrender) and charismatic. After a long period of silent waiting, messages would be delivered spontaneously through the inspiration of the Spirit.

Quakers of all types continue to be connected by a strong sense of history, as well as by a few unique elements, such as consensus decision making, a testimony to peace and gender equality, and an appreciation for the spiritual value of silence. The basis of all Quaker spirituality is a direct, unmediated experience of God. This may happen individually in the process of conversion and prayer, and communally in the experience of worship.

George Fox, founder of the Quaker movement whose *Journal* became a primary Quaker text, had numerous mystical encounters that he called "openings" when he was given revelations and new insights. He sometimes described such experiences as being "taken up into the love of God." One such insight, that everyone was "enlightened by the divine Light of Christ," became a key concept in Quaker spirituality. This Light, they claimed, was universal and "would work out the salvation of all, if not resisted." In later periods, Friends divided over the interpretation of this "inward light." Evangelically oriented Friends preferred to call it the Holy Spirit, and mystically oriented Friends, the "inner light," something divine in the soul.

Quaker spirituality initially developed around the idea of holiness, which they called perfection or union with God, a spirituality of radical optimism.

Perfection, always a work of grace, brought power to overcome sin, a new sense of spiritual freedom, and soul joy even amid suffering. Quaker theologian Robert Barclay (1648–1690), in his *Apology* (1678), called perfection the "holy birth … fully brought forth." Quakers always described perfection in biblical terms, such as "the life hidden with Christ in God" (Col. 3:3), "Christ in you, the hope of Glory" (Col. 1:27), to "participate in the divine nature" (2 Peter 1:4), and to be "one spirit" with the Lord (1 Cor. 6:17).

Early Quakers had a thoroughly biblical worldview and considered the Bible authoritative. However, Fox felt he was primarily called "to direct people to the Spirit that gave forth the Scripture." Quakers believed revelation was not closed nor confined to Scripture, but Scripture was the touchstone of truth and would confirm all direct, personal inspiration. The Bible and the practice of communal discernment became safeguards for self-deception.

Early Quakers, like many Puritans in their time, initially anticipated the imminent second coming of Christ, but when it did not happen literally, they recognized that Christ had come again spiritually within each person. Quakers then began to proclaim a "kingdom now" theology, preaching that the kingdom is within.

Quakers were evangelistic and prophetic, preaching good news to the poor and denouncing oppression — religious, social, and political. They became a missionary-oriented movement on a grand scale, adopting an itinerant, apostolic style of preaching. A concern for freedom of conscience, equality of all persons, and social justice were corollaries of their evangelism.

Early Quakers could arguably be called a grassroots Pentecostal movement. The experience of being "in the power," which meant being Spirit-filled and led, is one of the most recurring phrases in George Fox's *Journal* (1694). Early Friends often used the term *poured down* to describe whole meetings that were "in the power."

The first generation of Quakers were often harshly persecuted for their beliefs and thus identified themselves as belonging to the long line of martyrs for God's truth. Their experience of suffering was viewed positively as identification with Christ and brought redemptive meaning and purpose. The cross as a daily enacting of the suffering of Christ became a central symbol of Quaker spirituality. William Penn wrote in *No Cross, No Crown* (1682), a classic Quaker devotional text, "The bearing of thy daily Cross is the only true testimony."

Quaker Christology emphasized the inward Christ (the inward Light) and the cosmic Christ (the universal Light) more than the historical Jesus. Quakers proclaimed that Christ must be awakened and experienced inwardly, not simply believed in as a historic figure or event. Quaker preacher James Nayler testified to this Christology, the basis of incarnational holiness: "None can witness redemption further than Christ is thus revealed in them, to set them free from sin: which Christ I witness to be revealed in me in measure." Thomas Kelly, a twentieth-century Quaker spiritual writer, echoes this Christology in his classic text, *A Testament of Devotion* (1941): "Deep within us all there is an amazing inner sanctuary of the soul, a holy place, a Divine Center, a speaking voice…. Here is the Slumbering Christ, stirring to be awakened, to become the soul we clothe in earthly form and action. And He is within us all." For Quakers, the biblical phrase "in Christ" did not mean simply being "in the church" or being "saved," but signified a mystical relationship of divine indwelling and a complete transformation of being.

See also Fox, George; Shaker Spirituality; Unitarian Spirituality.

For Further Reading: M. Birkel, *Silence and Witness* (2004); P. Dandelion, *An Introduction to Quakerism* (2007); J. Punshon, *Encounter with Silence* (1987); *Quaker Spirituality: Selected Writings*, CWS (1984); C. Spencer, *Holiness* (2007).

Carole Dale Spencer

Quietism

The term *quietism* is sometimes used loosely to refer to any form of spirituality that minimizes the role of the will in the pursuit of the spiritual life. But historically, Quietism is associated with the names of Miguel de Molinos, Madame Guyon, François Fénelon, and Jean-Pierre de Caussade, among its better-known proponents. It arose in the 17th century in reaction to a highly regulated post-Tridentine church that had become deeply suspicious of mysticism and enthusiasm. Quietists taught that the only way to union with God is through infused contemplative prayer without the mediation of prayers involving the active response of the will, such as vocal prayers and discursive meditation. The error of Quietism is that it so stresses passivity that active ascetical prayers are regarded as inferior and even superfluous. Union with God or perfection comes from annihilation of the will and total indifference to self. According to François Fénelon, what ensues is "pure love, which leaves nothing to nature, by referring everything to grace." One should become wholly concerned with God even to the point of being indifferent to one's own eternal well-being. If this is pursued to its logical end, then one must not even be concerned about what God is concerned to do for people, namely, to draw them into union with himself. Quietism could ultimately become self-destructive. Passivity is pursued even to the point of total nonresistance toward temptation, since one could not sin if the will is nonactive. The obviously dangerous implications of Quietism led to its eventual condemnation by the Catholic Church in 1687.

Nonetheless, there are elements of truth in Quietism that account for its continuing attraction. First, by advocating the abandonment of self, it challenges complacent Christians who are easily satisfied with the bare minimum and exposes a common human tendency to desire the spiritual life for selfish ends. Second, it had seized upon a very important principle: passivity signals a higher level of Christian life. The Christian tradition of spiritual development has always included a place for passivity, stillness, and quiet at its higher end. In the West, spiritual growth is seen as a movement from active, vocal prayers and discursive meditation to passive or infused contemplation. In the East it can be found in the hesychastic tradition, especially in the use of the Jesus Prayer. But in hesychasm, "stillness" (*hesychia*) is preceded by disciplines like sorrow for sin and devotion to the name of Jesus.

Quietistic tendencies could be found in varying degrees in some Protestant movements. For the Quakers, silence prepares and purifies the heart for the Spirit to speak and act through them. The human will must be completely subject to the will of the Spirit, acting only as it is "moved." As one Quaker put it, "I am a white paper without any line or sentence, but as it is revealed and written by the Spirit, the revealer of secrets, so I administer." Closer to the Christian tradition is the Keswick Movement, known for promoting "the higher life" through an act of self-surrender and "reckoning." Reckoning, as Hannah Whitall Smith describes it, is not a particularly active pursuit but an unwavering act of trusting that God takes over completely the self that has been surrendered to him. Among the early Pentecostals, a kind of passive "waiting" or "yieldedness" was a means to receiving the baptism in the Holy Spirit. In most of the traditions, active pursuit or human response is not discounted but seen as a necessary part of or a prerequisite for spiritual growth.

Modern assessments of Quietism are mixed. The works of Madame Guyon have been favorably received by many Protestants, including Count von Zinzendorf, John Wesley, Hudson Taylor, and Jessie Penn-Lewis, partly because they exude a warm, personal piety that resonates with evangelicals. Not surprisingly, her works have become part of Keswick devotional literature, and through the towering influence of Watchman Nee, they were widely disseminated in Chinese churches. Protestants are also sympathetic to her works because they share her emphasis on "faith," a central Protestant principle. Knox, however, notes that in Madame Guyon faith is not contrasted with good works but with ascetical devotions. Faith is a kind of resting and a superior way to God. Dupré is perhaps more charitable compared to Knox. While recognizing that difficulties remain, he nonetheless argues that Quietism had traditional roots traceable to no less an esteemed figure than Francis de Sales and to the Rhineland mystics (Meister Eckhart, Johannes Tauler, and others).

See also Guyon, Madame; Fénelon, François.

For Further Reading: L. Dupré, "Jansenism and Quietism," in *Christian Spirituality: Post-Reformation and Modern,* WSEH (1989), 121–30; R. Knox, *Enthusiasm* (1950); G. Nuttall, *Studies in Christian Enthusiasm* (1948); H. Whitall Smith, *The Christian's Secret of a Happy Life* (1888).

Simon Chan

R

Rahner, Karl (1904–1984)

Prominent Roman Catholic theologian. A German Jesuit, Rahner was arguably the most important Catholic theologian of the 20th century. His theology reflects two critical presuppositions, one of which builds upon the other. First, Rahner understood this world to be infused with grace. Second, he believed that every human being has a subconscious or implicit openness to and awareness of God. Rahner was dissatisfied with neo-scholasticism, the type of theology dominant in Catholicism in the first half of the 20th century. He always considered his priestly role as his primary vocation and was very concerned that theology be intelligible to the modern person. Judging neo-scholasticism as insufficient for such a task, he crafted a theological system that wedded the theology of Aquinas to the philosophy of Kant. He was a theological adviser to Vatican II, during which his reputation shifted from a theologian who had faced church discipline for some of his writings to one whose work became widely respected.

Rahner's significance for spirituality lies in his assertion that the created order is infused with grace. This reality comes from the gratuitousness of God who chooses to reveal Godself to human beings. Rahner was concerned throughout his career to articulate the conditions under which human reception of divine revelation is possible. The graciousness of God in communicating to humanity, and the God-given ability of humans to receive divine communication, grounded his pastoral theology. His many publications include a collection of sermons and meditations entitled *The Great Church Year* (1994) and *Spiritual Writings* (2004).

For Further Reading: W. Dych, *Karl Rahner* (2002).

Mary M. Veeneman

Ramabai, Pandita (1858–1920)

Indian Christian social reformer, scholar, and mystic. Best known for her work to emancipate girls from sexual slavery, Ramabai was arguably the most prominent Christian woman in modern Indian history. She was born into a very high Braham caste and, unusually for the times, was taught Sanskrit by her father while still very young. Upon her graduation at age twenty-two, the University of Calcutta conferred on her the highest titles of Hindu learning: *Saraswati*, goddess of learning, and *Pandita*, expert in Hindu texts.

However, Ramabai grew disturbed by what these holy texts said about women, as well as low caste people and outcasts. Somehow she acquired a gospel of Luke and was profoundly moved by Jesus' very different relationships with women and the poor. This eventually led to her Christian conversion. After further studies at Cheltenham Women's College in England, she began rescuing girls from temple prostitution and brothels. She also begged Hindu parents to bring their unwanted female newborns to her, rather than practice infanticide. Hundreds of girls were rescued, and eventually the program developed into the Ramabai Mukti Mission.

Having acquired the biblical languages, she began in 1904 to translate the Bible into the local vernacular and finally completed this task just before her death in 1920. The dominant approach to Bible translation in India, then as now, was to employ high-caste Hindu and Aryan Sanskrit vocabulary. To the chagrin of other Bible translators, she consistently refused to use any terms with connotations of Hindu caste dominance over the oppressed.

Undergirding Ramabai's activist life was a passionate Christian spirituality, which she sought to pass on to the younger women under her charge. She spent many days in fasting and prayer, along with the hundreds of girls she rescued. In 1905 this resulted in many reports of ecstatic experiences. *The Indian Alliance* newspaper reported that Ramabai and her associates practiced "healing, the gift of tongues, visions, and dreams, the power to prophesy and pray the prayer of faith." This was a year prior to the famous Azusa Street Pentecostal revival in the United States, and the phenomena quickly spread to other parts of India.

In 1989 the government of India issued a commemorative stamp on the hundredth anniversary of the founding of her organization to liberate and empower Indian girls and women. She was formally recognized as "a social reformer, a champion of the emancipation of women, and a pioneer in education." Her many publications include an autobiography, *A Testimony to Our Inexhaustible Treasure* (1907).

See also Asian Christian Spirituality; Feminist Spirituality.

For Further Reading: S. M. Adhav, *Pandita Ramabai* (1979); R. Dongre and J. Patterson, *Pandita Ramabai* (1963).

R. Boaz Johnson

Rapture

The term *rapture* (Lat. *raptus*) conveys the sense of being transported or carried away. Its primary meaning in the context of Christian spirituality is joyful ecstasy—being carried beyond normal consciousness and quotidian preoccupations into an altogether different and self-forgetful experience of sustained and overwhelming delight. Echoes of rapture can be detected in the adjective *enraptured* and such familiar idioms as a fascinated audience being held in *rapt* attention. Usually *rapture* is pluralized (i.e., *raptures*) to describe a sustained series or waves of such phenomena.

Rapture is a familiar and desirable dimension of Christian experience, as in Bernard of Clairvaux's mystical experiences of *raptus*; the experience of eighteenth-century Nova Scotian revivalist Henry Alline, of whom it was said that he was "converted in a rapture; and ever after ... sought to live in a rapture; and judged of his religious condition by his enjoyments and raptures"; and the refrain to Fanny Crosby's nineteenth-century evangelical hymn "Jesus Keep Me Near the Cross": "In the cross, in the cross, be my glory ever; till my raptured soul shall find rest beyond the river." Some Christian writers have daringly utilized the erotic imagery of "ravishment" to describe the experience of rapture.

Jonathan Edwards, in his *Faithful Narrative of the Surprising Work of God* (1735) during the Great

Awakening, reported the rapturous experience of terrified sinners finally assured of divine grace, "filling the soul brim full, enlarging the heart, and opening the mouth in religion." Converts had "so great a sense of the glory of God and excellency of Christ, that nature and life … seemed almost to sink under it; and in all probability if God had showed them a little more of himself it would have dissolved their frame."

Recently Edith Humphrey, in *Ecstasy and Intimacy* (2006), has explored the contours of the Christian experience of deep spiritual communion and explained how some relinquishment of self is required to enter into ecstatic (or rapturous) union with God. The self-forgetfulness implicit in genuine religious rapture also serves as a firewall against its deterioration into pride or spiritual indulgence.

In the second place, however, the term *rapture* denotes the biblically predicted eschatological event in which living Christians will be "caught up" in the clouds together with recently resurrected saints to meet the Lord in the air, and then be with him forever (1 Thess. 4:16 – 18). Eager anticipation of this denouement is meant to keep Christians "looking up." This expectation is the underlying reason for the exuberant shout of hope found in the Christian liturgy — the *sursum corda*, "Lift up your hearts!" (cf. Luke 21:28).

Dispensationalist Christians (that is, those influenced by nineteenth-century Brethren leader J. N. Darby and the *Scofield Reference Bible* of 1909) have a distinct view of the rapture. They believe that Christ's second coming will take place in two stages. Most of the events foretold in prophecies of Christ's return will occur in the second stage, when Christ comes to the earth openly, in glory and as judge. But prior to this will be a secret return, an unseen event in which Christ will take his church away from the earth to be with him in heaven for a period of time prior to the final events. According to dispensational interpretation, Christ first returns *for* his saints, so that he can then return *with* his saints. Significantly, such a rapture

event could occur at any moment. The chief spiritual effect of such expectation is the sharp edge of immediacy it gives to Christian hope. It is also an incentive to vigilance, lest one be caught behaving badly, or worse still, be left behind.

See also Ecstasy; Fundamentalist Spirituality; Second Coming.

For Further Reading: A. Hultberg et al., *Three Views on the Rapture* (2010); G. Rawlyk, *Ravished by the Spirit: Religious Revivals, Baptists, and Henry Alline* (1984).

Fred Sanders and Glen G. Scorgie

Rauschenbusch, Walter (1861 – 1918)

American Baptist pastor and theologian of the Social Gospel movement. Born in Rochester, New York, to recent immigrants from Germany, Rauschenbusch studied in Germany for four years after completing high school. He later returned to study at the University of Rochester and Rochester Theological Seminary. After graduation in 1886, he assumed the pastorate of New York City's Second German Baptist Church in a depressed neighborhood known as Hell's Kitchen. While sharing life with poor immigrants and networking with pastors in similar situations, he began to explore the social teachings of the Bible over against the individualized faith of his tradition. He helped form the Brotherhood of the Kingdom, a fellowship of pastors dedicated to study, propagate, and demonstrate the kingdom of God. A study leave in Berlin in 1891 enabled him to further investigate the social teachings of the NT. In 1897 he became a professor of New Testament in the German department of Rochester Theological Seminary, and in 1902 he was offered the chair in church history, a position he held until his death in 1918.

His three best-known works are *Christianity and the Social Crisis* (1907), *Christianizing the Social Order* (1912), and *A Theology for the Social Gospel* (1917), which is still in print. Although he is most remembered as a social prophet, he maintained the deep piety of a prayer-filled life. His collection *Prayers of the Social Awakening* (1910) beautifully integrates love for God and a yearning for God's justice to be known on earth. His legacy was to correct a privatized religion by reigniting an understanding of the kingdom and its implications for all dimensions of life.

See also Kingdom of God; Social Justice.

For Further Reading: C. Evans, *The Kingdom Is Always But Coming: A Life of Walter Rauschenbusch* (2004); *Walter Rauschenbusch: Selected Writings*, SAS (1984).

Allan Effa

Reading, Spiritual

See **Spiritual Reading.**

Reconciliation

The theme of reconciliation presupposes that sin is estranging in its effects. In Christian spirituality, the theme is three-pronged. First, God in Jesus Christ became human in order to reconcile humanity to himself. The language of reconciliation is central to Paul's account of the good news in Jesus Christ. Reconciliation, which is made possible by the sacrificial death of Christ, brings about peace with God, that is, as Volf says, "reception into the eternal communion of God." Second, in what is often described as a horizontal dimension of reconciliation, the work of Christ becomes the ground to overcoming alienation among human beings and between human beings and the rest of creation. The former is dramatically displayed in the reconciliation of Jews and Gentiles into one body, the church (Eph. 2:11–22) and the latter in the vision of the eschatological time when the wolf will live in peace with the lamb and leopard with the goat, all being led by a child (Isa. 11:6–11). Meanwhile, the rest of creation still awaits the moment of its own

deliverance (Rom. 8:19; 2 Peter 3:13). Third, the NT takes the notion of reconciliation in Christ to a new height by suggesting a cosmic reconciliation whereby all things on earth and in heaven will be gathered up in Christ (Eph. 1:9–10; Col. 1:19–20).

Reconciliation in the NT is not only what Christ accomplished, but also the ministry entrusted to the church as a reconciled and reconciling community. Having been reconciled with God, believers, individually and collectively, are to act as ambassadors, appealing to the world on Christ's behalf to be reconciled with God (2 Cor. 5:18–20). This ministry becomes the occasion for a more intimate relationship with Christ, for even here reconciliation is still the work of God in Christ. Believers are ambassadors for Christ, for God makes his appeal for reconciliation through them. To be such ambassadors requires in the first place being open to God's grace in Christ, then ensuring that this reconciling power is continually modeled in the church's own corporate life, and finally becoming, individually and collectively, conduits of God's reconciling grace to others.

See also Forgiveness.

For Further Reading: E. Katongole and C. Rice, *Reconciling All Things* (2008); R. Schreiter, *Reconciliation* (1992); M. Volf, *Exclusion and Embrace* (1996).

Mabiala Justin-Robert Kenzo

Reform

See **Chapter 21.**

Reformation

See **Chapter 16.**

Reformed (Calvinist) Spirituality

Reformed spirituality is a Protestant tradition of piety rooted in the sixteenth-century theology of

John Calvin and his heirs. The term indicates that while Calvin was an important figure in shaping what became known as the Reformed (Calvinist) tradition, there was a Reformed spirituality in existence before and after him. Reformed spirituality begins with Zwingli and Bullinger in Zurich, extends to Calvin and his successors in Geneva, and includes, among others, English Puritans, Scottish Presbyterians, Dutch Calvinists, and in America, Jonathan Edwards and New England Puritanism, the Old Princeton School, and the Mercersburg Theologians. Classical Reformed writers did not use the modern word *spirituality*. They employed the older term *piety* to refer to the Christian life.

Reformed spirituality was shaped initially in reaction to popular late medieval Roman Catholic devotion with its emphasis on penitence, saints, relics, Mary, asceticism, and mysticism. It was also influenced by Renaissance humanism, which had a profoundly different way of looking at human knowledge and experience in the world. Following the Christian humanists, Reformed theologians emphasized God's transcendence over the world rather than God's immanence in human mystical experience. Deeply suspicious of the capacity of sinful humans to know God directly, Reformed spirituality stressed that God is known indirectly in God's words and actions.

Reformed spirituality is evangelical with an emphasis on grace and conversion, the need to confess one's sin (repentance) and trust in Christ alone (faith) for salvation—an emphasis found in Luther's doctrine of justification. But as a second-generation Reformer, Calvin also emphasized union with Christ and regeneration by the Holy Spirit as the basis of the Christian life. The spiritual life is a grateful response to God's gracious forgiveness. The purpose of life, as the seventeenth-century Westminster Shorter Catechism puts it, is "to glorify God and to enjoy him forever" (Q. 1). In the Reformed spiritual tradition, the Christian life is often portrayed as a pilgrimage marked by spiritual struggle and joyful obedience (e.g.,

John Bunyan's classic *The Pilgrim's Progress*). This emphasis on sanctification, the third use of the law, and the disciplined life sometimes led to legalism. Reformed spirituality has often been characterized by a rigorous stress on strict Sabbath observance, obligatory daily family devotions, the singing of the psalms, and private prayer.

Reformed spiritual practices have focused primarily on the means of grace, which the Westminster Shorter Catechism calls "the outward and ordinary means whereby Christ communicates to us the benefits of his redemption ... especially the Word, the sacraments, and prayer" (Q. 88). Accordingly, the Bible is central to Reformed piety. The spiritual life exists from hearing and believing the Word of God. The Reformed tradition teaches that this Word is the source of personal renewal and that God's Spirit uses the written Word to help believers grow in "the nurture and admonition of the Lord."

The theology and practice of the sacraments vary in the tradition. Baptism bestows Christian identity on believers and their children. Calvin spoke of the "true presence of Christ" in the Lord's Supper and emphasized the communion of the believer, by faith and the Holy Spirit, with the ascended Christ. The infrequent celebration of Communion in the later tradition (contra Calvin) emphasized the need for true repentance and faith. Reformed celebrations of Communion were normally preceded by preparatory services that focused on self-examination.

Reformed piety emphasizes the mind, heart, and will. In his *Institutes*, Calvin defined piety as "that reverence joined with love of God which the knowledge of his benefits induces." The Christian life is understood primarily as the cultivation of Christ-centered faith and godly knowledge in the service of God and neighbor. It does not exclude religious experiences either routine or ecstatic, but fostering experiences of the divine was not the primary focus. In addition to Bible reading, Reformed spiritual practices intended to encourage an educated growth in grace by catechetical training, diary keeping, and letter writing, and by reading spiritual autobiographies.

The Reformed spiritual tradition has generally eschewed the monastic and contemplative in favor of active engagement with the world. All of life is understood as belonging to God and to be lived under Christ's lordship. Christian piety is to find expression not only in the individual soul and the church, but in every realm—social, political, economic, and cultural.

Reformed spirituality is often deeply introspective and marked by anxiety, brooding, and spiritual heaviness. Such an ethos is rooted in a particular appropriation of the doctrine of predestination and the desire for assurance of salvation. The Puritans were the great spiritual doctors of the Reformed tradition who examined "the order of salvation." Spiritual disciplines in the Reformed tradition were never the means through which one earned salvation, but they often became the means through which one sought assurance of salvation.

In recent years, Reformed spirituality has been influenced by other great traditions of Christian spirituality, such as contemplative prayer. The ecumenical breadth, cultural diversity, and global expansion of the Christian movement, as well as the contemporary interest in spirituality, have all affected the spiritual practices of Reformed Christians.

See also Calvin, John.

For Further Reading: L. Bouyer, *History of Christian Spirituality,* vol. 3 (1969); H. Hageman, "Reformed Spirituality," in *Protestant Spiritual Traditions,* ed. F. Senn (1986), 55–79; T. Hall IV, "The Shape of Reformed Piety," in *Spiritual Traditions for the Contemporary Church,* ed. R. Maas and G. O'Donnell (1990), 202–21; H. Old, "What Is Reformed Spirituality?" *Calvin Studies* 7 (1994): 61–68; H. Rice, *Reformed Spirituality* (1991).

John A. Vissers

Regeneration

Regeneration is that work of God that provides new life and a new nature to the faithful, enabling them to relate to him with the compatible disposition he originally intended, and to live in full obedience to him.

God provides the supernatural gift of regeneration as a merciful response to humans' inability to achieve heartfelt and truly righteous character on their own (Rom. 3:9–20). Though converts cannot remain passive observers of the dynamics of conversion but must respond personally to God's grace, regeneration per se is monergistic—a work of God alone for humanity's benefit. This work, attributed particularly to the person of the Holy Spirit (John 3:5–8), is accomplished through the imparting of the resurrection life of Jesus Christ himself. Those who are born of the Spirit consequently become children of God (John 1:12–13) and members of his household (Eph. 2:19)— imagery that implies both familial belonging and an expectation of ever-clearer manifestations of "genetic similarities" to the divine parent (1 John 3:1–3).

The new life is neither the resuscitation of a previous life once lost nor merely a new start. It is, rather, a new creation (2 Cor. 5:17)—a being with a new nature that now is not only able to commune intimately with God, but is also outfitted with a new disposition that strives to respond rightly to him and to keep his commands (1 John). Consequently, the primary evidences of regeneration are faith in Jesus Christ, growing conformity to his character and disposition, and ready obedience and service—in short, a life marked by faith, hope, and love.

While the word *regeneration* (Gr. *palingenesis*) appears only twice in the NT (Matt. 19:28; Titus 3:5), the same idea is conveyed through a number of other phrases and analogies. These include, but are not limited to, "born again," "born of God," and "new creation." Furthermore, the idea is not peculiar to the NT but is found in the OT whenever God speaks of that day when he will renew the hearts of his people toward him (e.g., Jer. 31; Ezek. 11:19–20).

Some, including Calvin, have used the term *regeneration* to refer to the whole of the salvation experience. Following earlier Anabaptists, Pietists, and eighteenth- and nineteenth-century evangelicals, contemporary evangelicals tend to regard regeneration as the instantaneous and inaugural event of Christian experience that looks beyond itself to a life of continual growth in grace. In celebrating the mysterious transformation of becoming "born again," evangelicals are protected against a merely transactional, change-of-status notion of salvation.

See also Baptism of the Holy Spirit; Conversion.

For Further Reading: W. Best, *Regeneration and Conversion* (1975); P. Toon, *Born Again* (1987).

Bernie Van De Walle

Relics

Physical remains or possessions of a saint or holy person, said to be a source of spiritual power. God's grace, formerly at work in the life of the person, is ostensibly working for those who pray to the relic or venerate the memory of the saint. Relics of Jesus Christ such as the cross and burial sheet have been most prized.

Veneration of relics was an accepted practice of church fathers, with biblical precedence commonly cited from both testaments (e.g., 2 Kings 13:21; Acts 19:12). Reports of miracles were commonplace. Ambrose boasted that while others collected silver, Christians gathered the nails and blood of martyrs. Chrysostom said that God allowed the remains of saints to be gathered for purposes of leading in righteousness. Relics became staples in church buildings, which were often built on the sites of saints' graves. Caution was raised at times. Antony of Egypt demanded that he be buried in a secret place so his corpse would not become a target of piracy or worship. Athanasius concurred and disposed of relics given to him. Augustine bemoaned rampant commercialization of real and fictitious relics; nevertheless, he bore testimony to their miracles.

Medieval veneration reached scandalous commercial proportions, making the attack on relics a central tenet of the Reformation. Luther said that relics were "lifeless, dead things that can make no man holy." John Calvin's tract on relics was his most widely distributed. He lamented sarcastically that for each apostle there has been pawned the parts of four bodies, and bemoaned that while people should have been seeking Christ, they were instead chasing after his alleged garments. While Reformers purged relics, the Catholic Church confirmed their sacredness at the Council of Trent. Today the cult of relics is regulated through the Congregation for Divine Worship and the Discipline of the Sacraments.

There may be a mediating position. As Thomas Aquinas purported, the veneration of relics finds its parallel in the natural tendency to respect the bodies and belongings of the deceased. Coupled with the fact that God conveys spiritual truths through physical objects, there may have been a legitimate early impulse with relics that was contaminated by human idolatry. Meditating over Plymouth Rock may evoke the spirit of the Pilgrims, just as a signed copy of a saintly author's book may bring the reader into a heightened spiritual space. But such objects at best prompt for us what has already been authored by the triune God, the originator of all things spiritual and material, and the only worthy recipient of worship.

See also Primal Religions; Sacrament.

For Further Reading: J. Nickell, *Relics of the Christ* (2007); F. Chiovaro, "Relics," in *NCE*.

T. C. Porter

Religious Life

The Christian life involves committed response to a discerned calling. Every believer is called to follow Jesus in words of witness and deeds of love. Yet this shared calling is lived out in a great variety of vocations and endeavors. "Religious life," so-called, is an umbrella term for a cluster of vocations that have been very important and influential in the history of Christianity, especially within the Catholic and Orthodox traditions. The "religious" option designates a life characterized by poverty, celibacy, obedience, and prayer—each expressive of a radical devotion to the coming kingdom and to service of others. To realize such a life, men and women have for centuries withdrawn from the mainstream way of life to develop a new lifestyle in pursuit of Christian perfection. A life lived according to the aforementioned "evangelical counsels" requires a special calling and grace; it is not, in short, for everyone.

The "religious life" was nascent even in the 1st century and soon spread from the Middle East and central parts of North Africa throughout the entire Christian world. Some "religious" lived lonely, ascetic lives devoted to prayer, contemplation, and spiritual guidance. Others withdrew in small groups with a few companions, seeking solitude in community. Still others organized larger communities inspired by particular leaders or schools of spirituality and developed a common life structured by liturgical and personal prayer, studies, and practical work. Others followed the poor and homeless Christ as solitary wanderers or pilgrims committed to evangelization and the radical ideals of the coming kingdom.

Religious life is not a single, uniform tradition, but a diverse conglomeration of many "orders," each shaped by its own visionary founder and its distinct sense of mission, and reflective of the contexts in which it first came to life and later developed. By its very nature, religious life is both intentionally differentiated from the mainstream and passionate, and therefore it sometimes stands in ambivalent and uncomfortable relationship to the institutional church. Across the centuries, those who have embraced the religious life have richly resourced and influenced Christian spirituality in profound ways.

The Protestant Reformers rejected the religious life, or at least what it had become by the late Middle Ages. They regarded its withdrawal from ordinary social and family life to a presumably higher, more privileged way of prayer and Christian perfection as theologically invalid. For them the religious life implied that the Christian life was hierarchical—surely a false and spiritually damaging notion. It supported tendencies to privilege religious over lay, spiritual over material, and withdrawal and contemplation over engagement and work. This contradicted on every point basic theological convictions in Reformation theology and was therefore deemed unacceptable.

Today, in the context of a restless, stressful, consumption-focused culture, some of these issues are being reassessed. Basic Protestant doctrinal convictions are not being challenged, but there is a desire to explore the fullest range of viable and valid expressions of Christian discipleship. Perceptions of religious impoverishment and spiritual longing are prompting greater ecumenical openness and rapprochement. Aspects of the religious life, and its underlying commitments and rigor, are being selectively appropriated in many creative new ways. Among the hopeful signs in Western and Protestant traditions is the establishment of smaller communities of committed Christians, ecumenical retreat centers, pilgrim houses, and monasteries devoted to prayer, along with the realization of sacramental Communion and of social fellowship in service to a needy world.

See also Benedictine Spirituality; Monasticism; Rules, Religious.

For Further Reading: L. Cunningham and K. Egan, *Christian Spirituality* (1996); A. McGrath, *Roots That Refresh* (1995); P. Sheldrake, *Spirituality and History* (1995); R. Williams, *The Wound of Knowledge* (2002).

Leif Gunnar Engedal

Relinquishment

See **Surrender.**

Remembering and Forgetting

Christians who take the Bible seriously bear a significant challenge to sort through the various scriptural admonitions regarding remembering and forgetting. Both the Old and New Testaments contain a frequent theme of encouraging God's people to remember God's love and provision for them (e.g., Ex. 15; Josh. 24:17–18; Lam. 3:22–23; Mt. 6:25–34; Luke 15; John 10). God invites human beings to enter into a covenantal relationship, and many Scripture passages exhort us to remember God's faithfulness and to strive to remain faithful to God in return (e.g., Gen. 9; Deut. 11; many Pss., including 28, 37, and 66; Rom. 5; Heb. 8).

Memory is one of the hallmarks of human experience. The recollection of experiences and feelings is foundational to our identity and sense of self. We struggle to know how to relate to persons who have significant memory loss or damage. Pleasant memories sustain us through hardships and times of suffering. The well-known adage "Those who forget the past are doomed to repeat it" reinforces the importance of remembering the lessons of history on both individual and communal levels.

Christian spirituality is grounded in numerous rituals of remembrance, including the Christian liturgical calendar with the high points of Christmas and Easter and the regular observance of Communion in remembrance of the Last Supper. These rituals serve to strengthen and encourage believers to stay strong in the faith and to hold fast to the hope of heaven and the second coming of Christ. They are rooted in remembrance of God's faithfulness and care in the past, which gives hope for the future.

But the Christian message is not simply one of remembering God's goodness, faithfulness, and love. The gospel, the good news, is that God forgets — not in the fickle way that human beings forget (e.g., misplacing things, failing to recall important things, absentmindedly neglecting things); God intentionally forgets the worst about humans — our sinful, erring ways that cause God, ourselves, and other people so much pain. The overriding message of the gospel is that through Christ Jesus we are forgiven of all our sins, freed from the burden and guilt of sin, and God forgets about our past sinfulness so completely it is as if our sins are transported "as far as the east is from the west" (Ps. 103:12).

It may appear then that Christianity is simply a matter of remembering the good and forgetting the bad. However, it is considerably more complex than that. Survivors of genocide in the past century teach us that it is a complicated matter to heal from trauma — knowing what to forget while preserving the memory of what should never be forgotten. Ultimately, for Christians, remembering and forgetting are about healing and restoration, about forgiveness for the past and hope for the future, and about God's guidance in helping us discern when to remember and when to forget.

For Further Reading: B. Childs, *Memory and Tradition in Israel* (1962); C. Elliott, *Memory and Salvation* (1995); P. Gobodo-Madikizela, *A Human Being Died That Night* (2004); T. Kidder, *Strength in What Remains: A Journey of Remembrance and Forgiveness* (2009).

Myrla Seibold

Renewal

See **Chapter 21.**

Repentance

See **Penitence.**

Responsibility

The very use of the term *responsibility* in spiritual formation implies at least two things: human freedom and human intentionality. If humans are in some way responsible, then some level of human freedom is required. Subsequently, this implies that human persons are to some significant degree responsible for their spiritual formation. If this is true, than spiritual formation must also require responsible *intentionality* on the part of human persons.

Spiritual formation is indeed a matter of human responsibility even though it is only possible through the empowerment of the Holy Spirit. For this reason, it requires intentionality on the part of the believer. Throughout his writings, the apostle Paul used language that strongly indicated believers' responsibility to bring about ongoing spiritual transformation. He urged them with metaphorical phrases that advocate intention and resolve, including "putting to death," "ridding themselves," and "clothing themselves."

But responsibility, as it relates to spiritual formation, must always be kept in check; otherwise it may lead to a kind of "duty" fueled by nothing more than human willpower (*see* Perfectionism). Spiritual formation may be conceptualized in many ways, but at the very least it is a reorientation toward God and a rehabilitation of the human person—both ultimately made possible by God's grace. While humans are free to engage responsibly with God to bring about these changes, and while indeed God will not force his will on any person, it is God alone who creates this state of human freedom. The human capacity to respond to God's grace is paradoxically possible only *because* of God's grace. It is God who makes it possible for humans to be responsible and *response-able*.

Human freedom and personal responsibility, however, are not unlimited. Both can be severely impacted by genetics, upbringing, culture, race, gender, education, and even socioeconomic status. How truly free and responsible are persons suffering from mental illness and a history of trauma? How culpable are they for their behavior? Can a balance be struck between human freedom/responsibility and rigid determinism? Once again, it is the

gift of God's grace that empowers such persons, where they are, to bring about reorientation and rehabilitation. The testimony of Scripture, the church, and even the findings of contemporary psychotherapy suggest that even with severe qualifications on personal responsibility, some level of human liberty remains for cooperation with God's grace in bringing about transformation.

This transformation is not only an inward change, brought about by the twofold path of human responsibility and Spirit empowerment, but also includes one's lived life in the world. Believers are encouraged to walk by the Spirit (Gal. 5:16), which includes the fruits of the Spirit—love, joy, peace, patience, kindness, goodness, faithfulness, gentleness, and self-control (Gal. 5:22–23). Scripture also speaks of specific vices that should be left behind (e.g., Gal. 5:19–21; Col. 3:5–10) and specific virtues that should be taken up (Col. 3:12) in the ongoing journey of spiritual maturity. And perhaps most significantly, Jesus himself reminds believers that the spiritual path involves responsibility toward the other. The two greatest commandments, which sum up all the Law and the Prophets, include love of God and love of neighbor (Matt. 22:34–38; Mark 12:28–34; Luke 10:27). The responsibility (*response-ability*) of the believer, made capable by God's grace, will impact both the inward way of the heart as well as the outward way of living.

See also Accountability.

For Further Reading: J. Cobb, *Grace and Responsibility* (1995); E. Erikson, *Insight and Responsibility* (1964/1972); R. Maddox, *Responsible Grace* (1994); T. Oord and M. Lodahl, *Relational Holiness* (2005).

Brad D. Strawn

Resurrection

Christianity celebrates an empty tomb. The historical fact, the future promise, and the pervasive motif of resurrection are central to the Christian faith and its spirituality. Old Testament passages that speak of God's power to raise the dead (e.g., 1 Sam. 2:6; 1 Kings 17:22; 2 Kings 4:35; 13:21; Ps. 30:3) already anticipate it. The historic resurrection of Christ is highlighted in the Gospels, affirmed in the Epistles, and confessed in the ancient creeds. The crucifixion was the redemptive moment at which atoning sacrifice was made for humanity's sin, but the resurrection completed this redemptive act by triumphing over death, sin's ultimate penalty, and making new life possible for believers in Christ. The NT differentiates the historic resurrection of Christ from the promised resurrection of believers at the second coming. Yet these two resurrections are really inseparable, since the former ensures the latter. Together as a linked pair, they have formed the core of the gospel from its inception (1 Cor. 15:1–4).

The resurrection of Christ is the focal point of myriad formal and informal Christian spiritual practices. Easter is the high point of the liturgical year, and the Easter event is referenced in every major Protestant, Roman Catholic, and Eastern Orthodox liturgy throughout the year, in the Apostles' and Nicene creeds, in prayers, and in hymns. The memory of the resurrection is elicited in Christian baptism, marriage, and funerals, in formal ceremonies and personal devotions. It also calls to mind the doctrine of the incarnation, a closely related facet of Christian theology; for both presuppose the importance of material embodiment.

On a practical level, the resurrection shapes the Christian worldview. Without it, death would signal a final halt to individual human existence. With it, death becomes penultimate and provisional. The resurrection of Jesus acts as a compass to Christians, pointing them toward the Easter power of the Holy Spirit and the demonstrated faithfulness of God to his Son, and also, by implication, to those who likewise place their trust in him. The historical resurrection of Jesus is the preeminent sign that the *eschaton* has begun, that the kingdom of God has been inaugurated in the world, and God is bringing it ever closer to fulfillment. It empowers Christians to invest their lives boldly in that kingdom and alters their attitudes toward their present and anticipated circumstances.

When Christians encounter challenges and tragedies in life, the resurrection inspires them to hope nonetheless. The resurrection continues to anchor and stimulate the early Christian spirit of *Christus Victor* ("Christ is Victor!"). Whenever Christians encounter evil and death, they can look back to the resurrection of Christ and then forward to their own (and the assured complete defeat of evil) for comfort, encouragement, and enduring inspiration. With irrepressibly buoyant hearts, they claim "a living hope through the resurrection of Jesus Christ from the dead" (1 Peter 1:3). Such hope encourages them to live holy lives, knowing that they are persevering toward a real and enduring future.

The resurrection of the body in Christian spirituality is markedly different than the Hellenistic belief in the immortality of the soul. For the Christian, resurrection issues in an eternal embodied existence. At the end of the present age, believers' bodies will be raised from the dead and they will exist eternally with Christ. Because this affirms body-soul unity, Christian spirituality possesses a certain physicality—physical postures affect and encourage spiritual dispositions; practices that damage the body, such as promiscuity and substance abuse, are discouraged because they also damage the soul and dishonor the divine breath that first gave the body life; even basic functions take on new meaning as breath is used to help concentrate prayer and physical food becomes spiritual sustenance in the practice of Communion.

See also Afterlife; Body; Cross, The; Incarnation.

For Further Reading: M. Harris, *From Grave to Glory* (1990); N. T. Wright, *The Resurrection of the Son of God* (2003); idem, *Surprised by Hope* (2008).

Cynthia Cheshire

Retreats

The practice of spiritual retreat is modeled on Jesus' time in the wilderness as recorded in the Gospels.

During forty days of fasting, solitude, and prayer, Jesus was confronted by Satan with three specific temptations. He resisted all three. Later in the Gospels, Jesus is shown rising early and going apart to pray. Devout Christians have continued the practice of spiritual retreat throughout the centuries. Modern retreats are strongly influenced by Ignatius Loyola, founder of the Society of Jesus (the Jesuits). Ignatius composed his *Spiritual Exercises* over the years 1522–1524; this collection of prayers, meditations, and exercises is aimed at helping retreatants to draw closer to God, discern God's will, and choose to follow God's leading in their lives. The Ignatian exercises are designed to arouse the spiritual imagination. They help believers to sense the contrast between Jesus' influence on us and that of Satan. Loyola's *Spiritual Exercises* are adaptable. Divided into four segments, or "weeks," the exercises may be carried out in three days, seven days, thirty days, or even over a more extended time. However, the Ignatian exercises require that the individual be led by an experienced spiritual director. Since the early 1800s, the Ignatian retreat has been led by the Cenacle Sisters as well as the Jesuits themselves. The exercises have been adapted for use by Protestants as well as Catholics. Today non-Ignatian retreats are also offered in many Christian settings. One key element in the modern retreat is "going apart," or choosing a brief separation from the world, whether in the city or the country. Several retreat formats are in common use: the preached retreat, entailing a series of formal conferences; the silent retreat; and the directed retreat, which offers long periods of prayer and meetings with a trained spiritual director. Other important practices include devotion, confession, and worship. Both for laypeople and those in religious life, a retreat may be a life-changing experience.

See also Camps and Camping.

For Further Reading: W. Barry, *Finding God in All Things* (1991); E. Griffin, *Wilderness Time* (1997); J. Johnson, *Living in the Companionship of God* (2009); T. Jones, *A Place for God* (2000);

J. Tetlow, *The Spiritual Exercises of Ignatius Loyola* (2009); J. Vennard, *Be Still* (2000).

Emilie Griffin

Revival

Through the centuries, Christianity has experienced an ebb and flow in its fervor and intensity. Revivals—moments of upswing—are significant religious phenomena, characterized by powerful emotions (such as guilt and joy), contagious social dynamics, and lasting dispositional and behavioral effects. Beyond this, definitions of revival range from moments when the religious commitment of nominal Christians is renewed to events at which unbelievers embrace faith, to situations in which both of these outcomes (Christians refreshed and the lost saved) occur. Historian William McLoughlin has helpfully distinguished revivals from awakenings by noting that a revival is a local event with limited effects, while an awakening is a much larger, culture-wide revitalization movement. Even so, evangelical spirituality has been profoundly shaped by the powerful ripple effects of revivals. Often, for example, revivals stimulate evangelism, missions, and social reform for generations to follow.

Revivals continue to be significant in the global expansion of Christianity, just as they have been in the history of American Christianity. The phenomenon of revival was pervasive along the frontier but was not restricted to rural contexts or the relatively uneducated; it has also been felt in urban settings and among the highly educated (like Timothy Dwight, a president of Yale). During revivals religious truth claims enjoy heightened, self-authenticating plausibility. Colonial American theologian Jonathan Edwards observed during the Great Awakening, "The converting influences of God's Spirit very commonly bring an extraordinary conviction of the reality and certainty of the great things of religion" that does "more to convince [people] than reading many volumes of argument without it." He concluded that for revived individuals it was as though a strong blaze of light had overcome all their objections, and they "intuitively beheld, and immediately felt" its truth.

The doctrinal framework undergirding the revivals of the First Great Awakening was decidedly Calvinistic, while the doctrinal outlook informing the revivals of the Second Great Awakening was typically Arminian. The transition from the one to the other took about fifty years, but since then the latter theological orientation has shaped the greater part of revivalist preaching in America and around the world. Though revivals were seminal for historic evangelicalism, they were not an exclusively Protestant phenomenon, as Jay Dolan has pointed out. While paralleling much of Protestant revivalism, nineteenth-century Catholic revivalism developed its own approach through parish missions and innovative preaching.

Opinions differ on the primary cause or means of a revival. Sociological analyses can helpfully illuminate promising conditions and ensuing dynamics of revival; seldom do they adequately account for it. Some regard revivals as divinely initiated by a "surprising work of God" (Jonathan Edwards), while others see them made possible through skillful human orchestration of proven strategies and techniques. Charles Finney wrote in his *Revival Lectures* that a revival is not a miracle or the result of a miracle, but the predictable result of the right use of constituted means. In nineteenth-century America, no revivalist was more successful than Finney at evoking desired responses through his "new measures." Later revivalists adapted Finney's methods to their social contexts. While the appropriate means and the genuineness of response will continue to be debated, there is ample evidence that those caught up in a revival atmosphere experience strong emotions, which in turn produce changes in heads, hearts, and hands (that is, in thoughts, feelings, and deeds). Revivalists' appeal to feeling is compatible with recent psychological insights about the importance of emotion in altering neural networking and the default settings of the psyche.

Unfortunately, the shift from surprising work of God to orchestrated campaign has taken a toll on Christian spirituality. At its extreme, revivalism has sometimes earned a bad reputation for its indulgence in manipulative emotional hype, money grabbing, and the hypocritical lifestyles of some leaders (classically depicted in Elmer Gantry). Nonetheless, many people have been genuinely transformed through the ministries of faithful revivalists such as Dwight L. Moody and Billy Graham. The challenge is always to discern between genuine and false revivals. In evangelical spirituality, the historic revival motif has heightened regard for strong emotion experiences as validating evidence of a genuine work of divine grace. It has also meant that the Christian life is envisioned less as a smooth, progressive ascent and more like a chain of memorably decisive episodes.

For Further Reading: E. Cairns, *An Endless Line of Splendor* (1986); J. Dolan, *Catholic Revivalism* (1978); J. Edwards, *A Faithful Narrative of the Surprising Work of God* (1979); W. McLoughlin, *Revivals, Awakenings, and Reform* (1978); R. Mouw, *The Smell of Sawdust* (2000); T. Smith, *Revivalism and Social Reform* (1957).

Wayne S. Hansen and Glen G. Scorgie

Rewards

Though often misunderstood and sometimes denigrated, rewards are part of scriptural teaching about the Christian life. The promise of reward and the warning of judgment are two sides of the same biblical reality, with believers encouraged that their godly lives will not go unrewarded, nor will disobedience by a believer or unbeliever go unpunished.

In the NT, a great reward is promised to anyone who is persecuted and maligned for the cause of the kingdom of heaven (Matt. 5:11–12), while the rewards of a prophet and righteous person are promised to those who receive a prophet or righteous person; even the offer of a cold cup of water will not go unrewarded (10:40–42). Likewise, love of one's enemies will be met with great reward, as this action reveals one to be a son of the Most High (Luke 6.35). Rewards are also closely associated with the voluntary proclamation of the gospel (1 Cor. 9:17), with those active in reaping the spiritual harvest spoken of as already receiving their rewards/wages (John 4.36). All laborers for the Lord are assured that they will be rewarded according to their own works (1 Cor. 3:8), provided that their work survives the testing of fire (vv. 14–15).

Conversely, those who do their acts of righteousness (almsgiving, prayer, fasting) in public will not be rewarded by their Father in heaven but have their reward already in the form of human praise (Matt. 6:1–2, 5, 16). More ominously, false teachers will be paid back for the harm they have caused (2 Peter 2:15), while believers are warned not to lose the reward of eternal life for which they have worked (2 John 8). The Christian lives in the full knowledge that the time of eschatological reward and judgment draws near (Rev. 11:18) when Jesus himself brings his reward with him (Rev. 22:12).

While rewards serve both to motivate Christian living and to warn against a compromised Christian witness, the role of rewards in the life of the believer is far from a quid pro quo understanding of grace, for rewards are closely tied to activities of the believer that reflect the nature and mission of God. The dialectical relationship between grace and reward points to the divine-human cooperation essential to the godly life, an understanding nicely summed up in Revelation 19:8 where the clean linen garment given to the bride by God (or the Lamb) is described as the righteous acts of the saints.

For Further Reading: B. Charette, *The Theme of Recompense in Matthew's Gospel* (1992); W. Kroll, *It Will Be Worth It All* (1977).

John Christopher Thomas

Richard of St. Victor

See **Victorine Spirituality.**

Ritual

Ritual as a term first came into prominence in the Reformation era as a negative term describing "empty or mere ritual," that is, those actions that are done by rote and often out of ignorance if not fear. *Ritual* was not a complimentary term; it was what "those people" did, and certainly not your faith community. By the publication of the first edition of the *Encyclopedia Britannica* in 1771, *ritual* was defined in neutral terms as a book that directed the order of religious ceremonies, and then in the third edition (1797) this was expanded to describe the ceremonial actions themselves. And so it continues today with *ritual* serving as both a divisive term and a neutral term with variable breadth of meaning.

Ritual, as defined by many scholars in the field, is based on communication theory. We often accompany our spoken words with gestures, inflections of voice, body posture, and at times symbols or sounds. As any actor knows, the words in a script are only the beginning of the story; the interpretation of the words lies within the embodiment of the words. So too, ritual is considered to be a symbol enacted. The meaning is found not just in words, but in the intersection of words and actions. For example, one may pray with one's hands folded and eyes closed, one may pray lying prostrate on the floor, or one may pray with hands raised and body swaying. In each case, a person is praying, but one meaning of the prayer is conveyed by his or her body posture and another by the words prayed. One of the ways ritual studies can assist in the spiritual life of an individual or community is to assess the congruence of the words and actions.

Ritual scholars have also discovered that one learns inductively through ritual patterns of behavior and over time grows into their meaning. This is evident in children, who may not understand the value of food and that God is the source of all food, but grow into this understanding through a steady diet of the ritual of table blessing. This has lead to teaching spiritual practices, and specifically body postures for prayer, as a method of spiritual formation.

One must be careful not to confuse ritual with habitual. A ritual is an action with an intended meaning or meanings, often connected to a narrative that provides the meaning of the rite. A wedding is a ritual that has the specific function of joining a couple in marriage. It contains both the cultural narrative of marriage in that society and the narrative of the couple's relationship. Brushing one's teeth, however, is simply a habitual action, lacking intentional symbolic meanings for individual or society. Unfortunately, people often become ignorant of the meaning of rituals, and they disintegrate into mere ritual or obligation or habit. Rituals are inevitable in human life; the question is not "Do you have rituals?" but "How well do you do your rituals?" Intentionality in ritual practice is a spiritual issue for all Christians, regardless of their ritual patterns.

For Further Reading: H. Anderson and E. Foley, *Mighty Stories, Dangerous Rituals* (1998); P. Bradshaw and J. Melloh, eds., *Foundations in Ritual Studies* (2007); B. Cooke and G. Macy, *Christian Symbol and Ritual* (2005).

Todd E. Johnson

Rolle, Richard (1300 – 1349)

Late medieval English hermit. Richard Rolle was born at Thornton in Yorkshire about the year 1300. Information about Rolle's life is taken from an office (that is, a service in commemoration of a saint) of nine lessons that was drawn up for Rolle's canonization in the 1380s. The office, however, gives little information between the initial stages of Rolle's conversion to the eremitical life and the final days of his life. The first office lesson says that Rolle's parents provided for his education but were financially unable to send him to university. Thus, his university costs were paid by Thomas de Neville, the son of Ralph, Lord of Raby, who later became an archdeacon of Durham. Rolle began attending Oxford University at the age of thirteen or fourteen,

showing great interest in the study of theology and biblical studies. At nineteen, desiring knowledge of the Scriptures over secular knowledge, or so the office states, Rolle failed to return to Oxford University. Rather, he took up the life of a hermit by dressing in his sister's tunic, which he modified into his habit. He left home immediately, returning to his birthplace in Thornton. Subsequently, a patron proceeded to house Rolle in a cell in his house and to provide him with an appropriate habit and food. Rolle remained here "for a long time" according to the office, though he was likely only here for a few years. Where Rolle lived from the time that he left his patron to the final months of his life is unknown, though some scholars believe that he studied and taught at the Sorbonne in Paris. Two manuscripts record that Rolle was admitted as a student in 1320 and record that he died while living with the sisters of Hampole in Yorkshire. In another manuscript, he is included on a list of visiting scholars at the university from 1315 to 1320. Rolle died in September 1349 after living for thirty-one years as a hermit.

Rolle wrote spiritual works in both Latin and English. The earliest are his *Canticum Amoris*, a Latin rhyming and alliterative poem to the Virgin Mary, and the *Judica Me Deus*, a translation of a pastoral manual written by Rolle's contemporary, William of Pagula. His last work in English, *The Form of Living*, was intended for enclosed anchoresses and was probably written within a few months of Rolle's death. Rolle produced a number of commentaries, including *Commentary on the Readings in the Office of the Dead* taken from Job; *Commentary on the Canticles*; and two *Commentaries on the Psalter*, one in Latin and one in English, with a translation of the Latin Psalms into English. There is also a longer Latin *Treatise on Psalm 20*; a commentary on Lamentations (*Super Threnos*); a partial *Commentary on the Apocalypse*; and commentaries on the Lord's Prayer, Magnificat, and Apostles' Creed. Further, there is an English explication of the Ten Commandments, a comment on Proverbs 31:10 (*Super Mulierem Fortem*), and another on Psalm

88:2 (*De Dei Misericordia*). There are also two English *Meditations on the Passion*. The *Contra Mundi*, *Melos Amoris*, and *Incendium Amoris* all contain lyrical prayers to Christ or God. Rolle's four extant letters are all addressed to single recipients and contain similar material to his longer works.

Reminiscent of Augustine of Hippo's *Confessions*, Rolle frequently employs medical language when talking about God's work on our behalf—that is, we are spiritually sick and need medicine. As well, like Augustine, Rolle constantly requests God's grace and maintains a consistent emphasis on sin. Rolle employs visual imagery frequently, especially when he is meditating on the passion of Christ, and he frequently makes references to the five senses and their use in the spiritual life. Rolle practices and recommends an unceasing meditation on the wounds of Christ, holds a high view of Marian intercession, and is wont to employ nuptial imagery. The *Incendium Amoris*, oftentimes viewed as Rolle's greatest work, is concerned that all persons be "turned to God" so that they may experience contemplation of God. This is accomplished by one's ascent to a perfect love of God. Like Bernard of Clairvaux and Aelred of Rievaulx, he talks about the degrees of love, maintaining with Aelred that there are three degrees.

See also English Mystics; Julian of Norwich.

For Further Reading: R. S. Allen, "Introduction," in *Richard Rolle: The English Writings,* CWS (1988); R. Woolley, ed., *The Officium and the Miracula of Richard Rolle of Hampole* (1919).

Greg Peters

Roman Catholicism

See Chapter 19.

Romero, Oscar Arnulfo (1917–1980)

Salvadoran bishop and martyr. Romero left his small town on horseback at age fourteen to pursue his priestly vocation. He was ordained in 1942 and by 1977 was the archbishop of San Salvador. At first he was reticent to condemn structural injustice, but he was mobilized by the murder of his friend, Jesuit priest Rutilio Grande, on March 12, 1977. The next day, Romero celebrated Mass in Grande's parish, denouncing human rights violations. This experience marked a change in his pastoral approach, leading to his rediscovery of the church of the poor and his use of sermons to censure the violence carried out with impunity by paramilitary forces allied with rich and powerful Salvadorans. In his homily of March 23, 1980, transmitted by radio, he declared: "In the name of God, therefore, and in the name of this suffering people whose laments rise to the heavens each day with increasing tumultuousness, I beseech you, I beg of you, I command you in the name of God: Stop the repression!" The next day, while celebrating Mass, he was assassinated. He had predicted, "If I am killed, I will rise in the Salvadoran people." He is still remembered by Salvadorans of all faiths as the voice of the voiceless and a witness of God's solidarity with the poor.

See also Liberation Spirituality; Martyrdom; Social Justice.

Nancy E. Bedford

Rosary

A spiritual practice of meditative prayer using a set of beads. The practice of praying with beads originated with the desert fathers and mothers in the 3rd century. However, the form of the rosary developed in the Middle Ages as Irish monks divided the OT psalms into three sets of fifty, using a string of beads to count the psalms as each was prayed. Unfortunately, illiteracy during this period prohibited widespread use of this devotional exercise; therefore, prayers that were shorter, more familiar, and easier to memorize were needed. The Lord's Prayer and the Ave Maria became prominent in the repeated sequences that were substituted for the Psalms; by

1480 the original 150 meditations had been simplified usually to 50 prayers, and the function of the rosary changed from OT meditation to prayerful focus on Jesus Christ and Mary. During the Reformation, Luther did not abolish the rosary but allowed its use as an aid to meditation. Calvin and his followers forbade the rosary in favor of biblical literacy; this left the rosary as a predominantly Roman Catholic practice. Today rosary prayer can be structured in diverse ways and with varied content. The combination of repetitive patterns of prayer with meditation, however, has made the rosary a popular and enduring devotional aid. When practiced mindfully, it can help the practitioner focus on the life, death, and resurrection of Christ.

See also Meditation.

For Further Reading: N. L. Doerr and V. S. Owens, *Praying with Beads* (2007); G. Jensen, *The Rosary* (2006).

Johanna Knutson Vignol

Rule of Life

Christians who are free in Christ are not bound by rules, but they may adopt for themselves certain patterns of spiritual practice that they find healthy. These patterns of various practices may be called a "rule of life." The phrase comes from the "rule" that governed each religious order in the Roman Catholic Church. Among other matters, it described a pattern of life, a communal spirituality that came to distinguish a particular order from others. In the twelfth century, these rules of life came to be identified as core to the "spirituality" of each.

Protestant adaptation of the concept could be said to include a denominational, a congregational, and an individual component. Since there are no historic orders in Protestantism (with very few exceptions), denominations, congregations, and individuals are free to develop their own "rules." Denominations do not generally write explicit rules of life, but they do exemplify different emphases that are incorporated. Some Protestants emphasize silent prayer, others speaking in tongues. Some emphasize social action, others evangelism.

Congregations may be explicit about a rule of life, although perhaps most are not. Some congregations may call on new members explicitly to lead a life of prayer, worship, sacraments, and work for justice and peace. Others may ask for commitments concerning tobacco, alcohol, and evangelism. What is not written down may become evident through a program of preaching and teaching.

A personal rule of life is a written pattern of spiritual practices to which one is committed, not necessarily forever. One may begin to pray in a meditative fashion, consider hospitality, fasting, and advocacy as spiritual practices, and see the need for Scripture to balance these. Since personality types do influence the kinds of prayer we find most fruitful, individuals may choose to adopt kinds of prayer that are easy for them or more challenging styles. Care must be taken not to overload oneself with practices that are unsustainable, but instead take on a healthy yoke that is life giving. One may choose the discipline of being accountable for one's rule of life to an individual or to a congregation.

Thus, writing a rule of life is an exercise, led by the Holy Spirit, in which the Christian carefully determines a pattern of life, a structure, a set of spiritual habits that are seen to develop one's relation to God, to others, and to the creation.

See also *Lex Orandi, Lex Credendi.*

For Further Reading: Marjorie Thompson, "Putting It All Together: Developing a Rule of Life," in *Soul Feast* (1995).

Bradley P. Holt

Rule of St. Benedict

The Rule of St. Benedict was composed by Benedict of Nursia for his monastery in Monte Cassino c. AD 540. About the size of Matthew's gospel, it was quickly recognized as a legislative masterpiece, remarkable for its thoroughness, simplicity, brevity, humanness, and adaptability. The rule is a practical guide ("a little rule for beginners") for living the gospel and for cultivating Christian virtues in the daily life of the monastic community.

Benedict's Rule draws on the desert tradition, the Rule of Basil, the Rule of the Master, John Cassian, and Augustine. After the sack of Cassino (577), the fate of Benedict's Rule in Italy is a mystery; its future would be in Germanic kingdoms and especially in Gaul.

Benedict's Rule combined theoretical spiritual teaching in the first seven chapters (such as his description of humility) with practical regulations to govern the daily life of the monastery in the remaining sixty-six chapters. The latter dealt with the time and quantities of meals, sleep, and prayer; relations with the outside world; authority structures, such as the indispensable role of the abbot, the structure of communal prayer, and so on.

Benedict laced the entire rule with quotes from the Bible; only twelve of the seventy-three chapters have no biblical allusions. Benedict's Rule reflects an interpretation of Scripture that was applied to his single community that he describes in the prologue as "a school for the Lord's service"—a community in which one can learn the trade or skill of discipleship as a Christian apprentice who desires to seek, know, and love God.

Though it was meant only for the monks at Monte Cassino, the Rule of Benedict became the most influential document in the entire history of Western monasticism. Beginning with a decree of Charlemagne, it became *the* rule for Western monasticism from about 800 to 1200 (the "Benedictine centuries"), and it was copied more than any other piece of literature in the Middle Ages except the Bible. Though it borrowed heavily from the earlier and much longer but less adaptable Rule of the Master (by an unknown author around AD 500), it was esteemed because it was a masterful summary or synthesis of the whole preceding monastic experience.

Though some parts of the rule sound extreme to modern ears, a charitable reading reveals its balance, realism, and moderation. Given today's quest for authentic community and what some have called a "new monasticism," this text continues to provide rich resources to God's people.

See also Benedictine Spirituality; Benedict of Nursia; Rules, Religious.

For Further Reading: T. Kardong, *Benedict's Rule* (1996); *RB 1980: The Rule of St. Benedict in Latin and English with Notes*, ed. T. Fry (1981).

Dennis Okholm

Rules, Religious

Written sets of precepts that order life in a monastery or religious community. Religious rules do not comprise a consistent literary genre and often differ greatly in style and content, though most include both theoretical and practical components regarding prayer, worship, fasting, work, and the marking of sacred time and space in common life. At the beginning of the monastic movement in the East, many monks started as disciples to older hermits who instructed them in the ascetic lifestyle. As these communities grew, leaders like Pachomius began to put their guidelines into writing. As the movement spread from the East to the West, several major monastic founders left such "rules," often borrowing from one another's writings.

In the Eastern church, the writings of Basil of Caesarea have been most influential, though monasticism never became as organized or uniform as in the West. In the Roman Catholic Church, the Fourth Lateran Council of 1215 required all religious communities to use the Basilian, Augustinian, or Benedictine rule, though exceptions were later made for the Carmelite, Franciscan, and Jesuit orders. Since the 19th century, Anglican, Lutheran, and other Protestant monastic communities have often adopted rules from such founders as Benedict of Nursia, Augustine of Hippo, or Francis of Assisi.

A rule is different from an order, which refers to a network of communities bound together by both a common rule and a structure of leadership and accountability. Multiple orders may use the same rule; for instance, the Dominican order uses the Augustinian rule. A rule is also distinct from a community's constitutions, which are written guidelines added to the rule and adapted to the particular need or ministry of that community. Many religious societies and congregations founded since the 16th century have only constitutions.

A religious rule is not meant to be an end in itself, but a means to govern communal life, to help community members observe their vows of poverty, chastity, and obedience, and to establish a positive spiritual vision for the community. It also provides a tangible link to the larger monastic tradition. It has been said that a rule is "an introduction to a tradition," thus not a comprehensive guide to monastic spirituality, but a starting point for individuals pursuing such a vocation.

See also Benedictine Spirituality; Monasticism.

For Further Reading: W. Harmless, *Desert Christians* (2004); J. Hellmann, "Spiritual Writings, Genres of," in *The New Dictionary of Catholic Spirituality*, ed. M. Downey (1993); D. Moss, *Of Cell and Cloister* (1957).

Matthew Kemp

Russian Spirituality

Chroniclers date the beginning of the Christian faith in Russia as 988, when Prince Vladimir of Kiev was baptized. The primary reason was the Byzantine eucharistic liturgy as witnessed in the Hagia Sophia; "We knew not whether we were in heaven or earth ... we know only that God abides there." However, it is clear that the forgiveness of sin found at the altar was also crucial. Bouyer comments that "from the first, it was a feature of Russian Christianity that it was a [faith] of penitents."

The origins of Russian spirituality in high worship and individual repentance held sway for hundreds of years. The geographic isolation of the nation and people was exacerbated by the East-West church split in 1054 and the Mongol invasion and subjugation from 1237 to 1480. Rather than

liturgical Latin (Rome) or Greek (Constantinople), Slavonic was used in worship and theological discourse, separating Russia even more.

Initially influenced by the Greek tradition from Mount Athos, Russian monastics expanded their own influence deep into every level of Russian society. The monk Theodosius (1009–1074) lived an austere, penitential life admired by the masses, yet had access to the highest levels of the ruling families. Over the centuries, the church in Russia was bifurcated between the aristocratic official church and the faith of the commoners. The reforms of Peter I (1672–1725) created secular control at the highest levels of church structure, culminating in the absolute control of Catherine II (1729–1796), under whom church leaders became mere functionaries of the state. The growing alienation between the lay believers (now of the lower classes) and the tsarist/empress–controlled church officials resulted by the 1860s in a broad spectrum of the upper and middle classes becoming atheist or agnostic. This continued into the October Revolution of 1917 and the resulting attacks on Christianity. The official church structure permitted by the Communists after the massive waves of martyrdoms and church closures closely resembled the tsarist-controlled church.

Finally, two legacies of the Byzantine tradition that the Russian church made uniquely its own must be lifted up: hesychasm (quiet) and icons. Nilus of Sora (1433–1508) embraced the penitential emphasis of the Russian church and combined it with the cry of the Jesus Prayer from the Eastern fathers, "Lord Jesus Christ, have mercy on me, a sinner." This biblical prayer, repeated in silence, helped believers to "pray without ceasing" (1 Thess. 5:17 KJV) and experience God's presence in deep ways. The *Philokalia*, a collection of writings on hesychasm and the Jesus Prayer, was translated and made available to the laity. As can be seen in *The Way of a Pilgrim* (also known as *The Pilgrim's Tale*), the method was simple, but direction was still needed and provided by *starets* (spiritual directors).

Icons were embraced as aids to the spiritual life by the highest tier of the church, as well as those in the humblest homes of the steppes. An icon's meaning and power in the Russian tradition comes out of liturgy and prayer, created from within a community of worship and discipline, as did the work of iconographer Andrei Rublev (c. 1360–1430), which emerged from his monastic context. Icons are never to be worshiped, but are, as Henri Nouwen reminds us, "gateways to the divine . . . painted to lead us into the inner room of prayer." Thus, the icons of the saints, whether in the sanctuary or at home, remind the worshiper of that great cloud of witnesses who pray with all Christians, making each place of worship "heaven on earth."

Finally, from the beginning, Russian spirituality embraced the kenotic hymn of Philippians 2, and its theology is uniquely prevalent in Russia's history and culture. The self-emptying of Christ was manifested in the Russian spirit as surrender of privilege and acceptance of undeserved suffering and intentional poverty. Kenoticism, as this spiritual path is known in Russia, is present from the canonized monk Theodosius to the writings of great Russian novelists such as Dostoevsky, to theologian Elisabeth Behr-Sigel (1907–2005).

See also Hesychasm; Icons; Jesus Prayer.

For Further Reading: N. Arseniev, *Russian Piety* (1997); L. Bouyer, *A History of Christian Spirituality*, vol. 3, trans. B. Wall (1969); G. Fedotov, *A Treasury of Russian Spirituality* (1948); *Nil Sorsky: The Complete Writings*, CWS (2003); H. Nouwen, *Behold the Beauty of the Lord* (1987); M. Plekon, *Living Icons* (2002); *The Pilgrim's Tale*, CWS (1999).

Kelby Cotton

Rutherford, Samuel (c. 1600–1661)

Scottish theologian and devotional and political writer. Rutherford was controversial much of his life, and his Presbyterianism and strong desire for a covenantal form of church government clashed with the episcopacy of the Scottish church. He emphasized the importance of conversion and pastoral care in his congregation at Anwoth. Twice he was required to appear before the high commission for his nonconformist resistance. The second time he was deposed from his ministry and exiled to Aberdeen, a primary center of episcopacy, for a period of two years. The emotional and spiritual anguish of separation from his much beloved congregation became the impetus for almost two-thirds of his *Letters* (1664), for which he is best known today. These were not meant for publication but effectively reflect the importance of the spiritual practice of letter writing. While half of the letters are directed to women, some of whom had a mentoring relationship over Rutherford, the remaining letters to men reflect the same style that is representative of Bernard of Clairvaux, whom Rutherford occasionally quotes in his writings. Remarkably consistent throughout is the bridal imagery of spiritual marriage and the erotic love language of ravishment of the Song of Songs. The enduring value of these letters is no doubt found in the common themes of God's comfort and hope and intimacy with Jesus Christ even amid the numerous afflictions of life. His *Letters* became a devotional classic, influencing many, including Charles Spurgeon, Alexander Whyte, and Hudson Taylor. When the political climate changed in 1638, Rutherford was vindicated and became one of four Scottish delegates to the Westminster Assembly (1643–1647). During this period, he composed *Lex Rex* (1644), which defended the peoples' right to armed resistance against Charles I. This demonstrates that Rutherford's spirituality was not only personal but also public and political. The importance he attached to the Lord's Supper both personally and communally is another indicator of the balanced spirituality of the personal and public relationships with God.

See also Marriage, Spiritual; Puritan Spirituality; Reformed (Calvinist) Spirituality.

For Further Reading: A. Bonar, *Letters of Samuel Rutherford* (1891); J. Coffey, *Politics, Religion and the British Revolutions* (1997).

Tom Schwanda

Ruysbroeck, Jan van (1293–1381)

Leading Flemish mystic. Ruysbroeck took his name from the village in which he was born, not far from Brussels. He was ordained to the priesthood in 1317 and was vicar at the collegiate church of St. Gudela in Brussels for more than twenty-five years. In 1344, with two others, Ruysbroeck retired to a solitary life in the wooded valley of Groenendaal where they founded an Augustinian monastery. His widespread reputation as a discerning spiritual director drew many to seek his guidance, including Gerhard Groote, founder of the *Devotio Moderna*, and probably Johannes Tauler, the popular German mystic. Ruysbroeck was greatly influenced by Augustine, Bernard, and Richard of St. Victor.

Though he had little education, Ruysbroeck displayed a brilliant mind. With keen insight and theological precision, he wrote *The Espousels*, widely considered a masterpiece. It reflects the three classical stages of purification, illumination, and unification, to which he introduced an innovative fourfold movement: (1) see, (2) the bridegroom comes, (3) go out, (4) to meet him (Matt. 25:6). For Ruysbroeck, God's unceasing love awakens the drowsy soul to this fourfold response that is repeated in each of the three stages, culminating with the bridegroom achieving union with fallen human nature. His theology was eucharistic and profoundly Trinitarian. It synthesized Greek spiritual theology with the introspection of Augustine. Reflecting the view of the Greek fathers, Ruysbroeck taught that we are caught up into the dynamic communion and interpersonal movements between Father, Son, and Holy Spirit, which does not leave the soul in permanent rest and passive contemplation. In *The Sparkling Stone*, he argued for a cyclical movement from contemplation to action—the fruit of grace and becoming like Jesus. His other works include *Mirror of Eternal Blessedness* and *The Little Book of Clarification*.

Ruysbroeck opposed abuse and spiritual deadness in the church and wrote against the heresy of mystical pantheism that typified some contemporaries, including the Free Spirit movement. His writings influenced John of the Cross, the *Devotio Moderna*, and centuries later Evelyn Underhill. His feast is observed in Belgium, and he was beatified in 1908.

See also Ascent, Stages of Spiritual.

For Further Reading: L. Dupré, *The Common Life* (1984); *John Ruusbroec: The Spiritual Espousals and Other Works*, CWS (1985); P. Verdeyen, *Ruusbroec and His Mysticism* (1994).

L. Paul Jensen

S

Sabbath

The Sabbath is a day of rest. The English word *sabbath* comes from the Hebrew word *shabbat*, which is derived from a root that means "cease, pause, desist, rest, or stop." Genesis 2:1–3 describes God's rest on the seventh day after creating the world. The Sabbath command in the first version of the Ten Commandments refers to the creation account: "Remember the sabbath day, and keep it holy. Six days you shall labor and do all your work. But the seventh day is a sabbath to the LORD your God; you shall not do any work—you, your son or your daughter, your male or female slave, your livestock, or the alien resident in your towns. For in six days the LORD made heaven and earth, the sea, and all that is in them, but rested the seventh day; therefore the LORD blessed the sabbath day and consecrated it" (Ex. 20:8–11 NRSV).

In the second version of the Ten Commandments, the Sabbath command begins with similar instructions for observing the Sabbath day, but the reason for the command is different: "Remember that you were a slave in the land of Egypt, and the LORD your God brought you out from there with a mighty hand and an outstretched arm; therefore the LORD your God commanded you to keep the sabbath day" (Deut. 5:15 NRSV). These two versions of the Sabbath command evoke God's central roles in human life: Creator and Redeemer.

The Sabbath was a defining characteristic of the people of Israel in the OT, and the Sabbath continues to be a significant practice for Jews today. The Jewish Sabbath begins on Friday at sunset and continues until Saturday at sunset. Ceasing from paid work and traveling have been traditional components of the Jewish observance of the Sabbath. Exodus 35:3 mandates that a fire should not be lit on the Sabbath. This made cooking impossible, ensuring that women, slaves, and servants could enjoy a day of rest along with the men.

By the time of Jesus, the rabbis had codified the regulations for Sabbath observance. Jewish texts from around Jesus' time prohibited thirty-nine specific acts on the Sabbath, including sowing, plowing, reaping, threshing, winnowing, grinding, sifting, kneading, baking, spinning, weaving, hunting, slaughtering, building, hammering, and transporting.

Jesus and his disciples observed the Sabbath. In his first public appearance, on a Sabbath day, Jesus read a passage from Isaiah in the synagogue (Luke 4:16–20). The Gospels record five healings that Jesus performed on the Sabbath (Matt. 12:9–14; Luke 13:10–17; 14:1–6; John 5:1–18; 9:1–41), and one time his disciples plucked grain on the Sabbath (Matt. 12:1–8). These six incidents provoked conflicts with Jewish religious leaders about what is appropriate Sabbath behavior.

Acts and the Epistles mention the Sabbath very rarely. In Galatians 4:10, Paul condemns observing special days. Hebrews 4 argues that the sabbath rest is fulfilled in Christ. In the early church, Jewish converts to Christianity continued to observe the Sabbath while meeting on Sundays (the "Lord's Day," Rev. 1:10) to celebrate the resurrection. There is no evidence that Gentile Christians ever observed the Sabbath in Jewish form. Instead, over the centuries, Sunday began to have characteristics of the Sabbath, although that language was rarely used. In the 4th century, Constantine, the first Christian emperor, declared Sunday a day of rest. In the 16th century, John Calvin and Martin Luther insisted on the value of Sunday as a day of rest and worship, but they did not regard Sunday as the Christian fulfillment of the Jewish Sabbath.

After the Reformation, a small number of Christians came to believe that the fourth commandment had been neglected throughout Christian history. They grew into the Seventh-day Adventists and the Seventh Day Baptists, who argue for a Saturday sabbath in the OT tradition. Some Christians in England and Scotland, particularly the Puritans, proscribed strict rules for Sundays in order to avoid some of the excesses that had become common on the day of rest from work, such as gambling and drunkenness.

In the second half of the 20th century, many Western countries passed laws that removed the differences between Sunday and the other days of the week. The 24/7 lifestyle typical in so many countries at the beginning of the 21st century has precipitated an interest in rediscovering the wisdom of sabbath rest.

The two versions of the Sabbath command are increasingly seen as a call to enjoy God as Creator and Redeemer in the context of sabbath rest. Jesus' healings on the Sabbath are increasingly seen as a proclamation of the Sabbath day as a day of restoration, joy, and wholeness. Christians today more frequently ponder Jesus' statement that "the sabbath was made for humankind" and that he is "lord even of the sabbath" (Mark 2:27–28 NRSV). Many Christians are experimenting with new patterns of sabbath rest, even if it must take place on days other than Saturday or Sunday and even if the period of rest cannot last twenty-four hours. The Sabbath is a generous gift from God, affirming the simple joy of being God's beloved children, resting in the embrace of a good God who takes care of the world even when human work has ceased.

See also Lesiure and Play; Time, Sanctification of; Work.

For Further Reading: L. Baab, *Sabbath Keeping* (2005); M. Dawn, *Keeping the Sabbath Wholly* (1989); T. Edwards, *Sabbath Time* (2003); A. Heschel, *The Sabbath* (1951); W. Muller, *Sabbath* (1999); D. Postema, *Catch Your Breath* (1997).

Lynne M. Baab

Sacrament

A sacrament is a religious, symbolic rite or gesture ordained by Christ for the church and celebrated either on special occasions or on a regular basis, depending on their specific significance. Most Christians affirm at least two central sacramental actions: baptism and the Lord's Supper. But many Christian traditions practice other symbolic rites that they view as having been ordained by Christ and thus as having a certain sacramental character, including foot washing, the anointing of the sick, marriage, and ordination.

Baptism and the Lord's Supper are "sacraments" in that they are external expressions of internal realities. The theological principles that undergird such actions are three: that the created order is good and a means for God's self-revelation; that Christ Jesus himself took on human flesh and as the Incarnate One became, essentially, the sacrament of God; and that the church is the embodiment of the grace of God in the world, the "body" of Christ, and has been commanded of Christ to practice these rites as signs of God's grace to the church and through the church to its members and the world. Thus, in the sacraments, the church witnesses to the goodness of God in creation and the

grace of God in Christ through whom all things are being redeemed.

The church has over the centuries invested extraordinary energy in debating how effective the sacraments actually are; whether they are a means of grace; and whether the crucial factor is the faith of the church, the faith of the Christian who participates, or, in some cases, the power of the elements themselves (water, bread, or wine) when consecrated by a priest or pastor. But increasingly, Christians are recognizing that while we cannot discount the faith of the church or the individual Christian or the importance of words of consecration or indeed the significance of the elements, the crucial factor is not any of these, but rather the third person of the Trinity, the Spirit. Thus, the epiclesis—the prayer for the presence and anointing of the Spirit—is pivotal in the celebration of baptism, the Lord's Supper, and any other sacramental rite or practice.

See also Baptism; Lord's Supper.

Gordon T. Smith

Sacred and Secular

Sacred and *secular* are contrasting terms used to signify proximity to or distance from that which is divine or holy. Until at least the Renaissance and the Enlightenment, Christian cultures would not have questioned the existence of the sacred (Heb. *kadosh*, Gr. *hagios*) or distinguished sacred and secular spheres.

In the Hebrew Bible, God is holy, that is, set over against everything worldly or creaturely (Lev. 19:2; 21:8). God expects the people of God to be "a holy nation" (Ex. 19:6). Accordingly, cultic observances, the Sabbath (Ex. 20:8), places of worship such as the tabernacle (Ex. 29:43) or temple (Ps. 5:7) or Jerusalem (Isa. 27:13), the paraphernalia of worship, and all rites and rituals must be holy. In line with the OT, the rabbis of the 1st century counted holy the temple, priests, sacrifices, feast days, the Sabbath, the people of Israel, Palestine, and the rest. NT writers applied the term *holy* more reservedly to places, things, or observances. In addition to God, Jesus, the Holy Spirit, and angels, they used the term chiefly for the church and the life of Christians. Indicative of this shift, Paul and Luke designated all Christians *hagioi* (saints, holy ones). The sparse instances of "holy" applied to places, objects, or rites — holy city (Matt. 4:5; 27:53; Rev. 11:2; 21:2, 10), Holy Place (Matt. 24:15; Acts 6:13; Heb. 9:2), holy covenant (Luke 1:72), holy ground (Acts 7:33), Holy Scriptures (Rom. 1:2), holy law (Rom. 7:12), Most Holy Place (Heb. 9:2, 12, 24–25; 13:11), holy mountain (2 Peter 1:18), holy commandment (Rom. 7:12; 2 Peter 2:21) — reflected the continuing intersection of Jesus' and the early church's story within Judaism.

Sacralizing places, liturgical paraphernalia, relics, and other things took on new life as Christianity moved into the Roman world where the state cultus and oriental religions made them a central part of their existence. Martyrdoms may have put Christians on a fast track toward singling out holy persons, holy places, and holy things. After the authorities put the aged Polycarp, bishop of Smyrna, to death in 155, the faithful, according to the *Martyrdom of Polycarp*, "took up his bones, more precious than precious stones, and finer than gold, and put them where it was meet," an eyewitness recorded. "There the Lord will permit us to come together according to our power in gladness and joy, and celebrate the birthday of his martyrdom, both in the memory of those who have already contested, and for the practice and training of those whose fate it shall be." Christians studded their calendar with saints' days, erected churches in memory of martyrs, collected relics, made pilgrimages to holy sites, and did many other things to sanctify a hostile world and to point people to a benign world.

This outlook shifted in the Renaissance. Where in the Middle Ages people longed for a heavenly city, now they celebrated the one they lived in. Domes significative of this world replaced spires pointing toward the other world. Artists depicted

human bodies as the measure of the divine. Poets hymned nature in all its glory as God's glory. Had people of that day been able to peer deeply into the stream of European consciousness, they would have seen two streams beginning to emerge, a split between sacred and secular. Two centuries later as the Renaissance moved northward from Italy into other parts of Europe, the separate streams became more manifest in the reformation of the 16th century, Catholics reaffirming the medieval and Protestants repudiating many facets of it. In the Enlightenment, observers could not miss how far the divergence had proceeded. Bacon had signaled it in 1610 in the publication of his *Organon* defining scientific method; Descartes seconded him in 1633 with his *Methode*. Now many in Western society had a secular way to reach certainty and needed no longer to rely on the sacred. From this point onward, the streams would continue to flow farther and farther apart. In the mid-19th century, Western culture witnessed open conflict between sacred and secular realms. Religion not only suffered neglect but experienced deliberate attacks in critical biblical studies, in Marx's *Communist Manifesto* (1848), and in Kierkegaard's *Attack on Christendom*. It felt threatened with the publication of Darwin's *The Origin of the Species* (1859). Following two world wars in quick succession, many Europeans were ready to accept Nietzsche's pronouncement that God was dead. Fortunately, some hopeful signs have come along since the election of Roncalli as Pope John XXIII (1958–1963). Teilhard de Chardin strove to prove that sacred and secular, religious faith and modern science, are not polar opposites. Rather, "by virtue of the Creation and, still more, the incarnation, *nothing* here below is profane for those who know how to see."

See also Holiness; Secularization; World.

For Further Reading: P. Brown, *Society and the Holy in Late Antiquity* (1982); J. Delumeau, *Catholicism between Luther and Voltaire* (1977); *"Hagios,"* in *TDNT,* 1:88–110; M. Marty, *The Modern Schism* (1969); R. Otto, *The Idea of the Holy*, trans.

J. Harvey (1958); P. Teilhard de Chardin, *The Divine Milieu* (1960).

E. Glenn Hinson

Sacred Heart

Devotion to the Sacred Heart is a multifaceted mystical and liturgical response to the wounded, loving heart of Jesus. The intimate image of the beloved disciple resting on Jesus' breast (John 13:23–25) elicits, throughout the Catholic mystical tradition, the desire to be likewise loving and beloved. This longing is intensified by reflection on the piercing of Jesus' side, which caused "a sudden flow of blood and water" (John 19:34), the prophesied cleansing fountain of Zechariah 13:1.

Patristic theologians regarded this wound as the source of redemption and as the birthplace of the church and the Eucharist. Such medieval mystics as Mechthild of Hackeborn and Gertrude the Great (of Helfta) meditated on it as the human entryway to Christ's divine and sacred heart, a contemplation Bernard of Clairvaux popularized in his sermons (*On the Song of Songs*). Lutgardis (1182–1246) experienced an "exchange of hearts" with Christ, a betrothal union known also to Catherine of Siena and the mystical traditions of the Franciscans, Dominicans, Benedictines, Carthusians, and Jesuits.

An annual public feast of the Sacred Heart, initiated by Father Jean Eudes and approved by the Catholic bishops of France in 1672, marked the formal entry of the devotion into public worship. Its liturgical legitimization owes much to visions by the French Visitandine nun Mary Margaret Alacoque. In her first vision (1673), Christ drew her to rest "on his divine breast" and named her "Beloved disciple of my Sacred Heart." In her "great apparition" (1675), Christ requested specific eucharistic devotions and a feast of reparation. The feast was made universal by Pope Pius IX in 1856.

Evangelicals have echoed the Catholic devotion in their cross-centered piety, such as Fanny Crosby's refrain "Draw me nearer ... to Thy precious, bleeding side." Indeed, a Jesuit priest was once heard to remark that evangelicals are "Protestants who are devoted to the Sacred Heart."

See also Carthusian Spirituality; Images.

For Further Reading: H. Egan, *An Anthology of Christian Mysticism* (1991); W. Wright, "Transformed Seeing," *Studia Mystica* 22 (2001): 97–109.

Diane S. George Ayer

Sacred Space

Sacred space is any location that has been identified and designated as distinct from its surroundings, generally with religious or spiritual connotations attached. It is often looked upon as a place of encounter with the divine and therefore as a destination to which people go with clearly defined expected outcomes in mind.

Such places are not limited to the built environment or specific architectural structures such as church buildings, synagogues, mosques, or temples. Mountains, rivers, trees, and other elements of the cosmos frequently have been declared sacred locations as well.

Sacred space is generally saturated with story. Any study of it, therefore, must give careful attention not only to locative elements, but to narrative dimensions as well, and address the issue of what a sacred space says (meaning) in addition to what it does (function). Sacred space is ordinary space that has extraordinary meaning or history for some. It becomes "holy ground."

The function of sacred space exceeds the mere provision of shelter from the elements or a location for repeated ritualistic activity. It is also a vehicle through which meaning is conveyed. The Bible is replete with sacred places and spaces (mountains, monuments, cities, etc.) in which humans encountered the distinctive presence of God. Early Christians often met in graveyards, the intersection of earthly and eternal life. During the 4th through 16th centuries when the majority of the general public was illiterate, cathedrals served as highly effective tutors through which worshipers experienced the mystery and majesty of God. Through use of elements such as proportion, scale, and especially the manipulation of light, cathedral master builders were able to elicit subdued responses of awe conducive to participation in the ministries of the Word and sacrament. By stark contrast, churches that were informed by Reformed theology conveyed the message that invisible divinity was not accessible through the visible, material world.

The intrinsic sacrality of any given sacred space is very difficult to sustain scripturally. Sacred space is essentially a human construct in which a location is identified and set apart, often through some form of ritualistic activity, because of an extraordinary event, some manifestation of the sacred or divine (hierophany) that may have occurred or is anticipated there. In that sense, it is both created and discovered. "Surely the LORD is in this place, and I was not aware of it" (Gen. 28:16). The existence of sacred space is based in part on the assumption that the built environment has the capacity to affect a person's experience within that space. Generally, sacred spaces are intended to elicit certain responses from those immersed in that environment.

Interest in the responsive impact of sacred space has come from a variety of disciplines ranging from the social sciences to theological and biblical studies. Social and behavioral scientists, for example, have underscored the fact that personal response to sacred space is not exclusively contingent on the environment itself. What a person brings to a sacred space in terms of personality, personal history, and even theology all contribute to a person's experience. For that reason individual responses to the same built environment can be vastly different.

Conversely, there is compelling evidence that demonstrates how influential sacred space can be on a person's spiritual growth and openness to God. For example, advocates of the seeker-sensitive approach to ministry have established theaterlike venues void of any quintessential Christian symbols. Decisions such as these are born out of the conviction that environments laden with symbols requiring some degree of interpretation will profoundly affect visitors to the point of distraction.

Differences on the issue of sacred space often revolve around the tension between the immanence and transcendence of the divine. How does one reconcile the omnipresence of a transcendent God with the locative particularity of sacred space? In Christian thought sacred space does not inevitably attenuate the belief in God's omnipresence by limiting encounters with God's presence to specific places in which God has chosen to reveal himself, nor does it necessarily represent a regressive undermining of progressive revelation. Rather, it acknowledges God's divine sovereign prerogative to manifest himself in special ways in various ordinary places. Because of that, sacred space often fosters a sense of the numinous, an awareness of that which is beyond the mundane or ordinary yet at the same time present in it.

Sacred space reminds us that we live in a material world and that our spirituality is not limited to the realm of the ethereal. Christianity is an embodied, lived out spirituality rooted in the incarnation of Christ himself. It takes place somewhere. Therefore the "what" and "how" of Christian experience is intimately linked to the "where."

See also Geography, Spiritual.

For Further Reading: J. Kilde, *Sacred Power, Sacred Space* (2008); L. Nelson, ed., *American Sanctuary* (2006); P. North and J. North, *Sacred Space* (2007); P. Sheldrake, *Spaces for the Sacred* (2001); M. Torgerson, *An Architecture of Immanence* (2007); M. Visser, *The Geometry of Love* (2000).

William R. McAlpine

Saints

Saints are "holy ones." In the NT, especially in the writings of the apostle Paul, the term refers to all Christians, thereby highlighting both the justified status of believers and the goal of their ongoing moral transformation. It describes both who they already are and who they are destined to become. Subsequently, in the Christian tradition, the term *saint* has come to designate a very select minority of Christians recognized for their exceptional holiness, virtue, and Spirit-empowered achievements. The list of such (elite) saints begins with Mary, then many figures from the NT, especially apostles, followed by a tally of outstanding Christians ever since, men and women alike — creating in total a list that now numbers in the thousands and continues to expand. The memory of many such saints is kept alive by having days in their honor embedded in the annual church calendar, culminating in their collective remembrance on All Saints' Day (November 1 in the West). In the Catholic and Orthodox traditions, it is especially common to name children after saints.

The origin of the tradition of saints lies in the honor and respect the early church accorded to its martyred members. Later on such respect was extended to monastic figures who distinguished themselves by their self-sacrifice, devotion, and godly legacies, and still later to great missionary figures, among others. Over time the process by which a person qualified (always posthumously) as a saint became more complex and codified, with specific qualifying criteria (e.g., attested miracles) and sequential stages of recognition (beatification, canonization). Protocols vary by church communion and range from general consensus to precise legal requirements. Nonetheless, there has been an ecumenical consensus that the respect and reverence accorded to saints — that is, their *veneration* — must never encroach upon the worship that is due God alone. What is venerated is the manifestation of the glory of God through them.

Saints can function as powerful role models and examples of faithful Christian living. Thus, the stories of saints' lives can serve significant educational and inspirational purposes, and can be key to the formation of identity, virtue, and a sense of belonging to a tradition. Every spiritual tradition requires heroes. At the same time, the function of the saints in Christian spirituality has been enormously influenced by the Christian vision of "the communion of the saints," a seminal phrase embedded in the Apostles' Creed and signifying the living fellowship of all believers, past and present, alive together in Christ. From this it has often been inferred that communication with saintly persons is possible, and that their aid may properly be solicited in prayer, just as one might call upon a well-positioned, living family member for assistance in need. In their public worship, however, liturgical churches will usually direct such petitions only to officially recognized saints. Some saints have come to be regarded as patrons (i.e., attentive overseers) of particular localities (e.g., St. David for Wales) or functions (e.g., St. Christopher for travelers).

The Lutheran tradition recognizes the saints as worthy of emulation. However, Lutherans underscore that there is *one* mediator between God and humankind (1 Tim. 2:5), and therefore deny that prayers for help should be directed to saints. The Augsburg Confession, article 21, states that a Christian is to call upon the name of Christ, and Christ alone, in time of need. Most Protestant churches prefer the original NT idea that all Christians are called to be saints, thereby holding up the ideal of holiness as being applicable to, and potentially attainable by, all believers — even ordinary ones. Nonetheless, there is an intuitive awareness among Protestants generally, and evangelicals in particular, of a need to scan back through a neglected history for exemplars — for heroes who embody the highest ideals of their faith community. For evangelicals this function has most commonly been performed by the plethora of biographies of intrepid foreign missionaries.

See also Communion of Saints.

For Further Reading: R. Bertram, "A Constructive Lutheran Theology of the Saints," *Dialog* 31, no. 4 (1986): 265–71; P. Brown, *The Cult of Saints*

(1981); L. Cunningham, *The Meaning of Saints* (1980); D. H. Farmer, *Oxford Dictionary of Saints* (2004); K. Woodward, *Making Saints* (1996); M. Walsh, *A New Dictionary of Saints* (2007).

Alethea Savoy

Salesian Spirituality

See **Francis de Sales.**

Sanctification

Sanctification is that area of theology that treats the believer's process of becoming holy.

Sanctification is typically distinguished from justification. Justification is God's declaration that the believer has a right standing before God based on the imputed righteousness of Christ, while sanctification is the impartation of righteousness to the believer such that he or she actually possesses holiness. This impartation of actual righteousness is initiated by the sanctifying Spirit at regeneration, progresses throughout the believer's life, and culminates in glorification. Hence, it is correct to say that those who are "in Christ" *have been* made holy (regeneration), *are being* made holy (sanctification), and *will be* made holy (glorification). While each phase is part of the Spirit's overall sanctifying work, the theological category of sanctification (a subdivision of soteriology) addresses ongoing growth in holiness. So, taken in its doctrinal sense, sanctification refers to the Spirit-empowered process begun at regeneration and completed at glorification that increasingly conforms the believer's inner and outer life to the image of Christ (Rom. 8:28–29; cf. Col. 1:15). Since the image of God is gradually being restored in the believer, to become holy is to become the kind of person God originally intended human persons to be in thought, affect, will, character, relational capacity, and behavior (cf. 1 Thess. 5:23–24). It has not always been sufficiently acknowledged that sanctification is not only a natural reflection of new life within, but it is also an essential, rather than optional, dynamic in Christian living. The sanctification process is actually part of and key to Christian "salvation," inasmuch as it is the progressive means by which believers are being delivered (saved) in this life from the bondage and power of sin—which is the source of so much of the futility, pain, and suffering associated with being human.

It is important to note that the biblical terms for *holiness* (the Hebrew word group *qados* and to a lesser extent the Greek word group *hagios*) have a relational as well as a moral sense. The relational sense refers to believers being separated/set apart/consecrated to God, while the moral sense refers to intrinsic moral qualities that believers ought to possess as divine image-bearers. Developing a theology of sanctification emphasizing only moral holiness tends to disconnect the product of sanctification—moral character—from the relational process that brings such character about. Once the relational element drops out, the tendency is to view progress in holiness as mere moral improvement by natural powers alone. But if the concept of holiness is broadened to include the development of one's relationship with God, then a theology of sanctification involves both a discussion of how the believer grows in deeper dependence upon and love for God as well as the connection between such relational development and moral transformation.

While evangelicals are often eager to grow in Christ, an in-depth understanding of spiritual progress has often been lacking within evangelicalism. This is what church historian Richard Lovelace called "the sanctification gap." Lovelace's thesis is that the historical development of evangelicalism has predisposed it to overlook the doctrine of sanctification. Instead, evangelicals have specialized on justification/conversion, doctrinal correctness, and various external acts (e.g., church attendance, ministry involvement, etc.) that have been regularly identified with Christian maturity. The tendency has been to emphasize the product at the expense of the process. Unfortunately, in the absence of a robust theology of sanctification, various erroneous models of spiritual growth have emerged that confuse and disillusion many.

A crucial corrective when it comes to sanctification is the realization that human willpower alone cannot bring about conformity to the image of Christ. Christ himself did not live by autonomous human willpower, and so any characterological change that self-effort might bring about is not Christlike character change. Rather, formation in Christ can only be brought about by the empowering presence of the indwelling Spirit of Christ. Given that the human person was originally created to flourish in union and communion with God and that this nourishing relationship was severed through the fall, it should be no surprise that the inner life of the believer is regenerated and gradually reordered as the Spirit of God makes his home within the believer. The Spirit initiates the restoration of the divine-human relationship at conversion, and the believer continues to receive the life-giving influence of the Spirit (Eph. 5:18) as he or she learns to keep in step with the Spirit (Gal. 5:16 – 26).

While the Holy Spirit is the agent of sanctification, God allows believers the opportunity to cooperate intelligently with the Spirit through various means of grace (e.g., prayer, meditation on Scripture, spiritual friendship, etc.). As believers intentionally engage these means, they draw near to, interact with, and are enabled to receive the Spirit's gracious illumination of God's Word. People relate to one another through words that carry meaning, and the divine-human relationship is no different. God's Word contains transformational truths that the Spirit writes on believers' hearts (Jer. 31:33; John 17:17) as believers open their lives to the Spirit. In addition to the Word of God, the resources available through the varied gifts of the body of Christ serve as other essential means of grace.

Sanctification is easier said than done. Scripture makes clear that the world, the flesh, and the devil present serious obstacles to the believer's participation with the Spirit's transforming work (Eph. 2:1 – 3). In particular, "putting off" the old self (mortification of the flesh) with its ingrained tendencies to live independently from God, and "putting on" the new self (vivification by the Spirit) is a lifelong and oftentimes painful process (Eph. 4:17 – 24; Col. 3:1 – 17). It should not be taken lightly that sanctification involves death to oneself (Rom. 6:6 – 8) and an embracing of weakness (2 Cor. 12:9). Understanding the nature and dynamics of sanctification enables believers to respond to the narrowness of the way of Christ as Paul did: "Not that I have ... already become perfect, but I press on to take hold of that for which Christ Jesus took hold of me" (Phil. 3:12).

See also Baptism of the Holy Spirit; Holiness; Methodist Spirituality.

For Further Reading: G. C. Berkouwer, *Faith and Sanctification* (1952); B. Demarest, *The Cross and Salvation* (1997); M. Dieter et. al, *Five Views of Sanctification* (1996); G. Fee, *God's Empowering Presence* (1994); J. I. Packer, *Keep in Step with the Spirit* (1984); S. E. Porter, "Holiness, Sanctification," *Dictionary of Paul and His Letters* (1993).

Steve L. Porter

Sanders, J(ohn) Oswald (1902 – 1992)

Missionary statesman and devotional author. He was born in Invercargill, New Zealand, nurtured in a Brethren assembly, and greatly influenced by the Keswickian spirituality of the China Inland Mission (CIM), eventually dedicating himself to missionary service at a CIM spiritual awakening conference (1921). He earned a law degree (1922) but abandoned plans for a legal career to study at the Bible Training Institute (BTI) in Auckland, ultimately becoming its superintendent in 1933. Sanders gained a reputation as a skilled and gifted leader and administrator, leading CIM to name him its general director (1954 – 1969).

During his early work at BTI Sanders began a writing career that produced more than thirty-two books dealing with spiritual life and the dynamics of godly Christian leadership. In all his writing, as well as his preaching and ministry, Sanders was noted for his forthright nature, practical spirituality, and levelheaded, commonsense approach to life and faith. His most popular and enduring work, *Spiritual Leadership* (1967), emphasizes the central role that character, piety, and integrity must play in the life of the Christian leader, often expressing thoughts contrary to popular leadership theory and practice. Sanders maintained that true Christian leadership is the result of the Holy Spirit working with individuals' natural abilities to shape them into leaders consistent with biblical examples. The book concludes that "the church needs saints and servants, not 'leaders,' and if we forget the priority of service, the entire idea of leadership training becomes dangerous." *Spiritual Leadership* is frequently found in lists of "most influential" books by numerous Christian leaders, and was intended, along with *Spiritual Maturity* (1962) and *Spiritual Discipleship* (1990), to form a trilogy that addressed the issue of leadership and serious Christian discipleship.

See also Keswick Movement; Leadership, Spirituality of.

For Further Reading: R. Roberts, *To Fight Better: A Biography of J. Oswald Sanders* (1989).

John R. Lillis

Sayers, Dorothy L. (1893–1957)

Literary "accidental apologist." Dorothy Sayers was a British novelist, playwright, apologist, and translator. Best known for her Lord Peter Wimsey mystery stories (e.g., *Gaudy Night*), Sayers found a second career in writing apologetic essays and religious plays. Her BBC serial, *The Man Born to Be King* (1941), rescued Jesus and the disciples from the fusty language of the KJV, initially scandalizing straight-laced Protestant groups and then delight-ing the nation. Her friend C. S. Lewis read it every year during Holy Week. High Anglican in her own spirituality, Sayers wrote incisive apologetic essays, such as "The Dogma Is the Drama," clarifying the Great Tradition for layfolk and drawing many back to a moribund church. Her Penguin translation of Dante's *Divine Comedy* reached millions and highlighted the down-to-earth humor and vivid storytelling of that classic—her notes explaining the theology of the epic poem in clear, modern English. Sayers wrote effectively on the spirituality of work, vocation, creativity, and aesthetics, describing human creativity as a Trinitarian process (*The Mind of the Maker*) and insisting Christian artists work with quality and integrity. She was friends with G. K. Chesterton, with whom she helmed the still-active Detection Club, and Charles Williams, with whom she corresponded on Dante. Lewis called her one of the great modern letter writers: her letters are published in five volumes.

See also Imagination; Lewis, C. S.; Literature and Spirituality.

Chris R. Armstrong

Schuller, Robert H. (1926–)

Televangelist, pastor, and author. Robert Schuller's spirituality is centered in positive thinking, as promoted by his mentor Norman Vincent Peale. Schuller developed this theme further as possibility thinking, self-love, personal power, and self-esteem. This spirituality does not dwell on sin but emphasizes God's love and human value.

Schuller is a minister of the Reformed Church in America and founded his congregation in Southern California in 1955. Very early the services were offered as "drive-in" as well as "walk-in." The present glass church was completed in 1980 and named the Crystal Cathedral. It reflects an American desire for superlatives, among them (possibly) the largest organ in the world. The television ministry of this congregation, the *Hour of Power*, has been seen by millions and often includes interviews with celebrities. Schuller retired as senior pastor in 2006.

Schuller's many books are popular in style, bordering on the category of self-help tracts, but always with a Christian perspective. They reflect the popular culture of the United States in their concern for personal wellness and achievement. Schuller himself seems to live out his own philosophy by not thinking less of oneself than one ought to think. His congregation was among the early "seeker-friendly" megachurches with thousands of members. He also sees his teaching as bringing in a new era of church history, as seen in his title *Self-Esteem: The New Reformation*. His autobiography is *My Journey: From an Iowa Farm to a Cathedral of Dreams* (2002).

See also Peale, Norman Vincent.

Bradley P. Holt

Schweitzer, Albert (1875–1965)

Scholar and missionary of simple creed and extraordinary influence. A product of liberal Protestantism at its zenith, Schweitzer was raised by broad-minded parents in a Lutheran manse, earned doctorates in philosophy and theology, then became a popular Strasbourg professor and pastor whose lectures and sermons alike emphasized Jesus' ethical relevancy. His epochal *The Quest for the Historical Jesus* (1906) closed the first quest for the historical Jesus by exposing modern reconstructions of Christ as self-serving projections of liberal Protestant ideals; it also suggests why its author forsook academia for Africa, having entered medical school already in 1905 to train as a missionary doctor. Schweitzer depicted Jesus as an apocalyptic Jew, convinced he was divinely appointed to roll the wheel of history to its final halt in the messianic kingdom. But "the wheel rolls onward, and the mangled body of the one immeasurably great man ... is hanging on it still." For despite failure, Jesus' dying example resounds as an undying call to follow him for love's sake. This call beckoned Schweitzer in 1913 to Lambréné in present-day Gabon, where he toiled in a small missionary hospital most of the rest of his long life. The waxing of totalitarian ideologies and technological societies in the West, and his firsthand struggle in Africa against both the law of the jungle and the bitter colonial inheritance, compelled his famous principle of "reverence for life." Inspired by Jesus and Schweitzer's own mystical respect before nature, this worldview combines the trembling recognition that all living things will to live and have a right to live with active struggle against all life-denying forces. Universal, agnostic, and compellingly illustrated by the jungle doctor himself, "reverence for life" was thus perfectly pitched for the post-1945 world as a generic spiritual principle capable of rallying opposition to cultural decay, the nuclear arms race, overconsumption, and ecological degradation. A pop culture saint by life's end, Schweitzer received the Nobel Prize in 1953. See a collection of his essays, *The Teaching of Reverence for Life* (comp. 1965) and his autobiography, *Out of My Life and Thought* (1931).

For Further Reading: J. Brabazon, *Albert Schweitzer* (2000); M. Meyer and K. Bergel, eds., *Reverence for Life: The Ethics of Albert Schweitzer for the Twenty-First Century* (2002).

Todd Statham

Science and Spirituality

To be human is to be inescapably spiritual. Science, therefore, as a human activity, also has a latent spiritual dimension and potentiality. This is not news to many scientists for whom explorations of the natural world and human embodiment uncover orderliness and a layered complexity that inspires wonder and awe. For Christians, from Kepler, who "thought God's thoughts after him," and Newton, who believed planetary motion "could only proceed from the council and dominion of an intelligent and powerful Being," to modern scientists like John Polkinghorne and Francis

Collins, science is one way that God and God's ways are revealed to us.

While science can actually deepen explicitly Christian spiritual consciousness, it does not compel everyone in this direction. For Einstein, for example, science revealed a universe of "the profoundest reason and most radiant beauty," but his view of God was deistic at best. For atheist Richard Dawkins, "science is the poetry of reality." Indeed, many on both sides of the science-religion divide perceive an irreconcilable conflict between the two and are convinced that we must choose one or the other. This raises the question of what science *is*. Is it a "religious" metanarrative in its own right—that is, a comprehensive source of truth, meaning, direction, and hope? Or is it a powerful but limited tool, just one way of using our gifts to fulfill our calling to be creative and to be stewards of the creation?

Since the Enlightenment, the dominant Western view has been that science must replace faith. This view has elevated human rationality applied through scientific method until it has become the only way to obtain "objective truth" about reality. Theological or metaphysical knowing is disdained as naive. Because science has been spectacularly successful in granting knowledge of and control over natural processes, it has gained a dominance, status, and authority once held by the church. Influential public intellectuals like Richard Dawkins and Christopher Hitchens argue that science *must* replace ecclesial authority. According to them, only through human rationality unconstrained by "blind faith" can we achieve solutions to problems ranging from environmental destruction to armed conflict. Conversely, some Christians are equally suspicious of science. To them, science threatens, rather than contributes to, Christian faith and spiritual development. They value experientially apprehended and scripturally revealed knowledge over the scientific knowledge with which it sometimes appears to conflict.

A closer look at how science actually works undercuts both of these perspectives. Scientific knowledge is by nature tentative, provisional, and subject to perpetual revision. It is limited to the study of those properties of matter, energy, and their interactions that we can observe directly or indirectly. Scientific practice is also conducted within cultural contexts by people with deep commitments to extra-scientific assumptions and beliefs about the existence of an orderly world, the human capacity to understand that world, and the meaning and purpose of that pursuit.

Science also cannot single-handedly produce the transformation the world needs. First, it cannot answer questions about value and significance, or moral concerns about what should be rather than what is. It has been used for destruction as often as for good, *because* it is merely a tool wielded by humans with particular values, beliefs, and commitments. Moreover, scientific practice has led to a fragmentation of knowledge, spawning specialists in ever-narrowing areas of expertise, with no means internal to the scientific enterprise to weave these fragments together. Finally, too often scientists are inappropriately reductive, seeking to explain everything, including human experience, mechanistically. Whenever this happens, something essential—the understanding that (in Wendell Berry's words) "life is a miracle"—is lost.

Science only *appears* to offer a comprehensive accounting for reality when practiced by people with larger ideological commitments. But science practiced by Christians can be, instead, a wonderful tool through which to fulfill our calling. In any case, science is most effective if its users are aware of how their worldview shapes their scientific practice. While knowledge of a reality independent of ourselves is actually possible, it is also profoundly relational—shaped by the knower as well as what is becoming known. There is no completely objective perspective; scientific practice, as all of life, is lived in the context of deep commitments and relationships, whether to God or to other foundational beliefs.

Critical realists also argue that reality is stratified and claim that we must use methods appropriate to the nature of that which we are studying. This confers legitimacy on other ways of knowing and apprehending; they too are required if we are to approach a truer and fuller understanding of reality.

Indirectly, science also shapes the spiritual consciousness of Christians. The Christian faith and its lived expressions are rooted in and reflect a venerable historical tradition; and this enduring tradition, as it has developed in community, has been shaped by historical events and colored by cultural influences. Science is an important part of this host culture — a powerful shaping influence, and one that affects our "way of seeing" God and the cosmos, who we are becoming, and how we live out our vocations before God. In terms of its positive spiritual potential, science reveals that we, too, are creatures and that this planet is our home. This knowledge should engender humility and underscores the urgent need to live in right relation with God's creation. Leon Kass offers the reminder that "*only* in the discovery of our own lack of divinity comes the first real openness to the divine." It is hubris for us to believe that the practice of science will give us the power ultimately to resolve all our problems. It is also hubris for Christians to assume that their beliefs give them final and absolute knowledge of the truth about all of existence, allowing them to disregard the insights (and sometimes implicit challenges to conventional thinking) that scientific discoveries bring. It is only when we recognize that all our knowledge of truth is personal, relational, and embodied that we become humble and open to the guidance of the Holy Spirit. Then we can grow spiritually as we seek to apprehend God, understand his creation, and live in light of his wisdom, love, and grace.

See also Postmodernity; Technology and Spirituality.

For Further Reading: W. Berry, *Life Is a Miracle* (2000); R. Bhaskar, *The Possibility of Naturalism* (1998); H. A. Campbell and H. Looy, eds., *A Science and Religion Primer* (2009); P. Harrison, *The Fall of Man and the Foundations of Science* (2007); L. Kass, *Toward a More Natural Science* (1985); A. McGrath, *The Science of God* (2004); N. T. Wright, *The New Testament and the People of God* (1992).

Heather Looy

Scientology

The Church of Scientology is a new religious movement founded by L. Ron Hubbard. Hubbard was born in 1911 in Tilden, Nebraska. After wide travel and study at Georgetown University, Hubbard served in the U.S. Navy and became a popular writer of science fiction. In the late 1940s, he turned to the study of human psychology. He wrote *Dianetics* in 1950, and the Church of Scientology started in 1954. Hubbard led Scientology until his death in 1986.

Hubbard claimed that humans are thetans or spirit beings and said that he had discovered past lives and the way to achieve true human potential. The goal of each human is to become "clear" and follow his church's "bridge to freedom." Knowledge of our true identity has been blocked through karma in past lives. Scientologists use a device known as an e-meter in counseling sessions (auditing) to keep track of the inner mind. The ultimate goal in Scientology is to become an Operating Thetan (or OT), a being liberated from the boundaries of MEST (matter, energy, space, time).

Hubbard's naval background has impacted Scientology's spirituality in two ways. First, he chose a military model for his movement. Full-time members are part of the Sea Org, and the church adopts military dress, rankings, and nomenclature. Second, the mission of Scientology is pictured in terms of warfare, a fitting outlook given the ideological, political, social, and religious battles surrounding Hubbard, his views, and current leadership under David Miscavige. Scientologists live their faith in the context of enormous public critique of the movement, regardless of the public relations appeal of Tom Cruise and other celebrity Scientologists.

Scientology is best understood as a form of religious therapy. The regular trappings of ritual are minimized, and focus is on liberating the planet through the application of Hubbard's techniques. Chapel services, meditation, and prayer (often to a nameless force) are but secondary aspects of the mission. Scientologists claim compatibility with all religions though their esoteric teachings clearly offer a unique interpretation of human origins, spiritual demise, and the path of liberation. The Operating Thetan materials that provide relevant detail are viewed as confidential by Church of Scientology members.

For Further Reading: J. Atack, *A Piece of Blue Sky* (1990); M. Hedley, *Blown for Good* (2009); L. R. Hubbard, *Scientology* (2007); J. Lewis, ed., *Scientology* (2009); J. G. Melton, *The Church of Scientology* (2000); R. Miller, *Bare-Faced Messiah* (1987).

James A. Beverley

Second Coming

When Christ ascended into the clouds to take his seat at the right hand of the Father, the angels of the ascension declared: "This same Jesus, who has been taken from you into heaven, will come back in the same way you have seen him go into heaven" (Acts 1:11). The earliest Christian creeds enshrine this expectation of a future second coming, confessing that Christ shall "come again" from the Father's right hand "to judge the living and the dead." It will trigger a cluster of end-time developments that are foundational to Christian hope.

Belief in a real and physical second coming of Christ became a cause célèbre of the doctrinal conservationist movement (i.e., Fundamentalism) within Protestantism in the early 20th century. At its best it helped to sustain a worldview in which the supernatural remained plausible, while it also helped extend the horizon of Christian consciousness and concern beyond this life as a closed system of cause and effect. Since the mid-19th century,

the pessimistic conviction that the world will only grow worse prior to the second coming has gained ascendancy among evangelicals, and in some (but certainly not all) cases has encouraged passive indifference in the face of global challenges. At its millenarian extreme, hope of the second coming has occasionally led to excitable disregard for ordinary responsibilities and to rash, and inevitably disillusioning, predictions of dates.

The positive significance of the second coming for spirituality is classically stated in the Heidelberg Catechism's answer to the question of what comfort there is in this doctrine: "That in all my sorrows and persecutions, with uplifted head I look for the very same person, who before offered himself for my sake, to the tribunal of God, and has removed all curse from me, to come as judge from heaven: who shall cast all his and my enemies into everlasting condemnation, but shall translate me with all his chosen ones to himself, into heavenly joys and glory."

The Christian life, no matter what affliction it is marked by, takes place under the sign of confident expectation of a future encounter with the very person of the Savior. This encounter is not a beatific vision after death, but an event in future history; not an element of personal eschatology, but of cosmic. At his return, Christ will administer the judgment that has already been determined in his earthly ministry, in his self-offering advocacy of the believer's case and his bearing of the curse. His coming as Judge will also accomplish the final, righteous condemnation of all that is evil, resolving by action the problem of theodicy. And the return of Christ brings all the promises and plans of God to consummation, including the kingdom, the fulfillment of all longings for holiness, and the final goal of progress in sanctification. The expectation of such a decisive conclusion to history also infuses Christian endeavor with urgency and significance. The uplifted head, the characteristic posture of expectant believers, includes not only the eager watchfulness enjoined by Jesus, but also a participation in the "groaning" of the whole creation as it awaits the redemption of the body (Rom. 8:20–23). It also entails close attention to the conduct of life in the meantime, because the expectation of the second coming casts all of Christian existence in terms of "the meantime."

See also Rapture.

For Further Reading: D. Bebbington, *The Dominance of Evangelicalism* (2005); W. E. Blackstone, *Jesus Is Coming* (1908); G. Marsden, *Fundamentalism and American Culture* (1980).

Fred Sanders

Secularization

Secularization is the (usually gradual) process by which spheres and aspects of life are set apart or quarantined from the sacred. As the domain of the sacred atrophies, it becomes progressively marginal and irrelevant to the mainstream. The term itself comes from the Latin *saeculum*, meaning "belonging to this age." Secularization as a social and political phenomenon has emerged in the last several centuries in the West, in many cases actually advanced by Christians as a strategy for greater tolerance and peace. Its underlying premise is that faith is properly central in some spheres, while in others it can be divisive or even dangerous. There are at least three reasons for the rise of secularization in the past five centuries. The first is the failure to maintain a theological consensus in the West after the Protestant Reformation. The second is that increasingly Christians are obliged to coexist with people of non-Christian faith and ideologies. The third is a perception that historically religion has played an oversized role in precipitating global tensions, wars, and even genocide. For all these reasons, it is deemed prudent to carve out a "commons," or public domain, into which religion's potentially volatile influence will not intrude. A safe world is a world of privatized religions.

Secularization has served in many cases to advance the Christian ideal of freedom, since it undermines coercion and conformity in religious matters. Anabaptists, English Nonconformists, and European Free churches, for example, that suffered under government-enforced orthodoxy, have historically emphasized the need for liberty of conscience, social tolerance, and permission to dissent civilly. Secularization has thus preserved the rights and freedoms of those whose practices and beliefs lie outside of the majority. This underlies the practice in the United States of America of separation between church and state. Within this "secular" arrangement, voluntary religion in America has managed in the past, largely on the strength of a series of awakenings and revivals, to sustain an environment supportive of Christian spirituality.

Secularization has brought some good and even fostered some otherwise underdeveloped Christian virtues (e.g., humility and civility). But in other ways, it has been corrosive of spirituality. The ideological vacuum in the public domain has often been filled by alternative ideologies (e.g., communism, materialism) that are implicitly, if not overtly, hostile to living all of life before God in the transforming and empowering presence of his Spirit.

A world in which God is no longer imposed can easily become a world in which God is no longer acknowledged. As an extreme example, some today are advocating that the deepest spiritual needs of humans can better be addressed by a religion-free "secular spirituality." In the meantime, powerful socializing forces and secular plausibility structures have led to disastrous lapses and compromises by people whose practice of faith is largely reserved for Sunday mornings. And thus the survival of Christian spirituality in highly secularized contexts may depend in part on the ability of Christian communities to function as appealing, alternative "cultures" of formation for their members.

See also Modernity; Postmodernity; Public Life and Spirituality.

For Further Reading: R. Clapp, *A Peculiar People* (1996); A. McGrath, *The Twilight of Atheism*

(2004); J. Ratzinger and J. Habermas, *The Dialectics of Secularization* (2007).

Christopher Morton

Self

From God's revealed perspective, each person is a unique self, specifically intended, created in God's image, and unique in the history of humankind. From a psychological perspective, the self is a life force that continually defines how we understand our world and how we relate to it and shape it. Thus, the self is imbedded in a developmental process that is contingent on the physical, cognitive, and emotional states afforded us at any time in life. A newborn infant is faced with the task of developing a first sense of self; a person in midlife may deal with the reevaluation of what defines the sense of "I" at his or her core. An aging person may work on integrating the experiences that were piled up in the hectic pace of the past and try to forge a more coherent self.

A person with a healthy self has a sense of personal boundaries while still feeling connected to others. Psychologists call this healthy combination *differentiation*. It develops best within a nurturing environment. When hindered by negative circumstances, the results can be enmeshment or detachment; either way, further growth may be impaired. A healthy sense of self keeps us from excessive dependence on others; it also keeps us from isolation and encourages us to reconnect where bonds are strained or broken.

In order to experience psychological and spiritual health, people also need to possess self-efficacy (competence), the sense of "I can." This would also imply that "I can change myself" as compelled by need or human ambition. Developmental psychologists remind us that life is constantly unfolding and that in the best of cases, we experience within it freedom to evaluate and change in the direction of our perceived ideal self (the self we want to be). From a humanistic perspective, we are able to actualize our human talent, attain our goals, and define our success accordingly.

However, individuals may come to realize that their perceived ideal self is ultimately unattainable through their own effort and agency alone. In this way their carefully honed sense of self and self-efficacy begin to crumble. In such instances, the Holy Spirit may do at least three things: revise their false sense of self, recalibrate their ideal self, and redirect and empower their quest to attain the latter.

Ultimately the Christian's sense of self is grounded, not primarily in social feedback, but in God's declaration of who they are in his eyes — beloved and of infinite worth. Their ideal self is now defined by the paradigmatic person of Jesus Christ — the prototype of redeemed humanity — and supplemented by a divinely illuminated vision of what should be their own unique expression of this. And to these ends, God offers the possibility of a renewed self, one transformed by the inner work of his Spirit. This brings with it a heightened efficacy, reflected in the apostle Paul's testimony that "I can do everything through him who gives me strength" (Phil. 4:13). This inward renewal of the self also makes healthy, properly differentiated relationships with God and others more possible.

The Bible speaks of the need for believers to be "crucified" with Christ (Gal. 2:20) and to become "dead" to sin (Rom. 6–7). Some Christian traditions have tried to follow these admonitions by employing the language of "dying to self." This has too often fostered falsely negative perceptions of the self and excessive passivity in responding to one's responsibilities in an adult world. Christian spirituality should be grounded in a healthy regard for personal identity and self-efficacy. What is rightly emphasized is the rejection of self-*ishness*, of that fixation upon and preoccupation with one's own interests to the disregard of others and the claims of the Creator and Redeemer himself. This disposition lies at the core of human nature and constitutes the essence of sin. Motivated by love, Jesus relinquished his own self-interests to the higher claims of his Father's will; and now believers are invited to follow his example. As the saints of old testified, abundant life unfolds when the self is offered to the sacred.

See also Body; Sexuality; Soul.

For Further Reading: D. Benner, *The Gift of Being Yourself* (2004); T. Cooper, *Sin, Pride and Self-Acceptance* (2003); R. Kegan, *The Evolving Self* (1982).

Linde J. Getahun

Self-Control

Self-control, or temperance, is fundamental to Christian spirituality. Most of the spiritual disciplines, such as fasting, meditation, prayer, silence, solitude, and chastity, require it. Self-control is an inner disposition or virtue that enables a Christian to restrain "the flesh" in order to concentrate on higher goals. Self-control is a gift of grace to be developed through discipline into a habituated pattern of response.

Self-control is one of the four cardinal virtues. The original Greek term translated "temperance" (*sōphrosynē*) means "soundness of mind." In Greek literature, both it and *egkrateia* are sometimes translated "self-control." In Titus 2:2 (ASV), *sōphronās* is translated "sober-minded." A sober mind is one that is not overwhelmed by the "lust of the flesh, and the lust of the eyes, and the pride of life" (1 John 2:16 KJV). In 2 Peter 1:6, self-control is placed in a list between "knowledge" and "patience" or "perseverance." A person who practices temperance has patience to delay gratification and act according to knowledge.

Aristotle explained self-control as the appropriate balance between insensibility and self-indulgence. "Insensibility" would mean the elimination of all physical appetites and at its extreme would lead to death. The goal of Christian spirituality is not the elimination of desire but rather their control. Physical desires are essentially good. They are created by God and meant to be fulfilled. On the other hand, self-indulgence implies that a person has no control over his or her desires and becomes a "slave of the flesh." The essence of self-control is freedom to act according to one's highest values rather than being controlled by lower instincts or impulses.

Temperance is not a fixed standard of behavior that is the same for everyone. A child, an athlete, and an old person have different needs for food and exercise. Different cultures have different values concerning how human beings should control themselves. In Java, control of emotions and maintenance of everyone's honor in public situations is a high value. In contrast, Californians value honest and frank expression of feelings to build authentic relationships. Different cultures have different social goals, but all require self-control.

In Galatians the apostle Paul argues that we are not under the law, but rather under the Spirit. Self-control is listed among the fruit of the Spirit, with the concluding notation that "against such things there is no law" (5:23). Self-control is not inner fortitude to follow the law more strictly. Rather, it is a gift of God's grace that makes the law unnecessary. Temperance is not only a gift; it is also a skill that is perfected by practice. By the grace of God, every day from our birth we are learning to control our instincts. The positive virtue of temperance implies a sound mind that lives in the freedom of the Spirit.

See also *Apatheia;* Fruit of the Spirit.

For Further Reading: B. Adeney, *Strange Virtues* (1995); Aristotle, *Nicomachean Ethics* (many editions).

Bernard Adeney-Risakotta

Self-Knowledge

The Christian spiritual tradition has consistently affirmed that essential to spiritual health and vitality, and thus to wisdom in the Christian life, is a good measure of self-knowledge — which is, ultimately, to know ourselves as God declares us to be. Spiritual writers who call for self-knowledge often reference the words of Romans 12:3 and the call to "think of yourself with sober judgment." And what each writer consistently affirms is that self-knowledge is basic to wisdom, humility, and spiritual freedom.

Catherine of Sienna, for example, in *The Dialogue*, spoke of self-knowledge as true humility but then also stressed that the spiritual life rests on the appreciation of God's love for the self and that in knowing the love of God for our very selves, we are freed from self-love to love others as we have been loved.

Teresa of Avila also spoke of self-knowledge as essential disposition to prayer, for there is no humility without it. And she insisted in book 1 of the *Interior Castle* that self-knowledge is gained by the contemplation of the goodness of God.

John Calvin opened his *Institutes of the Christian Religion* with the oft-quoted observation that wisdom consists of two parts, "the knowledge of God and of ourselves," and that it is "not easy to determine which of the two precedes and gives birth to the other."

And then A. W. Tozer, in *The Pursuit of God*, was a more contemporary voice, insisting that freedom in the spiritual life comes by refusing to live by pretense, which he spoke of as the burden of hypocrisy — of living as though we are someone other than who we are.

What each of these spiritual authors witnessed to is (1) that self-knowledge is essential to humility and thus vital to the spiritual life; (2) that the knowledge of self is only possible by and through the interplay of knowledge of God; (3) that self-knowledge is only possible when one is confident of the goodness and love of God; and (4) that self-knowledge then frees a person to serve with generosity and love for others.

Thus, our approaches to spiritual formation and discipleship need to both free and guide Christians in this essential dimension of their spiritual journey; and parenting includes encouraging our children to be precisely who they are, in the grace and goodness of God. And one key expression of this: vocation, the work to which one is called, will be deeply consistent with one's identity. Indeed, self-knowledge necessarily precedes vocational discernment.

See also Examen.

For Further Reading: D. Benner, *The Gift of Being Yourself* (2004); G. Ten Elshof, *I Told Me So* (2009).

Gordon T. Smith

Service

Service refers to "ministry" or "support" or "work involved in worship." Three NT Greek words are translated into English as "service": *diakonia*, *leitourgia*, and *latreia*. First, *diakonia* means "ministry," that is, the spiritual gift of service (Rom. 12:7). A common belief is that members of Christ's body graced with the gift of service are supernaturally inclined to minister to others in a hands-on practical way. The spiritual gift of service can be distinguished from the spiritual gift of helps (1 Cor. 12:28) insofar as the former entails more leadership — this distinction being evidenced by the Greek word for the office of deacon (*diakonos*). In Romans 15:31, Paul uses the word *diakonia* more generally to speak of his "service in Jerusalem." Second, *leitourgia* means "support," as in financial support. The ministry of the Corinthians' "service ... is supplying the needs of God's people" (2 Cor. 9:12). *Leitourgia* also points to the service (i.e. support) of the Philippians' faith in God for Paul's sake (Phil. 2:17). Third, *latreia* means "work involved in worship" and refers primarily to the temple service that specially belongs to the Israelites (Rom. 9:4). In the OT the word *service* most commonly refers to the service of God in the context of worship in God's house. It appears most frequently in Numbers and 1 and 2 Chronicles, occurring more than a hundred times in the OT.

With regard to discipleship and spiritual formation, service is a primary discipline. Not only did Jesus set the ultimate example of greatness by washing the disciples' feet (John 13:14–15), but he also made it plain that "whoever wants to become great among you must be your servant ... just as the Son of Man did not come to be served, but to serve" (Matt. 20:26–28). Contemporary writer Richard Foster has said that being a servant enables a person "to say no to the world's games of promotion and authority." To serve is to humble oneself. When service seems like drudgery or when service is performed for the sake of notoriety or recognition, service is self-focused rather than others-centered as it ought to be. True Christian service is often hidden. To serve God cheerfully without the luxury of having control over the timing and situation of one's service — to serve in the context of complete surrender to God — that is what it means to serve in love.

See also Vocation.

For Further Reading: R. Foster, *Celebration of Discipline* (1978); W. Law, *A Serious Call to a Devout and Holy Life* (1728); H. W. Smith, *The Christian's Secret to a Happy Life* (1875).

Sarah Sumner

Seven Deadly Sins

See **Sins, Seven Deadly.**

Sexuality

Sexuality is an essential element of humanness that includes biological givens, role socialization, and social constructions about gender as well as sexual behavior. Humans are created as both transcendent beings and as embodied, gendered beings (Gen. 1:27). This embodiment is clearly intended by God as a gift, which is evident in God's declaration that humans were "very good" (v. 31). Thus, a focus on sexual health and wholeness is more consistent with creation than is a focus on sexual "should nots."

Sexual health and wholeness are characterized by the degree to which certain dynamics are present in a family, organization, congregation, or any other system, according to the late James Maddock, a family therapist who specialized in sexuality. First, sexually healthy systems demonstrate respect for both genders. Relational spirituality and sexual wholeness both require the capacity to value equally male and female ways of being in the world.

Second, sexually healthy systems are able to communicate effectively about sexuality. For some, this requires dealing with embarrassment or anxiety; for some, it requires acquiring new vocabulary and perhaps new, more accurate information about gender roles, physical development, and eroticism.

Sexually healthy systems also demonstrate clear, age-appropriate boundaries that allow persons to have sufficient privacy as well as sufficient connection with others. And finally, they are able to develop and implement a biblically based, culturally relevant system of sexual values and meanings that can be used to make decisions about sexual behavior. It is important to note that "culturally relevant" does not mean some kind of relativism in which prevailing cultural norms set the agenda for sexual decision making on the part of Christians. Rather, it suggests that the biblically based values and meanings that form a foundation for decisions are applied with a full awareness of the pressures and messages with which individuals live. For example, teaching children and adolescents about biblical expectations of purity most effectively includes discussion about how to live out those expectations in a hyper-sexualized environment of ubiquitous risqué media images and permissive, "anything goes" messages.

Persons who are single are often unintentionally ignored in discussions of sexuality, perhaps because of a tendency to think of sexuality primarily or only in behavioral terms. However, the essence of authentic sexuality, for both married and single persons, incorporates living lives of intimacy and passion. Deep knowing of others and being deeply known by others is not limited to sexually active persons, nor is finding and expressing passion beyond the physical realm. In fact, life in God invites and equips all for deep intimacy and thrilling passion.

Historically, Christians have tended toward a view of sexuality based more on the body as enemy than as gift. This view suggests residual influences of Gnostic dualism, in which the spirit was viewed as good and the flesh as the unfortunate evil container of that good spirit. More commonly (and especially in the monastic tradition, for example) Christians have tended to view the body not so much as evil as irremediably weak, vulnerable, and "earthen." While integrity in facing temptation is as important in sexual matters as in any other domain of life, an overemphasis on the dangers of embodiment tends to result in anxiety, shame, and objectification of others (seeing others either as commodities to be used for our own purposes or as frightening obstacles to our own right living). Guidelines for appropriate sexual expression and behavior exist because of the goodness of the gift, not the dangers of the gift.

Because sexuality is so intrinsic to the human self, woundedness in this area can be particularly challenging. Highly anxious responses to the power of sexuality (rigid rules, shaming messages, dismay at sexual development or curiosity) can complicate healing from the consequences of past decisions and behavior. Equally troubling is the impact of sexually inappropriate or abusive behavior of others on the development of a genuine sense of oneself as a chosen, holy, and dearly loved child of God (Col. 3:12). The trauma of sexual abuse or exploitation tends to create feelings of powerlessness and shame. When these feelings are met with the highly anxious reactions described earlier, survivors of sexual abuse or assault can feel inappropriate guilt and a misplaced sense of responsibility for the abuse. In the Gospels, Jesus modeled nonanxious engagement with the sexually wounded of his culture—the prostitutes and adulterers who were disdained by the religious and cultural elite—by seeing them, freeing them, and inviting them to new beginnings.

A significant contemporary challenge relates to the question of a right response to gay men and lesbians (and bisexual and transgendered persons). Denominations around the world have faced wrenching, divisive decisions about whether to ordain gay and lesbian clergypersons and whether to bless or affirm committed gay and lesbian relationships. Significant differences of opinion and interpretations of biblical teaching exist among Christians. For example, some evangelicals make a distinction between identity and behavior; others do not. And while some Christian therapists who work with gay and lesbian clients attempt to assist them in developing a heterosexual identity, others focus on helping gay men and lesbians reconcile their religious and sexual identities and make life choices that are congruent with their faith values.

See also Body; Celibacy; Chastity; Desire; Gender and Spirituality.

For Further Reading: J. K. Balswick and J. O. Balswick, *Authentic Human Sexuality* (2008); R. Bell, *Sex God* (2008); R. Clapp, *Families at the Crossroads* (1993); T. Gardner, *Sacred Sex* (2002); L. Smedes, *Sex for Christians* (1994).

Carla M. Dahl

Seymour, William Joseph (1870–1922)

African-American leader of the Azusa Street revival of 1906–1909. Born in Centerville, Louisiana, a formidable bastion of white supremacy, as the son of former slaves, Seymour grew up amid intense racial tension. Migrating to Houston in 1904, he sat under the teaching of former Topeka Holiness leader Charles Parham. Though seated outside the classroom, Seymour became convinced of Parham's message on Spirit baptism. He accepted a call to pastor the Apostolic Faith Mission in Los Angeles and there led a renewal many associate with the beginning of the Pentecostal and charismatic movements. He severed ties with Parham and proclaimed the Spirit of Pentecost as the great equalizer, thereby breaking racial, ethnic, and gender barriers. The revival received worldwide acclaim as people experienced newfound intimacy with Jesus and the power of the Spirit to proclaim the gospel around the world. Unfortunately, as the local revival waned and the movement found new expressions, Seymour fell into relative obscurity. While his hope for broken barriers experienced short-term and limited success, he was a man ahead of his time, a pioneer who helped move the theological axiom of a priesthood/prophethood of all believers beyond theory into reality.

See also African-American Christian Spirituality; Pentecostal Spirituality.

Martin Mittelstadt

Shaker Spirituality

Shaker spirituality pertains to the Shakers, formally known as the United Society of Believers in Christ's Second Appearing. "Spirituality" refers to their expressions of transcendent awareness of God as mediated through Jesus Christ and Mother Ann Lee (1742–1784), the founder. The group began with Ann Lee and her followers in 1780 near Albany, New York, after they arrived in 1774. After a peak of about four thousand members around 1840, living from New England to Kentucky, fewer than half a dozen Shakers continue today at Sabbathday Lake in Maine.

At the center of Shaker spirituality is the direct work of the Holy Spirit upon believers, both individually and gathered in union as celibate members of Shaker community. Jesus Christ and Mother Ann Lee are mediators of the spiritual manifestations. Mother Ann believed that the revelations she received from Christ, including mandatory celibacy for members, constituted Christ's second appearing, mediated through her. She also received songs and ecstatic movement (dance). Joseph Meacham organized ecstatic movement into orderly dances after 1787. Dance faded away in the early 20th century, but motions during some songs continue in Shaker worship. Song, whether with vocalized syllables, words, or unknown tongues, is equally central to spirituality. Confession of sin when joining the community and at later times is part of the Shakers' spiritual awareness of forgiveness in the present. Shaker spirituality assumes that each believer can experience the Spirit's work and will express it in a life of worship and work. These experiences are best shared in a community of spiritual unity and simplicity, where the role of female is balanced with the male. In Shaker spirituality, believers express to other Shakers and the world their experience through visions, song, dance, drawings, personal awareness, or other manifestations. Such experiences increased, sometimes to excess, during Mother Ann's Work, a time of revival from 1837 to the late 1840s.

Evangelicals often avoided Shaker spirituality because of the heightened role of Ann Lee and because of its emphasis on direct spiritual experience over biblical texts. Nonetheless, Shaker spirituality testifies that belief in Christ's appearing can transform the present, sometimes with dramatic, powerful expressions in the body; and that within a gathered community marked by unity, simplicity, and gender balance, "gifts of the Spirit" can abound.

See also Celibacy; Community, Experiments in; Quaker Spirituality.

For Further Reading: R. Bishop and S. Y. Wells, eds., *Testimony of the Life, Character, Revelations and Doctrines of Our Ever Blessed Mother Ann Lee* (1816); D. Patterson, *The Shaker Spiritual* (1979); *The Shakers: Two Centuries of Spiritual Reflection,*

CWS (1983); S. Stein, *The Shaker Experience in America* (1992).

Jeff Bach

Sheldon, Charles M. (1857 – 1946)

Social gospel novelist. Sheldon was a Congregationalist pastor and novelist who remains famous today for *In His Steps* (1896), the romanticized story that imagines what would happen if people started to ask, "What would Jesus do?" before making any important decision and then acting on the Spirit-led answer. Sheldon had his characters take on many of the social gospel causes of his own liberal theological training, as well as the more typically evangelical causes of evangelism and temperance. Pastor of a thriving Topeka, Kansas, Congregational church, Sheldon read *In His Steps* and his other novels (none nearly as successful) aloud serially at Sunday night services. He was no retiring dreamer: he not only wrote about but also participated in social gospel efforts and was a lifelong temperance advocate. Against the objections of some of his own congregants, he worked to bring the black community of Tennesseetown out of poverty by, among other things, founding the nation's first Black kindergarten there. In the late 20th century, the central question of Sheldon's most famous novel was abbreviated to WWJD and spawned a whole subindustry of Christian kitsch, including bracelets and decals.

See also Imitation of Christ.

Chris R. Armstrong

Shepherd of Hermas

Popular writing from the early decades of the 2nd century, reporting the teachings, visions, and parables received through angelic revelation by an untrained Christian layman. Some of the central themes in this work are repentance, detachment from vain worldly pursuits, service to the poor, prayer, fasting, vision, divine inhabitation, and angelic intercession. As such, the spirituality of *Shepherd* anticipates developments that come to full bloom in Christian monastic tradition.

Addressing the rigorist views prevailing in his community (possibly Rome), the author affirms a single chance of forgiveness for sins committed after baptism; however, the larger context of the *Shepherd* suggests that true repentance is always possible. The indwelling Spirit received at baptism intercedes on behalf of the believer; however, if one grieves and "oppresses" the Spirit, he intercedes *against* the sinner. For Hermas prayer is never an individual act, but a cooperation between the believer and the indwelling Spirit (or angel), which ensures that the well-pleasing service ("liturgy") of prayer becomes a sacrifice that reaches the heavenly altar.

The eschatological state is described as "being numbered with the angels," "dwelling with the Son of God," or "being granted entry with the angels"; this state, however, is anticipated by the ascetic Christian believers, whose place, says Hermas, "is *already* with the angels." This view is obviously not unrelated to the later monastic notion of the "angelic life."

Generally speaking, the *Shepherd* anticipates important elements of later Christian ascetic theory, such as prayer as an interior sacrifice, the link between the offering on the heavenly altar and the altar of the heart, and the connection between temple liturgy, interior liturgy, and the liturgy of the heavens. It is no wonder that subsequent generations — and perhaps especially the monastics who continued to copy the *Shepherd* — had good reasons to be deeply sympathetic to the ascetic theology of this work.

See also Apostolic Fathers; Monasticism.

For Further Reading: B. Bucur, "Observations on the Ascetic Doctrine of the *Shepherd of Hermas*," *Studia Monastica* 48 (2006): 7 – 23; C. Gieschen, "The Angel of the Prophetic Spirit," *Society of Biblical Literature Seminar Papers* 33 (1994): 790–803; C. Osiek, *Shepherd of Hermas* (1999).

Bogdan G. Bucur

Sider, Ronald J. (1939–)

Ethicist and founder of Evangelicals for Social Action. Born into a Canadian Brethren in Christ farm family, Sider completed seminary and doctoral studies at Yale, intending to become a historian and apologist. In the 1960s, as his growing awareness of racism and poverty merged with mounting conviction of a biblical mandate for social involvement, Sider and his wife, Arbutus, relocated to inner-city Philadelphia, where he taught college and led political advocacy. Sider chaired the 1973 Chicago Declaration of Evangelical Social Concern, insisting Christian discipleship demands repenting from neglect of the poor and confronting injustice—without losing passion for evangelism. To further this movement, Sider has long led Evangelicals for Social Action while also serving as professor of theology and public policy at Palmer Seminary.

Nourished by Anabaptist, Holiness, and African-American streams, his social ethic has defied facile categorization, drawing criticism and commendation across the political spectrum. He challenges both sides of the evangelical-mainline divide to abandon "one-sided Christianity," preoccupied only with saving souls or pursuing justice, and instead to practice a holistic faith in which word and deed, prayer and action, personal salvation and social transformation go hand in hand.

Named one of the twelve most influential persons in American religion in the 1980s, Sider's prolific speaking and writing—including more than twenty-five books, most notably *Rich Christians in an Age of Hunger* (1997)—have helped catalyze an evolving progressive evangelical movement. Yet his agenda is not a new social gospel but a revival of incarnational commitment to Christ. If Christians truly honored Jesus as Lord of "bedroom, board-room, and ballot box," he writes in *Living Like Jesus* (1999), they would change the world (and be changed). In *I Am Not a Social Activist* (2008), Sider describes his dangerous daily prayer—"Jesus, be the center." The inner journey toward the risen Savior drives and empowers social engagement and evangelistic witness, embodying God's restoration of his broken but beloved creation.

See also Social Justice.

For Further Reading: J. Fetzer and G. S. Carnes, "Dr. Ron Sider," in *Religious Leaders and Faith-Based Politics*, ed. J. R. Formicola and H. Morken (2001); T. Stafford, "Ron Sider's Unsettling Crusade," *Christianity Today*, April 27, 1992, 18–22.

Heidi Unruh

Silence

Silence is the spiritual discipline of withdrawing or abstaining from noise, words, and activity for a time to become more attuned to the voice of God. In silence we allow the noise of our own thoughts, human strivings, and inner compulsions to settle down so that we can hear and respond to the presence of God deep within. The discipline of silence confronts us with the fact that reliance on our own thoughts and words, even in our praying, can be one facet of our need to control things, to set the agenda, or at least know what the agenda is—even in our relationship with God. In silence we habitually release our own agendas and our need to control; we become more willing and able to give ourselves to God's loving initiative. In silence we cease striving and we create space for God's activity in our lives rather than filling every moment with our own.

Our understanding of this discipline derives from biblical passages such as Psalm 46:10, which instructs us to "Be still [or cease striving], and know that I am God." The Hebrew word translated "Be still" is *rapha*, which literally means "to let go of your grip." This verse indicates that silence as a spiritual practice is more than just the absence of noise; it involves a willingness to let go of all that we normally cling to — particularly the agendas and attachments we hold for ourselves, for others, and even for God himself. This is to *know* God at a whole new level. In Hebrew, the word for "to know" suggests a full, experiential knowing between subject and object rather than mere cognitive knowing that is purely intellectual. There is a difference between knowing someone and merely having information about them, and Psalm 46:10 is talking about the knowing that comes through experience that God is God in our lives.

In Psalm 62:1 the psalmist cries out, "My soul finds rest in God alone; my salvation comes from him." This verse indicates that there is a kind of salvation that comes in the silence that does not come through our attempts to act on our own behalf. This verse is reminiscent of Moses' instruction to the Israelites when they were trapped between the Red Sea and the pursuing Egyptians. His counterintuitive instruction was, "The Lord will fight for you; you need only to be still" (Ex. 14:14).

Psalm 4:4 teaches us that silence is a necessary discipline that helps us to cope with the disturbances of life in a fruitful and God-honoring way. "When you are disturbed, do not sin; ponder it on your beds, and be silent" (NRSV). And in 1 Kings 19, Elijah discovered that the Lord was not in the wind, the earthquake, or the fire, but in the "sound of sheer silence" (v. 12 NRSV). When Elijah experienced this silence that was "full" of the presence of God, he wrapped his face in his mantle, a sign of reverence in the presence of deity.

In the NT, the word *hesuchios*, which is translated "silence," is more literally "quiet" or "tranquillity arising from within." This meaning gives rise to a tradition of prayer that refers to the spirituality of the desert — men and women who seek solitude and silence as a way of coming to rest in God through unceasing prayer. This kind of quietness is pictured in Psalm 131 where the psalmist describes the soul at rest in God as being like a weaned child with its mother. In the NT, Jesus commended Mary for sitting quietly at his feet for the purpose of listening to his teaching (Luke 10:42).

The practice of silent prayer is referred to in Christian tradition by various terms, all with their own finer nuances: wordless prayer, centering prayer, contemplative prayer, prayer of the heart. All varieties have the same intent — to help us give up control, to experience the presence of God beyond words and concepts, to express our dependence on God, and to allow space for God to take the initiative in our lives. As William Shannon writes in his book *Silence on Fire*, "Wordless prayer ... is humble, simple prayer in which we experience our total dependence on God and our awareness that we are in God. Wordless prayer is not an attempt to 'get anywhere,' for we are already there (in God's presence). It is just that we are not sufficiently conscious of our being there."

Silence is the discipline that enables us over time to be more and more fully aware of where we are — in the presence of God. From the biblical references and the witness of spiritual seekers down through the ages, we learn that there is a wisdom that comes in the silence that does not come through words and the conceptualizations of the intellect mediated through words. There is a difference between *experiencing* God and just *knowing about* God. There is a kind of deliverance that comes in silent waiting upon God that is different than the solutions that come through striving on our own behalf. Silence invites us into the kind of emptiness that creates space for the fullness that is God.

See also Apophatic and Kataphatic Ways; Hesychasm.

For Further Reading: R. Barton, *Invitation to Solitude and Silence* (2004); T. Merton, *Contemplative Prayer* (1969); H. Nouwen, *The Way of the Heart* (1981); W. Shannon, *Silence on Fire* (1991).

Ruth Haley Barton

Silesius, Angelus
See **Angelus Silesius.**

Simeon, Charles (1759–1836)

Evangelical pastor-mentor. For more than fifty years, Simeon was the evangelical pastor of Holy Trinity Church in Cambridge and fellow of Cambridge University. He mentored some 30 percent of the Anglican ministers of his day (more than eleven hundred) through informal preaching seminars and "conversation parties" in his Cambridge rooms. Born of wealth, he also pulled strings to secure pulpits for many of his protégées. He was a man of difficult temperament, often impetuous and even arrogant, who struggled for sanctification through repeated lessons in humble contrition. For decades he was ostracized for his beliefs and foibles by Cambridge townfolk, undergraduates, and even many in his own congregation. But he published more than twenty-five hundred widely used "sermon skeletons," covering the entire Bible, sent countless chaplains to India, helped launch the hugely influential Church Missionary Society, and inspired the men who later founded the Cambridge Prayer Union, a precursor to today's Inter-Varsity Christian Fellowship. And he finished his race respected and beloved, having almost single-handedly renewed a Church of England in danger of losing all the benefit it had gained in the evangelical revival of the mid-1700s.

See also Anglican Spirituality.

For Further Reading: C. Armstrong, *Patron Saints for Postmoderns* (2009), chap. 7.

Chris R. Armstrong

Simplicity

Simplicity means focusing on priorities: "Seek first [God's] kingdom and his righteousness" (Matt. 6:33). John the Baptist lived in the wilderness, wearing rough clothing and eating "locusts and wild honey" (Matt. 3:4). In the Sermon on the Mount, Jesus counseled speaking the simple truth, warned against accumulating goods, and commanded us not to worry about daily practical details. The early church pooled possessions. Paul counseled contentment with little (Phil. 4:11–12). First Timothy 2:9 recommends that women should dress without "gold or pearls or expensive clothes."

Simplicity has been given priority by numerous Christian movements: Puritans, Moravians, Wesley and the Methodists, and the Salvation Army. Two streams are still particularly influential: monasticism and "plain," "Old Order" movements (e.g., Mennonites, Quakers, and Old German Baptist Brethren "Dunkers").

The most famous desert father, Antony of Egypt, disposed of his worldly goods after hearing Matthew 19:21: "If you want to be perfect, go, sell your possessions and give to the poor, and you will have treasure in heaven. Then come, follow me." Subsequent desert fathers and mothers earned their keep with manual labor. Later monasticism required adherents to hold things in common; eventually this was known as the vow of poverty. Ironically, monastic houses often grew wealthy. Renewal regularly involved a return to simple poverty: for example, Francis of Assisi and Discalced ("barefoot") Carmelites. Francis de Sales wrote, "There is no artifice as good and desirable as simplicity." Mother Teresa was a modern exemplar of poverty and simplicity.

Anabaptists (16th century) and Quakers (17th century) were known for priorities of simplicity, plainness, and nonconformity. They were suspicious of accumulating wealth. They advocated modest dress (undercutting class distinctions and hierarchy) and plain speech (honesty without oaths). Meetinghouses lacked ornamentation. Old Order practitioners now practice cautious restraint in the owning of complex technology.

Simplicity emerged as a counterculture priority in the 1960s and 1970s. Christian articulation came in the writings of E. F. Schumacher (*Small Is Beautiful*), Ron Sider (*Rich Christians in an Age of Hunger*), and Richard Foster (*Freedom of Simplicity*); periodicals such as *Sojourners* and *The Other Side*; and influential Mennonite books, *Living More with Less* and the *More-with-Less Cookbook*. They advocated voluntary simplicity, for example, people of privilege with choice and control over lifestyles.

Motives include rejecting materialism and consumerism, commitment to sustainability and appropriate technology, concern about poverty and injustice, and minimizing tax obligations that fund war. Time or money saved can be expended on central priorities — family, church, service, volunteering. Recent ecological expressions — especially in light of climate change — speak of environmental footprints, advocate growing and processing one's own food, eating locally (100-mile diet), ethical eating (vegetarian or vegan), and purchasing fair trade or secondhand goods. More recently, New Monasticism advocates and models simplicity.

Temptations associated with simplicity are scrupulosity (being overly concerned with one's sins), judgmental attitudes toward those who do not share one's standards, works righteousness, and a dour approach to life. Nevertheless, a nineteenth-century Shaker hymn reminds us of the call to the good life, full of joy: "'Tis a gift to be simple, 'tis a gift to be free, 'tis a gift to come down where we ought to be."

See also Benedictine Spirituality; Contentment; French (School of) Spirituality; Monasticism.

For Further Reading: S. Claiborne, *The Irresistible Revolution* (2006); V. Eller, *The Simple Life* (1973); A. Gish, *Beyond the Rat Race* (1981).

Arthur Paul Boers

Simpson, A(lbert) B(enjamin) (1843–1919)

Founder of the Christian and Missionary Alliance. Born in Canada and trained at Knox College, Toronto, Simpson served Presbyterian churches in Canada and the United States. A desire to reach "God's neglected people" coupled with a rejection of significant Presbyterian doctrines led him to establish the Gospel Tabernacle in New York City. Simpson and his supporters founded the Christian and Missionary Alliance in 1887 to promote both the deeper Christian life and world evangelization. His key writings include *The Gospel of Healing* (1885), *The Fourfold Gospel* (1887), and *Wholly Sanctified* (1890), all of which remain in print.

The Fourfold Gospel focuses on the appropriation, intensification, and expansion of dependence on the indwelling resurrected Christ as the source of fulfillment for all of one's needs. In particular, it identifies the indwelling Christ as the very content of one's regeneration, sanctification, and physical health. Each of these finds its fulfillment only with Christ's premillennial return when relationship with him will be unmediated and perfect.

Simpson taught that sanctification was a second work of grace subsequent to regeneration and appropriated by a distinct step of faith that provided the believer with power for ministry and holy living. Divine healing, likewise the consequence of the life of Christ within, provided the vitality necessary for holy living and ministry. In both cases, the Christian may be elevated to a plane beyond that of natural human capacity.

Convinced that the fullness of Christian experience would reach its perfection only at Christ's return, that this return could actually be hastened through the evangelization of the world, and that this task could be completed in his own lifetime, Simpson was deeply committed to the missionary cause.

Such thinking was widespread in late nineteenth-century evangelicalism and therefore was not unique to Simpson. He did, however, name it the Fourfold Gospel and served as its most visible proponent. This gestalt proved particularly influential in the birth and development of classic Pentecostal theology and spirituality, with some simply adding Spirit baptism to the gestalt while others substituted it for sanctification altogether.

See also Evangelism; Health and Healing; Holiness Movement; Pentecostal Spirituality.

For Further Reading: C. Nienkirchen, *A. B. Simpson and the Pentecostal Movement* (1992); R. Niklaus et al., *All for Jesus* (1986); B. Van De Walle, *The Heart of the Gospel* (2009).

Bernie Van De Walle

Sin

Sin is one of those concepts that, on first glance, would seem to need no explanation. What is more central to the Christian faith than the understanding that all have sinned and fallen short of the glory of God? Sin is, in short, the reason that we need a Savior to restore our relationship with our Creator. Like all powerful words, however, "sin" carries layers and subtleties of meaning that require further exploration. "Sin" commonly refers to willful acts of disobedience but can also refer to corporate and systemic moral transgressions, to a pervasive part of humanity's condition that leaves us estranged from God, and to a state of fallenness into which we are born. "Sin" can also refer broadly to the distortion of all of God's creation from what God intended it to be. Cornelius Plantinga notes that the word *sin* encompasses everything that violates God's shalom, the peaceful and just harmony that he intended for his creation. Christ followers, then, are to be shalom restorers.

To address sin for the purpose of spiritual formation, however, it is important to take a narrower vantage point. Sin in this context must be viewed, Plantinga tells us, as a "culpable and personal affront to a personal God." Dallas Willard notes that the frightening realization that we are responsible for our failure to meet God's standards leads us to build gospels of sin management. It is much easier to meet external behavioral requirements than it is to clean out the recesses of the human heart. Jesus repeatedly told his listeners, especially the Pharisees, that God is not as interested in rule following as he is in a humble and obedient heart.

The Bible tells us, though, that the heart is deceitful and difficult to know. Within the traditions of spiritual formation, it has long been known that sin begins in the heart. By the time it manifests itself in the form of disobedient behavior, sin has already sunk deep roots. Colomba Stewart noted that the desert fathers understood sin to consist primarily of deadly *logismoi*, or "thoughts," rather than behaviors. Their list of deadly *logismoi* evolved into the list that is today known as the seven deadly sins. Similarly, Oswald Chambers noted that the source of these sinful thoughts of the heart lies in the incurable suspicion we inherit through original sin: the suspicion that God is not good. In short, we sin out of self-protection.

See also Sins, Seven Deadly; Temptation.

For Further Reading: O. Chambers, *Biblical Psychology* (1994); M. Mangis, *Signature Sins* (2008); C. Plantinga Jr., *Not the Way It's Supposed to Be* (1995); C. Stewart, "The Desert Fathers on Radical Self-Honesty," *Vox Benedictina* 8 (1991): 6 – 53.

Michael Mangis and Brian Post

Singh, Sadhu Sundar (1889 – 1929)

Pioneer Indian evangelist and missionary to Sikhs, Hindus, and Tibetans. Singh was born into a Kshatriya (ruler, warrior) family; his father was a wealthy landlord, and his mother a devout woman. They were Sikhs, members of a religion whose founders (Gurus) were persecuted and martyred by the Muslim rulers of India.

As a young man, Singh persecuted Indian Christians and missionaries. At the same time, he was troubled and restless in his own life and religion. One morning, having planned to commit suicide, he prayed, "O God, if there is a God, wilt thou show me the right way, or I will kill myself." He explained, "At 4:30 a.m. I saw something of which I had no idea previously. In the room where I was praying, I saw a great light. I thought the place was on fire.... Then as I prayed and looked into the light, I saw the form of the Lord Jesus Christ. I heard a voice saying in Hindustani, 'How long will you persecute me? I have come to save you; you were praying to know the right way.'... So I fell at his feet and got this wonderful peace, which I could not get anywhere else. This is the joy which I was wishing to get."

Beginning with his conversion, Singh's spirituality began to take shape through an "Indianization" of Pauline thought and practice. First, he suggested that authentic Indian Christian spirituality must be located in genuinely Indian form, even, for example, in the life, expressions, worship pattern, and teaching methods of a wandering ascetic, a *Sadhu*. This he became. Second, he suggested that in every religion there is a spiritual vacuum, which only Christ and his gospel can fill. He diligently pursued the discovery of these spiritual vacuums and showed how Christ fills them. These convictions shaped his entire life and spirituality, and over the course of his relatively brief life, he won many devout Hindus, Sikhs, and Tibetans to Christ. Sundar Singh's Christian faith and experience were arguably unorthodox at points and highly mystical, yet authentically Christian and Indian. He described his mystical union with God as "a sponge which lies in water and the water fills the sponge ... it is the same when I immerse myself in God." His many writings included *At the Feet of the Master* (1922).

See also Asian Christian Spirituality; Hindu Spirituality.

For Further Reading: C. F. Andrews, *Sadhu Sundar Singh* (1934); K. Comer, ed., *Wisdom of the Sadhu* (2000); F. Heiler, *The Gospel of Sadhu Sundar Singh*, trans. O. Wyon (1927); S. S. Singh, *Essential Writings*, ed. C. Moore (2005).

R. Boaz Johnson

Singleness

Singleness refers to the state of being single: unmarried. This status can be voluntarily chosen or involuntarily imposed: never married, divorced, widowed, or due to a religious life calling or sexual orientation.

In the biblical story of creation, we read verses (e.g., Gen. 1:28; 2:18) generally interpreted as an indication that marrying and having children are part of the natural order. In the OT, there was no clear revelation about the afterlife, and continuity of oneself came through one's offspring. That meant that the choice not to have children was socially unacceptable, and the inability to have children was a tragedy.

When Jesus Christ became incarnate, he shone a new light on singleness as a state that is not only acceptable, but also equally whole and fulfilling. The Gospels revolve around this single man who is the example of perfect humanity. His life shows how to have healthy, intimate relationships with God and with others, and how to be fully dedicated to one's calling and ministry—as a single person.

In contrast with the common social view of singleness as atypical, a social oddity, or a temporary status, the apostle Paul contributed to a more positive view when he affirmed it, like marriage, as a gift from God (1 Cor. 7:7–8). Therefore, the biblical framework for love and intimacy is not limited to sex and marriage. We learn true intimacy within a personal relationship with God, and then we live it out with others. The monastic vocation has been just one example of this, among others, within the Christian tradition.

Sexuality is part of our identity as male and female individuals (Gen. 1:27), and impacts every aspect of our lives, encompassing much more than sexual intercourse. Healthy psychological development must not deny one's sexual needs, but embrace one's sexuality by finding appropriate ways of expressing it. Thus, the calling to celibacy is more than just abstinence: it includes an invitation to solitude, which fosters a holistic path to spiritual maturity.

Challenges to be overcome, such as issues of negative self-image, a lack of sense of belonging, the overall grief of not having a life partner or offspring, loneliness, or single parenthood, can lead to not knowing how one belongs or serves in the church. Therefore, one role of the local congregation is to create an environment that welcomes single children of God as integral and purposeful members of the community of faith. After all, marriage is temporal, whereas belonging to the family of God is eternal.

See also Celibacy; Chastity; Sin.

For Further Reading: C. Colón and B. Field, *Singled Out* (2009); D. Fagerstrom, ed., *Baker Handbook of Single Adult Ministry* (1997); D. Hoffeditz, *They Were Single Too* (2005); A. Hsu, *Singles at the Crossroads* (1997).

Minoa Chang

Sins, Seven Deadly

Evagrius's original list of eight evil thoughts (*logismoi*) — thoughts with which demons tempt us — became in John Cassian the eight principal faults — universal human tendencies from which sins result. Gregory the Great modified Cassian's list and enumerated the "seven principal vices," placing pride in a category by itself as the root of all sins, adding envy, and merging spiritual lethargy (*accidia*) with sadness (*tristitia*) into the single vice of sloth. These became our present-day list of the "seven deadly sins": gluttony, lust, greed, envy, anger, sloth, and vainglory.

As Thomas makes clear in the *Summa*, these are capital or chief or cardinal sins, but they are not necessarily always deadly sins. Each is a cardinal sin in part because it is the parent of "daughter" sins, but a capital sin becomes mortal when it opposes the love and grace of God in the sinner's life.

The order in which these sins are discussed reflects the fact that they are interconnected. For example, Cassian groups the vices in pairs; they form alliances against us, such as gluttony and lust, which are often found together. Anger is often the bedfellow of envy. Evagrius called for careful observation, description, and analysis of the precise nature of our thoughts in order for this knowledge to work to our advantage as we work with or against them and strange spirits. Some passages in the *Praktikos* even contain insights that it has taken our contemporaries decades to rediscover and record in psychological literature.

The first two, gluttony and lust, involve the body and the soul; they are the carnal sins. They are the first to be conquered, and along with greed, they belong to the concupiscible part of our existence. Anger is the first on the irascible list, which also includes sloth (*tristitia* and *accidia*); envy might also be here. Finally, vainglory and pride belong to the third category of principal thoughts — the rational (*logikon*). Some suggest the loss of *tristitia* as a distinctive is regrettable, as "despair" (different from laziness) is a common postmodern malady that undermines one's struggle against all others.

Specifically, in ascetic theology, gluttony is the first to be faced in the battle schema. Cassian compares our battle against these sins to Olympic and Pythian games with their qualifying heats; one who cannot conquer gluttony that has to do with the body will not be victorious in the contests against more insidious enemies that attack us in the spiritual arena.

Careful study of the "deadly sins" tradition is important in light of Thomas Oden's analysis showing that the roots of contemporary Christian psychology include Rogers, Jung, Freud, Maslow, Skinner, and Satir. Keeping in mind that roots determine fruits, concern over the neglect of centuries of Christian wisdom is apropos, particularly if the ascetic theologians and monastics cited in this article provide the church with a psychology that is not only specifically Christian in its orientation, but relevant to modern people if taken seriously. Quite often the classic analyses of the passions or deadly sins provide descriptions, etiology, and remedies that have since been borne out by the empirical observations of contemporary psychology.

See also Greed; Lust; Sloth.

For Further Reading: J. Cassian, *The Institutes*, trans. B. Ramsey (2000); *Evagrius of Pontus: The Greek Ascetic Corpus*, trans. R. Sinkewicz (2003); Gregory, *Morals on the Book of Job*, 3 vols., trans. J. Bliss (1850); T. Oden, *The Care of Souls in the Classic Tradition* (1984); S. Schimmel, *The Seven Deadly Sins* (1992); Thomas Aquinas, *Summa Theologiae*, 1.2 QQ 71–89 and 2.2 QQ 123–70.

Dennis Okholm

Sloth

Sloth is one of the seven "deadly sins," usually associated with *acedia* (weariness of the soul), though Gregory the Great linked it also with *tristitia* (sadness) when he rearranged a list of eight "thoughts" or "faults" into his list of seven. It is sometimes called the "noonday demon," referring to Psalm 91:6 and the desert monk's impatience for the three o'clock (*none*) position of the sun when he would eat his daily meal. More generally, early Christians associated it with deprivations of desires, failed plans, and impeded purposes, accompanied by anger. Its cousin with similar symptoms is what moderns call "depression," though there are differences.

Schimmel notes that of all the "deadly sins" this is the most explicitly religious. Aquinas identifies it as "an oppressive sorrow" that weighs the person down so much that he wants to do nothing. But it would be wrong to identify sloth merely with laziness. Cassian points out that it can also manifest itself as feverish activity that disguises a sluggishness of the soul. That is, it is a *spiritual* condition—an emptiness that encourages flight from spiritual discipline or purposeful, life-giving activity through indifference or distraction.

The early monastics implored others to encourage a slothful conferee, but to do so carefully, using Paul's tactful example in 1 Thessalonians 4:9–12 and remembering the advice in Proverbs 25:20 that singing songs to a heavy heart is like pouring vinegar on a wound. They insisted that the slothful person not run away, but stay in his cell with patience and resistance, meditating on Scripture and praying. In other words, the countermeasure was to maintain their regimen. They also encouraged manual labor for the sake of one's soul and to serve others (Acts 20:33–35; 1 Thess. 4:11–12). To avoid sloth, they urged the monk to stay away from those who were idle, restless, or busybodies (see 2 Thess. 3:6, 14–15); instead, one should meditate on what is "praiseworthy" (Phil. 4:8–9). Cassian and Gregory recommended keeping an eschatological perspective—specifically, living as if one will die tomorrow with God's final assessment of his work, but treating the body as if he will live for many years to come. In the end, the countervailing virtue to cultivate is passion in serving the Lord and others.

See also Sins, Seven Deadly.

For Further Reading: J. Cassian, *The Institutes*, trans. B. Ramsey (2000); Gregory, *Morals on the Book of Job*, 3 vols., trans. J. Bliss (1850); K. Norris, *Acedia and Me* (2008); S. Schimmel, *The Seven Deadly Sins* (1992).

Dennis Okholm

Small Groups

Small groups are intentional, face-to-face gatherings of a limited number of believers who come together regularly in a spirit of mutual commitment and accountability for spiritual growth. Such groups are effective contexts for a relational dynamic not always attainable in larger settings. Such a dynamic is vital to Christian spirituality with its focus on intentional, committed participation in authentic community (Gal. 6:10; Eph. 4:15–16; Heb. 10:24–25). Jesus often taught and preached to large crowds, but he also gathered an intimate group of twelve and taught them by word and example.

Throughout history small groups have contributed to the cultivation of Christian spirituality. The desert fathers and mothers, subsequent monastic movements, and later contemplatives such as Teresa of Avila used small groups to enhance spiritual growth. Evangelical Pietism arose in the context of small group meetings (*collegia pietatis*) held by Lutheran pastor Philip Jacob Spener for the study of the Bible, discussion of the Sunday sermon, and prayer. Calling these meetings "little churches within the church," Spener believed they promoted personal piety by allowing believers to discuss freely Scripture's meaning as well as its significance for their lives. Spener influenced other early Pietists, including Count von Zinzendorf, who in turn became an influential leader and sponsor of the Moravian movement. The Moravians contributed to spiritual revitalization through Europe, utilizing, among other things, small groups in which people studied Scripture, prayed, and held one another accountable for godly living. Zinzendorf and the Moravians also had a profound influence on John Wesley, who, after an extended visit with Zinzendorf in 1738, adopted the Moravian concept of small "bands" as a Methodist means of accountability for discipleship.

To succeed in promoting spiritual growth, a small group must be formed around a shared set of values as well as a well-defined and mutually accepted purpose. Individual members must be committed to mutual responsibility and accountability. This will involve willingness, when necessary, to honestly and biblically confront, encourage, reprove, and rebuke one another, with the goal of building up one another spiritually. There must also be freedom to disagree as well as express doubts. Such a dynamic is only possible as trust is earned and developed, and this requires that members understand and appreciate one another's life stories and experiences. Groups whose members also share a prior history and, hence, a common story can more easily attain this level of trust.

Even in the early days of Pietism, small groups were never intended to replace the regular meetings of the larger assembly or to supplant the believer's private, personal devotional life, nor should they

today. Rather, as Spener taught, they complement these activities by providing "a more extensive use of the Word of God among us," by introducing people to it "in still other ways than through the customary sermons on the appointed lessons."

For Further Reading: P. Deison, "Spiritual Formation through Small Groups," in *The Christian Educator's Handbook on Spiritual Formation* (1994); J. Gorman, *Community That Is Christian* (1993); G. Icenogle, *Biblical Foundations for Small Group Ministry* (1994); P. Spener, *Pia Desideria*, trans. T. Tappert (1964).

John R. Lillis

Smith, Hannah Whitall (1832 – 1911)

Author, preacher, women's suffragist, major voice in the Holiness movement, and cofounder of the Women's Christian Temperance Union (WCTU). In 1851 Hannah Tatum Whitall married Robert Pearsall Smith. Both were from a long line of Quakers. Though affirmed by the Quakers in her womanhood, she agonized over the legalism of her upbringing. It wasn't until the Noon-Day Prayer Meeting revival of 1858 that Hannah found spiritual satisfaction. Thereafter, she and Robert left the Quaker community, even at the cost of being shunned by their Christian families. Together they learned careful Bible study from the Plymouth Brethren and the doctrine of sanctification from the Methodists. Hannah was particularly influenced by the writings of Phoebe Palmer along with William Boardman's book *The Higher Christian Life*. Once the Smiths moved from Pennsylvania to New Jersey, they became prominent preachers in the Holiness movement. In England they were the top two speakers in the Higher Life movement. Hannah was also active in the women's suffrage movement in America. In 1874 she cofounded the Women's Christian Temperance Union (WCTU). In the course of her advocacy for women, she became lifelong friends with Francis Willard. Providentially, the same year that Robert's sexual misconduct was exposed, Hannah's bestselling book *The Christian's Secret of a Happy Life*, was released (1875), with two million copies being sold worldwide. Her book impacted luminaries as varied as E. Stanley Jones and Harvard philosopher William James. In 1888 Hannah and Robert moved to London where they were frequented by other intellectuals, including the famous atheists George Bernard Shaw and Bertrand Russell (who married their daughter Alys Pearsall). Of the Smiths' seven children, only three survived into adulthood. None chose to follow the Lord. In 1893 Hannah published *The Common Sense Teaching of the Bible*, and in 1903, her autobiography, which explains how she became a universalist.

See also Quaker Spirituality.

For Further Reading: M. Dieter, *God Is Enough* (2003); H. W. Smith, *The Unselfishness of God and How I Discovered It* (1903); B. Strachey, *Remarkable Relations: The Story of the Pearsall Smith Family* (1981).

Sarah Sumner

Sobrino, Jon (1938–)

Liberation theologian and Jesuit priest. Born in Barcelona, Spain, and of Basque origin, Sobrino joined the Jesuits when he was eighteen, moved to El Salvador in 1957, and since then has been identified with that Central American country. He studied engineering at St. Louis University in the United States and then theology in Frankfurt, Germany. Upon his return to El Salvador, he joined the faculty of the Roman Catholic University of Central America (UCA) as well as a group of Jesuits who in succeeding years became actively involved in asking for justice in relation to the "dirty war" waged by the Salvadorian government—a war that resulted in the murder of about seventy-five thousand "subversives," including famous archbishop Oscar Romero in 1980. In 1989 six of these Jesuits, together with their housekeeper and her daughter, were murdered; Sobrino was spared because on that day he was absent from the country.

The main focus of Sobrino's theology has been on Christology, but not as an end in itself. Rather, it is a way to discern what it means to follow Jesus Christ in a context of poverty and injustice. From his perspective, the essence of Christian spirituality is a discipleship that takes as its starting point the historical Jesus of Nazareth, whose life, actions, teachings, and attitudes spell out his understanding of the kingdom of God in terms of love and service to the poor, so as to create a world of justice and righteousness. To know him is to become practically involved in the same struggle for the liberation of the poor that he was involved in for the sake of the kingdom.

On November 26, 2006, the Vatican's Congregation for the Doctrine of the Faith issued a *Notification* saying that although Sobrino's "preoccupation ... for the plight of the poor is admirable," some of his doctrinal tenets are nevertheless "erroneous or dangerous and may cause harm to the faithful." As a result, he has been forbidden to teach or lecture as an official representative of the Roman Catholic Church and the *nihil obstat* has been removed from his writings. His many writings include *Christology at the Crossroads* (1978), *Jesus the Liberator* (1993), *The Principle of Mercy* (1994), and *Christ the Liberator* (2001).

See also Liberation Spirituality.

For Further Reading: S. Pope, ed., *Hope and Solidarity: Jon Sobrino's Challenge to Christian Theology* (2008).

C. René Padilla

Social Justice

Social justice is a condition when communities are characterized by harmonious and respectful relationships between members and when societies are ordered so there is adequate access to goods and services necessary for survival and human flourishing. Social justice is often codified in laws that protect human rights, safeguard human dignity, ensure the fair and equal treatment of persons, and distribute the goods of a society in an equitable manner. While social justice is an ideal, it is also a commitment that societies must continually guard in the continual examination, revision, and enactment of policies and practices that reflect the obligations that communities have to their members and members to their communities.

Social justice is an important part of Christian tradition. In Scripture there are important connections between justice, righteousness, and peace. In Hebrew, *mishpât* ("justice") and *tsâdaq* ("righteousness"), and in Greek, *dikaiosunē* ("righteousness" or "justification"), describe the process and status by which persons and circumstances are declared righteous and restored to goodness and virtuous conditions. These related terms connote the manner by which that which was broken is made whole and restored to an original position of harmony, peace, and right relationships. This kind of justice involving restoration and making things right found in Scripture is essentially relational because it is rooted in the purposes, character, and work of God. God does justice for humanity by restoring what was lost and broken due to sin. We do justice on God's behalf by working for the restoration of all creation guided by God's vision of shalom.

Social justice in Christian thought and practice is informed by God's desired shalom for the world. Shalom is the Hebrew concept for harmony, wholeness, completeness, and righteousness. It is a relational concept whereby persons are living in right relationships with others, with God, and with creation. Social justice in Christian faith starts with reflection on the creation narratives in the first two chapters of Genesis, where we ascertain God's purposes for creation. Humans were created to serve God in joyful obedience and were given responsibility to care for creation. Humans were created in

God's image, which grounds their own dignity and responsibilities to honor and protect the dignity of others. Human relationships were to be characterized by mutuality, equality, and sharing in serving the purposes of God. The creation narratives reflect the original conditions of social justice. The earth was habitable and safe, and its produce was abundant in sustaining human life. The work that God gave humans was designed to further God's purposes in caring for creation, meeting human needs, and honoring all that God created. Humans were in relationships that were life giving and fruitful. Humans were invited to be active participants with God in maintaining the quality of right relationships characteristic of justice.

This initial vision of shalom is reflected throughout the Scriptures where we see the intricate relationships between religious belief and moral obligations involving social justice. The OT law was given as a gift to the people of God to guide their religious practices and to give shape to their social life, which was to be characterized by right relationships and just actions. The law instructs persons to honor their neighbors in concrete ways: by telling the truth, by fulfilling promises, by sharing resources, by protecting the weak and vulnerable, and by caring for the land (Ex. 20:1–17; Lev. 25; Deut. 10:12–22). The vulnerable, marginalized, and powerless received particular attention because their lives were most at risk in the absence of justice. The prophets protested the injustices perpetrated by God's people, as well as surrounding nations. The prophets spoke against the oppression of the poor, the misuse of religion, violence, and the abuse of power. The prophets made justice a matter of worship and spirituality by reminding hearers of their covenant responsibilities to God and others, and the futility of sacrifices without justice and mercy (Mic. 6:6–8). Jesus' first public pronouncement in line with the prophetic concern for justice (Luke 4:14–30) highlighted that the gospel was good news for the poor, the prisoners, the outcasts, and the oppressed. The

Sermon on the Mount (Matt. 5–7) is steeped in Jesus' concern about the requirements of Christian discipleship to exceed and surpass a narrow form of piety and religion by embracing the righteousness and justice of the kingdom of God. The Bible ends with the grand eschatological vision of God's restoration of creation when all that has been wrong will be made right and "God will wipe away every tear from their eyes" (Rev. 7:17).

For Christians, social justice cannot be reduced to a political ideology or party politics. It cannot be limited to strict notions of distribution, retribution, equality, and impartiality. Social justice is a matter of spirituality that is a manifestation of one's relationship with God and commitment to other persons. The justice of God and the pursuit of justice by Christians go hand in hand. "Doing" justice is our response and witness to the grace, mercy, and compassion of God toward us in restoring what was broken. It is an indication that one has internalized and appropriated the implications of God's reconciling actions on behalf of humanity. A right relationship with God inspires and motivates service to others out of love, compassion, and generosity.

Justice is not an addendum to Christian faith and practice. It is central to spiritual formation in that it is a virtue learned through practice and spiritual disciplines. Through such disciplines as fasting, prayer, service, and giving, we learn what God requires of us. Spiritual disciplines foster practices that help us learn to focus on others. We acquire the virtues of Christian life as we practice generosity, mercy, compassion, and peacemaking, and by speaking out and working for social justice in our communities by attending to what humans need to survive and thrive. We pursue and do justice as persons who have been reconciled to God who are called to be God's ambassadors of reconciliation (2 Cor. 5:17–21), working to make all things new in God's creation by doing justice, loving mercy, and walking humbly with God (Mic. 6:8).

See also Beatitudes; Kingdom of God; Liberation Spirituality.

For Further Reading: W. Corbin Reuschling, *Reviving Evangelical Ethics* (2008); E. C. Gardner, *Justice and Christian Ethics* (1995); D. Gushee, ed., *Toward a Just and Caring Society* (1999); K. Lebacqz, *Justice in an Unjust World* (1987); D. Weaver-Zercher and W. Willimon, eds., *Vital Christianity* (2005); N. Wolterstorff, *Until Justice and Peace Embrace* (1983).

Wyndy Corbin Reuschling

Social Sciences

Social scientists focus on human nature in its social construction, contexts, and expression. Those interested in spirituality in broad terms attend to human existence and thriving, while Christian spirituality scholars focus their study on human spirituality as understood in relation to "the grace of the Lord Jesus Christ, and the love of God, and the fellowship of the Holy Spirit" (2 Cor. 13:14).

People are self-aware students of our own nature in a way that seems unique in the order of creation. We question, marvel, analyze, narrate, and theorize about ourselves. Moreover, as Scripture affirms, we assume dominion, take action, and individually and collectively shape the physical and social world into which new generations are born. While our predecessors molded the world chiefly with their hands, imaginations and minds form the ground of our reality. Efforts to study the fabric of our lives and our world, whether theologically or scientifically, are of perennial and boundless interest.

Science, the systematic accumulation and testing of knowledge through disciplined research by a community of experts, expands the scope of human comprehension and control, enabling us to imagine and effect what is invisible to our eyes, from neutrons and galaxies to what is perhaps most invisible: what C. W. Mills has described as the "interplay of man and society, of biography and history, of self and world." Social scientists offer people "a quality of mind that will help them to use information and to develop reason in order to achieve lucid summations of what is going on in the world and of what may be happening within themselves." Social science is hermeneutical, extending and weaving meaning, studying and informing social behavior, and enabling competent human comportment. It may be descriptive or analytic in intent, qualitative or quantitative in methodology, and as a secular pursuit, is scientifically neutral with regard to matters of religious belief. As a modern enterprise dating from the 18th century in the West, social science has concerned itself with large-scale social forms and movements, such as science and technology, industrialization, urbanization, religion, and globalization, as well as collective experiences and processes like alienation, anomie, and disenchantment. Its branches include anthropology, psychology, political science, economics, linguistics, and sociology, and branches continue to emerge, divide, and be engrafted into other disciplines.

The ancient enterprise of understanding social life was empirical but also practical and ethical. In his *Nicomachean Ethics*, Aristotle claimed that practical or social science is inherently concerned with morality: "Every art and every inquiry, and similarly every action and pursuit, is thought to be aimed at some good." Truth, morality, and interpretation entwined in Greek philosophy, as in the Judeo-Christian tradition. Modern social science aimed to disentangle truth from the latter two categories, a project now generally viewed as unsuccessful. The contemporary view of people is that we are self-defining, interpreting, evaluating thinkers and actors. Reason is understood as shaped by our humanity and therefore is an embodied, intersubjective, socially contextualized, practically embedded, and quotidian means of understanding human existence. Increasingly, the human sciences are seen as more than technical, epistemologically formal enterprises; they are viewed as fundamentally historical, practical, interpretive, value-responsive, and influential social enterprises situated in persons and communities.

In the late 1970s, certain philosophers and social scientists announced an "interpretive turn" in social inquiry (see, e.g., Hans-Georg Gadamer, Robert N. Bellah, Michel Foucault, Charles Taylor, and Clifford Geertz). Social science was brought into conversation with philosophy and philosophical methods, and dissociated from a strictly natural science model. The interpretive turn in modern social science occurred during the same years in which Christian spirituality (a subcategory of spirituality, and one that affirms the reference in the term to the Holy Spirit) was gaining more formal recognition within the academic community. In 1992, for example, the American Academy of Religion recognized Christian spirituality as a distinct sphere of inquiry and discipline.

Both contemporary social science and spirituality affirm the self-defining and developmental nature of human beings, the historical and prospective natures of the fields, the attention to everyday life (or "lived experience"), and the inextricable presence of the prescriptive within descriptive analyses. Spirituality, like social science, is a hermeneutical, self-implicating undertaking with moral heft.

The conjoined birth of contemporary interpretive social science and the legitimization—academic and popular—of spirituality (not only Christian) has changed our intellectual environment. The study of spirituality has flourished with scholars employing the term as distinct from religion and theology, and many in the field assuming no necessary transcendent referent. "Spirituality" as a broad term refers to the human search for meaning and well-being in everyday life, through insight and practice, both personal and corporate. Aristotle's principle of every inquiry aiming toward some "good" is now accepted in social science, and since 2000 we have seen the proliferation of positive psychology, interdisciplinary studies of resiliency, and research and university teaching on such subjects as gratitude, forgiveness, happiness, and the well-lived life.

There is a growing rapprochement between the domains of the intellectual and the spiritual in the academy and the seminary, both in academic content and in concern for the cultivation of health and character in students. With the gradual eradication of the intellectual barriers between spirituality and the social sciences, it is crucial that the rigor and substance of each be called upon to inform, challenge, and enhance the other. An intellectually emaciated spirituality that appropriates popular and piecemeal social science does not add scientific rigor to spirituality. Conversely, a social science that adopts a diffuse, solely affective, and privatized spirituality is bereft of the benefits a "mindful" study of human spirituality offers. Ideally, an increasingly correcting, illuminating relationship between spirituality and social science will advance understandings of human nature for the sake of persons, the academy, the church, and the culture. Christian spirituality will continue to benefit from this robust intellectual interchange.

See also Science.

For Further Reading: R. Bellah et al., *Habits of the Heart* (1985); P. Berger, *The Sacred Canopy* (1990); C. Mills, *The Sociological Imagination* (1959); P. Rabinow and W. Sullivan, *Interpretive Social Science* (1987); C. Taylor, *A Secular Age* (2007); R. Wuthnow, *After Heaven* (1998).

Susan S. Phillips

Solitude

Solitude is the discipline that calls us to pull away from life in the company of others for the purpose of giving our full and undivided attention to God. To enter into solitude is to take the spiritual life seriously. It is to take seriously our need to quiet the noise and constant stimulation of our lives, to cease the constant striving of human effort, to bring ourselves back from our absorption in human relationships *for a time* in order to give God full access to our souls. In solitude God begins to free us from our bondage to human expectations, for there we experience God as our ultimate reality—the one in whom we live and move and have our being (Acts 17:28). In solitude our thoughts and our mind, our will and our desires are reoriented Godward so we can become less and less attracted by external forces and can be more deeply responsive to God at work within us.

All the great ones of the Bible spent time in solitude and many of them for extended periods of time. All of them emerged from their times in solitude as changed people. Jacob wrestled with God's angel in the wilderness. Moses fled to the wilderness and remained out of the public view for forty years as preparation for leading the people of Israel out of Egypt. Elijah experienced the life-giving presence of God in solitude after he became so depleted in ministry that he was convinced he could not go on. Paul spent three days in the solitude of his blindness after God knocked him off his horse to get his attention. In solitude he experienced a radical conversion. And Jesus himself regularly left his life in the company of others to go to a solitary place and pray—sometimes all night! Whether it was on a mountain, in a garden, or on a beach, the practice of taking time to be alone with God seemed to be essential to Jesus' spiritual life.

Solitude is a "container" discipline. It is the time we set aside to be with God and God alone, but we have choices about how we will spend that time. For instance, silence deepens the experience of solitude, because in silence we withdraw not only from the demands of life in the company of others, but also from the "noise" of our own thoughts, words, and inner compulsions. Prayer with words emerges naturally in solitude as we allow ourselves more space for our souls to listen and respond to God. Reflection on Scripture, self-examination, journaling, spiritual reading, walking meditation, and worship are all spiritual practices that we can choose to incorporate into times of solitude. The key to engaging these practices effectively is to approach them as ways of making ourselves available to God, not as times of hard work and human striving. In solitude we choose whatever practices help us to give up control so that God can take the initiative with us.

Henri Nouwen, in *The Way of the Heart*, identifies solitude as "the furnace of transformation.... It is the place of the great struggle and the great encounter—the struggle against the compulsions of the false self, and the encounter with the loving God who offers himself as the substance of the new self." Indeed, in solitude we discover, first of all, how addicted we are to noise and activity and achievement as ways of shoring up our sense of identity and keeping us distracted from our own inner realities. What sounds so very easy—we are doing nothing, after all!—is actually quite challenging.

Solitude challenges us on every level of our being. It challenges us on the level of culture, because there is nothing in Western culture that supports us in entering into what feels like unproductive time for being (in God's presence) and listening (for God's voice). Solitude challenges our human relationships, because it calls us away from those relationships for a time so that we can be fully present to God. Solitude challenges the psyche, because without so much distraction, we become more aware of the inner dynamics we have been able to avoid by keeping ourselves so noisy and busy. Solitude draws us into spiritual battle, because in the stillness of solitude there is the potential for us to encounter God with such certainty that the competing powers of evil and sin and the ego self can no longer hold us in their grip. All the forces of evil band together to prevent us from knowing God in this way, because such knowing will bring an end to the dominion of those powers in our lives.

The practice of solitude opens us to the experience of being loved by God beyond all of our activity, our performance-oriented drivenness, and all that we think we can do for God. This experience of God's love is deeply transformative, for as we find ourselves loved unconditionally in God's presence, we are able to love others in return.

See also Monasticism; Silence.

For Further Reading: R. H. Barton, *Invitation to Solitude and Silence* (2004); A. Jones, *Soul Making* (1985); H. Nouwen, *Out of Solitude* (1974); idem, *The Way of the Heart* (1981).

Ruth Haley Barton

Song of Songs

The Song of Songs (sometimes Song of Solomon), a relatively brief book of OT wisdom literature, is devoted to the passionate love relationship between a king and his youthful bride. Ostensibly it is a celebration of love and intimacy, a canvas of desire and delight. It is written much like the script for a play, with dramatic speeches for both parties. Some interpreters discern not two, but actually three principal figures: the king (Solomon), the young woman, and her enigmatic shepherd lover (with the story turning out that instead of riches and position, she prefers the true love of the shepherd). Either way, the Song of Songs develops this romantic pairing (or triangle) in a tastefully sensuous style.

For a variety of reasons, some Jewish rabbis, and later Christian interpreters, have tended to downplay its literal sense and sexual explicitness, and instead opt for an allegorical interpretation of its contents. In this way, its amorous images have been regarded as descriptions of the love relationship between God and Israel (Jewish interpreters) or Christ and the church (Christian interpreters). Origen, one of the earliest Christian writers to address the volume, cautioned that it was fare only for the spiritually mature; those who still struggled with the temptations of the flesh would be too easily stimulated by its evocative imagery. Conscious of the NT image of the church as the bride of Christ, he proposed that the Song of Songs described God's love for his church collectively.

Later commentators speculated that the "spiritual" relationship in view was actually the one that exists between Christ and the individual believer. As such it expressed the yearning of the soul for union with God. Bernard of Clairvaux, perhaps the most famous medieval interpreter of the Song of Songs, saw significance in the book's canonical placement after Proverbs and Ecclesiastes. Those wisdom books properly addressed the Christian's proper attitude toward and conduct in the world; but after they were settled, it was time to move to higher things, namely, the matter of one's mystical union with God. Bridal mysticism, or spiritual marriage, became an important medieval paradigm for understanding the goal of the spiritual life.

This did not end with the Reformation. The spirituality of Zinzendorf, founder of the Moravians, was centered in a vision of marriage to Christ, the husband of each Christian soul. The potential of the Song of Songs to explicate the dynamics of the soul's relationship to God was also explored in depth by numerous Puritan writers, including Richard Sibbes, John Cotton, and James Durham. The pattern continued well into the 20th century, with ongoing contributions from such varied writers as Watchman Nee and Hannah Hurnard, whose bestselling *Hinds' Feet on High Places* (1955) and *Mountains of Spices* (1977) echo imagery from the Song. Such imagery of the spiritual life has generally been more meaningful to heterosexual Christian females than men.

In the past century or so, there has been a general shift in interpretation back to seeing the Song of Songs as a celebration of human love. Interpreting the Song literally, one may detect a didactic purpose of affirming human intimacy and sexual attraction as God's gifts to people. By such an account, the Song affirms human love, intimate relationship, sensuality, and sexuality. God thereby shows an interest in the whole person and not just the soul. The Song celebrates the enjoyment of physical touch, the elation of exotic scents, and other thrills of human intimate relationships. Spiri-

tuality is seen to be holistic; every aspect of being human, including relational intimacy, is God's gift and is good.

See also Allegorical Exegesis; Carmelite Spirituality.

For Further Reading: A. Astell, *The Song of Songs in the Middle Ages* (1990); *Bernard of Clairvaux: Selected Works*, CWS (1987); T. Longman III, *Song of Songs* (2001); E. A. Matter, *The Voice of My Beloved* (1990); R. Norris Jr., ed., *The Song of Songs: Interpreted by Early Christian and Medieval Commentators* (2003); G. Scheper, "Reformation Attitudes toward Allegory and the Song of Songs," *Modern Language Association of America Publications* 89 (1974): 551–62.

Joseph Shao and Glen G. Scorgie

Soul

Much has been written about the nature of the soul, yet scholars representing various disciplines stand divided in their comprehension of this mysterious phenomenon. As Phil Cousineau concluded, "Nobody really knows what the soul is, only that there are inscrutable depths that require tenacity of probing." After centuries of such probing, the soul remains a riddle insofar as a definitive theological and psychological grasp of it is concerned.

The Christian understanding of the self has evolved considerably beyond an early subscription to a dualistic Platonic notion (i.e., the material body and the immaterial soul are separate), and later widespread adoption of a Cartesian dualism, with its mechanistic stress on the distinction between the mind and the body). Today a (neo-Thomistic) concept of holistic (substance) dualism undergirds the widespread acceptance of the organic unity of personhood. The persistence through the centuries of dualistic conceptions of the soul is due in large part to the enduring influence of the ancient Greek philosophers who reckoned the mortal body as the prison house of the immortal soul.

The Hebraic take on the soul is, and has always been, opposed to such a dichotomy. Hebrew tradition consistently held the belief that soul corresponds to our total being. As humans, we don't possess a soul as much as we are a soul. According to Karl Barth, we are both embodied souls and ensouled bodies. More recently there has been a return to affirming the essential unity and indivisibility of human nature.

At the same time, within academic circles there continues to be debate over the real nature of the soul. On one side are *dualists* like J. P. Moreland and Scott Rae, who defend a more traditional Christian understanding of the soul. On the other side are the *monists* or "nonreductive physicalists" as they prefer to be called, who include Warren Brown and Nancey Murphy. Arguing against the commonly held notion of the immortality of the soul, they stress the functioning of the human brain, with its network of neural connections, as necessary to enable persons to consciously relate to God and others. Not that this position is entirely new; in the late 1950s Oscar Cullman published a polemic against the teachings of Socrates and Plato concerning the human soul.

Originally the word *psychology* designated the study of the human psyche or soul; over time its meaning shifted to the study of the mind, since it was regarded as more empirically defensible. During subsequent evolution of the discipline, according to David Fontana, "psychology first lost its soul and then its mind." Surprisingly, by the end of the 20th century, the concepts of "soul' and "psyche" had resurfaced once more in popular and academic contexts. For the most part, both concepts have been historically understood to underscore the insight that humans are personal, volitional, and emotional organisms possessing both conscious and unconscious cognition.

The Bible itself is not as crystal clear when it employs the term *soul*. Nonetheless, biblical scholars generally agree that *soul* has pointed reference to one's life and personality. Notwithstanding the attempts of some to offer a more concise scriptural definition, theologian Ray Anderson sensibly points out that the use of *soul* in Scripture appears to be more functional than "analytical or precise in a philosophical or semantic sense." In the familiar Genesis creation account, Adam became a living soul (or living being) after God breathed life into him. Little wonder Aquinas referred to the soul as the first principle of life, echoing Aristotle's classic definition of it as the "life-giving principle." Catholic theologian Ron Rolheiser adds that the soul represents not only the principle of energy that animates life, but also the principle of integration that holds our being together.

Biblically and theologically speaking, the reality of the soul represents the "self" as sustained in God. Since both are ontologically substantive in their formation and development, *soul* and *self* can thus be viewed, as Augustine did, almost synonymously. The soul's primary identity then is equated with the totality of the person created in the image of God.

See also Afterlife; Body; Dualism; Holistic Spirituality.

For Further Reading: R. Anderson, *The New Age of Soul* (2001); K. Barth, *Church Dogmatics* III/2 (1960); W. Brown et al., *Whatever Happened to the Soul?* (1998); J. Cooper, *Body, Soul, and Life Everlasting* (1989); P. Cousineau, *Soul* (1994); O. Cullman, *Immortality of the Soul or Resurrection of the Dead?* (1958); D. Fontana, *Psychology, Religion, and Spirituality* (2003); J. P. Moreland and S. Rae, *Body and Soul* (2000); P. Palmer, *A Hidden Wholeness* (2004); R. Rolheiser, *The Holy Longing* (1999); W. Rollins, *Soul and Psyche* (1999); R. Saucy, "Theology of Human Nature," in *Christian Perspectives on Being Human*, ed. J. P. Moreland and D. Ciocchi (1993), 17–52; R. Wise, *Quest for the Soul* (1996).

Wil Hernandez

Soul Care
See Care of Souls.

Spener, Philip Jacob (1635–1705)

Lutheran pastor and early leader of the Pietist movement. Born in Rappoltsweiler, Alsace, where his father was a jurist and adviser to the local aristocrat, Spener was raised in a deeply religious atmosphere, influenced by English Puritanism and the pietistic mysticism of Johann Arndt. In 1651 he entered the University of Strasbourg where he studied history and philosophy and later theology under the orthodox Lutheran J. K. Dannhauer. Completing his studies in 1659, he spent the customary academic wander years at four other universities. In 1663 he was appointed a "free pastor" (no fixed parish) in Strasbourg, received a doctorate the following year, and seemed headed toward a teaching career when, in 1666, he was called to Frankfurt to be a pastor and senior of the ministerial council.

Intense study of Luther's writings and his own parish experiences convinced Spener that Lutheran orthodoxy, with its dependence on political support from above and a carefully articulated doctrinal system to ward off heresy, could not bring genuine reform to the church. In 1670 he reemphasized the spiritual priesthood of all believers by holding small group meetings (*collegia pietatis*) in his home, where laypeople, both men and women, studied the Bible and instructed, encouraged, and admonished one another. He also proclaimed the hope of better times—Christ's return would occur once the church had been renewed and all scriptural promises to the church had been fulfilled. In 1675 he set forth his ideas in a foreword to a new edition of Arndt's *Postilla*, and the piece became so popular that he reissued it separately under the title *Pia Desideria* (*Pious Desires*). It had three parts—a review of the church's shortcomings in his day, an assertion that reform was possible, and six concrete proposals for achieving this goal. They were more extensive public and private use of the Scriptures, a larger degree of lay participation in the church, true faith to be expressed in deeds of love to one's neighbor, avoidance of theological disputation, a stress on spiritual life and the use of devotional literature in the training of ministers, and preaching oriented toward the inner life, thereby awakening faith and its fruits.

Holding private gatherings (conventicles) outside the official order of the church was unknown in Lutheranism, but the practice quickly spread. The orthodox feared (with some justification) that these private meetings would lead to schism and rejected Spener's broader devotional agenda, which they equated with radical pietism. Objections to his program rapidly mounted, even though little in it was original—Arndt, Boehme, and others before him had expressed reform ideas. Bitter controversy raged in spite of his efforts to restrain excesses within the movement.

In 1686 Spener became court chaplain to the Elector of Saxony, but troubles followed him to Dresden. His disciples were expelled from the University of Leipzig, his optimistic view of the future was attacked, and the Wittenberg University theological faculty charged him with 263 violations of the Augsburg Confession. In 1691 the Elector of Brandenburg invited him to Berlin to preach at St. Nicholas Church and join the consistory. Now in a more tolerant environment, he avoided the worst of religious polemics, endeavored to strengthen the position of Pietists elsewhere in Europe, and engaged in voluminous literary work. (His collected works [in German, 1979–1989] run to sixteen volumes.) The result was that his emphasis on the new birth, exemplary life, and religion of the heart undermined the position of scholastic orthodoxy and opened the way for revitalizing both German Lutheranism and Protestantism in Europe.

See also Pietism.

For Further Reading: E. Griffin and P. Erb, eds., *The Pietists: Selected Writings* (2006); C. Lindberg, ed., *The Pietist Theologians* (2005); P. Spener, *Pia Desideria*, trans. T. Tappert (1964); W. R. Ward, *The Protestant Evangelical Awakening* (1992).

Richard V. Pierard

Spirit, Human

Spirit (Heb. *nephesh*, Gr. *pneuma*) is something long understood to be characteristic of humans. It is that which makes humans spiritual beings. But whether people have spirits in the sense of a discreet component of their makeup is a matter of considerable ongoing discussion. Like "the will" or "the heart," "the spirit" may actually be the reification (or imaginative objectification) of certain capacities or characteristics of holistic human beings.

Moreover, the biblical authors did not always use the term *spirit* with precisely the same intent. Rather, *spirit* was employed, depending on the context, to convey a number of differently nuanced meanings. In Scripture, therefore, it is more a polyphonic metaphor than a tightly defined construct.

In both Hebrew (OT) and Greek (NT), the word for spirit serves double duty as signifier of breath and wind. The first belongs to living creatures, the second to the natural order. Both nuances are acknowledged and developed in biblical treatments of the topic. In Genesis the creation of the first human is depicted as God fashioning an inert body from the earth, and then breathing into it so that it became a living person (Gen. 2:7).

Two truths are hereby immediately established. The first is that spirit (as breath) is an animating life principle. As Job declared, "The Spirit of God has made me; the breath of the Almighty gives me life" (Job 33:4). Conversely, when God chooses to withdraw this breath, a person dies and returns to mere earthiness (Ps. 104:29). Echoes of spirit as *élan vital* can be detected in popular idioms such as "She is a spirited individual" or "We had a spirited conversation."

The second truth is that the life principle within humans comes directly from God. It is an animating energy directly from God's Spirit. This truth, already symbolized in Genesis 2 and acknowledged by Job, is sustained throughout the Scriptures. Ezekiel's valley of dry bones is resuscitated when the breath of God's Spirit comes on the four winds (Ezek. 37). Reflecting this same conceptual framework, the apostle Paul observed that while the first Adam became a living being (a recipient of life), the last Adam (Christ) was a life-giving spirit (1 Cor. 15:45). Regeneration (being born *again*) is the grand redux of God's original act of giving humanity life. Christ's promise of abundant life is really a promise of becoming more fully alive (John 10:10). For believers the Spirit of God becomes "the Spirit of life" (Rom. 8:2).

The connection between God's Spirit and the human spirit is thus unique and vital. It is more than mere coincidence that believers' inward assurance of belonging to God comes when God's Spirit bears witness with their spirits that it is so (Rom. 8:16). This locates the deep, critical place of meeting — the vortex, really — of the spiritual life. Where the capacity for such connection has deteriorated or atrophied, a person can be described (admittedly, somewhat hyperbolically) as "spiritually dead," in need of reanimation.

The idea of spirit as "wind," so explicitly connected to the Spirit of God at Pentecost (Acts 2), also illuminates the nature of human spirit (John 3:8). In both instances — human and divine — the imagery of wind underscores the fundamentally free, invisible, and mysterious nature of spirit. There is an autonomous dimension to humanity that transcends deterministic influences and a hidden aspect that defies empirical observation. In this deeper place, only the spirit of a person really knows what is going on (1 Cor. 2:11). But there is also an implication that what is buried there, beneath the surface level of performance and cosmetics, is most real and true. Jesus' observation that God is looking for those who will worship "in spirit and truth" (John 4:23) implies at the very least that such worship will be sincere and genuine.

Regarding the human spirit as a part of the self, to be differentiated from other "components," has often created a false restriction on the expansive scope and influence of "the spiritual life" on the whole of human experience. The language of human spirit, while presenting challenges, remains important. It is key to sustained awareness that there is more to human beings than meets the eye, and that our best hope of becoming fully alive depends on sustained and centered connection to the Spirit of God.

Glen G. Scorgie

Spiritual Direction
See **Direction, Spiritual.**

Spiritual Disciplines
See **Chapter 32.**

Spiritual Exercises
See **Ignatian.**

Spiritual Formation
See **Formation, Spiritual.**

Spiritual Geography
See **Geography, Spiritual.**

Spiritual Gifts
See **Gifts of the Spirit.**

Spiritual Journey
See **Journey, Spiritual.**

Spiritual Reading (*Lectio Divina*)

The term *spiritual* in "spiritual reading" has to do with the way we read the biblical text, not just the text that we are reading. Spiritual means that we read with our spirits participating in the spirit of the text. The word *spiritual* used this way insists that at their origin, words are alive — they come into being on the breath (spirit) of a person who is alive. It helps to know that the words in Hebrew (*ruach*), Greek (*pneuma*), and Latin (*spiritus*) translated "spirit" all mean "breath" or "air" or "wind." Words formed in lungs and throat, larynx and lips, have a life of their own. They come to life again when we receive them in the same spirit (the Holy Spirit) in which they were originally lived and then written. Another term for "spiritual" in this context is "resurrection" — resurrection reading.

We are not used to this. Most of us can read. But mostly we read to get information, to identify, define, explain. Or we read to learn how to build a house, balance a checkbook, cook a goose, or put a man on the moon. We bring to our reading of Scripture these expectations for getting information or learning how to do something.

Given our long training in reading to acquire information or master a technique that we can use on our own, a way of reading that places us under the text as obedient listeners instead of over the text is radical. In spiritual reading we do not take control of the text, we let the text take control of us.

A wise pastor-scholar, Austin Farrer, wrote of "the formidable discipline of spiritual reading" — formidable because it requires a total reorientation in the way we ordinarily read. We learn to receive the words of Scripture in their own voice, God's voice, to bring truth and holiness and salvation to life in us. This is in contrast to using the words of Scripture impersonally to defend God or explain God or get God to do what we want him to do.

In the twelfth century, an Italian monk, Guigo the Second, formulated the elements that for a thousand years had guarded the church against depersonalizng the biblical text into an affair of questions and answers, definitions and dogmas. He named it *lectio divina* (spiritual reading). His formulation continues to guide Christians in the practice of spiritual reading. He named four elements: reading (*lectio*), meditation (*meditatio*), prayer (*oratio*), and contemplation (*contemplatio*).

Reading is first reading what is there but only what is there. Because we know how to read—and it seems so effortless—it is common (and easy) to read into the text ideas of our own, meanings we have picked up in school or church or on the street. Exegesis is the common term that refers to careful and disciplined reading. Once we learn to love this text and bring a disciplined intelligence to it, we won't be far behind the very best Greek and Hebrew scholars. Exegesis is not pedantry; it is an act of love. Exegesis is about loving God enough to slow down and get the words right. Exegesis is a sustained act of humility.

Meditation is the discipline we give to keeping the memory active in the act of reading. Meditation moves from looking at the words of the text to entering the world of the text. As we take this text into ourselves, we find that the text takes us into itself. This world of biblical revelation is large; it is also coherent—everything is connected as in a living organism. Meditation is the aspect of spiritual reading that trains us to read Scripture as a connected, coherent whole, not a collection of inspired bits and pieces. No text, no sentence of Scripture, can be understood out of its entire context. The entire context is Jesus. Every biblical text must be read in the living presence of Jesus. We meditate to become empathetic with the text. We move from being critical outsiders to becoming appreciative insiders. The text is no longer something to be looked at with cool and detached expertise but as something to be entered into with the expectant curiosity of a child.

Prayer is language used in relation to God. The foundational presupposition of all prayer is that God reveals himself personally by means of language. Prayer is shaped by Jesus, in whose name we pray. It is a wonder that God speaks to us; it is hardly less a wonder that God listens to us. The biblical revelation is equally insistent on both counts: the efficacy of God's language to us, the efficacy of our language to God. Our listening to God is an on-again, off-again affair (that is, inconsistent and wavering); God always listens to us. The essential reality of prayer is that its source and character are entirely in God. We are most ourselves when we pray. The Scriptures read and prayed are our normative access to God as he reveals himself to us. The Scriptures are our listening post for learning the language of the soul.

Contemplation is the completing element in spiritual reading. It means living the read/meditated/prayed Scriptures in the everyday, ordinary world. It means getting the text into our muscles and bones, our oxygen-breathing lungs and blood-pumping heart. Contemplation means submitting to the biblical revelation, receiving it within ourselves, and then living it unpretentiously, without fanfare. It doesn't mean "quiet, withdrawn, secluded, serene." It has nothing to do with whether we spend our days doing the laundry or on our knees in a Benedictine choir. Contemplation means living what we read, using it up in living, not wasting or hoarding any of it. The assumption underlying contemplation is that Word and Life is at root the same thing. Life originates in Word. Word makes Life. There is no word of Scripture that God does not intend to be lived by us. All Scripture is capable of being incarnated because its words reveal the Word made flesh. Spiritual reading is not a methodical technique for reading the Bible. It is a cultivated habit of living the text in Jesus' name. This is the way that the Holy Scriptures become formative in the Christian church and become salt and leaven in the world.

See also Bible, Reading the; Memorization, Bible.

For Further Reading: A. Farrer, *The Glass of Vision* (1948); I. Illich, *In The Vineyard of the Text* (1996); C. S. Lewis, *An Experiment in Criticism* (1992); W. Ong, *The Presence of the Word* (1967); E. Peterson, *Eat This Book* (2006).

Eugene H. Peterson

Spirituals

The spiritual, as a musical genre, was a product of the African-American slave culture. The Second

Great Awakening brought the spontaneous "spiritual song" into the church revival and worship context, and by 1867 the term *spiritual* ("sperichil") had been attached to the slave song.

These spirituals carried many meanings with them. At times, they were songs of mutual encouragement. At other times, they provided rhythmic support for physical labor. Additionally, at times they contained mixed and coded messages. For instance, the term *train* often referred to the Underground Railroad or represented a means of getting to heaven. "Freedom" could represent freedom from slavery or the hope of heavenly freedom. Spirituals were sung socially in slave meeting halls as often as they were sung during times of worship.

The lyrical content of spirituals often retold biblical accounts of people seeking freedom from bondage. Inspiration came from stories that revealed God's provision, protection, and faithfulness in caring for his people. Jesus became Friend and Brother through his own suffering. Songs like "Daniel in the Lion's Den," "Joshua Fit the Battle of Jericho," "Go Down, Moses," "Paul and Silas Bound in Jail," and "Were You There?" are examples of spirituals reflecting biblical accounts. Hope that God was looking after the downtrodden was the common thread woven throughout the songs.

Musically, spirituals were initially sung a capella. The oral quality of the music lent itself to the familiar call-and-response style of singing, with a soloist initiating the song. Accompaniment was hand clapping, foot stomping, spoken words, tambourines, drums, and other percussion instruments made from available resources. As spirituals developed, more instruments were added, depending on the context.

As early as the 1870s, structured choral arrangements of spirituals were heard through the touring concerts of the Fisk Jubilee Singers. This group is credited with familiarizing a broader audience with the genre. William Dawson and Jester Hairston were popular composers whose spiritual arrangements became standard repertoire for both black and white churches, as well as for school, community, and professional choirs throughout the 20th century.

Black gospel style emerged at the end of the 19th century, along with ragtime, jazz, and blues. Composers like Thomas A. Dorsey utilized their jazz backgrounds to write spirituals that had congregational application. Dorsey's "Precious Lord, Take My Hand" became well known, was translated into fifty languages, and has been used by all denominations. In the mid-20th century, spirituals of social justice, such as "We Shall Overcome," provided powerful messages of solidarity in protest marches and church worship.

White spirituals are songs that developed in obscure, rural areas. The lining out, responsive, and antiphonal styles of singing were common in small churches and camp meetings. Singing schools, with their own systems of music reading (*fasola*, shaped notes), were also created, which helped further the songs from community to community. John Wyeth's *Repository of Sacred Music*, William Walker's *Southern Harmony*, and White and King's *Sacred Harp* all contain examples of white spirituals.

See also African-American Christian Spirituality; Hymns; Praise Music.

For Further Reading: W. Allen et al., *Slave Songs of the United States* (1951); A. Thomas, *Way Over in Beulah Lan': Understanding and Performing the Negro Spiritual* (2009).

Edwin M. Willmington

Spiritual Theology
See **Chapter 5.**

Sports and Spirituality

Sports are athletic activities requiring skill or physical ability, and usually of a competitive nature. Among other things, they provide biblical metaphors for the spiritual life. The apostle Paul used various sports images to help explain the truth of the Christian faith and how to live it out. These include the importance of hard training (1 Cor. 9:25; 1 Tim. 4:7–8), focus (1 Cor. 9:26), self-control (1 Cor. 9:27), perseverance (Heb. 12:2), and endurance (1 Tim. 4:8). Paul also uses sports to remind his audience of our goal in life, to win the imperishable crown (1 Tim. 4:8; 1 Cor. 9:25).

Historically, however, the Christian response to sports was guarded and restrained, if not negative, due to the coarseness of many sporting options and to a perception that life is a serious matter with little room for amusement and trivial pursuits. Sports especially collided with the Puritan (and general Protestant) idealization of a vigorous work ethic and respect for the Lord's Day.

All this was about to change. The Industrial Revolution triggered dramatic changes in male and female roles and forced reappraisal of male and female identities. Out of this nineteenth-century flux emerged "Muscular Christianity," with its celebrated ideal of a vigorous, strength-conscious masculinity. R. W. Conant, for example, in *The Manly Christ* (1904), expressed alarm about "the feminizing of Christianity." Many reacted against what they perceived to be, in Clifford Putney's phrase, "an overabundance of sentimental hymns, effeminate clergymen and sickly-sweet images of Jesus." In this context, an alliance, typified by the YMCA (1844), was forged between Christianity and sports, especially team sports, which has proved particularly enduring within evangelicalism. Athletic heroes of this movement include legendary English cricketer C. T. Studd, who joined the Cambridge Seven as a missionary to China, and American professional baseball player Billy Sunday, who became an evangelist.

Recreational sports were designed early on to help young people become healthy and physically fit and, in certain contexts, stay out of trouble. Great emphasis was also placed on the potential of participatory sports, especially team sports, to foster personal self-discipline, unselfishness, bravery, and various other Christian character traits. It was deemed crucial to personal formation and on this basis was incorporated into school curricula. All these insights are eminently compatible with a holistic understanding of Christian spirituality.

The 20th century saw increases in leisure time for many in the Western world and with that a proliferation of leisure sports and professionalized spectator sports. Capitalizing on societal enthusiasm for sports and the adulation of sports celebrities, evangelical Christians (especially organizations like Athletes in Action and Fellowship of Christian Athletes) have created sports-related forums for evangelism and missions. For example, every year thousands of Christian sports camps operate around the world, offering blended experiences of skill improvement, team camaraderie, and gospel witness.

Beyond these uses, and especially in the televised world, sports provide a forum for seeing the beauty of the human form and the gifting of God in physical talent. Across the globe, human beings of both genders and all colors have been gifted with various talents—talents that naturally call out to be displayed in the field of sports. Famous Olympic gold medalist from Scotland Eric Liddell said, "God made me fast. And when I run, I feel his pleasure." The physical gifts of God, especially when nourished by hard work and discipline, can bring glory to God on the athletic field and provide testimony to the existence of a remarkable Creator.

Three developments in sports are potential threats to a robust Christian spirituality. First, when sports become ubiquitous, they tend to crowd contemplative time and quiet out of life. Second, the intensification of competition—"winning is the only thing"—can seep over into everyday life and instinctively stifle sympathy, gentleness, and generosity. When such a mind-set becomes dominant, as S. J. Hoffman has observed, "the concrete trumps the symbolic; doing, achieving, and struggling are favored over mystery, joy, feeling, transport, and spiritual insight." Finally, the increase in bodily injurious violence in contemporary sports can no longer be dismissed as irrelevant to the spirituality of Christian participants and spectators.

See also Exercise, Physical Fitness; Leisure and Play; Work.

For Further Reading: S. J. Hoffman, *Good Game* (2010); T. Kluck, *The Reason for Sports* (2009); T. Ladd and J. Mathisen, *Muscular Christianity: Evangelical Protestants and the Development of American Sport* (1999); C. Putney, *Muscular Christianity: Manhood and Sports in Protestant America, 1880–1920* (2001).

Christopher Morton

Spurgeon, Charles Haddon (1834–1892)

English Baptist preacher. Spurgeon was the son of a Congregationalist minister in rural Essex. He had a striking conversion in a Primitive Methodist chapel in 1850 but subsequently became a Baptist. After his first pastorate in Waterbeach (1851–1854), a village to the northeast of Cambridge, he was called to pastor the historic New Park Street Chapel on the south side of the Thames in London. His ministry in this congregation (1854–1892) was remarkably successful. Two hundred attended the church when he first went there, but during the course of his ministry, more than fourteen thousand were added to the church. To accommodate the massive crowds that came to hear him, a new church building was erected, the Metropolitan Tabernacle. Plain by Victorian standards, his preaching was deeply indebted to the thought and piety of the Puritans, whose works he had read since his childhood. He differed from these seventeenth-century mentors, though, in that he refused to preach a series through a biblical book, fearful lest he grieve the Holy Spirit.

In many respects, Spurgeon's spirituality reflected the emphases of nineteenth-century evangelicalism: Bible-centered, ardently evangelistic, cross-centered, and seeking to make doers of good works out of his hearers. Unlike his contemporaries, however, he held to a Calvinistic view of the presence of Christ at the Lord's Supper (a perspective derived from the Puritans), and he could also advocate seasons of solitude spent in silence, fasting, and prayer so as to "inflame [the] soul with ardour" for Christ and his kingdom. His sermons and writings also display a pneumatological refrain that was especially due to his Calvinism and the influence of his Puritan mentors, most of whom had an abiding interest in the work of the Holy Spirit.

Typical of Spurgeon's early spirituality is *The Saint and His Saviour* (1857), in which he delineated the Christian life as a Christ-centered endeavor. Controversies, such as the Down-grade controversy in the 1880s, brought other themes to the fore. One of his final addresses, *The Greatest Fight in the World* (1891), succinctly depicted the spiritual vision of his final years: no compromise on the matter of biblical infallibility, the ecclesial nature of the Christian life, and the absolute necessity of the Spirit's power.

See also Baptist Spirituality; Reformed (Calvinist) Spirituality; Preaching.

For Further Reading: E. Bacon, *Spurgeon* (1967); L. Drummond, *Spurgeon* (1992); M. Nicholls, *C. H. Spurgeon* (1992); H. Thielicke, *Encounter with Spurgeon*, trans. J. Doberstein (1963).

Michael A. G. Haykin

Stages of Spiritual Ascent
See **Ascent, Stages of Spiritual.**

Steere, Douglas (1901–1995)

Quaker writer, educator, ecumenicist, peace advocate, and spiritual guide. He was a Rhodes scholar at Oxford from 1925 to 1926 and received his doctorate from Harvard University in 1931. He taught philosophy at Haverford College from 1928 to

1964. Steere attended the Second Vatican Council as an ecumenical observer and corresponded regularly with Thomas Merton and other prominent religious leaders of his time. Following the tradition of eminent Quaker ministers in the past, such as John Woolman, his deep inward life of prayer and contemplation was balanced by an outward life of service and action. He interrupted his teaching after World War II to work with the American Friends Service Committee, organizing relief work in Finland, Norway, and Poland. As clerk of the Friends World Committee for Consultation, Steere organized interfaith dialogues between Buddhist and Christian leaders in Japan, and Hindu and Christian leaders in India. Steere's understanding of Christ as the universal Light provided the theological basis for his interfaith dialogue. Steere held to the historical Quaker vision of the depth and breadth of God's loving purpose revealed in Jesus Christ to all humanity. He emphasized the indwelling Christ but held together the personal and the universal, the historical and the mystical dimensions of Christ.

Steere's writings focused primarily on spiritual disciplines, prayer, worship, and mysticism. His spirituality reflected optimism, hope, and the deep valuing of the "Other." He was known for his gift of truly listening "to confirm what was deepest in other persons." Steere was the author of more than ten books, including *On Beginning from Within* (1943), *On Listening to Another* (1955), *Work and Contemplation* (1957), and *Quaker Spirituality: Selected Writings* (1983).

See also Love; Peacemaking; Quaker Spirituality.

For Further Reading: E. G. Hinson, *Love at the Heart of Things: A Biography of Douglas V. Steere* (1998).

Carole Dale Spencer

Story

Story can be defined as a sequence of fictitious or nonfictitious events framed by a beginning, middle, and end. Most of Scripture comes to us in the form of story. Context and form of Scripture work together in an organic unity to reveal God's redemptive purposes for his creation. The Bible, while containing many genres, such as narrative, poetry and song, law and practical instructions, wisdom sayings and prophetic books, apostolic letters and fantastic visions, is held together by a great nonmodern metanarrative that gives coherence and understanding to individual books and sections of Scripture. This overarching narrative reveals to us that God is never abstract, detached, and general in his dealings with humanity but is intensely involved, always addressing specific people with real names in specific times, places, cultures, and communities. The biblical story and story in general call us to keep God's revelation personal and relational, loving and compassionate, protecting it against abstractions, impersonal generalization, privatization, and self-reliance. Story provides a relational and historical context for the ethical dimension of our Christian lives, keeping us from an overly compartmentalized and consequently fragmented life.

With the reception of Hegel's dictum, however—which state that story is the work of primitive people while philosophy and abstract thinking are the higher and more efficient way to accurate knowledge—Christians silently bought into an understanding of epistemology that is unbiblical and unstoried. While we have sought to be faithful in living in accordance to the content of Scripture, we have paid less attention to the form in which God's revelation comes to us and how this might inform the way we live and teach our faith. While more recent epistemologists have abandoned Hegel's dictum, there continues to exist an underlying suspicion toward story and a reticence to employ story for theology. The recognition of the storied nature of Scripture, storied preaching, the use of story in teaching theology and pastoral care will ensure that form and content continue to work together to communicate the gospel in accordance with Scripture and will bring persons before God.

See also Literature and Spirituality.

For Further Reading: R. Coles, *The Call of Stories* (1989); S. Hauerwas and L. Jones, eds., *Why Narrative?* (1989); D. Taylor, *Tell Me a Story* (2001); J. R. R. Tolkien, "On Fairy Stories," in J. R. R. Tolkien, *Tree and Leaf* (2001).

Gisela H. Kreglinger

Study of Spirituality

See **Chapter 2.**

Suffering

Suffering may be seen as a multidimensional experience of brokenness, which includes physical pain, psychological anguish, social degradation, and spiritual desolation. While any one of these dimensions of suffering may be excruciating by itself, the composite picture of affliction describes suffering in all of its complexity. Suffering in all of its horror must be faced up to squarely, and the Bible does not diminish the depths of sorrow that can be experienced in this life. The biblical view of a creation that groans under the strain of tragic brokenness anchors the evangelical perspective on the reason for suffering's existence in the world. While not offering an explanation for the "why" of suffering, the actual experiences of suffering are rooted in the fall of creation (Rom. 8:18–25). Since the creation is broken, we will experience all of these dimensions of affliction in this world.

In the evangelical tradition, the experience of suffering is most clearly depicted in the passion narratives of Christ's suffering, death, and resurrection. Since Christ has experienced in himself all of the sorrows of life, including death on a cross (Phil. 2:8), he is able to understand and sympathize with persons who are experiencing suffering in their own life. Evangelical thought on this subject includes both a commitment to the concrete experiences of suffering in all of their dreadful agony and the resolve to embrace the biblical vision of

hope, which is rooted in the resurrection of Christ. At times evangelical theology has leaned toward a triumphal view of suffering that emphasizes the hopeful dimension at the cost of fully recognizing the dark experiences of affliction and their ongoing effects in the lives of those who suffer. Such triumphal approaches may lead to what Dorothee Soelle has called the "premature acceptance of suffering." However, recent thought on the theme has recovered the biblical understanding of lament as an appropriate response to the experiences of suffering in our lives. The ability to lament is at the heart of a hopeful disposition in that one is able to cry in the dark for the companionship of God in one's own dark night of spiritual desolation.

Suffering is immense and difficult. The Scriptures consistently describe the experience of human anguish and suffering without minimizing the depths of sorrow. This realistic portrayal of suffering aids those who are in affliction to recognize that their tragedy and pain are not beyond the scope of God's concern. God is compassionate to those who suffer and near to the brokenhearted. God sees the oppression of those who have been unjustly hurt by life and responds to them with intimate concern and love.

Those who suffer experience themselves as forsaken by God, abandoned, and alone in the face of the daunting situation that has come upon them. Like Job they experience hope as being eroded away and diminished like the soil being taken downstream in a rushing river (Job 14:18–19).

Here the deeper question of God's presence or absence in suffering is revealed as a root concern. An all-powerful God who loves creation must be able to eliminate all suffering. The fact that suffering continues in massive scale would logically lead to the conclusion that either God is not all-powerful or he does not love creation. However, recent efforts in evangelical theology have reconsidered this way of setting up the riddle of suffering and prefer, rather, to see suffering as a reality to be confronted in cooperation with the triune God. Suffering is not something that is simply to be endured; it is something to be anguished, lamented, and protested. Lament is the sufferer's honest pouring out to God about his or her incapacity to endure the onslaught of serious affliction. Suffering leaves one mute and unable to articulate the depths of sorrow. Lamentation is the Bible's permission to declare that something is not right.

Evangelical spirituality has always encouraged pastoral consolation for sufferers, rooted in God's own comforting love and compassion (2 Cor. 1:3–4). God is revealed in the Bible as the "compassionate and gracious God, slow to anger, abounding in love and faithfulness, maintaining love to thousands, and forgiving wickedness, rebellion and sin" (Ex. 34:6–7). As the covenant community of God, the church is to live out this life of compassion and love to those in need (Col. 3:12–14; 1 John 3:16–18). The compassion of God is repeated in the character of those who know God and love God. "Compassion" literally means "to suffer with" (*pati cum*). Therefore, the scriptural call goes beyond mere sympathy and empathy to actions of solidarity and mercy that display the very compassion of God to those in great distress.

At the root of sorrow is the experience of disintegration. When life disintegrates, meaning fades, and what was once held with deep conviction can seem to melt away. This can result in the experience of spiritual desolation or what may be referred to as "the dark night of the soul." To understand the pronounced sense of absence of God in suffering is to inquire into a mysteriously deep realm. While God moves toward those who suffer, it is often impossible for the person who is in affliction to sense the nearness and care of God. Therefore, evangelical piety has always counted on the Christian community to represent God's presence to those who are afflicted and to uphold such sufferers in prayer as they move through their own experience of Gethsemane.

Tragedy and suffering are part of life in this broken world. In a sense, the experience of suffering touches on the ineffable. Here, without minimizing the seriousness of the anguished situation, the Christian community can enter into solidarity with those who suffer and in so doing, take up the sufferings of Christ (Col. 1:24). The Scriptures invite us to trust in this hopeful consolation: "God's dwelling place is now among the people, and he will dwell with them. They will be his people, and God himself will be with them and be their God. 'He will wipe every tear from their eyes. There will be no more death' or mourning or crying or pain, for the old order of things is passed away" (Rev. 21:3–4 TNIV). In the meantime, the Holy Spirit "intercedes for us with groans that words cannot express" (Rom. 8:26), and the Christian community is invited to live out the compassion of God to all who suffer.

See also Cross, Experience of the; Imitation of Christ; Martyrdom; Passion of Christ.

For Further Reading: K. Billman and D. Migliore, *Rachel's Cry: Prayer of Lament and Rebirth of Hope* (1999); P. Kreeft, *Making Sense Out of Suffering* (1986); B. Manning, *Ruthless Trust* (2000); D. Soelle, *Suffering* (1975); J. Thiel, *God, Evil, and Innocent Suffering* (2002).

Phil C. Zylla

Sufism

Sufism is a term used to describe Islamic mysticism (which probes the mystery of divine and human beings so that humans might commune with God). Its name is derived from *suf* (coarse wool), worn by Christian ascetics—hence the Arabic name for Sufism, *tasawwuf* (lit., "wearing the wool"). It stresses inwardness over externals and spiritual development over action. In contrast to the dogmatic theologians and jurists, who emphasize reason and the transcendence and justice of God, Sufis emphasize intuition and God's immanence and love.

The foundation of Sufism is traced to the practice of Muhammad (570–632) with his emphasis on prayer, his meditation on Mount Hira, and the story of his night journey to Jerusalem and ascent to heaven; the latter became a model of mystical ascent for his followers. During the first two centuries of Islam, pietists and ascetics reacted to the luxury and worldliness of the Muslim rulers and followed the practice of Christian monks — though the Qur'an, in an ambiguous verse (57:27), either does not prescribe monasticism for anyone or seems to proscribe it for Muslims. Here we have proto-Sufi pietists like Hasan al-Basri (642–728), who spoke of mutual love between God and humans, and Rabi'a (713–801), who remained celibate to focus her love on God.

In the next two centuries, schools of mystical thought developed in which stages were described on the "path" to God. These involve "stations" reached by human striving and "states" that are gifts of God. These stages, which have some counterparts in Christian experience, are ones in which the progressing soul is characterized as (1) *regenerate*, (2) *accusatory*, but not submissive, (3) *aspiring*, (4) *at rest* (the carnal mind having been subdued), (5) *God satisfied*, (6) *God satisfying*, and finally, (7) *sanctified*. A crisis between mystics on the one hand and the theologians and jurists on the other was reached when al-Hallaj (858–922) expressed his union with God and consequently was executed. Subsequently, only proximity to God or the vision of God has been considered orthodox.

Al-Ghazali (1059–1111) strove to bring orthodoxy and Sufism together, while philosophers like Ibn al-'Arabi (1165–1240), influenced by Greek philosophy, went beyond the union of God and humans expressed by al-Hallaj to voice the identity of the two, and Jalal al-Din al-Rumi (1209–1273) gave poetic expression to this monism. Such a spectrum of views led Sufism to be both accepted and condemned by the orthodox even as Sufi practices ranged from those expressing true piety to mere techniques to facilitate ecstasy.

From the twelfth century until today, Sufi orders have developed around the teachings and practices of various *shaykhs*, such as Abu al-Qadir Jilani (d. 1166), al-Shadhili (1196–1258), and al-Tijani (1737–1815). These have had a missionary role of spreading Islam even to some Western intellectuals, a social role of fostering unity, and a religious role of providing a faith that touches the hearts of common people even though reformers decry its excesses, especially when it has degraded into a shrine culture that venerates and seeks blessing from saints living and dead. Around the teachings of various founders, hundreds of orders have developed, with the Tajiniyya, Qadiriyya, Shadhiliyya, and Naqshabandiyya prominent among them.

See also Muslim Spirituality.

For Further Reading: S. H. Nasr, ed., *Islamic Spirituality*, 2 vols. (1987–1991); A. Schimmel, *Mystical Dimensions of Islam* (1975); M. Smith, *Studies in Early Mysticism* (1995), J. S. Trimmingham, *The Sufi Orders in Islam* (1971).

J. Dudley Woodberry

Sulpician Spirituality

Approach to the formation of seminarians taken from the Society of Saint-Sulpice. The Society was founded in 1642 by Jean-Jacques Olier, a Roman Catholic priest who had been influenced by Vincent de Paul, Charles de Condren, and Pierre de Bérulle. He began a school of religion out of his parish at Saint-Sulpice in Paris, from which the society takes its name. Early in their history they were given a land grant of most of the island of Montreal in the colony of New France, and they continue to this day to operate the Grand Seminary in that city.

The Sulpicians are not a religious order, but a society of diocesan priests who are bound by a simple promise, maintain personal property, and are subject to the authority of local bishops. The primary ministry of the Sulpicians is the education of seminarians for the priesthood. For this reason, priests in the society seek to have a visible presence at seminaries, residing and mingling with students as living models of the priesthood.

Olier and his followers were part of what is often called the French School of spirituality, a Roman Catholic movement that began in seventeenth-century France. For this reason, Sulpician spirituality cannot be understood apart from either the larger French School or the specific ministry of educating seminarians. Like the rest of the French School, Sulpicians give special emphasis to God, Christ, the priesthood, and the Virgin Mary. Olier famously wrote that there are three goals in the Christian life: to look at Jesus, to unite oneself to Jesus, and to act in Jesus. Thus, Sulpician spirituality focuses on God and Christ, not on humans or the world. In prayer there is an element of *via negativa*, in which one stands in awe before God's glory. Olier also emphasized the need to be open to grace and to the moving of the Holy Spirit, rather than setting one's own goals for spiritual growth.

The Sulpicians believe that the heart and spirituality of a priest are as important for ministry as knowledge and skills. While Sulpician schools teach theology, philosophy, and liturgy, they also seek to train students through mental prayer, spiritual direction, and Christian virtue. It is held that an "apostolic spirit" and a devotion to the Word and the Eucharist will lead to evangelistic zeal and love of pastoral ministry. Sulpician spirituality was practically normative for seminarians until the Second Vatican Council, and some Sulpician views on the priesthood anticipate the council's documents.

See also French (School of) Spirituality; Ignatiaon Spirituality.

For Further Reading: C. Noonan, "Sulpicians," in *NCE*; J. Olier, *Catechism of an Interior Life* (2009).
Matthew Kemp

Sung, John (1901–1944)

Chinese evangelist. Son of a Methodist pastor, he initially declared his Christian faith at age nine.

Subsequently, he studied in the United States, eventually earning a doctorate in chemistry from Ohio State University. While halfway through his first year at Union Seminary in New York, he had a series of spiritual crises that profoundly reawakened and deepened his Christian commitment and transformed his life. Rebelling against theological liberalism and what he viewed as the idolatry of intellectualism, he sparred with professors, burned theology books, and danced around campus in joy of the Lord, causing the seminary to admit him to a psychiatric hospital. During six months there, he read the Bible forty times—and never read another book again. Upon his release, he was ordered back to China, commencing a remarkable fifteen-year ministry.

According to Sung, the secrets of revival are public confession, prayer for the fullness of the Spirit, and witness for Christ. Sung was an exhaustive worker who preached, prayed, wrote in his journal, and read eleven chapters of the Bible every day, doing very little else. He preached the power of Jesus' blood, the efficacy of the cross, and the necessities of repentance, the new birth, and being filled with the Holy Spirit. By the late 1930s, cancer, tuberculosis, and other ailments were forcing him to travel less, and when he did, his message was shifting toward edification and comfort. He wrote many hymns and letters to the church. His allegories written in 1941 and published ten years later urged evangelists to attain commanding knowledge of Scriptures and strong character marked by a crucified and risen life. Throughout China and surrounding regions, usually under revivalist conditions, Sung introduced many thousands to Christ.

See also Asian Christian Spirituality; Evangelism.

For Further Reading: L. Lyall, *John Sung* (1964); W. Schubert, *I Remember John Sung* (1976); J. Sung, *The Journal Once Lost*, trans. T. Soon (2008).

T. C. Porter

Surrender

Surrender is an act corresponding to the inner attitude of humility. Both act and attitude arise spontaneously from realizing what Kierkegaard called the "infinite qualitative distinction" between God and humanity, without which there is no true religion. If humility is the chief virtue of the Christian life, surrender is its chief mode of expression. For example, in the Rule of Benedict, obedience (an act of surrender to a higher authority), reverential fear, and humility are seen as central to spiritual cultivation. The same is true in Bernard of Clairvaux's *Twelve Steps of Humility and Pride.*

The concept of total surrender is especially prominent in various Quietist traditions, although its roots are wider. For Jean-Pierre de Caussade, total abandonment or "passive surrender" to God's will "prompted by pure love" sums up the entire Christian life. It implies relinquishment of self-will and obedient response to God's overwhelming love. In the Keswick tradition, perhaps reflecting its Reformed heritage, "absolute surrender" comes from seeing one's own nothingness and God's greatness: "I a worm, God the everlasting and omnipotent Jehovah" (Andrew Murray). The early Pentecostals often spoke of "letting go" and "letting God," that is, letting go of self and letting God take over.

The significance of surrender can be seen specifically in relation to the concept of the love of complacence. This love characterizes the Trinitarian relationship. The Father, Son, and Holy Spirit exist in a relationship of mutual delight. In this relationship, the Son surrenders to the will of the Father. Francis de Sales's *Treatise on the Love of God* (1616), book 5, treats this topic. Whereas God's love of beneficence and benevolence is given for the creatures' well-being or benefit, love of complacence sees the objects of love as inherently beautiful and delightful. The Song of Songs is often cited in support (1:2; 2:14; 5:1; et al.). Such a love is extended to creatures, especially those that bear the *imago Dei.* They in turn respond in "complacency making us sweetly rest in the sweetness of the good which delights us." They take delight in God's infinite perfections rather than in what benefits he gives.

Such love is not purely passive (which makes it different from Quietism). According to Francis de Sales, the sign of self-surrender is repose rather than inertia. The soul satisfied by God's love continues yet to desire God's love: "When our will meets God it reposes in him, taking in him a sovereign complacency, yet without staying the movement of her desire, for as she desires to love so she loves to desire, she has the desire of love and the love of desire. The repose of the heart consists not in immobility but in needing nothing, not in having no movement but in having no need to move."

Love of complacence is usually understood as a higher order of love. It is similar to Bernard's third degree of love: loving God for God's sake; or to Jonathan Edwards's true or "saving" religious affections: a love that comes from insight into God's "beauty of holiness." According to Richard Baxter, the Christian may begin life motivated by fear but progresses "to the more high and excellent operations of complacential love." The prominence many spiritual traditions give to the practice of total surrender must be seen in the light of their high estimation of complacential love.

Perhaps another reason why absolute surrender is so highly valued is that it is seen as something within the reach of the ordinary Christian. Keswick writers are quite unanimous on this: God does not demand some extraordinary feats from us but "comes to work this absolute surrender in you" (Andrew Murray). Similarly, in the Catholic tradition, Thérèse of Lisieux's "little way," which portrays a little child in the arms of a loving father, totally restful, totally comfortable, is one that many ordinary Christians aspiring to a deeper life could readily identify with.

In a world that values self-fulfillment and exalts the Nietzschean "superman" (*Übermensch*), the spirituality of surrender is often interpreted as a sign of weakness. But it is not about capitulation in the face of overwhelming force; it is about a spontaneous response to an infinite love that both fascinates and inspires awe (Rudolf Otto).

See also Consecration; Humility.

For Further Reading: D. Benner, *Surrender to Love* (2003); J. P. de Caussade, *Abandonment to Divine Providence*, trans. J. Beevers (1975); A. Murray, *Absolute Surrender and Other Addresses* (n.d.); *Story of a Soul: The Autobiography of Saint Thérèse of Lisieux*, trans. J. Clarke (1996).

Simon Chan

Suso, Henry (c. 1295–1366)

German mystic. Suso (also known as Heinrich Seuse) was born around Konstanz; at the early age of thirteen, he entered a local Dominican monastery, an order dedicated to a life of poverty, study, preaching, and spiritual direction. Recognized as an unusually gifted scholar, he received extensive philosophical and theological studies (Augustine, Bernard of Clairvaux, Meister Eckhart). He returned to his monastery in Konstanz and for the next twenty years taught and continued his academic studies, seeking to reform his order to its original calling. An important turning point came when he was forty: he turned from self-imposed rigid ascetic practices and the life of a recluse to a new abandonment to God. This inner change was accompanied by a turn to the outer world, where Suso began an active preaching and spiritual direction ministry.

A wide variety of Suso's writings have survived. His *Vita*, *Little Book of Eternal Wisdom*, *Little Book of Truth*, and *Book of Letters* are found in an illustrated collection called *The Exemplar*. Further writings include the *Horologium Sapientiae*, an edited and expanded Latin version of his *Book of Eternal Wisdom*. His poetic, tender, and compassionate writings had a lasting impact on a wide range of

subsequent Catholic and Protestant movements, including the *Devotio Moderna* and German Pietism.

At a time of political unrest, famine, danger of flood, pestilence, and widespread spiritual sloth, Suso saw himself as a "servant of eternal wisdom," encouraging a wholehearted return to God. The focus of his pastoral writings is the mystical experience of the believer with God. The ascent to perfect (and incomprehensible) union with God happens in the three classical stages of purification, illumination, and union. A cruciform lifestyle, celebration of the Eucharist, meditation on the sufferings of Christ, and a sweet and knightly veneration of Mary are the way to mystical experiences and eventual union with God.

See also Union with God.

For Further Reading: *Henry Suso: The Exemplar with Two German Sermons*, CWS (1989).

Gisela H. Kreglinger

Swedenborg, Emanuel (1688–1772)

Swedish scientist and visionary. Swedenborg was the son of a Lutheran minister. Educated at the University of Uppsala, Swedenborg spent his early adult years in the study of mining, and he became a major inspector in the Swedish mining industry. He left behind his scientific pursuits after a spiritual crisis in 1743–1744. He claimed contact with the spiritual realm, and a diary records his frequent visits to heaven. His views are provided in the twelve volumes of *Arcana Coelestia* (Heavenly Secret), *Heaven and Hell* (1758), *Treatise on the Four Doctrines* (1760–1761), and *Conjugal Love* (1768), among other volumes.

Swedenborg's influence goes far beyond the few churches that bear his name. His teachings had a considerable impact on stellar figures of his time, including Goethe, Emerson, and Blake. Likewise, his esoteric reading of the Bible provided a resource for those who wanted a nontraditional version of Christian faith coupled with a respect for science and reason. Swedenborg has retained his image as both a man of science and a man of spirit. His most famous followers are Helen Keller and John Chapman (1774–1845). We know the latter as Johnny Appleseed.

Swedenborg avoided focus on the death of Christ and concentrated on Christ's transforming power on earth. Moreover, Swedenborg claimed that the Last Judgment took place in 1757 and the Second Coming of Christ on June 19, 1770. These epochal events heralded the arrival of the New Jerusalem, a new era for humanity—one in which all people are now called to be creatures of good will, even if they do not know or follow Swedenborg.

See also Contemporary Alternative Spiritualities.

For Further Reading: E. Benz, *Emanuel Swedenborg*, trans. N. Goodrich-Clarke (1949); G. Dole and R. H. Kirven, *Scientist Explores Spirit* (1992); *Emanuel Swedenborg*, CWS (1984); I. Jonsson, *Emanuel Swedenborg*, trans. C. Djurklou (1971); J. Williams-Hogan, "The Place of Emanuel Swedenborg in Modern Western Esoteric Tradition," in *Western Esotericism and the Science of Religion*, ed. A. Faivre and W. J. Hanegraaff (1998), 201–52.

James A. Beverley

Symbol

A symbol represents something else. Symbols are used throughout Scripture—for example, in the prophetic actions of Jeremiah smashing a pot (Jer. 19:10–11) or Ezekiel eating a scroll (Ezek. 3:1–3). Jesus used symbolic actions when he entered Jerusalem on a donkey (Mark 11:1–11), washed his disciples' feet (John 13:3–15), and took bread and said, "This is my body" (Mark 14:22). However, the OT ban on the use of graven images (Ex. 20:4–6) ensured that most Jewish symbolism is verbal, with a fertile and often metaphorical use of

language in referring to God and spiritual realities. In the fourth gospel, Jesus used symbols, such as vine, shepherd, bread, way, and door in his "I am" sayings; and Christian prayer and hymnody have continued to use linguistic symbolism as a way of communicating and appropriating realities that cannot be adequately communicated in analytical discourse. Theologian David Power distinguishes between the language of analysis, or dogmatic theology, and a more evocative means of reflecting on spiritual realities, "a language which can incite [a soul] to respond intersubjectively to God's call and to dispose of itself to God." The language of devotion will often use symbols because they enable a connection with the evoked reality that is more than simply intellectual. Thus, Jesus said that his followers need to take up their own cross (Mark 8:34), and many evangelists have invited their hearers to receive Jesus "into their hearts."

Despite the OT ban on images, the Christian church gradually came to represent spiritual realities and characters, including Jesus, in visual form. By the 3rd century, biblical images began to appear on the walls of the catacombs in Rome; and after Constantine, Christian art, with its inevitable and intentional symbolism, began to flourish openly. In the East, the church was divided in the 8th and 9th centuries by the Iconoclastic Controversy, but the Second Council of Nicea in 787 commended the use of icons and distinguished between their worship (which it condemned) and their veneration (which it commended). John of Damascus defended the use of icons by basing the use of material symbols on God's presence in the incarnation: "I do not worship matter; I worship the God of matter, who became matter for my sake, and deigned to inhabit matter, who worked out my salvation through matter."

The Puritans condemned the use of symbols in worship, and during the English civil wars of the mid-17th century, many churches were stripped of their statues and other works of art. Evangelicals have tended to follow this distrust of visual imagery, and their worship has been stripped of any visual symbolism; when images have been used devotionally, they have tended to be illustrative rather than symbolic. When images began to be used in evangelical places of worship in the latter years of the 20th century, they were often accompanied by words, as though the viewer couldn't be trusted to interpret the symbol of the image without verbal guidance. Nonetheless, there is currently an increased engagement by some evangelicals with cultural symbolism expressed, for example, through fine art and film. In this trend, we see a growing confidence in our material creatureliness, in which creativity is recognized as an aspect of the *imago Dei*, and an ecumenical openness to learn from the spirituality of other Christian traditions in which the Word has become flesh in material as well as verbal symbols.

See also Allegorical Exegesis; Apophatic and Kataphatic Ways.

For Further Reading: W. A. Dyrness, *Visual Faith* (2001); R. M. Jensen, *Face to Face: Portraits of the Divine in Early Christianity* (2005); *John of Damascus, On Holy Images*, trans. M. Allies (1898); D. Power, "Two Expressions of Faith," *Concillium* (1973): 95–103.

Christopher J. Ellis

Symeon the New Theologian (c. 949–1022)

Byzantine monk, one of the most important representatives of the Eastern Christian spiritual tradition. Initiated into the ascetical and mystical life by Symeon the Pious at the Studios monastery in Constantinople, Symeon the New Theologian preached and wrote at a time when the church felt secure in its orthodoxy, having its doctrine systematized, its sacred ritual in process of codification, and its monasticism well organized and highly regarded in society. In all his writings — *Catechetical Discourses, Theological Discourses, Ethical*

Discourses, Chapters, Epistles, and the poetic and highly personal *Hymns of Divine Love* — Symeon conveyed the same message: "Do not say that it is impossible to receive the Spirit of God, do not say that it is possible to be made whole without Him … do not say that men cannot perceive the divine light, or that it is impossible in this age!"

Symeon's insistence on the possibility of experiencing the divine light, his veneration of his monastic elder as an embodiment of such experience, and his first-person accounts of such experience scandalized the theologians and the ecclesiastical hierarchy. Understood as spiritual practice, Christianity is, for Symeon, a gradual but real and perceptible transformation of the entire human being — even of the flesh, with all its members — in the blazing fire of the Holy Spirit. Christian life is, therefore, a matter of discipleship, which requires the ministry of spiritual elders — persons whose sole qualification is the concrete experience of the divine light, regardless of their ordination to the clergy.

Symeon saw church ritual as a depiction of heavenly and eschatological realities but also of the interior life. He therefore criticized those who were satisfied with only the splendors of earthly celebrations. Yet sacred ritual and the sacraments are also instrumental in accomplishing the ongoing transformation of persons into members of Christ's body. This very goal is set forth, already accomplished, in the Eucharist, which therefore extends the incarnation and its deifying power to all those who receive Communion.

Nevertheless, Symeon applied the same high standard for the experience of eucharistic Communion and for that of the Holy Spirit in ascetic life: the divine presence must be experienced in a conscious and contemplative manner. Symeon's paradoxical articulation of God's simultaneous utter transcendence and complete immanence continues the theology of Pseudo-Dionysius; at the same time, his emphasis on God's luminous manifestation echoed Pseudo-Macarius and anticipated the doctrine of divine energies underlying Eastern Orthodox theology and spirituality.

See also Light.

For Further Reading: H. Alfeyev, *St. Symeon the New Theologian and Orthodox Tradition* (2000); A. Golitzin, "The Body of Christ," in *The Theophaneia School*, ed. B. Lourié and Orlov (2009), 106–27; idem, "Hierarchy Versus Anarchy?" *Saint Vladimir's Theological Quarterly* 34 (1994): 131–79; J. A. McGuckin, "Symeon the New Theologian and Byzantine Monasticism," in *Mount Athos and Byzantine Monasticism*, ed. A. Bryer and Cunningham (1996), 17–35.

Bogdan G. Bucur

Syrian Spirituality

The spirituality of Syriac-speaking Christians centered in Adiabene and Edessa during the early centuries of Christian history. Its most important shapers were Ephrem the Syrian and Aphraates (early 4th century), the first of the Syrian church fathers. Ephrem wrote exegetical, theological, apologetic, and ascetical writings, and his poems exerted much influence on both Syriac and Greek hymnography. Aphraates composed a survey of Christian faith titled *Demonstrations*. In the 5th century, Syrian spirituality also came under the influence of Evagrius of Pontus.

Notable features of Syrian spirituality included individualism, pronounced asceticism, strong symbolism, and use of feminine imagery.

Individualism. Syrian monasticism preferred hermitic or anchorite models in contrast to Egyptian, Cappadocian, and Western preference for the cenobite model of Pachomius. Even when they established communities, the Syrians made room for individuality. In the mid-4th century, a group called Messalians or Euchites emphasized personal religious experience and prayer as superior to sacraments and institutional life.

Asceticism. Ascetic tendencies stand out even more strongly. Until the 5th century, Syriac-speaking Christians preferred the *Diatessaron* of Tatian (c. 160), who edited the Gospels with deliberate efforts to enhance their rigorism. Tatian rejected marriage, owning property, eating meat, and drinking wine. Syrian monks held extremely pessimistic views of society. They practiced bizarre exercises to show their disdain for the body. Although they may not have associated the body with sin after the 3rd century, they asserted firm control of the body lest it hinder the upward movement of the lighter mind.

Symbolism. Early on, Syrian Christianity displayed a predilection for poetry. Already in the 2nd century, they made use of a collection of beautiful hymns, perhaps used in connection with baptism, titled *The Odes of Solomon*. In the 4th century, Ephrem the Syrian stepped forward as the master of Syrian poetry and put his stamp on all later Syrian writers, whether poets or not. His poetry cultivated a double vision in which the reader or the hearer would see both the visible world and the hidden realities of God concealed within it as conveyed through Scriptures, Christ, the church, and the sacraments. At the fourth-century councils, Syrian theologians resisted the effort to adopt precise theological formulas that would express the mystery of Christ.

Feminine imagery. Syrian poetry used feminine imagery with reference to God. Mary always held a special place in their devotion. Until the 4th century, the Syrians regarded the Holy Spirit as feminine; perhaps they compensated for their subsequent decline in emphasis on the Spirit by elevating Mary further.

See also Asceticism; Apophatic and Kataphatic Ways; Ephrem the Syrian.

For Further Reading: R. Bondi, "The Spirituality of Syriac-Speaking Christians," in *Christian Spirituality: Origins to the Twelfth Century*, WSEH (1985), 152–61; S. Brock, "The Syriac Tradition," in *The Study of Spirituality*, ed. C. Jones et al. (1986), 199–215; R. Murray, *Symbols of Church and Kingdom* (2006).

E. Glenn Hinson

T

Taizé

A celibate religious community in Burgundy, France. Established in 1940 by a Swiss Reformed pastor, (Brother) Roger Schutz (1915–2005), who sheltered refugees fleeing the violence of World War II, the ecumenical monastic community consists of more than one hundred Protestant and Roman Catholic brothers. Taizé's distinctive features include forging Christian community, reconciliation between denominations and peoples, and witness—in particular, to young people from many countries. Both young and old gather at Taizé in large numbers to explore the Christian faith and experience the unique form of worship. Pope John XXIII described the Taizé community as "a springtime of the church."

Well-attended contemplative liturgies of the community follow a rhythm of Scripture reading, repetitive chantlike songs taken from biblical texts, intercessory prayers, and periods of silence. The meditative music of Taizé, composed in various languages, is revered by Christians around the world. Mission communities in the Taizé tradition work with the poor and oppressed in many countries. During an evening prayer service on August 16, 2005, Brother Roger was assassinated by a deranged assailant. Brother Alois, a German-born Roman Catholic, assumed the position of prior of Taizé.

See also Monasticism; Reconciliation.

For Further Reading: J. Balado, *The Story of Taizé* (1980); R. Schutz, *Rule of Taizé* (1967); K. Spink, *A Universal Heart: The Life and Vision of Brother Roger of Taizé* (1986).

Bruce A. Demarest

Tauler, Johannes (c. 1300–1361)

German mystic. Johannes Tauler was born in Strasbourg to a bourgeois family; at fifteen he entered a Dominican monastery, an order dedicated to a life of poverty, study, preaching, and spiritual direction. After extensive philosophical and theological studies (Augustine, Thomas Aquinas, mysticism), Tauler's main responsibilities became preaching and giving spiritual direction to Beguine communities (pious laywomen) and Dominican and Franciscan nuns. Tauler's sermons, strongly influenced by Meister Eckhart's mysticism, combine theological reflection and practical wisdom for the everyday Christian life. About eighty of Tauler's sermons, delivered in High Middle German, have survived, and the contribution of these sermons to the German language, especially the powerful yet tender vocabulary relating to the interior spiritual life, is considerable. These sermons had a lasting impact on both future Catholic and Protestant traditions, and perhaps most notably on Martin Luther.

For Tauler the goal of the Christian life is mystical union with God. This union happens in the ground of the human soul (*grunt/abgrunt*) and cannot be grasped rationally. While this union is a gift of grace, it is the responsibility of each Christian to prepare the soul for the birth of God within. The context of a contemplative and ascetic life (*Abgeschiedenheit*) allows room for a turn to the inner life and increasing self-knowledge. The humble recognition and confession of sin, endurance of suffering, obedience, a growing prayer life, and the frequent reception of the Eucharist lead to a blossoming life in God, the inner detachment and freedom (*Gelassenheit*) from the outer and inner circumstances of life, and a loving service in the world. In a time and place torn by political unrest, revolts, hunger, money inflation, natural catastrophe, and the Black Death, Tauler's message was one of utter trust in God.

See also Union with God.

For Further Reading: *Johannes Tauler: Sermons*, CWS (1985).

Gisela H. Kreglinger

Taylor, J(ames) Hudson (1832 – 1905)

British evangelical missionary strategist. Born to a devout Methodist family, Taylor developed a missionary passion for China already in his childhood. In preparation for his future work, he pursued basic medical training, then sailed for China at the age of twenty-one under the Chinese Evangelization Society. Simple living, radical dependence on God's provision, and adoption of Chinese dress characterized the China Inland Mission, which he founded. Under his direction, more than eight hundred missionaries were recruited, from various denominational and national backgrounds, lay and clergy alike. Single females were accepted as equal partners in mission. After Taylor's death, the China Inland Mission became the largest Protestant mission agency in the world.

Taylor's influence grew primarily through his extensive speaking tours in Europe and North America. His determination to reach the multitudes of unreached millions in China stirred the consciences of Christians wherever he went.

Taylor joined other leaders in the Keswick Movement who advocated the spiritual pathway of "the exchanged life." Faced with numerous tragedies, loss of family members, and scandals that damaged the international reputation of his mission, Taylor sunk into a deep depression and self-hatred around 1868. Frustrated with ongoing temptations and sin in his life, he received a letter from a friend that highlighted the need to abide in the life of Christ who dwells within, rather than to strive in one's own strength against sin. This simple concept of dying to self and looking to Christ's life within became a powerful source of spiritual renewal that sustained him for the rest of his life.

His son, Howard, later popularized the concept in a widely circulated biographical account.

See also Evangelism; Keswick Movement.

For Further Reading: R. Steer, *J. Hudson Taylor: A Man in Christ* (1990); H. Taylor and G. Verwer, *Hudson Taylor's Spiritual Secret* (2009).

Allan Effa

Taylor, Jeremy (1613 – 1667)

Anglican clergyman, patristic scholar, and liturgist. Born and educated in Cambridge, Taylor was an avid defender of the *Book of Common Prayer* and the practice of organized formal prayer during a period of great religious upheaval in Cromwell's England. His stance led him to suffer imprisonment three times under Puritan rule. After the Restoration, in 1661 he became bishop of Down and Connor in Ireland. He also served as vice chancellor of the University of Dublin.

Taylor is best known for his sermons and devotional writings. Among his many books addressing theological and moral matters, the best known are *The Rule and Exercises of Holy Living* (1650) and *The Rule and Exercises of Holy Dying* (1651). These works, written in a rhythmic and vivid prose style, invite readers to consider the purpose of their lives in the face of inevitable death, offering practical advice on how to live well to acquire every virtue and to face one's end with hope and serenity. These writings had an enduring impact and were treasured by John and Charles Wesley a century later.

Taylor's family life was marred by tragedy. He buried not only his first wife, but all three of his sons. The day after his last surviving son's funeral, he caught fever from a sick person he visited, and after a ten-day illness, he died in Lisburn, Ireland, on August 13, which is the day the Anglican calendar commemorates his life.

See also Caroline Divines; Death and Dying.

For Further Reading: E. Gosse, *Jeremy Taylor* (1904); H. Hughes, *The Piety of Jeremy Taylor*

(1960); F. Huntley, *Jeremy Taylor and the Great Rebellion* (1970); *Jeremy Taylor: Selected Works*, CWS (1990); C. Stranks, *The Life and Writings of Jeremy Taylor* (1952).

Allan Effa

Taylor, Nathaniel (1786–1858)

American Congregational minister and chief architect of the New Haven theology. A revivalist and first professor of the newly formed Yale Divinity School (1822), he left a legacy that influenced such nineteenth-century figures as Charles Finney and D. L. Moody, and such twentieth-century figures as Billy Sunday (1862–1935) and Billy Graham.

Timothy Dwight, president of Yale and mentor to Taylor, influenced him to become pastor of New Haven's First Church (1811–22) and later professor at Yale Divinity School (1822–1857). From his position at Yale, Taylor developed a moderating theological position between strong Calvinism and Arminianism. Motivated by a desire to tone down the "harshness" of Calvinism and make it more compatible with revivalism, Taylor presented his modified views to a meeting of Congregational clergy in 1828 in a lecture entitled *Concio Ad Clerum*. His insistence that "sin was in the sinning" disconnected human depravity from Adam and made it a matter of individual choice. He affirmed that sin was inevitable but insisted that humans have "power to the contrary."

Believing that regeneration and conversion were possible through the exercise of the will, Taylor was energized in his fervor for evangelism by appealing to the human will to make decisions. This new approach attracted many involved in missions and church planning efforts on the frontier and helped ease tensions between those who employed the "new measures" and those who wished to preserve the Calvinist heritage. Charles Finney not only found Taylor's theology compatible with his evangelistic methodology, but also employed it "to support evangelical feminism, abolitionism, even Liberty Party politics." Taylor left a legacy that facilitated passionate evangelism, deep concern for individual spirituality, and living out the ethical implications of the Christian faith.

See also Reformed (Calvinist) Spirituality; Revival.

For Further Reading: S. Mead, *Nathaniel William Taylor, 1786–1858* (1942); D. Sweeney, *Nathaniel Taylor, New Haven Theology, and the Legacy of Jonathan Edwards* (2003).

Wayne S. Hansen

Tears

In Scripture, tears are associated with intense mourning, such as "Rachel weeping for her children" (Jer. 31:15; Matt. 2:18) and the psalmist's "tears have been my food" (Ps. 42:3). Since the desert fathers, and in later Christian spiritual tradition, penitents prayed for tears to accompany their devotion as a confirming physical evidence of true contrition. In John Climacus's seventh-century *Ladder of Divine Ascent*, tears are compared to one's baptism, inasmuch as both involve water and effect purification. The distinct power of tears is their ability, metaphorically speaking, to wash away *post*-baptismal sins. Week one of Ignatius Loyola's *Spiritual Exercises* involves meditation on one's sins and the desolations of hell. Compunction, heart-piercing regret for sins committed, produces tears of deep sorrow, firm repentance, and a desire for surrender to the will and way of God. During week three of the *Exercises*, participants are again guided to seek sorrow and tears, this time as means of apprehending more fully the sufferings of Christ.

Tears are pointers to a deeper inward reality. Human tears release one's grasp of power and control, and may signal a willingness to experience human emptying that mirrors the *kenosis* (emptying) of God in Christ (Phil. 2:1–11). Christian transformation, expressed in trusting dependence on God's mercy, requires this relinquishment, which will often be expressed with tears of surrender and acceptance.

The experience of redemption and the embrace of God's extravagant love and mercy will likewise be expressed in weeping tears of joy. Jesus said of the repentant woman who washed his feet with her tears that she had been forgiven much because she loved much (Luke 7:36–48). It is unclear whether hers were tears of remorse or gratitude—or both. Tears—as manifestations of overflowing emotion—may indeed accompany the joy that follows sorrow and grief (Pss. 30:5; 126:5–6; Eccl. 3:4; Luke 6:21). But such tearful moments are brief and transitional; at the inauguration of the new heaven and new earth, God will permanently wipe away every tear (Rev. 7:17; 21:4).

See also Grief; Joy; Lament; Penitence; Surrender.

For Further Reading: R. Foster, *Prayer* (1992); W. Frey, *Crying: The Mystery of Tears* (1985); M. Ross, *The Fountain and the Furnace* (1987); J. Skehan, *Place Me with Your Son* (1991).

Nancy R. Buschart

Technology and Spirituality

Technology denotes the tools and crafts created by humans and other species to help them adapt to their environment. It is derived from the Greek word *technologica*—*techne*, "art," and *logica*, "skill"—which refers to the artifacts and processes associated with creating and applying knowledge. Equating technology with spiritual language, qualities, and experience has a long tradition. Discussions on the philosophy and theology of technology often approach technology as a value-laden enterprise with social and moral implications, and thus employ spiritual language and concepts to debate the values of power, control, and efficiency seemingly promoted by technology. As Heidegger argued, attempts at human control over technology can be viewed as a spiritual act, inasmuch as

technology offers an avenue of "salvation" from the weaknesses of the human condition. Scholars such as Karl Marx, Walter Benjamin, and Lewis Mumford have alluded to the promises and perils of technology with religiouslike undertones, presenting technology as a powerful force with the potential to serve as a tool of either control by institutional structures or liberation in the hands of the people.

The human relationship to technology has often been framed as one of conflict and even a space of spiritual struggle. Jacques Ellul argued that human society has become dominated by *la technique* and the values of the scientific system of progress and efficiency. Thus, our technological society has created a value system that promotes a dependence on technology and forces society to conform to it. This conviction has promoted a general concern that technology use may encourage values antithetical to the Christian spiritual life. In an era of computers, the Internet, and other digital technologies, this concern has been heightened. Within discussions about the human relationship to technology, several common themes have emerged that have become tools for interpreting this complex relationship.

First, the innovative features of technology empower humanity in unique ways, offering humans a path to becoming divine, or at least to a form of redemption. Technology serves as a gateway to salvation from the brokenness of the world and human limitations. This outlook raises important questions about the nature of humanity, or what it means to be human in a technological world. Second, technology itself can be framed as a spiritual force. Here technology is presented as a magical and powerful medium, offering godlike qualities to create and communicate. Technology becomes a spiritual force guiding humanity, and so technology itself becomes a god to be worshiped. This outlook raises questions about the nature of technology and what role it plays in the created order. Third, engagement with technology is framed as offering humans a magical or spiritual experience. Here descriptions of technology are ingrained with religiouslike attributes so that technological use takes on an incarnational quality. It allows humanity to experience and understand the divine. This outlook raises questions about the extent to which humans should embrace or avoid them and the spiritual implications of technological engagement.

These questions and perceptions have evoked a variety of responses from different Christian communities. Ferre argues that historically, religious groups have conceived of and used technology, especially media technologies, in one of three ways. Some conceive of technology as a conduit, a neutral instrument that can be used for good or evil, dependent on the manner in which it is used. Since technology is thus simply a vehicle for delivering the message of a sender to a receiver, religious users are easily able to embrace it as a gift from God to do the work of the community. This discourse has been important for religious groups involved in producing religious media and especially evangelical groups promoting the use of technology for evangelistic purposes. Others see technology as a mode of knowing with its own set of biases and values. This implies that technology is all-powerful and thus promotes a cautious, if not negative, response from religious groups. Religious users are encouraged to be suspicious of technology lest engagement cultivates or encourages values through their interaction with media that run counter to their faith. This discourse has been common in the outspoken critiques of television or the Internet as seductive or even immoral technology. Finally, some perceive of media as a social institution. They understand that technology is neither a neutral nor a purely negative force, but a medium that is shaped both by systems of production and the desires and intents of its users. This encourages a reflective response toward media, encouraging religious groups to be both critical and purposeful in technology use. This is demonstrated by the work of the Pontifi-

cal Council on Social Communication and their numerous papers, which encourage Catholic media engagement while also critically reflecting on how media technology may impact their community. In summary, the relationship between technology and spirituality is complex and requires reflection on the nature of humanity as well as technology.

See also Internet; Postmodernity; Science.

For Further Reading: A. Borgmann, *Power Failure* (2003); J. Ellul, *The Technological Society* (1964); J. Ferre, "The Media of Popular Piety," in *Mediating Religion*, ed. J. Mitchell and S. Marriage (2003), 83 – 92; M. Heidegger, *The Question Concerning Technology and Other Essays*, trans. W. Lovitt (1977); L. Munford, *The Myth of the Machine*, 2 vols. (1967 – 1970).

Heidi Campbell

Teilhard de Chardin, Pierre (1881 – 1955)

Paleontologist, philosopher, and mystic. Born in Sarcenat, France, Teilhard developed early a love of "earth's blind matter." He was a brilliant student in the Jesuit school at Villefranche; his teachers included Henri Bremond (1865 – 1933). A historian of French Catholic spirituality, Teilhard decided in 1897 to become a Jesuit, entered the novitiate in 1899, and took his first vows in 1901. After studying chemistry and physics at a Jesuit college in Cairo, Egypt (1905 – 1908), he developed the first outlines of his theory reconciling Christian faith and evolution while studying theology at Hastings in England (1908 – 1912). During World War I, he served as a stretcher bearer, declining promotion to chaplain because he felt more useful among the troops. In 1918 he wrote that he wished to be "the apostle and, if I may ask so much, the evangelist of your Christ in the Universe." After pursuing a degree in natural sciences at the Sorbonne (1919 – 1922), Teilhard taught at Institut Catholique in Paris (1920 – 1923).

In 1923 his order dispatched him to Tientsin in China, marking a turning point in his theory of spiritual evolution. During a second trip there in 1926–1927, he wrote *The Divine Milieu*, his most important book on spirituality. Trying to help skeptical Europeans understand how Christianity still has meaning in an age ruled by science, he argued that all activities, not just religious ones, contribute to the completion of the universe in Christ, in whom "we live and move and have our being" (Acts 17:28). Evolution is evolution "in Christ" (*christogenesis*). What we must do is learn how to "see." For those who know how to see, nothing in this world is profane.

Following geological and paleontological work in Somaliland and Ethiopia (1928–1930), Teilhard returned to China, where he took part in the discovery of *Sinanthropus* (Peking man) and worked out the evolutionary model published as *The Phenomenon of Man* (1931–1938). Due to World War II, he was a virtual prisoner in Peking from 1939 to 1946. He patiently endured his order's refusal to let him publish any of his writings or to assume a professorship at the College de France. Suffering a heart attack in 1947, he spent most of his final years in the United States. His writings were published after his death, April 10, 1955, in New York City.

See also Ecological Spirituality.

For Further Reading: C. Cuénot, *Teilhard de Chardin* (1965); C. Mooney, *Teilhard de Chardin and the Mystery of Christ* (1966); R. Speaight, *The Life of Teilhard de Chardin* (1967).

E. Glenn Hinson

Temple, William (1881–1944)

Archbishop of Canterbury. William Temple is considered by some to be one of the greatest archbishops of Canterbury since the Reformation. He was a brilliant theologian and philosopher, author of *Nature, Man, and God* (1934), *Readings in St. John's Gospel* (1940), and *Christianity and Social Order* (1942), among many others. As a leader in the Anglican Communion, he was also active in the ecumenical movement leading to the founding of the World Council of Churches. Like many great scholars and church leaders, Temple wrote not only about doctrine but also about the Christian life. He wrote, "Religious faith does not consist in supposing that there is a God; it consists in personal trust in God rising to personal fellowship with God."

Temple grew up as the son of Frederick Temple, a clergyman who was also an archbishop of Canterbury (1896–1902). William attended Rugby School, where his father was headmaster, and Oxford University; he was an aristocrat. Yet throughout his life, people commented on his humanity, his democratic impulse, and his concern for social justice, especially for the unemployed.

Spiritually he always saw himself first as a Christian, and emphasized prayer, worship, and the Eucharist as central spiritual practices. He was a person who loved laughter and was a great listener and reconciler. He consistently demonstrated love of others, leaving his ego behind. He was strongly opposed to what he perceived as Pelagianism, emphasizing the role of grace in redemption and sanctification.

See also Anglican Spirituality.

For Further Reading: C. Lowry, *William Temple* (1982); W. Temple, *Daily Readings from William Temple* (1965).

Bradley P. Holt

Temptation

When God created humans, he made them in his image, with desires and wills of their own. Temptation can be triggered by many causes and beings—God himself being the notable exception, for he never tempts anyone (James 1:13). Indeed, temptation's defining feature is that it invites or encourages a person to act *in opposition to* God's will. But to be successful, such temptation must trigger an inward desire to acquiesce. When such desire is strong, the temptation becomes a powerful enticement and may feel almost irresistible. And so Jesus, with a discerning consciousness of his disciples' fallen human frailty, taught them to pray that they might be directed away from temptation and thereby delivered from the schemes of the evil one (Matt. 6:13).

When God instructed Adam and Eve not to eat from the tree of the knowledge of good and evil, the stage was set for the evil one to tempt them to sin. Traditionally it has been assumed that Satan had already succumbed to the desire to oppose God's will and had suffered the consequences. Oswald Chambers characterized the root of sin as an incurable suspicion that God is not good. From this perspective, the enemy exploited Adam and Eve's suspicion that a good God would not refuse to give them what they desired, especially when it appeared to be so good.

Temptations usually overwhelm when we experience needs or frailties and we do not have the confidence that God will sufficiently care for us. The temptation in such situations is to try to meet our own needs or to protect ourselves without trusting in God's wisdom and benevolence. There is no shame in being tempted; even Jesus was tempted (Heb. 4:15). Scripture is clear that every human is tempted to sin, though the particular triggers of temptation and their intensity will vary among persons, groups, and societies.

Since temptation to sin arises chiefly from the heart's suspicion that God is not good, an important way to combat temptation is to cultivate an ever-deeper awareness of God's goodness. The children of Israel commemorated occasions when God had proved his goodness by setting up piles of stones as memorials to those events. The recollection of past experiences of God's faithfulness remains to this day key to resisting temptation and therefore an important spiritual discipline. Likewise, one of the powerful dynamics of Christian corporate worship is *anamnesis*—rehearsing and remembering together what God is like, what he has already done, and what he has promised faithfully still to do.

Adam and Eve failed to resist temptation; so too did the children of Israel collectively during their wilderness wanderings (Deut. 6:13, 16; 8:3). But Jesus Christ, the second Adam and the fulfillment of Israel, successfully resisted the tempter during his own sojourn in the wilderness (Luke 4:1 – 14). Immediately before his spiritual triumph, the Spirit descended on him, and immediately afterward the Spirit still filled him—surely clues to how temptation is to be resisted by believers as well. One key is a renewed mind that has internalized true thoughts about God; another is access to the indwelling power of God's Spirit to resist what otherwise would surely overwhelm us (Col. 1:11).

See also Sin.

For Further Reading: O. Chambers, *Biblical Psychology* (1994); M. Mangis, *Signature Sins* (2008).
Michael Mangis and Brian Post

Teresa of Avila (1515 – 1582)

Catholic mystic and reformer. Teresa of Avila was one of the leading figures of the Catholic Reformation, though at the time her ministry was disparaged by many clerics—in part due to her gender. She was a tireless reformer and spiritual seeker whose writings have inspired generations of both Catholics and Protestants. Any warm feelings for Protestants on her part, however, would have been out of the question. She regarded the Reformation with contempt and was praised by the pope for ridding Spain of the "mischief and ravages those Lutherans had wrought in France."

Her devotion to the Catholic Church was not impeded by her Jewish ancestry—her grandfather having been coerced into converting to Christianity and later hounded by the Spanish Inquisition. Her father assimilated more easily, but it was through her pious mother that she inherited her devout faith, though not in her adolescence. She spent her days consumed with the fantasies of romance novels, or she was out with friends riding horses and dancing: "I began to deck myself out and to try to attract others by my appearance," she recalled, "taking great trouble with my hands and hair, using perfumes and all the vanities I could get." But the gaiety of her younger years came to a sudden end with the death of her mother and her own health issues—illness that brought to an end her education at a nearby convent. Then, influenced by the writings of Jerome, she left home at age twenty to become a Carmelite nun.

Her early years in the convent were complicated by illness and doubt: "I went through a life of the greatest conflict. On the one hand, God called me; on the other, I followed the world." Her definition of following the world was a failure to meet the most rigorous standard of asceticism—a standard of self-denial she insisted all Carmelite nuns should meet. She separated herself from the other nuns, refused visitors, and sometimes lashed herself until the blood flowed.

But despite her outward acts of devotion, Teresa did not progress spiritually until she began reading Augustine's *Confessions*: "When I got as far as his conversion and read how he heard that voice in the garden, it was just as if the Lord gave it to me." Her own "conversion" came one day while listening to the words of the liturgy that spoke of Christ's suffering and death. "So great was my distress when I thought how ill I had repaid Him for those wounds that I felt as if my heart was breaking, and I threw myself down beside him."

Now in her forties and still in poor health, Teresa began having visions: "A rapture came on me, so sudden that it snatched me out of myself.... I heard these words: 'Now I want you to talk no longer with men, but with angels.'" The visions came so often that she feared they might be due to some "troublesome disease." Others judged her insane or demonic. In time she became convinced that she had reached a mystical union with God, one that others could reach through four stages: tranquillity, union, ecstasy, and spiritual marriage.

The rapture for which Teresa is most remembered was an erotic sense of God's love during which time a fiery spear was plunged into the very core of her being, leaving her enflamed with love for God. She did not, however, equate this experience with true devotion: "Let everyone understand that real love of God does not consist in tearshedding, nor in the sweetness and tenderness for which we usually long, just because they console us, but in serving God in justice, fortitude of soul and humility." She expressed her own love for God most specifically through her far-reaching reform of the Carmelites. Within twenty years, she and dozens of followers established fifteen new convents and reformed many older ones.

If Teresa had imagined that her work would be appreciated by church authorities, she was mistaken. A papal official described her as a "restless gadabout, disobedient, contumacious woman who promulgates pernicious doctrine under pretence of devotion." She was carrying on in ways inappropriate for her sex: "She leaves her cloisters against the orders of her superiors contrary to the decrees of the Council of Trent." Further, "She is ambitious and teaches theology as if she were a doctor of the church in spite of St. Paul's prohibition." Even some of her own nuns questioned her propriety on occasion. When a sister came upon her devouring a large piece of chicken and wondered if she ought rather to be praying, Teresa retorted, "When I eat chicken, I eat chicken; when I pray, I pray."

The generations of time served Teresa well as disparagement turned to appreciation and veneration. She, with John of the Cross, is regarded the cofounder of the Discalced (barefoot) Carmelites, and in 1970 Pope Paul VI named her a doctor of the church. Her writings include *The Way of Perfection* and *Life* (1562), an autobiography to that point in her life; her *Interior Castle* (1577) remains one of the masterpieces of Christian mysticism.

See also Carmelite Spirituality; Dark Night; John of the Cross.

For Further Reading: S. du Boulay, *Teresa of Avila* (2004); C. Medwick, *Teresa of Avila* (2001); M. Starr, *Teresa of Avila* (2008).

Ruth A. Tucker

Teresa of Calcutta, Mother (1910 – 1997)

Renowned Catholic missionary to the indigent and dying. Born Agnes Gonxha Bojaxhiu to an Albanian peasant family in Skopje, Macedonia, Mother Teresa received world renown for her quest to bring God's love to the destitute. At age seventeen, she joined the Sisters of Loreto in Dublin and then went to Calcutta, where she remained until her death. In 1946, while serving as the principal at a high school for girls, she heard Jesus beseeching her to "satiate his thirst" by living among and loving the "poorest of the poor." Four years later, after a rigorous discernment process, she founded the Missionaries of Charity. To the usual vows of poverty, chastity, and obedience, she added "wholehearted and free service to the poorest of the poor." She founded homes for the abandoned, the dying, and lepers; and the ministry soon expanded throughout India and the world.

Mother Teresa became famous through Malcolm Muggeridge's *Something Beautiful for God* (1969). Nevertheless, Christopher Hitchens's BBC program *Hell's Angel* (1994) and subsequent book, *The Missionary Position* (1995), accused her of serious duplicity.

Mother Teresa: Come Be My Light by Brian Kolodiejchuk (2007) is a compilation of her letters with commentary, which describes her calling and subsequent struggles. It reveals that her supposed battle with depression was instead an experience, shared by mystics such as St. John of the Cross, of acute darkness as an intimately entrusted grace. Through the insight of a spiritual director, she saw her darkness as a way to live her own poverty more completely, because it enabled her to share in the abandonment experienced by Jesus on the cross. With this awareness, she came to love the darkness, though the suffering itself never left her.

Mother Teresa was often criticized by skeptics who thought she should direct her financial and personal efforts toward political change, but she staunchly believed that her call was to lovingly tend "the one" before her, for in so doing she was tending the wounds of Christ.

See also Compassion; Dark Night.

Diane S. George Ayer

Tersteegen, Gerhard (1697 – 1769)

Pietist teacher from the German Rhineland. His Reformed theology, influenced by the writings of Madame Guyon, centered on devout recognition of God's presence. Tersteegen taught that the state of perpetual prayer was an experience in which the believer basked in God's presence as the ground of his own soul. Tersteegen lived in constant tension between the established church and his own ministry as a teacher, leader of prayer meetings, and spiritual adviser. He did not encourage withdrawal from the churches, but his intense spirituality continually drew people into an orbit around him that took on incipient monastic forms. Tersteegen had himself lived as a solitary in early life, doing only enough business as a ribbon maker to meet his immediate needs.

Around 1727 Tersteegen formed a Pilgrim's Tabernacle community of people devoted to contemplative retreat and wrote a rule of life for them. Tersteegen's latter years saw both a widespread revival movement and the devastation of the Seven Years' War. He wrote thousands of letters of spiritual advice. He was a connoisseur of a wide range of mystical treatises, translating them and writing many of his own. His largest writing project was a series of twenty-five spiritual lives of saints, the *Selected Biographies of Holy Souls*, in which he

792 • Tertullian (c. 160–220)

identified lives of conspicuous holiness, featuring many Roman Catholics. Tersteegen was decidedly Protestant in his theology, but his primary interest was in the direct experience of contemplative awareness of God, and his nondogmatic temper led him to draw freely from all traditions. He also wrote over one hundred hymns, which have been influential in English translations by John Wesley, Catherine Winkworth, and others. His prose works have never been widely available in English.

See also Pietism.

Fred Sanders

Tertullian (c. 160–220)

Early African Christian theologian. Raised in pagan Carthage, Tertullian gained a rich classical education. By 197 he converted to Christianity. Later claims that he was a priest (Jerome) or lawyer and elder (Eusebius) are historically uncertain. Thirty-one surviving writings illustrate the issues of Tertullian's day, passions of an extraordinary Jesus follower, and a legacy befitting the "father of Latin theology."

Generations engaging his writings have struggled with his persona. Revered as masterfully orthodox (Cyprian) and rejected as heterodox (so not canonized), images abound: the sophist, the Puritan, the anti-intellectual, the misogynist, and the "snapping Tertullian." Yet contextualized, his spirit and understanding are revealed in five convictions or themes interwoven throughout his writings.

God is *Savior*, giver of life in time and eternity. *Against Praxeas* established the orthodox Trinitarian credo of "three persons, one substance." He defended God as Creator in *Against Hermogenes* and maintained this stance along with the centrality of Christ in *Against Marcion*. *On Baptism* (the first such treatise) presents "ichthus" as a confessional symbol for "little fishes."

Truth in *Scripture* grounds the knowledge of God, world, and self. Tertullian the "Bible reader" quotes an Old Latin NT version. His early *Apology* heralds the Scriptures' age, fulfilled prophecy, and unique character as a living Word: "One who listens [to it] will find God." *The Prescription against Heretics* locates Scripture in the church's apostolic tradition.

Sanctification is an imperative. Christians are freed from sin, imitating God's holiness. Called moralist or rigorist, Tertullian replied that he was a disciple. Treatises *On Patience, On Modesty,* and *On Monogamy* reveal deep convictions. *On the Shows* warns against entertainment culture. To accusing pagans, his *apologia* is that faithful Christians make good, useful citizens—and "the blood of the martyrs is seed." Closing a second letter *To His Wife* is a classic tribute to Christian marriage.

Simplicity favors virtue and removing distractions, and prefers divine realities. In his conversion, Tertullian made a simple, total choice—but past and surrounding complexities abounded: philosophers chattering, beauty defiled, heretics perverting, believers idolatrous. So rhetoric (Athens vs. Jerusalem), paradox (believing because absurd), humor ("'Christians to the lion'—all to just one?"), and confrontation (women as occasion for temptation) were all in the service of exhortation. His work *On the Soul* testifies that simplicity opens the way for divine life.

Life in the *Spirit* is the believer's daily, high calling. Tertullian's treatise *On Prayer* (the first) expresses this. Embracing Montanism (c. 207), Tertullian found a community of authority, vitality, and discipline to elevate his commitment. Perhaps a martyr (following Perpetua and *On Martyrdom*), years before Christian monasticism, Tertullian practiced a "bloodless martyrdom" of faith and practice that still challenges seekers, scholars, and would-be sedentary Christians today.

See also Asceticism; Montanism; Simplicity.

For Further Reading: T. Barnes, *Tertullian* (1971); G. Bray, *Holiness and the Will of God: Perspectives on the Theology of Tertullian* (1979); E. Osborn, *Tertullian* (1997).

James D. Smith III

Testimony

Testimony denotes that which is testified to, a record, a witness, a subjective account based on personal experience (Gr. *martyria/martyrion*, the English word *martyr* being a direct cognate). Forms of the word are used more than two hundred times in the NT. To offer a testimony is to bear witness to the truth, to something that has actually happened. Epistemologically, a testimony counts as a source of knowledge. Legally, a personal testimony is presented in court as formal evidence, especially when the testifier is an eyewitness. In ancient times and present, a testimony is given either to verify or disprove the evidence provided in a trial. A testimony can be true or false. Every genuine Christian has a story, starring Jesus, to share. The truthfulness of one's testimony in Christ liberates a person to resist the evil one (Rev. 12:11) and obediently bear witness to the world (Acts 1:8; 2:4; 2 Tim. 2:2). All along, the gospel has been spread by way of personal testimonies. The Bible says that John the Baptist "came as a witness" (*martyrian*) to "testify" (*martyreō*) (John 1:7–8, 15, 32, 34; 3:26) to the true Light. Jesus said John's testimony is "true" (John 5:32 NRSV). Mary, Jesus' mother, was the first to testify that Jesus is the Christ (Luke 1:46–55). The word *testimony* occurs seventy-six times in Johannine writings, ten times in Revelation alone. By far the most important and consequential testimony is that of Jesus Christ himself. Indeed, "the testimony of Jesus is the spirit of prophecy" (Rev. 19:10). Jesus, by his works, bore witness to the Father (John 5:36) who reciprocally bore witness to the Christ (v. 37). The whole OT is a testimony to Jesus (v. 39), and Jesus' whole life is a testimony to the living God (2 Tim. 1:8).

See also Evangelism; Witnessing.

For Further Reading: Augustine, *Confessions*, trans. R. Pine-Coffin (1961); G. Beale, *The Book of Revelation* (1998); R. Mounce, *The Book of Revelation* (1997).

Sarah Sumner

Thanksgiving

The act of thanking God for what he has done or given. Thanksgiving is exhorted in the OT both in invitations to worship and in commands to offer sacrifices (e.g., Lev. 7:11–15). Likewise, the psalmist commends both means: "Let them thank the LORD.... And let them offer thanksgiving sacrifices, and tell of his deeds with songs of joy" (Ps. 107:21–22 NRSV). Theologically, a clear distinction may be made between praise and thanksgiving. Both involve the giving of honor and worship to God, but whereas in praise God is honored for who he is, in thanksgiving God is thanked for what he has done. Inevitably these are often intertwined and interchanged (not confused!) in worship and prayer. So Psalm 100:4 exhorts, "Enter his gates with thanksgiving and his courts with praise." In the Gospels and Acts, thanksgiving is usually associated with prayer at a meal, such as Jesus' prayer in the upper room (Mark 14:23), and from here there is a straight line both to the continuing spiritual practice of giving thanks at a meal table, which acknowledges that all we have comes from God's gracious provision, and to the central prayer of the Eucharist, which is a prayer of thanksgiving for bread and wine and all that God has given in the death and resurrection of Jesus Christ. However, the Gospels also contain the story of the one leper who returned to Jesus to thank him for his healing (Luke 17:1–19) and the story of the sinful woman who anointed Jesus' feet (Luke 7:36–50). The dynamics of both of these stories suggests a view of Christian living in which the motive and quality of that living is a grateful response to the grace and forgiveness of God. This view may also be found in Paul (Col. 3:17), who exhorted his readers to give thanks whatever the circumstances (Eph. 5:20; 1 Thess. 5:18).

Thanksgiving is a golden thread running through much Christian hymnody and evangelical testimony of God's grace at work in people's lives. Yet there is more to be said. Not only is thanksgiving an action in which the believer transacts a response to God's goodness; it is also a spiritual discipline and communal practice, a formational pattern of behavior that influences the character of those who give thanks. By repeatedly giving thanks, the Christian sees the world as a gift of God and sees God as the gracious and generous Father (James 1:17). Theologically, to give thanks is to affirm the goodness and generosity of God. Devotionally, thanksgiving need not be only an expression of gratitude; it can also be a pattern of behavior that shapes and develops the attitudes and values of the believer.

See also Celebration; Worship.

For Further Reading: D. Bass, ed., *Practicing our Faith* (1997); D. Saliers, *Worship as Theology* (1994).

Christopher J. Ellis

Theologia Germanica

The *Theologia Germanica*, or the German theology, is a devotional work of fifty-six short chapters. The treatise was composed about 1350 by an anonymous author whom tradition identifies as a priest of the order of Teutonic Knights in Frankfurt, Germany. The *Theologia* reflects the ethos and teachings of the Friends of God, a contemplative and mystical renewal movement of the 14th and 15th centuries. The treatise broadly draws on emphases from Pseudo-Dionysius, Meister Eckhart, and more importantly Johannes Tauler. When Luther discovered the document, he added an introduction, published it in 1518, and gave it its current name. Through the centuries, some two hundred editions of the *Theologia* have been published in many languages.

In the treatise, God is depicted as "the one total and perfect Good" and "Light" from whose will the world came into being. To overcome human disobedience and to achieve redemption, God assumed human nature in the person of Jesus. Self-will is the supreme evil that must be overcome if a human being would know God and achieve loving union with him. "The more man follows after and grows in self-will, the further he is from God and the true Good." Indeed, "self-will is the most widespread commodity in hell." The soul escapes creaturely self-will by godly intention, disciplining the appetites, submission, and obedience.

The *Theologia* stresses experiential knowledge of God via the heart rather than external knowledge gained through formal learning and secondhand information. Other prominent themes in the *Theologia* include God's antipathy to sin, taking up Christ's cross in a life of suffering, poverty of spirit, Satan's seductions, divinization or becoming godlike, and service toward others in the world out of a posture of rest in the Lord. In short, the *Theologia Germanica* is a treatise on the life with God that translates into righteous and compassionate living in the world.

Luther highly valued the *Theologia*, claiming that it taught him more about God, Christ, and the pernicious effects of sin than any other work—save Scripture and the writings of Augustine. Sixteenth-century Lutherans as well as Anabaptists and Pietists also were supportive of the *Theologia*. Protestant Reformers, such as Farel, Calvin, and Beza, were unfavorable to the *Theologia* given its minimal theological rigor, mystical piety, and occasional quasi-pantheistic language (e.g., God as "the One who is All"). Roman Catholic interest in the treatise has been subdued by virtue of its aversion to Scholasticism.

See also Luther, Martin; Tauler, Johannes.

For Further Reading: A. Harnack, *History of Dogma*, 7 vols. (1899–1900), 6:84–149; A. Neander, *General History of the Christian Religion and Church*, 5 vols. (1859), 5:23–40; *The Theologia Germanica of Martin Luther*, CWS (1989).

Bruce A. Demarest

Theosis

See **Deification.**

Therapy

See **Chapter 27.**

Thérèse of Lisieux (1873–1896)

French Catholic mystic. Thérèse of Lisieux, known as the "Little Flower" (dying in the flower of her youth), has become a favorite saint of religious seekers — both Catholic and Protestant — since the publication of her *Autobiography* (also known as *The Story of a Soul*) in English. Pope Pius X regarded her "the greatest saint of modern times."

The daughter of a prosperous merchant, she followed her four older sisters into a nearby Carmelite convent with one goal: "I want to be a saint." With that in mind, she began writing her spiritual memoir, never imagining that her earthly pilgrimage would be over by age twenty-four. Hers is not so much the story of raptures and deep devotion. Rather, she speaks of loss of faith. During the months of suffering before she died, she battled doubt and depression. When she initially realized she was dying, "the hope of going to heaven," she wrote, "transported me with joy." But then she encountered the dark night of the soul: "In those days my faith was so clear and vigorous that I found perfect happiness in the thought of heaven.... But during those radiant days of Easter, Jesus ... allowed pitch-black darkness to sweep over my soul and let the thought of heaven, so sweet to me from my infancy, destroy all my peace and torture me. This trial was not something lasting a few days or weeks. I suffered it for months and am still waiting for it to end."

She struggled in explaining herself to others: "I wish that I could express what I feel, but it is impossible. One must have traveled through the same sunless tunnel to understand how dark it is.... The voice of unbelievers came to mock me in the darkness." Despite this darkness that engulfed her, she carried on with the motions of faith and recognizing the reality of God: "May God forgive me! He knows very well that although I had not the consolation of faith, I forced myself to act as if I had. I have made more acts of faith in the last year than in the whole of my life." Her openness and brutally honest spiritual reflections have endeared her to all who struggle in their faith.

See also Carmelite Spirituality; Dark Night.

For Further Reading: J. F. Schmidt, *Everything Is Grace: The Life and Way of Thérèse of Lisieux* (2007); *Thérèse of Lisieux, Autobiography*, trans. J. Beevers (1989).

Ruth A. Tucker

Third Orders

Third orders are lay groups, men or women, in various forms of life, living in the world under the rule of a religious order. In distinction to monks (first order) and nuns (second order), third orders are open to laypersons, as well as diocesan priests, clerics, and members of religious institutes not under vows, who thereby become *tertiaries*. Those who are part of a third order seek to live more perfect lives by following the spirit and rule of the religious order to which they belong. A third order can include a novitiate and an office, as well as some members who take vows of obedience and chastity.

There are multiple forms of third orders in multiple churches, including Catholic and Anglican traditions. These include the Augustinian Third Order, Third Order Secular of Our Lady of Mount Carmel, Dominican Third Order, Franciscan Third Order, Descalced Carmelites, Servites, and the Benedictine Oblates. The Order of St. Luke of the Methodist Church illustrates the expansion of the institution into the Protestant tradition as well.

Membership in a third order allows a tertiary to live a life in accordance with a rule such that he or she may find a more direct way to attain Christian perfection. The most important purpose of every third order is personal sanctification of its members as well as charitable works. Tertiaries share in prayers, masses, penances, and other good works of the order they belong to. No vows are taken for membership in a third order, and consequently a tertiary may later make the decision to return to the world. While tertiaries do not live in a monastery, they are often required to say certain prayers, attend a number of masses, and perform other duties or services.

Third orders gained popularity and, some will argue, existence in the 1200s. Impatient laity frustrated with the impious and scandalous lives of the clergy turned to preaching. This gave rise to the *Vaudois* (also known as the Waldensians—the name of a Christian evangelical movement in the late Middle Ages) and the *Fratres Humiliati* (an Italian religious order in the twelfth century). Eventually suspected of heresy and wrong dogma, these groups were forbidden. However, the idea of a secular order that followed a rule was not lost and was soon taken on by many who sought to live a holy life in the world.

See also Laypersons and Spirituality.

For Further Reading: P. Foley, *Three-Dimensional Living* (1962); K. Hennrich, *The Better Life* (1942); B. Tvedten, *How to Be a Monastic and Not Leave Your Day Job* (2006); F. Wendelli, *Perfection in the Market Place* (1958).

Alethea Savoy

Thomas à Kempis (1380–1471)

Author of the classic *The Imitation of Christ*. Thomas was also a late medieval member of the Augustinian Canons and associate of the Brethren of the Common Life (exemplars of the *Devotio Moderna*). Born Thomas Hammerken in 1380 in Kempen, near Düsseldorf in the Rhineland, he left home at age thirteen to join his older brother John at the school run by the Brethren in Deventer. In 1399 Thomas entered the monastery of Mount St. Agnes (St. Agnietenberg) of the Augustinian Canons in Zwolle (Holland). He made his final profession in 1407 and was ordained a priest in 1413 or 1414. Thomas would eventually write *The Chronicle of the Canons Regular of Mount St. Agnes*, providing a history for the monastery up to his death in 1471. Thomas's life in the monastery was primarily devoted to writing, preaching, and copying manuscripts, including a copy of the Bible, though he served for a time as sub-prior (in 1425 and 1448) and novice master. He is the author of a number of devotional and spiritual works, including *Prayers and Meditations on the Life of Christ, Meditation on the Incarnation of Christ, The Elevation of the Mind, On Solitude and Silence, On the Discipline of the Cloister, The Soliloquy of the Soul, Concerning the Three Tabernacles* (a treatment of poverty, humility, and patience), and *On True Compunction of Heart*. He also wrote biographical works on Gerhard Groote (founder of the *Devotio Moderna*) and Florens Radewijns (Thomas's spiritual father and successor of Groote) and a number of hymns.

Thomas's most influential work, however, remains *The Imitation of Christ*, which he wrote before he turned forty years old. It was first fully translated into English by Richard Whytford in 1556. Thomas's authorship of *The Imitation* has been the subject of much debate since the publication of the *editio princeps* at Augsburg in 1471. Other candidates for authorship put forward by scholars have included Jean Gerson, Gerhard Groote, Bernard of Clairvaux, and Walter Hilton. Most commentators today adopt the conclusion that Thomas is the author of the work.

The Imitation of Christ was likely intended as an instruction manual for young novices and is divided into four books, each with its own title derived from the first line of the book's first chapter: (1) "Counsels of the Spiritual Life"; (2) "Counsels on the Inner Life"; (3) "On Inward Consolation"; and (4) "On the Blessed Sacrament." The books are then subdivided into a total of 114 chapters. The work is heavily indebted to the thought and influence of Augustine of Hippo, Bernard of Clairvaux, and the Bible. In fact, there are more than a thousand direct biblical references in *The Imitation*.

In summary, the book considers topics that were of special importance to the followers of the Brethren of the Common Life, such as religious devotion, humility, denial of the world, silence, and meditation on the sufferings of Christ. In addition, *The Imitation* also serves as a brief manual on the monastic life, especially a kind of interiorized monasticism. According to Thomas, outward appearance does not make the monk, but "the transformation of one's way of life" is what characterizes the true monk from the false monk. This is in harmony with his conviction that one's "inner goodness" is always more important than one's outward behavior, since God searches the hearts of humankind. The need to cultivate one's inner monk is what makes it necessary for one to enter outwardly a monastery. Just like Jesus, all monks, writes Thomas, need to withdraw from the crowds to "live inwardly to God." Thus, despite having joined an active order of priests, Thomas was a strong advocate for a more traditional form of contemplative monasticism. This, too, was an identifying characteristic of the Brethren, whose founder, Groote, had spent a season of his early life in a Carthusian monastery.

In addition to his adulation of the monastic life, Thomas also wrote in exalted language about the priesthood. In *The Imitation*, he writes, "High the office, and great the dignity of a priest." Likewise, he understands God's admonition to "Be holy as I am holy" to be directed particularly to priests. Perhaps because he was a priest, Thomas was a strong advocate of frequent communion, believing that infrequent reception resulted in "sloth and spiritual dryness." For those unable to commune literally, Thomas promoted a "spiritual communion with Christ."

See also Brethren of the Common Life; *Devotio Moderna;* Imitation of Christ.

For Further Reading: A. de Reuver, *Sweet Communion* (2007); S. Kettlewell, *The Authorship of the Imitatione Christi* (1877); ibid., *Thomas à Kempis and the Brothers of Common Life* (1885); L. Sherley-Price, "Introduction," in *Thomas à Kempis: The Imitation of Christ* (1952).

Greg Peters

Thomas Aquinas (1224–1275)

Major theologian. Thomas is most widely known as a philosopher and theologian and, according to some, is the greatest (Roman Catholic) doctor of the church in history. He is the patron saint of all Catholic educational institutions. His best-known writings, *Summa Contra Gentiles* and *Summa Theologica* (1270s, also called *Summa Theologiae*), demonstrate the brilliance of his mind in the service of the Christian message. At a time when the faith was under threat from new ideas that polarized the church, he showed the way to using those ideas in the service of the faith.

The ancient philosophy of Aristotle (384–322 BC) appeared new and threatening to Western Europe in the 13th century. His books were not known there until they were introduced through Muslim philosophers in Spain. Thomas's accomplishment was to show how Aristotle's philosophy could be a medium of Christian understanding, instead of an enemy. He created a twofold system of thought in which reason and faith, philosophy and theology, science and religion, nature and grace were complementary.

Thomas's family was wealthy and influential; they had already planned from his early childhood that he should become the abbot of Monte Cassino, the historic Benedictine monastery. He went to this monastery as a boy but later studied at the University of Naples, where he first encountered the newly formed Dominican order. He entered that order at age nineteen but then underwent imprisonment by his own family, who wanted him to become a Benedictine abbot. It was a matter of prestige and wealth versus poverty and learning. According to legend, Thomas even resisted the temptation to have sex with a beautiful woman while in prison, and thus is known as a person of great personal steadfastness. Eventually his family relented, and he escaped, going to the intellectual center of the day, the University of Paris. There and in Cologne he worked with his learned mentor, Albertus Magnus (Albert the Great, 1193–1280). His fellow students had called him a "dumb ox" because he was both big and silent in class. But Albert reportedly said, "We call him the dumb ox, but in his teaching he will one day produce such a bellowing that it will be heard throughout the world."

In Thomas's biblical commentaries, we see the same gifts of clarity and organization that characterize his later works. In the discussion of the gifts of the Spirit in 1 Corinthians 12–13, he outlines the discussion and raises questions in a neat and orderly fashion. Most important, he sees the three central themes of love, faith, and hope as the key to the Christian life. Of these, as Paul says, love is the most important, for it unites us with God and lasts forever.

We see how Thomas the spiritual theologian makes use of this insight in the *Summa Theologica* 2.2, questions 1–27, where he uses the philosophical framework of Aristotle when naming the three themes as virtues, and his Christian understanding when adding that they are theological virtues, which transform and heal the cardinal virtues of temperance, justice, prudence, and fortitude. Faith, hope, and love unite us with God, for they are all gifts of grace. Questions 23–27 in particular describe the Christian life as a friendship with God and neighbor. According to Thomas, our first love is for God and for our neighbor, but it is right to love oneself and one's body in an ordered love.

When Thomas was nearing the completion of his greatest work, the *Summa Theologica*, in 1273, something happened that changed the course of his life. He is quoted as saying, "All that I have written seems like straw compared to what has now been revealed to me." From this time on, Thomas was able to carry on his rigorous spiritual practices but not his writing. Perhaps he had a taste of that beatific vision of God that he wrote of in his theology, and found it worth more than all the scholarly ideas he had been entertaining. He died just four months later.

Except for that very late dramatic change, Thomas did not seem to have crisis points in his spiritual life. His practice as a Dominican was a daily schedule of worship, prayer, teaching, and writing. It is obvious from his writing that he studied the Scriptures assiduously, for he seems to have the command of his own extensive mental concordance. His practice was clearly in the context of Roman Catholicism; he was a priest who confessed his sins daily, celebrated the Mass daily, and was obedient to the pope and other authorities.

A contemporary evangelical reader will find that Thomas's spirituality is, contrary to first impressions, focused on Jesus Christ and consists in a friendship with God through love.

See also Dominican Spirituality; Virtue.

For Further Reading: R. Barron, *Thomas Aquinas* (1996); Thomas Aquinas, *The Gifts of the Spirit: Selected Spiritual Writings*, ed. B. Ashley (1995); J. Weisheipl, *Friar Thomas D'Aquino* (1974).

Bradley P. Holt

Threefold Way

Humanity has long exhibited an interest in spiritual growth and maturity. Scripture affirms this necessity of growing in Christ (Eph. 4:12–16; Phil. 3:12–16; 2 Peter 3:18) and provides a paradigm contrasting spiritual immaturity with maturity (1 Cor. 3:13; Heb. 5:12–14). Significantly for this article, Scripture nowhere establishes a threefold pattern for spiritual growth. Origen was the first to advance a threefold way of the moral, natural, and contemplative stages based on the wisdom books of Proverbs, Ecclesiastes, and Song of Songs. Evagrius further refined this paradigm, speaking of beginners, proficients, and the perfect. In the 5th century, Pseudo-Dionysius named the three stages purgation, illumination, and union.

The continuing refinement and usage of this *triplex via* reveals variations in the nature and dynamics of each stage as well as the movement between the stages. Central to the understanding of the threefold way was a detailed system of various forms of prayer moving from the more elementary practice of discursive meditation to increasingly more challenging forms of contemplation. Broadly speaking, purgation begins once a person has been converted or justified by Jesus. Central to purgation is an emphasis on asceticism that intentionally employs spiritual disciplines to overcome the temptations of the world, the flesh, and the devil. Breaking the human will through surrendering one's life to God's grace is the primary goal of purgation. This reflects Jesus' command to deny self, take up one's cross, and follow him (Luke 9:23). Two specific tasks of purgation are detachment or offering up our desires to God and mortification, or putting to the death, those barriers that distort or deceive a believer from more fully following Jesus Christ. This involves a lengthy process of stripping the false perceptions a person has of God so that they might be replaced with a more biblically accurate image of God. The Holy Spirit, who is active in all three stages, leads a person into deeper participation of Christ's crucifixion.

The movement to the illuminative stage continues the purifying process with the persistent need to strip away false perceptions of God and of life and the world. The result is an increased awareness of God's presence. Prayer transitions to new forms of contemplative practices, and the experience of the dark night of the soul brings further detachment from the more dramatic spiritual experiences of God. This growing recognition of God leads one to a greater sense of mystery and the realization of how little one actually knows of God.

Some Christians will reach the third stage of union that introduces the believer to a habitual sense of God's presence. This oneness with God has been called spiritual or mystical marriage. The previous sufferings of the dark night of the soul lead one into deeper experiences of God's love. While the fullness of the unitive stage is reserved for heaven, one can experience spiritual ravishment, rapture, and other ecstatic forms of contemplative prayer as a foretaste of heaven. The result is an increasing desire for being with Christ in heaven and a deeper participation in the churches' mission of proclaiming the gospel.

The threefold way can appear very refined and structured, but in reality it is more a heuristic model than exact guide. Within Roman Catholicism one finds two distinct interpretations. The older school of Bonaventure understood these stages as three different but simultaneous movements of the overall process of sanctification. The latter approach, indebted to Teresa of Avila, perceived these three distinct stages as successive and progressive. Some contemporary evangelicals employ this schema with little awareness of its historical gap with Protestant theology. Many Protestants would be uncomfortable restricting union with God to the conclusion of the spiritual journey and rather place it at the start of one's pilgrimage. In recent decades, the threefold way has lost much of its earlier prominence though it has found new life in some areas, especially from a psychological perspective, due to the increased interest in stage and developmental theory (e.g., Groeschel).

Karl Rahner has argued that the threefold way is both inaccurate and unhelpful and tends to communicate that mystical experiences of God are not open to all believers. Philip Sheldrake succinctly condenses some of Rahner's critique: "An over-emphasis on separate, successive stages, with universal application, conflicts with a sense of the uniqueness of each person's spiritual journey as well as with the freedom of God and unpredictability of grace." And further, "By focusing exclusively on union with God as the final stage, we may miss the point that union with God is not so much a stage above and beyond all others as the precondition of all spiritual growth." However, the threefold way still possesses value in reminding people that the Christian life is not static, but dynamic, and that God expects believers to grow in maturity in Christ (2 Peter 3:18). Growth, while expected, is never guaranteed or possible through technique, but ever dependent on God's grace, which inspires human effort in growing in word and deed in love to God and one's neighbor.

See also Ascent, Stages of Spiritual; Conversion; Formation, Spiritual; Union with God.

For Further Reading: R. Garrigou-Lagrange, *Three Ways of the Spiritual Life* (1938); B. Groeschel, *Spiritual Passages* (1983); M. R. Mulholland, *Invitation to a Journey* (1993); D. Perrin, *Studying Christian Spirituality* (2007); K. Rahner, "Reflections on the Problem of the Gradual Ascent to Christian Perfection," in *Theology of the Spiritual Life*, vol. 3 of Theological Investigations, trans. K. H. and B. Kruger (1974), 3–23; P. Sheldrake, *Spirituality and History* (2007).

Tom Schwanda

Thurman, Howard (1899–1981)

Premier African-American mystic-activist. Spending the first twenty-five years of his life in Florida and Georgia and subsequent years traveling a racially divided nation, Thurman was drawn to a contemplative theology emphasizing the need for union with God coupled with a moral imperative to address public life. His theology was rooted in a core conviction that all life is one. Thurman's prophetic-leaning mysticism—forged in part by the black church, the Social Gospel, and Quakerism—was cultivated in the 1920s as he fought for integration while holding a prominent leadership role in the YMCA youth movement and as he studied philosophy at Haverford College under the Quaker mystic Rufus Jones.

While working in various educational capacities at Morehouse College, Spelman College, and Howard University in the 1930s, Thurman's quest to bridge the inner and outer life to assist in actual-

izing the kingdom of God inspired him to lead the first African-American contingent to India, where he met Gandhi. Thurman, like Martin Luther King Jr. after him, framed Gandhi's nonviolent ethic of resistance in Christian terms to preserve the integrity of the tradition and encourage a pacifist engagement in constructing a truly just democratic American experiment.

In the 1940s, both Thurman's classic *Jesus and the Disinherited* (1949) and his cofounding of The Church for the Fellowship of All Peoples in San Francisco were outgrowths of his appropriation of Gandhianism. After living for decades under the enormous shadow of King (whom he mentored) and other well-known leaders during the civil rights era, Thurman's own spiritual legacy is finally being seriously reassessed as a core contributor to the contemplative strain in African-American Christianity. He also wrote an autobiography, *With Head and Heart* (1979).

See also African-American Christian Spirituality; Gandhi, Mohandas Karamchand.

For Further Reading: W. Fluker and C. Tumber, eds., *A Strange Freedom: The Best of Howard Thurman on Religious Experience and Public Life* (1998); L. Smith, *Howard Thurman* (1981); H. Thurman, *Essential Writings* (2006).

Roy Whitaker

Time, Sanctification of

The sanctification of time must begin very simply: with learning to receive time itself as a gift from God, a part of his creation. "This is the day [an increment of time] the LORD has made," the psalmist writes; "let us rejoice and be glad in it" (Ps. 118:24). God stands above time, for he created it; yet he promises to be with us in time—moment by moment, hour by hour, day by day. In a contemporary culture where time is experienced as a thing to be managed rather than a thing to be enjoyed, a problem to be fixed rather than a blessing to be received, a place of scarcity rather than abundance, how do we receive time as the gift that it is, learning how to live faithfully in time, honoring God with the time of our lives? How do we experience time as something that is set apart for a holy purpose?

Several Christian practices aid us in the sanctification of time. The first is the practice of receiving each day—*this day*—as a gift from God. This might involve a morning prayer or other ritual that helps us to orient ourselves to God at the beginning of each day. One traditional morning prayer begins with rejoicing in God's activity that is already in progress as we are awakened from our night's rest. "God said, 'Let there be light,' and there was light. And God saw that the light was good. This very day the Lord has acted! Let us rejoice!" From there, our morning prayer or some other ritual act can help us express our intention to devote this day to God's Son, our Savior, Jesus Christ the Lord. We can, with words and with our attitude, invite God's presence into our day.

Closely associated with the practice of receiving the day is our attentiveness to the sacrament of the present moment. We cultivate our understanding and awareness that meets us in time, in the present moment. The past is gone, and the future is not yet here. God meets us in *this* moment and so we look for God and expect to find God right here right now. The examen of consciousness is a practice that helps us to reflect on God's presence at the end of every day so that we become more and more attuned to the presence of God in ordinary moments.

The Christian tradition of fixed-hour prayer helps us sanctify the different "hours" or segments of the day to God and his purposes. Although some communities recognize seven "hours" of the day that are marked by special times of prayer, Protestant Christians seem to do better with four—morning, midday, evening, and night. We "pray the hours" by setting aside a few moments to be quiet or to pray spontaneously at these hours, or we utilize written prayers of the church that have been recorded for us in Scripture and in various prayer books. A related practice is learning to live in and be shaped by seasons of the church year: Advent, Christmas, Lent, Easter, Pentecost, and Ordinary Time. Each of these times and seasons contains unique invitations for encountering God and being shaped by the great events and great themes of our faith. These invitations are contained in time that is marked by seasons.

Sabbath keeping calls us to steward our time and our energy by setting apart one day each week that is completely given over to rest, worship, and delight. The Sabbath is a sacred space in time that is holy unto the Lord. On this day, we give a portion of our time back to God, learning how to trust him with our time and with our very selves. We trust that the work we have done in six days is enough and that God can care for whatever else is needed. We allow God to run the world while we rest in him as he has instructed us to do.

This practice of tithing one-seventh of our time is affirmed throughout Scripture, beginning with God's rest on the seventh day of creation. Later on, when God called the Hebrew people to himself, a significant part of their national identity had to do with stewarding their time in this way. The prophet Isaiah promised that if we honor God with Sabbath time, we will find delight in God and we will be raised to new heights of intimacy in our relationship with him. Jesus affirmed the goodness of the Sabbath in the Gospels ("The sabbath was made for humankind, and not humankind for the sabbath" [Mark 2:27 NRSV]), and the significance of the Sabbath was highlighted by the writer of Hebrews, both as a current reality that we are to live now and that also points to a deeper rest in God that is to come. In Hebrews 4, the refusal to honor God by keeping a Sabbath was attributed to hardness of heart that stemmed from unbelief.

All of these practices having to do with sanctifying time can be spoken of as sacred rhythms—spiritual practices that help us to honor God with the minutes, hours, days, weeks, and years of our lives. These rhythms help us to orient ourselves toward God *in time* rather than being tyrannized by the passing of time. Scripture distinguishes between two different kinds of time: *chronos* time, which is measured by clocks and calendars, and *kairos* time, which is time characterized by spiritual fullness, a time when God's purposes and plans come to fruition. When the minutes, hours, days, and weeks of our lives are lived in sacred rhythms, we choose to order our lives around that which is of highest value and experience time in its fullness rather than its scarcity. We experience time as a precious gift that is set apart as holy unto the Lord, a sanctuary in which we encounter the presence of God.

See also Liturgical Year; Liturgy of the Hours; Sabbath.

For Further Reading: R. H. Barton, *Sacred Rhythms* (2006); D. Bass, *Receiving the Day* (2000); S. McKnight, *Praying with the Church* (2006); W. Muller, *Sabbath* (1999).

Ruth Haley Barton

Tithing

The act of giving a portion of one's earnings or wealth to either a human lord or deity is found in almost every culture, with the basic amount throughout history having been 10 percent due to the ease of counting by tens. However, its meaning in the Christian tradition is bound more closely to the relationship between God and his people.

The first biblical instance of a tithe is found in Genesis 14 when Abraham gives the Priest King Melchizedek a tenth of the spoils of his war with the captors of Lot. The Law later prescribed a tithe as part of the regular process of worship, with various operating procedures given for the support of the Levites and the poor, with the greater goal to remind the people to "learn to revere the Lord your God always." The tithe reminded the people that all they had was from God and that the return of the tithe (also synonymous with firstfruits) affirmed this reality and placed the people in an attitude of continued reliance upon the Lord. The people of God were to be totally devoted to God, and thus the failure to participate in the tithe was seen as robbing from God the worship due him (Mal. 3:8–11).

In the NT the tithe is mentioned, usually in connection with the actions of the Pharisees. Jesus turns the focus away from a particular amount and instead toward the attitude of the heart of the giver and the great blessings that the people of God have already received. In the parable of the talents Jesus tells his audience "To whom much is given, much is expected." This, along with the call to be joyful in one's giving, establishes the principles of NT giving and connects the Christian's spiritual maturity to the relationship of believers and their wealth.

Christians have historically taken different positions on tithing, at least with regard to the amounts and destinations of such gifts. Does the failure of the NT to reaffirm a strict tithe change the amount that the believer should give? Does the principle of "much given much expected" in fact increase the amount to be given? Does the presence of the Holy Spirit in the life of the believer mean that the amount given is based on the direction of the Spirit rather than the Law? Some believe that the full amount should be given only to the local church that one is a member of, basing this on the storehouse concept in Malachi 3. Still others indicate that since there is only one body of Christ, all who minister in light of the Gospel are eligible to receive portions of the tithe.

These various opinions do not negate the importance of giving as part of the Christian's spiritual growth. With money being a forum for the exhibiting of an individual's or a community's true beliefs and values it is easy to see why tithing has played an important role in evangelical spiritual growth.

See also Discipleship; Money.

For Further Reading: S. Olford, *The Grace of Giving* (2000); J. Stott, *The Grace of Giving* (2008).

Christopher Morton

Tolerance

Tolerance is both an attitude and an action, and it is always an issue in contexts of difference and diversity. Tolerance requires one to bear with people's otherness. It includes respect for the other, but it goes beyond respect. It is a willingness and resolve to endure lovingly the difficulties and stressors of diversity. In a religious context tolerance is important because it is one optional response in light of what one has concluded to be true or good. For example, evangelical Christians believe that Jesus Christ is "the way and the truth and the life" (John 14:6). But obviously not everyone shares this conviction about Jesus. An attitude of tolerance first of all recognizes and accepts that there are alternative perspectives on the truth.

In response, the tolerant person or group charts a middle course between persecution and passive indifference. Historically, Christianity has both suffered from persecution and persecuted others. During the first three Christian centuries, it was an illicit religion and many Christians were persecuted or even martyred for their faith. After Constantine, Roman imperial power began to support Christianity and its claims to truthfulness. The whole scene reversed, and some Christians began to show intolerance. The newer attitude is vividly captured in the Augustinian dictum with respect to heretics: Compel them to come in!

Tolerance also differs from passivity, which may reflect a relativist or indifferent spirit. Such familiar attitudes suggest that "it's impossible to know anyway" or "I simply don't care." Authentic tolerance, however, is compatible with deep personal conviction and caring. It is patterned after the prophetic witness and loving attitude of Jesus. Such tolerance is a virtue, in the sense that it always aims at the good. The apostle Paul hinted at this link between love and tolerance in his famous observation that love is patient and kind (1 Cor. 13:4). Tolerance is compatible with respectful, even vigorous, persuasion, but the posture of toleration ultimately is to *allow*. As such it stands in marked contrast to intolerance, which *demands*. True tolerance is undermined by fear and the need to control. It is nurtured by deep apprehension (necessarily sustained through meditative prayer) of the limits of one's own understanding, the volitional freedom and dignity of every other human being, and the sovereignty of God over human affairs. In the final analysis, tolerance dares to believe that love is more powerful than coercion. Civility is its grace-filled face in a pluralistic world.

See also Love.

For Further Reading: M. Albright, *The Mighty and the Almighty* (2006); B. Hostetler and J. McDowell, *The New Tolerance* (1998); R. Mouw, *Uncommon Decency* (1992); G. Niebuhr, *Beyond Tolerance* (2008); R. Wuthnow, *America and the Challenges of Religious Diversity* (2005).

Alan Kolp

Tolkien, J(ohn) R(onand) R(euel) (1892–1973)

Epic fantasy writer and Oxford philologist. J. R. R. Tolkien, as he came to be known, was born in Bloemfontein, South Africa. After his father died, his family moved back to England and soon converted to Roman Catholicism. As he grew, Tolkien developed a love for Old Norse myths, which informed many of the stories he later created. He was a trained philologist, and after serving in World War I was eventually appointed professor of Anglo-Saxon literature at Oxford University (1925–1959) where he became friends with another notable author, C. S. Lewis. Both Tolkien and Lewis were members of the literary group called the Inklings, a collection of friends who met regularly to read their fictional stories to one another. Tolkien's more notable works include *The Silmarillion* (1977), *The Hobbit* (1936), and *The Lord of the Rings* trilogy (1954–55). The latter has frequently earned "most favorite book" status in surveys conducted in Britain and other nations in the 21st century.

Tolkien's contribution to Christian spirituality comes through these epic works of fantasy fiction. Many Christian readers view them, especially *The Lord of the Rings*, as allegories of the Christian faith. Interpretations of this work range from the one ring representing sin, which desires to dominate the world, to elves as symbols of Christian believers. Although Tolkien acknowledged that *The Lord of the Rings* is thoroughly Catholic in nature, he denied that any of his works were written as allegories. For Tolkien, the reason his stories could possibly be understood to contain Christian themes was simply that as a Christian his writing was subconsciously informed by his Catholic view of God and the world. His death was deeply mourned by those who had grown to love the world of Middle Earth that he had so imaginatively created. The blockbuster success of the recent movie versions of *The Lord of the Rings* (2001–2003) appears to confirm that sometimes the most effective way to communicate spiritual truth is, in the poet Emily Dickinson's phrase, to "tell it slant."

See also Imagination; Lewis, C. S.; Literature and Spirituality.

For Further Reading: H. Carpenter, *J. R. R. Tolkien* (2000); T. A. Shippey, *J. R. R. Tolkien* (2002); idem, *The Road to Middle-Earth* (1982/2003).

David Frees

Tolstoy, Leo (1828–1910)

Pacifistic Russian novelist. Tolstoy was born into landed aristocracy in Yasnaya Polyana, in the Tula province of Russia. Both parents died during his childhood, and he was raised by a series of aunts. After a short stint—and rather lackluster performance—at the Kazan University, Tolstoy served the army in the Caucasus, where he began to write in earnest. His first book, *Childhood*, was an immediate success, and his later works—*War and Peace, Anna Karenina, Resurrection*—remain classics to this day.

Although a member of the Russian Orthodox Church, Tolstoy began to envision a new, "practical" Christianity more in accord with his Deist beliefs. He would later write his own Greek version of the gospel narrative, one that would be divested of its supernatural content. He also formed the cornerstones of Tolstoyism—nonviolence, a respect for all life, and the philosophy of "simplification."

Despite having been born into the elite, Tolstoy envied the simplistic faith he witnessed in the *muzhiks*. Ashamed of the fact that some members of society lived in abundance while others were exploited and impoverished, he rejected his wealth and aristocratic title, choosing instead the lifestyle of a peasant. In accordance with his nonviolent and pacifist beliefs, Tolstoy adopted a vegetarian diet, protested the bearing of arms, and advocated a nonviolent resistance to evil. Influenced by Christ's teachings in the Sermon on the Mount, Tolstoy adamantly believed that selflessness and universal love were the keys to humanity's salvation.

Tolstoy's fervent advocacy of his beliefs came at a cost. At the end of the 19th century, the Russian government regarded him as anarchic, and in 1901 the Russian Orthodox Church excommunicated him. However, his nonviolent philosophies had far-reaching effects, impacting the ideologies of Gandhi and Martin Luther King Jr.

See also Literature and Spirituality; Russian Spirituality.

For Further Reading: M. Muggeridge, *A Third Testament* (1976).

Sarah G. Scorgie

Tournier, Paul (1898–1986)

Swiss physician who eclectically integrated medical, psychiatric, and biblical wisdom in the healing of persons. Traumatized early in life through losing both parents by age six, Tournier found evangelical faith, wholeness, and a lengthy career in helping people encounter Jesus as part of their healing process. He was reared in the Swiss Reformed tradition and made an intellectual commitment to Jesus at age twelve when he also determined to practice medicine. In 1932 he began an association with Frank Buchman and the Oxford Group, which was key to his personal and professional transformation. He began daily meditation, sought detailed guidance from God, joined in group confession and moral encouragement, and began to see changes in his own life and in others. By 1937 this led to his professional decision to practice medicine a new way. He developed a view of "medicine of the person" that moved beyond technical medical knowledge to incorporate psychiatric and biblical insights on human beings, facilitated by careful attention to the complex interpersonal relationship between patient and physician. In this context he lived out his own version of holistic spirituality. He wrote two somewhat programmatic books: *Meaning of Persons* (1957) and *Healing of Persons* (1965) while other writings communicated spiritual wisdom on many life issues. Conservative evangelicals were unhappy with his views on hell and universal salvation, but even critics praised his joyful and gracious integration of biblical faith and science in serving others.

See also Counseling; Health and Healing; Oxford Group.

For Further Reading: G. Collins, *The Christian Psychology of Paul Tournier* (1973); J. Cox et al., eds., *Medicine of the Person* (2007); M. Peaston, *Personal Living: An Introduction to Paul Tournier* (1972).

Richard F. Kantzer

Tozer, A(iden) W(ilson) (1897–1963)

Conservative evangelical mystic. Tozer was a self-educated American who began his working life in an Akron, Ohio, rubber factory. Converted in 1915, he joined the Alliance, a Holiness denomination that became his lifelong church home. His first pastorate was in 1919; others followed, leading him eventually to Chicago's South Side (1928–1959) and Toronto, Canada (1959–1963). Temperamentally reclusive and poetic, Tozer was drawn to the writings of fourteenth- and fifteenth-century Christian mystics and seventeenth-century Quietists. He absorbed their visions and then, with a uniquely engaging style—half Jeremiah, half Mark Twain—passed along his discovered insights to countless appreciative fundamentalists and emerging evangelicals. He spoke reprovingly to a religious community that had become, in his judgment, largely disconnected from the authentic presence of God.

Two of Tozer's works, *The Pursuit of God* (1948) and *The Knowledge of the Holy* (1961), remain classics. Most of his writing consisted of clipped, pungent editorials for the *Alliance Witness*. He had three volumes of these reprinted, a practice perpetuated by later compilers and extended to his sermons. He also wrote *The Divine Conquest* (1950) and assembled *The Christian Book of Mystical Verse* (1963). He rejected both dispensationalism and what he regarded as Pentecostal emotional excess. For him the goal of life was the quiet, adoring contemplation of God's glory. This was an experience that evoked reverence and stimulated the transformation of the gazing soul.

American fundamentalism was always an awkward home for Tozer, though he shared its negative estimate of reason's sufficiency and its disposition toward detachment. He offered little guidance on spiritual formation practices or Christian vocation in the world, believing that "if our hearts keep right," such things will take care of themselves. His legacy was to reconnect conservative evangelicals with larger, ecumenical streams of Christian spirituality and to prod Biblicists to seek the God who dwells beyond the sacred page.

For Further Reading: L. Dorsett, *A Passion for God: The Spiritual Journey of A. W. Tozer* (2008); D. Fant Jr., *A. W. Tozer* (1964).

Glen G. Scorgie

Traditions, Major Christian

See **Chapter 19.**

Traherne, Thomas

See **Caroline Poets.**

Transcendentalism, American

American Transcendentalism is a literary and philosophical movement whose most significant writers are Ralph Waldo Emerson (1803–1882), Nathaniel Hawthorne (1804–1864), Henry David Thoreau (1817–1862), and Walt Whitman (1819–1892). The transcendentalists, initially centered in Concord, Massachusetts, bear monumental influences on modern American literature, politics, and religion. Akin to the Romantics in the British literary tradition, they privileged and sought the empowerment of the individual over the institutional in the social order: they replaced orthodox theological beliefs with concepts of transcendence emanating from the discovery of the self and its innate imaginative and spiritual possibilities.

Emerson posited the theoretical framework of transcendentalism in his essays and poetry; Thoreau diarized his personal embrace of its tenets; Whitman created the aesthetic expression of its private and public dimensions in his poems, especially in *Leaves of Grass* (1855); and Hawthorne immortalized its fictional heroes. With others, they articulated an idealism that propagated ideas and ideologies of the rights of the individual and the scrutiny of institutions that has been prized in American society since the gaining of its independence and the rise of its nationalism.

The influence of the transcendentalist writers, who also included Margaret Fuller, Elizabeth Peabody, Bronson Alcott, and other influential members of society, arose in apprentice friendships formed in the confluence of the economic, religious, and political turmoil of a new republic attendant to the American Revolutionary War and the testing of its human rights in the precipitation of the American Civil War. Transcendentalism has persisting value in articulating the American aspiration to "life, liberty and the pursuit of happiness" and in the seeking of an egalitarian social order.

The transcendentalists, although as diverse as any social movement, proposed various amalgamations of deism and Calvinism, positing a "unity of life in the metaphysical Absolute" (Emerson, "Nature"). They embraced all life as an expression of innate moral laws that impelled the individual to discover God as a creative intelligence in the universe, Christ as the highest demonstration of human potential, and the Holy Spirit as a pulsating life force in the cosmos. They can be interpreted to have perceived God as a unity rather than a trinity, constructing a paradigm in which God's immanence and human sacredness were made equivalent, intuition was privileged over reason as the guide to truth, and multiple sacred texts were made equivalent to Scripture. Although more erudite and deeply connected to the strong intellectual traditions of Greek thought and Western civilization, transcendentalism, in many ways, was the precursor to the New Age thought of today. It has also influenced the sometimes strongly individualistic practices of evangelicalism and the privileging of personal experience and preference over scriptural authority that is at the root of many schisms in present-day Christendom.

See also Nature Mysticism.

For Further Reading: P. Gura, *American Transcendentalism* (2007); B. Packer, *The Transcendentalists* (2007); A. Porterfield, *The Protestant Experience in America* (2006).

Lynn R. Szabo

Transcendental Meditation (TM)

Transcendental Meditation is a technique developed by Maharishi Mahesh Yogi (1918–2008), a follower of Swami Brahmananda Saraswati Maharaj, which the yogi introduced to the United States in 1959. It is a technique adapted from one of the *moksha* (paths to salvation) in Hinduism; specifically, from the *jnana marga*, the way of illuminated knowledge.

The Maharishi University of Management, located in Fairfield, Iowa, is the international center of TM. The university claims that TM is based on ancient Vedic traditions. An official statement reads, "Maharishi Mahesh Yogi—the representative in our age of the Vedic tradition—introduced the Transcendental Meditation technique to the world, restoring the knowledge and experience of higher states of consciousness."

It is suggested that TM be practiced twice a day, for about twenty minutes each time. An individual is given a Sanskrit word or phrase from the Upanishads, the sacred texts of Hinduism. He or she is to meditate on this phrase or word, which enables the person mystically to get in touch with the "transcendental consciousness." This transcendental consciousness is the same as the Upanishadic concept of ultimate reality, that is, Brahman. According to Maharishi Mahesh Yogi, TM is consistent with the Hindu motto *Aham Brahman tat tavam*—that is, "I am Brahman, the ultimate reality, and so are you." The transcendent Brahman is true reality; individuals are not. Through the technique of TM, individuals can realize oneness with the transcendental consciousness, the universal principle. An individual gains this incrementally through *TM-Sidhi*, or yogic flying, wherein a person has a series of out-of-body experiences until he or she finally merges with the transcendental principle—the ultimate goal of TM.

See also Hindu Spirituality.

R. Boaz Johnson

Transfiguration

Early Christian interpreters such as Irenaeus (*Against Heresies*) and Tertullian (*Against Praxeas*; *Against Marcion*) link the synoptic account of the transfiguration with Exodus 33: a more perfect vision of God than was available to Moses and Elijah on Mount Sinai was granted to them at the transfiguration, when they beheld the face of God (i.e., the Son, for Tertullian) in full glory. Evidently, Mount Tabor "fulfills the ancient promise" (Irenaeus) only on the assumption that Christ is the very one who summoned Moses and Elijah on Horeb/Sinai. Indeed, says Tertullian, it is the Son of God who "was visible before the days of his flesh" and "appeared to the prophets and the patriarchs, as also to Moses indeed himself." Linking the transfiguration account and the biblical visions on Sinai was crucially important for early Christians: it underlay their appropriation of the Scriptures of Israel as "Old Testament"; it highlighted the divine identity of Jesus Christ; and it lent itself to polemical use against the dualism of Marcion and against monarchianism. This exegesis of the transfiguration, also briefly mentioned by Origen in his commentary on the gospel of Matthew, was followed by Pseudo-Ephrem of Syria, Leo of Rome, and John of Damascus, and was eventually absorbed into Byzantine festal hymnography, thereby gaining wide acceptance in Byzantine theology.

Origen seems to have inaugurated a different strand of interpretation, epitomized by Augustine in the Latin tradition and by Pseudo-Dionysius and Maximus the Confessor in the Greek East. This approach uses the transfiguration account as a springboard for spiritual rumination by pondering the theological and spiritual significance of the details of the account. Thus, Tabor can be interpreted in a christological key (it reveals to the disciples the divinity of Jesus, so that they would later understand the majesty of the Crucified One); it sets forth the model, the icon, of what Christians are called to become here and now; it offers a sketch of the resurrection glory at the eschaton, when matter will be transfigured by the indwelling of God; and it maps out the spiritual journey of scriptural exegesis (the exegete being called to discern the glory of God in the various layers of Scripture). Byzantine monasticism consecrated Tabor as the fiery heart of

Orthodox theology by interpreting the Taboric light as a supersensual manifestation of God and by singling out the apostles' experience on Mount Tabor as the goal of ascetical and visionary practices.

For Further Reading: A. Andreopoulos, *Metamorphosis: The Transfiguration in Byzantine Theology and Iconography* (2005); B. Bucur, "Sinai, Zion, and Tabor," *Journal of Theological Interpretation* 4, no. 4 (2010): 33–52; J. E. Fossum, "*Partes Posteriores Dei*: The 'Transfiguration' of Jesus in the Acts of John," in J. Fossum, *The Image of the Invisible God: Essays on the Influence of Jewish Mysticism on Early Christology* (1995), 95–108; J. A. McGuckin, *The Transfiguration of Christ in Scripture and Tradition* (1986).

Bogdan G. Bucur

Transformation

See **Chapter 31.**

Trappists

Trappists, the customary name for the Order of Cistercians of the Strict Observance, the most radical cloistered order in Roman Catholic monasticism (and also found in female orders as Trappistines), can be traced to their foundation at La Trappe, France, in 1664. The order is rooted in the Christian orthodoxy of the desert fathers; the Rule of Benedict that guides the monastic life of work, prayer, and study; and the initial reforms of Abbot de Rancé (1626–1700) and later those based on the writings of Bernard of Clairvaux. Its vows are obedience, stability, and the conversion of manners that include poverty and chastity. Cistercians elect primarily to a contemplative life of silence, desiring to remain ever-present to God in order to receive and respond to the transforming work of the Holy Spirit in their lives. They commonly gather for prayer seven times daily, during which they sing, pray, and recite the Psalms. Architectural creativity, agricultural innovation, and erudite literature distinguish the work of many Cistercians, along with musical and liturgical excellence. The most famous North American Trappist abbey is Our Lady of Gethsemani near Louisville, Kentucky, where Thomas Merton, renowned American spiritual writer, made his vocation. It receives as many as five thousand retreatants annually, who come for prayer and private spiritual direction. Many Protestants, particularly evangelicals, are skeptical of a lifestyle that is so rigid in its demands and that is lived away from society, but the Cistercians do not presume to be a model for Christianity at large; rather, they are a demonstration of the extremities of penitence and sanctification to which God is free to call some of his people.

See also Cistercian Spirituality; Merton, Thomas.

For Further Reading: C. Lawrence, *Medieval Monasticism* (1984); T. Merton, *The Waters of Siloe* (1949); M. B. Pennington, ed., *The Cistercian Spirit* (1970).

Lynn R. Szabo

Trueblood, D(avid) Elton (1900–1994)

Quaker educator, theologian, philosopher, and adviser to presidents. Trueblood, whose Quaker ancestors had come to America in 1682, was born into an Iowa Quaker farming community. Educationally, he moved from this agrarian setting to William Penn College (Iowa) and on to Johns Hopkins and Harvard universities. Trueblood's Quaker heart was always evident during his years as chaplain at Harvard and Stanford and later as teacher of philosophy at Earlham College, a small Quaker College in Richmond, Indiana. That Quaker heart also was evidenced as he served as friend and adviser to U.S. presidents Hoover, Eisenhower, Nixon, and others. Trueblood used that tiny Earlham stage to speak to a nation and world about cultural problems and about how ordinary human beings might make meaning in their lives. His Quaker, Christ-centered faith had wide ecumenical appeal. Trueblood was a prolific writer, producing thirty-three books. His initial book, *The Essence of Spiritual Religion* (1936), began more than a half-century of public religious influence, rivaled only by the likes of his friend Billy Graham. Trueblood spoke to the war generation with *The Predicament of Modern Man* (1944). Arguably, his most famous work was a biography, *Abraham Lincoln* (1973). Trueblood brought what his biographer, James Newby, calls "rational evangelicalism" to countless people seeking to make Christianity speak to their condition in life. His dual emphasis on "the clear mind and the warm heart" made sense to Christians seeking deeper meaning. It was also an invitational message to those seeking alternative meaning to a consumer culture.

See also Quaker Spirituality.

For Further Reading: J. Newby, *Elton Trueblood* (1990).

Alan Kolp

Truth, Sojourner (1795–1883)

Evangelist, abolitionist, and suffragist. Sojourner Truth was born into slavery in 1797 in Ulster County, New York, and named Isabella Baumfree. Although she had received very little religious instruction, Isabella had a vision of Jesus, who became her great (and sometimes only) friend and intercessor.

Isabella was emancipated when New York State outlawed slavery in 1827. She then moved to New York City and worked as a domestic in several religious communes. In 1843, in response to another vision, Isabella changed her name to Sojourner Truth and traveled throughout the eastern seaboard preaching "God's truth and plan for salvation."

Sojourner later met and worked with abolitionists like William Lloyd Garrison and Frederick Douglas, and also became an ardent defender of women's rights. One of her most famous speeches was given at the Akron, Ohio, Women's Rights Conference in 1851. A number of men had been speaking against women's rights, some arguing that women were too delicate to assume such rights. This was too much for Sojourner, who pointed out that she had never been helped into a carriage but had worked hard in the fields. She had also seen most of her children sold off into slavery and asked, "When I cried out with my mother's grief, none but Jesus heard me! And ain't I a woman?"

During the Civil War, Sojourner carried donations of food to African-American soldiers. In the 1860s, she rode Washington, D.C., streetcars and argued that they should be desegregated. She spoke before Congress and two U.S. presidents. Her strong sense of God's calling gave her a confidence rare in any woman of her day, much less an uneducated woman born into slavery. As a woman who conversed with God, no man, whatever his earthly standing, could intimidate her.

See also African-American Christian Sprituality; Feminist Spirituality; Social Justice.

For Further Reading: C. Makee, *Sojourner Truth* (1993); R. Ruether and R. Keller, eds., *Women and Religion in America*, vol. 1 (1980).

Sharon Gallagher

Tutu, Desmond (1931 –)

Social justice activist and archbishop. Though Desmond Tutu is best known as a Nobel Peace Prize laureate (1984), his publications indicate a deep interest in the spiritual life. Many of his books are collections of sermons and prayers. It was his devotional life that sustained his very stressful and arduous campaign to end the apartheid system in South Africa. When Tutu was a young man, Trevor Huddleston, an English missionary opponent of apartheid, influenced him decisively. He became an Anglican priest, bishop, and later general secretary of the South African Council of Churches, and in these roles counseled nonviolent resistance. Finally, he became the Anglican primate, the archbishop of Cape Town. After the defeat of apartheid and the election of Nelson Mandela as president of South Africa, he advocated and then directed the Truth and Reconciliation Commission, a bold and controversial attempt to bring healing between black and white South Africans.

Tutu's *African Prayer Book* is a collection of short addresses to God from the African context, both Christian and pre-Christian. Some are his own composition, expressing compassion in situations of heavy suffering. All of them look to God for the strength to solve problems too large for any human being alone. *No Future without Forgiveness* contains reflections on the necessity of releasing the past in the light of God's forgiveness in Christ.

Tutu's spirituality can be characterized by the words *justice*, *mercy*, *passion*, and *humor*. Spirituality is not just an interior attitude for him, but an outer manifestation as well. Many of his years were spent calling for justice for oppressed people in his homeland and offering leadership for the split Christian community. Later he advocated mercy for people who had committed murder, torture, and other serious crimes, when they confessed their evil deeds. He is obviously a person who feels deeply about the Christian gospel and the need to preach it when "truth speaks to power." But through it all he has maintained a lively sense of humor. His humanity shines through his tears and laughter. His writings include *God Has a Dream* (2004), *Hope and Suffering* (1984), *The Rainbow People of God* (1994), and *The Words of Desmond Tutu* (1989).

See also African Christian Spirituality; Forgiveness; Reconciliation; Social Justice.

For Further Reading: J. Allen, *Desmond Tutu* (2006).

Bradley P. Holt

Twelve-Step Programs

The term usually refers to programs designed to address addictions and recovery. Pioneered by the cofounders of Alcoholics Anonymous, Bill Wilson and Dr. Bob Smith, Twelve-Step programs are based on a simple but ultimately revolutionary discovery: the recovering sick can heal the sick. In other words, a deep and profound therapeutic power can be found in people helping others who are similarly afflicted.

From Alcoholics Anonymous has come more than two hundred "fellowships" involving millions of people worldwide. These fellowships or meetings address not only alcoholism but a wide range of addictive behavior and human need. Often referred to as "self-help organizations," they are more accurately described as "mutual-help movements." Their power lies in how people find health through the help of others (often called "sponsors") similarly afflicted. They are movements because of their consistent avoidance of bureaucratic and organizational structures and their reliance on common principles to guide local meetings.

At the heart of Twelve-Step programs is the recognition that the fundamental problem is a spiritual illness — self-centeredness. The beginning of the Twelve-Step process involves individuals' recognition that they are powerless over their addiction and they need to turn their lives over to a Higher Power. Steps 4 and 5 require individuals to do a moral inventory of people and institutions they have harmed, and to confess those deeds to another human being. Steps 6 through 11 involve asking God to remove their shortcomings, making amends to those they have harmed, and keeping a continuing moral inventory. The goal is "a spiritual awakening" (Step 12) that involves a new and profound reorientation of individuals and their relationships to themselves, other people, and God (or "a Higher Power"), as well as a commitment to help others who are similarly afflicted.

Twelve-Step programs are similar to the basic patterns of Christianity and other major world religions in emphasizing that physical health is intimately related to, if not dependent on, spiritual health. The founders of Alcoholics Anonymous were deeply influenced by the Christianity of the Oxford Group and the Episcopal priest Samuel Shoemaker, as well as other religious movements of the 19th and 20th centuries that emphasized the relationship between spiritual and physical health. The cycle of "hitting bottom" and finding new life and meaning mirrors the religious model of repentance and rebirth. And yet Twelve-Step movements not only embrace a wide diversity of beliefs and faiths of religious institutions and organizations, but also consistently emphasize that they teach "a spiritual program." If people do not grasp the spirituality of the Twelve Steps, these movements declare, they miss the heart of the program.

See also Addictions and Recovery; Oxford Group.

For Further Reading: *Alcoholics Anonymous* (2001); E. Kurtz and K. Ketcham, *The Spirituality of Imperfection* (1992); *Twelve Steps and Twelve Traditions* (2002).

John M. Mulder

U

Unceasing Prayer

The Christian form of unceasing prayer may have been preceded by the psalmist David, who wrote, "I have set the LORD always before me" (Ps. 16:8). The apostle Paul encouraged believers in Thessalonica to "pray continually" (1 Thess. 5:17). This specific instruction may well have been intended in earlier Scriptures referring to continual prayer, such as Luke 18:1; 21:36; Acts 1:14; and Ephesians 6:18.

Around the 4th or 5th century, a tradition of "pure prayer," "prayer of the heart," or "Jesus prayer" was established. With its origin most likely in the Egyptian desert, which was settled by the monastic desert fathers and mothers in the 5th century, the prayer was defined as a short, formulaic prayer often uttered repeatedly. The earliest known mention is in *On Spiritual Knowledge and Discrimination* of St. Diadochos of Photiki (400–c. 486), a work found in the first volume of the *Philokalia*. John Climacus, in his *Ladder of Divine Ascent*, summarized the process: "The beginning of prayer is to banish oncoming thoughts as soon as they appear."

In later church history, the Celtic people believed that God was with them every moment of the day, so they used short prayers to communicate with God as they performed their chores. One Celtic writer explained, "They were the prayers of a people who are so busy from dawn to dusk, from dark to dark, that they have little time for long, formal prayers. Instead, throughout the day they do whatever has to be done carefully, giving it their full attention, yet at the same time making it the occasion for prayer."

Various forms of unceasing prayer have been used through the centuries, but the simplest is connected with breathing: breathing in Jesus as the gift of God's life, then breathing out Jesus as an offering back to God of the gift of life. Others attempted to synchronize the words "Lord Jesus Christ, Son of God, have mercy upon me, a sinner" with their heartbeat. Even today, this is an official prayer of Orthodox believers.

Contemporary writers such as Richard Foster see a more organized approach to unceasing prayer. The first step is outward discipline, followed by a move to the subconscious mind, then movement into the heart, and finally the permeation of one's whole personality with prayer. A more recent method of unceasing prayer is prayer walking. It takes one out of the head bowed and eyes closed repetition of familiar prayer phrases and locates the person where all five senses are operative while listening in an ongoing way to the promptings of the Holy Spirit.

Unceasing prayer, then, as defined in the NT, supported by the early church fathers, expanded in Orthodox literature, and adapted by current writers, is a significant aid to personal worship.

See also Brother Lawrence; Presence of God.

For Further Reading: Brother Lawrence, *The Practice of the Presence of God* (many editions); D. Crawford and C. Miller, *Prayer Walking* (2003); D. Farrington, *Unceasing Prayer* (2002); R. Foster, Prayer (1992).

Dan R. Crawford

Underhill, Evelyn (1875–1941)

Anglo-Catholic writer and mystic. Evelyn Underhill was a well-known early twentieth-century leader in the field of spiritual formation. She conducted retreats and offered spiritual direction to countless individuals during her decades-long ministry. Born in Wolverhampton, England, she was the only child of Alice and Sir Arthur Underhill, her father a wealthy barrister and yachtsman. Underhill grew up in a cultured world of high social status and often traveled abroad to visit art and architectural wonders of France and Italy.

In her early thirties, she married Hubert Moore, who, like her father, was a barrister and yachtsman. They had no children, but they doted on their cats and shared many common interests — though not spirituality. Before she was married, Underhill had written poetry and novels that broached spiritual topics and reflected her own growing interest in mysticism, influenced largely by her mentor Baron Friedrich von Hugel. In *The Lost Word* and *The Column of Dust* (1909), the heroine's experiences paralleled her own: "She had seen, abruptly, the insecurity of those defenses which protect our illusions and ward off the horrors of truth. She had found a little hole in the wall of appearances; and peeping through, had caught a glimpse of that seething pot of spiritual forces whence, now and then, a bubble rises to the surface of things."

An agnostic as a young adult, Underhill's love for art had drawn her toward Catholicism, and she eventually converted to Christianity despite her husband's objections. Then in 1921, in her midforties, she joined the Anglican Church. Her writings had a mystical bent with a significant focus on the Holy Spirit and contemplative prayer.

As a laywoman with no institutional or organizational ties, Underhill had a profound influence on Anglican spirituality during the early decades of the 20th century. Indeed, she was the most widely publicized female writer in the field of religion in that era. In addition to writing some thirty books (including her classics *Worship* and *Mysticism*), she frequently wrote religious pieces for the *Spectator*. She was acclaimed in academia — awarded an honorary doctorate from the University of Aberdeen, named a Fellow of King's College, and invited by Oxford University (as the first woman ever) to deliver lectures, later published as *The Life of the Spirit and the Life of Today* (1949).

See also Anglican Spirituality; Von Hügel, Friedrich.

For Further Reading: M. Cropper, *The Life of Evelyn Underhill* (2002); E. Underhill, *Radiance: A Spiritual Memoir*, ed. B. Bangley (2004).

Ruth A. Tucker

Union with God

Union with God describes the kind of relationship we can have with God through Jesus Christ. Christianity is founded on the principle that God made all things good and that he himself is the ultimate good. Boethius perceived that there is a yearning in each person to unite with what is good. The doctrine of union with God speaks to this innate human longing.

The fundamental biblical idea of God is that God is "one" (Deut. 6:4–5). "Oneness" means that Deity is not only "one in essence," but also "absolutely unique" among all beings. Therefore, nothing can compare with God, who alone is worthy of our complete longing and love. To love anything else so completely is to unite one's being with idols. The prophet Hosea chose the radical analogy of sexual union to describe the way the human soul unites with either God or idols. To love God is to be united to him in an intimate way that is analogous to the union of husband and wife. This is natural, because we are made in God's image; like is especially drawn to like. To love idols is equivalent to adultery—a "mixing" that is contrary to human nature. This is destructive, because we become what we love. Israel "followed worthless idols and became worthless themselves" (Jer. 2:5). In his *The Ascent of Mount Carmel*, the Spanish mystic John of the Cross noted that "love effects a likeness between the lover and the loved." The great command to love God is therefore essential to the completion, or perfection, of human personhood. It unites us to God, and from this union God's image in us is magnified.

In the NT, union with God is directly linked to the incarnation: Jesus, out of love for the Father and for humanity, united Deity to humanity in his flesh (Rom. 8:3). This opens up the door to unprecedented possibilities such as articulated by Maximus the Confessor and recorded in the *Philokalia*: "He becomes truly man so that by grace He may make us gods." According to Paul, every Christian is by definition "in Christ" through a faith encounter with Jesus. This means that everything that is true about Christ—his righteousness, his death and resurrection—is shared with each individual Christian and the church as a whole

(Rom. 6:1–11; 8:9–11; Eph. 1:3–14; 2:19–22). The practical outcome of this is that "God has poured out his love into our hearts by the Holy Spirit" (Rom. 5:5) so that we joyfully discover that we are empowered to live the great commandment to love God, which in our own power we could only fail to do.

Union is not only descriptive of all Christians, but also a process. The paradox is that we must become what we are (Eph. 5:1) and grow in understanding of what our union means. To this end Paul prays that "the eyes of your heart may be enlightened" (Eph. 1:18) and that we "may have the power to comprehend" our true position in Christ, which is too wonderful for words (Eph. 3:14–21 NRSV). Biblically, not only do we become what we love, but also, we become what we see. As Moses beheld the glory of God and was glorified with a glory that faded, Christians behold the glory of the Lord in Christ and are changed into his likeness with ever-increasing glory (2 Cor. 3:18, cf. 1 John 3:2). The apostle John uses the metaphor to "abide" in Christ as a description of this same union and process (John 15; 1 John 2:24–28), and those who "abide" share in the Trinitarian union that the Father, Son, and Holy Spirit enjoy (John 17:20–26). This is high theology indeed, but it is a reality extended to all and must not be dismissed because of its incomprehensibility. The Flemish mystic Ruysbroeck discerned that "all good [people] experience this; but *how* it is, this remains hidden from them all their life long if they do not become inward and empty of all creatures."

Though Christian mystics have used radical language to describe this experience of union, such as "annihilation of soul," "deification," "theosis," and "perfection," it is critical that these terms are not to be understood in a scientific sense. These words are suggestive, hinting about a transcendental state of being that is beyond words. Distinction is assumed between the individual and Deity. Union is not understood as an absorption into the divine and/or a loss of individuality, but rather as a realization of self and personhood distinct from God, though wholly penetrated by God. By way of illustration, John of the Cross uses the analogy of a glass in the light of the sun: a clean glass is not seen, though a dirty one is. The glass, though unseen, is still a separate entity from the sun, just as the person is distinct from God but participates in God's divine light.

In the Protestant world, the doctrine of justification by grace through faith has tended to eclipse the doctrine of union. Our judicial standing before God is critical, but it must be seen in the context of the whole order of salvation, of which union, along with glorification, is the great end. Without a goal, we become aimless. Grace not only justifies, but also invites and motivates the soul to the greatest of all human endeavors, union with God through Jesus Christ.

Some Protestants, however, have made the union theme central to their spiritual aspirations. Calvin founded his *Institutes* on it, albeit focused on the positional character rather than its transformative nature. Conversely, John Wesley taught the transformative potential of union as a radical "entire sanctification," an idea that fueled the Holiness movement and subsequent offshoots, such as the Keswick Conventions. The doctrine of union with God in Christ is very high and mystical, and it is inevitable that interpretations and experiences of it will vary. Be this as it may, meditation on this greatest of Christian themes has the unifying potential of drawing searchers into the vast riches of two thousand years of Christian spirituality, both East and West.

See also Formation, Spiritual; Marriage, Spiritual; Threefold Way.

For Further Reading: Boethius, *The Consolation of Philosophy*, trans. V. Watts (1969); O. Clement, *The Roots of Christian Mysticism*, trans. T. Berkeley (1993); R. Garrigou-Lagrange, *The Three Stages of the Interior Life*, 2 vols., trans. M. T. Doyle (1947); Gregory of Nyssa, *From Glory to Glory*, trans. H. Musurillo (1979); L. Smedes, *Union with Christ* (1983); J. van Ruysbroeck, *The Adornment of the Spiritual Marriage*, trans. C. Wynschenk (1916).

John E. Worgul

Unitarian Spirituality

Unitarianism is one of the unintended consequences of the Reformation. Luther and Calvin opened the door of protest against Rome, and within a generation, the earliest Unitarians followed suit on other matters. The formative leaders were Faustus Socinus (1539–1604) in Poland, Ferenc Dávid (1510–1579) in Transylvania, and John Biddle (1615–1662) in England. Unitarianism is now known chiefly through its American incarnation and its famous exponents, including William Ellery Channing (1780–1842) and Ralph Waldo Emerson (1803–1882).

Though Unitarians espouse no creed, common views emerge across the centuries, chiefly, of course, stress on the unity of God and the consequent denial of the Trinity. The divinity of Jesus is either denied or held in muted form. Human depravity is rejected along with affirmation of the Bible as the infallible Word of God. Over time Unitarian spirituality has broadened to include appreciation for Hinduism and Buddhism. This is in keeping with early trends toward universalism, though Unitarians can also be agnostic about life after death and even atheistic.

Worship in Unitarianism usually follows the patterns of Protestant worship, particularly its Reformed branch. Sermons are common, and Christian hymns are often used though the wording is altered where necessary to adapt to Unitarian ideals. An annual Water Communion is a popular alternative to the sacraments. The Unitarian emphasis on covenant and community is held alongside deep commitment to the individual and to the powerless. Unitarians have a deep sense of social justice, a trait shown by early struggles for abolition of slavery and the rights of women. Ultimately Unitarian spirituality is about the celebration of the human and the quest for goodness.

For Further Reading: R. Miller, *The Larger Hope*, vol. 1 (1979), vol. 2 (1986); W. Ross, *The Premise and the Promise* (2001); E. M. Wilbur, *A History of Unitarianism* (1945).

James A. Beverley

Urban Spirituality

The world is now well over 50 percent urban and continues its rapid march to the city. Yet the antiurban bias found deep in the history of the United States continues to find expression in many approaches to spiritual formation, reflected in the pastoral scenes found on the covers of much devotional literature. Despite this antiurban bias and discussions of the secular city, vibrant faith can be found in cities. African-American churches have thrived in urban areas, as have Roman Catholic churches, which have served successive waves of immigrants. In many poorer areas of the city, storefront Pentecostal churches create a lively presence. Immigrant churches reach out to their own as they arrive.

Urban spirituality can refer either to the spirituality of the people dwelling in cities or to the spirituality of the place called the city. Spirituality in and of the city challenges the assumption that the life of faith can be lived out in private, focused only upward in a relationship to God. Urban spirituality raises the question of what sustains people of faith in the context of urban life. Contemplative practices of attentiveness, the Jesus Prayer, and the Ignatian practice of "finding God in all things" enhance the life of the Spirit in the city. Some, like Carlo Carretto, have compared the urban context to the desert as the place of growth and transformation. Others have highlighted the need for spirituality as a foundation for an active life committed to social change.

Urban spirituality is also the spirituality of the place called a city. The built environment of a city demonstrates what is valued in that place. Spaces can be built to include or exclude. Cities are public places that challenge an exclusively private, interior understanding of life with God. Christian faith, especially in its evangelical expressions, has historically favored private worlds over public spaces. The city faces us with public spaces, places of difference and diversity. As the spiritual practice of everyday life is lived out, both friend and stranger are encountered in the heart of the city.

See also Geography, Spiritual; Marketplace Spirituality.

For Further Reading: C. Carretto, *The Desert in the City* (1970); H. Conn, *The American City and the Evangelical Church* (1994); J. Kotkin, *The City* (2008); H. Neumark, *Breathing Space: A Spiritual Journey in the South Bronx* (2002); P. Sheldrake, *Spaces for the Sacred* (2001).

Judith Tiersma-Watson

V

Vanier, Jean (1928 –)

Advocate for the disabled and marginalized. Vanier was born in Geneva, Switzerland, where his father was serving as a diplomat. Despite its privileged status, his family was humble, committed to justice, and devout. During World War II, Vanier had dreams of heroism and voiced his wish to enter the Royal Naval College. As Vanier narrates in *Our Life Together* (2008), his father's response was "I trust you." Though Jean was only thirteen, this experience of being trusted shaped his lifelong conviction that trust is necessary for any form of inclusion. Vanier left military life in 1950 in search of a different path to peace, one closer to "the roots."

Vanier's mother introduced him to Père Thomas Philippe, a Dominican who later became his spiritual father. After completing a Ph.D. dissertation in 1962 on Aristotle's *Ethics*, he taught briefly, but "the roots" continued to elude him, although he did discover a gift for proclaiming Jesus. He then moved to Trosly-Breuil, France, to join Père Thomas, who was living with thirty handicapped adults.

In 1964 Vanier purchased a home nearby and invited two handicapped men who were living in a squalid institution to live with him as family. Thus began L'Arche communities for disabled adults, which now number well over a hundred worldwide. Vanier founded L'Arche with the intention of doing good to the disabled, but, as he explains in *Drawn into the Mystery of Jesus* (2004), they were actually the ones blessing him—by reflecting the vulnerability, compassion, and tenderness of God. The L'Arche vision espouses poverty but not destitution and stresses the value of pilgrimage, celebration, and play as means of restoring joy and strengthening relationships.

Through his speaking engagements and numerous books, which also include *Becoming Human* (1998) and *Living Gently in a Violent World* (2008), Vanier persistently brings to light the deep pain that underlies violence, and proclaims that gentleness, not retaliation, is the only way to peace.

See also Disability.

For Further Reading: K. Spink, *The Miracle, the Message, the Story* (2006).

Diane S. George Ayer

Vatican II (1962–1965)

This most recent ecumenical council of the Roman Catholic Church was convened by Pope John XXIII and carried through by his successor, Pope Paul VI. It significantly shaped Catholic spirituality by giving greater emphasis to the ministry of the laity and by signaling its desire for more open communication with non-Catholic Christians, adherents of other religions, and the larger world. Additionally, the church emphasized its desire to engage in the problems facing the world, laying the groundwork for the explosion of liberation movements in Latin America.

The interpretation of the church's historical claim of *extra ecclesiam nulla salus* (there is no salvation outside the church) changed significantly at the council. While prior relations between Catholics and Protestants had been largely antagonistic, the council now referred to Protestants as "separated brethren" rather than those outside the church. Further, the council spoke of the possibility of non-Christians being "anonymous Christians," arguing that those who through no fault of their own had never heard the gospel might yet seek God to the best of their ability and attain salvation through Christ. Further, whatever goodness or truth existed among atheists could serve as preparation for the gospel.

Gaudium et Spes (Pastoral Constitution on the Church in the Modern World), one of the best-known council documents, opens with this declaration: "The joys and the hopes, the griefs and the anxieties of the men of this age, especially those who are poor or in any way afflicted, these too are the joys and hopes, the griefs and anxieties of the followers of Christ." It asserted the importance of the church's engagement with the challenges facing the world; in the context of the 1960s, it specifically condemned racism and nuclear proliferation.

Vatican II also instituted a number of liturgical reforms and significantly shifted the Catholic understanding of the church. Previously the church had been viewed as comprised chiefly of the hierarchy of clergy and the various religious orders. Now the council referred to the church as the whole "pilgrim people of God" and called for an increased role for the laity. Additionally, the council called for a significant revision of the liturgy and for offering it in the languages of the people.

Vatican II has led to a number of developments in Roman Catholic spirituality. Moral theology, at the center of the training of priests for hearing confessions, shifted from the use of manuals to using Scripture. Additionally, liturgical reforms resulted in greater lay participation in singing hymns (previously sung mostly by choirs) and by more often taking the Eucharist in both kinds (previously, the laity was usually offered the bread alone).

The shift in attitude toward other Christians also led to greater conversations between Catholics and Protestants in the area of Christian life and practice. One of the most significant examples of this is the growth of the Catholic charismatic renewal in the post–Vatican II period. Another example is the increase in Bible study groups in local Catholic parishes in the United States.

The decisions of Vatican II and subsequent efforts to implement them have not been uniformly received in all Catholic circles. A number of small groups either broke with the Roman Catholic Church or remained within the church while rejecting the authority of this particular council. Still other people remained in the church who agreed in principle with most of the decisions made but disputed the ways its decisions about liturgy were applied — particularly in the areas of church architecture, music used in the Mass, and the structure of the liturgy. Further, the reforms and directives of the council have not been uniformly interpreted and applied by the popes since John XXIII. Despite these disagreements surrounding Vatican II, it was the most momentous council to take place since the Council of Trent and arguably among the most significant ever.

See also John XXIII.

For Further Reading: A. Flannery, gen. ed., *Vatican Council II*, 3 vols. (1975 – 1996).

Mary M. Veeneman

Vaughan, Henry

See Caroline Poets.

Vegetarianism

Christians in increasing numbers have come to believe that one's food choices have spiritual ramifications, leading many Christians to choose vegetarianism as an expression of their Christian commitment. The reasons to eat vegetarian are rooted in good stewardship of our bodies and our planet, a desire to help alleviate worldwide hunger and poverty, and ethical concern for the welfare of animals. Our food choices have social, economic, political, and personal consequences, making vegetarianism one way to live out the Christian calling to be light and salt in the world.

A number of authors, including Young, Kaufman, and Braun, have investigated the topic of vegetarianism throughout the Bible, concluding that the Bible neither condemns meat eating nor requires vegetarianism. However, the relationship between food choices and one's spirituality does have a long tradition in Judeo-Christian faith. Examples include Daniel and his companions' refusal to eat the meat and delicacies of King Nebuchadnezzar's court, as well as the early Christian desert fathers who advocated simple lifestyles and abstention from meat, rich foods, and gluttony as means to promote one's spirituality. In his book *The Bloodless Revolution* (2006), T. Stuart chronicles the history of vegetarianism from 1600 to modern times, noting how over the years many Christians have made a connection between vegetarianism and their spirituality. Contemporary Christians tend to choose vegetarianism as one way to express tangibly their commitment to biblical principles of good stewardship of their bodies and the earth God has given humans to dwell on, concern for the impact of one's lifestyle and consumption patterns on others in the world who are hungry and living in poverty, and compassion for animals.

Numerous researchers and authors have alerted the public to the clear health benefits of eating a plant-based diet, based on decades of worldwide research. Cultures that eat fewer animal products and more plant foods enjoy significantly lower rates of obesity, cancer, heart disease, diabetes, and age-related health problems. Christians recognize that our bodies are a gift from God and we have a responsibility to care for our bodies as a way of honoring God, the Creator and giver of life. Vegetarianism promotes the health of our bodies, which Scripture tells us are "the temple of the Lord."

Meat consumption is known to contribute to worldwide poverty and hunger, because scarce food, water, and fossil fuel resources are channeled into meat production. It is estimated that 100 million people could be adequately fed if Americans reduced their meat intake by just 10 percent. Furthermore, meat consumption contributes to environmental deterioration as rain forests are demolished to produce more meat, and chemical and animal waste runoff from factory farms creates pollution that threatens water and air quality. Christians view vegetarianism as a spiritual response to these global issues.

Additionally, many Christians choose vegetarianism out of love for animals and a desire not to harm them. Abstaining from meat is a way to oppose the cruel and inhumane treatment of factory-farmed animals. Thus, vegetarianism is one way for Christians to care for their bodies, the earth, and the people and animals on earth—all of which honors God and God's creation.

See also Ecological Spirituality.

For Further Reading: T. C. Campbell, *The China Study* (2004); S. Kaufman and N. Braun, *Good News for All Creation* (2004); M. Scully, *Dominion* (2002); A. Spalde and P. Strindlund, *Every Creature a Word of God* (2008), R. A. Young, *Is God a Vegetarian?* (1999).

Myrla Seibold

Via Negativa, Via Positiva

See **Apophatic and Kataphatic Ways.**

Vianney, Jean-Baptiste Marie (1786–1859)

French Roman Catholic priest known principally for his pastoral intensity. Vianney did not have particular success as a student, lived through the difficult war years in France, and finally became a parish priest in the village of Ars. It was here that Vianney, known as the "Curé of Ars," saw that the French Revolution and Napoleonic wars had resulted in deep religious ignorance among the French population. Vianney set out to revive interest in Catholic devotion in the town with powerful appeals for spiritual renewal. Yet even more than his presence as celebrant and preacher, Vianney's pastoral presence was felt through conversations in the confessional. Finally, his own devout priestly asceticism, especially his almost constant investment in prayer, preaching, or sacraments, was well known among his contemporaries.

Soon Vianney's sermons, pastoral counsel, and devotion to Roman Catholic ritual bore fruit, motivating many to more intense spiritual commitment. A veritable revival began, allowing Vianney's reputation to become international. Historians note that the town received more than ten thousand pilgrims per year in the 1850s and, incredibly, that Vianney would regularly spend more than fifteen hours a day in the confessional in this last decade of his life. Several volumes of his sermons and remarks were collected and published posthumously.

See also Care of Souls.

For Further Reading: John XXIII, *Sacerdotii nostri primoridia* (1959); G. Rutler, *The Curé d'Ars Today* (1988); *The Sermons of the Curé of Ars*, trans. U. Morrissy (1960).

Jason Zuidema

Victorine Spirituality

This twelfth-century movement of monastic spirituality brought together the mystical traditions in monasticism with the practices of scholarship emerging in the schools of Paris. It is most notably associated with the writings of Hugh (c. 1096–1141) and Richard (c. 1123–1173), who were Augustinian canons in the Abbey of St. Victor in Paris. Founded by William of Champeaux in the early years of the twelfth century, the abbey soon attracted international attention and new recruits in the likes of Hugh (possibly Flemish, but probably a Saxon) and Richard (a Scot).

In Western Christianity, the twelfth century was important as a time of presentation and explanation of the inherited mystical and theological traditions. Although not alone in this systematization, the Victorines were one of the most significant movements. Both Hugh and Richard evidenced a spiritual fervor with deep contemplation that was closely tied to intellectual ardor. Indeed, it is the interrelationship of what might previously have been distinguished — scholarship, mystical experience, liturgy, ethics, among others — that was central to their spiritual vision. Scholarship, in particular, was not necessarily antispiritual but could be a critical part of a life of deep devotion. These themes are reflected in such extant writings as Hugh's philosophical *The Didascalion* and Richard's *The Twelve Patriarchs*, *The Mystical Ark*, and *Book Three of the Trinity*. Hugh's devotion is seen especially in his *On the Sacraments of the Christian Faith* (c. 1134). The work treats the sacraments, as the title promises, but it also invites readers to meditate on and ultimately contemplate all the important moments in the history of salvation.

A key theological influence in both thinkers was Augustine, but also Gregory the Great and certain Neoplatonists, who they felt best modeled this contemplative-intellectual way of life. The Victorines were appreciated by later monastics, particularly the Franciscans, but also by certain Reformers who noted their attachments to Scripture (and their valuation of its plain, historical sense) and Augustinian theology.

See also Holistic Spirituality.

For Further Reading: S. Chase, *Contemplation and Compassion* (2003); M. Girolimon, "Hugh of St. Victor's De sacramentis Christianae fidei," *Jour-nal of Religious History* 18, no. 2 (1994): 127 – 38; *Hugh of Saint-Victor: Selected Spiritual Writings* (1962); R. Petry, ed., *Late Medieval Mysticism* (1957); P. Rorem, *Hugh of Saint Victor* (2009); I. van't Spijker, *Fictions of the Inner Life* (2004).

Jason Zuidema

Vincent de Paul (c. 1580 – 1660)

Roman Catholic priest who put particular emphasis on serving the poor. Serving as both parish priest and chaplain to the nobility, Vincent is noted for having founded the Congregation of the Mission and cofounded the Daughters of Charity with Louise de Marillac. Affected particularly by the state of galley convicts, Vincent noted that they were in both spiritual and physical misery. Hence, to serve them spiritually, he also needed to serve them physically. He based his understanding on the common bearing of the divine image and sharing in the grace of God. Showing mercy to others reflected thankfulness that Christians ought to have for the mercy shown to them by God.

Following Vincent's death, the Congregation of the Mission, whose members are known as Vincentians or Lazarites, continued his work, emphasizing the religious instruction of the lower classes and the training of clergy. In the 19th and 20th centuries, Vincent's goals also inspired the Society of Saint Vincent de Paul, founded in 1833 by Frédéric Ozanam (1813 – 1853) and others, which shares Vincent's goal of serving the poor and less fortunate. Today the Society collects and redistributes goods to fund projects and practice wise stewardship of possessions.

See also French (School of) Spirituality; Poverty.

For Further Reading: P. Coste, ed., *The Life and Works of Saint Vincent de Paul* (1987); K. Moran, ed., *Saint Vincent de Paul* (1960); B. Pujo, *Vincent de Paul, the Trailblazer* (2003); *Vincent de Paul and Louise de Marillac*, CWS (1995).

Jason Zuidema

Violence

Wars, revolutions, human rights violations, and other social phenomena have generated many definitions for "violence." For our purposes, violence is "destruction to a victim by means that overpower the victim's consent." The NT contains several passages that address violence directly. Among the key texts are the teachings of Jesus in the Sermon on the Mount (Matt. 5–7; especially 5:38–48) and the exhortations of Peter (1 Peter 2:21–23). The theme of enduring violence rather than inflicting it runs prominently through the NT and is present in the Gospels and Epistles as well as in Acts and Revelation. Paul's reflections in Romans 12–13 on the roles of love and state responsibility have served as a sharp point of debate on the question of violence. Nevertheless, the pervasive call to imitate the cross-bearing Christ is central to the NT description of what it means to live all of life in obedience to God. The NT portrays a holistic spirituality that elevates sacrificial love above overpowering force.

Approaches to violence historically have been drawn along the lines of Christian pacifism (the rejection of violence in obedience to and imitation of God) and just war (the limited use of violence toward just ends). While there is evidence of Christians being soldiers from about AD 170, for the first three centuries no Christian writer expressed approval of Christian participation in state-sanctioned violence. Many early Christian writers, including Clement of Alexandria, Justin Martyr, Tertullian, Hippolytus, Cyprian, Lactantius, Origen, and Arnobius, provide arguments, derived from the NT, against violence.

Following the institution of Christianity as the official religion of the Roman Empire in the early 4th century, the question of Christian participation in military defense of the state became especially significant. Seeking to reconcile the Christian vocation to love with the forceful defense of justice, Augustine drew from Roman politics to formulate criteria for determining the legitimacy of violence. Augustine distinguished the personal calling of Christians to reject violence from the collective responsibility to defend justice. His set of criteria, later labeled the "just war theory," included legitimate civil authority, necessity to punish crime or uphold peace, and good intention. Similarly concerned with reconciling love for God and defense of justice, Thomas Aquinas added to these criteria several that determined not only the legitimacy of employing violence (*jus ad bellum*) but also the proper conduct within warfare (*jus in bello*).

In the Protestant Reformation, Martin Luther continued to draw the distinction between the duty of the state and the personal duty of the Christian, which he articulated in terms of two kingdoms in which believers participate faithfully. According to Luther, belonging to the kingdom of God does not exempt one from responsibility as a citizen of the kingdom of the world and the various vocations (soldier, magistrate, etc.) it demands. Likewise, John Calvin considered violence justifiable if the underlying intent is to love one's neighbor by protecting the common good.

Like the other Reformers, the early Anabaptists regarded Scripture as the origin and guide for theology and practice. But they insisted that following Jesus demands cross-bearing that makes the kingdom of God present in the lives of believers. On their view, violence is incompatible with both the example and exhortations of Jesus. The experience of God's grace empowers believers to resist the urge to make the world right through the use of violence. Further, because Jesus' rejection of violence derives not from a rule or principle but from his very nature, the use of violence is idolatrous. When we engage in violence, we reject Christ, cutting ourselves off from his life-giving Spirit and from his in-breaking kingdom.

Modern Christian pacifism emphasizes not only the call to obedience in rejecting violence, but also the effectiveness of nonviolent direct action in confronting injustice. Martin Luther King Jr. and the U.S. civil rights movement serve as a powerful example of effective nonviolent action grounded in

Christian spirituality that rejects violence out of love for the adversary. Violence within or between individuals, families, communities, and nations disrupts the life that God created humans to enjoy. For King and for his mentor Howard Thurman, nonviolent enemy love is the only way God heals both the rifts within the human community and the spiritual break between God and those who bear God's image. They emphasized that hatred is destructive both to the hater and to the hated; Jesus offers an alternative in the form of loving enemies in the way that God does.

Perpetrating violence can impact spirituality in several ways. Those involved in organized killing in war usually require extensive training and desensitization to cultivate their ultimate obedience to military authority. Some soldiers lose their faith; some are forced to set it aside for a time as they justify actions that they deem incompatible with following Jesus. Many veterans experience post-traumatic stress disorder for years after service, facing the psychological, emotional, and relational wounds of war in the form of guilt, depression, isolation, and substance abuse. Soldiers report the addictive and dehumanizing nature of violence that manifests itself in other areas of their lives. A high suicide rate exists among those who have engaged in the violence of war.

Stanley Hauerwas argues that our spiritual formation as nonviolent followers of Jesus must occur within a community. We learn in relationship with one another how to form habits that characterize all that we do, not simply our political stance on issues like war and capital punishment. This communal spiritual formation requires humility, as we recognize in each of us the capacity for cruelty, selfishness, and the drive to control one another. As our character is shaped in Christian community, we learn how to submit every area of our lives to the lordship of Christ.

The historical realities of religious and political wars, the Crusades, and the Holocaust, as well as ongoing violent conflicts, demand a faithful response. Recognizing a practical stalemate between the arguments for pacifism and just war, the theory of just peacemaking seeks to implement practices that prevent violent conflict and create peace. Regardless of their positions on the use of violence, all Christians can respond in obedience to Jesus' call to be peacemakers in a world in desperate need of transformation.

See also Cross, Experience of the; Love; Holy War; Peacemaking.

For Further Reading: L. Cahill, *Love Your Enemies* (1994); R. Clouse, ed., *War: Four Christian Views* (1991); M. L. King Jr., *A Testament of Hope*, ed. J. Washington (1986); G. Stassen, ed., *Just Peacemaking* (2008); J. H. Yoder, *The War of the Lamb* (2009).

Peter M. Sensenig

Virtue

Jesus said, "Blessed are the pure in heart, for they will see God" (Matt. 5:8). Virtue is an essential part of Christian spirituality because God is holy. Loving God and our neighbor requires virtue, not only so that we become holy as God is holy, but also because we are not holy and need humility, courage, and wisdom to approach God "just as I am, without one plea."

"Virtue" originally meant power or excellence (Gr. *arēte*) in achieving good ends. Virtue is determined by what end (*telos*) is desired. The virtue of a judge lies in her or his wisdom to assess the evidence in relation to the law and make a just judgment. Different people need different virtues at different times. Soldiers need courage, loyalty, and obedience; parents need gentleness, patience, and consistency. Spirituality is a virtue oriented to cultivating love of God.

"Virtue" (singular) means moral excellence or overall goodness of character, as in "a virtuous person." Specific qualities of moral character are referred to as "virtues." They are not particular acts, decisions, or rules regarding what is right and wrong, but rather settled dispositions of character that abide in a person. Some suggest that all the virtues are connected and that lack in one of the virtues will have a negative impact on all the others. For example, courage needs patience and patience needs wisdom, which needs gentleness, which needs honesty, which needs courage, and so on. Without love, all the virtues lose their potency (1 Cor. 13).

Plato argued that the most important virtues — that is, the cardinal virtues — were courage (fortitude), temperance (self-control), wisdom (prudence), and justice. Aristotle suggested a long list of virtues required by a Greek gentleman, including courage, self-control, generosity, magnificence, high-mindedness, gentleness, friendliness, truthfulness, wittiness, justice, and appropriate levels of ambition. Different cultures cultivate different sets of virtues, related to their material conditions, traditions, and stories. For example, heroic cultures, facing the threat of annihilation, valued courage above all other virtues. Countries of great diversity, like Indonesia, highly value gentleness, harmony, and cooperation.

Aristotle suggested that virtue was always the mean between two extremes. The mean is not the midpoint, but rather the proper balance between excess and deficiency, depending on individual circumstances. For example, the virtue of patience is neither too hasty nor too passive. A patient person has the virtue to know when to wait and when to act. Similarly, an honest person knows when to divulge information and when to keep silent. The right balance between frankness and reticence is determined by discernment of the proper ends of the communication. Virtues are always connected to ends.

If virtues are defined as the character traits needed to act appropriately (neither too much nor too little) to reach a good end, then there is no limit to the number of virtues. Some virtues may not even have a name. For example, the virtue needed to pass a course may include the right balance between the ability to concentrate on studies and the ability to take time off and relax. Such a virtue has no name in English.

In the Bible, there are many lists of virtues. The most famous is the "fruit of the Spirit": love, joy, peace, patience, kindness, goodness, faithfulness, gentleness, and self-control (Gal. 5:22–23). More powerful than any list are the many stories in both the Old and New Testaments that show how the virtues, or their lack, work out in the real lives of people. The obedience of Abraham, the hospitality of Rebekah, the humility of Moses, the honesty of David, the wisdom of Solomon, the faithfulness of Hosea, the courage of Jeremiah, the loyalty of Ruth, the endurance of Job, the boldness of Esther, the meekness of Mary, the sincerity of Peter, the love of Jesus, and the temperance of Paul are shown in stories of real human struggle and conflict. Above all, the life, suffering, and resurrection of Jesus tell an unparalleled story of the virtues, as displayed in a single person. For Christians, the virtues displayed in Jesus' life provide a compelling picture of what it means to be truly human.

Many writers have distinguished between the classical four cardinal virtues and the theological virtues of Christian life; namely, faith, hope, and love. Some, following Augustine, suggest that the classical virtues may be vices in disguise in that their hidden agenda is not the glory of God, but rather human glory. If so, then true spirituality consists in renouncing human, egocentric virtues, no matter how noble they appear, in favor of the virtues that come as a gift of God, through grace. In this view, virtue is totally a matter of grace and not the "excellence" or power that comes through human effort and conditioning. The heart and essence of all true virtue is to love God and your neighbor.

Thomas Aquinas synthesized Aristotle and Augustine, suggesting that the cardinal virtues are natural means of fulfilling human potential, while theological virtues are infused by God and totally by grace. Aquinas believed that grace is not in conflict with nature, but rather above it. The theological virtues are higher than natural virtues, but both are gifts of God.

Some evangelicals renounce the virtues as inconsistent with grace and a temptation to human pride. Others see virtue as a critical means of moving past the dichotomy between faith (motivation) and works (action) to a more fruitful emphasis on the human person who experiences spiritual transformation both by the Spirit of God and by obedience to God's will. All the virtues are learned by daily practice. All need the grace of God to prevent distortion. The distinction between cardinal and theological virtues disappears if all are seen as grounded in human potential but needing the grace of God to be realized in sinful human life. All of the virtues are grounded, ordered, and integrated in the Great Commandment.

See also Sins, Seven Deadly.

For Further Reading: B. Adeney, *Strange Virtues* (1995); Aristotle, *Nicomachean Ethics* (many editions); J. Crossin, *What Are They Saying about Virtue?* (1985); S. Hauerwas, *A Community of Character* (1981); A. MacIntyre, *After Virtue* (1984); J. Porter, "Virtue," in *Oxford Handbook of Theological Ethics*, ed. G. Meilaender and W. Werpehowski (2005).

Bernard Adeney-Risakotta

Vision of God

"Blessed are the pure in heart, for they will see God" (Matt. 5:8 NRSV). Can anyone see God and live? This is the question raised by the concept of the vision of God (*visio Dei*), known in Roman Catholic theology as the "beatific vision." On the one hand, Luther, referring to Moses' encounter with Yahweh in Exodus 33, affirmed that no one may see the face of God and live, and that at most, we have seen God's backside. On the other hand, scholastic theologians such as Thomas Aquinas

and Bonaventure maintained that after death the faithful will be able to see the face of God, and they left open the possibility that some might be given a special grace of "seeing" God in this lifetime, a mystical revelation akin to that implied by Paul in 2 Corinthians 12:2–4.

To discern the options raised by this concept, we must ask, as has been asked through the centuries, what one means by "seeing." Augustine of Hippo was among the early theologians to interpret the biblical passages referring to "seeing" God as "knowing" God, which is coming to a full understanding of who God is. The early fathers who had strong Greek philosophical ties dismissed the idea that God was corporal and could be seen (Plato) and that the face of God was the essence of God, which is perceived by the intellect not the eyes (Aristotle).

For evangelicals who neither limit what God can or cannot do, while not presuming what humanity is capable of understanding, sensing, or perceiving of God, a helpful resource is the work of Nicholas of Cusa titled *The Vision of God* (1453). Nicholas was a theologian and bishop who hoped to synthesize the various strains of medieval theology, both East and West, specifically the Augustinian and Pseudo-Dionysian traditions. Nicholas wrote this text for a Benedictine community and sent with the text an icon known as the *Omnivoyant*, or a face that appeared to be looking in every direction at once. This volume is a series of mediations that is rooted in the fact that God is able to see all things, and that it is only though God's grace that we are able to see (literally and figuratively) anything. Because we are seen, we are able to see. Because God is also omnipresent, we are able to see the presence of God in creation, a reflection of the divine image. Ultimately God, who was incarnate in Christ, allows us, through the ministry of the Holy Spirit, to see the presence of God in Scripture and the world, which will come fully into focus in our eternal state (1 Cor. 13:12). Nicholas's work offers a middle way between the rejection of the possibility of seeing God and the insistence that it must happen, and frames it as a spiritual practice.

See also Cappadocians.

For Further Reading: M. McIntosh, *Mystical Theology* (1998); Nicholas of Cusa, *The Vision of God*, intro. E. Underhill (1960).

Todd E. Johnson

Vocation

God calls people into every sphere and sector of society. Christian spirituality affirms that this calling is inherent in creation—Adam and Eve were given work to do; and work is a vital element of God's redemptive purposes for each person. Thus, vocation is not something supplemental or secondary to Christian spirituality. Spirituality is not merely a matter of prayer and the interior life—though it surely includes these; rather, it is about the whole of a person's life, lived in Christian community, in response to the call of Christ and in the power of the Spirit.

The Christian's fundamental calling, of course, is to be a follower of Christ. But it is helpful to appreciate that each individual, while living in community, can respond personally to the specific way in which Christ is calling him or her to live out a Christian identity in the world. And this "calling" or vocation is fulfilled as an integral dimension of one's spiritual life.

In speaking of the place of "vocation" in Christian spirituality, certain biblical principles apply. First, to speak of vocation is to affirm that work is good and that work is given to each person as a gift, as part of what it means to be created in the image of God. Just as God is a "worker," those created in the image of God are given meaningful work to do. Work, then, is part of the creation and thus necessarily part of the redemptive purposes of God.

Second, to speak of vocation is to recognize that the church cannot prioritize or assume that one kind of work is superior to, or more "sacred" than, another. While we recognize that work can be destructive and that some forms of engagement with the world are not redeemable (e.g., casino management), the Christian spiritual tradition recognizes the potential sacredness of all forms of human endeavor—business and commerce, the arts and education, work in the marketplace and work in the home. The particular challenge for many Christians has been to recognize and insist that religious or pastoral work is not inherently more sacred; and just as critical is the affirmation that manual work is to be equally valued and appreciated as so-called knowledge work. With this view and passion for vocation, then, the church becomes not so much the repository of people engaged in religious activities as a community of empowerment—equipping women and men, through teaching, prayer, mutual encouragement, and admonition, to fulfill their God-given vocations in the world.

Third, the language of vocation reflects a recognition that ultimately what is done is done not so much as an act of personal fulfillment or accomplishment, though it may well be this for some, as it is a response to the benevolent authority of Christ. The Christian acts in intentional response to the "call" of Christ." Christ is Lord; however satisfying one's work, in the end, whether it be in the garden or in the pulpit, in the classroom or in the studio, the Christian does this work at this time in response to the particular call of God. Consequently, the Christian accepts that the way may be difficult and marked with suffering, for as Christ's vocation took him to the cross, even so the Christian is called to bear the cross of Christ.

In addition to these fundamental assumptions, Christian spirituality has been enriched by a number of interdisciplinary conversations and perspectives on vocation, work, and career. Adult development theorists have highlighted the reality that young people and those in midlife and those in their senior years wrestle with the matter of vocational identity differently. Young people typically wrestle with matters of differentiation, those in midlife with accepting the limits of their time and talent, and those in their senior years with what it means to fulfill vocation by blessing the generation that follows.

Then also, one of the crucial elements of what Eugene Petersen has aptly called "vocational holiness" is that the Christian learns what it means to observe a Sabbath — to rest from one's work, to set it aside, for the work ultimately belongs to God, and to live not for one's work, but as a child of God in joyful embrace of God's providential goodness. Sabbath is an essential spiritual practice by which the Christian affirms that we live by God's provision and not by the work of our hands, that we live in trust and not fear, and that our work is ultimately God's and not ours. We undercut any propensity to treat work as a "god."

Therefore, one's work or vocation is not merely an expression of one's spirituality; it is also the essential context in which a Christian lives out his or her faith; it becomes the furnace where, as Christians, we grow in faith, develop patience, learn to serve with generosity and joy; it is that sphere of our lives where we learn what it means to embrace responsibility but also to let it go and allow others to pick up the baton. It is also, crucially, where we learn our limitations, for we cannot be all things to all people.

See also Call to the Ministry; Laypersons and Spirituality; Ordination; Service; Vows.

For Further Reading: J. Fowler, *Becoming Adult, Becoming Christian* (1984); P. Palmer, *The Active Life* (1990); E. Petersen, *Under the Unpredictable Plant* (1994); W. Placher, *Callings* (2005); D. J. Schuurman, *Vocation* (2004); G. Smith, *Courage and Calling* (1999).

Gordon T. Smith

Von Hügel, Friedrich (1852–1925)

Self-educated lay philosopher of religion and writer on Christian mysticism. He was the son of an Austrian diplomat and a Scottish mother who converted to Catholicism; after relocating to England, he was afflicted with typhus, which left him frail and nearly deaf. Financially independent, he devoted himself to writing, lecturing, and providing spiritual direction. An influential Catholic thinker, he dialogued with prominent bishops, scholars, professors, and theologians across Europe. His major work, *The Mystical Element of Religion* (1908), represents the fruit of a ten-year study of Catherine of Genoa, the fifteenth-century Italian noblewoman.

A broad-minded Catholic, von Hügel enjoyed cordial relations with Christians of other denominations. Jesus Christ, as the one who liberates from sin's bondage, occupied the supreme place in his thinking. Preferring Catholicism by virtue of its world-denying asceticism, strong mystical emphasis, and contemplative spirituality, he nevertheless believed that God's grace was operative in other Christian communions. He lobbied for creative change in the Roman Church, particularly in the areas of intellectual freedom and dissent.

He maintained in *The Mystical Element of Religion* that a mature spirituality should unite three foci: the institutional church with its beliefs, practices, and morality; mystical experience as direct apprehension of God through the Spirit; and critical thought reflected in great literature, history, and philosophy, both secular and sacred. In 1920 he was awarded a doctor of divinity degree from Oxford University, the first Catholic to be so honored since the 16th century. The inscription on his tomb is taken from Psalm 73: "Whom have I in heaven but Thee?"

See also Catherine of Genoa; Underhill, Evelyn.

For Further Reading: G. Greene, ed., *Letters from Baron von Hügel to a Niece* (1928); D. Johns, *Mysticism and Ethics in Friedrich von Hügel* (2004); E. Leonard, *Creative Tension: The Spiritual Legacy of Friedrich von Hügel* (1997); F. von Hügel, *Selected Letters* (1927).

Bruce A. Demarest

Vows

A vow is a promise, a giving of oneself to God, a cause, or another person. Though motives and reasons for vows vary, the making and fulfilling of them are directly related to one's character and standing before God and humanity. In the Bible, vows are a way of life. They affirm a paradoxical truth about human nature; though the will is weak and fundamentally unstable, it is nevertheless able, with the help of God, to fulfill promises made through the solemn declaration of a vow. Vows shape a person's life (Ps. 61:8) and, when made to God, become a joyful act of worship.

Leviticus, Israel's book of worship, illustrates the importance of vows. Sacrifice is at the core of worship, and the first seven chapters describe the sacrifices necessary for every Israelite to worship. The book concludes with voluntary acts of worship by special vows that go above and beyond what is required (chap. 27). Persons may be vowed as well as animals, houses, or lands. The Nazirite vow is an example of how one might separate oneself in a particular way to God for a specific time: refraining from products of the vine, shaving the head, and touching the dead (Num. 6). Hannah vowed to God her firstborn, Samuel, whose entire life seems to have been dedicated to God by this vow (1 Sam. 1:11). Her pure-hearted vow contrasts with Jephthah's vow that brought disaster upon himself, his daughter, and the nation (Judg. 11). Rash vows should not be made, but once made, should never be carried through (e.g., Matt. 14:7). Leviticus 27 makes provision for those who find that they cannot keep their vows.

There is nothing in the NT indicating that vows should not be a part of Christian worship.

Jesus' admonition in Matthew 5:33–37 is not against vows per se, but specifically addresses those who wish to confirm the verity of their word by extravagant oaths. Paul himself made a vow that seems to be a form of the Nazirite vow (Acts 18:18; 21:23). The earliest Christians vowed property as an act of worship (Acts 4:37). That this was taken seriously is evident by the swift judgment on Ananias and Sapphira, who must have vowed the land before the congregation, only to keep back some of the profit (Acts 5:1–11).

Men and women throughout church history have been inspired by Christ's words even to vow their chastity (Matt. 19:12), wealth (Luke 18:22), and positions of honor (Luke 14:7) as generous acts of worship. These three are called the evangelical counsels and are foundational to the ascetical spirituality that flowered into monasticism. It is this association with Catholicism that has set the Protestant world, by and large, against such vows, along with a deep distrust of human nature and its ability to keep vows. However, Calvin acknowledges a place for vows in the spiritual life. Vows bring stability to an otherwise unstable world and are an essential part of human integrity. We cannot live at our best without vows; they help bind us to the high ideals to which God has called us.

See also Covenant; Monasticism.

For Further Reading: J. Calvin, *Institutes of the Christian Religion*, 4.13; A. Vermeersch, "Vows," in *CE*.

John E. Worgul

W

Waiting

Waiting is a fundamental posture of the spiritual life. "Wait for the LORD," the psalmist exhorted; "be strong and take heart and wait for the LORD" (Ps. 27:14). Indeed, the Bible is filled with waiting. The patriarchs and matriarchs of Genesis waited for the promised plan of redemption to begin. The Israelites waited for release from slavery, for the Promised Land, for return from exile, and for the coming Messiah. Once the Messiah had lived, died, risen, and ascended, the disciples waited for the coming of the Spirit. The church, ever since, has been working and worshiping through the centuries, always anticipating Christ's return. To signify this, the first season of the church year is Advent, a time when believers await the celebration of Jesus' birth at Christmas, but also long together for the culmination of all things, when Christ will come again "to judge the living and the dead."

Long arcs of waiting characterize the human experience of God's plan in history, but waiting is also a strong theme in individuals' experiences of God. The Psalms contain frequent prayers for deliverance and expressions of patience, words that believers through the ages have repeated in times of waiting. Paul spoke of groaning inwardly as we "wait eagerly for our adoption," and he described hope as a matter of waiting patiently for what we do not see (Rom. 8:23, 25). One of the fruits of the Spirit is patience (Gal. 5:22).

When describing the experience of waiting, spiritual writers frequently affirm two biblical strains: waiting in desire, which is often compared to the waiting of the bride for her bridegroom; and waiting in suffering, which is often associated with an experience of God's absence. Simone Weil wrote eloquently about *hupomenē*, a deeply attentive waiting, which she compared to that of a servant waiting for a master's commands. "Attention animated by desire is the whole foundation of religious practices," she wrote. Another crucial image for spiritual waiting is pregnancy, so that Mary awaiting the birth of Jesus is an especially instructive model.

The most counterintuitive feature of spiritual waiting is the surrender of our human desire to work, try, earn. Instead, we must allow God to act, revealing actions and purposes beyond our perception or comprehension. This is particularly difficult for those living in cultures that prize striving and achievement. In such cultures, waiting may be the foundational aspect of faith most neglected in teaching, worship, and spiritual formation.

See also Chapter 11.

For Further Reading: H. Nouwen, *Reaching Out* (1975); S. Weil, *Waiting for God*, trans. E. Craufurd (1951).

Debra Rienstra

Wang, Ming Dao (1900–1991)

One of the most influential pastors in the history of modern Chinese churches. Born in Beijing, he founded in 1937 an indigenous church called the Christian Tabernacle, which operated primarily on the principles of "self-propagation, self-sufficiency, and self-dependency." Refusing to join the government-manipulated "Three-Self Movement" that took place across China after 1949, he was put in jail from 1955 to 1979. Wang has indeed won the respect of many and is highly regarded as a heroic image of the Chinese churches in the mainland and overseas.

Wang inherited both the essence of fundamentalist theology and the temperament of Chinese gentlemen (*chun-tze*), which implies courage and ethical merit. His teachings stuck strictly to those of the Bible. Christians were not permitted baptism unless they showed signs of true repentance. Good work was always expected prior to the public confirmation of faith. The kingdom of God was to be understood as separate from the kingdom of earth, and Wang believed strongly that the latter kingdom was under the control of Satan. There was no room for compromise between the two. Together Scripture and the Holy Spirit were adequate for making a servant of God. The only calling for Christians was to serve God, not to change society. A Christian must follow the Word of God strictly, especially its moral teachings. Christians should be prepared to pay the price to achieve perfection. For this reason, some scholars regard Wang as a religious moralist.

See also Asian Christian Spirituality; Persecution.

For Further Reading: T. Harvey, *Acquainted with Grief: Wang Mingdao's Stand for the Persecuted Church in China* (2002); W. Lam, *Wong Ming-Tao and the Chinese Church* (1982).

Hing-Kau (Jason) Yeung

War, Holy

See **Holy War.**

Ware, Kallistos (Timothy Richard) (1934 –)

Eastern Orthodox academic, bishop, and monk. Metropolitan Kallistos was born in Bath, England, and raised in the Anglican Church. In 1958, upon completing his studies at Oxford, he was received into the Greek Orthodox Church. Though deeply appreciative of Anglican music, he saw his encounter with Orthodoxy as initiating him into a world that was even more powerful, beautiful, and luminous. Henceforth, he directed his efforts at presenting Orthodoxy to the West. Most influential in this regard are his books *The Orthodox Church* (1963) and *The Orthodox Way* (1979).

Metropolitan Kallistos's academic career at Oxford as lecturer in Eastern Orthodox studies lasted from 1966 until 2001. His foremost academic achievements included research supervision of a generation of Orthodox (and non-Orthodox) scholars, and translation of Orthodox service books (*The Festal Menaion* and *The Lenten Triodion*) and a five-volume edition of the *Philokalia*, a collection of venerable monastic writings. The latter represents his lifelong commitment to ascetic theology and the monastic life.

Metropolitan Kallistos is also a pastor and spiritual father. In 1965 he was ordained deacon and given the name Kallistos. In 1966 he was ordained a priest, took vows as a hieromonk ("priest-monk"),

founded a parish, and served it until 2002. In 1982 he was consecrated titular bishop of Diokleia, and in 2007 was elevated to titular metropolitan of the patriarchal throne of Constantinople. Throughout his career, Metropolitan Kallistos has been active in the ecumenical movement and in efforts to establish an Orthodox communion in England.

For Further Reading: J. Behr et al., eds., *Abba: The Tradition of Orthodoxy in the West: Festschrift for Bishop Kallistos (Ware) of Diokleia* (2003).

Timothy J. Becker

Warfare, Spiritual

Metaphor for believers' conflict with the devil and demonic spirits. The expression is derived from Ephesians 6:12: "For our struggle is not against flesh and blood, but against the rulers, against the authorities, against the powers of this dark world and against the spiritual forces of evil in the heavenly realms." Accordingly, spiritual warfare is not a particular kind of prayer or ministry, but a way of viewing life that takes into account the reality and hostility of unseen spiritual forces.

The Bible affirms that demonic spirits exist and that they oppose God and his redemptive purposes. Satan, the leader of a vast number of evil spirits, was present at the very beginning of creation when he enticed the first couple to disobey an explicit command from God (Gen. 3). From that point forward, the people of God have struggled with demonic opposition. Evil spirits continue to tempt people to defy God, but they also deceive, inspire false belief systems, cause physical illness and emotional instability, and engage in other activities designed to disrupt and counter the good work of God.

This conflict with the kingdom of evil was a major focal point in Jesus' earthly ministry. In fact, the apostle John summarized what Jesus came to do as "to destroy the devil's work" (1 John 3:8). Immediately after the Holy Spirit came upon Jesus in his baptism, Jesus endured severe temptation by the devil (Matt. 4:1–11; Mark 1:12–13; Luke 4:1–13). Whereas Adam and Eve succumbed, Jesus was able to resist by the power of the Spirit. Throughout his ministry, Jesus encountered people who were profoundly affected by the presence of evil spirits. On each occasion, Jesus successfully drove out the tormenting spirits. Jesus attributed his ability to perform these deliverances not to his power as God incarnate, but to the empowering presence of the Holy Spirit in his life. He said, "If I drive out demons by the Spirit of God, then the kingdom of God has come upon you" (Matt. 12:28; Luke 11:20). His exorcisms were thus a sign of the kingdom's presence and also a model for future disciples on how to rely on the Holy Spirit's power to defeat the enemy when faced with intense manifestations of demonic power.

Jesus portrayed the mission of the church in terms of spiritual warfare. He said, "No one can enter a strong man's house and carry off his possessions unless he first ties up the strong man. Then he can rob his house" (Mark 3:27). The task of taking the good news of the gospel to a lost world (Matt. 28:19–20) was made possible by what Jesus did with respect to Satan. The cross represents a historic defeat for the devil and his spirits. The apostle Paul explained that Christ, "having disarmed the powers and authorities ... made a public spectacle of them, triumphing over them by the cross" (Col. 2:15). Although Satan's forces are still active and powerful, they have been severely limited in their ability to stop the church in its redemptive mission. All who are "in Christ" also share in Jesus' power and authority. Nevertheless, believers will continue to face great opposition until Jesus returns to deal the final blow to Satan and his realm.

Satan and demons are not the only form of spiritual opposition Christians face. Believers also face "the flesh" and "the world." When the apostle Paul spoke of "the flesh" (*sarx*; e.g., Gal. 5:19; Rom. 8:5; Eph. 2:3), he was referring to the inner bent to think and do evil—an inclination that is present in every person since the fall. The biblical notion of "the world" (Gr. *kosmos*) takes into account collective human rebellion against God that manifests itself in ungodly cultural trends, ideologies, organizations, philosophies, and various structures. While the world, the flesh, and the devil can be distinguished, it is often practically difficult to separate the three or to attribute a person's problem solely to one form and not the other two. This underlines the importance of a holistic approach to spiritual formation.

Throughout history, Christians have tried various techniques to resist and overcome the influence of demons. Before the Reformation, some Christian leaders thought practices like spitting, vomiting, making the sign of the cross, drinking holy water, saying the *Ave Maria*, and fasting (sometimes thought of as a way of depriving demons from enjoying the sensation of food) might help people suffering from demonic affliction. The Reformers (especially Zwingli and to some degree Luther) were convinced that a great deal of popular superstition had entered the church. They reasserted the importance of reading, hearing, and knowing the Word of God.

In more recent years, there has been a movement within the church to confront the demonic in terms of its influence on institutions, cities, territories, structures, and even whole nations. Practices such as "spiritual mapping" and "strategic-level spiritual warfare" have surfaced that endeavor to cast Satan out of these places and hinder his larger strategy.

As one assesses the merits of popular Christian belief and practices, it is important to realize that Scripture actually has much to say. Nevertheless, it does not provide believers with many details on how to engage the enemy and what practices are acceptable. Much can be learned from Christians who have gone before. It is wisest to emphasize the beliefs and practices that the Scripture emphasizes, to reject those that contradict it, and to be very cautious about advocating traditions and techniques that go beyond it.

Prayer is the principal means of resisting and defeating the work of demons. Jesus illustrated this by his own example, and the apostle Paul also stressed it (Eph. 6:18–20). This is only natural, because prayer represents a dependence on God's power and not one's own. The major blessing of the new covenant is the presence of the Holy Spirit. Consequently, learning to experience a greater closeness to the Spirit and to draw on the power of the Spirit is essential for countering the work of the evil one. Doing this involves engaging in the spiritual disciplines, especially worship, prayer, absorbing the Word of God, and gaining a better understanding of the truth of one's identity in the Lord Jesus Christ.

See also Angels; Devil, Demons, and the Demonic.

For Further Reading: C. Arnold, *3 Crucial Questions about Spiritual Warfare* (1997); L. Johns and J. Kraybill, eds., *Even the Demons Submit* (2006); A. S. Moreau, *Equipped for Battle* (1997); S. Page, *Powers of Evil* (1995).

Clinton E. Arnold

Water

Water is the colorless liquid in rain, rivers, lakes, and seas and is also a significant symbol of life, death, and cleansing in the Bible and in Christian history. Water is mentioned more than four hundred times in the Bible. In the arid climate of the Middle East, water is precious yet also dangerous, because dry land can easily flood.

God split the waters of the Red Sea to allow the Israelites to cross safely, but used those same waters to kill the Israelites' enemies (Ex. 14). God instructed Moses to strike a rock to provide water for the people (Ex. 17). Water cleanses, both physically and spiritually (Ps. 51:7). Streams of water nurture life and fruitfulness (Pss. 1:3; 104:10–13), and God brings water to parched desert lands (Isa. 35:6; 41:18). Water in its flood state causes suffering and death (Ps. 69:2, 15; Hab. 3:10).

Jesus was baptized in the waters of the Jordan River (Matt. 3:13–17). The apostle Paul linked the waters of baptism to both death and life when he wrote that through baptism, Christians participate in Jesus' death to receive new life through Jesus' resurrection (Rom. 6:3–5). Jesus changed water into wine (John 2:1–11), walked on water (Mark 6:47–52), and washed the disciples' feet (John 13:1–11). Jesus had a long discussion with a Samaritan woman about living water (John 4) and later said that rivers of living water will flow from a believer's heart, which the gospel writer equated with the Holy Spirit (John 7:37–39; cf. Isa. 44:3). The Bible ends with a vision of the heavenly city, where the river of the water of life nourishes the tree of life (Rev. 22).

Christians still baptize with water. Some Christians engage in foot washing. Increasingly, Protestants are joining with Roman Catholics and Eastern Orthodox Christians in using holy water or blessed water as a part of rituals of healing and spiritual cleansing. Water remains a powerful symbol of the flow of God's Spirit into the life of believers in Christ.

See also Baptism.

Lynne M. Baab

Watts, Isaac (1674–1748)

Pastor and hymnist. Born into the home of a Dissenting pastor, Isaac Watts was precocious in learning Latin, Greek, and Hebrew very early on. He once complained to his father that the psalmody sung in church was less than interesting. His father challenged Isaac to create lyrics of a higher caliber, to which Isaac responded willingly. He not only improved on the poetic nature of psalmody, but began to express his own faith in poetic form. This extrabiblical expression earned Isaac the title of "father of English hymnody."

Refusing to recant his Dissenting beliefs, Watts turned down an offer of more prestigious education in order to attend a Dissenting academy in

Stoke Newington. After graduation, he continued to write and took a pastorate, the duties of which he performed for almost fifty years. Recurring illnesses forced him to take long breaks from his preaching, but he continued to write. Watts not only wrote poetic literature but was also noted for his authorship and expertise in such disciplines as logic and theology.

The metrical psalms and hymns of Watts have become a standard over time, crossing denominational boundaries. For those who believed in psalm singing only, his hymns were controversial and summarily ignored. But just as David contextualized the Psalms for his time, so Watts did for his. As a result, his poetry reflected the world that he knew and tended to equate eighteenth-century England with the Israel of the Bible.

Watts's psalms and hymns crossed the Atlantic to America and were widely received in Puritan churches. The songs gained unparalleled acceptance on both sides of the Atlantic. In African-American churches, the hymns of "Dr. Watts" were broadly used, since his poetic phraseology lent itself to the lining out style of singing.

"When I Survey the Wondrous Cross," "Alas! And Did My Savior Bleed," "Joy to the World," "Jesus Shall Reign," and "O God, Our Help in Ages Past" are titles of Watts's hymns that demonstrate his central themes of personal devotion to Christ and his kingdom, as well as salvation through the suffering of Christ on the cross.

See also Hymns.

For Further Reading: D. Fountain, *Isaac Watts Remembered* (2003); I. Watts, *Hymns and Spiritual Songs* (1707).

Edwin M. Willmington

at different girls' schools, she gave most of her salary to the trade unions. She chose employment as a factory worker until ill health forced her to quit. She volunteered to fight in the Spanish Civil War in 1936, but her service there was cut short when she was accidentally burned with hot oil. During the time of recuperation, Simone had the first of her mystical encounters with Jesus. When the Germans took over France, she worked for the provisional French government in London. Owing to years of overexertion and a deliberately minimal diet, she died at the age of thirty-four. She wrote her spiritual reflections in letters, notes, and essays. They were collected and published posthumously, and include *Waiting for God* (1951) and *Gravity and Grace* (1952).

Weil regarded her calling as explaining the reality of divine love in the context of the horrific sufferings of the world. In creation God renounces himself so that the world can exist as distinct from God. The world is marked by these expressions of divine love: the absence of God, blind necessity, and human autonomy. The cross where God abandoned himself is the apex of divine love. To experience the love of God, we have to *decreate*, or renounce ourselves. In extreme sufferings, if we do not stop loving even when our souls are stripped bare and dying, we shall come face-to-face with the Crucified One. Other forms of decreation include learning to love the irresistible necessities of the world as beautiful, and learning to love persons without the slightest desire to dominate or benefit from them. For Weil, the root of our separation from God and social oppressions is the quest for power.

See also Suffering.

For Further Reading: M. Vetö, *The Religious Metaphysics of Simone Weil*, trans. J. Dargan (1994).

Kin-Yip Louie

Weil, Simone (1909 – 1943)

Modern mystic who joined suffering to God's presence. All her life, Parisian-born Weil fought against various forms of oppression. As a philosophy teacher

Wesley, Charles (1707 – 1788)

Cofounder (with his brother John) of Methodism. Charles Wesley was an Anglican clergyman and evangelist who became a patriarch of the eighteenth-century Methodist movement, and of the numerous churches that sprung from that root. Born in the Anglican manse of Epworth, England, he was educated at Westminster School (1716–1726) and Christ Church College, Oxford (1726–1735). In 1729 he founded a small group of students, sometimes called the Holy Club, in which spiritual disciplines like prayer, frequent Communion, fasting, alms-giving, prison visitation, and Scripture study were practiced. They also studied Christian classics such as *The Imitation of Christ* by Thomas à Kempis, *Holy Living and Holy Dying* by Jeremy Taylor, *The Life of God in the Soul of Man* by Henry Scougal, and *Christian Perfection* by William Law. These were not only works that the Holy Club read with gusto; they sought to implement the practices enjoined within them. In following the "method" of spiritual formation prescribed by their university with unusual rigor, this group of students earned, as Charles described it in an autobiographical letter, "the harmless nick-name of a Methodist." In embracing these disciplines, the Oxford Methodists believed they were following the pattern that had been laid down for them by the early church and the early church fathers. They believed that holiness (which they sometimes called "Christian Perfection") was the central aim and constitutive feature of Christian life.

After a brief and somewhat unsuccessful missionary stint in Georgia (1736), Charles returned to England an ill and disappointed man. During a serious illness, on May 22, 1738 (two days before John Wesley's more famous conversion), Charles Wesley experienced an evangelical conversion in which he realized and embraced the Reformation doctrine of justification by faith in Christ alone. Two days later, John Wesley had a similar experience, and together the Wesley brothers repudiated their earlier efforts at trying to achieve holiness by their own best efforts, and stressed—instead—that holiness of heart and life was the result of God's justifying grace, which was to be received by faith. So transforming was the infusion of grace into a person's life, that he or she was "born again" and embarked upon a life pilgrimage toward holiness.

Beginning in the summer of 1738, the Wesley brothers began preaching their "new" doctrines of justification by faith alone and holiness. Soon they found themselves excluded from Anglican churches; in response to this development, they began going more directly to the common people through the medium of open-air evangelism. Charles Wesley first preached out of doors on May 29, 1739; almost immediately he became a popular mass evangelist. The Wesleys soon added an itinerant form of ministry to the innovation of field preaching as a way of taking their gospel message to the masses. As they traveled across the British Isles, the Wesleys evangelized and urged people to participate in the Church of England, where they received the sacraments; established Methodist Societies, where gospel preaching was heard; and organized small groups that practiced spiritual disciplines.

Although Charles Wesley was an active and effective evangelist for more than fifty years, he is best known as writer of the Methodist hymns. The Wesleys had been a family of poets, and so it was not unusual for Charles Wesley to express his deepest feelings and heartfelt emotions through the medium of poetry. Two days after his conversion, Charles penned four hymns to celebrate the event, including "And Can It Be?" On the first anniversary of his conversion, he wrote the eighteen verses that would become his most famous hymn, "O for a Thousand Tongues to Sing." Charles had a remarkable ability to see God at work in all facets of human life, and so Charles Wesley penned poems that celebrate ordinary people and events as well as the great Christian holidays. For Christmas he wrote many hymns, including "Hark! the Herald Angels Sing." Our Easter celebrations would be bereft without his "Christ the Lord Is Risen Today."

Charles Wesley wrote no music, though he may have adapted classical and popular tunes to fit Methodist worship; his lyrics were his chief contribution to the Methodist movement. Establishing a discipline that must have amounted to writing one hymn or sacred poem every day during his frantic ministerial life, Wesley composed an estimated nine thousand hymns and sacred poems. Many were published in occasional hymnals, produced by his brother's editorship, over the course of their half-century of ministry together.

Charles Wesley was happily married to Sarah Gwynne in 1749; together they raised three children who lived to adulthood. After 1754 Charles traveled less and began to locate his ministry in the metropolitan centers of Methodism, first in Bristol and then in London after 1771. By this time, his hymns had begun traveling for him. The Wesleyan hymns became the congregational voice of Methodism. No only do they teach basic Bible doctrines and Wesleyan theology, but by using first-order, dramatic language, the hymns engendered the experiences of new birth, conversion, holy love, and inner cleansing that the lyrics spoke of. Methodist hymnbooks, most notably the standard *Collection of Hymns for the People Called Methodists* (1780), became the catechism, prayer book, and sound track for the Methodist experience.

See also Evangelism; Holiness; Methodist Spirituality; Revival; Wesley, John.

For Further Reading: *John and Charles Wesley*, CWS (1981); J. Tyson, *Assist Me to Proclaim: The Life and Hymns of Charles Wesley* (2008).

John Tyson

Wesley, John (1703 – 1791)

Church of England clergyman, leader in the evangelical revival, and a founder of Methodism. Wesley was born in Epworth rectory, Lincolnshire, England, the son of Samuel and Susanna Wesley. From an early age, the children were taught to pray and read Scripture and the *Book of Common Prayer*. Passive obedience and nonresistance to the ruling monarch were elements of the high-church Tory religious-political views that John Wesley adopted from his parents.

Wesley took his bachelor's degree at Christ Church, Oxford (1724). He was elected fellow of Lincoln College (1726) and took his master's degree (1727). Wesley was ordained deacon in the Church of England (1725) and later priest (1728). From 1729 he became a leader of Oxford Methodism, which consisted of several groups of students and townspeople who met for Christian fellowship and to encourage one another in devotional discipline and works of charity. Characteristic devotional practices included regular self-examination and prayer, meditation, devotional reading, fasting, and frequent partaking of Communion. Typical works of charity undertaken were care for the poor, the sick, and prisoners.

Wesley's reading at Oxford was wide-ranging, but with a particular focus on Anglican devotional writers of the 17th and early 18th centuries. Thomas à Kempis, Jeremy Taylor, and William Law were key influences on Wesley's conception and practice of holy living based on grace-enabled purity of intention and singular devotion to God. Wesley was also attracted to the writings of Continental mystics but later reacted particularly against their "quietism" while continuing to draw on their piety. From 1732, he increasingly concentrated his reading on the church fathers and high-church Anglican liturgical works. The high-church/nonjuror tradition, with its stress on restoring primitive Christianity, was dominant through 1737 and remained an influence on Wesley throughout his life. Wesley's high Anglican view of the eucharistic sacrifice and real presence of Christ in the sacrament was strengthened during this period and was later vividly represented in Charles Wesley's hymns.

Wesley served for two years as parish priest of Savannah, Georgia (1736 – 1737), where he implemented what he believed were the liturgical practices of the early church. By the time of his voyage back to England, he was undergoing severe doubts regarding the state of his soul. The Moravian emphasis on the Lutheran doctrine of justification by faith combined with their Pietist emphasis on assurance of salvation influenced Wesley on the way to his "heart-warming experience" on Aldersgate Street on May 24, 1738. Subsequently, Wesley placed an increased stress on the new birth, justification by faith, and assurance, with a continued emphasis on Christian perfection or entire sanctification as the goal of the Christian life, now understood and expressed more clearly as subsequent to justification and solely enabled by God's prevenient grace.

Wesley followed George Whitefield into itinerant open-air preaching, beginning in Bristol and later extending throughout the British Isles. Wesley organized Methodists into societies, bands (smaller groups of earnest Christians), select societies (for those seeking Christian perfection), and later class meetings (divisions of societies into smaller groups) for Christian fellowship with the aim of individual and communal growth in holiness and the renewal of the church from within. Evangelical preaching and hymn singing were central to the communal practice of Methodist societies. Society members were encouraged to attend their local parish church for worship and engage in works of charity and evangelism outside of the society. This outward orientation was also manifest in Wesley's controversial use of lay preachers.

Wesley's ability to minister to women was one of his greatest gifts. Women formed the majority of eighteenth-century British Methodists and were afforded limited opportunities to exercise spiritual leadership. They served as class leaders and were encouraged to speak about their spiritual experiences. In several "extraordinary" cases, Wesley allowed women to preach.

A central component of Wesley's spirituality was his unusual love for the poor and concurrent mistrust of riches. His ministry to the poor, prisoners, and women helped create space for them to explore and express their spiritual experience.

Wesley's *Journal* is primarily a catalog of his actions and a defense of Methodism, and therefore provides limited insight into his spiritual life. His diaries are somewhat more revealing of his devotional practices, but they are only extant for 1725–1741 (with some significant gaps) and 1783–1791. Wesley's letters, particularly those to Charles Wesley and female friends, provide a somewhat clearer window into his personal spirituality. Of his treatises, *A Plain Account of Christian Perfection* (1766) is the most important work for gauging his spirituality. Here perfection was defined as pure love toward God and neighbor.

Wesley's *Christian Library* (1749–55) and *Arminian Magazine* (from 1778) reveal the spirituality that he promoted among his fellow Methodists. Anglican, Puritan, Pietist, Catholic, and Eastern Orthodox models all feature prominently. The *Arminian Magazine* contains many accounts of Wesley's preachers that progress from conversion narrative to holy living and dying accounts.

The ascetical devotional practices of Oxford Methodism remained central to Wesley's life. He defined the chief means of grace as prayer, Scripture ("reading, hearing, and meditating" upon), and the Lord's Supper. Wesley spent time daily in private and public prayer (the latter generally drawn from the prayer book or extemporaneous) and devotional reading of Scripture, and during his lifetime he partook of the Lord's Supper more than once a week on average. Wesley's Aldersgate experience and subsequent leadership in the evangelical revival seems to have gradually led him to a more assured and steady Christian life with increased confidence in God's providential guidance. Nonetheless, the emotional spiritual experiences common to early Methodists were the exception rather than the norm for Wesley, which he at times admitted to correspondents. Wesley's spirituality is perhaps most clearly seen in what he did, that is, in his life of ceaseless evangelical activity in which he traveled over two hundred thousand miles and preached more than forty thousand sermons.

Wesley's clearest legacy is the subsequent creation of the Methodist and other Wesleyan churches present in most parts of the world. His stress on holy living cultivated through intimate and disciplined Christian fellowship has had a profound impact on Protestant spirituality. In addition to its continued significance in Methodist and Wesleyan churches, Wesley's emphasis on sanctification as the goal of the Christian life had (and remains) a major influence in the Pentecostal tradition, especially through its second blessing theology of Spirit baptism.

See also Evangelism; Holiness; Methodist Spirituality; Revival; Wesley, Charles.

For Further Reading: *John and Charles Wesley,* CWS (1981); H. Rack, *Reasonable Enthusiast* (2002); J. Walsh, *John Wesley 1703–1791: A Bicentennial Tribute* (1993); J. Wesley, *A Collection of Forms of Prayer* (1733); idem, *The Works of John Wesley,* Bicentennial ed., 16 of 35 projected vols. (1975–);

Geordan Hammond

Whitefield, George (1714–1770)

Church of England clergyman, evangelist, and leader of Calvinistic Methodism. Whitefield was born in Gloucester, England; educated at Pembroke College, Oxford, where he took his bachelor's degree; and then ordained a deacon (1736) and later priest (1739) in the Church of England. At Oxford he had became acquainted with the Wesley brothers and joined them and other students in "Methodist" spiritual practices, such as small group fellowship, regular self-examination and prayer, devotional reading, fasting, works of charity, and frequent partaking of Communion. After engaging in months of extreme asceticism, which drove him to severe illness and nearly to despair, Whitefield experienced a life-changing conversion in which reading Henry Scougal's *The Life of God in the Soul of Man* (1677) played an important role.

Following his ordination, Whitefield quickly became popular in London and Bristol on account of his powerful and effective preaching. Much is revealed about his spirituality in his first two published sermons of 1737 — "The Nature and Necessity of ... Religious Society" and "The Nature and Necessity of Our New Birth in Christ Jesus, in Order to Salvation." In these sermons he stressed the importance of the new birth/regeneration, justification by faith, experientially felt inward religion of the heart, real as opposed to nominal Christianity, striving after God, doing good works, using the means of grace (such as prayer, fasting, and Communion), and Christian fellowship.

With the support of the Countess of Huntingdon, Whitefield became a leader among Calvinistic Methodists, who formed a smaller but significant alternative to their Wesleyan counterparts. His spirituality was intimately bound up with his life as an itinerant evangelist. He preached perhaps eighteen thousand sermons and itinerated in England, Wales, Scotland (fourteen visits), Ireland (three visits), and America (seven visits), where he spent nine years of his life. Contemporaries, including Benjamin Franklin, remarked about his powerful voice, eloquence, anecdotes, dramatic gestures, tearful pleadings, and ability to preach as if he were speaking directly to them. Whitefield's preaching was marked by traditional Calvinist stress on the glory of God and mystical union with God, along with a firm commitment to election. While having a strong sense of God's providential guidance in his life and ministry, Whitefield possessed a profound personal humility; and although he helped erect several chapels to support his ministry, he showed a lack of concern with leaving behind a personal legacy. As one of the greatest preachers in the history of the church, Whitefield played a central role in the transatlantic Great Awakening. He died and was buried in Newburyport, Massachusetts.

See also Evangelism; Reformed (Calvinist) Spirituality; Revival.

For Further Reading: A. Dallimore, *George Whitefield,* 2 vols. (1970, 1979); *George Whitefield's Journals* (1960); F. Lambert, *"Pedlar in Divinity"*

(1994); *Letters of George Whitefield for the Period 1734–1742* (1976); *Works of the Reverend George Whitefield*, 6 vols. (1771–1772).

Geordan Hammond

Wilberforce, William (1759–1833)

British evangelical abolitionist. William Wilberforce was born to privilege in Hull, northern England, and was elected to Parliament at age twenty-one; later, in 1785, he experienced an evangelical conversion to Christ. This conversion, along with counsel from John Newton, a converted slave trader, contacts with abolitionists like Thomas Clarkston, and his close friendship with Prime Minister William Pitt, awakened Wilberforce to the urgent need for moral and political transformation, and the conviction that he was to live a useful life in politics. "God Almighty has set before me two great objects: the suppression of the slave trade and the reformation of manners [English morals]," he wrote in 1787.

Wilberforce and his influential associates, known as the Clapham Sect, called the country to weekly prayer and tirelessly led a movement to reform the state, the church, and the nation. Wilberforce wrote *A Practical View of the Prevailing Religious System of Professing Christians* (1797) (also known as *Real Christianity*) to promote "real Christianity" among the middle and upper classes. Starting in the 1790s, evangelical conversions abounded in all socioeconomic groups, and crime rates dropped. Despite repeated defeats at the hands of entrenched interests and his own poor health, Wilberforce, Clarkston, and colleagues finally prevailed in 1807 with Parliament banning the slave trade. Slavery itself was abolished three days before Wilberforce died. His personal charm and oratorical skills were crucial in evangelical efforts to foster social, moral, spiritual, and educational changes, and to establish foreign mission agencies.

Wilberforce's inner life fueled his public vocation. His spiritual disciplines included rising early each day for solitary meditation, Scripture reading and memorization, praying the Psalms, confession, and journaling. He also practiced annual summer sabbaticals (until his marriage in 1797), pilgrimages, retreats, participation in small groups, Sabbath observance, and fellowship. Each Sunday after church and dinner, he retired to his study for spiritual reading, solitude, and likely tending his "Friend's List," which was found posthumously among his papers. Next to names of his acquaintances on that list, Wilberforce had written potential steps toward a fuller life in Christ for which he had prayed. Wilberforce also wrote family prayers for his wife and children, which were subsequently published.

An estimated three-quarters of the world's population lived under forced labor in the late 18th century, while today the figure is less than a half percent. Wilberforce is buried in Westminster Abbey beneath his bust, which bears a moving tribute to his remarkable accomplishments.

See also Protest; Social Justice.

For Further Reading: K. Belmont, *Hero for Humanity* (2002); G. Lean, *God's Politician* (1987); J. Pollock, *Wilberforce* (1977); S. Thompkins, *William Wilberforce* (2007).

L. Paul Jensen

Will, Human

Human beings possess volition — the ability to choose, the power to decide for oneself. Such freedom is an aspect of the image of God — it is an important part of what makes humans godlike. As volitional creatures, people are able somehow to transcend the shaping influences that impinge upon them, so that such factors, though powerful and influential, can never absolutely determine how one will respond to a given challenge or situation. Volition enhances human dignity and makes people, in effect, responsible moral agents. The Christian view of persons, while sympathetic to the reality of conditioning influences, categorically rejects all forms of determinism.

Traditionally people were thought to possess a will, as though the will was a thing, a specific part or possession of a person. In fact, however, the notion of the will is simply a reification (or imaginary objectification) of the reality that humans, as complex and holistic beings, are mysteriously able to choose how they will respond to possibilities and what course of action they will take. Moreover, the exercise of volition is never entirely independent; over two hundred fifty years ago, Jonathan Edwards recognized that "all acts of the will are acts of the affections."

There is, of course, another "will" in the universe — the will of God; and the quality and the shape of a human life are determined by the degree to which personal volition is exercised in alignment with, or in defiance of, the higher will of God. Nevertheless, such alignment is never coerced, lest human dignity be violated and the voluntary nature of genuine love be trampled on. Obedience to God — though not just any obedience, but the kind expressive of heartfelt eagerness — stands at the heart of Christian spirituality.

How our power of volition is exercised determines the course of our actions and their consequences. What is perhaps less appreciated but equally true is how the exercise of our volition also shapes the contours of our own souls. Through our choices, we help to sculpt our own enduring character. As C. S. Lewis said in *Mere Christianity*, "Every time you make a choice you are turning the central part of you, the part of you that chooses, into something a little different from what it was before." Likewise, psychologist William May has observed, "We function not simply as agents producing deeds but partly as authors and coauthors of our very being." Doing affects being as much as the reverse. This two-way dynamic simply underscores the importance of the classic and biblical virtue of courage — the strength to choose the right, despite fear and in the face of risk.

Inevitably, volition is exercised according to the determining inward dispositions of persons — that is, according to their nature and affections. Given that humans possess volition, but are also naturally tainted by sin, the degree to which the human will is truly free has been a subject of considerable discussion and debate through the centuries. Three legendary rounds of debate stand out in history: Pelagius versus Augustine in the 4th century, Erasmus versus Luther in the 16th century, and Dutch Calvinists versus the followers of Jacob Arminius in the early 17th century.

The British monk Pelagius held that Adam's sin affected no one but Adam — his descendants are not morally debilitated by the transmission of his disposition to sin. It would be otherwise unfair, he reasoned, for God to expect of people behaviors of which they were constitutionally incapable. The early monastic writer John Cassian proposed a mediating position by suggesting that Adam's sin only weakened the moral abilities of his descendants but did not entirely incapacitate them. Augustine's contrary view, articulated in *On Grace and Free Will* (426) and elsewhere, was that original sin is so debilitating in its effects that only through a gracious intervention of God can constitutionally sinful human beings truly choose the good.

As an Augustinian monk, it is not surprising that Luther aligned with Augustine in opposition to the thesis of *The Freedom of the Will* (1524), written by Luther's humanist contemporary Erasmus. Luther's rejoinder, pointedly entitled *The Bondage of the Will* (1525), is a classic declaration of human inability to choose the right without enabling and regenerating grace. Later, Jacob Arminius affirmed much of what Augustine and Calvin had declared about the spiritual impotence of human beings in need of God's grace. However, he postulated the generous diffusion of "*preventing* grace" (also known as *prevenient* grace), which allegedly enabled sinful humans to be able freely to respond, should they so choose, to the call and commands of God.

The colonies of New England were founded by Puritans, who were Calvinist in outlook. In the next century, the American theologian Jonathan Edwards still processed the dynamics of the Great Awakening through this lens. However, the American cultural climate became increasingly hospitable to Wesleyan-Arminian appeals to the human will for decision — and this became in fact a defining feature of subsequent revivalism.

At stake in this tug-of-war over "freedom of the will" are two matters of abiding relevance to Christian spirituality: the degree to which life needs to be lived in dependence on God's enabling grace, and the degree to which we must take responsibility for our choices. Both points must be maintained, even when they appear to clash.

Happily, one theme unites Christians since Augustine. Through regeneration and the indwelling power of the Holy Spirit, it is now possible, no matter what the situation, not to sin (Lat. *posse non peccare*). The plight of the wretchedly conflicted man of Romans 6:1 – 14 no longer applies, for the Christian has access to spiritual resources that make him or her free "not to sin." There can be no more pleading of helplessness or posturing as victim. The choices believers make have enormous consequences; because of the moral empowerment available through the Spirit, even more can now be properly expected of grateful believers.

See also Conversion; Freedom of Choice; Obedience; Responsibility.

For Further Reading: D. Basinger and R. Basinger, eds., *Predestination and Free Will* (1986); J. Edwards, *Freedom of the Will* (1754).

Wayne S. Hansen

ings. He later oriented his life toward knowing the living Christ and making him known in the world. Initially, as a young man, however, he felt quite ignorant about God and matters of the soul; in fact, this so troubled him that he left a pastorate with the intention of returning after studying in the fields of psychology, philosophy, and religion. Later, however, he sensed a divine calling to serve the church through teaching in the academy, as a philosophy professor at the University of Southern California (since 1965) and as a distinguished lecturer at universities and seminaries around the world.

Known as a humble man of prayer with extraordinary intellectual and theological depth, Willard is respected for his philosophical writings on the phenomenology of Edmund Husserl, but especially for his contributions to evangelical spiritual formation literature. The influence of Thomas à Kempis, William Law, John Wesley, and other spiritual masters are evident in his many provocative articles and books on Christian spirituality. His major works — *In Search of Guidance* (1984), *The Spirit of the Disciplines* (1988), award-winners *The Divine Conspiracy* (1998) and *Renovation of the Heart* (2002), and *Knowing Christ Today* (2009) — offer guidance to evangelicals who desire to become what Willard calls "apprentices" of Jesus, that is, those who imitate his way of life with moral earnestness in God's kingdom here and now.

For Further Reading: *Journal of Spiritual Formation and Soul Care* 3.2 (Fall 2010); special issue about Willard; C. Scheller, "A Divine Conspirator," *Christianity Today*, September 2006, 44 – 48.

Natalie Hendrickson

Willard, Dallas Albert (1935 –)

Ordained Southern Baptist pastor, philosophy professor, Christian spiritual life author, and teacher. As a young boy, Willard was deeply impressed by Sunday school lessons about Jesus and his teach-

William of Saint-Thierry (1085 – 1148)

Benedictine abbot, then Cistercian monk, Trinitarian theologian of the mystical life. This confidant of Bernard of Clairvaux expanded his Augustinian theological heritage with study in both Latin and

Greek fathers. He developed his early anthropological explorations of the created image of God and the Spirit-restored likeness in two major works on the mystical life—*Mirror of Faith* and *Enigma of Faith*. Through prayer and ascetic, contemplative living, the soul may know God—now by grace-given exercise of faith, reason, and love, and eventually face-to-face (1 Cor. 13:12). The Spirit transforms this intellectual and affective knowledge, primarily focused on contemplation of the passion of Christ, into likeness and loving union with the triune Divine Lover. Human participation in the mystery of Trinitarian life in and through the Holy Spirit will be perfected only in the eschaton. William's *Golden Letter* continues to guide communal contemplatives in quest of the vision of God. William's exposition of Song of Songs (cf. Bernard's) expounds the individual's union with God. He left a biography of Bernard unfinished at his death.

See also Cistercian Spirituality.

For Further Reading: D. Bell, *The Image and Likeness: The Augustinian Spirituality of William of St Thierry* (1984); B. McGinn and P. McGinn, *Early Christian Mystics* (2003); M. B. Pennington, ed., *William of Saint Thierry: The Way to Divine Union: Selected Spiritual Writings* (1998).

Richard F. Kantzer

Will of God

God's will is God's intention for all he made and rules over. But more precisely, is the will of God what God *decrees* or what God *desires*? Evangelical spirituality answers yes to both. Some of the divine intention is manifested as God's sovereign control of what comes to pass, and some of it is expressed in his commands concerning what should come to pass—commands that moral agents can choose, at least for a time, to disobey.

Distinguishing God's "will of decree" from his "will of command," as John Piper puts it, helps a disciple of Jesus live in proper, faithful relation to both. Both dimensions of God's will are relevant to Christian spirituality. In the first place, we are called to live out God's desires by submitting to his sovereign and inexorable decrees (even when God does not reveal why, Deut. 29:29 says). Sustained trust in God's benevolent sovereignty, even in the face of difficult, tragic, or otherwise bewildering circumstances (cf. Job), is positively transformational. We are called secondly to live out God's desires by keeping his commands (his preceptive will, or "will of command"). And though we have freedom to ignore or rebel against divine commands, we will reap the consequences. So we need to repent when we do—readily, because often the consequences are painful and dehumanizing in our experience, and also contritely, because at a deeper level our heart owns its sin against our loving Creator-Redeemer.

Romans 12:1–2, a principal text for biblical spirituality, indicates that the (preceptive) will of God comes to us in the context of holistic worship ("Offer your bodies as living sacrifices") motivated by "God's mercy," and so transforming us that we "test and approve what God's will is"—an experiential process in which knowing, adoring, and submitting to God is the key to experiencing the goodness of God's plans for us.

The proper application of scripturally revealed divine commands to our individual lives and circumstances often requires discernment. The challenge of hearing the guiding voice of God may also involve attentiveness to biblically consistent and Spirit-directed messages from a myriad of supplementary sources, including reason, experience, communal consensus, tradition, wise counsel, dreams, visions, and more. (Many Christians in the West are less open to the nonrational and extraordinary methods of discerning God's will than Christians in places like Africa and Asia.) Often, however, the spiritual challenge greater than discerning the preceptive will of God is the courage to obey it—to be able to say, finally, with

Jesus, "Not my will, but yours be done" (Luke 22:42). Doing so enables the believer to experience the spiritual nourishment to which Jesus attested when he said: "My food is to do the will of him who sent me" (John 4:34).

See also Authority; Obedience; Predestination.

For Further Reading: T. Balzer, *Thin Places* (2007); Francis de Sales, *Finding God's Will for You* (1998); D. Morris and C. Olsen, *Discerning God's Will Together* (1998); R. Pritchard, *Discovering God's Will for Your Life* (2004).

David L. Rowe

Wimber, John Richard (1934–1997)

Founder of the Vineyard movement. Wimber was best known for his teaching on power evangelism, and signs and wonders. His contribution to evangelical spirituality lay in his unique blend of creative music, religious experience, and personal passion. His ministry reflected a blend of influences—from his early involvement with the Friends Church to his relationship with the Jesus People and Calvary Chapel movements. Wimber pastored the Anaheim Vineyard Christian Fellowship and finally led Vineyard Ministries International and the Association of Vineyard Churches. Wimber's *Power Evangelism* (1986) was included in *Christianity Today*'s 2006 list of the top fifty books that have shaped evangelicals.

For Wimber, Christian faith and practice are organic and are rooted in the transcendence and immanence of God. Christians are expressly empowered for the purpose of advancing the gospel (Matt. 28:18–20; Acts 1:4–8). This is understood as a mandate for all believers to participate in both the natural and supernatural practices of NT Christianity. According to Wimber, this kind of faith is risky, often resulting in spontaneous and situational empowerings of the Holy Spirit to minister in specific ways. This emphasis reflects his understanding of the kingdom of God as the dynamic rule and reign of God breaking into this present, earthly realm in tangible and sometimes dramatic ways. It ensured that "power encounters" and manifestations of the Holy Spirit became dominant expectations at Vineyard conferences.

Wimber's priority of intimacy in worship, along with his desire to embrace the larger body of Christ, provided Wimber with a platform for renewal. One of the most vital yet often resisted characteristics of Protestantism is the impulse for reform. Wimber sought to integrate the perspectives of charismatic, evangelical, and Pentecostal leaders in his quest for church renewal. While this provoked criticism and contributed to an identity crisis within the movement, it nonetheless expressed his personal desire for a more integrated and dynamic Christian paradigm.

For Further Reading: C. Wimber, *John Wimber: The Way It Was* (1999).

Gino Pasquariello

Wisdom

In the Scriptures, wisdom has anonymity (hidden in the mystery of God's omniscient counsel, calling aloud in the streets and yet unrecognized—Job 28:20–24; Prov. 1:20–33) and also synonymity (equated in Hebrew parallelism with the terms *understanding* and *knowledge*—Ex. 31:3; Ps. 49:3). Generally, this seemingly elusive jewel beyond all jewels called wisdom is holy discernment—the morally righteous understanding of life that originates in God and may be graciously given to humans who, like Solomon, ask (1 Kings 3:9; 4:29; James 1:5).

Though coming from the heart and mind of the Exalted One, who said, "My thoughts are not your thoughts" (Isa. 55:8), wisdom (or knowledge or understanding) becomes radically earthy, incarnate, and manifest in the gritty, dust-and-dreams, and everyday experience of the faithful. It is never mere shrewdness, "street smarts," or business acumen: wisdom characterizes the discerning heart that is both morally righteous and practically smart. This priceless gift, which Jesus said is "proved right by her actions" (Matt. 11:19), shows up (or doesn't) in the full gamut of daily life issues — friendship, conversational habits, drinking habits, relating to God, sexual behavior, leadership style, financial choices, and so on.

One finds all such issues addressed in what we know as the Wisdom Literature of the OT, preeminently the Psalms and Proverbs, and this literary tradition profoundly influences the NT teachings about discipleship "in Christ." Indeed, proverbial wisdom in its best biblical sense holds a crucial place in the tradition of evangelical spirituality: this wisdom begins with the fear of the Lord (reverent awe that takes God seriously — Ps. 111:10; Prov. 1:7), is contrasted with folly (fools, prideful and "wise" in their own eyes, despise God's wisdom and become morally deficient — Prov. 1:7; 13:10), proves redemptive and morally beneficial to our lives by saving us from the schemes and entrapments of the wicked (Prov. 2:12; 10:23), and is personified as Lady Wisdom in the Proverbs but finds fulfillment in the very person of Christ Jesus in the NT (the likenesses of these two show biblically they are one reality: Lady Wisdom is a type that reveals Christ). So Paul declares that Christ is "the wisdom of God," which means he is "our righteousness, holiness and redemption" (1 Cor. 1:24, 30).

This age of cell phones, satellites, Internet, and myriad other techno wonders is information rich yet wisdom poor, and we recognize this with special poignant force when we acknowledge the ethical dimension of wisdom. Isaac Asimov raised the issue this way: "Suppose that we are wise enough to learn and know — and yet not wise enough to control our learning and knowledge, so that we use it to destroy ourselves." Perhaps no time has ever been more vital for Christians to cultivate a life-redeeming spirituality of humble submission to "Christ … the wisdom of God" through disciplines of prayer and study of the Bible's Wisdom Literature.

See also Knowledge of God.

For Further Reading: W. Brown, *Character in Crisis* (1996); D. Estes, *Handbook on the Wisdom Books and Psalms* (2010); J. Houston, *The Creator* (2007).

David L. Rowe

Witnessing

The word *witnessing* is derived from the biblical term *martyreō* ("witness"). In Greek, *witness* is a legal term meaning "to attest to the facts or to assert the truth" (cf. Col. 4:5–6). Since the church's early centuries, some (e.g., Perpetua) have witnessed through a martyr's death, while others (e.g., Augustine) have done so through a transformed life. However, during the 20th century, *witnessing* came to mean a three-part process whereby a Christian engaged in a kind of stereotypical conversation with a non-Christian. This involved: (1) giving a "testimony," (2) followed by sharing a "plan of salvation" that describes how one becomes a Christian, and (3) ending with an invitation to "accept Jesus" by praying the so-called Sinner's Prayer.

The focus of the *testimony* is on one's personal conversion. Evangelicalism is characterized by an emphasis on conversion as the way into an authentic Christian life. Such testimonies, for interest's sake, tended to be condensed into a brief three- or four-minute format. Furthermore, the conversion experience was described in punctiliar terms (as an event that took place at a certain time and place), following the model of Paul's Damascus Road conversion, even though research has consistently indicated that no more than 30 percent of conversions are sudden.

The aim of the *plan of salvation* was to describe how to receive Jesus. Generally the focus in such a plan is on belief in Jesus and faith in his redemptive work. The most widely used plan of salvation was *The Four Spiritual Laws*, written by Bill Bright and used extensively by Campus Crusade for Christ. Other plans include the *Bridge to Life* (Navigators), which portrays the cross as that which bridges the chasm between the sinner and God, and the *Roman Road*, which uses verses from the book of Romans to guide the process of salvation (Rom. 3:23; 6:23; 5:28; 10:9; and 5:1). Newer renderings from InterVarsity Christian Fellowship include *Circles of Belonging* (Rick Richardson) and the *True Story* (James Choung), both of which seek to be more holistic gospel renderings. All are characterized by the attempt to encapsulate the gospel message in easy-to-grasp and pictorial terms.

The final step in the process of witnessing involved encouraging others to act on this information and then and there to "receive Jesus as Lord and Master" by praying a simple prayer, often referred to as the Sinner's Prayer, which acknowledges oneself as a sinner who by faith accepts Jesus' death on his or her behalf with thanks for eternal life.

In the twenty-first-century, postmodern world, there has been no small amount of reaction against such an approach that has come to be seen as simplistic (and not just simple), as monologue not dialogue (often delivered in a confrontational fashion), and as a faulty rendering of the gospel that leaves out the kingdom of God and makes becoming a Christian a matter of cognitive belief rather than full-orbed discipleship (which involves not only believing but also behaving in a new way, belonging to a new community, and becoming ever more conformed to the image of Christ).

In this new view, witnessing becomes a matter of an ongoing conversation that revolves around three stories: your story of God, my story of God, and God's story of Jesus. Such a view is posited on an understanding that all people are on spiritual pilgrimages (whether they are aware of this or not), and that those who have been involved in con-scious pilgrimage following the way of Jesus can be of help to those newly becoming aware of their own pilgrimages.

See also Conversion; Evangelism; Testimony.

For Further Reading: J. Brownson et al., *Stormfront* (2003); J. Choung, *True Story* (2008); R. Coleman, *The Master Plan of Evangelism* (1963); R. Peace, *Holy Conversation* (2006); R. Pippert, *Out of the Saltshaker and into the World* (1979).

Richard V. Peace

Womanist Spirituality

Womanist spirituality originated in the 1980s, when it emerged in the writings of African-American women in the field of religion and theology. The term *womanist* was coined by Alice Walker, an acclaimed African-American novelist, poet, and essayist, who set forth the definition in her collection of essays, *In Search of Our Mothers' Gardens* (1983). In short, *womanist* means "black feminist."

A bold and distinctive posture of advocacy for women is the foundation of womanist spirituality. It articulates bold expressions of love without being narrow or narcissistic. Womanist spirituality bears a strong component of affirmation, showing deep appreciation and concern for the well-being of community and the earth. This commitment to articulation and affirmation also mandates activism, the motivation to make a difference in the world in harmony with the spirit. The activist agenda of womanist spirituality is grounded in the liberation of black women, men, and children from discrimination and oppression based on race, class, and sex. Its historical perspective begins with the experience of slavery. Walker's definition recalls the spiritual activism of Harriet Tubman, a deeply committed Christian who helped three hundred persons escape from slavery to freedom prior to the Civil War.

African-American theologians who were also ordained clergy of Christian denominations and churches led the way in emphasizing spirituality within womanist scholarship. Katie Cannon, a Presbyterian minister and ethicist, pioneered the use of the womanist idea in theological reflection in her book *Black Womanist Ethics* (1988). However, womanist spirituality is inclusive of faiths and traditions other than Christianity, including the beliefs and practices of African traditional religions.

See also Feminist Spirituality; Gender; *Mujerista* Spirituality.

For Further Reading: K. Baker-Fletcher, *Sisters of Dust, Sisters of Spirit* (1998); C. Sanders, ed., *Living the Intersection* (1995); E. Townes, *In a Blaze of Glory* (1995); D. Williams, *Sisters in the Wilderness* (1995).

Cheryl J. Sanders

Women in the History of Christian Spirituality

From the 1st century until now, women have played an integral role in the development of a wide array of Christian spiritual traditions. Many women have been numbered among the great saints, mystics, and martyrs of the church. Their lives, teaching, and courageous leadership continue to bear witness to the love of God in the world and to shape the spirituality of Christians today.

While numerous faithful women are named in both the Old and New Testaments, the three who have left the greatest spiritual legacy are Mary, the mother of Jesus, and Mary and Martha of Bethany. In all Christian traditions, Mary, the mother of Jesus, is honored as exemplar of Christian discipleship. Mary has been venerated in Orthodox and Catholic traditions since antiquity, with a number of historical developments that have been resisted by Protestants, including the belief in Mary's immaculate conception. In Orthodoxy Mary is *Theotokos*, the Mother of God. Some feminists and liberation theologians today claim Mary as an exemplar of resistance to oppression through the politically subversive language of the Magnificat (Luke 1:46–55).

Mary and Martha of Bethany, two of Jesus' closest friends, for nearly two millennia have been archetypes for two basic expressions of Christian spirituality — contemplative and active. Thus, Mary represents devotion through practices of learning, prayer, and meditation, while Martha represents devotion through service. Both are necessary for a balanced spiritual life.

Many women were among the early martyrs of the church. Two of the most famous are Perpetua and Felicity, who were among a group of five catechumens martyred in 203, during the persecutions of Septimius Severus. Their story, including the prophetic visions and words of Perpetua, is told in *The Passion of St. Perpetua, St. Felicitas, and Their Companions*. Other female martyrs whose courage and tenacity continue to inspire Christians include Marguerite Porete, a Beguine mystic who was martyred in 1310, and Joan of Arc, a young visionary who was martyred in 1431. Modern examples include Orthodox martyr Maria Skobtsova, who died in Ravensbrück in 1945, and hundreds of thousands of other Christian women who have died in persecutions of Christians around the world in the 20th century. In many of these cases, the women's spirituality included a prophetic challenge against oppression and injustice in secular and ecclesiastical realms, major reasons for their martyrdom.

The spirituality of martyrdom, a willingness to lay down one's life in fidelity to Christ, is the ultimate expression of *kenosis*, or self-emptying in the manner of Christ. Thus, martyrdom by women or men is archetypal for Christian discipleship and for all forms of apophatic Christian spirituality.

Women have been part of monastic spirituality throughout the history of the church. From the desert mothers of the 4th century to contemporary Benedictine nuns, women have devoted their lives to prayer and service both in eremitic (solitary) and cenobitic (communal) monastic traditions. Many of these women founded new orders (Teresa of Avila, Mother Teresa of Calcutta), wrote spiritual books and poetry (Julian of Norwich, Hildegard von Bingen), and engaged in prophetic ministries of healing and justice (Catherine of Siena, Clare of Assisi).

The Beguines were an unofficial lay monastic movement that began among women in the 11th century in what is now Belgium. They worked among the poor and were self-supporting. Each Beguine house followed its own rule of life. Unlike other religious orders with permanent vows, Beguines were free to leave their communities to marry. Today women continue to be faithful leaders and participants in monasticism in Catholic, Orthodox, and Anglican traditions.

Women in Protestant traditions generally have not been able to join monastic orders or found convents, but in other ways they have shaped and led the spirituality of the church, especially in linking holiness with social justice. Margaret Fell (1614–1702) contributed immensely to the development of early Quaker spirituality along with her husband, George Fox, and is called the mother of Quakerism. Fell wrote many pamphlets and letters of spiritual direction, and spent significant time in prison for her faith. Quakers were among the first abolitionists and, from the beginning with Fell's scriptural arguments for the right of women to preach, were advocates for gender equality. Other significant Quaker women were nineteenth-century American abolitionists Sarah and Angelina Grimké.

Many women of the 19th and early 20th centuries were active in evangelism and missions, their spirituality being apostolic. They worked tirelessly to promote holiness of heart and life, which included dangerous and difficult social activism on behalf of abolition, temperance, women's rights, child protection laws, advocacy for the mentally ill and incarcerated, and more. These evangelists were often mystics, experiencing God's call through visions and dreams. They practiced rigorous spiri-

tual disciplines of prayer, Bible reading, fasting, and giving. Among these were Phoebe Palmer, the mother of the Holiness movement, who led more than twenty-five thousand people to Christ and wrote a landmark book on women's right to engage in public ministry; evangelist Julia Foote, whose parents were former slaves; suffragist leader Frances Willard; Catherine Booth, cofounder of the Salvation Army; Mary McLeod Bethune, founder of Bethune-Cookman College; and Amy Carmichael, missionary to India. Dorothy Day, founder of the Catholic Worker Movement, is a patron saint for the new monastic movement of the early 21st century.

During recent decades, the development of liberation theologies included women's contributions in feminist, womanist, *mujerista*, and *minjung* spiritualities. While diverse in expression and theological orientation, these spiritualities all arise from women's experiences of the gospel and the world, and all are concerned with the liberation and healing of the oppressed.

Since antiquity women have shaped liturgical spirituality through their composition of hymns, prayers, and other liturgical acts. Hildegard of Bingen was an extraordinary composer, whose music has been rediscovered in recent years. Other female hymn writers include Fanny Crosby, who wrote some nine thousand hymns, many of which continue to be favorites in the church. Contemporary composer Ruth Duck is renowned for her hymns, which express worship in the vernacular of the people and resonate with the healing and liberating themes of feminist Christian spirituality.

For Further Reading: M. Earle, *The Desert Mothers* (2007); P. L. Kwok, *Postcolonial Imagination and Feminist Theology* (2005); P. Palmer, *Promise of the Father* (1859); R. Tucker and W. Liefeld, *Daughters of the Church* (1987); J. Tyson, *Invitation to Christian Spirituality* (1999); L. Warner, *Saving Women* (2007); J. Wolski Conn, ed., *Women's Spirituality* (1996).

Elaine A. Heath

Wonder

At the popular level, to wonder is to doubt or feel unsure. But properly understood, it is a response of amazement, triggered by something unexpected and mysterious. Wonder per se contains elements of both surprise (thus, "wonder-struck") and puzzlement. The experience of wonder is always ambivalent, for the wonderer has two contradictory reactions: a longing for novelty and a fear of the unknown. Objects of wonder (that is, wonder-stimulating things) thus simultaneously attract and repel us. When the power of attraction predominates, wonder takes on the hue of admiration. Puzzlement moves on naturally to curiosity and the quest for explanation, and admiration leads forward to contemplation. This is not mindless languor, but an inner receptivity, a disciplined silence, an attentive listening. When wonder is sustained, these responses can and should lead eventually to celebration, where one can enjoy in an uninhibited way that which has been given to us so unexpectedly and inexplicably.

But, as noted earlier, wonder-struck individuals also fear the unknown. Out of a need for security and stability, the wonderer may very possibly choose to nip the dangerous thing in the bud and suppress the spirit of wonder at the outset. The status quo will be preserved, but the aborting of wonder robs such an individual of the deeper experiences of investigative adventure, admiration, contemplation, and celebration. Frederick Buechner, in his memoir *The Sacred Journey* (1982), urges that one should "never question the truth of what you fail to understand, for the world is filled with wonders." Wonder is indeed an important and fitting response to both the mystery of life and the story of redemption.

Wonder incorporates openness to novelty and stimulation of critical inquiry. On the one hand, it prevents us from suppressing the novelty that we do not fully understand and cannot fully control. On the other, it moves us beyond blank acceptance, beyond the shrug of boredom, to seek deeper comprehension. Wonder is the marvelous middle way between skepticism and credulity. It was the wisdom of the early church to put a fence around the mysteries of the faith. It is wisdom for Christians today neither to trample down those fences, nor to walk away from them. To extend the metaphor, we ought always to be bent over and peering through the slats.

Humility is basic to wonder, which is the antithesis of hubris (pride). It is opposed to the passion to control and stand in judgment over the world. Wonder involves a tacit concession that there is a profound reality over and against us, which exceeds our capacity to master it, and which must be accepted on its own terms and allowed to speak for itself. The true wonderer is always the marveling learner. Unfettered by pride, the wonderer is truly open to the world.

A number of benefits come with an infusion of wonder. One is that wonder serves as an antidote to skepticism. The Christian faith is irreducibly supernatural, its creed a declaration of shining incredibilities. A spirituality of wonder allows one to embrace and celebrate those features of the faith that can never be domesticated by the modern mind-set. Such wonder is not gullibility. Rather, it is a way to leave pried open the steel door of skepticism, which so often slams shut and seals us off from God and transcendent realities. It is humble openness to possibility; it is deferment of the decision to reject.

A sense of wonder lies at the heart of Christian spirituality. It is an eminently fitting response to our encounter with the mysterious ways of the God who stands above and beyond ourselves and our ways. Too often the efforts of theologians to make the faith plausible to themselves, and marketable to others, have robbed it of those dimensions for which (consciously or unconsciously) contemporaries still yearn. But wonder is the threshold of worship—an anticipation of that coming future when, in Charles Wesley's words, believers will finally cast their crowns before God, eternally "lost in wonder, love, and praise."

For Further Reading: K. Barth, *Evangelical Theology* (1963); C. Deane-Drummond, *Wonder and Wisdom* (2006); E. de Waal, *Lost in Wonder* (2003); R. Fuller, *Wonder: From Emotion to Spirituality* (2009); D. Hardy and D. Ford, *Praising and Knowing God* (1985); M. Inch, *The Wonder of It All* (2009); S. Keen, *An Apology for Wonder* (1969).

Glen G. Scorgie

Woolman, John (1720–1772)

Itinerant Quaker minister and writer. Woolman traveled widely throughout the American colonies, and England as well, to witness against slavery and social oppression. Largely through his efforts, slavery was all but eliminated within Quaker circles well before the abolition movement impacted the larger society.

Woolman was born near Mount Holly, New Jersey, and educated in Quaker schools. As a young man, he began a successful retail business, but was troubled by the lure of wealth. Led by the Spirit to relinquish his business and the need to strive for possessions, power, and prestige, he decided to make his living instead in a humbler way as an orchardist and tailor. This simpler lifestyle enabled him to pursue his true vocation as a traveling minister, and at age twenty-three he began the first of many missionary journeys.

Little would be known about Woolman if he had not kept a spiritual journal, a common practice among Quaker ministers. After his *Journal* was published posthumously in 1774, his influence spread far beyond Friends, and his thoughts on slavery as "a practice inconsistent with the Christian religion" became inspiration and fuel for the abolition movement of the next century. His *Journal* was heralded by many literary figures of the 19th century, such as John Greenleaf Whittier. Today it is considered one of the best examples of a Quaker journal and a classic of American literature.

Woolman's spirituality had both a mystical and a prophetic bent, in which inwardness led to outward action. In addition to his work to abolish slavery, he had a special concern for reconciliation with Native Americans and undertook a dangerous journey to meet with them face-to-face. He was an unwavering pacifist who recognized how oppression and exploitation through unjust social structures produced what he hauntingly called "the seeds of war."

Besides the fame of his *Journal*, Woolman is noted for several significant essays on social issues. He wrote two essays titled "On the Keeping of Negroes" (1754, 1762). The first was one of the earliest antislavery documents. His economic views and his methods for social change are outlined in his *A Plea for the Poor*, published posthumously in 1793. While traveling in England to promote his concerns for the poor, he died of smallpox at age fifty-two.

Woolman's writings reflect the core values and principles distinctive to traditional Quaker spirituality, which he sought to renew within the Society of Friends: obedience to God's call and inner promptings of the Spirit, and commitment to equality, peacemaking, nonviolence, reconciliation, and simplicity of lifestyle. Even his methods, such as war tax resistance and the boycott of products produced by slave labor, were grounded in his deeply mystical Quaker spirituality. His compassion extended beyond human life to all of God's creatures, and he is often cited as a proto-environmentalist. His striking insights, ingenuity, and resourcefulness continue to find relevance in our contemporary world. His love of God and belief in the sacredness of all of life permeate his writings.

For Further Reading: M. Birkel, *A Near Sympathy: The Timeless Quaker Wisdom of John Woolman* (2003); P. Moulton, ed., *The Journal and Major Essays of John Woolman* (1971).

Carole Dale Spencer

Work

A Christian spirituality of work begins with a correct theology of work. Three chief ideas form the starting point for such a theology. First, work was created by God to be part of the original perfection. "The LORD God took the man and put him in the garden of Eden to work it and keep it" (Gen. 2:15 ESV). Work is thus good in principle. Second, with the fall of the human race into sin, work was cursed (Gen. 3:17) and became toil, carried out "by the sweat of [man's] brow" (Gen. 3:19). A spirituality of work acknowledges the cursed nature of work in a fallen world. Third, the curse did not, however, eliminate work as a God-ordained and divinely sanctioned sphere of human life. God still commands people to work: "Six days you shall labor and do all your work" (Ex. 20:9).

A doctrine of calling or vocation completes a Christian spirituality of work. God calls people to their tasks in the world, as evidenced by the numerous times we read in the Bible that God "called" a person to a task. The NT answer to the question of how conversion affects one's vocation or task in the world is, "Let each person lead the life that the Lord has assigned to him, and to which God has called him" (1 Cor. 7:17 ESV; cf. also v. 20). By inference, then, to obey God's call in one's vocation is to serve God acceptably. The parable of the talents (Matt. 25:14–30) has served as a convenient paradigm for the idea of work as stewardship.

The Christian tradition that has most helpfully codified the implications of biblical ideas about work is the Reformed/Puritan tradition. The cornerstone of this tradition is the rejection of the sacred-secular dichotomy that claims that the spiritual life consists of withdrawal from work in the world to spiritual contemplation. In the Protestant tradition, all tasks and callings that a Christian carries out as a service to God and humanity are fully a part of the spiritual life. Inasmuch as God commands work, performing it is a spiritual act of obedience.

The practical outworking of these ideas about the spirituality of work is the ideal of experiencing God in the routines of life. Instead of escaping from the commonplace into the contemplative and transcendent, a person brings the transcendent into the commonplace. The shop, the kitchen, the school, and the nursery, not the monastery cell, become the locus of finding God and the life of the Spirit.

See also Benedictine Spirituality; Labor, Manual; Leisure and Play; Sabbath.

For Further Reading: R. Banks, *Redeeming the Routines* (1994); W. Boggs Jr., *All Ye Who Labor* (1961); J. Nelson, ed., *Work and Vocation* (1954); L. Ryken, *Redeeming the Time* (1995).

Leland Ryken

World, The

The term "world" (Gr. *kosmos*) is used in Scripture in both positive and negative ways, making spirituality vis-à-vis the world a rich and complex one. Positively, the world refers to God's creation (John 17:5, 24), the theater of God's revelation (Ps. 19:1; Rom. 1:20). It also refers to the people in the world, the object of God's love (John 3:16). It is used of the earth as distinguished from heaven (Gen. 1:1; Matt. 5:18; 6:10). A positive understanding of the world gives rise to different spiritualities of engagement. The world is an open book from which many spiritual lessons can be gleaned (e.g., Ps. 8:3–4; Prov. 6:6). It has been extensively treated in older spiritual writings by both Catholics and Protestants, for example, by Bonaventure (1221–1274), *The Mind's Road to God*, and Robert Bellarmine (1542–1621), *The Mind's Ascent to God by the Ladder of Created Things*; and by Puritans like Thomas Taylor (1576–1632), *Meditations from the Creatures*, and Joseph Hall (1574–1656), *The Invisible World, Discovered to Spiritual Eyes, and Reduced to Useful Meditation*. Its links to ecological concerns have been much exploited in recent times.

Under the influence of various cosmologies, engagement could mean participation in a world that is evolving toward its intended *telos* (Teilhard de Chardin). For others, it means participation in God's "original blessings" in creation apart from the question of sin and redemption (Matthew Fox).

The world also refers to organized humanity, a structure standing in opposition to God. Together with the flesh and the devil, it is one of the "enemies of the soul." This view is found predominantly in the Johannine and Pauline literature (John 15:18–19; 16:20; 1 Cor. 2:12; Gal. 6:14; 1 John 3:13; 5:19; et al.). It has generated two divergent responses. One is a spirituality of separation and detachment predicated on an ethical dualism: church versus world, the kingdom of light versus the kingdom of darkness. If the world in its orderly structure (*skēma*) is passing away, according to Paul, an attitude of detachment is called for (1 Cor. 7:29–31). The rejection of the evil world is thematized in certain practices, such as showing contempt for the world (*contemptus mundi*) and meditating on "the four last things" (death, judgment, heaven, and hell) and on the world's vanity and temporality. Some form of relative dualism is implicit in the biblical worldview, but its validity depends on the extent to which separation from the world is envisaged and practiced. A tendency toward docetism existed in more radical movements like the Cathari in the Middle Ages and among some Dutch Anabaptists who taught that Christ's "heavenly flesh" was born "in Mary" rather than "of Mary."

A second option is a spirituality of engaging the evil world in anticipation of its eschatological restoration. Liberation spirituality seeks to overcome structural evil to create a more just world. Various types of earth spirituality represent responses to the environmental and ecological crises. The validity of this option depends on how far the eschaton is believed to be realized. An overrealized eschatology could lead to utopianism.

The paradoxical nature of the "world" as good and fallen, as an object of both God's love and judgment, means that the Christian encounter with the world requires constant fine-tuning. Keeping the balance itself is part of the task of spiritual training. The key is the Spirit, who, as the firstfruits of the new creation, inaugurates the already–not yet tension in the world. Thus, the Spirit's work in creation (*Creator Spiritus*) has come to play an increasingly significant role in various cosmic spiritualities.

See also *Fuga Mundi*; Sacred and Secular.

For Further Reading: C. Braaten and R. Jenson, eds., *The Two Cities of God* (1997); C. Kauffman, "Incarnation of Christ," in *Mennonite Encyclopedia*, 5 vols. (1955–1990), 3:18–20; K. Kim, *The Holy Spirit in the World* (2007); G. Wainwright, "Types of Spirituality," in *The Study of Spirituality*, ed. C. Jones et al. (1986), 592–605.

Simon Chan

Worship

Frequently, spirituality is seen as an experience between the individual and God or is associated with extraordinary mystics, while worship is considered a routine communal activity. For Christians, however, worship is basic and not to be divided from spirituality. Jesus said to the Samaritan woman: "The hour is coming, and is now here, when the true worshipers will worship the Father in spirit and truth, for the Father is seeking such people to worship him" (John 4:23 ESV).

Jesus' startling words lead us to see worship as linked with himself as the Truth, and with the Holy Spirit. It is the communion of Father, Son, and Holy Spirit that makes true communion with God (that is, spirituality) possible, and that enables us to worship authentically. There is no play-off between the personal and the gathered community, nor are personal experiences of God more valuable than worship offered by the body of Christ, to which we are joined: these come together in God's plan.

When we consider the Old and New Testaments as well as the ongoing tradition of the church, both East and West, it becomes apparent that Christian worship is entrance into something larger than ourselves—a larger action, company, and space than the individual, or even the local community. We worship as part of "the communion of saints" (see Rev. 4–5).

Worship, then, is not foundationally a human creation, but something into which we are invited. This may seem counterintuitive in an age when creativity in worship is valued and when the Lord's people are always being taught "a new song." However, the drive for novelty has also been attended by tension in the churches today. It is not only true but also helpful to remember that worship is an ongoing action of God's creatures, which we join, especially when we gather together to celebrate. There are numerous OT texts where "entrance" into God's presence is a major theme: in Isaiah 6 the prophet joins the company of the angels singing "holy"; Psalms 95 and 132 exhort God's people to worship at his footstool and enter his dwelling place; in Exodus 24, Moses and the elders commune with a holy God; 1 Chronicles 16:29 enjoins us to "come before" and "worship the LORD in the splendor of his holiness"; in Exodus 40:34 and 2 Chronicles 7:1, God's glory is so thick that it makes a palpable impact upon the worshiper. This theme of entrance continues into the NT, which stresses the importance of worshiping in the communion of the apostles (Acts 2:42–47) and acknowledges that traditions of worship are passed down (1 Cor. 11:23, 26). In the apostolic church, the corporate and historic dimensions of worship did not vanish into a vague spirituality, but crystallized around Christ and his apostles, who witnessed to him. Christians worship together in a context that is startlingly huge—see the poignant drama of Hebrews 12:18–28 or the liturgical dynamic of the Apocalypse.

This approach is emphasized even more fully in the subsequent centuries of the church. The *Didache*, Justin Martyr, and the *Didascalia Apostolorum* register an understanding of corporate entry into a mysterious reality. This foundation was nurtured variously in the West and the East: the corporate "Amen" spoken at the high point of the service; the invocation of the Holy Spirit (*epiclesis*) and/or the repetition of Jesus' "words of institution," both of which place the worship under the guidance of the Lord himself; the recollection of sacred history and statements of corporate hope; the recognition of heavenly hosts in the "Glory to God in the highest" or the Trisagion ("holy, holy, holy").

Indeed, the Eastern liturgy is structured in terms of two great cycles of entrance—first by means of the Word, and then by Eucharist. In the West, Simeon's *Nunc Dimittis* or Mary's *Magnificat* have signaled that worshipers are entering into a drama far larger than their own small corner.

Such liturgical elements may seem removed from the contemporary worship of small emergent groups or megachurches in North American Christianity. However, worship leaders in those contexts endeavor to create an atmosphere of holiness or intimacy, thus bearing witness that worship is something bigger, of which we must be aware. Whenever prayers for healing take place at the Lord's Supper, whenever Christians remember the presence of the angels, whenever we see ourselves in continuity with the Scriptures, whenever we acknowledge the hosts of Christians before us and around the globe, the theme of entrance is recognized. This is so whether we worship together or in personal devotion. God sometimes nurtures us by solitary prayer but without calling us to isolation. When the Lord went "apart," his prayers concerned others—for example, choosing the Twelve, suffering for the world. In Luke 9:28–36, Jesus took three disciples to pray "alone": they met with Moses and Elijah, representatives of the people of God, and beheld Jesus. Learning to pray, they were transformed and witnessed to this in their ministry. Face-to-face with Jesus, the Christian is changed, becoming a "living sacrifice" (Rom. 12:1) for the sake of others.

In the current context of Christian "worship wars," it is helpful to remember that worship is not about individualist experience, good aesthetics, or relevance. Rather, it is entrance into the whole action of God's people, past, present, and future, who have "come to . . . the heavenly Jerusalem, the city of the living God" (Heb. 12:22). Our corporate unrest concerning worship will come to resolution as we nurture this sense and seek both to recover and to voice together the praises given to us by God and by our brothers and sisters in Christ.

See also Adoration; Celebration; Hymns; Praise Music.

For Further Reading: S. Chan, *Liturgical Theology* (2006); M. Dawn, *Reaching Out without Dumbing Down* (1995); D. Dix, *The Shape of the Liturgy* (1945); T. Howard, *Evangelical Is Not Enough* (1984); E. Humphrey, *Grand Entrance* (2010); A. Schmemann, *The Eucharist* (1987).

Edith M. Humphrey

Yoga

Yoga is a system of living as old as India itself. The earliest written description of the practice of yoga is the *Yoga Sutras*, attributed to Patanjali in the 3rd century AD. Archaeological evidence, however, from the Indus Valley civilization indicates that as early as 2500 BC yogic meditation was practiced. Barbara Stoler Miller, translator of the 195 Sanskrit aphorisms of the *Yoga Sutras*, claims that yoga is at the heart of all meditative practice in Asia, and in her commentary takes pains to show how heavily the Hindu Patanjali was influenced by Buddhist teachings, and how in turn Jain, Sufi, and Sikh spirituality have been shaped by yogic teaching.

Yoga is part philosophy, part meditative technique. The word *yoga* refers to both goal and method. As one of the six orthodox philosophies of India, its place as one way of knowing and living is secure. Yet yoga is also a detailed guide to living life, moving from moral prescription to ethical observances to physical training to breath control to sense perception management to three levels of higher meditative practice. Taken together, these constitute the eight ascending stages or "limbs" of Patanjali's system. The goal is "cessation of the turnings of thought," as Patanjali put it; or

as Eliade summarizes, yoga is "the effectual techniques for gaining liberation." It acknowledges the illusory symbiosis of spirit (*purusa*) and material world (*prakriti*) we all live with, recommending instead turning our materially entangled spirits to be trained to be liberated observers of the material world instead of slaves to it.

Yoga has become popular the world over. To observe it in the West, however, one would be convinced yoga is simply a set of physical stretching exercises. This perception has, in part, led to a controversy over whether yoga as a physical and mental training technique can be used by Christians to augment their spiritual, meditative practice. Too often this debate is carried on in ignorance of the total metaphysical system of yoga, which is based on principles sometimes at odds with the Christian worldview. Still, it would be a mistake to dismiss all we might learn from the wisdom of the yogis because of important disagreements. It has been the underlying root of Indian spiritual wisdom for millennia for good reason.

See also Hindu Spirituality.

For Further Reading: M. Eliade, *Yoga, Immortality and Freedom* (1969); B. Miller, *Yoga* (1996); S. Strauss, *Positioning* (2005); J. H. Woods, *The Yoga System of Patanjali* (1914).

Terry C. Muck

Z

Zen

Zen is a Buddhist religious tradition and a religious practice with a unique method of mind-body training whose aim is awakening (*satori*). Zen resembles other variants of Buddhist meditation in its form — sitting, breathing, posture. It is unique in its a-rational approach, fostered by sitting with an empty mind (*shikan-taza*), and the use of rationally unsolvable mind problems (*koans*) set in larger dialogues between Buddhist masters and disciples (*mondos*). Disciples, for example, are told to sit and contemplate "What is the sound of one hand clapping?" — one of the beginning koans. Other vehicles of expression, although not strictly speaking part of Zen training — such as haiku poetry, archery, flower arranging — are used to open disciples' minds to their true nature.

Zen (*ch'an*) was begun by an Indian bhikkhu in China, where it developed. It then took root in Japan, and today it has spread to the Western world. According to legend, a Hindu/Buddhist Brahman sage named Bodhidharma from India traveled to China in AD 527, where he sat in a monastery for nine years staring at a wall (wall gazing). He attracted the attention of the emperor, a Buddhist of the Tang Dynasty, who encouraged his innovations. Six patriarchs of Bodhidharma's disciple lineage developed the technique in what has become called the golden age of Zen. Collections of koans and mondos accumulated and were taken to Japan by a Chinese teacher, Eisei (founder of the Rinzai Zen movement), and Dogen, a Japanese who came to study Zen in China (and then became founder of the Soto Zen movement in Japan), where it is most dominant as a religious movement today.

Zen came to the West as a result of the Parliament of World Religions held at the Chicago World's Fair in 1893. A Japanese Zen teacher, Shaku Soen, was one of the presenters. Because of the popularity of his presentations, he was asked to stay in the United States and give Zen instruction. This has resulted in a form of Zen one might call Western Zen as a third stream added to the two principle Japanese sects, Rinzai and Soto.

Zen meditation has attracted the attention of Western Christians, some of whom (e.g., Thomas Merton) have encouraged sympathetic weddings of Zen Buddhist and Christian meditative techniques. Others have seen the Zen focus on an empty mind and the goal of emptiness of all being to be antithetical to the Christian teachings regarding human eternal souls and their relationship to God.

See also Buddhist Spirituality; Contemplation; Meditation.

For Further Reading: P. Kapleau, *Three Pillars of Zen* (1965); *Two Zen Classics*, trans. K. Sekida (1977); J. C. H. Wu, *The Golden Age of Zen* (1967).

Terry C. Muck

Zinzendorf, Nicholas Ludwig von (1700 – 1760)

German Pietist and leader of the Moravian Church. While trained as a lawyer, Zinzendorf also pursued theological studies. He was formed by Francke's Halle pietism and invited persecuted refugees of the Bohemian Brethren to his estate, becoming deeply involved in the revitalization of the *Unitas Fratrum*, or Moravian Church. Zinzendorf's theology of the heart was strongly Christocentric and emphasized resting in the wound of Christ's side. This was connected to his teaching on spiritual marriage to the crucified Christ, drawn in part from the Song of Songs, which envisioned Jesus as the husband of each Christian soul. This deeply inward experiential spirituality was combined with a fervent zeal for witness and missionary efforts.

Zinzendorf wrote more than two thousand hymns, many of which emphasize Christ's atoning sacrifice and love among Christians—including "Jesus, Thy Blood and Righteousness" and "Christian Hearts in Love United," which regularly appear in evangelical hymnals. Zinzendorf's strong leadership skills organized members into small groups or bands to study Scripture, pray together, and hold one another accountable as they sought to live under the guidance of Christ's love. Additionally, he encouraged renewal in worship through the introduction of love feasts and added times of singing and prayer. While grounding himself deeply within his own Lutheran roots, he was appreciative of Reformed and Roman Catholic theology. His ecumenical spirit, renewed by a strong sense of grace, created a relentless desire to encourage Christian unity through love in Jesus Christ. To promote the broadening expansion of Moravian communities, he introduced the *Daily Texts* of meditations on Scripture and hymns for each day of the year, which continues to the present.

Theological and economic tensions from outside Herrnhut caused Zinzendorf's expulsion from his Saxony estate, and for ten years he traveled widely throughout Europe, England, and America planting Moravian communities and developing missions. His influence on evangelicals was considerable. He especially influenced John Wesley. Among Zinzendorf's extensive writings, *Nine Public Lectures on Important Subjects in Religion* (1746) is the best English introduction to Zinzendorf.

See also Moravian Spirituality; Pietism.

For Further Reading: C. Atwood, *Community of the Cross* (2004); C. Podmore, *The Moravian Church in England, 1728–1760* (1998); J. R. Weinlick, *Count Zinzendorf* (1984).

Tom Schwanda

Share Your Thoughts

With the Author: Your comments will be forwarded to the author when you send them to *zauthor@zondervan.com*.

With Zondervan: Submit your review of this book by writing to *zreview@zondervan.com*.

Free Online Resources at

www.zondervan.com

Zondervan AuthorTracker: Be notified whenever your favorite authors publish new books, go on tour, or post an update about what's happening in their lives at www.zondervan.com/authortracker.

Daily Bible Verses and Devotions: Enrich your life with daily Bible verses or devotions that help you start every morning focused on God. Visit www.zondervan.com/newsletters.

Free Email Publications: Sign up for newsletters on Christian living, academic resources, church ministry, fiction, children's resources, and more. Visit www.zondervan.com/newsletters.

Zondervan Bible Search: Find and compare Bible passages in a variety of translations at www.zondervanbiblesearch.com.

Other Benefits: Register yourself to receive online benefits like coupons and special offers, or to participate in research.

ZONDERVAN®

ZONDERVAN.com/
AUTHORTRACKER
follow your favorite authors